Gun Digest®

1991/45th Annual Edition

EDITED BY KEN WARNER

DBI BOOKS, INC.

ABOUT OUR COVERS

Flashy looks and gadgets are just not in the vocabulary of the engineers at SIG Sauer. Form follows function is the order of business for this old and respected name in the firearms field.

Our covers show two great 9mm Parabellum double-action pistols from SIG Sauer that epitomize reliability, accuracy and ease of maintenance for law enforcement work and sport shooting.

On the right is the SIG Sauer P226, the high capacity model that holds 15 + 1 rounds (20 + 1 rounds with the optional magazine) and has a 4.41-inch barrel. The overall length is 7.71 inches, and the weight is 29.9 ounces (with magazine). Grips are of checkered high-impact composition for a secure hold.

On the left is the newest addition to the SIG Sauer line, the P228, a shorter and lighter gun ideally suited for off-duty or concealed carry but with the same high degree of performance built in. The P228 has a 3.86-inch barrel, measures 7.08 inches overall and weighs 29.1 ounces with magazine. Magazine capacity is 13 + 1 rounds. The grips are of stippled composition which is a departure from the usual style, but nonetheless an excellent touch. This model also does not have the hooked trigger guard of the other SIG Sauer guns.

Both pistols have double-action trigger systems with pull weights slightly over 12 pounds DA and 4 pounds SA, automatic firing pin locks, trigger-level magazine releases and matte black finishes.

Hundreds of U.S. law enforcement agencies, as well as the FBI's Hostage Rescue Teams and SWAT units, have made SIG Sauer their gun of choice because of quality, ruggedness, dependability and serviceability. In addition, thousands of civilian shooters have found these guns to be top-notch performers on the range. Imported from West Germany, the SIG Sauer line is available from Sigarms Inc.

Photo by John Hanusin.

GUN DIGEST STAFF

EDITOR-IN-CHIEF
Ken Warner

SENIOR STAFF EDITOR
Harold A. Murtz

ASSOCIATE EDITOR
Robert S.L. Anderson

EDITORIAL/PRODUCTION ASSISTANT
Jamie L. McCoy

ASSISTANT TO THE EDITOR
Lilo Anderson

CONTRIBUTING EDITORS
Bob Bell
Doc Carlson
Dean A. Grennell
Rick Hacker
Clay Harvey
Edward A. Matunas
Layne Simpson
Larry S. Sterett
Hal Swiggett
D.A. Warner
J.B. Wood

EUROPEAN CORRESPONDENT
Raymond Caranta

GRAPHIC DESIGN
Jim Billy
Mary MacDonald
Jamie L. McCoy

MANAGING EDITOR
Pamela J. Johnson

PUBLISHER
Sheldon L. Factor

DBI BOOKS, INC.

PRESIDENT
Charles T. Hartigan

VICE PRESIDENT & PUBLISHER
Sheldon L. Factor

VICE PRESIDENT—SALES
John G. Strauss

TREASURER
Frank R. Serpone

ISBN 0-87349-105-X   Library of Congress Catalog #44-32588

Goodbye, Omark; Hello, Blount

CCI, Speer, Outers, Weaver and RCBS fly the Omark flag no longer. They now constitute the Sporting Equipment Division of Blount, Inc. Since the name is pronounced "blunt," the punning season has long since opened.

In Our Blood

More than hunting, more than guns, more than Africa itself comes off the screen in "In the Blood," a George Butler ("Pumping Iron") film based on two safaris—one by Teddy Roosevelt in 1909, one in the '80s by his great-grandson accompanied by Teddy's rifle. It's in celebration of one of mankind's eternal rites of passage. (Venture Group Int'l. 203-350-8290.)

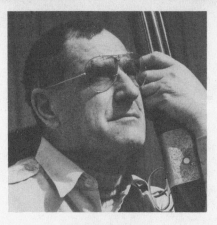

A SAFARI INTO THE PAST IN SEARCH OF THE FUTURE.

IN THE BLOOD

A Film by GEORGE BUTLER
The Director of "PUMPING IRON" and "PUMPING IRON II"

VGI
Venture Group International, Inc.

Colt Born Again

It is now "Colt's Manufacturing Company, Inc." and is owned by C.F. Holding Corp. of Hartford, Connecticut. The majority of the blue-collar workers will be returning members of the UAW union. Key players: Anthony D. Autorino of C.F. Holding; Richard F. Gamble, the new president; Ronald E. Stilwell, eighteen years at Colt, an executive vice president and chief operating officer.

Roger Barlow
1912-1990

Long-time GUN DIGEST contributor Roger Barlow died May 9, 1990, following a long and stout-hearted struggle with enough disabilities for three ordinary men. He had been a North Dakota farm boy, a Hollywood cinematographer, a dealer in foreign cars, a film maker in his own right, a respected writer in several fields, a country gentleman. To all those activities and to his personal life he brought warmth and wit and charm. Roger Barlow was a very good man.

Recalling 22 WMR A-Bolts

Owners of Browning A-Bolt rimfire rifles marked "A-BOLT 22 MAGNUM 22 WIN MAG CALIBER ONLY" should call, toll-free, 1-800-727-4312. The fix and shipping is free and there is definitely a problem.

Million-Dollar Shooter

Rob Leatham, six-time USPSA national champion and three-time IPSC champion, has a multi-year contract with Springfield Armory which will pay over $1,000,000. Leatham will anchor Team Springfield—an action-shooting competition team—and shoot only Springfield guns.

Dick Shaw
1906-1990

Fifty years ago, West Virginian Dick Shaw joined Bill Weaver in El Paso to sell scopes for thirty years. Thereafter, he was on the Board of Sturm, Ruger, Inc. Dick Shaw was the sort who made friends and deserved a lot of them, not least because he was a founding member of The Board of Governors of the National Shooting Sports Foundation.

More Longhunters

In just two years, the Longhunter Society begins to approach one-thousand members and nearly two hundred trophies have been registered for entry in the Society's Big Game Records. For $10, you can belong. Write: P.O. Box 67, Friendship, IN 47021. Recognize the town? Yep, the Longhunter Society is an NMLRA function.

Louis W. Seecamp

A successful gun designer who founded a father-son business, L. W. Seecamp spent his life devising the state of the art. That life ended, following a long illness, on September 6, 1989, but the name and the father-son business continue on—and no doubt will for a long time.

SCI Picks Morehouse

The new administrative director of Safari Club International is James A. Morehouse of Anchorage, Alaska. He will direct the club and staff in Tucson. Morehouse is a retired infantry officer, much decorated for twenty-two years of service. Besides two Bronze Stars for V, and numerous foreign awards, he has the Purple Heart and the Combat Infantryman's Badge.

CONTENTS

The Perfected Boxlock

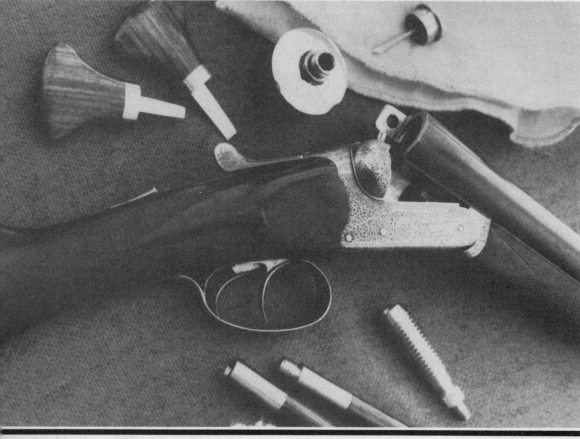

It can be better than the others.

Best quality boxlock shotgun by Hollis shows some good and some bad points. The treatment of the fences, the topstrap and the back of the action is excellent. Unfortunately, the stock has been ruined by unnecessary panels filled in with useless checkering. (Photo by the author)

by NIKITAS KYPRIDEMOS

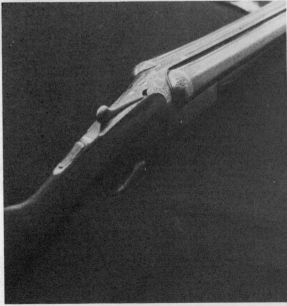

Shaping of the fences and topstrap of the Hollis is exemplary. Note the even flowing lines of the topstrap, the ball shape of the fences and the delicate bolster where the fences join the action body. (Photo by the author)

1900 could understand how a sidelock worked, and it also had a familiar shape inherited from the hammer gun his father had used, but the boxlock was new and different.

The opinions of the gun writers of the times came down greatly in favor of the sidelock. Sir Gerald Burrard leveled the most detailed criticism against the boxlock. It was weaker, he said, because of the necessity to take out so much metal from the action body under the standing breech in order to house the lock parts. The position of the lock parts made the achievement of crisp trigger pulls difficult and there were no lockplates for engraving. Also, the boxlock had no rebounding action which meant that it could remain striker bound, that is to say the firing pins do not retract after firing and sometimes they can lock into the primers and make opening the gun

FEW GUN ACTIONS have been with us as long as the Anson and Deeley boxlock. Patented 113 years ago, the boxlock has been used for every type of double-barreled arm imaginable, from knockabout 410s to 600 Nitro Express double rifles and everything in between. Gunmakers have adapted the boxlock to fit in with their ideas of quality, or their systems of mass production, but, strangely, none has taken it on himself to perfect this excellent action.

The improvements the boxlock needs to bring it to par with its more prestigious cousin, the sidelock, are few and, from a manufacturing point of view, easy to implement and inexpensive. At the same time, these improvements would do a lot to counteract much of the criticism that has been leveled at the boxlock over the years.

Some of the bad press the boxlock has received is technically valid, some is misinformed, while a major part is due to fashion. From its very inception the boxlock faced problems of status. It was patented in Birmingham in 1875 by Messrs. Anson and Deeley, both employees of the famous gunmaker Westley Richards. This was a time of great strides forward in gunmaking and the boxlock was certainly a stride forward. It provided a self-cocking action containing only five major parts per side. These parts were housed in recesses within the action body itself, making the boxlock what today's engineers would call an integrated design. What is more it could be easily built using then-perfected machine tools like milling machines and slotters, and it required less handwork than other actions. All this, however, happened in Birmingham when gunmaking pres-

Contrast this good quality Belgian boxlock with the Hollis. The fences of this gun are flat; the topstrap has none of the flowing sweep of the English gun and note the lines of the action sides and the stock which have been borrowed unquestioningly from the sidelock. (Photo by the author)

tige was epitomized by the words "London best quality sidelock."

Having started with the hammer gun, the process of developing the sidelock was a gradual one. First the hammers were moved to the inside of the locks and were renamed tumblers. Self-cocking and ejection mechanisms were added and eventually the ultimate in luxury, the self-opening mechanisms that removed all effort of opening the gun. It was, of course, up to a gentleman's loader to close it. The process was gradual and understandable, an important consideration in the gun trade where buying tastes are conservative. The average buyer in

very hard indeed. These criticisms were reflected by other writers of the times and are still valid today.

Of course, the criticisms did not prevent many gunmakers from making and selling boxlocks, some of superlative quality. Greener made a modified version of the boxlock which he had no trouble promoting. Greener was never at a loss for words when plugging his guns. He countered the claim of the boxlock's weakness by installing his famous Greener top extension. Westley Richards also made boxlocks. The highest quality of their guns remain to this day some of the most beautiful guns ever built, and they incorporated

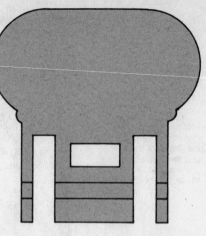

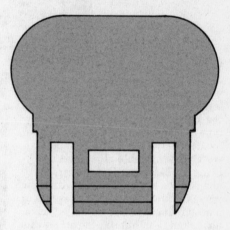

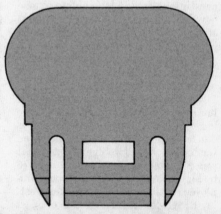

Cheap and nasty! This boxlock suffered from everything: bad design, second-rate material and faulty heat-treatment. It took only one baby magnum shell to break it in half. Note the wedge-shaped bar of the action, the slab-sided design and the flat fence. (Photo by the author)

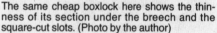

The same cheap boxlock here shows the thinness of its section under the breech and the square-cut slots. (Photo by the author)

The action of the boxlock can be as simple as this Greener action, composed of only three main parts—mainspring, tumbler (hammer), and sear. (Photo by the author)

Top: Section of typical cheap boxlock, this design offers 400 square millimeters of steel at the foot of the standing breech to resist the forces generated during firing. Middle: Design changes proposed by the late Gough Thomas increase the area of steel at the foot of the standing breech to 440 millimeters, an increase of 10 percent over the cheap gun, while the weight of the action actually drops by a small amount. Bottom: Design change proposed by author increases area of section under the breech to 508 square millimeters and incorporates rounded section and narrower action slots which further resist bending. The weight of the action remains the same as the cheap gun, the saving coming through the action being shallower by 4 millimeters. (Diagrams by the author)

detachable locks and single triggers. Even Burrard conceded that these guns deserved the title, "best."

However, this was a time when patents still applied and each maker was anxious to project originality and inventiveness. Witness the various reminders of the time: Greener's triple wedge fast, facile principe, Westley Richards patent, et al. The jealous guarding of patents was another factor that prevented the appearance of a perfected boxlock because no single maker could obtain the patents to all those ancillaries—e.g. a simple and reliable ejector mechanism—that could permit building a really fine boxlock.

When the patents had lapsed, around the beginning of our century, the lines had been firmly drawn. The sidelock was the best gun, the boxlock the poor relation. As one English book said, the sidelock is the "Rolls Royce of the shooting field with everything that this implies." The gunmakers who did enter the manufacture of boxlocks at this point were the Continental makers. They were not interested in making best guns, just in making many of them.

The boxlock was modified by the mass producers, not to make it better, but to make it easier and faster to make. The major modifications of the mass-produced boxlock were the abolition of the split bottom plate, so that the bottom plate incorporated the trigger plate as well—a nifty idea for cutting down machine time. Another modification was the wedge-shaped action body. Shallower at the front than the rear, it both eased machine manufacture and gave the boxlock a straight, angular look. These and several other touches applied by the hundreds of Spanish, Belgian and Italian makers combined to confirm the boxlock as the mass-producible cheap action.

On the other hand, the traditional makers of best boxlocks stuck to their designs in their entirety. Westley Richards to this day insists on installing their famous doll's head top extension and W. and C. Scott on making boxlocks with hinge pins machined from the solid. The first makes loading the gun unnecessarily difficult while the latter makes repair of a loosened shotgun a gunsmithing nightmare.

The amazing thing is that not a single gunmaker has seen his way to incorporate all those features and improvements that would perfect this venerable action and make it a real challenger to the sidelock. Today, there are no patent fetters to stop any maker from doing this; neither is the cost prohibitive since all the improvements can be easily incorporated during the machining stage. What's more, most of the needed improvements are known and have been used individually by some makers. All that's missing is the new, perfected boxlock.

Gough Thomas, the late gun editor of the UK's *Shooting Times*, was the first to perceive this situation and attributed it to mental inertia. He accused gunmakers of blindly following the sidelock as a guide to external shape while forgetting the inherent possibilities of the boxlock. In Thomas' opinion, the average gunmaker seems to feel that in order to sell boxlocks he must blindly imitate the external shape of the sidelock. So we get boxlocks with dummy sideplates that pretend to be sidelocks. When there are no dummy plates, the rear portion of the action bar is shaped like that of the sidelock and often the stock is made with panels and points as if it were intended to house the non-existent locks.

The alternative, Thomas believed, was to let function dictate the form. Let the boxlock be what it is, and it will gain beauty and elegance without any help from the sidelock. The guide to external shape, he said, should be the Dickson Round Action gun which "in terms of sheer thoroughbred lines yields nothing, nothing whatsoever, to the finest sidelock ever built."

Thomas' prescription for elegance was to make the bar of the action wider at the foot of the standing breech. This will leave more metal at the point of maximum stress and thus strengthen the gun. The bar should then be rounded, as in most Westley Richards guns, giving a pleasing rounded shape. Having achieved this rounded shape, the stock should blend with it by sweeping up to the metal with no flat areas.

The prescription certainly works. Whereas the normal action bar of a typical European boxlock is 38mm wide at the breech, one built to Thomas' specification is over 40mm. While the bar is widened, it is also shallower so that it gains in strength but not in weight.

The perfecting process, however, can go further. There is one more area under the standing breech that can provide more metal without too much trouble for the manufacturer. The slots in which the lock parts of the boxlock are housed are normally cut with a flat-nosed milling cutter. These slots are usually 6mm wide.

The way to do it here is by cutting a narrower slot using a round cutter at the part of the slot which is directly under the standing breech, the weakest part of the bar. The lock parts will then be made just 4mm thick which is ample as proven by the parts of the Westley Richards detachable-lock model. In addition, the round cutter used under the standing breech will allow more metal still to be left at this critical point and that metal will be shaped for strength, since a round section is much more resistant to bending than a square one. An external bolster can also be used to add even more strength.

If we contrast the present mass-produced boxlock with what is proposed here, it becomes evident that the proposed model has 25 percent more metal where it will do most work and that metal will be shaped to best advantage. Naturally, the top part of the tumbler (hammer) will have to be rounded to conform to the shape of the rounded slot but the alteration involved is not complicated and should not add more than a few cents to the cost of a medium-priced gun.

The additional strength derived from these simple machining stage alterations should do away with that abomination, the top extension. Top extensions make loading and unloading difficult; they make rebarreling difficult because they stand in the way during the fitting of the barrels to the face; and, most important, they do not allow the use of full-sized extractors. If you have ever had an extractor ride over the rim of a stuck cartridge you will appreciate the superiority of a full extractor.

But won't the new boxlock be heavier? The answer is "No," and it ties in with that other major element of side-by-side design, elegance. Elegance is usually treated as something which is beyond the mundane world of weights and measures, something undefinable. It isn't, really. The cheap mass-produced boxlock has no elegance because the manufacturer chose those lines of form that make his life easier. The topstrap in such a gun is absolutely straight. The action bar has a gradual taper, thickening toward the back where it meets the stock. Mass-produced actions have a depth of 23mm in the front deepening to 27mm under the standing breech. The bottom plate of the action is usually made in one piece incorporating the bottom and trigger plates. The unit bottom plate and the shape of the action bar dictate that the stock will meet the action at an angle. All these things are plain to the naked eye.

Now, let's take a look at the profile of an elegant boxlock. The action bar is the same depth throughout—23mm in the front, 23 in the back. The gun

Fully machined monoblock of a French Robust ready to receive the barrel tubes. The monoblock holds the tubes both by friction and the chemical bonding of the low melting point solder, unlike other barrel-making methods that rely on high temperature brazing. (Photo Marcos Xenakis)

Top of the line French Robust shotgun has split bottom plate, a feature that allows easy maintenance of the action parts. (Photo Marcos Xenakis)

has a split bottom plate, and its trigger plate is a straight line extension of the action. The stock curves down from a point behind the trigger guard and, naturally, the topstrap reflects this curve. Thus the metal that is saved by not making the action deeper is used to make it stronger, and more elegant.

This type of elegance should not cost more than the mass-produced wedge. The Spanish maker AyA incorporates a split bottom plate and some of the other features described here even in its cheapest boxlock costing a few hundred dollars. Going a few steps further in shaping the action can make it still prettier. The fences, those hemi-spherical projections that abut the barrel breeches, are a major point in the elegance of a gun. The tendency today is to go for a flat-topped fence, the Webley fence as it is called, because it is easier to shape and easier to polish by machine. It is also a lot less attractive than the ball-type fences used by Westley Richards and the Dickson Round Action. Farther back, the topstrap has its part to contribute to the elegance of a gun and again the same two makers seem to have hit the most elegant shape. A low top-lever complements the effect. The meeting of wood to metal is usually shaped in what is known as a scallop shape, but a straight line is not a bad idea either. And while on the subject of stocks, it is worth mentioning that the stock bolt is a much more practical way of securing the stock than the traditional and tricky stock screws through the grip.

Most guns have a removable hinge or cross-pin, the bolt onto which the barrels of a double shotgun hook. Some, like the Webley & Scott and the Westley Richards have cross-pins machined from the solid; that is to say, they can never be removed from the action. One gunsmith has called this a "manufacturing aberration." Considering he has retightened and rebarreled a few hundred of these guns, his opinion is worth noting. The normal way of tightening a shotgun that has shot loose—and the easiest—is by fitting a pin of larger diameter and refitting the barrels to the breech face. With solid pins this cannot be done; instead the barrel hook must be built up by welding, or soldering of shims, and a lot of intuition used in recutting the new radius. Rebarreling is not much fun either. A perfected boxlock, therefore, must have a removable cross-pin to provide for inevitable rebarreling and retightening.

That brings us to the barrels, the gun's engine rooms. For best guns, the traditional choice of barrels is chopper lump, called *demibloc* by the Continentals. In this system, the barrels are forged in one piece with the lumps and then the two barrels are brazed together. The proponents of chopper lump barrels claim their system is stronger because the lumps are in one piece with the barrels. However, the two barrels are brazed together and brazing is carried out at temperatures close to those that alter the structure of steel. Such barrels are bonded by a very thin layer of braze. Also at some point they might have to be repaired. The most common repair for chopper lump barrels is the sleeving method where the barrels are cut off just ahead

of the end of the chambers and new barrel tubes inserted into the bored-out breeches. It is easy to see that sleeved barrels are made up of a total of four pieces.

The other major method of barrel construction is the monoblock. Here a forged piece is machined to form the lumps, the barrel flats and the external shape of the breech end of the barrels. The barrels are then inserted into the monoblock and held there by friction and by low-melting-point solder. Note that the monoblock holds the barrels in place mechanically and chemically. The method is not used in best English guns; it is, however, used in the best Beretta and Perazzi trap and field guns and few guns have to take the pounding of trap guns. Rebarreling a monoblock gun is a fairly simple affair of knocking out the tubes and refitting new ones in their place.

But the reason for choosing monoblock is a more subtle one than strength and ease of repair. One of the great pleasures of best guns is their breathtaking balance. Handle one and you know it is a thing of quality; it literally feels alive. It has long been thought this balance comes about only through handwork. When a best gun is in the finishing stage, the barrel filer takes off metal from the last third or so of the barrels, where the pressures generated by the shell have fallen to manageable levels. Note that the barrel filer works on barrels that have already been joined, hence he takes metal away from the outside of the tubes only.

Assuming that the buyer of the perfected boxlock is happy to keep within the loads suitable to the weight of his gun, this breathtaking balance can be

The bottom rib on shotgun barrels does nothing to aid in holding the two barrels together and does not aid in pointing. Some makers abolished it long ago; this French Charlin has no bottom rib, its excellent handling resulting from the reduced weight up front. (Photo by the author)

incorporated into a mass-produced gun through the use of modern automated lathes and computers. The first requirement is to obtain the pressure curve of the intended loads, let us say field loads with an ounce or a little more of shot. We also obtain the elastic strength characteristics of our barrel steel and feed these into a computer so that we get a full table of minimum barrel thickness at any point along the length of the barrel. It is then a simple job to turn the barrel tubes on modern computer-controlled lathes so that they will have no more metal than absolutely necessary for safety. Needless to say this process can only be carried out if we use the monoblock process; you can't chuck *demibloc* barrels into a lathe. The barrels, when assembled, will be light and of equal thickness at any point of their circumference.

The technology for this end exists today and is being used by Ruger. The reason it has not yielded barrels of decent balance is because the policy of most makers is to offer barrels thick enough to stand any shell the buyer is likely to shove into his gun. Balance

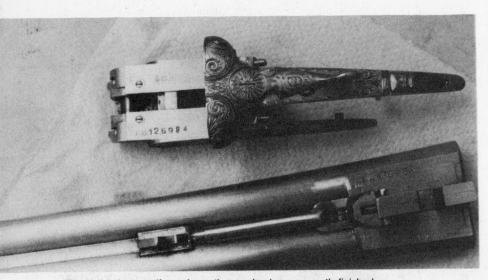

The Holland-type self-opening action mechanism on a partly finished Spanish sidelock. There is nothing to prevent this system from being installed on a boxlock. (Photo by the author)

has been sacrificed to reduce liability.

Ribs are another area that bear improvement. Traditionally, double shotguns have two ribs, top and bottom, held in place by solder. Soldering them in place is a tricky job and usually one of the first things to fail in service. The French have adopted some novel solutions on ribs that tend to point the right way. The famed Darne shotgun, for instance, has done away with the bottom rib on some models. That's a good idea when you consider that the bottom rib does not aid sighting, it adds dead weight, and it makes the space between the barrels inaccessible and prone to rust. Another French

the same time makes the trigger pull and travel less crisp than in a well-tuned sidelock. Much has been made of this facet of the boxlock design, and it should be stressed that boxlock trigger pulls can be regulated by competent gunsmiths to give the desired pull weights of 4 and 4.5 pounds. Correspondingly, there are sidelocks that are real dogs in this area.

Because the boxlock is less likely to go off accidentally, it does not have intercepting safeties—devices that catch

sor so that he can install a new mainspring, in case one breaks in some remote spot away from gunsmiths, along with the two prefitted springs marked clearly "left" and "right."

Here is the place to clarify one misconception regarding the boxlock. It is often said, by people who should know better, that the sidelock is the better gun because it "has two separate firing

The king of double guns, the Dickson Round Action is NOT a boxlock or a sidelock. Its thoroughbred lines, however, can be the starting point for a pretty and affordable boxlock. (Photo Geoffrey Boothroyd)

gun, the Ideal, has a solid "I"-section rib that combines top and bottom rib in one; it is easy to solder, but still has the weight problem. An improvement would be to abolish the bottom rib and make the top rib screw detachable. The adoption of the monoblock allows this. The rib can be screwed from the underside at the monoblock, the loop and then by the front sight. Thus the shooter can have almost instant choice of ribs: concave, flat, raised, or no rib at all.

Turning to the lockwork, there are three main considerations—safety, efficiency and trigger pull. Because of the nature of the design, the boxlock is unlikely to fire if dropped. The arrangement of tumbler and sear is such that during the let-off, the mainspring has to be compressed somewhat before the tumbler falls, a factor that makes accidental discharge unlikely but at

the hammer in case it falls without the trigger having been pulled. Putting these into a boxlock is no problem and some makes did incorporate them, notably the Charles Daly Prussian and the Churchill with the Smith action. Since we are talking about a perfected boxlock design, it might as well incorporate intercepting safeties. It is also easy to make the boxlock into a rebounding action by fitting it with inertia-type firing pins like the Colt Model 1911 pistol.

One touch of traditional class in shotguns has been the use of detachable locks. Among boxlocks these are found in best quality Westley Richards guns and lately in a Famars double. The problem with detachable locks is that they tend to get lost and stolen. They also prevent the use of intercepting safeties. Far better to provide the owner with a decent spring compres-

mechanisms." That is exactly what the boxlock has, two totally separate firing mechanisms and from the reliability point of view they are far less likely to go wrong than the intricate sidelock with its 19 parts per lock.

And now for the optional extras that will make the boxlock absolutely first class: self-opening and selective ejection. The Holland-type self-opening mechanism is a simple device that can be fitted to any double gun that breaks open. No maker has thought to install it on a boxlock gun even though this presents no apparent mechanical problem, which tends to corroborate Thomas' accusation of mental inertia. Selective ejection has been offered on a Miroku gun, and a neat little system for it in a side-by-side is described by Gough Thomas. Neither feature is absolutely necessary in any gun, but having gone so far toward perfecting the boxlock why stop short of a couple of small luxuries?

Except for the rounded section under the standing breech and the detachable ribs, all the other improvements mentioned have been used in some guns or have been proposed by authors in the past. It is also apparent these improvements can be accomplished within existing lines of production at no great additional cost. In fact, a couple of the ideas will reduce the cost of manufacture. On a gun retailing at present for $1000 the proposed features would add less than $100. (*This statement might mean $100 additional to the customer, which means the changes must cost the factory about $20, or it might mean $100 to the maker, which would run the total price up to $1400 or $1500. Sorry, but it's so. Editor.*) Considering that they would result in a stronger, safer and prettier gun, it is natural to ask why doesn't some maker adopt them?

This exact question was put to an Italian maker who produces a lot of boxlocks by machine. "Somebody must order a few hundred of these guns to make the changes worthwhile. The problem is that my orders do not come from the public, they come from importers and they do not care that much for exciting specifications" he says.

Would he build just one as a test?

As far as the external features go, yes; the internal changes were too much trouble for just one gun.

The gun was built using stock forgings for all its parts. Nothing had to be made especially for this design. The most troublesome part was the topstrap that had to be filed by hand. In 1982, the gun cost over $1000 including the signed engraving and top class walnut. And that will be another advantage of the perfect boxlock—even if you must resort to custom work, it will cost nowhere near the sidelock of equivalent quality. ●

The author's boxlock built in Italy along the principles discussed here, but, because of existing tooling, without the inside refinements. (Photo by the author)

This British Tolley illustrates the even depth of action which is one of the hallmarks of good boxlock design. (Photo by the author)

Bibliography

Greener, W.W. *The Gun And Its Development*

Burrard, Major Sir Gerald. *The Modern Shotgun*, Vol. I, II and III

Thomas, Gough. *Shooting Facts And Fancies*

Venner, Dominique. *Carabines et Fusils de Chasse*

Boothroyd, Geoffrey. *The Shotgun, History and Development*

STRAIGHT-PULL

by *FINN NIELSEN*

A Brief Overview

*Looking at and shooting the system
we might still use is fun.*

Author Finn Nielsen, a Canadian, may not shoot all his straight-pull rifles, but he shoots as many as he can. He likes them.

RIFLES:

Mannlichers—this is the Model 1889-90 Short Rifle—were early leaders in the straight-pull field.

Straight-pull rifle cartridges, left to right—11mm Mannlicher for 1886, 8x50R for 1888-90 and M95, 8x56R Hungarian for M95, 7.5mm Swiss Model 90/03, 7.5mm Swiss Model 1911, 236 or 6mm Lee Navy.

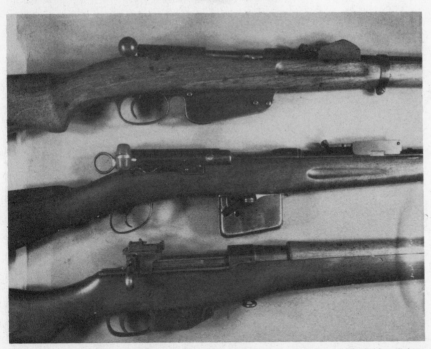

More and less successful military straight-pulls, from the top: Austrian 1886/90 Mannlicher; Swiss 1889 Schmidt-Rubin; Canada's 1910 (MKIII) Ross.

THERE ARE two basic types of bolt-action military rifles in existence. One is the turnbolt; the other, not often seen, is the straight-pull. Primary extraction and unlocking in the turnbolt is accomplished by the direct leverage of the bolt handle being transferred to the bolt and body and its camming surfaces by lifting up on and pulling back on the bolt handle. In the straight-pull, unlocking is accomplished by the conversion of the linear movement, without much leverage, into unlocking and extraction. There is very little camming action taking place during this process of movement. Generally speaking, straight-pull rifles are more complicated mechanically than the various turnbolt actions.

Today, of course, both types of rifles have been largely shelved for military use by the bigger countries. The turnbolt is still around in many configurations for sporting use, while the straight-pull has disappeared from the scene almost entirely. You see the little Browning 22 T-Bolt occasionally, but production is long past for that, too.

But the straight-pull had its run . . .

The country is Austria, and it is the year 1884. Germany has just rearmed its forces with the Model 71/84 turnbolt repeating rifle in 11mm Mauser. The prolific Austrian designer Ferdinand von Mannlicher has just introduced the first straight-pull locked breech bolt-action rifle. This was the Model 1884 chambered for the Austrian M77 11mm cartridge.

This Austrian rifle was unusual. It had a top-mounted, gravity-fed magazine, the first such magazine type for rifles. The design was the forerunner of the top-mounted light machinegun magazine. The rifle was made in limited quantities, but it is important because its bolt-action locking system was also used in the next Mannlicher rifle, the Model 1886 straight-pull.

The 1886 is especially noteworthy because here we see for the first time the use of the Mannlicher en-bloc clip system. The cartridge was still 11mm, but it was slightly modified from the earlier Werndl version. It was a state of the art blackpowder load and pushed a 370-grain paper-patched bullet at velocities between 1440–1600 fps.

To load the M1886 rifle, you first open the action by pulling straight back on the bolt handle. This action wedges the hinged locking block out of its abutment, making it possible to pull the bolt back until it strikes the bolt-stop lug. The loaded clip may now be inserted into the open magazine well. The rhomboid shape of the clip permits it to be loaded into the action in only one way. The upper sides of the clip are grooved so that even in dim light, the procedure can be carried out properly. Push the clip down into the magazine well until it locks in place. The clip lock is at the rear of the magazine well where the catch on the back of the clip can engage it. Pushing forward on the bolt will strip the top-most of the five cartridges into the chamber and the locking block will be forced down into the lock position. The rifle is now ready to fire.

This rifle was standard issue for several years in the Austrian army. When they discontinued its use, many found their way to the far-flung corners of the world. They were used by Italy following World War I, as many went there as part of war reparations. Some were still in use in World War II in three different 8mm chamberings. The M1886 Mannlicher is typical of the period. It is fairly heavy—9¼ pounds without its knife bayonet—and is 52 inches long without the bayonet, with a 31-inch barrel.

These rifles are fairly scarce today, especially in their original 11mm caliber. It is a sturdy, well-made rifle, but as with all military rifles of this vintage, care must be taken when you shoot them. Stick to original loading data if at all possible, and of course, insure that your rifle is in good condition before you do anything. Some of the M1886s were even converted to 8mm Mauser in the '20s for Oriental sales. I would advise extreme caution if you were planning to use surplus 8x57mm in one of those, or even the anemic 8mm Mauser sporting load. They were designed to hold the pressures of a low-intensity cartridge, so you should insure that this is the type of fodder they get.

Let me just digress for a moment. The period of the 1870s to the 1890s was tremendously important in the evolution of the military rifle. Efficient repeating rifles (the Model 71/84 Mauser) had been introduced, causing a small arms race between the nations of Europe. The French had just adopted their M1886 Lebel and, of course, Britain had the Lee system just about ready. The important invention was, of course, smokeless powder (Vieille in France) and the introduction of the jacketed rifle projectile (Rubin in Switzerland). These developments revolutionized small arms technology. The vastly improved ballistics of these new reduced-caliber projectiles, coupled with the absence of

Model 1886 11mm Mannlicher ready to be loaded. Note shape of clip and grooves at top to ensure proper loading. Clip drops out of bottom of magazine when the last round is chambered.

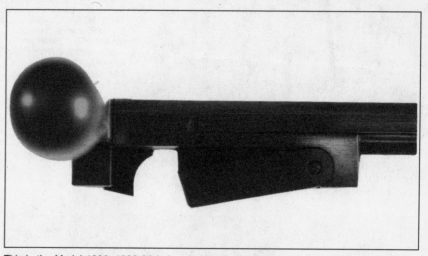

This is the Model 1886, 1888-90 bolt unit. Note how wedge is cammed down to lock. The principle is very similar to the present FN/FAL locking system.

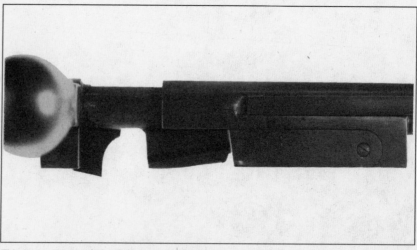

This is the Model 1886, 1888-90 bolt unit with the wedge unlocked. The system could well have been adapted to semi-automatic operation.

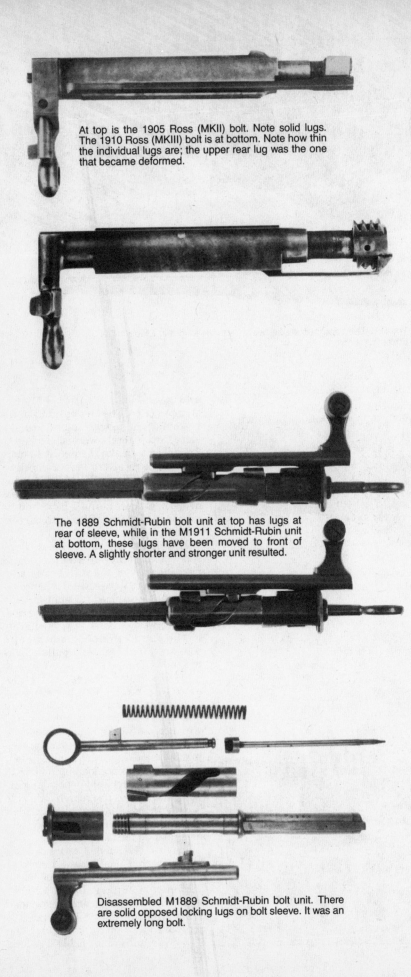

At top is the 1905 Ross (MKII) bolt. Note solid lugs. The 1910 Ross (MKIII) bolt is at bottom. Note how thin the individual lugs are; the upper rear lug was the one that became deformed.

The 1889 Schmidt-Rubin bolt unit at top has lugs at rear of sleeve, while in the M1911 Schmidt-Rubin unit at bottom, these lugs have been moved to front of sleeve. A slightly shorter and stronger unit resulted.

Disassembled M1889 Schmidt-Rubin bolt unit. There are solid opposed locking lugs on bolt sleeve. It was an extremely long bolt.

billowing clouds of powder smoke, greatly affected infantry tactics of the day.

Now, let us get back to Austria. Their version of a jacketed bullet rifle cartridge was the 8x50R. When first adopted, it used a blackpowder charge with a velocity of about 1700 fps. The M1886 rifles converted to handle the round were known as the M1888. This rifle was only used for 2 years, at which time smokeless powder was substituted for the black in the 8mm cartridge. The alteration of the sights to make efficient use of the ballistically improved cartridge also caused the change in the model designation. It became the M1888/90. It's a little-known fact that this rifle was the first modern small caliber rifle to see war use.

Just as today, there were lots of nasty little wars in the 19th century. In 1891, one such war was taking place in Chile. The dictator of Chile had ordered 3500 of these amazing new Austrian rifles. Unhappily, they fell into the hands of his opponents who used them with devastating effect against his troops. The rate of fire coupled with the tremendous range of the new cartridge threw terror into the forces of the government. The use of this new arm completely changed the balance of power in the country after only two successful engagements. There are many thousands of these rifles around today. The same caution applies to firing them as with the M1886.

Mannlicher recognized that the wedge locking system was not the best for these new cartridges. Accordingly, he and his designers soon had a new rifle ready for testing. It had two rotating opposing lugs mounted at the front of the bolt. The magazine system was still the same. Why mess with success? The action was that of a reciprocating bolt actuated by pulling straight back on the bolt handle. It was called the M1895 Mannlicher. It's probably the best known of all Austrian straight-pull rifles, if only because there were so many made.

The M1895 rifles and carbines were produced at arsenals in both Steyr and Budapest. This, of course, was prior to the dissolution of the Austro-Hungarian Empire at the conclusion of World War I. As already mentioned, the rifles were initially manufactured in 8x50R. Later, many were modified by Hungary to take their 8x56R cartridge. At the conclusion of World War I, thousands of M1895s were also given to the new nation of Yugoslavia. These were converted to 8x57mm Mauser. The Mannlicher magazine was changed into a box-type magazine,

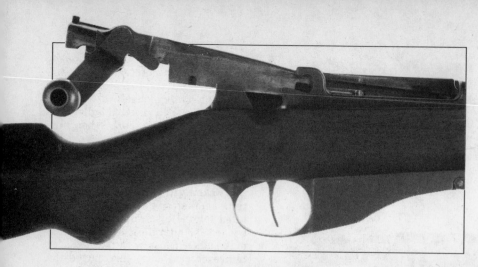

The M1895 Lee Navy action open. Note the large locking area on bolt—the square shoulder below the cam. (Harry Toye collection)

The U.S. Lee straight-pull rifle, which actually fought in China in the Boxer Rebellion.

The Lee closed up tight, operated smoothly, and but for extremely corrosive ammo might have had a long run.

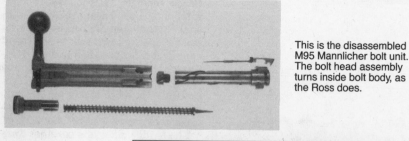

This is the disassembled M95 Mannlicher bolt unit. The bolt head assembly turns inside bolt body, as the Ross does.

This M95 Mannlicher was converted to 8mm Mauser by Yugoslavia. Note similarity of bolt assembly to 1905 Ross (MKII).

and it was loaded with '98 Mauser stripper clips. The clip opening in the bottom of the magazine box was also closed up. Barrels were shortened to 24 inches to make them a little more handy. The receivers were stamped either "STEYR" or "BUDAPEST," and below that marking, "M95M." These are sturdy rifles, and I have had no problems shooting them with current ammunition.

That is pretty well the end of the story of straight-pull rifles as far as Ferdinand von Mannlicher is concerned. There were several other countries that also used straight-pulls of their own design during this period. Let's go west of Austria very slightly to the land of cuckoo clocks and Schmidt-Rubin straight-pulls—Switzerland.

Lt. Col. Rubin was one of the pioneers in cartridge and projectile development. It was largely his work that caused the jacketed military rifle projectile as we know it to be developed. As early as 1883, he was working on a jacketed 7.5mm cartridge, albeit with a blackpowder loading. The 1886 invention of smokeless powder perfected the round. The search for a rifle to put it in ended when Colonel Rudolf Schmidt submitted his Model 1889 straight-pull for testing.

The first version of a series of rifles based on that design was long and clumsy. Chambered for the Model 90 7.5mm cartridge, it had a 12-shot magazine. The magazine was loaded using the uniquely Swiss six-shot cardboard and metal chargers. The M1889 is readily identifiable. The long

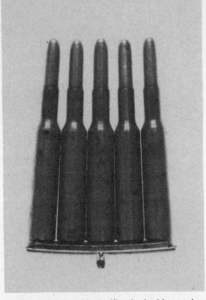

The issue clip for Lee Navy rifle as carried. (Harry Toye collection)

Issue clip for Lee Navy rifle, the locking spring shown in open position.

Issue clip for Lee Navy rifle, disassembled with its retaining spring shown.

magazine, roller coaster rear sight and the bolt/cocking handle of red fiber composition make it unique among this genre of military rifle.

The bolt mechanism of this model is different from any of the other designs. Pulling back on the cocking handle causes a lug connected to it to travel in a helical groove to rotate the bolt assembly, thus unlocking it. The locking lugs are found at the rear of the bolt body giving little support to the head of the cartridge. The bolt is also interesting in that it has to be one of the longest rifle bolts ever—8¾ inches overall.

Despite its length, this is a smooth, trouble-free action. One of the first rifles I ever owned was an M1889 that I had the good fortune to get for $10. It came with one magazine of cartridges, which, after I fired them, were tough to replace.

The initial cartridge which the M89 used was the 7.5mm M90. It had a 210-grain paper-patched bullet coming out at about 2000 fps. The round was upgraded in 1903; the primer was improved and it was designated M90/03. Much later came the spitzer boattail loading which was designated M90/23. I would be cautious in using these spitzers in the old codger. In fact, if you do not roll your own 7.5s, you should not use the current Swiss load in this rifle. It was not designed to handle the higher pressures of the newer loading.

In 1911, the old M89 and improved M89/96 were dropped and a newer version introduced. The position of the locking lugs was changed. They were moved up farther on the bolt body giving added strength. The magazine capacity was reduced to six cartridges, but it used the same clip. Lengthwise, there was no change from the M89. A carbine version was also produced, commonly called the Engineer Model, but also carried by the cavalry and artillery units. The rear sight on the M1911 rifle and carbine was also changed to conform with the improved ballistics of the new round. Again, these are nice rifles, beautifully made and extremely accurate. They are also not hard to find in good condition at fairly reasonable prices. The reason I suspect, as with all of the straight-pulls, is that ammunition is often not available, and the strange action will make most newer collectors and shooters shy away from them.

It should also be mentioned in passing that von Mannlicher did get into Switzerland. From March, 1896, until the end of production in 1905, some 3500 Mannlicher M93 carbines were made for the Swiss cavalry. The action is very similar to the M95 rifle, but the similarity ends there. No Mannlicher magazine was employed; instead a six-round detachable box magazine was added. Loading was as usual with the six-round packet. This carbine is rare. I don't think that I have seen more than half a dozen over the years. Despite the general lack of collector interest in straight-pulls, this little beauty always seems to fetch a big buck when it does emerge at gun shows.

The Swiss soldiered on with the M1911 rifle and carbine for years. In 1931, what was basically a new design came out. This was the Karbiner 31. Amongst the few things this rifle has in common with the others was the ammunition and its firing procedure. The bolt was shortened drastically, with a subsequent reduction in the length of the reloading cycle. The magazine (still six-shot) has been moved back to a position immediately in front of the trigger guard. The fit and finish of the parts is still superb. I wish some sporting rifles were finished half as well as these are. The rear sight is a tangent style akin to the K98. The red fiber bolt knob was changed to aluminum.

The K31 rifle is no longer in general issue in the Swiss army. It may still be found in limited use as the *Scharfschützengewehr 55*, or Sniper rifle 55. It is barely recognizable, having been fitted with a half stock with a pistol grip, bipod, muzzlebrake and a telescopic sight.

Not many K31s have shown up here. Rumors abound that they will shortly be released for sale. Apparently, the Swiss male at the end of his service, which spans most of his adult life, may elect to buy his rifle for a nominal sum. Many apparently did, which makes one wonder how many of the odd half-million made would be available when one considers that they have been in use from '31 to 1957 or '58 at least. A dealer out West did advertise some in 7.62mm NATO for $1000 some time ago. No doubt that would be a nice combination—available ammo coupled with a superbly accurate rifle—but it was a little too rich for me so I keep loading for, and shooting, my old 7.5mm K31.

As with everything else, there are straight-pull successes and straight-pull failures. I think that it may be said fairly that the various Mannlichers and Schmidt-Rubin straight-pull rifles were successful. Now let us look at what might be termed as the "failures."

When one mentions straight-pull rifles, the first name which invariably crops up is Ross. The stories about the Ross rifles and their troubles are familiar to most of us who have the pleasure of owning or shooting them. There is not enough space to go into all the various marks, models and modifications of the Ross rifles, so I will keep it simple.

I have owned and shot a number of Rosses over the years. Since I enjoy military rifles, I believe no military bolt-action collection is complete without a Ross. You have two basic choices to make when it comes to a Ross. Do you want solid lugs or the saw-tooth ones? (Remember, I am keeping it simple.) The solid lugs mean that you have a 1905 (MKII) Ross which were used briefly by the Canadian Army. The saw-tooth lugs mean you have a 1910 (MKIII) Ross which was also used by the Canadian Army under more unhappy circumstances. As far as the Ross is concerned, the 1910 model is the one which gave a not-bad rifle a black eye. The reasons are many.

It is possible to assemble the 1910 bolt so that it can appear to be closed correctly when replaced in the rifle, but, in fact, is not. Firing a rifle with an unlocked bolt is not a recommended practice. The Ross so-managed killed at least one shooter and caused many injuries.

In addition, its record in combat was not distinguished. The delicate mechanism did not stand up well under the muddy conditions found on the Western Front where it made its debut. The narrow bolt-stop tended to deform the edge of the locking lug which butted against it during the reloading cycle. This made the action almost impossible to open. The stories about entrenching tool handles being used to hammer open the action are true. By the time the defect was corrected, the 1910 Ross had its bad reputation and still has it. The lengthy Ross—just over 48 inches—made it very unwieldy in the trenches. Still, it was an accurate rifle and a sniper's version with the Warner-Swasey telescopic sight was in use long after the infantry issue had been withdrawn.

In terms of numbers manufactured, I suppose that it was a success (just over 400,000). The M1910 saw service again in World War II. World War I veterans who stayed home, this time guarding the prisoner-of-war sons of the fathers they had fought, must have felt a twinge of nostalgia or nausea when they were given a M1910 Ross to do it with. The last time we hear of the Ross was in Caracas, Venezuela, in the '50s where the Russians competed in the Running Deer event with heavily modified M1910 Rosses. These rifles had been issued to the White Russians in 1919, captured by the Reds, and finally found their way back across the pond.

I know that the simplified designations will make purists wince, but those who desire to know more can find it in a book on the Ross which came out fairly recently.

The next straight-pull failure belongs to the U.S.A. Yes, that's right, the Lee straight-pull. It was possibly not a failure as such, but merely a rifle which had the misfortune to use a cartridge in most ways ahead of its time.

The only service to adopt the Lee was the U.S. Navy. Their contract called for 10,000 rifles. The maker, Winchester, also had the rights to a sporting version of the military design.

As I said, the 6mm Lee cartridge was really many years ahead of its time. Today, we take small caliber military rifles for granted, but just prior to the Lee's period, there was grave concern over adopting a small-caliber rifle! The Lee's projectile was .244-inch in diameter. The 112-grain bullet traveled in the neighborhood of 2500 fps. This was reasonably fast when the closest competitors were the 30-30 or the 30-40, both moving along at about 2000 fps with heavier bullets. The speed of the Lee coupled with the great sectional density of its projectile made it an effective cartridge.

Mannlicher had covered his inventions with world-wide patents, so copying of his rotary bolt designs was out. James Paris Lee was not a man who needed to plagiarize anybody, and his straight-pull is completely different from all the others.

The bolt of his rifle did not rotate. It was basically a square configuration, and it locked into a recess in the receiver. Unlocking and extracting the cartridge case was accomplished by lifting up and back on the "bolt handle," which was really the handle of a cam which pushed the bolt forward and down to lock, or back and up to unlock.

Although it probably took some getting used to, it was a strong action which operated smoothly. Maintenance of this design was also easier than with the foreign models as there were fewer nooks and crannies for the dirt to gather in. The downfall of the Lee can be attributed only to the inefficient smokeless powder used which did not allow the cartridge to reach its full potential and which burned extremely hot. This quickly caused severe erosion and accuracy soon went by the board.

It is actually surprising that the conservative Navy bought the Lee at all. Perhaps interservice rivalries conspired against using the Krag, or perhaps there were not enough Krags to go around at this early date? At any rate, the small order was not renewed. The Lee was used at the siege of Peking (Beijing?) with no complaints. A number of them were also salvaged from the wreck of the *Maine* in Havana harbor. They were sold off by Bannerman's as surplus, and thus the shooter/collector of some 80 years ago benefited. I was fortunate enough to acquire a Lee at a point in my life when I did not fully realize what I had. It was one of the 1200 sporters made, and it came with a handful of neck-cracked FMJ cartridges in the clips.

The Lee clip is unique. At first glance it looks like the common Mauser-type charger, but it is not. The cartridges are held in place in the clip by a rotating wire clip mounted on its back. The whole is pushed into the magazine which unlocks the back of the clip, and it falls out of the bottom of the magazine. A little different, but it drew no Mannlicher lawsuits either.

The 220 Swift case is based on the 6mm Lee. So, if you are one of the lucky ones who own a Lee with a good bore, military or civilian, ammo can be made for it using the Swift cases. Load .243-inch bullets and take a journey into yesteryear in one of the few ways we are able to.

I must admit one of the reasons I have always had a soft spot for these rifles is that the straight-pulls are really a forgotten weapon system. If the semi-automatic rifle had never been perfected I would wager that there would still be straight-pull rifles in service today, at least in Switzerland.

Consider all the various designs we have discussed. Most of them would only need a method of bleeding gas from the barrel to move the bolt handle and a return spring to make them semi-autos. In fact, old Ferdinand made a few semi-autos on this system way back when. The only thing which denied him success was the crummy smokeless powder of the time. All the other ingredients were there.

And then there's this: when you shut off the gas supply on all of today's self-loaders, you get straight-pulls! ●

IT HAS BEEN more than 15 years since Charter Arms introduced the Standard Model Bulldog 44 Special. This fine gun is equipped with a 3-inch barrel, well designed fixed sights and weighs just 19 ounces. Charter Arms has since added three other 44 Special versions to the Bulldog line. The first was stainless steel. The Target Bulldog came next, with a 4-inch barrel and adjustable target sights. Then came the Bulldog Pug, with 2½-inch barrel, shrouded ejector and non-snagging fixed sights.

These guns have the same double-action mechanism as other Charter Arms revolvers. While factory single-

I have carried a 44 Special Target Bulldog hundreds of times while out hunting and keep one in the house in case I might be hunted. I can think of no weapon that is less obtrusive and more satisfying on the hip or on the dresser.

My immediate family owns two Target Bulldogs, one Standard Bulldog and one Pug. At least seven friends or acquaintances own one or another model. We are all completely satisfied. We have experienced few mechanical problems, and factory response has been more than generous.

I have twin sons, now 16, who began shooting Charter Arms Bulldogs at

age eight. (You should have seen the expression on my mother's face when son Jody said, "Grandma, I shot a Bulldog and it kicked!") My wife really enjoys shooting and I enjoy loading so a lot of 44 Special ammo gets used around here.

We own various other handguns and rifles, but by a wide margin we do more shooting with the Bulldogs than with any other centerfire guns. Part of this is their handiness—they always seem to be around when we are shooting—and part is by design. Since these are the most likely self-defense guns in our houses we all try to stay familiar with them. And finally: They are just

by M. L. McPHERSON

THE 44-CALIBER CHARTER

action trigger release is generally better than average, double-action trigger pull is no better than just tolerable—this reflects the state of the industry. With a little judicious tinkering a component pistolsmith can tune any Charter Arms revolver to achieve a very good double-action trigger pull.

Charter Arms uses a beryllium copper inertial firing pin—supposedly unbreakable—and a transfer bar safety. When the trigger is held to the rear, this transfer bar interposes between the hammer and the firing pin, otherwise the hammer rests on the frame and is held clear of the firing pin. This is a very good passive safety system. The chances of mechanical failure or some exotic circumstance causing or allowing one of these guns to fire inappropriately are very slim. While no safety can ever be entirely perfect this simple system comes close.

Charter Arms has designed a simple cylinder latching system whereby the cylinder is securely latched at both the front and rear, and as a bonus the ejector rod floats. On certain older revolver styles, a bent ejector could tie the gun up and make it impossible to fire. This cannot happen with Charter Arms revolvers. These and other features of the cylinder and lockwork are all very well thought out and combine to insure that these are both reliable and accurate revolvers. It is impressive that Charter Arms has been able to keep prices on these revolvers relatively low.

(Above) Suggested 44 Special loads for Bulldog revolvers. See text. From left: 180-grain Hornady JHP, 1130 fps; 200-grain Hornady JHP, 1050 fps; 200-grain Federal lead HP, 850 fps; 215-grain cast SWC, 775 fps; 240-grain cast SWC, 750 fps.

Now that is a full-size hole. Even empty, the 44 Charter is disconcerting.

Ten shots at 25 yards with a Target Bulldog and the 215-grain SWC produced this group.

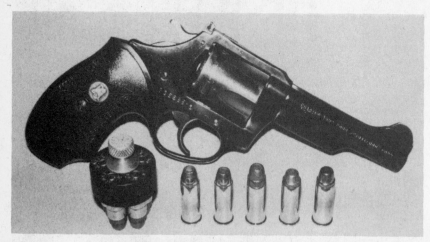

We equip a Charter Target Bulldog with Pachmayr Compac grips and HKS speed loader for all-round use.

plain fun to shoot. The majority of that shooting is of the plinking variety. When a 44 slug hits right under a can, the results are sometimes spectacular. In the desert country where we live,

44-caliber impacts are impressive even out at several hundred yards.

As an example of factory responsiveness, consider what happened with my first Bulldog. I purchased this

three-inch 44 Special new in 1975. Early Bulldogs lacked flame hardening, I was later told, of the recoil shield, that area around the firing pin hole in the frame behind the cartridge head. In 1980, after having fired over 6000 handloads and well over 1000 factory loads this gun developed a major problem. The last 300 rounds fired were old Winchester-Western loads with round head primers from the same lot.

We fired those during the course of an extended plinking session. As we shot, the action of the Bulldog became harder and harder to operate. We suspected fouling, but inspection of the gun revealed the recoil shield had failed and was being peened back into the gun.

I mailed a short letter to Charter Arms, explaining the history of that gun and what had happened to it. Included was a statement that I had fired thousands of handloads through it and that some of those were loaded to near SAAMI maximum 44 Special pressure. I requested an estimate for the cost to repair or replace the frame.

Charter Arms sent me back a letter asking that I return the gun for factory inspection. I did so. Two weeks later I received a new 44 Special Bulldog postpaid and gratis. Included was a letter explaining that a new process had been adopted, whereby the recoil shield was flame-hardened to prevent primer setback damage. They also generously explained that guns firing handloaded ammunition were not covered by warranty.

How could I have been treated more fairly? Sure, the gun failed with factory ammo; but it was six years old and Charter Arms had absolutely no legal obligation.

I am satisfied with Charter Arms quality, though I don't like the finish of barrel interiors. With lead bullets, barrel leading becomes a problem at pressures and velocities where many other guns give no trouble. Evidently, the barrel interior on Charter Arms 44 Specials is comparatively rough, and for the handloader shooting soft cast bullets it is discouraging.

Over the past 15 years, I have done considerable handloading for the Bulldog. I have tried many bullets and more powders than I care to remember. Much early testing was done while looking for a jacketed hollowpoint load that could be expected to give reasonable expansion without causing unreasonable expansion of the shooter's hand. Considerable other experimenting has been done in an attempt to find a low-recoil accurate load for plinking.

Much of this work has centered on 215- and 240-grain cast semi-wadcutter bullets. More on that later.

My first handloads for the Bulldog used high-quality commercial cast 250-grain Keith style SWC bullets and Unique powder. Loaded to about 850 fps, accuracy was exceptional, better than 2-inch five-shot groups at 25 yards. As a matter of fact, this is the best accuracy I've ever achieved with any 44 Special Bulldog.

Recoil was also good. In fact, it was so good I finally gave that load up permanently. I did manage to break the factory wood grip panels in the first 100 of those loads, so I got Pachmayr's excellent Compac grips. If you've never fired a wood-stocked double action that weighs 19 ounces shooting a 250-grain SWC at 850 fps, you probably want to keep it that way.

The Bulldog's heavy recoil could be significantly tamed if substantially lighter bullets were available. Unfortunately, lighter 44 bullets are generally not there. Lyman has recently introduced a wadcutter mould for a bullet of about 180 grains which might be just the ticket for those able and willing to cast their own.

We like Federal 44 Special brass because it has the thickest neck walls. This minimizes the possibility of bullet pull under recoil. Winchester-Western brass is OK. Remington-Peters brass tried early on had thin neck walls. I have no experience with R-P brass manufactured after about 1960.

We have tried many powders while looking for the ideal plinking load. We need uniform ballistics, clean burning, and minimum barrel leading. We tried Bullseye, Unique, Blue Dot and 2400; from Du Pont, we tried IMR-4227, SR-4756, SR-7625. We have also tried Accurate Arms AA-7, Winchester's 231 and Hodgdon HS-6. We have tested most of these with Federal 150, CCI 300 and CCI 350 primers.

One dominating fact led to 231 as the powder of choice for plinking loads with lead bullets in the 44 Special Bulldog. Of all powders tested, 231 is the only one that burns cleanly when loaded to provide the minimum velocity which achieves consistent accuracy. As a secondary consideration, it works perfectly through a powder measure and has been one of the least expensive powders available. It is possible that Accurate Arms #2 would work and be as clean or cleaner than 231. I am happy with 231, and it is unlikely I will ever do any more experimenting in this regard.

Much trial and error testing has lead us to the conclusion that the light-

The large 44 cartridge is particularly easy to handle, which could be a big help in a tense situation. I appreciate it during handloading and shooting sessions.

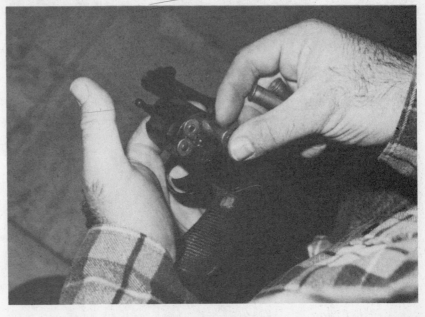

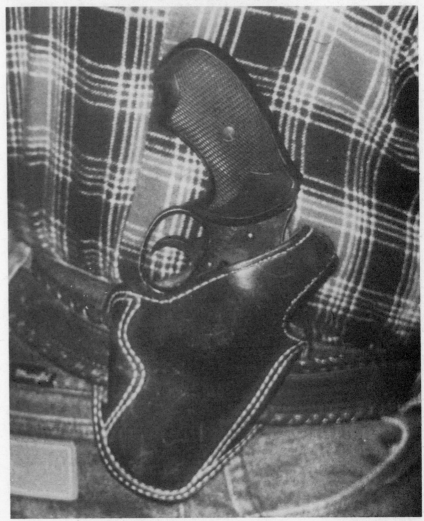

Standard Model Bulldog with Pachmayr Compac grips in handy Bianchi Thumb Break holster—not a great burden.

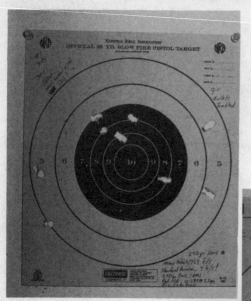

Wishful thinking won't do it. When the velocity falls below its threshold, bullets tumble. This 25-yard group was fired with 240-grain SWC bullets at 764 fps.

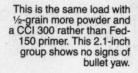

This is the same load with ½-grain more powder and a CCI 300 rather than Fed-150 primer. This 2.1-inch group shows no signs of bullet yaw.

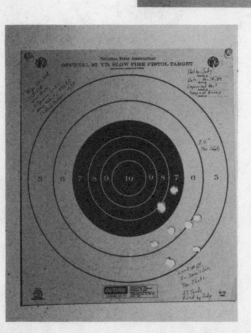

This 3.4-inch 10-shot group was fired at 25 yards with a 215-grain SWC load at 794 fps. This may not be world-class accuracy, but it is impressive for a 20-ounce 44 Special.

est load of 231 which provides consistent 25-yard accuracy in a 3-inch barrel Bulldog with the 215-grain SWC is 5.5 grains; for the 240-grain SWC it's 5.7 grains. Charges may have to be increased a few tenths of a grain for certain guns and for certain specific bullets. For use in the 4-inch Target Bulldog, charges can generally be reduced a few tenths of a grain.

With these loads we were able to achieve 2½-inch 25-yard five-shot off-hand groups in 4-inch Bulldogs. It takes a lot of practice to stay in form, especially with such a short and light gun, and it is always difficult to find time and money to do so. Regardless, it is evident that these guns are capable of fine accuracy.

Because of a slower burning rate, HS-6 gives less *felt* recoil than 231 for most people, when loaded to the same velocity. With cast SWC bullets in the 44 Special, HS-6 usually gives slightly better accuracy than 231. Unfortunately, at the pressure level of light 44 Special target loads HS-6 does not burn cleanly. Unburned powder can lead to a jammed gun during prolonged shooting sessions. For this reason we settled on 231 for all plinking and target loads. With 231 we got the best results with CCI 300 primers. We tried magnum primers with HS-6 in an attempt to clean the load up. No improvement.

As an example of loads tried and frustrations experienced consider what happened a few years ago: I bought a two-pound canister of Accurate Arms #7. I hoped this powder, praised by some for clean burning, might be just the ticket for 44 Special target loads. I loaded 240-grain commercial cast SWC bullets, five each with charges in ½-grain increments starting at about 600 fps and ending at about 750 fps. I loaded each charge weight with both standard and magnum primers.

I started targeting with the lightest charge and the standard primer; this load was very dirty and bullets tumbled. The same charge with the magnum primer was also dirty. Increasing the charge weight produced increasing accuracy and loads with magnum primers seemed to be somewhat cleaner. With the heaviest loads, accuracy went all to pieces. A look at the barrel revealed it had become uniformly plated with bullet metal. Barrel leading is a potential problem with the Bulldog.

Back to 231, this time to stay. I've tried at least ten powders and none work as well. My loads from a Dillon RL550B with 231 in Federal brass and

These are the components needed to make inexpensive—6 cents a shot—ammo for the 44 Special.

This Oehler 35P chronograph measured the ballistic detail of each tested load; the logbook ensures that things learned do not become information lost.

We have had the best results for 44 Bulldog loads using these commercially-available components. When 215-grain SWC bullets can be procured they are preferred because of reduced recoil.

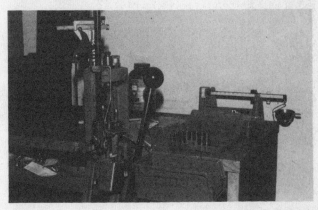

With a good progressive press even an improvised work station is sufficient for volume loading.

Selected Loads for the 44 Special Charter Arms Bulldog Revolver

Bullet Wgt. type	Powder Type	Charge Wt.	C.O.A. Length	Velocity 3"/4"	Impact 25 Yards	Accuracy*	Expansion*	Recoil*	Comments
180 HJHP	HS-6	12.5	1.455"	1065/1115	−4"	B	A	A	Maximum Load
200 HJHP	HS-6	11.5	1.455"	965/1035	0"	B	A	A	Maximum Load
215 SWC	231	5.7	1.350"	750/800	+2"	A	C	B	Hard cast bullet
240 SWC	231	6.0	1.485"	750/800	+7"	B	C	A	Hard cast bullet
Glaser	*****	****	***	***/1410	−14"	D	***	B	10", 25 yard group
200 STHP	*****	****	***	825/875	0"	B	A	B	
200 FLHP	*****	****	***	800/850	0"	A	B	B	Very consistent
200 RLHP	*****	****	***	1030	0"	***	***	***	Factory ballistics
246 LRN	*****	****	***	750/800	+10"	A/B	C	A	Accuracy varies

*Accuracy: A = very good, B = good, C = marginal, D = very poor.
Expansion: A = very good, B = good, C = non-existent.
Recoil: A = Very high, B = high.

The handloads listed in this table were assembled with CCI 300 primers in W-W brass trimmed to 1.147" and weighing 106 grs. If F-C brass are substituted reduce loads 0.2-gr. If Fed 150 or CCI 350 primers are used reduce loads 0.2-gr.

Abbreviations: HJHP Hornady Jacketed Hollow Point, 0.430"; SWC: Commercial Cast Semi-Wadcutter 0.430"; STHP: Winchester Silvertip Hollow Point; FLHP: Federal Lead Hollow Point; RLRN: Remington Lead Hollow Point; LRN: Remington or Winchester Lead Round Nose.

Notes: **1.)** Handloads in this table have been tested with both F-C and W-W brass, see text. **2.)** CCI 300 primers are recommended for these loads, see text. **3.)** High bullet pull is critical to all loads.

Special Note: The listed loads utilizing HS-6 are at or near SAAMI maximum pressure for the 44 Spcl. and should therefore be used with appropriate caution. These tend to put a lot of wear on the gun.

primers shooting 240-grain cast SWC bullets produce a standard deviation averaging 7.3 fps. This is remarkable consistency. What we need for target work is a 0.430-inch 180-grain swaged lead, hollow-base wadcutter. Loaded with such a bullet, one could practice all day with the Bulldog 44 Special without suffering permanent deformation of the physique. Such a load would produce one-half the recoil of a 240-grain load at the same velocity. One could possibly load such a bullet to even lower velocity, while maintaining accuracy, thus reducing recoil even further. In the Bulldog, reducing recoil for practice shooting makes a lot of sense.

In the early years, factory loads offered included the 246-grain lead round-nose by Winchester and a 246-grain lead round-nose by Remington—great selection. Soon after Sierra introduced their .4295-inch 180-grain JHP bullet, I loaded some at 970 fps out of my 3-inch Bulldog. Recoil was tolerable and accuracy was acceptable. Expansion was non-existent. Many recovered from a rocky hard-packed dirt backstop were virtually reusable! Designed for 44 Magnum velocities, that 180-grain Sierra bullet really is hard.

Since it was obvious this bullet would never do for the Bulldog and since several factory loads became available with 200-grain expanding bullets, I gave up the search for an expanding jacketed hollowpoint load for many years. A few years ago, I loaded up a few Hornady 200-grain JHP bullets with 10 grains of HS-6. This load gives 850 fps in the Target Bulldog, and therefore it recoils a little hard but shoots well. I was surprised to note good expansion in test media.

Thrilled, at the prospect of a jacketed hollowpoint load that would expand, I tested loads to 11.5 grains using CCI 300 primers in W-W brass. Velocity is 1050 fps in my Target Bulldog, and this load is certainly near maximum SAAMI pressure. This is an accurate, clean load. Recoil is severe, and I reserve these for serious use only.

I have taken one yearling mule deer buck with this load. This deer was shot at about 50 feet, the bullet centered the second vertebra in his neck and smashed it, penetrating to be trapped by the hide on the off side. Expansion was perfect at .65-inch and retained weight was 192 grains. I cannot imagine better performance.

For those a little more timid, Hornady's new 180-grain jacketed hollowpoint in front of 12.5 grains of HS-6 with Federal 150 primers in W-W brass gives 1130 fps in my Target Bull-

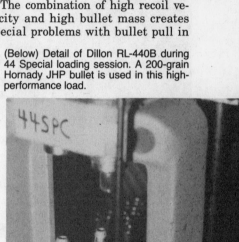

(Above) This is the kind of accuracy potential that every Charter Arms 44 I have ever seen has. Given the proper diet these guns will easily out shoot the average novice.

dog. This load recoils noticeably less than Hornady's 200-grain bullet at 1050 fps.

Compare these ballistics to modern 44 Magnum loads which produce 1350 fps with the 240-grain lead bullet and 357 Magnums at 1235 fps with the 158-grain JHP when fired from 4-inch vented test barrels. Muzzle energy for the 44 Magnum load is 970 foot pounds; for that 357 load, it's 535 foot pounds. Our 180-grain 44 Special load produces 510 foot pounds.

With most 44 Special loads in our

Bulldog revolvers, Federal 150 and CCI 350 primers about 20 fps higher velocity than CCI 300 primers. Loads in Federal brass cases, which weigh near 112 grains average about 20 fps higher velocity than W-W brass, which weigh near 106 grains each.

The combination of high recoil velocity and high bullet mass creates special problems with bullet pull in

(Below) Detail of Dillon RL-440B during 44 Special loading session. A 200-grain Hornady JHP bullet is used in this high-performance load.

Various grips, holsters and other accessories are available for the Charter Arms Bulldog revolvers—they are not orphans.

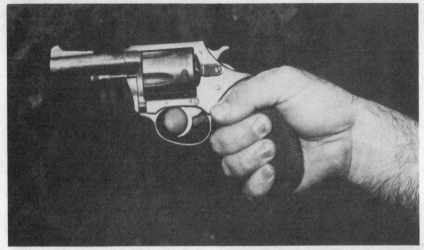

The bluing is almost gone, but not the utility. This comfortable hold with Pachmayr Compac grips keeps the thumb well down from the cylinder latch.

(Below) This is how not to do it. Note position of thumb—a sure way to open a knuckle.

our Bulldogs. A heavy crimp won't do the job. If case neck tension isn't high enough, bullets will pull. This can occur with any brass if too large an expander is used. A pulled bullet can tie the gun up; at best, it impairs accuracy.

In the past 15 years we have tested many bullets and powder combinations. Bullets tried include the Sierra 180-grain JHP, 180-grain and 200-grain Hornady JHP, two different 215-grain commercial cast SWCs, three different 240-grain commercial cast SWCs, 250-grain commercial cast SWC, and a 215-grain home cast SWC from a Lyman mould. This latter bullet is designed for gascheck, but we have used it very successfully sans gascheck, when cast of pure wheel weight metal. Well over 1000 jacketed bullets, over 6000 commercial cast bullets and a five-gallon bucket full of home cast slugs have been consumed by my family. We also tried round ball loads but were not able to get decent 25-yard accuracy.

Through the years, the various Bulldogs I have owned and shot have served me well. Price certainly is right; and where else can you get a 20-ounce five-shot 44 Special? Those limited to factory ammo can now choose from several good 200-grain, expanding bullet loads. I have no experience with Remington's new 200-grain load, but it should be good at a rated 1030 fps.

For those who want maximum power in a handy, lightweight, concealment sort of revolver, the 44 Special Bulldog is about the only show in town. These are fine guns for self-defense use, as a backup for police officers and for use on the trail. While they may not be ideal for informal target work, they can be accurate enough to surprise most shooters. Charter Arms has filled a small but important niche with these handy little revolvers. We're keeping ours. ●

The gun is loaded—any questions? You always know with a Charter.

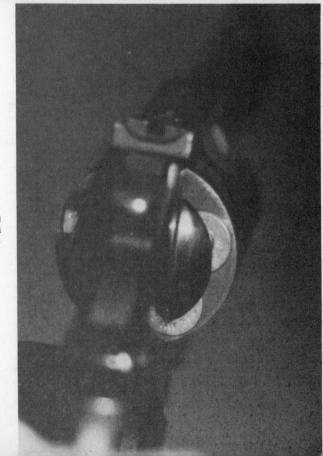

A CLASSIC CALLS HOME

by PEYTON AUTRY

(Top) In the grand manner, this American workmanship proved Autry's 1953 point—made in the U.S.A. ain't bad.

(Above) Severely classic, the Autry 375 offers some British proportioning.

It ALL STARTED about 1950 when I set out to see if I could job out and coordinate the various disciplines of craftsmanship in the U.S. to produce a big game sporting rifle equal to those of the great makers in England such as Holland & Holland, Westley Richards, Jeffery, and Rigby—as well as their special pre-war counterparts in the U.S. such as Griffin & Howe, Hoffman Arms and John Dubiel. At the time I started this project I was a regular correspondent and contributor to GUN DIGEST. John Amber was very interested in the project and asked me to write a feature article which appeared in the 1953 Seventh Edition of GUN DIGEST titled, "What Is A Custom Rifle?"

For several years afterward my old and dear friend the late Emery "Jock" Ellingson of Los Angeles would often visit me in Seattle, never failing to admire the "big gun" as he called it. Jock was in aviation, an official with the Civil Aeronautics Board and later with the Air Transport Association as well as a discerning arms collector. I always referred to him as a "gentleman's gentleman"; he called me "the Last of the Mohicans."

In the late 1950s I sold the handsome rifle to the admiring Jock. They both richly deserved each other. Near the end of his interesting life, the 375 went to his friend Chris Anderson and then to airline pilot Doug Faulkner, both in the southern California area. Later, Blaine Hutchison of El Cajon gave it a good home. Blaine is an enthusiastic collector who treasures it as a classic piece of arms customizing, and he has lately called to tell me the old rifle is alive and well.

A lot of water has gone under the bridge since that article in the 1953 GUN DIGEST, but I believe the conclusions I reached then are still true today. Perhaps even more true today than then. I can do no better than repeat a few lines from those conclusions verbatim:

In order to have a rifle made which was comparable to the finer British magazine models, the selection of American maker or makers was the one task which made or broke the whole job. This selection was based on both happy and disappointing personal experiences, experiences of friends and acquaintances and dozens of correspondents over several years on other jobs. The writer's conclusions are that the best way to build a comparable rifle using the skill of American gun craftsmen is

to select a specialist for each major part of the task. This is a ticklish operation involving much risk, since the entire rifle is not the responsibility of one maker.

The big difference, of course, is that pre-war British sporters were entirely made in one shop by two or three specialists. They were primarily made for use on big game in Africa and India by sportsmen and game controllers. The same one shop specialty or custom gunmaking, reflecting the same tastes practiced by the British, sprung up on a smaller scale in the U.S. in the '20s and '30s. Best known then were Griffin & Howe, Hoffman Arms, and John Dubiel.

In the immediate postwar era in which I began this 375 Magnum project, those makers had gone out of business with the possible exception of Griffin & Howe, whose activity, like the British makers, had diminished considerably over eight years of wartime activity. Here's what we said about that in 1953:

The postwar United States, with a few exceptions, builds the finest

Unadorned at the time, this trap grip cap came from a Rigby rifle.

quantity production sporting and target rifles for the money anywhere. I think that has always been quite generally true. As previously mentioned, the United States has for some time been producing more and more custom rifle makers until at the present time there are almost as many rifles being produced by custom riflemakers or "gunsmiths" as by the arms plants. There are hundreds of these shops throughout the land. The unfortunate truth is that the majority are simply not capable of surpassing a factory rifle by inherent workmanship. However, many of them will equal a factory job in general workmanship. The balance of these custom riflemakers are in the bracket which can and do surpass our own factory arms. Out of this latter bracket there are few who could be depended upon to equal the workmanship of a first quality British or Continental rifle.

The main reason for this proliferation of American custom riflemakers then was the availability of good bolt-action military rifles after the war. A profusion of Model 98 Mausers came into the country after the downfall of Germany and the Axis powers, brought here as souvenirs by GIs and then by surplus importers. The DCM released a large quantity of Springfield 1903s and Enfields when these were obsoleted early in the war by the Garand. Most small post-war American "custom" shops were really sporterizing Mauser 98s, Springfields and Enfields, fitting new stocks, sights, scopes, rechambering, rebarreling, etc. Today, custom makers are fewer and more sophisticated.

By the time I started the 375 project I had collected several high-quality British big game magazine sporters built on Magnum Mauser actions. So— I had a pretty darn good idea of what

I was trying to equal or surpass in an American-made counterpart. In the 1953 GUN DIGEST article I illustrated the comparison with a 404 Jeffery in my collection.

I have never believed in destroying an original collectible rifle for salvage. But in this case I still think I did the right thing. I had a 350 Rigby Magnum Mauser made by John Rigby, London. The action was sound and fully original, but the barrel was badly eroded and the stock badly split in the wrist. That action became the foundation for the project. The first step was the barrel. Let's see what I wrote in the 1953 GUN DIGEST on that:

> First the barrel job was initiated. This was turned over to Joe Pfeifer, well-known California barrel maker. Dimensions of the barrel were specified the same as a Hoffman 300 Magnum owned by the author, except length of 25″ was used instead of 26″. This was designed to give a total weight not less than 9 pounds and not over 9½ pounds. The barrel has 14″ twist (Pfeifer Premium Grade) with tight chamber and headspace.

Pfeifer was selected to do the barrel and chambering because in 1950 he was one of the best barrel makers in the business, aside from the fact that he displayed a knowledgeable appreciation of classic British big game ri-

(Below) The state-of-the-art sighting equipment, even in the heyday of the Lyman Alaskan scope, was still the precision aperture sight for many.

(Above) This buttplate was another item from the original Rigby rifle.

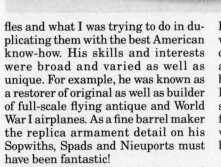

fles and what I was trying to do in duplicating them with the best American know-how. His skills and interests were broad and varied as well as unique. For example, he was known as a restorer of original as well as builder of full-scale flying antique and World War I airplanes. As a fine barrel maker the replica armament detail on his Sopwiths, Spads and Nieuports must have been fantastic!

The sights and barrel sling band were installed by W.F. Vickery of

Boise, Idaho. Vickery was not only widely known and respected as a high-caliber craftsman in metal work, but also as a rather prolific author. His book, *Advanced Gunsmithing* published by Samworth in 1940 is a classic. The front sight ramp is from a Jeffery-Farquharson single shot rifle with square top blade instead of the bead on the original sight.

The Lyman 48 micrometer rear sight is the only deviation from the typical British big-bore magazine ri-

Although Autry wanted a sense of Britishness, he wanted an *American* sense of it—therefore, the Lyman 48.

fle. The typical British rear sight is built into a ramp out on the barrel with a series of folding leaf sights regulated for the particular cartridge and a single bullet/powder weight combination. In other words one is stuck with a single bullet weight and a single charge of a given type of powder. If one departs from that, the point of impact will *also depart* from the line of sight!

The British big game magazine rifles were primarily designed for African hunting at short ranges and often at running game. I wanted my 375 sporter for use on North American big game such as elk and Alaskan bear. It is interesting to note that many of the British-style Mauser sporters built as custom rifles in pre-war U.S. were equipped with the classic high-quality Lyman 48 micrometer sight. The Lyman 48 is, or was, also a classic feature of the typical factory-produced American sporter, such as the Winchester Model 54 and Model 70 and the Model 52 (22) sporter, as well as the old Remington Model 30S sporter. Another reason for my using the Lyman 48 rather than the British fixed leaves is I wanted to use both the 270-grain and 300-grain bullet weights in 375 H&H Magnum factory ammo—as well as any handloads I might want to develop myself.

The deluxe grades of British rifles were tastefully engraved by artisans of long experience. I wanted this 375 of mine to be equal or better. I knew that a few excellent American engravers produced fine work in the pre-war years—men such as Rudolph Kornbrath–but in 1950 many had passed on or taken steady jobs doing special assignments for the American arms factories. However, there *were* two engravers of considerable experience and unique skill who had done unsurpassed work for me on earlier projects. These two were Alvin A. White of Attleboro, Massachusetts, and Arnold Greibel of Chicago, Illinois. For this 375 project I selected Alvin White and I'm sure anyone who has ever examined this rifle will attest I did not make a mistake.

I do have a regret. At the time White did the engraving, he said he feared an article showing his engraving in a prestigious publication like GUN DIGEST would deluge him with work he could not handle. My regret is that I did not try harder to persuade him to let me credit his fine work by name in the 1953 GUN DIGEST article. It was fully described and pictured as the high art that it is. I still to this day regret his name was not given in the article. His work stands as outstandingly classic in the history of the arms engravers art. I corrected that error in later articles—as did other writers who fully credited his fine work.

A bolt action does not lend itself to profuse engraving as well as a sidelock shotgun or double rifle or the receiver of a repeating arm. There just isn't that much sizable open area on a bolt action. Still, for a bolt action this 375 Magnum can be described as elaborately engraved. The bolt handle, bolt sleeve, safety, rear sight, receiver ring, barrel, floorplate, trigger guard and trap grip cap are cut with scroll and game scenes. The scene on the barrel just ahead of the receiver shows two rutting bull elk locking racks. That scene came from a painting which appeared as a full page color plate in a 1913 *National Geographic*—which I sent to Alvin White to use as a guide. He reproduced it faithfully in *steel*. The floorplate depicts an Alaskan brown bear confronting a hunter in a background typical of coastal Alaska. That scene was engraved from a pencil sketch I made and provided to Alvin White.

Some may ask "why engrave at all?" I think my reply to that question in 1953 applies today:

It is entirely a matter of taste, having only esthetic value. Yet, on the other hand, a fine rifle well-deserves a good engraving job, if you like engraving. Yet, there is nothing worse than a piece of junk that has been engraved. Engraving is not out of place on a gun for those who feel that a fine sporting weapon is something more than a rough tool which you can double up as a crutch or use to drive tent stakes. A finely finished rifle will stand as much rough use as any rough gun with the same care any rifle deserves. Engraving affects regular use in no way. There is the fellow who asks, "Why engrave it? It won't shoot any better." The late Capt. E. C. Crossman made a classic answer to this well worn remark, "You don't wear a tie to keep your neck warm, do you?"

The stock, of course, is a highly important major component, both from an aesthetic's viewpoint as well as practical successful use. The advantages of the most accurate barrel and chambering job in the world can be completely destroyed by a poorly bedded and inletted stock. Once again let me go back to what I wrote on this project in 1953:

Before the rifle is engraved or blued, it should be stocked in the white. The writer was not able to do this but it will be outlined here in the manner in which it should be done. A really good stocker can do a fine job without marring the metal but it is slow and unnecessary. If the action and barrel are not engraved or finished, the stockmaker is better able to fit and inlet the metal into the wood which is the primary mark of a good stock. The writer was fortunate in obtaining a fine blank of French walnut from Don Hopkins who procured it while in England. The stock was made by Tom Shelhamer, the well-known Michigan stockmaker, to the writer's specifications. These were intended to parallel the lines on British and German Magnum Mausers in the author's (then) collection. The Rigby trap grip cap and trap buttplate were used. The butt contains space for two cartridges and the grip cap will house spare front sight, screws, etc. Tom checkered the grip and forend using a pattern of 24 lines to the inch, which can be used in only the more dense and harder woods. The forend tip is real horn. Tom installed a cross bolt in the stock which he feels is a necessity on a rifle with heavy recoil, to take the thrust into the wood. Tom is an exceptionally good stockmaker and his stocks are fully as good as some of the best foreign stockmakers. His work is the exception in the United States today. He is not a newcomer, having made stocks at the pre-war Niedner Rifle Corp. for a number of years.

Tom Shelhamer passed on some years ago, but his work on rifle stocks remains a legend yet today. In my opinion he was probably the finest stockmaker in America during his practicing period. *All* of his stocks were *rifle* stocks. And they are treasured by knowledgeable collectors today. Tom loved rifles and rifle shooting. He had no use for shotguns from a personal standpoint. There is *one* exception. He did make a simply beautiful stock for a Winchester Model 21 shotgun for his best and most enduring customer, Dr. Russell Smith. Anyone else he would have turned down, even me, for whom he made several stocks as well as being his good friend.

There is even a *slight* exception to that, too. In the spring of 1954 I planned an Alaskan bear hunt on Kodiak and Afognak Islands. I had my heart set on using my 450/400 Jeffery double rifle, but only three months before the trip the stock wrist was completely snapped apart in an auto accident. Tom Shelhamer came to my rescue. Never one to gush or emote even in a distressful situation, "After all," he wrote, "it's *still* a rifle."

I supplied a beautiful Circassian blank which I had gotten from him earlier. He did a beautiful job and had it back to me in time for my hunt in Alaska. This double rifle was made by Francotte for the Jeffery 450/400-3-inch cartridge, and illustrated and described in my article, "The Double Rifle—Are We Missing a Bet?" appearing in the 1956 Tenth Edition of GUN DIGEST.

Tom Shelhamer specialized in stock-

ing and collecting British Farquharson single shots. Many of these were rebarreled to American factory loads as well as wildcat cartridges. He did custom Farquharson stocking for the writer as well as several others. Some of his more prolific Farquharson work was done for Dr. Russell Smith who, as I recall, also lived in Michigan. Another was Lowell Saunders. Still another was Roy W. Chamberlain. William Negley of San Antonio, next to Dr. Smith, probably had more stocks made by Shelhamer than any other man. Still another very avid Farquharson collector who had a number of fine Farquharsons stocked by Tom Shelhamer was Chris Pappas of Chicago, who made many personal visits to Shelhamer's home in Dowagiac,

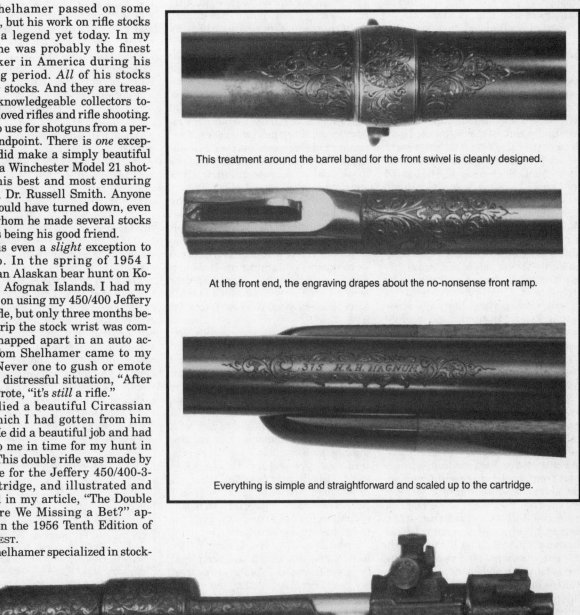

This treatment around the barrel band for the front swivel is cleanly designed.

At the front end, the engraving drapes about the no-nonsense front ramp.

Everything is simple and straightforward and scaled up to the cartridge.

Another thoroughly American touch is the style of the scroll engraving—the coverage is quite full.

Nicely laid out engraving aside, the Shelhamer flat is not often seen this big these days.

Michigan with barreled Farquharson actions needing exhibition stocks.

Many of Shelhamer's customers furnished their own high-grade blanks once the master had approved their use. On the other hand, Tom Shelhamer loved and collected wood like he loved Farquharson single shots. On several occasions he sold me wood as a favor—pure and simple. But I always eventually returned it to be used on a choice rifle project. The aforementioned Francotte double was stocked with a blank Shelhamer had treasured enough to have made a nice hinged wood box for its storage.

Another important aspect of Tom Shelhamer's expertise that may not be so well known was his intimate knowledge of single shot actions on the British Farquharson patent. He owned several himself, but more importantly he probably stocked more varieties of Farquharson actions than any other person. Each of these variations would be in his shop from several months to a year. Of the makers such as Gibbs, Westley Richards, Holland & Holland, Webley & Scott, Jeffery, etc., some had more than one pattern or size.

Shelhamer did stock work on two sizes of Jefferys for me. The first was a huge Jeffery-action complete original rifle in the 450 No. 2 Nitro Express and engraved by Alvin White. The second was the Jeffery medium-size action. I purchased this medium action unused in the white from W.F. Vickery. This action had been brought back from the Jeffery establishment in England many years earlier. I used this action to build a really high grade 257 Roberts single shot varmint rifle. It was barreled and chambered for the rimless Roberts case by A.W. Glaser of Zurich who also fitted barrel sights and a Hensoldt claw mount scope *to the barrel* (so the action was not drilled).

The action and barrel were beautifully engraved by Alvin White and stocked in high-grade European walnut by Shelhamer.

One of the reasons I had this action barreled in Europe was to get the best experience available in making a reliable rimless extractor. For all their expertise back in this time period (30 years ago and earlier) American riflesmiths did not have the years of experience of European makers in making reliable rimless extractors such as those used on European single shots and double rifles.

One of the reasons for this in the early postwar period was that most American riflesmiths worked on bolt actions. Barrel and chamber jobs on single shots like Winchesters, Sharps-Borchardt or Remington-Hepburn were rare, and few of them had ever seen a Farquharson, let alone provide a rimless or belted case extractor for it.

Most of the Shelhamer stocks and Alvin White engraving jobs I had made into custom rifles were described and pictured in various feature articles I wrote in past years for *The American Rifleman, Guns & Ammo, Guns, Guns & Game*, etc. Incidentally, now would be a good time to correct a persistent and common error regarding Shelhamer made by writers, editors and typesetters. His name is *spelled* Shelhamer (one "m"), but it's *pronounced* Shelhammer (two "m's"). He would really appreciate that correction and would surely be good for one of his famous chuckles!

I was asked by GUN DIGEST editor Ken Warner if the 375 had been fired by any of its owners. As I wrote earlier, my good friend Jock Ellingson was its regular visitor and admirer. He referred to it as that "beautiful cannon." Every time I mentioned an upcoming

elk hunt or a planned bear hunt in Alaska he would throw up his arms and wail in mock horror! "You are not taking this work of art into the freezing cold of Idaho or the wet woods of Washington much less ding it all to hell wading the streams and hip deep snow of Kodiak—*are you*?!"

So, it sat in my gun cabinet for a few short years, except for my shooting about a half dozen benchrest targets at 200 yards. These five-shot groups were about four to five inches, which isn't bad considering it was sans scope and had fairly healthy recoil. Thereafter, friend Ellingson became its proud owner, and I'm certain he never fired it or even considered it. I am also told that the other three later owners never fired the rifle. So it is still essentially mint inside and out.

The type of classic custom rifle defined in that 1953 GUN DIGEST article can still be built today. In fact, the disciplines to do it are still available in a new generation of artisans. There are some fine engravers, stockmakers and metalsmiths today. Indeed, there appear to be *more* good ones than there were back in 1953. That's my old rifle's message, I guess, brought over nearly forty years—it can still be done and it's still worth doing. ●

EDITOR'S NOTE

This was and is in every detail a distinguished rifle. Its presentation in these pages nearly forty years ago was immensely important to the craft of the gun in America. Do not think otherwise because you have seen recent work of higher refinement or better execution. This one—with some of its contemporaries—led that parade you are watching.

Ken Warner

Shelhamer laid a flat along the top and fit the metal in it squarely.

Smaller. Slimmer. Safer. Smoother.

The New Compact 9mm's from Smith & Wesson Any Way You Look at Them -- They're Better

You need a comfortably concealable compact 9mm -- but don't want to compromise capacity for size and weight. With the new Smith & Wesson compact models 3913 and 3914, you don't have to. These tough, reliable pistols pack a full eight-plus-one rounds, and are clearly. . .

Smaller than all other major 9mm compacts on the market today -- in short, 9mm power in a .380-sized package.

Slimmer than every other 9mm compact available from slide to grip girth.

Safer than any other make. Our unique three-safety system makes these the safest compacts you can carry.

Smoother than other models. You'll see it in the snag-resistant rounded edges and bobbed hammer -- and in the consistently smooth trigger pull that's ensured by our proprietary trigger pull monitor.

The new compacts from Smith & Wesson. Available in blue or stainless. With the quality -- and exceptionally reliable function -- you expect from a Third Generation pistol. Made in America and protected by our Lifetime Service Policy.

Any way you look at it, these are the compacts you'd expect from the company that always goes the extra mile.

Smith & Wesson
SPRINGFIELD, MASSACHUSETTS 01102

When it comes to building an argument for our 1894, we've got more than enough ammunition.

You see, the Marlin 1894's are chambered for more cartridges than most lever action rifles.

Which is important if you like the idea of using the same ammunition for both a rifle and a handgun.

Our 1894S, for instance, is available in two chamberings, 44 Magnum/44 Special (great for deer), and 45 Long Colt. Then there's the 1894CS. Besides being the perfect companion to the 357 Magnum or 38 Special revolver, it's hard to imagine a faster handling carbine. Or you might consider the nostalgic styling of the 1894CL. Chambered for the ven-

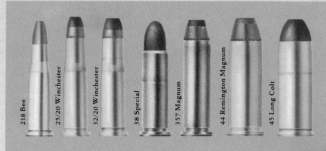

218 Bee   25/20 Winchester   32/20 Winchester   38 Special   357 Magnum   44 Remington Magnum   45 Long Colt

erable 218 Bee, 25/20 and 32/20 cartridges, the 1894CL is perfect for varmints and small to medium size game. With their straight grip stocks and square bolts, all the 1894's have the same look and heft of the original classic we first produced nearly 100 years ago.

Regardless of which 1894 rifle you pick, you can expect to get

Like the ideal rifle of the old west, the 1894's are chambered to be the perfect pistol companions.

solid steel forgings, then heat-treated for even greater strength. And genuine American black walnut stocks, each one individually fitted to its receiver. And our Micro-Groove® rifling, the secret behind Marlin's incredible accuracy.

See the entire line of Marlin 1894's at your favorite gun shop or sporting goods department. Or, for a free catalog, write Marlin Firearms Company, 100 Kenna Drive, North Haven, CT 06473.

A faithful reproduction of a classic original, the 1894CL is chambered for three famous old cartridges. The 218 Bee, the 25/20 and the 32/20.

the same exceptional level of craftsmanship, durability and attention to detail.

Like actions machined from

Marlin®

America's largest riflemaker

1870 120 YEARS OF GUN MAKING 1990

One Good Shot?
One Choice.
THE CONTENDER®

Once in a lifetime Big Horn Sheep taken by Clarence E. Vigre with a T/C Contender chambered for 6mmTCU. Shot in Western Montana at a range of 225 yards.

Let's face it, a whole hunting season can sometimes come down to "one good shot." When that opportunity arises, you need a handgun that is designed to do the job. . .one that handles hard hitting cartridges, with "Minute of Angle" accuracy.

Whether its varmint hunting with flat shooting cartridges like the 223 Rem., or anchoring big game at ranges out to 200 yards with the 7-30 Waters, you need the serious performance that only a Contender can give.

The T/C Contender is chambered for 19 cartridges; from 22 LR to 45/70 Gov't, including a .410 bore shotshell. It can handle conventional big bore handgun cartridges such as the 44 Mag. with the same ease it handles proven deer cartridges like the 30/30 or 35 Rem.

Instant barrel interchangeability allows you to tailor your Contender for a multitude of game by merely selecting the appropriate barrel/caliber combination. And, all T/C Contender barrels are drilled and tapped for easy scope mounting.

From shooting prairie dogs or coyotes in the spring, to knocking down a Whitetail in the fall, the Contender does it all. They don't come any more versatile than that.

160 lb. (dressed weight) Whitetail taken by Bill Aurand in central Pennsylvania. The 10 pt. buck was shot at 55 yds. with a 35 cal. T/C Contender. It scored 140 6/8 B&C points.

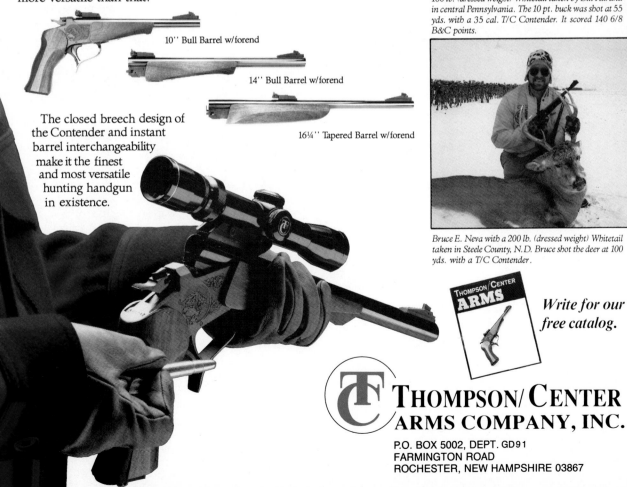

10'' Bull Barrel w/forend

14'' Bull Barrel w/forend

16¼'' Tapered Barrel w/forend

The closed breech design of the Contender and instant barrel interchangeability make it the finest and most versatile hunting handgun in existence.

Bruce E. Neva with a 200 lb. (dressed weight) Whitetail taken in Steele County, N.D. Bruce shot the deer at 100 yds. with a T/C Contender.

Write for our free catalog.

THOMPSON/CENTER
ARMS COMPANY, INC.

P.O. BOX 5002, DEPT. GD91
FARMINGTON ROAD
ROCHESTER, NEW HAMPSHIRE 03867

Expedition of Count Teleki to Lake Rudolf, East Africa 1886

A hunting tradition...

88B Safari .470 Nitro

88B Safari .375 H&H

SR 20 Trophy .270 with octagon barrel

SR 20 Alpine .30-06

SR 20 Classic Sporter (LH) .375 H&H

Express .416 Rigby

For the last 125 years, the firm of **Fredrich Wilhelm Heym** has made quality firearms. Rifles choosen by a select group of sportsmen and adventurers who need dependable firearms of the highest standard. Guns for hunting dangerous game.

Professional hunters prefer double rifles for two reasons: absolute reliability and speed of a second shot. The classic **Heym Model 88** represents the peak of design perfection for a double rifle. The purity and elegance of 19th century styling is wedded to modern engineering innovation. Modified Anson or full sidelock actions, sturdy Purdey-type double unlocking lugs, a Greener crossbolt extension, unbreakable coil springs, custom engraving; these are just a few of the features that go into making the **Heym Model 88** a unique rifle for our time.

Heym Model SR 20 bolt action rifles are made to the same high standard. More than 15 calibers are avaliable, including both standard and European chamberings.

Like every Heym firearm, barrels on **SR 20** rifles are made of special Krupp steel. Boring, honing, and cold-hammer forging on CNC machinery ensure all barrels are produced to exact tolerances. After stringent accuracy testing, rifles are proofhouse stamped by the German government. Actions are machined from a solid block of steel. Stocks for Heym rifles are made of fine walnut, hand checkered and oil finished; a balance of function with grace.

The big bore **Heym Express** is the definitive bolt action rifle designed especially for hunting dangerous game. The enlarged box magazine holds cartridges secure from recoil damage. Double traversal screws and large bedding surfaces in the stock provide the support needed for shooting large calibers. A magnun Mauser action guarantees strength for heavy-hitting cartridges up .500 Nitro.

For an elite class of hunting arms, choose a Heym rifle. Exclusively from Heckler & Koch, Tel. (703) 450-1900.

...you can stake your life on.

THE FIRST MAGNUM

by KEITH R. SCHMIDT

S&W offers the Model 27 in barrel lengths of 4, 6 and 8⅜ inches. Present production has neither recessed cylinders nor pinned barrels.

THE Smith & Wesson factory presented the first 357 Magnum revolver to J. Edgar Hoover, beginning a 50-year marriage between knowledgeable handgun enthusiasts and the large frame Smith & Wesson revolver that lasts today. Hoover's handgun was serial number 45768 but inside the cylinder yoke of this 8¾-inch barreled revolver was stamped No. 1. Each prewar Magnum carried individual registrations. Magnum number two went to Philip B. Sharpe, gunwriter and reloading expert, who worked with Winchester to develop the zippy original Magnum load. And, ZIP it did. Ads claimed 1515 feet per second under test conditions.

During those innocent days before it became fashionable to chamber rifle cartridges in long-barreled handguns, the 357 Magnum held first place for lots of leftover down-range foot pounds of energy. Even the name was new. Previously, the term magnum referred to a large wine bottle holding about two-fifths of a gallon.

Also creative were company advertisements barking: "THE MOST POWERFUL HANDGUN EVER MADE. The S&W Magnum has far greater shocking power than any .38, .44, or .45, ever tested." The new Magnum cost 60 Depression-era dollars which was about $15 above the price of any other S&W handgun made before World War II. Rich and famous handgun enthusiasts quickly filled out orders for the new revolver. Not so rich and famous shooters begged, borrowed or tried to steal one when they weren't busy dreaming about the Magnum

The Practical Pistol Course (PPC) was designed by agency instructors during the 1940s and the large-frame Smith & Wesson Magnum was a familiar sight on ranges. (National Archives photo)

and its previously unheard-of hand-held power. This first Magnum started American handgunners on a continual search for more powerful sidearms to reach farther and hit harder.

In part, the early Magnum's success came because it was a quality product presented to a shooting public beginning to emerge from dollar-scarce Depression days. Offered in any barrel length from 3½ inches to 8¾ inches with personalized registration, the Magnum owner bought power and prestige in his 40-odd ounces of richly blued and specially heat-treated nickel steel. Customers wanted steak for their money and S&W added the sizzle.

Also, the large frame 357 Magnum's development coincided with law enforcement needs. Officers faced well-armed gangs during the 1920s and '30s. Lawmen needed more pistol power to penetrate automobiles. Also, they wanted enough bullet *oomph* left over to perforate bottles of bootleg gin along with the bad guy behind the wheel. To meet this need, S&W first offered the 38/44 Heavy Duty revolver to handle a hot factory-loaded 38 Special cartridge. Also, Colt sold large numbers of the 38 Super Government Model autoloader that gained fame as a hot high-velocity round. However, both fell short of the new Magnum's ballistics.

Possessing the same frame size and other similarities to the 38/44 Heavy Duty revolver, the Magnum sported a distinctive new look. S&W engineers used stronger steel and recessed the cylinder for the powerful Magnum cartridge. A machined topstrap and ribbed barrel improved sighting under harsh light conditions. With the 3½-inch barrel, the Magnum often wore a fast draw ramp front sight developed by Capt. Frank Baughmann of the FBI. Baughmann later became head of the FBI's firearms training program where his pupils became intimately familiar with the large Magnum and other handguns. The Quantico, Virginia, FBI gun vault still retains early large frame Magnums with both 3½- and 5-inch barrel lengths.

Legendary law enforcement Magnum stories impressed. The bullet could rip through the trunk of an escaping felon's car; perforate the driver; then, destroy the engine's cylinder block bringing the auto to a slow clanking halt, they said. More a product of wishful thinking than fact, the new Magnum round did possess power and filled a need for lawmen.

Ed McGivern, the double-action revolver shooting wizard, who could accurately empty a double-action revolver faster than a heartbeat, called the large frame 357 Magnum the perfect lawman's handgun. McGivern owned several. He considered this revolver with Magnum loads effective to a range of 600 yards. Photos from McGivern's *Fast and Fancy Revolver Shooting*, published in 1935, proved a man-sized target at this distance wasn't safe from the Magnum . . . at least with someone like McGivern on the trigger.

"The large frame 357 Magnum that later became the Model 27 revolver in 357 Magnum was the company's top-of-the-line custom-ordered handgun of the 1930s," explains Roy Jinks, S&W historian. "Those early handguns cost a lot for the times, but received a great deal of attention and extra workmanship at the factory."

Early shooters of the Magnum included Major Douglas Wesson who hunted a variety of Wyoming's big critters during the 1930s to prove this handgun had the right stuff. The Magnum soon became a status symbol for the well-heeled sportsman, soldier and adventurer. Ernest Hemingway surreptitiously carried one to Spain when covering that country's Civil War during 1937.

A Magnum with ivory grips initialed GSP with a S&W grip adapter accompanied General George Patton through North Africa and Europe during World War II. Patton called the blued S&W with the 3½-inch barrel his "killing gun." An avid shooting enthusiast, Patton followed the Magnum's development and ordered one of the earliest. The factory shipped a Magnum with registration number 506 on October 18, 1935 to Patton's Fort Shafter duty station in Hawaii. Today, this revolver with its McGivern-style front sight of a large gold bead, assuring fast and accurate night

General Patton's early S&W Magnum wears McGivern gold bead front sights. (Patton Museum of Cavalry & Armor photo)

(Below) The large-frame Magnum offers superior control and durability. Fast repeat shots are easier with this handgun's heavy weight.

shooting, rests on display at the Fort Knox Museum of Cavalry and Armor in Louisville, Kentucky. The revolver shows extensive holster wear on the forward portion of cylinder and barrel. Present condition reveals extensive use, but that the Magnum received loving care.

Prior to World War II, S&W stopped using individual registration numbers, and the war soon halted Magnum production. Many handgun enthusiasts believe this prewar Magnum takes first place as the finest double-action revolver ever made.

After the war, a gun-hungry public happily saw the Magnum's reintroduction. Charlie Askins promoted the handgun and cartridge in a 1950 GUN DIGEST article comparing the Magnum to other handguns by shooting pine boards, paraffin blocks, sandbags, water-filled grapefruit cans, ice blocks and jackrabbits. "Here was truly power," wrote an ecstatic Askins while comparing this handgun's performance to a rifle.

The big Magnum became known as the Model 27 during the 1950s and barrel lengths standardized. This six-gun filled police holsters regularly. Western states in particular armed highway patrols with the Magnum.

"During the late 1950s, law enforce-

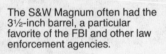

The S&W Magnum often had the 3½-inch barrel, a particular favorite of the FBI and other law enforcement agencies.

(Right and below) The Model 27 with a 5-inch barrel has been very popular with western and rural lawmen who appreciate a longer sighting radius, yet find a 6-inch barrel too cumbersome for the patrol car. They can hit with them, too.

The large-frame Magnum's big cylinder makes speed loading a snap; its action helps double-action use.

An older Model 27 357 Magnum with the 3½-inch barrel remains among my all-time favorite revolvers. From camping trips to my duties with a Texas Sheriff's department, the Magnum remains a proven performer. With many police departments emphasizing training and qualification with full-power Magnum loads, the Model 27 with its recoil soaking weight may find again an increased law enforcement following.

Times change. World wars, small wars, inflation, stock crashes and terrorism. But the 357 cartridge remains with us as an outstanding handgun development and the large Magnum, represented by the Model 27, still comes off the S&W assembly line.

"This handgun remains the 'glamour handgun' of the company," explains historian Jinks. "These days, a typical purchaser of the large frame 357 Magnum has a sense of the past and views a handgun as something much more than utilitarian." ●

(Left and below) Author and his large-frame S&W Magnum with Ajax stocks and an El Paso Saddlery holster and belt with floral carving—owners like to dress up Model 27s.

ment sales of the large magnum slowed," explains Roy Jinks, S&W historian. "In 1954, the Highway Patrolman revolver went into production which offered the same size and action but with a less expensive finish. A year later, the factory produced the Combat Magnum Model 19. With more competition, the more expensive large frame magnum became less popular."

A big handgun, the Model 27 weighs 42 ounces. The smaller Model 19 Combat Magnum weighs 6 ounces less. The weight difference is negligible except for a person who carries it on his hip all day. For the average police officer, carrying a lighter handgun with as much punch made sense.

Present sales figures for the large frame Model 27 357 Magnum rank distant third behind the popular Combat Magnum and more recently introduced L-frame. However, the large frame Magnum remains part of the S&W line due to its combination of handling characteristics, sturdiness with hot loads and its heavy weight. No other presently produced S&W handgun has a more interesting history than the Model 27 Magnum.

During 1986, S&W produced two special commemoratives of the Model 27 Magnum. One special issue celebrated the 50th anniversary of the first 357 Magnum. The other Model 27 honored the F.B.I. Five-inch barrels were standard on both. Presently, S&W offers the Model 27 Magnum as a standard part of their revolver line with barrel length choices of 4, 6 and 8⅜ inches. The company no longer offers the multitude of options available on the Magnum in years past.

The Weapons of
THE MAIL COACH

by WILFRID WARD

SOMEHOW, the Deadwood Stage and the British Mail Coach seem far more widely apart than the forty-odd years which separated them, yet the vehicles and their armaments have a lot in common. Both were horse-drawn, cumbersome and slow in country which was often lonely and bandit-ridden, and so both were tremendously susceptible to attack. The remedy was that of the Common Law, still the same in both countries, namely that a man was entitled to use his weapons to defend himself and his property. Thus, the guard of the Exeter Mail had a blunderbuss and pistols; on the Deadwood Stage they had Colts, Winchesters, and perhaps shotguns. The progress of firearms development increased firepower, but basically the problem was the same. This article tells of the means used to solve it in England when Englishmen were free to use pistols.

In Britain, the concept of a service of coaches running to a timetable had existed for a long time. The King's dispatches had been carried by horsemen since at least 1482, and a service for the public was officially approved during the 17th century, though the royal servants had long carried nonofficial letters "privately." All this traffic was transported by horsemen, and by 1770 the Bristol rider was robbed every week for five weeks. Presumably, these messengers were armed, but the situation had become so bad that devices such as a "robber proof" cart were tried. This was not a success (the keys got lost), and on August 2, 1784, John Palmer demonstrated a mail coach from Bristol to London, one which could outpace the normal passenger stage. It carried the mails and four in-

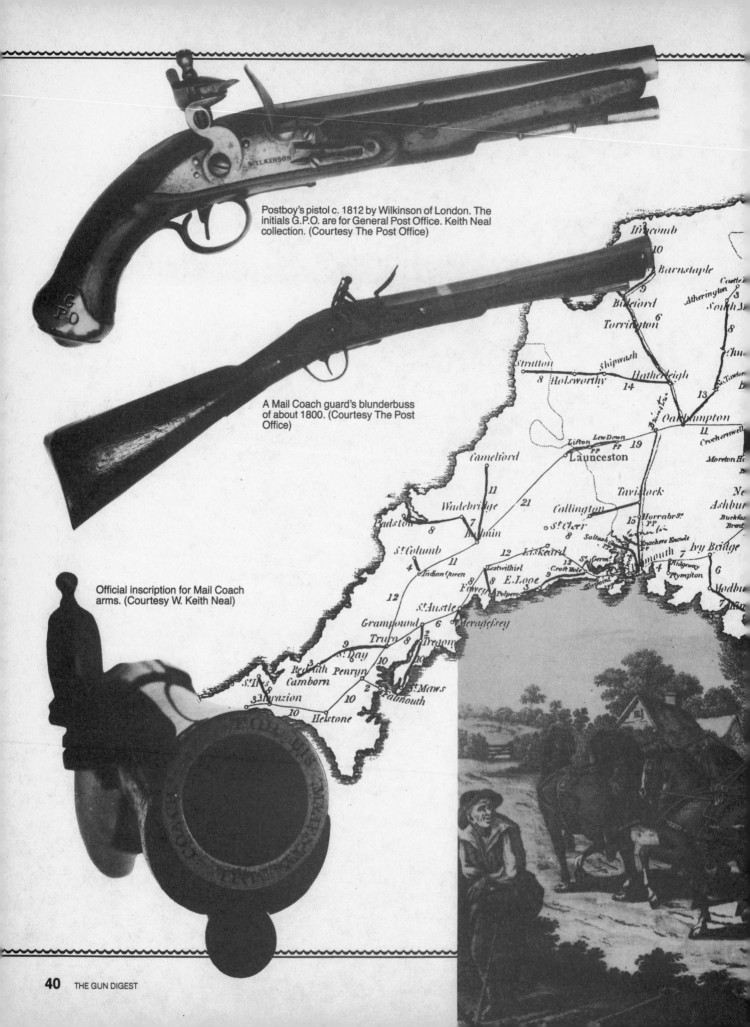

Postboy's pistol c. 1812 by Wilkinson of London. The initials G.P.O. are for General Post Office. Keith Neal collection. (Courtesy The Post Office)

A Mail Coach guard's blunderbuss of about 1800. (Courtesy The Post Office)

Official inscription for Mail Coach arms. (Courtesy W. Keith Neal)

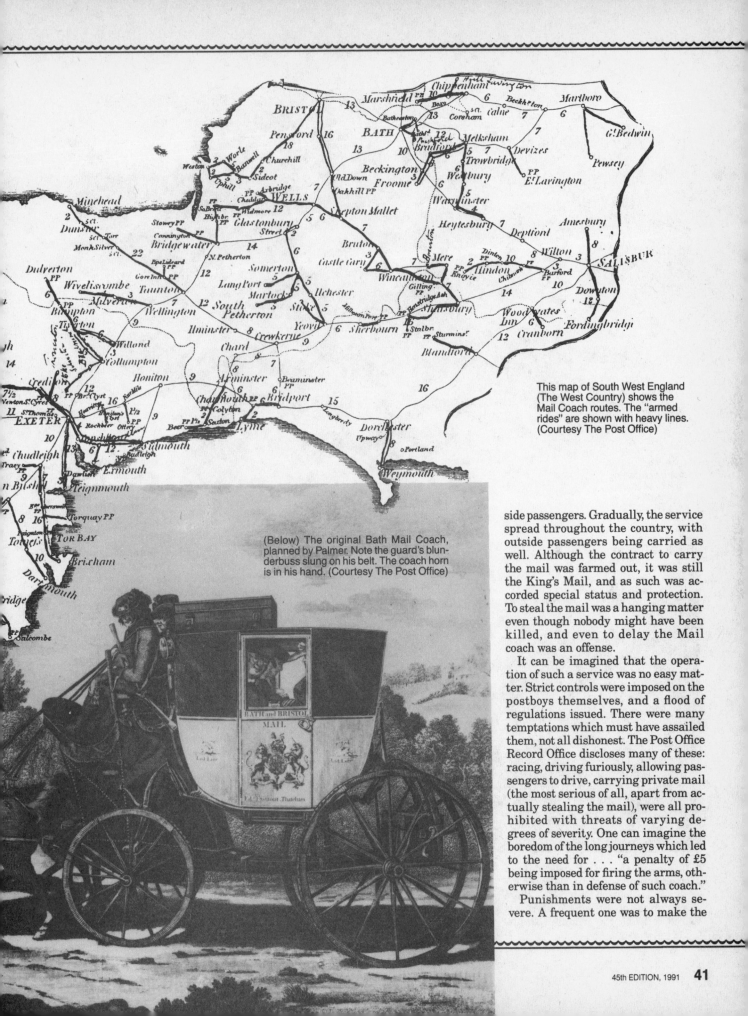

This map of South West England (The West Country) shows the Mail Coach routes. The "armed rides" are shown with heavy lines. (Courtesy The Post Office)

(Below) The original Bath Mail Coach, planned by Palmer. Note the guard's blunderbuss slung on his belt. The coach horn is in his hand. (Courtesy The Post Office)

side passengers. Gradually, the service spread throughout the country, with outside passengers being carried as well. Although the contract to carry the mail was farmed out, it was still the King's Mail, and as such was accorded special status and protection. To steal the mail was a hanging matter even though nobody might have been killed, and even to delay the Mail coach was an offense.

It can be imagined that the operation of such a service was no easy matter. Strict controls were imposed on the postboys themselves, and a flood of regulations issued. There were many temptations which must have assailed them, not all dishonest. The Post Office Record Office discloses many of these: racing, driving furiously, allowing passengers to drive, carrying private mail (the most serious of all, apart from actually stealing the mail), were all prohibited with threats of varying degrees of severity. One can imagine the boredom of the long journeys which led to the need for . . . "a penalty of £5 being imposed for firing the arms, otherwise than in defense of such coach."

Punishments were not always severe. A frequent one was to make the

General Post-Office,

Thursday, 6th December, 1798.

THE Postboy, carrying the Mail from Petworth to Hasle-mere, was stopped at a Place called North Heath, about two miles from Midhurst and six from Haslemere, between Seven and Eight o'Clock last Night, by two Men on Foot, dressed in White Round Frocks; one of them took hold of the Horse and threatened to blow the Boy's Brains out, if he was not quick in unstrapping the Mail.

The Robbers took away the Bags of Letters sent from Arundel, Petworth and Midhurst, of the 5th Instant, for London.

Whoever shall apprehend and convict, or cause to be apprehended and convicted, both, or either of the Persons who committed this Robbery, will be entitled to a Reward of TWO HUNDRED POUNDS, over and above the Reward of FORTY POUNDS for each Person, given by Act of Parliament for apprehending Highwaymen: Or if any Accomplice in the Robbery, or knowing thereof, shall surrender himself, and make Discovery, whereby both, or either of the Persons who committed the same, may be apprehended and brought to Justice, such Discoverer shall be entitled to the said Reward of TWO HUNDRED POUNDS, and will also receive His Majesty's most gracious Pardon.

By Command of the Postmaster-General,

FRANCIS FREELING,
SECRETARY.

SIR,

I HAVE the Honor of the Postmaster General's Commands, to direct you to be very attentive to your Arms, that they are clean, well loaded, and hung handy.

And further, that you do not suffer on any Account whatever, any Person except Superior Officers of this Department of the Post-Office, to ride on your Mail Box, which Mail Box you must never leave unlocked, when the Mail is therein.

If you are ever seen Sleeping while on Duty, you will be dismissed, you will be for disobeying any Part of these Orders.

THOMAS HASKER.

General Post-Office,
March 25th, 1793.

have been all given before; but I have now the Postmaster General to repeat them, r Instructions.

Order to Mail Coach guards reminding them to keep their arms clean and ready, not to allow riding on the Mail box, and never to sleep on duty. (Courtesy The Post Office)

Notice advertising armed robbery on the Mail Coach at Midhurst, Sussex. (Courtesy The Post Office)

(Below) Mail messenger's equipment. The arms are by H.W. Mortimer. (Courtesy The Post Office)

miscreant pay for an advertisement in a local paper in which he confessed his error and apologized for it. When there was an attack on a coach, no effort was spared to bring the criminals to justice, even to the extent of offering a reward and pardon to anyone who would turn King's Evidence and inform on his fellow criminals.

The new system drove the highway-men from the main routes to London to the cross-country roads, and on the former there were far fewer attacks. Nonetheless, such conditions would, one might have thought, have necessitated the arming of each and every Mail coach on every ride. As it was, the rides (a term dating from pre-coach days) were divided into armed and non-armed rides. I illustrate a map of the West of England, and it can be seen that the armed rides (marked with heavy lines) were the exception and not the rule. Although around London the reverse was true, the same applied in most of the country districts.

In those days, traveling of any kind was a notoriously dangerous business, and most but the very timid were likely to have some form of pistol for their self-defense. One of the many stories of Joseph Manton, the gunmaker, relates how on one occasion he was stopped by an armed highwayman when crossing Hounslow Heath near London. Looking at the pistols, he was able to identify them as of his own make. He confronted the highwayman with this, which the latter admitted,

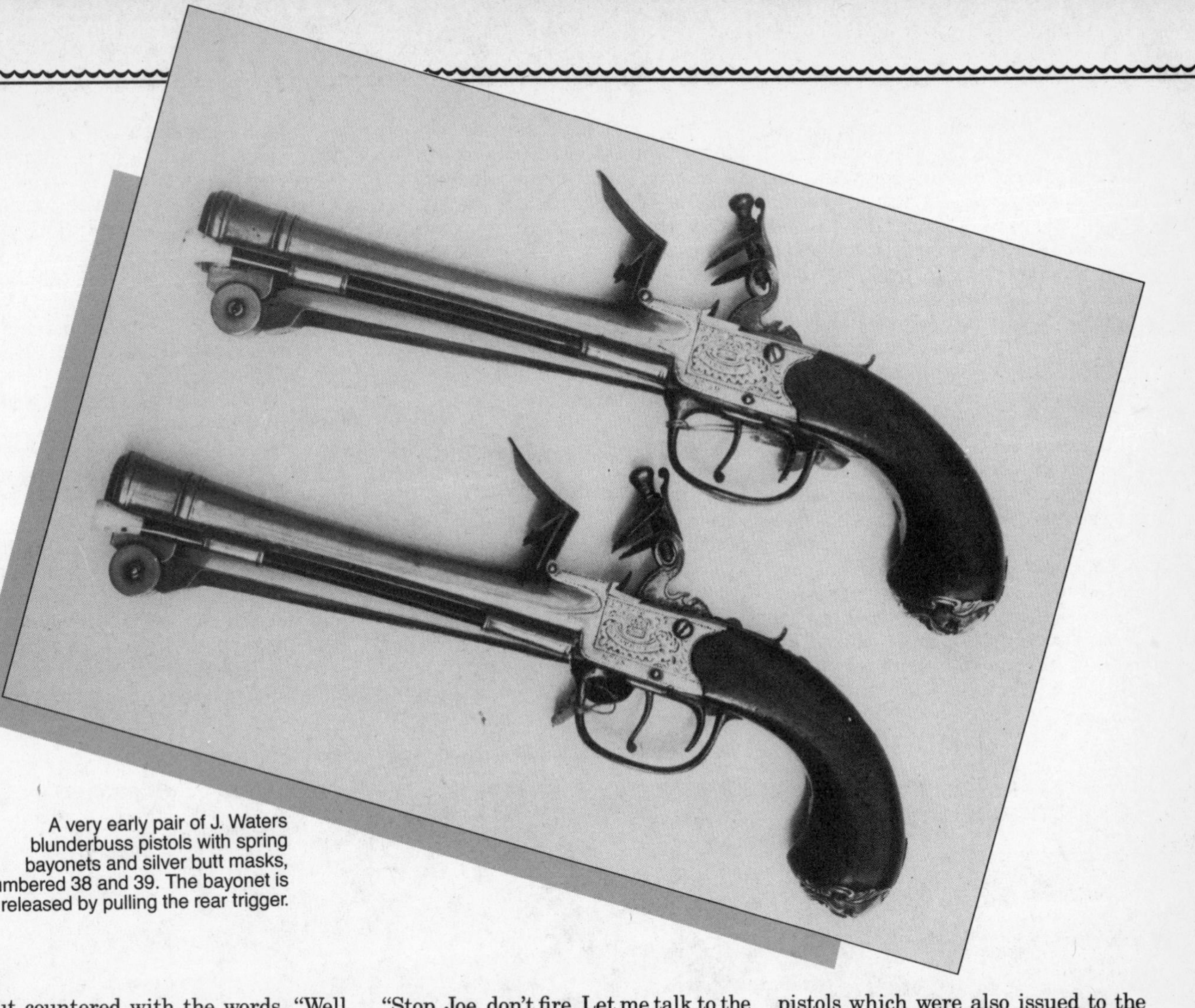

A very early pair of J. Waters blunderbuss pistols with spring bayonets and silver butt masks, numbered 38 and 39. The bayonet is released by pulling the rear trigger.

but countered with the words, "Well, you charged me ten guineas (£10.50) for this brace of pistols, which I call a damned swindle, though I admit they are a good pair of barkers. Now I mean to be quits with you. Hand over ten guineas and I'll let you go because I know you are Joe Manton, though I know you've got at least fifty pounds about you!"

Although Manton paid up, he did so reluctantly, and later made himself a short-barreled gun with only twenty-inch barrels. This he named "The Highwayman's Master." With it, he was supposed to have shot one highwayman, and mortally wounded another. This incident is related in Thormanby's *Kings of the Rod, Rifle and Gun*.

Gronow in his *Reminiscences and Recollections* refers to another occasion when Manton was traveling to Reading to assist Townshend, the Bow Street Runner (an early form of constable) in guarding the coach. Challenged by three footpads, Manton was about to use the gun again, but was restrained by the Runner saying,

"Stop, Joe, don't fire. Let me talk to the gentlemen." At the sound of his voice, the three fled but Townshend was able to identify them, and they were duly transported to Botany Bay. They were lucky on both counts, but probably didn't see it like that at the time.

In another famous incident, the standard weapon of the Mail coach, the coach's own blunderbuss, was used. It took place at an inn called The Pheasant on the night of Sunday, October 20, 1816, at Winterslow Hut near Salisbury in Wiltshire. My picture shows the guard of the Mail coach, Joseph Pike, about to fire at a lioness which had escaped from "the Caravan of an Exhibitor of Wild Beasts." She had flung herself at the offside leader injuring it badly, to the great consternation of inn guests and passengers alike. All but one passenger escaped to the safety of the inn. Though not savaged by the lioness, the experience rendered that one permanently insane. Additions have been made to the inn, but it is still active today, and has a large oil painting of the incident.

Post Office blunderbusses, and the

pistols which were also issued to the guards, seem to have been mostly made first by Henry Nock, and later by James Wilkinson, his son-in-law. They are marked, usually but not invariably, "For His Majesty's Mail Coaches," on the muzzle or the barrel. The pistols had "G.P.O." engraved on the butt caps. Their supply was part of a larger Post Office contract for providing and supplying warlike stores for the Post Office service, including its packet boats. The pistols used were a standard military pattern. A Post Office collection photograph also shows us the satchels, a pair of H.W. Mortimer pistols, a blunderbuss, and the timepiece carried by the early messengers. The Tower of London Collection contains a brass-barreled flintlock blunderbuss and a related brass-barreled pistol, both made by J. Harding of The Borough. The former is marked "1840 No 386" and the latter "1839 No 369." Both are marked "For Her Majesty's Mail Coaches." Not surprisingly, these two very late recruits to the Post Office service are in near perfect condition.

As in all services, the authorities found it difficult to ensure that their men kept their arms in good clean condition and ready for use. Thus, on March 25, 1793, Thomas Hasker had to issue an order reminding staff to "be very attentive to your Arms, that they are clean, well loaded, and hung handy." The penalty for disobeying this order, allowing anyone to ride on the Mail Box, or being seen asleep on duty, was dismissal.

The exact history and performance of the blunderbuss has been the subject of much controversy. In particular, the reason for its belled muzzle is undetermined. Experiments have shown that even using buckshot, the pattern is not noticeably wider than that produced by a shotgun of similar bore. Reasons offered for the belled muzzle vary between a device introduced for ease of loading to a mere method of inspiring fear in the potential victim.

To my mind, both theories have the ring of truth about them. Irrespective of ballistic performances, the sight of a blunderbuss, particularly a civilian one with a bayonet on it, certainly would inspire fear. Likewise, loading on a moving coach or horse cannot have been an easy matter. Vast amounts of nonsense have been written about what was loaded into a blunderbuss. Though old nails and the like may have been used on rare occasions, the proper load was dependent on the bore and would have comprised swan shot.

In his *Antique Firearms* (Doubleday & Co., New York, 1962), Frederick Wilkinson quotes a Post Office instruction of 1816 that eight to twelve pellets should be loaded with a capful of powder. This load approximates that of a fairly large bore shotgun. Although the spread would not have been that of a ducksfoot pistol, at any range at all the combination of a shot charge and

a short barrel must have given reasonable fear of injury to more than one member of a group of miscreants, which is precisely what must have been intended. At a time when only very few of even the very rich had a capacity to discharge more than four shots from a pair of pistols, the blunderbuss anticipated the functions of the Winchester and the Sten gun in the best available fashion. The Mail coach weapons, although they lacked the fine finish of the custom trade, must have been regarded as the best available, because it was with their finely finished counterparts that private carriages were defended.

As early as the days of Griffin, fine coaching carbines had been used for this purpose, and similar weapons continued to be used as long journeys were undertaken by private coach or carriage. The distinction between the Mail coach and the ordinary scheduled

The lioness attacks the Exeter Mail by Pollard describes an actual incident.

THE LIONESS ATTACKING THE HORSE OF THE EXETER MAIL COACH.

coach was an important one, not only because the near sacred Royal Mail was carried, but because the former was much faster and more expensive than the lumbering public coaches. Only by hiring his own postchaise could a traveler reach his destination faster. The Mail coaches were far more valuable prizes on account of both the Mail and the property of the richer passengers, but one interferred with them and their passengers at one's gravest peril.

Though they are not strictly the weapons of the mail coaches, it is worth comparing those of the private traveler with the government issue because the majority of those who could afford private travel by coach or chaise were probably so rich that their weaponry was the best that money could buy. I illustrate an example, which is an iron-barreled blunderbuss without a bayonet, made by the famous dueling

pistol maker Robert Wogdon. It is interesting to note how he has carried his simplicity of style to this different sphere and how, like his dueling pistols, it comes to the aim so well. Such pieces are seldom encountered, and doubtless were made for the richer and more discerning customer. As with volunteer weapons, possible patterns were legion, but Wogdon took his identifiable style with him to this patron's carriage.

Sometimes a set of arms was carried as part of the carriage's equipment. I remember encountering one such set carried in a handcrafted case of finest walnut, which must have survived the destruction of the carriage. Inside were baize-lined compartments for the weapons. Sadly, only the brass-barreled blunderbuss with spring bayonet had survived, albeit in factory new condition. No doubt the other two spaces would have been for pistols, per-

haps blunderbuss pistols, but we will never know any more of them than that they were not a pair, for the recesses were of different shape. For all of that, the whole was a delightful example of the combined cabinet-maker's and gun maker's arts. One cannot pronounce exactly upon the precise nature of the carriage blunderbuss for doubtless many of them doubled as home defense weapons as well. The probabilities are, however, that they were of similar size to the official examples which I illustrate.

In the sphere of pistols, the private trade seems to have diverted from the official type of arm. The Post Office kept to a Service-type pistol, although private customers seemed to prefer a blunderbuss-style pistol. This is surprising, since blunderbuss pistols had been known as long as blunderbusses, specimens existing from the late 16th century. By the period which we are

The Exeter Mail and other coaches at the Gloucester Coffee House in Piccadilly. The guard has his blunderbuss in his hand. (Photo courtesy Ackermann and Co.)

(Above and below) These brass-barreled blunderbuss pistols by Heylin were made about 1780. Typical traveling weapons. (Photo courtesy Sotheby's, London)

The Devonport to London Mail was the only named (The Quicksilver) Mail Coach, and was the fastest long distance coach. By the time of this print (1835), outside passengers were being carried. (Courtesy The Post Office)

(Right, above, opposite page) Wogdon blunderbuss made for either a private coach or home defense. Blunderbusses by the great duelling pistolmaker are very rare.

(Left) This 16-bore coaching carbine with bayonet is by H. Nock, late 18th century. (Photo courtesy Sotheby's)

discussing, blunderbuss pistols had long been popular for house defense, being the speciality of makers such as Heylin.

There was one maker whose product is worthy of special mention, and was without doubt especially suited to the needs of the traveler. In 1781, a Birmingham maker, John Waters, patented an outstanding brass boxlock blunderbuss pistol. He had patented a bayonet for use on pistols or blunderbusses in the name of Waters and Co. in 1776. Slab-sided butts and a spring-loaded bayonet which sprung from beneath the brass belled barrel, released by sliding the trigger guard, marked his cheaper model. The earlier and more expensive version boasted a silver butt mask, and the bayonet was controlled by a back trigger. On both, the ramrod was carried beneath the barrel. Spring-loaded bayonets are a source of danger to both the user and his opponent, as the writer can bear witness. Waters solved this problem, in as far as it could be solved, most competently. The pistols, which are made completely of brass apart from the lockwork, bayonet, and its spring mechanism, are sometimes encountered in pairs. All are numbered on the side of the lock. Both varieties handle extremely well, are rugged and forbidding, and yet have a very high standard of workmanship. The type was often copied in shorter and less attractive form by lesser makers, but

Waters, whose other weapons are also of a consistently well-made and attractive style, outdistanced them all and produced one of the most attractive weapons to be encountered "on the road."

Now that we have looked at the weapons most used on Britain's roads, we must ask ourselves whether, in the circumstances of the times, they were the right ones for the Mail coaches. Those times were rough and tough, but uncomplicated. Moreover, the gun trade had yet to provide more than single, or at most two-shot weapons, either pistols or rifles. It is hard to imagine that the postboys could have put any weapons to better use than they did. As at Waterloo, the British forces were as well armed as their opponents, though their weapons were muzzle-loading flintlocks. Those guarding the Mails were not outgunned by the highwaymen. Viewed overall, though they may have been simple, and even ugly to the eye, one can only conclude that the weapons of the Mail coaches served their purpose very adequately.

Now that they have passed into honorable retirement, they make a very interesting field for the specialized collector, albeit because of their scarcity the price may be high. They served in almost unaltered form from the inception of the service in 1783 to 1846 when the last horsedrawn Mail coach out of London returned from Norwich on the train and an era was over. Al-

though the inventions of the following thirty years were to change the whole concept of weaponry so much by the introduction of breechloader and magazine rifle, all this came too late for the men of the Mail coaches, though it came in very handy for the postboys of the Deadwood Stage. ●

Acknowledgements

I am grateful for all the assistance which I received at the Post Office Archives of 23 Glasshill Street, London SE 1, in my researches and for permission to reproduce photographs which are Post Office Copyright, to Mr. W. Keith Neil for permission to use his photograph of the muzzle of a Post Office blunderbuss, to Messrs. Christies and Sotheby's for permission to use illustrations from their sale catalogs and to Messrs. Ackermann for the right to use their picture of The West Country Mails, and also to Major D. Thomas R.A.

Further matter on relevant weapons of the period can be found in J. N. George's *English Pistols and Revolvers,* and *English Guns and Rifles,* Neal and Back's *The Mantons Gunmakers,* D. R. Baxter's *Blunderbusses,* and Frederick Wilkinson's *Antique Firearms.* Readers interested in the history of the Mail coaches are referred to *Carrying British Mails* by Jean Farrugia and Tony Gammons (National Postal Museum).
Wilfrid Ward

The Finally Proper

WE COULDN'T find the dead antelope.

This had never happened to me before, not while big game hunting. I'd lost birds, sure. Much as I hate to admit it, even with lots of conscientious searching and a good retriever to help me, I sometimes—not often but sometimes—fail to locate a duck or dove that I know fell solidly hit. But this was no inconspicuous bird in heavy cover. It was a sizable animal that was shot on the open plains of Montana, and we were almost certain that it was dead.

I'd fired from a steady prone position on the low ridge between two wide, grassy valleys. The shot, although moderately long, almost two hundred

yards, had felt good. I'd seen "my" antelope pull out of the herd and walk slowly away from us as the rest raced off; it had vanished abruptly into a dip in the landscape. My guide, Roy Rasmussen, watching through binoculars from his slightly higher vantage point kneeling behind me, had told me its sudden disappearance had been due to its falling dead—he'd actually seen it collapse—but the two of us had been zig-zagging systematically through the yellow prairie grass for the better part of an hour without finding it, and I was beginning to have serious doubts about my marksmanship and Roy's eyesight. . . .

Well, I reflected grimly as I made another long pass through the knee-

high grass, that was antelope hunting for you. Or at least for me. I'd never yet made a proper, one-shot kill on one of the elusive prairie goats. I'd hoped this was the time, but it was beginning to look as if my hopes were going to be frustrated again.

Some folks go hunting for big antlers; others travel to the ends of the earth to collect specimens of exotic game that few hunters have even heard of. My desires are simpler. Unlike the hunters who are out there to beat the book, I don't really care how large or small my target is, as long as it's legal. I figure that, at my age, I'm lucky to be hunting at all; I'm not about to make things difficult for myself by holding out for the mountain

Pronghorn
by DONALD HAMILTON

goat with the longest horns or the turkey with the longest beard. In fact, while I doubt that I'd have the strength of will to turn down a Boone and Crocket trophy if one stepped in front of me, I'd feel some conscience pangs as I took it, knowing that I should really leave it for some other hunter to whom it would mean a great deal more than it does to me.

The only trophy in which I'm really interested, in addition to a freezer full of venison, is the memory of an accurate shot and an instant, or almost-instant, kill—a hunting job done as cleanly and properly as a fine game animal deserves.

Which is why I was here in Montana for the second year in a row: last year

I'd put on an exhibition of lousy marksmanship that had really distressed me. Well, I suppose a gent who decides to take up rifle shooting again at the ripe age of seventy-something (never mind the exact figure), after a decade or two of nothing but shotgunning, is asking for trouble. However, I thought I'd done a pretty good job of reviving my rifle skills. I'd even bought a new rifle for my scheduled Montana antelope hunt since my old deer gun, a 308 Winchester M70 Featherweight, had seemed to kick a lot harder these days than it used to. To replace it I chose a 243 Ruger M77 that hardly kicked at all. I also blew myself to a 22 Anschutz 64MS for small-bore silhouette shooting and target practice. By the time

the antelope season rolled around that year, after expending a considerable amount of rimfire ammunition and even quite a bit of expensive centerfire stuff, I thought I was in pretty good shape as far as marksmanship was concerned.

Then fate took a hand. I'd had some accuracy problems with the 243 and various people had worked on it attempting to set it right. I'd even had it restocked, and it was finally shooting excellent groups but, perhaps as a protest against all this fiddling around, it suddenly decided to malfunction and had to be returned to the factory only days before I was scheduled to leave for Montana. After all my careful preparations, I wound up making the hunt with my ancient, hard-recoiling old 308.

As I've already indicated, it was a disaster. At the time, Montana allowed a hunter who'd drawn a buck-or-doe license to buy an extra permit entitling him to a doe or a fawn; but although antelope were plentiful and my outfitter and guide, Dave Moore (NeWest Outfitters, PO Box 6052, Helena, Montana 59604; 406-227-5798) knew just how to bring me within range, and did so time and again, I used up almost a full box of ammo (eighteen cartridges, to be exact) to get my two pronghorns. The fact was my somewhat arthritic shoulder just didn't take kindly to being belted that hard, retaliating with a violent flinch that should have been bottled and sent to the Smithsonian as a unique scientific specimen of its kind.

In my frustration, I'd wound up taking a rather small buck, thinking more about whether or not he was close enough for me to hit him than about what he was wearing on his head. It didn't bother me—I've already indicated that horns don't mean that much to me. However, Dave wanted to see me get a larger one, and I wanted to come back and see if I couldn't make a proper antelope hunt, one in which I didn't spend most of my time shooting holes in the landscape, so we made repeat arrangements for the following year. On the thousand-mile drive home I had plenty of time to think over what had to be done in the twelve months before the hunting season opened again.

I was going to have to cure that raging flinch; well, a lot of 22 practice with the Anschutz should take care of that. And I was going to have to get used to shooting at longer ranges. I had, as I've said, been playing around with small-bore silhouette shooting; but if I was going to start hitting those pronghorns out where they seemed to live, I'd better start entering the big-bore silhouette matches where you knock over—well, you're supposed to knock over—metal targets out to 500 meters, offhand. This meant getting a new rifle since the consensus around the gun club was that the 243 wasn't up to the job.

There was also the fact that my big-game horizons seemed to be expanding. Back in my younger days I'd shot a few strange critters like Swedish moose and Barbary sheep, but somehow I'd never managed to connect with a good, old-fashioned, American elk. Once I'd dealt with the antelope situation properly, I decided, it would be nice to close this glaring gap in my hunting record. Again, a more powerful cartridge was indicated.

Back home, I bought two cases of 22 target ammunition and embarked upon my marksmanship rehabilitation program, shooting almost daily at our club's outdoor range when weather conditions permitted and at a commercial indoor range when they didn't. Meanwhile, I did some research on rifles, looking for something halfway between the 243 that had too little energy at the muzzle end, and the 308 that had too much energy at the butt. However, my systematic, scientific approach got short-circuited by circumstances. One rainy day I was at the indoor range, doing the 60-round practice stint I'd set myself. They also sell guns there; and as I emerged from the rear of the building one of my salesmen friends called to me.

"This just came in, Don; maybe it's what you want."

He was unpacking a Ruger M77 that looked somewhat huskier than my 243. At least the barrel was considerably thicker.

I said, "Man, I'm going after antelope and elk; I don't need a varmint rifle!" I looked at the markings on the barrel. "What's a 25-06? I never heard of it."

"It's just a 30-06 case necked down to 25-caliber. Handles bullets up to 120 grains."

I hesitated.

"How much does this howitzer weigh, anyway?" I asked.

It weighed almost 8 pounds; and that was without a scope. Strangely, in spite of the weight it felt very good at my shoulder. Telling myself that I was crazy, this semi-bull-barrel job couldn't be the gun I was looking for, I nevertheless asked my friend to hold it for me overnight while I did some studying. Back home, I first made a couple of phone calls. A silhouette-shooting friend told me that once in a while the 25-06 might fail to knock over a ram at 500 meters, but it should take everything else cleanly. Well, I wasn't expecting to become the state champion, or even the local one; I could afford to lose an occasional target. An experienced hunting friend told me that it wasn't the caliber he'd choose for elk—he liked the 300 Winchester Magnum—but if I picked my shots, well, a lot of elk had fallen to much less powerful rounds like, for instance, the 30-30.

I checked my favorite reference work (initials GD) and learned that the 25-06 muzzle energy figures were almost exactly midway between those of the 243 and those of the 308, indicating that in guns of equal weight the recoil should split the difference between the comfortable nudge of the Ruger I already owned and the unbearable smash of the old Winchester. But it was not a question of guns of equal weight. With a scope suitable for silhouette work as well as hunting, the heavy-barreled 25-06 would weigh at least a couple of pounds more than the 308 Featherweight with its light Leupold

Returning to the ranch after shooting a small buck the author saw a better one near the road.

2x-7x variable, reducing its relative recoil even more. The big question was: while the almost-ten-pound 25-06 outfit might be gentle enough on my shoulder, and at the same time powerful enough for my needs, could I carry those extra pounds in the hunting field?

The answer was: *Carry them where?*

There's a theory to the effect that we elder statesmen of hunting need light guns because we're too feeble to pack heavy ones any distance. However, the fact is that we're not going any distance. Well, there may be some rawhide gents my age who still think nothing of loping twenty miles through tangled forests after deer, or climbing jagged 10,000-foot peaks af-

back to the factory to have the atrocious trigger pull reduced to about four pounds, and the low scope mounts that came with the gun replaced by higher mounts suitable for a big Bushnell 4x-12x varmint-type telescopic sight that, I hoped, would work reasonably well on the silhouette range as well as in the hunting field. It took a couple of weeks to get all the pieces together and assembled; then I headed for the outdoor range with a couple of boxes of each brand of ammunition I'd been able to find, Winchester and Remington with 120-grain bullets; Federal with 117-grainers.

I returned with a happy glow. The trigger pull was now reasonably crisp and light. The new scope was clear and

shoot better than a guy who doesn't know where the crummy musket is going to blow the next shot to, even if his hold is right on. Anyway, owning a truly accurate rifle is just plain fun, and we're all in this for enjoyment, aren't we?

As the summer wore on, I learned that my new gun wasn't quite perfect, of course. The high scope mounts made it necessary for me to build up the comb of the stock a bit to support my face, and a slip-on recoil pad was required to move me back far enough so the scope didn't rap me lightly on the nose in recoil when I got careless and crawled too far up the stock. The gun wasn't pretty with these add-ons, and sooner or later I'd get a new stock made to the right dimensions, but in the meantime it continued to shoot like a dream at all the ranges I tried. It couldn't quite perform miracles, however, and my shooting improved only slowly, but with constant practice it did improve. . . .

Then it was autumn and time to stop playing target games and get serious. When I reached Montana, the weather was fine, the scenery was as spectacular as always, and the antelope were very much in residence. This year, drawing a buck-or-doe license, as I'd done, entitled the applicant to purchase not just one, but two additional doe-or-fawn licenses; so I had three pronghorns coming.

"Get your buck first," Dave Moore had said after driving me to a likely spot where, after climbing a bit, I could keep watch over the junction of two canyons. "That way you've still got your doe tickets if you make a mistake. It has happened; they do bunch up. We can find you all the does you want later."

I'd equipped my Ruger with a Harris bipod, the tall model that let me shoot from a sitting position. Although I'd practiced with it at home, I had some difficulty getting it leveled in this rough terrain. Then I waited, and after an hour or so, there they came down the far side of the left-hand canyon, two bucks and six or eight does. They milled around in the brush for a moment almost opposite me; then a couple of the does started up the slope and ducked over the ridge out of sight. The remaining does, and the bucks, started to follow. Sitting cross-legged behind the bipod, the way I'd found worked best for me, I tracked the larger buck, a good-sized specimen, waiting for a clear shot. He disappeared behind some brush, reappeared, and I took him quartering away from me just as he reached the clear space at the top.

The author, with his rifle supported by a Harris bipod, sits in ambush waiting for a shot.

ter sheep or goats. If there are, I envy them; but these days I warn my guide at the start of each hunt not to expect any lengthy hikes or stalks or climbs from me, and certainly no mad sprints to cut 'em off at the pass, no matter what monster trophy he might spot out there. I'm not crippled, by any means, but I just don't move as fast as I used to, or as far. Since that's the case, it doesn't really matter whether my rifle weighs five pounds or fifteen. I'm only going to lug it short distances; and I'm better off with a gun I can shoot straight, no matter how heavy, than with one I can't.

At least that was my thinking that night; whether it was correct or not remained to be seen. In the morning I bought the gun—and promptly sent it

sharp, and the adjustments were positive. The recoil of the heavy gun, while somewhat more noticeable than that of the 243, was quite acceptable even at the benchrest. And the accuracy . . . Ah, the accuracy! The first three groups I'd fired after getting sighted in, with the three different brands of ammunition, were all well under 1-inch; one was almost a perfect half-inch cloverleaf. For a rifle right out of the box, with factory ammunition, it was unbelievable!

There's been a lot of idle chatter about how nobody really *needs* tack-hole accuracy in a hunting rifle. Well, maybe, but there's a lot of confidence to be had from owning a gun that puts its bullets exactly where you point it; and a confident marksman is apt to

In relative kicking order, from the left: the 308, 25-06, and 243.

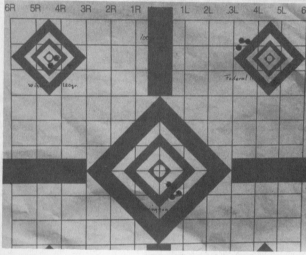

The author poses with his antelope buck; he should have shot the bigger one.

The first three 100-yard groups fired with the author's new Ruger 25-06. All groups were well under an inch.

The author sights in his new, heavy-barreled 25-06 Ruger M/77.

With the crash of the shot, he fell into the brush out of sight. Then he appeared again, sliding back down the steep slope toward me as he struggled to get to his feet. He managed it, and gave me a perfect broadside target for a moment. I fired again, and he dropped for good. Hurrying over there, I counted two hundred and eighty-three paces to where he lay. He'd been hit once rather high in the rear; the second 117-grain Federal boattail soft-point had got him right through the ribs, finishing the job. Not quite the clean execution I liked to see; but at least this year I seemed to be hitting what I shot at, for a change.

I guess I'm a marksman at heart, not a trophy hunter. Only after checking out the bullet holes did I think to look at the head. Then I laughed a bit grimly. My pronghorn jinx was still operative, it seemed. Milling around in the brush, they'd switched antelope on me. I'd got the little buck, not the big one. It didn't break my heart, but I knew that Dave Moore, who liked big horns for his hunters, was going to give me hell for it. He did.

But at least I had my buck. The following morning Dave went out with some hunters who didn't have theirs, leaving me with another guide, Roy Rasmussen, to get my two does. I missed the first one he found me, with every bullet in the gun, as it raced by me a hundred yards away. Then there was a bunch that got away while I was trying to get a good rest off a fence post. Considering that I'd just spent a year and around ten thousand rounds of ammunition practicing offhand shooting, and the pronghorns had appeared out of a wash only some fifty yards distant, this wasn't very bright. (An old Africa hand I once met said that the trouble with American marksmen was that they were all rest-happy; they'd be looking for something to steady the gun on even when a lion was chewing on the end of the barrel.)

We had a picnic lunch with the other guides and hunters in one of the ghost towns that dot those plains; only a few foundations and a great, weathered old granary remained. Leaving the place, Roy stopped the pickup and we got out to glass the broken, yellow-and-brown landscape.

"There's a good bunch," he said, pointing. He swung the binoculars to the right. "Dave's truck is heading that way. If we put you up on that rocky point, maybe he'll spook them right past you."

He did. I barely had time to climb up there and get settled—my ambush spot was too steep and cramped for the bipod, but I had some boulders to serve

as rests—when they came into sight at a run. There were at least a dozen of them. I judged they'd pass a little over a hundred yards away. With the scope set to 6x, I picked out a doe that had no bucks around her, waited until she made a nice big target in the glass and, remembering the other doe I'd missed earlier, behind every time, I pulled the trigger when the duplex crosshairs were a ridiculous distance ahead of her. But I'd overdone it; I saw a spurt of dust just in front of her. I worked the bolt, cut my lead and fired again. Behind, dammit. Desperately, still swinging with the running doe, I cranked in another cartridge, aimed at the end of her nose, and fired a third time. Down she came.

Standing over her, after scrambling down there, I saw that I'd made a perfect chest shot; but I knew that, hard as she'd been running, it was just a lucky accident and I could take little credit for it. Presently Roy came driving up; as soon as the doe was field-dressed and in the back of the pickup we set out to find me another. It took a couple of hours; then, driving up a wide valley we saw a sizable bunch moving ahead of us. They saw us coming at half a mile, broke into a trot, and swerved to cross a low saddle into the next valley, disappearing from sight. Roy spun the wheel and put the truck onto a small track leading toward another saddle just opposite us.

"If they swing to the right on the other side of the ridge we've lost them," he said. "But if they swing left, back toward us, maybe we can cut them off. . . . Quick now!"

So I wound up, after all, running like hell to cut 'em off at the pass. Reaching the top of the ridge, we peered cautiously over the crest to see the band just coming into sight single file. Near the front was a good buck, but I already had my buck. Lying on my stomach, I estimated the shot at 200 yards. No bipod this time, I'd left it off, and no rock for a rest, but my elbows were solidly planted in the stony soil. I'd caught my breath—well most of it—and the crosshairs were reasonably steady as I picked out a sizable doe with plenty of space around her and waited for her to come opposite us. Then the 25-06 crashed. I heard the slap of the striking bullet a moment later. The herd rushed off to the left, leaving "my" doe walking slowly away from us. Suddenly she disappeared.

"She's down!" Roy said behind me. "I've got her marked. That grass is pretty thick; I don't want to lose my bearing. You get the truck while I walk straight down to her. . . ."

But that had been almost an hour

ago. He'd walked his line all the way to the arroyo at the bottom of the valley without finding anything; and we were still hunting through the tall grass for some sign of a dead antelope. Roy even took a hike through the arroyo and up the far slope, just in case she could have sneaked away unseen and died over there. Waiting for him to return, I looked back at the ridge from which I'd shot, and found myself frowning. Something was wrong. I aimed the scope that way, and everything looked very small on the crest where we'd lain. I visualized an antelope up there, and realized that I'd have a very hard time hitting it.

It just hadn't been that long a shot, dammit!

I realized that we'd been searching much too far down the slope. I headed over to where I'd left the truck, after driving down here following Roy's long strides. I hiked along the tire tracks, back up the slope, until the ridge was only a reasonable rifle shot away. Then I started my search again. On the second cast I spotted the gleam of white rump hairs through the yellow prairie grass.

"Over here," I called. "I've got her!"

The 117-grain boattail had taken her in the ribs, leaving a pencil-sized entry hole and an exit hole almost 2 inches in diameter. The blood trail indicated that she'd come less than 20 yards from the spot where she'd been hit. Apparently, expecting to find her directly ahead of him, not looking very hard to the sides, Roy had just walked right by her in the thick grass. I felt the kind of satisfaction I suppose the trophy hunter feels when he comes up after the shot and sees the record-breaking antlers. But this was all the trophy I needed, at my age, the knowledge that I had at last managed to do it right, the way that it should be done. . . .

Lessons learned. The weight of the gun, as I'd expected, was not a factor. On the short hikes and climbs my guides had asked of me, I'd had no more problems with the heavy rifle I'd carried this year than with the light one I'd packed last year. As for the cartridge, the 117-grain 25-caliber bullets had done everything I'd asked of them; but there had never been any doubt that they could deal efficiently with game the size of antelope. The question was still, could they handle game the size of elk?

Unfortunately, it was a question that wouldn't be answered this year. Again, fate took a hand, and a death in the family kept me home at the time of my scheduled Colorado elk hunt. Next year?   ●

The Mini-Thirty . . .

by JOHN V. MILLER, JR.

"Realistically, this cartridge is best suited for small game and plinking." (Sierra Bullets Reloading Manual, Second Edition.)

"Well, it will undoubtedly kill deer when everything is right, but I am concerned that the light (for its caliber) bullet may not always have the necessary penetration for angling shots that are so common in thick cover. There are certainly many better deer cartridges." (Finn Aagaard, American Hunter, April 1987.)

Another 30-Caliber Success

"The M43 cartridge is an interesting one to experiment with, but like the M-1 Carbine cartridge, it has limited sporting usefulness. Powerwise, it is inferior to the 30-30. (Speer Reloading Manual #11.)

"The 7.62x39mm is just the right size and proportion to make a perfect medium-size hunting combination. The lightweight Mini-Thirty is the ideal rifle for extended carry and stalks in deer country. On target, the Mini-Thirty provides authoritative power with a light recoil, allowing for quick recovery." (Ruger Advertisement.)

"But as a woods rifle for small deer or varmints it can do the job if the shooter does his." (C.E. Harris, American Rifleman, April 1987.)

Author's daughter Sara, twelve, began deer hunting with the Mini-Thirty, found it easy to use, easy to shoot well.

THE RUGER Mini-Thirty and the 7.62x39mm cartridge it chambers have become controversial subjects in just a short time. Is the rifle and cartridge ideal for deer, an adequate but somewhat mediocre deer combination, or just an expensive plinker?

Intrigued by these questions, as well as by the little rifle itself and its short, fat cartridge, I set out to find the answers. After firing some 700 rounds across chronograph screens, several hundred more in target shooting, running three series of expansion tests, finishing 26 days of deer hunting and collecting eight deer, I feel I have the answers.

It's still true that the 7.62x39mm cartridge, which was developed in 1943, has been the principal small arms cartridge of the Warsaw Pact countries and has been chambered in an estimated fifty million firearms, until very recently has been almost unknown in the U.S. All that may be changing, however, partly because Ruger has modified the Mini-14 rifle to chamber the Soviet round and is advertising the result as the perfect deer rifle.

Everybody has read about the Mini-Thirty, but a few comments still seem to be in order. Most hunters would agree the little rifle makes a handy package. It comes with an excellent scope mounting system, a convenient safety and a hold-open device independent of the magazine follower, which makes it much easier and faster to load than other readily available U.S. autoloaders. It balances nicely and recoil is almost nonexistent. The comb of the stock should ideally be a little higher; the trigger is fair at best; and the little rifle is not a tack driver. In all, the Mini-Thirty has many assets and a few minor liabilities.

Compared with several other semi-automatic rifles I have used, the Mini-Thirty is a handloader's dream. In firing over 700 rounds in 136 different loads, I experienced only two jams—both with IMR-4227 powder. I experienced two more jams while hunting. The cause was the flat point of the 150-grain Sierra bullet catching on the rear edge of the barrel. Possibly the cold weather was a factor or the fact that the little rifle had not been disassembled for a thorough cleaning in over 500 rounds. I switched to the 150-grain Hornady round-nose bullet and since then have had no additional problems.

The standard 7.62x39mm cartridge is loaded with .311-inch bullets weighing 123 grains, produces approximately 2330 fps from an AKM rifle with a 16.4-inch barrel. Commercial ammunition with softpoint bullets is marketed by Federal, Hansen, PMC, Remington, and Winchester. All are loaded with 123- or 125-grain bullets of .311-inch diameter and all function reliably in my Mini-Thirty. These loads performed well in my expansion tests except the PMC shed its bullet jacket in the test medium and failed to penetrate adequately. Remington lists a load with softpoint bullets, but I was unable to obtain any.

Choices for the reloader are almost limitless. The Ruger Mini-Thirty has a standard .308-inch barrel, so any standard 30-caliber bullet of 170 grains or less can be used—theoretically.

There are six basic categories of 30-caliber bullets. These are: (1) Premium big game bullets; (2) High-velocity big game bullets such as 150-grain spitzers; (3) High-velocity varmint bullets like the 125-grain Sierra spitzer; (4) 30-30 rifle bullets, including the 125-grain Sierra flat nose hollowpoint; (5) Single shot pistol bullets such as the 130-grain Hornady; (6) Bullets specifically designed for the 7.62x39mm, one of which is the 123-grain Hornady .311-inch softpoint.

These choices can be narrowed, of course. The premium bullets are obviously designed for high velocity and tough game as are high-velocity big game bullets. High-velocity varmint bullets have been used successfully on deer in single shot pistols at velocity ranges similar to that produced by the 7.62x39mm. Factory ballistics can be duplicated with the 125-grain spitzer bullets by Sierra and Nosler. The Nosler Ballistic Tip bullet will open up faster but the Sierra softpoint spitzer will retain more weight. (See Table II.) I did not try either of the 110-grain bullets or the 130-grain hollowpoints. The 110 I feel is too light and hollowpoints often give unreliable expansion at low velocities.

The various 30-30 bullets appear to be top choices for deer-size animals in the Mini-Thirty. The 7.62x39mm will not push them quite as fast, but the difference is only about 100 feet per second with 150-grain bullets in a carbine length barrel. My 7.62x39mm handloads with 150-grain bullets produced expansion and penetration comparable to 150-grain, 30-30 factory loads fired in a Winchester carbine when tested in wet newspapers. (See Table II.) The 130-grain Speer and 170-grain Hornady bullets would appear from my tests to give more penetration and less expansion than the 125-grain Sierra hollowpoint, the 150-grain Sierra flat point and the 150-grain Hornady round-nose bullets.

Bullets for the single shot pistols have only recently appeared. The 130-grain Hornady and 135-grain Sierra bullets are the only choices at this writing. They are designed for expansion at the velocities obtainable by this cartridge and their spitzer form allows them to retain this velocity at longer ranges. A ballistician from Sierra told me the 135-grain bullet was the only bullet in their line he would recommend without reservation for use in deer hunting with the 7.62x39mm cartridge.

Both the Hornady and Sierra functioned well in my expansion tests. They cannot be given a great deal more velocity than the 150-grain bullets, but they do retain that velocity better and consequently retain substantially more energy at 100 yards than the 150-grain flat-point bullets. In the wet newspapers these pistol bullets gave performance very similar to the 30-30 bullets.

The 123-grain Hornady softpoint bullet performed fairly well in my tests. This is possibly the only logical bullet to use in 7.62x39mm rifles that have .311-inch bores such as the SKS and AK-type rifles. For the Ruger, the 308 bullets are better choices.

In selecting powders, the handloader must keep in mind that the 7.62x39mm has very limited case capacity so a dense powder on the fast burning end of the rifle powder spectrum is indicated. WW680 meets these criteria, but I found it touchy to work with in this cartridge—pressure appears to rise quickly with very small additions of powder.

Dense Accurate Arms 1680 ball powder was designed for this cartridge. It was much less touchy to work with than WW680. It produced excellent velocity, but did not prove to be very accurate in my gun.

The *Sierra Manual* recommends IMR-4227. I did develop one reliable load with the 125-grain Sierra bullet, but the cartridge cases ejected rather weakly. There are certainly much better powders for the 7.62x39mm.

IMR-4198 powder proved to be one of the best—providing very uniform results with all bullet weights tested. I recommend anyone start with IMR-4198 in the 7.62x39mm. Velocities increase in very uniform steps as the charge weight is increased with this powder and it is difficult to use too much. Many of the loads recommended are heavily compressed. This caused no problem other than the inconvenience of using a long drop tube to get the powder in the case.

IMR-3031 powder also gave very

TABLE I
Loading Data for the Mini-Thirty
7.62x39mm

Bullet	Charge (grs.)	Powder	Velocity (fps)	Extreme Spread (fps)	Case	Overall Length (ins.) C-Crimp	Group (ins.)
Hansen 123-gr. FP	(Factory)		2449	61			4⅛
Hansen 123-gr. SP	(Factory)		2353	61			4⅛
BELL 123-gr. FP	(Factory)		2421	58			5⅜
PMC 122-gr. FP	(Factory)		2334	103			8
PMC 125-gr. SP	(Factory)		2150	114			7⅝
Federal 123-gr. SP	(Factory)		2313	36			6⅞
Federal 124-gr. FP	(Factory)		2326	27			6⅜
Winchester 123-gr. SP	(Factory)		2301	31			4½
Hornady	23.7	IMR-4198	2119	34	BELL	2.19 C	3
123-gr.	24.6	IMR-4198	2212	32	BELL	2.19 C	3½
SP	25.0	IMR-4198	2221	23	BELL	2.19 C	3⅞
	25.5	IMR-4198	2266	38	BELL	2.19 C	4½
	27.2	H322	2110	78	BELL	2.19 C	2⅞
	28.5	H322	2209	62	BELL	2.19 C	3⅜
	25.4	RL-7	2172	31	BELL	2.19 C	5
	26.6	RL-7	2297	39	BELL	2.19 C	3⅛
Sierra	22.0	WW680	2304	57	PMC	2.19	6
125-gr.	23.5	AA1680	2236	70	BELL	2.19	
Spitzer	24.0	AA1680	2260	45	BELL	2.19	6⅛
	24.5	AA1680	2300	43	BELL	2.19	6¼
	24.5	IMR-4198	2122	57	PMC	2.19	6¼
	25.0	IMR-4198	2179	34	PMC	2.19	4½
	25.0	IMR-4198	2193	52	BELL	2.19	5¼
	25.5	IMR-4198	2205	20	PMC	2.19	2
	25.9	RL-7	2234	16	PMC	2.19	3¼
	26.3	RL-7	2288	44	PMC	2.19	3⅜
	26.6	RL-7	2323	40	PMC	2.19	6⅜
Nosler	22.0	WW680	2358	60	PMC	2.20	4¼
125-gr.	26.5	IMR-4198	2381	67	PMC	2.20	4⅝
Ballistic	26.6	RL-7	2355	46	PMC	2.20	3½
Tip							
Sierra	22.5	IMR-4227	2274	12	PMC	2.05	6½
125-gr.	21.0	WW680	2140	100	BELL	2.05	5⅝
Flat Nose	21.5	WW680	2217	76	BELL	2.05	6
HP	22.0	WW680	2295	128	BELL	2.05	11¼
	24.0	IMR-4198	2076		PMC	2.05	
	24.5	IMR-4198	2140		PMC	2.05	
	25.0	IMR-4198	2170	27	PMC	2.05	
	25.5	IMR-4198	2209	51	PMC	2.05	2½
	26.0	IMR-4198	2264	35	PMC	2.05	2⅜
	26.5	IMR-4198	2316	27	PMC	2.05	3¾
	27.0	H322	2067	18	BELL	2.05	4
	27.5	H322	2093	33	BELL	2.05	3½
	28.0	H322	2124	29	BELL	2.05	3½
	28.5	H322	2174	47	BELL	2.05	3¾
	29.0	H322	2204	43	BELL	2.05	2⅛
	29.5	H322	2243	29	BELL	2.05	3
	25.5	RL-7	2171	62	PMC	2.05	3⅞
	26.0	RL-7	2214	36	PMC	2.05	6⅛
	26.5	RL-7	2246	26	PMC	2.05	5⅜

Bullet	Charge (grs.)	Powder	Velocity (fps)	Extreme Spread (fps)	Case	Overall Length (ins.) C-Crimp	Group (ins.)
Speer	24.0	IMR-4198	2074	15	PMC	2.035 C	3⅜
130-gr.	24.5	IMR-4198	2118	43	PMC	2.035 C	5
Flat Nose	25.0	IMR-4198	2137	11	PMC	2.035 C	3¼
	25.5	IMR-4198	2186	49	PMC	2.035 C	3¾
	26.0	IMR-4198	2300	27	PMC	2.035 C	
	28.5	H322	2177	51	BELL	2.035 C	2¾
	27.0	IMR-3031	2036	65	PMC	2.035 C	
	27.5	IMR-3031	2076	25	PMC	2.035 C	2⅜
	28.0	IMR-3031	2117	39	PMC	2.035 C	4⅜
	28.5	IMR-3031	2154	54	PMC	2.035 C	5¾
Hornady	20.0	WW680	2014	119	BELL	2.19	
130-gr.	20.5	WW680	2146	172	BELL	2.19	10½
SP	21.0	WW680	2163	40	BELL	2.19	10⅝
(Pistol)	21.5	WW680	2270	143	BELL	2.19	
	23.0	AA1680	2193	73	BELL	2.19	7¾
	23.5	AA1680	2211	60	BELL	2.19	5⅛
	24.0	AA1680	2236	73	BELL	2.19	8
	25.0	RL-7	2152	53	BELL	2.19	5½
	25.5	RL-7	2209	37	BELL	2.19	4⅞
	26.0	RL-7	2248	17	BELL	2.19	5⅝
	28.5	H322	2158	30	BELL	2.19	5¼
	25.0	IMR-4198	2186	14	BELL	2.19	4¾
	25.5	IMR-4198	2218	24	BELL	2.19	3¾
	26.0	IMR-4198	2256	42	BELL	2.19	3¾
Sierra	22.0	AA1680	2015	144	BELL	2.19	8⅜
135-gr.	22.5	AA1680	2118	101	BELL	2.19	10½
Spitzer	23.0	AA1680	2149	78	BELL	2.19	6½
(Pistol)	23.5	AA1680	2214	32	BELL	2.19	5½
	24.0	IMR-4198	2094	42	BELL	2.19	6⅞
	24.5	IMR-4198	2142	36	BELL	2.19	3⅛
	25.0	IMR-4198	2167	47	BELL	2.19	3⅞
	24.0	RL-7	2039	59	BELL	2.19	3½
	24.0	RL-7	2143	12	PMC	2.19	
	24.5	RL-7	2060	54	BELL	2.19	2¼
	24.5	RL-7	2162	33	PMC	2.19	
	25.0	RL-7	2107	47	BELL	2.19	3¾
	25.0	RL-7	2181	47	PMC	2.19	3
Sierra	24.5	IMR-4198	2111	24	PMC	2.012 C	
150-gr.	28.0	H322	2071	21	PMC	2.012 C	4
Flat Point	28.5	H322	2101	25	PMC	2.012 C	4
	29.0	H322	2123	15	PMC	2.012 C	2⅜
	24.5	IMR-3031	1845	14	PMC	2.012 C	2¼
	25.0	IMR-3031	1873	33	PMC	2.012 C	4
	25.5	IMR-3031	1918	33	PMC	2.012 C	5
	26.0	IMR-3031	1948	63	PMC	2.012 C	2
	26.5	IMR-3031	1995	65	PMC	2.012 C	5
	27.0	IMR-3031	2000	53	PMC	2.012 C	4½
	27.5	IMR-3031	2041	29	PMC	2.012 C	3⅞
	28.0	IMR-3031	2064	71	PMC	2.012 C	4⅜
	28.0	BL-C(2)	1855	19	PMC	2.150	3¼
	28.5	BL-C(2)	1887	33	PMC	2.150	1⅞
	28.5	BL-C(2)	1948	33	PMC	2.012 C	6
	29.0	BL-C(2)	1961	33	PMC	2.012 C	
	29.5	BL-C(2)	1976	36	PMC	2.012 C	2¼
Hornady	28.5	H322	2116	17	PMC	2.035 C	2¼
150-gr.	27.0	AA2460	1930	61	BELL	2.19	4½
Round-Nose	27.5	AA2460	1965	38	BELL	2.19	6½
	28.0	AA2460	1982	72	BELL	2.19	5
	28.5	AA2460	2003	59	BELL	2.19	6½
Speer	24.0	IMR-4198	2055	37	PMC	2.26	6
150-gr.	24.5	IMR-4198	2085	24	PMC	2.26	3⅜
Spitzer							
Hornady	24.0	IMR-3031	1781	32	PMC	2.05 C	3¾
170-gr.	24.5	IMR-3031	1820	34	PMC	2.05 C	3⅛
Flat Point	25.0	IMR-3031	1838	50	PMC	2.05 C	4
	25.5	IMR-3031	1835	48	PMC	2.05 C	3⅞
	26.0	IMR-3031	1855	38	PMC	2.05 C	2⅛

Velocities are instrumental at 7.5 feet. All loads use Winchester-Western Large Rifle primers and were fired in a Ruger Mini-Thirty rifle with a 18½-inch barrel. Velocities were measured with a Tepeco chronograph. Temperatures ranged from 54 to 85 degrees Fahrenheit.

consistent results, although this powder is too slow-burning to give adequate velocity in the 7.62x39mm cartridge except with the heavier bullet weights. H322 and Hercules Reloder 7 are both small-grain extruded powders and both perform well in this cartridge. Results with both were uniform, and they measure very accurately. Again, many loads are heavily compressed.

Hodgdon BL-C(2) can be used quite satisfactorily with the heavy bullet weights. I could not get quite as much velocity with this powder as I could with IMR-4198 or IMR-3031 but it measures very uniformly so it would be a good choice for the handloader who consumes a large amount of ammunition. I tried AA 2460 with the 150-grain bullets and experienced no particular problems. But to obtain adequate velocity, the charge has to be compressed more than I consider desirable.

New unprimed cartridge cases are available from Eldorado Cartridge Corp.; Federal, Winchester and Hansen cases are apparently only available in loaded ammunition, therefore, I used them very sparingly in my tests. The Eldorado (PMC and B.E.L.L.) cases performed very well though not very attractive as they came from the factory. They had not received a final polish and many of the flash holes were not punched through cleanly. A 5/64-inch drill served to clean out the flash holes and after a trip through the case tumbler the cases looked and functioned like other quality brass. Incidentally, the Eldorado cases I used were not headstamped in any way. This creates an interesting cartridge to pass around among your friends. Case life has been very good for a semi-automatic. After five firings, I have had almost zero case failures.

There is a substantial difference in weight among the various brands of cases for such a small cartridge (see Table III). As my testing progressed, I was surprised by the small velocity difference between identical loads in B.E.L.L. and PMC cases that differ substantially in weight. So I ran the test series recorded in Table IV. To eliminate variables caused by barrel heating, I fired one shot with each case, followed by a second shot with each case, etc., until the series was completed. The greatest velocity difference among the five cases was only 20 fps.

No special problems were encountered in reloading for the Mini-Thirty. Since the cartridge can be loaded with either .311- or .308-inch bullets, it is

Cases by B.E.L.L., Chinese (brand unknown), Federal, Hansen, PMC, and Winchester. All are reloadable except the surplus Chinese ball which has steel cases and Berdan primers.

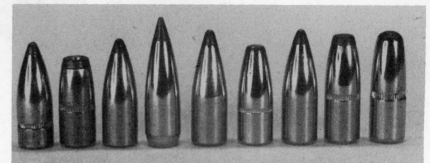

The author recommends these bullets for deer hunting with the Mini-Thirty, from left: the 123-grain (.311-inch diameter) Hornady softpoint; 125-grain Sierra hollowpoint; 125-grain Sierra spitzer; 125-grain Nosler Ballistic Tip; 130-grain Hornady single shot pistol; 130-grain Speer flat point; 135-grain Sierra single shot pistol; 150-grain Sierra flat nose and 150-grain Hornady round-nose.

Factory 7.62x39mm ammunition is manufactured by a number of companies in the United States and abroad. Federal, Hansen, Winchester, and PMC softpoints are shown on the left. Surplus Chinese (brand unknown), Federal, PMC, B.E.L.L., and Hansen ammunition with full metal jacketed bullets are on the right.

Here's a variety of powder to suit the 7.62x39mm: fast-burning ball powders AA1680 and WW680 work for light bullets; medium-burning extruded powders RL-7 and H322 (and IMR-4198, not shown) are useful for a variety of loads. Slower burning powders like IMR-3031 (extruded) and BL-C(2) (ball) work with heavy weight bullets.

The Mini-Thirty has a standard .308-inch barrel so a large number of bullet types are suitable. Reloaders for 7.62x39 rifles with .311-inch barrels will find the Hornady .311-inch diameter 123-grain softpoint bullets (on the left) most suitable.

important to use an expanding plug suitable to the bullet diameter. The Lee die set that I used includes expanding plugs for both bullet diameters. It is important that the bullets are gripped tightly by the case neck. I encountered no problems with the bullet being forced into the case neck during the loading cycle, and I did not find crimping to be necessary. I did crimp the 123-grain Hornady softpoint, the 130-grain Speer flat nose and the 150- and 170-grain bullets intended for the 30-30. I did not crimp the 125-grain Sierra hollowpoint because to do so requires an overall length of 1.910 inches. This seats the bullet base below the neck of the case and reduces the available powder space. The proper overall length for the 7.62x39mm cartridge is generally listed as 2.19 inches and I found this length quite satisfactory with all the pointed bullets.

There are so many promising loads for the Mini-Thirty that selecting one for hunting can be perplexing. In order to assist in load selection I prepared Table V to study the retained velocity and energy of representative bullets at 100 yards. It is quite evident that the pointed bullets retained their energy much better even at this modest range than did the flat-nosed bullets. This is graphically illustrated by comparing the 100-yard energy figures for the 125-grain Sierra flat nose hollowpoint and the 125-grain Sierra spitzer, both starting at 2300 feet per second muzzle velocity. At 100 yards the Spitzer bullet carries approximately 40 percent more energy than the flat nose bullet. From an energy standpoint the 150-grain Speer Spitzer is a clear winner, but one must also consider the effect of bullet construction on terminal ballistics. What the bullet actually does once it strikes the animal is more dependent on the bullet construction than on the velocity or energy of the bullet.

Among the factory loads, there is little difference in performance between the Hansen, Federal and Winchester softpoints. All should prove very satisfactory on whitetail deer under normal conditions. I do not recommend the PMC load since it did not perform well in either the accuracy or expansion tests.

The first year we used the Mini-Thirty for deer hunting I chose to load the 150-grain Sierra flat point in front of 29.0 grains of H322 for a muzzle velocity of 2123 feet per second. I chose the 150-grain load because it closely duplicates the time-proven 30-30 load and because some writers expressed concern over the penetration of the cartridge with lighter bullets.

TABLE II: Bullet Performance in Wet Newspapers

Bullet	Average Penetration (ins.)	Average Weight Retention (grs.)	Percentage Weight Retention	Average Expanded Diameter (ins.)
Hornady 123-gr. Softpoint	10¼	89.3	72.6	.574
Sierra 125-gr. Spitzer	11¼	120.6	96.5	.653
Nosler 125-gr. Ballistic Tip	11	79.0	63.2	.539
Sierra 125-gr. Hollowpoint	9¼	92.2	73.8	.610
Hornady 130-gr. (Pistol)	11⅞	112.2	86.3	.622
Speer 130-gr. Flat Nose	13⅛	110.2	84.8	.565
Sierra 135-gr. Spitzer (Pistol)	12¾	130.5	96.7	.591
Sierra 150-gr. Flat Point	11½	145.2	96.8	.671
Hornady 150-gr. Round-Nose	10¾	134.9	89.9	.697
Speer 150-gr. Spitzer	13⅜	130.9	87.3	.615
Hornady 170-gr. Flat Point	12	150.0	88.2	.590
Federal 123-gr. Softpoint (Factory Load)	10¾	105.5	85.7	.693
Hansen 123-gr. Softpoint (Factory Load)	10¾	111.1	90.3	.648
Winchester 123-gr. Softpoint (Factory Load)	10½	91.2	74.1	.605
Remington 150-gr. Softpoint Core-Lokt 30-30 (Fired in Winchester Carbine)	12⅜	125.8	83.8	.599

All loads were fired into tightly packed and thoroughly soaked newspapers at 50 yards. A single layer of heavy canvas and two layers of 4-mil polyethylene in front of the newspapers simulated skin. Expanded diameter was measured at the widest point.

Bullets tested for expansion and penetration in wet newspapers include, from left: 123-grain Hornady softpoint; 125-grain Sierra flat nose HP; 125-grain Sierra spitzer; 125-grain Nosler Ballistic Tip; 130-grain Hornady softpoint (SS pistol); 135-grain softpoint (SS pistol); 130-grain Speer flat point; 150-grain Sierra flat nose; and 150-grain Hornady round-nose.

TABLE III
Average Weight of Once-Fired Cases

Case	Weight (grs.)	Range of Weight (grs.)
BELL	129.9	1.0
Winchester	129.1	1.5
Federal	124.4	2.9
PMC	121.6	1.6
Hansen	110.9	3.3

TABLE IV
Velocity of Test Load in Different Cases

Case	Velocity	Range of Velocity
Winchester	2193	21
BELL	2183	22
Federal	2180	34
Hansen	2173	58
PMC	2173	31

Shots were fired in rotation. (First shot from each load was fired, followed by second shot from each load, etc.) Load was 26.0-grs. Reloder 7, 125-gr. Sierra Softpoint spitzer, and Winchester Large Rifle primers.

From left, factory softpoints by Federal, Hornady, and Winchester performed well in expansion tests in wet newspapers. PMC softpoint (on the right) shed its jacket and therefore did not penetrate well.

(Above) The Ruger Mini-Thirty is shorter than either the Winchester Model 70 lightweight carbine at the top or the Winchester Model 94 Carbine at the bottom.

Simple, strong scope mount.

Hold-open device separate from the magazine carrier.

These features add to the usefulness of the Mini-Thirty as a deer rifle.

Convenient safety.

My daughter Sara took two deer with the 150-grain load and I added three more. Unfortunately our shooting was not the best and two of these deer were shot too low and too far back. The 150-grain Sierra flat-point bullets expanded well even in this soft tissue area. Both deer were recovered after long and careful tracking. Another deer was hit through both shoulders at about sixty yards. He dropped instantly. A fourth deer was shot from above at about forty yards. The bullet took out part of the backbone and demolished one lung. He also fell on the spot. The final deer was standing broadside and was shot behind the shoulders, the bullet passing through both lungs. That deer took two or three jumps and stopped, looking very droopy. My daughter shot him again in the same general area, and he collapsed. All bullets penetrated completely.

The next year we tried the light bullet approach and used the 125-grain Nosler Ballistic Tip bullets driven to 2355 feet per second by 26.6 grains of Reloder 7 and the 125-grain Sierra Spitzer in front of the same powder charge. We bagged two deer with the Nosler bullet and another with the Sierra bullet. All were shot broadside from distances ranging from thirty to fifty yards, and all collapsed after a short run. Two bullets penetrated the heart and one lung, the other penetrated both lungs. Again all bullets exited. I believe the Nosler Ballistic Tip bullet opened up a little faster and produced slightly more destruction than the Sierra softpoint, but the difference was slight. Both bullets performed well.

In the final analysis I found little difference between the performance of the 125-grain and 150-grain bullets on deer. Deer that are reasonably well hit with either bullet drop quickly; deer that are poorly hit often run long distances regardless of what cartridge or bullet is used.

I started my third daughter deer hunting with the Mini-Thirty a few days after her twelfth birthday. We are often admonished not to mix kids and autoloaders for safety considerations. However, I instructed her in basic safety procedures and supervised her closely while shooting on the range and while hunting. She had no problems learning safe gun handling. The action of the Mini-Thirty can be manipulated easily by a youngster of limited strength, and the safety is readily visible to both the child and the adult instructor. These are important features in a first rifle for a youngster.

My oldest daughter began deer hunting with a standard weight bolt-action 243 Winchester. She could manipulate the action without difficulty but the weight of the rifle made it difficult for her to handle. My second daughter began with a lever-action 44 Magnum. The exposed hammer on this rifle proved to be very difficult for a child of limited strength to manipulate, particularly during the unloading cycle. The loading gate also proved to be difficult for a twelve-year-old to function, and the tubular magazine necessitates feeding the cartridges through the action to unload, creating an obvious safety problem. Based on this experience, the Mini-Thirty is a good choice as a first deer rifle for a child of limited strength.

So in the final analysis how do the Mini-Thirty and the 7.62x39mm cartridge stack up for deer hunting? I would have to agree from the standpoint of pure efficiency there are several rifles on the American market of the same general weight, length and price of the Ruger Mini-Thirty that are better stocked, have better triggers, are more accurate and fire cartridges that are much more powerful. However, none of the competition fires repeated shots by simply pulling the trigger and none produces less recoil. Therein lies the attractiveness of the Mini-Thirty. It is the only short, light semi-automatic on the American market firing a cartridge of light recoil that is fully adequate for 90 percent of the shots taken at whitetail deer.

I can remember some forty years ago hearing a wise old deer hunter who had used the 30-30 extensively (my Father) say, "If some company will just make a lightweight semi-automatic for the 30-30 cartridge, they will sell a million of them." Ruger has essentially done just that, and I predict that Ruger will indeed sell a million Mini-Thirties. I hope so. I like them.

●

TABLE V
Retained Velocity and Energy at 100 Yards

Bullet	Muzzle Velocity	Muzzle Energy	100-Yd. Velocity	100-Yd. Energy
Hornady 123-gr. Softpoint	2300	1445	1967	1057
Sierra 125-gr. Flat Nose HP	2300	1468	1733	833
Sierra 125-gr. Spitzer	2300	1468	2053	1169
Hornady 130-gr. Softpoint (Pistol)	2250	1461	1981	1131
Speer 130-gr. Flat Nose	2300	1526	1976	1127
Sierra 135-gr. Spitzer (Pistol)	2180	1424	1951	1140
Sierra 150-gr. Flat Point	2100	1469	1643	899
Hornady 150-gr. Round-Nose	2100	1469	1684	945
Speer 150-gr. Spitzer	2100	1469	1900	1201
Hornady 170-gr. Flat Point	1800	1223	1441	784

WW680 powder can be tricky. Case at the right blew the primer with the same load as the other and normal round.

KALTHOFF'S

by GAD RAUSING

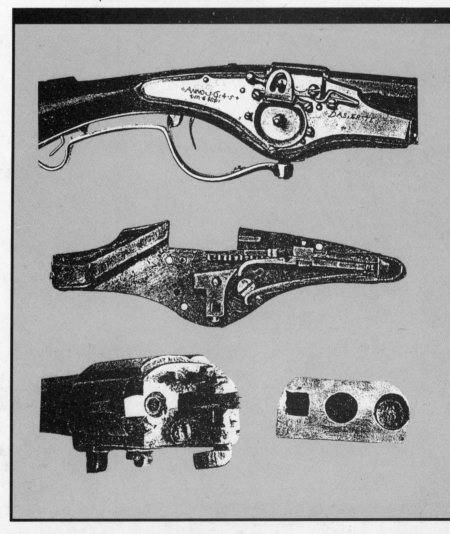

Fig. 1: (Below) Here is "Das Erste" (The First), a wheellock repeater dated 1646, made by Peter Kalthoff; also shown are the backside of the lockplate and the breech and breechlock.

ALTHOUGH snipers had used rifles ever since the middle of the 16th century, such weapons were still rare in the regular armies of the 17th century. In Sweden as well as in the Danish border province of Scania, farmers when called to arms would use their own firearms. By the second half of the 16th century these were mostly small-bore snaphaunce rifles. Inspired by the feats of these militiamen, Christian IV, king of Denmark, equipped his guards with wheellock rifles. These are simple, utilitarian arms with plain stocks. The rear third of the barrel is octagonal, the main part round. The barrel is 965mm (36½ inches) long with a bore of 15.9 to 16.1mm (0.594- to 0.634-inch). The barrels are stamped with a crowned C and carry dates from 1611 to 1622. Most of these rifles were made in Copenhagen.

In the Thirty-Years' War (1618-1648) rifles were considered so dangerous that any rifleman captured was killed on the spot. In spite of this, rifles became more common, particularly in the Swedish and Danish services, and efforts were made to design breech-loading rifles and even repeaters.

Here the Danish gunmaking family Kalthoff excelled and many breech-loaders signed by members of this family have been preserved in the Danish Royal Armoury, the "Töjhus-museum." On June 7, 1641 Peter Kalthoff obtained a Dutch patent for a repeating rifle with a capacity of 21 rounds. *(Archief Staten-General, Ak-*

FLINTLOCKS...
...the Repeaters of 1657

tenboek 1639-42, (inv. no. 3336,) Fol. 176 ff. Algemeen Rijksarchief, Haag.) The very first Kalthoff repeater was a wheellock, now in the Royal Armoury in Copenhagen, no. B 180, (Fig. 1.) but later ones are all flintlocks. (Fig 2. Royal Armoury, Copenhagen, No. B 184). The rifles preserved have bores from 10mm to 20mm (0.40- to 0.80-inch) and are dated from 1644 to 1647.

Not until brass cartridge cases were adopted was it possible to design a gas-tight breech-loading action and thus the great problem which the early designers of magazine arms had to solve was that of preventing a flash-back from the chamber to the powder magazine. The Kalthoffs solved this in an ingenious manner, by separating the powder magazine completely from the

Fig. 2: (Below) This flintlock repeater by Kalthoff is also dated 1646; within a dozen years, Fredrik III was issuing such rifles for the Scanian Guard.

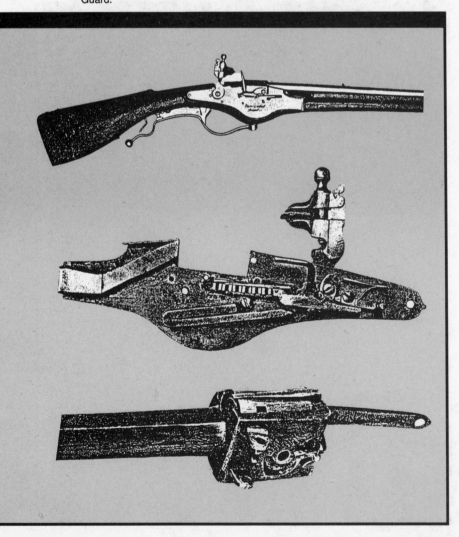

action, placing it in the butt.

The prismatic breechblock, which slides horizontally in a frame into which the barrel is welded, is equipped with a rack which meshes with a cogwheel on the rotating trigger guard. Turning the trigger guard will thus move the breechblock. (Fig. 3.) This has three chambers, drilled from the front. The left chamber (3: 1a) receives the ball from a magazine in the foreshaft. The breechblock is then slid to the right. The central chamber receives the powder charge and the right-hand chamber the priming charge from a powder measure on the trigger guard.(3: 2b, 2c.)

A duct from the powder magazine in the butt, leads to an ingenious valve beneath the grip. The powder measure on the trigger guard is also closed by a valve, which corresponds to that in the grip. The valves are spring-loaded, and open each other. (3: 6, 7.) Thus, with the trigger guard in its normal position, powder can flow from the magazine in the butt into the powder measure. As the trigger guard is rotated out of this position both valves close. At the same time the hammer is cocked by a lever connecting it with the trigger guard, and a ball slides into the left chamber of the breechblock. The breechblock is then moved to the right by the cogwheel until the chamber containing the ball is in position behind the barrel and the ball is pushed into the barrel by a plunger activated by the trigger guard.

The balls in the magazine are prevented from falling out by a spring. When the trigger guard has been turned 180 degrees, the powder measure lines up with a valve and duct in the forestock, through which the powder slides into the powder chamber and the priming chamber in the breechblock.

When being returned to its original position, the trigger guard slides the breechblock back, lining up the powder chamber behind the barrel and permitting the priming charge to slide into the pan. Thus, to load and cock

hunting use.

How many of the military repeaters were made? We know that the 100 guardsmen carried such weapons. Some of the surviving rifles have numbers cut in the wood, the highest being 108 and 110. The inventory of the Royal Armoury in the years 1696 and 1718 mention 60 different lots of arms in the Royal Armoury, one of which comprised no less than 137 repeating rifles. Evidently the Guards had discarded them before 1696. The Armoury's inventory of 1775 still listed 133 of them. By that time they were already venerable antiques but still technically far ahead of the time. ●

The author's special thanks to Arne Hoff, from whose book *Aeldre Dansk Bössemageri* these illustrations were drawn.

the rifle the shooter simply rotates the trigger guard half a turn, forwards and back.

Although it was far from gastight, the action worked well for the first few rounds. It became increasingly stiff to operate as powder residue built up, and it was extremely complicated and expensive in the first place.

When Fredrik III had succeeded his father Christian IV in 1648, he decided to equip his Scanian Guards—100 men—with Kalthoff repeaters, the first repeating firearms to be adopted by any army. They were issued in 1657 or soon after, at a time when the musketeers of all the great powers still carried smoothbore matchlock muskets, since in that year the Swedish ambassador reported home that "they will soon be equipped with repeating rifles" *(Becker, E. Samlinger til Danmarks Historie under Fredrik III. 1.p 194.)* and since two letters from the king, both dated 1659, stated that one company of the Guards now carried such rifles. *(Nielsen, O. Kjöbenhavns Diplomatarium V, p. 605 ff.)* They were still used in 1674 and 1675, when ammunition was issued. *(Royal Armoury Accounts.)*

These weapons were probably made by Peter Kalthoff who was first mentioned in 1641, and died in 1672, and by Mathias Kalthoff, who was first mentioned in 1656, when he was already a master, and died by 1681. Some may have been made by Hans Boringholm, mentioned as a master in 1670, who died shortly before 1700, a pupil of Mathias Kalthoff's, and also by Anders Mortensen, who was a master by 1677, and was still alive in 1717, Hans Boringholm's pupil. At least, the latter two men made repeaters for

Fig. 3: (Below) This diagrams the Kalthoff action. At top is the breechblock; then the ball-loader; at bottom the powder vent.

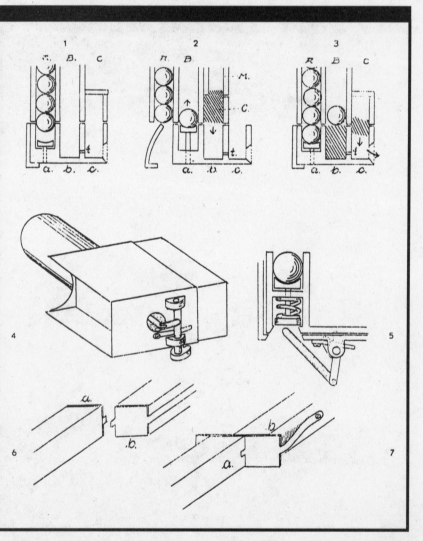

IF YOU THINK OUR PRODUCTS ARE DURABLE, THEN TAKE A LOOK AT OUR GUARANTEE.

At RCBS, we make over 5,000 different products for reloaders. From dies and presses to scales, bullet moulds and accessories.

Yet our main concern isn't how many we make, but how well we make them. Carefully. Meticulously. For reloaders, by reloaders. The same way we've done it for over four decades.

RCBS.
EVERYTHING WE MAKE IS GUARANTEED FOR LIFE OR FOREVER: WHICHEVER COMES FIRST.
If your RCBS equipment breaks or doesn't work, we'll fix it or replace it. Free. No time limit. No questions asked.
GUARANTEE

And that's not just idle talk. We back up our words with the most far-reaching guarantee in the reloading business.

But the real beauty of our lifetime guarantee isn't its simplicity or its extent. It's the simple fact that you will probably never need to use it.

RCBS®
YOUR SHOOTING PARTNER.
CCI · SPEER · RCBS · OUTERS · WEAVER

The new Double Eagle™ state-of-the-art shooting system. Only from the leader. Colt.

THE EAGLE HAS LANDED.

Our new double action delivers large-bore punch. It's reliability with an edge: A choice of double or single action firing. An 8-round magazine. A beveled magazine well. Three-dot sight system. Non-reflective stainless steel. Available in 45ACP and 10mm Auto.

For personal protection, law enforcement, or competition, fly with the Eagle. The new Double Eagle from Colt, the leader in 45ACP and 10mm pistols.

COLT®

MADE ONLY IN THE USA≈

THE ONE FOR THE BIG FIVE.

You can see the freshly broken branches. The spotters have your quarry in sight. You're closing in on the trophy of a lifetime.

When you only get one shot at glory, don't take it with anything less than a Weatherby® Mark V® Safari® Grade rifle.

For more than 40 years, the Weatherby name has been synonymous with power and accuracy in big game hunting. We pioneered the first high-velocity magnum rifle back in 1945. And we've been perfecting it ever since.

Designed for the hunter who desires simple elegance and high quality in a custom rifle, the Safari Grade is an outstanding example of Weatherby perfection. Painstakingly crafted from hand-selected French walnut, its stock features handsome, fine-line checkering. Its action is customized and hand-honed for smoothness.

Choose from five Weatherby® magnum calibers best suited for the safari hunt: .300, .340, .378, .416 and .460.

Best of all, like all Weatherby Mark V rifles, the Safari Grade's performance is as remarkable as its appearance. From a cold barrel, it's guaranteed to shoot a 1½″ or less, 3-shot group at 100 yards.

So when you're in the market for today's finest safari rifle, set your sights on the awesome Weatherby Mark V Safari Grade.

It's everything you're shooting for.

Weatherby®
Always ahead of the game.

NSSF:

30 Years on the Line

by STEVE LIGHTFOOT

Biathlete Mary Ostergren of Vermont uses Summer Biathlon as a training tool; thousands now run and shoot it for itself alone.

OUTSIDE of a day in September for the yearly observance of National Hunting and Fishing Day, most shooters don't come in direct contact with the National Shooting Sports Foundation. Or do they?

The NSSF celebrates its diamond anniversary this year: 30 years of promoting a better understanding of and a more active participation in the shooting sports. And, if you look around, you'll probably see a few of their gems in action.

Don't be surprised if on your next trip to the shooting range, someone in designer running shoes and bright-colored, stretchy knit shorts turns up next to you on the firing line. It's quite possible you're seeing a Summer Biathlon competitor sharpening his or her shooting skills for an upcoming race. The NSSF conceived this warm weather spin-off of the popular Winter Olympic sport to attract new shooters. And it has certainly done that, with over fifty races across the country held last year alone, including an International Series featuring Olympic athletes from Russia and East Germany.

A combination of running and shooting, Summer Biathlon is administered by the U.S. Biathlon Association under a grant from the NSSF. But what Summer Biathlon is really about is favorable publicity for shooting: With stories in the *New York Times,* the *Los Angeles Times, USA Today,* they have achieved that objective in spades.

You may have seen another of the NSSF's most ambitious new shooting programs, the Chevy Truck/Sportsman's Team Challenge, on ESPN, in a recent edition of *Sports Afield* maga-

zine, or possibly in person at your local gun club. This new competition is designed to recognize the country's best all-round shooters with three-man teams competing in pistol, rifle and shotgun events and to recognize their accomplishments with cash purses exceeding $100,000.

If you're seeing new faces at your local range, it could be as a result of any number of NSSF promotions. Recently, the Foundation gave some ten million outdoor enthusiasts who read *Field &*

(Below) The string finished—
they are knockdown targets—
the rifle is left and away goes
the runner.

(Above) A Summer Biathlon event
is mostly running—up to ten kilo-
meters.

(Above) Runners are running between shooting stations, where
they get a standard arm to shoot.

Stream magazine information about over 900 places to shoot nationwide by running its "Directory of Public Shooting Ranges" in the publication.

Those new shooters at your range might also be taking the NSSF up on its invitation to sportsmen to see: "How Well Do You Shoot?" This program enables hunters to compare their shotgun, rifle and pistol shooting skills with those of the "average" sportsman nationwide. For example, NSSF determined that the average score among hunters in trap was 13x25 and in Skeet, 11x25. On average, the scores improved by about two birds if a second round was shot. Testing in the rifle event had each hunter fire 20 shots offhand with a 22 rimfire from 50 yards. The target used was a

For a decade, NSSF has worked to educate young people about hunting and conservation, and placed almost 85,000 sets of educational videos and filmstrips in our nation's schools.

Here it is, shooting's biggest apple, the Shooting, Hunting and Outdoor Trade (SHOT) Show, which draws thousands of manufacturers, distributors, dealers and members of the media together each year.

standard 50-yard small-bore rifle target. The average score in this event was 95x200. Handgun testing was shot at standard NRA targets for both 25-yard slow fire and 25-yard rapid fire events. Twenty shots with a 22 rimfire handgun shot from the offhand position was the standard for testing. The average slow fire score was 92x200, while the rapid fire score averaged 125x200.

Then, again, those newcomers to the gun club may have been spurred by an article on shooting in their local paper or favorite magazine. Each year, the NSSF provides information about the shooting sports to over 3800 outdoor communicators across the country through press releases, public service advertisements and radio and video news releases. Information ranges from how to get started in trap, Skeet or silhouette, to how much Pittman-Robertson federal aid to wildlife funds were raised through excise taxes on the shotshells fired at the Grand American.

Other major NSSF activities encompass development of new shooters and places to shoot. The Foundation's literature program features over forty publications on topics ranging from firearms safety and hunter ethics to the role of the hunter in conservation, as well as such down-to-earth subjects as "How To Start A Gun Club" and "When Your Youngster Wants A Gun."

The NSSF has taken an active involvement in helping to ensure sportsmen will have a place to shoot in the future by sponsoring projects such as: a National Range Development Symposium; producing a quarterly "problem-solver" newsletter, *The Gun Club Advisor,* for gun clubs and shooting ranges; and underwriting a comprehensive pamphlet for the Wildlife Management Institute titled: "How To Develop New Places To Shoot."

Since its inception, the NSSF has maintained a commitment to providing young people with information about and opportunities for shooting. In the last ten years, the Foundation has placed over 85,000 sets of educational materials in our nation's schools—free of charge. As a result, recent surveys have shown that those programs have resulted in a 40 percent improvement in young people's attitudes toward hunting. Coincidentally, almost a quarter million dollars has been raised for NSSF's educational programs through annual SHOT Show auction guns and prints.

The Foundation also sponsors "hands-on" shooting promotions for youngsters through 4-H and Boy Scouts of America and contributes to the collegiate shooting ranks, as well, through sponsorship of ACU-I competition.

Over the last 30 years, the NSSF's programs have responded to the needs of the times. But the Foundation's goals have never changed: To help every hunter and shooter; help make ours a safer, more satisfying sport; and assure that the sons, daughters and grandchildren of today's sportsmen and women will be able to enjoy the shooting sports in the future.

The NSSF Promotional Materials Catalog describes instructive booklets, posters, filmstrips, slides, videotapes, publications and other useful materials available at nominal cost to all hunters and shooters. For a free copy of this catalog, write to: National Shooting Sports Foundation, 555 Danbury Road, Wilton, CT 06897. ●

Editor's Note: The National Shooting Sports Foundation is also the guiding light behind the world's greatest shooting trade show. Each year for four days in January, the entire industry, worldwide, can be found at NSSF's Shooting Hunting and Outdoor Trades (SHOT) Show, wherever it is.   Ken Warner

The NSSF is actively involved in promoting youth shooting instruction through groups such as 4-H and the Boy Scouts of America.

by DONALD M. SIMMONS

Model 66MB Mohawk Brown

Model 66AB Apache Black

Model 66BD Black Diamond

Model 76MB Mohawk Brown

Model 11 bolt action—box magazine

Model 12 bolt action—tubular magazine

Those Plastic Remingtons

Best Wishes
to a Good
Sportsman—
Tom Frye
Remington Arms Co Inc

WORLD 22 RIFLE
AERIAL SHOOTING RECORD
100,010 WOOD BLOCKS—6 MISSES
SET BY TOM FRYE
REMINGTON ARMS COMPANY, INC.
1959

IN THE SPRING of the dark Depression year of 1933, E.I. Du Pont de Nemours & Company took a sick Remington Arms Company under its wing. Remington at that time not only made firearms, which were their principal product, but also controlled a large ammunition company and had been dabbling in such things as cash registers, typewriters, and pocketknives.

Du Pont sent over some of its top management people to help get Remington back on its feet. Their first task was to modernize the existing Remington line and all popular Remington rifles went through a face-lifting process. For example, in the high-powered line, the slide-action Model 14 and autoloading Model 8 were cosmetically upgraded to the Models 141 and 81. So, too, in the line of repeating 22-caliber rifles: the autoloading Model 24 was renamed the Model 241 and the popular slide-action Model 12 became the Model 121. All this was accomplished in the Depression days of 1936.

The arrival of World War II more or less put sporting arms on the back burner, but with the coming of peace, new guns began to come out of Remington's Research and Development department. A new philosophy of having an entire line of firearms sharing a large number of parts and even sharing in common some of the more complicated subassemblies was instigated at Remington.

And during the late 1950s, spurred by Du Pont, Remington began to plan an almost entirely plastic rifle. This rifle was to be an autoloading 22 weighing less than five pounds, and was to be priced near to that of competition. Remington asked the chemical engineers at Du Pont to come up with a plastic that could replace both the wooden stock and the receiver. This was a tall order and here are the specs given to the Du Pont chemical development department:

1. The material must be capable of forming any shape desired.
2. It must have a high tensile impact and flexural strength.
3. It must have high abrasion resistance.
4. It must have high resistance to heat distortion.
5. It must be resistant to cold temperatures.
6. It must, if exposed to a flame, not continue to burn when that flame is removed.
7. It must be impervious to solvents, oils, mild acids, alkalis,

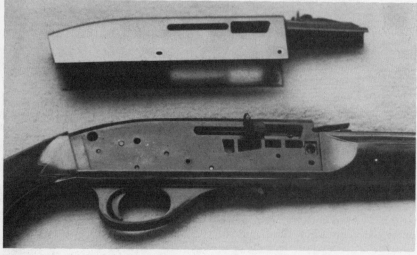
Remington's guarantee of the Nylon stock; this decal was on each one.

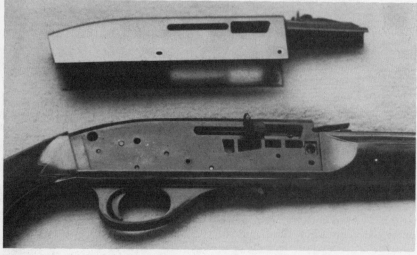

Right side Mohawk 10-C, cover removed.

fungus, rodents, and insects.

8. It must have a finish that is easy to repair.
9. It must be light in weight.
10. It must hold permanent colors.
11. It must have no corrosive effect on other parts.
12. It must be self-lubricating and dimensionally stable.

In less than four months, Du Pont's engineers came up with Nylon Zytel-101. This wonderful plastic had all of those prerequisites and then some. Because of mould cost, the first model was not moulded; instead, a nylon prototype was machined out of bar nylon, and this amazing rifle was able to be fired 75,000 times. This initial testing established the feasibility of using plastic in the manufacture of a gun.

The new Remington family of plastic rifles began with an autoloading 22 rifle called their Model 66. Nylon Zytel-101 only came in basic colors like red, blue, black and yellow but the engineers at Remington found that they could mix these colors and arrive at a wood-like shade. The wood-colored mixture was called Number 66, thus the name of the rifle. Production began in November of 1958. The Model 66 has been so popular that a dead-ringer copy has been imported from Brazil by Firearms Import & Export Corp. (F.I.E.) of Hialeah, Florida.

The Remington Model 66 has a moulded Zylon-101 stock, which is injection moulded in two halves, of which one half has a tongue and the other a groove. They are later bonded together to form a strong hollow assembly replacing three normal sections, the buttstock and forearm, of course, are two; the middle section is the rifle's receiver. Remington calls Color Number 66 "Mohawk Brown." The buttplate, the forearm tip, and the pistol grip cap are all black plastic bonded in place. Each has an attractive white spacer. There are two reinforcing screws with nuts under the receiver cover, and there is one more under the ivory-white diamonds on each side of the forearm. The magazine is in the butt of the rifle, loaded through the buttplate, holding 14 22 Long Rifle standard or high-speed cartridges.

The striker (hammer) is either an investment steel casting or a forging which requires no machining, except for the two-diameter hole down its center; the bolt appears to be a steel machined forging. The two parts run in grooves in the self-lubricating nylon receiver. The other parts are either stainless steel or mild steel stampings or, like the trigger guard and the trigger itself, are also plastic.

The barrel measures just over 19½ inches, and is clamped to the receiver by a screw-secured barrel bracket in a cradle formed within the stock. When, rarely, the gun needs cleaning, the barrel can be easily removed and cleaned from the breech.

One of the main advantages of the Model 66 from a manufacturer's point of view is that the gun could be assembled with little or no hand fitting. The total weight is about 4½ pounds, and the initial price was $49.95. In spite of the lack of hand fitting, trigger pulls of all the plastic Remington rifles I've seen have been excellent.

In 1959, the Armalite Corporation of Costa Mesa, California, introduced their AR-7 which had a plastic stock, into which the entire rifle could be stored. One of the two big differences between the AR-7 and the Remington 66 is the fact that the 66's bolt runs in a nylon receiver but the bolt of the AR-7 is in a metallic die-cast receiver. The second difference is that the size of the mould required to make the entire Remington stock is much larger. The AR-7 is still made today by Charter Arms Corp. of Stratford, Connecticut.

In the early 1970s, Winchester offered their Model 270, a slide-action, tubular magazine, 22-caliber rifle with a Cycolac plastic stock and forearm. Again, as in the case of the Armalite gun, the mould size of the Model 66 overshadows the Winchester; this rifle never seemed to be very popular with the plastic and was discontinued in the mid-1970s.

Today we hear much about the plastic Austrian Glock 9mm pistols; someone stirred up the feeling they might be able to pass through airport security without detection. However, the Remington Nylon 66 rifle never caused a ripple to the delicate sensitivity of the Ban the Gun groups. It had a steel bolt that recoiled in a plastic receiver, not as in the Glock 17 a steel slide running in steel clips, albeit a plastic frame, too. Both the Glock and the Remington rifle in its later box magazine model appear to have plastic magazines in which only the magazine spring and the cartridges themselves are visible under X-ray. The Glock 17 also has a detectable sheet metal liner while the Remington is all plastic, save for only a small metal "U" clip that holds the top rear of the magazine lips together. The most remarkable point is that the production of the Remington plastic rifle preceded the Glock plastic pistol by almost 30 years!

At the time Remington introduced the Model 66, they still had two other autoloading 22s on the market: the old Model 550-1 and the newer Model 552. The Model 550-1 was on its way out, but the 552 is still in the Remington catalog today. At the time of the Model 66's introduction, the 550-1 sold for $46.75, and the 552 sold for $52.25. The Model 66 acted as a sort of "middle of the line" gun at $49.95.

Sales figures for the Model 66 and its spinoffs are remarkable; at no time through 1981, where my year-to-year production figures end, did it sell under 20,000 rifles per year, and in the year after its introduction, 1959, almost 80,000 were produced. The average yearly production was almost 40,000 rifles. What led to the almost

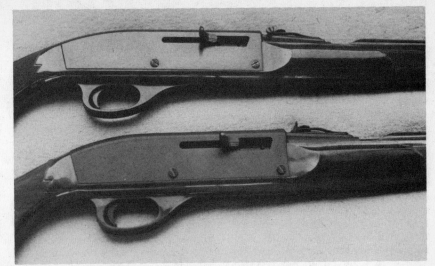

Detail of the early (top) and late covers and rear sights.

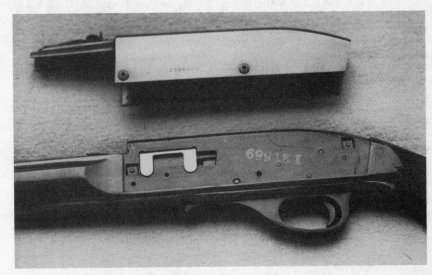

Left side Mohawk 10-C, cover removed.

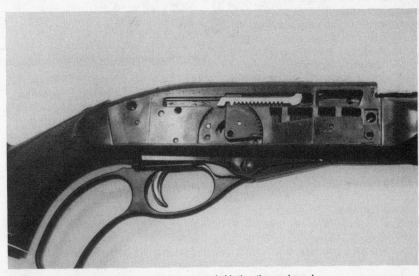

Detail of the Model 76 with its cover removed. Notice the rack and pinion action—most ingenious.

The two correct tools for disassembling—a 50 Centavo Mexican coin and a round-ground screwdriver.

instant public acceptance of this revolutionary rifle? I think the answer is its reliability. Ever since the first 22 autoloading rifle came on the market, there has been a great doubt in the public's mind about performance. The first American autoloader was the Winchester Model 1903 which was a quality rifle, but even with its own special ammo, it could occasionally malfunction, especially if it was not cleaned often enough. The Remington Model 66, dirty or clean, wet or dry, just kept rolling along. With this well-earned reputation, it is easy to see why shooters bought it in large quantities.

The Model 66 has been used to establish endurance records in aerial target shooting. In 1959, Mr. Tom Frye, a representative for Remington, made history as an aerial shooter by firing a set of three Remington Model 66 rifles for 100,010 rounds in 14 days. He only missed six of the hand-thrown wooden blocks in all those shots, a record that still stands today. Each rifle fired 33,000 times and none had a malfunction. This also stands as a testimonial to the sound design of the Remington plastic rifle.

In order to avoid shooter rejection of their PLASTIC gun because of its plastic receiver, the designers at Remington covered the nylon receiver with a blued steel stamping. They must have decided that as long as they were going to disguise the receiver with a steel shell, they might as well make the shell serve some useful purpose. With this in mind, the receiver cover has the rear sight assembly riveted to it. The rear sight is screw-adjustable for both windage and elevation, which is unusual for a rifle in this price range. The cover is grooved so a scope can be mounted. It has been found that when a scope is mounted and the gun is too-rigidly gripped the point of impact may be changed. The steel cover also holds the ejector into the receiver. Finally, the flat spring that tensions the cartridge feed guide is mounted by a rivet to the cover's underside. The original receiver cover had no serial number stamped on it until 1968, when the

federal law required that all guns have serial numbers. This requirement must have given Remington a fit, because their receiver was plastic and completely covered. They ended up with the cover stamped instead on the left side.

The serial numbering of the Model 66 and its spinoffs started in 1967 at S/N 400000 and went to 419011, but at that time the number was stamped on the underside of the barrel just aft of the front sight. In 1968 the S/N started with 419012 and went to S/N 473710. In December of 1968, the serial was changed to 2100000, which accounts for the seemingly high serial numbers seen. When this series of serial numbers reached 2599999 in February of 1977, the letter "A" was added and the S/N went back to A2100000 again. In the last production year of 1988, the serial numbers would be in the A2360000 range. Also, today's numbers are stamped much deeper than they had been previously, for longer and clearer legibility. These serial numbers indicate that even in the last year of production, Remington was making an average of whopping 27,000 Nylons per year!

There is one item on a true blowback action that is nonfunctional—the extractor. When a blowback gun cycles, the shell acts as a piston, driving the

bolt rearward without the extractor doing anything. The extractor *is* functional, of course, when an *unfired* cartridge is withdrawn from the gun's breech manually. To verify this, I removed the extractor from one and the rifle functioned perfectly. If the Model 66 is to be fired as a single shot, a loaded cartridge is laid in the ejection port with the rifle slightly slanted. The bolt is retracted and released and the round will automatically be chambered. Also, no matter if the rifle is held right side up or upside down or any place in between it will keep firing.

The Model 66 was just the beginning of a family of 22-caliber plastic rifles

Model	Years Introduced	List Price Then
66	1958	$49.95
66SG	1959	$49.95
66AB	1962	$54.95
66GS	1962	$59.95
76	1962	$59.95
11	1962	$36.95
12	1962	$39.95
10	1962	$25.95
150 Year Commemorative	1966	
77	1970	$54.95
Mohawk 10-C	1971	$54.95
Bi-Centennial Commemorative	1976	$84.95
Black Diamond	1978	$84.95
Apache 77	1987	$109.95

to be made by Remington Arms. The first change, begun in early 1959, was not in the model of the rifle, but rather in the addition of a new color for its stock. "Seneca Green" was the name given to the new stock's mottled dark olive color; this color was discontinued in 1961. The model was called 66SG. Still retaining the basic Model 66, the Apache Black color was added in late 1962, and called the Model 66AB; it was also called the "Presentation" grade. This new variation to the 66 was black-stocked with the receiver cover and the barrel chromium-plated—an impressive combination of colors. The plating of the steel parts was discontinued in 1983, but the black stock was available as the Model 66BD, "Black Diamond."

In the momentous year of 1962, four new models were added to Remington's Nylon gun line. A lever-action repeater in 22 Long Rifle only, the Model 76, was dubbed the Trail Rider. This gun has an extremely short throw on its lever and was available in Mohawk Brown and Apache Black. The internal mechanism is something to behold. The designers of this spinoff had

nounced a low cost Nylon-stocked single shot bolt-action rifle, the Model 10, which, as a safety feature, went on safety each time it was cocked. Strangely, with Remington's great interest in interchangeability, none of the bolt-action rifles shared parts with the Model 66 that could have been the same. As an example, the white diamond that covers the screw in the bolt-action line is entirely different from the one used in the others.

None of these spinoffs really caught

ical shooting gallery hardware) are added. In 1966 Remington made the Model 66 a Commemorative celebrating Remington's 150th year; it had an embossed receiver cover. Lastly, and probably the rarest, was the smooth bore 22 Nylon Model 10 single shot, a bolt-action shotgun.

A lot of confusion exists as to which model plastic rifle is which, all of which can be readily resolved by looking at any rifle's black pistol grip cap where the full model nomenclature will be found. There is also the Remington bolt-action single shot handgun with a nylon plastic stock, the Model XP-100, which was introduced in 1963.

The next spinoff from the Model 66—in 1970—was the Model 77, a 5-shot box magazine, autoloading Nylon rifle. This magazine, with the exception of its spring and strength clip discussed before, is all plastic. The shooting public seemed to want more magazine capacity and a 10-shot magazine was soon offered as an accessory. In 1971 the Model 77 was renamed the Mohawk 10-C and came with a 10-shot magazine as standard equipment. The original Model 77 was phased out in 1971 and the Mohawk 10-C lasted until 1978. It was a promotional rifle offered to the distributors in large quantities at special discount. At this writing, the only surviving Model 66

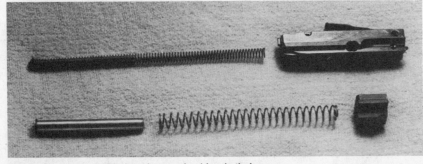

Bolt and hammer, with their springs and guides, in their correct positions.

Plastic trigger guard detail.

to work with what they had, using the Model 66 stock and bolt. They came up with a locked-breech lever-action rifle starting from an autoloader. They created a very short stroke—about 30 degrees—lever action with a rack and pinion reminiscent of the old Bullard lever-action rifle. The only fly in the ointment of interchangeability was that the barrel, the magazine, and the sights were the only parts borrowed as-is from the Model 66. Could they have gone on from there and substituted a pump forearm for the lever? I would guess Remington had this in mind, but the lack of Model 76 sales changed their plans.

The other new models were bolt actions, but with the Model 66 type of stock and sights, and there the similarity ended. The Nylon Model 11 has a steel detachable box magazine, six-shot, 22 Short, Long, or Long Rifle—later there was a 10-shot magazine. The Model 12 is the same type of rifle with a 22 Short or 15 Long Rifle-length tubular magazine under the barrel. In late 1962, Remington an-

Model	Years Made	Quantity
66	1958-To Date	(By 1981) 956062
66 Seneca Green	1959-1962	42500
76	1962-1964	26947
11	1962-1964	22423
12	1962-1964	27551
10	1962-1964	10670
150 Year Commemorative	1966	3792
77	1970-1973	15327
Mohawk 10-C	1971-1975	(By 1972) 5601
Bi-Cent Commemorative	1976	

on and by 1964 all four models were dropped. Some rare combinations were also sold; the bolt-action Nylons were occasionally made with Seneca Green stocks, and also unusual was the Model 66, made to shoot 22 Shorts (only) called the "Gallery Special Model". . . . 66GS; this rifle, in a world that had forgotten the small town carnival. These relatively rare rifles were introduced in 1962 and terminated in 1981. The "Gallery Special" uses a lot of different parts in its manufacture, the bolt and the striker and their respective springs are different for functional reasons, while a counter chain retainer and a cartridge deflector (typ-

is the promotional rifle called the Apache 77 which today is being sold at discount houses such as K-Mart for about $109.95. These latest of the Nylons have their metal parts finished in a jet black with a black sand-blasted painted finish on the external metal parts and the stock/receiver is a dark olive blue-green; there is a 10-round magazine. In September 1987 these new rifles, a cross between the rebirth of the Mohawk 10-C and the Black Diamond were on sale at K-Mart for the low price of $84.97, a real bargain!

One can see by my compilation of list prices that Remington was competitive, but the shooting public didn't

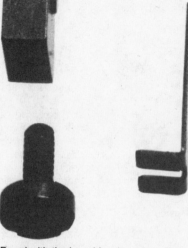

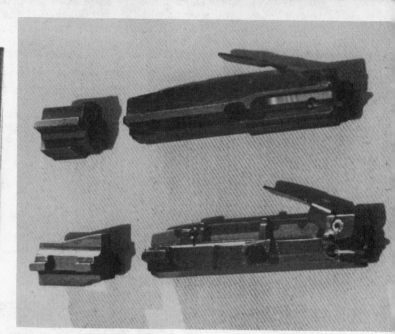

Barrel with the barrel bracket assembled in the correct mounting position.

Bolt and striker of a regular Model 66 over the special lightened parts of a Gallery Special.

take to the other plastic rifles like they did to the Model 66. Also note every price was 5 cents short of the next highest dollar.

The two U.S. patents issued to Remington Arms to cover the Model 66 and the subsequent spinoffs are 3,023,527 and 3,027,811, and they cover both the use of plastics to form combination stock/receiver, and the disconnector system used in this fine rifle. Patent number 3,023,527, applied for in January of 1956, was issued on March 6, 1962. It covers the rifle and could be considered the basic specific patent for the whole family of rifles that it eventually spawned. The patent is in the joint names of Wayne E. Leek, of Ilion, New York, which is the town where Remington is located, and Charles H. Morse of Herkimer, New York, which is a smaller town just south of Ilion. These men were the leaders of a design team which put together the Model 66.

The second patent, referred to in detail in the first patent, is number 3,027,811 filed April 29, 1958 and issued April 3, 1962. The patent is in the name of Homer W. Young of Ilion, New York, and covers the ingenious sear

and disconnector system using sheet metal stampings as found in the Model 66 et al.

Both patents were assigned to Remington Arms Co., as these men were employees, and both patents make for very interesting reading, although like all patents, you have to read and reread them to get the meat of their disclosures. In the Leek/Morse patent, there is one section that restates in a few words the entire principle of the Young patent so that you don't have to be looking at the two patents all the time. Also in the Leek/Morse patent there is a very interesting section describing the competitor's plastics that could be used to make the rifle's stock/receiver instead of using Du Pont's Zytel. Also here we are told that Du Pont's Teflon could be used but it was then too expensive and too difficult to mould.

There is always a lot to learn in reading patents. In all the drawings included in the patents, there is no cartridge feeder guide shown because, obviously, it had not yet been found necessary to the smooth feeding of the autoloading rifle. Also, from the pat-

ents we see that Remington was not sure whether to use a more or less standard cross-bolt manual safety behind the trigger or the top of the pistol grip sliding shotgun-type safety. They ended up with the latter.

The Leek/Morse patent shows an extremely complicated adjustable rear sight that was replaced in production by a much simpler and more efficient one. The patent shows a double screw-adjustable windage setup, while the early production sight had two wheels, one for adjustment of elevation and the other windage; later the windage wheel was replaced by a very small slotted screw. Both the screws are peened over so they can't fall off during shooting.

The action of the 66 is very interesting in that it uses a sear block mechanism. In this system the sear itself is free to pivot out of engagement with the striker against its own spring tension. This is because it is over-ridden by the much stronger cocked striker spring tension. All this above movement is prevented by the disconnector/sear block stopping any unlocking movement of the sear. When the trigger is pulled, the disconnector/sear block moves forward and unlocks the sear which releases the striker. When the bolt, after firing, blows rearward driving the striker back, the disconnector/sear block is detached from the trigger, which allows the striker to be locked in the cocked position. In addition to the normal function just described, the disconnector/sear block prevents accidental jar firing of the rifle.

A design patent was also issued to three men, Robert P. Kelly, James S. Martin, and Wayne E. Leek. This type of patent is good for 14 years and this partially explains why the F.I.E. rifle can look so much like the Remington Model 66!

The quantities of these various models of Nylon guns made are very interesting in that the numbers of some of the models are quite, quite low. On the other hand, all the Nylons would have passed 1 million rifles in 1983 at the previously established rate of 40,000 per year.

Various magazines for Apache 77, 10-C, 11, 77, 581.

In writing about the Remington plastic rifles, I really don't need to proof fire them because both I and so many others have tested them so often that everybody knows of their reliability. I did have two Mohawk 10-Cs in my collection that I thought would interest the readers to test. That is because one of them went back to the factory very often for repairs and the other is perfect. The older Mohawk is serial number 2398803 and was assembled by the factory in March of 1974. No later than April, 1974, it went back to the factory for repairs; in December of 1974, it returned to the factory again. Again in November of 1978, same old thing—back again. Finally, in March of 1982, it went to the factory again. One would think by this time the rifle would be perfect, but, alas, it was not to be, for the gun still jams occasionally with a loaded 22 cartridge partially in the chamber— about once in every 25 rounds. I cured

it by replacing the entire receiver cover assembly; I suspect the cover-mounted cartridge feed guide spring was not putting quite the required tension on the guide itself.

The other Mohawk is serial number 2417818 made in June of the same year, 1974, and is unmarked as ever having been returned for repairs. It has never malfunctioned in firing hundreds of rounds. Thus we have two Mohawk 10-Cs made within four months of each other; one is a good guy and the other is a black sheep, a rare one.

Changes in the logo stamped on the Nylon Remington barrels: The original logo stamped on the barrel in the open space just in front of the rear sight was "PAT. PEND." over "22 L.R. ONLY" plus the date code and the final inspector's stamp. Later the PAT. PEND. was dropped as the patent was granted and the stylized word "Remington" was added. Most Nylons I have seen also have the oval stamp with "REP" on the right rear of the barrel. This, we understand, means "Remington's English Proofed." In the early 1980s, Remington started to use a much larger stamp on the barrel behind the front sight. It read: "REMINGTON 22 LONG RIFLE ONLY." The date code and inspection stamps remained where they were. Late-manufactured Remington Nylon rifles like the Model 66 and the Black Diamond, and their newest promotional rifles, the Apache 77, carry the cryptic, and now universal, "Warning—read instruction book for safe operation—free from" (over) "Remington Arms Company, Inc., Ilion N.Y. USA" on the barrel just behind the front sight. At the breech, the Remington logo is replaced with just "22 LONG RIFLE ONLY," with the date code and the approval stamps.

Variations in the Model 66 and its spinoffs are relatively rare. The legend or logo changes on the barrel have already been covered. The front sight's material changed in about 1962 from

a steel investment casting to a nonferrous die casting. This material change lasted only until about 1964 and then the sight went back to steel again. The front sight cross-sectional shape varied to a more upright line on the sight's post, giving a more conventional sight picture. The barrel at its breech had two gas relief cuts added very soon after production started. In the event of a ruptured shell casing, these cuts allow the hot gases to escape in a vertical direction, thus not hurting the shooter. The bolt's forward face had no spot facing cut as originally fabricated; soon a semi-circular end mill cut was added. The original cartridge feed guide piece was held in the bolt through its two hook-like arms by a roll pin. Later on, the surface area of the arms was increased and the hooks became two holes which completely enclosed the pin. The windage adjustment screw on the early rifles up to 1964 was a small coin-slotted knob; because it was so exposed and easily bent, it was replaced by a conventional headless screw. The original striker spring sleeve was made from seamless steel tubing; this was replaced by an open seamed tube in the very early production guns. The earliest strikers were machined all over and appear to have been made from steel bar stock; later the strikers were made from an investment steel casting with little or no machining. The fore and rear ends of the ribs of the striker are much more beveled in the cast ones. In the very earliest Model 66s, the barrel bracket and the later separate barrel support were one piece. Next, in order to use up the stock of thick barrel brackets, a milling cut was taken on one side to make room for the new barrel support. In early examples of the Model 66, on the inside of the plastic stock in the area under the receiver cover, there was a large boss on the right side of the foremost edge of the outer magazine tube which was later deleted from the mould of the right-hand stock piece. Lately, Remington Nylon rifles have their receiver's covers finished in the crinkly black described earlier on the Model Apache 77.

The basic differences between the tubular Model 66s and the box magazine Model 77s and others of its ilk are found obviously in the magazines and the area of the stock where those magazines are mounted. The thing not so apparent is that the bolts of the two types of rifles are very different and can't be interchanged. The 77 bolt has a feed rib at the bottom and this rib is not found on a 66. Also, the contour of the ejectors on the two rifles change.

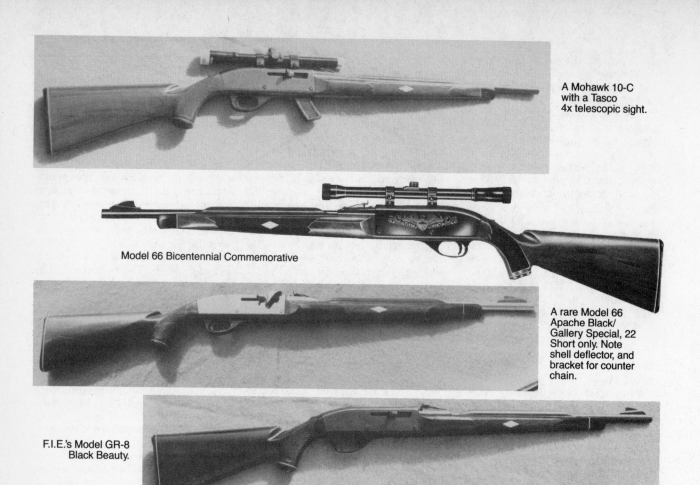

A Mohawk 10-C with a Tasco 4x telescopic sight.

Model 66 Bicentennial Commemorative

A rare Model 66 Apache Black/Gallery Special, 22 Short only. Note shell deflector, and bracket for counter chain.

F.I.E.'s Model GR-8 Black Beauty.

To help identify the two items, the one with two holes is used in the tubular Model 66; the one with three is for the box magazine rifles.

F.I.E. (Firearms Import and Export Corp.) of Hialeah, Florida, imported a Remington Model 66 look-a-like from Brazil. The actual manufacturer is CBC (Cia Brasileire Cartuchos, Brazilian Cartridge Company) of Santo Andre, Brazil, SA. The CBC rifle was sold here as the "Black Beauty," usually priced lower than the Remington it was patterned after. In the 1930s Remington Arms owned a minority interest in CBC and with the help of Remington's engineering and production personnel they manufactured Remington guns for the Brazilian market. When, in 1981, the Brazilian government nationalized the company, doing away with Remington's interest in CBC, the Brazilian company was left with the tooling and know-how which enabled them to make a copy of the Remington Model 66.

I have been very satisfied with my Brazilian copy. There are some small differences between the two rifles. The F.I.E. gun has a black stock with black buttplate, pistol grip cap, and forearm tip. Each of these pieces is bonded to the stock with the typical white spacer.

There is also a white diamond covering the forearm stock bolt. These add-ons in the F.I.E. are very neatly bonded to the stock with no rough edges at the bonding point. The front sight is a nonsteel die casting, without the typical Remington white dot. The rear sight still has a knob on the windage adjustment screw.

Internally, the parts that are in the Remington left in the white are blued in the F.I.E. The fit of the bolt in the nylon receiver in the F.I.E. import is a little more loose than in the Remington, but this seems to have no effect on the function of the rifle. The Brazilian gun's external metal parts are well polished and then blued in a deep black color. Many of the internal parts are steel investment castings including the trigger, and show little or no machining; the rest are, like in the Remington, steel stampings.

While the rifling in the F.I.E. offers the same six lands and grooves and clockwise twist as in the Remington, the actual rifling is quite different in cross-section. The lands in the F.I.E. are rounder on top, and the grooves are deeper. The barrel and the receiver cover are both serial numbered, which is a good idea; the F.I.E. rifle's muzzle is not crowned as in the Remington 66.

Like the Remington, the F.I.E. has a bright yellow follower in the magazine that will protrude and can be readily seen when the bolt is drawn rearward. This acts as a very important safety feature, telling the shooter the magazine is empty. F.I.E.'s follower is about 1/8-inch longer than the Remington and can be seen much more easily.

The most remarkable difference, in my mind, is found in the manual that comes with the F.I.E. There are NO instructions on how to field-strip the rifle, let alone disassemble it. Since it is so like the Remington, I just started to take it apart in a similar manner, but things didn't come apart as easily. The receiver cover front retaining screw was very difficult to remove from its hole, and the bolt cocking handle had to be pried from the bolt with two screwdrivers and a great deal of force. The barrel bracket that secures the barrel in the stock fits very tightly around the barrel, and had to be driven out of the slot in the barrel with a drift punch. Adding to the feeling that this rifle is never to be field-stripped is the fact that the barrel support, which in a Remington is marked "FRONT," is marked "FRENTE," Spanish for front.

I don't know whether the F.I.E. people who wrote the manual don't want the shooter to ever take the rifle apart or if they think that it will never need to be thoroughly cleaned, but I have seen Remington Nylons that were never cleaned by their former owners and they were full of carbon deposits and grit and sand. Although the guns still worked, they are subject to unwarranted wear because of the dirt. In the initial testfiring of the F.I.E. I used both 22 Long Rifle standard and high velocity. The standard ammo had trouble cycling the action with a full magazine on the first two or three series, when the gun was brand-new. After some series of both standard and high speed, the action functioned better.

While in general one would expect the foreign product to undersell our domestic one, this does not seem to be the case in the printed advertising literature for the F.I.E. and the Remington. In the 42nd GUN DIGEST, the Remington 66 was shown at $124 and the F.I.E. Black Beauty at $124.95. Even stranger is the fact that at the recent sale at K-Mart the promotional Remington Apache 77 was $84.97, as mentioned above, and the F.I.E. Black Beauty at that time and store was $96.95.

In preparation for this article on the Remington plastic rifles, I telephoned many people who had advertised a Nylon for sale; almost without exception these were collectors of Remingtons in general and Nylons in particular. In most cases what they had for sale were duplicates. While I knew that these revolutionary rifles interested me, I had no idea how many other collectors were out there. I was also surprised to find that many of these collectors knew much more than I did before I picked their brains.

Jack Heath of Remington Arms wrote me that the Model 66 was to be dropped from the Remington catalog in the year 1988, because the dies that make the plastic stock were wearing out and Remington does not feel justified in replacing them. The Apache 77 will still be available to large quantity buyers. In a gun-using world, where in the military the use of wood is virtually passe, and in a civilian shooting world where walnut stocks have become a luxury and where the climatic stability of plastics is just coming into its own, don't we now see that Remington was way ahead of their time? Don't we also find in a shooting world that no longer feels that gun cleaning and maintenance are important to the function of a firearm that Remington was a quantum jump ahead of its competition? The Remington Model 66 and the type of guns it gave birth to will become more and more common in the near future. •

Acknowledgements

Mr. Jack Heath, Remington Arms Co., Wilmington, Delaware.
Mr. Richard F. Dietz, Remington Arms Co., Wilmington, Delaware.
Mr. Bud Dumsteg, Remington Arms Co., Wilmington, Delaware.
Mr. Ron Vogel, F.I.E., Miami, Florida.
Mr. Leonard Hunter, fellow nylonophyle.
Mr. Steve Adrio, who helped.
Mr. J. D. Anderson, another nylonophyle.
Mr. Michael Sheehan, photographer.
Mrs. Celeste Kelly, photographer.
Mr. John Raynor, one of the biggest nylonophyles.

Remington Nylons
April 16, 1988

MODEL	CODE	DATE	S/N	MODEL	CODE	DATE	S/N	MODEL	CODE	DATE	S/N
66MB	KF	MAY 59	NONE	76MB	PK	JUN 63	NONE	10-C	OZ	JUL 75	2515406
66MB	OF	JUL 59	NONE	12	PK	JUN 63	NONE	10-C	OZ	JUL 75	2521005
66SG	OF	JUL 59	NONE	76AB	DK	SEP 63	NONE	10-C	OZ	JUL 75	2522884
66SG	OF	JUL 59	NONE	76MB	DK	SEP 63	NONE	10-C	OZ	JUL 75	2523885
66SG	BG	JAN 60	NONE	11	BL	JAN 64	NONE	10-C	WZ	AUG 75	2537357
66SG	LG	FEB 60	NONE	11	KL	MAY 64	NONE	66AB	WZ	AUG 75	2538095
66SG	XG	DEC 60	NONE	12	KL	MAY 64	NONE	BI-CENT	LI	FEB 76	2562604
10	?J	62	NONE	12	PL	JUN 64	NONE	BI-CENT	CI	APR 76	2590335
11	BJ	JAN 62	200359	76MB	PL	JUN 64	NONE	BI-CENT	PI	JUN 76	2590747
11	BJ	JAN 62	NONE	76MB	DL	SEP 64	NONE	BI-CENT	LO	FEB 77	2594453
76MB	LJ	FEB 62	NONE	150TH	AN	MAR 66	NONE	66AB/GS	LO	FEB 77	A2107369
12	AJ	MAR 62	NONE	66AB	BR	JAN 68	421705	66AB	AQ	MAR 78	A2152054
76MB	AJ	MAR 62	NONE	66AB	LR	FEB 68	425707	66BD	EQ	OCT 78	A2152530
11	BJ	JAN 62	NONE	66GS	KR	MAY 68	2165148	66BD	PA	JUN 80	A2211592
11	BJ	JAN 62	NONE	77MB	KT	MAY 70	2170597	66BD	PA	JUN 80	A2211807
76MB	J	62	NONE	77MB	KU	MAY 71	2207843	66BD	BB	JAN 81	A2227503
76MB	J	62	NONE	10-C	BW	JAN 72	2233022	66MB	KB	MAY 81	A2241291
11	KJ	MAY 62	NONE	66MB	CW	APR 72	2253118	66AB	WB	AUG 81	A2250227
11	KJ	MAY 62	NONE	10-C	?	?	2273043	66AB	LC	FEB 82	A2261678
76MB	KJ	MAY 62	NONE	10-C	BX	JAN 73	2301825	66BD	RE	NOV 84	A2305651
76MB	PJ	JUN 62	NONE	10-C	PX	JUN 73	2329907	APACHE 77	KH	MAY 87	A2335160
12	PJ	JUN 62	NONE	10-C	RX	NOV 73	2362289	APACHE 77	KH	MAY 87	A2335167
12	OJ	JUL 62	NONE	66MB	LY	FEB 74	2382331	66MB	OH	JUL 87	A2341424
76MB	DJ	SEP 62	NONE	10-C	AY	MAR 74	2398803	66BD	DH	SEP 87	A2366106
76AB	RJ	NOV 62	NONE	10-C	PY	JUN 74	2401364				
12	XJ	DEC 62	NONE	10-C	PY	JUN 74	2417810				
11	BK	JAN 63	NONE	10-C	OY	JUL 74	2419996				
76MB	LK	FEB 63	NONE	66GS	WY	AUG 74	2421905				
11	CK	APR 63	NONE	66AB	AZ	MAR 75	2486977				
76AB	PK	JUN 63	NONE								

F.I.E.

MODEL	CODE	DATE	S/N
GR-8			GR-14918
GR-8			GR-76616

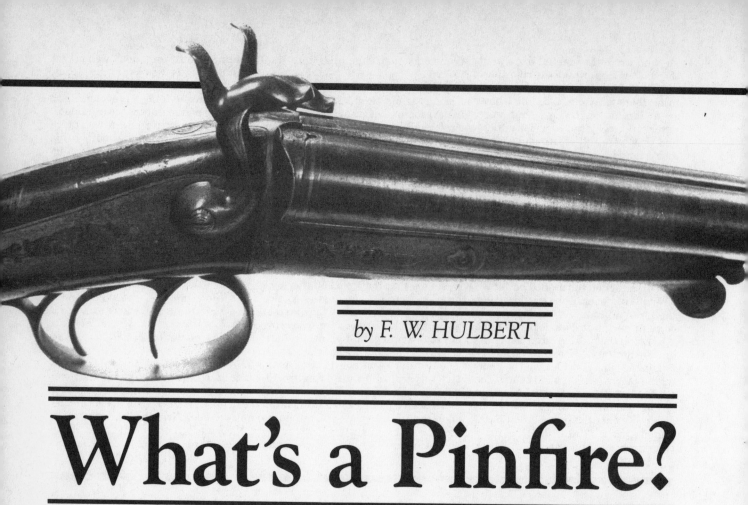

by F. W. HULBERT

What's a Pinfire?

MANY YEARS ago, when I first began to collect pinfire arms, I would walk the gun shows with a sign hung around my neck. The sign read: "Wanted, pinfire arms and ammunition."

Approaching a sales table I was often greeted with the question: "What's a pinfire?" Apparently there are a great many people out there who are not acquainted with one of the most important firearms developments of all time.

The pinfire was born March 31, 1835, sired by a Frenchman, Casimir Lefaucheux (1802-1852), in the fourth

(Above) A 20-gauge pinfire shotgun, with shell, by Auguste Francotte (left).

This group of pinfire cartridges is discussed in the text.

(Right) This circa 1850 12mm pepperbox was made by Casimir Lefaucheux.

(Left) A sectioned 9mm pinfire cartridge—the pin rests on the cap.

addition to his patent number 5525 of January 28, 1833. The concept began as a double shotgun using a cartridge very similar to the modern shotgun shell, with a copper base and a rolled paper body. The obvious difference was the pin which projected from the head of the case at a right angle to the case body, just forward of the rim. In loading, this pin was located in a slot in the chamber or cylinder which placed it directly below the hammer. Pulling the trigger released the hammer which fell on the projecting pin. The pin was forcefully driven down into the case to explode a percussion cap secured there which, in turn, ignited the powder and propelled the shot charge.

No longer was there a separate operation for hurrying fingers to carefully place a cap on the nipple. The cap had now moved inside the case where it became one of the four elements of a self-contained round: case, primer, powder and shot.

Neither Lefaucheux's revolutionary pinfire shotgun, nor any other breechloader, won the favor of the traditional British sportsman easily. Breechloaders were thought unsafe and lacking in hitting power, the Lefaucheux once being termed ". . . the French crutch

gun . . . ." It took a series of trials held by *The Field*, a British sporting paper, in the 1850s and 1860s to prove the superiority of the pinfire over the muzzleloader.

In the 1858 trials, 20 of the 26 guns were muzzleloaders. Just 8 years later, the trials of 1866 showed 23 of 35 to be pinfires which took five of the top 10 places. By that time pinfires were being made in England by Pape, Lang and others, and there can be little doubt that it was the pinfire which ended the dominance of the muzzleloader on the British sporting scene.

A typical pinfire shotgun, by Auguste Francotte, is shown, with shell, in a photo nearby.

By the 1840s, Casimir Lefaucheux had designed a Mariette-style pepperbox, still using the paper-bodied cartridge. There is a picture of one of these rare, early handguns. Note the distinct ridge at the forward end of the chamber which was intended to prevent the paper tube from moving down the barrel. Casimir Lefaucheux received a medal when he displayed a very similar arm, much more highly ornamented, at the London Exhibition of 1851.

Following Casimir's death, his son

Eugene Lefaucheux (1833-1892) improved the pinfire handgun round by replacing the paper body with a metal case. In the pictured group of pinfire cartridges we show (from left): 5mm ball (.196-inch), 7mm ball (.276-inch), 9mm ball (.354-inch), 9mm shot, 12mm ball (.472-inch), 15mm ball (.590-inch) and 20-gauge shotgun. Another photo shows a sectioned 9mm pinfire revolver cartridge. The pin can be seen resting on the cap, ready to receive the hammer blow and ignite the charge.

The pinfire has many firsts to its credit: the first practical self-contained breech-loading shotgun shell, first practical self-contained metallic handgun cartridge and the first metallic handgun cartridge to be adopted as a military issue arm by any nation. This was Lefaucheux's Model of 1854 which was adopted by the French Navy in 1857 and became known as the Navy Revolver Model 1858. This was fully 15 years before the United States Army adopted the Colt Model 1873. Incidentally, there are many similarities between the two: large caliber (45 and 47), six-shot, single action only with loading gate and side rod ejection. We show a commercial M1854 which is, except for markings, identical to the 1858 Navy model.

The revolver was the most popular style of pinfire arm. It was made until well after the turn of the century in calibers ranging from 5mm to 15mm, and quality from horrible to excellent, for either military or civilian use. The most often encountered type of pinfire revolver is a six-shot 7mm with 3- to 4-inch barrel and folding trigger. They are often nickel-plated and lightly engraved and usually unmarked except for the Liege proof house mark of the letters ELG surmounted by a star and the whole enclosed in an oval. These were sometimes sold with fanciful legends engraved on the cylinder such as: "The Guardian American Model of 1878." They are reminiscent of the spur trigger Suicide Specials made and sold in the United States in the same period and marketed under such names as: "Tramps Terror," "Swamp Angel" and many others.

Today most people refer to all pinfire arms as "Lefaucheux's," but, in fact, comparatively few were actually the product of Lefaucheux's own factories

A commercial Lefaucheux M1854, identical except for markings, to the French Navy M1858.

A fine example of the most common pinfire revolver, not often found this fancy.

A Dolne "knuckleduster" with the Parisian "Apache" sort of appeal.

and these were well marked as such on the barrel and/or frame and are serial numbered. Most of the "serial numbers" found on pinfire arms are not that at all. They are simply assembly numbers intended to keep parts of the same gun together during the largely hand filed and fitted manufacturing process. Most of the names found on the barrels are not makers' names either, but are wholesale agents' or dealers'. It is always nice to find a name-marked pinfire because most of them were not. Some, depending on when and where made, do not even have proof markings.

Another very popular early form of pinfire handgun was the pepperbox, a sort of revolver with an over-long cylinder and no barrel. The design had been around since the flintlock. Ranging in caliber from the tiny 5mm to the impressive 12mm, with 7mm and 9mm being the more common, they were produced by scores of French and Belgian makers, most of whom did not trouble to sign their efforts. Some models of these are sometimes called "Apache" or "fist pistols." The term "Apache" does not refer to the American Indian tribe, but rather to French street gangs of the period who were said to favor such guns. In the photo of a typical pre-1877 Belgian-made pepperbox, the small knob at the bottom of the butt is the head of the separate ejector rod.

In the 1880s, such a pepperbox was combined with a folding dagger and brass, iron or German silver knuckles to create a multi-purpose weapon often called a knuckleduster or Apache knuckleduster. We show a 7mm Dolne made in Belgium, fully open for use as a pepperbox/dagger. The grip portion (knucks) can be folded forward under the frame for use as knucks and dagger. Only two of the three functions were usable at one time.

There was also what is often termed a "square frame knuckleduster." We

This is the square frame Delhaxhe knuckleduster, again tagged with the Apache label.

(Right) An ornate example of a relatively scarce 7mm pinfire pepperbox.

Getting serious, this 12-shot 7mm pinfire offers a folding dagger, too.

They got big as well. This is a 12mm pinfire revolving rifle of Spanish origin.

(Below) This 12-shot pinfire revolver offers the weight-saving hollowed-out cylinder.

show a later type by Delhaxhe, also 7mm and Belgian-made. The improved design of the Delhaxhe, with only the blade folding, allowed the user instant choice among all three functions without further folding or unfolding. Quite a handy gadget in a street fight!

Although the design of the pinfire cartridge precluded the use of detachable magazines in which cartridges are stacked, such as autoloading pistols, the possibilities of increased firepower did not escape notice. There was a 12-shot 7mm revolver with a folding dagger blade, and you see it here. Other pinfire revolvers are known with cylinders carrying up to 20 rounds. No doubt bulky, but what a friend in a firefight! Some of these large capacity cylinders had hollow centers.

The first pinfire was a double barrel shotgun, but single barrel and revolving cylinder shotguns were to follow in all popular gauges. From the plainest to the most ornately inlaid and en-

graved specimens, their styles depended only on the taste and purse of the customer.

The pinfire cartridge was also adapted to rifles in the same configurations of single and double barrel and revolving cylinder. We show a typical 12mm, six-shot single-action revolving rifle with 26-inch barrel marked Jose Unzueta, Eibar. Some revolving rifles were engraved, but very few show the degree of ornamentation found on shotguns. Apparently then, as now, the shotgun was the more favored object of adornment.

Gunmakers, presented with a practical self-contained cartridge, were free to make almost anything patrons could imagine. Single shot pistols or double barrel shotguns, revolvers or rifles, military or commercial, plain or fancy. In whatever form, the pinfire is often overlooked, but it provided an important and very interesting chapter in firearms history and evolution.

So what's a pinfire?

It's damn near anything!

by FRANK MARSHALL, JR.

For Mine, It's an Old 45 Carbine

However, in spite of that slight hypocrisy, thanks to firearms proficiency impressed to be a responsibility in a free country by my forebears, I survived the fight from Omaha Beach to Munich in one piece picking up four Combat Stars in the process and I'm sure Gramps and Will rest comfortably.

Marshall is a shooter; if he deigns to pull its trigger, a rifle will shoot.

MOST BONAFIDE gun buffs, usually quite early in this fascinating pursuit, become aware that they have a particular affinity to some rifle, handgun or shotgun on their rack for reasons not always based on rhyme or reason, fame or fortune. There's a fond attraction that persists, undefinable.

Most men, who live long enough and are lucky, can relate also to a similar sensitivity for one woman in this life that defies any logical explanation of why or wherefore.

In my case, from the gun hypnosis viewpoint, a common M1873 Springfield rifle, caliber 45-70, cut off to a handy 19-inch carbine and resighted with sporting rear and front is the one. The forearm is finished off to standard carbine contour with a walnut dowel filling the cleaning rod cut.

To start at the beginning, I came into this world as spawn of a shooting clan, law-abiding and respectful of the rights of all people and bound to uphold that principle. On my 10th birthday, grandpa, "Commander Jim," a strong 80 in spite of the Civil War wear and tear 60 years earlier, and some post-war Western escapades, announced that we would walk "down street" and see if we might find a clean-barreled 45 Springfield which the local surplus store had in abundance at $1.00 per piece.

This was on a fine 15th of May day, 1925, and we each carried one home that trip. Grandpa was fondest of the trapdoor action among single shots. The 577 Snyder conversion also held a place of high esteem on Gramp's military rack, along with the "rear cleaner" Remington rolling block.

At the formal cake-cutting in honor of my having made the magical first decade unscratched, which was not as common then as today and thus a *cause celebre* in our clan circles, Uncle Will of WW I "horroics," at the price of lung and leg anguish thereafter, presented me with a Mill's "lucky" dogshead-buckle 45-round web belt. It was fully loaded with issue 45-70 carbine ammo. That was 55 grains of black and a 405-grain lead bullet at 1050 fps.

In retrospect, 65 years later, I can conclude firmly that was the complete birthday, never since quite matched.

It was not exactly my first firearm experience, but rather my elementary gunnery graduation present, so to speak. I had passed the required programs up to that point of time including reloading chores short of charging the primed cases.

To discourage any solo sortie to our river plink and picnic utopia with "my own" 45-70, unattended by Uncle Will or Gramps, the firing pin was removed and held by my tutors, except on family expeditions. When I fully appreciated beyond any question the glory and fury of the 45-70 carbine load, with equal respect also to any firearm from a Flobert 22 BB cap up and all inclusive, things would change.

The Springfield stock, at my insistence, was not cut for a perfect fit while Gramps was expertly wielding his saws and files. He made my "citizen's" carbine in about one hour that afternoon in our carriage house refuge. The three-leaf sporter rear and standard front sight are the original job by Gramps, drawn from his treasure chest of parts. The notable fact is that he guessed the height of the selected front sight would be "about right" for "about on" at our normal big game range of 60 yards, using the carbine load.

This, surprisingly to me, although Gramps didn't bat an eye, was in fact the case and has been to this day with any reasonable facsimile of that original load. It even works with my modern smokeless lead load components.

Further satisfying, but never predicted, the second leaf is on at 125 yards and the third leaf cuts it good at an even 200 yards, which about covers any requirement in a 45-70 carbine for a citizen.

I can't report cloverleaf groups even from the bench with this home-cut carbine, but there are never wild flyers from the reload groups it will shoot consistently. It's fully adequate for beer cans at 60 paces or our big Blue Ridge bucks. That's as far as anyone ever earns a shot at those shadows in our woods.

This 19-inch stiff barrel can handle a .465-inch round ball in front of enough Unique to make 1100 fps, which puts it on at 45 yards with the standard sight. It can also do the 500-grain nonstop Express load at 1100

Over his "Speaking Frankly" column in the Cast Bullet Association paper "The Fouling Shot" appears this guileless Celtic face.

fps. I get that at low pressure using 4198, which also matches the low sight, but at 75 yards.

For my standard all-utility favorite load duplication, I use the 400-grain Lyman 457124 bullet cast of 1-40-tin-lead, at 1050 fps. Old reliable Unique has given consistent confidence over fifty years of full satisfaction on range or afield. That's my standard, but one other load deserves special mention.

That is the notorious old Gould 330-grain hollowpoint bullet which, in my carbine from a picnic table, could hit the hanging 12-inch steel gong target with fair regularity across our river. This distance was judged variously as from 175 to 250 yards by eyeballers, but geometry put the one-foot plate exactly 209 yards out. From rest, using my tallest leaf and holding at six o'clock on the left edge of plate line into the prevailing west wind, I could

ring the bell with an orange flash from the added fireworks of the 22 black-powder blank cartridge inserted snugly into the Gould bullet's 22-caliber hollownose.

To say that form of plinking was spectacular is to put it mildly. Nothing in my peacetime shooting repertoire could even approach that blank bomb effect. On a miss, the amount missed was clearly visible by the orange flash on the cliff wall. That was not much less exciting than a ringer. This shootout was a winner with never a dull lull, although a 45-round belt didn't last long with that kind of sheer fun and festivity.

Lest some reader may think that form of gun fun was wild, I will point out that old Gramps owned both sides of the river and the cliff of sheer granite was the most natural lead load backstop I've known. In some future time, the lead splotches and pock holes from our bomb loads will be a source of wonder to the viewer.

Uncle Will believed ardently that bigger is better. With a couple cases of 577 Snyder on hand, which was the way they did things then, in no time Will had cut off the noses of the Snyder bullets and precisely reamed out cavity to take a 32 rimfire blank.

That added a new dimension to our picnic plinkouts, except Will could only hit the plate about half as often with his Snyder 577 as Gramps and I could with our 45-70 bombers. The 577 was an awesome piece of breechloading ordnance and really only slightly less accurate than our 45-70, judging from the near-miss fireworks I can recall as if yesterday.

Those days flew by; it seems on looking back though there were actually years of unforgettable all-out shooting pressure.

Myriad rifles have graced my rack since, but the 45 carbine was never retired. The only birthdays on which I failed to shoot this, my everlasting old faithful fusil, were due to World War II. Besides leaving my girls behind, I missed that 45 carbine and Hodge's hot and generous roast beef chips on a hard roll. Hodge's was on old 9th Street north of Pennsylvania Avenue in the District of Columbia, right around the corner from gunshop row, all gone now, but that's what we fought for.

My old citizen's carbine is the only thing unchanged in any way and that, I suppose, is the wonder of it all. Why one gun can grab hold, so the sentimental memories are always peaceful and pleasant, I don't know. But I'm glad it works that way. ●

Yes, the woods, and yes, the dinner table, but most of all, the bench.

MY 25 YEARS WITH A WINCHESTER 52

A GOOD GUN does what it is supposed to do and keeps on doing it, year after year. A superb gun goes the good gun one better. Mine is a Model 52B Winchester bolt-action 22 with a 28-inch standard weight barrel. At 10 pounds and 46 inches overall, this is a *big* 22. The rifle—#46045—was made in 1940 about the same time I was. We did not meet, however, until 1964.

At age 15, I thought my shooting days, along with a lot of other things, were over after I blew off both hands fooling about with homemade explosives. Later, unable to feed cartridges into my little single shot 514 Remington, I traded it in on the first of what was to become a series of 22 autoloaders, which seemed the sensible sort of rifle for someone equipped with a set of hooks. The problem with the autoloaders was they didn't some of the time and in terms of accuracy they also left much to be desired. I once wrote a funny article explaining exactly *how* these autoloaders didn't. Several editors explained to *me* how such writing was not good for their advertising.

My final autoloader was traded in 1964 for a used 52B Winchester. Ninety dollars seemed a lot for a previously owned 22 in those days, but I was desperate for something accurate that would function *all* the time and to hell with fast shots. The previous owner had been a park ranger who gave the rifle good care and plenty of use. The blue was off here and there and the finish on the stock was crazed and flaking. I dithered; then took it.

My first discovery was I had a rifle that could group under ½-inch at 50 yards and would stay at an inch out to 75, even with high-velocity hollow-

Working with hooks instead of hands made autoloaders attractive, but accuracy outweighs convenience.

James dithered, then bought this heavy 22 full of virtues twenty-five years ago.

by C. RODNEY JAMES

points. I'd never had an autoloader that would group better than 1½ inches at 50 yards on a very good day and most ran well over that. My new rifle deserved a sling and a scope.

The man at the gun show saw me coming. His bargain scopes carried the brand name "Eagle." A 6x with a fine crosshair seemed like a good buy at about $25. I have since heard these were one of the bargains of the century, with clarity and ability to hold zero far beyond many of the more expensive name brands. In the 25 years I've had it, I've no complaints.

As with anyone who writes about firearms, I have had a good many pass through my possession, but right from the start I knew the 52 was a keeper. I touched up the blue, steamed out the

The 52, I found, was a connoisseur of ammunition, at times as finicky as Morris, the cat. It loved the expensive match fodder (naturally), but also had preferences for Stingers and Mini-Mag solids, occasionally turning in ³⁄₁₀-inch groups at 35 yards, right up there with the match-target stuff. It does not care for the Mini-Group—standard-velocity loading—never grouping at much under an inch at that range. The 52 positively hated the old Western Xpert, which piled up lead in the barrel as did some of those chain store brands whose names have drifted into oblivion.

Other interesting phenomena included the opening of groups if the bore was not swabbed out every 100 rounds or so. And just as C.S. Landis said,

½-inch at 50 yards. Yellow Jackets did nearly as well, but with the same sight setting grouped to the right at 100 yards.

Lest I give the impression my 52 is simply a paper puncher, let me say that when I moved to the country in 1974, it proved the most useful gun on the farm. I operate three feeders for song birds and a chain of bluebird houses, all of which attract unwanted starlings, grackles, cowbirds and such. The 52 converted these nuisances into fine entertainment. The one year I kept count by dropping the spent cases of successful shots in a Mason jar, the tally added up to 367, and there

No rifle that will shoot twelve consecutive Stingers mostly inside an inch at 75 yards is bad.

Any gun James shoots needs a gadget or two and the 52 is no exception.

After twenty-five years, even the offhand technique falls right into place.

dents and refinished with tung oil. Shooting a good gun, over a period of years—really *working* with it—is an education in itself. I learned that gilt-edged accuracy has its price—in the careful selection and testing of ammunition and in frequent cleaning of the rifle. Owning the 52 started me reading the works of Henry Stebbins, E.C. Crossman and the grand master of the 22—C.S. Landis. I had always considered the 22 Long Rifle to be, at best, a 50-yard cartridge; that is, so I thought until I read how Landis used it on squirrels and woodchucks to 100 yards and beyond, once taking a chuck at better than 150 yards. Before you turn to the next article, reader, let me emphasize that this sort of shooting cannot be done with a light sporter, no matter how big a scope is mounted on it, nor with just any old ammunition.

"Some ammunition does not shoot well over the fouling of other types."

During the 4 years I spent in Canada, the 52 adapted well to the CIL/Dominion product, delivering match-target results with their standard-velocity Canuck brand, once clustering five consecutive shots in ²⁄₁₀-inch at 35 yards. That stuff is sadly missed, but some Mexican-made Navy Arms 22s recently turned up that look promising. Perhaps the best news, on my returning to the U.S., was the introduction of the hyper-velocity cartridges. To my delight, the 52 took to both Stingers and Yellow Jackets, grouping the Stingers at ½-inch at 35 yards and keeping them in an inch out to 75, and just a shade over 2 inches at 100 yards with a drop of 2.5 inches with the sight zeroed for 75 yards. This setting zeros again at 25 yards, rising a little over

weren't many misses. The 52 has accounted for quite a few squirrels in the beech woods and pigeons off the barn roof in addition to woodchucks and crows around the back garden. No, I did not make any of those C.S. Landis shots, taking the above from ranges of 30 to 60 yards.

The nearest I have come to that level of marksmanship was on two occasions. The first was a downhill shot from a second-story window at a grackle who was muttering taunts and insults from atop a cornstalk in the north field. I held over a bit and squeezed one off, drilling him with a Yellow Jacket. The distance was 70 paces. The second time was during pheasant season when a large cock, which had been hanging around the area, came pussyfooting along the hedge bordering the north side of the yard. I loaded the rifle with some old EZXS it favored and slipped to the back porch, where I eased open a window to take a rest on the sill. Unsure of the sight setting, I placed the hairs on the bird's neck. At the time I was unaware that a pheasant's neck, minus the feathers, is about as thick as a little finger—smaller than a chicken's. The rifle gave a soft pop and the bullet whiffed . . . it must have been *very* close, but at the same moment a hawk swooped in and the pheasant tipped his head, more concerned by the raptor than "whiffs" in the air. The next shot hit the neck close to center. The range

costs. Could a shooter expect more?

I guess I did and the 52 delivered. The ammunition was a gun show bargain sold to me as *standard* velocity. It was a French-made Gevelot, a type I'd had no experience with so I assumed the pasted blue labels, listing the weight of the powder and priming charges and sealing the individual boxes, was simply the way they did it. The cases were copper, which used to be the norm for standard- and target-velocity ammunition. The cracking reports, however, did not seem in keeping with that sort of fodder. Since I had only recently acquired the rifle and

sense enough to stop shooting when I realized what the trouble was.

Could anyone ask for more? Or better? There was the time lightning took the top out of a locust tree, except for an axe-handle-thick piece holding it up there. A tree company wanted $150 to take it out, but I did the job with a box of cartridges.

The Model 52C was the last repeater in the line and had something called a "Micro-Motion" trigger. If a standard-barrel 52B was accurate, a heavy-barreled model with one of those super triggers would . . . well, one dreams. Heavy, even bull barrel, 52Cs along

Ten shots with Mini-Mag solids at left; four with Navy Arms imports at right—all at 35 yards.

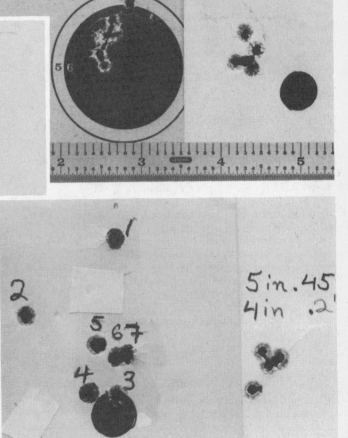

This is the kind of 35-yard group it takes—⁴⁄₁₀ of an inch—to stand a chance of a "Landis shot" on woodchucks.

The effect of noncompatible fouling—Stinger over EZXS. It was not until the fifth shot that the group tightened up. The group on the right is Stinger over its own fouling. Both groups were fired at 35 yards.

was a little over 30 yards.

The accuracy of the 52 made it an invaluable research tool when I began a study of the ballistics of richochets. The standard 22 is a marvelous chambering—capable of handling everything from a BB cap to the Stinger, and I used all of them to examine the behavior of various bullet shapes, weights and velocities in richochet. Since that time, the 52 has been a dependable workhorse, unfailingly delivering the ballistic goods needed to turn out a number of technical articles, at a bargain price in ammunition

suspected there might be some fault with *it,* I persisted through a couple dozen rounds, cursing split rims and burst heads until a complete head separation jammed the magazine, bursting the crimps holding it together. The problem? They were high-pressure *proof loads.* The 52 had digested nearly half a box and I still had my face and eyesight intact. Old friend, I do mightily apologize for my stupid abuse. Some years later I again encountered case ruptures—a result of defective ammunition. There were no problems, just split rims, and I had

with 52Ds, Bs, As and even the originals occasionally turn up on those gun show tables, *but* they are all attached to price tags that cause the throat to tighten, eyes to bulge and breathing to become difficult until a clear area—away from Winchester tables—is reached. Such is the power of higher mathematics!

As I grow older, will my eyesight become keener, my nerves more steady? Do I really need a "Micro-Motion" trigger? And what if the one I swapped mine for turned out to be not *quite* as good? When I'm rich I'll have *two!* ●

My Model 12:

GOOD, BUT

IT'S GOOD, but there is no way my Model 12, in 16-gauge, can be called fancy. I got it as a high school graduation present almost 20 years ago, out of an ad in the classified. The gun was still available when I called, one of the few times that has happened. My father made the actual purchase, forking over $35, the same price he paid for a new 12-gauge Model 12 in the 1930s. I was still a few days shy of my 18th birthday.

The Model 12 wasn't pretty then, either, not to anybody but me. The barrel had been bobbed a little and a Poly Choke added sometime. Much of its blue was gone and the stock was scratched and short of finish in spots. It hasn't become any prettier since.

I used it first for chasing grouse. The cover in Michigan's Upper Peninsula can be thick and the Model 12 picked up dings and dents there. Later, in an effort to improve my wing-shooting, I had a Weaver Qwik Point optical sight mounted. That's why a Winchester collector I showed the gun to, shortly after I got it, just laughed. With the holes for the Weaver in the receiver, and the sight itself spoiling whatever classic lines the old 16 has managed to retain, he'd probably cry now.

Bobbed, butchered and looking slightly sandblasted, the Model 12 still is a shooter. I asked the guy we bought it from how it had worked afield and what it had been used for. He said his dad had hunted deer with it. I already owned a 30-06 and, since the U.P. is rifle country in November, I thought hunting deer was a strange thing to do with a shotgun.

It took me almost 10 years to change my mind. In the meantime, my Model 12 took grouse, squirrels, geese, blackbirds, clay birds and more informal targets. It did fine on all of them.

I started considering the shotgun as a deer gun after, carrying a rifle, I missed an eight or ten-foot chance at a doe jumped in a cedar swamp one year. Later that same opening day, I raced a bigger deer to the junction of two skid trails. We tied, but again I found the rifle I carried too slow. The deer seemed to be moving as fast as

Winchester Model 12 16-gauge—scratched, battered and added onto, but a gun to keep. (Munch photo)

It once had to have some springs replaced, but the old 16 is spitting them out fine here. (Munch photo)

by LEE H. ARTEN

NOT FANCY

One Good Gun

A rifled slug unrolled this water-filled can.
(Munch photo)

(Above) Not very pretty anymore, but the author still admires it—often in the woods. (Munch photo)

This smoothbore works—Arten has just set a can soaring with a slug; will now whack it again with shot. (Munch photo)

hunting on a doe permit, making my way down a trail with my Contender holstered, when a small doe appeared 30 yards ahead. It was sleeting and snowing and the woods were noisy with dripping water, but the walking was quiet. I was trying to protect the Contender, and in that kind of weather, of course, I should have been carrying the shotgun. It doesn't need protection and would have been right there, in my hands when the deer showed. Shortly, she would have been right there on the ground. The holstered handgun was a different story. In the time the deer gave me, I couldn't draw it, uncover the scope, line up and shoot.

Besides being a fair to middling deer gun, the old smoothbore also works as a plinker, if you don't mind the recoil. There are other possibilities, too. I keep a 45 semi-auto as a house gun and lately a 30 Carbine has been the gun I'd send my wife for if someone was breaking in. The 16-gauge and a box of duck loads used to be what I would tell her to get. You could make a case that the shotgun would still be the best choice.

The Model 12 is nice to have around because it works. Since I've had it, the gun has been to the gunsmith twice. Once to have the Qwik Point installed and once to get some springs replaced. The gun, which a Winchester collector places in early post-WW II production, was exhibiting occasional ejection problems. Besides switching springs, the 'smith told me, "Be sure to pump it hard enough." I took the advice and we both have been doing much better since.

We have more rabbits than burglars in my small town. I don't really need the Model 12 for either (or for deer since I just bought a Ruger 77 lightweight). If I never shot it at anything but clay and cans again, I'd still keep it.

It may be true that only accurate rifles are interesting, but you can't say only pretty firearms are worth notice. With its scars, blemishes, and add-ons, my Model 12 looks like a gun with stories to tell. That look is something good guns just have to have. ●

any grouse.

The next season, I carried the shotgun into the cedars. Deer were scarce for the next few years due to a series of bad winters. After they rebounded, I took a spike from a blind with my 30-06. The next buck was killed on the edge of a swamp with the Model 12. I got a little excited, and shot more than

once, but the deer didn't move from where it stood when I shot. The old smoothbore did very well, particularly since the deer shot with the rifle ran about 25 yards.

I brought the shotgun with me the next year, too, but elected to use a scoped 357 Maximum handgun instead. That choice cost me a deer. I was

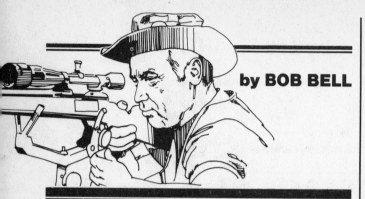

by BOB BELL

SCOPES AND MOUNTS

COLT Woodsman . . . Hoppes #9 . . . . Model 70 Winchester . . . Lyman Alaskan All-Weather . . . . Certain words—names—are the keys to special compartments in the minds of older American shooters. They conjure up images of long gone hunts, long gone friends, days on distant windswept mountain ridges or in green-shadowed swamps in our almost forgotten yet never to be forgotten pasts. Just overhearing them in fragments of passing conversations, or seeing them on a printed page, sends shivers along our spines. And we are saddened by the knowledge that the reality on which they are based is gone forever.

Forever? Forever is a long time. And sometimes, what goes around comes around.

Leaving the handguns and rifles for others to contemplate, let's think for a moment about the Alaskan. That's how I always thought of it, how all of us always referred to it, back in the old days: simply, the Alaskan. And those old days are pretty old. It's more than a half-century since the Alaskan appeared in 1937, yet I can still visualize the ads in an older relative's *American Rifleman,* plain yet perfectly executed line drawings. And I can still remember the price: $50.

Now, $50 during the Great Depression was, to a kid, an amount beyond comprehension. A lot of men worked several sixty-hour weeks for less than that—if they were lucky enough to have a job at all. Back then, I don't think I ever even dreamed of having an Alaskan

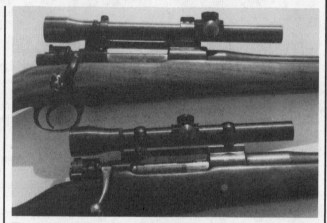

The original Alaskan at top is replicated in spirit and simplicity if not in detail by Leupold's new Alaskan.

of my own. If I did, it was the impossible dream. I was lucky—damn lucky—to have a little Weaver 29S on my Winchester 22, and I knew it and was grateful.

Then World War II came along, and there were rumors that the Alaskan was being used as a sniper scope on the Springfield rifle, but all I ever saw in that capacity in Europe was the Weaver 330C, which the Army called the M73B1. Later, Al Wardrop, my longtime gunsmith/shooting buddy, told me he had seen a few Alaskans on M54 Winchesters in combat areas of southern Europe. They were probably rigged up by unit armorers rather than of general issue. One outstanding rifleman, John George, took his Alaskan-scoped M70 to Guadalcanal and Burma with Merrill's Marauders, and later wrote about it in one of that war's great books, *Shots Fired*

in Anger. But apparently the Alaskan was never officially used as a sniper scope. It was, however, used by many well-known riflemen such as Elmer Keith and Phil Sharpe, and most knowledgeable hunters of the day regarded it as the best scope in America.

After the war, many things changed, and in the early '50s Lyman introduced their All-American line, abandoning several excellent but too-expensive-to-manufacture big game scopes, including the Alaskan. I never could understand why they even gave up on the name. It was perfectly descriptive; it created visions of far-off gamefields; it had already become a legend. The All-Americans were fine scopes—I have a complete line and still use them often—but the name had no relationship to hunting. It just

made me think of football. But be that as it may, the Alaskan was gone.

So why do I spend so much time on it now? Because the Alaskan is back.

Obviously, I was not the only rifleman who regretted the Alaskan's passing, but one of the others was in a position to do something about it. He is Jack Slack, and he's the honcho at Leupold, and that's a good position to be in if you want to get something done in the scope field.

During the '40s, Slack had done a lot of hunting with an Alaskan-scoped Springfield. For him, too, it was something special. Undoubtedly that's why a photo of him and his gun and a nice bunch of mule deer trophies grace the cover of the announcement of the Leupold Alaskan. And quite likely he's the reason the copy reads: "Before there was a state, there was

a scope. The Alaskan. The Alaskan was to scopes what Mt. McKinley is to North American mountains: more handsome, more rugged, more steeled against the weather, and more or less above it all . . ."

And so the Alaskan is back. I have no idea what arrangement with Leupold permitted Leupold to introduce their new version of this great scope. That's their business. But Mike Slack told me it was settled with a handshake, and that's another pleasant image in this day and age.

The Leupold Alaskan is a near-twin of the original. It's built on a 22mm steel tube; it's tough (it's been tested to withstand as many as 15,000 impacts with a force of 750 Gs); and it incorporates the advances which have been made in scopes during the past half-century. Those details are covered under the Leupold entry, below. Now, I just want to say that I'm grateful for the Alaskan's return. I hope to put one to good use this fall.

Zeiss is usually the last entry in this review, but this year, just to be different, we're presenting them in reverse alphabetical order, so it's leading off. Seems only fair, since on the scope scene it would be hard to find a manufacturer with more seniority.

Zeiss has been producing a four-scope line of hunting models for the American market since early 1983—the Diatal C 4x, 6x and 10x and Diavari C 3-9x. In the years since, I've had a fair amount of experience with the 4x and 10x, using the latter mostly on a 223 Remington for sit-still varmints such as chucks and prairie dogs, the former on one big game rifle or another. The last few seasons it's been atop a M77 Ruger Ultra Light 308.

This past December it gave a pair of quick kills under the kind of conditions for which such an outfit is made. Both shots had to be taken quickly—short-range chances at whitetails running through the brush. By short range I mean 30-35 yards, at which distance the 4x Zeiss' field was about ten feet. But that was more than enough, for I've altered the Ruger's stock so it fits me perfectly when wearing lots of wool and a down jacket, and it was easy to keep the Z-Plex reticle where I wanted it. A 165-grain Speer spitzer boattail loaded to 2750 fps centered the neck of one deer; the other smashed through both shoulders of the second.

The important thing about this shooting, I believe, is that it shows a 4x has enough field for fast shooting at close range if the rifle fits well, and of course it has enough magnification for precise aiming at any big game as far as most of us should be shooting. All of which explains why it's still a fine choice for the hunter who wants a straight-power scope.

For those who prefer a small variable, so they can have an extremely wide field at bottom power and enough magnification for all but the longest shots at big game, Zeiss introduced their Diavari-C 1.5-4.5x18T* sometime back. Like the other Zeiss Cs (American style) and Zs (European style), this one has multicoating to provide a brilliant color-accurate image, excellent adjustments and weatherproof construction.

We also have it on good authority that there will be a new European-style line of Zeiss scopes by this summer. Specs have not been released at this writing.

Bell and the V10-700 rig he shot these targets with.

Weaver scopes are now available from Blount, Inc., a Lewiston, Idaho, corporation which also includes CCI, Speer, RCBS, and Outers, names all well-known to shooters.

Currently, nine Weavers are available—two rimfire models and seven big game and varmint scopes. These range from the most modern versions of the legendary K2.5 and K4 scopes, which originally appeared just after WWII, on up to the KT15, an action-mounted, large-objective (1.65-inch) target/varmint rig which has proved deadly on my heavy 25-06 in the woodchuck meadows.

Three big game variables are

also made and pretty well cover any shooting situation. The V9 and V10, 3-9x and 2-10x respectively, are about the same size and weight, approximately 13 inches and 12 ounces, with 1.5-inch unobstructed objective units. The V3 is a 1-3x which is only 9.5 inches long and 9.5

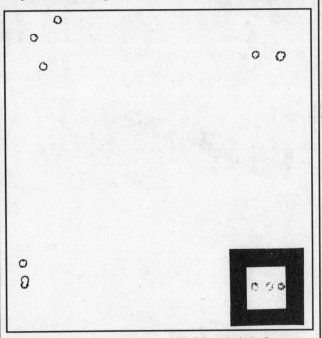

Clicking around a square proves the V10 follows its helm fine.

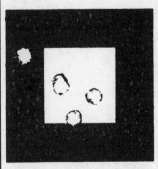

Five shots, each at its own power setting.

ounces. With a 95-foot field at bottom power, it seems an ideal choice for a dangerous-game rifle. In tough situations, a big field and non-critical eye relief—in this case about 4 inches—are of utmost importance. It would be hard to find another scope with better specs for such usage than this little V3.

I've reported on the V9 before. This year I put the V10 on a varmint-weight M700 Remington 223, to check adjustment values, point of impact stability, etc. I had some prairie dog loads left—50-grain Sierra spitzers, 27/748 and 116 primers—so used them. They usu-

ally group in about .75-inch, which seemed good enough for this little test.

It was dry here on March 5, but cold and a bit windy. I zeroed in at 100 yards, then shifted to a clean target and fired four three-shot groups, moving twenty clicks after each shot so that the groups were located at the corners of a square. The clicks are valued at .25-inch, so the centers of the group should have been 5.0 inches apart. Actual measurement put them at 5.8, 5.5, 5.2 and 5.6, which gives an average click value of .27, or some .02 greater than listed. The four three-shot groups measured .50, 1.12, .62 and .69, for an average of .73. The way I see it, considering the weather and the likelihood of human error, this is as close as anyone can reasonably expect.

I then fired a five-shot group, changing the magnification after each shot to cover the entire power spread. It measured 1.06. The first four shots went into .50, the final one from 2x opening it up a bit. Again, I'm dubious about blaming the scope as at that low power I was having trouble holding on the small target.

To wrap things up, I put on eight clicks to give me a varmint-shooting zero of +2 inches, then fired a five-shot group at 10x. Zero was perfect and the group measured .75-inch.

Everything considered, I find these Japanese-built Weavers impressive. Group sizes ran about the same after much clicking as they did without any—certainly so close that any variation would be unnoticeable in the field. Images at all powers were excellent—clean and sharp.

Weaver scopes now have solid-tube construction, including the adjustment housings. Also new are the Pro View mounts, in which the base and lower ring section are formed into one integral unit. The top ring section, which securely fastens to the bottom with four screws, encloses 210 degrees of the scope tube circumference, rather than 180 degrees as most do. The old but still popular QD mounts are still available, as are the See-Thru and Imperial designs.

Weatherby scopes haven't been mentioned here for awhile, so for new readers we'll say that four big game models are available. Two of these Supreme models, a 4x and a 3-9x, have 44mm objectives to maximize light supply. For those desiring smaller scopes, there is a 2-7x with 34mm objective, an excellent choice for all-round

This is the V3, sitting in B&L mounts a bit high.

use, and 1.7-5x with 20mm objective. I've used this model on several rifles in recent years and found it excellent for Eastern woods hunting.

The Supreme models have Lumiplex reticles, which appear black against light backgrounds and seem to lighten against dark backgrounds. All air-glass surfaces are multicoated, and each scope is pressure tested to ensure proper sealing. All four models have the Weatherby Autocom system which automatically compensates for trajectory.

Thompson/Center Arms has been increasing its line of Recoil Proof scopes suitable for pistols and rifles. All have constantly centered duplex reticles, tubes are nitrogen-filled, and turrets have all weather caps. In some models the reticle can be illuminated by a rheostat-controlled battery, for precise aiming when light conditions are truly bad.

T/C pistol scopes are available in several straight and variable power models, black or silver finish, with mounting rails or to accept conventional rings. Rifle models come in compact 4x, 1½-5x, 3-9x with standard duplex reticle, while other models can have a lighted duplex or an Electra Dot. The 4x Compact Electra Dot can be had with a rail mount that will attach directly to the grooved receivers found on many rimfire 22s.

T/C also has a new Quick Release mounting system for their muzzle-loading rifles, Contender pistols and Carbines, and TCR'87 Hunter Model rifles. It consists of a one-piece base which accepts an integral set of rings equipped with a spring-loaded plunger. To remove the scope, you simply pull it and the rings to the rear, tilt up the front and lift off. It is claimed that zero will be maintained when scope is remounted—assuming, of course, no adjustments have been made.

Tasco has such an extensive line that I doubt all their scopes are listed in their own catalog. So there's no way I can mention them all here. But their latest offerings are a pair called the Titan models, a 1½-6x with field of 59-20 feet and a 3-9x with 37-13 feet.

The Titans are Tasco's premium line. They feature one-piece 30mm tubes (with enlarged objectives—42mm—and eyepieces, of course), five-layer multicoating, indicators which show where the reticle is lo-

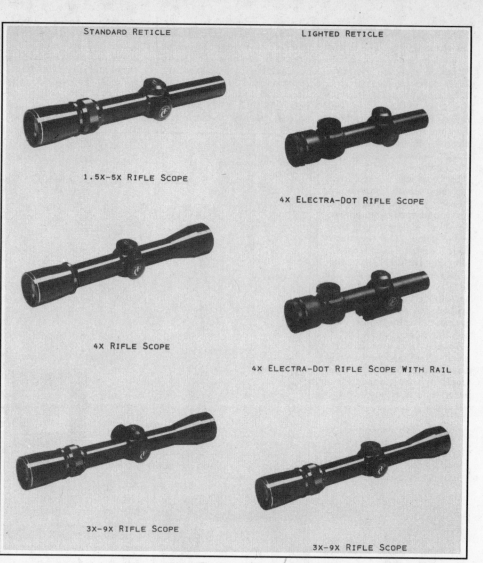

STANDARD RETICLE   LIGHTED RETICLE

1.5X–5X RIFLE SCOPE

4X ELECTRA-DOT RIFLE SCOPE

4X RIFLE SCOPE

4X ELECTRA-DOT RIFLE SCOPE WITH RAIL

3X–9X RIFLE SCOPE

3X–9X RIFLE SCOPE

Thompson/Center scopes—with and without electric reticle.

The T/C Hunter package—gun, case, sling, mount and scope.

cated within the adjustment range, a fast-focusing eyepiece, a titanium gimbal system which holds the inner assembly of the scope together and prevents recoil from changing windage or elevation adjustments, and a quad-reticle pattern which provides four aiming points. The reticle is placed in the scope's first focal plane, which means there can be no change of zero when magnification is changed. Adjustments are quarter-minute, silent, and finger movable—no coin or screwdriver needed. A set of 30mm steel rings is included with each Titan scope.

Schmidt & Bender fixed-power scopes from Leica include 1½x, 4x and 6x.

Among other Tasco scope lines are the World Class, some of which have electronic reticles for low light use and non-removable windage and elevation screws; the Traditional, which has Opti-Centered range-finding reticles; the Mag-IV, variables, which have a 4-1 zoom ratio; the TR, which computes range and trajectory, and the TS, which is designed for target and silhouette shooting.

Swarovski Optik has been making high quality scopes and binoculars since the late '40s. Their Habicht Nova line consists of four straight powers (1½x20, 4x32, 6x42, 8x56) and four variables (1½-6x42, 2.2-9x42, 3-12x56, and 3-12x50). Note that the Habicht variables have a 4-1 zoom ratio and the objectives are large enough in all cases to give exit pupils as big as the human eye can accept in almost any light. All of these except the 1½x20 are offered with either steel or alloy tube, the 1½x being steel.

There is also an "A" line of Swarovskis—4x32A, 6x36A and 3-9x36A. The latter has its reticle in the second focal plane (as is typical of most American/Japanese variables); therefore, it appears smaller at the higher powers than at the lower. The middle (mounting) portion of the A model tubes measures 1-inch, compared with 26mm for the straight power Habichts and 30mm for the variables. All Swarovskis have compressible eyepieces to reduce the chance of injury if one should hit the eyebrow.

Over the years some friends and I have had the chance to test and use a number of Swarovski scopes in 4x, 6x and 8x, and there isn't the slightest doubt that their optics are outstanding. In fact, one veteran hunter insisted the 4x32 was the best scope of that power he'd ever used. He was a bit annoyed when I told him I had to return it after the test period; he probably intended to finagle it off me somehow.

Simmons continues to expand—and improve—its extensive scope line. This year four Whitetail Classic models have been added to the earlier Gold Medal, Silver Medal, Deerfield and Whitetail lines. As mentioned last year, coating systems on these ranged from multi to single, the Whitetail having the least. The Whitetail Classics are at a higher level. Offered in 4x, 1½-5x, 2½-8x and 3½-10x, the WCs have multicoated lenses, Monotube (one-piece) construction, and what they call a BlackGranite finish, which is a nonreflective surface that tends to disappear among the shadows in typical whitetail country.

Also new this year are Gold Medal silhouette-varmint scopes in 12x44, 24x44 and 6-20x44. These are action-mounted scopes measuring about 14½ inches and weighing 18¼-19½ ounces. They have a new internal erector tube and a synchronized windage and elevation indexing system. And for pistol shooters who prefer glass sights, Simmons has four new Gold models—1½-4x28, 2½-7x28, 2x20 and 4x32. As with the rifle models, these have what Simmons calls the Truplex reticle, better known as Duplex.

Shepherd DRS (Dual Reticle System) scopes are made in a number of sizes and magnification spreads, from the 1.5-5x32 Carbine model through the 3-10x for centerfire loads, plus a rimfire model. This scope is too complex to describe in detail in the space available here (see GD 38, 1984 ed., for complete coverage). We'll just take a moment to explain how the Shepherd's two independently adjustable reticles (one in each focal plane) make it easy to zero in, often with only one shot.

To begin with, have both reticles in alignment; that is, one overlying the other. Then from a sandbag rest carefully fire a shot at a 100-yard target. Note where the bullet hits. Holding the rifle motionless on the bags, reticle on the aiming point, adjust the second reticle so that it aims directly at the bullet hole while the first is still on the aiming point. Next, adjust the first reticle so it overlays the second (which will of course also align it with the bullet hole). If the cold barrel shot from your rifle is usually in the middle of the group, the rifle is now zeroed—with only one shot fired. If your rifle doesn't have that quality, fire a three-shot group before doing any adjusting, then use the center of the group as your basic impact and go from there.

Schmidt & Bender, a company named for its founders, Helmut Schmidt and Helmut Bender, both precision engineers, was founded in West Germany in 1957. For two decades they manufactured scopes to be sold by wholesalers under various trade names. All this time they worked toward higher and higher quality, their primary objective being the best optics possible in the most durable unit. In 1978, when they believed their scopes were among the best in the world, they began marketing them under their own names, Schmidt & Bender. In the years since, shooters around the world have come to recognize that the S&Bs deserve such rating. This is further indicated by the fact that they are now available from Leica USA.

For some time now, S&Bs have been available in straight power models from 1½x to 12x, with either steel tubes for conventional mounting or hardened aluminum with rails (except 12x). The steel tubes have a five-step finishing process which includes grinding and polishing, copper-plating, nickel-plating, black chrome plating, and a final baked satin enamel coating of low reflective characteristics.

The 1½x15 has a 90-foot field, so will do the job on anything where fast shooting at close range is necessary. The 4x32 and 6x42 are logical big game choices in either average or open terrain, while the 8x56 is a more specialized unit for treestand use, morning or evening, when the shots tend to be long. The 12x42, of course, is intended for varmints or perhaps silhouette shooting.

The latest Schmidt & Bender variable is a 4-12x42, which makes a good power spread available in a smaller lighter scope than their 2½-10x56, which is more appropriate to stand hunting than conventional use. Twilight factor with the 4-12x runs from 13.0-22.5, compared with the 2½-10x's 7.5-23.6, so there's no significant difference despite the newer model's smaller objective.

Schmidt & Benders have one-piece tubes, 1-inch or 26mm in the straight powers, 30mm in variables, centered reticles in a choice of numerous styles, and quick-focusing cushioned eyepieces.

Redfield has only one new scope this year, a 1-4x intended for use on shotguns using rifled slugs. That's no big surprise, as they currently have the Ultimate Illuminator line, built on 30mm tubes with 56mm objectives; the Illuminators, with either Widefield or Traditional construction eyepieces and 1-inch tubes; the Golden Five Stars in both conventional and Compact styles; Low Profile Widefields; the Trackers; Pistol scopes and Specialty scopes. Various reticles are available, including the Accu-Trac for shooting over long unknown ranges, and various finishes such as matte, glossy, and nickel. Obviously, with such choices, and powers running from 1+x to 18x, there's little room to squeeze in any new ones.

The 1-4x Shotgun model has an eye relief of 6 inches, which puts it in the intermediate category. With Redfield's Mag Mount base that fits most vent-rib shotguns, including doubles and over/unders, a rifled slug shooter can doubtless find some combination that will work for him. The Mag Mount base accommodates Weaver-style rings and is also available for many handguns. Installation requires no gunsmithing.

This shotgun scope has plenty of field despite its long eye relief—48 to 16 feet. It would have been great to have such a scope in the late '40s, when so many 98 Mausers and '03 Springfields were being converted to sporters, as the eyepiece could have been positioned low and centrally ahead of the as-issued bolt handle, eliminating the need for alteration. Fact is, such an arrangement would be highly practical on the military Mausers which are making a comeback on the hunting scene today. Mounting might take some jury-rigging, as it has been decades since anyone thought in these terms, but I'm sure it could be accomplished.

Speaking of mounts, Redfield has been marketing their Rotary Dovetail system since 1916 or thereabouts, and it's still going strong. I've been using them since the late '30s, have more of them on my guns than any other make, and doubt if there's anything better to be found, despite their antiquity. In one combination or another, most any scope can be installed on most any shoulder arm with a Redfield mount. Also on a lot of handguns.

Pentax has added a pair of variable power rifle scopes to its line this year, both toward the upper end of the magnification spread. The first is a 4-12x Mini, a slightly larger version of their earlier 3-9x which was offered in both Mini and conventional sizes. The new Mini is about an inch longer and 2 ounces heavier than the 3-9x version, going 11.3 inches and 15 ounces. Its field is also decreased—as is normal when power goes up.

The 6-18x is in a noticeably different category. Obviously, its primary usage will be as an

all-round varmint scope, with some possibility of doubling as a pronghorn glass. It has a 40mm objective, 4mm larger than the 4-12x Mini's, and a field spread of 16-7 feet. The internal adjustments are quarter-minutes in both, and in several Pentax models we've tried have been very accurate. The 6-18x is just under 16 inches long and weighs 18½ ounces. Like the 4-12x Mini, it has a high-gloss finish. All of the lower power Pentax models offer a choice of Pro-Finish to reduce the possibility of spooking game. Their two pistol scopes, 2x and 1½-4x, can be had with high-gloss or satin-chrome finish.

Pentax scopes haven't been available as long as some makes, but they come from a highly respected optical company, and the several that we've used have been very impressive.

Nikon has added three scopes to its line, a 6.5-20x40 and two pistol models, a 2x20 and a 1.5-4.5x24. The rifle scope is obviously intended to cover all varmint shooting needs as well as having some benchrest application. Like the 4-12x40 which has been available from Nikon for years, this bigger variable also has an adjustable objective system for exact focusing at any distance from less than 50 yards to infinity. All other Nikons have Nikoplex (Duplex) reticles, but this 6.5-20x has a fine crosswire. "Fine" is the correct word, too, as it subtends only 0.17 MOA at the 6.5x setting, 0.05 at the top power. This means that, when properly focused, a shooter can easily quarter a 22-caliber hole in a 100-yard target—or a chuck's ear orifice way out yonder.

Eye relief is about 3½ inches,

which means it can be used on a big game outfit if desired, perhaps for pronghorns. Length is 14.8 inches, weight 19.6 ounces, and adjustment values are ⅛-minute. A number of scopes in this power category are now available with ⅛-minute clicks, which I suppose has some interest to bench shooters, but it can't be significant for varmint hunters. So far as I'm concerned, if the ⅛-minutes are more difficult or costly to manufacture, I'd prefer staying with the ¼-minutes.

The handgun scopes have large exit pupils (10mm in the 2x20, 16-5+ in the variable) which means they are not too difficult to align with the eye even with the arm extended (maximum eye relief is better than 24 inches). It also means they have good brightness, even at 4½x in the variable as it has a slightly enlarged objective.

All Nikons have aluminum alloy one-piece tubes; rifle models are offered with black luster or matte finish, the handgun models with black or silver. I've used a number of Nikon scopes since they first came on the market and, as with my old Nikon F and Nikkormat cameras, they always perform better than I do.

Leupold, as pointed out in the opening of this review, has introduced a new version of the old Lyman Alaskan scope. Actually, three versions, as 4x and 6x models are being offered as well as the 2½x of the original Lyman. All are built on ⅞-inch (22mm) tubes, and all have enlarged eyepieces with external tube diameters of 1.3 inches. The 4x and 6x (actually 3.7x and 5.8x) also have enlarged objective lenses to keep the light supply up at these higher powers.

These new Alaskans have nonreflective blued steel tubes

which give a solid feel in the hand. Eye relief is 4 inches, plus or minus a whisper according to power, and fields of view are 34+, 24 and 15+ feet. Adjustment dials are marked in minutes of angle, but are friction (non-click) type, so smaller adjustments are simple to make. The Duplex reticle is used in all. Mounting rings are offered in three heights: super low, .550-inch; low, .650-inch; and medium, .770-inch. I'd suggest the lowest that will permit the bolt to clear the eyepiece; this, coupled with a tube diameter that's smaller than normal these days, will make a neat looking combination that seems to blend rifle and scope into one unit.

Also new from Leupold this year is a 3.5-10x with a 50mm objective. (An older 3.5-10x40 is still available.) The new scope has a 5mm exit pupil at 10x, which is as large as the human eye can accept under most circumstances. The image is very bright, with a twilight factor of 22. Few scopes match that. In addition, Multicoat 4 coating is now applied to this and all other Vari-X IIIs, including the 6.5-20x and the 6x42mm. Multicoa-

ting improves light transmission and aids color accuracy, qualities which are particularly notable when ambient light is bad. The new 3.5-10x50 can be had with either standard or heavy Duplex reticle.

Back this year is the Vari-X II 1-4x, whose 70-foot field is the largest in the entire Leupold line. And the straight 4x has had its objective lens diameter increased by 5mm, from 28mm to 33mm, its overall length decreased ½-inch.

I don't know how long I've been using Leupold scopes. I

Bushnell Trophy 3x-9x has
European styling, amber
coating, ¼-MOA adjustment.

Bushnell Compact 22 scope is
3x-9x, has 32mm objective and
50-yard parallax setting.

Upgraded ScopeChiefs
are now Bausch & Lomb.
This is the 3x-9x.

started with models which vanished from their line many years ago, and more of my current rifles carry Leupolds than any other make. I guess that indicates that I've been happy with them. I like equipment that works.

K-Loc Mounts, a low profile, see-through design created by Vietnam vet Larry Lockert, are currently produced for a number of rifles including the AK47, stamped or milled receiver, SKS, Ruger 10/22 and Mini 14/30, and AR 15/M16, as well as a custom version for the 30-caliber M-1 Carbine. Most of these require the drilling/tapping of two holes in the left side of the receiver to attach a steel bracket. The mount is then fastened to the bracket with two large-head thumbscrews. Parts are machined from steel. The K-Loc Mount allows use of the iron sights while scope is installed.

Kimber rifles, from rimfires to rhino-wallopers, are known for their beauty as well as their efficiency. Perhaps a bit overlooked are the excellent scope mounts they also make. A slightly revised version of the unit created by the late Len Brownell, a renowned rifle builder and stockmaker—essentially the same mount—is available in either a quick detachable or a solidly installed version. In the QD style, the vertically split rings are secured to dovetail bases by fin-

ger-operated levers. A recoil shoulder at the front end of each base prevents any slippage between rings and bases. In the solid version, a sturdy Allen head screw replaces the lever in each ring and binds it to the base. In efficiency and appearance, these mounts belong on the Kimber rifle.

Hertel & Reuss have four Macro 200 scopes intended for the American market—4x32, 6x40, 2-7x32 and 3-9x40. This West German company has been in the optical field for 63 years, and they have a good idea of what many hunters over here prefer in scopes. In addition to fitting American 1-inch mounts, they have binocular-type focusing, which is quick and easy; rubber eyepiece rings; constantly centered reticles (not true of all European scopes); coated optics; and a choice of four reticles: crosswire, post and crosswire, duplex and center dot. I haven't used a current H&R, but have examined several. They give the impression of solid quality. Numerous other Supra and Macro scopes are available in Europe and possibly here by special order. All have alloy tubes with integral rail mount, while most

are available without the rail and some are fabricated with steel tubes. Powers run from 1x15mm to 4-16x56mm.

Bushnell has quite a bit of news this year. First is a completely new line of scopes called the Trophy Series. Six wide angle rifle models (round, not rectangular eyepieces) are included—4x40, 1.7-5x32, 2-7x32, 3-9x40, 4-12x40 and 6-18x40. All have the European-style fast-focusing eyepiece, one-piece nitrogen-filled tube, amber-coated optics that filter out blue light rays to increase contrast, low-profile adjustment housings, and quarter-minute clicks with raised finger tab instead of coin slot. All Trophy scopes are built to waterproof/fogproof specs. The line includes a pair of handgun models, 2x32 and 2-6x32, blued or silver, with eye relief of 9-26 inches, and a 1.7-5x shotgun scope. Eye relief on this one is 3½ inches, which means it must be action—rather than barrel—mounted; that also means it will make a fine woods rifle scope.

All the Trophies have quarter-minute clicks, which is conventional on rifle models though I don't see the necessity

on a handgun scope. Half-inch clicks would do all that's necessary here—in fact, all that's necessary on a big game rifle. I sometimes wonder whether the coarser value might allow making these units stronger. I suppose by now, though, everyone expects quarter-minute adjustments—or finer—on everything.

Don Robertson loaned me a first production sample 3-9x40 Trophy to try. As expected, the optics were excellent and it was handy to have the binocular-type eyepiece adjustment to focus the reticle for my getting-older eyes. I put it on a M700 7mm Magnum, but big game season was closed so I couldn't actually use it hunting. Had a slight problem in mounting. I prefer scopes as close to the gun as possible, so used low Redfield rings. With the scope as far forward as it would go without the power adjusting ring hitting the base, the objective bell just touched the barrel, an unacceptable situation. There should be at least ⅛-inch clearance here. It pays to check out such things before ordering a specific combination. Higher rings are available, of course. With luck, I might get to use this rig on game this season. In the meantime, I can say that the collimator showed no discernible change in point of impact when going through all the powers, and adjustment values were very close.

In another move, the Bushnell ScopeChief series—always an excellent line—has been upgraded even more to meet Bausch & Lomb's performance standards. A one-piece tube is used for strength and to assure alignment of the multicoated optics. Point of impact shift during power change in the variables is said to be nonexistent because tolerances in the moving parts are held to .0003—that's three ten-thousandths of an inch, or about one-tenth the thickness of a human hair. (Blonde, I assume.) Things sure have changed—for the better—since variables first flooded the market back in the '50s. In a way, it's too bad that many shooters are too young to appreciate how good they've got it now, compared to the good ol' days.

This ScopeChief line (series VII???) includes a straight 4x40mm and four variables—1.5-4.5x32, 2-7x32, 3-9x40, and 4-12x40—the last having an adjustable objective for exact focusing and thus parallax elim-

Burris mounts for Dan Wesson, Python and S&W revolvers work with no tapping, no drilling.

ination.

Bushnell also has added three scopes to their Sportview line, a 4-12x40mm and two compact rimfire models, 4x32 and 3-9x32. The rimfires are parallax-free at 50 yards and come with mounting rings to fit grooved receivers. It's good to see high-quality RF scopes like these being marketed for the many fine 22-caliber rimfire rifles now on the market. It makes it easy for youngsters to get started with excellent equipment that will let them gain proficiency quickly and thus maintain their interest in shooting.

Burris has added a pair of variables to their Signature Series introduced last year, one at each end of the power spectrum. At the lower end is a 1½-6x, which has a slightly enlarged objective—29mm—to give excellent light transmission even at its 6x setting. Field varies from 62-20 feet and, interestingly, windage and elevation adjustments are in half-minutes, with maximum adjustment of 110 inches at 100 yards. This is the most of any scope in the Burris line, and more than is available in many other makes.

The other new variable is a 6-24x44mm. It is, of course, much bigger than the 1½-6x (16 inches and 23 ounces vs 10.7 inches and 13 ounces) and field varies from 17-6 feet. These are consistent with the intended usages of these models: all-round big game hunting with one, all-round varmint use, with some benchrest application, for the other. The 6-24x has ⅛-minute adjustments and is fitted with the Light Collector system introduced in the 3-12x last year. This feature allows the shooter to reduce the objective aperture via a ring (much as a good camera lens can be opened and closed) to reduce the light intensity when appropriate—such as at midday in July in a prairie dog town.

I haven't used this system in

the 6-24x, but have had it in the 3-12x for about a year now. It's on my 40XB-BR 222, and under the conditions mentioned, it helps. However, my personal feeling, after using it in only the one scope, is that I would like to be able to close down the aperture even more at times. This would be more helpful in the 3-12x than the 6-24x, of course, as simply boosting the power in the latter automatically decreases the size of the exit pupil. But this is a quibble. The Light Collector is an interesting feature and at times can be helpful.

The 6-24x is offered with a one-piece tube body, is nitrogen filled, has either dot or plex reticle, and either target knobs or low profile adjustments. Lenses are multicoated, of course. The Signature Series has internal lenses which, despite the conventional 1-inch scope tube, have as much as 40 percent greater area than many scopes, even some with 30mm tubes. Reticles available in Burris scopes include regular and fine plex, crosshair, dot, and interestingly in this day and age, yesteryear's flat-top post and crosshair. Not all reticles are available in all scope models.

The 1½x XER Scout model, which is mounted in front of the action, now can be had with a heavy German three-post reticle, long popular in other parts of the world for fast use on dangerous targets at close range. And for handgunners, Burris has a new solid steel magnum handgun mount base that installs without drilling and tapping. Made to fit Dan Wesson, Colt Python and Smith & Wesson K, L and N frames with 6-inch or longer barrels, this base accepts any height Burris rings and incorporates windage adjustment.

Bausch & Lomb has in a sense increased their available models by absorbing improved versions of the Bushnell Scope-Chief scope line (discussed under the Bushnell entry, above). The new ScopeChiefs wear the Bausch & Lomb name, which isn't assigned lightly, so shooters now have a choice of B&L lines.

Bausch & Lomb Target mod-

els continue to be available in 36x and 24x with either fine crosswires or ⅛-minute dot, and the Balvars in 12-32x and 6-24x (one of my pet varmint jobs). All of these have ⅛-minute clicks; all other B&L's have quarter-minutes. Hunting models include variables from 1.5-6x to 2.5-10x, plus a pair of Compacts and two handgun models.

During the past year we've had a chance to use the 2.5-10x, which offers a 4-1 power spread. Though less than an inch longer than the 3-9x Balvar and weighing the same, 16½ ounces, the 2½-10x gives a noticeably more useful field at bottom magnification (43+ vs 36 feet) and much greater internal adjustment range, ±50 MOA vs ±30 for the 3-9x. With the same eye relief, 3¼ inches, this newer model would seem to be a more logical choice when buying an all-round big game scope.

B-Square keeps expanding their no-gunsmithing mount line. New this year is a base that straddles the slide of Smith & Wesson's recent 9mm autoloader and clamps to the trigger guard. It incorporates an elevation adjustment. Its top surface is a standard dovetail base which accepts scope rings, lasers, and electronic sights. A similar version is made for the Glock 9mm and by the time you read this will be available for the Colt 45 ACP. The position of all these mounts permits use of the iron sights.

B-Square now has a receiver mount for Ruger's Mini-14 that is installed by replacing the bolt-stop cover on the 181 and later series. A single knob attaches the mount base to a cover plate. It positions the scope high enough to use the metallic sights. One-inch rings are included. Other new B-Square military mounts are now made for the British SMLE, SKS 56, AR180, SIG 550, and Colt AR-15/16.

Armson Day/Night Trijicon scopes offer a different approach to bad-light shooting: reticles that glow in the dark. These are not battery-illuminated, but rather self-luminous. They are fabricated by encapsulating tritium in microscopic glass tubes. Under gloomy conditions, the reticle of the Trijicon 4x32 scope glows red, offering good contrast against a dark animal, though under daylight conditions it appears a conventional black.

Trijicon Spectrum scopes are

available in 4x40, 6x56, 1-3x20, 3-9x40 and 3-9x56. These have a selector ring located near the rear of the eyepiece which allows the shooter to choose a reticle color of green or amber, for greater contrast at dawn or dusk or over moonlit snow.

The military applications of this design are obvious, and there is a Trijicon 4x32 ACOG (Advanced Combat Optical Gunsight) for use on the M16. Doubtless there are numerous occasions when police would find such an outfit useful.

Action Arms Ltd. offers a line they call the Micro-DOT scopes—four variables of 1.5-4.5x, 2-7x, 3-9x, and a long eye relief handgun model also of 1.5-4.5x. These are conventional-appearing scopes, except for a small turret on the eyepiece. This is a battery compartment which contains one Duracell DL 2032. It provides the power to project a glowing red dot at the intersection of the duplex crosswires for use as an aiming point when light conditions are bad. Intensity of the dot can be varied greatly by turning the cap of the battery turret. Battery life is listed at 20-4500 hours, which seems like quite a spread. No matter; it should be plenty for any season as it will be used only for short periods. Under reasonable lighting conditions, the regular duplex unit will serve perfectly. Dot diameter is listed at 3-1 minutes in the smallest variable, 2.0-9⁄16 in the 2-7x, and 1.3-7⁄16 in the 3-9x. I don't think this is particularly important, as the only time the illuminated reticle is likely to be used is at short range on big critters. The important aspect is that it's highly conspicuous. I haven't had the chance to hunt with a Micro-DOT scope, but have several samples and have tested them in late evening, and can say that dot is visible—right now.

Action Arms also has a short, light, no-magnification Ultra DOT unit suitable for handgun, shotgun or short-range rifle use. Far as that goes, an archer could doubtless rig it up on a bow. It, too, features a battery-powered red dot (there is no other reticle) of variable intensity. At 5 inches and 4 ounces, it's fairly unobtrusive. Internal adjustments are valued at ½-minute, which seems awfully fine for such an outfit, but that's no matter; the important thing is to be able to zero in. Comes with attachable polaroid filter and dovetail mounting rings. ●

Remember that money you were saving for a rainy day?

When we designed our spotting scopes, we had our heads in the clouds.

Rain clouds.

After all, Leupold's idea was to make spotting scopes that are guaranteed waterproof. And we have.

With our plant smack dab in rain country, we're well aware of the need for waterproofing. But Leupold didn't settle for a walk in the rain to test these spotting scopes. Because compared to the Proof Test, Oregon rain is a spit bath.

One hundred percent humidity. One hundred twenty degrees Fahrenheit. Ten thousand feet of altitude. These are the conditions simulated by the Leupold Proof Test.

Each spotting scope is submerged in a special tank of water, which creates a vacuum that makes the pressure inside the nitrogen-filled scope greater than that of the surrounding water. If a seal fails, as indicated by escaping bubbles, the scope won't get the Leupold Proof Mark. And it won't be sold.

Having licked the moisture problem, we turned our attention to eye relief. Leupold spotting scopes sport nearly an inch of it.

Out of respect for people with glasses.

Likewise, Leupold spotting scopes respect your need for mobility in the field. They're compact. Light. Still, they have all the ruggedness you'd expect from Leupold.

Also as you'd expect, Leupold's unmatched optics are sharp, clear and distortion-free.

But a picture-perfect image is useless without a tripod to steady things. We have three new heavy-duty tripods that feature adjustable, locking legs.

Each is strong yet light, thanks to sturdy aluminum construction.

Leupold spotting scopes come in black satin finish or rubber armor finish, in four models: 30x60mm, 25x50mm, 20x50mm, and the armored 25x50mm with a crosshair. (When sharing the scope, the crosshair makes it easy to pinpoint objects in the field for others.)

For more details, see your Leupold dealer. Or write for our free, full-color catalog. Whichever model you choose, it'll be worth the money.

Whatever the weather.

LEUPOLD®
Performance starts on the inside.®

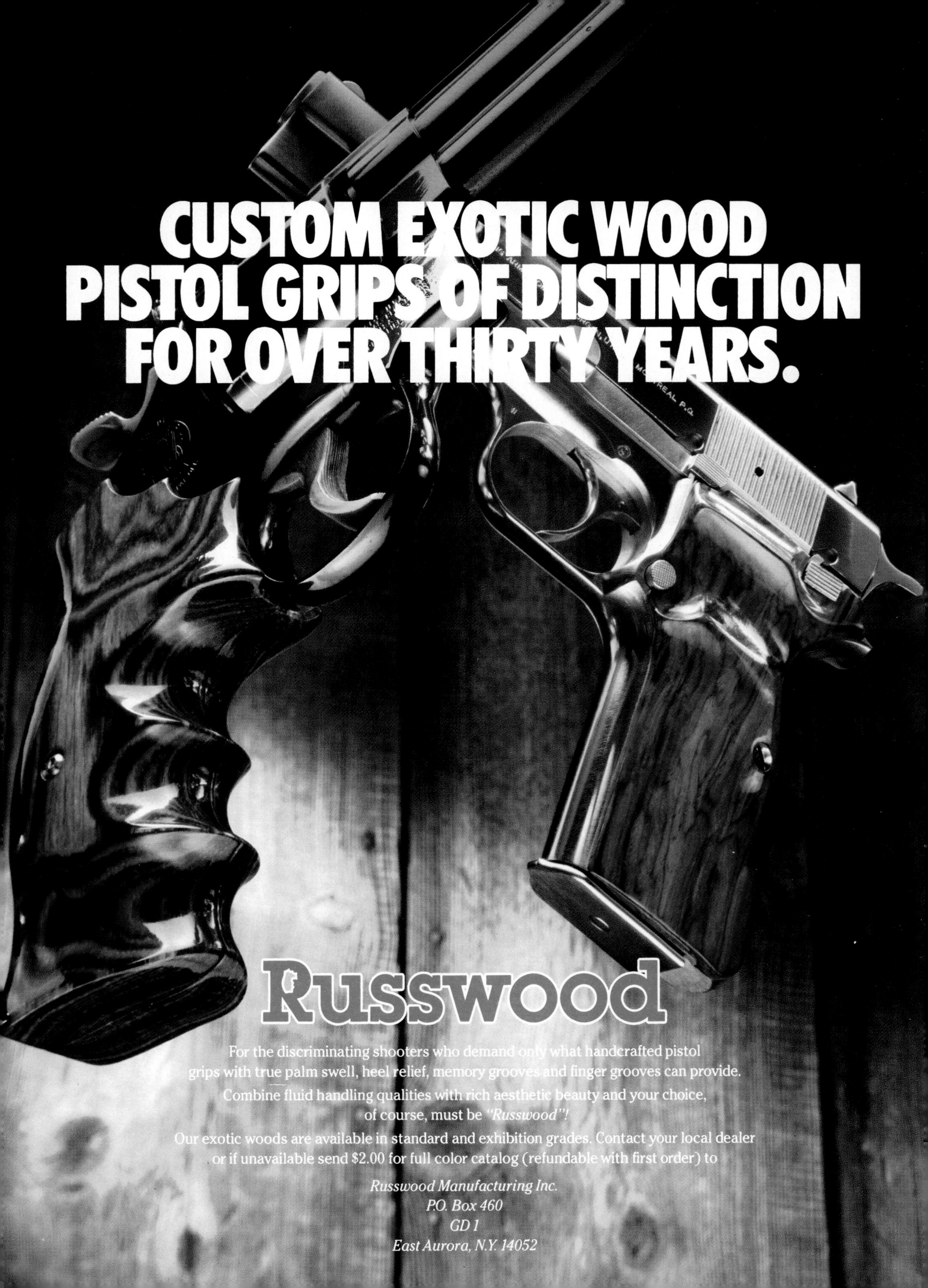

CUSTOM EXOTIC WOOD PISTOL GRIPS OF DISTINCTION FOR OVER THIRTY YEARS.

Russwood

For the discriminating shooters who demand only what handcrafted pistol grips with true palm swell, heel relief, memory grooves and finger grooves can provide.

Combine fluid handling qualities with rich aesthetic beauty and your choice, of course, must be *"Russwood"*!

Our exotic woods are available in standard and exhibition grades. Contact your local dealer or if unavailable send $2.00 for full color catalog (refundable with first order) to

Russwood Manufacturing Inc.
P.O. Box 460
GD 1
East Aurora, N.Y. 14052

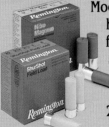
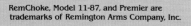

Shooting the

SMOOTHBORE RIFLE

by SAM FADALA

One of Sam's special four-shot groups first shot dry from an oily bore, next three dry. The ball from the oily bore struck high center. The three-shot cluster is about 2 inches center-to-center from 50 yards.

"DON'T SHOOT 'til you see the whites of their eyes, boys!"

So Bunker Hill soldiers were cautioned, if you believe history books. It wasn't so much that Command distrusted infantry marksmanship; the officers simply lacked faith in the accuracy of the smoothbore muskets in the hands of the Revolutionary soldiers—or any other shooter. Smoothbores have been defamed by most authorities since the day Kollner or Kotter got the idea of rifling the bore. However, even though smoothbores were discredited after rifling appeared, guns without rifling remained popular.

A few great latter-day hunters preferred smoothbores. William Cotten

Oswell, who died in 1893, hunted tuskers for ivory as a young man. S. W. Baker said Oswell was absolutely the first white man to show up in certain parts of South Africa. And when Oswell did show up, he was carrying a smoothbore made by Purdey—10 pounds, 10-gauge, charged with "six drachms of fine powder," according to Baker, who borrowed the piece from Oswell for an African hunt. A *drachm* is a dram—27.34 grains weight—so the load was about 164 grains of powder. Baker claimed to have great success with Oswell's smoothbore. He said, "There could not have been a better form of muzzleloader than this No. 10 double-barrel smoothbore. It was very accurate at 50 yards . . ." (*Big Game Shooting*, 1902.)

Oswell had learned to pre-patch round balls for his 10-bore, wrapping them in either "waxed kid" (leather) or linen. The "object of the smoothbore was easy loading," said Baker. The pre-patched ball was rolled tightly in cloth or leather with the excess trimmed close so the wrapping became a part of the projectile. The powder charge was also premeasured and carried in a paper cylinder, "the end of which could be bitten off," says Baker. The whole package of powder, paper and all, was thrust downbore after the end was nipped off, followed by the pre-patched ball rammed home with a "powerful loading rod."

Even though Baker admired his mentor's smoothbore, he found it lacking for long-range shooting, preferring the rifle for his own big game hunting in Africa and Ceylon. And later, in his book, *The Rifle and the Hound in Ceylon*, S. W. Baker cuts the smoothbore up with an abrupt tongue-lashing: "Smoothbores I count for nothing, although I have frequently used them," said he.

Another hunter, J. H. Walsh, "Stonehenge" to his friends, also distrusted the smoothbore for hunting. In his book, *Modern Sportsman's Gun & Rifle* (now reprinted by Wolfe Publishing Company), Walsh warned: "If, however, the six-inch circle at 50 yards could be depended on, I should be ready to admit that for large game it (a smoothbore) is a most useful weapon; and with this view I have repeatedly tested smoothbores by various makers, but the trial has invariably ended in disappointment. Sometimes the first or second, but oftener further on in a short trial, a wild shot occurred, and of course this wild shot may be the one to cost a sportsman his life, when charged by any kind of large game."

Stonehenge was not alone in his distrust of the smoothbore; however, military men, while not applauding the accuracy of the smoothbore, often chose it over the rifle. Our own General Washington often replaced rifles with muskets, believing the smoothbore a better tool of battle. They were easier to keep in repair, simpler to reload for rapid fire, and the musket carried a fixed bayonet better than a rifle, Washington believed.

The Brown Bess smoothbore musket remained Britain's first choice of arms, too, for a very long time, firing a .753-inch ball (11-bore) with 70 grains of powder. General George Hanger, said to be the best shot in the British Army (he served with Hessian Jaegers during the Revolution), reported that "a soldier's musket, if not exceedingly ill-bored (as many of them are), will strike the figure of a man at eighty yards; it may even at 100 . . .," but he concluded that "firing at a man at 200 yards with a common musket, you may just as well fire at the moon." (*American Rifleman*, August, 1947.) Hanger still thought smoothbores more manageable than rifles, hence better for battle.

In spite of controversy, many hunters did choose the smoothbore well into the era of rifled longarms. We may think of our own early Far West adventurers as riflemen, but indeed many carried smoothbores. The "fusil" was a smooth bore arm, referred to as far

Two 56-caliber T/C round balls, 252-grain weight, and a 36-caliber round ball. Smooth bore power means big balls.

Bill Fadala takes a shot with the T/C 56-caliber smoothbore. Sights made good ball placement a reality.

back as 1515 in French hunting ordinances, and still in use during the 19th century in one form or another.

I became intrigued with all of this for two reasons. First, the historical pull was magnetic. If muskets were so bad, at least in terms of accuracy, why did they hang on for so long, even after rifles were widely available? Second, some places today require smoothbores must be used for certain black-powder hunts. Can hunters packing smoothbores cleanly drop deer at woods ranges of 50 or 60 yards? After all, even the longbow outshot the common musket back in 1792 in a match on Pacton Green, Cumberland. The range was "over 100 yards" and the bowman placed sixteen arrows out of twenty on target—size not given. Meanwhile, the best musketeer only hit the target twelve for twenty tries.

As Karl Foster (of rifled slug fame) said in the *American Rifleman*, "Round balls in smooth barrels have lacked accuracy since guns were first made" (p. 23, October, 1936).

What could be expected from a smooth bore firearm today? In Scotland, 1803, soldiers practiced to meet Napoleon by firing their muskets. However, they were content when ". . . every fifth or sixth shot is made to take place in a target of three feet diameter at the distance of 100 yards." (*American Rifleman*, August, 1947, p. 8.) When I presented this quote to one of my buckskinner friends who had recently laid out a fat wad of greenbacks for a custom rifle with a smoothbore, he replied, "Must have been damn poor shots." And he went on to tell me that if ever I was in need of venison steaks for supper, just let him get within 75 yards of a buck and, "We'll be in meat with my smoothbore." Then he added, "Of course, I stalk for close shots. You do remember stalking don't you? That's where you get close before you shoot," he added sarcastically.

It was a puzzlement.

My first attempt to unravel the mystery came with a double-barreled shotgun shooting patched round balls. I was caressed with success and slapped with failure simultaneously. The shotgun was 12-gauge, a side-by-side caplock, and 80 grains of GOEX FFg gave 927 fps MV average from its 28-inch tubes. The load was mild, even behind a .695-inch patched ball, which averaged 502 grains weight, so I progressed to a flat 100 grains of the same powder for a MV of 1190 fps, along with three quarters of a ton muzzle energy (1579 foot-pounds). However, a target a foot across was safe forty paces away—power enough, but poor accuracy. I was disenchanted with the cluster, not the thump. The big round ball penetrated a couple feet of test media at 50 yards, bettering the "wound channel" I'd gotten from a couple of 30-06 handloads.

I tried the old trick of filing the muzzles to register the barrels, because even with double shotgun beads for "sights," the left barrel could be counted on to drop its projectile into the black at forty paces with some semblance of consistency, while the right would sail its bullet right off target, missing everything, including the target *frame*. Filing, which cut away the inside edge of the right-hand muzzle, did bring the ball over a little, but nothing close to true bore regulation resulted. I gave up—the muzzle looked as if a mean kid with a hacksaw attacked it.

This 100-yard group won't win any benchrest competitions, but it's a far cry from Fadala's first 100-yard attempts, and better than old-timers claimed.

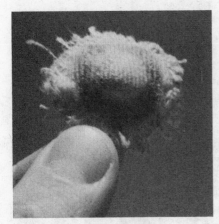

Hornet nest as a buffer keeps the patch intact even with 100 grains of FFg.

Fadala found a bristle brush with cleaning patch worked better than the jag provided with the rifle.

Why was the lead sphere inaccurate from a smoothbore when from a rifled barrel (with test scope mounted) I'd managed so many one-inch five-shot groups with patched round ball at 100 yards? Ballistics said the ball's center of mass would rotate on its axis the same as a conical, so imperfections in the ball itself would cause the projectile to leave the bore at a different angle of departure each shot. Matter in motion moves in a straight line, so the "heavy" part of the projectile would determine the initial line of flight of the round ball. An imperfect ball would tend to travel on a tangent from the line of the axis. In other words, static imbalance would ruin accuracy. I began to wonder just what sort of static balance—the actual precision of the projectile in terms of mass distribution—was present in those old missiles of the past, where the boys felt lucky to infrequently hit a three-foot target at 100 paces?

A sphere needs less rotational stabilization than a conical. W. W. Greener said, "Rifling, therefore, is of greater importance when a conical or elongated projectile is used than when the bullet is spherical." (*The Gun*) The principle of rotating an elongated missle for stabilization was a phenomenon tested hundreds of years ago. There are even relics of crossbow bolts which had been grooved to create a spiral motion.

The big ball had mass going for it, too. The greater the mass, the greater the inertia. The heavier the projectile, the less rotation on its axis necessary to stabilize it, and for big game hunting with the smooth bore muzzleloader, ½-inch missiles prevail. The .690-inch ball for the 12-gauge, for example, weighs 454 grains. Thompson/ Center's 56-caliber ball (more on that in a moment) is 252 grains heavy on my scale.

The smaller ball gains more advantage from rifling than the larger. The large round ball would be inherently stable, if made right. Ezekiel Baker, well-known court ballistician who wrote a gunnery treatise for George IV said in his 11th editions of the work, "The Honorable Board of Ordnance being anxious to ascertain if rifling a large piece would have the same advantage over smooth barrels which rifles possess over muskets, and would be equally effective in carrying the ball, the experiment was tried at Woolrich [on May 15, 1806] with two wallpiece barrels of equal dimensions, one rifled, the other not rifled."

The barrels were 4 feet 6 inches long, each weighing 20 pounds. The projec-

tiles were 5-gauge round balls. The advantage of the rifled piece was not nearly as pronounced as it had been with smaller round balls of 20-gauge size. What was not tried, however, was very careful sorting of round balls in the 20-gauge and smaller smooth bore firearms. It was long known that swaged balls were the more uniform; however, I found no test in which the smoothbore was fired with very carefully weighed round balls. Would *balanced* spherical missiles make a difference in the smoothbore? Static

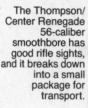

The Thompson/ Center Renegade 56-caliber smoothbore has good rifle sights, and it breaks down into a small package for transport.

Bill Fadala takes down the Thompson/Center Renegade smoothbore for cleaning—another thing that is easier and simpler with smoothbores.

The percussion lock of the Thompson/ Center 56-caliber smoothbore is reliability-prone. They've made tens of thousands and know how to do it.

stability would be improved, for certain, which should improve dynamic stability.

In this century, Dr. F. W. Mann concluded, after thousands of experiments, that precision of projectiles was the most important single aspect of accuracy. The sphere, if perfect, would theoretically fly true, would it not? Even from a smoothbore. Round ball perfection wasn't possible. But precision was. Rifling vastly improved round ball accuracy because it "averaged" the imperfections in the ball on a common axis. Example—a ball heavier on one side than the other. Rifling twist equalizes lopsidedness on the axis through rotation. In my later tests, I pre-sorted round ball projectiles, which improved accuracy.

When I turned to the T/C factory 56-caliber ball, sorting was not necessary. The greatest variation in random sampling of ten balls was only .9-grain weight. The heaviest in the string was 252.1 grains, the lightest 251.2. The micrometer gave an average diameter of .552-inch. If the T/C ball were pure lead, it would weigh 253 grains. Weighing proved that the T/C ball was precise, and it was not an alloy. Homogenity was not proved by weighing, but uniformity was.

Besides, target accuracy wasn't the object of smooth bore testing. Deer hunting accuracy was. The sightless shotgun, with careful loading and pre-sorted missiles, could be counted on to strike a six-inch bull at forty paces, but it was the Thompson/Center Renegade 56-caliber smoothbore, with adjustable rear sight, that became my test firearm. This rifle—and it will be referred to as a rifle even though by strict definition perhaps it's a musket—was created to give the blackpowder hunter a reliable firearm where law or desire called for a non-rifled bore. Sights at last! I had been spinning my wheels, even with a good benchrest, trying to remove extraneous variables while aiming with shotgun beads for sights.

About the T/C rifle—it proved totally reliable, with 100 percent ignition using CCI No. 11 caps. The test run included the firing of eighty .550-inch T/C cast "265-grain" projectiles, which were actually closer to .551-.552-inch average diameter, weighing about 252 grains.

Loads were selected from the T/C manual, *Shooting Thompson/Center Black Powder Guns.* Three were given, all using T/C patch material, a No. 11 cap, and Maxi-Lube. My tests included three patch types and three lubes. The shooting patches were .005-inch, .010-inch and .013-inch, the first two from Gunther Stifter's West German supply house, the last of my own cut, pure Irish linen. The .010-patch proved best of the three, only because it loaded with comparative ease, and still offered a tight bore fit. While a patch is not a true gasket—no cloth patch by itself seals hot expanding powder gas behind the ball—it's still best to have a tight ball/patch fit to hold the ball on the powder charge and maintain a consistent load pressure. My direct load pressure on the ramrod (an N&W steel

loading rod) was 45 pounds as maintained by a special tool a reader of mine built for me, which spring-collapses when 45 pounds pressure is reached.

The lubes were grease, cream and liquid—RIG, Young Country Lube 103 and Falkenberry Juice. All three worked equally in terms of accuracy. Initially, shooting from the 50-yard bench, the balls struck the black with a 6-inch center-to-center group. My early 100-yard tests were folly. Test-shooting with open iron sights, coupled with initially large groups, did not warrant 100-yard shooting. That would change. Boring the reader with details of continued failures is pointless, so I'll get to the method which gave best accuracy.

No accuracy difference was found among the three allowed powder charges, 80, 90 and 100 grains of FFg, so the latter was used. It only developed about 6000 LUP. Recoil was comparatively mild. And muzzle velocity averaged 1366 fps. Thompson/Center tests averaged 1300; however, powder lots can vary, and I was shooting 6000 feet above sea level with a temperature of 85 degrees Fahrenheit. The muzzle energy of this load was a bit over a half ton—1044 foot-pounds—with a 252-grain projectile. At 50 yards, my chronograph (shooting through the large Oehler Skyscreens) showed a retained velocity of 1101 fps for the 56-caliber ball, with a retained energy of 678 foot-pounds, which doesn't sound like much, but is certainly ample for deer when coupled with a half-inch *entrance* hole.

The ball-shooting smoothbore proved amply accurate for deer hunting in woods and timber. Scattergun-like clusters shrank to consistent 100-yard 8-inch groups. That's with iron sights, remember. Hundred-yard potential may be higher. At 50 yards, 3-inch groups became common, however, only after installing regimen in the loading process. First, as stated above, I assured that the missile was good. T/C commercial cast ball proved its precision; I stayed with it. Second, I got consistent powder charges by overfilling the measure, tapping the barrel ten times, then swiping off excess kernels of powder by swinging the funnel section of the measure in line. Third, a buffer was placed between the patched ball and charge. I used hornet nest, which is my favorite in the muzzleloader rifle with hunting loads. It does not ignite and it saves the patch from burnout. Moreover, the buffer between patch and charge acted to absorb excess lube which might attack

the powder charge.

The fourth step proved important—wiping the bore free of excess lube after the load was seated. I fired several groups with the bore untouched after seating the ball and several with the bore wiped with a cleaning patch after seating the ball. The latter were always more accurate in my particular test rifle. Point of impact changed though. Final sight-in was with a lube-free bore.

Another T/C muzzleloader came to my attention—the New Englander, a single-barrel 12-gauge shotgun with auxiliary rifled 50-caliber barrel. My interest was with the 12-gauge smooth bore barrel, firing a .690-inch round patched ball, using the loading sequence mentioned above, with hornet nest buffer. The powder, however, was not black, but rather was Golden. A new batch of Golden Powder had arrived for my testing, so a charge of 80 grains bulk was used in the New Englander. In spite of the no-sight shotgun barrel (bead only), results were extremely pleasing from the 50-yard bench. Big 69-caliber holes peppered the bullseye with groups averaging about eight inches. One group was well under half that size. I took a photo of that one! Carefully loaded, the New Englander smoothbore could be counted on to strike the chest area of a deer in a brush or timber setting with close-range shooting the rule. Naturally, bench shooting is one thing; shooting from the offhand posture is another. So I shot offhand at the 50-yard target and no ball flew outside of a 12-inch circle. Most clustered under ten inches center-to-center, which seems to be good enough.

The smoothbore, with precise spherical missiles, proved sufficiently accurate for woods/brush deer hunting, at least with the 56-caliber T/C Renegade and the 12-bore New Englander test arms. As for those old shooters feeling lucky about hitting a man-sized target at 100 yards, I can only say they should have put some better sights on their rifles, pre-sorted their projectiles, maintained a uniform powder charge, as well as uniform ramrod pressure on the seated patched ball, and they should have wiped the bore clear of excess lube prior to firing.

I've been shooting too long to believe in panaceas, but these methods did work in one test rifle. Of course, most of these rules would have been impossible in battle. But all of them are possible in modern hunting. And the present-day blackpowder smoothbore rifle is for hunting, not target shooting and certainly not for war. ●

THE LOSER'S GUN

THE ERA OF the adult TV Western, spanning approximately ten years from the mid-1950s, produced a number of professional exhibition shooters who toured the country demonstrating Fast Gun skills. Such legends as Dee Woolem, four-time National Fast Draw Champion and holder of the "Fastest Gun Alive" title, Joe Bodrie of Colts Patent Firearms Company, Rodd Redwing, famous movie gun coach and technical adviser, and Joe Bowman, who is still active today, were among them. Unique among these professional fast guns for his use of the modern double-action police revolver was former U.S. Border Patrol officer Bill Jordan.

Jordan remains well known among handgunners today for his design of the Jordan holster as made by Don Hume, his Jordan Trooper revolver stocks as produced by Herrett's Stocks, his classic combat handgunning book, *No Second Place Winner*, the 1976 Outstanding American Handgunner Award he received and his monthly writing. While he developed his fast draw and hip shooting skills out of necessity along the Border early on, it wasn't until he became a supervisory patrol officer that he developed his formal Fast Draw act. The act was developed to fulfill his duties in answering requests for after-dinner speakers. With the burgeoning interest in Fast Draw generated by the TV Westerns, many TV shows were looking for Fast Guns. The Border Patrol detailed Jordan to appear with such stars as James Arness of *Gunsmoke*, Richard Boone of *Have Gun, Will Travel*, and Clint Walker of *Cheyenne*. Bill also appeared on *To Tell The Truth, You Asked For It, I've Got A Secret* and *Wide, Wide World*. His act was so well-received that Jordan was soon using his annual leave touring for the Knife and Fork Clubs and Executive Clubs as a professional speaker.

I saw Jordan's shooting exhibition two different times. His waist-level point shooting was the finest I've witnessed. He hit two-inch cedar wafers to start with and worked down to a final hit on a saccharin tablet, shooting wax bullets in his S&W Model 19 at a distance of 10 feet. It was, beyond that, his speed from the leather that fascinated me. To prove that he was both fast AND accurate, Bill would drop a Ping-Pong ball from the back of his gun hand held waist-high, draw and fire, hitting the falling ball before it reached the floor. A good hit with the wax bullet would split the Ping-Pong ball into two pieces.

In order to demonstrate sheer speed, Jordan performed what Fast Guns know as the "beat the drop." To do this, one must draw and fire, beating someone who already has his gun drawn and pointed. That's when he used the "loser's gun." A Colt Single Action revolver, it was given to a volunteer from the audience, loaded with primed cases. The volunteer was instructed to squeeze the hair-trigger on the already cocked SA as fast as possible after seeing Bill start to draw. The trick here is to be able to perform a self-started (no reaction time) draw in less than the volunteer's reaction time, which is the time it takes him to see the Fast Gun's move and react by squeezing the trigger. Bill beat the drop with ease, making the volunteer the "loser," the Colt the "loser's gun."

As illustrated on page 69 of *No Second Place Winner*, the loser's gun has a 4¾-inch barrel. Jordan says it is a parts gun he had assembled to his specs for use in his act. Built on a blackpowder frame originally produced in 1887, the original barrel and cylinder have been replaced with 357 Magnum parts so the old Colt uses the same wax bullet or primer-only loads as Jordan's Model 19. Jordan's giant hands (size thirteen gloves are far too small) required the original grip frame be replaced with one from a Colt 1860 Army revolver, ½-inch longer than the original unit. The stocks are of guayacan, a hardwood growing in southern Texas and Mexico, and made by Steve Herrett. To prevent sight drag, the original front sight was reversed on the barrel, offering a semi-ramped shape. The mainspring has been lightened for an easier cocking action and the checkering has been removed from the hammer spur. These are all standard modifications on Fast Draw Colts.

I was recently in the right place at the right time, caught Bill Jordan in the right mood, and I added his loser's gun to my collection.

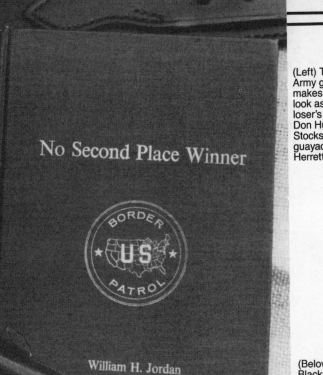

(Left) The 1860 Colt Army grip frame makes a different look as Jordan's loser's gun sits in a Don Hume holster. Stocks are of guayacan by Herrett.

(Below) Blackpowder frame, 357 barrel and cylinder, de-toothed hammer spur are other changes Jordan's act demanded.

by BOB ARGANBRIGHT

The final chapter in the story sounds like it came right out of Hollywood. On July 14, 1978, Rock Springs, Wyoming, chief police officer Ed Cantrell shot and killed undercover narcotics agent Michael Rosa. Located in Sweetwater County, Rock Springs was caught up in a county-wide drug, prostitution and graft crime wave which went with the recent oil boom. Rock Springs' reputation as a boom town had inspired a two-part *60 Minutes* national TV show which in turn led to a state-wide grand jury investigation. Cantrell was the scapegoat the state had been looking for and he was charged with murder. The prosecution charged Cantrell had killed Rosa to silence him before he could talk to the grand jury. Cantrell pled self-defense, claiming that Rosa had reached for a gun.

Cantrell retained famous trial lawyer Gerry Spence for his defense. Spence has won some of the most important criminal and civil cases of our time and is described as another Clarence Darrow. While Spence was able to show that Rosa was on medication which had side effects of insomnia, hallucinations and depression, the case hinged on the fact that the shooting occurred so fast that, though two other police officers were present, neither saw it happen.

Bill Jordan and the loser's gun were instrumental in Cantrell's defense. The complete story of the Cantrell case, the biggest murder case in the history of Wyoming, is told in attorney Gerry Spence's autobiography titled, *Gunning for Justice*. Three pages are devoted to a description of Jordan's testimony. The newspapers had identified Cantrell as the last of the old-time gunfighters, as he had spent years practicing the fast draw with his old S&W Model 10 revolver. Spence had Jordan demonstrate the fast draw for the jury. Quoting from *Gunning for Justice*:

We enlisted a surprised deputy from the door of the courtroom. The jury was enthralled as we took two pistols out of a box, and His Honor became intensely interested. I took the guns to His Honor and asked him to inspect them. He was obviously familiar with sidearms. The guns were empty and safe except for the blanks we intended to use. Jordan buckled on a holster for his revolver. He carried it high on his right hip. I put the cocked single-action .45 (sic) in the hands of the deputy and told him to point the gun at the old man's belly. He only had to touch the hair trigger when he saw Jordan go for his holstered gun, that's all—just touch it. 'Pull the trigger the moment I make my move,' Jordan instructed the deputy. The deputy grinned sheepishly—the gun pointed at Jordan, trigger finger tense and ready. The sixty-nine-year-old Jordan went on talking and then, suddenly, made his move. His weapon flashed from his holster, exploding. The deputy stood there, open-mouthed, unmoving—he never had a chance, Jordan told the jury."

While later telling me of this experience, Jordan said that was the fastest draw he had ever made. He felt that the life of his old friend might hang on this demonstration of his gun speed. The jury found Ed Cantrell innocent of all charges. Bill Jordan's loser's gun had given one last show. Loaded with a blank it never fired, the old Colt was instrumental in saving the life of Ed Cantrell, the last of the old-time gunfighters. ●

This is the current look of the all-out Fred Wells shop-made Mauser.

CUSTOM GUNS

DENNIS ERHARDT
(Above and below) Shortened and recontoured Model 98 in 250-3000 has Shilen barrel, Grisel grip cap and swivels, French walnut and its own look.

KLAUS HIPTMAYER
Mauser 98 in 270 Weatherby Magnum has Shilen barrel, English walnut, Heidi Hiptmayer engraving. Owner: Michael Lacroix.

GEORGE BEITZINGER
(Above and below) Ruger in 7×57 has Douglas Premium barrel, quarter-rib, stock in California English walnut that holds 26 lpi checkering.

ROBERT M. WINTER
Model 77 Ruger 270 in California English is slimmed with blind magazine, checkered with fleurs-de-lis.

KENT BOWERLY
(Above and below) Mannlicher styling suits this G 33-40 Mauser action in 7×57 caliber, stocked in California English walnut, with metalwork by Larry Brace.

STEPHEN NELSON
(Below) Personal elk rifle, a 338 in an FN Mauser 98 action, is detailed for horseback hunting, stocked in Claro walnut with 24 lpi checkering. (Utesch photo)

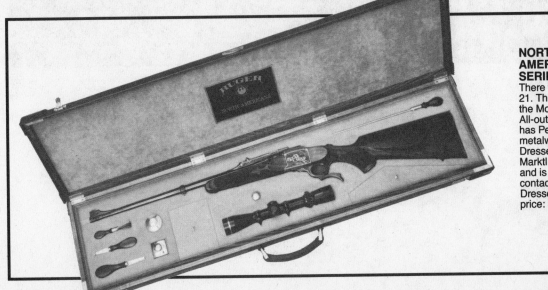

NORTH AMERICAN SERIES
There were to be 21. This is No. 2, the Mountain Lion. All-out Ruger No. 1 has Penrod metalwork, Paul Dressel wood, Marktl engraving and is for sale: contact Paul Dressel. Asking price: $48,000.

JAMES A. TERTIN/JAEGER
(Above and below) This Oberndorf Mauser in 7mm-06 has an Obermeyer barrel, English walnut, all the latest metalwork touches.

WILLIAM G. TALMAGE
The California style lives on this FN Mauser-actioned 7mm Remington Magnum. Stock is mesquite, checkering skip-a-line. (Merrick photo)

MAURICE OTTMAR
Flat-top Brno in 257 Roberts has slim blind-magazine stock in Turkish walnut, shotgun guard, Burgess scope rings. (Callie photo)

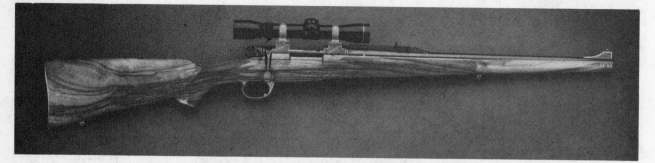

PAUL G. DRESSEL, JR.
(Above) All-out 358 Winchester has Grisel action, Donnelly barrel, Butler engraving, all in Oregon English walnut with detail inletting, serious checkering and high style. (Bilal photo)

DICK DEVEREAUX
Long Sako action holds 375 H&H. Feather crotch California English stock has scroll pattern checkering, weighs 8¾ pounds.

AL LIND
Dakota 76 holds 416 Hoffman in Moroccan walnut. Scope shown is a Leupold 1x4. Pad is a Pachmayr Decelerator, leather-covered. (Bilal photo)

JAY McCAMENT
Classic styling in a light, quick sporter with Herman Waldron metalwork throughout, stocked in French walnut. (Bilal photo)

DARWIN HENSLEY
Wells-actioned 308 Winchester has Griffin & Howe metalwork, Bayer and Evans engraving, splendid Turkish walnut stock. (Bilal photo)

JERE EGGLESTON
Talley metalwork and clean style in a 280 Remington done up in English walnut with trademark schnabel and ribbon checkering.

DARWIN HENSLEY
Gibbs-Farquharson in 225 Winchester has Heilmann metalwork, Evans engraving, Mazur metal finish, Moroccan walnut and great looks. (Bilal photo)

DON KLEIN
Once shown on a book cover, this Winchester high wall is a 30-30 built for Bud McCollum—engraved by Steve Huff, stocked in French walnut.

SHARON FARMER-DRESSEL
(Above and below) Commissioned by the North Carolina chapter of the National Wild Turkey Federation, this 12-gauge Browning Citori is cased by Marvin Huey, engraved by Jon Robyn. All wood and metalwork by Farmer-Dressel. (Bilal photos)

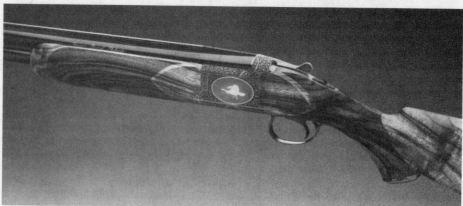

STEPHEN NELSON
(Below) This Bolognini 12-gauge over/under is stocked in black walnut with leather-bound pad. Awaits engraving. (Hughes photo)

WILLIAM G. TALMAGE
Remington 870 has full-court press in fancy black walnut, skip-line checkering, grip cap with spacers.

L. KORTZ
Weight is not a factor in these Elko rifles. Kortz goes for strength.

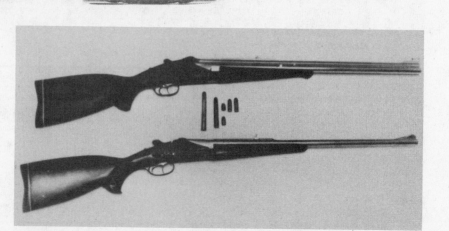

BILL HOLMES
The falling block rimfire at top has a round breechblock—seen at left above—and worked out so well Holmes built the other rifle with a square block for centerfires. One expectation is that the one-piece stock will improve accuracy. The round-block version has also been built as a 410 shotgun. Holmes intends to concentrate on single shots now.

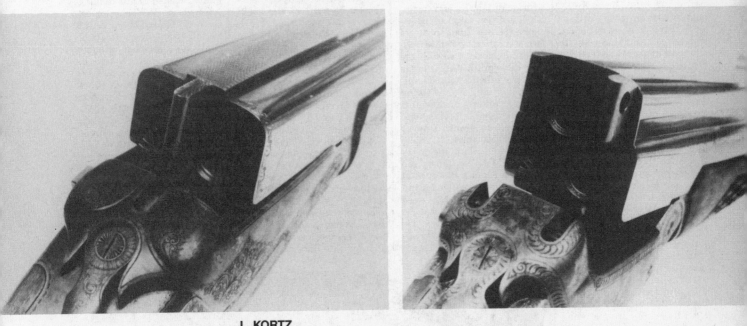

L. KORTZ
Massive breeches are only one of the idiosyncrasies of Elko Arms Belgian bench-made guns. Usual caliber: 458 Elsa Magnum.

by LAYNE SIMPSON

RIFLE REVIEW

THE WAY it sometimes works in the firearms industry is if you can't think of something new to introduce the reintroduction of something old is about as good. All of which is fine because if somebody didn't do something, people like me wouldn't have anything to write about. Probably next best is to modify something fairly new and call it brand new. And so it goes with rifles, one way or another, throughout this great land for 1990.

Front page news for big game hunters is the introduction of a new version of an old centerfire rifle. Simply put, it combines the best of the new with what some shooters will always believe was the best of the old. They used to even go so far as to call it "The Rifleman's Rifle," and perhaps now they will do so once more. Moving out West, another company that seems to always manage to stay a step or two ahead of the rest is now offering us "Tomorrow's Bolt Action 22 Rimfire Today." Which brings me to the third largest producer of rifles in the U.S. and a stainless steel bolt-action option that big game hunters who hunt come rain or shine are sure to find appealing. Which also brings up the fact that any major rifle company who does not have stainless steel or rust resistant metal coatings on their drawing boards had better wake up before the race is over.

In the chamberings department, a mild mannered little varmint cartridge, one introduced in a lever-action rifle back in 1938, has been snatched from its grave once more and given another chance in somebody else's lever-action rifle. As 22 rimfires go, one rifle company dropped Winchester's Magnum version, another rifle company added it to its list of options.

Last, but certainly not least, two rifle companies who got caught in the financial storm seem to have struggled through to find a ray of sunshine peeping from behind dark clouds. Here's hoping they find smoother waters ahead.

Now for a review of exciting things another fruitful year promises to bring us in rifles.

Anschutz

Last year, Anschutz introduced its new 6¼-pound Model 1700 FWT (featherweight) with a McMillan fiberglass stock. In 1990, the stock will be available with McMillan's Fibergrain finish. It is a very nice looking little 22 rimfire. Incidentally, I own several custom rifles with McMillan stocks, two with the new Fibergrain finish. I was sold on synthetic-stocked hunting rifles long before using them became the fashionable thing to do and, believe me, handsome is a word I never thought I'd find myself using to describe one. That's exactly what the McMillan Fibergrain finish is. From a distance of about two feet, most find it impossible to tell which is wood and which is glass.

Browning

Back in 1924, Winchester decided to "discontinue" its little Model 1892 lever action, make a few minor modifications to it and call it the "new" Model 53. Available in 25-20, 32-20, and 44-40, the Model 53 differed mainly from the Model 92 by its round 22-inch barrel, shotgun-type buttstock, checkered steel buttplate, and integral front sight base. After slightly fewer than 25,000 were produced, the Model 53 was discontinued in 1932, only to be snatched from its grave the very next year and renamed the Model 65. Less than 6000 Model 65s were made in 218 Bee, 25-20, and 32-20 before it was dropped in 1947.

For 1990, Browning is introducing a limited run of Model 53 reproductions in 32-20 only.

I used this Model 70 Super Grade prototype to bag this whitetail during mid-1989.

Offered only in the Deluxe Grade configuration with checkered wood, the Browning 53 follows the design of the Winchester 53 quite closely, right down to its button magazine. It has a 22-inch barrel with 1 in 20 twist and is said to weigh 6½ pounds. Only 5000 are to be made.

Last year Browning announced its limited production Model 65 reproduction in 218 Bee. As I understand it, only 3500 Grade I and 1500 High Grade Bees were made. This year rifle and production numbers remain the same, but the caliber is 25-20. Its 24-inch barrel has a rifling pitch of 1 in 16 inches.

Before you put away the bug spray, be aware of the fact that the 22 Hornet has invaded yet another rifle factory. The fine little Hornet is now the eighth cartridge option for the A-Bolt Micro-Medallion. The others are 223, 22-250, 257 Roberts, 7mm-08, 284, 308, and 243.

David Gentry

Can't afford to pay $2500 for one of Gentry's custom double square bridge Mauser actions? I talked with him in January, and he says he has found a way to trim a few frills away and come up with an action at a much lower price. If he does, you'll eventually read about it in GUN DIGEST.

Kenny Jarrett

A few things have been cooking down in a sleepy little place called Jackson, South Carolina. One is a new wildcat called the 358 Shooting Times Alaskan, or 358 STA for short. The 35 has, off and on, been such a neglected caliber (until Remington made the 35 Whelen honest, that is), I figured it was time it soaked up a bit more limelight. And too, a number of firms, both large and small, have introduced marvelous new big game bullets of this caliber. Just to name a few we have Nosler 225-grain Partition, the Speer 250-grain Grand Slam, the Sierra 225-grain spitzer boattail, the Hornady 250-grain spire point (reintroduced), the Barnes 250-grain Super Solid and 240-grain X-Bullet, the Orion 225-, 250-, and 265-grain partitioned bonded, and the Swift 225- and 250-grain A-Frame. Trophy Bonded, and Alaska Bullet Works also offer excellent 35-

The fine little 218 Bee has found a new home in Marlin's Model 1894 Classic.

Lisa Jarrett bagged this August buck with (naturally) a Jarrett rifle in 300 Winchester Magnum and its 8x56mm Swarovski scope.

The 358 STA, by the way, is the 8mm Remington Magnum case necked up (or the 416 Remington Magnum case necked down) and fireformed to minimum body taper and a 35-degree shoulder angle. You might say it is a chubby version of Griffin & Howe's 1920s vintage 350 Magnum, the one James Howe developed after big game hunter Leslie Simpson told Townsend Whelen it was what was needed for hunting African game like lion, leopard, and the larger antelope such as sable, greater kudu, and the ton-size eland. Incidentally, my new Jarrett rifle is a switch-barrel gun. Its other barrel is a 24-inch Schneider in 7mm STW. That enables me to also push 140- and 160-grain spitzers along at 3500 and 3300 fps with the same rifle.

Forgive me, Hal Swiggett, for saying so here, but another project Jarrett and I have been involved in is what I suggested he call the XP-1-Hunter. It's a switch-barrel, switch-scope XP-100 with an SSK Industries T'SOB mount, three Burris scopes, and three Shilen benchrest grade rifle barrels chopped back to 16 inches (22-250 Improved) and 14 inches (7mm SGLC and 358 Winchester). The 7mm and 358 barrels have George Vais' muzzlebrakes. The 22-250 Improved kicks a 55-grain spitzer along at close to

3600 fps, the 7mm does 2700 fps with the Nosler 140-grain Ballistic Tip, and Hornady's new 180-grain spire point leaves the muzzle of the 358 at close to 2550 fps.

The 22 averages less than .250-MOA with Euber bullets (on those rare occasions when I can hold it that close); the 7mm averages in the neighborhood of .400-MOA, but I haven't shot the 358 enough to say how accurate it is. What we have here is one of Jarrett's benchrest rifles with short barrels and no buttstock. The XP-1-Hunter is also available in a repeating version.

While I'm on the subject of accuracy, I visited the Jarretts last August 14th, the day before opening day of deer season in the South Carolina low country. Lisa Jarrett (Kenny's spouse) invited me to try her new 300 Winchester Magnum at the 100-yard benchrest. My first 100-yard three shot group with IMR-4350 and Nosler's 150-grain Ballistic Tip measured less than 0.400-inch, which is by no means the best accuracy I have squeezed from a Jarrett rifle. But, it was not bad for a load chosen at random and good enough to enable Lisa to later plaster a nice buck standing on yon side of a vast soybean field with one shot. Someday I might write for GUN DIGEST an opus entitled "The Mid-Summer

caliber bullets.

First I sent 358 STA chamber dimensions to David Manson at Clymer to be used in grinding the reamer. Then I ordered a benchrest grade 24-inch stainless steel barrel with 1 in 12-inch twist from Dan Lilja, a fiberglass stock from Kelly McMillan, a muzzlebrake from George Vais, and a Dual-Dovetail mount and a 1/5-5x Vari-X III from Leupold. Jarrett threw everything into the pot along with a Remington Model 700 action and, as happens about 100 times each year in Jackson, came up with one of his superbly accurate rifles. His doing so enabled me to send fireformed cases to Jay Postman at RCBS for full-length resizing and bullet seating dies.

As a result of all that effort by so many good people, I can now push a 250-grain bullet out the muzzle at just over 3000 fps. The 358 STA simply thrives on big doses of Reloder 19. I call it the Alaskan because, God willing and the creek don't rise, it and I will have accounted for one of the giant bears there by the time you read this. And since it seems to rain more often than not in some parts of Alaska, I sent the barreled action to Jim Dedmon of Armoloy

of Forth Worth for the application of an extremely durable and rust-resistant satin finish to all metal.

Remington's lightweight Model 700AS is now available in Weatherby's 300 Magnum, a combination of power and portability.

Left-handers will probably like the looks of the Model 700BDL-LH in 22-250 and 338 Winchester Magnum with the bolt handle on the right side, so to speak.

The 7x57mm Mauser is the Model 700 Mountain Rifle's latest chambering—some old soldiers never die.

Remington's limited edition Model 700 Classic is available in the classic 25-06, but only during 1990, like all the others.

Southeastern Deer Hunter's Survival Manual," but in the meantime, something you should know about August deer hunting in South Carolina is that a T-shirt, short pants and leather boots thick enough to shed a big diamondback's strike are all the wardrobe you'll need; you avoid some of the heat by hunting only during afternoons; you never forget to take a gallon each of iced tea and bug dope to your stand, and flat-shooting bolt actions with Schmidt & Bender and Swarovski scopes and their 56mm objective lenses absolutely rule the roost.

Kimber

Kimber has new ownership and a few new plans. One is the new Hunter Grade Models 82, 84, and 89 rifles. They are standard grade configurations of what Kimber fans like to describe as the most deluxe factory rifles available. Like the earlier Model 84 Ultra Varminter, the Hunter Grade rifles have stocks of laminated wood and a matte metal finish.

The Model 89 African in 375 H&H, 404 Jeffery, 416 Rigby, 460 Weatherby Magnum, and 505 Gibbs is in Kimber's 1990 catalog, but I don't see it on the dealer price list. Which may mean that the 416 Rigby I took to Zambia a couple of years back was one of very few Kimber Africans ever built. The price list does contain two Model 89 variations, roundtop receiver, and double square bridge receiver, both available in twelve chamberings: 257 Roberts, 25-06, 7x57mm Mauser, 270, 280, 30-06, 7mm Remington Magnum, 300 Winchester Magnum, 300 H&H Magnum, 338 Winchester Magnum, 35 Whelen, and 375 H&H Magnum.

The Model 84 is still available in four variations: Deluxe, Super America, Ultra Varminter (laminated birch stock and stainless steel barrel), and Super Varminter. The Ultra Varminter is available in Remington's 222 and 223 while the others are offered in those two plus the 17-caliber member of the same family.

The Model 82 rimfire has survived in a number of variations: Deluxe Righthand, Deluxe Lefthand, Super America, Government Target (26-inch bull barrel) and new for 1990, the All American Match with a 25-inch medium heavy barrel. I expect the latter will enjoy some popularity among small-bore me-

tallic silhouette shooters.

Perhaps Kimber's new Star Grade version of the Model 82 Government Target calls for a bit of explaining. Sometime back, Uncle Sam awarded Kimber a contract to build 20,000 target rifles. Before each rifle could be shipped, it had to be capable of shooting ten shots with Eley Tenex ammunition into .700-inch at 50 yards. While the rifles were being accuracy tested at Kimber's indoor range, one would occasionally come through that averaged .300-inch or less. They were set aside, identified by a star stamped on their receivers, and reserved for sale to civilian shooters like you and me.

Something I see missing from the Kimber lineup this year is the 22 WMR chambering in the Model 82 rifle.

Marlin

According to my pal Bill Brophy's wonderful 696-page book, *Marlin Firearms,* the Marlin Model 1894 lever action was, as its model designation implies, introduced in 1894. Prior to being dropped from production in 1935, the 94 served as a second home for revolver cartridges with romantic sounding names like 25-20, 32-20, 38-40, and 44-40. Then came 1956 and gunsmiths throughout the land rejoiced as hunters and shooters sent old Marlin 94s and Winchester 92s to be rebarreled or rechambered and rebored to a new revolver cartridge called the 44 Remington Magnum. Figuring to get in on some of the action, Marlin eventually offered its Model 336 in 44 Magnum, only to discover that long actions and short cartridges are not the most compatible of combinations.

In 1969, Marlin did it the right way by bringing back a lever-action rifle designed for short cartridges. Called the Model 1894, it was basically the old 1894 carved from stronger steel. Introduced in 44 Magnum, the new Model 94 family has since grown to include the 22 WMR, 357 Magnum, 41 Magnum, 45 Colt, 25-20, 32-20, and brand new for 1990, the sweet little 218 Bee. Winchester still makes the ammunition, and Speer has just introduced a new 46-grain flatnose bullet with a thin jacket and soft lead core so it will expand at Bee impact velocities. On top of all that, its cannelure is located exactly where it should be for Marlin's 1894.

Like its litter mates in 25-20,

and 32-20, the Model 1894CL (Classic) in 218 Bee bears a strong resemblance to Marlin's Model 1894 Baby Carbine of yesteryear. The straight buttstock (with no whiteline spacer), and square finger lever make the 1894CL look the way a classic lever-action rifle ought to look. The 1894CL weighs a nominal 6¼ pounds and measures 38¾ inches overall. The half-magazine hanging beneath its 22-inch, six-groove barrel holds six rounds. The only thing I see missing are eyes for detachable sling swivels.

I mounted a Burris 4-12x Mini on my new 94CL and tried it at the 100-yard benchrest with Speer's equally new 46-grain flatnose, a bullet designed specifically for 218 Bee lever actions. Powders tried included SR-4759 (reduced-velocity turkey and small game loads), AA-2460, Reloder 7, Hercules 2400, W680, IMR-4227, H-4227, W296, H110, H4198, and IMR-4198. The overall aggregate for 22 five-shot groups was 2.17 inches, with 1.60 and 3.24 inches the smallest and largest averages. Old (and no longer available) Remington and Winchester Super-X 46-grain loads averaged respective muzzle velocities and accuracy of 2831 and 2866 fps and 2.11 and 1.74 inches. The current Winchester WW Super load averaged 2589 fps and 3.65 inches. A very nice rifle, this little 218 Bee. Pick up a Marlin 94, swing it to your shoulder, gaze across its sights, squeeze its trigger on varmint, small game, paper target, or tin can, and you won't be able to get along without it.

Mitchell Arms

I have never been one to get overly excited about foreign-built replicas of various Winchester lever-action rifles, but will have to admit that a brief examination of three being imported by Mitchell Arms left me highly impressed. One is called the 1858 Henry; the other two are designated as 1873 Winchester and 1886 Winchester. The 1858 is available only in 44-40; the 1873 and 1886 come in 22 Long Rifle, 38 Special, 44-40, and 45 Colt. All wear rather large price tags, but that's what it takes to get quality better than commonly seen in firearms of this type.

New England Firearms

In case you haven't already noticed, a company called New

England Firearms is manufacturing some of the old Harrington & Richardson shotguns, revolvers, and single shot rifles. A number of rifle variations are available, all of tipping breech, exposed hammer design.

First there's the Handy-Rifle with a 22-inch barrel in 22 Hornet, 30-30, 45-70, and for 1990—the 223, 243 and 30-06. I never thought I'd ever see the old H&R single shot available in such powerful chamberings. The Handi has walnut-finished hardwood, has a drilled and tapped barrel for scope mounting, and comes with quick-detach sling swivel studs, one on the buttstock, another out on the barrel. The 223, 243, and 30-06 have no open sights but do come with a scope mount. A Southwestern rancher pal of mine has one of these in 30-30. For whitetails, and coyotes, he loads the Nosler 125-grain Ballistic Tip to about 2500 fps. He says it is, (if you'll pardon his pun) about the handiest little rifle in Texas.

The Handi-Gun Combination has two 22-inch barrels, one rifled, one smoothbore, and two metal finish options, blued and nickel-plated. The shotgun barrel is available in 20- or 12-gauge, both with 3-inch chambers. Rifle barrel chambering options are the same as for the regular Handi-Gun.

Everybody who reads this should buy at least one Handy-Rifle and one Pardner shotgun. If we don't, the only type of rifle and shotgun a farm lad like I once was could afford to buy may disappear forever from the hunting scene.

Precision Imports

Remember the Voere centerfire rifle once imported into the U.S. from Germany? As I understand it, Mauser Werke of Oberndorf, West Germany now owns the manufacturing rights to that rifle and it is being imported by Precision Imports of San Antonio, Texas. Called the Mauser Model 99, it features an adjustable trigger (1½ to 7 pounds); three locking lugs at the front of its bolt (60-degree bolt lift) that mate with a stellite insert in the receiver ring; extremely fast lock time (said to be 1.6 milli-seconds); tang safety (locks bolt rotation, sear, and trigger); steel bottom metal; detachable magazine; free-floating barrel and oil-finished European walnut stock with cut checkering. The Model 99 is available with two styles of stocks, Classic with cheekrest and schnabel-style forend or American Monte Carlo with rosewood gripcap and forend tip, both available with oil or high-gloss finishes. Available chamberings are 243, 25-06, 6.5x57mm, 270, 7x57mm, 7x64mm, 308, 30-06, 7x57mm, and 7x64mm, all with 24-inch barrels. Chamberings with 26-inch barrels include belted magnums such as the 257 Weatherby, 270 Weatherby, 7mm Remington, 300 Winchester, 300 Weatherby, 338 Winchester, 375 H&H, and beltless magnums called the 5.6x57mm, 8x68S, and 9.3x 64mm Brenneke.

Precision Imports is also bringing back the Mauser Model 66 switch barrel gun with interchangeable barrels in most of the chamberings I have mentioned for the Model 99, plus the 458 Winchester Magnum. The Model 66 is presently available in four configurations, Stutzen (fullstock and 21-inch barrel), Standard (standard chamberings with 24-inch barrel), Magnum (magnum chamberings with 26-inch barrel), and Safari with 26-inch barrel. Nominal weights for the four rifles are 7½ pounds for the Stutzen and Standard, 7.9 pounds for the Magnum, and 9.3 pounds for the Safari.

The new Model 201 Mauser, a 6½-pound bolt action in 22 Long Rifle or 22 WMR with twin locking lugs and dual extractors at the front of its bolt is actually the extremely accurate Voere rifle I "Testfired" in the 1985 GUN DIGEST, but with a new name. In fact, when Texan Robert Kleinguenther imported it several years ago, he called it the K-22. Its detachable magazine holds five rounds; an optional eight-shot magazine is also available. Barrel and overall lengths are 21 and 40 inches respectively. The receiver has dovetail grooves as well as holes drilled and tapped for various scope mounts. The standard model has a stained beechwood stock while the Luxus stock is European walnut. Both models are available with or without open sights and both stocks are of the Bavarian style.

Remington

Compared to the past few years, the 1990 edition of the *Green Gazette* is rather a thin one. As rifles go, the only news is fine old cartridges added to the option lists of existing rifles. First there's the limited edition Model 700 Classic in yet another classic chambering, the

25-06 with 24-inch barrel and 1 in 10-inch rifling twist. This, by the way, is the third quarter-incher to appear in this limited production series of rifles. First came the 257 Roberts in 1982, followed two years later by Charlie Newton's even older 250-3000 Savage. Moving on to Remington's highly successful Model 700 Mountain Rifle, the 7x57mm Mauser joins the 243, 270, 280, 7mm-08, 308, and 30-06.

Roy Weatherby's magnificent 300 Magnum is now available in last year's Model 700AS, the rifle that replaced the Models 700RS and 700FS. Its other

The new Model 70 Super Grade has one of the most handsome, best feeling stocks I have held in my hands.

chamberings are the 22-250, 243, 270, 280, 7mm Remington Magnum, 308, and the 30-06. For the benefit of those who aren't familiar with this rifle, the 700AS is called that because its stock is made of Arylon, a synthetic material developed by Du Pont. As I understand it, Arylon is a fiberglass reinforced thermoplastic said to retain the inert characteristics of other synthetics used in moulding rifle stocks (including great strength), but it is lighter than most. One thing is certain, my new 700AS in 30-06 is noticeably lighter than my old 700RS in the same

caliber. Can the 700AS be improved? I believe so. Using the Model 700 Mountain Rifle barreled action instead of the heavier standard Model 700 barreled action would cause the 700AS to shed even more ounces.

Depending on whose statistics you choose to believe, anywhere from eleven to sixteen of every 100 people shoot rifles from the opposite side. Left-handers who shoot groundhogs at breathtaking distances and those who plan to tiptoe through the alders in search of salmon-eating grizzly bears will probably cry out with glee when they see the Model 700 BDL-LH in its new 22-250 and 338 Winchester Magnum chamberings. I won't exactly faint from shock to someday see a Model 700AS in 338.

Ruger

The Ruger Model 77 Mark II has now grown to include a rather large family of bolt-action centerfires. First came the Mark II with a short action in 223, followed by the promise of an extremely long magnum action in 375 H&H Magnum and 416 Rigby.

For 1990, Ruger has announced additional chamberings for the short-action 77 Mark II, the 243 Winchester, the 6mm Remington, and the 308 Winchester. Also slated for introduction during mid-1990 is a medium action Mark II in both right- and left-hand versions in 270, 7mm Remington Magnum, 30-06, and 300 Winchester Magnum. All major component parts of the all-

This is that Winchester Model 70 Super Grade—best described as a combination of the best of the new with what some shooters consider to be the best of the old.

Metallic silhouette competitors might be interested in the Model 70 Varmint with a 26-inch heavy barrel in 308 Winchester.

The Winchester 94 now has the old ramped front sight and a smoother action. This is the Big Bore version.

weather version are made of 400 series stainless steel. The synthetic stock is almost a spitting image of the stock introduced on the stainless Model 77/22RSP last year. The stock is an injection moulding of Du Pont Zytel with the Ruger name and logo formed into its sides. Grooved side panels at the wrist and forearm are made of General Electric Xenoy, the same synthetic material Colt chose for the grip panels on its new Double Eagle autoloader.

The Model 77 Mark II is supposed to be available initially in the following styles: M77-MKIIR (22-inch barrel, no sights, 223, 243, 6mm, and 308); KM77-MKIIRP (stainless steel, synthetic stock, no sights, 22-inch barrel in 223, 243, and 308); M77-MKIIRS (22-inch barrel, open sights, 243 and 308); M77-MKIIRL (Ultra Light 20-inch barrel, no sights, 223, 243, 308); M77-MKIIRLS (Carbine, 18½-inch barrel, 243 and 308).

There are many things I like about Ruger's Mark II series of centerfires, one at the top of the list being the three-position safety switch. I am also extremely pleased to see Ruger introduce a dependable and affordable stainless steel rifle for those of us who hunt come rain or shine. I see one detail that could stand some improvement, though. The synthetic stock needs quick-detach sling swivels. Permanent swivels went out of style many hunting seasons ago when it was discovered that one does not leave the sling on a rifle for certain hunting conditions.

Ruger's 1990 dealer price sheet for the Model 77RS lists the 35 Whelen among its seven chamberings. The grand old cartridge is not, however, listed in the Ruger 1990 catalog. This probably means they intend to make only a few rifles chambered for James Howe's old wildcat and Remington's new factory cartridge.

Last year's Model 77/22 all-weather rifle with its stainless steel barreled action and synthetic stock is slated for introduction in 22 WMR during 1990. A nice little no-nonsense rifle this one is.

Savage

Challenger International Limited has announced that as of November '89, it became the owner of the following Savage Industries, Inc. product lines: the Model 110, the Model 99, the Model 24, and the Model 72.

Challenger has also purchased the Savage tradename and formed a new corporation called Savage Arms, Inc.

According to the 1990 Savage catalog, the Model 110 is available in a number of configurations: 110G with either right- or left-hand action, open sights, walnut finished hardwood stock with cut checkering, in 223, 22-250, 243, 270, 7mm Remington Magnum, 308, 30-06, and 300 Winchester Magnum; 110GX (same as 110G but with integral scope mounting base and no open sights); 110F and 110FX (same as 110G and 110GX, but with black Rynite stock); 110B (same as 110G, but with laminated wood stock); 110GV (same as 110G, but with heavy 24-inch barrel in 22-250 and 243 only.

Savage has also introduced the Model 110FP, a rifle said to be designed as an anti-sniper tool for police departments, but I see no reason why it wouldn't work just as well on four-legged creatures. Available in 223 or 308 with a heavy 24-inch barrel, the 110FP has a Rynite stock with two Uncle Mike's quick-detach sling swivel studs on the bottom of its forearm. The front stud is for attaching a Harris bipod, the rear one is for the sling swivel. All metal has nonreflective finish and the nominal weight is 8 pounds.

The grand old Model 99 lever action is still with us, but only with Monte Carlo style buttstock and detachable magazine and only with a 22-inch barrel in 243 and 308. Long gone are the slim stock, the rotary magazine, the cartridge counter in the side of the receiver, and the 250-3000 and 300 Savage cartridges. As an old hunting chum of mine might say, the 99 sure don't look like no classic no more. Kinda sad, don't you think? On the brighter side, at least one of our most beloved hunting rifles still lives in some form.

The new Savage catalog also has pictures of the Models 24F and 389 over/under guns. The Model 24F-20 has a 22 Hornet, 223, or 30-30 barrel on top and a 20-gauge barrel at the bottom. The 24F-12 is the same, but as its model designation implies, its smoothbore barrel is 12-gauge. Both are available only with black Rynite buttstocks and forearms. The 24F-T Turkey also has the Rynite, but finished in a camo pattern. It is available in 22 Hornet or 223 over 12-gauge. Last but not least, the Model 389 comes with

a 12-gauge barrel on top and a 222 or 308 barrel on the bottom. It has three interchangeable choke tubes (Full, Modified, and Improved Cylinder), and walnut with cut checkering. All Model 24F and Model 389 guns come from the factory with an extra safety device Savage calls a gun lock, a good idea for gun owners who constantly hear the patter of little feet in their homes. Incidentally, the Model 389 reminds me of the Savage over/under of the 1970s, the one built for Savage in 20-gauge over 222 or 308 by the Finnish firm of Valmet.

Ernie Simmons

Ernie Simmons Enterprises, the importer of Nichols telescopic rifle sights, SKB shotguns, and the source for Old Ern outdoor clothing, has reintroduced the Sauer rifle to U.S. hunters and shooters. Manufactured by the famed J.P. Sauer & Sohn of West Germany, today's bolt-action Simmons Sauer will look quite familiar to those who own yesteryear's Colt Sauer rifles. The Sauer is presently offered in a number of chamberings, including the 22-250, 243, 25-06, 270, 280, 308, 30-06, and belted magnums such as the 300 Weatherby, 300 Winchester, 338 Winchester, 375 H&H, 416 Remington, and 458 Winchester. Several variations will be available, including Mannlicher-style half-stock carbine, and rifles with high-gloss or satin-finished walnut. A synthetic-stocked Sauer is being considered for introduction sometime in the future. The rifles I looked at and held in my hands were very nice.

SSK Industries

Last year I mentioned a barrel in 416 Rigby I had ordered from SSK for my Thompson/Center TCR '87 single shot rifle. My first shooting session with the new barrel was occasionally interrupted by an extraction problem, so I bundled it up and shipped it back to SSK. Shortly thereafter, the gun was extracting cases as smoothly as silk and I was again burning large quantities of powder with each squeeze of its trigger. With my favorite charge of H-4831 pushing the A-Square 400-grain Monolithic Solid and Hornady's soft-nose of the same weight along at 2400 fps, the SSK-TCR averaged slightly less than two inches at 100 yards for five shots. Darned good for such a

big boomer and an innocent country boy.

The SSK barrel is 25 inches long, and measures 0.880-inch in diameter at the muzzle. With a Leupold mount holding a Bausch & Lomb 2-8x Compact atop the monobloc, the rifle weighs precisely 10 pounds. That plus the SSK Arrestor muzzlebrake makes the rifle quite comfortable to shoot. Everything including the scope mount is protected from the elements by a handsome coat of SSK Khrome, an industrial grade chrome plating with a satin finish—like the one you see on Sears, Roebuck tools. Overall length is 42½ inches, a bit shorter than most bolt actions with the same barrel length.

I have a rather large soft spot for the old 416 Rigby cartridge in bolt guns, but I believe I would prefer a rimmed, or as the British describe it, a flanged cartridge in the TCR rifle. Which brings up the 470 Nitro Express, another cartridge SSK builds TCR and Ruger No. 1 rifles for. I spent a brief range session with an SSK-TCR '87 with a 24-inch barrel in 470. It came with iron sights so I shot it that way at 50 yards with Federal's Premium Safari loading of the Woodleigh 500-grain softnose. As Elmer Keith seemed to be fond of saying, the rifle consistently shot silver dollar-size groups every time I squeezed its trigger five times. The Federal load did not quite live up to its rated bullet speed of 2150 fps, but it still generated over 4600 foot-pounds of punch and, wow, was it ever so accurate in the SSK rifle. I also fired a few rounds of ammunition with the Barnes 500-grain soft-nose and Super Solid bullets. It was loaded by Custom Hunting Ammo & Arms of Howell, MI. Neither load was quite as accurate in the SSK gun as the Federal loads, but both easily managed minute-of-Cape-buffalo.

Thompson/Center

The Contender Carbine with a 21-inch barrel, the featherweight mini-rifle youngsters and oldsters just love to shoot, is now available with optional black Rynite buttstock and forearm. This makes three variations, the other two having walnut, one a youth model with 16¼-inch barrel and shorter length of pull. They are available in 22 Long Rifle, 22 WMR, 22 Hornet, 223, 7mm T/CU, 30-30, 35 Remington, 357 Maximum, 44 Magnum, 45 Colt/410, 410 smoothbore, and 45-70 Government.

The TCR '87 single shot rifle is now available with the light sporter (23-inch) and medium sporter (25⅞-inch) barrels in 22 Hornet, 222, 223, 22-250, 243, 270, 7mm-08, 308, 32-40, 30-06. If you want a complete rifle or a barrel for your TCR '83 or '87 in other chamberings

Ultra Light Arms

Nothing new up in Granville, West Virginia this year. Melvin Forbes showed me a "new" Model 20 single shot varmint rifle in 6mm PPC with a solid bottom receiver, but he's tried the same trick for getting my money for the past 2 years. Dave Petzal, and another chap who works with the company that

Ultra Light. My order is in for either a 280 with an extra barrel in 338-06, or a 7mm STW with an extra barrel in 358 STA. We'll see.

USRAC

Now for the biggest and certainly the most handsome news of the year 1990. After quite a few years of listening to thousands of requests for the re-

best described as a combination of the best of the new Model 70 with what many hunters and shooters believe is the best of the old Model 70. First of all, it has the new Model 70 receiver. In laymen's language, this means its receiver is more concentric than the Pre-'64 receiver and its slightly greater length is better suited for full-length belted magnums such as

Mitchell Arms' new 1873 in 22 LR, 44-40 and 45 Colt is a very nice reproduction of Winchester's old 1873.

The new Ultramark is but one of several Mark V variations now available from Weatherby. This one has the Supreme 3-9x44 scope in a Buehler mount.

The first Weatherby bolt action in 22 LR and 22 WMR has classic Weatherby styling, a detachable magazine, and dual locking lugs at the front of its bolt.

such as 17 Remington, 22 PPC, 6mm PPC, 25-06, 280 Remington, 35 Whelen, or 45-70, you'll have to place an order with the TC Custom Shop through your local dealer. TCR shotgun barrels with choke tubes now available include the 3½-inch 10- and 12-gauge. Slug barrels with open sights come with the 3-inch 12-gauge chamber and are available with smooth or rifled bore. Thompson/Center has also introduced a quick-detach scope mount for the TCR '87, Contender, and various muzzleloaders.

makes a funny looking bullet called the Partition, and I recently cornered smiling Melvin and threatened to reveal to the world that his Model 20 rifle really is made by anemic elves—if he doesn't start building takedown models before next hunting season. As we gently explained to Melvin, one nice thing about an Ultra Light takedown rifle is you could pack it in your duffle bag without inviting the whole world to steal your elk gun. Another nice thing about this particular takedown rifle is it would be an

turn of the Pre-'64 Winchester Model 70, and watching other manufacturers steal its more popular design features, those clever fellows at U.S. Repeating Arms have built a new rifle that may prove to be far better than the old rifle. Unlike some of the other rifles that have been introduced with certain Model 70-type features (like its three-position safety), the Super Grade is an affordable rifle. On top of all that, it's a genuine Winchester.

Called the Winchester Model 70 Super Grade, the new rifle is

the 375 H&H. The Super Grade also has the new Model 70 barrel which means it will, on average, be somewhat more accurate than run-of-mill Pre-'64s.

Like the Pre-'64 Model 70, the new Super Grade bolt has Charlie Newton's ejector and the Mauser-type nonrotating extractor, but the bolt is a bit longer simply because the Post-'64 receiver is a bit longer than the Pre-'64 receiver. The Super grade has also inherited the breeching system of the Pre-'64 rifle. Back in the 1920s when

Winchester technicians were designing the Model 54 bolt gun, they incorporated the coned breech of the 1903 Springfield in all calibers except the 30-30 and 22 Hornet. The same type of breeching system was used in the old Model 70 until it was replaced by the new Model 70 in 1964. It is now back in the new Super Grade rifle. Everything else about the new rifle is also pure Model 70, inclusive of a three-position safety lever atop the bolt shroud, a bolt release located aft of the left-hand receiver bridge wall, and the two-piece trigger bow/floorplate assembly with a floorplate release button protruding from the front of the trigger bow. All bottom metal is genuine blued steel.

The Winchester Super Grade wears the most handsome and best feeling Model 70 stock I have ever wrapped my hands around. Carved from a piece of select grade walnut, it is of classic form with cheekrest but no Monte Carlo hump, satin finished, cut checkered, and fitted with a solid (in lieu of ugly ventilated) red recoil pad. A steel throughbolt located between the trigger housing and magazine box cutouts in the stock serves as a reinforcement to keep the stock from splitting in that area when it is asked to absorb high levels of recoil generated by powerful cartridges. A trace of engraving on the exposed heads of the throughbolt and "Super Grade" stamped on the hinged floorplate add subtle touches of class to what I consider to be the most handsome big game rifle introduced in many years. For now, the Super Grade's standard chamberings are belted magnums only, Remington's 7mm and Winchester's 300 and 338.

Available on special order from the USRAC Custom Shop are Super Grade rifles in those three calibers but with a higher grade of walnut, engine turned bolt body and magazine follower, plain bolt handle knob, hand-lapped locking lugs, and hand-lapped bore. Also available from the Custom Shop are Super Grade Express rifles in 375 H&H Magnum, 416 Remington Magnum, and 458 Winchester Magnum. The Express version has the old Pre-'64 style detachable sling swivels and an express-type rear sight with one fixed and two folding leaves. Since the Super Grade is not presently available in 270 and 30-06, one can only assume that

The Mauser Model 99 is available in four variations, from top to bottom: oil-finished stock with schnabel forend, high-gloss stock with schnabel forend, oil-finished Monte Carlo style stock, and high-gloss Monte Carlo style stock.

The Mauser rimfire 201 is made in these four variations, from the top: 22 WMR with open sights, 22 WMR without sights, 22 LR with sights, 22 LR without sights.

Jack O'Connor is looking on with great dismay. Once demand stops outpacing supply, other chambering options including Jack's two favorites will be added to the list. Something else I hope to eventually see on all Super Grade receivers is the Pre-'64 matte finish.

I received an experimental model of the Super Grade in 300 Winchester Magnum in June of '89 and even went so far as to shoot a whitetail buck with it about two months later. To see what the rifle would do on paper, I shot it at the 100-yard benchrest with Winchester 150-, 180-, 190-, and 220-grain factory loads, as well as nine handloads. The handloads were chosen at random and were not worked up specifically for the rifle. Aggregate accuracy for two five-shot groups with the factory loads was 2.37 inches. Eighteen five-shotters with my handloads averaged 1.90 inches. The handload I used on the whitetail consisted of IMR-4350 behind Nosler's 150-grain Ballistic Tip. Developed specifically for the rifle, it averaged less than 1.25 MOA, with some individual groups measuring less than an inch.

New chamberings in other Model 70s for 1990 are the 25-06 in the Sporter and 308 in the Varmint. During the summer of '89, I invaded several Montana prairie dog towns with a Model 70 Varmint in 223. Later, I spent a number of hours at the 100-yard benchrest with it and another in 243. When fed Watson and Euber custom bullets, both rifles averaged close to half an inch for five shots. Like I said before, USRAC's Model 70 is, on average, considerably more accurate than the one Winchester stopped producing back in 1963.

For a couple of years, a plain blade (with no contrasting bead) dovetailed to the barrel had replaced the long familiar ramped front sight on all variations of the Winchester Model 94. The dovetailed blade still lives on the Model 94 Ranger and the Trapper Carbine, but the ramped front sight (with contrasting bead) is back on the WinTuff (laminated wood), the Big Bore (307 and 356), the 94CW (checkered walnut), and the 94W (standard walnut). Also new for 1990, tolerances of various moving parts have been tightened and a link pin and set screw have been added to the lever. These modifications are said to reduce noise and increase smoothness of the Model 94 action.

Quiz time: What's the finest and most useful factory cartridge ever developed for lever-action hammer guns with tubular magazines? If you said 307 Winchester, go sit at the front of the class. The 307 gives today's woods hunters 300 Savage power from a rifle originally designed to give yesteryear's woods hunters 30-30 power. Many years ago, deer hunters used to ask for that quite often, but by the time

Winchester got around to furnishing the answer, most hunters had forgotten what the question was. In other words, the 307 came along about two decades too late.

In case you haven't noticed lately, the handsome little easy-to-take down, extremely accurate, Model 9422 is available in 22 Long Rifle or 22 WMR with WinCam, WinTuff, or standard walnut buttstocks and forearms. All have cut checkering at the wrist and out front.

Weatherby

For many years the name Weatherby has been synonymous with double-barrel shotguns, autoloading shotguns, slide-action shotguns, a 22 rimfire autoloader, and bolt actions chambered for a number of cartridges that were designed to leave the competition choking in their dust. Even so, Weatherby had never offered a bolt-action 22 rimfire. That is, not until the Accumark was introduced in 1990. Available in Deluxe (shiny wood) or Classic (oil-finished wood) grades, the Accumark is a German-made bolt-action repeater with five-shot detachable magazine and 21-inch free-floated barrel. An optional eight-round magazine is also available. The hammer forged barrel is rifled with six lands and grooves. Overall length is 40 inches and its weight is 6½ pounds. Unlike most 22 rimfire bolt actions that lock up at the rear, the Accumark has twin locking lugs at the front of the bolt. The receiver has dovetail grooves and is drilled and tapped to give its new owner several options in scope mounting. The weight of the Accumark's trigger has an adjustment range of 1½ to 7 pounds. And I don't see the Mark XXII autoloader in Weatherby's 1990 catalog.

In last year's Rifle Review, I mentioned that as rumor had it, a Weatherby side-by-side double rifle was in the works. What was rumor has turned out to be factual. A prototype Weatherby double in 470 Nitro Express has been built and chances of the rifle progressing onward to the production stage are quite good. How much will it cost? As the old saying goes, if you have to ask, you probably can't afford it. I did and the old saying is absolutely correct—I can't.

The Mark V Ultramark and two new Vanguard variations were introduced in 1989, but too late to be included in the previous Rifle Review. The Ul-

tramark has select grade Claro walnut with basket weave checkering pattern, a hand-honed and jeweled bolt body, and "Weatherby Ultramark" engraved on its floorplate. It is available with right- or left-hand actions in 30-06 as well as Weatherby magnums 240, 257, 7mm, 300, and 340. This makes six different models of the Mark V rifle. The others are Deluxe, Euromark (my personal favorite), Lazermark, Fibermark, and Safari Grade (the most handsome factory Weatherby ever built). Extra cost options for all models include shorter or longer than standard stock length of pull, more checkering coverage at the wrist, engine turned bolt body, checkered bolt handle knob, hand-honed action, owner's initials engraved on floorplate, and open sights. A lot of shooters probably don't realize that Mark V barreled actions (with no stock) in all Weatherby chamberings plus the 30-06 have long been available.

The Roy E. Weatherby Commemorative rifle is a Mark V in 300 Magnum with engraving by Richard Boucher (including a gold bust of Roy on the floorplate), high grade Claro walnut stock with hand checkering, 3-9x Weatherby scope with engraved Buehler mount, and various tools and accessories, all fitted into a leather case built by Marvin Huey. Its serial number is REW001, meaning there will be only one of these. The money will go to the Roy E. Weatherby Foundation, a non-profit organization dedicated to educating the public on the value to society of wildlife and the beneficial role of ethical sport hunting in wildlife conservation. The minimum bid is $20,000.

Probably the second most handsome standard production Weatherby rifles ever built are the Vanguard Classic I and Classic II. Both have oil-finished, classic-style stocks. About the only differences between the two are a black forend tip and grip cap and a bit more checkering on the Classic II. The Classic I is available with a 24-inch Number 2 contour barrel in 223, 243, 270, 7mm-08, 7mm Remington Magnum, and 30-06. The Classic II is offered with the same weight and length barrel in those chamberings plus 270 Weatherby Magnum, 300 Weatherby Magnum, 300 Winchester Magnum, and 338 Winchester Magnum. The Classic II

is also available with a heavier Number 3 contour barrel in 22-250.

I've been having lots of fun with a Mark V Deluxe in 416 Weatherby Magnum. I'm able to do that because the Vais muzzlebrake I installed on its 24-inch barrel tames recoil to a level comparable with a 10-pound 338 Magnum. Just as its maker George Vais said it would do, the brake also directs propellant gas away from my face rather than toward it as some brakes are prone to do. The Weatherby factory loads with 400-grain Hornady softnose, Swift A-Frame, and A-Square Monolithic Solid bullets averaged less than two inches at the 100-yard benchrest. Two slightly exceeded their rated bullet speed of 2400 fps, one fell short by only a few fps. Any way you look at it, Weatherby's 416 churns up over six tons of crunch each time its trigger is squeezed. I have also put quite a few rounds of handloads through the Mark V. Muzzle velocities with various 300-, 350-, and 400-grain bullets averaged 3050, 2900, and 2700 fps respectively. As I discovered several months before Hercules told me so in its new *Reloader's Guide,* Reloder 22 is THE powder for Weatherby's 416 Magnum, especially when loading the 400-grain bullets.

In preparation for an upcoming safari in Zambia during 1990, I removed the factory stock from my 416 and sent the barreled action to Kelly McMillan so he could fit one of his new Griffin & Howe-style fiberglass stocks to it. I also specified the Fibergrain finish and no sling swivel stud on the forearm. Next I ordered a T'SOB scope mount from SSK Industries, the one that utilizes Kimber quick-detach rings but has a deep mortice for each ring rather than a thin recoil shoulder. Then I sent the rifle out to South Gate so one of the Weatherby gunsmiths could equip it with the barrel band-type sling swivel and the quarter rib and open sights of the Mark V Safari Grade. The folks at Weatherby also applied the Safari Grade matte finish to all the metal. Haven't fully decided which scope I will mount on the rifle, but the new 1.4-4.5x Swarovski I recently attached to it looks like just the thing to have on such a rifle. Next time we meet, I'll tell you how this swiftest and most powerful of the 416s works on lion and Cape buffalo. ●

Gun Finishes For the 21st Century

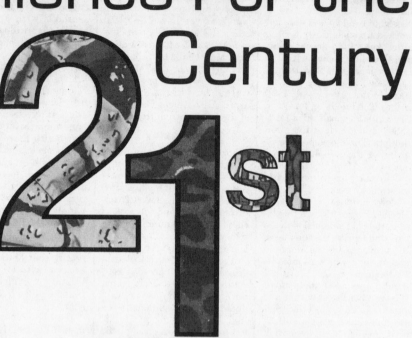

by HOLT BODINSON

Lots more to meet the eye.

THERE IS a quiet revolution going on in the firearms industry. It's still in its infancy, but the end result for millions of shooters will be firearms that for all practical purposes will be totally corrosion resistant AND self-lubricating.

It is said that the blue or blackened oxide metal finish which is so ingrained in our minds as the ultimate fine firearm finish was developed centuries ago in the armor-making trade. When Damascening or inlaying metal armor with gold and silver linework, early armorers found that corrosion developing under the inlays would loosen them in time. That was until some observant craftsman discovered that blackening the armor in a charcoal fire (temper bluing) created an oxidized finish that reduced corrosion sufficiently so that the process became a widespread practice.

Interestingly, the browning or blackening of firearms by either heat or chemical means was not common until the latter half of the 18th century. And while the Brown Bess and the brown-barreled Kentucky rifle went up against each other in the 1770s, the Blue and the Gray were still clinging to brightly polished muskets as late as the 1860s.

The blue or black firearms finish we so cherish today is not really a very good metal finish. Under military specifications (mil specs), it is considered a "decorative" finish. As anyone knows who has maintained a firearm, a blued finish is not particularly corrosion resistant. In fact, it rusts quite readily in the presence of a little moisture or humidity. Bluing is also not very durable and readily wears off and scratches under normal use. Yes, it's classic; it's traditional. But from a practical standpoint, about the kindest thing you can say about bluing is that it has provided an after-market industry for hundreds of brands of firearms preservatives and thousands of refinishers. Protecting or replacing the famous blued finish is BIG business.

While stainless steel receivers and barrels coupled with synthetic stocks are making inroads in the gun business, stainless guns represent a small portion of the firearms in actual use. And even stainless has its unique

Bodinson expects his pet Tefloned Sako to still be good-looking in the year 2001.

problems. From a hunting viewpoint, many sportsmen object to the silver color of stainless in the field—and with reason. Except over snow, stainless is more visible than darker finishes. And as stainless steel firearms' owners have discovered, even stainless steel will rust if totally neglected.

Today, however, there are a variety of finishes for metal firearms as exciting and useful as any recent development in the gun field. Some of these are a result of the aerospace industry's continuing search for better metal protection under the most demanding environmental and wear conditions. Most are finishes that have been used for industrial applications other than firearms until someone put two-and-two together. One of the greatest forces now active in the development and use of better firearms finishes is the military (particularly special operations units) and law enforcement establishments. What is significant is that the cost of many of these superior finishes is now competitive with traditional

The new Detonics mini-45 can be had as here, with electroless nickel frame and a slide finished in NP3.

blued finishes. In addition, there are more specialized finishing companies than ever before willing to take on firearms work from individual customers.

Basically, the new finishes can be divided into several types. There are non-metallic finishes such as black Teflon, Polymax or Z-Coat which are sprayed on and cured. There are electrolytically applied finishes, usually hard industrial chrome, such as Armaloy and Metalife. There are electroless applied finishes—the most common being electroless nickel. And there are conversion process finishes such as traditional bluing and the more improved forms known as chrome-sulfide and phosphating or Parkerizing. Finally, there are hybrid combinations of these such as NP3 which combines Teflon and electroless nickel. There are probably many more, but these seem to cover the most common modern finishes now available to the average gun owner. Their essential purpose is to provide superior protection from corrosion. In addition, many of these finishes have the added advantage of exhibiting a natural lubricity that "slicks up" working parts, minimizing the need for lubrication and routine maintenance while reducing wear.

The companies which apply these sophisticated coatings are a diverse group indeed. Few advertise. Most are involved in larger industrial coating businesses and firearms make up only a small share of their overall business activity—and the bulk of that from military and law enforcement contracts. Some offer gun owners one specific process such as Armaloy while others like Robar offer a half-dozen or more finish options. Some offer their finishes strictly through your local dealer; most are quite willing to work directly with a gun owner. Some are

This McMillan Safari Grade rifle in 375 H&H has a Polymaxed receiver and barrel and a dead-serious look.

After more than fifteen-hundred rounds and three years in the field, the Sako's only discernible wear is on the bolt lugs.

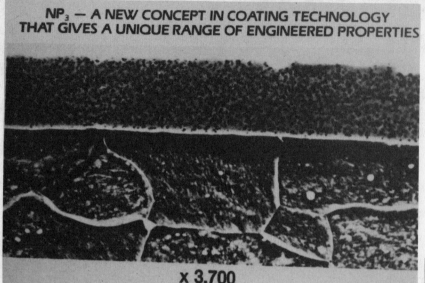

NP₃ — A NEW CONCEPT IN COATING TECHNOLOGY THAT GIVES A UNIQUE RANGE OF ENGINEERED PROPERTIES

x 3,700

corrosion resistance. More importantly in terms of modern finishes, phosphating is also used as a porous base to provide a better grounding for other finishes such as the polymers, Teflon or even the painted finishes on office furniture, automobiles, and such. Be aware that the last step in the original Parkerizing process called for the parts to be dipped in linseed or vaseline oil. So if you have a Parkerized firearm, keep that spongy finish oiled! Average cost for a handgun is $75 and $90 for rifles. (*About the time Bodinson entered the public school system, we used to run smoothly Parkerized guns through the bluing process. It looked nice. Editor*)

reluctant to talk too specifically about their proprietary processes, so comparisons among finishes are sometimes hard to make.

For comparison purposes and when available, standard salt spray test data is included which tells one approximately how many hours a coating will prevent corrosion from developing on a standard underlying metal surface when subjected to a heated salt spray fog. Called an "accelerated corrosion test," it normally consists of a 5 percent salt solution sprayed at 95 degrees Fahrenheit. But in all fairness, sporting firearms are not subjected to such harsh environmental conditions so the value of the test is only relative, and for some finishes the data simply is not readily available. Furthermore, desirable values in a firearms finish such as adhesion, lubricity, and impact resistance are not reflected in a comparative accelerated corrosion test.

The alternative gun finish options available today are intriguing. While no list is complete, the following compilation of various modern coatings is a brief overview, but one which I hope will stimulate greater gun owner interest in this rapidly developing field. And hopefully lead the way to more corrosion resistant, more reliable, less wear-prone, and generally more satisfactory sporting firearms.

The Conversion Processes:

Bluing or Blacking

Whether the metal parts are cold rust-blued or hot-dipped, one of the interesting observations bluers seem to agree upon is that the corrosion resistant qualities of blued finishes are en-

(Above) This is how an electron microscope sees NP3 deposited on steel. Below the horizontal boundary line are steel molecules; above the line is the NP3 composite of sub-micron Teflon particles and electroless nickel.

hanced by the degree of preliminary polishing. In short, highly polished steel presents less surface area to the corrosive process than do sand or glass bead-blasted matte finishes, and consequently, is less prone to rust—all other factors being equal. And yet, matte finishes are "in" because sportsmen and the military and law enforcement establishments are demanding non-reflective, low sheen field finishes on their firearms. In any case, blued finishes when compared to other current options are more decorative than functional, wear and scratch easily, and provide a minimal degree of corrosion resistance.

Phosphating or Parkerizing

Here is the finish that the military establishment made famous. In practice, it changes the surface of the steel to a sponge-like manganese or zinc phosphate. While it is more corrosion and abrasion resistant than bluing, its greatest value lies in its spongy surface which better entraps oils and other preservatives than plain surfaces and therefore exhibits greater

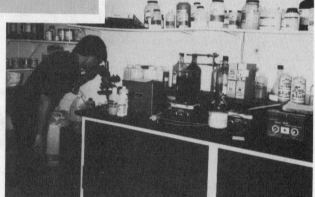

(Above) To provide consistent results, a plater must maintain fully-equipped testing facilities. Solutions must be constantly monitored.

Stainless Steel Blacking

If you like stainless steel firearms, but dislike their color or shine, blacking them through a "chrome sulfide" process being marketed by Robar may be your salvation. The process converts the chrome on the surface of the stainless steel or chrome-moly steel to a chrome sulfide, resulting in a very attractive black non-reflective finish. In addition, the process increases corrosion resistance to 96 hours of salt spray and helps prevent galling. It is also economical—costing approximately what a "blue" job costs, or about $85 for pistols and $105 for rifles.

Non-Metallic Coatings

Polymax

Offered by Robar, Polymax is a sprayed-on-and-cured polymer finish which is applied over a phosphated base finish. I recently tested a McMillan Safari Grade 375 H&H rifle which had been Polymaxed. The finish is non-reflective satin black in appearance. It has tested out to 500 hours in a 5 percent salt spray and 100 hours in total water immersion. Its qualities are excellent adhesion, impact, water and chemical resistance, and Polymax can be applied to all external parts of a firearm including the scope and stock. Robar does not recommend it for internal moving parts. The cost averages $115 for handguns and $120 for rifles.

Black Teflon

Black Teflon (polytetrafluoroethylene) was one of the first of the modern super finishes I ever met. I had had Bill Wiseman fit a stainless steel barrel in 7mm-08 to a factory-blued Sako action. The resulting finished color combination wasn't what I was looking for and Wiseman recommended we ship the barreled action and scope rings off to Walter Birdsong to have them Tefloned. The result was one of the nicest and slickest black non-reflective finishes I have ever seen. Now, after approximately 1500 rounds, the rifle shows finish wear only on its locking lugs. What is intriguing is that every internal part of the rifle action including the trigger assembly and springs have been coated through the Birdsong process. Basically, Birdsong creates a phosphated base finish which is then air brushed with the coating and finally cured with heat. The black Teflon finish will go at least 500 hours in a salt spray test, is highly adhesive and resistant to water and chemicals, and is naturally lubricating. Available in black or olive drab color, it can also be applied to aluminum parts. The application price is approximately $160 for rifles and $125 for handguns.

Z-Coat

Z-Coat is a proprietary coating and the company is very tight-lipped about its chemistry. It appears to be a member of the Teflon family, but I can't confirm that fact. Highly resistant to water and chemicals and having a natural lubricity, Z-Coat is applied over a bead-blasted metal finish for better adhesion and can be applied to all external parts of the firearm as well, including scopes and stocks. What is remarkable about Z-Coat is that it can be had in virtually any imaginable color or color combination including all variations of modern camouflage patterns, black, gold, stainless, hot pink—you name the color, Z-Coat can probably furnish it. The Z-Coat Company, however, works only through local dealers so no standard retail prices are quoted.

Electroless Hard Finishes

Electroless Nickel

Probably no process has lately had a greater impact on firearms coating than electroless nickel. Not only is electroless nickel an exceedingly satisfactory firearm finish in practically all respects, but, because it does not require expensive electrical plating equipment, it has been adopted by some of the smallest of gunmaking shops. A high phosphorous electroless nickel coating is durable—a 1/1000-inch thick deposit will withstand approximately 1000 hours of salt spray. It plates evenly on complex surfaces and does not present the build-up problems which sometime occur in areas like sharp corners during electrolytic plating processes. It is highly adhesive and can pass a 180-degree bend test without peeling off the underlying base metal. It has a Rockwell hardness of C48-55 and exhibits a low friction and lubricity which results in smoother firearm functioning. And it is relatively inexpensive. Typical prices from commercial plating houses run approximately $150 for a pistol to $165 for a rifle. On the other hand, electroless nickel comes in one color only—silver to silver gray. One important point when ordering an electroless nickel job is to specify HIGH PHOSPHOROUS nickel, for it is far superior to standard electroless nickel.

NP3

NP3 is a five-year-old patented process requiring a license to apply. The only plater offering it extensively for firearms today is Robar. NP3 is a unique coating process in which electroless nickel and Teflon are co-deposited at the same time. Under an electron microscope, one can actually see the sub-micron particles of Teflon imbedded in the electroless nickel matrix. As a result, an NP3 finish exhibits high lubricity and is ideal for working parts under the most harsh extremes. A 1/1000-inch coating endures 240 hours of salt spray. And to increase NP3's corrosion resistance and adhesion, it is routinely deposited over a high phosphorous electroless nickel base. Dull gray in color, NP3 can be applied to aluminum, stainless steel and titanium as well as common gun steel alloys. How would one utilize NP3? Probably as the coating for the internal, high friction operating parts of a firearm. The exterior of the gun could then be coated with any of the highly corrosion resistant finishes such as electroless nickel, Polymax, black Teflon, Z-Coat, Armaloy or Metalife. It is the most expensive of the new finishes and currently costs $165 for a handgun and $215 for a rifle, but of course, small or internal parts are less expensive.

Electrolytic Hard Finishes

Armoloy

Armoloy is an electrolytic hard chrome plating process which coats steel with a 99 percent pure chrome surface approximately 2/10,000 thick. Armoloy has a Rockwell hardness of 70-72 and exhibits a natural lubricity. It is very adhesive and corrosion resistant, having been tested out to 96 hours under a salt spray. Silver gray in color, it has been an exceedingly successful hard chrome finish for handguns and long guns. Armoloy is the

A modern coating facility takes a lot of tankage to handle a variety of fine firearms finishes. This is the workspace at Robar in Phoenix, Arizona.

only company contacted which states right in its literature that it will plate the interior of a bore. Other companies, regardless of the process being promoted, bluntly said they would not. Armoloy also uses a mechanical vapor hone process rather than a chemical process for cleaning firearms parts immediately before plating, thereby eliminating the potential problem of hydrogen embrittlement of the steel. In fairness to the other coaters, most stress-relieve or normalize all plated parts in mild ovens to drive out any lingering hydrogen that might result from the process used. Armoloy's plating price for pistols is approximately $105 and for rifles $115.

Metalife

Metalife is another electrically deposited, industrial hard chrome, silver gray finish that has found particular favor with handgunners. Having a Rockwell of C68-72, Metalife provides a high degree of wear and corrosion resistance, and a natural lubricity. Metalife prices start at approximately $88 for handguns and $120 for rifles.

Deciding Upon a Finish

With the variety of super finishes available today, how does one go about selecting one over the other? Making the decision-making process harder is one's ability to mix various finishes on the same gun.

The qualities inherent in the new finishes are corrosion resistance, wear resistance, impact resistance, abrasion resistance, fatigue resistance and lubricity or a lowered coefficient of friction. They also range in thickness which is commonly stated in ten-thousandths of an inch or *mil*. In some cases there is a minimum thickness which is essential for the coating to work effectively and there are even some coatings that can be built up to tighten or restore worn surfaces. There are coatings that are recommended for external surfaces only and coatings that can be applied to every part of the firearm. These are the qualities that permit one to compare the characteristics of one finish to another.

Strange as it might sound, since all the newer super finishes provide far superior corrosion resistance and lubricity to traditional blues and blacks, the color of the finish may be the basic choice. If you don't care for the silver or silver gray tones of nickel and chrome-plating, you will probably be looking at Teflon, Polymax or Z-Coat.

At the top, tiger stripe; in the middle is mossy oak; and above is the clever concealment finish called undercover white. These and a zillion others are Z-Coat.

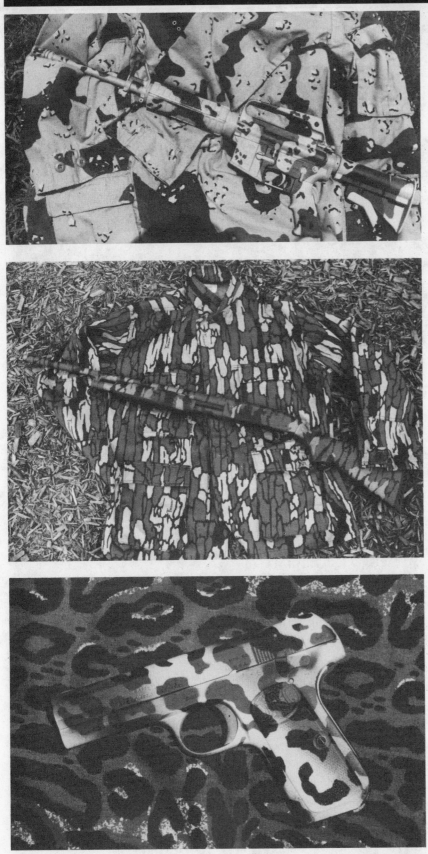

But then again, you can coat the outside of the firearm including stocks and scopes with one of the pigmented coatings and coat the inside working parts with electroless nickel, chrome, NP3, or whatever. Or, if you own a stainless steel firearm and don't appreciate its sheen, you can have it easily blackened through the chrome-sulfide process.

On the other hand, if a silver to silver gray color is acceptable, you can just about mix and match any of the electroless nickels and hard chromes.

When dealing with a coater or plater, by all means stick with well-known firms that have established reputations for excellent work on firearms. This is not work for fly-by-nights. The firm should provide a guarantee for its work. Ask for references and study their catalogs, literature, and technical data. It is an education in itself. For example, the Armoloy catalog even quotes prices for plating bullet moulds and reloading die sets.

Today's super firearms finishes are just that. They are so superior in all respects to our traditional blues that one can only say, "The blue is dead. Long live the blue. Or whatever." ●

ROBAR
21438 North 7th Ave., Suite B
Phoenix, Arizona 85027
(602) 581-2648
Coatings: NP3, Polymax, electroless nickel, black stainless, Parkerizing.

W. BIRDSONG & ASSOCIATES
4832 Windermere
Jackson, Mississippi 39206
(601) 366-8270
Coating: Black Teflon.

Z-COAT GROUP, INC.
3915 U.S. Highway 98 South
Lakeland, Florida 33813
(813) 665-1734
Coating: Z-Coat.

ARMOLOY
204 E. Daggett Street
Fort Worth, TX 76104
(817) 332-5604
Coating: Armoloy.

METALIFE
P.O. Box 53
Mong Ave.
Reno, Pennsylvania 16343
(814) 436-7747
Coating: Metalife, electroless nickel.

More, and more dramatic, Z-Coating. At top, GI desert pattern; middle, the ubiquitous tree bark; above an eye-fooler they call cheetah. You could have hot pink—or even a nice blue.

ON THE AIR-POWER FRONT

Some are slick, and some are awesome.

The Air Powered Sabot Cannon looks like an anti-tank rocket launcher and can fire single or multiple projectiles.

by J.I. GALAN

Daisy's Power Line Model 45 is a spittin' image of the legendary Colt self-shucker, shoots 13 pellets really quick, and is powered by CO_2.

Air-soft guns are still available on a limited basis. The slick Robocop model (top) and Desert Eagle replica are both gas-powered and a lot of plinking fun.

WE ARE STILL in an airgun revolution. Technological developments have created whole new subdivisions within this ever-expanding field. A prime example is field target shooting. This sport, now a major airgun competitive event originating in England, has been the direct result of the development of magnum-class air rifles, particularly those employing the pre-charged pneumatic power-plant. Field target shooting is now gaining wide acceptance here in the colonies following its tremendous success in England.

There are other directions as well, such as the incredibly detailed replicas of real firearms currently produced in Japan. Called air-soft guns because they shoot 6mm plastic BBs at velocities generally below 250 fps, these truly delightful airguns have become somewhat scarce—there are now some hysterically-conceived anti-replica laws.

Another entire new activity that grew out of nowhere involves paintball guns. These often bizarre-looking CO_2-powered paint blasters are in great demand by those who play the immensely popular tag or "survival" games. The guns lob relatively large— 68-, 62-, or 50-caliber—gelatin spheres containing water-soluble paint. When the paintballs strike a solid object, they burst with a most satisfying splattering of paint all around the point of impact. Incredibly, paintball guns have been banned from display at the SHOT Show, beginning in 1990. The SHOT Show Committee apparently felt that these fun-guns did not meet any legitimate sporting purpose, despite the fact that they make terrific plinking guns as well.

With so much expansion and so many changes, it is natural to expect new and sometimes unusual models coming down the pike. Such is certainly the case now, and we will discuss some of them, but first let's take a close look at one extremely interesting and unique type of airgun:

The Airrow Series 8 gun appeared in 1989. Developed by **Swivel Machine Works, Inc.** (Suite 286, 167 Cherry Street, Milford, CT 06460), this decidedly novel gun looks a lot like a CAR-15 assault carbine and shoots short crossbow-style aluminum bolts at

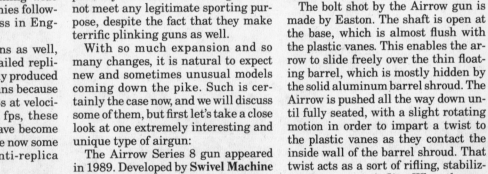

The Beeman/FWB C5 rapid-fire CO_2 pistol is the latest world class offering from Feinwerkbau of West Germany.

muzzle velocities that can reach nearly 500 fps, with accuracy. The Airrow can be powered by either compressed air or CO_2 and far exceeds the velocities produced by even the most powerful conventional hunting crossbows currently available. Constructed mostly of stainless steel and aluminum, the Airrow Series 8 gun is high-tech all the way, and its original retail price of more than $1,200 reflects that fact.

The bolt shot by the Airrow gun is made by Easton. The shaft is open at the base, which is almost flush with the plastic vanes. This enables the arrow to slide freely over the thin floating barrel, which is mostly hidden by the solid aluminum barrel shroud. The Airrow is pushed all the way down until fully seated, with a slight rotating motion in order to impart a twist to the plastic vanes as they contact the inside wall of the barrel shroud. That twist acts as a sort of rifling, stabilizing the arrow as it flies. When the gun fires, a charge of CO_2 or compressed air is released *inside the arrow*, pushing against its front end and propelling it out of the gun with considerable velocity and precision.

The high retail price seriously limited the gun's marketing potential, so, while still producing the Series 8, as well as harpoon and line-throwing Series 10 guns, a new more affordable model is at hand, the Series 6. This Airrow model is basically a handgun. It converts to a carbine by adding a 7-ounce CO_2 bottle that doubles as a shoulder stock. It also works with compressed air, including a scuba tank hook-up that conjures up James Bond-style possibilities. Its base price is $499.

The Airrow Series 6 design is modular. The shooter can switch easily from the standard 10¾-inch barrel to a 16-inch or even 20-inch barrel. The longer barrels allow the use of longer and heavier arrows. The Series 6 is not as powerful as the Series 8. Its muzzle velocity runs from 225 fps to perhaps 375 fps, depending upon barrel length, arrow type and whether CO_2 or compressed air is the power source. The latter produces higher velocity; CO_2 delivers better consistency. Mind you, even the low end figure above is still impressive. A short 11- or 16-inch bolt with a razor-sharp multi-blade broadhead up front moving at 225 fps is a fearsome customer by any standard, certainly capable of bringing down deer-sized animals with a well-placed shot. The higher velocities simply mean flatter trajectories and greater effective range.

Incidentally, arrows with tranquilizer syringes for capturing large and/or dangerous animals are also available from Swivel Machine Works for the Series 6 model. These tranquilizer arrows require special barrels—also available at extra cost—and reportedly increase the effective delivery range of the drug to approximately twice that of conventional CO_2-powered capture guns.

I have tested both the Series 8 and Series 6 guns and found them awesome. The Series 8 had a Redfield

Tracker 2x-7x scope and no open sights. The Series 6 pistol had an adjustable Williams open rear sight and a removable shotgun-style bead up front.

The Airrow guns provide a peculiar trigger system. It requires a bit of getting used to. There is no conventional sear mechanism; the trigger acts directly on the valve to release the air or CO_2. The traditional slow squeeze is out of the question; the quick snap is in. The Series 8 trigger/grip assembly is like those on various anti-tank rocket launchers; the Series 6 trigger

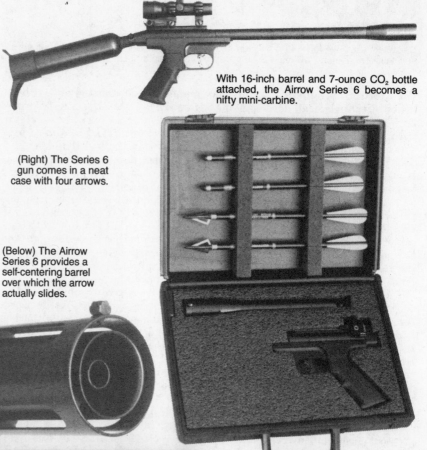

(Right) The Series 6 gun comes in a neat case with four arrows.

With 16-inch barrel and 7-ounce CO_2 bottle attached, the Airrow Series 6 becomes a nifty mini-carbine.

(Below) The Airrow Series 6 provides a self-centering barrel over which the arrow actually slides.

is conventional-looking, but still requires a quick snap.

Shooting the Airrows is unique. They are powerful and can hit at all practical ranges, which in the Series 8 means as far as 80 to 100 yards—roughly half that for the Series 6. The latter gets forty shots from a full 7-ounce CO_2 bottle, can also operate with regular 12-gram CO_2 cartridges and get three to four shots each or special 16- and 25-gram CO_2 cartridges available at marine supply outlets. Recoil is about the same as a 22 rimfire; the report is like a high-power pneu-

matic or CO_2 pellet rifle. The guns are both sold in compartmented waterproof carrying cases which include several arrows.

This is another decidedly new category, with the advantages of compressed air or CO_2 and elements of archery. They *are* airguns—an exalted breed, to be sure, but airguns, nonetheless.

What else is there? Well, there are

The Airrow Series 8, shown here working from a 7-ounce CO_2 bottle, is a truly wicked looking gun that can produce muzzle velocities of nearly 500 fps.

The Beeman-Webley Eclipse is an elegant spring-piston underlever model intended to compete with the hugely successful Weihrauch HW77.

more new magnum air rifles:

Air Rifle Specialists (311 E. Water St., Elmira, NY 14901) now sells the superb Weihrauch HW90. This elegant model has Weihrauch quality, a gas-ram powerplant—in which compressed gas, not a coil spring, propels the piston—developed by **Theoben Engineering** in Britain several years ago.

ARS also imports several Theoben models directly from Britain, such as the exquisite and powerful Imperator Field Target and the Grand Prix SLR 88. The latter, available in 22-caliber only, has a seven-shot magazine that can chamber a pellet when the rifle is cocked. Definitely at the high end, Theobens are outstanding examples of current high-power air rifle technology.

Beeman Precision Arms, Inc. (3440 Airway Drive, Santa Rosa, CA 95403) is one of the undisputed leaders in the field of precision adult airguns in the U.S. The new Beeman RX is a magnum-class rifle, offers West German craftsmanship and the power and vibration-free performance of the Theoben-designed gas-ram. The RX is available in 177, 20, 22 and 25 calibers, so that the potential owner is really spoilt for choice. In 177, the RX can be adjusted to produce a remarkably consistent muzzle velocity of

Crosman's new Outbacker single-stroke pneumatic will suit grownups as well as kids.

The Model 262 Sporter—Crosman's first CO_2-powered pellet rifle in more than a decade.

around 1200 fps.

Beeman is also distributing the Webley Eclipse spring-piston air rifle. This underlever-cocking model competes directly with the Weihrauch HW77. The Eclipse certainly has the hot performance.

Crosman Air Guns leads the kiddie parade with three new models. The first is Crosman's CO_2 comeback, after more than a decade. The Crosman 262 Sporter is a 177, combines affordability performance enough for a general-purpose pellet rifle. With open sights,

rifled barrel and oil-finished hardwood stock, the 262 Sporter can deliver approximately fifty shots at around 550 fps from one 12-gram CO_2 Powerlet.

Crosman's Black Diamond is also CO_2-powered, shoots both BBs and pellets as a manual repeater. The Black Diamond also gets approximately 550 fps. It's a real backyard plinker's delight, with a reservoir that holds 195 BBs—plus 21 in its magazine. Pellets are loaded in new five-shot clips.

Crosman's Outbacker is a single-pump pneumatic and can handle both BBs and 177 pellets. Among several interesting features, the Outbacker sports a novel Pinpoint Sight developed by Crosman. Then there's the detachable compass in the pistol grip, which also contains an Adventure Guide; and in the hollow buttstock there's a special canteen. On top of that, the Outbacker produces about 450 fps at the muzzle.

Dynamit Nobel-RWS, Inc. is the sole U.S. source for Dianawerk guns from West Germany. Two nifty new Diana models are intended for serious junior shooters. Models 70 and 72 are basically mini-versions (complete with diopter match sights) of full-fledged 10-meter target air rifles. Model 70 is a standard recoiling model; the 72 incorporates the famous Giss contra-piston recoilless system. Their suggested retail prices are $170 and $310, respectively.

Marksman Products, now a major player, has introduced the #1750 BB/pellet air rifle. With the skeletonized

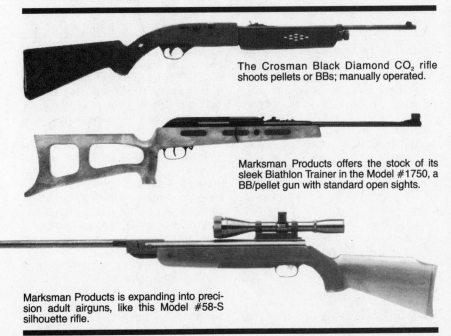

The Crosman Black Diamond CO_2 rifle shoots pellets or BBs; manually operated.

Marksman Products offers the stock of its sleek Biathlon Trainer in the Model #1750, a BB/pellet gun with standard open sights.

Marksman Products is expanding into precision adult airguns, like this Model #58-S silhouette rifle.

How about an air-soft replica of the M16A2 assault rifle? Why not, indeed.

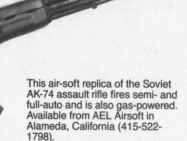

This air-soft replica of the Soviet AK-74 assault rifle fires semi- and full-auto and is also gas-powered. Available from AEL Airsoft in Alameda, California (415-522-1798).

stock first introduced with the Marksman #1790 Biathlon Trainer, the #1750 has a simple, adjustable open rear sight, a smooth bore barrel and an 18-shot forced-feed BB magazine. Pellets are loaded singly, by hand. This spring-piston fun-gun produces a rather sedate 450 fps at the muzzle.

One new shoulder-fired airgun way beyond the ordinary is the megablaster developed by **Airpower Sabot Cannons** (707 Wells Road, Suite 2, Boulder City, NV 89005). The company's name really says it all, because the gun is basically a portable artillery piece powered by compressed air. The latter is obtained from an inexpensive foot-operated bicycle pump, a scuba tank, or even from an air compressor. Looking like an anti-tank rocket launcher, the air cannon can fire a variety of projectiles either singly or shotgun-fashion. Imagine, for instance, shooting a 140-grain 50-caliber steel ball at approximately 500 fps, or a shot charge capable of bringing down ducks at 30 to 40 yards.

The air cannon is constructed mostly of PVC and is electrically fired. It packs ample power, but shooting it accurately requires a good bit of practice. It is a very interesting concept with some practical applications.

In air pistols, **Beeman**, for instance, has just introduced **Feinwerkbau's C5**, a CO_2-powered pistol developed for international-style rapid fire competition. Although such an event did not exist officially at the time that this pistol was developed, all indications are that it is currently in the process of being incorporated as a regular ISU discipline. At any rate, the Beeman/FWB C5 can fire five 177-caliber pellets at 510 fps as fast as the trigger can be pulled and with match precision.

Walther has its own CO_2-powered rapid fire pistol, dubbed the CP5. This one is also full of refinements, including an absolutely superb electronic trigger. The Walther CP5 is available from **Interarms** (10 Prince St., Alexandria, VA 22314).

Another world-class air pistol, first seen at the 1990 SHOT Show, is Steyr's CO_2 model. This is not a rapid-fire version but a regular single shot 10-meter pistol that can deliver razor-sharp accuracy. The production prototype that I examined certainly looked the part of a medal-winner.

Among the general-purpose sporting air pistols, **Daisy** offers the Power Line 45, a 177 pellet-firing spittin' image of the legendary 1911 Colt autoloader. The CO_2-powered Model 45 has a magazine with capacity for 13 match-style pellets, all of which can be fired real quick at an average muzzle velocity of around 400 fps.

And a British outfit, **Phoenix Arms Company, Ltd.** of Kent, has resurrected none other than that great American classic of the 1950s, the Hy-Score Sporter air pistol. The British-made Hy-Score is close, except the original had a long, tapered barrel and the British one has a stubby barrel that makes the gun a lot more compact. Frankly, I like it a lot this way, especially with its easily changed micro-grooved barrel liners in 177 and 22 calibers. This hard-hitting spring-piston air pistol may soon be available in the U.S. ●

"Based on the demonstrated performance of the M9 pistol, and the failure of the two other candidates to meet the minimum performance requirements, the Department of the Army... announced today that the M9 pistol manufactured by Beretta U.S.A. is the winner in the recompetition for the 9mm handgun."

— Official Statement   Department of the Army   May 22, 1989.

In 1985, the Beretta M9 (92F) pistol was selected to be the U.S. military's standard 9mm handgun.

Rigorous testing proved that it was the best in the world. Bar none.

That didn't sit well with other gun manufacturers who repeatedly challenged Beretta's contract. They even asked Congress for a second chance. And got it.

There was another round of tests. And now it's been proven again: The Beretta 92F pistol is simply the best in the world. As the Army stated, "The performance of the Beretta USA M9 pistol was significantly better than either of the competing weapons."

The 92F, the most tested gun in the world, is in a class by itself. It's tough. It's reliable. And it can't be beaten.

The best there ever was, is still the best there is.

Beretta U.S.A.

Beretta U.S.A. Corp.   17601 Beretta Drive
Accokeek, Maryland 20607   (301) 283-2191

Ten Breakthroughs That Count.

Any way you add it up, the semi-automatic Desert Eagle is a firepower breakthrough. The pistol packs ten rounds in .357 Magnum, nine in .44 and .41 Magnum. And the soon-to-be-available .50 Magnum Action Express will have the capacity to unleash eight rounds of the most powerful ammo available for a pistol.

The Desert Eagle Pistol is the only Magnum-caliber pistol that won't chew up your hand — even if you shoot all day long. The gas operation and breakthrough design will almost eliminate recoil and muzzle flip from your shooting vocabulary. You'll enjoy quick second shot, excellent pointability and reassuring reliability.

Ask your dealer about the Desert Eagle, its unparalleled stopping power and the rip-roaring Desert Eagle video, which you can also order directly from Magnum Research for $12.95 (plus $1.00 postage and handling) for each VHS-format tape.

The Desert Eagle Pistol. A firepower breakthrough you can count on.

Invented, patented and marketed by

MAGNUM RESEARCH

7110 University Avenue N.E.
Minneapolis, MN 55432
(612) 574-1868

.357/.41/.44 and .50 Magnum

Manufactured and developed by
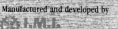

The group pictured was shot with nine rounds out of a scoped .44 Magnum Desert Eagle with a 14" barrel (6" barrel pictured). Remington 180-grain semi-jacketed hollow-point ammunition was used. The steel plate is 1/4-inch thick.

WARNING: Shooting at metal plates is very dangerous and should only be attempted with extreme caution under controlled conditions and with professional assistance.

The complete line-up.

Benelli M1 Super 90 A defensive firearm, a utility shotgun, or a dependable sporting arm, all describe the M1 Super 90. The Benelli inertia recoil operating system means fast-firing, reliable function with all types of 12 gauge shells, from light 2 3/4 inch field loads to the most potent 3 inch magnums. Special ghost ring sights are now options on the M1 SLUG and DEFENSE models. The M1 Super 90 FIELD model unites the quick handling M1 receiver and tough polymer stock with a wide choice of sporting barrels. A complete set of screw-in chokes gives the M1 FIELD unmatched versatility for hunting under the toughest conditions imaginable.

The **Benelli Black Eagle** is a premium grade sporting shotgun that combines the advanced technology of the M1 and Montefeltro Super 90 system with the classic design of vintage Benelli shotguns. The special two piece receiver of steel and aluminum means unmatched strength and enhanced balance. A distinctive high gloss walnut stock and gold plated trigger round out the fine lines of this select class shotgun. Black Eagles come in a variety of barrel lengths with a complete set of tough screw-in chokes. A new Black Eagle SLUG gun is now available with a 24 inch rifled barrel and scope mounting base on the receiver top cover.

Benelli Montefeltro Super 90 A direct descendent of the M1, the Montefeltro uses the same simple and reliable operating system. There is no complicated gas system to collect grime and powder residues. No complex linkages or pistons to clean or maintain. Like all Benelli shotguns, the Montefeltro disassembles completely without tools for easy cleaning and maintenance. The unique Benelli loading system lets you change a shell in the chamber without emptying the entire magazine. Something you'll appreciate if you need to change loads or want to safely unload the chamber. With the special buttstock adjustment kit the Montefeltro and Black Eagle shotguns can be easily custom-fitted to any shooter.

The **Benelli M3 Super 90 Combination Pump/Auto** joins the unique features of semi-automatic Benelli shotguns with a traditional pump action favored by many law enforcement agencies. Rugged, reliable, and easy to operate, the M3 can be quickly converted from auto-loading to pump by flipping a single spring-loaded ring in the forearm. The M3 functions with all standard shotgun loads as well as gas grenades, flares, and rubber ammunition. Designed to operate under the most demanding conditions, the M3 is now available with a tough folding stock and special ghost ring sights for fast target acquistion.

M1 Super 90 Field (short magazine), one of 11 models

Black Eagle with 26" barrel, one of 5 models

Montefeltro Super 90 Standard Hunter, one of 7 models

M3 Super 90 Combination Pump/Auto, one of 4 models

Advanced semi-automatic shotguns for sporting, law enforcement, and defense use. Available only at your Authorized HK Dealer, for the location nearest you call (703) 450-1900.

In a world of compromise, some don't.

by HAL SWIGGETT

HANDGUNS TODAY:

SIXGUNS AND OTHERS

IT'S going to be a *good* year! A b-i-g, long-awaited snake; a single shot pistol only 1⅛ inches longer, overall, than its barrel; a reincarnation; another new cartridge and l-o-n-g-cylindered double action to handle it; a don't-be-surprised-if-you-see-it big single action making its reentrance; a Beauty and Beast combo; a somewhat redesigned bronze-framed six-pound 45-70 single action out for sure; a blackpowder single shot capable of handling real hunting charges; and a single shot pistol with a single-action ejection rod.

Yes, it is going to be a *good* year.

Colt

Anaconda it's called, Colt's finally-made-it-through-the-gate 44 Magnum. A bit of a misnomer in that, in real life, pythons can be larger than anacondas. Anacondas are, however, definitely heavier of body. My source: Dr. Raymond L. Ditmars, more than forty years on the staff of the New York Zoological Society and world-renowned as the authority on snakes.

So be it. Anaconda it's called and it is a *big* stainless steel Python. From its full-length ejector rod housing to its vent rib and slightly protruding proboscis. Barrel length, for the moment, is 6 inches and the weight 53 ounces. The grip is black neoprene combat-style with finger grooves. There are offset bolt notches. The company claims mid-year avail-ability, so we will get a chance to see for ourselves this year.

Competitor

About the single shot pistol only 1⅛ inches longer than its barrel: it's called Competitor and is cannon-like in that the receiver overlaps the barrel by 1-inch and extends 1⅛ inches beyond. It is about 1⅞ inches in diameter. In use the left hand holds the pistol while the right grasps the knurled ring and twists to the right. This cocks the pistol, extracts and ejects the empty (both actions can be felt as it works). Insert a fresh cartridge, turn back to the left until closed—and fire. There is a safety button on the rear. It *is not* automatic. Another safety is in the trigger. This one must be depressed (this is an automatic action as the trigger is pulled) for the gun to fire.

Barrel lengths are 10 to 18 inches (optional) and interchangeable. Calibers offered include 22 rimfire to most any belted magnum the shooter might want. Up to the short 458 Winchester Magnum have been used to date. The pistol in hand is chambered for the ancient, highly-honored, always competent 30-30.

Sights are fixed ramp front, Williams rear. The company has its own scope base of novel and extremely practical design. A four-holer with only three claimed necessary to use. It is so made that it can be reversed for an extended inch of eye relief. And, it is made to accept not only Weaver-type rings but Burris, Leupold, Redfield or

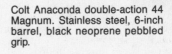

Colt Anaconda double-action 44 Magnum. Stainless steel, 6-inch barrel, black neoprene pebbled grip.

any similar rings. An honest-to-goodness jack-of-all-trades.

Three stocks are offered: synthetic, walnut and resin impregnated camo. As to weight, a 14-inch 223 with synthetic weighs 59 ounces; walnut 64 ounces and resin impregnated 72. The test pistol in hand wears the heavier stock and is dressed with a 14-inch 30-30 barrel. It weighs 74 ounces on my postal scale. The grip is ambidexterous. The receiver is vented away from the shooter's face. All critical parts are made

from hardened 4140 or 8620 steel. Trigger pull on our test Competitor is 4½ pounds and the serial number is CC000012. This pistol will be marketed by New England Firearms.

American Derringer

Long famous for their derringers, American Derringer Corp. has reincarnated High Standard's great little derringer in both calibers: 22 Long Rifle and 22 WMR. As with the original, barrel length is 3½ inches, weight 11 ounces, over/under and blue finish with black grips (my original has white—the only difference). A companion derringer, very similar in appearance, is a double-action 38 Spec. or 9mm Luger.

Colt's Anaconda was chained down or Swiggett might have tried to walk out with it.

Another resurrection by Bob Saunders' American Derringer Corp. is the Mini COP. This is the little four-barreled double-action 22 WMR. Barrel length is 2.85 inches and the weight 16 ounces. This one, and the 38 Special or 9mm Luger, is stainless steel.

Dan Wesson

So new only a prototype was shown at the SHOT Show, Bob Talbot, Dan Wesson's chief engineer, held out, for my inspection, a 5-pound behemoth of a double-action revolver. It is one of their Super Mags stretched another .495-inch. Barely short of ½-inch.

American Derringer's new High Standard-type 22 LR and 22 WMR and a similar 38 Special and the cute four-barrel COP 22 LR.

Why?

To hold their new cartridge, the 7mmx357 Super Mag. Bob's choice of bullet is 160 grains. He claims 1515 feet per second (fps) out of a 7½-inch barrel. The extended-length cylinder is still only 30 thousandths longer than a seated bullet.

DW's 445 is off and running. It's been a hit with silhouette shooters. The 445 Super Mag is simply a magnum 44 Magnum. Out later this year will be its stablemate, the 414 Super Mag which came about the same way—a magnum 41 Magnum.

Their long-talked-about 45 Colt finally made its appearance. My test revolver is of the heavy format with 6-inch barrel. Loaded with rather heavy handloads using 260- and 300-grain hard-cast bullets, it is a "shootin' dude." At a gathering of "The Shootists" in Wyoming last summer it was *the* favorite. Having just arrived, my regulation 260-grain loads made the trip. Since then I've changed to 300-grain 45-70 bullets sized down to .451. They, without a doubt, are here to stay.

Rod Herrett, following in the mighty big footsteps of his father, has designed a great two-piece grip for DW guns. They fit together via a plastic insert and display the usual Herrett Stocks quality.

North American Arms

Remember North American Arms' 45 Winchester Magnum/450 Magnum Express (page 124, 1986 Gun Digest 40th Annual Edition)? It IS coming back. This was a dual cylinder

This is the breech of the Competitor from New England Arms.

single action that had at least two strikes against it because of the cartridge(s) selected. Ken Friel, NAA executive, wouldn't say for sure about the new chambering, but indicated it would be a superb hunting single action. It will be a currently available cartridge, however. It was called N.A.A. SAS. The first three are obvious. The remainder indicates "single-action stainless."

Another remember? Last year NAA introduced their Mini-Master 4-inch heavy vent barrel 22 WMR. It's a five-shooter with adjustable sights. Now cataloged is a 2-inch version—a real cutie.

SSK's Beauty and the Beast

Starting with a Ruger Super Redhawk, in this case one with a 9½-inch barrel, "Beauty" now wears a tapered octagon 7½-inch, measuring only ¹¹/₁₆-inch at the muzzle. Four Mag-na-port slots finish off that end.

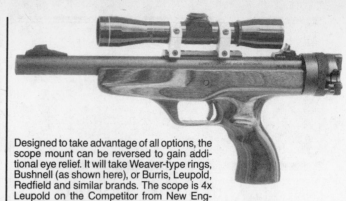

Designed to take advantage of all options, the scope mount can be reversed to gain additional eye relief. It will take Weaver-type rings, Bushnell (as shown here), or Burris, Leupold, Redfield and similar brands. The scope is 4x Leupold on the Competitor from New England Arms.

There is no front sight. This is probably an option. The company knows I'm a user of scopes. Trigger pull is the smoothest 38 ounces I've ever pulled. There is absolutely no movement until it breaks.

On the bottom of the frame, up front, there is a tiny threaded hole. A witness mark is on the face of the frame and barrel. Now you know the secret. SSK has turned this Super Redhawk into an interchangeable barrel revolver. Back the screw off a bit, turn out the 7½-inch octagon barrel, and "Beast" gets to perform. It is 6⅛ inches in length and ¹⁵/₁₆-inch at the muzzle. In other words no taper. Matte finished, "Beauty" is highly polished; a "shocking pink" blade sits atop the sight base 1³/₁₆ inches back from the muzzle. The reason: there is a ¾-inch cutaway just back of the muzzle—SSK's muzzlebrake. It works, I'd best add.

Ruger's great Super Redhawk has never been accused, threatened with, or even hinted at being good looking. Until a scope is mounted. With its integral scope mounting system it was obviously intended that way. SSK Industries' "Beauty and the Beast" interchangeable barrel conversion changes all that. Plus the trigger job, all by itself, is worth your gun's trip to Ohio.

Golden Bison

Super Six Limited builds this 6-pound giant of a single-action revolver. First shown on page 91 of 1988 Gun Digest 42nd Annual Edition, there have been a few changes. A young fellow by the name of Albert Marti is Production Manager. The name comes from its manganese bronze frame, trigger guard, backstrap, loading gate, trigger and hammer. Truly "golden" in appearance.

The "big" six-gun is designed to handle full powder charges under 500-grain bullets. It is beautifully built. The fit and finish are what one would expect in/on an expensive gun. Not a mass-produced item, the company's intent is to turn out the best. It would appear they have done that. Initially planned to be more of a collectors' plaything, Marti has seen to it the gun is fully usable. To an old single-action almost-fanatic who still isn't convinced the 45 Colt and 45-70 cartridges aren't the best ever, this one could be a dream come true.

The Scout

Only mentioned in passing here because a thorough review is in the Testfire section, Thompson/Center's new Scout muzzle-loading pistol *is* a pistol. The first blackpowder handgun capable of digesting hunting charges. One hundred grains of FFg under T/C's prelubed 370-grain 50-caliber Maxi-Ball clocked, over Ken Oehler's Model 35P Chronograph, right at 1200 fps. Pyrodex RS 100-grain equivalent charges went a bit over 1300. Though these first Scout pistols are 50-caliber, I'm told they will eventually be produced in both 45 and 54.

Dan Wesson's new 7mmx357 Super Mag, cylinder lengthened by .495-inch to accept 160-grain bullets.

Herrett's two-piece Dan Wesson grip.

Those 260-grain 45 bullets have retired. Swiggett now shoots this 300-grainer.

North American Arms 4-inch Mini-Master now has a 2-inch partner.

M.O.A. Maximum

Richard Mertz' M.O.A. Corporation has become a trademark name in production silhouette shooting with many appearances in the winner's circle. His falling block lever-action pistol is now available in 22 rimfire with what looks like a single-action revolver's ejection rod to shove out empties. It's a bit different—for sure. With the hammer back, drop the block, use the ejection rod same as with a revolver, insert a fresh cartridge, close the action, move the transfer bar down to its firing position (the pistol can't be loaded with the transfer bar in firing position) and fire when ready.

Simplicity at its best and surprisingly fast once the procedure is mastered. Trigger pull on number 89-000927 is glass-breaking crisp at 26 ounces. Adjustable sights are Millett. With that behind us let's go alphabetical.

ARMSCOR of the Philippines

Squires Bingham, a trading firm founded in 1905 by two Englishmen, Roy Squires and William Bingham, has grown into ARMSCOR of the Philippines. Manufacturing a full line of firearms, our interest here concerns three double-action revolvers. The Detective Chief is 2½-inch barrel, six-shot (as are all three models), full shroud and 38 Special. The Police is 4 inches of barrel, half shroud and 38 Special. Thunder Chief is also with 4-inch barrel, full shroud, adjustable sights (the other two are fixed) and 38 Special plus 22 Long Rifle and 22 WMR. These are blue guns with floating firing pins, safety transfer bars and wide, serrated hammer spurs. Grips are checkered on the 4-inchers and rubber on the 2½-inch model.

Anschutz

Dieter Anschutz hasn't conceded yet, but we are working on it. I still feel this Anschutz Exemplar bolt-action pistol is ideally suited to the 22 WMR cartridge. His concern is accuracy. He feels the cartridge isn't up to his standards for this great pistol. Available in both 22 Long Rifle and 22 Hornet, triggers are factory set at 9.85 ounces. Stocks are European walnut with stippled forends and grip. Left-hand models, meaning the bolt is on the right, are now available as are 14-inch barrels. I recently used my right-hand (bolt on left) 22 Long Rifle 10-inch to help prove a scope. The pistol shot five perfect 1-inch squares at 40 yards then turned in a 5/16-inch six-shot group at that same distance. Not unusual for the Anschutz Exemplar, but here the pistol was proving the scope: one shot each at 2.5, 3, 4, 5, 6 and 7x. It was a new model to be offered by Simmons. Imported by Precision Sales International, Inc.

Charter Arms

Still a leader for Charter Arms is their Bonnie and Clyde set, 2½-inch barreled, blue, with color coordinated Select-A-Grips. Bonnie is in 32 Magnum, Clyde 38 Special. Each is delivered in its own, identified by name, gun rug.

Target Bulldog, stainless steel 5½-inch revolvers are offered with adjustable sights in three chamberings: 357 Magnum, 9mm Federal and 44 Special.

With the current obsession for 9mm cartridges, Charter's rimmed 9mm Federal load is a natural. Along with the longer barreled target model the Pit Bull 9mm Federal is available in 2½- or 3½-inch. These too are stainless steel guns. Grips are black neoprene.

Cimarron Arms

A new kid on the block, Cimarron Arms imports the entire Aldo Uberti & C. line of replica firearms. Catching my eye, in particular, was their U.S. Artillery Model 5½-inch 45 Colt. The reason: I have an original with *all* serial numbers matching, other than the barrel. These were, when first issued, 7½-inch six-guns. Cavalry Models. Recalled, they were stripped down, 5½-inch barrels installed and parts picked from the bench with no effort to keep numbers together. Even the one-piece grip on mine matches. Only the barrel is a different number. Not only do I have the gun—a letter

Swiggett used the 450 Magnum Express to take several head.

SSK's two-barrel Beauty and the Beast is a Super Redhawk plus a lot of machine time.

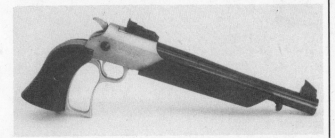

Six pounds of six-shooter: the 45-70 Golden Bison.

from Colt documents it.

Now I can get a "shooting version."

These replicas are stamped US and with RAC, Rinaldo A. Carr, the inspector's stamp, plus all U.S. government proof marks. Both versions are listed in their catalog and are described as color case-hardened steel, just like the originals.

Also in the line: the 1875 Remington single action, 1890

M.O.A.'s new 22 rimfire with the single-action-type ejection rod.

ARMSCOR of the Philippines revolver lineup: Thunder Chief, Police and Detective Chief—all 38 Specials.

Army S.A. "Police" revolver; Sheriff 3- and 4-inch model; the original Peacemaker; Buntline; on and on with most in 357 Magnum, 44-40 and 45 Colt. Most of the long guns of that period are also included for those interested in shooting versions. Few of us are willing to shoot our originals.

Erma

Even the Germans are running scared. There is a lengthy paragraph up front in their Erma-Werke catalog on firearms safety. Nevertheless they still offer their double-action revolvers with instructions on how to adjust both trigger pull and stop. Erma's Model 777, 772 and 773 are 357 Magnum, 22 Long Rifle and 32 S&W Long, in that order. The 357 offers a choice of 4- or 5½-inch barrel. The 22 and 32 are of 6-inch length. All are six-shot. The rear sight is micrometer adjustable.

These are match-quality revolvers. Both front and rear sight blades are interchangeable. All testing in the Dachau plant is with match ammunition. This to the degree their catalog says, ". . . .so-called high-speed cartridges have a poorer target accuracy than the ammunition especially produced for competition."

Erma revolvers are delivered with standard wood grips but, on request, match grips for right- or left-hand shooters are available. Imported by Precision Sales International, Inc.

F.I.E.

A couple of new items. Make that three. F.I.E.'s new Silhouette Pistol Model 722TP is bolt action, 22 Long Rifle, both six- and ten-round magazines are included, and with a four-way adjustable trigger, not counting for tension. Forward or back-ward, left or right, up to about 25 degrees. Tension is adjustable down to 20 ounces. The globe front sight comes with a match post insert but interchangeable with several choices. The rear sight is fully adjustable with match grade micro-click wheels. This is removable should the shooter prefer the two-piece scope mount included as a standard feature. Barrel length is 10 inches.

A new American-made line of standard revolvers, double action, includes 2- and 4-inch barrels in 22 Long Rifle, 22 WMR, 32 Magnum and 38 Special. The 2-inchers are available in blue, chrome or gold finish. Only blue in 4-inch guns. Cylinder capacity: eight rounds in 22s, seven in 32 and six in 38. Built in F.I.E.'s Miami, Florida, factory these revolvers have an internal safety device making it impossible to fire unless the trigger is pulled.

The third: F.I.E.'s Custom Shop offers Gold Rush single-action 22s, WMR and Long Rifle, or combo, with two gold-filled barrel bands, one at the muzzle, the other at the frame end. There are three gold-filled cylinder bands and six gold-filled index notches. Both the backstrap and trigger guard are gold-plated. All that plus delivery in F.I.E.'s exclusive Doskocil "Gun Guard" pistol case.

Freedom Arms

Commissioned by the United States Marshal's Foundation and the Wyoming Centennial Wagon Train Committee, Freedom Arms has produced commemorative revolvers befitting both organizations. The revolvers: a 3-inch as customarily worn by early day frontier marshals and a 7½-inch reminiscent of handguns used by cowboys, trappers and explorers during that period. All, had best be said, in 454 Casull chambering.

Only 250 Centennial Wagon Train revolvers will be built. It's buyer's choice as to fixed or adjustable sights. All will be 7½-inch. These will be Premier Grade, serial numbered WCWT 001-WCWT 250. Special gold markings on the gun and WCWT logo on the cylinder. An 11x16-inch walnut case, French fit for the gun, wears a 3x5-inch stainless steel plaque suitably photo engraved

Steve Comus shoots the Anschutz 22 Hornet.

with gold-filled lettering.

Five hundred U.S. Marshal revolvers, with 3-inch barrels and choice of fixed or adjustable sights will be produced. Numbers will be USM 001-USM 500. A French fit 9½x14-inch hardwood case will house the revolver and silver Marshal Buckle. A similar stainless plaque, suitably photo engraved and gold filled, is on top. Baron Technology is doing the engraving on both issues. The short version U.S. Marshall revolver is accompanied by a 3-inch holster.

Handrifle

Often referred to these past few years, but Falling Block Works selected that as the name for their new single shot pistol. Barrel length is 14½ inches. Rigged for shooting, as the one on my desk is, it weighs 68 ounces. Sights are Williams FP receiver rear and Williams Streamlined ramp front with ¹⁄₁₆-inch gold bead or Williams scope mount with 1-inch rings.

Screws are Allen, no slotted heads. The barrel is chrome-moly steel as is the frame, block and lever. Stock and fore-end are walnut. The trigger is adjustable for sear engagement and overtravel.

The hammer spur is almost square, ⅝x¾-inch and deeply checkered. Open the action and the safety automatically moves over to block the firing pin. It is deeply serrated on top so sliding to the right for firing is easily accomplished.

Charter Arms 9mm Federal Pit Bull is off and running.

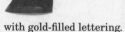

F.I.E.'s Silhouette Pistol offers six- and ten-round magazines, adjustable trigger.

My single complaint, there might be others as I shoot it more but don't believe so at the moment, is the lever length. It extends almost an inch below the stock. I find this, for maybe a reason I can't really justify, objectionable. So far I can't fault anything that's happened. Cock the hammer, drop the block, insert a cartridge, close the block, slide the safety to the right if shooting, lower the hammer if carrying. Simplicity straight down the line.

I've not tried any of my more-potent-than-maybe-they-should-be handloads made up for my SSK Custom T/C barrel. Factory-loaded Remington and Federal 45-70s are doing a fine job. Those 300-grain bullets will handle, quite easily, all the rocks, stumps, cactus leaves and paper targets I've encountered as they would most North American game animals at reasonable distances.

Current chamberings, along with the 45-70 in hand, are 7x30 Waters, 30-30 and 44 Magnum. This Handrifle is "Model T" according to Leo E. Fix. He should know. He built it.

Riggs. It looks like stainless and *very* vicious. Made in Spain, as are all Astra handguns, the real cutie is a blue, 3-inch barrel revolver with interchangeable cylinders: one for 357 Magnum and the other chambering 9mm Parabellum cartridges via the use of full-moon clips.

X-Caliber

Ithaca Gun officials still insist their X-Caliber single shot pistol will be out, redesigned and ready to go, this year. Last year it was talked about as 44 Magnum in 10- or 15-inch and 22 Long Rifle in 10-inch. This time around the claim includes that pair plus 22 WMR, 218 Bee, 35 Remington and 375 Winchester. The barrels *will not* be interchangeable.

Aldo Uberti's U.S. Artillery Model 45 Colt is authentic—from Cimarron Arms.

Cimarron's 1890 Remington is offered in 44 WCF or 45 Colt.

Mitchell Arms

New for this year Mitchell Arms is offering the 1875 Remington revolver in 45 Colt or 357 Magnum. It is royal blue in finish with color case-hardened frame. Walnut grips and a solid brass trigger guard make this Remington counterpart in the Colt 45 era a fine looking six-gun. Also added to his line, Don Mitchell is offering dual cylinders for his Single Action Army: 45 Colt/45 ACP and blue/color case-hardened or nickel.

New England Firearms

Paul Senecal heads up this company. It is what used to be Harrington & Richardson. He is adding to the line each year. In handguns, his new catalog lists four revolvers: the Standard in 22 Long Rifle with 2½- or 4-inch barrel and blue or nickel finish. Another Standard with 2½- or 4-inch barrel is in 22 WMR and blue only. A third Standard has the same barrel lengths and choice of blue or nickel finish and is chambered for the started on Industrial Rowe (their address) 32 H&R Magnum. Number four is dubbed Ultra Revolver.

It is blue finish only and 3 or 6 inches of barrel. Chamberings are 22 Long Rifle, 22 WMR or 32 H&R Magnum.

In all models 22 Long Rifle are nine-shot, 22 WMR six-shot and 32 H&R Magnum five-shot. I first started using Harrington & Richardson revolvers more than 50 years ago—on a trap line. They, under the name of New England Firearms, are still mighty good for that or any other field or plinking purpose.

Pachmayr

The Dominator, Pachmayr's single shot conversion for Colt-type Government Model frames, is now offered as a complete unit. Mine was set up by Carl Cupp, Pachmayr's Chief Engineer, for the *Handgun Hunting With Hal Swiggett* video. It is chambered for the really great 7mm-08 cartridge and is a tack driver. Trigger pull is 1½ pounds. Obviously a slide could not be mounted on it.

Conversion units are still offered, as is the completed pistol, in 22 Hornet, 223, 7mm-08, 308, 35 Remington and 44

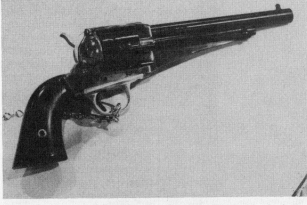

Mitchell Arms' newest is a Remington single-action, 357 Magnum or 45 Colt.

Erma 357 Magnums, 32s and 22s are match quality, sold by Precision Sales International.

Interarms

Both Rossi and Astra revolvers come through this Alexandria, Virginia based company. The Rossi line includes the Model 511, a stainless steel 22 Long Rifle 4-incher; Model 89, 32 S&W 3-inch stainless steel; Model 971, stainless steel 4- or 6-inch or 3-inch blue 357 Magnum and at least four other 38s. You really need their catalog.

Astra 44 Magnum revolvers are stainless steel and 6 inches of barrel. One of my constant companions is one chopped to 2¾ inches in blue, an early version of this big six-gun, then was electroless nickeled by Jim

Llama

Nothing new in Stoeger's Llama revolver line. It's still the Comanche 357 Magnum in blue or satin chrome and 4- or 6-inch barrels and the Super Comanche in 357 Magnum or 44 Magnum with 4-, 6-, or 8½-inch barrels. Llama revolvers have what they claim to be a foolproof eccentric cam system on which the hammer pivots making an accidental discharge virtually impossible. It is fascinating to watch as the hammer rises to fire.

Falling Block Works' new pistol wears a 14½-inch barrel, weighs 68 ounces chambered for 45-70.

Remington Magnum Hornet and 44 barrels are 10½ inches. All others are 14.

Remington

Remington's press release reads: "The latest development for 1990, of a Model XP-100 repeater, was almost predictable. Its time had come." To that I can only add, Amen! Kicking around since 1963, built on the Model 600 bolt-action rifle action, single shot XPs have been chambered, rechambered, re-

This javelina and a 55-grain 223 bullet got together at about 120 yards, introduced by Remington's new XP-100.

barreled to most everything from 17s to 50s. Successfully, I might add.

The new XP-100R—it's stamped on the receiver designation—is from the Custom Shop. Based on their already proven Model Seven action, it is a five-shooter in 7mm-08 Remington and 35 Remington and six in 223 Remington. Along with being a repeater, it has a new look. Described as rear-handle, the synthetic Du Pont Kevlar stock positions the grip at the rear of the gun, directly beneath the bolt. This eliminates the transfer bar between a forward trigger and rear assembly, creating a crisper trigger pull and faster lock time.

This new XP-R will be delivered with a dull finish, minus sights. To aid any possible use it will be drilled and tapped for scope mounting to include holes up front for silhouette shooters. All will wear a standard-weight 14½-inch barrel.

The pistol I've been testing is chambered for the very useful 223 Remington cartridge. To take advantage of its possibilities a Redfield base and rings firmly hold Burris' great 7x scope. Sighted in 2 inches high

New XP-100 has a bolt release.

at 100 yards, less than 1-inch three-shot groups are common-place. Most are about ¾-inch.

All single shot Model XP-100 pistols in existing calibers will continue to be available, both production-grade and custom. Oh yes, an added feature to the

New England Firearms Model R73 6-inch 32 H&R Magnum and Model R22 3-inch 22 Winchester Magnum.

"R." No longer is a tiny-bladed screwdriver necessary to remove the bolt. There is now a release in the trigger guard, in front of the trigger.

Ruger

It's here!

Ruger's new SP101, six-shot 22 Long Rifle revolver. Stainless steel, same as its parents, grandparents and great grand-parents. That's right. This format started with the Super Redhawk 44 Magnum. Next came the GP100 357 Magnum followed by SP101 38 Special. Barrel lengths for this 22 Long Rifle version are 2 and 4 inches.

Built to the same quality as its forerunners, it has all of the family features: strong frame design, floating firing pin, swing-out cylinder with a double frame-lock and the traditional transfer-bar safety.

You won't have to wait for this SP101 22 Long Rifle revolver. Unlike many of Ruger's an-

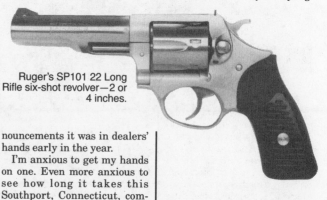

Ruger's SP101 22 Long Rifle six-shot revolver—2 or 4 inches.

nouncements it was in dealers' hands early in the year.

I'm anxious to get my hands on one. Even more anxious to see how long it takes this Southport, Connecticut, company to discover the very excellent handgun cartridge known as the 22 Winchester Magnum Rimfire. This SP101 22 revolver is a natural. Are you listening, Bill?

Smith & Wesson

All sorts of goodies. Some out a while, others close. Let's go by

model number: Model 16 is a reincarnation of the K-32 (32 S&W Long) match revolver, this time chambered for the 32 H&R Magnum, which means it will also digest 32 S&W Long ammo. It is blue, square butt, adjustable sights and in choice of 4-, 6-, or 8-inch barrel. As with almost all the others to be named, it features a full-length lug.

Model 17 is the K-22 Masterpiece in 4-, 6- and 8-inch barrels. In blue only. A top target revolver of yesteryear this new Model 17 should be even better. I own a very early K-22 so am looking forward to comparing the two side by side. The Model 617 is as above except in stainless steel. These "17" models are 22 Long Rifle.

Always a favorite, the Model 27 357 Magnum has been modernized into the Model 627, meaning it is stainless steel. Dubbed "Mountain Revolver" because of its easy-carrying qualities this Model 629 44 Magnum 4-incher is stainless steel and the single new one without a full under lug.

"Back by popular demand," to quote their literature but with an added word. Now it is the New Model 640 Centennial. This five-shot 38 Special with the fully-concealed hammer was introduced in 1952 to celebrate S&Ws' 100th anniversary. It has been a collector's item since 1974. Weighing in at a paltry 20 ounces in all of its satin stainless steel glory, it could well be the perfect "pocket" revolver.

And now there are Magna-Classics. Model 29 and 629. Barrel length is 7½ inches. Grips are ergonomic Goncalo Alves. Finish is Hi-Bright blue or Hi-Bright stainless. A limited edition, serial numbers will be MAG0001 to MAG3000. Only 3000 will be issued.

Sights are many and varied: the 29 comes with a red ramp front, the 629 with black ramp. A sight box accompanies the revolver. In it are six other front sights: gold bead, white dot, and four Patridge sights for distances from 50 to 200 yards. All of this in a gold-embossed leather lid cherrywood case. Along with a Certificate of Authenticity signed by the president of Smith & Wesson.

Yes, things are looking up in Springfield, Massachusetts.

Taurus

Reading through the Taurus catalog I find an even dozen revolver offerings: Models 65, 66, 669, 669VR, 73, 80, 82, 83, 85, 86, 94 and 96. These run the gamut from 22 Long Rifle through 357 Magnum in variations to fit every need. This includes punching holes in tin cans through precision target shooting with their Model 86. This match model is offered in 22 Long Rifle, 32 S&W Long and 38 Special. It features a contoured target grip, adjustable counterweight, fully adjustable rear sight with interchangeable front sight inserts and in single or double action. Another match version, the 669VB6L and 669VSS6L offer Laser Aim Sight with all accessories and in a custom case.

For the moment our interest is in their new Model 94 SS4. It's a stainless steel nine-shot 22 Long Rifle with 4 inches of barrel. A micrometer adjustable rear sight matched with a

Smith & Wesson Model 16 32 H&R Magnum, the K-32 improved.

Smith & Wesson Model 617 Stainless—a heavier K-22.

Smith & Wesson Model 629 44 Magnum in stainless—the Mountain Revolver.

Model 640 Smith & Wesson Centennial five-shot 38 Special.

serrated ramp up front allow proper sighting in. Weighing in at 25 ounces, it is small enough to keep handy yet with sufficient accuracy to prove its worth every time the trigger is pulled. Taurus handguns are guaranteed with an Exclusive Lifetime Repair Policy. Made in Brazil, true, but better said well-made in Brazil.

Thompson/Center

The Contender Hunter is new to Thompson/Center's catalog. A special 12-inch barrel equipped with their Muzzle Tamer recoil reducer. Sling swivels, a nylon sling and a 2.5x T/C Recoil Proof scope with lighted reticle complete the package. Seven calibers are offered: 223 Remington, 7x30 Waters, 30-30, 357 Remington Maximum, 35 Remington, 44 Remington Magnum and 45-70 Government. This is a complete package for the handgun hunter. All that's needed is ammunition.

T/C introduced their Super "16" barrels last year, but there wasn't time to try one out before this section went in. I have been shooting a 22 WMR and 45-70, one extreme to the other. Both have done a magnificent job. I've found the 22 WMR cartridge to be a great handgun round in shorter barrels. Only a little more potent than Long Rifle cartridges in long guns. This 16-inch makes it almost rifle-like.

Thompson/Center Contender Hunter comes fully dressed: 2.5x T/C scope, Muzzle Tamer, and nylon sling.

Taurus' new Model 94 22 weighs 25 ounces.

Ultra Light Arms pistols come in 22-250 to 308.

The really new item from T/C is their Quick Release Scope Rings and Mount. Once a scope/barrel combo is sighted-in, the scope can be removed by unscrewing the locking screw, pulling the scope and rings slightly rearward and lifting the scope off the base. When reinstalled on the same base and barrel, the scope's zero is maintained precisely.

Thompson/Center Assn.

If you are into Thompson/Center Contender handguns you should know about the Thompson/Center Association (TCA). This is not a company-sponsored organization but a group interested in T/C Contenders, their multitudes of variations, their collectible possibilities. A well-put-together quarterly publication keeps members informed. One of the advantages of being a member is that the group gets limited numbers of not otherwise offered barrels/calibers. Currently they have had a few over a hundred 12-inch octagon 22 Jet barrels made. About half are with sights, the remainder scope models. These will never be cataloged by T/C. Like I've said, if you are into T/C Contenders you are a good candidate for the TCA (P.O. Box 792, Northboro, MA 01532).

300 Gunsmith Service

My favorite Model 29 S&W 44 Magnum is 20 years old. It was put together for me at the S&W factory on an order from Elmer Keith—and so states on the right sideplate. Two decades back quality was excellent, triggers were good, little was necessary to improve its shootability. Or so I thought. A

year or so ago Allan Duckworth hit me up at the NRA Show. We talked guns a bit then came his proposition: send me your M29 (we had talked about this particular gun). If you like what we do to it—write it up. If you don't, write that up too, if you want, or skip it. Whatever, there will be no hard feelings.

I took him up. Several months later I shipped my 56-ounce s/a trigger pull, 12-13 pounds double-action, M29 to Englewood, Colorado (6850 S. Yosemite Ct., 80111). Several weeks later it came back. With a single visible change. The accompanying letter said, "No parts have been changed; your gun still contains all of the original parts as it came from the factory." Only a trigger stop was added.

Internally the action was modified to remove the stack and heavy trigger. The difference: my M29 now smoothly pulls through at barely 7 pounds. A fraction over half of the factory pull. Single action it almost requires a magnifying glass to see the movement. I know; it has to move to fire. This one is so slight, at an even 40 ounces, it can't be felt.

The one visible difference: long a believer in smooth, rounded triggers I had no idea their thinking was the same. Tim Gerhardt, Service Manager and the man who did my gun, described it as "having been contoured to a special elliptical curve designed by 300 Gunsmith to provide the best finger-to-trigger contact." He is absolutely and positively correct.

Allan set me up when he said, "If you like it, write it up; if you don't, write that up too." That's

The cylinder houses nine 22 Long Rifle cartridges.

Model 94 rear sight is adjustable.

what I call being sure of yourself. And your staff.

Ultra Light Arms

Melvin Forbes has settled on 22-250 through 308 Winchester as standard for his Model 20 REB bolt-action pistol. He does concede, however, that most silhouette and other calibers are available on request. He uses 14-inch Douglas No. 3 barrels, composite Kevlar, graphite re-

inforced stocks with Du Pont Imron paint. Colors are green, brown, black and camo. His triggers are Timney adjustable. Finish is matte or bright for both stock and metal. It's the customer's option. Magazine capacity is five rounds. Left- or right-handed makes no difference and delivery is in a hard case.

Yes, 1990 IS going to be a good year.   ●

GAIL WAS born a Montana girl so it was only natural to buy her a new hunting rifle when we were married. We spent a Saturday morning in July looking through the gun shops in town. She tried on 243s, 270s, 30-30s and 30-06s in lever- and bolt-actions, in long and short barrels and in heavy and light rifles. One rifle caught her eye.

She asked me what I thought of the

Gail liked the rifle. "It's a natural pointer," she said.

I wrote a check for the rifle and a set of Weaver scope rings, and Gail walked out of the store with her wedding present. I mounted a Weaver 4x scope on it. That summer Gail practiced on gophers, and that October, she shot an antelope 230 yards across an alfalfa field. The next month she tracked a mule deer buck in the snow

times as much, is just as light and handy as custom-made fiberglass stocked carbines and has all the power it takes for whitetail in the brush and antelope across the prairie. Unfortunately for Remington and the Model 600, there were not enough hunters who agreed.

The Model 600 started out as a deer rifle. A January 1964 Remington newsletter stated the nation's deer

TOO GOOD TOO SOON

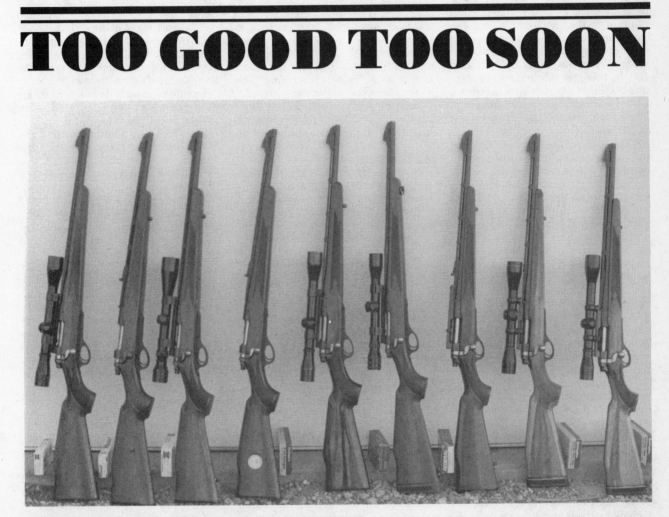

This is a complete collection of original Model 600 carbines made by Remington. From left to right—222, 223, 243, Montana Centennial in 6mm, standard 6mm, 308, 35 Remington, 6.5 Remington Magnum and 350 Remington Magnum.

by JOHN HAVILAND

Remington. I did not know what to think. The rifle was light and the barrel was short. The bolt handle looked like a dog's hind leg. The plastic trigger guard/floorplate looked cheap. I did like the fact the rifle was chambered in 6mm Remington, because I had heard it was a good big game cartridge. What I had not heard of, though, was "Mohawk 600" stamped on the receiver.

and shot it 60 yards away through the trees.

That was thirteen years ago. Gail has taken more big game, and countless gophers, since with her 600. You cannot tell her there is a better cartridge than the 6mm Remington or rifle than the Model 600.

Once a season I take Gail's 600 deer hunting. I paid $99 for it, and it shoots better than other rifles that cost three

population was at an all-time high, and there was an increased demand from hunters who hunted in thick cover for lightweight, easy-to-carry, easy-to-handle rifles with the accuracy and power to drop a buck in heavy brush.

In response to this demand Remington introduced the Model 600 in 6mm Remington, 308 Winchester and 35 Remington. The rifle was also chambered in 222 Remington to make it "tough on coyotes," according to Remington. The rifle was truly compact — it measured 37.25 inches from one end to the other. Not to leave anybody out, the newsletter continued, "the compact power package should also be popular with ranchers and others who hunt in open country." The 243 Winchester was added a year later, in 1965.

Also in 1965, the Model 600 Magnum was introduced along with a new cartridge, the 350 Remington Magnum, to fit the short 600 action. The magnum was made with a laminated stock of walnut and beech and was the same overall length as the standard 600. In 1966, the 6.5 Remington Magnum, another short bolted cartridge, was chambered in the 600 Magnum. The 6.5 was the 350 case necked down to .264-inch.

The weight of the standard 600 was first annouced as "5½ well-balanced pounds." Two years later the weight inched up to 6 pounds. The same thing happened with the 600 Magnum. The weight started at 6.2 pounds and was then upped to 6.5 pounds.

Hunters did not care about the ounces one way or another and stayed away from the 600 rifles in droves. Remington dropped the 600 in 1968, and that same year brought out the Model 660 and 660 Magnum. The 660 was chambered in 222 Remington, 6mm Remington, 243 Winchester and 308 Winchester. The magnum version was made in the 6.5 and the 350 Remington Magnum.

The standard and magnum 660 weighed 6.5 pounds. Their 20-inch barrels lacked the plastic rib that distinguished the 600. The 660 also had a black forearm tip and pistol grip cap. White-line spacers, which every rifle had to have to sell, garnished the forearm tip, grip cap and buttplate. The magnum version came with a laminated stock of beech and walnut, detachable swivels and a carrying strap.

The 660s did not please anyone. The 20-inch barrel was too long for carbine fans and too short to qualify as a full-size rifle. The 660 lasted only three years, until it was dropped in 1971.

Remington returned to the 18.5-inch barrel and brought out the Mohawk 600 in 1972. The Mohawk looked similar to the original standard 600, but without the ventilated rib. The Mohawk weighed about 6.5 pounds, a pound more than the 600. Most of the extra weight was in the barrel of the Mohawk.

The Mohawk was chambered in 222 Remington, 6mm Remington, 243 Winchester and 308 Winchester. Ac-

cording to a Remington advertisement, the Mohawk was "economically priced and built to take tough 'carbine country' use." Not many hunters must hunt in "carbine country," because even the low price of the Mohawk could not help it sell, and the rifle was discontinued in 1978.

Like the song goes, "You don't know what you got 'til it's gone." Most hunters could have cared less about Remington's carbine while it was in production. But the minute the 600 was taken off the market, hunters tripped all over their boot laces looking for Remington 600s. The rifle instantly went into that expensive category known as a "collector's item." The price of 600s shot up accordingly.

Mike Burton is a collector of Remington 600s and also a hunter who appreciates light mountain rifles with plenty of power for elk. Burton hunts in the steep mountains around his home in the Bitterroot Valley of Montana. Those steep mountains made him appreciate the light weight of the Model 600. Burton started seriously collecting 600s fifteen years ago.

A couple rare 600s, however, may thwart even determined collectors. Four years ago Burton heard about the 600 in 223. The collector's grapevine reported only 315 600s were made in 223. Burton made a few long distance phone calls and contacted a collector on the East Coast who had a 223 for sale. After some creative trading, Burton had his 223. According to Remington, these 223s were never listed in a catalog and were sold only to police departments. Remington does not have an exact number of how many 600s in 223 were made.

Another rare 600 is the Montana Centennial, built to commemorate Montana's territorial centennial in 1964. According to Burton, Remington made 1,500 Model 600s in 6mm. A gold-colored medallion inscribed "Montana Territorial Centennial 1864-1964" is inletted in the side of the stock, below the comb. Again, Remington does not have an exact figure on how many Montana Centennial rifles they made.

"If you can even find a 600 in a Montana Territorial Centennial or a 223, the price is way up there and it is anybody's guess how much they are worth," Burton said.

Burton said a 600 in common calibers, like 243, 6mm and 308, sells for around $325. A 600 in 222 and 35 Remington is harder to come by, and sells in the neighborhood of $500. The 6.5 and 350 600 magnums sell for $650. Burton says you will be lucky to

even find a rifle in one of these short magnums.

The number of 600 series rifles made is not known because, at times, the serial numbers were mixed in with the Remington Model 700.

Since Remington introduced the Model Seven, another carbine rifle, in 1983, the price of 600s has leveled off. In fact, a 600 in the same calibers available in the Model Seven sells for about the same price as a new Model Seven.

"The price is not going up like it once did," Burton said. "Maybe that is because of the introduction of the Model Seven. But at the same time the price for 600s hasn't gone down either."

Burton says 600s do not turn up on used gun racks. "People are holding on to their rifles," he said.

Dick Dietz, of Remington, said the Model Seven is a better rifle than the 600. He said the Model Seven has a better stock, a better bolt release and is a more attractive rifle than the 600.

Unlike my wife, I was never a fan of the Model 600 stock design. The square corners of the forearm reminded me of a railroad tie. The tree trunk pistol grip never fit my hand. The bolt release, hidden in the left rear of the action, was impossible to push without a tool. The crooked bolt handle, with only half a knob, was awkward. A Remington advertisement said the handle was made that way so it would hug the stock. The same news release said the rifle's ventilated rib formed "a quick sighting line that helps shooters to get on targets faster."

Jim Carmichel, the shooting editor of *Outdoor Life*, said the rib was "as useful as mud flaps on a sledge hammer." I have seen five 600s with the rib removed, because the owners thought they were so odd looking. About the only thing the rib did was distinguish the rifle from other models on a gun rack.

The plastic rib and other inexpensive features may not have endeared the 600 to all riflemen. But the 600's beauty is not for the eye. The 600 is a utilitarian rifle that is handy to carry and quick to point. I shot my biggest whitetail buck with Gail's 6mm as the buck weaved through the willows 175 yards away.

I have never met anyone who complained about the accuracy of their 600. Most 600 rifles will print five shots into one inch at 100 yards. Some will shoot tighter. The free-floating 18.5-inch on the 600 has its weight in its diameter and that helps accuracy. My wife's Mohawk measures a thick .62-inch at the muzzle, unlike most carbine rifles with barrels pared down to save weight. After three shots, these thin barrels are so hot they start waving like sheets on a clothesline.

Oddly, the limited number of 600s in 223 do not shoot accurately. Burton said the only explanation he had heard was the 223s had the wrong twist. This is all academic, however, because 600s in 223 are so rare and expensive they are seldom fired.

The 600s that *are* bought to be fired, however, are the 350 and 6.5 Remington Magnums. These two cartridges are one thing the 600 was all about— power in a small package. There are hard-core elk hunters out there who think all cartridge development started and stopped with the 350. I once met three brothers elk hunting. All three were carrying 600s in 350. They said the short 600 combined with the 350 launching a 250-grain bullet

was the best they had found for hunting elk in lodgepole thickets.

Burton says a full-size rifle feels awkward after he has packed his 350 around the mountains. When Burton carries his 350 on a sling over his shoulder, he does not worry about the short barrel catching on branches or brush. "Honest to God, that 350 shoots and handles well in the brush," he said.

If you cannot live without a short 350, but cannot find one, don't pout. Remington's custom shop will make you a Model Seven in 350. Leave plenty of room on the check, though, because this special Model Seven costs over $700. Dick Dietz, of Remington, said the custom shop does a brisk business in Model Seven 350s.

The 350 was developed especially for the 600's short action, but not enough hunters wanted that power in a short

action and as a commercial venture, the 350 is dead. I guess nobody will ever know if the 350 made the 600 Magnum as popular as it was or if the short 600 made the 350 as successful as it was.

Remington used to load 250- and 200-grain bullets for the 350. Now, only the 200-grain is loaded. I suspect the big bullet was dropped because of the recoil it generated. Burton loads 200-grain round-nose Sierra bullets to around 2700 feet per second in his. Because of the 600's short magazine, pointed and round-nose bullets catch on the loading ramp. "All the calibers in the 600, not just the 350, have a tendency to catch the bullet on the loading ramp," he said. "I have never had a round jam, they just stick and you have to give the bolt a bit more of a push."

The 350 has never had any problem with bad press. One article called the 350 in the 600 rifle the "most versatile and practical hunting package developed in this century." Another stated it was "the best elk rifle in the universe."

For all the praise, though, the 350's range is limited to 300 yards. But come to think of it, when was the last time you shot an elk over 300 yards?

Burton's two brothers were hunting elk one season in the steep Sapphire Mountain Range in Montana. Long shots are common in the Sapphires. One brother was carrying a 350 and the other a 338 Winchester Magnum. They spotted a bull "a long ways" across a canyon. They each found a solid rest and on the count of three, fired across at the bull. Both shots went low. All this story tells is that the 350 is not a cartridge for shooting from one mountain canyon to the next.

Several articles on the 350 and the Model 600 stated recoil was the main reason the rifles failed to sell. A rifle weighing 6.5 pounds, shooting a 250-grain bullet is going to kick. Remington announced the 600 Magnum in 1965 as "the most powerful package, pound for pound, of any carbine on the market today." If that was not enough to make buyers flinch, Remington made the magnum model with a laminated stock "for greater strength" and a bracket at the front of the receiver as a support for the scope "when shooting powerful, large caliber loads."

The 350 is not a rifle for the faint of heart. "Face it," Burton said. "You're going to pay the price for having that much gun in such a small package."

The hardest recoiling 600, though, is one in 308 Winchester. The 308 came

Mike Burton with his favorite elk rifle, a 600 in 350 Magnum, naturally.

in the standard rifle and does not have a recoil pad, like the magnum models. "The 308 has a nasty, sharp crack to it," Burton said.

The 6.5 Remington in the 600 is also a handful. Remington made the 6.5 by simply necking down the 350. They developed the round to give the ballistic performance of the 270 Winchester in a short case. In fact, the 6.5 and the 270 use the same amount of 4350 powder with a 140-grain bullet.

The rarest 600 is one of these made in 223 Remington. Only 315 were made.

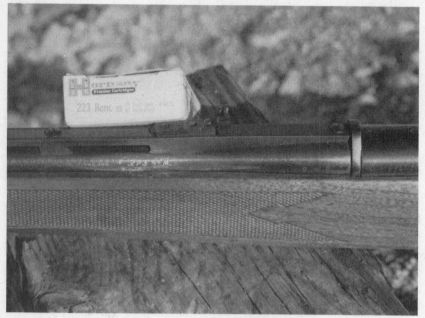

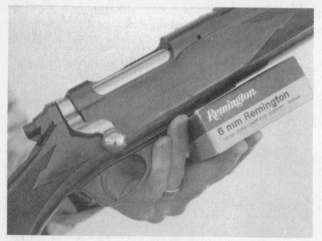

The Haviland family experience with 600s is with the 6mm.

Of all the calibers in the 600, Burton's favorite is the 6.5 Remington Magnum, which makes him one of the few—the 6.5 was a sales flop.

Out of all the calibers in the 600, Burton's favorite is the 6.5. He considers it just as good a cartridge as the 270 Winchester.

For three seasons in a row Burton used his 6.5 to shoot his mule deer buck from the same point on the Judith River breaks on the Montana prairie. Each year the deer were feeding far below in an alfalfa field. And each year the herd moved up in the breaks toward Burton. Each year again the deer always stopped and bedded down 400 yards from where Burton sat waiting. On each of the three bucks he held too high the first shot because he overestimated the range. He killed each buck on the second shot, after he aimed lower. "I'm a 270 fan," Burton says, "and I consider that little 6.5 right up there with the 270."

A Remington advertisement stated the 6.5 was "ideally suited for long-range big game hunting." It was, but nobody believed it. The cartridge and the rifle were short and fat, just what hunters consider ideal for hunting in the thick stuff. The combination of the 600's short action and long 140-grain 6.5 bullets also did not work. The heaviest bullets that work in the 6.5 short case and action are 120 grains. So, hunters reasoned, the 600 in 6.5 was not a brush cartridge because of its light bullet and not a plains rifle because of its carbine length. The 6.5 fell, brain dead, just out of the starting gate.

Another reason the magnum 600s failed was they were made 6.5 and 35-caliber. Americans, for some back-of-the-brain reason, do not like these calibers. Consider how quick the 264 Winchester, 358 Winchester and 358 Norma took sick. And ponder why the various 6.5s are popular in Europe—even militarily—but unknown in North America.

Yet another reason, probably the main reason, more hunters did not buy the 600 was the 600's strange looking stock. Shooters passed up the rifle for something more traditional. Others thought the concept of a compact rifle was beautiful, but the rifle itself was ugly. They bought 600s for the actions, turned down the barrels, fitted fiberglass stocks and made even lighter rifles.

Today, the trend is toward lightweight rifles. Everybody wants one, and every rifle company makes at least one light model.

That was the main reason the 600 died. It just was not in fashion . . . then. Like many good ideas that fail, it was slightly ahead of its time. ●

by BOB ARGANBRIGHT

THE FINEST holsters in the world have been produced in the United States for over ninety years. At the turn of the century, holsters of superior design and quality were produced by such holster makers as S.D. Myres of El Paso, Texas, and H.H. Heiser of Denver, Colorado. Such holsters were made of heavy saddle leather which was blocked (wet fit to a wooden block the approximate size and shape of the gun it was to carry) for a correct fit.

In the 1950s, New York City holster designer/manufacturer Chic Gaylord pioneered the new breed of holster produced from a high-quality lightweight molding leather. Gaylord holsters were trimmed of all excess material and given extensive wet molding to the exact make and model of gun they were to carry. And in the 1980s, we have seen the nylon revolution with Uncle Mike's introducing an economical soft padded nylon holster. The nylon holsters are light, economical, easy to clean, waterproof and wear-resistant.

Yet, with all these advances in holsters, there remain handguns for which it is difficult to obtain a proper holster. These tend to fall into three classes: the very small handgun, such as the Freedom Arms and North American Arms mini-revolvers, derringers, and the small 22- and 25-caliber pocket autos; the very large handguns such as Ruger's 10½-inch Super Blackhawk, the long Redhawks, Smith & Wessons, and Dan Wessons in 44

(Above, left) Ruger SP101 works with this Uncle Mike's inside-the-pants nylon holster. And this Brauer Brothers nylon belt slide (below, left) carries an SP101, too. (Right) And when the custom Rybka Bearpaw for the Ruger SP101 got there, it worked, too.

HOLSTERING THE

HARD-TO-HOLSTER

Magnum; and the Thompson/Center Contender with its barrels up to 14 inches long, and other big single shots. Holstering this class of handgun is often complicated by its including a scope. And then the unusual or custom handgun, the one-of-a-kind that is hard to holster. In this article we will look at what is available in holsters for these three classes of handguns.

The first place to look is among the popular padded nylon holsters. Chances are pretty good Uncle Mike's or Bianchi International will make a soft padded nylon holster which will work. However, it will be a compromise. It won't fit your gun perfectly, as we have come to expect the finer leather holsters to do. Nylon holsters are made in several sizes, where each size fits several guns. This is called *generic fit*. This means that the holster may be longer than necessary, or for a slightly larger framed handgun, which isn't as bad as it may sound. One of the attributes of the padded nylon construction process is that the holster tends to shape itself to the gun it carries. And this doesn't require any laborious fitting process. Merely insert the handgun in the holster, adjust any safety or retaining strap for proper secure fit, and leave the gun in the holster overnight.

Handguns that have just been introduced, such as the Ruger SP101 small

frame 38 Special and 22 revolvers, often reach the market before the holster makers can produce holsters for them. I found Uncle Mike's soft nylon inside-the-pants holster to work satisfactorily in such cases. This holster is available in only one size, for 2- to 3-inch barreled small and medium-frame revolvers. This means it works satisfactorily, but not the best, with the 2¾-inch Ruger Speed-Six, my 2½-inch Charter Arms Bulldog Pug, and the new Ruger SP101 in either 2¼- or 3-inch version.

Another circumstance where the padded nylon holster works well is for

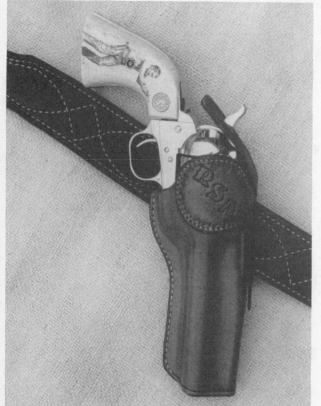

(Above) This Uncle Mike's duty holster, made for 4-inch DA revolvers, also works with the author's favorite 4¾-inch Colt Single Action 44, and maybe with one you own, too.

This custom crossdraw for Colt Single Action is from The Gunfitters, which would charge the same or close for a Webley-Fosbery.

the customized handgun, such as the Mag-na-port Mini-Magnum versions of the Smith & Wesson Model 29 44 Magnum with 2½-inch barrel. One of my favorite double-action handguns is a Colt New Service revolver in 45 Colt, now being given the "Fitz" treatment. Named for J.H. "Fitz" Fitzgerald, a legendary Colt employee of pre-WWII fame, a Fitz Special was made like Fitzgerald's personal New Service revolvers with 2-inch barrels, round butts, open trigger guards and spurless hammers. No one offers a holster for 2-inch New Services. I will settle at first for a padded nylon holster for a large framed 4-inch revolver, then if the project comes out as nice as I hope, I will have a custom leather holster made.

The one-size-fits-several approach of the padded nylon holster has advantages. Often holsters can be adapted to guns not meant for them. My favorite handgun is the Colt Single Action revolver in 4¾-inch barrel. While I prefer the Hollywood-style Fast Draw holster, it doesn't offer enough security for a stroll through the Missouri woods. Recently, while testing an Uncle Mike's duty holster for medium-frame 4-inch double-action revolvers, I

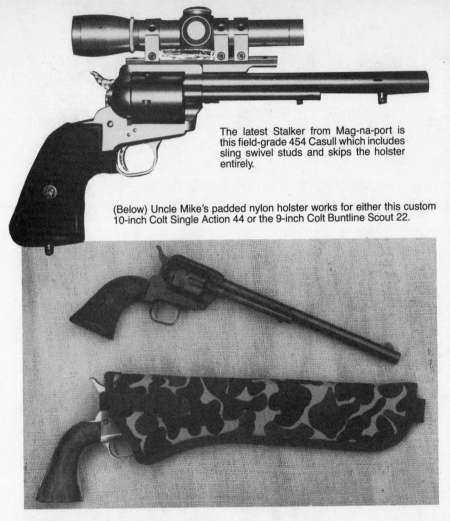

The latest Stalker from Mag-na-port is this field-grade 454 Casull which includes sling swivel studs and skips the holster entirely.

(Below) Uncle Mike's padded nylon holster works for either this custom 10-inch Colt Single Action 44 or the 9-inch Colt Buntline Scout 22.

was pleased to find it would accept my 4¾-inch Colt SA. This holster encloses the trigger guard and includes a thumb-break retaining strap. The pouch is split partially down the front edge, held closed with elastic. The gun is drawn by rocking the butt forward against the elastic until the trigger guard clears and then withdrawing it normally. This makes a fast and secure field holster which, due to its soft padded construction, provides maximum protection for my pet Colt.

Both Uncle Mike's and Bianchi International offer padded nylon shoulder holsters for the large handguns used for hunting big game. Versions are available for normal underarm carry, with or without a scope attached to the handgun. They also offer versions attached to a bandoleer-type harness, with the gun carried toward the front of the chest. Several of these are available with detachable full flaps for maximum protection when in the hunting field. I have been using a Bianchi Model 4100 Ranger Hunting Shoulder Holster with my Ruger 7½-inch Super Blackhawk. This rig is very comfortable with this relatively heavy revolver and is just the ticket for the

Missouri whitetail deer handgun hunter.

This is a good place to mention the carry system worked out by Larry Kelly of Mag-na-port Arms for the large scope-mounted hunting handgun. Kelly has been more successful in taking big game with the handgun than any other hunter. He offers, through Mag-na-port Arms, Inc., his "Stalker" revolver. This is the customer's choice of a Ruger Super Blackhawk, Redhawk, Smith & Wesson 629 or field-grade Freedom Arms 454 Casull. The "Stalker" conversion has the barrel shortened to 8⅜ inches, crowned and ported (Mag-na-port process), an action job, and scope attached. Swivel studs are attached to the underside of the barrel and the gun butt. After trying many holster systems for these large handguns, Kelly went to a carry sling exclusively. He told me the prototype for this system consisted of using boot laces to sling an early "Stalker" from his shoulder in order to drag the kill back to camp.

I have been involved in "action shooting" since the mid-1970s. (Actually, Arganbright is a genuine fast-draw champion, having won several titles in national competition. Editor) My Colt-Wilson Accucomp 45 auto pistol has proven to be one of the most accurate and reliable handguns I have ever shot. But with its compensated slide, the only holsters available are those meant for action shooting competition. These are superb holsters though they are not practical for field carry of this great field gun. Recently, I have been carrying it in a Ted Blocker's Custom Holsters nylon TAC holster. Developed for police and military specialty teams, this is a low-hanging strong side hip holster suspended from a waist belt and supported by a wide

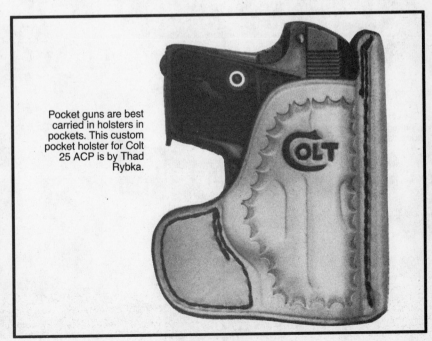

Pocket guns are best carried in holsters in pockets. This custom pocket holster for Colt 25 ACP is by Thad Rybka.

(Right) This Rybka crossdraw holster for short-barreled Colt Bisley Sheriff Model includes piggyback ejector rod.

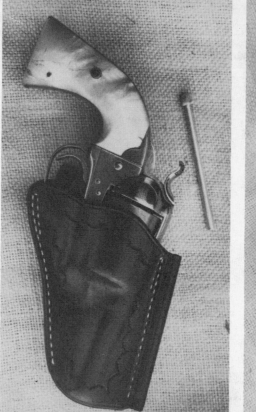

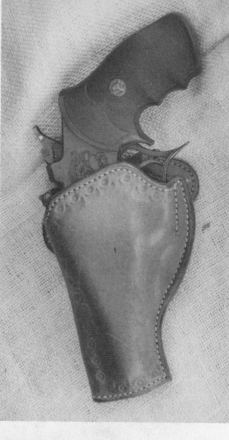

(Far right) Even a 6-inch Contender can find a home— this one in a southpaw rig.

(Below) Single actions with barrels shorter than 4⅝ inches are hard to find holsters for. Center holster is from Old West Reproductions, that at left by the author, that at right from El Paso Saddlery.

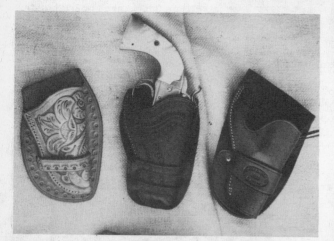

(Below) This western swivel holster from Ted Blocker's makes carrying big, heavy handguns easy.

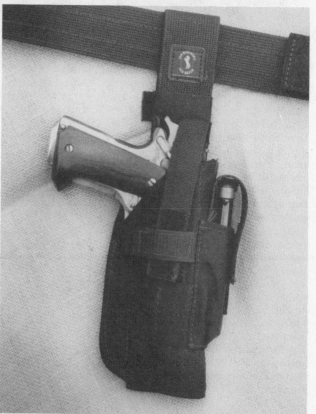

This soft nylon Tactical holster from Ted Blocker's Custom Holsters works well with this Wilson compensated Colt 45 ACP pistol.

thigh strap. The belt, holster and thigh strap are constructed of ballistic nylon and the holster includes a pouch on its face for an extra magazine. This holster is light in weight, secure, and comfortable when carrying this relatively large and heavy handgun.

One final nylon holster deserves attention. This is the belt slide, as made by Ted Blocker's Custom Holsters and by El Paso Saddlery. This is a simple open-ended ballistic nylon pocket with belt loops on both front and back sides. This makes it ambidextrous, as well as allowing one to wear it between the belt and trousers for better security. Because belt slides are not designed to cover the barrel or forward portion of the slide on a handgun, barrel length is unimportant. So the nylon belt slide will work with any handgun not too big to go in or so small it falls through. I usually have one of these in my shooting bag. Brauer Brothers has just introduced a nylon belt slide and I have been using one when I go to the range to shoot my Colt auto pistols, as it works equally well with the Officer's ACP, the standard Government Model or my long compensated Wilson Accucomp.

If none of the nylon holsters fill your needs, and a factory leather holster isn't available for your handgun, a custom holster maker is the answer. The custom maker can make a holster for any handgun. As a last resort, you can ship your gun to the holster man and he can fit the holster to your personal handgun.

Starting with the small pocket guns, such as the mini-revolvers, 25 ACP and 22 auto pistols and derringers, the best way of holstering these is with a pocket holster. The pocket holster protects the mini-gun from the contents of the pocket such as lint, dirt, coins, etc., and also keeps the gun from working around and ending up upside down when one reaches for it. Both Thad Rybka and Ken Null make excellent pocket holsters. I have been using a Rybka holster to carry a Colt hammerless 25 ACP auto and it works perfectly. This beautiful example of the holster makers' art includes an extended welt on the front edge which is used as a "push rod" in order to push the holster off the gun with the thumb as the gun is drawn from the pocket. I have found it easier to brush the holster loose with the middle finger against the tab which extends from the trigger guard edge. This tab is meant to prevent the holstered gun from rotating in the pocket, so that it is oriented correctly when one reaches for it. DeSantis and Galco offer pocket

holsters for the Hi-Standard Derringer which look like a wallet and allow one to fire the gun without removing it from the wallet-holster. Pockets are convenient for carrying very small handguns, and pocket holsters are the best way to carry a gun in a pocket.

The custom holster maker is the answer for holsters for custom guns. Guns such as the mini-conversions of the S&W Model 29/629 44 Magnum from Mag-na-port may require custom work. A friend purchased a Freedom Arms Single Action revolver, legendary for its power when chambered for 454 Casull, in 44 Magnum with 10½-inch barrel. This is the most accurate revolver I have had the pleasure of shooting, but after using it on a Missouri deer hunt, my friend decided he wanted a shorter barrel. He returned his gun to Freedom Arms, and they shortened the barrel to a non-standard 6½ inches with express sights. For use without a scope, he wanted a Western-style hip holster, but no one offered one for this non-standard barrel length. A custom maker provided exactly what he wanted, hand fit to his gun. When using it with scope in place, my friend wanted to carry his 44 in a high, behind the hip "cavalry draw" holster. This is a reverse draw holster with extreme angle. It is easy to draw from, yet out of the way. Once again, the custom maker was the answer, and my deer hunter friend ended up with what he wanted in a holster. Two holsters, in fact.

A prairie dog hunting friend wanted to carry a handgun for the occasional close shot, as well as for protection against rattlesnakes on his Wyoming prairie dog safaris. His favorite handgun is the T/C Contender, so he had one set up with a 6-inch barrel in 357 Magnum. After checking different makers' catalogs for an appropriate holster, he ended up with a custom holster for his custom Contender.

El Paso Saddlery is a company which specializes in copies of Old West and GI leather. Their holsters are of superb quality, and they are one of the few shops still offering full hand-carved floral decoration. They are also willing to do custom work. With the relaxed import laws and the influx of thousands of surplus handguns, we will be seeing a need for holsters for some of these imports. Thousands of broomhandle Mausers are available at reasonable prices on the import market, for instance. El Paso Saddlery would be a good bet for a holster for a shootable broomhandle.

A hard-to-holster handgun is the

Colt Sheriff's Model, with its shorter-than-normal barrel. With the Colt custom shop currently producing Sheriff's Models, plus the various Italian replica makers offering Sheriff's Models, there are a lot of them around. El Paso Saddlery and Old West Reproductions catalog holsters for the Sheriff's Model revolver. Old West Reproduction's hip holster is a copy of a Mexican loop style, with one or two loops attaching the pouch to the full skirt. El Paso Saddlery makes several hip holsters, in addition to their "M1895 Hardin" shoulder holster, for the Sheriff's Model. The last is a copy of a rig originally made for legendary Texas gunfighter John Wesley Hardin.

The long-barreled, large-frame handguns used for hunting big game are usually carried in shoulder holsters. The best of these, in leather, are the ones which are designed so the underarm pouch swivels forward to allow the gun to be drawn easily. DeSantis, Roy's and Alessi all manufacture swivel shoulder holsters for these large handguns. I have used an iron-sighted Ruger Super Blackhawk with such rigs and they worked well. However, for such large, heavy, scoped handguns, I find a shoulder holster, regardless of the design, to be uncomfortable. An option seldom seen, which works well with these heavy guns, is the Western-style swivel hip holster. This is a low hanging holster which ties to the thigh and is attached to a wide gunbelt with a swivel. These are available with or without a full flap, and the wide belt worn around the hips comfortably carries these heavy handguns. My sample is from Ted Blocker's Custom Holsters and is cataloged as the Grizzly 745. Bruce Nelson also makes a superb swivel field rig. I prefer this type of rig for carrying the big handguns.

A unique carrying system for the large hunting handgun is the Rybka "Packmule." This is a leather full-flap gun case which may be worn on the belt or attached to a shoulder strap. It includes a double flap to protect the scope, as well as pouches on the face for spare ammunition and a folding knife. The "Packmule" was designed for the Mag-na-port 8⅜-inch scoped 44 Magnum "Stalker."

We have looked at several options for holstering the hard-to-holster handgun. The generic fit nylon holster is easily modified, or one can opt for the finest in holsters, the handmade custom holster. If you have an out-of-the-main-stream handgun and want a holster for it, don't give up. They are available.

●

When the Canada honkers are on the make, the shotgun range may well be this side of sixty yards.

THE MAKING OF

I SUPPOSE there are almost as many methods of downing a goose as there are gunners, but there is just about one good way of coming to terms with a high flyer. When the fabulous English gunner of the early 19th century said he would rather see a gunner miss in good style than hit in poor style, both being accidents, he touched upon a gunning truth that still has application. When shooters talk of sustained lead in shooting high-flying Canada honkers, they forget one very important essential: While the average speed of a high-flying goose is about 45 miles an hour, this is seldom the basis upon which actual lead is cal-

culated. The gunner must always base his lead on the *apparent* speed of his quarry—anything from 10 miles an hour on up to 45.

Actually, there are only two shots where that 45 miles per hour speed is the basis for the lead—a direct passer and an incomer. And to the confusion of the experts punditing on sustained lead, the incomer is always blotted out as the shot is taken. Where then the lead?

I have gunned with my hunting partner Jack Morgan on many goose shooting expeditions when he made out his limit of five geese with as many shots. During a week's gunning, he

maybe missed two or three shots. And, let it be whispered, I have equalled his gunning, often taking shot for shot. By the same token, I have watched other hopeful gunners use up a box of heavy wildfowling loads and maybe scratch down a goose or two.

The difference is that gunners like Jack Morgan know that the telling shot doesn't begin with the flight overhead, the wild music of Canada honkers calling. The beginning of all successful shooting starts long before the blind is occupied. It starts with the gun, of course, but not from the standpoint of ranging, though that is important. It starts with gun responsive-

by FRANCIS E. SELL

A GOOSE DINNER

ness—something that is often lacking in pass-shooting guns. If a gunner comes to his pass-shooting blind with a shotgun that isn't correct for him in every way, he has a shooting handicap tough to overcome.

Take proper gun weight as a prime example. If a gun feels heavy, it is too heavy. If a gun feels light in hand, it is too light. When a gun feels neither light nor heavy, it complements the gunner's pointing ability, furthers it in fact. While all this sounds downright simple, it takes plenty of gunning savvy to come up with the right weight. In my own case, I handle best a gun weighing between 6½ pounds,

to not more than 7¼ pounds. My ideal gun weight is a fraction under 7 pounds.

Gun weight, of course, is only one element of proper gun pointing, though an important one. For example, the shotgun rib is seldom given the consideration it deserves. Most shotgun ribs serve better as an aiming device rather than a pointing element, and there is a great difference in aiming and pointing on a goose pass.

After a lot of shooting, testing, experimenting, I developed a tapered rib that took all the aiming out of my gunning. This rib, used on my double, tapered from 5/16-inch at the breech to

a trim 3/16-inch at the muzzle. This is complemented by a flat front sight tapered so it appears part of the rib. Its chief function in gunning is to prevent over and under shooting.

Looking down this rib, the converging sides seem to reach infinity at about forty yards. There is not an aiming element in it, but it is a beautiful pointing element. The stocking, of course, complements the pointing. When a gunner brings his gun to shoulder, he should be looking down that rib, all elements of gun mounting attended to. This, of course, is even true of rifles designed for off-hand snap-shooting. In short, any sporting

Balance just 4 inches in front of the forward trigger is an element many heavy wildfowling guns miss, but not this 20-gauge magnum stocked by Sell for his own use.

arm designed for shooting off-hand should come up already aligned.

I recall that the editor of this journal of shooting enlightenment examined a rifle I developed for off-hand deer shooting when he paid a visit to my wilderness hideout. He, to put it mildly, was much impressed. Said he, "I know this is the first rifle I ever had in hand I feel I could take a running deer with, off-hand."

A flight is coming over my hideout. I judge the range to be around sixty yards, though I do not make the estimate in yards. My assessment is more personal and consists of a basic proposal. Is the flight in or out of range? If those geese are actually flying within eighty yards of my hideout, I would consider them in range—a proposition confirmed by a lot of shotgun testing especially of the line of guns I developed and shoot. The 20-gauge magnum I use will put a five-pellet hit of #2 shot on a goose-size target at this extreme distance, if I do my part correctly.

All this brings up a crucial point—

how to judge range against a stormy winter sky, a flight of Canada honkers coming over. With me, the problem of range judgment is more or less solved by how the bird appears at extreme range, as well as the size. Unless the color pattern is distinct and clear cut, the targets are out of range for me. I sometimes make a further estimate by gun pointing. If the wing spread more than covers the twin barrels of my double, that goose is well out of range. A goose is large. At 150 yards he will appear bigger than a mallard at 50 yards and invite a lot of futile banging away by the sky-scraping pass-shooter. So the first essential is the question—in range or out?

Leading a winging target is essential. More geese are missed by improper lead than any other factor. There is no possible way to use that sustained lead so beloved of the experts. The apparent speed may vary from a mere 15 miles an hour from the standpoint of the gunner to, on a few occasions, the actual speed of the target.

Actual lead is more or less a personal problem of the gunner, different from gunner to gunner. In support of this particular gunning contention, I say that *my lead* seems about the same for all wildfowling ranges. This lead, regardless of range, *seems* about three feet. Obviously, a goose winging by my hideout at sixty yards range needs more than this. That extra lead requirement is made up by the overthrow—the time consumed in actually getting off the shot. This overthrow is automatically lengthened as the range is extended—when I am doing the shooting, anyway.

Once, while a number of people in the community thought that I might employ my time to better purpose, I spent days measuring my personal overthrow at all ranges out to eighty yards. I did this by making the shot as I swung by the target after what appeared to be three feet. The lead was progressively lengthened as the range was increased. What looked like three feet at forty yards was much shorter than what appeared to be three feet of lead at seventy yards.

This overthrow is different for different gunners as it is based on personal reaction time. In teaching gunners wing-shooting, one of the fundamental problems is to get them to develop lead based on their personal reaction time. Usually when I had them shoot as they always did, in order to get their gunning problems in perspective, they took what they called sustained lead on targets thrown by their stand at a 90-degree angle, then they stopped their guns as they pulled. To show them what they did wrong, I had them swing by a stationary target set in the river. Here, if they actually hit the target, which they usually did, it was because they stopped their gun swing. Some of the more stubborn cases spent weeks shooting over these water targets before they managed to consistently make the shots with a dynamic moving gun. After that, the rest was easy. Several sessions at those fast claybirds thrown at 90 degrees and they were better than average wildfowlers.

The only problem they collectively had to overcome was selecting a gun within a weight limit with which they were familiar. Previously, they came to the passes with those heavyweight magnum 10 and 12 gauges tipping the scales at nine to as much as eleven pounds. The extra weight played hob with their timing and, while they may have added a few yards of extra range, they had better trade those extreme distances for a gun they could handle.

Even at the expense of reiteration, let's take a look at the pass guns I developed, a 20- and 12-gauge. A good starting point is Jack Morgan's gun. When I first knew Jack, he shot a

Author with a 20-gauge Newman double, 30-inch barrels. Field-shooting whitefront geese, this gun with 1¼ ounces of Winchester-Western copper-plated 4s proved deadly.

heavy 12-gauge magnum. He got his share of geese, but he didn't turn in an outstanding performance by any means. Then one day, he used a 20-gauge double, a gun I had developed and personally stocked to my own specifications. Jack was about my size, so there was no big problem of fit.

I missed one shot that day—got my feet tangled up in the tulies and slowed my swing enough to get a few tail feathers for my effort. I finished the day with five honkers for six shells. Jack ran his limit of five without a miss with that 20. He said nothing. But as the flight continued, he would swing on them, take down the gun, look at it, shake his head.

Back in camp, he carried the gun to his trailer, and later that evening he brought it over to me all cleaned and polished.

"Spud, I have been looking through those barrels. Everything seems different, forcing cones, choke cones—the whole shooting match."

I nodded, remembering.

My first experimental work on the 20 and 12 gauges started with the forcing cones. The conventional short cones left a lot to be desired. As I lengthened the cones, the patterns improved, became more uniform. Eventually, I found that a forcing cone length of 1½ inches gave maximum results in both gauges, once the chokes were properly adjusted. Both the 12 and 20 gauges are usually adjusted with 7½ shot size. In adjusting the chokes for the 20-gauge, I found that several thousandths of choke could be removed for top performance with size 4 and size 2 shot. In the gun he tried that day, the right barrel carried .020-inch for choke; the left barrel had .022-inch. The barrel carried an overbore of .003-inch, checking out at .618-inch.

Then I give the choke cones the same 1½-inch length as the forcing cones. The choke parallels were long enough to contain the entire shot charge before the launch. My highest percentage of 2s and 4s in a killing 30-inch circle was obtained in the 20-gauge when that several thousandths of choke was removed. With 1¼ ounces of 2s or 4s, I found 4s shot tightest in the left barrel, and when 2s were shot, the right barrel gave the higher percentage, putting an average of 55 pellets in a 30-inch circle at 80 yards.

So there you have it. What it takes to down one of those high flying Canada honkers on a pass starts a long way back of the actual shooting, not when the wild music of their calling fills the gray winter sky, and you toe the line for the shot. Think of it. ●

SIGNS

by JIM PECK

FOR DECADES, handloaders have used certain "signs" as guides to the pressure generated by smokeless powder in their firearms. Since pressure in a firearm is only generated when a shot is fired, knowing what pressure signs to look for after you fire a shot can be pretty important.

To observe the signs of pressure, you will need three things which are normally at the range with you: your handloaded ammo, your firearm and your target. The signs of pressure will appear most reliably if you have a commercial bolt-action or single shot firearm. These signs are not reliable for semi-automatics, revolvers or military-based actions.

(Top right) A reduced load produces this sort of primer in a 30-06 case. (Above) A normal load can be read from the primer in a 30-06 case. (Right) A warm load is indicated by the primer in this 30-06 case.

One of the most visible and reliable signs of pressure available to the average handloader is the changing appearance of the primer as pressure increases. Since primers from different manufacturers will change their appearances at different rates, we highly recommend that you stick to one brand of primer while working up your loads. We are going to divide primer appearance into five categories corresponding to the types of loads which produce them: reduced, normal, warm, hot and destructive.

OF PRESSURE

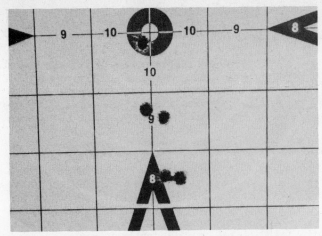

Target #1—a starting load using 57 grains of IMR 7828 in a pressure-sensitive, short-throated 270 Winchester.

Target #2—four loads later, 60 grains of IMR 7828 in the same rifle, on the same day. Good enough.

Reduced loads generate low to moderate pressure and produce a rounded primer with a pushed-in center. The firing pin dimple has a rounded bottom and rounded sides which often form a curve across the top of the primer. The top surface is also curved as it rolls over the outer rim of the primer toward the edge of the primer pocket, but may have a small flat area on top representing a mild load, such as the one pictured. Reduced loads usually do not produce much pressure-related deformation in a primer or place any strain on a firearm. Such loads, with a small charge of fast to medium-burning powder, are quiet and can produce excellent accuracy. They are for use on fur-bearing animals, local pests, and with cast bullets for all of the above plus hunting and benchrest competition. A case used for reduced loads may be reloaded over 50 times if shot in a well-chambered rifle.

Normal loads represent an increase in force, power and pressure compared to reduced loads. This is the pressure level for which the firearm and the loading components were designed. The normal load leaves the outer edge of the primer rounded as pictured. The top surface of the primer has usually been flattened to some degree by the bolt face and the center has a smooth indentation where the firing pin hit. This indentation does not appear as deep or as rounded as in the reduced load, but is more sharply defined at its outer edge. Normal loads produce good to excellent accuracy. Velocity is usually close to factory specifications for a given bullet weight. Case life is excellent, often exceeding 10 or 20 reloads in many calibers.

Warm handloads produce the first signs of deformation on the primer due to higher than normal pressure. Warm loads usually flatten the top of the primer so that the outer edge next to the case has very little, if any, rounded appearance. The firing pin indentation in the center of the primer will be well defined. Different rifles tend to flatten primers to various degrees, but the firing pin indentation will often have a thin raised edge or lip around its margin like the ones pictured. Warm loads represent the marginal upper limit of safety in handloading. This is not an ideal operating condition for any rifle. Accuracy in some rifles is good, but in most it is beginning to fall off. Case life is shorter than with normal loads but may still be acceptable. Some warm loads when fired on warm or hot days may become hot loads.

The hot load often produces a primer with a large flattened surface which may spread completely across the primer pocket. Pressure is so high that the primer metal and often the brass case itself is being deformed. The entire primer surface looks as if it has been slammed back against the bolt face and firing pin, which is exactly what happened. The outer edge of the primer may appear sharp and occa-

Target #3—too much powder, the group opened up and the primer went from normal to warm at 61 grains of IMR 7828.

These are the warm and normal loads that correspond to targets #2 and #3. Not much gained by the pressure increase.

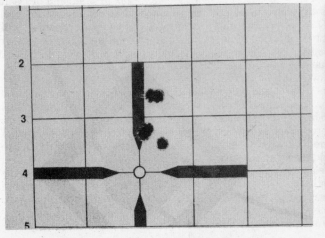

Typical firearms in which one can reliably read signs of pressure. Less tightly breeched models produce different signs.

sionally is raised where it has been forced beyond the primer pocket onto the base of the brass case. Sometimes a black smudge of burned powder will ring the outer edge of the primer and may extend onto the base of the case. The dimple in the center has been driven back against the firing pin and has formed around it, making a crater with a raised rim you can feel and see. The bottom of the dimple is often raised like the center of an impact crater. High pressure in the case has forced the thinned metal in the center of the dimple to follow the firing pin back for a short way, leaving a small raised area in its center. The brass case

Normal and very warm primers in 243 Winchester seem grotesque at this enlargement, but they are very real.

head, which usually has slightly rounded surfaces, is sometimes flattened.

Top accuracy was achieved before the warm load, and is now gone for all practical purposes. Case life is very limited and in some cartridges may be only one shot. The hot primer condition represents a potentially dangerous situation. The temperature of the firearm as it heats up from shooting can raise the already dangerous pressure to the destructive level where damage to the firearm and shooter are possible. Pull the bullets from all hot loads and lower the powder charge to a safe level or work up new loads with different components.

Destructive pressure is seldom noticed on the primer. When it is, the totally flattened primer often has a black smudge of burned powder around the outer edge and is perforated. Perforation is a black hole in the center of the primer where the firing pin hit it. Perforation is caused by the excessive pressure in the brass case overcoming the yield strength of the metal in the primer and causing it to blow out. A perforated or missing primer can allow the excessive chamber pressure to blow back toward the shooter at initial pressures often exceeding 55,000 pounds per square inch. In most modern well-designed actions, this gas is diverted away from the shooter. I recently saw a Remington Model 700 which had been destructively overloaded. The hot high-pressure gasses that had escaped from the ruptured case were diverted down away from the shooter and had blown the magazine follower through the bottom of the stock. The bolt on this rifle had to be hammered open to extract the case. The shooter was OK but pretty shook up and the event was testimony to a well-designed action and a foolish handloader.

A noticeable increase in the effort required to open the action of your firearm after firing a shot is a sign that

forebodes trouble. It is the first feel of truly excessive and potentially dangerous pressure. This feel or stiffness upon opening the action is often experienced after shooting a load which produced a warm to hot primer. Check the primer. If it's normal, have a gunsmith check out the firearm. If the primer looks warm or hot, stop shooting those particular loads. Pull the bullets, dump the powder and go back to a known load that gives you good accuracy, or work up a fresh set of loads with different components.

The target should be the object which shows the results of your handloading efforts. When shooting from a bench or steady rest, the size of the groups should get smaller (all else being equal) as the right load for your firearm is approached. Once pressure has passed this right load, the groups will usually start to open up. This happens because the increased pressure generated by additional powder gets beyond what we might call the comfort zone of your firearm, and it shows this by throwing the bullets into a larger pattern. The loads preferred by most firearms will occur in a range of normal pressures, prior to the warm primer. If your best groups don't seem to be small enough and the primer is starting to look warm, change powder type, and work up a fresh set of loads. Most rifles will do their best with only a couple of different load combinations. In loading for practical accuracy, it is worthwhile to try several different powder, primer and bullet combinations. Don't load past a warm primer.

A good loading manual is an absolute necessity for reliable, accurate and safe handloading. A manual should tell you a bit about your cartridge, give specific guidelines to follow in choosing the best powder(s), bullet weight(s), primers and brass. It should also point out any special tips, loading hints or hazards which will help you in loading your particular cartridge.

The objective of most handloading, aside from cost savings, is to find the ideal balance between accuracy and velocity for a particular firearm, and to do so safely. Once a series of loads have been put together, the only pressure signs most of us have to follow are the appearance of the primer, the feel of the action as it is opened and the group on the target, once a series of shots have been fired. These signs have been used for decades with good success. They should work for you. ●

by J. B. WOOD

HANDGUNS TODAY:

AUTOLOADERS

The experimental 50 Auto (left) with a 45 Winchester Magnum. Formidable!

THE USE of injection-moulded polymers (we no longer say "plastic") for handgun grip frames is not startlingly new. It has been done in the past by Heckler & Koch, Glock, and others. Now it's the way Gaines Chesnut has done it and it's absolutely brilliant. The pistol is called the Syn-Tech, and the chambering is for 22 Long Rifle.

An aerospace alloy receiver and a polymer-sheathed barrel, along with the polymer grip frame and magazine, keep the weight to 21 ounces in this full-sized pistol. The magazine, with its ribbon-type constant-force spring, holds 15 rounds. A spring of the same type powers the sear, giving a superb trigger pull.

The grip shape is unusual, tapering toward the bottom. Many shooters who have handled the pistol say that this

shape gives better control. For those of the old school, a more conventional grip frame will be offered as an option. Another option, in the near future, will be a fully-adjustable Millett rear sight. And an entirely-contained 25-round magazine is also in the works.

In the same category—that is, having a non-metal grip frame—is the new P-30 from **Grendel, Incorporated**. It is the second commercially-made pistol in 22 WMR chambering (the AMT/IAI Automag II was the first). In its own way, the P-30 is also a remarkable engineering achievement. The operating parts are made of high-grade steel, and the grip frame is formed out of glass-reinforced Zytel.

The removable magazine holds 30 rounds of 22 WMR, and the magazine release is reversible for left-handers. There will be three versions of the gun: a standard model with a 5-inch barrel; the P-30M with a 5.6-inch barrel and muzzle-brake; and the P-30LM, with an 8-inch barrel and provisions for mounting scopes and other accessories. In the standard P-30 model, the dimensions are about the same as for any 22 Long Rifle trail gun.

The Automag III from **Irwindale Arms** in 30 Carbine has now been joined by a version in 9mm Winchester Magnum, one of the two rounds that were originally developed for the Wildey. I have fired the new 9mm WM gun with handloads devised by Walt Jones of IAI,

and the performance is impressive. If you like the Automag III, and consider the 30 Carbine to be too small, then here is an option. Or, you can go to the Javelina in 10mm.

On more than one occasion, I have asked Harry Sanford of IAI whether he would ever consider bringing back the original Automag, not in 44 AutoMag, but in 45 Winchester Magnum. According to Harry, the production cost would make the retail price outrageous. Now, though, he *has* done something with that cartridge: It's called the Automag IV, a beautiful monster in 45 Winchester Magnum chambering.

It is a long-slide gun, with a 6½-inch barrel, and it weighs in at 46 ounces. I haven't fired it yet, but I have handled the prototype, and it has excellent balance. As with all IAI guns, it's made of stainless steel, and in

news this year from **Glock**. First, there is the Glock 20, in 10mm Auto. In that chambering, the magazine holds 15 rounds. In overall dimensions, it is very slightly larger than the standard Glock 17. And, there is the long-awaited version in 45 Auto, the Glock 21. It will have a 13-round magazine, and production was scheduled for mid-1990. Dimensional data were not available at the time this was written.

So many new items from **Smith & Wesson** that there's room here for only a brief description of each one: There's the 9mm Model 3913, a small and flat pistol with an eight-shot magazine, and its counterpart for the ladies, a LadySmith version. The latter has a different frame shape and other special points to make it user-friendly for the female shooter.

Partly as a result of their

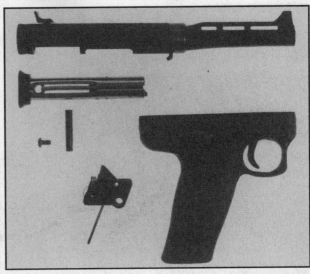

The new 22 LR Syn-Tech pistol from Ram-Line is full-sized, but weighs only 21 ounces.

The Ram-Line Syn-Tech, field-stripped.

that material these people are artists. The grips are carbon fiber, and the sights are by Millett. The magazine capacity is seven rounds.

There were two items of big

work on a 10mm pistol for the FBI, Smith & Wesson now has two new pistols in the same general caliber-category. One is the Model 1006, a 10mm pistol with, appropriately, a 10-shot

The new Glock 20 in 10mm Auto holds 15 rounds.

capacity (nine in the magazine). It is offered with either a straight or curved backstrap, depending on which Delrin wraparound grip is chosen. As the "06" suffix will tell you, the pistol is in stainless.

The other pistol, and the newest addition, is the Model 4006. It is chambered for a new cartridge, made by **Winchester**, the 40 S&W. The gun has the appearance of a reduced-size Model 1006. This is sort of appropriate, as the same description could be applied to the cartridge, a very slightly scaled-down 10mm. The magazine of the Model 4006 holds 11 rounds, and the 40 S&W cartridge has muzzle figures of 990 fps and 392 fpe.

The steel/alloy 22 Long Rifle sport pistols from S&W have now been joined by an all-stainless-steel version, the Model 2206. For those who like this neat plinking/target gun, but who want a bit more weight, there you are. The Model 2206

tional Rifle Association. A World War II Marine Ace and Medal of Honor winner, Foss certainly deserves this tribute. Only 2500 pieces will be made, appropriately cased, and the announced price was $1,375.

The ruggedly reliable **Ruger**

weighs 35 ounces with the 4½-inch barrel, and 39 ounces in 6-inch. It is offered with either a fixed or a fully-adjustable rear sight.

Last year in this space I predicted that the little 380 Mustang would soon be offered by **Colt** in stainless steel. Now, it is, in both the regular and the Plus II versions. Over the past few weeks, I have been shooting a Colt 45 Double Eagle, and I have found it to be everything you expect from a Colt pistol—reliable, and extremely accurate. In fact, on paper targets from a casual rest, the Double Eagle delivered smaller groups than my "old" single-action Colt pistol.

The Colt Custom Shop announced a limited edition engraved version of the classic Government Model in honor of Joe Foss, president of the Na-

Browning has a new version of the 22 Buck Mark, called the Target 5.5—the number referring to the .900-inch diameter bull-type 5½-inch barrel. It's like the Silhouette version, but with a shorter barrel. The hooded sights are on a track

The 22 LR P-98 pistol from American Arms and a test target.

The PSP-25 from K.B.I., a finely-made copy of the 25 Browning Baby, made in the U.S.

(Far left and left) This is the P9C, the compact 9mm from Springfield Armory, Wood shot very well.

P-85 has been around a relatively short time, but there are already two new versions. One of these is of all-stainless construction, and it proves that the P-85 can not only work well, but also look handsome. The other new P-85, developed with police use in mind, is the "Decocker" version. Instead of the regular safety system, the lever on the slide safely drops the hammer, then springs back to its original position. Aside from the law enforcement applications, there will be many other shooters who may prefer this system.

that also adapts to scope mounting, and the contoured walnut grips have a comfortable thumb rest. Shooters who want a match-quality 22 pistol at an affordable price should check this one out.

The **Taurus** 92-series pistols and the compact versions are expected soon in 41 Action Express, with 9mm convertibility. In the meantime, Taurus Firearms and **Emerging Technologies** have teamed up to offer the first factory pistol-laser package in the industry. In either finish, blue or satin nickel,

The LadySmith S&W Model 3913 has its own frame.

all length to 6½ inches, and shorten the grip-frame accordingly. To keep it flat, put in a seven-round single-row magazine. Change the safety to a frame-mounted type, with ambidextrous levers. Give it checkered rubber grips and a fully-adjustable rear sight, make it all-steel, and keep the weight to just over 30 ounces. Got all that? It's the Firestar from **Interarms**. I haven't fired it yet, but it looks marvelous.

I have recently been shooting a pistol that is difficult to cate-

9 is in 9mm Para. chambering, but others are offered. The Göncz company is located in North Hollywood, California.

American Arms of North Kansas City, Missouri, is now making or importing most of the excellent ERMA line, and the most recently added item is worthy of note—it's the 22 Long Rifle P-98, an almost perfect replica of the famed Walther P-38 in slightly reduced size. I fired the prototype of this pistol in 1989, and it was extremely accurate. It also worked per-

The Grendel P-30M pistol is ambitious though not pretty.

The standard Grendel 22 WMR P-30 is field-stripped here.

the Taurus PT92 is available with a matching-finish Laser Aim LA1 sight, complete with mount, rings, charger, and a custom case. The underside mount allows the use of regular sights, or a scope.

Springfield Armory continues to offer their regular and custom versions of the time-tested Model 1911-A1, and the multi-caliber Omega. In their version of the Italian CZ75 copy, the P9, there is now a long-slide model with a ported barrel and slide, called the P9LSP. For some time now I have been shooting the smaller version, the P9C, and in close-range combat-style shooting I have found its performance to be superb. It is the most accurate pistol of its size that I have ever fired.

Now that the **Wildey** company has begun to catch up on all of the back-orders, some new items are being offered. One of these is an optional 12-inch barrel in 45 Winchester Magnum or 475 Win. Mag. For handgun hunters who may find the nice Wildey polish to be too reflective, there is now an optional matte finish. Grips of smooth uncheckered walnut are available. For those who want it, there's a squared guard. And, a sight rib that mates with a B-Square scope

mount. My own standard 45 Win. Mag. Wildey performs flawlessly.

The **New Detonics** company, now located in Phoenix, Arizona, offers four restyled guns in 45 Auto—the small Combatmaster, the mid-sized Servicemaster, the full-sized target Scoremaster, and the Compmaster, the last-named with a built-in compensator. Also new this year is the Ladies' Escort, which is essentially a Combatmaster that has been modified to make it just right for the lady who wants 45 power. With the use of aerospace polymer finishes, it is even offered in a choice of three color combinations, with gold accents.

There's a new pistol that looks Walther-ish, but has a single-action trigger system. It is just over 5½ inches long, and comes in 32 or 380 chambering. It's made by **Accu-Tek** in Chino, California, and the AT-32 and AT-380 that I have examined are well-made little pistols. The safety is a firing-pin-block style, located on the slide, and the magazine holds five rounds in either caliber. They, also, have a prettied-up version for the ladies.

Someone at the **Star** factory had a brilliant idea: Take the Model 30 9mm, and make it single action. Reduce the over-

gorize. Its general "look" and 18-round magazine tend to place it among the assault pistols, but for several reasons it doesn't belong there. It is the **Göncz** High-Tech, and a look at its construction shows that some high technology, indeed, went into its making. Ergonomically perfect, it has a firing mechanism that is beautifully simple. Precision is evident everywhere, the sights are fully adjustable, and the accuracy is outstanding. My GA-

fectly with six different cartridges. Also new this year from American Arms is the 22 Long Rifle Woodmaster, a re-creation of the old Woodsman pistol.

One fine ERMA pistol that is not handled by American Arms is the serious target gun, the ESP-85A. Convertible from 22 LR to 32 S&W LWC, it has all of the accoutrements of the international competition pistol, including a firing pin block that allows unlimited dry-firing for practice. The trigger is adjust-

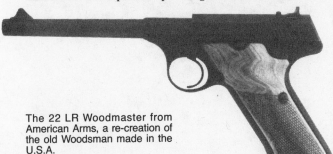

The 22 LR Woodmaster from American Arms, a re-creation of the old Woodsman made in the U.S.A.

Wood's regular-production Wildey in 45 WM, with the 10-inch barrel.

The 380 Bersa Model 85 (below) has a 13-round magazine; Model 83 holds seven (bottom).

able five ways. The U.S. importer is **Precision Sales International** of Westfield, Massachusetts, and the price is less than you might think.

Magnum Research is testing a Desert Eagle that is chambered for an experimental 50-caliber auto pistol round. If this one goes into production, it will be the first selfloader to have a ½-inch bore. I have no data on the 50 Auto round, but I have a sample cartridge, and it is a monster! I have been shooting a 9mm Bernardelli P018, also imported by Magnum Research, and it has become one of my favorite nines. The British-designed Victory pistol from Magnum Research is still in the works.

A gun reported on here last year has a new name. It was called the "Maverick," but that trademark was already being used by a shotgun maker. So, it's now the Model JS-9mm by **Stallard Arms**. It has a blowback action and is of average large-frame size, with a substantial weight—48 ounces. Striker-fired and single action, it has an eight-round magazine. I have tried the pistol, and it works fine. For the person who wants a "full nine" at a price of only $140, it's a good choice.

The SIG/Sauer P228, announced last year in Europe, has now reached our shores, and **Sigarms** has it. A reduced-size version of the popular P226, it has a 13-round magazine. Mechanically and in operation, it has the same features as the other SIG/Sauer pistols. Its size would make it ideal for law enforcement back-up or off-duty use, or for personal defense among licensed-carry civilians. Sigarms just moved into new quarters in Exeter, NH.

From both **Beretta** and **Heckler & Koch**, the news involves medium-frame pistols in 380 chambering. These guns were announced last year, and have now become generally available. Beretta has the Model 84F and Model 85F, bringing their 380 pistols closer in looks and

There is now a 380 version of the little Davis pistol.

The Göncz High-Tech GA-9 in 9mm Parabellum has an 18-round magazine.

Wood likes the Göncz a lot.

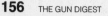

operation to the 9mm Model 92F of the U.S. military forces. In like manner, the Heckler & Koch P7K3 is very much like their P7M8 and P7M13 in 9mm Para. The P7K3 is convertible from 380 to 22 Long Rifle and 32 Auto, and I can state that these conversions work.

Speaking of conversions, a 10mm unit is now available for the **L.A.R. Grizzly**, and it has worked well on my gun. **Auto-Ordnance** also has a 10mm kit for 1911-A1-pattern guns, and now offers their Thompson pistol in that chambering. Another item from Auto-Ordnance is a "completion kit" for those who

have the increased-capacity frame from **Para-Ordnance**. And that Canadian company is now making a line of complete 45 pistols in three sizes, with 12-, 13-, and 14-round magazines. Para-Ordnance also has a new 10mm with a 16-round

magazine, the P16-10.

Action Arms Ltd., whose Evan Whildin invented the 41 Action Express cartridge, finally has their AT-88 series of pistols in that chambering, with 9mm Para conversions. **F.I.E. Corporation** got there

Browning's 5.5 Target Buck Mark—their newest 22.

The 10mm S&W Model 1006 comes as shown with straight grip, or in a curved version.

The S&W Model 4006 chambers the new 40 S&W cartridge.

The IAI Automag IV pistol shoots the 45 Winchester Magnum.

The 10mm Javelina from IAI has that handsome long-slide look.

The Norinco Tokarev in 7.62x25mm is now offered with a conversion to 38 Super Auto.

China Sports' Model 59 is the Chinese version of the Russian Makarov.

first with a 9mm/41AE package, in their TZ75 Series 88. I have fired one of these extensively, and its performance was perfect, with really fine accuracy. F.I.E. also has the 9mm TZ75/88 in two ported longslide Competition Models. In their TA90 version of the Italian pistol, **Excam** has a pretty custom piece with the slide and frame in color case-hardened finish.

The **Bersa** pistols from Argentina have been around for a while, in 22 Long Rifle and 380 Auto, and I have always liked

Another entry in the convertible category is the new Jericho Model 941 from **K.B.I., Incorporated** of Harrisburg, Pennsylvania. As its model designation implies, it can change from 9mm Para. to 41 Action Express, and it comes in a kit with spare magazines and other accessories. Attributed to IMI of Israel, the Jericho has some similarity to the Italian versions of the CZ75, but there are several differences. Another really fine little pistol from K.B.I. is the PSP-25, an exact re-creation of the 25 Browning

The Colt Double Eagle 45 Auto double action—at last.

The Colt Mustang Plus II, now in stainless steel, has the long grip.

The first Colt Mustang, now in stainless steel, has a short grip.

them. They offer high quality at reasonable cost, and they work. In recent years, the finish and workmanship of these guns has been excellent. They are now marketed in the U.S. by **Eagle Imports** of Ocean, New Jersey, and there are two new 380 models. The Model 83 has a single-row seven-round magazine, and the Model 85 has a double-row 13-round magazine. The slide hold-open system is internal.

Baby, in regular steel, with a superb blue finish. The PSP-25 is made by **Precision Small Parts** of Charlottesville, Virginia, and their name says it all.

China Sports, Incorporated, importer of the pistols made by Norinco, now has the Type 59, the Chinese-made version of the Russian Makarov. It is chambered for the 9x18mm cartridge, which is between the

380 Auto and the 9mm Para. in size and power. The Chinese version of the Tokarev pistol is now offered in 7.62x25mm with a conversion barrel and recoil spring for 38 Super Auto. This news made me smile, as I had converted a Tokarev in this manner about twenty years ago, and I still shoot it.

Armscorp of America has the G90 (full-sized) and the G91 (compact) 9mm pistols from

Gamba of Italy. These appear to be nicely made, and seem to be the same as the other Italian CZ75-types. Armscorp still has the ugly-but-excellent little 9mm SD9 pistol from Israel, and they are also importing a good Argentine-made version of the FN Hi-Power.

TD Arms of New Baltimore, Michigan, has the 9mm Zastava CZ99, a pistol that combines some of the features of the SIG/

The SIG/Sauer P228—a reduced-size version of the P226.

This limited edition tribute to Joe Foss is from the Colt Custom Shop.

The Bernardelli P018 9mm can be had with hand-checkered walnut grips.

The Ruger P-85 is now available in stainless steel.

This is the new Decocker version of the Ruger P-85.

You can get F.I.E.'s TZ75/88 in 9mm with components for 41 Action Express conversion.

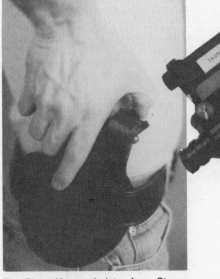
The Piece-Keeper holster from Strong Holsters has a unique safety latch.

The Taurus PT92 pistol, with the LaserAim sight installed.

The new rear sight from Pachmayr is low-profile and rounded.

Sauer and the Walther P88. It is not Czech, as the "CZ" might imply, but is Yugoslavian.

The well-made and inexpensive **Davis** P-32 now has a 380 counterpart, the P-380, with no increase in size. The **Jennings/ Bryco** company also has an equally-good pair in the same two chamberings, in similar small size, with both the 32 and the 380 called Model 38. Larger guns from both makers are still in the works. Meanwhile, **Raven Arms** still makes the utterly reliable MP-25, now with a new rotary safety and hi-tech-looking grips that have vertical-diagonal grooving.

Fully-adjustable replacement rear sights by **Millett** and **MMC** are well-known, and now there's another: **Pachmayr** has a new low-profile sight with rounded edges that is made for most of the popular 9mm-sized pistols. It is available in plain black, white outline, or with twin white dots for three-dot sight systems. CNC-machined from solid steel, it should be practically indestructible.

The **Strong Holster Company** is offering a new holster called the "Piece-Keeper," with a safety latch on the thumb-break that is easily operated (if you know the trick) to free the pistol. The design of the latch, for which a patent is pending, is beautifully simple. The applications for law enforcement use are obvious. ●

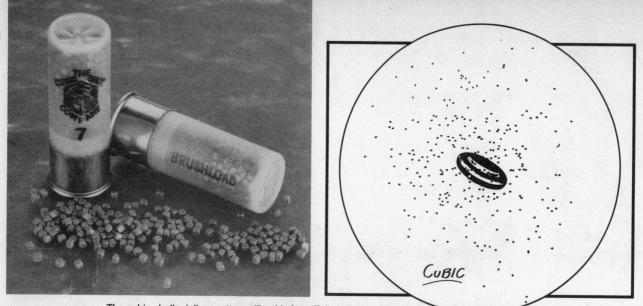

The cubic shells deliver patterns like this from Full chokes at 20 yards.

SPECIAL PURPOSE SHOTSHELLS

In Europe, shooting close-up game is handled simply. Your French or Italian shooter simply buys short-range shells—what we used to call spreader loads. Indeed, I am told that in a certain warehouse belonging to a certain U.S. shotshell producer there is a pile of spreader loads, all boxed, awaiting an upturn in the spreader market.

And there is a small business in Ohio ardently seeking those shooters in the U.S. who get caught out with tight chokes and short shots. The name is Cubic Shotshell Co. (P.O. Box 118, Youngstown, OH 44501) and the game is square—that is, cubical—shot.

Does it work? Yes. The little cubes don't fly very well so they spread fast, enough to take a Full choke out to spreads like Improved Cylinder. And when those cubes hit, they kill.

The cubic loads come in 20, 16 and 12 gauges and in a couple of short lengths—65mm and 67.5mm—if wanted. That makes them sensible in older tight-choked guns. Prices are higher than standard, but not exorbitantly so.

Over on the other side of the mountain, Rhino Replacement Parts (P.O. Box 669, Seneca, SC 29679) is furnishing 12-gauge flechette rounds, somewhat like Uncle used to make. There are twenty $1/16$-inch darts in each round, delivered, Rhino says, at 1550 fps.

The technical claims are impressive. Rhino says a Cylinder-bore 12 will put 78 percent of its twenty darts in a 30-inch circle at 40 yards. Rhino does not discuss terminal results, but in Southeast Asia flechette rounds were highly thought of for use in the jungle.

Of course, nothing is easy. Rhino quotes $19.50 for the standard packet of five rounds. They are 2¾-inch standard shells to be shot through ordinary 12-gauge guns—the darts are encased in a poly wad and packed therein in granular polyethylene.

Ken Warner

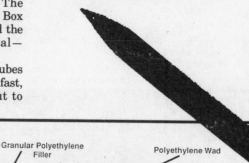

Polyethylene Flechette Container
Granular Polyethylene Filler
Polyethylene Wad
Flechettes (20)
Aluminum Disc Base
Cardboard Spacer Wad
Powerful Propellant

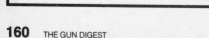

The deadly flechette can fly again, but not at tourist-class prices.

SOMEDAY ALL HANDGUNS WILL BE THIS GOOD.

While other companies were improving upon the technology of the past, GLOCK was busy perfecting the technology needed for the 21st Century.

Polymer technology.

You can see it in the complete line of GLOCK 9mm, semi-automatic pistols. Hailed by police and sportsmen alike, these remarkable handguns fire even the most advanced ammunition with unfailing accuracy.

Find out for yourself what makes the GLOCK so good. And why it's been setting new standards for simplicity, reliability, cost effectiveness and safety.

Contact your nearest dealer for a free GLOCK brochure. Or write or call GLOCK, INC. today.

·SEMI-AUTOMATIC·ＧＬＯＣＫ

Perfection

GLOCK,®INC.
P.O. Box 369 • Smyrna, Georgia 30081 • (404) 432-1202
Telex: 543353 Glock Atl UD • Fax: (404) 433-8719

When 2nd Place Won't Do No Other Slug is BRI Tough!

New for the '90s!

BRI's state-of-the-art Sabot Slug ammo has just gotten better! For the 1990s, BRI has introduced new, improved Sabot Slug loads in 12 and 20 gauge.

Slug shooters worldwide have accepted the fact that the BRI Sabot 500 Series slugs can't be beat—at the bench, or in the field! The new 500 Series 12 and 20 ga. offerings make your slug choice even easier. For extended range, pin-point accuracy, and outstanding penetration, the new 500s will continue to set the standard by which all others are measured.

Want proof? At the second annual Shotgun Slug World Championships, BRI Sabot 500s placed No. 1 at benchrest. Or, consider the fact that 12-gauge BRI Sabot 500s were used to set a prestigious **world record** for slug-gun accuracy at 100 yards—three shots, .745-inch center to center.

For the field, just ask an experienced hunter who has run BRI 500 Series Slugs through his favorite rifled-barrel slug gun— BRI stands the test. In fact, it's the only slug of its type known to have taken record-class whitetail, mule deer, elk, caribou, Dall sheep and nilgai. On game like this you don't get a second chance.

When accuracy, power and penetration are a must, no other slug is No. 1—No Other Slug is BRI Tough!

BRi

Ballistic Research Industries
Attn: Ballistics Department
953 "A" Tower Place ■ Santa Cruz, CA 95062
(Fax: 408-476-0113)

HK/Benelli Black Eagle

If you are looking for the top-of-the-line slug gun, look no further. The HK/Benelli Black Eagle has it all! Coupled with BRI Sabot slugs, the groups, the penetration and extended range will fill the bill for sportsmen looking for the best.

Each Black Eagle slug gun features a 24-inch precision rifled barrel chambered for 3-inch Magnum (handles 2¾-inch Mag-num as well). If you're looking for flexibility, the Black Eagle has it—interchangeable upland barrels are readily available. No drilling or tapping required for scope mounting—each Black Eagle comes complete with an installed scope mount base that's easily removable. Checkered walnut stocks fore and aft; and, the buttstock is fully adjustable for drop!

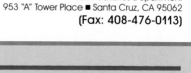

Contact your nearest HK/Benelli dealer for more information, or call HK at **703-450-1900.**

Savage Arms

Savage Arms, Inc.
Springdale Road
Westfield, MA 01085

MAKE A MULE MINIÉ:

If that's what it takes to get a replica to shoot.

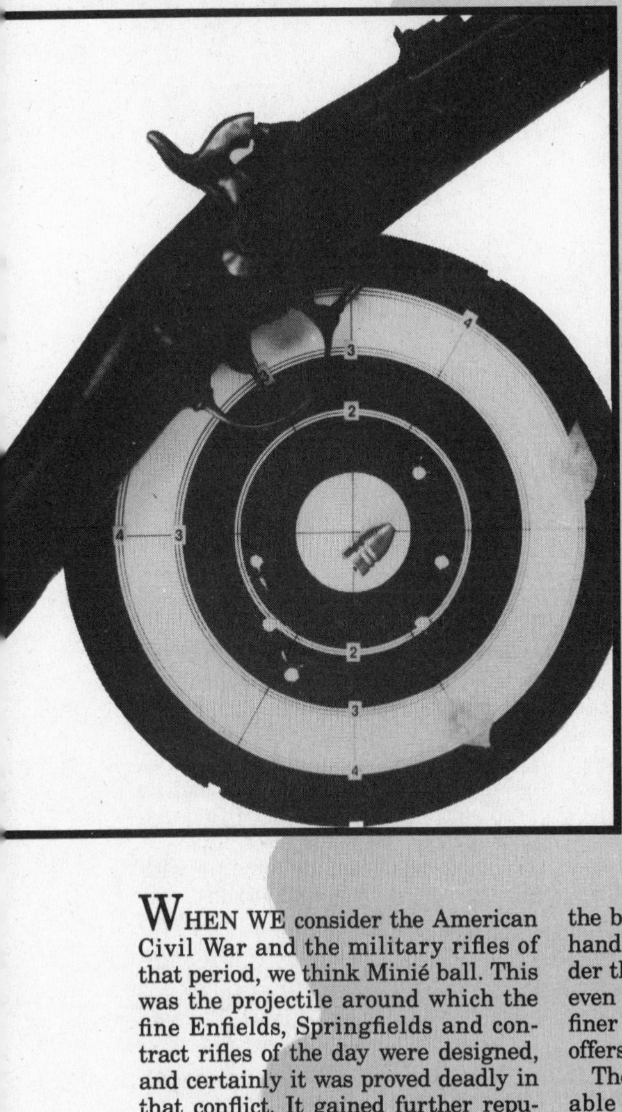

Two good groups from Mule Minié bullet #3 and the Zouave.

by ROBERT K. SHERWOOD

W HEN WE consider the American Civil War and the military rifles of that period, we think Minié ball. This was the projectile around which the fine Enfields, Springfields and contract rifles of the day were designed, and certainly it was proved deadly in that conflict. It gained further reputation for effectiveness in some of Britain's arguments abroad during the mid-19th century.

The Minié ball musket was both fast-loading and accurate, according to all historical wind and ink, and many of us who have fired an original rifled musket, using Minié projectiles and the original service charge of powder have verified this. Five rounds fired off the bench will usually go under your hand at 100 yards, and sometimes under the end of a beer can. They might even go tighter, using sights a little finer than those the military musket offers.

There are not many originals available now, and those you find cost to beat hell. Most of us don't want to shoot them; we want them to be around to look at forever. So we turn to replicas. And when we try to use Minié balls in many of these, we find accuracy is elsewhere.

To some, this presents only minor problems. Said replicas shoot well using the patched round ball and a somewhat huskier charge of powder. I have won some beer and money using a modern Zouave that way. I have even killed some animals with a round ball out of a rifle-musket barrel. It works as well from a Zouave replica as it does from a Hawken replica.

However, there are those of us who want to shoot a historically correct load, and there are matches where the rules demand it. Hunters may want the 60 percent advantage in knockdown that a Minié offers over a round ball, and certainly it is there. It can be a major consideration when hunting elk or bears with a musket.

The first solution to the problem is to purchase the one brand of replica that does shoot the Minié as well as

Navy Arms Zouave replica finally came to terms after tons of tinkering.

any original. The Parker-Hale Company, of Birmingham, U.K. produces exact copies of several models of the Enfield Rifled Musket of 577-caliber. These were used by the British, the Confederate, and the United States Armies in the middle of the 19th century, and they were popular with all users. I have one, and I am numbered among the admirers.

They are not inexpensive. They cost measurably more than other military replicas, and they aren't found on every shelf. One may, however, already have a Zouave or Springfield replica that he likes and wants to do business with it. Is he out of luck?

No, he isn't necessarily. But if he has no luck, he must have a great will to experiment.

To solve such a problem, one must first understand it. An original rifle-musket or a Parker-Hale replica is rifled with tapered-depth grooves. The grooves were cut to a depth of .015-inch at the breech end of the barrel and gradually decreased to a depth of .005-inch at the muzzle. The lands also tapered; they were about .003-inch higher at the muzzle than at the breech. The skirt of the hollow-based bullet flared into the grooves on firing and then was trued and swaged down, and a tighter gas seal was formed as the bullet traveled down the constricting sleeve of the barrel. The riflings got a good tight bite on the projectile, starting in about the first inch or so of travel, and getting tighter and more true as it went. The bullets came out true and threw to the same path each firing.

From left: Mule Miniés 1 and 2, and the successful Mule #3, cast by changing mould parts.

This rifling pattern was used at Enfield Lock, by the American military arsenals, and by those firms furnishing arms on contract to both of our Civil War armies. Parker-Hale uses the original gauges for specifications for their military musket replicas; they borrow them from the Tower of London, and they rifle in exact copy.

No other replica military musket is rifled in the aforesaid fashion. Those I have measured average about .004-inch in groove depth, with about a turn for every six feet of barrel. They cannot get the grip on the bullet that the aforementioned muskets do, obviously, and there is little if any truing action. If the bullet starts a little cockeyed, it continues that way, off toward Bill Jones' barn.

Leading and powder fouling are serious problems in such barrels. The grooves of an original or a Parker-Hale can suffer considerable clogging and still keep a good bite on bullet skirts. When the shallow-grooved and flat-rifled replica barrel gets gunked and groove-plugged, it is easy for the bullet to get jumped across the lands and the results are more funny than fun. The

corrective factor of the tightening bore is missing.

And then many replica muskets have rough bores. Shining a penlight down the muzzles of mine reveals a number of tool marks, except for the Parker-Hale, which is lapped smooth as any original. Leading and fouling problems increase in degree in a rough bore.

Someone is going to come up with the statement that his flat-rifled replica shoots Miniés into a six-inch circle at 100 yards. It can happen, especially if the barrel is long. I had a 42-inch-barreled Springfield 1863 replica that would shoot one pattern of Minié into about five inches. A friend had a twin to it that would not shoot the next Minié within four feet of the one just fired.

None of the above is a guarantee that your flat-rifled replica rifle-musket will not shoot some combination of Minié ball, charge weight, and lubricant into a five-inch circle at 100 yards, but there is probably only one such combination and what works for one musket may not do well in another apparently like it. Powder charge weight will be extremely critical, and limited by narrow parameters. Usually only one granulation class of powder will work, and lube type and base will be equally critical. Perhaps my experiences and experiments will serve to illustrate this.

I joined the long-search club in 1975 with the purchase of a Navy Arms 58 Zouave, one of the classier military replicas in appearance and finish. It was rifled with three rather shallow grooves and low lands, of no more than .004-inch difference.

The basic integrity of the iron was quickly established with patched round balls. It would throw five .575-inch balls patched with light denim lubed with Hodgdon's Spit-patch into a three-inch circle, using 90 grains of FFg to get it there. This was off a concrete bench, using sandbags under forearm and toe. It might have grouped them tighter; the iron sights and my aging visual equipment were probably greater limiting factors than any faults of the rifle-musket. I took a few prizes and a lot of beer in local matches with it.

It used Minié balls, however, to no advantage whatsoever in early trials. I tried some ready-mades before buying a mould; the first of these was a Tennessee Thunderball weighing 500 grains. I could not cover the average three-shot group of these with a Jeep can with any powder charge tried. I went to a short 315-grain bullet of the same brand, with somewhat better results, since thrown stones were more effective in terms of accuracy than the first Minié. Anyway, the Zouave would throw three out of five into three inches off the bench—and the other

two out of five went barely into Bonneville County. And 60 grains of FFg was the only charge that would get such a good result. Occasionally I could actually get a decent string of five, but most of the time I average 40 percent fliers. Leading with both Thunderballs was swift and heavy. I was lubing them with Crisco, and it didn't appear to do enough of that. Subsequent lube trials with other materials on these bullets decreased the leading but did nothing for accuracy, and they furnished other complications, to be described later.

Most good sense told me to give up my Minié quest, but every so often a Zouave owner would show up at the matches and throw a bucketful of hollow-bases through the right part of the paper. They did this without any explanation whatsoever; that right combination was some unadvertised otherwhere. This was a heavy incentive to disregard the laws of probability, and I set out to find a Minié ball load that my Zouave would group in four inches at 100 yards.

I had an RCBS mould for a 500-grain Minié. It was nearly a duplicate of the Lyman 575213 projectile. I obtained moulds for the Lyman 575494, the 575213 Old-Style, and the 577611 Minié balls.

Then I considered the lubrication situation. This is going to have a critical bearing on successful use of any cylindrical bullet in a muzzle-loading rifle. Commonly available were Crisco, Hodgdon's Spit-patch, Hodgdon's Spit-Ball revolver lube, automotive chassis lube grease, Marfak water-pump grease, Thompson/Center Maxi-Lube, beeswax, paraffin, and various Lyman

On this recovered Mule #3 Minié, the shallow grooves evidence the light bite of shallow rifling on these projectiles.

revolver bullet lubes. I had a few tubes of Lock-Eze powdered graphite.

Crisco and Spit-Patch were too thin for adequate lubrication of a bullet's travel down a 32-inch barrel. They permitted leading, and they tended to run in hot weather and cripple powder charges.

The petroleum derivatives prevented leading, but they apparently bonded with the powder fouling residue, producing a thicker layer faster that was extremely hard to scrub out. Accuracy was impossible to maintain after just six or seven shots without scrubbing the bore with a wire brush and Household Cleaner 409. Beeswax and the pistol-bullet lubes had the same fault, though not to the degree as did the petroleum based greases. Paraffin had some promise, but it wouldn't stay in the grease grooves of the bullets if they were jostled a bit.

Spit-Ball and Maxi-Lube worked reasonably well; they did permit some leading in sustained fire. I finally settled on a mixture of Spit-Ball and the powdered graphite. I would squeeze a tube of Spit-Ball into a bowl and stir two of the Lock-Eze tubes into it. The resulting black goo did all the good needed by any rifle-musket, and I use it today.

Powder charges are very critical. Too light a charge will fail to swell the Minié's basal skirt into the rifling grooves, and too hefty a load will jump the ball across the lands and strip it. It will also deform or demolish the skirt as the Minié leaves the muzzle. I could not approach accuracy with my Zouave using a lighter charge than 60 grains or a heavier load than 70 grains of FFg.

Eley musket caps were used for all trials; I wanted a big hot ignition spark.

At center is the successful Mule Minié #3, flanked by its parents, 577611, left, and Old-Style, right.

(Above) Author shooting Zouave, which he did a lot of before he made it shoot a Minié ball.

From left: Lyman 577611, RCBS 500-grain, Lyman 575213 Old-Style, and Lyman 575494. All are Miniés, but all don't shoot well in replicas.

I started shooting trials with projectiles from the afore-named moulds. It was, in general, a disappointing exercise. The first bullet tried was the Lyman 575494. It was the shortest bullet tried and should have been the best for the slow-twist rifling of the Zouave. Three or four of every five shots went down the middle; one or two went to Jones' place. Or Houlihan's. The fliers never went to the same barn twice. This could be partly explained by the fact that the Zouave had an oversize bore. It went .5848-inch across lands and .5840-inch across grooves. Short Miniés could get a lopsided start in such a bore, and certainly any .575-inch diameter bullet risked an angled launch. Both American and British standards required a somewhat tighter sleeve in their militaries; .5820-inch was maximum groove diameter at the muzzle.

The 577611 bullet should have performed more impressively than it did. It was .002-inch larger in diameter than other Minié balls tried, with a heavier, thicker skirt. It was designed for the heaviest powder charges, for use on large game. The Zouave shot it; that is, it got the projectile out the end of the barrel, but I might as well have used Tarot cards to predict the fall of shot. It was the heaviest Minié tried, weighing 530 grains, and would have been an excellent hunting projectile, had I been able to group it on the shadow of a Clydesdale horse in late afternoon. I used powder charges ranging from 55 to 120 grains without getting any pattern smaller than four feet per string of five. It performed splendidly in the Parker-Hale with a 100-grain charge of FFg, by the way.

The RCBS 500-grain gave better performance. I could keep them all on target (24″x24″) and I got two groups of about ten inches diameter with it.

At 50 yards it was hunting accurate—almost.

The Lyman 575213 Old-Style was the most consistent of the conventional Miniés tried. I got eight-inch groups with frequent bore-swabbing (wire brush and solvent after every third round); it leaded and fouled badly. The inaccuracy may have been due to the very short bearing surface back of the last grease groove. The driving bands were quite narrow, and proper upset and rifling grip may not be possible in the shallow grooves of the Zouave, especially with fouling and lead deposits clogging them.

By swapping base plugs with mould blocks never intended for them, I then produced three hybrid or "mule" Minié bullets, whence our title here. The first of these was formed by mating the 577611 tail plug with the 575494 blocks. This union produced a massive thick skirt weighing 520 grains. It lacked adequate grease groove area and interspersal and leaded badly. Like the burned buffalo, it wasn't just wild, it was stompin' bawlin' hogwild.

Using the base plug from the Old-Style in the 577611 blocks produced a 485-grain bullet that looked better than it performed. It was on an accuracy par with the Old-Style in the Zouave, although it leaded the bore more rapidly. Another grease groove might have done something for this one.

The mating of the tail plug from the Old-Style with the blocks of the thick-skirt 577611 produced a mule bullet of 495 grains, and it was a true blue Jenny. Pushed by 65 grains of FFg, a string of five or six would all go into the black of the 100-yard target. I got repeated groups miking 3 inches across centers, and shot one memorable cluster of 4 inches in diameter standing up in the infantry pose of 1864. The hybrid bullet was named

Mule #3. With this bullet and that 65 grains in the Zouave, it became a big game rifle and a skirmish tool.

I seldom find a complete explanation for performance of a given load in any muzzleloader, and this last was harder than most to interpret. I could but examine the evidence and speculate. Recovered bullets showed heavy land cuts on only the basal driving bands. Rifling marks were very light on the forward driving bands. The indication was that the swelling or "upset" of the bullet was only adequate on the aft third of the skirt. The rear driving band was the only complete seal area, and stabilization of the bullet depended on the grip of the lands on that single strip of lead.

The rear band on Mule #3 was 5/32-inch wide, apparently the right width. The parent 577611 bullet had too thick a skirt to expand properly into the rifling grooves. The hybrid Mule #1 had too wide a skirt for adequate lubrication; thus it leaded badly and accuracy went somewhere else in sustained fire. Both the other hybrids and the cast-as-writ Miniés had inadequate rear driving band surface to form an adequate gas seal, and the rail grip surface was too thin to stabilize them. They probably skidded and jumped the lands too often to establish any consecutive string of intended hits.

Until a better engineer and/or physicist—many of these there be—furnishes me a better explanation, I shall say that the driving band width of Mule Minié #3, its .002-inch greater diameter, and its thin skirt combined to make it an accurate bullet for my Zouave. The ancient unexplained maxim that decrees a mule will do bigger things better than will either parent, amateur and professional scientists notwithstanding, remains unexplained. ●

by CLAY HARVEY

SECURITY GUNS

the long-gun market, and is especially easy and comfortable to shoot.

My test gun—purchased retail from Randy Melton of Southern Firearms, Greensboro, North Carolina—left much to be desired. It shot and extracted OK, with both lengths of shells as advertised, and recoil was so mild it must be experienced to be appreciated. Feeding was another matter. I tried both Winchester and Federal shells, in several shot sizes as well as slugs, and about 20 percent of the time the next shell due out of the magazine would hang up on the cartridge interrupter assembly, just to the rear of the magazine opening in the bottom of the action. Not good.

I called Mossberg and was told that I could send the gun to a service center, or home to Connecticut for repairs if needed. The first ten rounds I fired fed without a hitch. Many

users, at best, will fire a like number of rounds to get a feel for the gun, then load it and retire it to a hidey-hole for emergency use. If I had done that with my test gun, any emergency that might have arisen would have brought with it an unpleasant CLICK instead of a BOOM. That type of surprise I can do without.

On the other hand, my test gun hit exactly on point of aim at 25 yards using Federal ⅖-ounce slugs. Accuracy was poor—groups ran around 11 inches for five shots—but since this gun/bore is a very short-range proposition, I'll take point-of-aim hits over tight grouping any time.

Incidentally, Mossberg does *not* sanction slugs for home defense, recommending instead #2 or #4 shot to prevent any chance of over-penetration. For use hard-off-the-muzzle, I agree. However, should your assailant be at the opposite end of

THE attrition rate in the security-gun market has been marked. Ill-conceived government intervention blew some companies and guns right out of the picture. Nonetheless, there are still many viable alternatives out there. Let's look at some.

Mossberg has brought forth a neat and handy little 410 pump bedubbed the Home Security 410. It holds five rounds—including one in the chamber—and will take either 2½- or 3-inch shells. The diminutive shotgun boasts an innovative pistol-grip forend, twin action bars, a muzzle compensator to reduce felt recoil—and appears from the front to be of larger bore than it is—a "spreader" choke, a short 13-inch length of pull to enable easy manipulation by teen or distaff users, a soft rubber recoil pad, and a synthetic stock and forend. The gun hefts but 6¼ pounds, wears an 18.5-inch barrel, and has a steel-to-steel lockup between barrel and barrel extension.

Additional features are a top tang safety convenient to one's thumb, twin extractors for yanking the odd recalcitrant case from its moorings, and a Mossberg Cablelock. Also provided in the cardboard container is a video that, as might be expected, is somewhat more than modestly anti-handgun in its message. It's as handy a home defender as can be had in

The SAR-4800 thumbholer makes a sporter out of the basic FN-FAL layout, doesn't it?

The SAR-8 is a thumbhole rendition of the basic HK-91 sort of action—a robust sporter.

The Saturn 30 is a stateside rendition, sporter style, of the AKM design to be produced by Feather Industries.

The SR-9 is H&K's own sporter version of the HK-91 with a bull barrel.

Harvey hunted the SAR-8 sporter and slew a hog—no problems.

curity use." This is an excellent idea that other makers will doubtless copy. Kudos to Mossberg.

Although the UZI carbine is no longer available, the tradition continues through the UZI pistol from **Action Arms**. And while the tube-fed, Timber Wolf 357 pump carbine may not be deemed by all to be a typical security arm, it's as viable for that purpose as, for example, a Marlin Camp Gun, in my view. It is quick to load, holds ten rounds of effective ammunition, fires as quick as a flick of the wrist, is light and maneuverable, and can be handled easily by smaller members of the family.

The Ultra-Dot optical sight from Action Arms is perhaps the most compact unit of its type. It offers no magnification, but boasts an illuminated red dot that makes hitting easy, and without all the tremor associated with typical handgun optics.

New from U.S. **Repeating Arms Company** is a corrosion-resistant Sandstrom 9A phosphate coating on the alloy-receiver Model 1300 Stainless Marine pumpgun. In addition to the receiver, 41 internal parts are coated with the substance, which the factory

The popular Defender pump shotgun can be had with a 28-inch vent rib barrel fitted with Winchokes for the household protector who might like to hunt with his defense shotgun. The M1300 Defender Combo comes with both barrels.

Beretta is now offering the Model 1200FP auto shotgun, a short-recoil mechanically-operated 12-bore weighing just under 6½ pounds unloaded. It comes with a matte black synthetic stock, matte black metal work, and the ability to handle both high- and low-base shells. The handsome gun sports a 20-inch barrel, six-round magazine, adjustable sights, and a Cylinder choke.

The RS 202P is a 20½-inch-barreled pump with wood stock and extended six-round mag. Weight is 7 pounds and the foresight is said to be "fluorescent," whatever that means. Sling swivels are installed by Beretta, a good thing. These pumps are built on alloy receivers, and fire only 2¾-inch shells, something to take into consideration.

Beretta has an excellent reputation for quality. I'd give these guns a close look were I in the market for a security shotgun.

Feather Industries, Inc., pro-

This is what a slide-action 357 looks like. It's the Timber Wolf from Action Arms.

a long hallway, or shooting at you from amongst the rose bushes, or aiming at you from the seat of a pickup truck with which he just ran you off the road, I'd take slugs over birdshot.

Federal's little 96.7-grain, .385-inch diameter, hollow-base, hollowpoint (in name only) soft lead slug chronographed 1600 feet per second on the nose, average of five shots. That's good for 550 foot-pounds of energy and should prove lethal if well placed, about like a 110-grain 357 Magnum fired from a long-barreled revolver.

I will highly recommend one of these bitty Mossberg pumps if they can get them to feed. They're convenient, relatively inexpensive, and accommodate serious but light-kicking loads. Good combo, this should be, in a reliable example. A laser-sight permutation of the HS 410 is cataloged, for the affluent.

Also new from O.F. Mossberg

is a series of nine-shot pump shotguns. They can be had in the normal configuration Model 590, the Model 590 Bullpup, and the Model 590 Mariner.

Mossberg is one of the first major shotgun producers to be savvy enough to offer a "ghost ring" rear sight on factory security scatterguns. Their literature proclaims the front element, a simple and sturdy blade dovetailed into a ramp, to be "adjustable." The rear aperture is adjustable for both windage and elevation and is provided with "tough duty (sic) protective side plates" designed "to prevent damage during se-

claims to have been widely used on military guns in Southeast Asia. According to the new catalog, "This coating not ony resists the effects of moisture, but components coated with this substance benefit from its lubricating properties which are suspended in an epoxy resin system that provides not only lubrication but extends the life of the coated parts." The catalog also refers to Sandstrom 9A as a "corrosion inhibiting dry film lubricant." I am consequently unsure whether Sandstrom 9A is a true finish or a dry lubricant, but what do I know?

The Marine's stainless steel barrel is said to have a "multiple-plated chrome finish." Wow. Bet *that* tube won't rust easily!

ducers of the well-known AT-9 (9mm Luger) and AT-22 (22 Long Rifle) semi-auto carbines are planning for late in 1990 the introduction of an AK clone built here in the United States. Actually, the rifle looks more akin to the Israeli-built Hadar sporter that was imported in 308 Winchester persuasion by Action Arms, complete with bulky thumbhole stock, cumbersome forend, and thick recoil pad.

The new gun will feature an adjustable rear sight, sling swivel studs, composite stock, and will be drilled and tapped for scope mounting. The action, of course, is gas-operated. Chambering's the excellent 7.62x39, in a barrel 19½ inches long. Complete with five-round mag, the rifle is claimed to weigh 8½ pounds unloaded.

Optional are a walnut stock, scope mount with 1-inch rings, sling and swivels, and padded nylon case. No large-capacity magazines are to be available from the manufacturer. If you're interested in one of these rifles, ask for the Feather Saturn 30.

Springfield Armory, ever innovative, is offering two "new" centerfire sporters. The SAR-4800 is a copy of the FAL/LAR complete with forged-steel parts and a hammer-forged chrome-lined barrel. Standard equipment is a thumbhole sporter stock and an unsuppressed muzzle with thread protector. Optional is an accurizing package that includes a flash suppressor and a black synthetic pistol-grip stock. In addition to the full-length rifle, a shorter "Bush Model" is planned.

The new SAR-8 is a rendition

There are no catalog changes to the excellent line of M-1A service rifles, including the fine little Bush Rifle. Few autoloading rifles provide the combination of accuracy, reliability, portability, balance, fit, and good looks of the M-1A. In fact, only one modern gun comes close, and it is provided only in 223 chambering.

I recently purchased one of the new 18-inch-barreled **Remington** Model 870 Police riot guns. The shorter tube makes it handier to tote muzzle down—dangling at the end of one's shooting arm—without plowing a furrow deep enough to plant radishes. It also renders the five-shot 12-bore easier to poke in and out of a vehicle. Metal on barrel and receiver is Parkerized to thwart the elements and absorb instead of reflect light. The forend is grooved circumferentially, and, like the buttstock, is made of walnut-colored hardwood. There is a

Over on the shotgun side, H&K will deliver the Benelli M3 Super 90, the folding stock being only the latest of the Benelli's bells and whistles.

tube, for about the same outlay as a Police version with slug barrel *only,* and no rear sight. Not bad, huh?

My pal Don Beamon, hunting partner of long standing, gun enthusiast, ex-Ranger and Vietnam combat vet, and one of the honchos of famed **Jim's Gun Jobbery** of Fayetteville, North Carolina, brought to my household not long ago one of the

as is a rubber buttpad. My spec sheet gives no weight, but I'll bet this sporter weighs like a Packard.

More exciting is the Black Eagle Slug Gun, 12-gauge only, that comes with a 24-inch *rifled* barrel and a two-piece receiver intended for scope mounting. No vent rib, no iron sights, no Ping Pong-ball front bead mar the Black Eagle's barrel plain. Weight is listed at 7 pounds 5 ounces, and overall length is 45½ inches. The stock and forend are of high gloss, checkered walnut; the buttstock features a drop adjustment kit.

This appears to be a fine rig, one I look forward to testing. Or even seeing.

The Montefeltro autoloader is now produced in a mirror-image left-hand version, plus a new slug/riot iteration that provides for forward scope mounting atop the barrel, Scout-rifle style. Finish on metal is matte black; on stock and forend, matte wood. The bore is not rifled on the Montefeltro slugster, so buckshot is a viable option. H&K is making it easy for any shotgun aficionado to find a suitable home-defense device. Their scatterguns are well built, unparalleled in reliability, affordable, and available. Further, the acquisition of several different barrels enables one firearm to serve a multiplicity of purposes well, with scant need of compromise.

Ruger is finally shipping quantities of the stainless steel Ranch Rifle Mini-14. I have been shooting one; it's a honey. Standard now is the 1:7-inch twist, which stabilizes the new heavy-bullet 223 loadings nicely, and does no harm I can see when handling the normal 55-grain fare. For example, my test gun grouped its best with 69-grain Federal Match hollowpoint boattails, with five five-shot strings going 2.85 inches at 100 yards. Runner-up was the short-bullet 52-grain hol-

Beretta's 1200 FP is a lean and mean police machine—has rifle sights, holds eight rounds.

H&K can do a slug-gun setup for scopes in their Benelli Black Eagle line.

of the famed Heckler & Koch Model 91. As with the SAR-4800, chambering is 308 Winchester only, there is no suppressor provided as standard, and the wood stock boasts a thumbhole. An accuracy package is cataloged, complete with synthetic pistol grip stock and suppressor. The roller-lock action and fluted chamber design of the original German firearm is present, as well as the distinctive front and rear sights.

I have used these guns in accurized form on more than one hunt. They are sufficiently accurate for varminting to 200 yards or so; past that point, clean-kill accuracy is not sufficient for woodchuck-sized critters. On big game, the Springfields work fine, thanks.

thick recoil pad but no sling accoutrements.

My test gun had a reasonable trigger, stiff action that slicked up through use, absolute reliability so far, and hit close to point of aim when using the crude front bead (no rear sight). This one's my personal choice among slide-action anti-personnel smoothbores. An extra Rem-Choked 28-inch barrel is not out of my financial reach, so I can plug for three-shot capacity and hie off to the dove fields to make a fool of myself.

A similar matte-finished (not Parkerized) version of the five-shot M870 comes with iron sights, checkered stock, and for less money. In fact, the Express Combo includes both a vent rib Modified barrel and the slug

hard-to-find **Heckler & Koch** Model SP89 9mm assault pistols. To the range we went.

Note: The gun is quite well made, heavy, and gifted with a spongy trigger. Note: It is not cheap. Note: It will *not* function with Blazer aluminum-cased ammunition. Note: The test gun proved moderately accurate with Hornady FMJ ball, printing just over 2½ inches for five-shot strings at 25 yards, from the bench.

H&K is now offering a 308 Winchester-chambered sporter benamed the SR-9 Orion. Standard are a Precision Marksman trigger group, thumbhole stock of Kevlar-reinforced fiberglass, adjustable iron sights, and a 19½-inch "bull" barrel. Five-round magazines are standard,

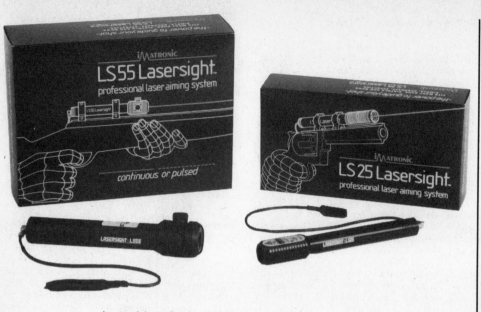

Imatronic's professional aiming systems provide for short or long guns.

lowpoint rendition from Black Hills Ammunition, going into 3.85 inches.

My favorite hunting load is the Hirtenberger 55-grain Nosler softpoint, which clocked a sizzling 3165 feet per second instrumental speed (12 feet) from the Ruger's stubby 18½-inch barrel. Grouping is not especially noteworthy—about 4¼ inches for the average—but slaying power is.

Hunting with Gerald Almond (Goldmine Hunting Preserve, Route 2, Box 95C, Stanfield, NC, [704] 786-0619) last month, I decked a wild hog at just under sixty yards—with it

running its little porcine legs to nubs—by sticking through its bellows the speedy Hirtenberger/Nosler softpoint. Never have I seen a galloping porker hit the deck with such finality; all I saw upon impact were legs and snout and Carolina redclay dust, all aclump. Penetration was fine; the bitty bullet nabbed both lungs after negotiating the gristle shield, leaving a red mess in its wake.

Eagle International, Inc. offers high-capacity magazines for your Mini-14, as well as lots of other stuff. For example, 18-round magazines for the Ruger Mini-Thirty are now available,

and new Low-Profile Base Pad boxes for the 1911 45, in both stainless and black versions. Flash hiders and QD scope mounts are currently cataloged, as is a ventilated barrel shroud with swivel.

From **MPI Stocks** comes a completely finished fiberglass stock for the Ruger Mini-14. As with all MPI work I have examined, quality is excellent. A recoil pad is included, and the length of pull has grown an inch over Ruger's specs.

Imatronic Limited is offering two laser sights. The LS25 is intended for use on handguns; the LS55 mounts on automatic

weapons, shotguns, rifles, airguns, and crossbows, according to my press material. The handgun optic is 6½ inches long with a ¾-inch tube; the LS55 is 7 inches in length and of 1-inch diameter. Both offer a 6⅞-inch cable and pressure switch to be affixed to a convenient part of the firearm (or crossbow). Wave length is said to be 670mm (blood red). A pair of AAA Alkaline batteries will give up to eight hours of continuous operation, or 6500 five-second bursts. The sight is attached to the firearm by conventional scope mounts. Dot size increases, as would be expected, with beam travel. At 50 meters, beam diameter is 55mm—just over two inches.

Barrett Firearms Manufacturing, Inc.'s Model 90, a 22-pound bolt-action bipod-mounted rifle chambered for the 50 Browning, is now available in some stores. If rapid-fire capabilities are important to you, there's the Barrett Model 82A1 Light 50, a semi-auto reamed to the same round. Accuracy is said to be minute-of-angle to one-thousand yards, so this gun is just the ticket for true *long*-distance sniping. Ammo? Why, both **PMC** and **Samson** (from Action Arms) catalog the load!

Speaking of **PMC**, the Barnes "X" bullet is now being loaded in two popular paramilitary/defense cartridges, the 308 Winchester (7.62 NATO) and the 30-06. According to Rick Jamison and Ross Seyfried, these new homogeneous bullets are devastating in flesh, penetrating deeply as well.

Starfire handgun bullets are due from PMC soon, these developed by the same gent who gave us Hydra-Shok, Peter Pi. I've seen these things used—44 Magnum persuasion—by several hunters, on wild boar. Impressive.

Federal Cartridge Company has given owners of SMLE military rifles a shot in the arm by adding a 150-grain 303 British loading to their queue, at a quoted 2690 muzzle speed. Shades of pre-war 30-06 ballistics! Such a load makes the ancient 303 into a genuine 300-yard cartridge, assuming a competent shooter and a rifle with a good barrel. Good move.

The 308, everyone's favorite battle cartridge, is now proffered by Federal in 180 Nosler Partition format. For all-round use, this is a great idea. Look for it under the Premium label. ●

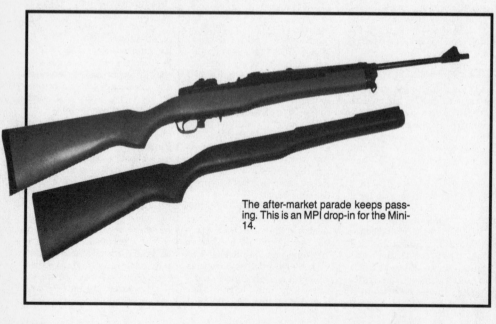

The after-market parade keeps passing. This is an MPI drop-in for the Mini-14.

by DON ZUTZ

It Is
What You Use
That COUNTS

A year is not complete for Zutz until some squirrels meet his old Model 37 16-gauge.

Maybe most of the time, the gun makes the day.

WHEN I began hunting back in the 1940s and started spouting all sorts of gun talk and ballistics, my elders patiently counseled me that, "It ain't a matter of what you hit 'em with—it's where you hit 'em that counts!"

I respected their advice, but I went on to become a teenage gun nut, anyway. I traded everything from cap pistols and air rifles to shotguns for that traditionally classic purpose of seeing what the next piece could do. Indeed, everything I'd read as a kid had been slanted toward an age of scientific specialization, so why shouldn't I apply the prevailing trend to sorting out the calibers, cases, gauges, designs and other stuff to make certain I'd be ready for each hunting and shooting niche as we roared toward the age of space.

Sure, I'd gotten my first small game with a bolt-action 410, and I'd dropped my first deer with a 30-30. But like every other budding gun nut, I was beset by the overpowering question: Might I have done it a little better with sporting ordnance more suited for the specific condition?

My elders shook their heads sadly. It was a negative shake. To them, a piece of meat on the table was a piece of meat, and they philosophized, "Deer steaks don't taste any different if you hit them with a 38-40 or a 250-3000."

After years of putting my feet under their dining tables, I readily admitted

(Above) Why does the kid with the ripped pants, torn shirt, and busted gun always get the game? Are gun nuts making too much of the guns and loads? Naw!

The writer loves fine doubles, but must admit that he shoots the Model 1100 as well as, or better than, any of the world's great-name side-by-sides and over/unders.

course. It's the gun that makes the day.

And why not? They tell us we don't have enough game to pile it high in the duck skiff these days, and habitat is shrinking. So why not derive some pleasure from doing special things with special guns and loads? It may not be the thing practical sportsmen would do, but who's to say that using the theoretically right gun/load tandem for any given hunt isn't really the personification of practicality because of the way it gets things done so efficiently when the chance presents itself? An open-bored 20 is indeed a better grouse gun than is a pragmatist's 30-inch Full-choke pump gun. So, too, will a scope-topped 40XR lay squirrel-head-sized groups at 50-60 yards far better than the rusty hammer pump

the truth of their convictions. The first Hungarian partridge I folded with a hail of 6s from the 410 had tasted the same as the last one I reached out for with my expensive Merkel over/under and copper-plated 6s launched from a plastic shotcup. For a hunter who's only interested in filling a freezer, then, there's a lot to be said for the pragmatism of the, "It's-not-what-you-use-but-where-you-hit-'em" school of thought. Since I once did see a white-tail buckled by a punk 38-40, and since I've seen some big rooster pheasants knocked toenails over tea kettle by centered hits with a pee-wee 410, I can appreciate that where you hit 'em is a factor in making clean, sporting kills.

Nevertheless, I still took a different fork in the road. While my father and Uncle John fussed with dogs and told the same hunting tales over and over, I dug deeper into guns, loads, ballistics, and primitive performance experiments. I wanted to know the strong and weak points of everything, how they actually worked, and when and where the respective stuff should be used for optimum effectiveness. In that sense, I don't think I was much different than the other kids of my rural neighborhood; they also got deeply interested in things, but their attention centered on such things as cars and airplanes. I scoffed at their discussions, because new cars already cost $695 whereas air rifles went for $2.95. And who wanted to tear down a '33 Chevy when there was some hunting to do?

The major difference between being

a dedicated gun nut and a practical hunter, then, is one's frame of mind. What counts the most for some is not just bagging game, but bagging it according to all sorts of refined concepts and hair-splitting arguments. Traditions also play a role, and the impact of modern advertising isn't insignificant. Put them all together, and you've got folks who aren't happy unless they have a 20-gauge side-by-side for grouse, a 10-gauge magnum for geese, a tubed over/under for Skeet, a 25-06 for antelope on the flat and a 7mm magnum for mule deer or elk up the slope. If they go to Africa, the 458 is no longer any good; they must, simply *must,* have a 416 something or other. For such, even a day spent in the hardwoods waiting for gray squirrels isn't complete without a fancy Kimber, an Anschutz, or a Remington Model 40XR—all of them sporting 1-inch scopes corrected for parallax, of

22 that stands behind the barn door. Buffered shotshell loads will pattern tighter than discount-store stuff, and handloads "engineered" to wring the best from any sporting arm will add another degree of personal satisfaction.

Before you can understand the gist of this piece, then, you've got to tolerate the human psyche. Some of us just like to adjust to the total environment differently than others. It's more fun doing it a *certain* way rather than merely doing it. Let me give you an example . . .

Several seasons back, I was grouse hunting with a young man who had a flair for the finer things in life. If he didn't exactly own them, he at least knew what they were. But finances being what they were, he hunted with a 12-gauge autoloader when he thought he should be using a neat double. Well, he bagged some birds anyway, and then he made a fuss when I wanted to take some photos. Didn't want his picture snapped while he held an autoloader. No self-respecting sport should be caught without a trim double, he opined. Then, some years later, he hunted with a Parker and was only too glad to stand before the lens. Now it was all different: the Parker fit the scene; at least, in his mind it did.

From that last paragraph one might detect a note of the gun nut snob. Not necessarily. I might be termed somewhat of a snob because of the way I've written about the finer break-action shotguns, but there are times each year when my fun comes from a Winchester Model 37 single shot in 16-gauge. I've got handloads that print tight patterns from the M37, and I like it for my squirrel hunting in areas where habitations make the 22 unsafe. And it has accounted for a grouse or two each year since I've had it. Indeed,

whenever I pull off a nice shot with that single of yesteryear, I feel a pleasant tingle that can't be topped by a limit dropped by a thousand-dollar item. It was, for that moment, exactly what I wanted to use, an enjoyable link with the past.

A second episode pivots upon a trombone gun standing in the corner. I am absolutely no true fan of pump guns, but there is nevertheless one slide action that has caught my fancy—a Winchester Model 12 Heavy Duck Gun. This breed was first fashioned for the market in 1934 when it became the initial magnum-grade repeater on the American gun dealers' shelves. At the time, many of the 3-inch shells were loaded with nothing

more than 1⅜ ounces of shot, but things changed and we can now launch 2 full ounces of lead from the 3-inch 12. More importantly, however, is the fact that this particular gun fits me and swings smoothly. And there are days when you couldn't tempt me to use anything else. I'm not especially sure how the M12s will respond to steel shot, but that won't stop me from giving it some air this autumn. There will be misty mornings when only the Heavy Duck Gun will seem appropriate in the slough. And when I bring down the ol' honker or greenhead, the gun will get the glory.

Using a specific rifle can also make the day, even if the same bag of bushytails could probably have been garnered by practically any gun. For me, that special 22 is a Winchester Model 67 single shot that I badly defaced as a kid. During severe winter cold spells, I tried to carve a jumping buck deer

on the stock; and after receiving a Christmas gift of a checkering tool, I also tried to work a hitherto unknown pattern onto both its stock and forearm with disastrous results. However, a couple times each season I'll entertain nothing but a lazy afternoon with it in the hardwoods. The bag is unimportant. It's just fun being out with the knockabout from my younger days. Here, again, the gun is the focal point. The pleasure of the day derives from what I used, not how I used it. Gunnutitis tinged with nostalgia? Perhaps. But one of life's little pleasures nevertheless.

The point I've been driving at, of course, is that the gun and/or the load are often more important to the hunter than they are to the overall success of any outing. We know that everything from a 222 Remington to the 600 Nitro can bag a deer *pronto* with a hit in a vital place, yet gun nuts and handloaders focus entirely on one or two pet cartridges or handloading recipes for those rounds. When I went on my first antelope hunt, I *had* to use the 257 Roberts. The cartridge had interested me since I first began reading about sporting arms and ammo as a kid, and if I hadn't used the Roberts the hunt would have been a failure regardless of the trophy. The cartridge made the hunt.

A gun nut's dream come true: a cloverleaf group at 100 yards out of a 25-284 wildcat. If the group had been shot with a factory cartridge, it would be long forgotten. The 25-284 was special and that's what counts!

(Below) The ol' 30-30 is probably enough gun if the hunter places his shots, but how many modern gun nuts enjoy such plebian stuff?

Later on, I whomped up a 25-284 wildcat, thinking that its more compact body (rebated rim design) would provide better ignition and combustion than the lengthy 25-06 case, and nothing could have replaced it on a hunt in eastern Montana. Nothing. Finding an antelope on that bleak, gently rolling plain was tough that fall, and my reload with the 115-grain Nosler dropped only a so-so buck. Yet, the hunt was a total success because the 25-284 had scored. Forget the fact that the shot was basically inside 30-30 range when I finally got around to sneaking up on a herd. Indeed, had I actually piled up that same pronghorn with a 30-30, I'd have long ago forgotten the hunt. At that moment, there was only the 25-284.

Shortly after I got out of college, Remington brought out a new rifle and cartridge known as the Model 725 and 280 Remington, respectively. I liked the idea of utilizing the versatile and aerodynamically efficient 7mm projectiles in a 30-06 case, but at the time I simply couldn't afford every gun set on the market. The years languished, and the 280 Remington spun its wheels. It didn't excite the public, which isn't very astute about ballistic matters anyway, and the Model 725 folded before I amassed a bankroll. However, I didn't forget; I tended to remember that the M725 may very well have been the finest non-custom gun Remington ever put on the market, including the finest checkering. And the barrels were a stiff steel and button rifled, not cold forged, and had reputations for super hunting accuracy. The more I thought on it, the more I *needed* a Model 725 in 280, and finally got one.

The very first time I hunted with the M725 I bagged the biggest buck in our camp. Tell me it wasn't the gun and the load. Just try. Some other guys might have bagged bigger bucks with shotgun slugs through beat-up hand-me-down klunkers and thrown the gun into the bushes while attending the game, but that wouldn't have been any way to treat the 280 in its classic M725 form. It continues to receive TLC. To date, no other rifle or cartridge has supplanted it on my rack.

At a time when it's fashionable for gun scribblers to boom the elegant break actions, I must confess to having an affair with the Model 1100 Remington. There has always been a mystical air about the M1100 and its great pointing qualities and its ability to score. There were over three million Model 1100s made before Remington brought out the more versatile Model 11-87, but when I get serious about wanting to hit something I reach for the M1100, not a leaned-out side-by-side. It's gotten to the point where the Model 1100 and my Merkel are the workhorses around here, and a hunt doesn't seem the same without them. I enjoy using them.

Last season I received an *el cheapo* slide action to use as the basis of a magazine review, and I disliked having to swing it. In fact, my long-range duck shooting suffered. Then one day when the ducks were holding quite high I aborted the trial, switched back to the old favorite M1100 Magnum, and began feeling much better about the hunt. The M1100 brought confidence. It also brought down two of the highest mallards I'd tried all season. Call it confidence, if you wish, or maybe familiarity. Whatever. But always understand that what you use does count!

Casual shooters, armchair experts, and occasional hunters like to believe that a good shooter should be able to score with any gun. No way. If that were so, the All-American trap shooters of today could be using L.C. Smith, Parker, Fox, and Baker single shots. But you'll seldom ever see any of those guns in tournament trap, because they don't score as easily as do the modern designs. For Skeet and trap perfection, the gun becomes vitally important. I once watched as a standout American trapman missed targets repeatedly with a new gun that had been gifted to him. After the round, he went back to the car for his old gun.

Perhaps the entire gist of this article can be summed up in a short tale that comes out of the faded 1950s when I was first beginning to hang around clay target clubs. In those days, a local conservation club held an annual mid-summer poultry shoot. Each test was over ten targets, Skeet or trap, winner take the plucked and frozen bird. And we all snickered slightly when a little old gent limped slowly to the trap line carrying a long-barreled double with dog-leg stock. Poor guy didn't know what he was getting into!

We smiled broadly as he called "Pull" and tracked the targets almost to the end of their flights before shooting. This was in direct contrast to the snap-'em-up technique of the young sharpies on the line with him. They'd holler "Pull!" and *Bang!* the target would be clobbered practically before it got out of the trap house. Then the old gent would call for his target rather meekly, ride it up and out, and finally let go practically as the target settled into the grass. Quite entertaining.

What we weren't doing, however, was writing down the score. For the young sharpies did miss, whereas the old deadeye didn't. His choke barrel reached out a mile to chip and chunk every target. He shot three events, won three chickens against all comers, and suddenly had a fan club that rivaled Elvis Presley's, a singer who was getting started about then. When somebody asked the old-timer if he'd like to try one of the newer trap guns, the old boy hefted a couple with Monte Carlos and elevated ribs, set them down gently, and quietly said, "Well, no, thanks. I always enjoyed shooting my double the best even if I do miss once in a while."

And so saying, he backed his 1939 DeSoto out of the parking lot, spun its wheels in the gravel, and disappeared into the late afternoon sun.

Now, who's to say the old gent didn't have it all wrapped up in that one sentence? It's what you use that does count in sport shooting—to you! There is a place in sport shooting for the fun and games of pet loads, favorite guns, treasured memories, dreams of hunts to come and tournaments to shoot, fantasies, vicarious experiences, and hair-splitting arguments. All you've got to do is become a practicing gun nut to enjoy 'em all. ●

For a lot of us, it's not a quail hunt without a 20-gauge side-by-side. What you use counts—at least in your own mind!

by LARRY S. STERETT

SHOTGUN REVIEW

EACH passing year sees fewer single shot break-action shotguns in the low price range being available. Even the number imported has decreased. New England Firearms is the sole U.S. manufacturer, picking up the H&R line after that firm folded; Savage sold their single shot tooling overseas; Iver Johnson quit years earlier. However, up at the high-priced end, Remington Arms has gotten into the business with a new, and for them a first, target grade single shot—the 90-T, a break-action with false sideplates. If the production guns are as good as the prototypes examined at the 1989 Grand American, it promises to be some shotgun.

The "super mag" 12-gauge shotshell measuring 3½ inches in length has been around for at least three decades, but it is really catching on now. Mossberg was the first, and now has three versions of the Ultra-Mag; Federal was the first to produce ammunition in recent years, and neither Remington nor Winchester have it cataloged at present, nor do any importers. A number of other firms do have 12-gauge shotguns so chambered, and there are at least a dozen models available, most of which are over/under or side-by-side designs. Included are Armsport, American Arms, Bernardelli, Browning has both their BPS pump and Citori over/under, Laurona, New England Firearms, and SKB. It is doubtful Remington or U.S. Repeating Arms will jump on the bandwagon, unless, of course, Remington or Winchester decide to start manufacturing 3½-inch shotshells.

Fixed choke shotguns are getting scarce, and are available mostly in cheaper single shots, riot guns and as an option on some over/under and single-barrel target models. Such barrels may, indeed, become special order options.

Sporting Clays is the name of the game, and no shotgunning game has caught on as rapidly with U.S. shooters, or as well, since Skeet was introduced back in 1926. Early in the '80s the shotguns were mainly field guns, and the shotshells field or target loads. Today, nearly every major manufacturer or importer has at least one model available with the "sporting clays" label attached to it, or "suitable for sporting clays," and Browning leads the pack. American Arms has a couple of new models; Armsport has three new "sporting clays" models in two versions—with or without sideplates. Beretta has a new Sporting Clays Combo in addition to earlier sporting clays models; Bernardelli has at least four such models; Browning at least ten; Laurona has the Silhouette Sporting Clays model; Savage has a new 312SC over/under so designated; and so does Antonio Zoli USA.

Here, name by name, are more details:

American Arms

The Black Magic series of semi-automatic and over/under shotguns by Franchi was announced in 1989, but did not actually appear until late in the year. Five models—Game, Skeet, Trap, Sporting Hunter and Lightweight Hunter—are available and all feature checkered walnut stocks and forearms. The semi-auto Game model is available in 12- or 20-gauge, with a choice of 24-, 26-, or 28-inch Multichoke barrel chambered for standard length and 3-inch shells, interchangeably. The Skeet model is available only in 12-gauge, and has 26-inch ported barrel with Tula choke and standard length chamber; the Trap model, also with 2¾-inch chamber, has a 12-gauge 30-inch Multichoke barrel.

The Sporting Hunter and Lightweight Hunter are over/unders with single selective triggers, Multichoke barrels and automatic selective ejectors. Extra barrels, including slug versions, are available for the autoloaders.

Also new are the Silver Lite—6 pounds in 12-gauge and 5 pounds, 13 ounces, in 20-gauge with 26-inch Multichoke barrels—and the Silver Sporting in 12-gauge only with 28-inch Multichoke barrels. The former has a super lightweight alloy receiver; both have single selective trigger, selective automatic ejectors, and checkered walnut.

Armsport

Armsport's three-barrel gun is back as the "Trilling." It has three 12-gauge barrels with automatic ejectors and is obviously the shotgun for the man

The new Remington Model 90-T single barrel trap gun offers 30-, 32- or 34-inch over-bored barrels; shown is the 30-inch barrel.

The Mossberg Model HS 410 has a special spreader choke, synthetic stock and pistol grip forearm.

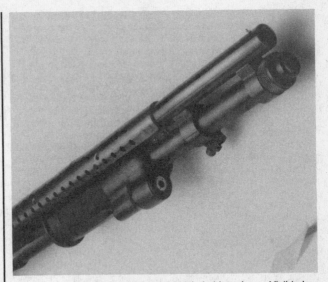

This Mossberg Model 590 Intimidator has a Visible Laser Module built in on the right side of the slide handle; comes in a six- or nine-shot capacity.

Beretta's new Model 686 over/under (top) and Model 626 side-by-side Onyx shotguns are chambered for the Super Mag 12-gauge shotshells measuring 3½ inches long.

who has everything. See our Testfire, page 199.

Elsewhere by Armsport, Models 2746 and 2747 are chambered for the 12-gauge Super Mag shells, and come in a choice of 28- or 32-inch lengths with three interchangeable choke tubes. The Boss-type actions have single selective triggers. There are also three new sporting clays shotguns, with counting the Trilling, Armsport has eighteen new shotguns available. That's a fair number of shotguns, and all but five carry prices of under $700.

Beretta U.S.A.

Beretta shotguns have done well on the clay target fields in recent years, including Skeet, trap and sporting clays. The 1989 Grand American Handi-

guns have the same engraved game scenes as the standard 687L guns, but with the blackened receiver, while the 687EL Onyx guns sport engraved false sideplates. Onyx barrels all have the Mobilchoke system, capable of handling steel shot; stocks and forearms are American walnut, with black rubber recoil pads and special Onyx grip caps. There are two new

case-hardened finish, hand-engraved game scenes, classic scroll or floral patterns, gold inlays, monograms, or custom designs. The sidelocks are hand-detachable, and single or double triggers are options. The wood is specially selected European walnut, with choice of stock style built to measure. There is now a Premium Grade Model 452 side-by-side Holland & Holland-style sidelock in 12-gauge only and, indeed, a similar double rifle.

Bernardelli/Magnum Research

Bernardelli shotguns have been available to American shooters since the 1920s. The current line, imported by the Minnesota firm of Desert Eagle fame, includes almost every double barrel a shotgunner could wish for, plus a folding single barrel and a semi-auto 9mm carbine with smoothbore barrel. (Yes, Virginia, they do manufacture 9mm shotguns in Europe, and have for decades past.) Hammerless, boxlock, sidelock, single trigger, double triggers, hammer guns, sporting clays guns, trap, Skeet, field, and slug guns are all available, as are pistol grip stock, straight (English-style) and half-pistol grip stocks. Gauges available include 12 and 20 in most models, plus 16 and 28 in many.

The four slug guns are available only in 12-gauge, as are the competition guns—trap, Skeet, and sporting clays—and the Holland & Holland-type sidelock side-by-sides. At the top of the line, you can spend $44,635, with a single trigger costing $455 extra. The Model 192 Waterfowler over/under and the Model 112 Waterfowler side-by-side are chambered for the 3½-inch Super Mag 12-gauge, have single selective triggers, ejectors, and come with three Multichoke tubes.

Bernardelli's folding shotgun is the only one currently available in seven different chamberings—12, 16, 20, 24, 28, 32, and 36 (.410)—for the shooter who wants something a bit different. Shells for the 24- and 32-gauge are a bit difficult to locate, but not impossible.

BRNO/T.D. Arms

This Michigan firm has BRNO's 12-gauge ZP 49 side-by-side in plain and engraved grades, the 12-gauge ZH 300 over/under in field, Skeet, and trap grades, or as an eight-barrel Combo set in 12- and 16-

The new Savage Model 312SC over/under 12-gauge shotgun, designed for shooting sporting clays, features 28-inch barrels with ventilated side ribs, top rib and interchangeable choke tubes.

The Black Magic Sporting Hunter by Franchi is suitable for game shooting or sporting clays.

or without sideplates, in 12-gauge with 28-inch barrels and 20-gauge with 26-inch barrels. Five choke tubes are provided with each shotgun, and extra tubes are available. Two have selective automatic ejectors. Armsport has dropped one single-barrel 12-gauge model, as well as the 12-gauge over/under Slug Gun with 20-inch barrels, but the 10-gauge over/unders are still selling well.

There's also a new line of side-by-sides in 12, 20, 28 and 410 alongside new over/unders in the same gauges. Barrel lengths are 26 and 28 inches, depending on the gauge, and the chokes are fixed, with the 410 in Full and Full. There are also two new 12-gauge Competition Trap over/unders with 30-inch barrels. The shotgun-rifle combination Turkey Gun has been discontinued, but

cap, Clay Target Championship for America, the Doubles Championship, and the All-Around Championship winners shot Beretta, as did five of the All-American First Team Skeet shooters. Thus, it is not surprising to see the Beretta shotgun line expanded even further.

The semi-auto Model 1200 FP, with aluminum-zirconium alloy receiver, has been adopted by the North Carolina Highway Patrol as their service shotgun. The Onyx line has been expanded by a dozen new models, including the 626 side-by-side and 686 over/under models chambered for the 3½-inch 12-gauge Super Mag shells. There are other Model 626 Onyx side-by-sides with 28-inch barrels in 12- or 20-gauge; four 687L over/under models in 12- or 20-gauge; and four similar 687EL over/unders. The 687L Onyx

687EL small bores—28-gauge and 410—with smaller proportioned, low-profile receivers.

For sporting clays shooters, the new Model 682 Sporting Combo has matte black barrels, silver receiver with light scroll engraving, a sliding single selective trigger for perfect length-of-pull fit, and two interchangeable Multichoke barrel assemblies in 28- and 30-inch lengths. For International-style pigeon and competition shooters there's a Pigeon Grade 682.

Beretta's new Premium Grade shotguns and rifles are custom-fitted, styled, and accessorized to meet any shooter's specific desires for sporting arms. The SO9 Series of over/under shotguns can now be obtained in 12-, 20- and 28-gauge, plus 410-bore, built on true proportionate receivers, with color

gauge, including four rifle-shot-gun barrel assemblies (talk about versatility). There is also the BRNO 500 over/under 12-gauge in field grade, the CZ 581 over/under in 12-gauge and the BRNO Super over/under in 12-gauge field, Skeet, trap or Combo grades with a choice of single or double triggers. The ZP 49 side-by-side and the BRNO Super over/under models are true sidelock designs, while the others are boxlocks. The ZP 49, ZH 300, and BRNO Super shotguns tested in the past have been good, solidly constructed sporting arms representing good value for the money, even though the stocks are definitely European styles.

Browning

Counting grades and chamberings and different models, this Utah firm has more *new* shotguns—over thirty—than any of the U.S. firms. The BPS pump action is now available as a Hunting Buck Special in both 10-gauge and 12-gauge with 24-inch barrel chambered for 3½-inch shells. Intended for use with rifled slugs or buckshot, the Buck Special models have screw-adjustable rear sights and ramp fronts with gold beads. The Limited Edition Model 12 slide action is available in 20- and 28-gauge.

In the autoloading line, the new A-500G and A-500R will handle all 12-gauge loads from those containing 1-ounce of shot to the 3-inch magnums. They look alike, except the A-500G is gas-operated, with a rounded pistol grip stock, choice of 26-, 28-, or 30-inch Invector choke barrels; the A-500R is a short-recoil gun with a full pistol grip stock, choice of 26-, 28-, or 30-inch Invector choke barrel, and a 24-inch Invector choke Buck Special barrel with rifle-type sights to boot.

Last year the BT-99 Plus Single Barrel Trap Special was introduced. This year there's the Citori Plus Trap Grade I over/under with, or without, ported 32- or 34-inch Invector Plus barrels. It has total stock and ventilated rib adjustability, and actually costs slightly less than the single barrel BT-99 Plus.

Also in the Citori line are ten slightly different sporting clays over/unders, including ported and unported versions of the GTI Invector Plus, Grade I Special Sporter Invector Plus, Grade I Special Sporting Set Invector Plus with extra barrels, the Grade I Lightning

The Orvis/Ruger over/under shotgun provides a slim forearm, straight grip stock with leather-covered recoil pad, and less weight than regular Rugers.

Sporting Invector Plus, with choice of high or low ventilated rib. All sporting clays models come with three different trigger shoes having different surfaces, and adjustable for three different positions to alter the length of pull. Barrel lengths range from 28 to 32 inches, depending on the model, and the barrels are back-bored to 0.745-inch.

Those shotgunners wanting a Browning from Belgium will find the B-25 over/under—the original Browning Superposed by John M.—and the B-125 available from the Custom Shop. There are fifteen versions available, which can in turn be engraved, carved, or altered to the customer's specifications. In

interim the firm has moved to South Carolina, and production models now include a choice of 243 or 308 rifle barrel coupled with the 12-gauge barrel. The barrel lengths are 18½ inches for the rifle, plus brake, and 20 inches for the shotgun. Magazine capacity is seven rounds for the shotgun, and twenty for the rifle, while the action is pump activated, gas-operated with dual rotating bolts. All parts, except the bolts, which had a bright chromed finish on the gun examined, have a nonreflective matte black finish, including the synthetic Du Pont Zytel stock. The sight system has been changed to a universal Weaver-type mounting rail to permit the use of open sights,

tory.

There are not likely to be, F.I.E. says, over/unders for a while, but both U.S.-made and imported repeating shotguns will be on hand.

Franchi

At this writing, Franchi's plans for distribution of their

The Avanza by Marocchi of Italy is a fast handling gun for field use and sporting clays. It's available in 12- and 20-gauge.

The Bernardelli Model 112 above has half-pistol grip, splinter forearm, and single triggers; barrel length is 28 inches. For the bird hunter, the Model 192 over/under (below) has single selective trigger, auto ejectors, and choice of barrel length.

12- or 20-gauge only, trap or hunting, the B-125 is available in A, B, or C styles, while the B-25 can be obtained in Pigeon, Pointer, Diana, or Midas Grades, with or without a second set of barrels. Production time is from four to six months, depending on the options, and could be even longer.

Crossfire/SSAM

The Crossfire Model 88P was mentioned last year, but in the

telescope, laser, or Aimpoint-type, making the 1990 Crossfire even more versatile.

F.I.E. Corp.

F.I.E. no longer sells Franchi guns. They continue with the Brazilian CBC-made Hamilton & Hunter single barrels in 12, 20, and 410. And they hope to import the Atis (see page 189) box-magazine police configuration 12-gauge pump as well as other models from the same fac-

well-received shotguns are unannounced. However, the excellent SPAS-12, SAS-12 and LAW-12, the standard sporting autoloaders and the rest of the line will no doubt be on hand in the same well-stocked gun stores they have been.

Hastings

The barrel people have replacement barrels—smoothbore, rifled, fixed choke, interchangeable choke tubes, etc.—

The New England Pardner single-barrel break-action shotgun with the Double Back Up stock holding two spare shells. This feature is available on 12-gauge Pardner, Protector, and Shark Repeller versions, plus two 20-gauge versions.

for many Franchi, Ithaca, Browning, Remington, and Winchester shotguns, in addition to some barrels from the original manufacturers, including Smith & Wesson. Now they have a new 50-caliber rifled blackpowder barrel to fit Remington Model 870, 1100, and 11-87 shotguns.

In use, this new 50-caliber barrel replaces the regular shotgun barrel, and is secured with the same magazine tube cap. With the safety "on," a suitable charge of Pyrodex is poured into the muzzle of the barrel, followed by a projectile of desired weight, seated using the ramrod which comes with the barrel. The ramrod is secured between the open rear sight and front sight, and retained by a latch on the front sight. Next, a regular 209-size shotshell primer is inserted into the special breech plug, the action closed, and the shotgun is ready to fire. The test barrel was 24 inches long, with a rifling twist of 1 turn in 34 inches, and was made in France by Verney-Carron for the Hastings firm. The shotguns function as straight-pull bolt-action single shots. The ejection port permits access to the breech plug to install and remove the primer. This creative Hastings barrel permits a shotgunner to have the familiar feel of his or her favorite shotgun when hunting with a muzzleloader.

Hatfield

Down in the Ozark country they produce some top grade side-by-side English-style grouse guns, complete with XXX fancy grade walnut stock and splinter forearm. Their 20-gauge Uplander, for instance, chambered for 3-inch shells, weighs 5¾ pounds. Available in a choice of 12-, 20-, or 28-gauge, with 26-inch barrels, boxlock action and single nonselective trigger, the Hatfield Uplander is produced in eight grades—I through VIII—plus a Collector's Grade within each. For example, the Grade I Uplander currently lists at $1,295, while the Collector's Grade I lists at $1,625. Each grade differs from

the previous one in the amount of engraving, stock checkering, carving, and gold inlays, with the Grade VIII Uplander Top Hat going at $17,500 and the Grade IV Uplander Golden Quail, complete with flushing quail inlaid in gold, along with the Hatfield name and gold outlining, carrying a tab of $5,500.

Heckler & Koch

The Benelli line of 12-gauge autoloading shotguns has been expanded to include ten new versions. The M1 Super 90 is now available as a Slug gun with Ghost-Ring sighting system, as a Defense gun with Ghost-Ring sighting system, and as an Entry gun for police use, plus a Field gun with choice of 21- or 24-inch ventilated rib barrel and short magazine tube. The M3 Super 90 is available with a barrel length of 19¾ inches in two options—with Ghost-Ring sighting system and pistol grip stock, or with a folding stock—and as a law enforcement model only with 14-inch barrel. The Montefeltro Super 90 is now available with a satin finish stock and 24-inch slug barrel featuring a long eye relief scope mount, while the Black Eagle is available with a 24-inch rifled barrel and receiver scope mount. Since the government curtailing of the HK-91/93 rifle sales, H&K can be expected to place more emphasis on their line of shotguns, as indicated by this year's ten new versions.

IAC/Ithaca Gun

The firm at Kings Ferry has held the line with prices on the various grades of the Model 87 available. In addition to the original Deerslayer II with Monte Carlo stock and 12-gauge 25-inch rifled barrel, there are two new versions—one in 12-gauge and one in 20-gauge, both with 20-inch barrels, but otherwise the same as the 25-inch barrel version. The four Deluxe Combo Model 87s in 12- and 20-gauge, furnished with extra 20- or 25-inch rifled barrel, have been discontinued; shooters apparently didn't re-

alize what a deal they had, as the rifled barrel cost only an additional $33 over the Combo with the 20-inch smoothbore barrel. The regular Deluxe Combo is still available in a choice of 12- or 20-gauge, and a 20-inch rifle-sighted barrel.

K.B.I., Inc.

The Kassnar line of shotguns has been trimmed a bit, since the Churchill line is now available through another firm. The Kassnar 12-gauge over/under is available only as a Grade I with a choice of blued standard receiver with hardwood stock and forearm, or with deluxe chromed receiver and walnut stock and forearm. Side-by-side models are available in Grade I featuring gauges 10, 12, 16, 20, 28 and 410-bore with choice of barrel lengths and chokes. All Grade I versions have double triggers, extractors, antiqued silver finished receiver, automatic tang safety, hand-checkered European walnut pistol grip stock with recoil pad, and choice of fixed choke or interchangeable choke tube barrels. The Grade II side-by-sides have double hinged triggers, extractors, English-style stocks of European walnut, splinter forearm, and case-hardened receiver finishes. Gauges for the Grade II range from 12 to 410-bore, but not the 10 and 16.

Laurona/Galaxy Imports

The Laurona Silhouette Trap and Sporting Clays models were mentioned last year. The new Ultra-Mag, built on the same receiver, but with barrels chambered for the 3½-inch 12, is now available, and there's a new single shot for trapshooters. Designed as a true single shot, and not as an over/under with a single over barrel, the new Laurona has the same "black chrome" finish that is said to be sixty-three times more resistant to corrosion than ordinary bluing. Originally, they planned an unsingle barrel, but the over-barrel design seems to be more popular, and by the time you read this their production guns should also have overbored barrels.

Mandall Shooting Supplies/Bretton

The lightweight Bretton over/under shotguns are not exactly new to the U.S. shores, but reliable sources have been difficult to find. Now this well-known Arizona firm has the Baby Sprint model available in 12-gauge, with a 20-gauge magnum version available on special order. All have choke tubes—a rifled tube can be obtained—and the actual barrels can be changed in seconds. There are three grades—Standard, Elite, and Luxe—although not all may be in stock, and three buttstock styles—pistol grip, half-pistol grip, and English—and all come with ventilated rubber recoil pads. The 20-gauge magnum version is a bit different in design and comes as a Sprint Fair Play model in Standard or Luxe grade. All models and grades have double triggers and extractors, and an empty weight of 5 pounds in the 12-gauge versions; weight may vary slightly depending on the stock density and grip style, but the Bretton is the lightest 12-gauge over/under available today.

Marocchi/Precision Sales

This Massachusetts firm has a new line of over/under shotguns—the Avanza by Marocchi. Available with a choice of 26- or 28-inch barrels, and fixed or detachable Interchoke tubes, the Avanza is currently available in 12- and 20-gauge, both chambered for 3-inch shells. The 12-gauge version is built on a 20-gauge frame to reduce weight, making it suited to upland shooting. Guns in either gauge weigh under 7 pounds, and single selective triggers, automatic selective ejectors, automatic safeties, and selected grade walnut, with cut checkering, are standard, as are recoil pads.

Maverick Arms

A fifth version of the Model 88 pump-action shotgun has been added to the original line from Eagle Pass, Texas. With a 24-inch Cylinder-bore barrel with rifle sights, and the synthetic field-style stock and forearm, the latest version handles all regular length and magnum (3-inch) 12-gauge shells. Maverick shotguns are now all furnished with a Mossberg Cablelock.

O. F. Mossberg

Every year Mossberg comes

Benelli Montefeltro Super 90 slug gun with smooth bore barrel.

Benelli M1 Super 90 Field with short magazine tube (12-gauge).

up with more new models, or different versions of the same model, and this year is no exception. The Model 5500 12-gauge autoloader is available as a MKII Combo with 28-inch Accu-II and Accu-Steel vent rib barrels, one for standard length shells, one for magnum steel shotshells. The Model 835 Ulti-Mag Camo is available with a 24-inch Accu-Mag vent rib barrel, and as a Limited Edition "Waterfowl U.S.A." with 28-inch Accu-Mag vent rib barrel. Also available for the 835 are a 24-inch rifle-sighted Cylinder-bore barrel, and a 24-inch rifled barrel, also with rifle-type sights.

In the 500 line, there's a new 12-gauge Combo with 28-inch Accu-II vent rib barrel and a 24-inch barrel with rifle-type sights, plus a Ghost-Ring version in six-shot or nine-shot capacity and 18½- or 20-inch barrel, depending on the shell capacity desired. The Ghost-Ring sight system consists of an adjustable front blade sight, and a protected aperture rear receiver sight adjustable for windage and elevation. The name is new, but the concept is the same as the old peep . . . looking through the large rear aperture causes it to fade out, permitting the eye to focus on the front sight and the target. The Ghost-Ring Model 500 is available with blued or Parkerized finish.

The other big news from North Haven is in the security line, starting with the HS 410 featuring a barrel length of 18½ inches with special spreader choke, synthetic stock and special pistol grip slide handle. It is also available with an integral laser sight built in, so the shot charge strikes what

the "red dot" touches. Intended for home security, it delivers more punch than the 44 Magnum, but with a larger impact area, depending on the distance. Also new is the 12-gauge Model 590 Intimidator, available with blue or Parkerized finish, six- or nine-shot capacity, 18½- or 20-inch barrel, and a Visible Laser Module built into the forearm on the right side. The Laser uses a 7-volt battery, which will provide 1¼ hours of continuous use or up to 4 hours of intermittent use. The red beam has a diameter of approximately 3 inches at 100 yards, with a range of 50 yards indoors during daylight hours and 300 yards outdoors at night.

New England Firearms

The Pardner single barrel break-action shotgun is available in nine new versions, plus a couple of new rifle barrel calibers—243 Winchester and 30-06 for the Handi-Gun Combinations. The Pardner additions include three 12-gauge versions—one chambered for the Super Mag (3½ inches) and two Double Back Up designs featuring a special buttstock holding two spare shells.

There are two 20-gauge Double Back Up versions, plus two Youth models, one each in 20-gauge and 410 with 22-inch barrels and shortened stock with recoil pad. The 12-gauge Double Back Up Protector and Shark Repeller versions feature a blue and nickel metal finish, respectively, and barrel lengths of 18½ inches. The barrels are all chambered for 3-inch shells.

Orvis

This Manchester, Vermont,

firm has had custom-built shotguns available for many years, but now has a special Orvis/Ruger over/under in 12- or 20-gauge with 28-inch barrels in the 12-gauge and 26-inch barrels in the 20-gauge. Lighter in weight than regular Ruger over/under shotguns, the Orvis/Ruger model has a special slim forearm and a straight grip stock of American walnut with leather-covered recoil pad. Designed to handle steel shot, the over/under comes with five screw-in choke tubes, single selective trigger, and a polyurethane stock finish that resembles hand-rubbed oil.

For sporting clays shooters, Orvis also has a new trap with double arms. Capable of throwing from one to four clay targets, the trap can be cocked using two fingers, and takes a mere one-quarter turn to reset for the next throw. It's adjustable for speed and elevation, and it's American-made. Orvis has several shotshell loads, including an English Light 12 featuring a 2½-dram equivalent load containing 1 1/16 ounces of size 8 shot in a 2½-inch long case, plus a new Duo-Shot 12-gauge load having 1⅛ ounces of sizes 8 and 9 shot. Designed for shooting sporting clays and upland bird hunting, the new Duo-Shot load is manufactured in England exclusively for Orvis.

Remington

The big news from Ilion is the new Model 90-T single barrel break-action trap gun, a first for Remington. The firm has produced many trap guns over the years, including over/under models, but not a break-action single shot. It's so new it is not even listed in the 1990 catalog, although there is a partial view

in a promotion of Remington's Shooter's Sweater.

Available in 12-gauge only, with a choice of 30-, 32-, or 34-inch over-bored ventilated rib barrel, and fixed or an interchangeable "trap choke" system, the Model 90-T should become a trapshooter's delight. Factory porting and a heavier-than-standard 34-inch barrel will be optional. All metal finish will be a non-glare, matte-style, with a high luster blued finish as an option. Sideplates conceal the dropout trigger mechanism, and the plates can be custom engraved if desired. The semi-fancy American walnut stock is available as a standard straight comb, or with a Monte Carlo, and a length of pull of 14⅜ inches. Both the buttstock and semi-beavertail forearm have cut checkering at 20 lines-per-inch, and concealed cavities for the addition of weight, if desired. Custom-made stocks with special dimensions, as well as adjustable stocks, will be available on special order, as will extra trigger assemblies, and extra barrels. Price of the 90-T is under $2,600 for the standard grade.

In the regular shotgun line the Model 11-87 SP Magnum autoloader is now available with a 28-inch Rem Choke barrel chambered for 3-inch shells, as is the Model 870 SP. The autoloading SP-10 and cantilever scope mount Models 870 and 11-87 are just starting to become available as this is written, and they were announced last year.

Savage Arms

The latest Savage firm has a new over/under shotgun available only in 12-gauge, but in three different grades—the

Mossberg's Limited Edition Waterfowl U.S.A. Model 835 Ulti-Mag Camo features a 28-inch Accu-Mag vent rib barrel, and a special bronze medallion inlaid in the stock. For each of these sold during 1990, Mossberg will contribute $10 to Waterfowl U.S.A.

The Remington Model 870 SP Magnum is now available with a 28-inch Rem Choke barrel chambered for 3-inch 12-gauge shells.

The new Orvis trap will throw from one to four clay targets of any size, and can be cocked with the use of two fingers. Designed for sporting clays use, it is adjustable for target throwing speed and elevation.

312T with 30-inch barrels for trapshooters, the 312SC with 28-inch barrels for sporting clays, and the field grade 312F with a choice of 26- or 28-inch barrels. All grades come with interchangeable choke tubes, ventilated rib barrels chambered for standard and 3-inch shells, American walnut stock with recoil pad, and forearm, a satin chrome finished receiver and a single selective trigger.

New SKB/Ernie Simmons Enterprises

The SKB Single Barrel Trap gun announced here back in 1988 still has not made an appearance. It was supposed to be similar to the old SKB Century Single, but with a lighter barrel threaded for SKB interchangeable choke tubes.

Prices have increased considerably on all other models, and the over/under Model 885, with engraved sideplates, is now available in field, trap, Skeet and sporting clays grades, including combos and a three-barrel Skeet set. The regular 505 and 605 models are available in the same grades, in addition to an over-barrel trap version. In the autoloader department the Model 1300 is available in Upland Mag and Slug grades.

U.S. Repeating Arms

Shotgun slug shooting has grown considerably in recent years, and USRA has come up with five new slug versions of the Model 1300 and 1400 shotguns. The 12-gauge autoloading Model 1400 Walnut Slug Hunter receiver has steel inserts drilled and tapped for a scope mount; its 22-inch smooth bore barrel has a rifled sabot tube and rifle-type sights.

The Model 1300 12-gauge pump-action Walnut Slug Hunter is also drilled and tapped for scope and has a 22-inch rifled barrel with rifle-type sights. Identical, except for the laminated stock, is the Model 1300 WinTuff Slug Hunter, plus there's a Model 1300 Walnut Slug Hunter with smooth bore barrel and rifle sabot choke tube.

The 1400 with walnut stock is available in 20-gauge with 28-inch ventilated rib barrel, while the 1400 Ranger with hardwood stock can be obtained with a 22-inch Cylinder-bore barrel in 12-gauge, and as a Deer Combo in 12-gauge with 28-inch ventilated rib Winchoke barrel and extra 22-inch Cylinder-bore barrel with rifle sights. For turkey hunters there's a new Model 1300 NWTF Turkey Gun WinCam Series II—new receiver engraving, laminated stock, and 22-inch ventilated rib Winchoke barrel. There is a similar Model 1300 Ladies/Youth Gun, but with walnut stock and forearm, and the regular Model 1300 Walnut is now available in 20-gauge with 28-inch ventilated rib Winchoke barrel.

The Marine Defender Pump Action Model 1300 has an 18-inch multiple-plated chrome finished stainless steel barrel, corrosion-resistant finish on the receiver and major parts, and synthetic stock and forearm. There is a "cruiser" pistol grip version. Magazine capacity is seven standard 12-gauge rounds, or six magnum rounds.

Valmet/Tikka/Stoeger

The Tikka, Valmet, and Sako firms have been merged into one company, Sako Ltd., and what was formerly the Valmet shotgun line is now the Tikka line, with production having been transferred from Finland to Italy. There is complete interchangeability of parts between firearms formerly produced in Finland, and those now produced in Italy, according to the manufacturer. Currently the Stoeger firm is importing the Model 412S in a 12-gauge field grade, with a choice of 26- or 28-inch barrels chambered for 3-inch shells, plus a shotgun/rifle combination gun, and a double rifle. Extra barrels for trap and Skeet are available, and interchangeable.

Antonio Zoli USA

Zoli shotguns, available to U.S. shooters for many years, now offer eight new models. The Z-90 is available in Trap (over/under), Trap Mono (over-barrel), Skeet (over/under) and Sporting Clays (over/under), in 12-gauge only. With Turkish Circassian walnut stock and forearm, single selective trigger adjustable for length of pull, and ventilated rib barrels with interchangeable choke tubes, the Z-90 boxlock action provides engraved sideplates on the Sporting Clays version. There is also a Silver Falcon model over/under in a choice of 12- or 20-gauge, chambered for 3-inch shells, having interchangeable choke tubes. The Silver Falcon is suitable for field use or for sporting clays. For slug shooters there's the Woodsman, a 12-gauge over/under featuring single selective trigger—the European version has double triggers. The 23-inch barrels have a raised quarter-rib with pop-up rifle-type sights and interchangeable choke tubes.

For shotgunners who like side-by-side designs there are two boxlock models—the Uplander and the Silver Fox. Both offer choice of 12- or 20-gauge, chambered for 3-inch shells, with selective automatic ejectors, single selective triggers, and English-style wood. The Uplander receiver is color case-hardened, houses 25-inch barrels choked Improved Cylinder and Modified. The Silver Fox is considered a Best Grade, with an engraved, polished and gold-inlaid receiver, and specially selected wood. ●

TRADITIONAL lever actions and bolt actions comprise the two most popular rifle types here in the States and Canada. They create an interesting paradox—the former is decidedly

(Below) From left—Browning Model 71 Carbine with 20-inch barrel, Grade 1; Winchester Model 71 rifle, 24-inch barrel, standard grade; and, Browning Model 71 rifle, 24-inch barrel, Grade 1.

the more complicated mechanism, yet is easier and simpler to load and fire.

Energies created during the cycling of the lever action maintain a vertical axis which assists in bringing the rifle back on target faster. This results in timely aimed and accurate fire.

The bolt-action rifle is certainly the simpler machine with fewer parts, is often more inexpensive to produce, yet is more difficult and far more inefficient to operate, certainly when speed is critical. Bolt actions demand the user exert lateral energies when cycling the action that twist the gun well off vertical and horizontal axes.

Contrary to what some critics of the lever guns proclaim, the lever actions are bought because they offer the user ease of operation, speed, and accurate fire. And no ideal bolt-action-type rifle exists commercially. None preclude

odd balance and pointability, awkward reloading and manual cycling techniques disturbing to the sight picture and concentration.

There are, on the other hand, some quite ideal lever actions. Those most noted have been and are the Winchester Model 1886 (produced from 1886 to 1935 in quantity of about 160,000), and Winchester Model 71 which replaced it (Nov. 2, 1935 to 1957 in quantity of 47,254-plus).

The Model 71 utilized the Golden Jubilee (50-year celebration updating and revision of the Model 1886) action and was produced in state-of-the-art metallurgy in Deluxe (checkering, pistol grip cap, sling, low profile swivels) and Standard (sans the above features) grades, both affected by minor manufacturing variations (tang length, comb shape and length, sights, mag-

THE ERGONOMIC 71

by KARL BOSSELMANN

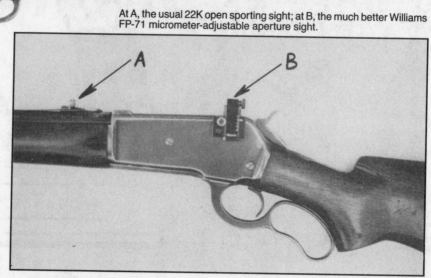

Here are the two best sporting firearms safeties going, both ergonomically sound—the tang slide safety and the external hammer.

azine tube caps, barrel stamping and crown, trigger block safety, and hammer serrations to name most). Rifles with 20-inch carbine-length barrels were first offered on Jan. 14, 1937, later dropped in 1947, with the standard being the 24-inch barrel. Caliber was 348 WCF only, one of the most powerful of lever gun calibers. Production quality slightly declined from initial prewar to the late postwar guns. The Model 71 proved to be a decided favorite with many hunters in Alaska, Canada, and the Pacific Northwest. Numbers of guides used it for reliable backup duty, especially with the 250-grain bullet loading. The rifle remains popular to this day in those regions.

The 71 incorporated several new features of that particular firearms transition era: thicker buttstocks with reduced drop, shotgun buttplate, and pistol grip; a wider forearm—not too thin for comfort nor too thick to be handy; thinner, round barrels to cut muzzle weight and overall heft; coil springs for smoother action as well as the ultimate in serviceability.

The 348 WCF is a powerful cartridge with very manageable, non-abusive recoil levels, and it certainly amassed some fine field results. The rifle itself and its factory cartridge may be enhanced by some big-bore wildcatting to a wide variety of calibers on that superbly constructed case which has an exceptionally strong and thick web section. These can make the 71 the rifle of choice on large, dangerous, thin-skinned game such as the big

With aesthetically pleasing lines and highly functional flat profile, the 71 is easily carried in the field; the action is very strong and operates with incredible smoothness.

(Below) A Special Order Deluxe Model 1886 Winchester in 45-70, produced in 1887.

At A, the usual 22K open sporting sight; at B, the much better Williams FP-71 micrometer-adjustable aperture sight.

bears, jaguar, African lion and leopard. The most notable such wildcat is the 450 Alaskan by Harold Johnson of Cooper Landing, Alaska, developed in the early 1950s.

Some wildcatters found that flat-point bullets—which the tubular magazine demands—weren't always available in their chosen calibers, so existing projectiles would be modified or used as-is, the latter by loading just one cartridge in the magazine in addition to the one chambered. I did that for some years in two 40-caliber wildcats. It's no real handicap even against

The 71's tubular magazine can be recharged while a loaded round remains in the chamber, a sizable advantage.

the big bears since reloading is so fast and effortless.

Present-day condemnations of the 71 exist, so let's examine the most popular ones to gauge their validity:

- The rifle won't take high-pressure ammunition. So what? Since when are high pressures desirable or even necessary, especially for dangerous game? The factory 348 round is loaded to not exceed 43,200 CUP; the successful British elephant-category cartridges for the big double guns only produce about 29,000 CUP. High pressures, except for flat trajectories in long distance shooting, are just not desirable.
- The rifle won't allow a top-mounted scope. I'm right-handed and have had several customized 71s with scopes mounted on the off-side (right side) of the receiver. This in no way affects loading, and cheeking the stock a bit harder doesn't cause any problems with me. Furthermore, many of us who constantly hunt in brush and timber don't care for optics at all.
- The tubular magazine requires flat-point bullets. Excellent! On a world-

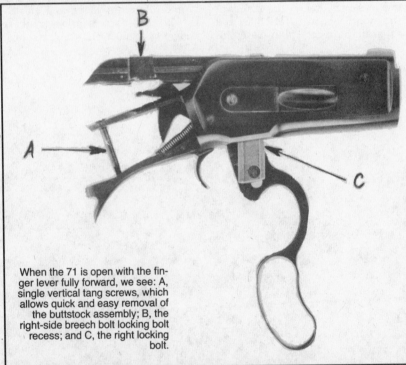

When the 71 is open with the finger lever fully forward, we see: A, single vertical tang screws, which allows quick and easy removal of the buttstock assembly; B, the right-side breech bolt locking bolt recess; and C, the right locking bolt.

Loading just one quickly is easy with the 71.

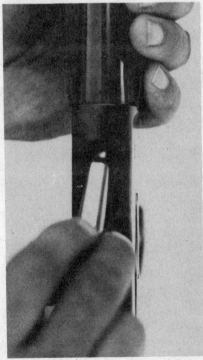

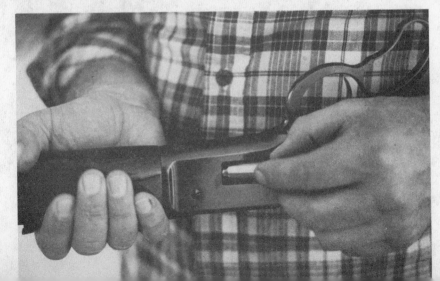

There is also a fast and easy reloading technique for southpaws—it really is ergonomic.

wide basis, most sporting shots average well under 150 yards; such closeness makes spitzer projectiles unnecessary. The various flat-points are superior for the bigger, tougher varieties of game in that their shock potentials are increased; and they produce better, *more consistent,* straighter and larger wound channels than pointed styles do.

- They're grossly inaccurate. Balderdash! No such thing. I've used and collected the 71s—and 1886s—since I was in grade school and have fired tens of thousands of rounds through them in the process. Don't treat them like target rifles; mount sights you like; shoot *three-shot strings.* In a properly set-up 71 with tailored loads, a 2-inch, 100-yard average group size is certainly feasible.

Reliability of the Model 71 has proven to be absolutely excellent throughout the years. I fired those thousands of rounds through a variety of 71s without parts breakage of any kind or jams attributable to anything but poor quality handloads. John Kronfeld has recently completed a series of tests with a new Browning 71 he later wildcatted to 348 Ackley Improved, as well as with a companion Winchester-made gun in 450 Alaskan caliber. He reports that no malfunctions of any sort occurred during the shooting of thousands of rounds.

In my last two years of high school, I purchased a custom 450 Alaskan postwar 71 from Dick Williams of the Williams Gun Sight Company. It had an ideal 22-inch, medium-heavy, straight-taper barrel with a 21-inch rifling twist; serial #40365. In practice and plinking, I fired about two thousand rounds through it, then used it for culling bison one season. Later, I fired another accumulated fifteen hundred rounds or so, then sold it to a friend who abused it with an additional 36,000-plus rounds over the course of several years. His standard loading was 65 grains of IMR 3031 and a 400-grain hard-cast, plain-base bullet. No parts broke; no malfunctions other than those attributable to incorrect handloads ever occurred; one magazine spring was the only part ever replaced to my recollection. This is good service.

(Author's Note: To adapt that rifle to the heavier recoil of this wildcat cartridge [400-grain bullet at about 2100 fps], the buttstock had to be solidly bedded to the receiver; also, the forearm tip had to be modified to a band-type arrangement, the tenon soft-silver-soldered to the barrel, and the forearm appropriately glass-bedded to the front of the receiver and the forearm tip or the whole forearm assembly would continually shoot loose.)

Throughout decades past, objective writers reviewing the Model 71 refer to it in such terms as, " . . . tops in a lever action; a first class hunting rifle; has superb balance; classic; a favorite of many hunters young and old; the very best lever action for powerful cartridges suitable for larger game; busi-

Beau Hickory shoots rapid-fire with the 71.

This is an Improved 416x348. A 348 WCF case is at right.

2.255"

Useful components include: A, Hornady 200-grain (#3410), cannelured; B, Barnes 250-grain (#34810), cannelured; C, LBT (Lead Bullets Technology), unsized, 250-grain flat-nose gascheck; D, NEI (Northeastern Industrial), unsized, 275-grain flat-nose gascheck (experimental); E, Hoch-sized 300-grain flat-nose gascheck (experimental); F, Winchester factory-loaded Silvertip Cartridge.

A   B   C   D   E   F

nesslike in appearance; nicely balanced; a delight to handle; capable of extremely fast repeat shots; effortless to use; very smooth handling . . ." Many noted authorites as well as a great number of hunters and shooters agree today.

An accomplished man with this lever gun can chamber a cartridge during recovery from recoil, and his aimed fire is only slightly slower than that of a double rifle shooter. An additional benefit of the 71 is that it carries three more rounds than the double and it has no down-time when reloading provided a cartridge remains in the chamber. While the hammerless, sidelock double rifle remains the epitome of the big and dangerous game sporting rifle, most especially against Cape buffalo, rhino, and elephant in Africa, I'm convinced the 71 beats it in Alaskan, Canadian, and Pacific Northwest game fields and even in Africa when used against such as lion and leopard, especially when big-bore wildcatted.

Another appreciable design fact of the Model 71 is that the owner need not be a genius to dismantle or service

it in the field. If I have any complaint concerning this rifle, it's that it has never been produced by any factory in a larger caliber.

Certainly, nothing is now being produced that does the Model 71 jobs bet-

ter. Shooting the Model 71 is an exercise in flowing motions and energies. Ergonomically sound, of super quality and aesthetics, it remains " . . . . the finest of the lever actions." And of sporting repeaters. ●

Displayed is the comfortable shouldering and the unstrained position of the hand/wrist/forearm the 71 provides.

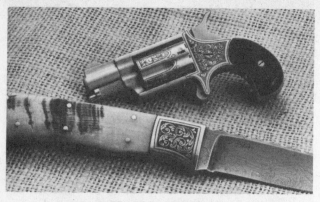

SCOTT PILKINGTON

JOHN J. ADAMS

The Art of The Engraver

ROGER SAMPSON

GEOFFROY R. GOURNET

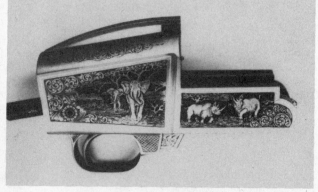

HOWARD V. GRANT

ROGER SAMPSON

RACHEL WELLS

SCOTT PILKINGTON

SCOTT PILKINGTON

TERRY THEIS

HEIDEMARIE HIPTMAYER

HEIDEMARIE HIPTMAYER

ROGER KEHR

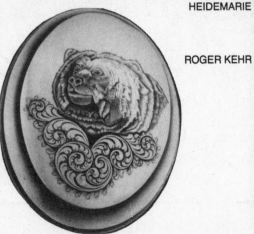

1912   Edward Clark Prudhomme   1990

Another of the grand old men has left us. E. C. Prudhomme died February 25, 1990, in a hospital in Rochester, Minnesota, and was buried March 2 in Forest Park Cemetery, Shreveport, Louisiana. He was seventeen years a professional wrestler, three years a soldier, and thirty-five years an engraver, during which time he embellished over three-thousand firearms. Prudhomme was a tireless promoter of the art of engraving and the NRA and his work appeared in these pages many times. His kind are rare, which is why they're always missed when they're gone.

BILL JOHNS

BILL JOHNS

JOHN KUDLAS

JOHN KUDLAS

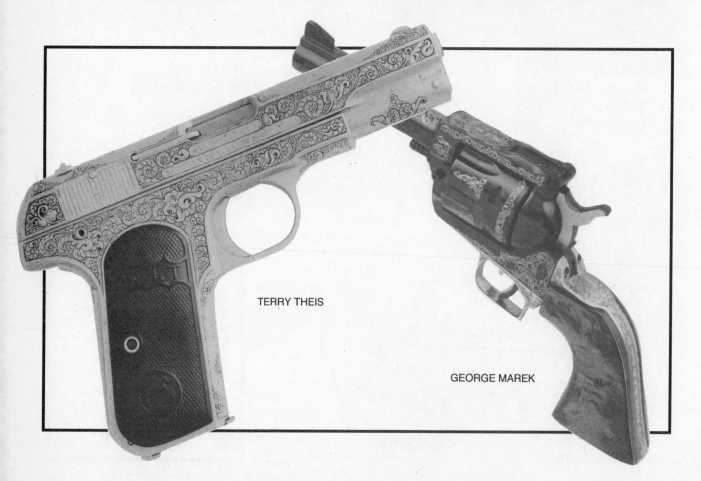

TERRY THEIS

GEORGE MAREK

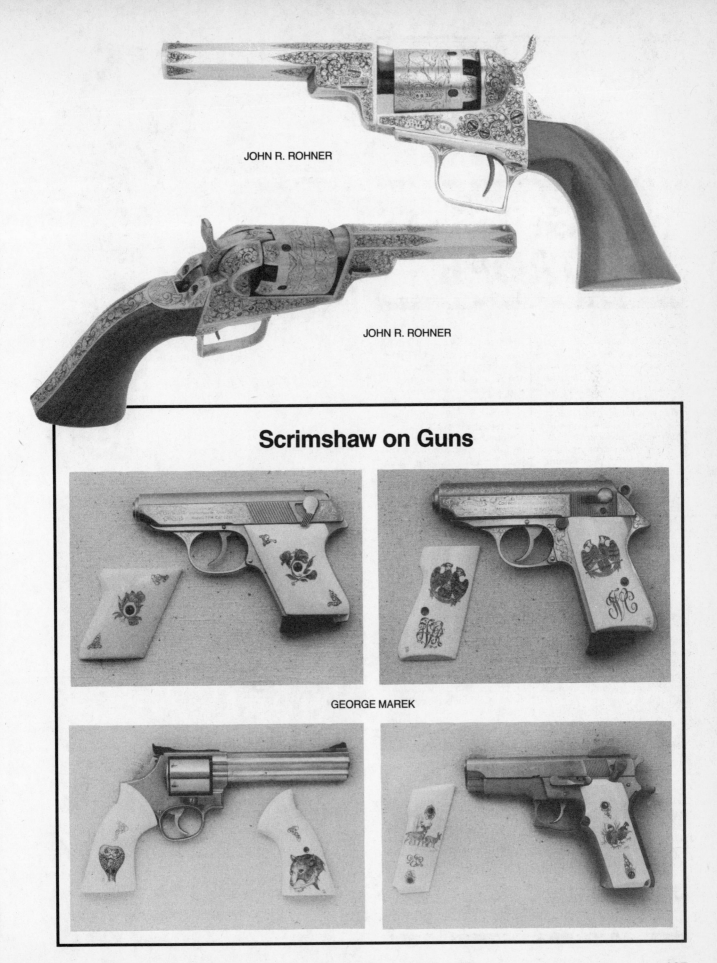

JOHN R. ROHNER

JOHN R. ROHNER

Scrimshaw on Guns

GEORGE MAREK

by RAYMOND CARANTA

THE GUNS OF EUROPE

THE situation has little changed since last year in Western Europe; the firearms market is still quite soft. More and more, we see exotic ammunition made in East European countries, Israel, Brazil and the Far East, with low prices and distribution in supermarkets.

About restrictive gun laws: just as the government commission in charge was gathered in a Paris palace to initiate new regulations in accordance with the international Schengen agreements, a huge demonstration of angry hunters passed under their windows which, in conjunction with the results of European elections where hunter candidates obtained unexpected successes, convinced the honorable members that they were not becoming popular and, temporarily, they have postponed any measure. The Government of France, at least, has turned its activity toward the immigration problems, which seems a much sounder attitude.

We have noted about 20 new automatic shotgun variations, this year, from Beretta, Breda, Browning-FN, Franchi, Lanber and Verney-Carron, but none of major technical interest. Of European pump-action guns, only the new prismatic magazine-fed Atis is worth notice.

More than 40 over/under variations or new products, this year, from Beretta, Browning-FN, Chapuis, Franchi, Gamba, Investarm, Marocchi, Raznoexport (Soviet), Felix Sarasqueta, Tecni-Mec and Verney-Carron. And there are 46 new or modified side-by-sides from Arrieta, Bruchet, Chapuis, Ego, Fabarm, Ferlib, Francotte, Garbi, Gaucher, Marocchi, Powell, Raznoexport, Wolf and Zanardini.

The world's gun industry has shown the European market about 90 new, modified or rechambered repeating rifles this year, from 33 manufacturers. The most important achievements in this field seem to be American, with the exception of the small Israeli pump-action rifle.

Austrian SPOWA Ultramatic 9mm Luger 19-shot double-action pistol.

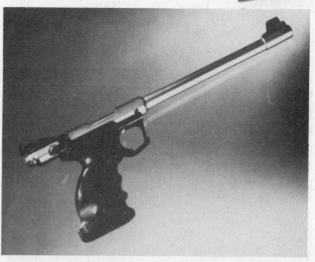

Practical shooting SIG P-210 9mm pistol customized by Morier in Switzerland.

Gaucher GN 1 Silhouette single shot rimfire pistol of the type now popular and legal in France.

Erma's EP 882 22 Long Rifle automatic pistol—not quite as big as a P-38.

Editor's Note

Raymond Caranta's work appears more in GUN DIGEST now than ten years ago, but a lot has happened to our European Correspondent over those ten years, so a little updating is in order: He has retired from Aeronautique du Sud, France's principal helicopter manufacturer, and replaced that effort with high-level and unofficial investigative police work, as among other things, one of two arms and crime experts accredited to the Courts of Appeal of France. His Guillaume Tell, a French GUN DIGEST, has undergone a change to an annual product review, a process which pleases him and no doubt a number of thousands of French citizens and Francophones everywhere. It pleases us, too, for now he has the time to seek and find the unusual in Europe and bring it to GUN DIGEST.

Ken Warner

The Beretta Model 98 F target pistol is chambered in 30 Luger for the Italian market.

The Benelli MP 90 S system comprises three ISU competition pistols—22 Short, 22 LR, 32 SW Long WC.

This is Star's Firestar M-43 eight-shot 9mm Luger compact pistol.

products were the new ISU competition Benelli line, the Erma 22 LR Luger conversion and their clever 22 LR P-38 imitation, the six Peters Stahl practical pistols, the new Polish service pistol, the SIG-Sauer P228, the Austrian SPOWA 9mm 19-shot system, the five new Tanfoglios, the French Unique silhouette pistol and the four Yugoslav Zastava handguns.

In revolvers, the main activity was with Franchi, Gamba, Manurhin, Mateba, Morier and Zastava, which has extended its line. And we saw about 20 new replicas from Ardesa, Dikar, Pedersoli and Uberti.

There are new air and CO_2 pistols from FAS, FEG (Hungary), Feinwerkbau, El Gamo, Merkuria (Czech) and Walther. Of these, the most impressive were the Feinwerkbau, Merkuria and Walther Olympic Rapid Fire CO_2 five-shot automatic training pistols.

Among European guns new or changed since last year, not intended for a large distribution in the United States or of some peculiar interest for the American reader, we have noted:

Anschütz . . . .

. . . . has generated 15 new versions of sporting and top-level competition rifles this year in rimfire calibers, 22 Hornet and 222 Remington.

Ardesa . . . .

. . . . provides eight new percussion rifles, one percussion shotgun and a percussion "Parker Match" pistol. Among the rifles, the Creedmoor Match and Henry Target in caliber 451 are the most original from this Spanish manufacturer.

Atis . . . .

. . . . presented a new Atis P.M. pump riot gun fed by a prismatic six-shot box magazine. Contrary to other Italian box magazine riot guns, this one is actually available at a reasonable price on the European market.

Benelli . . . .

. . . . showed a set of superb ISU competition automatic pistols respectively chambered in 22 Short, 22 Long Rifle, and 32 S&W Long labeled MP 90 S for Olympic rapid fire, standard pistol and sporting pistol events. Their new shotguns are exported to the United States.

Beretta . . . .

. . . . announced several new chamberings in the "SO" luxury line of over/unders. The other classic shotgun and pistol variations introduced this year are already available on the American market with, perhaps, the exception of the 30 Luger Model 98 F pistol.

The Frankonia Model 98 trigger widely distributed in Europe.

In the popular rimfire and competition rifle field, European activity has been quite limited, but there are a good dozen new or modified match rifles from Anschütz, Diana, Feinwerkbau, Keppeler, Raznoexport, Sako, Sauer and Unique. The situation is about the same for express rifles and *Drillinge* with new items from Ego, FIAS, Francotte, Gamba, Gaucher, Heym, Ripamonti, Zanardini and Antonio Zoli. Many of the 27 new air or CO_2 rifles are American, but BSA, Diana, Feinwerkbau, El Gamo, Norica, Raznoexport, Steyr and Walther did have new things to show.

Among handgun offerings, more than 100 new automatic pistol variations were shown by about 50 companies, many of them American. Among the most significant European

The Atis Trusty P.M. 3 prismatic box magazine riot gun in 12-gauge.

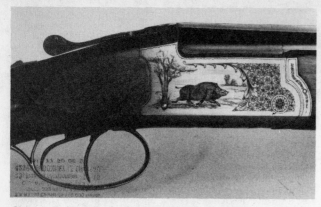

Chapuis Alpha-2 over/under with a frisky boar on view.

Chapuis Progress side-by-side, intended for woodcock.

Double express rifle with Louis XVI style engraving by Auguste Francotte.

Brenneke . . . .

. . . . has expanded the chamberings in their high-quality bolt-action rifle.

Bruchet . . . .

. . . . now makes in Saint Etienne five different versions of the famous French Darne side-by-side fixed-barrel shotguns. Prices range from about $2,000 to $6,000 on the French market, including an internal tax of 18.6 percent.

B.S.A. . . . .

. . . . showed the new fixed-barrel "Superstar" air rifle.

Chapuis . . . .

. . . . simply showed improvements on their Alpha over/unders and Progress side-by-sides.

Diana . . . .

. . . . has made detail changes in Models 100 (pre-compressed air), 820 F and 820 L 22 LR rifles.

EGO . . . .

. . . . marketed their new Anglia sidelock side-by-side hammerless shotgun, a Hammerlux external hammer model and a classic side-by-side express rifle chambered in 9.3x74R and 375 H&H Magnum.

Erma . . . .

. . . . now has an interesting conversion in 22 LR for the German Luger and an eight-shot 22 LR replica of the service P-38, slightly undersized, but offering double action.

FAS . . . .

. . . . has launched the AP-606 pre-compressed air competition pistol for ISU regulation showing.

FEG . . . .

. . . . says its new Patronett target CO_2 pistol, using conventional 12-gram sparklets, will shoot at least the 70 shots required for shooting the ISU 10-meter match on one loading.

Feinwerkbau . . . .

. . . . introduced the fascinating C5 automatic CO_2 five-shot pistol for Olympic Rapid Fire training; C10 single-shot CO_2 pistol; Model 100 single shot pre-compressed air pistol; Model 601 air rifle; and Model 2600 ISU free 22 LR rifle. It's a big FWB year.

Fias . . . .

. . . . has moved to 10 chamberings, from the 222 Remington to the 9.3x74R in their 340 Express over/under.

Francotte . . . .

. . . . continues to show its fantastic custom guns ranging from about $5,000 to $25,000.

Frankonia . . . .

. . . . has now designed a clever trigger for Model 98 rifles costing about $80 in France. They have sold 10,000 of them in five years.

Renato Gamba . . . .

. . . . now can make the Bayern 88 over/under combination gun chambered in 12-gauge for one barrel and many rifled calibers for the other one, including 222 Remington and 30-06. However, their best offering is the Safari King side-by-side express rifle available in 375 H&H Magnum, 470 Nitro-Express and 458 Winchester Magnum.

French Bruchet V 22 side-by-side fixed-barrel shotgun.

Sagittaire Express rifle by Verney-Carron, in 7x65R or 9.3x74R, with *battue* sights.

(Above and above right) Plume Grand Becassier Special over/under by Verney-Carron—a woodcocking gun.

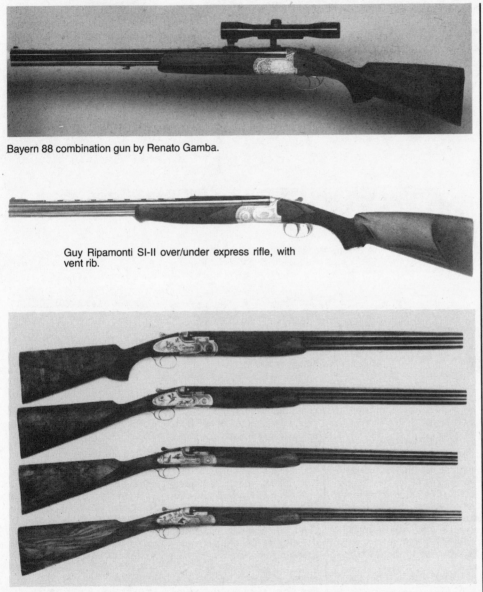

Heym three-barrel Model 35 available in a wide range of calibers; barrel layout at left.

Bayern 88 combination gun by Renato Gamba.

Guy Ripamonti SI-II over/under express rifle, with vent rib.

These are the sidelock Beretta S0-9 over/under shotguns. From top: 12, 20, 28 and 410 bore.

Keppeler . . . .

. . . . can provide, from Germany, a complete line of competition rifles for ISU 300-meter shooting on request.

Merkuria . . . .

. . . . is selling, from Czechoslovakia, a highly sophisticated five-shot CO_2 training pistol for Olympic Rapid Fire and a nice competition single shot CO_2 model for the ISU 10-meter match. Both use 12-gram sparklets and avoid the cylinder refilling of German guns.

Morier . . . .

. . . . has a specialty in fitting special barrels with muzzle-brakes to Smith & Wesson revolvers chambered in 357 and 44 calibers (from $90 to $105 ex Works). The Swiss Saint Sulpice firm also customizes Colt Government and SIG P210 pistols for practical shooting.

Pedersoli . . . .

. . . . has marketed, in honor of the French Revolution Bicentenary, a wonderful service musket Model 1777 with bayonet which is selling quite well in spite of its high $832 (retail, inclusive of purchase tax) price tag.

Raznoexport . . . .

. . . . seems to have found *glasnost* and is now mailing gun catalogs. They have also introduced, since 1986, 18 new models of target pistols, rifles and shotguns.

Ripamonti . . . .

. . . . has added, from Saint-Etienne, a combination rifle-shotgun sold, according to the grade, from $3,000 to $5,000 in France (tax must be deducted for export) and offers new chamberings for his side-by-side SE VII and over/under SI-II express rifles.

SPOWA . . . .

. . . . announced it is offering a practical shooting 19-shot 9mm Ultramatic pistol of original design (system Gabriel-Vojta).

Gaucher . . . .

. . . . is meeting pistol silhouette shooters' needs. No gun license is required in France for single shot rimfire pistols over 11 inches long, so silhouette shooting is expanding fast and Gaucher now has a nice GN 1 Silhouette model.

Gex-Dumez . . . .

. . . . is a French company which introduced the Crapahute bullpup bolt-action rifle chambered in 7x64, 270 Winchester, 30-06 and 8x68S Magnum.

Heym . . . .

. . . . introduced this year an Express Big Bore bolt-action rifle chambered in 404 Jeffery, 416 Rigby, 500 Nitro-Express, 450 Ackley, 460 Weatherby Magnum and 500 A-Square. Heym is also making an interesting three-shot combination rifle-shotgun sold, in France, at $9,000, inclusive of the 18.6 percent purchase tax.

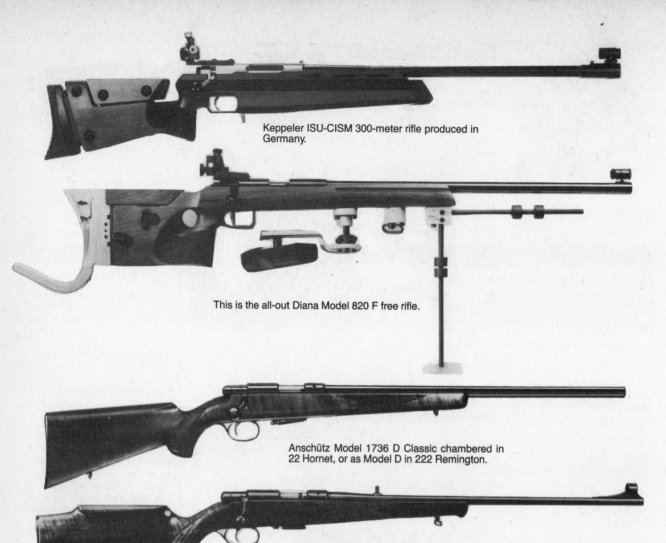

Keppeler ISU-CISM 300-meter rifle produced in Germany.

This is the all-out Diana Model 820 F free rifle.

Anschütz Model 1736 D Classic chambered in 22 Hornet, or as Model D in 222 Remington.

Anschütz Model 1712 bolt-action rifle, one of the most prized European rimfires.

The new Austrian firm created a stir with its internal bolt sliding in a receiver, recoil compensator and adjustable selective double-action trigger. The single-action let-off is set at 3.3 pounds and the double-action weight is 8 pounds. The grip pitch is 72 degrees.

Star . . . .

. . . . displayed this year its Firestar M-43, a small 9mm Luger pistol and a small 25 ACP Starlite which cannot be exported to America. The Starlite M-43 is a progressive single-action

sign of all-steel construction weighing 28 ounces empty.

Verney-Carron . . . .

. . . . offers four new variations of their automatic shotguns (two long recoil and two gas-operated), five light over/unders, a combination rifle-shotgun, the Sagittaire mixte, chambered in 12-gauge and 7x65R or 9.3x74R, and a Sagittaire Express rifle in the same calibers.

Voere . . . .

. . . . showed a Combat 9mm Parabellum 15-shot self-loading rifle, which raised much interest. Austrian guns are doing that these days.

Walther . . . .

. . . . offers, beside the impressive CP 5 Olympic Rapid Fire CO_2 training pistol, a new electronic trigger mechanism in the FP free pistol and introduced the LG-90 pre-compressed air competition rifle along the lines of the CG 90 CO_2 model. Moreover, two ESK 30 and ESK 60 9mm submachine gun prototypes featuring *axial*

30-shot and 60-shot magazines attracted plenty of visitors at IWA.

Zastava . . . .

. . . . now markets, from Yugoslavia, improved versions of the Tokarev pistol chambered both in 7.62mm and 9mm Luger and fitted with fixed or adjustable sights, plus hammer-drop safeties. They also make similar variations of the 32 ACP and 380 ACP police pistols and have introduced sporting revolvers chambered in 357 Magnum and 9mm Luger. ●

Pedersoli's Model 1777 replica French service musket.

You Don't Really Own an Over & Under Unless You Own a Browning.

Uncasing a Browning is the perfect beginning to a successful hunt. That's because — unlike other over and under shotguns — a Browning Citori offers an instant sense of exceptional quality, careful craftsmanship, and functional elegance.

It is well worth your time to consider the following points when you are ready to purchase your over and under.

Insist on a full-width hinge pin that fully bridges the receiver for strength. Look for a *tapered* locking bolt that seats deeper into the barrel lugs as your shotgun "shoots in" over the decades. You want your over and under to wear in, not wear out.

Make sure that metal surfaces are polished fully before blueing. This extra measure of attention is identified by extraordinary richness and deepness of the blued finish. Check wood-to-metal fits. They should be tight and consistent in contour. Inspect all working parts, right down to the ejectors, to assure they possess tight tolerances. Settle for no less than select walnut embellished by sharp cut checkering.

Don't stop there: inspect the rib, feel the trigger, open and close the action. Listen carefully. Shoulder and swing. Only the finest over and under will feel like an extension of your body.

If it passes the test, odds are it's a Browning.

For more details that will make your decision even easier, write for our 116 page catalog with more on the 110 different Citori models and other Browning hunting and shooting gear. Please send $2.00 to Browning, Dept. J013, Morgan, Utah 84050.

BROWNING®
The Best There Is.

See what you've been missing.

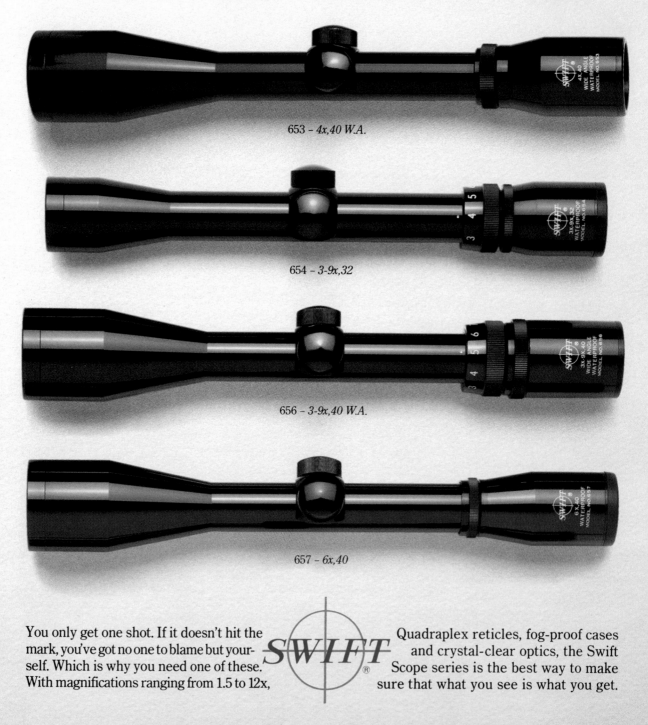

653 – 4x,40 W.A.

654 – 3-9x,32

656 – 3-9x,40 W.A.

657 – 6x,40

You only get one shot. If it doesn't hit the mark, you've got no one to blame but yourself. Which is why you need one of these. With magnifications ranging from 1.5 to 12x,

SWIFT

Quadraplex reticles, fog-proof cases and crystal-clear optics, the Swift Scope series is the best way to make sure that what you see is what you get.

Swift Instruments, Inc., 952 Dorchester Ave., Boston, MA 02125 • P.O. Box 562, San Jose, CA 95106

Go for the GOLD!

A winning tradition. Legendary quality. Springfield Armory's gold medal pistols are winners, every one.

1911-A1 PISTOL

The Springfield 1911-A1 pistol is the choice of the world's top action shooters, including three time IPSC World Champion and six time USPSA National Champion Rob Leatham. Winners choose winners, and the Springfield 1911-A1 is "The Winners' Choice".

P9 DOUBLE ACTION PISTOL

The 9mm Springfield P9 is the premium quality version of the famed Czech CZ-75. With a high capacity fifteen-round magazine, slim profile grips, a selective double/single action that allows it to be carried "cocked and locked", and a superior fit and finish, the P9 is the "the best of the best". There's even two sizes—standard and compact—and a new LSP model (Long Slide Ported) that's ideal for competition. Want to be a winner at the 9mm game? Say "Czechmate", and the game is yours.

OMEGA 10MM PISTOL

The Springfield OMEGA was the first production pistol capable of effectively handling high performance 10mm ammunition. Optional .38 Super and .45 ACP are also available, and dual extractors make interchangeability of calibers a reality. The Springfield OMEGA. It's the "Perfect Ten".

1911-A2 S.A.S.S.™

Springfield's patented design for an affordable, single shot tack driver is the perfect choice for hunting or metallic silhouette shooting. With interchangeable barrels in eight calibers and two different lengths, and a choice of either a complete S.A.S.S.™ pistol or a S.A.S.S.™ conversion unit for your own 1911-A1 frame, S.A.S.S.™ is the perfect choice—all in one shot.

See the complete line of Springfield Armory gold medal pistols and rifles at any Authorized Springfield Retailer. Or, send $3 for our 1990 four-color catalog.

Safety and instruction manuals available from Springfield Armory. Always wear eye and ear protection when using any firearm. Use only factory recommended ammunition. Ask your Authorized Springfield Retailer for details on Springfield's generous across-the-board warranty and service after the sale.

The Oldest Name In American Firearms

SPRINGFIELD ARMORY ®

Section SV-28 ■ 420 West Main Street ■ Geneseo, Illinois 61254 ■ (309) 944-5631

by DOC CARLSON

BLACKPOWDER REVIEW

IN THE late 1960s a rebirth began. Muzzle-loading, which had lain dormant for many years, began to awaken. This renewal of interest was directed mostly along traditional or historical lines. The interest seemed to stem from a rekindling of interest in early American history—probably brought on to a great extent by the centennial of our Civil War. The interest literally exploded in the 1970s, reaching a peak by the end of that decade.

The rapid expansion of the market for muzzle-loading arms and accessories brought with it an explosion in the number of companies making and selling these products. There were some bad effects, however, as is possible with any explosion. There were many products on the market that were shoddy, poorly designed and made, and, in many cases, downright dangerous. It was an interesting time, but confusing and fraught with danger for the consumer. Because of this, the peak of the interest passed quickly and muzzle-loading quieted down. It still was a very viable market but the big push subsided.

Then, about five years ago, a second rebirth began, a much more healthy, long lasting type. There is a balance between many facets of this muzzle-loading game that will make it a marathon runner instead of a sprinter. Nowhere has this trend been more in evidence than at the Shooting Hunting and Outdoor Trade (SHOT) Show held each year in January.

The driving force of this new muzzle-loading interest seems to be the hunter and the guns and accessories that are aimed at this large market. Tradi-

tional interest is still there and growing, however, and there seems to be a real trend to better quality reproductions, especially top-drawer target-type firearms.

Hunting firearms dominated the SHOT Show again this year. The in-line type of action, coupled with a modern stock shape, is definitely a growing species of muzzle-loading firearm. There were in-line muzzleloaders in the 1800s and reports of an even earlier flintlock in-line on exhibit in a museum in Europe, the modern styling is certainly a recent innovation. Traditionalists are not impressed with the looks of these rifles, but it is hard to argue with the functionality of the guns.

The Knight Rifle, by Modern Muzzle Loading, Inc., started it all a few years back. They continue to expand their line from the 45-, 50- and 54-caliber basic rifles. Two new ones should stir interest.

The first of these is the Back Country Carbine, with a 20-inch barrel. It is available in stainless steel with a black laminate stock or in blued steel with a wood laminated stock in a pleasing brown wood tone. There is the 45-caliber with a 1-in-24-inch twist, the 50 or 54 with 1-in-28-inch twist. The gun is intended for slug-type projectiles. The receiver is drilled and tapped for scope mounts and the rifle comes with adjustable open sights. The trigger is adjustable, similar to those of modern centerfire rifles. There is a thumb safety and a second safety that blocks the striker from hitting the cap on the nipple. This device also allows dry firing, something not simple with traditional actions.

The second rifle is called the

BK-89 Squirrel Rifle. In 36-caliber, the little gun has a 24-inch barrel with a 1-in-24-inch twist, intended for shooting patched round ball, conical-type bullets or jacketed bullets using a plastic sabot. The sabot is available. There is a walnut stock of modern-type configuration and blued barrel and action. It tips the scales at a light 5½ pounds and comes with adjustable open sights. A peep or aperture sight is easily mounted.

Ultra Light Arms is now

making their new M-90 muzzle-loading rifle, their first foray into the muzzle-loading market. The rifle is an in-line style with totally modern lines and feel, in a typical Ultra Light stock of Kevlar and graphite. It is finished in brown with a leaf pattern. The rifle is a trim 6 pounds; the 28-inch barrel is button-rifled and has a 48-inch twist which should make it reasonably accurate with either patched round ball or conical projectile. Ultra Light says it will shoot under 2 inches at 100 yards, plenty good enough. The rifle comes with detachable-type sling swivels, recoil pad and a protective hard case. The blued steel receiver is topped with an adjustable peep-type rear sight and a front bead on a ramp.

The Ultra Light Model 90 striker is cocked with a knurled knob. The trigger is the tried-and-true Timney. At a suggested retail of $950, this is not a cheap rifle. However, it is built to the same standards as the

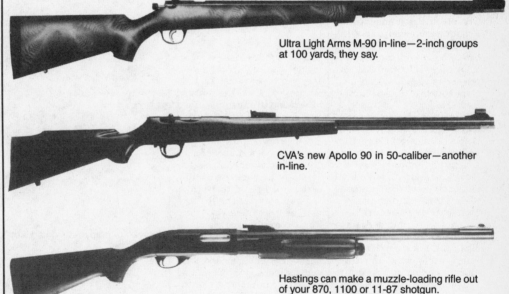

Ultra Light Arms M-90 in-line—2-inch groups at 100 yards, they say.

CVA's new Apollo 90 in 50-caliber—another in-line.

Hastings can make a muzzle-loading rifle out of your 870, 1100 or 11-87 shotgun.

rest of the Ultra Light line—definitely custom grade. It's light and well balanced with the handling features that one wants in a modern-style hunting rifle.

Before leaving the modern styling let's look at one more. Called the Apollo 90, the rifle is Connecticut Valley Arms' first step into the in-line type of rifle. It is available in two grades, standard with a hardwood stock and the Premier Grade that features a walnut stock, and chrome-lined bore and action. Pricing is $387.95 and $513.95 respectively.

The action is an in-line percussion with a pull-back bolt of stainless steel. The bolt is cocked with a side-mounted handle. The blued receiver is octagonal with a tapered round barrel in 50-caliber, rifled with one turn in 32 inches intended for slug-type projectiles, obviously. There is a typical CVA open hunting sight, adjustable

The ramrod is housed on top of the barrel under the open sights. The rear sight is adjustable for windage and elevation.

The advantage of this setup is that the occasional muzzle-loading hunter can use his familiar shotgun as a muzzle-loading deer rifle and the safety button, etc. will be familiar to him. He'll have to remember that pumping the 870 action will have no reloading effect

pistol with a 12-inch barrel are available in 50- and 54-caliber and are rifled to handle either the T/C Maxi-type bullets or patched round ball. The barrels are readily interchangeable so that calibers can be changed easily by merely changing the barrel. See the Testfire report, page 199.

Hornady has been swaging lead round balls for the muzzle-loading shooter for some time.

this market also with their new hollowpoint XTP pistol bullets prepackaged with plastic sabots for various muzzle-loading calibers. The XTP pistol bullet is also a new innovation of the Hornady people. Developed to give controlled expansion and deep penetration without breaking up at a wide variety of velocities, this bullet was picked by Hornady for use in muzzle-loading arms.

On a more traditional note, I stopped by the Taylor & Co. booth and what I saw should be good news for Civil War reenactors and those who just like to shoot Civil War-type arms. Sue Hawkens, the honcho at Taylor, was showing a new 1861 Springfield they import from Italy. The rifle is a dead ringer for the original, well fitted and finished. The lock is crisp and correctly marked; all metal work is finished bright; the barrel has the nipple bolster forged in one piece with the barrel. The rifling, while three lands and grooves, as original, is not ta-

(Above and below) New configuration for Thompson/Center provides a slick carbine or a powerful pistol.

for windage and elevation, teamed with a ramped bead. The stock has a cheekpiece, rubber recoil pad and sling swivel studs. There is a sliding action cover which provides a sealed ignition area. Gas and powder residue are vented out of the bottom of the action, away from the shooter.

While not everyone's cup of tea, it appears the in-line muzzleloader is here to stay. They definitely have a following among the hunting fraternity using the muzzleloader to hunt one more season. These hunters seem to prefer the familiar look and feel of the modern rifle.

How about a muzzle-loading rifle barrel to fit your favorite shotgun? It's here. Hastings Barrels has come up with a muzzle-loading rifle barrel to fit Remington 1100, 870 or 11-87 shotguns. Darndest idea I ever heard of, but it seems to work out fine.

Barrels are French-made for Hastings of chrome-moly steel using the hammer forge technique. Rifling is one turn in 34 inches, .008-inch depth grooves for use with either slug-type bullets or jacketed bullets with a plastic sabot. Made in 50-caliber only at present, each barrel is serial numbered and proofed by the French Govt. proof house.

The special breech plug uses standard 209 shotgun primers for ignition; otherwise it is loaded like any muzzleloader.

and his hunting buddies might look at him slightly askance if they see him loading an 1100 Remington from the muzzle; otherwise it appears to be a very innovative way of getting into the muzzle-loading hunting sport with a reasonable cash outlay of just under $220.

Thompson/Center Arms has a totally new muzzle-loading carbine and pistol that bridge the gap between the in-lines and the more traditional guns. The T/C carbine and pistol use essentially the same action/receiver which has two moving parts—the hammer and trigger. The hammer is center hung and strikes a nipple set in the rear of the barrel. Nothing very new so far. Here's where the new ideas come in, however. The nipple is set with the base a fraction of an inch from the actual end of the barrel, causing the flash from the cap to jump a short distance and ignite the powder charge through a touch-hole-type arrangement similar to a flintlock. The T/C folks say that this produces less pressure variation shot to shot and, therefore, more accuracy. The entire gun can be taken down to its parts by the removal of one screw which makes cleaning a snap. Both the carbine with a 21-inch barrel and the

Now they are swaging lead slug-type projectiles. These bullets, available in 45, 50 and 54 calibers, have proven to be very accurate and dependable performers on game.

Many rifle makers are recommending jacketed pistol bullets with plastic sabots and Hornady has moved to serve

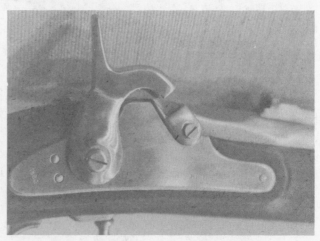

Hornady's prepackaged sabot bullets for muzzle-loading hunters.

Taylor & Co. Richmond Civil War Musket has the classic lines and style.

pered. It's a good looking rifle, accurate and definitely a shooter.

Taylor also had something for the Rebs, a very nice reproduction of the Confederate States Richmond Rifle Musket made from 1861 to 1865 at the Richmond Armory. This rifle-musket is made with the same attention to detail as their 1861 Springfield, nipple bolster forged in one piece with the barrel and all. There is a brass nose cap and buttplate, as is typical of the originals. Caliber is, of course, 58.

Buffalo Bullet Company has introduced a 58-caliber Minie bullet swaged of pure lead. It comes in two designs, a hollow-base semi-pointed style very similar to the standard Civil War issue in shape, and a hollowpoint version with a much thicker rear skirt to combat over-expansion and therefore bullet deformation when using heavy charges. The thinner skirt bullet is intended to expand to fill the grooves of the bore with standard charges of 60 to 65 grains of blackpowder in the Civil War-type muskets.

Given the trouble that it is to hand-cast target quality Minie bullets, these should be a real hit with shooters. They are packaged in protective foam boxes of 16 and come pre-lubed. The major deviation from the old design is that the grease grooves are gone, replaced by a knurled banding to hold the grease. They surely do look good and I would expect them to shoot as well as they look.

Buffalo now makes swaged pure lead round balls in .440, .451, .490, .495, .530 and .565. These bullets are packaged 100 to a reusable plastic box. There are, as well, two new slug-type bullets. One, for 50-caliber, is a 350-grain hollowpoint, hollow-base bullet and the other is also hollowpoint, hollow base in 54-caliber that tips the scales at 390 grains.

Thompson/Center is selling a carded package that has two plastic tubes each containing five Maxi Hunter bullets. These are available in 45, 50 and 54 calibers. The tube fits well in a pocket or pouch and, with the removable end caps, allows the carrying of pre-greased bullets

with a minimum of mess. The samples I saw were supplied ungreased. I like this idea. Greased Maxi-type bullets are a real mess in the field.

T/C also has a small, pocket-sized capper for #11 caps. It is about half the length of the standard capper and much easier to carry in either pouch or pocket while hunting. It's very well made.

Lyman Products was showing a new carbine that also bridges the gap between modern and traditional. The new carbine is basically the half-stock rifle; what is different is that the butt has less drop and a rubber recoil pad, more in line with what the modern rifle shooter expects. Sights are a white bead front and a folding rear adjustable for both windage and elevation. The tang is drilled and tapped to take the

fine #57 Lyman receiver sight. Called the Lyman Deerstalker, it can be had in either flint or percussion, with a choice of 50 or 54 calibers. Pricing is $285 for percussion and $310 for flint. This one should find favor among hunters and shooters, I would imagine.

Lyman has packaged a starter kit for the muzzleloader shooter who wants to start casting his own bullets. Priced at $89.95, the kit contains Lyman's 400 watt, Mini-Mag casting furnace, a long-handled casting dipper, flux, and the round ball or Maxi Ball mould of your choice in 45-, 50- or 54-caliber. The whole deal is complete and ready to begin casting on arrival. The Mini-Mag furnace will heat 8 pounds of lead to casting temperatures in about 30 minutes.

On a very traditional note,

Buffalo Bullets has two new 58-caliber slugs, as well as round balls in several calibers.

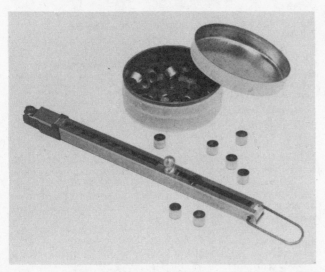

Thompson/Center's pocket-size capper really does carry easily.

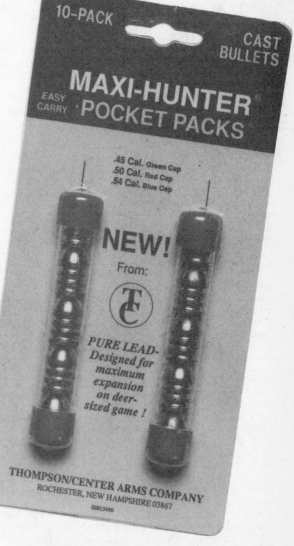

10-PACK

CAST BULLETS

MAXI-HUNTER® POCKET PACKS

EASY CARRY

.45 Cal. Green Cap
.50 Cal. Red Cap
.54 Cal. Blue Cap

NEW!
From:

TC

PURE LEAD—
Designed for maximum expansion on deer-sized game!

THOMPSON/CENTER ARMS COMPANY
ROCHESTER, NEW HAMPSHIRE 03867
00015490

These pocketable bullet selections make real hunter sense.

Lyman's Deerstalker takes the traditional line as near as it can to 1990 efficiency.

The Classic Turkey Double by CVA offers something new in buttstocks, but nice old-timey high-rise hammer.

Connecticut Valley Arms single-barrel Trapper Shotgun brings the convenience of screw-in chokes—three are furnished—to muzzle-loading.

Traditions, Inc. was showing a Kentucky-style rifle that, for a production gun, captures the look of this venerated rifle quite well. The walnut full stock has an oil-type finish, nicely set off by brass inlays at the wrist and forestock, as well as brass buttplate, trigger guard and patchbox. The octagon barrel is 40½ inches long and uses a 1-in-66-inch twist for patched round ball.

The rifle is 57½ inches overall and weighs 9 pounds. The barrel is ⅞-inch across the flats which makes the gun balance well and point as it should. Lock and barrel are blued, which surprisingly doesn't take away from the "look" of the gun, although I would prefer to see it browned. Double set, double throw triggers, fully adjustable for let-off, complete the outfit. Sights are primitive-type with the rear being adjustable for elevation and, of course, windage by moving it in its dovetail. The front sight is typical brass blade. This is one of the few Kentucky reproductions OKed by the Brigade of the American Revolution for use in reenactments. The style is the typical Roman nose Kentucky of the mid to late era. The gun is available in either flint or percussion and 45- or 50-caliber. Pricing is $410 and $387 respectively. All in all a very nice looking gun with lots of brass, but done so it looks right, not glitzy.

New this year from the Traditions folks is a pistol that is a very decent reproduction at $208 of one made by William Parker of London in the early 1800s. This is a half-stock gun with the percussion lock and barrel finished bright. Nonadjustable sights, typical of the era, sit atop the ¹⁵⁄₁₆-inch octagon barrel. The 10⅜-inch type is rifled with one turn in 18 inches, right for a pistol. All Traditions barrels are made by the cold-drawn process which produces the outside octagon, the rifling and exact bore dimensions all in one operation. It makes for a very smooth interior of the barrel promoting accuracy and ease of cleaning.

This pistol has set triggers and a half-stock of walnut nicely checkered at the grip. The base of the grip has the flare often seen on dueling and target-type pistols of this era. The triggers will fire set or unset and are fully adjustable as is the sear engagement of the lock. A brass cap guard, to keep cap flash from burning the stock, completes the picture. The balance and feel of this pistol makes it a natural for target shooting. Accuracy is good, from the reports I hear.

Target shooters certainly haven't been left out of this year's lineup. **Navy Arms Co.** has been catering to the target folks and this year they offer the Tryon Target model. This half-stock rifle is patterned after the Tryon rifles of the mid-1800s. This particular rifle has a 33-inch octagon barrel rifled with

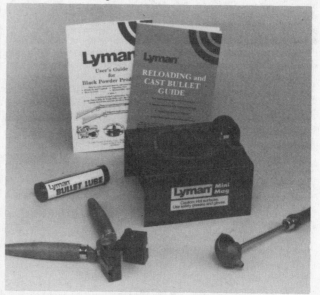

The new muzzleloader bullet casting kit from Lyman has all it takes.

a one in 20 twist for slug shooting. The groove depth is .006-inch and caliber is 451. Sighting equipment combines a hooded front with an adjustable Vernier tang sight. It sports all blackened hardware and sling swivels.

This rifle was used by the United States Team at the 13th World Muzzleloading Championships in Pforzheim, West Germany in 1989 and was a gold medal winner. Rifles for this competition must pass rigid standards of authenticity and must be very close copies of an existing original. Obviously this one is a very fine reproduction and a shooter, too. The

price of $495 is reasonable.

More and more folks are discovering the fun of hunting with the front-stuffer scattergun. As a result there are several good quality shotguns on the market and have been for some time.

Connecticut Valley Arms has combined both old and new styling in coming up with a couple of smooth bores for the hunter. The first is a side-by-side double with classic English lines, but with a rubber recoil pad. The Classic Turkey Shotgun also has a beavertail forend. Locks are typical V-spring front-action percussion locks, finished with a case-hardened appear-

The Ball Buster Combination tool provides about six functions.

ance that is most pleasing on a gun of this style. The 12-gauge barrels are blued, 28 inches long, and have the hook breech. Priced at $428.95 suggested retail, this one should be popular with the hunting crowd.

The second CVA gun for this year is the Trapper Shotgun. Single barreled, its lock is color case-hardened; its stock English style, again with a rubber recoil pad. The 28-inch 12-gauge barrel has screw-in chokes—Improved Cylinder, Modified and Full.

The sport of muzzle-loading fosters more accessories than

any other sport I can think of. These come and go; some make it, some don't. I ran into a few that just might be around for awhile:

The Ball Buster Combination tool, put out by **Cousin Bobs Mountain Products**, and invented by Robert Jones, provides many functions in a package weighing less than six ounces. Basically a bullet starter, it screws apart. The shaft of the tool holds two different screwdrivers, a vent or nipple pick, a stubby short starter and three powder measures. The hardwood ball handle is useful as a hammer also. The entire tool is very well machined and finished, a handy

addition to your hunting gear.

D&H Products Co. has been making a soft scope cover for some time, and just added a cover for flintlocks. It's soft and rubbery with a lot of stretch. It fits over the lock in the half-cock position and effectively keeps rain and snow from falling on the pan and freezing. Neither it, nor any other lock cover I ever saw, will stop water from running down the barrel and into the pan; it will effectively keep water off the lock.

How about a rack to hold your rifle while you are cleaning or working on it? **MTM Molded Products**, the folks that make all the CaseGard cartridge cases for modern cartridges, tackle boxes and other moulded plastic products for shooters, have come up with one that is a real winner. They have a combination tray and rifle rack that will either stand alone or will set on top of their large Shooter's Accessory Box. Between the accessory box and the tray, you'll have everything that you could possibly need at the range. The padded gun forks in the tray snap out and lay down for transportation. I have built similar setups of wood for years, but this one is better designed and handier than mine.

Shiloh Sharps Company has reproduced a lithographed print of the original Sharps Ri-

The D&H flintlock cover is short on looks, tall on performance.

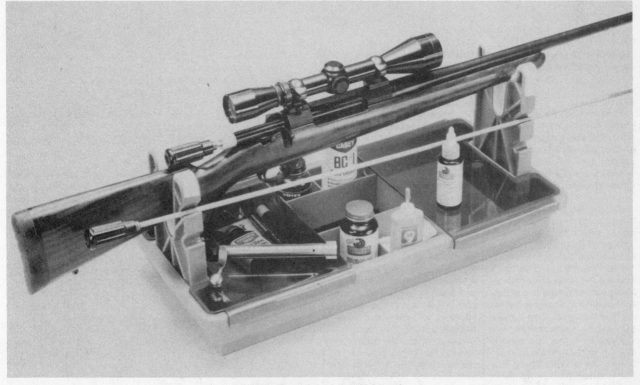

MTM's rifle rack and cleaning stand
is better than wood, and lighter, too.

fle Company bullet board that was used to display all the different cartridges that the Sharps was chambered for. The beautifully done print is 25¼ x 32⅝ inches in size and costs $25 prepaid from Shiloh. I'm sure tickled with mine.

A couple of other things that I ran onto:

CVA has a screw-in funnel that fits the spout threads on most powder flasks. It makes filling powder flasks a very easy operation. I, personally, have spilled enough powder to fight a good portion of the Civil War in attempts to fill flasks. A funnel like this would have sure saved me some time and aggravation.

The CVA flask-filling accessory—saves powder, and it's safer.

They also make a tool that operates as a nipple wrench for all sizes of nipples and has a couple of screwdrivers, all in a compact pouch.

They make a Swiss army knife-type tool that fits in the pocket or pouch and has a wedge puller, ball starter, cap holder, nipple wrench, screwdriver, nipple pick, knife blade and adapter to turn it into a ramrod handle. Heck of a deal.

There's a new kid on the block making some nice carry bags and pouches. These are different, made of a very solid canvas or duck material. Don't make my mistake. I assumed we were dealing with the lightweight cloth bag that won't hold its shape. These are nothing like that. These bags hold their shape very well even when heavily loaded—something

that leather won't always do, by the way. The star of the collection is the Uplander which is a large shotgunner's bag, and measures 11 x 9½ by 4 inches deep. It has three outside pockets, a main compartment with smaller outside compartment and double flaps to help separate them. It is very well designed with shotgunners and all the wads, etc. they have to carry in mind. All edges are bound and the workmanship is really good with leather trim and solid brass hardware. Pricing is from $40 to around $60 depending on the style of bag. Called the Great Miami Sport Bags by **E. Christopher Manufacturing**, this type of bag would have been right at home on the shoulder of the gentleman hunter of years gone by.

Mountain States Muzzleloading has added a nipple to their line that is supposed to stop errant misfires. Called the

Spitfire Magnum Nipple, the Mountain States folks claim it gets a much hotter flame to the powder than any other type of nipple design. Hodgdon Powder Co. tested it and found it to indeed give a hotter flash than conventional nipples, so Hodgdon recommends them for use with their slightly-harder-to-ignite Pyrodex.

One other shooting thing really took my eye: New glasses frames from Australia. Those of us into bifocals and trifocals fight the lines of magnification constantly. If I get a pair of glasses set up to be comfortable for reading, working in the shop or shooting, they sit too high for just walking around. This new frame uses a nose piece that slides up and down and allows the positioning of the magnification spot exactly where you want it for the job at hand. It's the greatest idea for shooters and those who like to fool around with mechanical things I have seen for some time. I or-

dered a pair and I wouldn't trade them for an original Paterson Colt—at least I wouldn't if I couldn't get another pair—well, I don't think I would. They are imported by Decot Hy-Wyd Sport Glasses, Inc. They can be purchased direct, or your optometrist can probably get

them for you.

The muzzle-loading sport is alive and well and is getting a maturity that is showing itself in the quality of things that are being offered for sale to the enthusiast. Your local dealer has some good new stuff on his shelves. ●

Heavy duck hunting bags from E. Christopher Manufacturing— nothing flimsy or soft here.

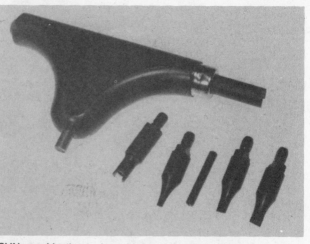

CVA's combination tool provides real leverage with its own profile.

by LARRY S. STERETT

Armsport's Trilling

The muzzle end of the Trilling is impressive.

three-barrel shotgun with smooth barrels.

Measuring 44½ inches overall, its barrels are 26¹³⁄₁₆ inches long and it weighs 7½ pounds. The boxlock action has three trigger-plate-mounted hammers cocked by a single rectangular bar; this bar is activated by a single lug on the forend iron when the shotgun is opened.

The trigger is inertia-set; the forward trigger will fire all three barrels in sequence—under, right, and left—if the recoil is sufficient to set the mechanism. However, if the recoil is too light, as with some target loads,

left barrel required a pull of 5½ pounds.

The Trilling hammers are powered by coil springs, with the center hammer spring (under barrel) encased in a hollow steel cylinder. Firing is accomplished using the double triggers, identical to those found on conventional side-by-side shotguns with double triggers.

The Trilling has monobloc barrel construction; and the monobloc has a divided rear lump to permit underbolt locking and allow the one-piece cocking bar to pass underneath. At the forward edge of the monobloc is a slight

The Armsport Model 2900 Trilling has a streamlined appearance and nicely-figured walnut in the stock and forearm.

BOTH over/unders and side-by-sides are common today, and most dedicated shooters have seen a few drillings, with either two shotgun barrels over a rifle barrel, or less commonly, two rifle barrels over a shotgun barrel. But three-barrel shotguns are definitely uncommon, as are four-barrel shotguns, only a few of which have been manufactured.

Now there's a three-barrel shotgun available here. Manufactured in Italy by Armi Silma, and imported and distributed in the U.S. by Armsport, Inc., of Miami, Florida, it's simply labeled the Trilling. In Germany, it would be a *Flintendrilling drei Schrotläufe*, or

the forward trigger will fire the under barrel, and the rear trigger will fire the left barrel, leaving the right barrel unfired, unless the recoil from the second shot was sufficient to set the mechanism, permitting the right barrel to be fired using the forward trigger. If the left barrel is to be fired first, the rear trigger must be used, after which the forward trigger must be used to fire the under and right barrels in sequence.

Trigger let-off on the test gun measured 5½ pounds, 3¼ pounds, and 6½ pounds for the forward trigger when used in sequence to fire all three barrels. Using the rear trigger to fire the

forward lump, with hooks on each side of the leading edge to engage the hardened steel trunnions on the inner walls of the receiver. These trunnions permit barrel pivoting, and on the test gun they each measured 0.474-inch in diameter. This design allows a trim receiver shape; on the test gun the maximum width of the receiver, at the recoil shields, measured 2.095 inches, while the maximum depth measured 2.618 inches.

Slightly above and a bit forward of the trunnions are recesses in the receiver wall to engage lugs on the arms of the stirrup-type extractor; the recesses cam the lugs forcing the ex-

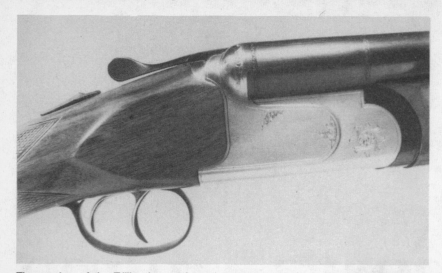

The receiver of the Trilling has sculptured side panels with a minimum amount of engraving on the sides, recoil shields, and the bottom, forward of the trigger plate. It is actual engraving, not etching.

checkering was good, with fewer flat-topped diamonds than on the forearm. No cap graced the base of the pistol grip, which had a smooth, slightly convex surface. A thin, ventilated, black rubber pad having a screened surface and black base completed the stock. As on many European shotguns, the Trilling has sling swivels suitable for a ¾-inch carrying strap.

Metal finish on the test gun was good. The barrel assembly, forearm iron and latch plate assembly, trigger guard, and top lever had a deep, well-polished blue-black luster, while the receiver and trigger plate were finished in the white, providing some contrast. The double triggers were gold-plated, while the cast safety slide had

tractor rearward as the shotgun is opened. On the test gun the shells—loaded and fired—were raised 0.355-inch by the extractor, allowing easy manual removal. The extractor takes different bites on the shell rims for each barrel.

The barrels are joined at the monobloc and at the muzzle with a single top rib between the over barrels. This permits air to circulate around the barrels, but it also allows moisture and grime to enter, requiring careful cleaning after use in inclement weather. A single 0.123-inch diameter brass bead graced the muzzle end of the top rib, and for this shooter the sight picture consisted of a bit of rib showing, along with the bead, above the top lever post.

The barrels on the test gun were not marked as to choke, but the under barrel was stamped CAM.70, indicating 70-millimeter (2¾ inches) chambers, and 18.3 for the bore diameter in millimeters. The right barrel was stamped 18.3 on the underside, and the left barrel was stamped 18.5 in the same approximate location. Actual bore diameters for the under, right, and left barrels measured 0.722-inch, 0.722-inch, and 0.728-inch, respectively. The amounts of constriction for each barrel in sequence were 4 points, 24 points, and 38 points, respectively, or Improved Cylinder, Modified, and Full.

The forearm and stock on the test gun were of select walnut with a good amount of figure and hard glossy finish. The U-shaped forearm measured 10⅙ inches long, with a maximum width of 1¾ inches. The tip of the fore-

The monobloc of the Trilling has short forward and rear lumps and underbolt locking. A single extractor raised all chambered shells—fired or not—for manual extraction. Cocking of the three hammers is accomplished via a single cocking bar sliding within the floor of the receiver.

arm had a slight schnabel, and the sides were covered with hand checkering in a wraparound pattern of 20 lines per inch, plus a two-line border. Quality of the checkering was fair, with few runouts, but many of the diamonds were flat-topped near the edges, and the stock finish had been applied after the checkering was done, making it more decorative than functional.

The buttstock had a length of pull of 15¼ inches, measured from the forward trigger, with drops at the comb and heel of 1⅝ and 2²¹⁄₃₂ inches, respectively. The nose of the comb was rounded, with wide flutes on each side, and the circumference of the grip at its minimum measured 5¹³⁄₁₆ inches. A palm swell graced the right side of the pistol grip, both sides of which had hand checkering at 20 lines per inch, with a two-line border. Quality of the

a charcoal gray finish. Metal-to-metal fit was better than average, with those surfaces that were supposed to be flush actually flush.

To obtain an idea of where the Trilling would center its patterns and exactly what the chokes were, the test gun was patterned at 40 yards using the Fiocchi VIP heavy (3, 1⅛, 7½) load containing an average of 392 pellets per shell by actual count. Five shots were put through each barrel to obtain an average, and the 16-field pattern was used as a standard for comparison. Regulating two-barrel shotguns to center patterns to the same point of aim is a time-consuming task; adding a third barrel creates a whole new problem.

It was assumed the Trilling would throw its patterns high, which it did, so the aiming point was placed on the lower half of the 48-inch square pattern sheets. The under barrel centered its patterns 7¾ inches above the point of aim, and just over 2¾ inches to the left. Average for the five shots was 34.2 percent with 44.1 percent of this total within the four center fields. The generally accepted percentages for an Improved Cylinder choke is 35 to 45 percent.

Averaging 66.1 percent, of which 35.9 percent was within the four center fields, the right barrel centered its patterns just over 14 inches above and 2¼ inches to the right of the point-of-aim. Modified choke patterns average from 45 to 60 percent of the shot charge in a 30-inch circle, depending on the reference source, so the right barrel was actually producing Im-

The Trilling takes down into basic assemblies as shown. If transporting, the forearm would be attached to the barrel.

Shells raised by the single extractor for manual removal get well out there within reach.

factory loads and handloads, for a session with the Champions and White Flyers. The gun shot a bit higher than do many trap guns, but the rising targets could still be broken, even though the puffs of black dust did not appear as frequently as liked, indicating the pattern fringes were catching some of the targets. No malfunctions were encountered, other than some of the light target loads, particularly those with an ounce of shot or less, would fail to set the trigger mechanism. The heavier loads never failed.

The Trilling feels lighter in the hands than it actually weighs, with the center of gravity located at a point

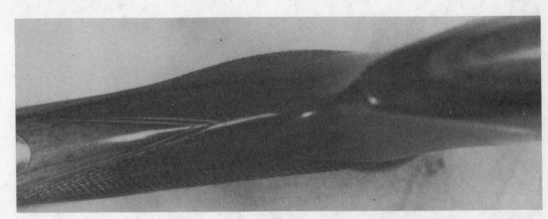

The "palm swell" on the right side of the pistol grip is evident here.

proved Modified patterns with this particular load.

The left barrel centered patterns 14 inches high and 6½ inches to the left of the point of aim. Averaging 68.1 percent, with 37.1 percent of this total

located in the center fields, the left barrel patterns with this load as Improved Modified.

Following the patterning session, the Trilling was taken to the practice range, along with an assortment of

½-inch to the rear of the hinge pin center. It handled well in use, and produced acceptable patterns, some a bit high. It definitely has lots of possibilities. The $2900 price is not out of line for the type. ●

T/C's SCOUT

by HAL SWIGGETT

T/C SCOUT muzzle-loading pistol has that frontier flavor.

SMOKE covered the Oehler 35P chronograph screens 8 feet in front of the muzzle. In fact, it seemed to reach all the way to my 25-yard target.

No, it wasn't accidental.

I was testing Thompson/Center's all-new SCOUT muzzle-loading guns. The two used here were 50-caliber. Eventually, I'm told, both will also be offered in 45 and 54.

The SCOUT is simple for something new. Pistol barrel length is 12 inches and it is 7/8-inch at the muzzle. There is a brass trigger guard and frame and an adjustable rear sight and a weight of 4 pounds 6 ounces. I didn't measure the carbine before returning the guns. Obviously, my main interest was in the pistol.

The guns in my hands for a few days were prototypes. The out-when-you-read-this models may differ a bit but should be close.

Looking like the back end of a single-action Colt, the trigger mechanism has only two parts, the trigger and hammer. It is so designed (Pat. #4,854,065) that the hammer can't reach the nipple unless the trigger is all the way back—an automatic safety.

The nipple is in-line with the chamber. This in-line ignition system, according to T/C, increases both accuracy and overall performance. My first reaction was, "How do I get the nipple out?"

My muzzle-loading experience dates back a lot of years, back to when a shot failed to fire after two or three caps, we took the nipple out, dribbled in a few grains of FFFFg, put it back and fired the gun. The SCOUT doesn't permit this and even if it did, it wouldn't work.

To get the nipple out, either gun must be broken down into its four parts: the forend is removed; the barrel assembly lifted out; and the frame sep-

Firing 100 grains of FFg under T/C's 370 Maxi drove smoke almost to the 25-yard target.

arated from the grip and trigger assembly. This requires a screwdriver and a ³/₁₆-inch hex wrench. On each side of the barrel/frame—they interlock—in front of the nipple is a vent hole. When I mentioned my concern about not being able to remove the nipple, Ken French, designer of the SCOUT, informed me my dribbling in FFFFg wouldn't work anyway because of those vents.

So be it.

My powder supply still included a can of FFg and one of FFFFg along with a bit of early Pyrodex. Knowing some changes had been made with Pyrodex, a pound each of RS and P were acquired. The only bullets set aside for testing were 370-grain T/C Maxi-Balls and 385-grain Hornady Great Plains Maxi-Hunters. Both are pre-lubed. The T/C has a gooey grease and the Hornady is dry and much, much nicer to work with. Ken French tells me there are some changes being made and I hope so.

I started off with 80 grains of FFg and the carbine. Only Remington #11 caps were used. Three shots averaged 1269 feet per second (fps) and produced a 25-yard group of 1.1 inches. The barrel was cleaned, then three shots with 90 grains of the same powder turned in 1363 fps and a .60-inch group. Another cleaning, then 100 grains put three shots in .641-inch at 1440 fps. All this with T/C's Maxi-Ball and that's all I did with the carbine because that's enough to convince anyone it is, in fact, a true hunting carbine.

T/C's gooey 370 Maxi alongside Hornady's 385 dry-lubed Maxi-Hunter.

My real interest was in the SCOUT pistol because there has never been a muzzle-loading handgun capable of more than small game hunting. Round balls, ever so much lighter, were not considered. I want to take big game with a frontloader pistol like I had with rifles a lot of years ago, game up to an American bison (buffalo), possibly the first buffalo killed in modern times with a muzzleloader. I used Navy Arms' 58-caliber Buffalo Hunter and a 505-grain Minie ball. The charge, as I recall it, was 110 grains of FFg. This took place shortly after Val Forgett added the 58 to his catalog more than two decades ago.

Still, with FFg and the 370 T/C Maxi, 80 grains put three balls from the pistol in .95-inch at 1055 fps. Adding 10 grains increased velocity to 1119 fps and group size to 1.94 inches. Another 10 grains—100 this time—recorded 1187 fps with a 1.29-inch group. The pistol was cleaned after each three shots throughout this testing, even with Pyrodex, to assure each load an equal chance.

Going to Pyrodex RS (their equivalent of FFg) and using the blackpowder measuring scale, 80 grains listed 1213 fps with a .931-inch group. Remember, all of this is at 25 yards and with 370-grain T/C Maxi-Balls. Ninety grains gave 1221 fps and 1.9 inches. The top load, 100-grain equivalent RS, did a beautiful cloverleaf measuring .54-inch while clocking 1319 fps.

Pyrodex P, a pistol powder, was used according to Hodgdon's recommendation by reducing the charge in rifles by 10 percent. Though the SCOUT is a pistol, it is rifle-like and was being handled as such. Setting my blackpowder scale on 72 grains, the P reached 1136 fps with a .89-inch group.

Here's the pair, but Swiggett likes the short one better.

At 81 grains equivalent, 1167 fps printed 1.93 inches. Going on to the full charge of 90 grains equivalent gained only 3 fps to 1170 and printed .82-inch. I feel confident heavier charges of Pyrodex P could be used but find it prudent to follow directions where powders are concerned and urge you to do the same.

Hornady's 385-grain Maxi-Hunter is ever so much nicer to use because of its dry lube. Not once did I pick up a paper towel. (I can't help but wonder how our forefathers founded this country without paper towels, styrofoam cups and paper clips.) *(Not to mention Band-Aids, Scotch tape and Xerox machines. Editor)* T/C's Maxis demanded the use of a towel each time a bullet was picked up.

Pyrodex RS 80-grain equivalent put the Hornady in 1.2 inches and averaged 1156 fps for the three. Upping the charge 10 grains produced a 1.38-inch group at 1234 fps. The 100-grain charge developed 1309 fps with a group measuring 2.2 inches.

FFg—80 grains—went 1059 fps and printed in .895-inch. The 90-grain charge recorded 1197 and measured .742-inch. On up to the full charge of 100 grains, my three shots measured 1.67 inches at 1237 fps.

All this really proved very little, but it did convince me the T/C SCOUT pistol was, in fact, a hunting handgun, so I proceeded to take it hunting. A trip to the Y.O. Ranch, near Mountain Home, Texas, provided the setting. An eight-point whitetail buck cooperated. He weighed a bit over a hundred pounds and measured right at nineteen inches.

His mistake was he assumed a cedar was sufficient concealment and a T/C 370-grain Maxi-Ball over 100 of FFg proved it wasn't. The distance was close, give or take a few feet, about forty yards. I don't know how long it stayed in the air, nor how far it traveled, but neither that buck's right shoulder nor his left shoulder blade stopped the 370-grain Maxi.

Remember, this T/C SCOUT is a prototype. I'm confident the production guns, carbine and pistol, will be at least as good. It is of simple design, foolproof to dismantle for cleaning (when old fumble-fingers—me—can do it anyone can), and built to handle hunting charges of blackpowder or its equivalent.

Handgun hunters are going to find a whole new field to conquer. I do have one regret. Make that an apology. Years ago I wrote that I had cleaned my *last* blackpowder gun.

I'm sorry folks—but I lied.

The SCOUT breaks down into four parts: barrel, forend, frame and trigger assembly/grip.

The nipple that can't be removed without total dismantling. Don't fret over the chipped edges. This *is* a prototype.

What you see is what you get. The trigger and hammer are the only two parts in this assembly.

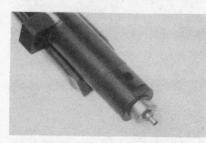

To get this view of the SCOUT's nipple you have to break down the entire pistol.

The SCOUT test guns were 50-caliber but 45 and 54 will be available later.

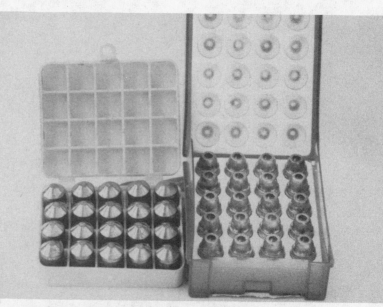

The T/C 370-grain Maxi-Ball, left, and Hornady 385-grain Great Plains Maxi-Hunter were the test bullets.

Hämmerli 280

by RAYMOND CARANTA

The Hämmerli 280 will be winning past 2001, Caranta predicts.

HÄMMERLI has been famous in Europe since the Lyon international rifle match of 1897, which foreshadowed modern ISU World championships. Franck Jullien, the Swiss winner, used a rifle featuring a Martini action made by the Lenzburg company. Since, Hämmerli has won many international honors along the years; U.S. national shooting teams have often used Hämmerlis. Major technological improvements have significantly upset the gunsmith art during recent years, but Hämmerli has maintained its renown, and built on it with the introduction of new lines of perfected handguns. Lately, Hämmerli has introduced the Model 150 (mechanical trigger) and 152 (electronic trigger) free pistols; Olympic rapid-fire pistols chambered in 22 Short, the Models 230 and 232; and, in 1988, their two-caliber Model 280 instantly convertible to 22 Long Rifle for the Standard pistol event, or to 32 S&W Long WC for the Sport pistol events. Calibers are simply shifted by fitting a new upper assembly unit (barrel, upper housing and slide) and magazine.

The 280 is ultra-modern. Its slide is enclosed in an upper housing unit also bearing the removable barrel, a modular trigger mechanism with a fully adjustable trigger and a magazine located in front of the trigger guard, al-

light balance weights made of carbon fiber-reinforced high tensile strength synthetic material, which has been used for many years in the manufacture of main rotor blades and structural components of French helicopters. As black is the natural color of this material, eventual scratches are easily blended by local polishing.

In order to check stress computations for validity, the Hämmerli staff submitted four production pistols—two of each caliber—to an endurance test of 50,000 rounds per gun. Each pis-

The Hämmerli 280 22 LR pistol with its basic accessories—it all comes in one box.

lowing for entire freedom as far as the grip size and configuration are concerned. Field-stripping is very easy and gives proper access to the bolt recess and barrel chamber areas which are critical for maintaining perfect reliability. Moreover, the complete disassembly procedure for repairs and part replacements is outlined in the technical manual accompanying the gun, written in German, French, English and Spanish.

From a production point of view, the Hämmerli 280 is as close to a Third Millenium gun as possible with its upper housing, receiver, magazine and

tol was shot at the rate of 1500 rounds per day and cleaned in the evening for several weeks, using twelve different brands of ammunition in 22 Long Rifle, and five in 32 S&W Long WC.

As a first step and every 10,000 rounds thereafter, accuracy was bench-tested at 25 meters through five comparison five-shot groupings for every type of ammunition involved. At the same time, a new electronic device analyzed trigger pulls and the mainspring, recoil spring and magazine spring for condition, while the barrel chamber and bore dimensions were accurately measured. At the end of the

The Hämmerli 280 22 field-strips like this for most maintenance.

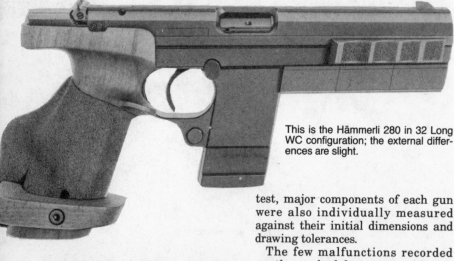

This is the Hämmerli 280 in 32 Long WC configuration; the external differences are slight.

Fitting the grip at the Lenzburg factory on production Hämmerli 280 pistols.

test, major components of each gun were also individually measured against their initial dimensions and drawing tolerances.

The few malfunctions recorded mostly resulted from ammunition or mishandling. The total malfunction rate was .08 percent over 200,000 rounds; four extractors and five hammer pins were changed during the shooting. All major components finished the test in good condition without any significant wear marks. With the rimfire ammunition, groups were better after 50,000 rounds than after 10,000; in 32 S&W Long, accuracy didn't change.

We fired our 22 Long Rifle 280 Hämmerli over a slow fire shooting run of 30 rounds at 25 meters, off-hand, using Remington standard velocity ammu-

nition. Our score was 279/300, a 93/100 average. For us, that's quite good.

The gun is delivered in a nice cardboard box with a Hämmerli medal, two cleaning rods with solid bronze and hair brushes, a spare magazine, three metal and three synthetic balance weights, a quick-loader device, a dummy round for 22 Long Rifle dry firing, four Allen wrenches and a multi-blade screwdriver.

The amazingly light synthetic magazine can be filled without undue difficulty and the slide is smoothly operated. The gun is provided with a manual hold-open device and there is no thumb-safety. The magazine stop is easy to operate with the forefinger.

The grip is made of sanded walnut. It has a fixed thumbrest and adjustable palm-rest, and comes in two sizes as well as for both right- and left-handers. This grip is excellent; it puts the forefinger correctly on the trigger, more especially as the latter can be moved lengthwise nearly half an inch.

Weight can be varied from 2.04 to 2.6 pounds with ten balance combinations, thanks to three metal receiver attachments of 3 ounces each and three half-ounce synthetic ones.

Its sights are just 1.18 inches above the hand, undercut and click adjustable for windage and elevation (one click = .4-inch at 25 meters). Both front and rear sights are available in three widths, readily interchangeable without effect on the point of impact. We particularly like the .142-inch wide sights.

Two trigger pull settings are available in accordance with ISU regulations—1 kilogram for the Standard pistol and 3 pounds for the Sport pistol. The trigger is fully adjustable for the weight of slack and pull, let-off travel, backlash and length, for each ISU option. We found the second pull excellent as factory set, but the first pull was quite stiff. It is adjustable, of course.

Shooting off-hand, 27 of the 30 impacts were contained in a group 2.55 inches high and 3.46 inches wide at 25 meters, the way they are measured in Europe. Our best ten-round run was a 94/100.

The Hämmerli 280 is currently one of the most sophisticated sporting automatic pistols in the world, both from the design and production standpoints, and its virtues have already been confirmed on the range. Its price is quite reasonable for the performance level offered and we feel this gun is well qualified to supersede the glorious but expensive Hämmerli 208 by the end of the century. ●

A Tough Simmons Scope

by HAL SWIGGETT

Simmons new 2.5-7x handgun scope is 8¾ inches long and weighs 8½ ounces.

WHAT DOES a gunwriter do when he has come down hard, real hard, on a manufacturer, then receives another of that company's products in the mail—with a note saying "Destroy this one if you can." It wasn't in those exact words, but that's the meaning of the letter.

It all started with some sample handgun scopes from Simmons which I felt didn't come up to par. I wrote bad things to the point the company zeroed in on their customer service department and re-designed their handgun scope line. At least to some extent.

With the new scope came a letter saying it had already been broken in with a good many 44 Magnum and 375 JDJ rounds. The scope was a 2.5-7x, 8¾ inches in length. Both ends measured 1⅜ inches in diameter; the tube was 1-inch. Adjustments were listed as ¼-inch at 100 yards. Weight 8½ ounces. There was no tech sheet, no printed data; everything you read here is as I found it to be. We'll know later, when they release the scope, how close I've come to their description.

At 2.5x, eye relief was easily full circle between 14 and 21 inches. I considered it usable on down to 9 inches and out to 22. On the other hand, at 7x, it offered an excellent field of view from about 11 on out to 16 or even 17 inches.

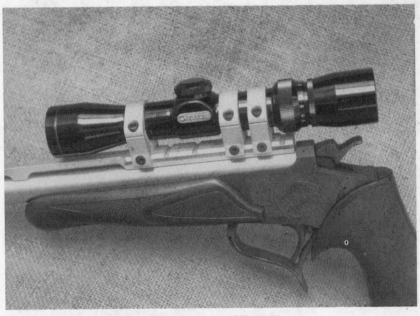

For sheer punishment, Swiggett mounted it on his SSK 45-70 Contender barrel in a T'SOB mount.

This new scope was mounted on my Remington XP-100 7mmBR and fired forty times to get the feel of it, and to check out its adjustments. My XP 7mmBR is a consistent ½- to ¾-inch shooter. The first twenty were fired getting on paper and then at rocks and other interesting targets. The second box was used up by putting a hole in the paper then moving twenty clicks right for another hole. Down twenty then left twenty, then back up completed a square. This was done five times and each group was within the accuracy of the gun and at the right place.

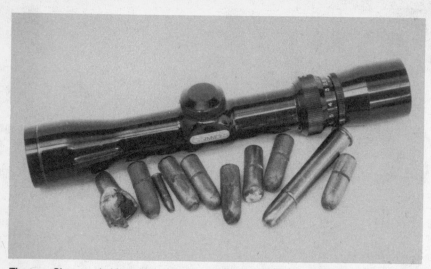

The new Simmons held together through 107 rounds of heavy-charged 500-grain Hornady FMJ bullets at 1554 fps, some of which were dug out of the dirt backstop.

For a final test of adjustments Hal used his 22 Long Rifle Anschutz pistol, and the Simmons steered correctly.

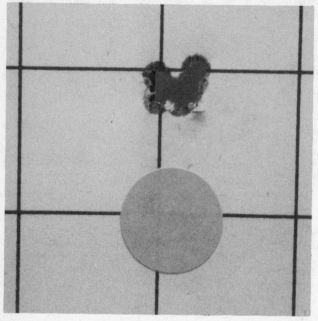

This 5/16-inch, 6-shot group was shot at 40 yards—one each at 2.5x, 3x, 4x, 5x, 6x, and 7x.

Knowing it had been atop 44 Magnum and 375 JDJ rounds, my first thought was to submit it to my 7½-inch 454 Casull in which I shoot 300-grain bullets at 1900+ feet per second. Rethinking the project, I knew it would have to end up on my 45-70 12-inch SSK Contender barrel—so why bother with the 454? That made sense.

Scrounging for empties, 107 were located, cleaned and made ready for loading. My charge: 47.5 grains of H322 under Hornady's great 500-grain full metal jacket bullet and set off with Winchester primers. This is the bullet used by many dangerous game hunters in their 458s.

The first ten, all I felt like carefully aiming, clocked 1554 fps over Ken Oehler's 35P screens. The remaining ninety-seven were simply fired into a dirt bank. The entire shooting fiasco used up about ninety minutes. An hour and a half. A sure enough test of scope and gun, along with positive proof of my stupidity. It ended up pure torture.

Rather large chunks of skin and flesh were removed from my trigger finger and the forefinger of my left hand which was given the chore of helping hold on to the gun. I'm not sure when it happened, but it finally dawned on me I was pulling the trigger with my middle right finger. Both my wrist and elbow ached for several days.

Once things settled down, a final test was made. The prototype 2.5-7x Simmons was put on my Anschutz 22 Long Rifle pistol to go over the adjustments again. Five near-perfect 1-inch squares were shot. At 40 yards. The adjustments were still performing as they had before brutality took over.

A final test—one I had failed to try earlier—went like this: the 22 Long Rifle Anschutz pistol, under the new Simmons 2.5-7x scope, shot at 40 yards into 5/16-inch, six-shot group.

What's so unusual about that?

How about one shot each at 2.5, 3, 4, 5, 6 and 7x?

It's getting more crowded. We've had Leupold for a long time. We've had Burris for a lot of years. Bausch & Lomb joined up a few years ago. If Simmons' production scopes can hold up the way this one has, we now have four companies putting out quality scopes capable of withstanding big bore punishment.

I also realize this 2.5-7x Simmons could have given up on shot number 108. I do not believe it would have because the adjustments still functioned perfectly. This new one from Simmons, a variable—the most delicate of all—has certainly proved itself to me. ●

by DEAN A. GRENNELL

HANDLOADING UPDATE

BEFORE LAUNCHING this annual discussion, I'd like to offer a few comments on the business of assembling home-brewed ammunition. I've been thus engaged for nigh onto forty years, roughly sixty percent of my ongoing lifespan, and it seems as if I should be able to offer some noteworthy observations after all this while.

To the best of my knowledge, I'm the guy who first suggested a small crank handle for twirling inside/outside case neck deburring tools. I sent the idea to Pacific, when they were operating out of Lincoln, Nebraska, and they added the gizmo to their tool offering. They sent me one for my troubles and I think I still have it, somewhere out in the shop. Several other firms market the same basic tool today and they certainly are handy.

For a time, I thought my brother Ralph and I had in-vented and publicized the fitted mandrels that can be chucked into electric hand drills or drill presses to spin empty cartridge cases so as to scrub them clean with fine-grade steel wool. These gadgets are just addictively handy. I wrote them up in various publications, giving them the catchy name of K-Spinners.

Some helpful reader out there sent me an ad that had appeared in some gunzine of about the mid-'30s, showing the identical device and, as Ken Warner is my witness, marketed under the name of K-Spinner!

The useful K-Spinner—whatever its origins—remains in production and readily available down to the present. Hanned Precision can supply them in virtually any desired diameter and offers a stepped set with ¼-inch shanks capable of handling nearly any centerfire rifle or pistol cartridge apt to be encountered in normal reloading procedures.

Long ago, I gave up the happy idea that I was going to dream up something that would make me rich and famous, not necessarily in that order. I've known guys who kept getting bright ideas and who'd hardly boggle at pawning their wife's good tooth to raise money for getting the given example of sheer genius patented. Not for me and no, thank you very much.

If I get what sounds like an interesting idea, I just buck it along to someone with the facilities to put it into production, wish them well and settle back to scheme up something else. Look, Ma: no stomach ulcers!

I hereby toss one such idea onto the table for anyone deft enough to grab it first. The cordless screwdriver is an established art form. How about an accessory attachment with a simple rubber cup tapering to about ⅞-inch? When you want to remove a loading die, you grab the cordless screwdriver, press it down onto the die, hold down the switch and—*ffzzoottchtt*—out it comes. Reverse the switch and you can turn the next die into place, just as quickly and with as little ex-

This is the new RCBS electronic scale and—ever the wordsmith—Grennell wants desperately to be the first in print to call it a Blount instrument.

RCBS has a new primer tray.

This is a micrometer headspace/bullet seating depth gauge by RCBS.

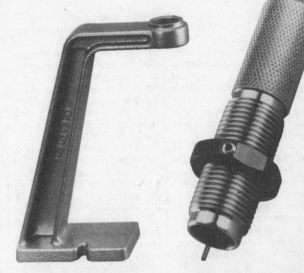

For when your powder measure must go piggyback from RCBS.

The sensible RCBS universal de-cap die.

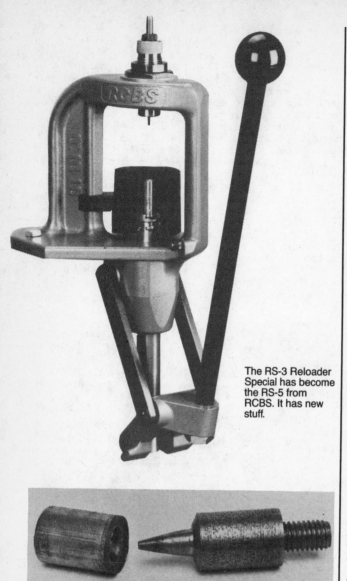

The RS-3 Reloader Special has become the RS-5 from RCBS. It has new stuff.

A mysterious Grennell missile called the 357 Spelunker can be seated comfortably only with this plug in an M-die.

pended effort.

Ideas such as this are spawned by what I like to think of as creative discontent. I seem to spend endless amounts of time turning dies out of presses and back into presses. *(Poor Dean. He's describing a simple accessory to the now-popular battery-operated shotgun choke tube changers! KW)*

Of all the ideas I wish I'd had first, the Lyman M-die comes foremost to mind. It's so simple and so painfully obvious, once it came along. All it is is a case mouth expanding plug, with the lower tip slightly smaller than bullet diameter and the upper shank some few thousandths larger than bullet diameter.

When installed and correctly adjusted, the Lyman M-die expands the top sixteenth-inch or so of the case mouth, just barely large enough to accept the base of the bullet for a smooth and precise seating when you get that far. The M-type expander plugs are secured to the die punch by a shank threaded 10-32NF and are quite easy to produce, given access to a metal lathe. My collection of the plugs numbers forty or more, most of them homemade, housed in a box prominently labeled "M-Dies" on all six sides for ease in keeping track of its whereabouts. I would be desolately lost without them.

Veteran hull-stuffers are painfully aware of the occasional difficulties encountered in getting the base of the bullet comfortably started into the neck of the charged case. If you try to seat the bullet by main force, you're apt to end up with the case neck hopelessly scrooched out of shape.

By way of coping with such a dilemma, I dreamed up a tapered steel pin with a shank for installing it in the chuck of the drill press. The tapered portion has an included angle of about twelve degrees and I ended up knocking out two of them. One has a taper that runs from about caliber 17 through 358 and the other goes from there through .458-inch or so.

I passed the basic concept along to Ed Wosika, of Hanned Precision, and he embodied it in a tool he calls the Nexpander. It's just a piece of aluminum bar stock with a tapered steel pin at each end. If you can't get the base of the bullet to start into the case neck, you dump the powder charge back into the reservoir of the powder measure, apply the appropriate end of the Nexpander, rap the head of the case smartly against a clear space atop the bench a time or two and—*Shazam!*—no more problems. Replace the powder charge and proceed with the loading.

In writing up Wosika's Nexpander for the department at hand a few years back, I said it would handle anything from caliber 17 through caliber 50 and I was wrong in so stating. This was brought to my attention by a justifiably irate reader up in Canada who'd bought a Nexpander on my say-so, only to find its capabilities ended at about caliber 475 or so.

My ongoing philosophy is that contented readers are the finest kind and my response was to produce a customized Nexpander with maximum ex-

pansion capabilities to .635-inch. Actually, I knocked out two of them and sent one to the disgruntled Canuck with my compliments and best wishes, adding the other to my own trove of unlikely hardware and tooling. The aggrieved party responded with a note saying he was quite happy with the replacement; in a word, gruntled. It will expand case mouths up through 600 Nitro Express, and if one wishes to work with brass cases for the 4-gauge, at a diameter of roughly 1.05208 inches, all bets are off.

With the foregoing notes duly noted, let us see what the various makers have been up to in recent times.

Blount, Inc., is the new parent entity for **CCI, Speer, RCBS, Outers** and **Weaver,** superseding **Omark.** You might assume Blount rhymes with count, but I'm told it's pronounced "Blunt," and my informant added, "Thank goodness we don't make knives!"

RCBS has modified their Uniflow powder measure so one rotor now does it all, handling charge weights from 0.5-grain of Bullseye up to 110.0 grains of IMR-4350. They have a new square primer tray to handle the larger primer packaging in current use.

The RCBS RS-3 Reloader Special press has been modified to the RS-5 model, changing the plastic grip to a round ball and adding a primer seating arm to replace the ram-prime unit for the RS-3.

RCBS now has a universal decap die for depriming uncleaned and unlubricated cases of virtually every size and cal-

These are K-Spinners for 38 Special and 45 ACP cases. The 45 case is just half-polished.

iber from 22 through 45 without need for adjustment.

Another new RCBS item is their cartridge micrometer, called the Precision Mic. By checking a fired case, you get a precise measurement of the chamber's head to shoulder dimension, comparing it to the SAAMI recommendation for that caliber. It becomes possible to adjust your sizing die for the best fit of cartridge to chamber, thus improving accuracy, with longer case life and safer loads. A further ability is that of assuring a precise and predictable amount of bullet "jump" before engaging the rifling. The gauge reads off the lands so the setting does not change with different bullet shapes. Initially, the Precision Mic is available in twelve popular rifle cal-

ibers.

The new RCBS flash hole deburring tool is designed to remove any irregularities around the front of the flash hole and it is supplied with a case pilot stop for the given bullet diameter, to help steer the tip into the flash hole. Pilot stops are available in all sizes from 22- to 45-caliber.

The RCBS powder checker die is intended for use with progressive loading presses to verify the presence of a powder charge and comparison to assure it is the proper powder charge. The die has the standard ⅞-14 thread and can be installed between the powder charging station and the bullet seating station.

Last but far from least, there's the new RCBS electronic scale, with a capacity of up to

500 grains and a zeroing or Tare adjustment to permit using a powder pan or doing without it. Re-zeroing, combined with the scale's ability to display negative numbers, permits selection of a bullet as a reference to sort other bullets rapidly by weight. It can be used indoors or—at least to some extent—outdoors. A set of batteries is said to be good for fifty hours of normal use.

Corbin Manufacturing & Supply have two new bullet swaging presses. One is a beefed-up redesign of the original Mity Mite press, open at the top for maximum convenience of operation. The other is a husky vertical design, with an optional bench mount that puts the working area up about the eye level of the operator.

Also new to the Corbin line are dies for producing your own gaschecks and/or bullet base washers to minimize or eliminate bore fouling. If desired, the washer die can be dimensioned for a precise fit to a specific bore and Corbin recommends that as the better way to go. At the moment, Corbin doesn't have a catalog, but offers a comprehensive handbook at $6 per copy, postpaid.

Dillon Precision has just added a new press to their line, the Model RL 450 Jr. It addresses the basic problem of starting out with a single-stage loader and learning the basics before graduating to a progressive machine: Namely, what do you do with your old single-stage? The RL 450 Jr. can be operated as a single-station

This is Lee's Automator which, together with other gadgets, automates almost any press.

Lee can do this to nearly any single-station reloading press, which makes that press a progressive.

The Lee Speed Die replaces the normal three-die set for almost all pistol calibers; offers carbide sizing.

Grennell thinks this Hensley & Gibbs No. 352—a 44-caliber conical-point wadcutter—has potential.

Here are six mid-weight Hensley & Gibbs designs for the 45-70.

press, or, by adding the B Conversion Kit, it becomes a progressive, retaining the option to return to single-station mode at any time the operator wishes. The basic Dillon RL 450 Jr. goes for $94.50 complete with carbide die set in your choice of one pistol caliber. The B Conversion, with powder measure, cartridge ejection and collection box is $25, or both items are $119 as a package.

Next up the scale is the Dillon Square Deal B, or SDB, at $172.50, set up with tooling for one pistol caliber, including carbide sizing die. Unlike the RL 450 Jr., the SDB indexes its shell plate with each stroke of the operating handle. It has a linkage to prevent jamming of the powder measure slide and a strident buzzer that lets you know when the primer feed tube approaches empty. How strident? I can hear it, even without my hearing aid. *(It's LOUD, then. KW)*

Up one more notch and we come to my personal favorite in the Dillon lineup, the RL550B, at $259.95, factory direct, less dies. It has the same fail-safe powder feed as the SDB and the same primer early warning system, with the primer feed tube enclosed by a hefty steel tube, just in case. The primer feed system is the nicest I've ever seen and I find I'm much prone to use the rig to full-length resize and deprime cases, installing fresh primers on the downstroke.

Like the RL 450 Jr., the shell plate of the RL550B does not advance until the operator is darned good and ready for it to do so. At that point, said operator extends a thumb and motivates the manual sprocket by one-quarter turn and that's it.

My quease and unease

around automated reloading equipment is a matter of painfully redundant record. I am intensely concerned that there be at least one specified charge of powder in each and every round, but absolutely no more than one. This tracks back to my formative years, when I used to reload for assorted police departments, in their 38 Special brass, for a princely $35 per thousand. Long since, I've shifted to reloading for myself and no other, but I'm a very concerned and demanding consumer.

As reloaders go, I am a purebred and pedigreed maverick. Most of the equipment I continue to use and cherish has not been made for a matter of some few decades. However, a Dillon RL550B is the youngest recruit in the production line, and its operating handle is well polished by extensive and appreciative use. It is the first progressive loader I've ever encountered with which I feel comfortable. As always, I've modified it a little, to hew to my eccentric tastes. For example, I've inked in a plus and minus sign on either side of the powder slide adjustment screw to remind me which way to turn it when I want more or less powder.

There's at least one more level of attainment in the form of the Dillon RL1050 at $895, and, for that, you get an electric case feeder, dies and powder measure. Other handy hardware from Dillon includes the Dillon Super Swage, engineered for getting those infernal stamped crimps from around the primer pockets of military brass. One model copes with both large and small primer pockets, all for $45, factory direct.

Then there's the Dillon RT1200B electric case trimmer, ready and eager to bring 223, 308 or 30-06 brass back down to its prescribed length at the same time it's being resized. There's a connection for attaching the hose from a vacuum cleaner to whisk away the brass shavings, but the catalog gently advises that the vacuum cleaner is not included. What you do get, however, is one steel size/trim die and the RT1200B for $125.

Hensley & Gibbs produce moulds—or molds, as they prefer to spell it—for production of handgun bullets. Within the past year, it was brought to their attention that the 45-70 Government has come to be regarded by a great many shooters as a handgun cartridge, and they have responded by adding several new designs to their offering.

There are six basic designs—numbers 344, 345, 346, 347, 348 and 349—in the length and weight class generally regarded as suitable for the 45-70 cartridge, plus another, the 78BB, which is a bevel-based semi-wadcutter of a length and weight perhaps better suited to the 45 Colt cartridge, except that it comes from the mould at a diameter permitting it to be lube/sized to the requisite .458-inch diameter for employment in the 45-70 case. Thus, the 45-70 fan now has access to a lightweight bullet that can be used for casual plinking, without unnecessary expenditure of casting alloy and with a welcome reduction in felt recoil.

Each of the heavier H&G 45-70 bullets can be had in a variety of weights. As examples, the No. 344 moulds can be set up to drop bullets weighing 275, 340 or 405 grains; the No.

345 at 275, 325 or 395 grains and so on. Wayne Gibbs is working up another design I regard with considerable interest. It's their #352, a conical-point semi-wadcutter in 44 size that will be available in a wide variety of bullet weights, both plain base and with gaschecks. That should be available by about the time you read this.

Lee Precision has never forgotten the entry-level reloader and one of the latest offerings is

The Dillon RL 450 Jr. opts up and down, single-stage or progressive, with a $25 conversion package.

the carbide Speed Die; a system in which one die replaces three in normal use. While the concept may seem puzzling, it's actually quite simple in use. The seating stem and decapping/expanding plug are removed from the die and the carbide sizing ring is left attached to its lower end. Run the press ram to top of its stroke and turn the die down until the sizing ring is snug against the shellholder, locking it in that adjustment. Proceed to resize all the cases, then remove the carbide sizing ring by turning it off the lower end of the die and install the decap/expand pin from the top of the die, holding it in place

The Square Deal B from Dillon has all the bells and the whistle is a primer inventory buzzer loud enough for deaf people.

with the bullet seater stem.

Adjust the die to get the desired amount of case mouth expansion, lock it in its setting and decap/expand all the cases. New primers have to be seated, but the die does not handle that. A dipper-type powder measure and card of load data is included with the Speed Die, together with a shellholder of the proper size.

With the case primed and charged, the decap/expand pin is removed and the bullet seating stem is reinstalled and adjusted. It will handle nearly any typical bullet nose config-

This is the Dillon RL550B, a very twin of which works right alongside Grennell at his own reloading bench.

uration. The amount of case neck crimp is obtained by turning the die body up or down in the press head, locking it in the desired adjustment.

Speed Dies are available for most pistol calibers, at $19.98 a set, and they're furnished in a neat plastic box that stacks to save storage space.

Nearly any conventional single-station reloading press with a vertical ram now can be converted into a progressive press with the Lee Automator, at $39.98, not including the Lee shell plate carrier, which must be used with it. Also available is a case feeder and a case collator to keep all four tubes filled.

Requested by a great many customers, Lee now has a lever-operated bench stand for use with their Safety Disk powder measure, supplied with a complete set of four six-cavity disks and a chart giving the charge from each cavity for most powders, at $27.98.

Other new products include a line of taper crimp dies from 32 S&W Long up through the 7.62x39mm and 308 Winchester, all at $8.98 each. Several calibers have been added to the limited production die sets and the Lee collet dies now are available in 17 Remington, 22 PPC and 6mm PPC. Eight new Micro Band bullet moulds have been added to the existing line;

four each in two-cavity and six-cavity types.

Lyman Products Corporation has added three new bullet mould designs. The #356632 is for the 9mmP, weighing 100 grains, with a single grease groove and a truncated cone point. Quite similar but slightly heavier is the #356634, weighing 130 grains and intended for those 9mm fans who feel a need for heavier bullets. It looks as though it should perform quite well in the 38 Super, also. The #401633 is a 200-grain design for the 10mm Auto, with two grease grooves and a moderate bevel base, still retaining much the same truncated cone nasal profile as the first two.

Also new to the Lyman line is their Liquid Alox bullet lube for coating bullets without sizing. Then there's the Pop-Top case polisher with a transparent dome so you can check the progress visually and a Qwik Spray case lube. In the loading die department, they have new universal carbide four-die pistol sets in 9mmP, 38 Special/357 Magnum, 10mm Auto and 45 ACP for $43.95 a set.

The Old Western Scrounger has a loading press called the Rock Crusher, a big, burly monster well suited for loading large cartridges such as the 50 Browning MG, the 55 Boyes, 7.92x107mm Polish, 12.7x107 Russian or 15x103 Besa, to name but a few. His catalog, giving full details, is $2 per copy, postpaid, from Old Western

Scrounger, 12924 Highway A-12, Montague, California 96064.

Nosler Bullets has published the third edition of their Nosler Reloading Manual; 516 pages of eminently readable commentary on reloading, with a great many listings of load data for rifle and handgun cartridges. It's available from your local Nosler dealer or direct from Nosler if not otherwise available.

Sierra Bullets has put forth their third edition of the *Sierra Manual* and, as with the second edition, it comes in two volumes, covering rifles in one and handguns in the second. Someone has burned a lot of midnight oil on this revision. It has a great many listings of new cartridges, with a lot of loads for powders seldom covered in similar books by others. Velocities and the corresponding charge weights are given in vertical columns and they've taken the handy step of giving the equivalent energy in foot-pounds at the bottom of each column. One or both volumes can be had from your local Sierra dealer, or from the factory if not obtainable locally.

Volume I of the *Handloaders' Bullet Making Annual* is off the press and priced at $6.95 per copy from Wolfe Publishing, 6471 Airpark Drive, Prescott, Arizona 86301. It covers 122 pages with myriad aspects of bullet production, authored by a great many writers who know whereof they speak. ●

Nosler's third manual on rifle and handgun reloading runs 516 readable pages.

Sierra, too, publishes for the third time—a giant in two volumes full of product of squeezed midnight oil.

by EDWARD A. MATUNAS

AMMUNITION, BALLISTICS AND COMPONENTS

(Above) New Winchester 40 Smith & Wesson is a shortened 10mm round.

Mushroom Express Bullet Co.

Muzzle-loading bullets in 50- and 54-caliber are available from Dave Harris' new bullet company. They weigh 345 and 410 grains respectively and feature two-piece construction. There is an internal hollow cavity in the nose of the bullet, formed by swaging a round-nose front section with a hollow base. A rear section is then seated into the hollow base leaving a generous internal hollow area beneath the round

(Below) A new 308 Supreme 150-grain Silvertip boattail has been added.

I N THIS field, one could easily succumb to pessimism if it were important that all be as claimed, advertised, or suggested. However, it is a heap more fun to be aware that some folks don't always deliver. One can even sit back and grin a bit, sometimes laugh out loud. In defense of a few, some discrepancies are only the net outcome of trying too hard to do that which has not yet become practical to do.

In the *oops* department, be aware there may be a good amount of factory loaded 458 500/510-grain loads which were assembled using bullets that keyhole. This generally makes the ammo unsuitable for the intended purposes. Some component bullets are also involved. Don't head for Africa unless samples of your 458 ammo have been carefully checked in your rifle by, of course, shooting it.

Winchester

A brand new round to go with a variation of a popular handgun is the 40 Smith & Wesson. Basically a shortened 10mm, its 180-grain bullet is tentatively scheduled for a velocity of 990 fps. Tis said, by Winchester, that this load meets all of the FBI requirements for penetration and expansion. I'll bet it will be a heap easier on handguns than the high pressure Ten.

A 12-gauge 2¾-inch load with 1⅝ ounces of 4, 5, or 6 shot will be available for turkey hunters. Too, No. 6 shot has been added to the 10-gauge 2¼-

ounce loadings. A 3-inch 20-gauge No. 3 buck load has been added to the Olin lineup.

New steel shot loads include 10- and 12-gauge with F, T, and BBB size shot. A 10-gauge 1¾-ounce load of No. 1s should be about perfect for effective steel shot duck hunting. Two 16-gauge steel loads with ⅞-ounce of 2s or 4s are now available.

The fresh additions to the Supreme rifle ammo line are a 160-grain 7mm Remington Magnum and a 150-grain 308 Winchester—Silvertip boattails both. There is also a 280 Remington with a 160-grain Silvertip boattail.

A much needed 16-gauge component wad will, hopefully, become available sometime this year. And in keeping with the changes necessitated by a

(Above) If buckshot in 3-inch 20-gauge shells interests you, investigate the new Winchester load with No. 3 Buck.

(Above) The 7mm Remington Magnum with a 160-grain Silvertip boattail is a new Supreme item.

raw material change, another new Ball Powder is being offered called Super Field. The 452AA and 473AA are no longer cataloged by Winchester.

(Above) Also new to Winchester's Supreme line is a 160-grain 280 Remington loading.

nose. The bullet base is hollow to ensure adequate obturation and the best possible accuracy.

I suspect that the two-piece construction might tend to detract from accuracy unless production controls are tightly maintained. Shooting on game revealed one bullet did separate into two pieces, though devastation to the animal was immediately fatal. It is a lot of bullet for $6.95 per 10.

Federal Cartridge Co.

Federal has not slowed its new product development and a

gaggle of new items appear in this year's catalog. New shotshell items include Sporting Clays loads in both 12- and 20-gauge. These have biodegradable "paper" wad columns, and are loaded with hard No. 7½ or 8 shot. And a premium grade 16-gauge 1¼-ounce shell is now being loaded in 4s and 6s.

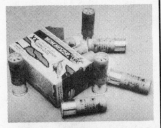

These 1⅝ ounces of shot in a 12-gauge 2¾-inch case from Winchester should help turkey hunters.

New international clay pigeon and Skeet regulations specify 1-ounce shot loads, and Federal is making a number of target loads that meet specifications. Twelve-gauge loads at approximately 1300 fps using 7½, 8, and 9 shot are being produced under the International Target Load logo. For international Skeet there is a load using extra hard 2mm diameter shot at 1350 fps.

Pocket pistol fans will be interested in the new 380 ACP load using a 90-grain Hydra-Shok bullet. At an advertised velocity of 1000 fps, this should be among the top performing loads in this caliber. Even if you actually only get about 900 or so fps from your favorite Colt or PPK, it will still be a hot performer. We will report on actual performance of this load in next year's pages if we can get the ammo.

As the 10mm continues the struggle to become an accepted cartridge, even in the face of Plus-P 45 ACP loads for competition, new loadings are continually surfacing. Federal's 180-grain Hydra-Shok 10mm loading is listed at a believable 950 fps, which equates to about 360 foot pounds of muzzle energy. And now the 44 Magnum has been loaded with Hydra-Shok bullets—a 240-grain bullet at 1180 fps and 740 foot pounds.

Four new, and much needed, rifle loadings using Nosler Partition bullets are now available. These include a 100-grain 243, 180-grain 308 Winchester, 180-grain 300 H&H Magnum, and a 300-grain 375 H&H Mag-

Steel 16-gauge loads? They're in production now from Winchester.

num. These will greatly enhance the game-taking potential of each of these classic rounds. The 243 and 308 Winchester loads are being sold under the Premium logo, while both H&H loads are sold under the Premium Safari trade name. There are also, in Federal's Hi-Power line, a new 150-grain 280 Remington and a 150-grain 303 British.

Hornady

Hornady has redesigned their handgun bullets and dubbed the results XTP, short for Extreme Terminal Performance. These are available in both hollow or softpoint configurations in .251, .312, .355, .357, .400, .410, .431, .451, and .452-inch diameters. There is also a new 147-grain 9mm full metal jacket bullet.

The goals of the XTP handgun bullets include deeper penetration and bullet expansion to 1½ times original diameter. They are to answer the charge that many handgun bullets just don't go deep enough for the deadly serious applications of police or personal protection. We have yet to try samples.

The Great Plains Maxi-Bullet line has been expanded to give muzzle-loading enthusiasts even more choice. This line now includes: 45-caliber 285-grain HBHP and 325-grain HBRN, 50-caliber 385-grain HBHP and 410-grain HBRN, and a 54-caliber 425-grain HBHP. And Hornady is now offering pistol bullets already placed into plastic sabots in 45, 50 and 54 calibers.

Nosler Bullets

Noslers continue to be among the very finest premium grade hunting bullets. When combined with their affordable price (about twice the cost of an ordinary bullet) these are indeed a solution to getting the

most out of any given caliber bullet weight combination. This year, Nosler has added two new bullets to this fine line—the 7mm 175-grain and a 35-caliber 225-grain, spitzers both. We received some limited samples in time to dispatch a few head of game with a 35/338 magnum. As always, performance was perfect and accuracy more than hoped. If I could hunt with only one style bullet, it might well be the Partition.

Also new from Nosler is a Ballistic Tip bullet in 25-caliber weighing 85 grains. This may well prove to be the best-ever varmint bullet for quarter-inch bores. I'm looking forward to doing in some prairie dogs with these.

A 90- and a 115-grain 9mm hollowpoint have been added to the handgun bullet line and the .224-inch 55-grain spitzer sans cannelure is back. Added too are 200- and 240-grain .429-inch bullets. A 185-grain JHP for the 45 ACP is also new. Finally, there is an extensively updated handbook, Nosler's third edition; it's a good one.

Buffalo Bullets

Buffalo Bullets continue to produce their superb muzzle-loading bullets and we continue

Hollow-cavity round-nose bullets for the muzzle-loading shooter are available from Mushroom Express Bullet Company in 50- and 54-caliber.

(Above) Federal still likes the 303 British cartridge; now offers a 150-grain softpoint.

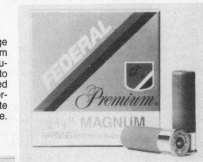

(Right) Now 16-gauge 1¼-ounce magnum loads are being manufactured by Federal to satisfy some renewed interest in this otherwise almost obsolete bore.

(Left) A new sporting clays load using biodegradable wads has been introduced by Federal in both 12 and 20 gauges.

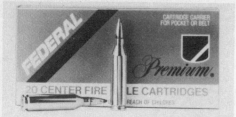

A much needed load for the 243 is Federal's Premium load with a 100-grain Nosler Partition bullet.

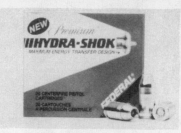

Hydra-Shok loads for the 380 auto will help keep this personal defense round a valid selection.

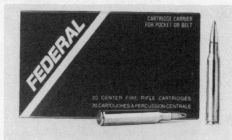

In the standard line, Federal now loads a 150-grain 280 Remington cartridge.

With the 300-grain Nosler Partition bullet, the Federal Premium Safari 375 H&H load will let this cartridge do some really effective work.

to have nothing but perfect one-shot kills with them—four nice deer during this past season. But there is something entirely new from Buffalo this year—metallic cartridges loaded with prefragmented bullets.

These are not the usual bullet jackets simply filled with small shot. They are jacketed bullets fitted with a supply of small shot on top of which is seated a light lead core. As a result, these will penetrate to an effective depth while not dangerously over-penetrating; and the chance of ricochet is notably reduced.

The new prefragmented Core-Shot loads are available in such calibers as: 223 Remington—47 grains; 25 ACP—36 grains; 308 Winchester—129 grains; 32 ACP—53 grains; 380 ACP—74 grains; 9mm Luger—100 and 147 grains; 38 Special—91 grains; 357 Magnum—120 grains; 10mm—156 grains; 41 Remington Magnum and 41 Action Express—162

grains; 44 Special—150 grains; 44 Magnum—180 grains; and 45 ACP—144 grains. Prices for 6 rounds range from about $14 to $20.

Hodgdon

Hodgdon Powder Co. has for the past several years been engaged in the formulation of tighter and tighter product acceptance specifications, according to Bob Hodgdon. However, new product introduction has not been totally ignored. To this end the folks from the Shawnee Mission sector of Kansas are now offering a super-slow burning propellant called H1000. It has a burning speed somewhere between H4831 and H870 in some applications. Generally, Hodgdon states that it is slightly slower than IMR 7828. Data is included in Hodgdon's #25 reloading manual and covers such calibers as 22-250 Remington, 220 Swift, 243 Winchester, 6mm Remington, 25-06 Remington, 257 Weath-

erby Magnum, 270 Winchester, 7mm Remington Magnum, 30-06 Springfield, and various 30-caliber magnums. For those who favor Winchester 452AA powder and may soon find it difficult to locate, Hodgdon will continue to sell their equivalent Trap 100. This may save the necessity to develop a new shotshell or handgun target load.

Accurate Arms Co.

Accurate's newest propellant offering is Nitro 100. It is a shotshell propellant of flake geometry. Designed to compete with IMR's "Hi-Skor" 700-X and Hercules' Red Dot, it is aimed at a large potential market share. Pricing may entice shotgunners to give it a try. It will also have some handgun cartridge loading applications. There are now 11 propellants available from Accurate, who import their products from IMI of Israel.

Garret Cartridges

Garret is offering several very heavy and very hard cast bullet loadings for the 44 Magnum and the 45-70 Gov't. The 44 Magnum loads use 280- and 320-grain extra hard lead alloy bullets. The newer 45-70 loads are rated as Plus-P type and as such are unsuitable, I presume, in the old Springfield Trapdoor rifles and carbines, or any similar strength firearms.

The 45-70 loads have 410- or 520-grain bullets with listed velocities of 1850 and 1650 fps respectively. Hardness rating for both is BHN 25. Leading surely should not be a problem.

I have used the 44 Magnum loads and found them to be all as claimed. Thus I look forward to having a go with the new rifle ammo.

Trophy Bonded Bullets

New, in this custom-made bullet line, is a true solid bullet made from homogeneous naval bronze, in .458-inch diameter.

It is a 400-grain bullet that will offer 458 Winchester Magnum loaders the capability of loading many propellants without the need to use heavily compressed loads, as compared to a like bullet of the typical 500-grain weight. That's good because many compressed loads tend to provide erratic performance after long-term storage.

The Bear Claw Trophy Bonded bullets are highly praised for their ability to penetrate and retain almost all of the original bullet weight. The Sledgehammer solids enjoy a reputation for positive penetration without bullet failures.

54 cal. 425 gr. HBHP   50 cal. 385 gr. HBHP   45 cal. 285 gr. HBHP

Hornady has expanded their muzzle-loading bullet line to include a variety of selections in 45-, 50- and 54-caliber.

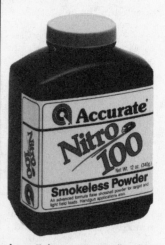

Accurate's newest propellant is a shotgun type, called Nitro 100.

Blount (CCI/Speer)

There is more new from Speer this year than there has been for quite a few years. There are a dozen new standard bullets and that many more Grand Slam and African Grand Slam bullets. It all starts with a blunt-nosed 46-grain 22-caliber bullet for the new and old lever-action 218 Bee rifles.

Kudu and Partition bullets go well together. That's me behind the 50 inches of horn bagged with a Nosler.

Also, in the same diameter are a 50-grain TNT (a fast expander), a 52-grain match-grade hollowpoint, a 62-grain hollowpoint and a 68-grain match-grade boattail hollowpoint.

For the lever-action 25-20s, there is a 75-grain flat-nosed, cannelured bullet. Need a 120-grain 7mm bullet? You have it. How about a .311-inch of 125 grains? You bet. New handgun bullets are 9mm 115-grain and two styles at 147-grains; 10mm 180-grain; .429-inch 300-grain; and .451-inch 300-grain.

In Grand Slam premium grade bullets there is a new 6mm 100-grain and a .257-inch 120-grain bullet. Also a 7mm 125-grain and .308-inch 150-grain Grand Slam styles are now available. There is even a Grand Slam in .358-inch—a 250-grain weight.

In standard heavy caliber bullets a 225-grain .338-inch, a 270-grain .375-inch, and a 350-grain 458 Winchester Magnum have been added. I hope the latter truly turns out to be a magnum grade bullet as I have been disappointed in other similar so-called magnum bullets which disintegrated on very small animals.

Finally there is a new line of bullets—African Grand Slams. These will include softpoints in .416-inch 400-grain and .458-inch 500-grain. Solids in this line will be in .375-inch 300-grain, .416-inch 400-grain and .458-inch 500-grain. The solids will have a very heavy jacket turned from gilding metal and a core of a dense hard material that looks as though it might be carbide. These solids would appear to offer the potential of low fouling characteristics, and shorter length than some other true solids (at the same weight). All of which makes me anticipate their use, both on the test range and during the next safari.

New ammo from CCI includes 22 Long Rifle Pistol Match, with sub-sonic velocity and positive pistol functioning. Other rimfire additions are 22 Long Rifle Mini-Mag + V (a between-high-and-hyper-velocity 32-grainer), and 22 Long Rifle

SGB (small game bullet). A 22 WMR Maxi-Mag + V adds hyper velocity to the 22 Magnum. It has a light 30-grain bullet moving at a claimed 2200 fps—wow! There is also a 9mm Luger shot load containing #11 pellets. New Blazer loads (that

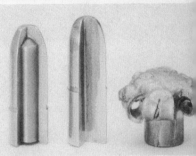

Cutaway of the Speer unique solid and softpoint African Grand Slam bullets, along with an expanded softpoint—all 458-500-grainers.

A new line of African Grand Slam bullets from Speer consists of, from left to right: 338-275-grain solid, 375-300-grain solid, 416-400-grain softpoint and solid, and 458-500-grain softpoint and solid.

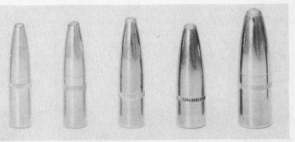

Speer has expanded their Grand Slam Premium bullet line to include, from left to right: 243-100-grain, 257-100-grain, 284-145-grain, 308-150-grain, and 358-250-grain.

New Speer handgun bullets include, from left to right: 9mm 115-grain PHP, 147-grain PHP, 147-grain TMJ, 10mm 180-grain PHP, 451-300-grain PSP, and 429-300-grain PSP.

New Speer 22 bullets include, from left to right: 46-grain FPSP, 50-grain TNT, 52-grain BTHP, 62-grain HP and 68-grain BTHP.

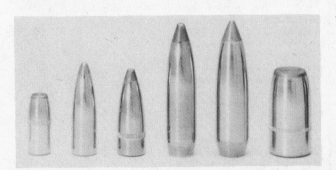

More Speer bullets new to the line are, from left to right: 257-75-grain FPSP, 284-120-grain SP, 311-125-grain SP, 338-BTSP, 375-270-grain BTSP, and 458-350-grain FPSP.

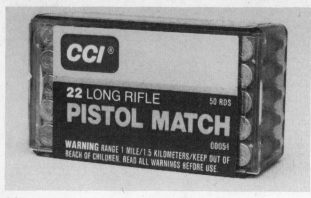

CCI's new pistol match grade 22 Long Rifle ammo.

good-shooting, inexpensive, non-reloadable handgun ammo) include a 147-grain 9mm Luger and a 180-, as well as a 200-grain, 10mm Auto round.

Remington

This year saw the expensive move of Remington's rimfire ammunition production capability from Bridgeport, Connecticut to Lonoke, Arkansas, which puts all Remington's ammo in one plant. There will be benefits to the rimfire line as a result of being part of a very sophisticated manufacturing facility.

There is increasing interest in making the 9mm a more effective cartridge, but time and expanding usage of the round is simply showcasing its shortcomings. Various new loadings to make the cartridge more effective in desperate situations offer heavier, slower bullets which expand well.

Thus, Remington handgun ammo now includes a 9mm Luger loading using a 147-grain jacketed hollowpoint at a muzzle velocity of 990 fps and muzzle energy of 320 foot pounds. Time will tell.

Steel shot applications continue to point out, to me at least, its shortcomings. This year Remington has five new loads, which makes more than 50 variations you may choose from in the familiar green boxes. BBB and T steel pellet sizes in 1⅜-ounce payloads are now offered in the 3-inch 12-gauge shell. In the shorter 12-gauge, BB, BBB and T sizes are now being produced in a 1¼-ounce shot weight. These larger pellets are finding favor among some waterfowlers who find that going two shot sizes larger (when switching from lead to steel pellets) is simply not sufficient to produce the desired results. These oversized pellets are not, by the way, legal for use in some jurisdictions, such as my home state of Connecticut.

Other new loads include lead pellet types for the Nitro Mag buffered shotshells. For the first time there are now 10-gauge 3½-inch selections (to go with the Remington SP10 semi-automatic shotgun) including 2, 4 and 6 size pellets in 2¼ ounces. For the 12-gauge 3-inch, No. 6 shot in a 1⅞-ounce load is another turkey special. A duplex target load using 7½ and 8 shot

is the final new Remington shotshell offering.

Barnes Bullets Inc.

Barnes bullets have been around for as long as I can remember, though we have never before discussed them in these pages. They manufacture bullets in almost every conceivable diameter starting with the 22 and on up to the 600 Nitro Express.

Barnes tends to offer bullets in the medium to ultra heavy weights in any given diameter. They have their traditional softpoint line with numerous nose

A shot load for the ubiquitous 9mm Luger is now available from Speer.

profiles. These include some not very common types, such as bullets for the 348, 38-55 and 401 Winchester rounds. Quite a few English calibers are covered, too. There are some traditional full metal case bullets in this line.

For those who hunt truly dangerous game in Africa, Barnes offers a complete line of true "solids" of the monolithic-type construction. These are of a solid bronze alloy and have a reputation among serious African pros as being the best type of solid for very serious applications. But this line also includes tiny 22-caliber bullets as well as the giant 577 and 600 cartridges. There are a lot of hard-to-find diameters.

The new Barnes X-Bullet is a unique solid copper bullet that expands on game in a very uniform manner without any notable loss of original bullet weight. Originally available in 27-, 28- and 30-caliber, Barnes has added .338, .375, .411 and .416-inch diameters. And by the time you read this there will be .243, .257, and .264-inch di-

ameter X-Bullets. Perhaps there will be opportunity to report further on this line in next year's pages. There is more than a gross of different bullets to play with.

ACTIV

A new nickel-plated shot load has been added to meet International Target shooting specifications for a 28-gram maximum. Changes have been made to all tournament 1-ounce loads to ensure compliance with the new regulations.

The ACTIV catalog/data book is a super source of reloading data for the ACTIV shell. Loads for Hercules, IMR, Hodgdon, and Scot powders are included. Also shown are some tips on adjusting your reloading press to handle the ACTIV case.

If you use a 2¾-inch chamber 12-gauge shotgun for any heavy-duty application (such as turkey or very long range pheasants) you should know about ACTIV's Penetrator series shot loads. These offer a full 1⅝ and 1¾ ounces of shot in sizes 2, 4, 6, and 7½. These are weights otherwise found only in 3-inch shells. The large internal case volume of the ACTIV shell makes these very heavy loads possible in their 2¾-inch loadings. And they are a heap less expensive than a new 3-inch shotgun. And effective, too.

PMC

If you're having a hard time locating a source of brass that can supply you with all your needs from a single lot, one answer is to get your dealer to fetch you up some PMC brass cases. These are packed 200 cases to a box, plenty to keep even a big user going for a while without the hassle sometimes associated with constant lot changes. ●

Remington 10-gauge shells with 2¼ ounces of shot may prove a very effective load for turkey.

New aluminum-cased CCI Blazer ammo includes, from left to right: 9mm 147-grain TMJ, 10mm 180-grain PHP, 10mm 200-grain TMJ, and 45 Colt 200-grain JHP.

The 44 Magnum is being loaded with Federal's successful Hydra-Shok bullet; this one is 240 grains.

Last-Minute ABC News

For shotshells, Winchester now offers Super-Field AA, a ball powder.

(Right) There are one-hundred and ten rifle bullets, fifty-two pistol bullets, forty-six rifle cartridges, thirty-nine pistol cartridges, seventeen round balls, and five Great Plains bullets on Hornady's new 1990 bullet chart.

(Below) Hornady's 9mm 147-grain HP/XTP is boattailed for deep loading in law enforcement applications.

Federal now has a Premium 308 Winchester load with the 180-grain Nosler Partition, a fine hunting bullet.

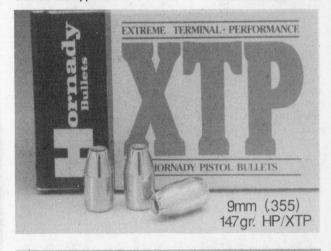

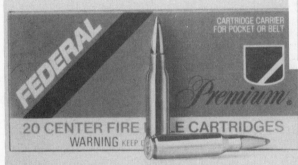

Winchester's sub-sonic 9mm is a 147-grain Silvertip hollowpoint at under 1000 fps.

Remington's sub-sonic 9mm Luger loads meet the new requirements of many law enforcement agencies.

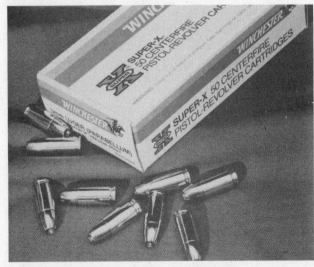

(Below) Winchester's choice for their Supreme in 280 Remington is a 160-grain Silvertip boattail at 2850 fps.

ACTIV keeps adding new stuff—here all-purpose loads in three gauges.

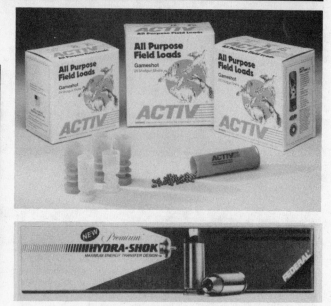

Federal's 10mm Hydra-Shok load has a 180-grain hollowpoint bullet.

For target shooters who cannot decide on a shot size, Remington's Duplex has a mix of 7½s and 8s.

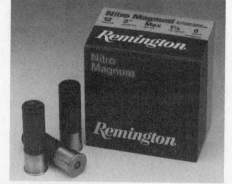

Many turkey hunters will favor Remington's new Magnum 12 load with 1⅞ ounces of #6 shot.

Winchester has added a 10-gauge load with 2¼ ounces of #6 shot, undoubtedly for turkey hunters.

Accurate Arms
40 S&W Loading Data

The 40 S&W is going to gain dramatic acceptance as soon as guns and components are available. We are developing data for several of our powders in this cartridge. This data includes all the .400-inch bullets we have on hand. The data is pressure tested; pressures were kept slightly below the proposed SAAMI maximum level.

The listed loads were determined to be maximum. Reduce .5- to 1.0-grain for a start charge. Cartridge length for all loads was 1.120 inches, maximum is listed at 1.135 inches. Velocities were obtained from a Cameron Hopkins reworked Colt with 5¼ inches compensated Bar-Sto barrel (Ed Brown Mini-Comp).

For those interested in IPSC style shooting, all loads listed make major power factor. No. 5 will allow the shooters to develop loads from the plinking range to full-house competition loads, for all present bullet weights.

CAST BULLET DATA

Bullet	Max. Charge	Powder (grains)	Velocity (feet/sec.)
164 CP	8.2	No. 5	1150
172 Lee	7.5	No. 5	1095
177 CP	6.9	No. 5	1030
185 Colorado	6.5	No. 5	992

JACKETED BULLET DATA

Bullet	Max. Charge	Powder (grains)	Velocity (feet/sec.)
150 Sierra	8.7	No. 5	1204
155 Hornady	8.6	No. 5	1180
170 Hornady	7.7	No. 5	1040
170 Nosler	8.0	No. 5	1083
180 Sierra	7.2	No. 5	1000
190 Sierra	7.0	No. 5	977
190 Speer	7.2	No. 5	964
200 Hornady	6.5	No. 5	911

AVERAGE CENTERFIRE RIFLE CARTRIDGE BALLISTICS AND PRICES

Caliber	Bullet Wgt. Grs.	—VELOCITY (fps)— Muzzle	100 yds.	200 yds.	300 yds.	400 yds.	—ENERGY (ft. lbs.)— Muzzle	100 yds.	200 yds.	300 yds.	400 yds.	—TRAJ. (In.)— 100 yds.	200 yds.	300 yds.	400 yds.	Approx. Price per box
17 Remington	25	4040	3284	2644	2086	1606	906	599	388	242	143	+2.0	+1.7	-4.0	-17.0	$ 14
22 Hornet	45	2690	2042	1502	1128	948	723	417	225	127	90	0.0	-7.7	-31.0	NA	$ 25
218 Bee	46	2760	2102	1550	1155	961	788	451	245	136	94	0.0	-7.2	-29.0	NA	$ 42
221 Fireball	50	2800	2137	1580	1180	988	870	507	277	155	109	0.0	-7.0	-28.0	NA	$ 13
222 Remington	50	3140	2602	2123	1700	1350	1094	752	500	321	202	+2.0	-0.4	-11.0	-33.0	$ 11
222 Remington	55	3020	2562	2147	1773	1451	1114	801	563	384	257	+2.0	-0.4	-11.0	-33.0	$ 11
22 PPC	52	3400	2930	2510	2130	NA	1335	990	730	525	NA	+2.0	-1.4	-5.0	NA	NA
223 Remington	40	3650	3010	2450	1950	1530	1185	805	535	340	265	+2.0	+1.0	-6.0	-22.0	$ 13
223 Remington	55	3240	2748	2305	1906	1556	1282	922	649	444	296	+2.0	-0.2	-9.0	-27.0	$ 12
223 Remington	64	3020	2621	2256	1920	1619	1296	977	723	524	373	+2.0	-0.2	-9.3	-23.0	$ 12
223 Remington	69	3000	2720	2460	2210	1980	1380	1135	925	750	600	+2.0	+0.8	-5.8	-17.5	$ 17
222 Rem. Mag.	55	3240	2748	2305	1906	1556	1282	922	649	444	296	+2.0	-0.2	-9.0	-27.0	$ 12
225 Winchester	55	3570	3066	2616	2208	1838	1556	1148	836	595	412	+2.0	+1.0	-5.0	-20.0	$ 15
224 Wea. Mag.	55	3650	3192	2780	2403	2057	1627	1244	943	705	516	+2.0	+1.2	-4.0	-17.0	$ 27
22-250 Rem.	40	4000	3320	2720	2200	1740	1420	980	660	430	265	+2.0	+1.8	-3.0	-16.0	$ 13
22-250 Rem.	55	3680	3137	2656	2222	1832	1654	1201	861	603	410	+2.0	+1.3	-4.0	-17.0	$ 13
220 Swift	50	4110	3570	3080	2640	2240	1875	1415	1055	775	555	+2.0	+2.8	-7.0	NA	$ 23
22 Savage H.P.	71	2790	2340	1930	1570	1280	1225	860	585	390	190	+2.0	-1.0	-10.4	-35.7	$ 24
6mm BR Rem.	100	2550	2310	2083	1870	1671	1444	1185	963	776	620	+2.5	-0.6	-11.8	NA	$ 19
6mm PPC	70	3140	2750	2400	2070	NA	1535	1175	895	665	NA	+2.0	+1.4	-5.0	NA	$ 22
243 Winchester	60	3600	3110	2660	2260	1890	1725	1285	945	680	475	+2.0	+1.8	-3.3	-15.5	$ 15
243 Winchester	80	3350	2955	2593	2259	1951	1993	1551	1194	906	676	+2.0	+0.9	-5.0	-19.0	$ 15
243 Winchester	85	3320	3070	2830	2600	2380	2080	1770	1510	1280	1070	+2.0	+1.2	-4.0	-14.0	$ 17
243 Winchester	100	2960	2697	2449	2215	1993	1945	1615	1332	1089	882	+2.5	+1.2	-6.0	-20.0	$ 15
6mm Remington	80	3470	3064	2694	2352	2036	2139	1667	1289	982	736	+2.0	+1.1	-5.0	-17.0	$ 15
6mm Remington	100	3100	2829	2573	2332	2104	2133	1777	1470	1207	983	+2.5	+1.6	-5.0	-17.0	$ 15
240 Wea. Mag.	87	3500	3202	2924	2663	2416	2366	1980	1651	1370	1127	+2.0	+2.0	-2.0	-12.0	$ 27
240 Wea. Mag.	100	3395	3106	2835	2581	2339	2559	2142	1785	1478	1215	+2.5	+2.8	-2.0	-11.0	$ 36
25-20 Win.	86	1460	1194	1030	931	858	407	272	203	165	141	0.0	-23.5	NA	NA	$ 29
25-35 Win.	117	2230	1866	1545	1282	1097	1292	904	620	427	313	+2.5	-4.2	-26.0	NA	$ 19
250 Savage	100	2820	2504	2210	1936	1684	1765	1392	1084	832	630	+2.5	+0.4	-9.0	-28.0	$ 16
257 Roberts	100	2980	2661	2363	2085	1827	1972	1572	1240	965	741	+2.5	-0.8	-5.2	-21.6	$ 18
257 Roberts	117	2780	2411	2071	1761	1488	2009	1511	1115	806	576	+2.5	-0.2	-10.2	-32.6	$ 17
257 Roberts	120	2780	2560	2360	2160	1970	2060	1750	1480	1240	1030	+2.5	+1.2	-6.4	-23.6	$ 22
25-06 Rem.	87	3440	2995	2591	2222	1884	2286	1733	1297	954	686	+2.0	+1.1	-2.5	-14.4	$ 17
25-06 Rem.	90	3440	3043	2680	2344	2034	2364	1850	1435	1098	827	+2.0	+1.8	-3.3	-15.6	$ 17
25-06 Rem.	100	3230	2893	2580	2287	2014	2316	1858	1478	1161	901	+2.0	+0.8	-5.7	-18.9	$ 17
25-06 Rem.	117	2990	2770	2570	2370	2190	2320	2000	1715	1465	1246	+2.5	+1.0	-7.9	-26.6	$ 17
25-06 Rem.	120	2990	2730	2484	2252	2032	2382	1985	1644	1351	1100	+2.5	+1.2	-5.3	-19.6	$ 17
257 Wea. Mag.	87	3825	3456	3118	2805	2513	2826	2308	1870	1520	1220	+2.0	+2.7	-0.3	-7.6	$ 27
257 Wea. Mag.	100	3555	3237	2941	2665	2404	2806	2326	1920	1576	1283	+2.5	+3.2	0.0	-8.0	$ 38
257 Wea. Mag.	120	3300	3056	2823	2599	2388	2902	2489	2124	1800	1520	+2.5	+2.2	-4.1	-18.4	$ 38
6.5x50mm Jap.	139	2360	2160	1970	1790	1620	1720	1440	1195	985	810	+2.5	-1.0	-13.5	NA	$ 24
6.5x50mm Jap.	156	2070	1830	1610	1430	1260	1475	1155	900	695	550	+2.5	-4.0	-23.8	NA	$ 24
6.5x52mm Car.	139	2580	2360	2160	1970	1790	2045	1725	1440	1195	985	+2.5	0.0	-9.9	-29.0	$ 24
6.5x52mm Car.	156	2430	2170	1930	1700	1500	2045	1630	1285	1005	780	+2.5	-1.0	-13.9	NA	$ 24
6.5x55mm Swed.	139	2850	2560	2290	2030	1790	2515	2025	1615	1270	985	+2.5	+1.2	-6.8	-23.3	$ 24
6.5x55mm Swed.	156	2650	2370	2110	1870	1650	2425	1950	1550	1215	945	+2.5	0.0	-10.3	-30.6	$ 24
6.5 Rem. Mag.	120	3210	2905	2621	2353	2102	2745	2248	1830	1475	1177	+2.5	+1.7	-4.1	-16.3	$ 20
264 Win. Mag.	140	3030	2782	2548	2326	2114	2854	2406	2018	1682	1389	+2.5	+1.4	-5.1	-18.0	$ 22
270 Winchester	100	3430	3021	2649	2305	1988	2612	2027	1557	1179	877	+2.0	+1.0	-4.9	-17.5	$ 17
270 Winchester	130	3060	2776	2510	2259	2022	2702	2225	1818	1472	1180	+2.5	+1.4	-5.3	-18.2	$ 17
270 Winchester	140	2960	2753	2554	2365	2183	2724	2356	2029	1739	1482	+2.5	+1.6	-4.8	-17.4	$ 24
270 Winchester	150	2850	2585	2336	2100	1879	2705	2226	1817	1468	1175	+2.5	+1.2	-6.5	-22.0	$ 17
270 Wea. Mag.	100	3760	3380	3033	2712	2412	3139	2537	2042	1633	1292	+2.0	+2.4	-1.2	-10.1	$ 27
270 Wea. Mag.	130	3375	3119	2878	2649	2432	3287	2808	2390	2026	1707	+2.5	+2.9	-0.9	-9.9	$ 38
270 Wea. Mag.	150	3245	3036	2837	2647	2465	3507	3070	2681	2334	2023	+2.5	+2.6	-1.8	-11.4	$ 38
7mm BR	140	2215	2012	1821	1643	1481	1525	1259	1031	839	681	+2.0	-3.7	-20.0	NA	$ 19
7mm Mauser	140	2660	2435	2221	2018	1827	2199	1843	1533	1266	1037	+2.5	0.0	-9.6	-27.7	$ 17
7mm Mauser	145	2690	2442	2206	1985	1777	2334	1920	1568	1268	1017	+2.5	+0.1	-9.6	-28.3	$ 17
7mm Mauser	154	2690	2490	2300	2120	1940	2475	2120	1810	1530	1285	+2.5	+0.8	-7.5	-23.5	$ 17
7mm Mauser	175	2440	2137	1857	1603	1382	2313	1774	1340	998	742	+2.5	-1.7	-16.1	NA	$ 17
7x30 Waters	120	2700	2300	1930	1600	1330	1940	1405	990	685	470	+2.5	-0.2	-12.3	NA	$ 17
7mm-08 Rem.	120	3000	2725	2467	2223	1992	2398	1979	1621	1316	1058	+2.0	0.0	-7.6	-22.3	$ 17
7mm-08 Rem.	140	2860	2625	2402	2189	1988	2542	2142	1793	1490	1228	+2.5	+0.8	-6.9	-21.9	$ 17
7x64mm Bren.	154	2820	2610	2420	2230	2050	2720	2335	1995	1695	1430	+2.5	+1.4	-5.7	-19.9	NA
284 Winchester	150	2860	2595	2344	2108	1886	2724	2243	1830	1480	1185	+2.5	+0.8	-7.3	-23.2	$ 21
280 Remington	120	3150	2866	2599	2348	2110	2643	2188	1800	1468	1186	+2.0	+0.6	-6.0	-17.9	$ 17
280 Remington	140	3000	2758	2528	2309	2102	2797	2363	1986	1657	1373	+2.5	+1.4	-5.2	-18.3	$ 17
280 Remington	150	2890	2624	2373	2135	1912	2781	2293	1875	1518	1217	+2.5	+0.8	-7.1	-22.6	$ 17
280 Remington	165	2820	2510	2220	1950	1701	2913	2308	1805	1393	1060	+2.5	+0.4	-8.8	-26.5	$ 17
7x61mm S&H Sup.	154	3060	2720	2400	2100	1820	3200	2520	1965	1505	1135	+2.5	+1.8	-5.0	-19.8	NA
7mm Rem. Mag.	140	3175	2923	2684	2458	2243	3133	2655	2240	1878	1564	+2.5	+2.0	-3.4	-14.5	$ 21
7mm Rem. Mag.	150	3110	2830	2085	2320	2085	3221	2667	2196	1792	1448	+2.5	+1.6	-4.6	-16.5	$ 21
7mm Rem. Mag.	160	2950	2730	2520	2320	2120	3090	2650	2250	1910	1600	+2.5	+1.8	-4.4	-17.8	$ 21
7mm Rem. Mag.	165	2950	2800	2650	2510	2370	3190	2865	2570	2300	2050	+2.5	+2.0	-3.4	-14.4	$ 21
7mm Rem. Mag.	175	2860	2645	2440	2244	2057	3178	2718	2313	1956	1644	+2.5	+1.0	-6.5	-20.7	$ 21
7mm Wea. Mag.	140	3400	3163	2939	2726	2522	3593	3110	2684	2309	1978	+2.5	+3.0	-0.6	-9.2	$ 38
7mm Wea. Mag.	154	3260	3023	2799	2586	2382	3539	3044	2609	2227	1890	+2.5	+2.8	-1.5	-10.8	$ 27
7mm Wea. Mag.	160	3200	3004	2816	2637	2464	3637	3205	2817	2469	2156	+2.5	+2.7	-1.5	-10.6	$ 38
7mm Wea. Mag.	175	3070	2879	2696	2520	2351	3662	3220	2824	2467	2147	+2.5	+1.8	-2.7	-13.1	$ 27
7.5x55 Swiss	180	2650	2450	2250	2060	1880	2805	2390	2020	1700	1415	+2.5	+0.6	-8.1	-24.9	$ 26
30 Carbine	110	1990	1567	1236	1035	923	977	600	373	262	208	0.0	-13.5	NA	NA	$ 27
303 Savage	190	1890	1612	1372	1183	1055	1507	1096	794	591	469	+2.5	-7.6	NA	NA	$ 21
30 Remington	170	2120	1822	1555	1328	1153	1696	1253	913	666	502	+2.5	-4.7	-26.3	NA	$ 17
30-30 Win.	55	3400	2693	2085	1570	1187	1412	886	521	301	172	+2.0	0.0	-10.2	-35.0	$ 16
30-30 Win.	125	2570	2090	1660	1320	1080	1830	1210	770	480	320	+2.0	-2.6	-19.9	NA	$ 13
30-30 Win.	150	2390	1973	1605	1303	1095	1902	1296	858	565	399	+2.5	-3.2	-22.5	NA	$ 13
30-30 Win.	170	2200	1895	1619	1381	1191	1827	1355	989	720	535	+2.5	-5.8	-23.6	NA	$ 13
300 Savage	150	2630	2354	2094	1853	1631	2303	1845	1462	1143	886	+2.5	-0.4	-10.1	-30.7	$ 17
300 Savage	180	2350	2137	1935	1754	1570	2207	1825	1496	1217	985	+2.5	-1.6	-15.2	NA	$ 17
30-40 Krag	180	2430	2213	2007	1813	1632	2360	1957	1610	1314	1064	+2.5	-1.4	-13.8	NA	$ 17
307 Winchester	150	2760	2321	1924	1575	1289	2530	1795	1233	826	554	+2.5	-1.5	-13.6	NA	$ 16
7.65x53mm Arg.	180	2590	2390	2200	2010	1830	2685	2280	1925	1615	1345	+2.5	0.0	-27.6	NA	$ 24
308 Winchester	55	3770	3215	2726	2286	1888	1735	1262	907	638	435	+2.0	+1.4	-3.8	-15.8	$ 19
308 Winchester	150	2820	2533	2263	2009	1774	2648	2137	1705	1344	1048	+2.5	+0.4	-8.5	-26.1	$ 17
308 Winchester	165	2700	2440	2194	1963	1748	2670	2180	1763	1411	1199	+2.5	0.0	-9.7	-28.5	$ 17
308 Winchester	168	2680	2493	2314	2143	1979	2678	2318	1998	1713	1460	+2.5	0.0	-8.9	-25.3	$ 17
308 Winchester	180	2620	2393	2178	1974	1782	2743	2288	1896	1557	1269	+2.5	-0.2	-10.2	-28.5	$ 17
30-06 Spfd.	55	4080	3485	2965	2502	2083	2033	1483	1074	764	530	+2.0	+1.9	-2.1	-11.7	$ 19
30-06 Spfd.	125	3140	2780	2447	2138	1853	2736	2145	1662	1279	953	+2.0	+1.0	-6.2	-21.0	$ 17
30-06 Spfd.	150	2910	2617	2342	2083	1853	2820	2281	1827	1445	1135	+2.5	+0.8	-7.2	-23.4	$ 17
30-06 Spfd.	165	2800	2534	2283	2047	1825	2872	2352	1909	1534	1220	+2.5	+0.4	-8.4	-25.5	$ 17

AVERAGE CENTERFIRE RIFLE CARTRIDGE BALLISTICS AND PRICES (con't.)

Caliber	Bullet Wgt. Grs.	—VELOCITY (fps)— Muzzle	100 yds.	200 yds.	300 yds.	400 yds.	—ENERGY (ft. lbs.)— Muzzle	100 yds.	200 yds.	300 yds.	400 yds.	—TRAJ. (in.)— 100 yds.	200 yds.	300 yds.	400 yds.	Approx. Price per box
30-06 Spfd.	180	2700	2469	2250	2042	1846	2913	2436	2023	1666	1362	+2.5	0.0	− 9.3	−27.0	$ 17
30-06 Spfd.	220	2410	2130	1870	1632	1422	2837	2216	1708	1301	988	+2.5	− 1.7	−16.0	NA	$ 17
308 Norma Mag.	180	3020	2820	2630	2440	2270	3645	3175	2755	2385	2050	+2.5	+ 2.0	− 3.5	−14.8	$ 31
300 H&H Magnum	180	2880	2640	2412	2196	1990	3315	2785	2325	1927	1583	+2.5	+ 0.8	− 6.8	−21.7	$ 22
300 Win. Mag.	150	3290	2951	2636	2342	2068	3605	2900	2314	1827	1424	+2.5	+ 1.9	− 3.8	−15.8	$ 22
300 Win. Mag.	180	2960	2745	2540	2344	2157	3501	3011	2578	2196	1859	+2.5	+ 1.2	− 5.5	−18.5	$ 22
300 Win. Mag.	200	2830	2680	2530	2380	2240	3560	3180	2830	2520	2230	+2.5	+ 1.6	− 4.7	−17.2	$ 24
300 Win. Mag.	220	2680	2448	2228	2020	1823	3508	2927	2424	1993	1623	+2.5	0.0	− 9.5	−27.5	$ 22
300 Wea. Mag.	110	3900	3441	3028	2652	2305	3714	2891	2239	1717	1297	+2.0	+ 2.6	− 0.6	− 8.7	$ 27
300 Wea. Mag.	150	3600	3307	3033	2776	2533	4316	3642	3064	2566	2137	+2.5	+ 3.2	0.0	− 8.1	$ 38
300 Wea. Mag.	180	3300	3077	2865	2663	2470	4352	3784	3280	2834	2438	+2.5	+ 2.6	− 1.8	− 6.8	$ 38
300 Wea. Mag.	220	2905	2498	2126	1787	1490	4122	3047	2207	1560	1085	+2.5	+ 1.2	− 6.8	−23.4	$ 27
32-20 Win.	100	1210	1021	913	834	769	325	231	185	154	131	0.0	−32.3	NA	NA	$ 21
303 British	180	2460	2124	1817	1542	1311	2418	1803	1319	950	687	+2.5	− 1.8	−16.8	NA	$ 17
7.62x39mm Rus.	123	2300	2030	1780	1550	1350	1445	1125	860	655	500	+2.5	− 2.0	−17.5	NA	$ 14
7.62x54mm Rus.	146	2950	2730	2520	2320	NA	2820	2415	2055	1740	NA	+2.5	+ 2.0	− 4.4	−17.7	$ 20
7.62x54mm Rus.	180	2580	2370	2180	2000	1820	2650	2250	1900	1590	1100	+2.5	0.0	− 9.8	−28.5	$ 20
7.7x58mm Jap.	180	2500	2300	2100	1920	1750	2490	2105	1770	1475	1225	+2.5	0.0	−10.4	−30.2	$ 20
8x57mm JS Mau.	165	2850	2520	2210	1930	1670	2965	2330	1795	1360	1015	+2.5	+ 1.0	− 7.7	NA	NA
32 Win. Special	170	2250	1921	1626	1372	1175	1911	1393	998	710	521	+2.5	− 3.5	−22.9	NA	$ 14
8mm Mauser	170	2360	1969	1622	1333	1123	2102	1464	993	671	476	+2.5	− 3.1	−22.2	NA	$ 17
8mm Rem. Mag.	185	3080	2761	2464	2186	1927	3896	3131	2494	1963	1525	+2.5	+ 1.4	− 5.5	−19.7	$ 25
8mm Rem. Mag.	220	2830	2581	2346	2123	1913	3912	3254	2688	2201	1787	+2.5	+ 0.6	− 7.6	−23.5	$ 25
338 Win. Mag.	210	2830	2590	2370	2150	1940	3735	3130	2610	2155	1760	+2.5	+ 1.4	− 6.0	−20.9	$ 32
338 Win. Mag.	225	2780	2572	2374	2184	2003	3860	3305	2845	2383	2004	+2.5	+ 0.6	− 7.5	−22.8	$ 26
338 Win. Mag.	250	2660	2456	2261	2075	1898	3927	3348	2837	2389	1999	+2.5	+ 0.2	− 9.0	−26.2	$ 26
340 Wea. Mag.	210	3250	2991	2746	2515	2295	4924	4170	3516	2948	2455	+2.5	− 1.9	− 1.8	−11.8	$ 46
340 Wea. Mag.	250	3000	2806	2621	2443	2272	4995	4371	3812	3311	2864	+2.5	+ 2.0	− 3.5	−14.8	$ 46
338 A-Square	250	3120	2799	2500	2220	1958	5403	4348	3469	2736	2128	+2.5	+ 2.7	− 1.5	−10.5	$ 34
357 Magnum	158	1830	1427	1138	980	883	1175	715	454	337	274	0.0	−16.2	−33.1	NA	$ 24
35 Remington	150	2300	1874	1506	1218	1039	1762	1169	755	494	359	+2.5	− 4.1	−26.3	NA	$ 15
35 Remington	200	2080	1698	1376	1140	1001	1921	1280	841	577	445	+2.5	− 6.3	−17.1	−33.6	$ 15
356 Winchester	200	2460	2114	1797	1517	1284	2688	1985	1434	1022	732	+2.5	− 1.8	−17.1	NA	$ 25
358 Winchester	200	2490	2171	1876	1619	1379	2753	2093	1563	1151	844	+2.5	− 1.6	−15.6	NA	$ 26
350 Rem. Mag.	200	2710	2410	2130	1870	1631	3261	2579	2014	1553	1181	+2.5	− 0.2	−10.0	−30.1	$ 27
35 Whelen	200	2675	2378	2100	1842	1606	3177	2510	1958	1506	1145	+2.5	− 0.2	−10.3	−31.1	$ 17
35 Whelen	250	2400	2066	1761	1492	1269	3197	2369	1722	1235	893	+2.5	− 4.2	−21.3	NA	$ 17
358 Norma Mag.	250	2800	2510	2230	1970	1730	4350	3480	2750	2145	1655	+2.5	+ 1.0	− 7.6	−25.2	NA
9.3x57mm Mau.	286	2070	1810	1590	1390	1110	2710	2090	1600	1220	955	+2.5	− 2.6	−22.5	NA	NA
9.3x62mm Mau.	286	2360	2089	1844	1623	NA	3538	2771	2157	1670	1260	+2.5	− 1.6	−21.0	NA	$ 56
9.3x64mm	286	2700	2505	2318	2139	1968	4629	3984	3411	2906	2460	+2.5	+ 2.7	− 4.5	−19.2	$ 59
9.3x74Rmm	286	2360	2089	1844	1623	NA	3538	2771	2157	1670	NA	+2.5	− 2.0	−11.0	NA	$ 59
38-55 Win.	255	1320	1190	1091	1018	963	987	802	674	587	525	0.0	−23.4	NA	NA	$ 20
375 Winchester	200	2200	1841	1526	1268	1089	2150	1506	1034	714	527	+2.5	− 4.0	−26.2	NA	$ 22
375 Winchester	250	1900	1647	1424	1239	1103	2005	1506	1126	852	676	+2.5	− 6.9	−33.3	NA	$ 22
375 N.E. 2½″	270	2000	1740	1507	1310	NA	2398	1815	1362	1026	NA	+2.5	− 6.0	−30.0	NA	$ 89
375 Flanged	300	2450	2150	1886	1640	NA	3998	3102	2369	1790	NA	+2.5	− 2.4	−17.0	NA	$ 68
375 H&H Magnum	250	2670	2450	2240	2040	1850	3955	3335	2790	2315	1905	+2.5	− 0.4	−10.2	−28.4	$ 40
375 H&H Magnum	270	2690	2420	2166	1928	1707	4337	3510	2812	2228	1747	+2.5	0.0	−10.0	−29.4	$ 27
375 H&H Magnum	300	2530	2171	1843	1551	1307	4263	3139	2262	1602	1138	+2.5	− 2.0	−16.2	NA	$ 29
375 Wea. Mag.	300	2700	2420	2157	1911	1685	4856	3901	3100	2432	1891	+2.5	− 0.4	−10.7	—	$ 50
378 Wea. Mag.	270	3180	2976	2781	2594	2415	6062	5308	4635	4034	3495	+2.5	+ 2.6	− 1.8	−11.3	$ 48
378 Wea. Mag.	300	2929	2576	2252	1952	1680	5698	4419	3379	2538	1881	+2.5	+ 1.2	− 7.0	−24.5	$ 48
375 A-Square	300	2920	2626	2351	2093	1850	5679	4594	3681	2917	2281	+2.5	+ 1.4	− 6.0	−21.0	$ 39
38-40 Win.	180	1160	999	901	827	764	538	399	324	273	233	0.0	−33.9	NA	NA	$ 35
450/400-3″	400	2150	1932	1730	1545	1379	4105	3316	2659	2119	1689	+2.5	− 4.0	− 9.5	−30.3	$ 70
416 Taylor	400	2350	2117	1896	1693	NA	4905	3980	3194	2547	NA	+2.5	− 1.2	−15.0	NA	$ 59
416 Hoffman	400	2380	2145	1923	1718	1529	5031	4087	3285	2620	2077	+2.5	− 1.0	−14.1	NA	$ 50
416 Rigby	410	2370	2110	1870	1640	1440	5115	4050	3165	2455	1895	+2.5	− 2.4	−17.3	NA	$106
416 Rem. Mag.	400	2380	2145	1923	1718	1529	5031	4087	3285	2620	2077	+2.5	− 1.0	−14.1	NA	$ 66
416 Wea. Mag.	400	2700	NA	NA	NA	NA	6476	NA	NA	NA	NA	NA	NA	NA	NA	$ 42
404 Jeffery	400	2150	1924	1716	1525	NA	4105	3289	2614	2064	NA	+2.5	− 4.0	−22.1	NA	$ 53
425 Express	400	2400	2160	1934	1725	NA	5115	4145	3322	2641	NA	+2.5	− 1.0	−14.0	NA	$ 59
44-40 Win.	200	1190	1006	900	822	756	629	449	360	300	254	0.0	−33.3	NA	NA	$ 33
44 Rem. Mag.	240	1760	1380	1114	970	878	1650	1015	661	501	411	0.0	−17.6	NA	NA	$ 13
444 Marlin	240	2350	1815	1377	1087	941	2942	1753	1001	630	472	+2.5	−15.1	−31.0	NA	$ 18
444 Marlin	265	2120	1733	1405	1160	1012	2644	1768	1162	791	603	+2.5	− 6.0	−32.2	NA	$ 18
45-70 Govt.	300	1810	1497	1244	1073	969	2182	1492	1031	767	625	0.0	−14.8	NA	NA	$ 19
45-70 Govt.	405	1330	1168	1055	977	918	1590	1227	1001	858	758	0.0	−24.6	NA	NA	$ 19
458 Win. Mag.	350	2470	1990	1570	1250	1060	4740	3065	1915	1205	870	+2.5	− 2.5	−21.6	NA	$ 42
458 Win. Mag.	465	2220	1999	1791	1601	NA	5088	4127	3312	2646	NA	+2.5	− 2.0	−17.7	NA	NA
458 Win. Mag.	500	2040	1823	1623	1442	1237	4620	3689	2924	2308	1839	+2.5	− 3.5	−22.0	NA	$ 52
458 Win. Mag.	510	2040	1770	1527	1319	1157	4712	3547	2640	1970	1516	+2.5	− 4.1	−25.0	NA	$ 35
450 N.E.-3¼″	465	2190	1970	1765	1577	NA	4952	4009	3216	2567	NA	+2.5	− 3.0	−20.0	NA	$ 70
450 N.E.-3¼″	500	2150	1920	1708	1514	NA	5132	4093	3238	2544	NA	+2.5	− 4.0	−22.9	NA	$ 70
450 No. 2	465	2190	1970	1765	1577	NA	4952	4009	3216	2567	NA	+2.5	− 3.0	−20.0	NA	$ 96
450 No.2	500	2150	1920	1708	1514	NA	5132	4093	3238	2544	NA	+2.5	− 4.0	−22.9	NA	$ 96
458 Lott	500	2300	2062	1838	1633	NA	5873	4719	3748	2960	NA	+2.5	− 1.6	−16.4	NA	$ 59
450 Ackley Mag.	500	2320	2081	1855	1649	NA	5975	4085	3820	3018	NA	+2.5	− 1.2	−15.0	NA	$ 59
460 Short A-Sq.	500	2420	2175	1943	1729	NA	6501	5250	4193	3319	NA	+2.5	− 0.8	−12.8	—	$ 45
460 Wea. Mag.	500	2700	2404	2128	1869	1635	8092	6416	5026	3878	2969	+2.5	+ 0.6	− 8.9	−28.0	$ 53
500/465 N.E.	480	2150	1917	1703	1507	NA	4926	3917	3089	2419	NA	+2.5	− 4.0	−22.2	—	$ 70
470 Rigby	500	2150	1912	1693	1494	NA	5132	4058	3182	2478	NA	+2.5	− 4.0	−23.0	NA	NA
470 Nitro Ex.	480	2190	1954	1735	1536	NA	5111	4070	3210	2515	NA	+2.5	− 3.5	−20.8	NA	$170
470 Nitro Ex.	500	2150	1890	1650	1440	1270	5130	3965	3040	2310	1790	+2.5	− 4.3	−24.0	NA	$170
475 No. 2	500	2200	1955	1728	1522	NA	5375	4243	3316	2573	NA	+2.5	− 3.2	−20.9	NA	$ 98
505 Gibbs	505	2300	2008	1741	1501	NA	6166	4702	3532	2625	NA	+2.5	− 3.0	−20.0	NA	$ 98
500 N.E.-3″	600	2150	1927	1721	1531	NA	6158	4947	3944	3124	NA	+2.5	− 4.0	−22.0	NA	$ 75
495 A-Square	600	2280	2050	1833	1635	NA	6925	5598	4478	3562	NA	+2.5	− 2.0	−17.0	NA	$ 48
500 A-Square	600	2380	2144	1922	1766	NA	7546	6126	4920	3922	NA	+2.5	− 3.0	−17.0	NA	$ 49
500 A-Square	707	2250	2040	1841	1567	NA	7947	6530	5318	4311	NA	+2.5	− 2.0	−17.0	NA	$ 49
577 Nitro Ex.	750	2050	1793	1562	1360	NA	6990	5356	4065	3079	NA	+2.5	− 5.0	−26.0	NA	$ 98

Notes: NA in velocity or energy column = This data not available from manufacturer;
NA in trajectory column = Bullet has fallen more than 3 feet below line or sight and hold-over is not practical—in any column means the data was not available at press time
Wea. Mag. = Weatherby Magnum
Spfd. = Springfield
A-Sq. = A-Square
N.E. = Nitro Express
Some manufacturers do not supply suggested retail prices. Others did not get their pricing to us before press time. All pricing can vary dependent on the exact brand and style of ammo selected and/or the retail outlet from which you make your purchase. Pricing has been rounded to the nearest dollar and represents our best estimate of average pricing.

CENTERFIRE HANDGUN CARTRIDGES—AVERAGE BALLISTICS AND PRICES

Caliber	Bullet Wgt. Grs.	Velocity (fps) Muzzle	50 yds.	100 yds.	Energy (ft. lbs.) Muzzle	50 yds.	100 yds.	Mid-Range Traj. (in.) 50 yds.	100 yds.	Bbl. Length (in.)	Approx. Price/box
22 Rem. Jet	40	2100	1790	1510	390	285	200	0.3	1.4	8⅜	NA
221 Rem. Fireball	50	2650	2380	2130	780	630	505	0.2	0.8	10½	$13*
25 Automatic	45	815	730	655	65	55	40	1.8	7.7	2	$18
25 Automatic	50	760	705	660	65	55	50	2.0	8.7	2	$16
30 Luger	93	1220	1110	1040	305	255	225	0.9	3.5	4½	$29
30 Carbine	110	1790	1600	1430	785	625	500	0.4	1.7	10	$27
32 S&W	88	680	645	610	90	80	75	2.5	10.5	3	$15
32 S&W Long	98	705	670	635	115	100	90	2.3	10.5	4	$16
32 Short Colt	80	745	665	590	100	80	60	2.2	9.9	4	$15
32 Long Colt	82	755	715	675	100	95	85	2.0	8.7	4	NA
32 H&R Magnum	85	1100	1020	930	230	195	165	1.0	4.3	4½	$21
32 H&R Magnum	95	1030	940	900	225	190	170	1.1	4.7	4½	$18
32 Automatic	60	970	895	835	125	105	95	1.3	5.4	4	$22
32 Automatic	71	905	855	810	130	115	95	1.4	5.8	4	$19
380 Automatic	85/88	990	920	870	190	165	145	1.2	5.1	4	$22
380 Automatic	90	1000	890	800	200	160	130	1.2	5.5	3¾	$19
380 Automatic	95	955	865	785	190	160	130	1.4	5.9	4	$19
38 Automatic	130	1040	980	925	310	275	245	1.0	4.7	4½	NA
38 Super Auto +P	115	1300	1145	1040	430	335	275	0.7	3.3	5	$24
38 Super Auto +P	125/130	1215	1100	1015	425	350	300	0.8	3.6	5	$20
9mm Luger	88	1500	1190	1010	440	275	200	0.6	3.1	4	$22
9mm Luger	95	1300	1140	1010	350	275	215	0.8	3.4	4	$21
9mm Luger	115	1155	1045	970	340	280	240	0.9	3.9	4	$23
9mm Luger	123/125	1110	1030	970	340	290	260	1.0	4.0	4	$24
9mm Luger	140	935	890	850	270	245	225	1.3	5.5	4	$22
9mm Luger	147	990	940	900	320	290	265	1.1	4.9	4	$11*
9mm Luger +P	115	1250	1115	1020	400	315	265	0.8	3.5	4	$23
9mm Federal	115	1280	1130	1040	420	330	280	0.7	3.3	4V	$24
38 S&W	145	685	650	620	150	135	125	2.4	10.0	4	$17
38 Short Colt	125	730	685	645	150	130	115	2.2	9.4	6	$17
38 Special	110	945	895	850	220	195	175	1.3	5.4	4V	$26
38 Special (Multi-Ball)	140	830	730	505	215	130	80	2.0	10.6	4V	$9*
38 Special	148	710	635	565	165	130	105	2.4	10.6	4V	$18
38 Special	158	755	725	690	200	185	170	2.0	8.3	4V	$18
38 Special	200	635	615	595	180	170	155	2.8	11.5	4V	NA
38 Special +P	95	1175	1045	960	290	230	195	0.9	3.9	4V	$27
38 Special +P	110	995	925	870	240	210	185	1.2	5.1	4V	$22
38 Special +P	125	945	900	860	250	225	205	1.3	5.4	4V	$22
38 Special +P	129	945	910	870	255	235	215	1.3	5.3	4V	$11*
38 Special +P	158	890	855	825	280	255	240	1.4	6.0	4V	$19
357 Magnum	110	1295	1095	975	410	290	230	0.8	3.5	4V	$24
357 Magnum (med. vel.)	125	1220	1075	985	415	315	270	0.8	3.7	4V	$23

Caliber	Bullet Wgt. Grs.	Velocity (fps) Muzzle	50 yds.	100 yds.	Energy (ft. lbs.) Muzzle	50 yds.	100 yds.	Mid-Range Traj. (in.) 50 yds.	100 yds.	Bbl. Length (in.)	Approx. Price/box
357 Magnum	125	1450	1240	1090	585	425	330	0.6	2.8	4V	$24
357 Magnum (Multi-Ball)	140	1155	830	665	420	215	135	1.2	6.4	4V	$9*
357 Magnum	140	1360	1195	1075	575	445	360	0.7	3.0	4V	$23
357 Magnum	145	1290	1155	1060	535	430	360	0.8	3.5	4V	$29
357 Magnum	158	1235	1105	1015	535	430	360	0.8	3.5	4V	$24
357 Magnum	180	1145	1055	985	525	445	390	0.9	3.9	4V	$24
357 Rem. Maximum	158	1825	1590	1380	1170	885	670	0.4	1.7	10½	$12*
357 Rem. Maximum	180	1555	1330	1155	965	705	530	0.5	2.5	10½	NA
10mm Automatic	170	1340	1165	1045	680	510	415	0.7	3.2	5	$30
10mm Automatic	175	1290	1140	1035	650	505	420	0.7	3.3	5½	$15*
10mm Automatic	200	1160	1070	1010	598	510	450	0.9	3.8	5	$28
41 Rem. Magnum	170	1420	1165	1015	760	515	390	0.7	3.2	4V	$30
41 Rem. Magnum	175	1250	1120	1030	605	490	410	0.8	3.4	4V	$15*
41 Rem. Magnum (Med. Vel.)	210	965	900	840	435	375	330	1.3	5.4	4V	$26
41 Rem. Magnum	210	1300	1160	1060	790	630	525	0.7	3.2	4V	$13*
44 S&W Special	200	1035	940	865	475	390	335	1.1	4.9	6½	$12*
44 S&W Special	246	755	725	695	310	285	265	2.0	8.3	6½	$25
44 Rem. Magnum	180	1610	1365	1175	1035	745	550	0.5	2.3	4V	$13*
44 Rem. Magnum	210	1495	1310	1165	1040	805	635	0.6	2.5	6½	$25
44 Rem. Magnum (Med. Vel.)	240	1000	945	900	535	475	435	1.1	4.8	6½	$13*
44 Rem. Magnum (Jacketed)	240	1180	1080	1010	740	625	545	0.9	3.7	4V	$13*
44 Rem. Magnum (Lead)	240	1350	1185	1070	970	750	610	0.7	3.1	4V	$32
44 Rem. Magnum	250	1180	1100	1040	775	670	600	0.8	3.6	6½V	NA
45 Automatic	185	1000	940	890	410	360	325	1.1	4.9	5	$13*
45 Automatic (Match)	185	770	705	650	245	204	175	2.0	8.7	5	$27
45 Automatic	230	830	800	675	355	325	300	1.6	6.8	5	$26
45 Automatic Shot	Shot	This data not available									NA
45 Automatic +P	185	1140	1040	970	535	445	385	0.9	4.0	5	$27
45 Win. Magnum	230	1400	1230	1105	1000	775	635	0.6	2.8	5	$12*
45 Auto. Rim	230	810	775	730	335	305	270	1.8	7.4	5½	NA
45 Colt	225	960	890	830	460	395	345	1.3	5.5	5½	$12*
45 Colt	250/255	860	820	780	410	375	340	1.6	6.6	5½	$10*

Notes: Blanks are available in 32 S&W, 38 S&W, and 38 Special. V after barrel length indicates test barrel was vented to produce ballistics similar to a revolver with a normal barrel-to-cylinder gap. Ammo prices are per 50 rounds except when marked with an * which signifies a 20-round box. Not all loads are available from all ammo manufacturers. Listed loads are those made by Remington, Winchester, Federal, and others.

RIMFIRE AMMUNITION—BALLISTICS AND PRICES

Cartridge Type	Bullet Wt. Grs.	Type	Velocity (fps) 22½" Barrel Muzzle	50 Yds.	100 Yds.	Energy (ft. lbs.) Muzzle	50 Yds.	100 Yds.	Velocity (fps) 6" Barrel Muzzle	50 Yds.	Energy (ft. lbs.) 6" Barrel Muzzle	50 Yds.	Approx. Price Per Box 50 Rds.	100 Rds.
22 CB Short (CCI & Win.)(1)	29	solid	727	667	610	34	29	24	706	—	32	—	NA	$4.50
22 CB Long (CCI only)	29	solid	727	667	610	34	29	24	706	—	32	—	NA	4.50
22 Short Match (CCI only)	29	solid	830	752	695	44	36	31	786	—	39	—	NA	5.07
22 Short Std. Vel. (Rem. only)	29	solid	1045	—	810	70	—	42	865	—	48	—	NA	2.26
22 Short H. Vel. (Fed., Rem., Win.)	29	solid	1095	—	903	77	—	53	—	—	—	—	2.26	NA
22 Short H. Vel. (CCI only)	29	solid	1132	1104	920	83	65	55	1065	—	73	—	NA	4.33
22 Short H. Vel. HP (Rem. only)	27	HP	1120	—	904	75	—	49	—	—	—	—	NA	NA
22 Short H. Vel. HP (CCI only)	27	HP	1164	1013	920	81	62	51	1077	—	69	—	NA	4.50
22 Long Std. Vel. (CCI only)	29	solid	1180	1038	946	90	69	58	1031	—	68	—	NA	4.17
22 Long H. Vel. (Fed., Rem.)	29	solid	1240	—	962	99	—	60	—	—	—	—	2.36	NA
22 LR Match (Rifle) (CCI only)	40	solid	1138	1047	975	116	97	84	1027	925	93	76	NA	8.61
22 LR Std. Vel.	40	solid	1138	1046	975	115	97	84	1027	925	93	76	2.17	4.34
22 LR H. Vel.	40	solid	1255	1110	1017	140	109	92	1060	—	100	—	2.17	4.34
22 LR H. Vel. HP	36-38	HP	1280	1126	1010	131	101	82	1089	—	95	—	2.54	5.09
22 LR-Hyper Vel. (Fed., Rem., Win.)(2)	33-34	HP	1500	1240	1075	165	110	85	—	—	—	—	2.56	NA
22 LR-Hyper Vel.	36	solid	1410	1187	1056	159	113	89	—	—	—	—	NA	NA
22 Stinger (CCI only)	32	HP	1640	1277	1132	191	115	91	1395	1060	138	80	3.46	NA
22 Win. Mag. Rimfire	40	FMC or HP	1910	1490	1326	324	197	156	1428	—	181	—	7.61	NA
22 LR Shot (CCI, Fed., Win.)	—	#11 or #12 shot	1047	—	—	—	—	—	950	—	—	—	5.71	NA
22 Win. Mag. Rimfire Shot (CCI only)	—	#11 shot	1126	—	—	—	—	—	1000	—	—	—	3.34	NA
22 Win. Mag. Rimfire	50	JHP	1650	—	1280	300	—	180	—	—	—	—	7.61	NA

Please Note: The actual ballistics obtained from your gun can vary considerably from the advertised ballistics. Also, ballistics can vary from lot to lot even with the same brand. All prices were correct at the time this chart was prepared. All prices are subject to change without notice.

(1) per 250 rounds   (2) also packaged 250 rounds per box.

SHOTSHELL LOADS AND PRICES

Winchester-Western, Remington-Peters, Federal

Dram Equivalent	Shot Ozs.	Load Style	Shot Sizes	Brands	Average Price Per Box	Nominal Velocity (fps)
10 Gauge 3½″ Magnum						
4½	2¼	Premium[1]	BB, 2, 4, 6	Fed., Win.	$31	1205
4¼	2	H.V.	BB, 2, 4, 5, 6	Fed.	$21	1210
Max.	1¾	Slug, rifled	Slug	Fed.	$7	1280
Max.	54 pellets	Buck, Premium[1]	4 (Buck)	Fed., Win.	$7	1100
Max.	18 pellets	Buck, Premium[1]	00 Buck	Fed., Win.	$7	1100
Max.	1¾	Steel shot	BB, 2	Win.	$26	1260
4¼	1⅝	Steel shot	BB, 2	Fed.	$26	1285
12 Gauge 3″ Magnum						
4	1⅞	DuPlex Premium	BBx4-2x6	Rem.	NA	1210
4	1⅞	Premium[1]	BB, 2, 4, 6	Fed., Rem., Win.	$20	1210
4	1⅝	Premium[1]	2, 4, 5, 6	Fed., Rem., Win.	$18	1280
4	1⅞	H.V.	BB, 2, 4	Fed., Rem.	$18	1210
4	1⅝	H.V.	2, 4, 6	Fed., Rem.	$17	1280
4	Variable	Buck, Premium[1]	000, 00, 1, 4	Fed., Rem., Win.	$5	1210 to 1225
3½	1¼	DuPlex Premium	BBx2-BBx4-2x6	Rem.	NA	1375
3½	1⅜	Steel shot	BB, 1, 2, 4	Fed.	$18	1245
3½	1¼	Steel shot	F, T, BBB, BB 1, 2, 4	Rem., Win.	$17	1375
4	2	Premium[1]	BB, 2, 4, 6	Fed.	$21	1175
Max.	1	Slug, rifled	Slug	Rem.	$4	1760
12 Gauge 2¾″ Hunting & Target						
3¾	1½	DuPlex Premium	BBx4-2x6	Rem.	NA	1260
3¾	1½	Premium[1], Mag.	BB, 2, 4, 5, 6	Fed., Rem., Win.	$17	1260
3¾	1½	H.V., Mag.	BB, 2, 4, 5, 6	Fed., Rem.	$15	—
3¾	1¼	H.V., Premium[1]	2, 4, 6, 7½	Fed., Rem.	$13	1330
3¾	1¼	H.V., Promo.	BB, 2, 4, 5, 6 7½, 8, 9	Fed., Rem., Win.	$10	1330
3¼	1¼	Std. vel., Premium[1]	7½, 8	Fed., Rem.	NA	1220
3¼	1⅛	Std. vel., Premium[1]	7½, 8	Fed., Rem.	NA	1255
3¼	1⅛	Std. vel.	4, 5, 6, 7½, 8, 9	Fed., Rem., Win.	$9	1255
3¼	1	Std. vel., Promo.	6, 7½, 8	Fed., Rem., Win.	$7	1290
Max.	1¼	Slug, rifled, Mag.	Slug	Fed.	$5	1490
Max.	1	Slug, rifled	Slug	Fed., Rem., Win.	$4	1560
Max.	1	Slug, rifled, hi-vel.	Slug	Rem.	NA	1680
4	Variable	Buck, Mag., Premium[1]	00, 1, 4 (Buck)	Fed., Rem., Win.	$4	1075 to 1290
3¾	Variable	Buck, Premium[1]	000, 00, 0, 1, 4 (Buck)	Fed., Rem., Win.	$8	1250 to 1325
3¾	1⅜	H.V.	2, 4, 6	Fed.	NA	1295
3¼	1¼	Pigeon	6, 7½, 8	Fed., Win.	NA	1220
3	1⅛	Trap & Skeet	7½, 8, 9	Fed., Rem., Win.	NA	1200
2¾	1⅛	Trap & Skeet	7½, 8, 8½, 9	Fed., Rem., Win.	NA	1145
2¾	1	Trap & Skeet	7½, 8, 8½	Fed., Rem., Win.	NA	1180
3¾	1¼	Steel shot	BB, 1, 2, 4, 6	Fed., Win.	$17	1275
3¾	1⅛	Steel shot	1, 2, 4, 6	Fed., Rem., Win.	$15	1365
3¾	1⅛	DuPlex Premium	BBx2-BBx4, 2x6	Rem.	NA	1365
16 Gauge 2¾″						
3¼	1¼	H.V., Mag., Premium[1]	2, 4, 6	Fed., Win.	$16	1260
3¼	1⅛	H.V., Promo.	4, 5, 6, 7½, 9	Fed., Rem., Win.	$10	1295
2¾	1⅛	Std. vel.	4, 6, 7½, 8, 9	Fed., Rem., Win.	$9	1185
2½	1	Std. vel., Promo.	5, 7½, 8	Fed., Win.	$7	1165
Max.	⅘	Slug, rifled	Slug	Fed., Rem., Win.	$4	1570
Max.	12 pellets	Buck	1 (Buck)	Fed., Rem., Win.	$4	1225
20 Gauge 3″ Magnum						
3	1¼	Premium[1]	2, 4, 6	Fed., Rem., Win.	$15	1185
3	1¼	H.V.	2, 4, 6, 7½	Fed., Rem.	$14	1185
Max.	18 pellets	Buck	2 (Buck)	Fed.	$4	1200
Max.	1	Steel shot	2, 4, 6	Fed., Rem., Win.	$15	1330
20 Gauge 2¾″ Hunting & Target						
2¾	1⅛	Premium[1], Mag.	4, 6, 7½	Fed., Rem., Win.	$13	1175
2¾	1⅛	H.V., Mag.	4, 6, 7½	Fed., Rem.	$13	1175
2¾	1	H.V., Premium[1]	4, 6	Fed., Rem.	$12	1220
2¾	1	H.V., Promo.	4, 5, 6, 7½, 8, 9	Fed., Rem., Win.	$10	1220
2½	1	Std. vel., Premium[1]	7½, 8	Fed., Rem.	NA	1165
2½	1	Std. vel.	4, 5, 6, 7½, 8, 9	Fed., Rem., Win.	$9	1165
2¼	⅞	Promo.	6, 7½, 8	Fed., Rem., Win.	$7	1210
Max.	¾	Slug, rifled	Slug	Fed., Rem., Win.	$4	1570
Max.	20 pellets	Buck	3 (Buck)	Fed., Rem., Win.	$4	1200
2½	⅞	Skeet	8, 9	Fed., Rem., Win.	NA	1200
2¾	¾	Steel shot	4, 6	Fed., Win.	$14	1425
28 Gauge 2¾″ Hunting & Target						
2¼	¾	H.V., Premium[1]	6, 7½	Fed., Rem., Win.	$12	1295
2	¾	Skeet	9	Fed., Rem., Win.	NA	1200
410 Bore Hunting & Target						
Max.	11/16	3″ H.V.	4, 5, 6, 7½, 8	Fed., Rem., Win.	$10	1135
Max.	½	2½″ H.V.	4, 6, 7½	Fed., Rem., Win.	$9	1135
Max.	½	2½″ target	9	Fed., Rem., Win.	NA	1200
Max.	⅕	Slug, rifled	Slug	Fed., Rem., Win.	$3	1815

[1] Premium shells usually incorporate high antimony extra hard shot and a granulated polyethylene buffer to increase pattern density at long ranges. In general, prices are per 25-round box. Rifled slugs and buckshot prices are per 5-round pack. Premium buckshot prices per 10-round pack. Not every brand is available in every shot size. Price of Skeet and trap loads may vary widely.

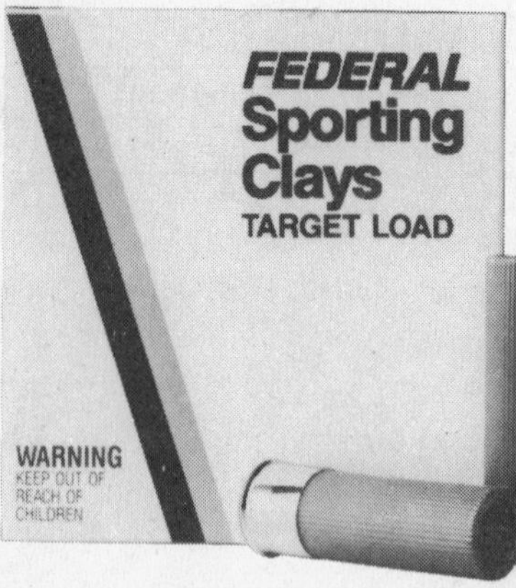

Federal 12- and 20-gauge Sporting Clays loads.

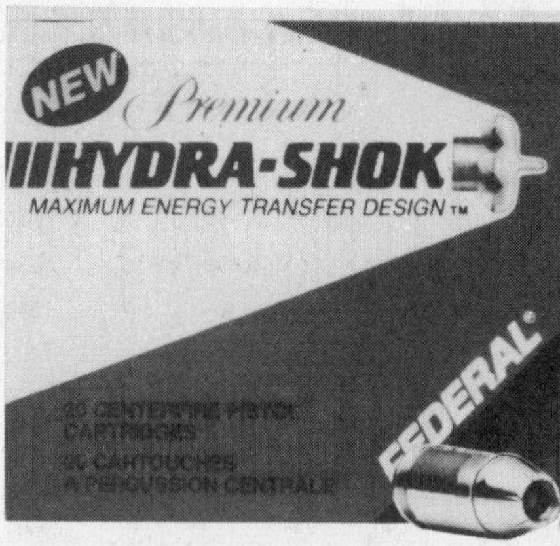

Federal 380 ACP with 90-grain Hydra-Shok bullet.

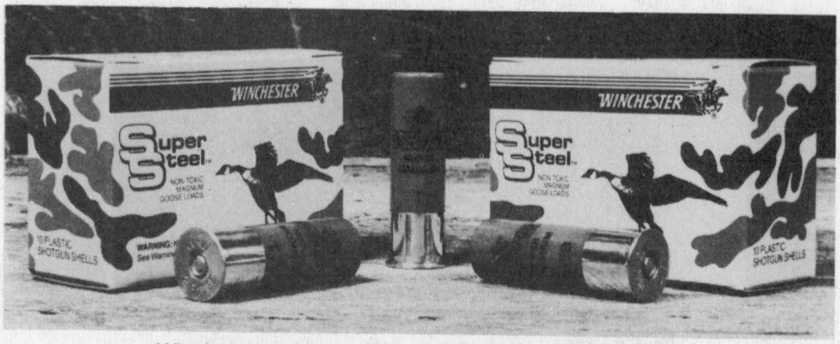

Winchester 12-gauge goose loads, T and BBB steel shot.

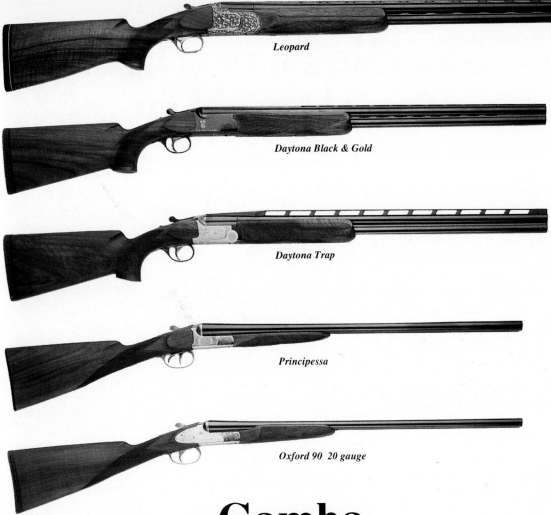

Leopard

Daytona Black & Gold

Daytona Trap

Principessa

Oxford 90 20 gauge

Gamba.
A generation of excellence.

As a preeminent shooter and sportsman, your position in society and your success in life demonstrates your pursuit of excellence in all things, a quality you share with Renato Gamba, president of Societa Armi Bresciane, Renato Gamba Firearms.

For the past 30 years, the firm of Renato Gamba has been committed to the principle of excellence in the design and manufacture of elite class shotguns.

Gamba shotguns are not for everyone. In the tradition of vintage firearms, many Gambas are custom-fitted to individual shooters. Using the highest quality materials and advanced manufacturing processes, expert gunmakers create a firearm that blends old world precision craftsmanship with modern metallurgy. Master engravers transform these classic shotguns into works of art.

For the competitive shooter, Gamba offers a full range of deluxe options with the Daytona Over & Under Trap model.

Modern sidelock and boxlock side-by-side shotguns from Renato Gamba have the same classic look as other guns in their class but with the addition of many premium features.

For competition, hunting, and shotgun sports, invest in excellence. Gamba elite class shotguns. Exclusively from Heckler & Koch, Inc. USA. For your nearest dealer call (703) 450-1900.

Hoppe's makes the perfect case for safe travel, storage and proper maintenance.

INTRODUCING HOPPE'S "SECURITY PAC" SERIES.
A GUN CASE WITH A PROBLEM-PROOF SYSTEM.

It's a "how to" system designed especially for the traveling sportsman, and only Hoppe's offers it.

At no extra cost, the owner gets the "Security Pac" which contains the following:

• A Hoppe's "Guide to Gun Care"—a booklet every shooter should have and read.

• A special "Maintenance Checklist"— important tips for storage, and a handy chart for logging in periodic inspections.

• A Hoppe's treated silicone cloth— indispensible for proper maintenance.

"Security Pac" is designed to give the shooter confidence that his gun is well-secured in a lockable case. And security in the knowledge that his gun is well maintained.

WHATEVER YOUR SHOOTING NEEDS, HOPPE'S HAS A "SECURITY PAC" PROTECTO CASE FOR YOU.

The "Security Pac" series represents the most popular gun cases in the Hoppe's line. We offer 14 combinations of colors and sizes. For example, you can get just about any conceivable combination of case for rifles, handguns and shotguns—and you can choose between Deluxe Black and Hunter Brown.

HOPPE'S PROTECTO CASES. BUILT TO BE SUPER TOUGH.

We've taken the latest high-strength materials and combined them with a THERMO PRESSURE process for added strength and stiffer corners.

The color won't chip, crack or peel because it's fused into the body material. The case is lined with polyurethane egg-crate foam—the best protection available. The handles are crackproof, and the case closes with a satisfying snug fit—because of a tight-fitting tongue and groove valance.

We're talking one tough case.

HOPPE'S MAKES A TIGHT CASE FOR SECURITY.

We designed Hoppe's Protecto cases—and the "Security Pac" program with the traveling sportsmen in mind.

These tough cases have proven themselves all over the world in the most demanding conditions.

They are fully lockable, and they meet all state and airline requirements for safety and security.

And armed with "Security Pac," the shooter gets everything he needs to know for traveling, storing and caring for his valuable firearms.

HOPPE'S 9

THE GUN CARE PEOPLE.

A Division of Penguin Industries Inc.
Airport Industrial Mall—Coatesville, PA 19320

SHOOTER'S MARKETPLACE

NEW ELECTROCHEMICAL BORE CLEANER

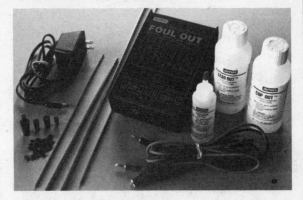

Outers® Foul Out™ electrochemical bore cleaner is a revolutionary new cleaning system that removes lead and copper fouling from rifle, pistol and shotgun bores. Lead deposits require tedious brushing. Copper wash is just as detrimental since it affects accuracy and promotes rust and pitting.

The Foul Out™ patented process removes metallic fouling in a manner similar to electroplating. Copper and lead are electronically stripped from the bore using specially formulated chemicals plus other accessories. As fouling builds up on the bore rod, lights on the electronic control unit will indicate which stage the cleaning process has reached, eventually reaching "zero."

Write for more info.

BLOUNT, INC., SPORTING EQUIP. DIV./OUTERS® PRODUCTS

SIGHT-IN TARGETS

Easy-to-use, "Precision Squares"™ targets from Birchwood Casey offers hunters, bench rest and varmint shooters a superior and highly visible, non-glare paper target for accurate sighting-in, load evaluation or target practice.

A fluorescent red and diamond center allows exact dead-center reticle or dot placement while the black corner squares function as side bars to eliminate crosshair canting.

Your choice of three different sizes for use with scopes of all magnifications, small or large bore rifles and hand-guns.

Suggested retail price of $4.50 per package.

See your dealer or write for a free catalog on these and other Birchwood Casey products.

BIRCHWOOD CASEY

NEW RIFLE BULLET SEATING DIE

Ponsness/Warren's new CAL-DIE eases and speeds bullet seating. Assembly complete with housing, large and small bullet seating pins, and 308 bullet retaining sleeve. Eliminates pinched fingers and the fatigue of seating bullets. Speeds process by 25%. Standard ⅞x14 die set.

Only one housing required for all calibers—merely change bullet retaining sleeves for different bullet diameters.

Price: $24.95; additional bullet retaining sleeves $6.95 ea.

Calibers available include: 22, 243, 244, 6mm, all 25s, 6.5mm, 270, 280, 284, 7mm, all 30s (30-30, 30-06, 308, etc.), 32 Spl., 8mm, 338 and all 35s.

Write for more info.

PONSNESS/WARREN

See manufacturer's addresses on page 246.

SHOOTER'S MARKETPLACE

HIGH-RIDE AUTO HOLSTER

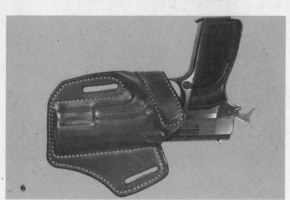

According to the folks at Milt Sparks Leather, the response to their 60TK Roadrunner High-Ride concealment rig has been tremendous! Metal reinforcement stabilizes the top of the Roadrunner and the detailed hand molding provides a perfect fit and reduces bulk. Comfortable, all-day carrying is a prime feature.

Dual belt slots allow you to position the holster over belt loops and pull the pistol close to your body for better concealment.

The 60TK also has a full-length front sight track. Available for the Colt Govt., Commander, Officers Model ACP, Browning Hi-Power, S&W 645 and Beretta 92F.

Send $2.00 for a brochure of Milt Sparks Leather's complete line of products.

MILT SPARKS LEATHER

CHALLENGING PRACTICE GAME

The Hunter's Game #2010 is a challenging, educational, and fast paced target shooting game for one or two shooters, and can be used with rifles, handguns and airguns.

The game consists of two sets of five different targets featuring a deer in wilderness scenes. A scoring grid is on the buck, showing the proper "hit" zones. Maximum points are awarded for center hits, and lesser points for off-center shots.

The kit includes all targets, practice grids, scorecards, target holders and sells for $6.95.

The Hunter's Game improves shooting skills while teaching the proper hunting shots. Ideal for a preseason tune-up, or a challenging target for year-round shooting fun!

MARKSMAN PRODUCTS

NEW LASER SIGHT

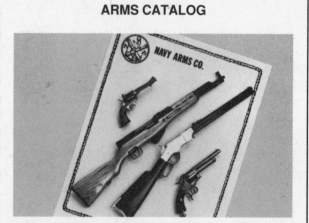

B-Square's new BSL-1 Laser Sight is compact (2¾" long, ¾" dia.), and weighs in at about 2 oz. Complete line of mounts available. Features internal adjustments, so it's interchangeable from gun to gun. It is one of the first laser sights to use a third generation laser diode—the most powerful laser diode available.

The BSL-1 is a self-contained, moisture proof system with built-in shock absorbers and a long-life battery that's easily charged while the sight's mounted. Features direct-beam steering and internal locking adjustments not found on other laser sights.

The BSL-1 Laser Sight mounts over/under the barrel, to any mounted scope or to any standard dovetail mount. Write for more info.

B-SQUARE COMPANY

ARMS CATALOG

The new 36-page Navy Arms Company catalog has something to offer every collector, shooter and re-enactor. Over 230 years of firearms, from the Brown Bess of the American Revolutionary War to the modern European styled shotguns of today.

Long established as a source of high quality muzzleloading firearms and accessories, Navy Arms now offers many surplus guns, modern shotguns, handguns, ammo and accessories. Over 220 guns, kits, and cannons are available. The selection of ammo ranges from new commercial boxer primed, special pistol ammo, blanks, military surplus FMJ, soft point hunting cartridges and new manufactured military ball FMJ to round balls and bullets for muzzleloading guns. Send $2.00 for a full color catalog.

NAVY ARMS COMPANY

See manufacturer's addresses on page 246.

SHOOTER'S MARKETPLACE

NEW GRUNT DEER CALL

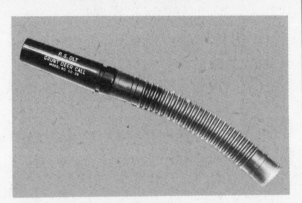

The P.S. Olt Company, Pekin, Illinois, is now manufacturing a new grunt deer call. The new deer call produces the grunting sounds made by rutting bucks tending does in the estrus. These sounds cause jealousy in other bucks in the area, and bring them in to fight. The new model will be called the GD-26 Grunt Deer Call. The GD-26 is molded in moistureproof and durable ABS Cycolac, and uses a long-lasting Mylar reed for years of troublefree performance. It is furnished with a grunt tube, but can be blown without the tube for variations in sound. Easy to blow with good volume. The Olt GD-26 Grunt Deer Call will be furnished in hangup packaging. The 1990 List Price: $13.95.

Write for more information.

P.S. OLT COMPANY

NEW SCOPE MOUNTS

Weaver® Pro-View™ and See-Thru scope mounts are newly designed and will fit most popular rifles.

Each style has symmetrical steel caps and four hardened screws for extra strength and holding power on big-caliber rifles. A reversible feature lets mounts be turned around for adaptation to the newer, more compact scopes. Both styles attach directly to rifle receivers.

Pro-View™ mounts have a low profile that help keep a shooter's cheek on the stock for quicker sight alignment and better accuracy. See-Thru mounts allow the hunter to switch between scope and iron sights instantly.

Write the manufacturer direct for more information on these new mounts.

BLOUNT, INC., SPORTING EQUIP. DIV./WEAVER® PRODUCTS

RIFLED SHOTGUN BARRELS

The Hastings Paradox Rifled Slug Barrel, for the shotgun hunter who insists on the accuracy only a rifled bore can provide, is the only off-the-shelf rifled shotgun barrel designed to be an exact replacement on popular makes of shotguns.

Each barrel is produced with a high finish, exacting tolerances and precise contours, and is available in 20" or 24" lengths with either rifle sights or special scope mounts installed.

Hastings Paradox slug barrels are available at fine gunshops, or directly from Hastings. Hastings also manufactures the Choke-Tube II system, integral choke barrels and specialized trap and Skeet barrels, and offers a full range of smithing services. Write or call for more info.

HASTINGS BARRELS

GUNSMITH SUPPLIES CATALOG

Since 1939, Brownells has been furnishing tools, supplies, fixtures and chemicals to professional gunsmiths and serious hobbyists world-wide. Their 200 page Catalog features the finest gunsmithing equipment available for rebuilding, re-pairing, accurizing, engraving, checkering, bluing or building a complete gun. All shipments made from in-stock inventories. Professional gunsmiths available for technical support. As Bob Brownell says, "Our products, service, quality and reliability are guaranteed to satisfy you, our customer, 100%—period!"

The catalog is free to qualified, full or part time gunsmiths and dealers; $3.75 to others—refunded on first $35.00 order. Brownell's accepts MC/Visa, COD or check.

BROWNELLS, INC.

See manufacturer's addresses on page 246.

SHOOTER'S MARKETPLACE

NEW SCOPE MOUNTS

Imperial Bench Rest Kwik-Mounts are another great innovation from Kwik-Site Co.

They are ideal for the hunter that is looking for strong, rigid low mounts for use in open country.

This rugged, lightweight aluminum mount features an integral one-piece base and ring. Installation time is cut in half compared to most popular makes. It uses existing factory holes in the gun's receiver, comes with precision machined allen head screws and wrench. With its bright finish and good looks it complements the finest scopes and rifles.

Kwik-Site Imperial Bench Rest Mounts are available for all popular rifles.

Write for more info.

KWIK-SITE CO.

RIFLE PRIMER ADAPTER

Accra-Shot eliminates hangfires and misfires! Accra-Shot replaces percussion nipples on muzzleloaders and allows the use of regular Small Rifle primers instead of percussion caps. The hotter spark of rifle primers allows more flame to reach the powder. The result is sure-fire ignition and increased velocity!

Hunters get only one shot with a muzzleloader. You can make it count with Accra-Shot. Available in all popular thread sizes, Accra-Shot is available at your dealer or direct from Anderson Manufacturing for $17.95 postpaid. If ordering direct please specify make and model of your gun.

VISA/MC orders are accepted by Anderson Manufacturing. Write for more info.

ANDERSON MANUFACTURING CO.

SHOOTERS NEWSPAPER

Established in 1946 THE SHOTGUN NEWS is a leader in its field.

It offers some of the finest gun buys in the United States. More than 180,000 persons read, enjoy and profit from its columns 3 times each month.

THE SHOTGUN NEWS has aided thousands of gun enthusiasts locate firearms, both modern and antique—rifles, pistols, shotguns, scopes, etc...all at money saving prices.

The money you save on the purchase of any of the more than 10,000 listings appearing 3 times a month could more than pay for the $18.00 (36 issue) annual subscription cost.

As it says on the cover, it's "the trading post for anything that shoots."

THE SHOTGUN NEWS

TOTAL FIREARMS CARE PRODUCT

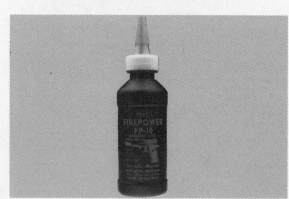

This year MPC is emphasizing their "Firepower FP-10" for blackpowder cleaning/lubrication.

It has been proven to be one of the leading products for the care and feeding of the primitive or modern-day muzzleloader. It's a patch lube that removes fouling every time the "frontstuffer" is loaded. It protects, removes lead and fouling, dramatically improves lubrication, restores stock finishes, improves accuracy, and removes light rust from bluing.

Won't harm blued or browned finishes. Used as a final bore cleaner, FP-10 eliminates traditional messy clean-up and the need to "bathe" the smokepole in soapy water!

Suggested retail price is $5.99 per 4oz. bottle.

MUSCLE PRODUCTS CORPORATION

See manufacturer's addresses on page 246.

FORSTER/BONANZA CATALOG

This catalog features a wide range of reloading, gunsmithing and muzzleloading tools. It is one of the most useful catalogs in the shooting sports business because of the unique problem solving tools available.

Some of the most popular tools are the Bench Rest® rifle reloading dies, gunsmith screwdriver kits, the Universal Sight Mounting Fixture®, chamber headspace gauges, powder measures and scales, the Co-Ax® reloading press and Forster case trimming tools.

Forster products have earned an enviable reputation and are acknowledged to be superior in many aspects of design and workmanship.

Write today and mention *Shooter's Marketplace* for your free catalog.

FORSTER PRODUCTS

ELECTRONIC SCALE

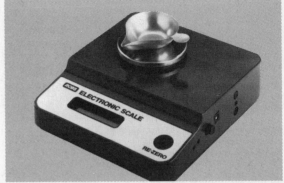

The RCBS Electronic Scale brings solid state electronic accuracy and convenience to handloaders at a reasonable price.

The LCD digital readings are ideal for weighing bullets and cases and provide the ultimate convenience for checking powder charges.

The scale gives readings in grains; and the range of 0-500 grains is ample for most handloading applications. Can be used at home or at the shooting range.

Comes with an AC adaptor, or operates on 8 AA batteries (not included).

The RCBS Electronic Scale has a two-year warranty against defects in workmanship or materials and carries a suggested retail price of $375.00.

BLOUNT, INC., SPORTING EQUIP. DIV./RCBS PRODUCTS

SAFETY SLUG AMMUNITION

Available in calibers from 25 ACP to 30-06, the Glaser Safety Slug represents the state-of-the-art in high performance ammunition and has been the choice of police professionals since its introduction. The unique pre-fragmented bullet is loaded to hypervelocities, giving far greater impact energy and barrier penetration than high performance hollow-points. The design of the Glaser delivers unequalled stopping power and provides maximum overpenetration safety by virtue of the projectile's fragmentation into over 300 pieces upon impact.

According to the manufacturer, the tested ricochet danger of the Glaser line of Safety Slugs is the lowest of any ammunition.

Write for free brochure!

GLASER SAFETY SLUG, INC.

UNIMAT PC

The UNIMAT PC from Blue Ridge Machinery & Tools, Inc. is shown here with optional accessories.

The new UNIMAT PC allows the gunsmith to design (CAD) on an IBM or compatible PC (640 Kb RAM minimum) and see the design become a finished part at the touch of a button (CAM).

The UNIMAT PC is unique even as a manually driven lathe.

The advantages are numerous. The UNIMAT PC exhibits maximum precision in machining, convenient operation, versatility, and up-to-date technology.

Call a member of Blue Ridge's sales staff and mention GUN DIGEST to receive a free color brochure on this incredible machine, the UNIMAT PC.

BLUE RIDGE MACHINERY AND TOOLS, INC.

See manufacturer's addresses on page 246.

Shooter's Marketplace

DOUBLE ACTION DERRINGERS

High Standard Double Action derringers are now being made by the American Derringer Corp. The DA 38 is available in two calibers, 38 Special and 9mm Luger. The DA 38's barrel, receiver, and internal parts are made from high strength stainless steel; the grip frame is made out of aluminum. Weight is 14.5 oz., the overall Length is 4.85" with a barrel length of 3". The finish is satin and the grips are rosewood. The suggested retail price is $235.00.

The DA 22 is available in two calibers, 22 LR and 22 Magnum and weighs in at 11oz. The overall length is 5" with a 3" barrel length. The finish is blue with black plastic grips. (Rosewood grips are available for $10 extra). Suggested retail price is $139.95. Write or call for more information.

AMERICAN DERRINGER CORP.

LINSEED RUBBING OIL

OLD WORLD Oil Products has been offering best-quality linseed oil for over a decade. Long recognized as *the* professional gun stock finish, linseed oil brings out the full character and quality of a walnut gun stock.

This superior linseed oil is available in red or amber shades. Serves perfectly for the expert refinishing of old gun lumber or the complete and total enhancement of a brand new gun stock.

This particular product is also ideal when it comes to the maintenance of original, oil-finished stocks.

Each bottle of this excellent linseed oil comes complete with instructions. Simply send $6.00 for your postpaid 4 oz. bottle of red or amber OLD WORLD Linseed Oil. No catalogs.

OLD WORLD OIL PRODUCTS

NEW COMPACT CHRONOGRAPH

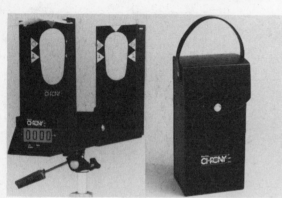

The Chrony is a new approach in Chronographs; you might say it's the "Volkswagen" of the Chronographs. Suggested Retail Price: $99.95 U.S., but some mail order houses sell for less. It folds up into a 7.5" x 2.5" x 4" (19cm x 7cm x 10cm) package, that weighs less than 2.5 lbs. (1.14kg) and fits into a custom carrying case that sells for $18.95. Any camera tripod and two minutes is all it takes to set up, ready to shoot. Measures velocities from as low as 70 fps (21 m/s) to 9,999 fps (9,999 m/s) with an accuracy of better than 99.5%. Ideal for measuring velocities of bullets, arrows, shot, pellets, paintballs. A ½" high LCD display lets you read from a distance; muzzle blast on high powered rifles requires the Chrony to be set up 10-15 ft. (4-5 m) down range.

SHOOTING CHRONY, INC.

PATENTED RIFLE SLING

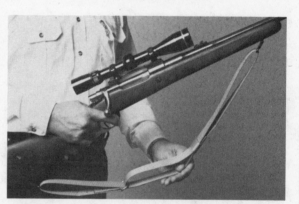

The unique, patented design of The Super-Sling® rifle sling permits rapid one-hand adjustment to any desired position. No snaps, buckles, etc., to manipulate when opening or closing The Super-Sling. The infinite one-hand adjustment provides the shooter with a "quick sling" for any shooting position. It greatly improves steady holding of a rifle. The sling is fully assembled with or without detachable swivels.

The Super-Sling is manufactured from superior quality Mil-Spec. type webbing available in 1" or 1¼". A choice of colors/patterns is available: Brown, Tan, Black, Gray, OD Green, Day-Glo Orange, Woodland Camo, Trebark Camo, Realtree Camo, or Arctic White.

THE OUTDOOR CONNECTION, INC.

See manufacturer's addresses on page 246.

SHOOTER'S MARKETPLACE

NEW WALTHER P-38 ADJUSTABLE SIGHT

MMC's new option sight package for the P-38 is *the* long-awaited accessory shooters have always wanted. Importation in quantity, and the current interest in 9mm pistols, has reaffirmed the value of this fine pistol—at the shooting range or as a practical sidearm.

Use MMC's #15000 P-38 rear sight with the original front sight; or, order sight combo #15500 (New .125" wide front and new rear sight) for a better "modern" sight picture. The front and rear sight Combo is shown above.

Easy installation, no machining, no alteration of the pistol.

Change back to original sights at any time. Free catalog!

MINIATURE MACHINE COMPANY

NEW HANDGUN AMMUNITION

CCI—a pioneer in alternative case technology—recently announced the introduction of four new Blazer® centerfire ammo products. The new loads are a 9mm, 147 grain Totally Metal Jacketed™ bullet at 1000 fps, a 45 Colt loaded with the Speer® 45 caliber, 200 grain JHP bullet at 1000 fps, and two new 10mm Auto loadings that round out CCI's Blazer lineup.

The 10mm loads are a 200 grain Totally Metal Jacketed bullet at 1050 fps, and a new 180 grain PHP (plated hollow point) which eliminates the problem of core-jacket separations. Nominal velocity is 1150 fps.

The new Blazer loads certainly increase the flexibility of these three fine calibers.

Write for more information.

BLOUNT, INC., SPORTING EQUIP. DIV./CCI PRODUCTS

PELLET FIRING CONVERSIONS

Loch Leven Industries' Convert-a-Pell kit enables the shooter to convert his favorite handgun to shoot inexpensive pellets. Available for any caliber from 380 through 45LC, each Convert-a-Pell kit contains a barrel adapter tube (to convert one's firearm bore to 177 caliber) and six brass "cartridges". No special tools, no disassembly, and no reloading expertise required.

Will not harm bore, action, or component parts of any handgun. A 22 Centerfire rifle version of the Convert-a-Pell kit and complete line of accessories is also available.

You can practice year round, indoors or out, when shooting with Convert-a-Pell. Suggested retail price: Handgun Kit $39.95. Write for more info.

LOCH LEVEN INDUSTRIES

CHECKERING TOOLS

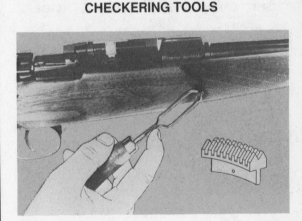

FULL-VIEW checkering tools have been on the market since 1949. The tool features a split shank (which allows the gunsmith to fully view his work at all times), and an adjustable head which lets him checker at any desired angle. FULL-VIEW cutters are made of the highest quality tool steel and come in sizes 16, 18, 20, 22, 24, 26, and 32 lines per inch. The teeth are self-cleaning and cut equally well backwards and forwards. FULL-VIEW checkering tools include holders; spacing, single line, superfine, skipline, and border cutters; and short corner tools. A special checkering kit sells for $22.00 (plus $3.00 for shipping). Send for a free descriptive folder that comes complete with prices and hints for better checkering.

W.E. BROWNELL CHECKERING TOOLS

See manufacturer's addresses on page 246.

SHOOTER'S MARKETPLACE

HANDY POWDER MEASURE

The Quinetics Powder Measure offers handloaders a number of advantages. Most importantly, it incorporates a patented feature which enables the user to achieve a superior degree of charge-throw accuracy.

This fact can be appreciated immediately by anyone using the Quinetics Powder Measure in strict adherence to their operational and maintenance procedures.

The spring-action charge bar is design-engineered so that powder grains are not caught between surfaces in opposition to one another. Thus, shearing is prevented!

It's a real space saver, requiring only a 14" x 18" table area for entire operation.

A free brochure is available upon request!

QUINETICS CORPORATION

SHOOTING ACCESSORY PLANS

Make your own portable benchrest, and stool to go with it, from a half sheet of plywood and metal hardware. Easy to carry, sturdy, stable and compact—fits into any car. Easy to make, plywood top and stool, pipe legs, assembles/disassembles in seconds. Now you can have your own benchrest—anytime, anywhere.

This unique portable benchrest accommodates right or left-handed shooters. Plans complete with measurements, materials list, and step-by-step instructions with photos. Portable benchrest and stool; shooting sticks and stools; or, pedestal rest and front and rear shooting bags—each set of plans, $5.00. Loading bench plans—$10.00. Add $2.00 per set for shipping and handling.

RICK JAMISON'S PLANS

SHOTGUN BARREL PORTING SERVICE

The patented Pro-Port process is a result of more than 25 years of research by Larry Kelly of Mag-na-port Fame.

Pro-Porting is accomplished with Electrical Discharge Machining, a surgically precise method of removing metal. The ports will dissipate shock and, because of their design and their barrel placement, redirect muzzle energy to dramatically reduce muzzle lift.

For slug shooting, waterfowling, trap, Skeet and law enforcement, the patented Pro-Port goes a long way toward reducing perceived recoil and muzzle lift.

If you would like to have more information and prices on the Pro-Porting service, write for a free brochure.

PRO-PORT LTD.

45 AUTO RIG

The Deputy Marshall is a lawman rig cut from rich natural saddle leather and lined with silicone suede. The belt is ranger style in the standard 2¼" width. The holster rides medium-high for comfort when driving. A double magazine pouch complements this rig which is available in black or russet.

The holster, which is made to fit 45 Colt automatics, is available with or without hammer strap and is 100% American made by Kirkpatrick which has been serving the police, military and sportsmen for over a quarter-century.

Specify waist size, color, gun model, barrel length, right or left hand, with or without hammer strap. Write or call manufacturer for current retail price.

Send $3.00 for a catalog. Dealer inquiries invited.

KIRKPATRICK/AMERICAN SALES & MFG. CO.

See manufacturer's addresses on page 246.

SHOOTER'S MARKETPLACE

HI-CAPACITY MINI-30 MAG.

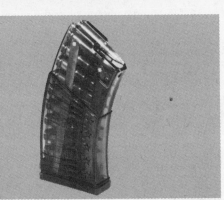

Eagle is now offering its new 18-round high-capacity magazine for the Ruger MINI-30. Made of strong, transparent polymer (safety of quick shell count at a glance), the BETA-MAG 3015 is ruggedly built to provide reliable functioning under hard use and adverse conditions. It incorporates Eagle's patented "no-jam" spring design. It also facilitates loading, making the last round as easy to load as the first. Other features include an easily removable base-pad that facilitates cleaning of the magazine and a lifetime guarantee.

Suggested retail price: $18.95.

Eagle International's catalog which normally sells for $1.00 is available free to *Shooter's Marketplace* readers.

EAGLE INTERNATIONAL, INC.

NEW BULLETS FROM 22 - 458 CAL.

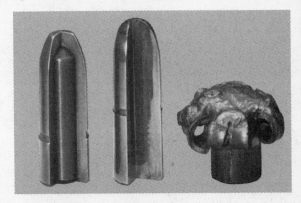

Since the late '40s Speer bullets have been earning their place on reloading benches of the shooting fraternity time and time again.

Over the years, Speer has increased their bullet lineup dramatically. This year is no exception.

Speer has just introduced 28 new bullets that are sure to please the reloader. From the new 22 "TNT" varmint bullet to the new 458 "African Grand Slam" solid with its tungsten carbide core for the world's most dangerous game.

Shown above in cut-away is the new 458-300 gr. African Grand Slam solid, soft point and expanded soft point.

Write the manufacturer direct for more information on the new bullets.

BLOUNT, INC., SPORTING EQUIP. DIV./SPEER PRODUCTS

GUN PARTS CATALOG

THE GUN PARTS CORPORATION, World's Largest Supplier of Gun Parts, (formerly Numrich Arms Corp.) is offering a brand new, updated (500+ Pages) 15th Edition catalog.

You'll find complete listing and pricing of the more than 300 million gun parts they currently have in stock.

This is a standard reference for gunsmiths, shooters, collectors and military organizations worldwide.

It consists of machine guns, military, U.S., foreign, commercial and antique gun parts—all of which they stock. This catalog contains hundreds of schematic drawings. To order, simply send $5.95. (Foreign surface mail orders: $10.95—Write for Airmail quote.)

THE GUN PARTS CORPORATION

SHOOTER'S PUNCH SET

Lyman has just introduced a nifty shooters' Punch Set. Although intended primarily for use by shooters, gunsmiths will appreciate the quality and convenience of a readily portable set of basic punches. The American-made set includes a center punch, $\frac{1}{8}$" brass drift punch, and five hardened steel punches; $\frac{1}{16}$", $\frac{3}{32}$", $\frac{1}{8}$", $\frac{5}{32}$", and $\frac{3}{16}$". It's invaluable when working on sights, trigger assemblies, ejectors, cocking pieces, safeties, firing pin assemblies, etc.

Comes in a redwood storage case. It's also offered in a combo-pack with the Lyman Brass Tapper gunsmith's hammer which features interchangeable nylon, brass and steel heads. Suggested Retail Price, $19.95; With Brass Tapper, $37.95. Send for a free Lyman mini-catalog!

LYMAN PRODUCTS CORPORATION

See manufacturer's addresses on page 246.

Shooter's Marketplace

DAMASCUS CUTLERY STEEL

Damascus Cutlery Steel is the steel of choice from the masters in antiquity right through today. Great stress resistance, superior cutting capability and stunning beauty are the basic qualities responsible for Damascus' reputation in legend and historical fact.

Having received the "American Design," "American Made," and "Knives Of The Year" awards at the world's largest knife show, they are beautiful, but more importantly, they're functional.

Featuring Forged-to-Shape Damascus Steel (not the much simpler and less costly "stock-removal" method), these knives are 100% hand-made, from anvil forging through final finishing. Send $3.00 for brochure.

DAMASCUS-U.S.A.

NEW COMPETITION HOLSTER

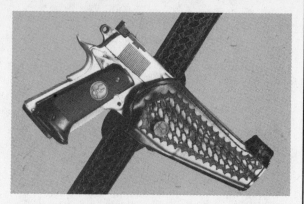

Team Safariland enjoyed an excellent 1989 IPSC Championship season. That season was highlighted by the fact that their 008 Final Option holster was selected for competitive IPSC use by world-class shooters Rob Leatham and John Pride.

Safariland's 008 Final Option Holster features a patented trigger guard lock system that grips the trigger guard and prevents the handgun from rocking forward.

When the 008 Final Option is used in conjunction with Safariland's Gunfighter belt, the shooter can easily adjust the mounting angle of the holster to suit his own requirements.

A full-color 64-page catalog is available from Safariland for $1.00.

SAFARILAND LTD., INC.

QUALITY CAST BULLETS

The people at Lane Bullets put a great deal of work and quality into their consistently high-quality line of handgun bullets, batch after batch. Lane Bullets were used by the 1989 Camp Perry winner (Sharpshooter Class). Additionally, the Missouri State PPC Championship was won by shooters using Lane Bullets in 1985, '86, '87 and '88. Write for a free brochure. Here's their lineup:
- 380—95 RN
- 9mm—115 SWC, 125 RN & 147 FP
- 38—148 DEWC, 150 SWC, 158 SWC & 158 RN
- 41—210 SWC
- 44—240 SWC
- 45—185 SWC, 200 SWC, 230 RN & 255 SWC
  (for Long Colt)

LANE BULLETS, INC.

TRITIUM NIGHT SIGHTS

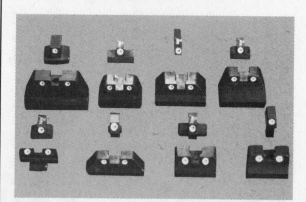

Trijicon self-luminous iron sight blades are the strongest and brightest night sights available for handguns. These 3-dot sight systems are proven faster and much more accurate than instinctive shooting in low light. When the gun cannot be seen or the sights are silhouetted against the target, the 3-dots are quickly aligned with the target. Polished sapphire windows give bright, crisp round edges to the glowing green dots.

Inlaid white rings around each sapphire window make the sights stand out like standard white dots in daytime.

No exposure to daylight or any artificial light needed.

See your dealer/distributor. Write for more info.

TRIJICON, INC.

See manufacturer's addresses on page 246.

SHOOTER'S MARKETPLACE

REAMERS & GAUGES

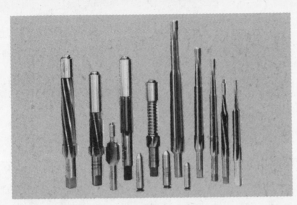

As a leader in the field of chambering reamers and headspace gauges for the gunsmith and serious shooter, Clymer Manufacturing Co., Inc., continues to expand its line of tooling available from stock. Reamers and gauges are offered in all popular rifle, pistol, and shotgun calibers. Many other tools are also available to alter factory-standard firearms to meet an individual shooter's requirements.

Clymer Manufacturing will help the wildcatter in designing a new cartridge and will gladly provide technical assistance in design and manufacture of specialized tooling not normally carried in stock. A 40-page catalog is available for $4.00 (refunded on first $30.00 order).

Call Clymer direct.

CLYMER MANUFACTURING CO., INC.

RELOADING PRESS CONVERSION UNIT

The RCBS Piggyback Conversion Unit allows handloaders to utilize their single stage presses for fully automatic, progressive reloading. The Piggyback Unit can be quickly and easily mounted onto a Rock Chucker, Reloader Special-3 or Reloader Special-5 press.

Features include automatic indexing, priming, powder charging and loaded-round ejection. Piggyback uses a five-station shell plate (numbered the same as RCBS shell holders), standard $7/8 \times 14$ dies and an RCBS Uniflow Powder Measure, all sold separately.

The RCBS Piggyback Conversion Unit has a suggested retail price of $130.00. Five-station shell plates are $26.50.

BLOUNT, INC., SPORTING EQUIP. DIV./RCBS PRODUCTS

STEEL SHOT LOADS

ACTIV Industries, Inc. recently announced four new loads in Triple BB ("BBB") for the ACTIV Steel Shot line.

ACTIV now offers shooters twenty-four different 12 gauge Steel Shot loads to go along with two 20 gauge Steel Shot loads.

ACTIV's larger internal hull volume prevents high pressures in its Steel Shot loads. The right amount of powder without high pressure results in outstanding velocity making the brass-free ACTIV hull the right choice when choosing steel shot ammo for your favorite type of waterfowling.

Write for more information on ACTIV Steel Shot and the entire ACTIV line of shotshell ammunition and reloading data.

ACTIV INDUSTRIES, INC.

NEW LIGHTWEIGHT BIPOD

At less than 6 ounces, (half the usual weight), the Glaser/Cherokee bipod offers the discriminating shooter the ultimate in strength (lifetime guarantee) and sleek beauty. A frontal area 4.5 times smaller than other bipods reduces snag hazards and uneven terrain is automatically compensated for up to 33 degrees. Deployment and retraction are single, silent, one-hand movements taking less than a second. The bipod readily fits all sporter, varmint and most para-military firearms. The basic mount permits front or rear mounting to the forearm rather than the barrel (for target accuracy) and accessories are available for hidden or quick detachable, custom mounts.

Write for free brochure!

GLASER SAFETY SLUG, INC.

See manufacturer's addresses on page 246.

SHOOTER'S MARKETPLACE

SEE-THRU SCOPE MOUNTS

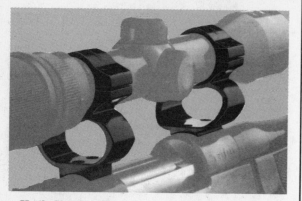

Kwik-Site See-Thru Scope Mounts are among the finest mounts on the market.

With their forward look, they are lowest to the receiver and have the largest viewing area of any see-thru scope mount made today. Popular in dense bush and forest their low profile and wide "see-thru" design gives hunters the immediate option of using iron sights or scope.

Made of high strength bright black anodized aluminum alloy, Kwik-Site mounts install in minutes using supplied allen wrench and screws.

Kwik-Site mounts are available for all popular centerfire rifles, shotguns, muzzleloaders and 22 rimfire rifles.

Write for more info.

KWIK-SITE CO.

NEW COMPOSITE STOCK

Clifton Arms' composite stock utilizes laminates in Kevlar, uni-directional graphite and fiberglass cloth, with integral pillars and cross-bolts. This precisely-inletted, classic stock is manufactured for most popular bolt-action rifles.

Available exclusively, on a composite stock manufactured by Clifton Arms, is an optional, integral, retractable bipod which stows flush with the contour of the stock. The bipod features a 40-degree pivot, which steadies aim and provides a consistent shooting platform regardless of terrain. Because the device does not bear on the barrel or interfere with sling mounts, point of impact remains unchanged.

Other offerings include blanks, installations, and complete rifles. Send $3.00 for full-color brochure.

CLIFTON ARMS, INC.

45 AUTO MAGS.

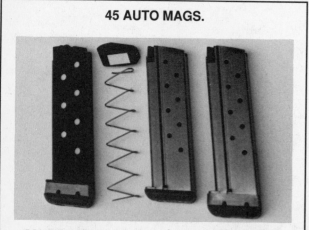

MAG-PACK CORP. has developed the following Magazines for the Colt Model 1911 Pistol:

• 8-round 45 ACP Standard Magazine: Stainless or Blued, with Pad; Lead Spacer added in Comp. Model.

• 8-round 45 ACP Concealment Carry Magazine: Blued, with Pad, and short Floor Plate to eliminate the Magazine from digging into clothes.

• 7-round 45 ACP Officer's Model Magazine: Blued, with or without Pad.

• 8-round 45 ACP Follower Pack: converts 7-round Magazines.

• 10-round 38 Super Magazine: Stainless, with Pad; Lead Spacer added in Competition Model.

• 10-round 38 Super Follower Pack: converts 9-round Mags. Free brochure. Dealers welcome.

MAG-PACK CORPORATION

HIGH-MELT BULLET LUBE

Rooster Labs now offers a choice of hardnesses in high-melt cannelure lubricants. ZAMBINI is the hard tough version.

It comes in 2" x 6" sticks for the commercial reloader, and 1" x 4" hollow and solid sticks. Lube-sizer must be warmed.

HVR is soft but firm, and applies more easily. 1" x 4" sticks only.

Meant for high velocity pistol and rifle—both lubes melt at 220°F—neither will melt and kill the powder.

Rooster Red lubes now enable the individual to make professional quality bullets. 2" x 6" sticks cost $4.00. 1" x 4" suggested retail $3.00, $135.00 per bulk pack of 100 sticks. Write Rooster Laboratories direct for more information.

ROOSTER LABORATORIES

See manufacturer's addresses on page 246.

SHOOTER'S MARKETPLACE

COLORCASE HARDENING

Doug Turnbull of Creekside Gun Shop offers Bone Charcoal Colorcase Hardening. This unique process duplicates the same fine colors that are found on guns manufactured by Parker, LC Smith, Colt, Winchester and other celebrated makers. With over 20 years of experience in colorcase work, Turnbull is able to get the natural colors that are notable on fine collectible firearms. Price: $60.00 (Colt SAA) and up.

To help complete the restoration work, Rust Blueing of soft-soldered, double-barrels is available for your shotgun. Prepare your parts personally or, with your direction, Turnbull will be glad to give your parts the care in preparation needed to make your project complete.

Send $2.00 for color brochure.

DOUG TURNBULL/CREEKSIDE GUN SHOP

NEW RIMFIRE PRODUCTS

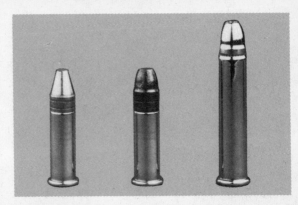

CCI has three new rimfire loads for the serious rimfire hunter.

The 22 LR SGB™ (Small Game Bullet) features a 30 gr. unplated lead bullet with a flat point for better penetration and less meat damage than a hollow point, but more shock than a round nose. Next is the Mini-Mag +V™, which bridges the velocity gap between Mini-Mag and Stinger. A 36 gr. *solid* truncated cone bullet at 1425 fps gives a flat trajectory and reduced meat damage.

There's also the Maxi-Mag +V™, the *first* hyper-velocity 22 WMR load. A 30 gr. hollow point with CCI's exclusive Penta Point™ design leaves the rifles's muzzle at 2200 fps, making Maxi-Mag +V the ultimate rimfire varmint round.

BLOUNT, INC., SPORTING EQUIP. DIV./CCI PRODUCTS

IMPROVED 60mm SPOTTING SCOPE

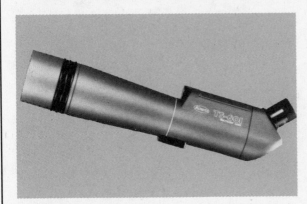

INNOVATION in 60mm Conventional Spotting Scope!

The TS-601 is equipped with a multi-coated lens that lets the shooter see a clear, brighter and sharper target than any other conventional 60mm spotting scope.

Bayonet mounting is included for simple eyepiece changing.

Also optional photo capability. Available in 20x Wide, 25x, 25x Long Eye Relief, 40x, 20x-60x zoom.

Manufacturer's suggested retail: $479.90 for TS-601 with 25x eyepiece. Straight type also available.

For more information on the TS-601 Spotting Scope and other Kowa Optimed products, write or call the manufacturer direct.

KOWA OPTIMED, INC.

CHOKE TUBE SERVICE/INSTALLATION

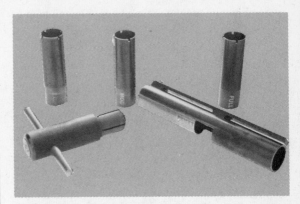

Hastings offers installation of the Briley Long Choke System for any shotgun gauge, all single barrel shotguns and most over/unders and side-by-sides. For double barrel guns, tube series are carefully matched to the barrel wall diameter, and special fixtures and instruments are used to provide a degree of concentricity between bore and choke that will satisfy the most discriminating shooter. Most series are suitable for use with steel shot, but check with them to be sure of the right choice. For barrels that fall short of the minimum wall thickness requirements (many over/unders, side-by-sides and some single barrels), they make special tubes. Give them a call. Screw chokes can be installed in all gauges, including 10, 12, 16, 20, 28, and 410 bore.

HASTINGS BARRELS

See manufacturer's addresses on page 246.

RIGID BASE SCOPE MOUNTS

The J.B. Holden Company's most recent scope mount innovation is a line of rigid-base, solid-top mounts designed to fit most popular hunting rifles. Like all Holden mounts, the PlainsMaster™ line is precision crafted from the highest strength alloys available for durability and strength.

The base and ring connect points commonly used in a number of older style mounts has been effectively eliminated in the PlainsMaster™. The result is an uncomplicated, lightweight scope mounting system which offers superior performance and appearance at an economical price.

Write or call for a free catalog on these and other fine products available as part of the company's 25th Anniversary.

J.B. HOLDEN COMPANY

PORTABLE SHOOTING TABLE

The precision shooters ultimate aide. SSC's Portable Field Shooting Table is designed to be used and perform like a stationary bench.

Triangulated design provides strength and stability with no leg interference. Features capped ends, extra heavy hinges with full welds, 3/8" pivots and self-locking nuts for adjustable hinge resistance. Carefully selected quality materials with specially selected coatings provide function and durability. Ambidextrous design suitable for both rifles or pistols. 30" wide by 36" long, legs fold to a compact 4", self-contained package weighing only 26 pounds.

Comes fully assembled.

Price: $149.95 freight included. Send $1 for brochure of SSC products.

SPORTSMAN SUPPLY COMPANY

NEW SYNTHETIC SHOULDER HOLSTER

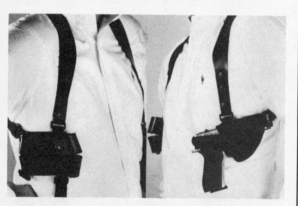

Bianchi International's new synthetic Model 4613 "Shark"™ concealment shoulder holster offers the ultimate in light-weight durability and comfort. Two tough layers of abrasion-resistant ballistic weave fabric make up the holster body. A metal reinforced safety strap features a wraparound double strap closure for sturdy gun retention.

The tough, 1-inch web nylon harness attaches at four points on a pivoting DuPont Hytrel synthetic back piece. The off-side ammo pouch accommodates two single or double-stacked magazines.

Send for their full color 66-page product catalog; normally $3, now only $2 if you mention *Shooter's Marketplace*.

Dealer inquiries welcome.

BIANCHI INTERNATIONAL

QUALITY FIREARM FINISHING

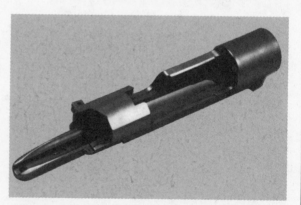

Precise Firearm Finishing offers a unique rifle-action service. They will precision surface grind the exterior of most rifle action surfaces (Mauser Action seen here), and insure clean, crisp lines as well as precise mounting surfaces for scope mounts, etc. They also offer Rockwell testing of Mauser and other actions and they will evaluate your action for suitability of use.

Additionally, Precise Firearms Finishing can hand finish your action and components. They can also heat-treat your action to meet the standards of today's modern cartridges.

Send $2.00 for a current brochure and price list that fully outlines Precise Firearms Finishing's specialized services.

PRECISE FIREARM FINISHING

See manufacturer's addresses on page 246.

SHOOTER'S MARKETPLACE

ANTI-SEIZING CHOKE-TUBE LUBE

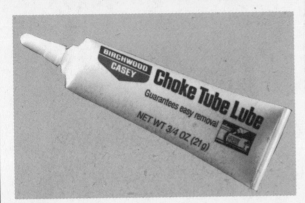

Birchwood Casey Choke Tube Lube™ prevents stuck shotgun choke tubes caused by rain or saltwater corrosion, high stress of steel shot loads, and extreme temperatures and pressure from repeated shooting.

Contains metallic particles of nickel, aluminum and graphite in a non-evaporating lubricant that will withstand heat and prevent seizure up to 2600°F.

Guarantees ease in choke-tube removal for all regular and stainless steel tubes. Also excels as a universal lubricant and eliminates galling on stainless steel.

Suggested retail price for a ¾-ounce tube is $4.00.

See your dealer or write for a free catalog on this and other Birchwood Casey products.

BIRCHWOOD CASEY

SHOOTING GLASSES APERTURE

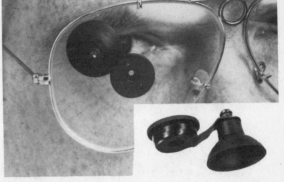

Pistol shooters can now see their sights and target clearly with the Merit Optical Attachment and its instantly adjustable diameter aperture.

An aperture (pinhole) will increase your eyes' depth of field (range of focus) dramatically.

The optical attachment is instantly adjustable from .022- to .156-inch diameter aperture to accommodate different light conditions. The sights and target will be in clear focus.

Additionally, using an aperture distinctly improves the shooter's concentration by actually helping the shooter maintain a consistent position of the head. This device works equally well for bifocals, trifocals or plain lensed shooting glasses.

Contact Merit for a free brochure.

MERIT CORPORATION

PROFESSIONAL HUNTER BULLETS

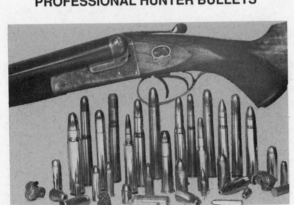

Professional Hunter Supplies has been making, testing and supplying custom bullets to hunters for six years, but specifically for heavy dangerous game in Africa. These bullets have been and are being used by professional hunters of government agencies for elephant, cape buffalo and other animal control. These bullets are also used by many professional hunters guiding and "backing up" clients on African safari. Bullets incorporating ideas from continuing field research are actually tested on dangerous game.

Professional Hunter Supplies offers various solids and soft nose bullets in calibers from 7mm through 600 N.E. including 12 bore. Individual customer specifications may be special ordered. Prices start at $22.50 per 25 bullets. Write for free brochure.

PROFESSIONAL HUNTER SUPPLIES

COTTON FLANNEL CLEANING PATCHES

Real, 100% pure cotton flannel gun cleaning patches in money saving Bulk Paks of 1000. Originally added to Brownells line to satisfy the needs of their high-usage gunsmith customers, they're perfect for shooters too. Soft and absorbent, they carry solvents and oils into barrels, and fouling back out, far better that synthetic or synthetic blend patches. Available in square or round shapes and four sizes to handle everything from 22 to 12 gauge. For complete, 200 page Catalog, filled with more than 14,000 items for the gunsmith and hobbyist, send $3.75 (free to qualified gunsmiths/dealers). And, if you'd like to get your FFL, just ask and they'll send free info on the licensing procedures. Brownells accepts MC/Visa, COD or check.

BROWNELLS, INC.

See manufacturer's addresses on page 246.

SHOOTER'S MARKETPLACE

BLACK POWDER SCOPE BASE

Holden scope mount bases are designed to fit most popular black powder rifles (pictured here is the T/C Hawken Rifle). Each adapter base utilizes factory drilled and tapped holes (no gunsmithing).

To complement the MuzzleMaster™ line of black powder bases, two styles of scope mounting systems are available; the Holden Ironsighter® Model 710 see-through mount and the MuzzleMaster Weaver Adapter and Ring Set Model MMWA.

These new bases are precision-machined from high tensile strength aluminum alloy to provide maximum scope rigidity and strength. A rear sight, adjustable for windage and elevation, is an integral part of each base. Write or call for a free catalog.

J.B. HOLDEN CO.

FASHION-DESIGN HOLSTERBAG

Created from fine top-grain leather and a durable matching liner, this designer handbag offers the ultimate in protection. A hidden velcro-sealed compartment with holster conceals your handgun, up to a 4" barrel, holstered and ready for easy access in emergencies. Straps are reinforced with steel mesh so cutting is virtually impossible. Handbag size is a comfortable 12½" x 11" and is available in black, gray, taupe, tobacco, navy, light denim and bone white (seasonal).

The GML Products Holsterbag is available direct from the manufacturer for $99.95 plus $5.00 for shipping and handling. GML requests you use their 800 number for orders only. Visa and Mastercard are both accepted.

GML PRODUCTS

LEAD REMOVER

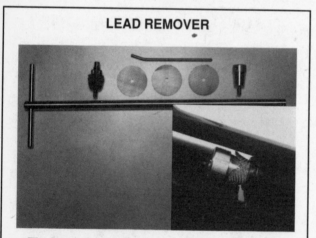

The Lewis Lead Remover is an effective method for removing lead deposits from the barrel, forcing cone and cylinder of revolvers.

The Lewis Lead Remover is also ideal for removing lead deposits from autoloading pistol barrels.

It was invented by a pistol shooter and contains nothing that will harm the chamber or bore of your handgun.

Available in 38/357/9mm, 41, 44 and 45 calibers. (16" handle available at extra cost.)

The original Lewis Lead Remover from L.E.M. Gun Specialties has been on the market for over 36 years and has been endorsed by many of the nation's top shooters.

Write for more info.

L.E.M. GUN SPECIALTIES, INC.

NEW SHOTSHELL PROPELLANT

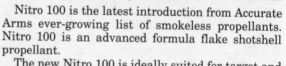

Nitro 100 is the latest introduction from Accurate Arms ever-growing list of smokeless propellants. Nitro 100 is an advanced formula flake shotshell propellant.

The new Nitro 100 is ideally suited for target and light field loads.

Accurate offers a full line of propellants. Five for handgun applications: No. 2, No. 5, No. 7, and No.9. Six for rifles: 1680, 2230, 2460, 2520, 3100, and 8700.

Accurate Arms has plans to introduce several more powders in the near future.

If you would like to have a copy of Accurate Arms Company's Loading Guide, it's yours for free to *Shooter's Marketplace* readers.

Write for more information.

ACCURATE ARMS COMPANY, INC.

See manufacturer's addresses on page 246.

SHOOTER'S MARKETPLACE

NEW SHOOTING BENCH

Joe Hall's Shooting Products has announced the addition of complete plans for a portable/adjustable shooter's bench. This unique product is vertically and angularly adjustable to 8 different positions and is adaptable to all shooters and terrain.

Joe Hall's shooting experts have designed a bench which enables the rifle and handgun shooter to practice and repeat "off-hand" shooting positions both on the range and in the field. The bench, when folded, carries like a suitcase and measures about 48" x 18" x 6" deep.

Plans include all dimensions and complete list of materials.

Plans are available at $9.95 plus $2.50 shipping and handling.

JOE HALL'S SHOOTING PRODUCTS, INC.

ADJUSTABLE PEEP SIGHT DISC

Shooting under varying light conditions, with a peep sight, can be highly frustrating.

Merit Corporation has come up with a solution—an adjustable peep sight disk that allows you to keep your front sight and target in clear focus.

As lighting conditions vary, shooters can now instantly adjust the aperture diameter of the Merit Iris Rifle Disc to maintain a clear sight picture.

The Iris aperture is adjustable from .022- to .125-inch diameter opening and has an internal click spring to maintain its setting.

The Master Disc includes a 1½-inch diameter replaceable light shield and is available in a lens disc model that will hold a prescription ground lens.

Contact Merit for a free brochure.

MERIT CORPORATION

CUSTOM PRE-FINISH STOCK

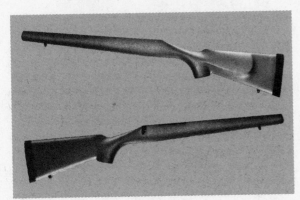

The Custom Pre-Finish stock is a Classic style hunting stock made for most factory barreled actions. Made in a dark gray, textured finish, the Custom Pre-Finish has a standard length of pull and a standard pad.

Weight is a light 1½ pounds.

Inletting is precisely fitted using a duplicate factory action. Add 10-15 minutes to bolt together the rifle with the epoxy compound included, and maximum performance is combined with the stability of synthetics. The Custom Pre-Finish stock is guaranteed for *all* calibers, and highly recommended for magnums.

Write for free stock brochure; or, send $2.00 for catalog.

BROWN PRECISION, INC.

SHOOTER'S PRODUCT CATALOG

The Fed Ord Product Catalog includes the entire Ranger Pistol line including the Alpha linkless multi-caliber auto, the Ranger Lite, the 10mm PSP-07 Combat Compensator, and a full array of 1911 accessories. Also covered are the popular accessory lines for the Mini-14, Mini-30, 10/22, AR-15, M1 Carbine, Garand and more! Only $1.00.

Fed Ord's "Surplus Gazette," covers U.S. and foreign military rifles, pistols, cleaning gear, ammo and more! Only $1.00.

Fed Ord also offers "The Mauser Broomhandle Catalog"—a comprehensive, commercial reference for the classic C96, collectible carbines, cased sets, and customizations. Only $2.00. You can get all three catalogs for $3.00.

FEDERAL ORDNANCE, INC.

See manufacturer's addresses on page 246.

SHOOTER'S MARKETPLACE

RIMFIRE BANANA CLIPS

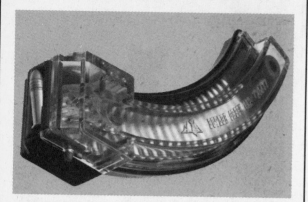

Say goodbye to bad feeding habits, say hello to Butler Creek's unique HOT LIPS 25/22 Banana Clip—one of the hottest high capacity feed systems available for Ruger's 10/22 and AMT's Lightning.

What makes this magazine so hot is the radical new one-piece feed lip design that vastly improves feeding reliability. What makes it so unique is the ease of operation plus features not found on "similar" products.

The Lexan housing is virtually indestructible! A single, constant-force spring insures uniform tension and means easy loading and no more sore fingers. Space Age polymers—uniform, self-lubricating, long life! Feeds all brands of 22 ammo. Butler Creek guarantees your satisfaction.

BUTLER CREEK CORPORATION

NEW ELECTRONIC RED-DOT SIGHT

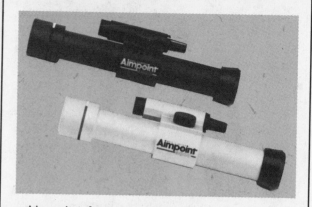

Aimpoint has recently introduced it's new electronic, red-dot sight, the 3000 series.

It's a small, lightweight sight that's easy to mount on all firearms and has a sharp adjustable red dot that covers 2.5" of the target (100 yards). Available in two versions: the short model for pistols and revolvers, and a long version (pictured) for shotguns, air rifles and bows. The 3000 incorporates the best features from earlier models; a mil-spec switch built to withstand heavy recoil and a small battery pack which decreases the weight while increasing the shooter's field of view. Suggested retail price is $259.95. Write for more information on the Aimpoint 1000, 3000, Laserpoint and complete Aimpoint line of mounting systems.

AIMPOINT

GUN BOOK SPECIALISTS

RAY RIFLING ARMS BOOKS CO., "America's oldest mail order Arms Book Speciality Company," is now in its third generation with 50 years of prompt, efficient and personalized service.

They feature one of the largest, carefully selected stocks of new, out-of-print, used and rare books on Firearms, Hunting, Edged Weapons, Armor and related subjects.

They also specialize in Fine Bindings, Limited Editions, and offer unbeatable values and bargain books on every listing.

If a book is worth reading it is worth buying from Ray Riling Arms Books Co. Their 50th Anniversary catalog will be sent free with mention of the *Shooter's Marketplace*.

RAY RILING ARMS BOOKS COMPANY

CUSTOM RELOADING TOOLS

The folks at Custom Products/Neil Jones have twenty years experience in designing and building the most accurate reloading tools available. Their design allows them to custom fit all cartridges including wildcats; and, they are available in ⅞x14 threaded dies and the straight line hand dies preferred by benchrest shooters.

Their micro powder measure is second to none in accuracy and repeatability with even the toughest powders. All tools are designed to do the best job possible with improved accuracy as the goal. Jones will personally assist customers with unusual or difficult handloading problems.

Readers of *Shooter's Marketplace* can send for a free catalog.

CUSTOM PRODUCTS/NEIL JONES

See manufacturer's addresses on page 246.

SHOOTER'S MARKETPLACE

HIGH QUALITY BULLET MOLD

NEI recently introduced the ultimate combination for the serious cast bullet maker, a line of precision-machined tool steel molds with ¼-inch anodized aluminum sprue plate. These molds are designed for the commercial caster as well as the serious enthusiast.

The new NEI catalog is also ready for delivery. With over 500 styles & sizes of bullets, NEI is the world's most complete manufacturer of molds made of aluminum, brass, cast iron, and now steel.

They also have molds for virtually all calibers and bore sizes—whether pistol, rifle, shotgun or muzzleloader.

Send $1.00 to NEI/Tooldyne for their comprehensive tool catalog.

NEI/TOOLDYNE

ADJUSTABLE DISC APERTURE

When hunting, you are faced with continually changing light conditions. A receiver sight with a fixed aperture is adequate for only one light condition.

The Merit Hunting Disc aperture is instantly adjustable from .025- to .155-inch in diameter, allowing you to maintain a clear sight picture under changing conditions.

The aperture leaves are supported to withstand recoil from heavy calibers and the shank is tapered to provide solid lock-up of the Disc to your receiver sight.

Contact Merit Corporation for a copy of their free brochure describing this and other sighting aids for shooters.

MERIT CORPORATION

CAMO STOCK FOR SKS

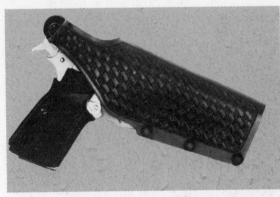

CARBELITE gun stocks by B & C for semi-automatic rifles, bolt action rifles and shotguns are composed of fiberglass and Kevlar, with random strands of glass throughout.

For added strength, B & C Deluxe bolt action rifle stocks also include graphite and additional fiberglass.

Impervious to weather, all stocks are available in two beautiful, realistic woodgrain finishes or durable baked-on enamel finishes in gray, black or camo.

B & C also maintains a fully staffed service department for custom fitting these stocks to customers' actions.

Send $2.00 for further information on the ultimate laminated composite gun stocks by B & C.

B & C (BELL & CARLSON, INC.)

CONTOUR BASKETWEAVE HOLSTER

The patented Pachmayr® basketweave-design holster looks like leather, but has none of the disadvantages of leather or cordura® nylon.

This Contour-Fit™ holster is manufactured from an inert synthetic material which is impervious to moisture, solvents, fuels, heat or cold.

It won't shrink, mildew, sweat, unravel, tear, or break. Each model is made to fit the handgun for which it was designed—no sloppy loose fitting "generic" sizes. Your handgun is carried comfortably in a very secure, protective, lightweight, easy-to-draw, thumb-break holster.

Models available for Browning Hi-Power, Colt Gov't. 45, S&W "K" and "L" frames. For more information, write Pachmayr directly.

PACHMAYR, LTD.

See manufacturer's addresses on page 246.

CARTRIDGES FOR COLLECTORS

Tillinghast's famous *Cartridges for Collectors List* is $2.00 sent prepaid. Lists over 1000 cartridges for sale: Patent Ignition, rimfires, pistol, rifle, shotgun; American and Foreign: books, catalogs. Also includes a 300 lot *Mail Order Cartridge Auction.* Send $8.00 for the next five Cartridge and Auction Lists, a real "bargain." Special—*Antique Ammunition Price Guide #1,* 8½ x 11, 64 pages, well illustrated, Regular: $6.00; Special: $3.50 sent prepaid.

Cartridge list is free with a purchase of the Ammunition Price Guide. Wanted—cartridge collections, accumulations, box lots, rare singles of all types.

Tillinghast purchases gun catalogs, gun powder tins, gun and ammunition related advertising.

JAMES C. TILLINGHAST

PROFESSIONAL GUNSMITHING TOOLS

Professional gunsmithing tools manufactured by Thomas W. Menck have been in use world-wide for years. They are designed for the professional law enforcement armorer, journeyman gunsmith or advanced hobbyist.

As a professional gunsmith and gun-tool designer, Menck insures that each precision-made tool is solidly built of first-quality materials for a lifetime of dependable service. A copy of Tom Menck's current catalog is available for $3.00, the price being fully deductible from the first order.

Menck's catalog lists quality tools for Browning, Ithaca, Remington, Ruger, Winchester and other makes of firearms, as well as generic tools for 22 rimfires and shotguns.

THOMAS W. MENCK, GUNSMITH

SLUG SIGHTS

Slug Sights are simple, rugged, and easy to attach. They're available for both ventilated ribbed and plain single-barreled shotguns.

They allow for the precise sighting necessary for the accurate use of slugs in shotguns, without drilling, soldering or interfering with the gun's action.

Made of a tough non-marring black nylon, Slug Sights actually stretch and lock to the shotguns' rib or barrel. The Sights are low-profile featuring a Blaze Orange front sight blade, and are adjustable for elevation and windage.

Only $9.95, Slug Sights are available for plain barrels in 12, 16, and 20 gauges, and for 5/16" and 3/8" wide ventilated ribs. To order or find the dealer nearest you, call or write the manufacturer.

INNOVISION ENTERPRISES

RUBBER BAND PRACTICE GUN

The Regal Ranger Rapid Fire Target Rubber Band Gun comes in four different kits: One gun (G1-$10.95), one gun and metallic targets (G1S-$15.90), two guns (G2-$19.90) and two guns and targets (G2S-$23.95).

Each Regal Ranger comes with twelve rubber bands.

The guns are guaranteed for a year.

Extra ammo is available for $1.50 per package. (A package contains 18 Magnum rubber bands.) Shipping and handling is $3.00 per order (no limit). Range is up to 25 feet. Made for adults, but great entertainment and practice for young and old alike.

Free brochures upon request. Dealer inquiries welcome.

LEFTHANDER'S HEAVEN, INC.

See manufacturer's addresses on page 246.

COLLECTIBLE KNIFE CATALOG

W.R. Case & Sons, first choice of knife collectors, offers a complete selection of collectible knives in their new Case Centennial Catalog, a collector's piece in itself.

You'll find patterns from Case's early years, including reproductions of rare patterns with handles in such unusual materials as India stag horn, red bone, Rogers bone and goldstone.

This Case Centennial Catalog is a must for serious knife collectors looking for something unusual, beginners looking for a place to start, or dealers looking for their customer's needs.

To order, send $3.95. (Foreign surface mail orders: $6.95—Write for Airmail quote.) Mention *Shooter's Marketplace* when ordering.

W.R. CASE & SONS CUTLERY COMPANY

LEARN GUN REPAIR

Modern School has been teaching gun repair the home study way since 1946 to over 45,000 students. All courses are Nationally Accredited and Approved for VA/GI benefits. Courses are complete and include all lessons (including how to get your FFL), Tool Kit, Powley Calculator and Powley Computer, *Gun Digest*, Gun Parts Catalogue, Mainspring Vise, School Binders, Brownell's Catalogue, Pull & Drop Gauge, Trigger Pull Gauge, Two Parchment Diplomas ready for framing, free Consultation Service plus much more. Here's how you can get into a career where you can enjoy what you are doing! Find out how you can start your own business and make money in your spare time too. No previous experience needed. Write or call for free information.

MODERN GUN REPAIR SCHOOL

RELOADER'S SUPPLY CATALOG

HUNTINGTON DIE SPECIALTIES is this nation's *foremost* supplier of hard-to-get reloading products plus standard RCBS, CCI, Speer, Bell cases, Sierra bullets and other products. They also manufacture the well-known Huntington Compac Press.

If you're a serious handloader who's looking for something unusual, a beginner who's looking for a place to start, or a dealer who's trying to fill a customer's needs, the Huntington catalog is a must. It's the sort of reloader's "tool" that quickly becomes part of the bench. Both the Retail and Dealer's Catalogs (FFL required) normally sell for $3.00 each. If you'll mention you saw it in *Shooter's Marketplace,* it's yours for the asking.

HUNTINGTON DIE SPECIALTIES

SHARPENING TOOLS

W.R. Case & Sons Cutlery Company offers one of the finest selections of sharpening tools and knife accessories available, from pocket size to gift sets.
- #904 Tri-Hone Set in Cedar Box, suggested retail $45.99.
- #914 Pocket Sharpener, suggested retail $13.49.
- #922 (4-3) 3" Pocket Mini-Steel Rod, suggested retail $10.99.
- #938 Pocket Size Crock Stick, suggested retail $6.99.
- #924 Sportsman's Honing Kit, including 2 stones, oil, plastic storage case, suggested retail $14.50.

Free brochure with order. Send $2.95 for full color Case Sporting Goods Catalog. Mention *Shooter's Marketplace*. Dealer inquiries welcome.

W.R. CASE & SONS CUTLERY COMPANY

See manufacturer's addresses on page 246.

SHOOTING ACCESSORIES

Parker-Hale's famous quality shooting accessories are once again available in the U.S., imported from England by Precision Sports, a Division of Cortland Line Company.

British-made throughout, the following Parker-Hale accessories provide the knowledgeable shooter with a standard of excellence equal to his choice of fine guns.

- Presentation Cleaning Sets
- Snap Caps
- Rosewood Shotgun Rods
- Steel Rifle Rods
- Phosphor Bronze Brushes
- Jags, Loops, and Mops
- Youngs "303" Cleaner
- Express Oil
- Rangoon Oil
- 009 Nitro Solvent
- Black Powder Solvent
- Comet Super Blue

Write now for a free color catalog.

PARKER-HALE/PRECISION SPORTS

SIDE-BY-SIDE SHOTGUNS

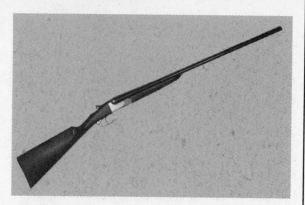

Long favorites in Great Britain, the Parker-Hale "600" series of side-by-side shotguns is finally available in America.

Custom crafted in Spain, these classic doubles are available in five field models, with either English or American styling.

Traditional "game-gun" design and craftsmanship throughout.

Parker-Hale doubles are offered in 10, 12, 16, 20 and 28 gauges and 410 bore.

Additionally, each Parker-Hale 600 series side-by-side shotgun comes with a Lifetime Operational Warranty.

Parker-Hale's color catalog is available free to *Shooter's Marketplace* readers.

PARKER-HALE/PRECISION SPORTS

MANUFACTURERS' ADDRESSES

ACCURATE ARMS, INC.
Dept. SM'91
Box DB
McEwen, TN 37101

ACTIV INDUSTRIES, INC.
Attn: Dept. SM'91
P.O. Box 339, 1000 Zigor Rd.
Kearneysville, WV 25430 (304-725-0451)
(Fax 304-725-2080)

AIMPOINT
Dept. SM'91
203 Elden St., Suite 302
Herndon, VA 22070 (703-471-6828)

AMERICAN DERRINGER CORP.
Attn: Dept. GD'91
127 N. Lacy Dr.
Waco, TX 76705 (817-799-9111)

AMERICAN SALES & MFG. CO.
Attn.: Dept. SM'91
P.O. Box 677
Laredo, TX 78042-0677 (512-723-6893)

ANDERSON MANUFACTURING COMPANY
Attn: Dept. GD'91
P.O. Box 4218
Federal Way, WA 98063 (800-541-4242 or 206-838-4299, Fax 206-838-4130)

B & C (BELL & CARLSON, INC.)
Dept. GDM
509 N. 5th
Atwood, KS 67730

BIANCHI INTERNATIONAL
100 Calle Cortez, Dept. GD
Temecula, CA 92390 (800-854-8545 or 714-676-5621; Fax 714-676-6777; Telex 288553 BNCI UR)

BIRCHWOOD CASEY
Attn: Dept. SM'91
7900 Fuller Road
Eden Prairie, MN 55344 (612-937-7933)

BLOUNT, INC., SPORTING EQUIPMENT DIV.
See CCI, Outers®, RCBS, Speer and Weaver®

BLUE RIDGE MACHINERY AND TOOLS, INC.
Dept. SM'91
P.O. Box 536, 2806 Putnam Ave.
Hurricane, WV 25526
(1-800-872-6500; in WV 304-562-3538)

BROWN PRECISION INC.
P.O. Box 270GD
Los Molinos, CA 96055 (916-384-2506)
(Order line 1-800-543-2506)

W.E. BROWNELL CHECKERING TOOLS
Dept. GD-91
3356 Moraga Pl.
San Diego, CA 92117

BROWNELLS, INC.
Dept. SM'91
222 West Liberty
Montezuma, IA 50171

B-SQUARE CO.
Attn: Dept. SM'91
P.O. Box 11281
Fort Worth, TX 76110-0281 (817-923-0964)

BUTLER CREEK CORPORATION
Dept. SM'91, 290 Arden Dr.
Belgrade, MT 59714 (406-388-1356)
(Fax 406-388-7204)

W.R. CASE & SONS CUTLERY COMPANY
c/o Sales & Marketing Div., Dept. SM'91
P.O. Box 22724
Knoxville, TN 37933 (615-690-5200)
(Fax 615-694-5922)

CCI PRODUCTS
Attn: Dept. SM'91
P.O. Box 1538
Lewiston, ID 83501

CLIFTON ARMS, INC.
Dept. GD-SM
P.O. Box 531258
Grand Prairie, TX 75053 (214-647-2500)

CLYMER MANUFACTURING CO., INC.
Dept. SM'91
1645 West Hamlin Rd.
Rochester Hills, MI 48309-3368 (313-853-5555)
(Fax 313-853-1530)

CUSTOM PRODUCTS/NEIL A. JONES
Attn: Dept. GD'91
R.D. 1, Box 483-A
Saegertown, PA 16433

DAMASCUS-U.S.A.
Attn: Dept. SM'91
P.O. Box 448
Edenton, NC 27932

EAGLE INTERNATIONAL, INC.
Attn: Dept. SM'91
5195 W. 58th Ave.
Arvada, CO 80002

FEDERAL ORDNANCE, INC.
Attn: Dept. SM'91
1443 Potrero Ave., P.O. Box 6050
S. El Monte, CA 91733 (818-350-4161)
(Fax 818-350-1538)

FORSTER PRODUCTS
Dept. SM'91
82 E. Lanark Ave.
Lanark, IL 61046 (815-493-6360)

GLASER SAFETY SLUG, INC.
Attn: Dept. GD'91
P.O. Box 8223
Foster City, CA 94404

GML PRODUCTS
Attn: Dept. SM'91
1634A Montgomery Hwy, Suite 196
Birmingham, AL 35216 (800-345-BAGS [orders]
or 205-979-GUNS [inquiries])

THE GUN PARTS CORPORATION
Successors to Numrich Arms Corp.
P.O. Box SMP-91
West Hurley, NY 12491 (914-679-2417)

JOE HALL'S SHOOTING PRODUCTS INC.
443 Wells Road
Doylestown, PA 18901 (215-345-6345)

HASTINGS BARRELS
Dept. SM'91
Box 224
Clay Center, KS 67432 (913-632-2184)

J.B. HOLDEN CO.
Attn: Dept. SM'91
P.O. Box 320
Plymouth, MI 48170 (313-455-4850)

HUNTINGTON DIE SPECIALTIES
Attn.: Buzz Huntington
P.O. Box 991
Oroville, CA 95965 (916-534-1210)

INNOVISION ENTERPRISES
Attn: Dept. SM'91
728 Skinner Dr.
Kalamazoo, MI 49001 (616-382-1681)

RICK JAMISON'S PLANS
Attn: Dept. SM'91
P.O. Box 691
Springfield, OR 97477

KOWA OPTIMED, INC.
Attn.: Dept. SM'91
20001 S. Vermont Ave.
Torrance, CA 90502 (213-327-1913)

KWIK-SITE CO.
Attn: Dept. SM'91
5555 Treadwell
Wayne, MI 48184

LANE BULLETS, INC.
Attn: Dept. SM'91
1011 S. 10th St.
Kansas City, KS 66105 (800-444-7468 Ext.#3)

LEFTHANDER'S HEAVEN, INC.
Attn: Dept. GD'91
P.O. Box 1544
Albany, OR 97321 (800-782-5388 [orders],
503-928-1077 [other] or Fax 503-967-8034)

L.E.M. GUN SPECIALTIES, INC.
Attn: Dept. GD'91
P.O. Box 87031
College Park, GA 30337

LOCH LEVEN INDUSTRIES
Dept. GD'91
P.O. Box 2751
Santa Rosa, CA 95405 (707-573-8735)

LYMAN PRODUCTS CORPORATION
Route 147, Dept. 790
Middlefield, CT 06455

MAG-PACK CORPORATION
Attn: Dept. SM'91
P.O. Box 846
Chesterland, OH 44026 (216-423-4681)

MARKSMAN PRODUCTS
5622 Engineer Dr., Dept. GD'91
Huntington Beach, CA 92649 (714-898-7535)

THOMAS W. MENCK, GUNSMITH
Attn: Dept. SM'91
5703 S. 77th St.
Ralston, NE 68127

MERIT CORPORATION
Attn.: C.M. Grant
Dept. SM'91 Box 9044
Schenectady, NY 12309 (518-346-1420)

MMC (MINIATURE MACHINE CO.)
Dept. P38
210 E. Poplar
Deming, NM 88030

MODERN GUN REPAIR SCHOOL
Attn: Dept. GEB91
2538 N. 8th Street, P.O. Box 5338
Phoenix, AZ 85010 (602-990-8346)

MUSCLE PRODUCTS CORPORATION
Dept. SM'91
188 Freeport Road
Butler, PA 16001 (800-227-7049)

NAVY ARMS COMPANY
Dept. PR, SM'91
689 Bergen Blvd.
Ridgefield, NJ 07657 (201-945-2500)

NEI/TOOLDYNE
Attn: Dept. GD'91
9330 N.E. Halsey
Portland, OR 97220

OLD WORLD OIL PRODUCTS
Dept. SM'91
3827 Queen Ave. North
Minneapolis, MN 55412 (612-522-5037)

P.S. OLT CO.
Dept. GD-91
P.O. Box 550
Pekin, IL 61554

THE OUTDOOR CONNECTION, INC.
201 Douglas, P.O. Box 7751
Waco, TX 76712-7751
(817-772-5575, or, 800-533-6076)

OUTERS® PRODUCTS
Attn: John Wiggert, S.M.
Dept. SM'91, P.O. Box 39
Onalaska, WI 54650

PACHMAYR, LTD.
1875 S. Mountain Ave.
Monrovia, CA 91016

PARKER-HALE/PRECISION SPORTS DIV.
Mr. Greg Pogson
Dept. SM'91
P.O. Box 708-5588
Cortland, NY 13045-5588 (607-756-2851)

PONSNESS/WARREN
Attn: Dept. SM'91
S. 763 Highway 41, P.O. Box 8
Rathdrum, ID 83858

PRECISE FIREARM FINISHING DIVISION
EZ Tool Corp.
Attn: Dept. SM'91
P.O. Box 3186
Des Moines, IA 50316

PROFESSIONAL HUNTER SUPPLIES
Dept. SM'91
P.O. Box 608, 660 Berding St.
Ferndale, CA 95536 (707-786-4040)

PRO-PORT LIMITED
Dept. SM'91
41302 Executive Drive
Mount Clemens, MI 48045-3448 (313-469-7323)

QUINETICS CORPORATION
Dept. SM'91
P.O. Box 13237
San Antonio, TX 78213 (512-684-8561)
(Fax 512-684-2912)

RCBS PRODUCTS
Attn: Dept. SM'91
Oro Dam Blvd.
Oroville, CA 95965 (800-533-5000)

RAY RILING ARMS BOOKS CO.
Dept. SM'91
6844 Gorsten St., P.O. Box 18925
Philadelphia, PA 19119 (215-438-2456)

ROOSTER LABORATORIES
Attn.: Dept. SM'91
P.O. Box 412514
Kansas City, MO 64141 (816-474-1622)

SAFARILAND LTD., INC.
Attn: Dept. GD'91
1941 So. Walker Ave.
Monrovia, CA 91016 (818-357-7902)

SHOOTING CHRONY, INC.
Attn: Dept. GD'91
2480 Cawthra Rd., Unit 22
Mississauga, Ont., CANADA L5A 2X2

THE SHOTGUN NEWS
Attn.: D. Clark
Dept. SM'91
P.O. Box 669
Hastings, NE 68902

MILT SPARKS LEATHER
Attn: Dept. SM'91
P.O. Box 187-1
Idaho City, ID 83631

SPEER PRODUCTS
Attn: Dept. SM'91
P.O. Box 1538
Lewiston, ID 83501

SPORTSMAN SUPPLY CO.
Attn: Dept. GD'91
714 East Eastwood, P.O. Box 650
Marshall, MO 65340

JAMES C. TILLINGHAST
P.O. Box 27GD
Hancock, NH 03449-27GD (603-525-6615)

TRIJICON, INC.
Attn: Dept. SM'91
P.O. Box 2130
Farmington Hills, MI 48333 (313-553-4960)

DOUG TURNBULL
Creekside Gun Shop
County Road #30, P.O. Box 100
Holcomb, NY 14469 (716-657-6338)

WEAVER® PRODUCTS
Attn: Dept. SM'91
P.O. Box 39
Onalaska, WI 54650

THE COMPLETE COMPACT CATALOG

It's not a trick phrase, you know. This really is a complete catalog of legal firearms available through trade channels in the U.S. It shows them all in just 248 pages, which is certainly compact. So you definitely are looking at a complete compact catalog. And this year, there's quite a bit more of it.

There's more catalog because there are more and more models of guns out there, particularly rifles. It seems that factories just can't make too many different models.

A catalog like this one, even a 45-year-old catalog, is not an automatic perennial. It does not just happen each year; it's made to happen.

We start with last year's catalog and we send tearsheets to all the gun sources listed. We ask for new model notes, for new photos, for the manufacturer to tell us what he's discontinued. As soon as we hear of a new gun, its maker goes on the list.

With the data in our offices, the work starts—it all has to get into its proper place. That's called, in publishing, "production work." However, in this case, it can't be turned over to what, in publishing, are called "production people." To get such a gun catalog straight takes what we call "gun people."

We have them and they do it.

This many—there are 240 or so here—pages of dense-packed information have to be organized properly or they're useless. What worked fine when there were only 120 pages of catalog does not serve when there are 248. We make new categories; we combine old ones; we change the order of things—the change is constant.

We want you to depend on this catalog and use it—like always—and enjoy it—like always. That's why we do it; that's why we change it. *The Editors*

GUNDEX R

A listing of all the guns in the catalog, by name and model, alphabetically and numerically.

Includes models suitable for several forms of competition and other sporting purposes.

AA ARMS AP9 AUTO PISTOL
Caliber: 9mm Para., 20-shot magazine.
Barrel: 5".
Weight: 3.5 lbs. **Length:** 11.8" overall.
Stocks: Checkered plastic.
Sights: Adjustable post front in ring, fixed open rear.
Features: Matte blue/black or nickel finish. Lever safety blocks trigger and sear. Fires from closed bolt. Introduced 1988. Made in U.S. by AA Arms, Inc.
Price: Matte blue/black $259.00
Price: Nickel finish $294.00

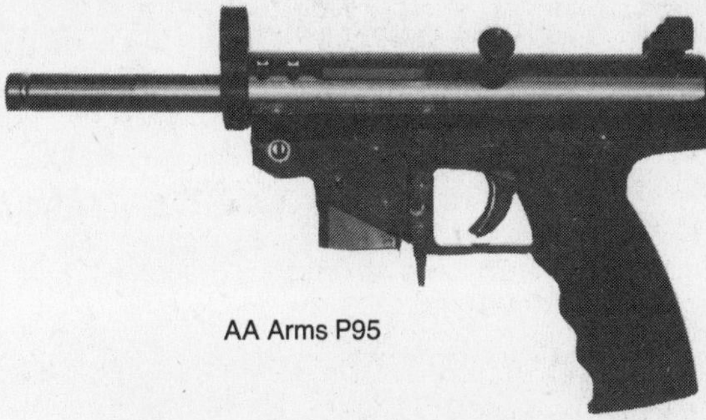

AA Arms P95 Pistol
Similar to the AP9 except does not have vented barrel shroud. Comes with 5-shot magazine; 20- and 30-shot magazines available. Introduced 1989.
Price: Matte blue/black finish $249.99
Price: Nickel finish $279.99

AA Arms P95

ACCU-TEK MODEL AT-380 AUTO PISTOL
Caliber: 32 ACP, 380 ACP, 5-shot magazine.
Barrel: 2.75".
Weight: 16 oz. **Length:** 5.6" overall.
Stocks: Black combat or wood.
Sights: Blade front, rear adjustable for windage.
Features: External hammer, manual thumb safety with firing pin block and trigger disconnect. Black or chrome finish, also Lady 380 (chrome with gray bleached oak grips). Introduced 1990. Made in U.S. by Accu-Tek.
Price: $250.00

Accu-Tek AT-380

ACTION ARMS AT-88S DA PISTOLS
Caliber: 9mm Para., 15 shots; 41 Action Express, 10 shots.
Barrel: 4.8".
Weight: 35.3 oz. **Length:** 8.1" overall.
Stocks: Checkered walnut.
Sights: Blade front, rear drift-adjustable for windage.
Features: Double action; polished blue finish. Comes with 9mm and 41 A.E. barrels. Introduced 1987. Imported from England by Action Arms Ltd.
Price: $595.00
Price: Model 88P with both barrels (3.7" bbl., 7.3" o.a.l., weighs 32.1 oz., and has 13/8-shot magazine) $595.00
Price: Model 88H with both barrels (3.5" bbl., 6.9" o.a.l., weighs 30.5 oz. and has 10/7-shot magazine) $595.00

Action Arms AT-88S

AMERICAN ARMS PX-22 AUTO PISTOL
Caliber: 22 LR, 7-shot magazine.
Barrel: 2.85".
Weight: 15 oz. **Length:** 5.39" overall.
Stocks: Black checkered plastic.
Sights: Fixed.
Features: Double action; 7-shot magazine. Polished blue finish. Introduced 1989. Made in U.S. From American Arms, Inc.
Price: $189.00

AMERICAN ARMS CX-22 DA AUTO PISTOL
Caliber: 22 LR, 8-shot magazine.
Barrel: 3⅓".
Weight: 22 oz. **Length:** 6⅓" overall.
Stocks: Checkered black polymer.
Sights: Blade front, rear adjustable for windage.
Features: Double action with manual hammer-block safety, firing pin safety. Alloy frame. Has external appearance of Walther PPK. Blue/black finish. Introduced 1990. Made in U.S. by American Arms, Inc.
Price: $179.00
Price: CXC-22 (as above with chrome slide) $189.00

AMERICAN ARMS MX-9 AUTO PISTOL
Caliber: 9mm Para., 9-shot magazine.
Barrel: 3¾".
Weight: 27 oz. **Length:** 6⅞" overall.
Stocks: Checkered composition.
Sights: Blade front, rear adjustable for windage.
Features: Single-action, locked-breech design with manual hammer-block safety. Blue finish. Introduced 1990. From American Arms, Inc.
Price: $299.00

American Arms PX-22

CAUTION: PRICES CHANGE, CHECK AT GUNSHOP.

AMERICAN ARMS MODEL P-98 AUTO PISTOL
Caliber: 22 LR, 8-shot magazine.
Barrel: 5".
Weight: 25 oz. **Length:** 8⅛" overall.
Stocks: Grooved black polymer.
Sights: Blade front, rear adjustable for windage.
Features: Double action with hammer-block safety, magazine disconnect safety. Alloy frame. Has external appearance of the Walther P-38 pistol. Introduced 1989. Made in U.S. by American Arms, Inc.
Price: $225.00

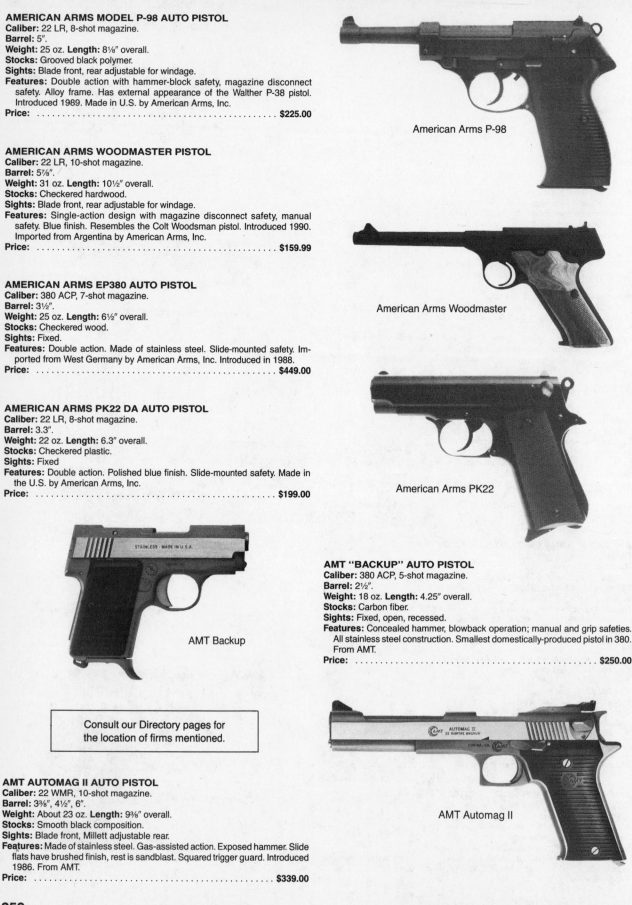

American Arms P-98

AMERICAN ARMS WOODMASTER PISTOL
Caliber: 22 LR, 10-shot magazine.
Barrel: 5⅞".
Weight: 31 oz. **Length:** 10½" overall.
Stocks: Checkered hardwood.
Sights: Blade front, rear adjustable for windage.
Features: Single-action design with magazine disconnect safety, manual safety. Blue finish. Resembles the Colt Woodsman pistol. Introduced 1990. Imported from Argentina by American Arms, Inc.
Price: $159.99

American Arms Woodmaster

AMERICAN ARMS EP380 AUTO PISTOL
Caliber: 380 ACP, 7-shot magazine.
Barrel: 3½".
Weight: 25 oz. **Length:** 6½" overall.
Stocks: Checkered wood.
Sights: Fixed.
Features: Double action. Made of stainless steel. Slide-mounted safety. Imported from West Germany by American Arms, Inc. Introduced in 1988.
Price: $449.00

AMERICAN ARMS PK22 DA AUTO PISTOL
Caliber: 22 LR, 8-shot magazine.
Barrel: 3.3".
Weight: 22 oz. **Length:** 6.3" overall.
Stocks: Checkered plastic.
Sights: Fixed
Features: Double action. Polished blue finish. Slide-mounted safety. Made in the U.S. by American Arms, Inc.
Price: $199.00

American Arms PK22

AMT Backup

AMT "BACKUP" AUTO PISTOL
Caliber: 380 ACP, 5-shot magazine.
Barrel: 2½".
Weight: 18 oz. **Length:** 4.25" overall.
Stocks: Carbon fiber.
Sights: Fixed, open, recessed.
Features: Concealed hammer, blowback operation; manual and grip safeties. All stainless steel construction. Smallest domestically-produced pistol in 380. From AMT.
Price: $250.00

Consult our Directory pages for the location of firms mentioned.

AMT Automag II

AMT AUTOMAG II AUTO PISTOL
Caliber: 22 WMR, 10-shot magazine.
Barrel: 3⅜", 4½", 6".
Weight: About 23 oz. **Length:** 9⅜" overall.
Stocks: Smooth black composition.
Sights: Blade front, Millett adjustable rear.
Features: Made of stainless steel. Gas-assisted action. Exposed hammer. Slide flats have brushed finish, rest is sandblast. Squared trigger guard. Introduced 1986. From AMT.
Price: $339.00

CAUTION: PRICES CHANGE, CHECK AT GUNSHOP.

AMT 45 ACP HARDBALLER LONG SLIDE
Caliber: 45 ACP.
Barrel: 7". **Length:** 10½" overall.
Stocks: Wrap-around rubber.
Sights: Fully adjustable rear sight.
Features: Slide and barrel are 2" longer than the standard 45, giving less recoil, added velocity, longer sight radius. Has extended combat safety, serrated matte rib, loaded chamber indicator, wide adjustable trigger. From AMT.
Price: **$539.00**

AMT 45 ACP HARDBALLER
Caliber: 45 ACP.
Barrel: 5".
Weight: 39 oz. **Length:** 8½" overall.
Stocks: Wrap-around rubber.
Sights: Adjustable.
Features: Extended combat safety, serrated matte slide rib, loaded chamber indicator, long grip safety, beveled magazine well, adjustable target trigger. All stainless steel. From AMT.
Price: **$504.00**
Price: Government model (as above except no rib, fixed sights) **$459.00**

ASTRA A-90 DOUBLE-ACTION AUTO PISTOL
Caliber: 9mm Para. (15-shot), 45 ACP (9-shot).
Barrel: 3.75".
Weight: 40 oz. **Length:** 7" overall.
Stocks: Checkered black plastic.
Sights: Square blade front, square notch rear drift-adjustable for windage.
Features: Double or single action; loaded chamber indicator; combat-style trigger guard; optional right-side slide release (for left-handed shooters); automatic internal safety; decocking lever. Introduced 1985. Imported from Spain by Interarms.
Price: Blue **$500.00**

Astra Constable

Astra A-60 Double-Action Pistol
Similar to the Constable except in 380 only, with 13-shot magazine, slide-mounted ambidextrous safety. Available in blued steel only. Introduced 1980.
Price: **$435.00**

AUTO-ORDNANCE 1911A1 AUTOMATIC PISTOL
Caliber: 9mm Para., 38 Super, 9-shot; 10mm, 45 ACP, 7-shot magazine.
Barrel: 5".
Weight: 39 oz. **Length:** 8½" overall.
Stocks: Checkered plastic with medallion.
Sights: Blade front, rear adjustable for windage.
Features: Same specs as 1911A1 military guns—parts interchangeable. Frame and slide blued; each radius has non-glare finish. Made in U.S. by Auto-Ordnance Corp.
Price: 45 cal. **$368.95**
Price: 9mm, 38 Super, 10mm **$404.25**

Auto-Ordnance ZG-51 Pit Bull Auto
Same as the 1911A1 except has 3½" barrel, weighs 36 oz. and has an overall length of 7¼". Available in 45 ACP only; 7-shot magazine. Introduced 1989.
Price: **$404.25**

AMT Long Slide

ARGENTINE HI-POWER 9MM AUTO PISTOL
Caliber: 9mm Para., 13-shot magazine.
Barrel: 4²¹⁄₃₂".
Weight: 32 oz. **Length:** 7¾" overall.
Stocks: Checkered walnut.
Sights: Blade front, adjustable rear.
Features: Produced in Argentina under F.N. Browning license. Introduced 1990. Imported by Century International Arms, Inc.
Price: About **$450.00**

Astra A-90 Pistol

ASTRA CONSTABLE AUTO PISTOL
Caliber: 22 LR, 10-shot; 380 ACP, 7-shot.
Barrel: 3½".
Weight: 26 oz.
Stocks: Moulded plastic.
Sights: Adjustable rear.
Features: Double action, quick no-tool takedown, non-glare rib on slide. 380 available in blue, stainless steel, or chrome finish. Engraved guns also available—contact the importer. Imported from Spain by Interarms.
Price: Blue, 22 . . . . **$365.00**
Price: Chrome, 22 . . . . **$375.00**
Price: Blue, 380 . . . . **$350.00**

Auto-Ordnance 1911A1

BEEMAN MODEL P-08 AUTO PISTOL
Caliber: 22 LR, 8-shot magazine.
Barrel: 4".
Weight: 25 oz. **Length:** 7¾" overall.
Stocks: Checkered hardwood.
Sights: Fixed.
Features: Has toggle action similar to original "Luger" pistol. Action stays open after last shot. New feeding mechanism. Has magazine and sear disconnect safety systems. Imported from West Germany by Beeman.
Price: **$389.50**

Beeman Mini P-O8

BEEMAN MINI P-08 AUTO PISTOL
Caliber: 380 ACP (5-shot).
Barrel: 3.5".
Weight: 22½ oz. **Length:** 7⅜" overall.
Stocks: Checkered hardwood.
Sights: Fixed.
Features: Toggle action similar to original "Luger" pistol. Action stays open after last shot. Has magazine and sear disconnect safety systems. New feeding mechanism. Imported from West Germany by Beeman.
Price: **$389.50**

Bernardelli PO 18

BERNARDELLI PO18 DA PISTOL
Caliber: 9mm Para., 16-shot magazine.
Barrel: 4.8".
Weight: 36.3 oz. **Length:** 6.2" overall.
Stocks: Checkered, contoured plastic standard; walnut optional.
Sights: Low profile combat sights.
Features: Manual thumb safety, half-cock, magazine safeties, auto-locking firing pin block safety; ambidextrous magazine release. Introduced 1987. Imported from Italy by Magnum Research, Inc.
Price: With plastic grips **$499.00**
Price: With walnut grips **$539.00**
Price: Compact model (4" bbl., 14-shot) **$519.00**

Bernardelli Model USA

BERNARDELLI MODEL USA AUTO PISTOL
Caliber: 22 LR, 10-shot; 380 ACP, 7-shot.
Barrel: 3½".
Weight: 26½ oz. **Length:** 6½" overall.
Stocks: Checkered plastic with thumbrest.
Sights: Ramp front, white outline rear adjustable for w. & e.
Features: Hammer-block slide safety; loaded chamber indicator; dual recoil buffer springs; serrated trigger; Inertia-type firing pin. Imported from Italy by Magnum Research, Inc.
Price: **$289.00**
Price: Model AMR (as above except has 6" bbl., target sights) **$309.00**

Beretta Model 87

BERETTA 80 SERIES DA PISTOLS
Caliber: 380 ACP, 13-shot magazine; 22 LR, 7-shot (M87).
Barrel: 3.82".
Weight: About 23 oz. (M84/85), 20.8 oz. (M87). **Length:** 6.8" overall.
Stocks: Glossy black plastic (wood optional at extra cost).
Sights: Fixed front, drift-adjustable rear.
Features: Double action, quick takedown, convenient magazine release. Introduced 1977. Imported from Italy by Beretta U.S.A.
Price: Model 84 (380 ACP) **$479.00**
Price: Model 84 wood grips **$505.00**
Price: Model 84 nickel finish **$545.00**
Price: Model 85 nickel finish **$500.00**
Price: Model 85 plastic grips **$440.00**
Price: Model 85 wood grips **$467.00**
Price: Model 87, 22 LR, 7-shot magazine, wood grips **$447.00**
Price: Model 87 Long Barrel, 22 LR, single action **$460.00**
Price: Model 89 Sport Wood, single action, 22 LR **$620.00**

Beretta Model 86

Beretta Model 86
Similar to the 380-caliber Model 85 except has tip-up barrel for first-round loading. Barrel length is 4.33", overall length of 7.33". Has 8-shot magazine, walnut or plastic grips. Introduced 1989.
Price: **$480.00**

BERETTA MODEL 92F PISTOL
Caliber: 9mm Para., 15-shot magazine.
Barrel: 4.9".
Weight: 34 oz. **Length:** 8.5" overall.
Stocks: Checkered black plastic; wood optional at extra cost.
Sights: Blade front, rear adjustable for w.
Features: Double action. Extractor acts as chamber loaded indicator, squared trigger guard, grooved front- and backstraps, inertia firing pin. Matte finish. Introduced 1977. Made in U.S. and imported from Italy by Beretta U.S.A.
Price: With plastic grips **$600.00**
Price: With wood grips **$625.00**

Beretta Model 92FC Pistol
Similar to the Beretta Model 92F except has cut down frame, 4.3" barrel, 7.8" overall length, 13-shot magazine, weighs 31.5 oz. Introduced 1989.
Price: With plastic grips **$620.00**
Price: With wood grips **$645.00**

Beretta Model 92FS Pistol
Similar to the Model 92F except has enlarged hammer pin head and a groove cut into the slide rail. Developed to modify the military M9 pistol to meet special military operational requirements. Introduced 1990.
Price: **$600.00**

Beretta Model 92SB Compact Type M Pistol
Similar to the Model 92FC except has thinner grip, straight 8-shot magazine. Weighs 30.8 oz., has 1.25" overall width. Introduced 1989.
Price: **$605.00**

BERETTA MODEL 950 BS AUTO PISTOL
Caliber: 22 Short, 6-shot; 25 ACP, 8-shot.
Barrel: 2.5".
Weight: 9.9 oz. (22 Short, 10.2 oz.) **Length:** 4.5" overall.
Stocks: Checkered black plastic.
Sights: Fixed.
Features: Single action, thumb safety; tip-up barrel for direct loading/unloading, cleaning. From Beretta U.S.A.
Price: Blue, 22, 25 . . . . **$161.00**
Price: Nickel, 22, 25 . . . . **$189.00**
Price: Engraved **$230.00**

Beretta Model 21 Pistol
Similar to the Model 950 BS. Chambered for 22 LR and 25 ACP. Both double action. 2.5" barrel, 4.9" overall length. 7-round magazine on 22 cal.; 8-round magazine on 25 cal.; 22 cal. available in nickel finish. Both have walnut grips. Introduced in 1985.
Price: 22 cal. **$215.00**
Price: 22 cal., nickel finish **$237.00**
Price: 25 cal. **$215.00**
Price: EL model, 22 or 25 . . . . **$255.00**

BERSA MODEL 23 AUTO PISTOL
Caliber: 22 LR, 10-shot magazine.
Barrel: 3.5".
Weight: 24.5 oz. **Length:** 6.6" overall.
Stocks: Walnut with stippled panels.
Sights: Blade front, notch rear adjustable for windage.
Features: Double action; firing pin and magazine safeties. Available in blue or nickel. Introduced 1989. Imported from Argentina by Eagle Imports, Inc.
Price: Blue **$263.95**
Price: Nickel **$291.95**

BERSA MODEL 85 AUTO PISTOL
Caliber: 380 ACP, 13-shot magazine.
Barrel: 3.5".
Weight: 25.75 oz. **Length:** 6.6" overall.
Stocks: Walnut with stippled panels.
Sights: Blade front, notch rear adjustable for windage.
Features: Double action; firing pin and magazine safeties. Available in blue or nickel. Introduced 1989. Imported from Argentina by Eagle Imports, Inc.
Price: Blue **$366.95**
Price: Nickel **$374.95**
Price: Model 83 (as above, except 7-shot magazine), blue **$263.95**
Price: Model 83, nickel **$291.95**

Beretta Model 92F

Beretta 92SB Compact

Beretta Model 950

Bersa Model 85

BERSA MODEL 90 AUTO PISTOL
Caliber: 9mm Para., 13-shot magazine.
Barrel: 4²¹/₃₂".
Weight: 32 oz. **Length:** 7³/₄" overall.
Stocks: Checkered walnut.
Sights: Blade front, rear adjustable for windage.
Features: Polished blue finish. Introduced 1990. Imported from Argentina by Eagle Imports.
Price: **$383.95**

BRNO CZ 75 AUTO PISTOL
Caliber: 9mm Para., 15-shot magazine.
Barrel: 4.7".
Weight: 35 oz. **Length:** 8" overall.
Stocks: Checkered wood.
Sights: Blade front, rear adjustable for w.
Features: Double action; blued finish. Imported from Czechoslovakia by TD Arms.
Price: $599.00

BRNO CZ 85 Auto Pistol
Same gun as the CZ 75 except has ambidextrous slide release and safety-levers, is available in 9mm Para. and 7.65, contoured composition grips, matte finish on top of slide. Introduced 1986.
Price: $655.00

Browning Buck Mark Plus

Browning Buck Mark Varmint

Browning Buck Mark Target 5.5 Pistol
Same as the Buck Mark Silhouette except has a 5½" barrel with .900" diameter. Has hood sights mounted on a scope base that accepts an optical or reflex sight. Rear sight is a Millett Gold Cup #360, front sight is an adjustable post that customizes to different widths, and can be adjusted for height. Contoured walnut grips with thumbrest. Matte blue finish. Overall length is 9⅝", weight is 35½ oz. Has 10-shot magazine. Introduced 1990. From Browning.
Price: $353.95

Browning Hi-Power

BRNO CZ 83 DOUBLE-ACTION PISTOL
Caliber: 32, 15-shot; 380, 13-shot.
Barrel: 3.7".
Weight: 26.5 oz. **Length:** 6.7" overall.
Stocks: Checkered black plastic.
Sights: Blade front, rear adjustable for w.
Features: Double action; ambidextrous magazine release and safety. Polished or matte blue. Imported from Czechoslovakia by TD Arms.
Price: $425.00

BROWNING BUCK MARK 22 PISTOL
Caliber: 22 LR, 10-shot magazine.
Barrel: 5½".
Weight: 32 oz. **Length:** 9½" overall.
Stocks: Black moulded composite with skip-line checkering.
Sights: Ramp front, rear adjustable for w. and e.
Features: All steel, matte blue finish, gold-colored trigger. Buck Mark Plus has laminated wood grips. Made in U.S. Introduced 1985. From Browning.
Price: Buck Mark $218.95
Price: Buck Mark Plus $265.95

Browning Buck Mark Silhouette
Same as the Buck Mark except has 9⅞" heavy barrel with .900" diameter; hooded front sight with interchangeable posts, Millett Gold Cup 360 SIL rear on a special top sighting plane. Grips and forend are solid walnut. Introduced 1987.
Price: $370.95

Browning Buck Mark Varmint
Same as the Buck Mark except has 9⅞" heavy barrel with .900" diameter and full-length scope base (no open sights); black multi-laminated wood grips, with optional forend. Overall length is 14", weight is 48 oz. Introduced 1987.
Price: $334.95

Browning Buck Mark 5.5

BROWNING HI-POWER 9mm AUTOMATIC PISTOL
Caliber: 9mm Para., 13-shot magazine.
Barrel: 4²¹⁄₃₂".
Weight: 32 oz. **Length:** 7¾" overall.
Stocks: Walnut, hand checkered, or black Polyamide.
Sights: ⅛" blade front; rear screw-adjustable for w. and e. Also available with fixed rear (drift-adjustable for w).
Features: External hammer with half-cock and thumb safeties. A blow on the hammer cannot discharge a cartridge; cannot be fired with magazine removed. Fixed rear sight model available. Ambidextrous safety available only with matte finish, moulded grips. Imported from Belgium by Browning.
Price: Fixed sight model, walnut grips $473.95
Price: 9mm with rear sight adj. for w. and e., walnut grips $517.95
Price: Standard matte black finish, fixed sight, moulded grips, ambidextrous safety $436.95

Browning BDA-380

BROWNING BDA-380 DA AUTO PISTOL
Caliber: 380 ACP, 13-shot magazine.
Barrel: 3¹³⁄₁₆".
Weight: 23 oz. **Length:** 6¾" overall.
Stocks: Smooth walnut with inset Browning medallion.
Sights: Blade front, rear drift-adjustable for w.
Features: Combination safety and de-cocking lever will automatically lower a cocked hammer to half-cock and can be operated by right- or left-hand shooters. Inertia firing pin. Introduced 1978. Imported from Italy by Browning.
Price: Blue $474.95
Price: Nickel $499.95

BRYCO MODEL 38 AUTO PISTOLS
Caliber: 22 LR, 32 ACP, 380 ACP, 6-shot magazine.
Barrel: 2.8".
Weight: 15 oz. **Length:** 5.3" overall.
Stocks: Polished resin-impregnated wood.
Sights: Fixed.
Features: Safety locks sear and slide. Choice of satin nickel, bright chrome or black Teflon finishes. Introduced 1988. From Jennings Firearms.
Price: 22 LR, 32 ACP $109.95
Price: 380 ACP $129.95

Bryco Model 48

Calico Model 110

CALICO MODEL M-950 AUTO PISTOL
Caliber: 9mm Para., 50- or 100-shot magazine.
Barrel: 6".
Weight: 2.25 lbs. (empty). **Length:** 14" overall (50-shot magazine).
Stocks: Glass-filled polymer.
Sights: Post front adjustable for w. and e., fixed notch rear.
Features: Helical feed 50- or 100-shot magazine. Ambidextrous safety, static cocking handle. Retarded blowback action. Glass-filled polymer grip. Introduced 1989. From Calico.
Price: $552.00

BRYCO MODEL 48 AUTO PISTOLS
Caliber: 22 LR, 32 ACP, 380 ACP, 6-shot magazine.
Barrel: 4".
Weight: 19 oz. **Length:** 6.7" overall.
Stocks: Polished resin-impregnated wood.
Sights: Fixed.
Features: Safety locks sear and slide. Choice of satin nickel, bright chrome or black Teflon finishes. Announced 1988. From Jennings Firearms.
Price: 22 LR, 32 ACP $139.00
Price: 380 ACP $139.00

CALICO MODEL 110 AUTO PISTOL
Caliber: 22 LR, 100-shot magazine.
Barrel: 6".
Weight: 3.7 lbs. (loaded). **Length:** 17.9" overall.
Stocks: Moulded composition.
Sights: Adjustable post front, notch rear.
Features: Aluminum alloy frame; flash suppressor; pistol grip compartment; ambidextrous safety. Uses same helical-feed magazine as M-100 Carbine. Introduced 1986. Made in U.S. From Calico.
Price: $232.00

Calico Model 950

Colt Government Model

COLT GOV'T MODEL MK IV/SERIES 80
Caliber: 9mm, 38 Super, 45 ACP, 7-shot.
Barrel: 5".
Weight: 38 oz. **Length:** 8½" overall.
Stocks: Checkered walnut.
Sights: Ramp front, fixed square notch rear.
Features: Grip and thumb safeties and internal firing pin safety, grooved trigger. Accurizor barrel and bushing.
Price: Blue, 45 ACP $624.95
Price: Bright stainless, 45 ACP $729.95
Price: 9mm, blue only $629.95
Price: 38 Super, blue $669.95
Price: Stainless steel, 45 ACP $659.95

Colt 10mm Delta Elite

Similar to the Government Model except chambered for 10mm auto cartridge. Has three-dot high profile front and rear combat sights, rubber combat stocks with Delta medallion, internal firing pin safety, and new recoil spring/buffer system. Introduced 1987.

Price: Blue **$689.95**
Price: STS **$699.95**
Price: BSTS **$769.95**

Colt Combat Elite MK IV/Series 80

Similar to the Government Model except in 45 ACP only, has stainless frame with ordnance steel slide and internal parts. High profile front, rear sights with three-dot system, extended grip safety, beveled magazine well, rubber combat stocks. Introduced 1986.

Price: **$759.95**

COLT 380 GOVERNMENT MODEL

Caliber: 380 ACP, 7-shot magazine.
Barrel: 3¼".
Weight: 21¾ oz. **Length:** 6" overall.
Stocks: Checkered composition.
Sights: Ramp front, square notch rear, fixed.
Features: Scaled-down version of the 1911A1 Colt G.M. Has thumb and internal firing pin safeties. Introduced 1983.

Price: Blue **$399.95**
Price: Nickel **$449.95**
Price: Stainless **$429.95**

Colt Mustang 380, Mustang Pocket Lite

Similar to the standard 380 Government Model. Mustang has steel frame (18.5 oz.), Pocket Lite has aluminum alloy (12.5 oz.). Both are ½" shorter than 380 G.M., have 2¾" barrel. Introduced 1987.

Price: Mustang 380, blue **$399.95**
Price: As above, nickel **$449.95**
Price: As above, stainless **$429.95**
Price: Mustang Pocket Lite, blue **$399.95**

Colt Mustang Plus II

Similar to the 380 Government Model except has the shorter barrel and slide of the Mustang. Introduced 1988.

Price: Blue **$399.95**
Price: Stainless **$429.95**

COLT COMBAT COMMANDER AUTO PISTOL

Caliber: 9mm Para., 38 Super, 9-shot; 45 ACP, 7-shot.
Barrel: 4¼".
Weight: 36 oz. **Length:** 7¾" overall.
Stocks: Checkered walnut.
Sights: Fixed, glare-proofed blade front, square notch rear.
Features: Grooved trigger and hammer spur; arched housing; grip and thumb safeties.

Price: Blue, 9mm **$629.95**
Price: Blue, 45 . . . . **$624.95**
Price: Blue, 38 Super **$629.95**

COLT SERIES 90 DOUBLE EAGLE DA PISTOL

Caliber: 45 ACP, 8-shot magazine.
Barrel: 5".
Weight: 39 ozs. **Length:** 8½" overall.
Stocks: Black checkered Xenoy thermoplastic.
Sights: Blade front, rear adjustable for windage. High profile three-dot system.
Features: Made of stainless steel with matte finish. Checkered and curved extended trigger guard, wide steel trigger; decocking lever on left side; traditional magazine release; grooved front strap; bevelled magazine well; extended grip guard; rounded, serrated combat-style hammer. Introduced 1989.

Price: About **$679.95**

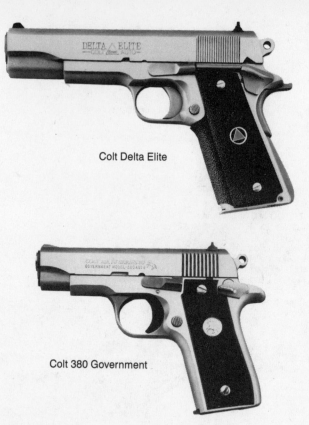

Colt Delta Elite

Colt 380 Government

COLT OFFICERS ACP MK IV/SERIES 80

Caliber: 45 ACP, 6-shot magazine.
Barrel: 3½".
Weight: 34 oz. **Length:** 7¼" overall.
Stocks: Checkered walnut.
Sights: Ramp blade front with white dot, square notch rear with two white dots.
Features: Trigger safety lock (thumb safety), grip safety, firing pin safety; grooved trigger; flat mainspring housing. Also available with lightweight alloy frame and in stainless steel. Introduced 1985.

Price: Matte finish **$605.50**
Price: Blue **$624.95**
Price: L.W., matte finish **$624.95**
Price: Stainless **$659.95**
Price: Bright stainless **$729.95**

Colt Lightweight Commander Mark IV/Series 80

Same as Commander except high strength aluminum alloy frame, wood panel grips, weight 27½ oz. 45 ACP only.

Price: Blue **$624.95**

Colt Double Eagle

CAUTION: PRICES CHANGE, CHECK AT GUNSHOP.

COONAN 357 MAGNUM PISTOL
Caliber: 357 Mag., 7-shot magazine.
Barrel: 5″.
Weight: 42 oz. **Length:** 8.3″ overall.
Stocks: Smooth walnut.
Sights: Open, adjustable.
Features: Unique barrel hood improves accuracy and reliability. Many parts interchange with Colt autos. Has grip, hammer, half-cock safeties. From Coonan Arms.
Price: Model B (linkless barrel, interchangeable ramp front sight, new rear sight) **$680.00**

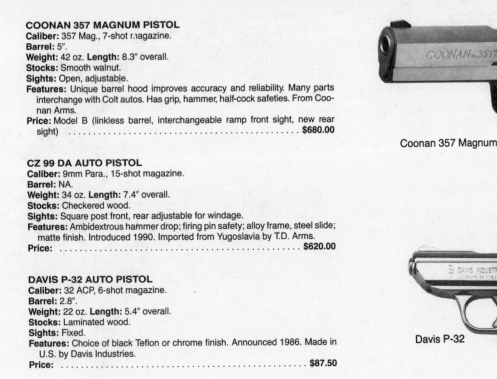
Coonan 357 Magnum

CZ 99 DA AUTO PISTOL
Caliber: 9mm Para., 15-shot magazine.
Barrel: NA.
Weight: 34 oz. **Length:** 7.4″ overall.
Stocks: Checkered wood.
Sights: Square post front, rear adjustable for windage.
Features: Ambidextrous hammer drop; firing pin safety; alloy frame, steel slide; matte finish. Introduced 1990. Imported from Yugoslavia by T.D. Arms.
Price: $620.00

DAVIS P-32 AUTO PISTOL
Caliber: 32 ACP, 6-shot magazine.
Barrel: 2.8″.
Weight: 22 oz. **Length:** 5.4″ overall.
Stocks: Laminated wood.
Sights: Fixed.
Features: Choice of black Teflon or chrome finish. Announced 1986. Made in U.S. by Davis Industries.
Price: $87.50

Davis P-32

Desert Eagle 357

DESERT EAGLE MAGNUM PISTOL
Caliber: 357 Mag., 9-shot; 41 Mag., 44 Mag., 8-shot.
Barrel: 6″, 10″, 14″, interchangeable.
Weight: 357 Mag.—52 oz. (alloy), 62 oz. (steel); 41 Mag., 44 Mag.—56 oz. (alloy), 66.9 oz. (stainless). **Length:** 10¼″ overall (6″ bbl.).
Stock: Wrap-around soft rubber.
Sights: Blade on ramp front, combat-style rear. Adjustable available.
Features: Rotating three-lug bolt; ambidextrous safety; combat-style trigger guard; adjustable trigger optional. Military epoxy finish. Satin, bright nickel, hard chrome, polished and blued finishes available. Imported from Israel by Magnum Research, Inc.
Price: 357, 6″ bbl., standard pistol **$789.00**
Price: As above, alloy frame **$789.00**
Price: As above, stainless steel frame **$839.00**
Price: 41 Mag., 6″, standard pistol **$799.00**
Price: 41 Mag., alloy frame **$799.00**
Price: 41 Mag., stainless steel frame **$849.00**
Price: 44 Mag., 6″, standard pistol **$839.00**
Price: As above, alloy frame **$839.00**
Price: As above, stainless steel frame **$889.00**

Desert Ind. Double Deuce

Consult our Directory pages for the location of firms mentioned.

DESERT INDUSTRIES "WAR EAGLE" PISTOL
Caliber: 9mm Para., 14-shot magazine; 10mm, 13-shot; 45 ACP, 12-shot.
Barrel: 4″.
Weight: NA. **Length:** NA.
Stocks: Rosewood.
Sights: Fixed.
Features: Double action; matte-finished stainless steel; ambidextrous safety. Announced 1986. From Desert Industries, Inc.
Price: $650.00

DESERT INDUSTRIES "DOUBLE DEUCE" PISTOL
Caliber: 22 LR, 6-shot; 25 ACP, 5-shot.
Barrel: 2½″.
Weight: 15 oz. **Length:** 5½″ overall.
Stocks: Rosewood.
Sights: Fixed.
Features: Double action; stainless steel construction with matte finish; ambidextrous slide-mounted safety. From Desert Industries, Inc.
Price: 22 . . . . **$325.00**
Price: 25 (Two-Bit Special) **$325.00**

ENCOM MP-9, MP-45 ASSAULT PISTOLS
Caliber: 9mm, 45 ACP, 10-, 30-, 40- or 50-shot magazine.
Barrel: Interchangeable 4½", 6", 8", 10", 18", 18½".
Weight: 6 lbs. (4½" bbl.) **Length:** 11.8" overall (4½" bbl.).
Stocks: Retractable wire stock.
Sights: Post front, fixed Patridge rear.
Features: Blowback operation, fires from closed breech with floating firing pin; right- or left-hand models available. Made in U.S. From Encom America, Inc.
Price: 9mm or 45 ACP, standard pistol **$329.95**
Price: As above, Mini Pistol (3½" bbl.) **$319.95**
Price: Carbine (18½" bbl., retractable wire stock) **$399.95**

ENCOM MK IV ASSAULT PISTOL
Caliber: 45 ACP, 30-shot magazine.
Barrel: 4.5", 6", 8", 10" optional.
Weight: 6 lbs. **Length:** 12.6" overall (4.5" barrel).
Stocks: Black composition.
Sights: Fixed.
Features: Semi-auto fire only. Side-loading magazine. Interchangeable barrels. Optional retractable stock available with 18½" barrel. Made in the U.S. by Encom America, Inc. Introduced 1988.
Price: **$329.95**

ERMA SPORTING PISTOL MODEL ESP 85A
Caliber: 22 LR, 8-shot; 32 S&W Long, 5-shot.
Barrel: 6".
Weight: 41 oz. **Length:** 10" overall.
Stocks: Checkered walnut with thumbrest and adjustable left- or right-hand shelf.
Sights: Interchangeable blade front, micro. rear adjustable for windage and elevation.
Features: Interchangeable caliber conversion kit; adjustable trigger, trigger stop. Comes with lockable carrying case. Imported from West Germany by Precision Sales Int'l. Introduced 1988.
Price: 22 LR **$1,119.00**
Price: 32 S&W Long **$1,169.00**
Price: 22 LR, chrome **$1,200.00**

F.I.E. "TZ-75" SERIES '88 DA AUTO PISTOL
Caliber: 9mm Para., 16-shot magazine; 41 Action Express, 11-shot magazine.
Barrel: 4.72".
Weight: 35.33 oz. **Length:** 8.25" overall.
Stocks: Smooth European walnut. Checkered rubber, Micarta and polymer optional.
Sights: Undercut blade front, open rear adjustable for windage.
Features: Double-action trigger system; squared-off trigger guard; frame-mounted safety. Introduced 1988. Imported from Italy by F.I.E. Corp.
Price: 9mm, blue **$519.95**
Price: 9mm, satin chrome **$539.95**
Price: 9mm, blue slide, chrome frame **$539.95**
Price: Combo, 9mm and 41 A.E., blue **$708.95**
Price: Combo, 9mm and 41 A.E., satin chrome **$737.95**
Price: Combo, 9mm and 41 A.E., blue slide, chrome frame **$737.95**
Price: 9mm, 5" bbl., ported bbl. and slide, blue **$708.95**
Price: 9mm, 6" bbl., compensated expansion chamber, blue **$803.95**

F.I.E. "Government Model" TZ-75 DA Pistol
Similar to the standard TZ-75 except available only in 9mm Para., 13-shot magazine. Barrel length of 3⅗", overall length of 6⅞", and weighs 33.5 oz. Smooth European walnut grips; checkered rubber optional. Introduced 1990. Imported from Italy by F.I.E. Corp.
Price: Matte blue **$519.95**
Price: Satin chrome **$539.95**
Price: Blue slide, chrome frame **$539.95**

F.I.E. "TITAN E-28" PISTOL
Caliber: 25 ACP, 6-shot magazine.
Barrel: 2⁷⁄₁₆".
Weight: 12 oz. **Length:** 4⅝" overall.
Stocks: Smooth walnut.
Sights: Fixed.
Features: External hammer; fast simple takedown. Made in U.S.A. by F.I.E. Corp.
Price: Blue **$59.95**
Price: Dyna-Chrome **$64.95**
Price: 24K gold and bright blue frame, smooth walnut grips **$104.95**
Price: Titan Tigress Lady 25 . . . . **$159.95**

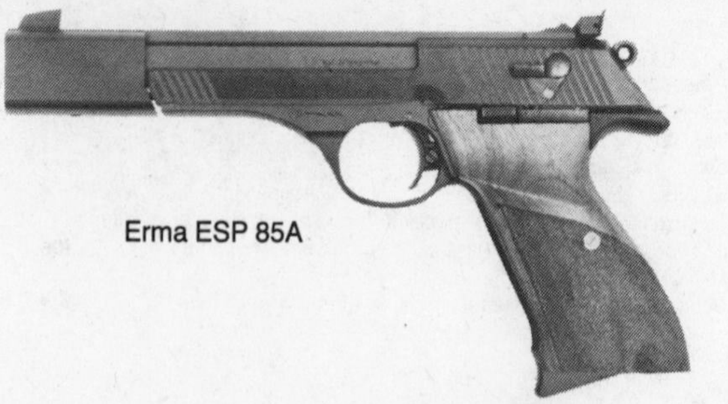
Erma ESP 85A

F.I.E. Series '88 TZ-75

F.I.E. T2-75 "Government"

F.I.E. "Titan E-28"

F.I.E. "SSP" AUTO PISTOL
Caliber: 32 ACP, 380 ACP.
Barrel: 3⅛".
Weight: 25 oz. **Length:** 6¼" overall.
Stocks: Smooth European walnut.
Sights: Blade front, rear adjustable for windage.
Features: Single action. External hammer, magazine safety with hammer, trigger and firing pin block. Available in blue, chrome and Lady models. Introduced 1990. Made in U.S. by F.I.E. Firearms Corp.
Price: 32 or 380, blue **$144.95**
Price: As above, chrome **$164.95**
Price: Lady model **$249.95**

CAUTION: PRICES CHANGE, CHECK AT GUNSHOP.

F.I.E. Spectre

Glock Model 20

GONCZ GA HIGH-TECH PISTOLS
Caliber: 30 Mauser, 9mm Para., 38 Super (18- or 36-shot); 45 ACP, 10mm (10- or 20-shot).
Barrel: 9.5″.
Weight: 3 lbs., 2 oz. **Length:** 15.1″ overall.
Stocks: Moulded composition.
Sights: Adjustable post front in ring, open rear adjustable for windage.
Features: Telescoping bolt, floating firing pin. Safety locks the firing pin. Sight radius of 14.1″. Target model (GAT) has tuned action, adjustable trigger. Made in U.S. From Goncz Co.
Price: GA High-Tech Pistol $500.00

Goncz High-Tech GS Pistols
Similar to the GA pistols except has 5″ barrel, 10.5″ overall length, and weighs 2 lbs., 10 oz. Barrel has ¾-10 UNC thread for screw-on flash suppressor, sound suppressor. From Goncz Co.
Price: $465.00

Grendel P-10

F.I.E. SPECTRE DOUBLE-ACTION AUTO PISTOL
Caliber: 9mm Para., 30-shot magazine; 50-shot optional.
Barrel: 8″.
Weight: 2.2 lbs. **Length:** 13.7″ overall.
Stocks: Black composition grip.
Sights: Post front, flip rear.
Features: Double-action mechanism fires from closed bolt. Introduced 1989. Imported by F.I.E. Firearms Corp.
Price: $724.95

GLOCK 17 AUTO PISTOL
Caliber: 9mm Para., 17-shot magazine.
Barrel: 4.49″.
Weight: 21.9 oz. (without magazine). **Length:** 7.21″ overall.
Stocks: Black polymer.
Sights: Dot on front blade, white outline rear adjustable for w. and e.
Features: Polymer frame, steel slide; double-action trigger with "Safe Action" system; mechanical firing pin safety, drop safety; simple takedown without tools; locked breech, recoil operated action. Adopted by Austrian armed forces 1983. NATO approved 1984. Imported from Austria by Glock, Inc.
Price: With extra magazine, magazine loader, cleaning kit $511.60
Price: Model 17L (6″ barrel) $773.53

Glock 19 Auto Pistol
Similar to the Glock 17 except has a 4″ barrel, giving an overall length of 6.74″ and weight of 20.99 oz. Magazine capacity is 15 rounds. Introduced 1988.
Price: $511.60

Glock Model 20 10mm Auto Pistol
Similar to the Glock Model 17 except chambered for 10mm Automatic cartridge. Barrel length is 4.60″, overall length is 8.27″, and weight is 27.5 oz. (without magazine). Magazine capacity is 15 rounds. Comes with an extra magazine, magazine loader, cleaning rod and brush. Introduced 1990. Imported from Austria by Glock, Inc.
Price: $598.00

Goncz GA-9

GRENDEL P-10 AUTO PISTOL
Caliber: 380 ACP, 10-shot magazine.
Barrel: 3″.
Weight: 15 oz. **Length:** 5.3″ overall.
Stocks: Checkered polycarbonate metal composite.
Sights: Fixed.
Features: Double action only with a low inertia safety hammer system. Magazine loads from the top. Matte black, electroless nickel or green finish. Introduced 1987. From Grendel, Inc.
Price: Black finish $150.00
Price: Green finish $155.00
Price: Electroless nickel $165.00
Price: Nickel-green $167.00

HAMMERLI MODEL 212 AUTO PISTOL
Caliber: 22 LR, 8-shot magazine.
Barrel: 4.9″.
Weight: 31 oz.
Stocks: Checkered walnut.
Sights: Blade front, rear adjustable for windage only.
Features: Polished blue finish. Imported from Switzerland by Beeman.
Price: $1,525.00

Heckler & Koch SP89

Heckler & Koch P7-M8

Helwan "Brigadier"

HECKLER & KOCH SP89 AUTO PISTOL
Caliber: 9mm Para., 15- or 30-shot magazine.
Barrel: 4.5″.
Weight: 4.4 lbs. **Length:** 12.8″ overall.
Stocks: Black high-impact plastic.
Sights: Post front, diopter rear adjustable for windage and elevation.
Features: Semi-auto pistol inspired by the HK94. Has special flash-hider for-end. Introduced 1989. Imported from West Germany by Heckler & Koch, Inc.
Price: $1,193.00

HECKLER & KOCH P7M8 AUTO PISTOL
Caliber: 9mm Para., 8-shot magazine.
Barrel: 4.13″.
Weight: 29 oz. **Length:** 6.73″ overall.
Stocks: Stippled black plastic.
Sights: Fixed, combat-type.
Features: Unique "squeeze cocker" in frontstrap cocks the action. Gas-retarded action. Squared combat-type trigger guard. Blue finish. Compact size. Imported from West Germany by Heckler & Koch, Inc.
Price: P7M8 . . . . $908.00
Price: P7M13 (13-shot capacity, matte black finish, ambidextrous magazine release, forged steel frame) $1,132.00

Heckler & Koch P7K3 Auto Pistol
Similar to the P7M8 and P7M13 except chambered for 22 LR or 380 ACP, 8-shot magazine. Uses an oil-filled buffer to decrease recoil. Introduced 1988.
Price: $908.00
Price: 22LR conversion unit $474.00

HELWAN "BRIGADIER" AUTO PISTOL
Caliber: 9mm Para., 8-shot magazine.
Barrel: 4.5″.
Weight: 32 oz. **Length:** 8″ overall.
Stocks: Grooved plastic.
Sights: Blade front, rear adjustable for windage.
Features: Polished blue finish. Single-action design. Cross-bolt safety. Imported by Interarms.
Price: $275.00

IAI AUTOMAG III PISTOL
Caliber: 30 Carbine, 9mm Win. Mag., 8-shot magazine.
Barrel: 6⅜″.
Weight: 43 oz. **Length:** 10½″ overall.
Stocks: Carbon fiber.
Sights: Blade front, Millett adjustable rear.
Features: Stainless steel construction. Hammer-drop safety. Slide flats have brushed finish, rest is sandblasted. Introduced 1989. From Irwindale Arms, Inc.
Price: $674.00

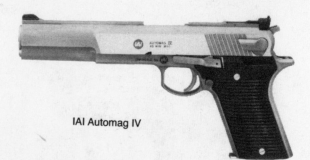

IAI Automag IV

IAI JAVELINA 10MM PISTOL
Caliber: 10mm Auto, 8-shot magazine.
Barrel: 5″ or 7″.
Weight: 40 oz. **Length:** 10½″ overall (7″ barrel).
Stock: Wraparound rubber.
Sights: Blade front, Millett adjustable rear.
Features: All stainless construction. Brushed finish. Introduced 1989. From Irwindale Arms, Inc.
Price: About $600.00

IAI AUTOMAG IV PISTOL
Caliber: 45 Winchester Magnum, 7-shot magazine.
Barrel: 6.5″.
Weight: 46 oz. **Length:** 10.5″ overall.
Stocks: Carbon fiber.
Sights: Blade front, Millett adjustable rear.
Features: Made of stainless steel with brushed finish. Introduced 1990. Made in U.S. by Irwindale Arms, Inc.
Price: $695.00

CAUTION: PRICES CHANGE, CHECK AT GUNSHOP.

INTRATEC TEC-9 AUTO PISTOL

Caliber: 9mm Para., 32-shot magazine.
Barrel: 5".
Weight: 50 oz. **Length:** 12½" overall.
Stock: Moulded composition.
Sights: Fixed.
Features: Semi-auto, fires from closed bolt; firing pin block safety; matte blue finish. Comes with 1" black nylon sling. From Intratec.
Price: **$266.95**
Price: TEC-9S (as above, except stainless) **$328.95**

Intratec TEC-9M Pistol

Similar to the TEC-9 except smaller. Has 3" barrel, weighs 44 oz.; 20-shot magazine.
Price: **$244.95**
Price: TEC-9MS (as above, stainless) **$306.95**

INTRATEC TEC-22T AUTO PISTOL

Caliber: 22 LR, 30-shot magazine.
Barrel: 4".
Weight: 30 oz. **Length:** 11³⁄₁₆" overall.
Stocks: Moulded composition.
Sights: Protected post front, rear adjustable for windage and elevation.
Features: Ambidextrous cocking knobs and safety. Matte black finish. Accepts any 10/22-type magazine. Introduced 1988. Made in U.S. by Intratec.
Price: **$217.95**
Price: TEC-22TN (as above, nickel finish) **$241.95**
Price: TEC-22 (as above, non-threaded bbl.) **$201.95**

ISRAELI KAREEN AUTO PISTOL

Caliber: 9mm Para., 13-shot magazine.
Barrel: 4¾".
Weight: 32 oz. **Length:** 8" overall.
Stocks: Checkered walnut.
Sights: Blade front, rear adjustable for windage.
Features: Blued steel frame. Introduced 1990. Imported from Israel by Century International Arms, Inc.
Price: About **$425.00**

Intratec TEC-9

Intratec TEC-22T

Israeli Kareen

JENNINGS J-22, J-25 AUTO PISTOLS

Caliber: 22 LR, 25 ACP, 6-shot magazine.
Barrel: 2½".
Weight: 13 oz. (J-22). **Length:** 4¹⁵⁄₁₆" overall (J-22).
Stocks: Walnut on chrome or nickel models; grooved black Cycolac or resin-impregnated wood on Teflon model.
Sights: Fixed.
Features: Choice of bright chrome, satin nickel or black Teflon finish. Introduced 1981. From Jennings Firearms.
Price: J-22, about **$75.00**
Price: J-25, about **$89.95**

Jennings J-25

JERICHO 941 MULTI-CALIBER PISTOL

Caliber: 9mm, 16-shot; 41 A.E., 11-shot magazine.
Barrel: 4⅜".
Weight: 33 oz. **Length:** 8⅛" overall.
Stocks: High impact black polymer.
Sights: Blade front, rear adjustable for windage; three tritium dots.
Features: Double action; all steel construction; polygonal rifling; ambidextrous safety. Comes with one box each of 9mm and 41 A.E. ammunition, RIG cleaning kit, four magazines, conversion unit, carrying case. Introduced 1990. Produced in Israel by Israel Military Industries; distributed by K.B.I., Inc.
Price: **$849.00**

Jericho Model 941

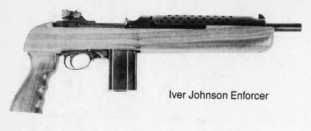

Iver Johnson Enforcer

Iver Johnson TP22

L.A.R. Grizzly Win Mag

IVER JOHNSON ENFORCER MODEL 3000 AUTO
Caliber: 30 M-1 Carbine, 15- or 30-shot magazine.
Barrel: 10½".
Weight: 4 lbs. **Length:** 18½" overall.
Stocks: American walnut with metal handguard.
Sights: Gold bead ramp front. Peep rear.
Features: Accepts 15- or 30-shot magazines. From Iver Johnson.
Price: Blue finish $374.95

IVER JOHNSON TP22, TP25 AUTO PISTOLS
Caliber: 22 LR, 25 ACP, 7-shot magazine.
Barrel: 2.85".
Weight: 14½ oz. **Length:** 5.39" overall.
Stocks: Black checkered plastic.
Sights: Fixed.
Features: Double action; 7-shot magazine. Introduced 1981. Made in U.S. From Iver Johnson.
Price: Either caliber, blue $165.00

L.A.R. GRIZZLY WIN MAG MK I PISTOL
Caliber: 357 Mag., 357/45, 10mm, 45 Win. Mag., 45 ACP, 7-shot magazine.
Barrel: 5.4", 6.5".
Weight: 51 oz. **Length:** 10½" overall.
Stocks: Checkered rubber, non-slip combat-type.
Sights: Ramped blade front, fully adjustable rear.
Features: Uses basic Browning/Colt 1911A1 design; interchangeable calibers; beveled magazine well; combat-type flat, checkered rubber mainspring housing; lowered and back-chamfered ejection port; polished feed ramp; throated barrel; solid barrel bushings. Available in satin hard chrome, matte blue, Parkerized finishes. Introduced 1983. From L.A.R. Mfg., Inc.
Price: 45 Win. Mag. $775.00
Price: 357 Mag. $800.00
Price: Conversion units (357 Mag.) $198.50
Price: As above, 45 ACP, 10mm, 45 Win. Mag., 357/45 Win. Mag. . . . $183.00

L.A.R. Grizzly Win Mag 8" & 10"
Similar to the standard Grizzly Win Mag except has lengthened slide and either 8" or 10" barrel. Available in 45 Win. Mag., 45 ACP, 357/45 Grizzly Win. Mag., 10mm or 357 Magnum. Introduced 1987.
Price: 8", 45 ACP, 45 Win. Mag., 357/45 Grizzly Win. Mag. $1,250.00
Price: As above, 10" $1,313.00
Price: 8", 357 Magnum $1,275.00
Price: As above, 10" $1,337.00

LLAMA LARGE FRAME AUTO PISTOL
Caliber: 38 Super, 45 ACP.
Barrel: 5".
Weight: 40 oz. **Length:** 8½" overall.
Stocks: Checkered walnut.
Sights: Fixed.
Features: Grip and manual safeties, ventilated rib. Imported from Spain by Stoeger Industries.
Price: Blue $385.00
Price: Satin chrome, 45 ACP only $499.00

LLAMA COMPACT FRAME AUTO PISTOL
Caliber: 9mm Para., 9-shot, 45 ACP, 7-shot.
Barrel: 4⁵⁄₁₆".
Weight: 37 oz.
Stocks: Smooth walnut.
Sights: Blade front, rear adjustable for windage.
Features: Scaled-down version of the Large Frame gun. Locked breech mechanism; manual and grip safeties. Introduced 1985. Imported from Spain by Stoeger Industries.
Price: Blue only. $385.00

LLAMA M-82 DA AUTO PISTOL
Caliber: 9mm Para., 15-shot magazine.
Barrel: 4¼".
Weight: 39 oz. **Length:** 8" overall.
Stocks: Matte black polymer.
Sights: Blade front, rear drift adjustable for windage. High visibility three-dot system.
Features: Double-action mechanism; ambidextrous safety. Introduced 1987. Imported from Spain by Stoeger Industries.
Price: $975.00

Llama Compact Frame

Llama M-82

CAUTION: PRICES CHANGE, CHECK AT GUNSHOP.

Llama Small Frame Auto

LORCIN AUTO PISTOL
Caliber: 25 ACP, 7-shot magazine.
Barrel: 2¼".
Weight: 13.5 oz. **Length:** 4.75" overall.
Stocks: Smooth composition.
Sights: Fixed.
Features: Available in choice of finishes: black and gold, chrome and satin chrome or black. Introduced 1989. From Lorcin Engineering.
Price: **$79.95**

NEW DETONICS "SERVICEMASTER" DUTY PISTOL
Caliber: 45 ACP, 7-shot magazine.
Barrel: 4½", recessed crown.
Weight: 32 oz. **Length:** 7⅞" overall.
Stocks: Checkered walnut with rubber mainspring housing.
Sights: Ramp front, adjustable rear.
Features: All stainless steel construction; patented self-centering cone barrel system; lengthened and lowered ejection port; beveled magazine well; patented, cushioned, counter-wound dual spring recoil system; hand-fit tolerances; redesigned thumb safety; matte black stainless slide with dual serrations; extended beavertail grip safety; improved magazine release; skeletonized trigger and hammer. Comes with gun rug and two spare magazines. Introduced 1990. From New Detonics Mfg. Corp.
Price: **$998.00**

New Detonics "Combat Master" Concealable Duty Pistol
Similar to the "Servicemaster" except has 6-shot magazine, 3½" barrel, weighs 28 oz., and measures 4½" overall. Checkered walnut grips with rubber mainspring housing. Ramp front sight, fixed combat rear. Other features same as "Servicemaster." Introduced 1990. From New Detonics Mfg. Corp.
Price: **$768.00**

New Detonics "Ladies' Escort" Auto Pistol
Same as the "Combat Master" except has reduced grip frame size, shortened trigger reach and space-age color polymer finishes. Introduced 1990. From New Detonics Mfg. Corp.
Price: "Royal Escort" (iridescent purple slide, blackened stainless frame and gold-plated hammer and trigger) **$968.00**
Price: "Jade Escort" (jade-colored slide, satin stainless frame) **$918.00**
Price: "Midnight Escort" (black slide, satin stainless frame) **$868.00**

Norinco Type 54-1

LLAMA SMALL FRAME AUTO PISTOLS
Caliber: 22 LR, 32, 380.
Barrel: 3¹¹⁄₁₆".
Weight: 23 oz. **Length:** 6½" overall.
Stocks: Checkered plastic, thumbrest.
Sights: Fixed front, adjustable notch rear.
Features: Ventilated rib, manual and grip safeties. Imported from Spain by Stoeger Industries.
Price: Blue **$325.00**
Price: Satin chrome, 22 LR or 380 .... **$399.00**

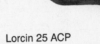

Lorcin 25 ACP

New Detonics Servicemaster

New Detonics Ladies Escort

NORINCO TYPE 54-1 TOKAREV PISTOL
Caliber: 7.62x25mm, 38 Super, 8-shot magazine.
Barrel: 4.5".
Weight: 29 oz. **Length:** 7.7" overall.
Stocks: Grooved black plastic.
Sights: Fixed.
Features: Matte blue finish. Imported from China by China Sports, Inc.
Price: .... **NA**

NORINCO M1911 AUTO PISTOL
Caliber: 45 ACP, 7-shot magazine.
Barrel: 5".
Weight: 39 oz. **Length:** 8.5" overall.
Stocks: Checkered wood.
Sights: Blade front, rear adjustable for windage.
Features: Matte blue finish. Comes with two magazines. Imported from China by China Sports, Inc.
Price: .... **NA**

NORINCO TYPE 59 MAKAROV DA PISTOL
Caliber: 9x18, 8-shot magazine.
Barrel: 3.5".
Weight: 21 oz. **Length:** 6.3" overall.
Stocks: Checkered plastic.
Sights: Blade front, adjustable rear.
Features: Blue finish. Double action. Introduced 1990. Imported from China by China Sports, Inc.
Price: .... **NA**

NORINCO TYPE 77B AUTO PISTOL
Caliber: 9mm Para., 8-shot magazine.
Barrel: 5".
Weight: 34 oz. **Length:** 7.5" overall.
Stocks: Checkered wood.
Sights: Blade front, adjustable rear.
Features: Uses trigger guard cocking, gas-retarded recoil action. Front of trigger guard can be used to cock the action with the trigger finger. Introduced 1989. Imported from China by China Sports, Inc.
Price: .... **NA**

Norinco Type 59

OMEGA AUTO PISTOL
Caliber: 38 Super (9-shot), 10mm (8-shot), 45 ACP (7-shot).
Barrel: 5", 6".
Weight: 42.8 oz. (5" barrel).
Stocks: Wraparound checkered rubber.
Sights: Blade front, fully adjustable rear.
Features: Convertible between calibers; ported barrels. Based on 1911A1 but with improved barrel lock-up. Introduced 1987. From Springfield Armory.
Price: Single caliber, 38 Super, 10mm or 45 ACP **$849.00**

PSP-25 AUTO PISTOL
Caliber: 25 ACP, 6-shot magazine.
Barrel: 2⅛".
Weight: 9.5 oz. **Length:** 4⅛" overall.
Stocks: Checkered black plastic.
Sights: Fixed.
Features: All steel construction with polished finish. Introduced 1990. Made in the U.S. under F.N. license; distributed by K.B.I., Inc.
Price: Blue **$249.00**
Price: Hard chrome **$329.99**

Omega Auto

PARA-ORDNANCE P14.45 AUTO PISTOL
Caliber: 45 ACP, 13-shot magazine.
Barrel: 5".
Weight: 28 oz. (alloy frame). **Length:** 8.5" overall.
Stocks: Textured composition.
Sights: Blade front, rear adjustable for windage. High visibility three-dot system.
Features: Available with alloy, steel or stainless steel frame with black finish (silver or stainless gun). Steel and stainless steel frame guns weigh 38 oz. (P14.45), 35 oz. (P13.45), 33 oz. (P12.45). Grooved match trigger, rounded combat-style hammer. Double column, high-capacity magazine gives 14-shot total capacity (P14.45). Beveled magazine well. Manual thumb, grip and firing pin lock safeties. Solid barrel bushing. Introduced 1990. Made in Canada by Para-Ordnance.
Price: P14.45 .... **$716.25**
Price: P13.45 (12-shot magazine, 4¼" bbl., 25 oz., alloy) **$716.25**
Price: P12.45 (11-shot magazine, 3½" bbl., 24 oz., alloy) **$716.25**
Price: Steel frame pistols, as above **$708.75**

K.B.I. PSP-25

Para-Ordnance P14.45

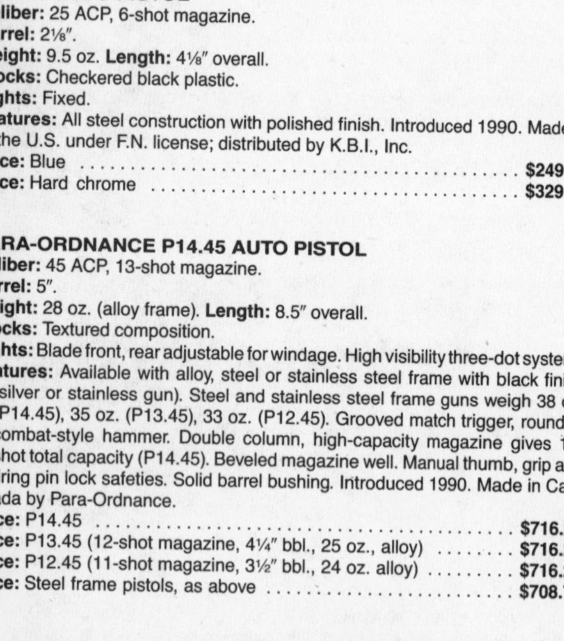

Partisan Avenger

PARTISAN AVENGER AUTO PISTOL
Caliber: 45 ACP, 30-shot magazine.
Barrel: 6¼".
Weight: 5 lbs., 7 oz. **Length:** 11" overall.
Stocks: Smooth composition.
Sights: Protected blade front, fixed rear.
Features: All steel construction; cam-activated striker; chamber loaded indicator. Easy takedown. Semi-auto only. Fires from a closed bolt. Uses standard M-3 "Grease Gun" magazine. Introduced 1988. Made in U.S. From Patriot Dist. Co.
Price: **$445.00**

CAUTION: PRICES CHANGE, CHECK AT GUNSHOP.

Ram-Line Syn-Tech

RAM-LINE SYN-TECH AUTO PISTOL
Caliber: 22 LR, 15-shot magazine.
Barrel: 5.5".
Weight: 21 oz. **Length:** 9.75" overall.
Stocks: One-piece impact resistant polymer.
Sights: Moulded ramp front with .150" blade, fixed rear.
Features: Injection moulded grip frame, alloy receiver, hybrid composite barrel. Constant force sear spring for smooth trigger pull. Thumb safety isolates the sear and bolt. Semi-transparent magazine. Introduced 1990. Made in U.S. by Ram-Line, Inc.
Price: $199.97

RANGER 1911A1 45 AUTO PISTOL
Caliber: 45 ACP, 7-shot magazine.
Barrel: 5".
Weight: 38 oz. **Length:** 8½" overall.
Stocks: Checkered walnut.
Sights: Millett MK.I front and rear.
Features: Made in U.S. from 4140 steel and other high-strength alloys. Barrel machined from a forged billet. Introduced 1988. From Federal Ordnance, Inc.
Price: Standard model $439.95
Price: With extended slide release and safety $449.95
Price: With ambidextrous slide release and safety $459.95

Raven MP-25

RAVEN MP-25 AUTO PISTOL
Caliber: 25 ACP, 6-shot magazine.
Barrel: 2⁷⁄₁₆".
Weight: 15 oz. **Length:** 4¾" overall.
Stocks: Smooth walnut, ivory-colored or black slotted plastic.
Sights: Ramped front, fixed rear.
Features: Available in blue, nickel or chrome finish. Made in U.S. Available from Raven Arms.
Price: $69.95

Ruger P85

RUGER P85 AUTOMATIC PISTOL
Caliber: 9mm Para., 15-shot magazine.
Barrel: 4.50".
Weight: 32 oz. **Length:** 7.84" overall.
Stocks: Grooved "Xenoy" composition.
Sights: Square post front, square notch rear adjustable for windage, both with white dot inserts.
Features: Double action with ambidextrous slide-mounted safety which blocks firing pin and disengages firing mechanism. Slide is 4140 chromemoly steel, frame is a lightweight aluminum alloy, both finished matte black. Ambidextrous magazine release. Blue or stainless steel. Introduced 1986; stainless introduced 1990.
Price: P85, blue $357.50
Price: P85DA (as above, double action only) $357.50
Price: P85C, blue, with extra magazine, plastic case $390.50
Price: P85DAC (as above, double action only) $390.50
Price: K-P85 (stainless steel) $397.50
Price: K-P85C (as above with extra magazine, plastic case) $430.50
Price: K-P85DAC (as above, double action only) $430.50

Ruger P85D Decocker Automatic Pistol
Similar to the standard P85 except has a decocking lever in place of the regular slide-mounted safety. The decocking lever blocks the hammer from the firing pin while simultaneously blocking the firing pin from forward movement—allows shooter to decock a cocked pistol without manipulating the trigger. Conventional thumb decocking procedures are therefore unnecessary. Blue or stainless steel. Introduced 1990.
Price: P85D $357.50
Price: P85DC (as above with extra magazine, case) $390.50
Price: K-P85D (stainless steel) $397.50
Price: K-P85DC (as above with extra magazine, case) $430.50

Ruger P85D Decocker

CAUTION: PRICES CHANGE, CHECK AT GUNSHOP.

Ruger Mark II Stainless

Safari Arms Matchmaster

SEECAMP LWS 32 STAINLESS DA AUTO
Caliber: 32 ACP Win. Silvertip, 6-shot.
Barrel: 2", Integral with frame.
Weight: 10.5 oz. **Length:** 4⅛" overall.
Stocks: Black plastic.
Sights: Smooth, no-snag, contoured slide and barrel top.
Features: Aircraft quality 17-4 PH stainless steel. Inertia-operated firing pin. Hammer fired double action only. Hammer automatically follows slide down to safety rest position after each shot—no manual safety needed. Magazine safety disconnector. Polished stainless. Introduced 1985. From L.W. Seecamp.
Price: $350.00

SIG P-210-2 AUTO PISTOL
Caliber: 7.65mm or 9mm Para., 8-shot magazine.
Barrel: 4¾".
Weight: 31¾ oz. (9mm). **Length:** 8½" overall.
Stocks: Checkered black composition.
Sights: Blade front, rear adjustable for windage.
Features: Lanyard loop; matte finish. Conversion unit for 22 LR available. Imported from Switzerland by Mandall Shooting Supplies.
Price: P-210-2 Service Pistol $1,895.00

> Consult our Directory pages for the location of firms mentioned.

SIG P-210-6 AUTO PISTOL
Caliber: 9mm Para., 8-shot magazine.
Barrel: 4¾".
Weight: 36.2 oz. **Length:** 8½" overall.
Stocks: Checkered black plastic; walnut optional.
Sights: Blade front, micro. adjustable rear for w. and e.
Features: Adjustable trigger stop; target trigger; ribbed frontstrap; sandblasted finish. Conversion unit for 22 LR consists of barrel, recoil spring, slide and magazine. Imported from Switzerland by Mandall Shooting Supplies.
Price: P-210-6 . . . . $1,900.00
Price: P-210-5 Target $1,900.00

RUGER MARK II STANDARD AUTO PISTOL
Caliber: 22 LR, 10-shot magazine.
Barrel: 4¾" or 6".
Weight: 36 oz. (4¾" bbl.). **Length:** 8⁵⁄₁₆" (4¾" bbl.).
Stocks: Checkered hard rubber.
Sights: Fixed, wide blade front, square notch rear adjustable for w.
Features: Updated design of the original Standard Auto. Has new bolt hold-open device. 10-shot magazine, magazine catch, safety, trigger and new receiver contours. Introduced 1982.
Price: Blued (MK 4, MK 6) $224.75
Price: In stainless steel (KMK 4, KMK 6) $299.25

SAFARI ARMS MATCHMASTER PISTOL
Caliber: 45 ACP, 7-shot magazine.
Barrel: 5".
Weight: 44 oz. **Length:** 8.7" overall.
Stocks: Walnut.
Sights: Combat adjustable.
Features: Beavertail grip safety, ambidextrous extended safety, extended slide release, Commander-style hammer, threaded barrel bushing; throated, ported, tuned. Finishes: Parkerized, matte black, or stainless steel. Available from Olympic/Safari Arms, Inc.
Price: $702.00

Safari Arms Enforcer Pistol
Shortened version of the Matchmaster. Has 3.8" barrel, 6-shot magazine, overall length of 7.7", and weighs 36 oz. (standard weight), 27 oz. in lightweight version. Other features are the same. From Olympic/Safari Arms, Inc.
Price: $684.00

SEDCO SP-22 AUTO PISTOL
Caliber: 22 LR.
Barrel: 2½".
Weight: 11 oz. **Length:** 5" overall.
Stocks: Simulated pearl, white or gray.
Sights: Fixed.
Features: Available in polished chrome, satin nickel or black Teflon finish. Rotary safety blocks sear and slide. Made in U.S. by Sedco Industries.
Price: $68.50

Seecamp LWS 32

SIG P-210-6

CAUTION: PRICES CHANGE, CHECK AT GUNSHOP.

SIG SAUER P220 "AMERICAN" AUTO PISTOL
Caliber: 9mm, 38 Super, 45 ACP (9-shot in 9mm and 38 Super, 7 in 45).
Barrel: 4⅜".
Weight: 28¼ oz. (9mm). **Length:** 7¾" overall.
Stocks: Checkered black plastic.
Sights: Blade front, drift adjustable rear for w.
Features: Double action. De-cocking lever permits lowering hammer onto locked firing pin. Squared combat-type trigger guard. Slide stays open after last shot. Imported from West Germany by SIGARMS, Inc.
Price: "American" (side-button magazine release, 45 ACP only) ... **$720.00**
Price: "European" **$695.00**
Price: "American," 45 ACP, Siglite night sights **$820.00**

SIG-Sauer P220 American

SIG SAUER P225 DA AUTO PISTOL
Caliber: 9mm Para., 8-shot magazine.
Barrel: 3.8".
Weight: 26 oz. **Length:** 7³⁄₃₂" overall.
Stocks: Checkered black plastic.
Sights: Blade front, rear adjustable for windage. Optional Siglite night sights.
Features: Double action. De-cocking lever permits lowering hammer onto locked firing pin. Square combat-type trigger guard. Shortened, lightened version of P-220. Imported from West Germany by SIGARMS, Inc.
Price: **$750.00**
Price: With Siglite night sights **$850.00**

SIG Sauer P226 DA Auto Pistol
Similar to the P-220 pistol except has 15-shot magazine, 4.4" barrel, and weighs 26½ oz. 9mm only. Imported from West Germany by SIGARMS, Inc.
Price: Blue **$780.00**
Price: With Siglite night sights **$880.00**

SIG Sauer P228 DA Auto Pistol
Similar to the P226 except has 3.86" barrel, with 7.08" overall length and 5.35" height. Chambered for 9mm Para. only, 13-shot magazine. Weight is 29.1 oz. with empty magazine. Introduced 1989. Imported from West Germany by SIGARMS, Inc.
Price: Blue **$780.00**
Price: Blue, with Siglite night sights **$880.00**

SIG-Sauer P228

SIG SAUER P230 DA AUTO PISTOL
Caliber: 32 ACP, 8-shot; 380 ACP, 7-shot.
Barrel: 3¾".
Weight: 16 oz. **Length:** 6½" overall.
Stocks: Checkered black plastic.
Sights: Blade front, rear adjustable for w.
Features: Double action. Same basic action design as P-220. Blowback operation, stationary barrel. Introduced 1977. Imported from West Germany by SIGARMS, Inc.
Price: Blue **$495.00**
Price: In stainless steel (P-230 SL) **$575.00**

SIG-Sauer P230

SKORPION AUTO PISTOL
Caliber: 9mm Para., 12 and 32-shot magazine.
Barrel: 4.63".
Weight: 3.5 lbs. **Length:** 12.25" overall.
Stocks: Stained polymer. Oak grip available.
Sights: Fixed, open.
Features: Semi-auto fire only. Comes with one 12-round magazine, magazine loading tool, cleaning tool. Top port ejection, machined receiver and bolt, ambidextrous side cocking knobs. Accessories available. Made in U.S. Introduced 1988. From Armitage International, Ltd.
Price: **$399.50**

Skorpion Pistol

SMITH & WESSON MODEL 422 AUTO
Caliber: 22 LR, 10-shot magazine.
Barrel: 4½", 6".
Weight: 22 oz. (4½" bbl.). **Length:** 7½" overall (4½" bbl.).
Stocks: Checkered plastic (Field), checkered walnut (Target).
Sights: Field—serrated ramp front, fixed rear; Target—Patridge front, adjustable rear.
Features: Aluminum frame, steel slide, brushed blue finish; internal hammer. Introduced 1987. Model 2206 introduced 1990.
Price: 4½", 6", fixed sight **$206.00**
Price: Model 622 (stainless) **$266.00**
Price: As above, adjustable sight **$257.00**
Price: As above, stainless (Model 622) **$316.00**

CAUTION: PRICES CHANGE, CHECK AT GUNSHOP.

Smith & Wesson Model 2206 Auto
Similar to the Model 422/622 except made entirely of stainless steel with non-reflective finish. Weight is 35 oz. with 4½" barrel, 39 oz. with 7½" barrel. Other specs are the same. Introduced 1990.
Price: With fixed sight $299.00
Price: With adjustable sight $355.00

Smith & Wesson 3904

SMITH & WESSON MODEL 3904/3906 DOUBLE ACTIONS
Caliber: 9mm Para., 8-shot magazine.
Barrel: 4".
Weight: 28 oz. **Length:** 7.5" overall.
Stocks: Delrin one-piece wraparound, arched backstrap, textured surface.
Sights: Post front with white dot, fixed or fully adjustable rear with two white dots.
Features: Smooth .365" trigger, .260" serrated hammer. Introduced 1989.
Price: Model 3904, blue, fixed sight $520.00
Price: As above, adjustable sight $545.00
Price: Model 3906, stainless, fixed sight $570.00
Price: As above, adjustable sight $596.00

Smith & Wesson 5904/5906 Double-Action Autos
Same as the Models 3904 and 5904 except with 14-shot magazine (20-shot available), and available with straight backstrap. Introduced 1989.
Price: Model 5904, blue, fixed sight $570.00
Price: As above, adjustable sight $596.00
Price: Model 5906, stainless, fixed sight $621.00
Price: As above, adjustable sight $651.00

Smith & Wesson 3913

SMITH & WESSON 3913/3914 DOUBLE ACTIONS
Caliber: 9mm Para., 8-shot magazine.
Barrel: 3½".
Weight: 26 oz. **Length:** 6¹³⁄₁₆" overall.
Stocks: One-piece Delrin wraparound, textured surface.
Sights: Post front with white dot, Novak LoMount Carry with two dots, adjustable for windage.
Features: Aluminum alloy frame, stainless slide (M3913) or blue steel slide (M3914). Bobbed hammer with no half-cock notch; smooth .304" trigger with rounded edges. Straight backstrap. Introduced 1989.
Price: Model 3913 . . . . $541.00
Price: Model 3914 . . . . $493.00

Smith & Wesson Model 3913/3914 LadySmith Autos
Similar to the standard Model 3913/3914 except has frame that is upswept at the front, rounded trigger guard. Comes in either deep blue matte finish with black grips or frosted stainless steel with matching gray grips. Both grips are ergonomically correct for a woman's hand. Both have Novak LoMount Carry rear sight adjustable for windage, smooth edges for snag resistance. Introduced 1990.
Price: Model 3913-LS, stainless $541.00
Price: Model 3914-LS, blue $493.00

Smith & Wesson 3913LS

SMITH & WESSON MODEL 4006 DA AUTO
Caliber: 40 S&W, 11-shot magazine.
Barrel: 4".
Weight: 36 oz. **Length:** 7½" overall.
Stocks: Delrin wraparound with checkered panels.
Sights: Replaceable post front with white dot, Novak LoMount Carry fixed rear with two white dots, or micro. click adjustable rear with two white dots.
Features: Stainless steel construction with non-reflective finish. Straight backstrap. Introduced 1990.
Price: With adjustable sights $701.00
Price: With fixed sight $674.00

SMITH & WESSON MODEL 4506/4516 AUTOS
Caliber: 45 ACP, 7-shot magazine (M4516), 8-shot magazine (M4506).
Barrel: 3¾" (M4516), 5" (M4506).
Weight: 34½ oz. (4516). **Length:** 7⅛" overall (4516).
Stocks: Delrin one-piece wraparound, arched or straight backstrap on M4506, straight only on M4516.
Sights: Post front with white dot, adjustable or fixed Novak LoMount Carry on M4506, fixed Novak LoMount Carry only on M4516.
Features: M4506 has serrated hammer spur; M4516 has bobbed hammer. Both guns in stainless only. Introduced 1989.
Price: Model 4506, fixed sight $674.00
Price: Model 4506, adjustable sight $701.00
Price: Model 4516 . . . . $674.00

Smith & Wesson 4006

CAUTION: PRICES CHANGE, CHECK AT GUNSHOP.

Smith & Wesson Model 1006 Double-Action Auto

Similar to the Model 4506 except chambered for 10mm auto with 9-shot magazine. Available with either Novak LoMount Carry fixed rear sight with two white dots or adjustable micrometer-click rear with two white dots. All stainless steel construction; one-piece Delrin stocks with straight backstrap; curved backstrap available as option. Has 5" barrel, 8½" overall length, weighs 38 oz. with fixed sight. Rounded trigger guard with knurling. Introduced 1990.
Price: With fixed sight $695.00
Price: With adjustable sight $747.00

Smith & Wesson 6904/6906 Double-Action Autos

Similar to the Models 5904/5906 except with 3½" barrel, 12-shot magazine (20-shot available), fixed rear sight, .260" bobbed hammer. Introduced 1989.
Price: Model 6904, blue $539.00
Price: Model 6906, stainless $589.00

SPORTARMS TOKAREV MODEL 213

Caliber: 9mm Para., 8-shot magazine.
Barrel: 4.5".
Weight: 31 oz. **Length:** 7.6" overall.
Stocks: Grooved plastic.
Sights: Fixed.
Features: Blue finish, hard chrome optional. 9mm version of the famous Russian Tokarev pistol. Made in China by Norinco. Imported by Sportarms of Florida. Introduced 1988.
Price: Blue, about $196.95
Price: Hard chrome, about $226.95

SPRINGFIELD ARMORY P9 DA PISTOL

Caliber: 9mm Para., 15-shot magazine.
Barrel: 4.72".
Weight: 35.3 oz. **Length:** 8.1" overall.
Stocks: Checkered walnut.
Sights: Blade front, open rear drift-adjustable for windage; three-dot system.
Features: Patterned after the CZ-75. Frame-mounted thumb safety. Magazine catch can be switched to opposite side. Commander hammer. Introduced 1989.
Price: Parkerized $467.00
Price: Blued $493.00
Price: Duotone $545.00

Springfield Armory P9 Compact Pistol

Similar to the standard P9 except has 3.66" barrel, 7.24" overall length, and weighs 32.1 oz. Has 13-shot magazine. Introduced 1989.
Price: Parkerized $485.00
Price: Blued $511.00
Price: Duotone $563.00

Springfield Armory P9 LSP Long Slide Pistol

Same as the standard P9 except has 5.03" ported barrel, 8.38" overall length and weighs 38.4 oz. Rubber stocks. Introduced 1990.
Price: Parkerized $493.00
Price: Blued $519.00
Price: Duotone $571.00

Smith & Wesson 1006

Smith & Wesson 6906

Springfield P9

SPRINGFIELD ARMORY 1911A1 90s EDITION PISTOL

Caliber: 9mm Para., 38 Super, 10-shot magazine, 45 ACP, 8-shot.
Barrel: 5".
Weight: 36 oz. **Length:** 8½" overall.
Stocks: Checkered walnut.
Sights: Fixed low-profile combat-style.
Features: Beveled magazine well. All forged parts, including frame, barrel, slide. All new production. Custom slide parts available. Introduced 1990. From Springfield Armory.
Price: Parkerized $454.00
Price: Blued $487.00
Price: Duotone (blue slide, hard chrome frame) $532.00
Price: 45 to 9mm conversion unit, Parkerized $169.00
Price: As above, blued $177.00

Springfield Armory 1911A1 Commander

Similar to the standard 1911A1 except slide and barrel are ½" shorter. Has low-profile three-dot sight system. Comes with Commander hammer and walnut stocks. Available in 45 ACP only; choice of blue or Parkerized or Duotone finish. Introduced 1989.
Price: Blue $545.00
Price: Parkerized $514.00
Price: Duotone $592.00

Springfield Armory 1911A1

Springfield Compact

Springfield Commander

Springfield Armory 1911A1 Defender
Similar to the standard 1911A1 except has fixed combat-style sights, beveled magazine well, extended thumb safety, bobbed hammer, walnut stocks, serrated frontstrap, and comes with two stainless steel magazines. Available in 45 ACP only, choice of blue or Parkerized finish. Introduced 1988.
Price: Blue $601.00
Price: Parkerized $567.00

Springfield Armory 1911A1 Compact
Similar to the Commander model except has a shortened slide with 4.25" barrel, 7.25" overall length. Magazine capacity is 6 shots. Has low-profile three-dot sight system, checkered walnut grips. Available in 45 ACP only. Introduced 1989.
Price: Blued $545.00
Price: Parkerized $514.00
Price: Duotone $592.00

STALLARD JS-9MM AUTO PISTOL
Caliber: 9mm Para., 8-shot magazine.
Barrel: 4.5".
Weight: 48 oz. **Length:** 7.72" overall.
Stocks: Textured acetal plastic.
Sights: Fixed, low profile.
Features: Single-action design. Scratch-resistant, non-glare blue finish. Introduced 1990. From MKS Supply, Inc.
Price: $139.95

STAR FIRESTAR AUTO PISTOL
Caliber: 9mm Para., 7-shot.
Barrel: 3.39".
Weight: 30.35 oz. **Length:** 6.5" overall.
Stocks: Checkered rubber.
Sights: Blade front, fully adjustable rear; three-dot system.
Features: Low-profile, combat-style sights; ambidextrous safety. Available in blue or weather-resistant Starvel finish. Introduced 1990. Imported from Spain by Interarms.
Price: Blue $405.00
Price: Starvel finish $435.00

Star Firestar

STAR MODEL 30M & 31PK DOUBLE-ACTION PISTOLS
Caliber: 9mm Para., 15-shot magazine.
Barrel: 4.33" (Model M); 3.86" (Model PK).
Weight: 40 oz. (M); 30 oz. (PK). **Length:** 8" overall (M); 7.6" (PK).
Stocks: Checkered black plastic.
Sights: Square blade front, square notch rear click-adjustable for windage and elevation.
Features: Double or single action; grooved front- and backstraps and trigger guard face; ambidextrous safety cams firing pin forward; removable backstrap houses the firing mechanism. Model M has steel frame; Model PK is alloy. Introduced 1984. Imported from Spain by Interarms.
Price: Model M or PK $535.00

Star PD

Star Model 30 PK

STAR MODEL PD AUTO PISTOL
Caliber: 45 ACP, 6-shot magazine.
Barrel: 3.94".
Weight: 28 oz. **Length:** 7⁷⁄₁₆" overall.
Stocks: Checkered walnut.
Sights: Ramp front, fully adjustable rear.
Features: Rear sight milled into slide; thumb safety; grooved non-slip frontstrap; nylon recoil buffer; inertia firing pin; no grip or magazine safeties. Imported from Spain by Interarms.
Price: Blue $450.00
Price: Starvel $495.00

CAUTION: PRICES CHANGE, CHECK AT GUNSHOP.

Star Model BM

TANARMI TA90/TA41 DOUBLE-ACTION PISTOL
Caliber: 9mm Para. (16-shot); 41 AE (11-shot).
Barrel: 4.50″.
Weight: 38 oz. **Length:** 8.25″ overall.
Stocks: Black neoprene.
Sights: Notch rear adjustable for windage; three-dot system.
Features: Forged barrel and slide; hammer drop safety system; full-length sight rib; extended slide release. Available in matte blue or matte chrome. Imported from Italy by Excam.
Price: Matte blue, 9mm $449.99
Price: Matte chrome, 9mm $469.00
Price: Matte blue, 41 AE $509.00
Price: Matte chrome, 41 AE $520.00

Tanarmi TA90CH/TA41CH Double-Action Pistol
Same as the standard TA90/TA41 except comes with checkered walnut grips, and frame and slide are color case-hardened. Imported from Italy by Excam.
Price: Either caliber $559.00

TARGA MODELS GT22, GT32, GT380 AUTO PISTOLS
Caliber: 22 LR, 10-shot; 32 ACP or 380 ACP, 6-shot magazine.
Barrel: 4⅞″.
Weight: 26 oz. **Length:** 7⅜″ overall.
Stocks: Walnut.
Sights: Fixed blade front; rear drift-adjustable for w.
Features: Chrome or blue finish; magazine, thumb, and firing pin safeties; external hammer; safety-lever takedown. Imported from Italy by Excam, Inc.
Price: 22 cal., blue $200.00
Price: 22 cal., nickel $215.00
Price: 32 cal., blue $200.00
Price: 32 cal., chrome $215.00
Price: 380 cal., blue $212.00
Price: 380 cal., chrome $220.00

TARGA GT380XE PISTOL
Caliber: 380 ACP, 11-shot magazine.
Barrel: 3.88″.
Weight: 28 oz. **Length:** 7.38″ overall.
Stocks: Smooth hardwood.
Sights: Adjustable for windage.
Features: Blue finish. Ordnance steel. Magazine disconnector, firing pin and thumb safeties. Introduced 1980. Imported by Excam.
Price: 380 cal., blue $235.00

TARGA MODEL GT27 AUTO PISTOL
Caliber: 25 ACP, 6-shot magazine.
Barrel: 2⁷⁄₁₆″.
Weight: 12 oz. **Length:** 4⅝″ overall.
Stocks: Smooth walnut.
Sights: Fixed.
Features: Safety-lever takedown; external hammer with half-cock. Assembled in U.S. by Excam, Inc.
Price: Blue $56.00
Price: Chrome $69.00

STAR BM, BKM AUTO PISTOLS
Caliber: 9mm Para., 8-shot magazine.
Barrel: 3.9″.
Weight: 25 oz.
Stocks: Checkered walnut.
Sights: Fixed.
Features: Blue or chrome finish. Magazine and manual safeties, external hammer. Imported from Spain by Interarms.
Price: Blue, BM $375.00
Price: Blue, BKM only $395.00
Price: Starvel, BM only $425.00

SUNDANCE MODEL A-25 AUTO PISTOL
Caliber: 25 ACP, 7-shot magazine.
Barrel: 2″. **Length:** 4⅞″ overall.
Weight: 14 oz.
Stocks: Grooved black ABS or simulated smooth pearl.
Sights: Fixed.
Features: Rotary safety blocks sear. Bright chrome, satin nickel or black Teflon finish. Introduced 1989. From Sundance Ind.
Price: $65.00

Tanarmi "Baby" TA90 Compact DA Pistol
Similar to the TA90 except available only in 9mm Para. (13-shot), has 3.50″ barrel and overall length of 7″. Weighs 34 oz. No sight rib on slide. Imported from Italy by Excam.
Price: Matte blue $449.00
Price: Matte chrome $469.00

Tanarmi TA90SS/TA41SS Competition Model
Similar to the standard TA90/TA41 except has 5″ barrel with EDM porting, overall length of 8.50″, and weight of 40 oz. Adjustable rear sight. Frame-mounted cocked and locked safety system; hand-honed double-action trigger and serrated front and backstraps. Full-length sighting rib on slide. Matte chrome frame with matte blue slide. Imported from Italy by Excam.
Price: Either caliber $610.00

Targa GT380XE

Targa GT26

Targa GT26 Auto Pistol
Similar to the GT27 except has steel frame, push-button magazine release and magazine disconnect safety. Contoured smooth walnut grips. Satin blue finish. Imported from Italy by Excam; assembled in U.S.A.
Price: $115.00

TARGA GT22T TARGET AUTO
Caliber: 22LR, 12-shot.
Barrel: 6".
Weight: 30 oz. **Length:** 9" overall.
Stocks: Checkered walnut, with thumbrest.
Sights: Blade on ramp front, rear adjustable for windage.
Features: Blue finish. Finger-rest magazine. Imported by Excam.
Price: $200.00

TAURUS MODEL PT-92AF AUTO PISTOL
Caliber: 9mm Para., 15-shot magazine.
Barrel: 4.92".
Weight: 34 oz. **Length:** 8.54" overall.
Stocks: Brazilian walnut.
Sights: Fixed notch rear. Three-dot sight system.
Features: Double action, exposed hammer, chamber loaded indicator. Inertia firing pin. Imported by Taurus International.
Price: Blue $446.00
Price: Blue, Deluxe Shooter's Pak (extra magazine, case) $471.00
Price: Nickel $482.00
Price: Nickel, Deluxe Shooter's Pak (extra magazine, case) $507.00

Taurus/Laser Aim 9mm Pistol Package
Includes the Taurus Model PT-92AF pistol (blue or satin nickel finish) and the Taurus/Laser Aim LA1 laser sight with appropriate mount and rings in matching finish, the LA1C 110-volt charger and LA9C 9-volt field charger, and a sturdy high-impact case. Below-barrel mount allows the use of conventional sights or a scope. Introduced 1990.
Price: $668.00

TAURUS PT-99AF AUTO PISTOL
Similar to the PT-92 except has fully adjustable rear sight, smooth Brazilian walnut stocks and is available in polished blue or satin nickel. Introduced 1983.
Price: Blue $483.00
Price: Blue, Deluxe Shooter's Pak (extra magazine, case) $508.00
Price: Nickel $523.00
Price: Nickel, Deluxe Shooter's Pak (extra magazine, case) $548.00

> Consult our Directory pages for
> the location of firms mentioned.

TAURUS MODEL PT58 AUTO PISTOL
Caliber: 380 ACP, 13-shot magazine.
Barrel: 4.01".
Weight: 30 oz.
Stocks: Brazilian walnut.
Sights: Integral blade on slide front, notch rear. Three-dot system.
Features: Double action with exposed hammer; inertia firing pin. Introduced 1988. Imported by Taurus International.
Price: Blue $399.00
Price: Satin nickel $427.00

UZI® PISTOL
Caliber: 9mm Para.
Barrel: 4.5".
Weight: 3.8 lbs. **Length:** 9.5" overall.
Stocks: Black plastic.
Sights: Post front with white dot, open rear click-adjustable for windage and elevation, two white dots.
Features: Semi-auto blowback action; fires from closed bolt; floating firing pin. Comes in a moulded plastic case with 20-round magazine; 25- and 32-round magazines available. Imported from Israel by Action Arms. Introduced 1984.
Price: $750.00

Taurus Model PT-91AF Auto Pistol
Same as the Model PT-92AF except chambered for the 41 Action Express with 12-shot magazine. Introduced 1990. Imported by Taurus International.
Price: Blue $446.00
Price: Blue, Deluxe Shooter's Pak (extra magazine, case) $471.00
Price: Nickel $482.00
Price: Nickel, Deluxe Shooter's Pak (extra magazine, case) $507.00

Taurus PT99AF

Taurus PT58

UZI Pistol

VICTORY MC5 AUTO PISTOL
Caliber: 9mm Para., 38 Super (17-shot magazine); 41 Action Express (12-shot); 45 ACP (10-shot).
Barrel: 4⅜", 5⅞", 7½", interchangeable.
Weight: 45 oz. **Length:** 8½" overall (4⅜" barrel).
Stocks: High-impact plastic.
Sights: Patridge three-dot system; ramped non-snag front, rear adjustable for windage with different heights available.
Features: Double-action auto; chamber loaded indicator; exposed hammer; ambidextrous safety, magazine catch, slide release; open-top slide. Introduced 1988. Imported from England by Magnum Research, Inc.
Price: MC5 . . . . $499.00
Price: Extra barrels $100.00
Price: Extra magazines $25.00

CAUTION: PRICES CHANGE, CHECK AT GUNSHOP.

WALTHER PP AUTO PISTOL
Caliber: 32 ACP, 380 ACP, 7-shot.
Barrel: 3.86".
Weight: 23½ oz. **Length:** 6.7" overall.
Stocks: Checkered plastic.
Sights: Fixed, white markings.
Features: Double action; manual safety blocks firing pin and drops hammer; chamber loaded indicator on 32 and 380; extra finger rest magazine provided. Imported from Germany by Interarms.
Price: 32 . . . . $850.00
Price: 380 . . . . $875.00
Price: Engraved models . . . .**On Request**

Walther PPK/S American

Walther American PPK/S Auto Pistol
Similar to Walther PP except made entirely in the United States. Has 3.27" barrel with 6.1" length overall. Introduced 1980.
Price: 380 ACP only $549.00
Price: As above, stainless $549.00

Walther American PPK Auto Pistol
Similar to Walther PPK/S except weighs 21 oz., has 6-shot capacity. Made in the U.S. Introduced 1986.
Price: Stainless, 380 ACP only $549.00
Price: Blue, 380 ACP only $549.00

Walther P-38 Auto Pistol

WALTHER P-38 AUTO PISTOL
Caliber: 9mm Para., 8-shot.
Barrel: 4¹⁵⁄₁₆" (9mm); 5¹⁄₁₆" (22 LR).
Weight: 28 oz. **Length:** 8½" overall.
Stocks: Checkered plastic.
Sights: Fixed.
Features: Double action; safety blocks firing pin and drops hammer. Matte finish standard, polished blue, engraving and/or plating available. Imported from Germany by Interarms.
Price: 9mm $995.00
Price: Steel frame $1,400.00
Price: Engraved models . . . .**On Request**

Walther P-5 Auto Pistol
Latest Walther design that uses the basic P-38 double-action mechanism. Caliber 9mm Para., barrel length 3½"; weight 28 oz., overall length 7".
Price: $895.00
Price: P-5 Compact $1,100.00

Walther P-88

WALTHER P-88 AUTO PISTOL
Caliber: 9mm Para., 15-shot magazine.
Barrel: 4".
Weight: 31½ oz. **Length:** 7⅜" overall.
Stocks: Checkered black composition.
Sights: Blade front, rear adjustable for w. and e.
Features: Double action with ambidextrous decocking lever and magazine release; alloy frame; loaded chamber indicator; matte finish. Imported from Germany by Interarms.
Price: $1,285.00

WALTHER MODEL TPH AUTO PISTOL
Caliber: 22 LR, 6-shot magazine.
Barrel: 2¼".
Weight: 14 oz. **Length:** 5⅜" overall.
Stocks: Checkered black composition.
Sights: Blade front, rear drift-adjustable for windage.
Features: Made of stainless steel. Scaled-down version of the Walther PP/PPK series. Made in U.S. Introduced 1987. From Interarms.
Price: $419.00

Walther TPH

Wildey Auto

Wilkinson "Linda"

WILDEY AUTOMATIC PISTOL
Caliber: 10mm Wildey Mag., 11mm Wildey Mag., 45 Win. Mag., 475 Wildey Mag., 357 Peterbuilt.
Barrel: 5", 6", 7", 8", 10" (45 Win. Mag.); 8", 10" (all other cals.). Interchangeable.
Weight: 64 oz. (5" barrel). **Length:** 11" overall (7" barrel).
Stocks: Polished hardwood.
Sights: Ramp front, fully adjustable rear.
Features: Gas-operated action. Made of stainless steel. Has three-lug rotary bolt. Double action. Polished and matte finish. Made in U.S. by Wildey, Inc.
Price: **$1,175.00**

WILKINSON "LINDA" PISTOL
Caliber: 9mm Para., 31-shot magazine.
Barrel: 8⁵⁄₁₆".
Weight: 4 lbs., 13 oz. **Length:** 12¼" overall.
Stocks: Checkered black plastic pistol grip, maple forend.
Sights: Protected blade front, aperture rear.
Features: Fires from closed bolt. Semi-auto only. Straight blowback action. Cross-bolt safety. Removable barrel. From Wilkinson Arms.
Price: **$682.00**

Wilkinson "Sherry"

WILKINSON "SHERRY" AUTO PISTOL
Caliber: 22 LR, 8-shot magazine.
Barrel: 2⅛".
Weight: 9¼ oz. **Length:** 4⅜" overall.
Stocks: Checkered black plastic.
Sights: Fixed, groove.
Features: Cross-bolt safety locks the sear into the hammer. Available in all blue finish or blue slide and trigger with gold frame. Introduced 1985.
Price: **$160.00**

COMPETITION HANDGUNS

Models specifically designed for classic competitive shooting sports.

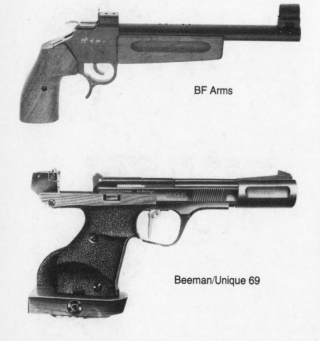

BF Arms

Beeman/Unique 69

BF ARMS SINGLE SHOT PISTOL
Caliber: 222 BF Rimmed, 7mm Super Mag., 7mm International Rimmed, 32-20 (30-20), 30 Herrett, 30-30 Win., 357 Mag., 357 Super Mag. (Maximum), 357 Herrett, 375 Super Mag., 7mm ET Gates (7mm/375 Super Mag.), 270 Ren, 7x30 Waters; single shot.
Barrel: 10", 12", 14¾".
Weight: 46 oz. (10" bbl.).
Stocks: Plain and finger-grooved, ambidextrous; oil-finished walnut and forend.
Sights: Hooded front, fully adjustable match rear.
Features: Falling block short-stroke action, automatic case ejection. Wilson or Douglas air-gauged match-grade barrel. Flat black oxide finish. Drilled and tapped for standard scope mounts. Introduced 1988. Made in U.S. by BF Arms.
Price: 10" Silhouette, with sights **$331.00**
Price: 14¾" Unlimited Silhouette, with sights **$354.00**
Price: 12" Hunter, no sights **$336.00**

BEEMAN/UNIQUE D.E.S. 69 TARGET PISTOL
Caliber: 22 LR, 5-shot magazine.
Barrel: 5.91".
Weight: 35.3 oz. **Length:** 10.5" overall.
Stocks: French walnut target-style with thumbrest and adjustable shelf; hand-checkered panels.
Sights: Ramp front, micro. adj. rear mounted on frame; 8.66" sight radius.
Features: Meets U.I.T. standards. Comes with 260-gram barrel weight; 100, 150, 350 gram weights available. Fully adjustable match trigger; dry-firing safety device. Imported from France by Beeman.
Price: Right-hand **$1,298.00**
Price: Left-hand **$1,375.00**

CAUTION: PRICES CHANGE, CHECK AT GUNSHOP.

Beeman/Unique 2000-U

BEEMAN/UNIQUE MODEL 2000-U MATCH PISTOL
Caliber: 22 Short, 5-shot magazine.
Barrel: 5.9″.
Weight: 43 oz. **Length:** 11.3″ overall.
Stocks: Anatomically shaped, adjustable, stippled French walnut.
Sights: Blade front, fully adjustable rear; 9.7″ sight radius.
Features: Light alloy frame, steel slide and shock absorber; five barrel vents reduce recoil, three of which can be blocked; trigger adjustable for position and pull weight. Comes with 340-gram weight housing, 160-gram available. Imported from France by Beeman. Introduced 1984.
Price: Right-hand $1,398.00
Price: Left-hand $1,480.00

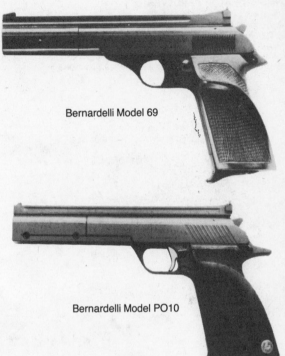

Bernardelli Model 69

BEEMAN/UNIQUE D.E.S. 32U RAPID FIRE MATCH
Caliber: 32 S&W Long wadcutter.
Barrel: 5.9″.
Weight: 40.2 oz.
Stocks: Anatomically shaped, adjustable stippled French walnut.
Sights: Blade front, micrometer click rear.
Features: Trigger adjustable for weight and position; dry firing mechanism; slide stop catch. Optional 120, 220, or 320-gram sleeve weights. Introduced 1990. Imported from France by Beeman.
Price: Right-hand $1,378.00
Price: Left-hand $1,475.00

BERNARDELLI MODEL 69 TARGET PISTOL
Caliber: 22 LR, 10-shot magazine.
Barrel: 5.9″.
Weight: 38 oz. **Length:** 9″ overall.
Stocks: Wrap-around, hand-checkered walnut with thumbrest.
Sights: Fully adjustable and interchangeable target-type.
Features: Conforms to U.I.T. regulations. Has 7.1″ sight radius, .27″ wide grooved trigger with 40-45 oz. pull. Manual thumb safety and magazine safety. Introduced 1987. Imported from Italy by Magnum Research, Inc.
Price: $459.00

Bernardelli Model PO10

BERNARDELLI PO10 TARGET PISTOL
Caliber: 22 LR, 5- or 10-shot magazine.
Barrel: 5″.
Weight: About 40.5 oz.
Stocks: Anatomically shaped walnut with thumbrest.
Sights: Fully adjustable and interchangeable target-type.
Features: External hammer with safety notch; pivoted, adjustable trigger; matte black finish. Meets U.I.T. specs. Introduced 1989. Imported from Italy by Magnum Research, Inc.
Price: $519.00
Price: With case $579.00

CHIPMUNK SILHOUETTE PISTOL
Caliber: 22 LR.
Barrel: 14⅞″.
Weight: About 2 lbs. **Length:** 20″ overall.
Stock: American walnut rear grip.
Sights: Post on ramp front, peep rear.
Features: Meets IHMSA 22-cal. unlimited category for competition. Introduced 1985. From Oregon Arms, Inc.
Price: $149.95

Chipmunk Silhouette

Colt Delta Gold Cup

COLT GOLD CUP NAT'L MATCH MK IV/Series 80
Caliber: 45 ACP, 7-shot magazine.
Barrel: 5″, with new design bushing.
Weight: 39 oz. **Length:** 8½″.
Stocks: Blue has checkered walnut, gold-plated medallion; stainless has black walnut.
Sights: Ramp-style front, Colt-Elliason rear adjustable for w. and e., sight radius 6¾″.
Features: Arched or flat housing; wide, grooved trigger with adjustable stop; ribbed-top slide, hand fitted, with improved ejection port.
Price: Blue $799.95
Price: Stainless $859.95
Price: Bright stainless $924.95
Price: Delta Gold Cup (10mm, stainless) $889.95

COMPETITION HANDGUNS

COMPETITOR SINGLE SHOT PISTOL
Caliber: 22 LR, 223, 7mm TCU, 7mm Int., 30 Herrett, 357 Maximum, 41 Mag., 44 Mag., 454 Casull, 375 Super Mag. Others on special order.
Barrel: 10.5", 14".
Weight: NA **Length:** NA.
Stocks: Smooth walnut with thumbrest.
Sights: Ramp front, open adjustable rear.
Features: Interchangeable barrels of blue ordnance or bright stainless steel; ventilated barrel shroud; receiver has integral scope mount. Introduced 1987. From TMI Products.
Price: With 10.5" bbl. $562.50
Price: With 14" bbl. $578.50
Price: Extra barrels, 10.5", standard calibers $93.75
Price: Special calibers, add $62.50

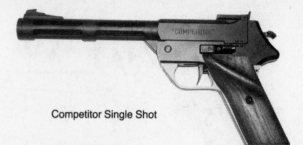

Competitor Single Shot

ERMA ER MATCH REVOLVERS
Caliber: 22 LR, 32 S&W Long, 6-shot.
Barrel: 6".
Weight: 46 oz. **Length:** 11.2" overall.
Stocks: Stippled walnut, adjustable match-type.
Sights: Blade front, micrometer rear adjustable for windage and elevation.
Features: Polished blue finish. Introduced 1989. Imported from West Germany by Precision Sales International.
Price: 22 LR or 32 S&W Long $1,225.00

FAS 602 MATCH PISTOL
Caliber: 22 LR, 5-shot.
Barrel: 5.6".
Weight: 37 oz. **Length:** 11" overall.
Stocks: Walnut wrap-around; sizes small, medium or large, or adjustable.
Sights: Match. Blade front, open notch rear fully adjustable for w. and e. Sight radius is 8.66".
Features: Line of sight is only ¹¹⁄₃₂" above centerline of bore; magazine is inserted from top; adjustable and removable trigger mechanism; single lever takedown. Full 5-year warranty. Imported from Italy by Mandall Shooting Supplies.
Price: $1,295.00

FAS 601 Match Pistol
Similar to SP 602 except has different match stocks with adjustable palm shelf, 22 Short only for rapid fire shooting; weighs 40 oz., 5.6" bbl.; has gas ports through top of barrel and slide to reduce recoil; slightly different trigger and sear mechanisms.
Price: $1,295.00

FAS 601

Glock Model 17L

GLOCK MODEL 17L COMPETITION AUTO
Caliber: 9mm Para., 17-shot magazine.
Barrel: 6.02".
Weight: 23.3 oz. **Length:** 8.7" overall.
Stocks: Black polymer.
Sights: Blade front with white dot, adjustable rear.
Features: Polymer frame, steel slide; double-action trigger with "Safe Action" system; mechanical firing pin safety, drop safety; simple takedown without tools; locked breech, recoil operated action. Introduced 1989. Imported from Austria by Glock, Inc.
Price: $773.53

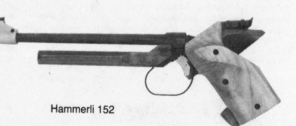

Hammerli 152

HAMMERLI MODEL 208s PISTOL
Caliber: 22 LR, 8-shot magazine.
Barrel: 5.9".
Weight: 37.5 oz. **Length:** 10" overall.
Stocks: Walnut, target-type with thumbrest.
Sights: Blade front, open fully adjustable rear.
Features: Adjustable trigger, including length; interchangeable rear sight elements. Imported from Switzerland by Mandall.
Price: $1,755.00

HAMMERLI MODEL 150 FREE PISTOL
Caliber: 22 LR, single shot.
Barrel: 11.3".
Weight: 43 oz. **Length:** 15.35" overall.
Stocks: Walnut with adjustable palm shelf.
Sights: Sight radius of 14.6". Micro rear sight adjustable for w. and e.
Features: Single shot Martini action. Cocking lever on left side of action with vertical operation. Set trigger adjustable for length and angle. Trigger pull weight adjustable between 5 and 100 grams. Guaranteed accuracy of .78", 10 shots from machine rest. Imported from Switzerland by Mandall Shooting Supplies.
Price: About $1,980.00
Price: With electric trigger (Model 152), about $2015.00

HAMMERLI MODEL 152 MATCH PISTOL
Caliber: 22 LR.
Barrel: 11.2".
Weight: 46.9 oz. **Length:** 16.9" overall.
Stocks: Match.
Sights: Changeable post front, micrometer rear.
Features: Electronic trigger. Introduced 1990. Imported from Switzerland by Beeman.
Price: $1,998.00

CAUTION: PRICES CHANGE, CHECK AT GUNSHOP.

COMPETITION HANDGUNS

Hammerli 208

HAMMERLI STANDARD, MODELS 208, 211, 215
Caliber: 22 LR.
Barrel: 5.9″, 6-groove.
Weight: 37.6 oz. (45 oz. with extra heavy barrel weight). **Length:** 10″.
Stocks: Walnut. Adjustable palm rest (208), 211 has thumbrest grip.
Sights: Match sights, fully adjustable for w. and e. (click adjustable). Interchangeable front and rear blades.
Features: Semi-automatic, recoil operated. 8-shot clip. Slide stop. Fully adjustable trigger (2¼ lbs. and 3 lbs.). Extra barrel weight available. Imported from Switzerland by Mandall Shooting Supplies, Beeman.
Price: Model 208, approx. (Mandall) $1,399.00
Price: Model 211, approx. (Mandall) $1,295.00
Price: Model 215, approx. (Mandall) $1,295.00
Price: Model 208 (Beeman) $1,615.00
Price: Model 211 (Beeman) $1,669.00
Price: Model 215 (Beeman) $1,420.00

HAMMERLI MODEL 232 RAPID FIRE PISTOL
Caliber: 22 Short, 6-shot.
Barrel: 5″, with six exhaust ports.
Weight: 44 oz. **Length:** 10.4″ overall.
Stocks: Stippled walnut; wrap-around on Model 232-2, adjustable on 232-1.
Sights: Interchangeable front and rear blades, fully adjustable micrometer rear.
Features: Recoil operated semi-automatic; nearly recoilless design; trigger adjustable from 8.4 to 10.6 oz. with three lengths offered. Wrap-around grips available in small, medium and large sizes. Imported from Switzerland by Beeman, Mandall. Introduced 1984.
Price: Model 232-1, about $1,500.00
Price: Model 232-1 (Beeman) $1,435.00
Price: Model 232-2 (Beeman) $1,530.00

LLAMA M-87 9MM COMP
Caliber: 9mm Para., 14-shot magazine.
Barrel: 6″.
Weight: 47 oz. **Length:** 9.5″ overall.
Stocks: Polymer composition.
Sights: Patridge front, fully adjustable rear.
Features: A match-ready Comp pistol. Built-in ported compensator, over-size magazine and safety releases, fixed barrel bushing, bevelled magazine well, extended trigger guard. Introduced 1989. Imported by Stoeger Industries.
Price: $1,450.00

NEW DETONICS "COMPMASTER" COMPETITION PISTOL
Caliber: 45 ACP, 7-shot magazine.
Barrel: Two barrels supplied: 5.6″ compensated match and 5″ match with recessed crown.
Weight: 42 oz. **Length:** 9¾″ overall.
Stocks: Pachmayr rubber wrap-around.
Sights: Ramp front, positive-click adjustable rear.
Features: Same features as "Scoremaster" pistol. Introduced 1990. From New Detonics Mfg. Corp.
Price: $1,650.00

NEW DETONICS "SCOREMASTER" TARGET PISTOL
Caliber: 45 ACP, 7-shot magazine.
Barrel: 5″ match barrel with recessed crown.
Weight: 36 oz. **Length:** 8⅞″ overall.
Stocks: Checkered walnut with rubber mainspring housing.
Sights: Ramp front, positive-click adjustable rear.
Features: All stainless steel construction. Patented self-centering cone barrel system; lengthened and lowered ejection port; beveled magazine well; patented, cushioned counter-wound dual spring recoil system; hand-fitted National Match tolerances; redesigned thumb safety; blackened slide top; dual slide serrations; extended beavertail grip safety; improved magazine release; skeletonized trigger and hammer. Comes with gun rug and two spare magazines. Introduced 1990. From New Detonics Mfg. Corp.
Price: $1,178.00

HAMMERLI MODEL 280 TARGET PISTOL
Caliber: 22 LR, 6-shot, 32 S&W Long WC, 5-shot.
Barrel: 4.5″.
Weight: 39.1 oz. (32). **Length:** 11.8″ overall.
Stocks: Walnut match-type with stippling, adjustable palm shelf.
Sights: Match sights, micrometer adjustable.
Features: Sight radius of 8.8″. Comes with barrel weights, spare magazine, loading tool, cleaning rods. Introduced 1990. Imported from Switzerland by Mandall Shooting Supplies.
Price: ....NA

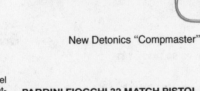

Llama M-87 Comp

New Detonics "Compmaster"

PARDINI FIOCCHI 32 MATCH PISTOL
Caliber: 32 S&W Long, 5-shot magazine.
Barrel: 4.9″.
Weight: 38.7 oz. **Length:** 11.7″ overall.
Stocks: Stippled walnut match-type with adjustable palm shelf.
Sights: Match. Undercut blade front, fully adjustable open rear.
Features: Match trigger. Recoil compensation system. Imported from Italy by Fiocchi of America.
Price: $750.00

PARDINI FIOCCHI RAPID FIRE MATCH
Caliber: 22 Short, 5-shot magazine.
Barrel: 5.1″.
Weight: 34.5 oz. **Length:** 11.7″ overall.
Stocks: Stippled walnut, match-type.
Sights: Post front, fully adjustable rear.
Features: Alloy bolt. Has 14.9″ sight radius. Imported from Italy by Fiocchi of America.
Price: $750.00

Pardini Fiocchi Rapid Fire

Pardini Fiocchi Free Pistol

Remington XP-100 Silhouette

Ruger Government Target

Ruger Mark II Bull Barrel

Same gun as the Target Model except has 5½" or 10" heavy barrel (10" meets all IHMSA regulations). Weight with 5½" barrel is 42 oz., with 10" barrel, 52 oz.

Price: Blued (MK-512, MK-10) **$280.50**
Price: Stainless (KMK-512, KMK-10) **$355.25**

SMITH & WESSON MODEL 29 SILHOUETTE

Caliber: 44 Magnum, 6-shot.
Barrel: 10⅝".
Weight: 58 oz. **Length:** 16³⁄₁₆" overall.
Stocks: Over-size target-type, checkered Goncalo Alves.
Sights: Four-position front to match the four distances of silhouette targets; micro-click rear adjustable for windage and elevation.
Features: Designed specifically for silhouette shooting. Front sight has click stops for the four pre-set ranges. Introduced 1983.
Price: **$536.00**

SMITH & WESSON MODEL 41 TARGET

Caliber: 22 LR, 10-shot clip.
Barrel: 5½", 7".
Weight: 44 oz. **Length:** 9" overall.
Stocks: Checkered walnut with modified thumbrest, usable with either hand.
Sights: ⅛" Patridge on ramp base; S&W micro click rear adjustable for w. and e.
Features: ⅜" wide, grooved trigger; adjustable trigger stop.
Price: S&W Bright Blue, satin matted top area **$657.00**

PARDINI FIOCCHI STANDARD PISTOL

Caliber: 22 LR, 5-shot magazine.
Barrel: 4.9".
Weight: 37 oz. **Length:** 11.7" overall.
Stocks: Match-type stippled walnut.
Sights: Match-type undercut blade front, fully adjustable open rear.
Features: Match trigger. Matte blue finish. Comes with locking case. Imported from Italy by Fiocchi of America.
Price: **$730.00**

PARDINI FIOCCHI FREE PISTOL

Caliber: 22 LR, single shot.
Barrel: 4.9".
Weight: 37 oz. **Length:** 11.7" overall.
Stocks: Walnut, special hand-fitting free-pistol design.
Sights: Post front, fully adjustable open rear.
Features: Rotating bolt-action design. Has 8.6" sight radius. Imported from Italy by Fiocchi of America.
Price: **$820.00**

REMINGTON XP-100 SILHOUETTE PISTOL

Caliber: 223 Rem., 7mm BR Remington, 35 Remington, single shot.
Barrel: 14½".
Weight: 4½ lbs. **Length:** 21¼" overall.
Stocks: Brown nylon, one piece, checkered grip.
Sights: None furnished. Drilled and tapped for scope mounts.
Features: Universal grip fits right or left hand; match-type grooved trigger, two-position thumb safety.
Price: 7mm BR Rem. **$406.00**
Price: 223 Rem. **$398.00**
Price: 35 Rem. **$419.00**

RUGER MARK II TARGET MODEL AUTO PISTOL

Caliber: 22 LR, 10-shot magazine.
Barrel: 6⅞".
Weight: 42 oz. **Length:** 11⅛" overall.
Stocks: Checkered hard rubber.
Sights: .125" blade front, micro click rear, adjustable for w. and e. Sight radius 9⅜".
Features: Introduced 1982.
Price: Blued (MK-678) **$280.50**
Price: Stainless (KMK-678) **$355.25**

Ruger Mark II Government Target Model

Same gun as the Mark II Target Model except has higher sights and is roll marked "Government Target Model" on the right side of the receiver below the rear sight. Identical in all aspects to the military model used for training U.S. armed forces except for markings. Comes with factory test target. Introduced 1987.
Price: Blued (MK678G) **$324.25**

Smith & Wesson 29 Silhouette

Smith & Wesson Model 41

COMPETITION HANDGUNS

SMITH & WESSON 38 MASTER Model 52 AUTO
Caliber: 38 Special (for mid-range W.C. with flush-seated bullet only), 5-shot magazine.
Barrel: 5".
Weight: 40 oz. with empty magazine. **Length:** 8⅝" overall.
Stocks: Checkered walnut.
Sights: ⅛" Patridge front, S&W micro-click rear adjustable for w. and e.
Features: Top sighting surfaces matte finished. Locked breech, moving barrel system; checked for 10-ring groups at 50 yards. Coin-adjustable sight screws. Dry-firing permissible if manual safety on.
Price: S&W Bright Blue **$834.00**

Smith & Wesson Model 52

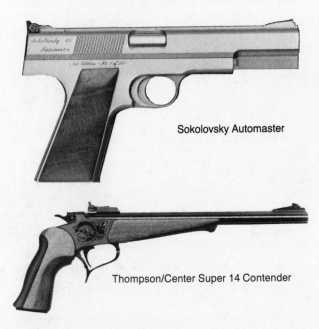
Sokolovsky Automaster

Thompson/Center Super 14 Contender

SOKOLOVSKY 45 AUTOMASTER
Caliber: 45 ACP, 6-shot magazine.
Barrel: 6".
Weight: 3.6 lbs. **Length:** 9½" overall.
Stocks: Smooth walnut.
Sights: Ramp front, Millett fully adjustable rear.
Features: Intended for target shooting, not combat. Semi-custom built with precise tolerances. Has special "safety trigger" next to regular trigger. Most parts made of stainless steel. Introduced 1985. From Sokolovsky Corp.
Price: **$4,500.00**

TAURUS MODEL 86 MASTER REVOLVER
Caliber: 38 Spec., 6-shot.
Barrel: 6" only.
Weight: 34 oz. **Length:** 11¼" overall.
Stocks: Oversize target-type, checkered Brazilian walnut.
Sights: Patridge front, micro-click rear adjustable for w. and e.
Features: Blue finish with non-reflective finish on barrel. Imported from Brazil by Taurus International.
Price: **$290.00**

THOMPSON/CENTER SUPER 14 CONTENDER
Caliber: 22 LR, 222 Rem., 223 Rem., 7mm TCU, 7x30 Waters, 30-30 Win., 35 Rem., 357 Rem. Maximum, 44 Mag., 10mm Auto, 445 Super Mag., single shot.
Barrel: 14".
Weight: 45 oz. **Length:** 17¼" overall.
Stocks: T/C "Competitor Grip" (walnut and rubber).
Sights: Fully adjustable target-type.
Features: Break-open action with auto safety. Interchangeable barrels for both rimfire and centerfire calibers. Introduced 1978.
Price: **$355.00**
Price: Extra barrels, blued **$165.00**

Thompson/Center Super 16 Contender
Same as the T/C Super 14 Contender except has 16¼" barrel. Rear sight can be mounted at mid-barrel position (10¾" radius) or moved to the rear (using scope mount position) for 14¾" radius. Overall length is 20¼". Comes with T/C Competitor Grip of walnut and rubber. Available in 22 LR, 22 WMR, 223 Rem., 7x30 Waters, 30-30 Win., 35 Rem., 44 Mag., 45-70 Gov't. Also available with 16" vent rib barrel with internal choke, caliber 45 Colt/410 shotshell.
Price: **$360.00**
Price: 45-70 Gov't **$375.00**
Price: Extra 16" barrels (blued) **$170.00**
Price: As above, 45-70 . . . . **$185.00**
Price: Super 16 Vent Rib (45-410) **$385.00**
Price: Extra vent rib barrel **$195.00**

UBERTI "PHANTOM" SA SILHOUETTE
Caliber: 357 Mag., 44 Mag.
Barrel: 10½".
Weight: NA. **Length:** NA.
Stocks: Walnut target-style.
Sights: Blade on ramp front, fully adjustable rear.
Features: Hooked trigger guard. Introduced 1986. Imported by Uberti USA.
Price: **$518.00**

WALTHER GSP MATCH PISTOL
Caliber: 22 LR, 32 S&W wadcutter (GSP-C), 5-shot.
Barrel: 5¾".
Weight: 44.8 oz. (22 LR), 49.4 oz. (32). **Length:** 11.8" overall.
Stocks: Walnut, special hand-fitting design.
Sights: Fixed front, rear adjustable for w. and e.
Features: Available with either 2.2 lb. (1000 gm) or 3 lb. (1360 gm) trigger. Spare mag., bbl. weight, tools supplied in Match Pistol Kit. Imported from Germany by Interarms.
Price: GSP, with case **$1,450.00**
Price: GSP-C, with case **$1,700.00**
Price: 22 LR conversion unit for GSP-C (no trigger unit) **$750.00**
Price: 22 Short conversion unit for GSP-C (with trigger unit) **$925.00**
Price: 32 S&W conversion unit for GSP-C (no trigger unit) **$950.00**

Walther OSP Rapid-Fire Pistol
Similar to Model GSP except 22 Short only, stock has adjustable free-style hand rest.
Price: **$1,600.00**

Walther GSP Match

COMPETITION HANDGUNS

Walther Free Pistol

WALTHER FREE PISTOL
Caliber: 22 LR, single shot.
Barrel: 11.7".
Weight: 48 oz. **Length:** 17.2" overall.
Stocks: Walnut, special hand-fitting design.
Sights: Fully adjustable match sights.
Features: Special electronic trigger. Matte finish blue. Introduced 1980. Imported from Germany by Interarms.
Price: $1,700.00

DAN WESSON MODEL 40 SILHOUETTE
Caliber: 357 Maximum, 6-shot.
Barrel: 6", 8", 10".
Weight: 64 oz. (8" bbl.). **Length:** 14.3" overall (8" bbl.).
Stocks: Smooth walnut, target-style.
Sights: 1/8" serrated front, fully adjustable rear.
Features: Meets criteria for IHMSA competition with 8" slotted barrel. Blue or stainless steel.
Price: Blue, 6" $508.32
Price: Blue, 8" $525.19
Price: Blue, 10" $543.41
Price: Stainless, 6" $568.97
Price: Stainless, 8" slotted $595.13
Price: Stainless, 10" $609.03

Dan Wesson Model 40

DAN WESSON MODEL 22 TARGET REVOLVER
Caliber: 22 LR, 6-shot.
Barrel: 10", regular vent or vent heavy.
Weight: 53 oz.
Stocks: Combat style.
Sights: Patridge-style front, .080" narrow notch rear.
Features: Single action only. Available in blue or stainless. Introduced 1989. From Dan Wesson Arms, Inc.
Price: Blue, regular vent $430.00
Price: Blue, vent heavy $448.42
Price: Stainless, regular vent $458.43
Price: Stainless, vent heavy $484.53

Dan Wesson 445 Supermag Revolver
Similar size and weight as the Model 40 revolvers. Chambered for the 445 Supermag cartridge, a longer version of the 44 Magnum. Contact maker for complete price list. Introduced 1989. From Dan Wesson Arms.
Price: Blue, 6" $574.55
Price: Blue, 8" $605.25
Price: Blue, 10" $596.88
Price: Stainless, 6" $608.98
Price: Stainless, 8" $629.86
Price: Stainless, 10" $650.09

WICHITA MK-40 SILHOUETTE PISTOL
Caliber: 22-250, 7mm IHMSA, 308 Win. F.L. Other calibers available on special order. Single shot.
Barrel: 13", non-glare blue; .700" dia. muzzle.
Weight: 4½ lbs. **Length:** 19⅜" overall.
Stock: American walnut with oil finish.
Sights: Wichita Multi-Range sighting system.
Features: Aluminum receiver with steel insert locking lugs, measures 1.360" O.D.; three locking lug bolts, three gas ports; flat bolt handle; completely adjustable Wichita trigger. Introduced 1981. From Wichita Arms.
Price: $1,100.00

DAN WESSON ACTION CUP/PPC COMPETITION REVOLVERS
Caliber: 38 Spec., 357 Mag., 6-shot.
Barrel: Extra heavy 6" bull shroud with removable underweight.
Weight: 4 lbs., 7 oz. (PPC, with weight).
Stocks: Pachmayr Gripper.
Sights: Tasco Pro Point II on Action Cup; Aristocrat with three-position rear on PPC model.
Features: Competition tuned with narrow trigger, chamfered cylinder chambers. Action Cup available in stainless only, PPC in bright blue or stainless. Introduced 1989.
Price: Action Cup $913.30
Price: PPC, blue $779.83
Price: PPC, stainless $857.48

WICHITA SILHOUETTE PISTOL
Caliber: 22-250, 7mm IHMSA, 308. Other calibers available on special order. Single shot.
Barrel: 14¹⁵/₁₆".
Weight: 4½ lbs. **Length:** 21⅜" overall.
Stock: American walnut with oil finish. Glass bedded.
Sights: Wichita Multi-Range sight system.
Features: Comes with left-hand action with right-hand grip. Fluted bolt, flat bolt handle. Action drilled and tapped for Burris scope mounts. Non-glare satin blue finish. Wichita adjustable trigger. Introduced 1979. From Wichita Arms.
Price: Center grip stock $1,100.00
Price: As above except with Rear Position Stock and target-type Lightpull trigger $1,100.00

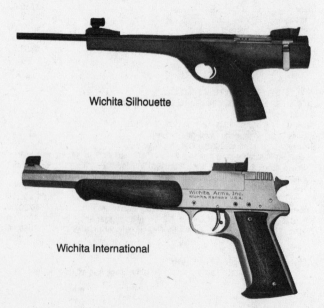

Wichita Silhouette

Wichita International

WICHITA INTERNATIONAL PISTOL
Caliber: 22 LR, 22 WMR, 7mm INT-R, 7x30 Waters, 30-30 Win., 32 H&R Mag., 357 Mag., 357 Super Mag., single shot.
Barrel: 10½", 14".
Weight: 3 lbs. 13 oz.
Stocks: Walnut grip and forend.
Sights: Target front, adjustable rear.
Features: Made of 17-4PH stainless steel. Break-open action. Grip dimensions same as Colt 45 auto. Extra barrels are factory fitted. Introduced 1983. Available from Wichita Arms.
Price: International 10" $484.95
Price: International 14" $525.00
Price: Extra barrels, 10" $295.00
Price: Extra barrels, 14" $325.00

CAUTION: PRICES CHANGE, CHECK AT GUNSHOP.

THE BEST HANDGUN ACTION AROUND

6 BIG ISSUES A YEAR FEATURING...

- In-depth reviews of auto pistols, revolvers, and single-shot handguns — including *exclusive first looks* at the newest guns on the market
- Handloading how-to's that help you squeeze maximum accuracy out of every shot
- Special reports on handgun hunting, competitive shooting, law enforcement, and more
- Accurate info on how factory loads perform on the range and in the field
- Modifications you can make at home to turn your factory handgun into a custom shooting piece
- The nation's *best* handgun writers, including Dick Metcalf, Charles E. Petty, Rick Jamison, Layne Simpson, Kerby Smith, and James Clark

TRY IT FREE!

If you like it, you'll get a full year for just $17.⁹⁵

Send for your *FREE ISSUE* now!

SHOOTING TIMES HQ HANDGUN QUARTERLY FREE ISSUE OFFER

❑ **YES!** Please send me a free trial issue of **HQ**. If I like it and want more, I'll pay the $17.95 invoice for a full year of handgun action — 6 big issues (5 additional).

Or I may return the invoice, marked "cancel." The trial issue is mine to keep — *FREE!*

KGGD8

Please Print

Name _____

Address _____ Apt. _____

City _____ State _____ Zip _____

Offer expires July 1, 1991.
Your first issue will arrive in two to ten weeks. Outside U.S., add $8 postage, payable in U.S. funds drawn on a U.S. bank.

GET MORE OUT OF HANDGUNS

There's always something new in the handgunning world. New state-of-the-art handguns. New cartridges that can improve your performance on the range and in the field. New accessories to turn your factory handgun into a custom shooting piece.

HQ keeps you on top of the excitement and the challenge of your favorite handgun sports.

Be the first to see the latest handguns on the market — often months ahead of the competition. Know how specific handguns perform under actual field conditions. And get more out of handgunning with valuable tips from the **HQ** experts.

Just drop this postage-paid card in the mail today. You'll get the newest issue of **HQ** to read and examine — *FREE.*

6 big issues a year including the exclusive Handgun Buyer's Guide

Essential reading for anyone who's thinking of buying a handgun. **HQ**'s exclusive catalog section features complete specs and suggested prices for more than 100 handguns.

Includes models suitable for hunting and competitive courses for fire, both police and international.

Armscor 38

ARMSCOR MODEL 200 REVOLVER
Caliber: 22 LR, 22 WMR, 38 Spec., 6-shot.
Barrel: 2½", 4".
Weight: 26 oz. (4" barrel). **Length:** 8⅞" overall (4" barrel).
Stocks: Checkered mahogany or rubber.
Sights: Ramp front, fully adjustable rear on 200TC, fixed rear on 200P.
Features: Blue finish. Introduced 1990. Imported from the Philippines by Armscor.
Price: Model 200P (38 Spec.) **$189.95**
Price: Model 200TC (22 LR or 38 Spec.) **$204.95**

Astra 357

ASTRA 357/9mm CONVERTIBLE REVOLVER
Caliber: 357 Magnum, 6-shot.
Barrel: 3", 4", 6", 8½".
Weight: 40 oz. (6" bbl.). **Length:** 11¼" (6" bbl.).
Stocks: Checkered walnut.
Sights: Fixed front, rear adjustable for w. and e.
Features: Swing-out cylinder with countersunk chambers, floating firing pin. Target-type hammer and trigger. Imported from Spain by Interarms.
Price: **$395.00**

Astra Model 44, 45 Double-Action Revolver
Similar to the 357 Mag. except chambered for 44 Mag. or 45 Colt. Barrel length of 6" only, giving overall length of 11⅜". Weight is 2¾ lbs. Introduced 1980.
Price: **$450.00**

CHARTER ARMS BULLDOG
Caliber: 44 Special, 5-shot.
Barrel: 2½".
Weight: 19 oz. **Length:** 7¾" overall.
Stocks: Checkered walnut, Bulldog.
Sights: Patridge-type front, square-notch rear.
Features: Wide trigger and hammer; beryllium copper firing pin.
Price: Service Blue, 2½" **$242.00**
Price: Stainless steel, 2½" **$290.00**

Charter Arms Bulldog Tracker
Similar to the standard Bulldog except chambered for 357 Mag., has adjustable rear sight, 2½" bull barrel, ramp front sight, square butt checkered walnut grips. Available in blue finish only.
Price: **$250.00**

CHARTER ARMS POLICE BULLDOG
Caliber: 32 H&R Mag., 38 Special (6-shot), 357 Mag., 44 Special (5-shot).
Barrel: 32 H&R Mag., 44 Spec.—3½"; 38 Special, 357 Mag.—4".
Weight: 23.5 oz. (44 Spec.) to 28 oz. (357 Mag.)
Length: 8½" overall (357 Mag., 4" bbl.).
Stocks: Checkered neoprene; walnut or neoprene on 44 Special.
Sights: Blade front, fixed rear on 4", adjustable on 3½" barrel.
Features: Stainless steel or Service Blue. All have full barrel shrouds. Made in U.S. by Charter Arms.
Price: Stainless, 32 H&R Mag., about **$285.00**
Price: Stainless, 38 Special, about **$275.00**
Price: Stainless, 357 Mag., about **$299.00**
Price: Stainless, 44 Spec., about **$307.00**
Price: Service Blue, 32, 38, 3½" barrel, about **$260.00**
Price: Service Blue, 32, 38, 4" barrel, about **$235.00**
Price: Service Blue, 44 Spec., about **$260.00**

CHARTER ARMS UNDERCOVER POLICE SPECIAL
Caliber: 38 Special, 5-shot.
Barrel: 2.1".
Weight: 21 oz. **Length:** 6.5" overall.
Stocks: Smooth combat-style of laminated wood.
Sights: Blade front, fixed rear.
Features: Stainless steel or Service Blue. Double action mode only. Spurless hammer. Full ejector rod shroud. Made in U.S. by Charter Arms.
Price: Service Blue, about **$184.00**
Price: Stainless, about **$264.00**

CHARTER ARMS BULLDOG PUG
Caliber: 44 Special, 5-shot.
Barrel: 2½".
Weight: 19 oz. **Length:** 7¼" overall.
Stocks: Bulldog walnut or neoprene.
Sights: Ramp front, notch rear.
Features: Shrouded ejector rod; wide trigger and hammer spur. Introduced 1986.
Price: About **$250.00**

Charter Police Bulldog

Charter Undercover Police

Charter Arms "Bonnie" and "Clyde" Revolvers
Similar to the Undercover Police Special except in blue only with 2½" full-shroud barrel; one gun barrel is marked "Bonnie," the other "Clyde." Grips of laminated wood in choice of nine colors: Rosewood, Camo, Oak, Burnt Orange, Golden Brown, Aqua, Scarlet, Ebony, Blonde. Both have fixed sights. Introduced 1989.
Price: **$259.00**

CHARTER ARMS PATHFINDER REVOLVER
Caliber: 22 LR, 6-shot.
Barrel: 3½".
Weight: 26 oz. **Length:** 8¼" overall.
Stocks: Checkered neoprene.
Sights: Blade front, adjustable rear.
Features: Stainless steel or Service Blue. Full-length ejector rod shroud. Made in U.S. by Charter Arms.
Price: Service Blue (does not have shroud), about **$230.00**
Price: Stainless, about **$282.00**

CHARTER ARMS UNDERCOVER REVOLVER
Caliber: 38 Special, 5-shot.
Barrel: 2".
Weight: 16 oz. **Length:** 6¼" overall (2").
Stocks: Checkered walnut.
Sights: Patridge-type ramp front, notched rear.
Features: Wide trigger and hammer spur. Steel frame. Police Undercover, 2" bbl. (for 38 Spec. +P loads) carry same prices as regular 38 Spec. guns.
Price: Polished blue, about **$216.00**
Price: Stainless, about **$272.00**

CHARTER ARMS TARGET BULLDOG
Caliber: 357 Mag., 9mm Federal, 44 Spec., 5-shot.
Barrel: 5½", vent. rib, full shroud.
Weight: 29 oz. **Length:** 10" overall.
Stocks: Walnut, smooth target-type.
Sights: Blade front, adjustable rear.
Features: Made of stainless steel. Shrouded ejector rod. Made in U.S. by Charter Arms.
Price: **$375.00**

CHARTER ARMS PIT BULL REVOLVER
Caliber: 9mm Federal, 5-shot.
Barrel: 2½", 3½".
Weight: 24.5 oz. (2½" bbl.). **Length:** 7¼" overall (2½" bbl.).
Stocks: Checkered neoprene.
Sights: Blade front, fixed rear on 2½", adjustable on 3½".
Features: Stainless steel or Service Blue. Both barrels have full-length ejector rod shroud. Made in U.S. by Charter Arms.
Price: Service Blue, 2½", about **$286.00**
Price: Service Blue, 3½", about **$293.00**
Price: Stainless, 2½", about **$300.00**
Price: Stainless, 3½", about **$307.00**

COLT ANACONDA REVOLVER
Caliber: 44 Rem. Magnum, 6-shot.
Barrel: 6".
Weight: 53 oz. **Length:** 11⅝" overall.
Stocks: Combat-style black neoprene with finger grooves.
Sights: Red insert front, adjustable white outline rear.
Features: Stainless steel; full-length ejector rod housing; ventilated barrel rib; offset bolt notches in cylinder; wide spur hammer. Introduced 1990.
Price: . . . . **NA**

> Consult our Directory pages for
> the location of firms mentioned.

COLT KING COBRA REVOLVER
Caliber: 357 Magnum, 6-shot.
Barrel: 2½", 4", 6", 8" (STS); 2½", 4", 6" (BSTS); 2½", 4", 6" (blue).
Weight: 42 oz. (4" bbl.). **Length:** 9" overall (4" bbl.).
Stocks: Checkered rubber.
Sights: Red insert ramp front, adjustable white outline rear.
Features: Stainless steel; full-length contoured ejector rod housing, barrel rib; matte finish. Introduced 1986.
Price: STS, 2½", 4", 6", 8" **$419.95**
Price: BSTS, 2½", 4", 6" **$456.95**
Price: Blue, 2½", 4", 6" **$395.95**

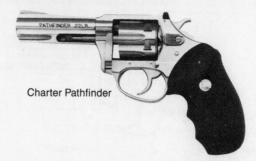

Charter Pathfinder

Charter Arms Off-Duty Revolver
Similar to the Undercover except 38 Special or 22 LR, 2" barrel, Mat-Black non-glare finish. This all-steel gun comes with Red-Dot front sight. Also available in stainless steel. Introduced 1984.
Price: Mat-Black finish, about **$184.00**
Price: Stainless steel, about **$241.00**

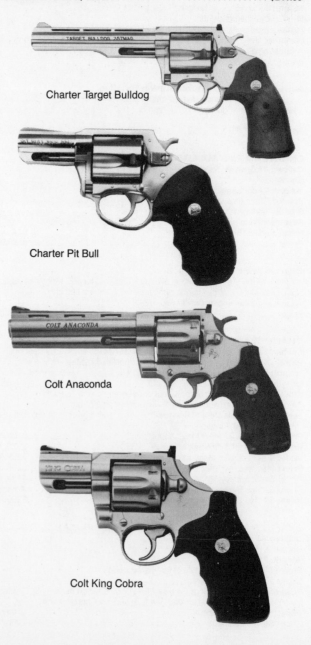

Charter Target Bulldog

Charter Pit Bull

Colt Anaconda

Colt King Cobra

COLT PYTHON REVOLVER
Caliber: 357 Magnum (handles all 38 Spec.), 6-shot.
Barrel: 2½", 4", 6" or 8", with ventilated rib.
Weight: 38 oz. (4" bbl.). **Length:** 9¼" (4" bbl.).
Stocks: Checkered walnut, target-type.
Sights: ⅛" ramp front, adjustable notch rear.
Features: Ventilated rib; grooved, crisp trigger; swing-out cylinder; target hammer.
Price: Blue, 2½", 4", 6", 8" $759.95
Price: Stainless, 2½", 4", 6", 8" $849.95
Price: Bright stainless, 2½", 4", 6", 8" $879.95

Colt Python

ERMA ER-777 SPORTING REVOLVER
Caliber: 357 Mag., 6-shot.
Barrel: 4", 5½", 6".
Weight: 44 to 48 oz. **Length:** 9½" overall (4" barrel).
Stocks: Stippled walnut service-type.
Sights: Interchangeable blade front, micro-adjustable rear for windage and elevation.
Features: Polished blue finish. Adjustable trigger. Imported from West Germany by Precision Sales Int'l. Introduced 1988.
Price: $1,093.00

Erma ER-777

F.I.E. ARMINIUS REVOLVERS
Caliber: 38 Special, 357 Mag., 32 S&W, 22 WMR, 22 LR.
Barrel: 4", 6".
Weight: 35 oz. (6" bbl.). **Length:** 11" overall (6" bbl.).
Stocks: Checkered plastic; walnut optional.
Sights: Ramp front, fixed rear on standard models, w. and e. adjustments on target models.
Features: Thumb-release, swing-out cylinder. Ventilated rib, solid frame. Interchangeable 22 WMR cylinder available with 22 cal. versions. Imported from West Germany by F.I.E. Corp.
Price: . . . . $159.95 to $254.45

F.I.E. "Arminius"

F.I.E. "TITAN TIGER" REVOLVER
Caliber: 38 Special.
Barrel: 2" or 4".
Weight: 27 oz. **Length:** 6¼" overall (2" bbl.)
Stocks: Checkered plastic, Bulldog style. Walnut optional.
Sights: Fixed.
Features: Thumb-release swing-out cylinder, one stroke ejection. Made in U.S.A. by F.I.E. Corp.
Price: Blue $174.95

F.I.E. "STANDARD" REVOLVER
Caliber: 22 LR, 22 WMR, 22 LR/WMR combo, 32 H&R Mag., 38 Spec., 6-shot.
Barrel: 2" or 4".
Weight: 23 oz. (2" barrel). **Length:** 6¼" overall (2" barrel).
Stocks: Magnum-style round butt; checkered plastic.
Sights: Ramp front, fixed square notch rear.
Features: One-piece solid frame; checkered hammer spur, serrated trigger; blue finish. Introduced 1989. Made by F.I.E. Firearms Corp.
Price: . . . . $99.95 to $139.95

F.I.E. "Standard"

KORTH REVOLVER
Caliber: 22 LR, 22 Mag., 357 Mag., 9mm Parabellum.
Barrel: 3", 4", 6".
Weight: 33 to 38 oz. **Length:** 8" to 11" overall.
Stocks: Checkered walnut, sport or combat.
Sights: Blade front, rear adjustable for windage and elevation.
Features: Four interchangeable cylinders available. Major parts machined from hammer-forged steel; cylinder gap of .002". High polish blue finish. Presentation models have gold trim. Imported from Germany by Mandall Shooting Supplies.
Price: . . . . NA

Llama Super Comanche

LLAMA COMANCHE III REVOLVERS
Caliber: 357 Mag.
Barrel: 4", 6".
Weight: 28 oz. **Length:** 9¼" (4" bbl.).
Stocks: Checkered walnut.
Sights: Fixed blade front, rear adjustable for w. and e.
Features: Ventilated rib, wide spur hammer. Satin chrome finish available. Imported from Spain by Stoeger Industries.
Price: Blue finish $339.00
Price: Satin chrome $395.00

Llama Super Comanche IV Revolver
Similar to the Comanche except: large frame, 44 Mag. with 6", 8½" barrel, 6-shot cylinder; smooth, extra wide trigger; wide spur hammer; over-size walnut, target-style grips. Weight is 3 lbs., 2 oz. Blue finish only.
Price: 44 Mag. $440.00

NEW ENGLAND FIREARMS R92, R22, R73 REVOLVERS
Caliber: 22 LR (9-shot), 22 WMR (6-shot), 32 H&R Mag. (5-shot).
Barrel: 2½", 4".
Weight: 25 oz. (22 LR, 2½"). **Length:** 7" overall (2½" bbl.).
Stocks: American hardwood.
Sights: Fixed.
Features: Choice of blue or nickel finish. Introduced 1988. From New England Firearms Co.
Price: . . . . **NA**

NEW ENGLAND FIREARMS ULTRA REVOLVER
Caliber: 22 LR (9-shot), 22 WMR (6-shot), 32 H&R Mag. (5-shot).
Barrel: 5", 6".
Weight: 32 oz. (5" bbl.). **Length:** 8⅝" overall (5" bbl.).
Stocks: Walnut-finished hardwood.
Sights: Blade front, fully adjustable rear.
Features: Blue finish. Bull-style barrel with recessed muzzle, high "Lustre" blue/black finish. Introduced 1989. From New England Firearms.
Price: . . . . **NA**

New England Ultra

ROSSI MODEL 68 REVOLVER
Caliber: 38 Spec.
Barrel: 2", 3".
Weight: 22 oz.
Stocks: Checkered wood.
Sights: Ramp front, low profile adjustable rear.
Features: All-steel frame, thumb latch operated swing-out cylinder. Introduced 1978. Imported from Brazil by Interarms.
Price: 38, blue, 3" **$180.00**
Price: M68/2 (2" barrel) **$190.00**
Price: 3", nickel **$195.00**

Rossi Model 68

ROSSI MODEL 88 STAINLESS REVOLVER
Caliber: 32 S&W, 38 Spec., 5-shot.
Barrel: 2", 3".
Weight: 22 oz. **Length:** 7.5" overall.
Stocks: Checkered wood, service-style.
Sights: Ramp front, square notch rear drift adjustable for windage.
Features: All metal parts except springs are of 440 stainless steel; matte finish; small frame for concealability. Introduced 1983. Imported from Brazil by Interarms.
Price: 3" barrel **$215.00**
Price: M88/2 (2" barrel) **$220.00**
Price: M89 stainless (3", 32 S&W **$215.00**

Rossi Model 951

ROSSI MODEL 951 REVOLVER
Caliber: 38 Special, 6-shot.
Barrel: 3", 4", vent. rib.
Weight: 30 oz. **Length:** 9" overall.
Stocks: Checkered hardwood, combat-style.
Sights: Colored insert front, fully adjustable rear.
Features: Polished blue finish, shrouded ejector rod. Medium-size frame. Introduced 1985. Imported from Brazil by Interarms.
Price: M951, blue **$233.00**
Price: M851 (as above, stainless, 3", 4") **$253.00**

Rossi Model 971

ROSSI MODEL 971 REVOLVER
Caliber: 357 Mag., 6-shot.
Barrel: 4", heavy.
Weight: 36 oz. **Length:** 9" overall.
Stocks: Checkered Brazilian hardwood.
Sights: Blade front, fully adjustable rear.
Features: Full-length ejector rod shroud; matted sight rib; target-type trigger, wide checkered hammer spur. Introduced 1988. Imported from Brazeil by Interarms.
Price: **$250.00**
Price: M971 stainless, 4", 6" **$280.00**

Rossi Model 511

ROSSI MODEL 511 SPORTSMAN'S 22 REVOLVER
Caliber: 22 LR, 6-shot.
Barrel: 4".
Weight: 30 oz. **Length:** 9" overall.
Stocks: Checkered wood.
Sights: Orange-insert ramp front, fully adjustable square notch rear.
Features: All stainless steel. Shrouded ejector rod; heavy barrel; integral sight rib. Introduced 1986. Imported from Brazil by Interarms.
Price: **$235.00**

CAUTION: PRICES CHANGE, CHECK AT GUNSHOP.

RUGER GP-100 REVOLVERS
Caliber: 38 Special, 357 Magnum, 6-shot.
Barrel: 3", 3" heavy, 4", 4" heavy, 6", 6" heavy.
Weight: 3" barrel—35 oz., 3" heavy barrel—36 oz., 4" barrel—37 oz., 4" heavy barrel—38 oz.
Sights: Fixed; adjustable on 4" heavy, 6", 6" heavy barrels.
Stocks: Ruger Cushioned Grip (live rubber with Goncalo Alves Inserts).
Features: Uses all new action and frame incorporating improvements and features of both the Security-Six and Redhawk revolvers. Full length and short ejector shroud. Satin blue and stainless steel. Introduced 1988.
Price: GP-141 (357, 4" heavy, adj. sights, blue) **$393.75**
Price: GP-160 (357, 6", adj. sights, blue) **$393.75**
Price: GP-161 (357, 6" heavy, adj. sights, blue) **$393.75**
Price: GPF-330 (357, 3"), GPF-830 (38 Spec.) **$378.00**
Price: GPF-331 (357, 3" heavy), GPF-831 (38 Spec.) **$378.00**
Price: GPF-340 (357, 4"), GPF-840 (38 Spec.) **$378.00**
Price: GPF-341 (357, 4" heavy), GPF-841 (38 Spec.) **$378.00**
Price: KGP-141 (357, 4" heavy, adj. sights, stainless) **$425.25**
Price: KGP-160 (357, 6", adj. sights, stainless) **$425.25**
Price: KGP-161 (357, 6" heavy, adj. sights, stainless) **$425.25**
Price: KGPF-330 (357, 3", stainless), KGPF-830 (38 Spec.) **$409.50**
Price: KGPF-331 (357, 3" heavy, stainless), KGPF-831 (38 Spec.) . . **$409.50**
Price: KGPF-340 (357, 4", stainless), KGPF-840 (38 Spec.) **$409.50**
Price: KGPF-341 (357, 4" heavy, stainless), KGPF-841 (38 Spec.) . . **$409.50**

RUGER SP101 REVOLVER
Caliber: 22 LR, 38 Special +P, 5-shot.
Barrel: 2¼", 3".
Weight: 2¼"—25 oz.; 3"—27 oz.
Sights: Fixed.
Stocks: Ruger Cushioned Grip (live rubber with plastic inserts). Goncalo Alves wood inserts are available as an accessory.
Features: Incorporates Improvements and features found in the GP-100 revolvers into a compact, small frame, double-action revolver. Full-length ejector shroud. Stainless steel only. Introduced 1988.
Price: KSP-821 (2½", 38 Spec.) **$388.50**
Price: KSP-830 (3¹⁄₁₆", 38 Spec.) **$388.50**
Price: KSP-221 (2¼", 22 LR) **$388.50**
Price: KSP-240 (4", 22 LR) **$388.50**
Price: KSP-241 (4" heavy bbl., 22 LR) **$388.50**

Ruger GP-100

Ruger SP101

RUGER REDHAWK
Caliber: 41 Mag., 44 Rem. Mag., 6-shot.
Barrel: 5½", 7½".
Weight: About 54 oz. (7½" bbl.). **Length:** 13" overall (7½" barrel).
Stocks: Square butt Goncalo Alves.
Sights: Interchangeable Patridge-type front, rear adjustable for w. and e.
Features: Stainless steel, brushed satin finish, or blued ordnance steel. Has a 9½" sight radius. Introduced 1979.
Price: Blued, 41 Mag., 44 Mag., 5½", 7½" **$436.75**
Price: Blued, 41 Mag., 44 Mag., 7½", with scope mount, rings **$473.00**
Price: Stainless, 41 Mag., 44 Mag., 5½", 7½" **$492.25**
Price: Stainless, 41 Mag., 44 Mag., 7½", with scope mount, rings . . **$530.75**

Ruger Super Redhawk Revolver
Similar to the standard Redhawk except has a heavy extended frame with the Ruger Integral Scope Mounting System on the wide topstrap. The wide hammer spur has been lowered for better scope clearance. Incorporates the mechanical design features and improvements of the GP-100. Choice of 7½" or 9½" barrel, both with ramp front sight base with Redhawk-style Interchangeable Insert sight blades, adjustable rear sight. Comes with Ruger "Cushioned Grip" panels of live rubber and Goncalo Alves wood. Satin polished stainless steel, 44 Magnum only. Introduced 1987.
Price: KSRH-7 (7½"), KSRH-9 (9½") **$561.00**

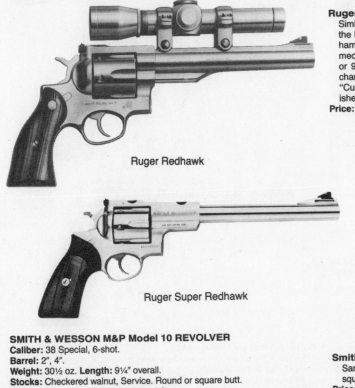

Ruger Redhawk

Ruger Super Redhawk

S&W Model 10

SMITH & WESSON M&P Model 10 REVOLVER
Caliber: 38 Special, 6-shot.
Barrel: 2", 4".
Weight: 30½ oz. **Length:** 9¼" overall.
Stocks: Checkered walnut, Service. Round or square butt.
Sights: Fixed, ramp front, square notch rear.
Price: Blued **$333.00**

Smith & Wesson 38 M&P Heavy Barrel Model 10
Same as regular M&P except: 4" heavy ribbed bbl. with ramp front sight, square rear, square butt, wgt. 33½ oz.
Price: Blued **$333.00**
Price: Nickeled **$345.00**

SMITH & WESSON Model 13 H.B. M&P
Caliber: 357 and 38 Special, 6-shot.
Barrel: 3" or 4".
Weight: 34 oz. **Length:** 9⁵⁄₁₆" overall (4" bbl.).
Stocks: Checkered walnut, Service.
Sights: ⅛" serrated ramp front, fixed square notch rear.
Features: Heavy barrel, K-frame, square butt (4"), round butt (3").
Price: Blue $339.00
Price: Model 65, as above in stainless steel $368.00

SMITH & WESSON MODEL 15 COMBAT MASTERPIECE
Caliber: 38 Special, 6-shot.
Barrel: 4", 6".
Weight: 32 oz. **Length:** 9⁵⁄₁₆" (4" bbl.).
Stocks: Checkered walnut. Grooved tangs.
Sights: Front, Baughman Quick Draw on ramp, micro-click rear, adjustable for w. and e.
Price: Blued, 4", 6" $361.00

SMITH & WESSON MODEL 16 FULL LUG REVOLVER
Caliber: 32 Magnum, 6-shot.
Barrel: 4", full lug.
Weight: 42 oz. **Length:** 9⅛" overall.
Stocks: Square butt Goncalo Alves, combat-style.
Sights: Patridge-style front, adjustable micrometer click rear.
Features: Polished blue finish. Semi-target model has .375" semi-target hammer, .312" smooth combat trigger. Model 16 Target has .500" target hammer, .400" serrated trigger, and is available with either 6" or 8⅜" barrel. Introduced 1990.
Price: Model 16, Semi-target $368.00
Price: Model 16 Target, 6" bbl. $403.00
Price: Model 16 Target, 8⅜" bbl. $414.50

SMITH & WESSON MODEL 17 K-22 FULL LUG
Caliber: 22 LR, 6-shot.
Barrel: 4", 6", 8⅜".
Weight: 39 oz. (6" bbl.). **Length:** 11⅛" overall.
Stocks: Square butt Goncalo Alves, combat style.
Sights: Patridge front with 6", 8⅜", serrated on 4", S&W micro-click rear adjustable for windage and elevation.
Features: Grooved tang, polished blue finish, full lug barrel. Introduced 1990.
Price: 4", 6" bbl. $379.00
Price: 8⅜" bbl. $427.00

Smith & Wesson Model 617 Full Lug Revolver
Similar to the Model 17 Full Lug except made of stainless steel. Has semi-target .375" hammer, .312" smooth combat trigger on 4"; 6" available with either .312" smooth combat trigger or .400" serrated trigger and .500" target hammer; 8⅜" comes with .500" target hammer and .400" serrated trigger. Introduced 1990.
Price: 4" $400.00
Price: 6", semi-target hammer, combat trigger $400.00
Price: 6", target hammer, target trigger $430.00
Price: 8⅜", target hammer, target trigger $440.00

SMITH & WESSON COMBAT MAGNUM MODEL 19
Caliber: 357 Magnum and 38 Special, 6-shot.
Barrel: 2½", 4", 6".
Weight: 36 oz. **Length:** 9⁹⁄₁₆" (4" bbl.).
Stocks: Checkered Goncalo Alves, target. Grooved tangs.
Sights: Front ⅛" Baughman Quick Draw on 2½" or 4" bbl., Patridge on 6" bbl., micro-click rear adjustable for w. and e.
Features: Also availabe in nickel finish.
Price: S&W Bright Blue, adj. sights, from $355.00
Price: Nickel, 4", 6" only $375.00

SMITH & WESSON MODEL 25 REVOLVER
Caliber: 45 Colt, 6-shot.
Barrel: 4", 6", 8⅜".
Weight: About 46 oz. **Length:** 11⅜" overall (6" bbl.).
Stocks: Checkered Goncalo Alves, target-type.
Sights: S&W red ramp front, S&W micrometer click rear with white outline.
Features: Available in Bright Blue or nickel finish; target trigger, target hammer. Contact S&W for complete price list.
Price: 4", 6", blue $429.00
Price: 8⅜", blue or nickel $437.00

S&W Model 15

S&W Model 16 Full Lug

S&W Model 17 Full Lug

S&W Model 19

S&W Model 25

Smith & Wesson Model 625-2
Similar to the Model 25 except chambered for 45 ACP, is made of stainless steel. Has pinned black front sight ramp, micrometer rear with plain blade, semi-target hammer, combat trigger, round butt Pachmayr stocks, full lug barrel. Available in 3", 4", 5" barrel lengths. Introduced in 1989.
Price: $535.00

SMITH & WESSON 357 MAGNUM M-27 REVOLVER
Caliber: 357 Magnum and 38 Special, 6-shot.
Barrel: 4″, 6″, 8⅜″.
Weight: 45½ oz. (6″ bbl.), 44 oz. (4″ bbl.). **Length:** 11⁵⁄₁₆″ overall (6″ bbl.).
Stocks: Checkered walnut, Magna. Grooved tangs and trigger.
Sights: Serrated ramp front, micro-click rear, adjustable for w. and e.
Price: S&W Bright Blue, 4″ $451.00
Price: As above, 6″ $423.00
Price: 8⅜″ bbl., sq. butt, target hammer, trigger, stocks $431.00

Smith & Wesson Model 627 Revolver
Similar to the Model 27 except comes only with 5½″ full lug barrel with straight cross-hatched rib, and is made of stainless steel. Has target hammer and .400″ smooth trigger, black pinned ramp with red insert front sight, adjustable rear; round butt combat-style Goncalo Alves grips. Barrel marked: ".357 MAGNUM Model 1989." Overall length is 10.25″; weight is 50 oz. Introduced 1989.
Price: $530.00

SMITH & WESSON 44 MAGNUM MODEL 29 REVOLVER
Caliber: 44 Magnum, 44 Special or 44 Russian, 6-shot.
Barrel: 4″, 6″, 8⅜″, 10⅝″.
Weight: 47 oz. (6″ bbl.), 44 oz. (4″ bbl.). **Length:** 11⅜″ overall (6″ bbl.).
Stocks: Oversize target-type, checkered Goncalo Alves. Tangs and target trigger grooved, checkered target hammer.
Sights: ⅛″ red ramp front, micro-click rear, adjustable for w. and e.
Price: S&W Bright Blue or nickel, 4″, 6″ $482.00
Price: 8⅜″ bbl., blue $492.00
Price: 10⅝″, blue only (AF) $536.00
Price: Model 629 (stainless steel), 4″, 6″ $510.00
Price: Model 629, 8⅜″ barrel $527.00
Price: As above with scope mount $562.00

S&W Model 629 MagnaClassic

SMITH & WESSON 1953 MODEL 34, 22/32 KIT GUN
Caliber: 22 LR, 6-shot.
Barrel: 2″, 4″.
Weight: 24 oz. (4″ bbl.). **Length:** 8⅜″ (4″ bbl. and round butt).
Stocks: Checkered walnut, round or square butt.
Sights: Front, serrated ramp, micro-click rear, adjustable for w. and e.
Price: Blued $366.00
Price: Model 63, as above in stainless, 4″ $402.00

SMITH & WESSON BODYGUARD MODEL 38
Caliber: 38 Special, 5-shot.
Barrel: 2″.
Weight: 14½ oz. **Length:** 6⁵⁄₁₆″ overall.
Stocks: Checkered walnut.
Sights: Fixed serrated ramp front, square notch rear.
Features: Alloy frame; internal hammer.
Price: Blued $379.00
Price: Nickeled $392.00

SMITH & WESSON 38 CHIEFS SPECIAL & AIRWEIGHT
Caliber: 38 Special, 5-shot.
Barrel: 2″, 3″.
Weight: 19½ oz. (2″ bbl.); 13½ oz. (Airweight). **Length:** 6½″ (2″ bbl. and round butt).
Stocks: Checkered walnut, round or square butt.
Sights: Fixed, serrated ramp front, square notch rear.
Price: Blued, standard Model 36, 2″ $338.00
Price: As above, nickel, 2″ $349.00
Price: Blued, Airweight Model 37 . . . . $358.00
Price: As above, nickel $372.00

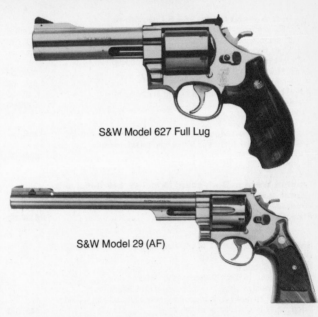

S&W Model 627 Full Lug

S&W Model 29 (AF)

Smith & Wesson Model 29, 629 MagnaClassics
Similar to the standard Model 29 and 629 except comes only with 7½″ full lug barrel, highly polished finish, and in a cherrywood case with gold-embossed leather lid, fitted velvet interior, and with a black leather sight box. Has .500″ target hammer, .400″ serrated target trigger. Comes with replaceable black ramp (M629) and red ramp (M29) front sight and post with white dot, post with gold bead, and four black Patridge sights. Grips are ergonomic Goncalo Alves, finger-grooved, combat-style with Carnuba wax finish. Guns are accurized at the factory. Serial numbers run from MAG0001 to MAG3000; barrels marked "1 of 3000" with laser etching. Comes with test target and certificate of authenticity. Introduced 1990.
Price: . . . . NA

SMITH & WESSON 32 REGULATION POLICE MODEL 31
Caliber: 32 S&W Long, 6-shot.
Barrel: 2″, 3″.
Weight: 18¾ oz. (3″ bbl.). **Length:** 7½″ (3″ bbl.).
Stocks: Checkered walnut, Magna.
Sights: Fixed, ¹⁄₁₀″ serrated ramp front, square notch rear.
Features: Blued.
Price: $365.00

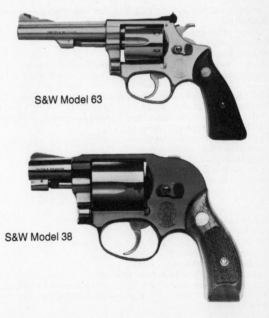

S&W Model 63

S&W Model 38

Smith & Wesson Model 36-LS LadySmith

Similar to the standard Model 36. Available with 2" or 3" barrel. The 2" comes with smooth, contoured rosewood grips with the S&W monogram; 3" has smooth, finger-grooved Goncalo Alves grips. Each has a speedloader cutout. Comes in a fitted carry/storage case. Introduced 1989.

Price: Model 36-LS $379.00
Price: Without case $352.00
Price: Model 60-LS (as above except in stainless) $427.00
Price: Without case $400.00

S&W 36 LadySmith

Smith & Wesson Model 60 Chiefs Special Stainless

Same as Model 36 except: 2" bbl. and round butt only.
Price: Stainless steel $386.00

Smith & Wesson Bodyguard Model 49, 649 Revolvers

Same as Model 38 except steel construction, weight 20½ oz.
Price: Blued, Model 49 .... $359.00
Price: Stainless, Model 649 .... $408.00

SMITH & WESSON 41 MAGNUM MODEL 57 REVOLVER

Caliber: 41 Magnum, 6-shot.
Barrel: 4", 6" or 8⅜".
Weight: 48 oz. (6" bbl.). **Length:** 11⅜" (6" bbl.).
Stocks: Oversize target-type checkered Goncalo Alves.
Sights: ⅛" red ramp front, micro-click rear adjustable for w. and e.
Price: S&W Bright Blue or nickel, 4", 6" $427.00
Price: 8⅜" bbl. $442.00
Price: Stainless, Model 657, 6" $455.00
Price: As above, 8⅜" $471.00

S&W Model 57

SMITH & WESSON MODEL 64 STAINLESS M&P

Caliber: 38 Special, 6-shot.
Barrel: 2", 3", 4".
Weight: 34 oz. **Length:** 9⁹⁄₁₆" overall.
Stocks: Checkered walnut, Service style.
Sights: Fixed, ⅛" serrated ramp front, square notch rear.
Features: Satin finished stainless steel, square butt.
Price: $417.00

SMITH & WESSON MODEL 66 STAINLESS COMBAT MAGNUM

Caliber: 357 Magnum and 38 Special, 6-shot.
Barrel: 2½", 4", 6".
Weight: 36 oz. **Length:** 9⁹⁄₁₆" overall.
Stocks: Checkered Goncalo Alves target.
Sights: Front, Baughman Quick Draw on ramp, micro-click rear adjustable for windage and elevation.
Features: Satin finish stainless steel.
Price: From $404.00

S&W Model 66

SMITH & WESSON MODELS 586, 686 DISTINGUISHED COMBAT MAGNUM

Caliber: 357 Magnum.
Barrel: 4", 6", 8⅜", full shroud.
Weight: 46 oz. (6"), 41 oz. (4").
Stocks: Goncalo Alves target-type with speed loader cutaway.
Sights: Baughman red ramp front, four-position click-adjustable front, S&W micrometer click rear (or fixed).
Features: Uses new L-frame, but takes all K-frame grips. Full-length ejector rod shroud. Smooth combat-type trigger, semi-target type hammer. Trigger stop on 6" models. Also available in stainless as Model 686. Introduced 1981.
Price: Model 586, blue, 4", from $401.00
Price: Model 586, nickel, from $413.00
Price: Model 686, stainless, from $422.00
Price: Model 586, 6", adjustable front sight, blue, ... $436.00
Price: As above, 8⅜" $423.00
Price: Model 686, 6", adjustable front sight $461.00
Price: As above, 8⅜" $479.00

S&W Model 586

SMITH & WESSON MODEL 640 CENTENNIAL

Caliber: 38 Special, 5-shot.
Barrel: 2".
Weight: 20 oz. **Length:** 6⁵⁄₁₆" overall.
Stocks: Round butt Goncalo Alves.
Sights: Serrated ramp front, fixed notch rear.
Features: Stainless steel version of the original Model 40 but without the grip safety. Fully concealed hammer, snag-proof smooth edges. Introduced 1990.
Price: $408.00

S&W Model 640 Centennial

SPORTARMS MODEL HS38S REVOLVER
Caliber: 38 Special, 6-shot.
Barrel: 3", 4".
Weight: 31.3 oz. **Length:** 8" overall (3" barrel).
Stocks: Checkered hardwood; round butt on 3" model, target-style on 4".
Sights: Blade front, adjustable rear.
Features: Polished blue finish; ventilated rib on 4" barrel. Made in West Germany by Herbert Schmidt; imported by Sportarms of Florida.
Price: About **$150.00**

Sportarms HS38S

TAURUS MODEL 66 REVOLVER
Caliber: 357 Magnum, 6-shot.
Barrel: 3", 4", 6".
Weight: 35 oz.
Stocks: Checkered walnut, target-type. Standard stocks on 3".
Sights: Serrated ramp front, micro-click rear adjustable for w. and e. Red ramp front with white outline rear on stainlees models only.
Features: Wide target-type hammer spur, floating firing pin, heavy barrel with shrouded ejector rod. Introduced 1978. From Taurus International.
Price: Blue **$258.00**
Price: Nickel **$272.00**
Price: Stainless steel **$328.00**
Price: Model 65 (similar to M66 except has a fixed rear sight and ramp front), blue, 3" or 4" only **$235.00**
Price: Model 65, satin nickel, 3" or 4" only **$249.00**

Taurus Model 66

TAURUS MODEL 73 SPORT REVOLVER
Caliber: 32 S&W Long, 6-shot.
Barrel: 3", heavy.
Weight: 22 oz. **Length:** 8¼" overall.
Stocks: Oversize target-type, checkered Brazilian walnut.
Sights: Ramp front, notch rear.
Features: Imported from Brazil by Taurus International.
Price: Blue **$210.00**
Price: Satin nickel **$230.00**

Taurus Model 73

TAURUS MODEL 80 STANDARD REVOLVER
Caliber: 38 Spec., 6-shot.
Barrel: 3" or 4".
Weight: 31 oz. (4" bbl.). **Length:** 9¼" overall (4" bbl.).
Stocks: Checkered Brazilian walnut.
Sights: Serrated ramp front, square notch rear.
Features: Imported from Brazil by Taurus International.
Price: Blue **$204.00**
Price: Satin nickel **$218.00**

TAURUS MODEL 82 HEAVY BARREL REVOLVER
Caliber: 38 Spec., 6-shot.
Barrel: 3" or 4", heavy.
Weight: 33 oz. (4" bbl.). **Length:** 9¼" overall (4" bbl.).
Stocks: Checkered Brazilian walnut.
Sights: Serrated ramp front, square notch rear.
Features: Imported from Brazil by Taurus International.
Price: Blue, about **$204.00**
Price: Satin nickel, about **$218.00**

Taurus Model 85

TAURUS MODEL 83 REVOLVER
Caliber: 38 Spec., 6-shot.
Barrel: 4" only, heavy.
Weight: 34½ oz.
Stocks: Oversize checkered walnut.
Sights: Ramp front, micro-click rear adjustable for w. and e.
Features: Blue or nickel finish. Introduced 1977. Imported from Brazil by Taurus International.
Price: Blue **$215.00**
Price: Satin nickel **$228.00**

Taurus Model 669-VR

TAURUS MODEL 85 REVOLVER
Caliber: 38 Spec., 5-shot.
Barrel: 2", 3".
Weight: 21 oz.
Stocks: Checkered walnut.
Sights: Ramp front, square notch rear.
Features: Blue, satin nickel finish or stainless steel. Introduced 1980. Imported from Brazil by Taurus International.
Price: Blue **$223.00**
Price: Satin nickel, 3" only **$242.00**
Price: Stainless steel **$280.00**

TAURUS MODEL 669 REVOLVER
Caliber: 357 Mag., 6-shot.
Barrel: 4", 6".
Weight: 37 oz., (4" bbl.).
Stocks: Checkered walnut, target-type.
Sights: Serrated ramp front, micro-click rear adjustable for windage and elevation.
Features: Wide target-type hammer, floating firing pin, full-length barrel shroud. Introduced 1988. Imported by Taurus International.
Price: Blue **$268.00**
Price: Stainless **$337.00**

CAUTION: PRICES CHANGE, CHECK AT GUNSHOP.

Taurus/Laser Aim 357 Revolver Package
Includes the Taurus Model 669VR revolver (6" barrel, blue or satin nickel finish) and the Taurus/Laser Aim LA1 laser sight with appropriate mount and rings in matching finish, the LA1C 110-volt charger and LA9C 9-volt field charger, and a sturdy high-impact case. Below-barrel mount allows the use of conventional sights or a scope. Introduced 1990.
Price: From **$668.00**

TAURUS MODEL 94 H.B. REVOLVER
Caliber: 22 LR, 9-shot cylinder.
Barrel: 3", 4".
Weight: 25 oz.
Stocks: Checkered Brazilian hardwood.
Sights: Serrrated ramp front, click-adjustable rear for w. and e.
Features: Floating firing-pin, color case-hardened hammer and trigger. Introduced 1989. Imported from Brazil by Taurus International.
Price: **$235.00**
Price: Stainless **$280.00**

UBERTI "INSPECTOR" REVOLVER
Caliber: 32 S&W Long, 38 Spec., 6-shot.
Barrel: 3", 4", 6".
Weight: 24 oz. (3" bbl.). **Length:** 8" overall (3" bbl.).
Stocks: Checkered walnut.
Sights: Blade on ramp front, fixed or adjustable rear.
Features: Blue or chrome finish. Introduced in 1986. Imported from Italy by Uberti USA.
Price: Blue, fixed sights **$413.00**
Price: Blue, adjustable sights, 4", 6" only **$450.00**
Price: Chrome, fixed sights **$441.00**
Price: Chrome, adjustable sights, 4", 6" only **$481.00**

DAN WESSON MODEL 44V, 45V REVOLVERS
Caliber: 41 Mag., 44 Mag., 45 Colt, 6-shot.
Barrel: 4", 6", 8", 10"; Interchangeable.
Weight: 48 oz. (4"). **Length:** 12" overall (6" bbl.).
Stocks: Smooth.
Sights: ⅛" serrated front, white outline rear adjustable for windage and elevation.
Features: Available in blue or stainless steel. Smooth, wide trigger with adjustable over-travel; wide hammer spur. Available in Pistol Pac set also. Contact Dan Wesson Arms for complete price list.
Price: 41 Mag., 4", vent **$412.80**
Price: As above except in stainless **$461.98**
Price: 44 Mag., 4", blue **$431.45**
Price: As above except in stainless **$507.30**
Price: 45 Colt, 4", vent **$431.45**
Price: As above except in stainless **$507.30**

DAN WESSON MODEL 8-2 & MODEL 14-2
Caliber: 38 Special (Model 8-2); 357 (14-2), both 6-shot.
Barrel: 2½", 4", 6", 8"; interchangeable.
Weight: 30 oz. (2½"). **Length:** 9¼" overall (4" bbl.).
Stocks: Checkered, interchangeble.
Sights: ⅛" serrated front, fixed rear.
Features: Interchangeable barrels and grips; smooth, wide trigger; wide hammer spur with short double-action travel. Available in stainless or Brite blue. Contact Dan Wesson for complete price list.
Price: Model 8-2, 2½", blue **$267.15**
Price: As above except in stainless **$311.38**
Price: Model 714-2 Pistol Pac, stainless **$516.68**

DAN WESSON MODEL 22 REVOLVER
Caliber: 22 LR, 22 WMR, 6-shot.
Barrel: 2½", 4", 6", 8", 10"; interchangeable.
Weight: 36 oz. (2½"). 44 oz. (6"). **Length:** 9¼" overall (4" barrel).
Stocks: Checkered; undercover, service or over-size target.
Sights: ⅛" serrated, interchangeable front, white outline rear adjustable for windage and elevation.
Features: Built on the same frame as the Dan Wesson 357; smooth, wide trigger with over-travel adjustment, wide spur hammer, with short double-action travel. Available in Brite blue or stainless steel. Contact Dan Wesson for complete price list.
Price: 2½" bbl., blue **$337.64**
Price: As above, stainless **$366.07**
Price: With 4", vent. rib, blue **$369.97**
Price: As above, stainless **$398.41**
Price: Stainless Pistol Pac, 22 LR **$689.01**

Taurus Model 669-VR Revolver
Same as the Model 669 except has full-length ventilated barrel rib. Available in blue or stainless steel. Introduced 1990. From Taurus International.
Price: Blue, 4" or 6" **$279.00**
Price: Stainless, 4" or 6" **$349.00**

Taurus Model 94

Uberti Inspector

Dan Wesson 44 Magnum

Dan Wesson Model 32M

Dan Wesson Model 15 Gold Series
Similar to the Model 15 except has smoother action to reduce DA pull to 8-10 lbs.; comes with either 6" or 8" vent heavy slotted barrel shroud with bright blue barrel. Shroud is stamped "Gold Series" with the Dan Wesson signature engraved and gold filled. Hammer and trigger are polished bright; rosewood grips. New sights with orange dot Patridge front, white triangle on rear blade. Introduced 1989.
Price: 6" **$543.59**
Price: 8" **$554.26**

Dan Wesson 9-2, 15-2 & 32M Revolvers
Same as Models 8-2 and 14-2 except they have adjustable sight. Model 9-2 chambered for 38 Special, Model 15-2 for 357 Magnum. Model 32M is chambered for 32 H&R Mag. Same specs and prices as for 15-2 guns. Available in blue or stainless. Contact Dan Wesson for complete price list.
Price: Model 9-2 or 15-2, 2½", blue **$337.64**
Price: As above except in stainless **$366.07**

Both classic six-shooters and modern adaptations for hunting and sport.

CENTURY MODEL 100 SINGLE ACTION
Caliber: 30-30, 375 Win., 444 Marlin, 45-70, 50-70.
Barrel: 6½" (standard), 8", 10", 12". Other lengths to order.
Weight: 6 lbs. (loaded). **Length:** 15" overall (8" bbl.).
Stocks: Smooth walnut.
Sights: Ramp front, Millett adjustable square notch rear.
Features: Highly polished high tensile strength manganese bronze frame, blue cylinder and barrel; coil spring trigger mechanism. Calibers other than 45-70 start at $1,500.00. Introduced 1975. Made in U.S. From Century Gun Dist., Inc.
Price: 6" barrel, 45-70 . . . . **$750.00**

Century Model 100

CIMARRON U.S. CAVALRY MODEL SINGLE ACTION
Caliber: 45 Colt.
Barrel: 7½".
Weight: 42 oz. **Length:** 13½" overall.
Stocks: Walnut.
Sights: Fixed.
Features: Has "A.P. Casey" markings; "U.S." plus patent dates on frame, serial number on backstrap, trigger guard, frame and cylinder, "APC" cartouche on left grip; color case-hardened frame and hammer, rest charcoal blue. Exact copy of the original. Imported by Cimarron Arms.
Price: **$459.00**

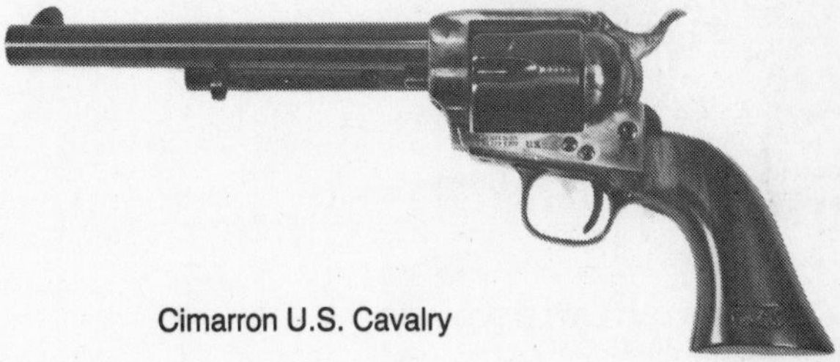

Cimarron Artillery Model Single Action
Similar to the U.S. Cavalry model except has 5½" barrel, weighs 39 oz., and is 11½" overall. U.S. markings and cartouche, case-hardened frame and hammer; 45 Colt only.
Price: **$459.00**

Cimarron U.S. Cavalry

CIMARRON 1873 PEACEMAKER REPRO
Caliber: 22 LR, 22 WMR, 38 WCF, 357 Mag., 44 WCF, 45 Colt.
Barrel: 3", 4", 4¾", 5½", 7½".
Weight: 39 oz. **Length:** 10" overall (4" barrel).
Stocks: Walnut.
Sights: Blade front, fixed or adjustable rear.
Features: Uses "old model" blackpowder frame with "Bullseye" ejector or New Model frame. Imported by Cimarron Arms.
Price: Standard model (Old Model or New Model) **$389.00**
Price: "A" engraving (30 percent coverage) **$589.00**
Price: "B" engraving (50 percent coverage) **$699.00**
Price: "C" engraving (100 percent coverage) **$1,099.00**

Cimarron 1873 Peacemaker

CIMARRON SHERIFF MODEL SINGLE ACTION
Caliber: 22 LR, 22 WMR, 38 Spec., 357 Mag., 44 WCF, 45 Colt.
Barrel: 3" or 4".
Weight: 38 oz. **Length:** 10" overall.
Stocks: Walnut.
Sights: Fixed.
Features: Patent dates on frame; serial number on backstrap, trigger guard, frame and cylinder. Modern or old-style blue. Uses blackpowder frame. Imported by Cimarron Arms.
Price: **$389.00**

Cimarron 1875 Remington

CIMARRON 1875 REMINGTON
Caliber: 357 Mag., 44-40, 45 Colt, 6-shot.
Barrel: 7½".
Weight: 44 oz. **Length:** 13¾" overall.
Stocks: Smooth walnut.
Sights: Blade front, notch rear.
Features: Replica of the 1875 Remington S.A. Army revolver. Brass trigger guard, color case-hardened frame, rest blued, or nickel finish. Imported by Cimarron Arms.
Price: **$349.00**

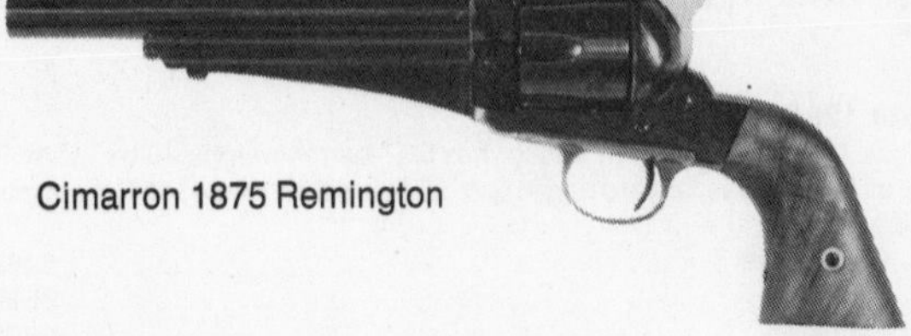

CIMARRON 1890 REMINGTON REVOLVER
Caliber: 357 Mag., 44-40, 45 Colt, 6-shot.
Barrel: 5½".
Weight: 37 oz. **Length:** 12½" overall.
Stocks: American walnut.
Sights: Blade front, groove rear.
Features: Replica of the 1890 Remington single action. Brass trigger guard, rest is blued, or nickel finish. Lanyard ring in butt. Imported by Cimarron Arms.
Price: **$349.00**

DAKOTA SINGLE-ACTION REVOLVERS
Caliber: 22 LR, 22 WMR, 357 Mag., 30 Carbine, 32-20, 32 H&R Mag., 44-40, 44 Spec., 45 Colt, 45 ACP.
Barrel: 3½", 4⅝", 5½", 7½", 12", 16¼".
Weight: 45 oz. **Length:** 13" overall (7½" bbl.).
Stocks: Smooth walnut.
Sights: Blade front, fixed rear.
Features: Colt-type hammer with firing pin, color case-hardened frame, blue barrel and cylinder, brass grip frame and trigger guard. Available in blue or nickel-plated, plain or engraved. Imported by E.M.F.
Price: 22 LR, 30 Car., 357, 44-40, 45 Colt, 4⅝", 5½", 7½" $450.00
Price: 22 LR/22 WMR, 45 Colt/ 45 ACP, 32-20/32 H&R, 357/9mm, 44-40/44 Spec., 5½", 7½" $580.00
Price: 357, 44-40, 45, 12" $520.00
Price: 357, 44-40, 45, 3½" $520.00

Dakota Single Action

Dakota Bisley

DAKOTA 1875 OUTLAW REVOLVER
Caliber: 357, 44-40, 45 Colt.
Barrel: 7½".
Weight: 46 oz. **Length:** 13½" overall.
Stocks: Smooth walnut.
Sights: Blade front, fixed groove rear.
Features: Authentic copy of 1875 Remington with firing pin in hammer; color case-hardened frame, blue cylinder, barrel, steel backstrap and brass trigger guard. Also available in nickel, factory engraved. Imported by E.M.F.
Price: All calibers $450.00
Price: Nickel $495.00
Price: Engraved $570.00

Dakota Hartford Model Single-Action Revolvers
Similar to the Dakota Single-Action revolvers except available with 5½" barrel (Artillery) or 7½" (Cavalry); or with 4⅝" barrel. Identical to the original Colts with inspector cartouche on left grip, original patent dates and U.S. markings. All major parts serial numbered using original Colt-style lettering, numbering. Bullseye ejector head and color case-hardening on frame and hammer. In 45 Colt only (for Cavalry and Artillery), or 22 LR, 357, 38-40, 44 Spec., for 4⅝". Introduced 1990. From E.M.F.
Price: $500.00
Price: Cavalry or Artillery $550.00
Price: Nickel plated $560.00
Price: Cattlebrand engraved $680.00
Price: Engraved nickel $730.00

Dakota 1890 Police Revolver
Similar to the 1875 Outlaw except has 5½" barrel, weighs 40 oz., with 12½" overall length. Has lanyard ring in butt. Calibers 357, 44-40, 45 Colt. Imported by E.M.F.
Price: All calibers $485.00
Price: Nickel $520.00
Price: Engraved $600.00

F.I.E. "COWBOY" SINGLE-ACTION REVOLVER
Caliber: 22 LR, 22 LR/22 WMR, 6-shot.
Barrel: 3¼" or 6½".
Weight: 28 oz. (3¼" barrel).
Stocks: Smooth nylon.
Sights: Blade front, fixed rear.
Features: Floating firing pin, hammer block safety. Available as combo with extra cylinder. Made in U.S. by F.I.E. Firearms Corp.
Price: 22 LR $94.95
Price: 22 LR/22 WMR combo $114.95

DAKOTA BISLEY MODEL SINGLE ACTION
Caliber: 22 LR, 22 WMR, 32-20, 32 H&R Mag., 357, 30 Carbine, 38-40, 44 Spec., 44-40, 45 Colt, 45 ACP.
Barrel: 4⅝", 5½", 7½".
Weight: 37 oz. **Length:** 10½" overall with 5½" barrel.
Stocks: Smooth walnut.
Sights: Blade front, fixed groove rear.
Features: Colt-type firing pin in hammer; color case-hardened frame, blue barrel, cylinder, steel backstrap and trigger guard. Also available in nickel, factory engraved. Imported by E.M.F.
Price: All calibers, bbl. lengths $540.00
Price: Combo models—22 LR/22 WMR, 32-20/32 H&R, 357/9mm, 44-40/44 Spec., 45 Colt/45 ACP $600.00
Price: Nickel, all cals. $640.00
Price: Engraved, all cals., lengths $700.00

Dakota Hartford Cavalry

Dakota 1890 Police

F.I.E. "Cowboy"

F.I.E. "TEXAS RANGER" REVOLVER
Caliber: 22 LR, 22 WMR.
Barrel: 4¾", 6½", 9".
Weight: 31 oz. (4¾" bbl.). **Length:** 10" overall.
Stocks: American walnut.
Sights: Blade front, notch rear.
Features: Single action, blue/black finish. Introduced 1983. Made in the U.S. by F.I.E.
Price: 22 LR, 4¾" **$109.95**
Price: As above, convertible (22 LR/22 WMR) **$129.95**
Price: 22 LR, 6½" **$109.95**
Price: As above, convertible (22 LR/22 WMR) **$129.95**
Price: 22 LR, 9" **$114.95**
Price: As above, convertible (22 LR/22 WMR) **$134.95**

F.I.E. "Texas Ranger"

F.I.E. "Yellow Rose"

F.I.E. "Little Ranger" Revolver
Similar to the "Texas Ranger" except has 3¼" barrel, bird's-head grips. Introduced 1986. Made in U.S. by F.I.E.
Price: 22 LR **$109.95**
Price: 22 LR/22 WMR convertible **$129.95**

F.I.E. "YELLOW ROSE" REVOLVER
Caliber: 22 LR/22 WMR.
Barrel: 4¾".
Weight: 32 oz. **Length:** 10" overall.
Stocks: Walnut.
Sights: Blade front, fixed rear.
Features: Slide spring ejector. Positive hammer block. Imported from Italy by F.I.E.
Price: "Yellow Rose," gold, 22 convertible **$159.95**
Price: "Yellow Rose of Texas" Presentation Model **$324.95**

F.I.E. "HOMBRE" SINGLE-ACTION REVOLVER
Caliber: 357 Mag., 44 Mag., 45 Colt.
Barrel: 6" or 7½".
Weight: 45 oz. (6" bbl.).
Stocks: Smooth walnut with medallion; ivory polymer optional.
Sights: Blade front, grooved topstrap (fixed) rear.
Features: Color case-hardened frame. Bright blue finish. Super-smooth action. Introduced 1979. Imported from West Germany by F.I.E. Corp.
Price: **$264.95**
Price: 24K gold-plated **$349.95**

FREEDOM ARMS 454 CASULL
Caliber: 44 Mag., 45 Colt, 454 Casull, 5-shot.
Barrel: 3", 4¾", 6", 7½", 10".
Weight: 50 oz. **Length:** 14" overall (7½" bbl.)
Stocks: Impregnated hardwood.
Sights: Blade front, notch or adjustable rear.
Features: All stainless steel construction; sliding bar safety system. Lifetime warranty. Made in U.S.A.
Price: . . . . **$1,044.75 to $1,149.75**
Price: Field Grade, adjustable sight, (matte stainless finish, Pachmayr Presentation grips, 4¾", 7½", 10") **$929.00**
Price: Field Grade, fixed sights, 4¾" only **$847.00**

MITCHELL SINGLE ACTION ARMY REVOLVERS
Caliber: 357 Mag., 44-40, 44 Mag., 45 ACP, 45 Colt, 6-shot.
Barrel: 4¾", 5½", 6", 7½", 10", 12", 18".
Weight: NA. **Length:** NA.
Stocks: One-piece walnut.
Sights: Serrated ramp front, fixed or adjustable rear.
Features: Color case-hardened frame, brass or steel backstrap/trigger guard; hammer-block safety. Bright nickel-plated model and dual cylinder models available. Contact importer for complete price list. Imported by Mitchell Arms, Inc.
Price: Fixed sights, 357, 45 Colt, 4¾", 5½", 7½" **$309.95**
Price: As above, steel backstrap, trigger guard **$349.95**
Price: Fixed sights, dual cyl. 45 Colt/45 ACP, 4¾" **$374.95**
Price: As above, bright nickel **$399.00**
Price: Adjustable sights, 44 Mag., 4¾", 6", 7½" **$349.00**
Price: As above, dual cyl., 44 Mag./44-40 . . . . **$379.00**
Price: Silhouette Model, 44 Mag., 10", 12", 18" **$395.00**
Price: 1875 Remington, 357 Mag., 44-40, 45 Colt, 7½" **$350.00**
Price: 1890 Remington, 44-40, 45 Colt, 5" **$350.00**

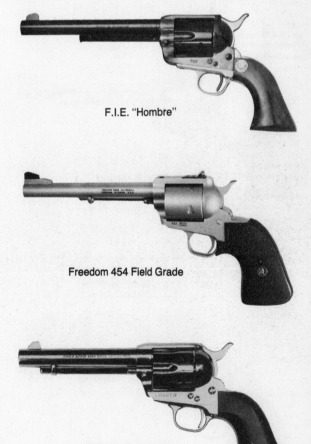

F.I.E. "Hombre"

Freedom 454 Field Grade

Mitchell Single Action

CAUTION: PRICES CHANGE, CHECK AT GUNSHOP.

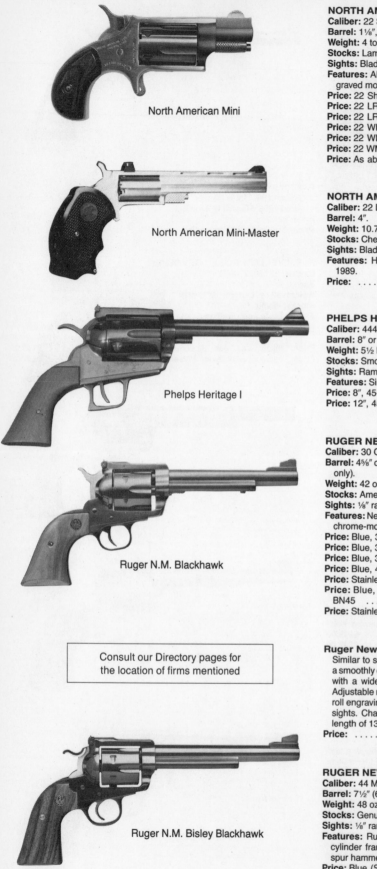

North American Mini

North American Mini-Master

Phelps Heritage I

Ruger N.M. Blackhawk

Consult our Directory pages for
the location of firms mentioned

Ruger N.M. Bisley Blackhawk

NORTH AMERICAN MINI-REVOLVERS
Caliber: 22 S, 22 LR, 22 WMR, 5-shot.
Barrel: 1⅛″, 1⅝″, 2½″.
Weight: 4 to 6.6 oz. **Length:** 3⅝″ to 6⅛″ overall.
Stocks: Laminated wood.
Sights: Blade front, notch fixed rear.
Features: All stainless steel construction. Polished satin and matte finish. Engraved models available. From North American Arms.
Price: 22 Short, 1⅛″ bbl. $148.00
Price: 22 LR, 1⅛″ bbl. $149.00
Price: 22 LR, 1⅝″ bbl. $149.00
Price: 22 WMR, 1⅝″ bbl. $170.00
Price: 22 WMR, 2½″ bbl. $188.00
Price: 22 WMR, 1⅛″ or 1⅝″ bbl. with extra 22 LR cylinder $203.00
Price: As above, 2½″ bbl. $221.00

NORTH AMERICAN MINI-MASTER
Caliber: 22 LR, 22 WMR, 5-shot cylinder.
Barrel: 4″.
Weight: 10.7 oz. **Length:** 7.75″ overall.
Stocks: Checkered hard black rubber.
Sights: Blade front, white outline rear adjustable for elevation.
Features: Heavy vent barrel; full-size grips. Non-fluted cylinder. Introduced 1989.
Price: $265.00

PHELPS HERITAGE I, EAGLE I REVOLVERS
Caliber: 444 Marlin, 45-70, 6-shot.
Barrel: 8″ or 12″, 16″ (45-70).
Weight: 5½ lbs. **Length:** 19½″ overall (12″ bbl.).
Stocks: Smooth walnut.
Sights: Ramp front, adjustable rear.
Features: Single action; polished blue finish; safety bar. From Phelps Mfg. Co.
Price: 8″, 45-70 or 444 Marlin, about $765.00
Price: 12″, 45-70 or 444 Marlin, about $790.00

RUGER NEW MODEL BLACKHAWK REVOLVER
Caliber: 30 Carbine, 357 Mag./38Spec., 41 Mag., 44 Mag., 45 Colt, 6-shot.
Barrel: 4⅝″ or 6½″, either caliber, 5½″ (44 Mag. only), 7½″ (30 Carbine, 45 Colt only).
Weight: 42 oz. (6½″ bbl.). **Length:** 12¼″ overall (6½″ bbl.).
Stocks: American walnut.
Sights: ⅛″ ramp front, micro-click rear adjustable for w. and e.
Features: New Ruger interlocked mechanism, independent firing pin, hardened chrome-moly steel frame, music wire springs throughout.
Price: Blue, 30 Carbine (7½″ bbl.), BN31 . . . . $300.25
Price: Blue, 357 Mag. (4⅝″, 6½″), BN34, BN36 . . . . $312.25
Price: Blue, 357/9mm (4⅝″, 6½″), BN34X, BN36X $327.25
Price: Blue, 44 Mag. (5½″), S45N $360.50
Price: Stainless, 44 Mag. (5½″), KS45N $394.00
Price: Blue, 41 Mag., 44 Mag., 45 Colt (4⅝″, 6½″), BN41, BN42, BN44, BN45 . . . . $312.25
Price: Stainless, 357 Mag. (4⅝″, 6½″), KBN34, KBN36 . . . . $384.75

Ruger New Model Bisley
Similar to standard New Model Blackhawk except the hammer is lower with a smoothly curved, deeply checkered wide spur. The trigger is strongly curved with a wide smooth surface. Longer grip frame has a hand-filling shape. Adjustable rear sight, ramp-style front. Available with an unfluted cylinder and roll engraving, or with a fluted cylinder and no engraving. Fixed or adjustable sights. Chambered for 357, 41, 44 Mags. and 45 Colt; 7½″ barrel; overall length of 13″. Introduced 1985.
Price: $372.25

RUGER NEW MODEL SUPER BLACKHAWK
Caliber: 44 Magnum, 6-shot. Also fires 44 Spec.
Barrel: 7½″ (6-groove, 20″ twist), 10½″.
Weight: 48 oz. (7½″ bbl.), 51 oz. (10½″ bbl.). **Length:** 13⅜″ overall (7½″ bbl.).
Stocks: Genuine American walnut.
Sights: ⅛″ ramp front, micro-click rear adjustable for w. and e.
Features: Ruger interlocked mechanism, non-fluted cylinder, steel grip and cylinder frame, square back trigger guard, wide serrated trigger and wide spur hammer.
Price: Blue (S-47N, S-411N) $360.50
Price: Stainless (KS-47N, KS-411N) $394.00

CAUTION: PRICES CHANGE, CHECK AT GUNSHOP.

Ruger Small Frame New Model Bisley

Similar to the New Model Single-Six except frame is styled after the classic Bisley "flat-top." Most mechanical parts are unchanged. Hammer is lower and smoothly curved with a deeply checkered spur. Trigger is strongly curved with a wide smooth surface. Longer grip frame designed with a hand-filling shape, and the trigger guard is a large oval. Dovetail rear sight drift-adjustable for windage; front sight base accepts interchangeable square blades of various heights and styles. Available with an unfluted cylinder and roll engraving, or with a fluted cylinder and no engraving. Weight about 41 oz. Chambered for 22 LR and 32 H&R Mag., 6½" barrel only. Introduced 1985.
Price: **$313.00**

Ruger Bisley Single-Six

RUGER NEW MODEL SUPER SINGLE-SIX CONVERTIBLE REVOLVER

Caliber: 22 LR, 6-shot; 22 WMR in extra cylinder.
Barrel: 4⅝", 5½", 6½", or 9½" (6-groove).
Weight: 34½ oz. (6½" bbl.). **Length:** 11¹³⁄₁₆" overall (6½" bbl.).
Stocks: Smooth American walnut.
Sights: Improved Patridge front on ramp, fully adjustable rear protected by integral frame ribs.
Features: Ruger interlocked mechanism, transfer bar ignition, gate-controlled loading, hardened chrome-moly steel frame, wide trigger, music wire springs throughout, independent firing pin.
Price: 4⅝", 5½", 6½", 9½" barrel **$267.75**
Price: 5½", 6½" bbl. only, stainless steel **$337.00**

Ruger New Model Single-Six Revolver

Similar to the Super Single-Six revolver except chambered for 32 H&R Magnum (also handles 32 S&W and 32 S&W Long). Weight is about 34 oz. with 6½" barrel. Barrel lengths: 4⅝", 5½", 6½", 9½". Introduced 1985.
Price: **$257.00**

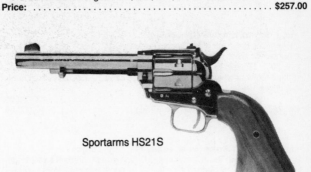

Sportarms HS21S

SPORTARMS MODEL HS21S SINGLE ACTION

Caliber: 22 LR or 22 LR/22 WMR combo, 6-shot.
Barrel: 5½".
Weight: 33.5 oz. **Length:** 11" overall.
Stocks: Smooth hardwood.
Sights: Blade front, rear drift adjustable for windage.
Features: Available in blue with imitation stag or wood stocks. Made in West Germany by Herbert Schmidt; Imported by Sportarms of Florida.
Price: 22 LR, blue, "stag" grips, about **$80.00**
Price: 22 LR/22 WMR combo, blue, wood stocks, about **$110.00**

SUPER SIX GOLDEN BISON 45-70 REVOLVER

Caliber: 45-70, 6-shot.
Barrel: 8", 10½", octagonal.
Weight: 5 lbs., 12 oz. (8" bbl.) **Length:** 15" overall (8" bbl.).
Stocks: Smooth walnut.
Sights: Blaze orange blade front on ramp, Millett fully adjustable rear.
Features: Cylinder frame and grip frame of high tensile manganese bronze; hammer of manganese bronze with a hardened steel pad for firing pin contact; all coil springs; full-cock, cross-bolt interlocking safety and traveling safeties. Choice of antique brown or blue/black finish. Lifetime warranty. Comes in a fitted walnut presentation case. Made in the U.S. by Super Six Limited.
Price: Golden Bison (8" bbl.) **$2,595.00**
Price: Golden Bison Bull (10½" bbl.) **$2,595.00**

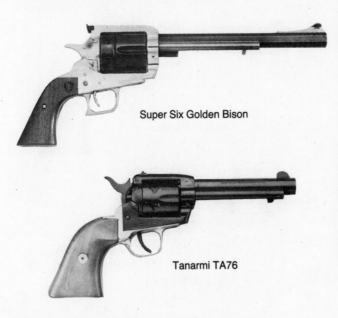

Super Six Golden Bison

Tanarmi TA76

TANARMI S.A. REVOLVER MODEL TA76/TA22

Caliber: 22 LR, 22 WMR, 6-shot.
Barrel: 4¾", 6", or 9".
Weight: 32 oz. **Length:** 10" overall.
Stocks: Walnut.
Sights: Blade front, rear adjustable for windage.
Features: Manual hammer block safety. Imported from Italy by Excam.
Price: 22 LR, blue, 4¾" **$95.00**
Price: Combo, blue, 4¾" **$105.00**
Price: 22 LR, chrome, 4¾" **$99.00**
Price: Combo, chrome, 4¾" **$121.00**
Price: Combo, blue, 6" **$115.00**
Price: Combo, blue, 9" **$115.00**

TEXAS LONGHORN GROVER'S IMPROVED NO. FIVE

Caliber: 44 Magnum, 6-shot.
Barrel: 5½".
Weight: 44 oz. **Length:** NA.
Stocks: Fancy AAA walnut.
Sights: Square blade front on ramp, fully adjustable rear.
Features: Music wire coil spring action with double locking bolt; polished blue finish. Handmade in limited 1,200-gun production. Grip contour, straps, oversized base pin, lever latch and lockwork identical copies of Elmer Keith design. Lifetime warranty to original owner. Introduced 1988.
Price: **$985.00**

Texas Longhorn Grover's No. 5

TEXAS LONGHORN RIGHT-HAND SINGLE ACTION
Caliber: All centerfire pistol calibers.
Barrel: 4¾".
Weight: NA. **Length:** NA.
Stocks: One-piece fancy walnut, or any fancy AAA wood.
Sights: Blade front, grooved topstrap rear.
Features: Loading gate and ejector housing on left side of gun. Cylinder rotates to the left. All steel construction; color case-hardened frame; high polish blue; music wire coil springs. Lifetime guarantee to original owner. Introduced 1984. From Texas Longhorn Arms.
Price: South Texas Army Limited Edition—handmade, only 1,000 to be produced; "One of One Thousand" engraved on barrel **$1,500.00**

Texas Longhorn Arms Texas Border Special
Similar to the South Texas Army Limited Edition except has 3½" barrel, bird's-head style grip. Same special features. Introduced 1984.
Price: **$1,500.00**

Texas Longhorn Arms Cased Set
Set contains one each of the Texas Longhorn Right-Hand Single Actions, all in the same caliber, same serial numbers (100, 200, 300, 400, 500, 600, 700, 800, 900). Ten sets to be made (#1000 donated to NRA museum). Comes in hand-tooled leather case. All other specs same as Limited Edition guns. Introduced 1984.
Price: **$5,750.00**
Price: With ¾-coverage "C-style" engraving **$7,650.00**

Texas Longhorn Arms West Texas Flat Top Target
Similar to the South Texas Army Limited Edition except choice of barrel length from 7½" through 15"; flat-top style frame; ⅛" contoured ramp front sight, old model steel micro-click rear adjustable for w. and e. Same special features. Introduced 1984.
Price: **$1,500.00**

UBERTI 1873 CATTLEMAN SINGLE ACTIONS
Caliber: 38 Spec., 38-40, 357 Mag., 44 Spec., 44-40, 45 Colt/45 ACP, 6-shot.
Barrel: 4¾", 5½", 7½"; 44-40, 45 Colt also with 3".
Weight: 38 oz. (5½" bbl.). **Length:** 10¾" overall (5½" bbl.).
Stocks: One-piece smooth walnut.
Sights: Blade front, groove rear; fully adjustable rear available.
Features: Steel or brass backstrap, trigger guard; color case-hardened frame, blued barrel, cylinder. Imported from Italy by Uberti USA.
Price: Steel backstrap, trigger guard, fixed sights $361.00
Price: As above, adjustable sight $385.00
Price: Brass backstrap, trigger guard, fixed sights $333.00
Price: As above, adjustable sight $358.00

Uberti 1873 Buckhorn Single Action
A slightly larger version of the Cattleman revolver. Available in 44 Magnum or 44 Magnum/44-40 convertible, otherwise has same specs.
Price: Steel backstrap, trigger guard, fixed sights $371.00
Price: As above, brass $343.00
Price: Convertible (two cylinders) add $40.00

UBERTI 1875 SA ARMY "OUTLAW" REVOLVER
Caliber: 357 Mag., 44-40, 45 Colt, 6-shot.
Barrel: 7½".
Weight: 44 oz. **Length:** 13¾" overall.
Stocks: Smooth walnut.
Sights: Blade front, notch rear.
Features: Replica of the 1875 Remington S.A. Army revolver. Brass trigger guard, color case-hardened frame, rest blued. Imported by Uberti USA.
Price: $343.00
Price: Nickel-plated $378.00

Texas Longhorn Sesquicentennial Model Revolver
Similar to the South Texas Army Model except has ¾-coverage Nimschke-style engraving, antique golden nickel plate finish, one-piece elephant ivory grips. Comes with handmade solid walnut presentation case, factory letter to owner. Limited edition of 150 units. Introduced 1986.
Price: **$2,500.00**

Texas Longhorn Border Special

Texas Longhorn Flat Top

Uberti Cattleman

Uberti 1875 Army

UBERTI 1890 ARMY "OUTLAW" REVOLVER
Caliber: 357 Mag., 44-40, 45 Colt, 6-shot.
Barrel: 5½".
Weight: 37 oz. **Length:** 12½" overall.
Stocks: American walnut.
Sights: Blade front, groove rear.
Features: Replica of the 1890 Remington single action. Brass trigger guard, rest is blued. Imported by Uberti USA.
Price: $357.00
Price: Nickel-plated $399.00

Specially adapted single-shot and multi-barrel arms.

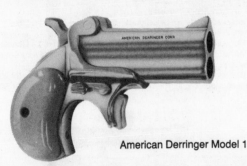

American Derringer Model 1

American Derringer Model 10 Lightweight

Similar to the Model 1 except frame is of aluminum, giving weight of 10 oz. Available in 45 Colt or 45 ACP only. Matte gray finish. Introduced 1989.

Price: 45 Colt $295.00
Price: 45 ACP $235.00
Price: Model 11 (38 Spec., aluminum bbls., wgt. 11 oz.) $187.00

American Derringer Texas Commemorative

A Model 1 Derringer with solid brass frame, stainless steel barrel and rosewood grips. Available in 32 H&R Mag., 38 Speical, 44-40 Win., or 45 Colt. Introduced 1987.

Price: 32 Mag. or 38 Spec. $200.00
Price: 44-40 or 45 Colt $307.00

AMERICAN DERRINGER DA 38

Caliber: 38 Spec.
Barrel: 2½".
Weight: 14 oz. **Length:** 4.8" overall.
Stocks: Checkered plastic.
Sights: Fixed.
Features: Double-action only; two-shots. Manual safety. Made of satin-finished stainless steel and aluminum. Introduced 1989. From American Derringer Corp.

Price: $225.00

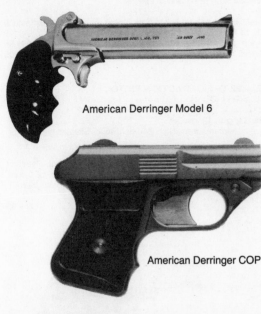

American Derringer Model 6

American Derringer COP

American Derringer Mini COP Derringer

Similar to the COP 357 except chambered for 22 WMR. Barrel length of 2.85", overall length of 4.95", weight is 16 oz. Double action with automatic hammer-block safety. Made of stainless steel. Grips of rosewood, walnut or other hardwoods. Introduced 1990. Made in U.S. by American Derringer Corp.

Price: .... NA

AMERICAN DERRINGER MODEL 1

Caliber: 22 LR, 22 WMR, 22 Hornet, 223 Rem., 30 Luger, 30-30 Win., 32 ACP, 38 Super, 380 ACP, 38 Spec., 9x18, 9mm Para., 357 Mag., 357 Maximum, 10mm, 40 S&W, 41 Mag., 38-40, 44-40 Win., 44 Spec., 44 American, 44 Mag., 45 Colt, 45 ACP, 410-bore. (2½").
Barrel: 3".
Weight: 15½ oz. (38 Spec.). **Length:** 4.82" overall.
Stocks: Rosewood, Zebra wood.
Sights: Blade front.
Features: Made of stainless steel with high-polish or satin finish. Two-shot capacity. Manual hammer block safety. Introduced 1980. Available in almost any pistal caliber. Contact the factory for complete list of available calibers and prices. From American Derringer Corp.

Price: 22 LR or WMR $235.00
Price: 22 Hornet, 223 Rem. $375.00
Price: 38 Spec. $199.00
Price: 357 Maximum $250.00
Price: 357 Mag. $235.00
Price: 9x18, 9mm, 380, 38 Super $187.50
Price: 10mm, 40 S&W $235.00
Price: 44 Spec., 44 American $307.00
Price: 38-40, 44-40 Win., 45 Colt, 45 Auto Rim $307.00
Price: 30-30, 41, 44 Mags., 45 Win. Mag. $375.00
Price: 45-70, single shot $312.00
Price: 45 Colt, 410, 2½" $312.00
Price: 45 ACP, 10mm Auto $235.00
Price: Lady Derringer .... $225.00 to $695.00

AMERICAN DERRINGER MODEL 3

Caliber: 38 Special.
Barrel: 2.5".
Weight: 8.5 oz. **Length:** 4.9" overall.
Stocks: Rosewood.
Sights: Blade front.
Features: Made of stainless steel. Single shot with manual hammer block safety. Introduced 1985. From American Derringer Corp.

Price: $115.00

American Derringer Model 4

Similar to the Model 1 except has 4.1" barrel, overall length of 6", and weighs 16½ oz.; chambered for 3" 410-bore shotshells or 45 Colt. Can be had with 45-70 upper barrel and 3" 410-bore or 45 Colt bottom barrel. Made of stainless steel. Manual hammer block safety. Introduced 1985.

Price: 3" 410/45 Colt (either barrel) $350.00
Price: 3" 410/45 Colt or 45-70 (Alaskan Survival model) $375.00

American Derringer Model 6

Similar to the Model 1 except has 6" barrels chambered for 3" 410 shotshells or 45 Colt, rosewood stocks, 8.2" o.a.l. and weighs 21 oz. Shoots either round for each barrel. Manual hammer block safety. Introduced 1986.

Price: High polish or satin finish $369.00
Price: Gray matte finish $337.50

American Derringer Model 7

Similar to Model 1 except made of high strength aircraft aluminum. Weighs 7½ oz., 4.82" o.a.l., rosewood stocks. Available in 22 LR, 32 S&W Long, 32 H&R Mag., 380 ACP, 38 S&W, 38 Spec., 44 Spec. Introduced 1986.

Price: 22 LR or 38 Spec. $195.00
Price: 38 S&W, 380 ACP, 32 S&W Long $169.00
Price: 32 H&R Mag. $169.00
Price: 44 Spec. $500.00

AMERICAN DERRINGER COP 357 DERRINGER

Caliber: 38 Spec. or 357 Mag., 4-shot.
Barrel: 3.14".
Weight: 16 oz. **Length:** 5.53" overall.
Stocks: Rosewood.
Sights: Fixed.
Features: Double action only. Four shots. Made of stainless steel. Introduced 1990. Made in U.S. by American Derringer Corp.

Price: .... NA

American Derringer Semmerling

AMERICAN DERRINGER SEMMERLING LM-4
Caliber: 9mm Para., 7-shot magazine; 45 ACP, 5-shot magazine.
Barrel: 3.625".
Weight: 24 oz. **Length:** 5.2" overall.
Stocks: Checkered plastic on blued guns, rosewood on stainless guns.
Sights: Open, fixed.
Features: Manually-operated repeater. Height is 3.7", width is 1". Comes with manual, leather carrying case, spare stock screws, wrench. From American Derringer Corp.
Price: Blued $1,250.00
Price: Stainless steel $1,500.00

ANSCHUTZ EXEMPLAR BOLT-ACTION PISTOL
Caliber: 22 LR, 5-shot; 22 WMR, 22 Hornet, 5-shot.
Barrel: 10", 14".
Weight: 3½ lbs. **Length:** 17" overall.
Stock: European walnut with stippled grip and forend.
Sights: Hooded front on ramp, open notch rear adjustable for w. and e.
Features: Uses Match 64 action with left-hand bolt; Anschutz #5091 two-stage trigger set at 9.85 oz. Receiver grooved for scope mounting; open sights easily removed. Introduced 1987. Imported from West Germany by PSI.
Price: 22 LR $395.00
Price: 22 LR, left-hand $405.00
Price: 22 LR, 14" barrel $419.50
Price: 22 Hornet $744.50

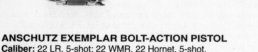

Anschutz Exemplar Hornet

DAVIS DERRINGERS
Caliber: 22 LR, 22 WMR, 25 ACP, 32 ACP.
Barrel: 2.4".
Weight: 9.5 oz. **Length:** 4" overall.
Stocks: Laminated wood.
Sights: Blade front, fixed notch rear.
Features: Choice of black Teflon or chrome finish; spur trigger. Introduced 1986. Made in U.S. by Davis Industries.
Price: $64.90

Davis Derringer

F.I.E. Model D-86

F.I.E. Model 722 TP

F.I.E. D-86 DERRINGER
Caliber: 38 Special.
Barrel: 3".
Weight: 14 oz.
Stocks: Checkered black nylon, walnut optional.
Sights: Fixed.
Features: Dyna-Chrome or blue finish. Spur trigger. Tip-up barrel; extractors. Made in U.S. by F.I.E. Corp.
Price: With nylon grips $94.95
Price: With walnut grips $104.95

F.I.E. MODEL 722 TP BOLT-ACTION PISTOL
Caliber: 22 LR, 6- and 10-shot magazines.
Barrel: 10⅜".
Weight: 3.4 lbs. **Length:** 19" overall.
Stock: Walnut-finished anatomically-shaped hardwood. Stippled grip and forend.
Sights: Hooded front, micro. adjustable target rear (removable).
Features: Bolt action. Fully adjustable (six-way) match trigger. Receiver grooved for scope mounting and comes with two-piece high-base mount. Comes with both magazines. Introduced 1990. Imported from Brazil by F.I.E. Firearms Corp.
Price: $259.95

FEATHER GUARDIAN ANGEL PISTOL
Caliber: 9mm Para., 38 Special.
Barrel: 3".
Weight: 17 oz. **Length:** 5½" overall.
Stocks: Black composition.
Sights: Fixed.
Features: Uses a pre-loaded two-shot drop-in "magazine." Stainless steel construction; matte finish. From Feather Industries. Introduced 1988.
Price: $139.95

Feather Guardian Angel

GAUCHER GN1 SILHOUETTE PISTOL
Caliber: 22 LR, single shot.
Barrel: 10".
Weight: 2.4 lbs. **Length:** 15.5" overall.
Stock: European hardwood.
Sights: Blade front, open adjustable rear.
Features: Bolt action, adjustable trigger. Introduced 1990. Imported from France by Mandall Shooting Supplies.
Price: About $290.00

HIGH STANDARD DERRINGER
Caliber: 22 LR, 22 WMR, 2-shot.
Barrel: 3.5".
Weight: 11 oz. **Length:** 5.12" overall.
Stocks: Black composition.
Sights: Fixed.
Features: Double action, dual extraction. Hammer-block safety. Blue finish. Introduced 1990. Made in U.S. by American Derringer Corp.
Price: . . . . NA

High Standard Derringer

Ithaca X-Caliber

ITHACA X-CALIBER SINGLE SHOT
Caliber: 22 LR, 44 Mag.
Barrel: 10", 15".
Weight: 3¼ lbs. **Length:** 15" overall (10" barrel).
Stocks: Goncalo Alves grip and forend on Model 20; American walnut on Model 30.
Sights: Blade on ramp front; Model 20 has adjustable, removable target-type rear. Drilled and tapped for scope mounting.
Features: Dual firing pin for RF/CF use. Polished blue finish.
Price: 22 LR, 10", 44 Mag., 10" or 15" $270.00
Price: 22 LR/44 Mag. combo, 10" and 15" $365.00
Price: As above, both 10" barrels $365.00

MANDALL/CABANAS PISTOL
Caliber: 177, pellet or round ball; single shot.
Barrel: 9".
Weight: 51 oz. **Length:** 19" overall.
Stock: Smooth wood with thumbrest.
Sights: Blade front on ramp, open adjustable rear.
Features: Fires round ball or pellets with 22 blank cartridge. Automatic safety; muzzlebrake. Imported from Mexico by Mandall Shooting Supplies.
Price: $125.00

Maximum Single Shot

MAXIMUM SINGLE SHOT PISTOL
Caliber: 22 LR, 22 Hornet, 22 BR, 223 Rem., 22-250, 6mm BR, 6mm-223, 243, 250 Savage, 6.5mm-35, 7mm TCU, 7mm BR, 7mm-35, 7mm INT-R, 7mm-08, 7mm Rocket, 7mm Super Mag., 30 Herrett, 30 Carbine, 308 Win., 7.62 x 39, 32-20, 357 Mag., 357 Maximum, 358 Win., 44 Mag.
Barrel: 8¾", 10½", 14".
Weight: 61 oz. (10½" bbl.), 78 oz. (14" bbl.). **Length:** 15", 18½" overall (with 10½" and 14" bbl., respectively).
Stocks: Smooth walnut stocks and forend.
Sights: Ramp front, fully adjustable open rear.
Features: Falling block action; drilled and tapped for M.O.A. scope mounts; integral grip frame/receiver; adjustable trigger; Douglas barrel (interchangeable); Armoloy finish. Introduced 1983. Made in U.S. by M.O.A. Corp.
Price: 8¾", 10", 14" $499.00
Price: Extra barrels $139.00
Price: Scope mount $49.00

New Advantage Derringer

> Consult our Directory pages for the location of firms mentioned.

RANDALL BOLT-ACTION PISTOL
Caliber: 9mm shot, single shot.
Barrel: NA.
Weight: 2.4 lbs. **Length:** 16.5" overall.
Stock: European hardwood.
Sights: Bead front.
Features: Bolt action, blue finish. Introduced 1990. Imported from France by Mandall Shooting Supplies.
Price: $225.00

NEW ADVANTAGE ARMS DERRINGER
Caliber: 22 LR, 22 WMR, 4-shot.
Barrel: 2½".
Weight: 15 oz. **Length:** 4½" overall.
Stocks: Smooth walnut.
Sights: Fixed.
Features: Double-action mechanism, four barrels, revolving firing pin. Rebounding hammer. Polished blue finish. Reintroduced 1989. From New Advantage Arms Corp.
Price: 22 LR $199.00
Price: 22 WMR $199.00

RPM XL SINGLE SHOT PISTOL

Caliber: 22 LR, 22 WMR, 225 Win., 25 Rocket, 6.5 Rocket, 32 H&R Mag., 357 Max., 357 Mag., 30-30 Win., 30 Herrett, 357 Herrett, 41 Mag., 44 Mag., 454 Casull, 375 Win., 7mm UR, 7mm Merrill, 30 Merrill, 7mm Rocket, 270 Ren, 270 Rocket, 270 Max., 45-70.

Barrel: 8" slab, 10¾", 12", 14" bull; .450" wide vent. rib, matted to prevent glare.

Weight: About 60 oz. **Length:** 12¼" overall (10¾" bbl.).

Stocks: Smooth Goncalo with thumb and heel rest.

Sights: Front .100" blade, Millett rear adjustable for w. and e. Hooded front with interchangeable post optional.

Features: Polished blue finish, hard chrome optional. Barrel is drilled and tapped for scope mounting. Cocking indicator visible from rear of gun. Has spring-loaded barrel lock, positive hammer block thumb safety. Trigger adjustable for weight of pull and over-travel. For complete price list contact RPM.

Price: Regular ¾" frame, right-hand action **$750.00**
Price: As above, left-hand action **$775.00**
Price: Wide ⅞" frame, right-hand action **$800.00**
Price: Extra barrel, 8"-10¾" **$230.00**
Price: Extra barrel, 12"-14" **$300.00**

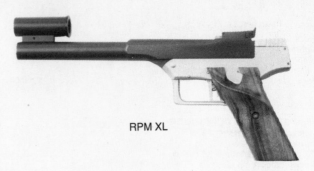

RPM XL

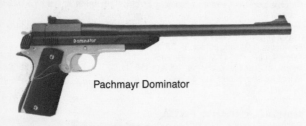

Pachmayr Dominator

PACHMAYR DOMINATOR PISTOL

Caliber: 22 Hornet, 223, 7mm-06, 308, 35 Rem., 44 Mag., single shot.

Barrel: 10½" (44 Mag.), 14" all other calibers.

Weight: 4 lbs. (14" barrel). **Length:** 16" overall (14" barrel).

Stocks: Pachmayr Signature system.

Sights: Optional sights or drilled and tapped for scope mounting.

Features: Bolt-action pistol on 1911A1 frame. Comes as complete gun. Introduced 1988. From Pachmayr.

Price: Either barrel **$524.50**

Remington XP-100 Varmint Special

REMINGTON XP-100 "VARMINT SPECIAL"

Caliber: 223 Rem., single shot.

Barrel: 10½", ventilated rib.

Weight: 60 oz. **Length:** 16¾".

Stock: Brown nylon one-piece, checkered grip with white spacers.

Sights: Tapped for scope mount.

Features: Fits left or right hand, is shaped to fit fingers and heel of hand. Grooved trigger. Rotating thumb safety, cavity in forend permits insertion of up to five 38-cal. 130-gr. metal jacketed bullets to adjust weight and balance. Included is a black vinyl, zippered case.

Price: Including case, about **$398.00**

Remington XP-100 Custom Long Range Pistol

Similar to the XP-100 "Varmint Special" except chambered for 223 Rem., 7mm-08 Rem., 35 Rem., 250 Savage, 6mm BR, 7mm BR. Offered with standard 14½" barrel with adjustable rear leaf and front bead sights, or with heavy 15½" barrel without sights. Custom Shop 14½" barrel, Custom Shop English walnut stock in right- or left-hand configuration. Action tuned in Custom Shop. Weight is under 4½ lbs. (heavy barrel, 5½ lbs.). Introduced 1986.

Price: Right- or left-hand **$943.00**

Remington XP-100R

Remington XP-100R Repeater Pistol

Similar to the Custom Long Range Pistol except chambered only for 223 Rem., 7mm-08 Rem., and 35 Rem., and has a blind magazine holding 5 rounds (7mm-08 and 35), or 6 (223 Rem.). Comes with a rear-handle, synthetic stock of Du Pont Kevlar to eliminate the transfer bar between the forward trigger and rear trigger assembly. Fitted with front and rear sling swivel studs. Has standard-weight 14½" barrel with adjustable leaf rear sight, bead front. The receiver is drilled and tapped for scope mounts. Weight is about 4½ lbs. Introduced 1990. From Remington Custom Shop.

Price: **$798.00**

SPRINGFIELD ARMORY 1911A2 S.A.S.S. PISTOL

Caliber: 22 LR, 223, 243, 7mm BR, 7mm-08, 308, 357 Mag., 358 Win., 44 Mag., single shot.

Barrel: 10¾" or 14.9".

Weight: 4 lbs. 2 oz. (14.9" bbl.). **Length:** 17.2" overall (14.9" bbl.).

Stocks: Rubberized wraparound.

Sights: Blade on ramp front, fully adjustable open rear. Drilled and tapped for scope mounting.

Features: Uses standard 1911A1 frame with a break-open top half interchangeable barrel system. Available as complete gun or as conversion unit only (requires fitting). Introduced 1989.

Price: Complete pistol, 15" bbl. **$519.00**
Price: As above, 10¾" bbl. **$519.00**
Price: Conversion unit, 15" bbl. **$259.00**
Price: As above, 10¾" **$259.00**
Price: Interchangeable barrel, 15" **$128.70**
Price: As above, 10¾" **$128.70**

Springfield S.A.S.S.

CAUTION: PRICES CHANGE, CHECK AT GUNSHOP.

HANDGUNS—MISCELLANEOUS

TEXAS LONGHORN "THE JEZEBEL" PISTOL
Caliber: 22 Short, Long, Long Rifle, single shot.
Barrel: 6".
Weight: 15 oz. **Length:** 8" overall.
Stocks: One-piece fancy walnut grip (right- or left-hand), walnut forend.
Sights: Bead front, fixed rear.
Features: Handmade gun. Top-break action; all stainless steel; automatic hammer block safety; music wire coil springs. Barrel is half-round, half-octagon. Announced 1986. From Texas Longhorn Arms.
Price: About $250.00

Thompson/Center Contender

Thompson/Center Contender Hunter Package
Package contains the Contender pistol in 223, 7-30 Waters, 30-30, 357 Rem. Maximum, 35 Rem., 44 Mag. or 45-70 with 12" barrel with T/C's Muzzle Tamer, a 2.5x Recoil Proof Long Eye Relief scope with lighted reticle, q.d. sling swivels with a nylon carrying sling. Comes with a suede leather case with foam padding and fleece lining. Introduced 1990. From Thompson/Center Arms.
Price: $595.00

UBERTI ROLLING BLOCK TARGET PISTOL
Caliber: 22 LR, 22 WMR, 22 Hornet, 357 Mag., single shot.
Barrel: 9⅞", half-round, half-octagon.
Weight: 44 oz. **Length:** 14" overall.
Stocks: Walnut grip and forend.
Sights: Blade front, fully adjustable rear.
Features: Replica of the 1871 rolling block target pistol. Brass trigger guard, color case-hardened frame, blue barrel. Imported by Uberti USA.
Price: $294.00

ULTRA LIGHT ARMS MODEL 20 REB HUNTER'S PISTOL
Caliber: 22-250 thru 308 Win. standard. Most silhouette calibers and others on request. 5-shot magazine.
Barrel: 14", Douglas No. 3.
Weight: 4 lbs.
Stock: Composite Kevlar, graphite reinforced. Du Pont Imron paint in green, brown, black and camo.
Sights: None furnished. Scope mount included.
Features: Timney adjustable trigger; two-position, three-function safety; benchrest quality action; matte or bright stock and metal finish; right- or left-hand action. Shipped in hard case. Introduced 1987. From Ultra Light Arms.
Price: $1,300.00

THOMPSON/CENTER ARMS CONTENDER
Caliber: 7mm TCU, 30-30 Win., 22 LR, 22 WMR, 22 Hornet, 223 Rem., 270 Ren, 7x30 Waters, 32-20 Win., 357 Mag., 357 Rem. Max., 44 Mag., 10mm Auto, 445 Super Mag., 45/410, single shot.
Barrel: 10", tapered octagon, bull barrel and vent. rib.
Weight: 43 oz. (10" bbl.). **Length:** 13¼" (10" bbl.).
Stocks: T/C "Competitor Grip." Right or left hand.
Sights: Under-cut blade ramp front, rear adjustable for w. and e.
Features: Break-open action with automatic safety. Single-action only. Interchangeable bbls., both caliber (rlm & centerfire), and length. Drilled and tapped for scope. Engraved frame. See T/C catalog for exact barrel/caliber availability.
Price: Blued (rimfire cals.) $345.00
Price: Blued (centerfire cals.) $345.00
Price: Extra bbls. (standard octagon) $155.00
Price: Quick Release scope base $18.50
Price: 45/410, internal choke bbl. $160.00

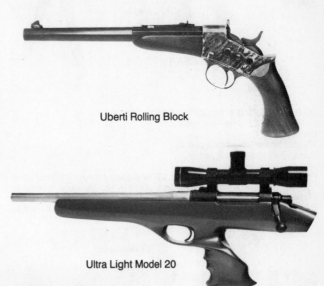

Uberti Rolling Block

Ultra Light Model 20

WICHITA CLASSIC PISTOL
Caliber: Any, up to and including 308 Win.
Barrel: 11¼", octagon.
Weight: About 5 lbs.
Stock: Exhibition grade American black walnut. Checkered 20 lpi. Other woods available on special order.
Sights: Micro open sights standard. Receiver drilled and tapped for scope mount.
Features: Receiver and barrel octagonally shaped, finished in non-glare blue. Bolt has three locking lugs and three gas escape ports. Completely adjustable Wichita trigger. Introduced 1980. From Wichita Arms.
Price: $2,950.00
Price: Engraved, in walnut presentation case $4,850.00

CENTERFIRE RIFLES—MILITARY STYLE AUTOLOADERS

Suitable for, and adaptable to, certain kinds of competitions as well as sporting purposes, such as hunting.

Prices shown were correct at presstime, but may not reflect current market trends.

Thompson M1

AUTO-ORDNANCE MODEL 27 A-1 THOMPSON
Caliber: 45 ACP, 30-shot magazine.
Barrel: 16".
Weight: 11½ lbs. **Length:** About 42" overall (Deluxe).
Stock: Walnut stock and vertical forend.
Sights: Blade front, open rear adjustable for windage.
Features: Recreation of Thompson Model 1927. Semi-auto only. Deluxe model has finned barrel, adjustable rear sight and compensator; Standard model has plain barrel and military sight. From Auto-Ordnance Corp.
Price: Deluxe $735.00
Price: 1927A5 Pistol (M27A1 without stock; wgt. 7 lbs.) $704.00
Price: Lightweight model $707.00

Auto-Ordnance Thompson M1

Similar to the Model 27 A-1 except is in the M-1 configuration with side cocking knob, horizontal forend, smooth unfinned barrel, sling swivels on butt and forend. Matte black finish. Introduced 1985.

Price: $712.50

AMAC LONG-RANGE RIFLE

Caliber: 50 BMG.
Barrel: 33″, fully fluted, free-floating.
Weight: 30 lbs. **Length:** 55.5″ overall.
Stocks: Composition. Adjustable drop and comb.
Sights: Comes with Leupold Ultra M1 20x scope.
Features: Bolt-action long-range rifle. Comes with Automatic Ranging Scope Base. Adjustable trigger. Rifle breaks down for transport, storage. From Iver Johnson.

Price: $4,468.00

Barrett Model 82 A-1

BARRETT LIGHT-FIFTY MODEL 82 A-1 AUTO

Caliber: 50 BMG, 10-shot detachable box magazine.
Barrel: 29″.
Weight: 28.5 lbs. **Length:** 57″ overall.
Stock: Composition with Sorbothane recoil pad.
Sights: Open, iron and 12x scope.
Features: Semi-automatic, recoil operated with recoiling barrel. Three-lug locking bolt; muzzlebrake. Self-leveling bipod. Fires same 50-cal. ammunition as the M2HB machinegun. Introduced 1985. From Barrett Firearms.

Price: From $4,995.00

BARRETT MODEL 90 BOLT-ACTION RIFLE

Caliber: 50 BMG, 5-shot magazine.
Barrel: 29″.
Weight: 22 lbs. **Length:** 35″ overall.
Stock: Sorbothane recoil pad.
Sights: Scope optional.
Features: Bolt-action, bullpup design. Disassembles without tools; extendable bipod legs; match-grade barrel; high efficiency muzzlebrake. Introduced 1990. From Barrett Firearms Mfg., Inc.

Price: From $3,350.00

Colt AR-15A2 H-BAR

Similar to the AR-15A2 Delta H-BAR except has heavy barrel, 800-meter M-16A2 rear sight adjustable for windage and elevation, case deflector for left-hand shooters, target-style nylon sling. Introduced 1986. **Law enforcement sales only.**

Price: $899.95

Colt AR-15A2 Rifle

Colt AR-15A2 Delta H-BAR Match

Similar to the AR-15A2 Government Model except has standard stock, heavy barrel, is refined and inspected by the Colt Custom Shop. Comes with a 3-9x rubber armored scope and removable cheekpiece, adjustable scope mount, black leather military-style sling, cleaning kit, and hard carrying case. Pistol grip has Delta medallion. Introduced 1987. **Law enforcement sales only.**

Price: $1,424.95

COLT AR-15A2 GOVERNMENT MODEL TARGET RIFLE

Caliber: 223 Rem., 5-shot magazine.
Barrel: 20″.
Weight: 7.5 lbs. **Length:** 39″ overall.
Stock: Composition stock, grip, forend.
Sights: Post front, aperture rear adjustable for windage and elevation.
Features: Five-round detachable box magazine, standard-weight barrel, flash suppressor, sling swivels. Has forward bolt assist. Military matte black finish. Model introduced 1989. **Law enforcement sales only.**

Price: $859.95

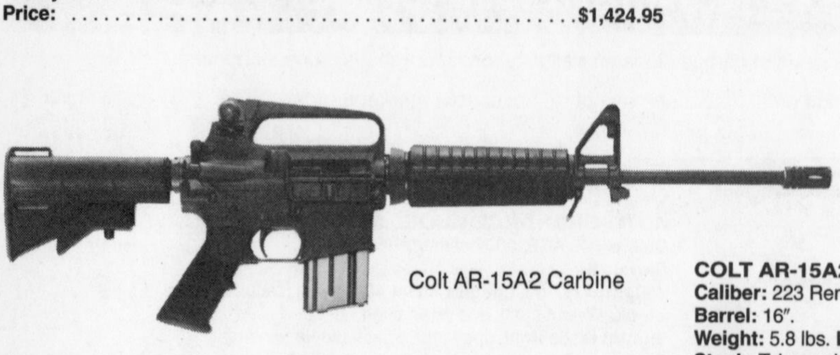

Colt AR-15A2 Carbine

COLT AR-15A2 GOVERNMENT MODEL CARBINE

Caliber: 223 Rem.
Barrel: 16″.
Weight: 5.8 lbs. **Length:** 35″ overall (extended).
Stock: Telescoping aluminum.
Sights: Post front, adjustable for elevation, flip-type rear for short, long range, windage.
Features: 5-round detachable box magazine, flash suppressor, sling swivels. Forward bolt assist included. Introduced 1985. **Law enforcement sales only.**

Price: $879.95

Feather AT-9

FEATHER AT-9 SEMI-AUTO CARBINE
Caliber: 9mm Para., 25-shot magazine.
Barrel: 16".
Weight: 5 lbs. **Length:** 35" overall (stock extended); 26½" (closed).
Stock: Telescoping wire, composition pistol grip.
Sights: Hooded post front, adjustable aperture rear.
Features: Semi-auto only. Matte black finish. From Feather Industries. Announced 1988.
Price: $499.95

FEDERAL XC-900/XC-450 AUTO CARBINES
Caliber: 9mm Para., 32-shot magazine; 45 ACP.
Barrel: 16.5" (with flash hider).
Weight: 8 lbs. **Length:** 34½" overall.
Stock: Detachable tube steel; adjustable stock optional.
Sights: Hooded post front, peep rear adjustable for w. and e.
Features: Quick takedown for transport, storage. All hell-arc welded steel construction. Made in U.S. by Federal Engineering Corp.
Price: Complete package contains gun, case, extra magazine, sling and q.d. swivels, receiver cap $636.00

Federal XC-900/XC-450

HECKLER & KOCH HK-91 AUTO RIFLE
Caliber: 308 Win., 5- or 20-shot magazine.
Barrel: 17.71".
Weight: 9½ lbs. **Length:** 40¼" overall.
Stock: Black high-impact plastic.
Sights: Post front, aperture rear adjustable for w. and e.
Features: Delayed roller-lock action. Sporting version of West German service rifle. Takes special H&K clamp scope mount. Imported from West Germany by Heckler & Koch, Inc. **Law enforcement sales only.**
Price: HK-91 A-2 with plastic stock $960.00
Price: HK-91 A-3 with retractable metal stock $1,131.00
Price: HK-91/94 scope mount with 1" rings $357.00

Heckler & Koch HK-91

Heckler & Koch HK-93 Auto Rifle
Similar to HK-91 except in 223 cal., 16.13" barrel, overall length of 35½", weighs 7¾ lbs. Same stock, forend. **Law enforcement sales only.**
Price: HK-93 A-2 with plastic stock $960.00
Price: HK-93 A-3 with retractable metal stock $1,131.00

HECKLER & KOCH HK-94 AUTO-CARBINE
Caliber: 9mm Para., 15-shot magazine.
Barrel: 16".
Weight: 6½ lbs. (fixed stock). **Length:** 34¾" overall.
Stock: High-impact plastic butt and forend or retractable metal stock.
Sights: Hooded post front, aperture rear adjustable for windage and elevation.
Features: Delayed roller-locked action; accepts H&K quick-detachable scope mount. Introduced 1983. Imported from West Germany by Heckler & Koch, Inc. **Law enforcement sales only.**
Price: HK-94-A2 (fixed stock) $960.00
Price: HK-94-A3 (retractable metal stock) $1,131.00
Price: 30-shot magazine $24.00
Price: Clamp to hold two magazines $29.00

Heckler & Koch HK-94

Iver Johnson PM30HB

IVER JOHNSON PM 30HB CARBINE
Caliber: 30 U.S. Carbine
Barrel: 18" four-groove.
Weight: 6½ lbs. **Length:** 35½" overall.
Stock: Glossy-finished hardwood or walnut.
Sights: Click-adjustable peep rear.
Features: Gas-operated semi-auto carbine. 15-shot detachable magazine. Made in U.S.A.
Price: Blue finish, hardwood stock $312.43
Price: Blue finish, walnut stock $365.00

Ruger Mini Thirty

RUGER MINI-14/5R RANCH RIFLE
Caliber: 223 Rem., 5-shot detachable box magazine.
Barrel: 18½".
Weight: 6.4 lbs. **Length:** 37¼" overall.
Stock: American hardwood, steel reinforced.
Sights: Ramp front, fully adjustable rear.
Features: Fixed piston gas-operated, positive primary extraction. New buffer system, redesigned ejector system. Ruger S100RH scope rings included. 20-, 30-shot magazine available only to police departments and government agencies only.
Price: Mini-14/5R, blued $504.50
Price: K-Mini-14/5R, stainless $552.50

Ruger Mini Thirty Rifle
Similar to the Mini-14 Ranch Rifle except modified to chamber the 7.62x39 Russian service round. Weight is about 7 lbs., 3 oz. Has 6-groove barrel with 1-10" twist, Ruger Integral Scope Mount bases and folding peep rear sight. Detachable 5-shot staggered box magazine. Blued finish. Introduced 1987.
Price: $504.50

Ruger Mini-14/5
Same as the Ranch Rifle except available with folding stock, checkered high impact plastic vertical pistol grip. Over-all length with stock open is 37¾", length closed is 27½". Weight is about 7¾ lbs.
Price: Blued ordnance steel, standard stock, Mini-14/5 . . . . $468.00
Price: Stainless, K-Mini 14/5 . . . . $516.00

Springfield Armory M1A

SPRINGFIELD ARMORY M-1A RIFLE
Caliber: 7.62mm NATO (308), 243 Win., 5-, 10- or 20-shot box magazine.
Barrel: 25¹⁄₁₆" with flash suppressor, 22" without suppressor.
Weight: 8¾ lbs. **Length:** 44¼" overall.
Stock: American walnut with walnut colored heat-resistant fiberglass handguard. Matching walnut handguard available. Also available with fiberglass stock.
Sights: Military, square blade front, full click-adjustable aperture rear.
Features: Commercial equivalent of the U.S. M-14 service rifle with no provision for automatic firing. From Springfield Armory. Military accessories available including 3x-9x56 ART scope and mount. Optional accurizing packages available.
Price: Standard M1A rifle, about $1,045.00
Price: Match Grade, about $1,269.00
Price: Super Match (heavy premium barrel) about $1,525.00
Price: M1A-A1 Bush Rifle, walnut stock, about $1,066.00

SPRINGFIELD ARMORY BM-59
Caliber: 7.62mm NATO (308 Win.), 20-shot box magazine.
Barrel: 19.3".
Weight: 9¼ lbs. **Length:** 43.7" overall.
Stock: Walnut, with trapped rubber buttpad.
Sights: Military square blade front, click adjustable peep rear.
Features: Full military-dress Italian service rifle. Available in selective fire or semi-auto only. Refined version of the M-1 Garand. Accessories available include: folding Alpine stock, muzzlebrake/flash suppressor/grenade launcher combo, bipod, winter trigger, grenade launcher sights, bayonet, oiler. Extremely limited quantities. Introduced 1981.
Price: Standard Italian model, about $1,950.00
Price: Alpine model, about $2,275.00
Price: Alpine Paratrooper model, about $2,275.00
Price: Nigerian Mark IV model, about $2,340.00

Consult our Directory pages for the location of firms mentioned.

Steyr A.U.G. Rifle

STEYR A.U.G. AUTOLOADING RIFLE
Caliber: 223 Rem.
Barrel: 20".
Weight: 8½ lbs. **Length:** 31" overall.
Stock: Synthetic, green. One-piece moulding houses receiver group, hammer mechanism and magazine.
Sights: 1.5x scope only; scope and mount form the carrying handle.
Features: Semi-automatic, gas-operated action; can be converted to suit right- or left-handed shooters, including ejection port. Transparent 30- or 42-shot magazines. Folding vertical front grip. Introduced 1983. Imported from Austria by Gun South, Inc. **Available on limited basis only to law enforcement officers.**
Price: Right- or left-handed model $1,375.00

Includes models for hunting, adaptable to and suitable for certain competition.

Browning High Power Rifle

Browning Magnum Semi-Auto Rifle
Same as the standard caliber model, except weighs 8⅜ lbs., 45" overall, 24" bbl., 3-round mag. Cals. 7mm Mag., 300 Win. Mag., 338 Win. Mag.
Price: Grade 1, with sights **$658.50**
Price: Grade 1, no sights **$643.50**

CALICO MODEL M-900 CARBINE
Caliber: 9mm Para., 50- or 100-shot magazine.
Barrel: 16".
Weight: 3.7 lbs. (empty). **Length:** 28½" overall (stock collapsed).
Stock: Sliding steel buttstock.
Sights: Post front adjustable for w. and e., fixed notch rear.
Feature: Helical feed 50- or 100-shot magazine. Ambidextrous safety, static cocking handle. Retarded blowback action. Glass-filled polymer grip. Introduced 1989. From Calico.
Price: **$582.00**

Feather Saturn 30

FEATHER SATURN 30 AUTO RIFLE
Caliber: 7.62x39, 5-shot detachable magazine.
Barrel: 19.5".
Weight: 8.5 lbs. **Length:** 39.5" overall.

GONCZ HIGH-TECH GC CARBINE
Caliber: 30 Mauser, 9mm Para., 38 Super (18- or 36-shot), 45 ACP, 10mm (10- or 20-shot).
Barrel: 16.1".
Weight: 4 lbs., 9 oz. **Length:** 31.7" overall.
Stock: Walnut.
Sights: Adjustable post front in ring, open rear adjustable for windage.
Features: Telescoping bolt, floating firing pin. Safety locks the firing pin. Sight radius of 20.1". Accepts same magazines as Goncz High-Tech pistols. Can be equipped with scope, Aimpoint, halogen light or laser sighting device. Made in U.S. From Goncz Co.
Price: GC High-Tech Carbine **$560.00**
Price: With halogen light **$765.00**
Price: With laser sight **$1,500.00**

BROWNING HIGH-POWER SEMI-AUTO RIFLE
Caliber: 243, 270, 280, 30-06, 308.
Barrel: 22" round tapered.
Weight: 7⅜ lbs. **Length:** 43" overall.
Stock: French walnut p.g. stock and forend, hand checkered.
Sights: Adj. folding-leaf rear, gold bead on hooded ramp front, or no sights.
Features: Detachable 4-round magazine. Receiver tapped for scope mounts. Trigger pull 3½ lbs. Imported from Belgium by Browning.
Price: Grade 1, with sights **$608.50**
Price: Grade 1, no sights **$593.50**

Calico Model 900

Calico Model M-951 Carbine Deluxe
Similar to the M-900 Carbine except has an adjustable forward grip, long compensator, and 13" barrel. 9mm Para., 50- or 100-shot magazine. Introduced 1990. Made in U.S. by Calico.
Price: **$625.00**

Stock: Composite, thumbhole type.
Sights: Protected post front, fully adjustable rear.
Features: Gas-operated semi-automatic. Receiver drilled and tapped for scope mounting. Recoil pad. Swivel studs. Walnut stock, scope mount and rings, sling, swivels, extra, magazines available as options. Announced 1990. From Feather Industries, Inc.
Price: **$694.95**

Goncz GC

HECKLER & KOCH SR-9 ORION RIFLE
Caliber: 308 Win., 5-shot magazine.
Barrel: 19.7", bull.
Weight: 11 lbs. **Length:** 42.4" overall.
Stock: Kevlar reinforced fiberglass with thumbhole; wood grain finish.
Sights: Post front, aperture rear adjustable for windage and elevation.
Features: A redesigned version of the HK91 rifle. Comes standard with bull barrel, PSG1 Marksman trigger group. Uses HK clawlock scope mounts. Introduced 1990. Imported from West Germany by Heckler & Koch, Inc.
Price: **$1,269.00**

H&K SR-9 Orion

Marlin Model 45

Marlin Model 45 Carbine
Similar to the Model 9 except chambered for 45 ACP, 7-shot magazine. Introduced 1986.
Price: $330.95

MARLIN MODEL 9 CAMP CARBINE
Caliber: 9mm Para., 4-shot magazine (12-shot available).
Barrel: 16½", Micro-Groove® rifling.
Weight: 6¾ lbs. **Length:** 35½" overall.
Stock: Walnut-finished hardwood; rubber buttpad; Mar-Shield® finish.
Sights: Ramp front with red post cutaway Wide-Scan™ hood, adjustable open rear.
Features: Manual bolt hold-open; Garand-type safety, magazine safety; loaded chamber indicator; receiver drilled, tapped for scope mounting. Introduced 1985.
Price: $330.95

Remington 7400

Consult our Directory pages for the location of firms mentioned

REMINGTON MODEL 7400 AUTO RIFLE
Caliber: 243 Win., 270 Win., 280 Rem., 308 Win. and 30-06, 4-shot magazine.
Barrel: 22" round tapered.
Weight: 7½ lbs. **Length:** 42" overall.
Stock: Walnut, deluxe cut checkered p.g. and forend.
Sights: Gold bead front sight on ramp; step rear sight with windage adj.
Features: Redesigned and improved version of the Model 742. Positive cross-bolt safety. Receiver tapped for scope mount. 4-shot clip mag. Introduced 1981.
Price: About $487.00
Price: Carbine (18½" bbl., 30-06 only) $487.00
Price: D Grade, about $2,383.00
Price: F Grade, about $4,910.00
Price: F Grade with gold inlays, about $7,364.00

Springfield SAR-8

SPRINGFIELD ARMORY SAR-8 SPORTER RIFLE
Caliber: 308 Win., 20-shot magazine.
Barrel: 18"
Weight: 8.7 lbs. **Length:** 40.3" overall.
Stock: Black composition forend, wood thumbhole butt.
Sights: Protected post front, rotary-style adjustable rear.
Features: Delayed roller-lock action, fluted chamber; matte black finish. Introduced 1990. From Springfield Armory.
Price: $1,229.00

Springfield SAR-4800

SPRINGFIELD ARMORY SAR-4800 RIFLE
Caliber: 7.62mm NATO (308 Win.), 20-shot magazine.
Barrel: 21".
Weight: 9.5 lbs. **Length:** 43.3" overall.
Stock: Fiberglass forend, wood thumbhole butt.
Sights: Protected post, adjustable peep rear.
Features: New production. Introduced 1990. Optional accurizing packages available. From Springfield Armory.
Price: Standard Sporter model $1,229.00
Price: "Bush" Sporter rifle, 18" barrel $1,229.00
Price: Compact model, 18" bbl. $1,233.00

WILKINSON TERRY CARBINE
Caliber: 9mm Para., 31-shot magazine.
Barrel: 16³⁄₁₆".
Weight: 6 lbs., 3 oz. **Length:** 30" overall.
Stock: Maple stock and forend.
Sights: Protected post front, aperture rear.
Features: Semi-automatic blowback action fires from a closed bolt. Bolt-type safety and magazine catch. Ejection port has automatic trap door. Receiver equipped with dovetail for scope mounting. Made in U.S. From Wilkinson Arms.
Price: $725.00

Both classic arms and recent designs in American-style repeaters for sport and field shooting.

Action Arms Timber Wolf

ACTION ARMS TIMBER WOLF PUMP RIFLE
Caliber: 38 Spec./357 Mag., 10-shot magazine; 44 Mag., 8-shot magazine.
Barrel: 18.5".
Weight: 5.5 lbs. **Length:** 36.5" overall.
Stock: Walnut.
Sights: Blade front, adjustable rear.
Features: Push-button safety on trigger guard; integral scope mount on receiver. Blue finish. Introduced 1989. Imported from Israel by Action Arms Ltd.
Price: **$475.00**

Browning Model 53

BROWNING MODEL 53 LEVER-ACTION RIFLE
Caliber: 32-20, 7-shot magazine.
Barrel: 22", round, tapered.
Weight: 6 lbs., 8 oz. **Length:** 39½" overall.

Stock: Full pistol grip with semi-beavertail forend of select walnut with high gloss finish. Cut checkering on grip and forend. Metal grip cap.
Sights: Post bead front, adjustable open rear.
Features: Based on the Model 92 Winchester with half-length magazine. Blue finish, including trigger. Limited to 5000 guns. Introduced 1990. Imported from Japan by Browning.
Price: **$675.00**

Browning Model 65

BROWNING MODEL 65 LEVER-ACTION RIFLE
Caliber: 218 Bee, 7-shot magazine.
Barrel: 24" round tapered.
Weight: 6 lbs., 12 oz. **Length:** 41.75" overall.
Stock: Select walnut. Full pistol grip, semi-beavertail forend.

Sights: Hooded ramp front, adjustable buckhorn-style rear.
Features: Reproduction of the Winchester Model 65 with half-length magazine, uncheckered wood, blue finish. High Grade model has better wood with cut checkering and high gloss finish; receiver has grayed finish with scroll engraving and game scenes—a coyote on the left side, bobcat on the right, both gold-plated, as is the trigger. Production limited to 3500 Grade I guns, 1500 High Grades. Introduced 1989. Imported from Japan by Browning.
Price: Grade I **$550.00**
Price: High Grade **$850.00**

Browning BLR

BROWNING BLR MODEL 81 LEVER-ACTION RIFLE
Caliber: 222, 223, 22-250, 243, 257 Roberts, 7mm-08, 308 Win. or 358 Win., 4-shot detachable magazine.
Barrel: 20" round tapered.
Weight: 6 lbs. 15 oz. **Length:** 39¾" overall.
Stock: Checkered straight grip and forend, oil-finished walnut.
Sights: Gold bead on hooded ramp front; low profile square notch adj. rear.
Features: Wide, grooved trigger; half-cock hammer safety. Receiver tapped for scope mount. Recoil pad installed. Imported from Japan by Browning.
Price: With sights **$472.50**

Cimarron 1873 "Short"

CIMARRON 1873 "SHORT" RIFLE
Caliber: 22 LR, 22 WMR, 357 Magnum, 44-40, 45 Colt.
Barrel: 20" tapered octagon.
Weight: 7.5 lbs. **Length:** 39" overall.
Stock: Walnut.
Sights: Bead front, adjustable semi-buckhorn rear.
Features: Has half "button" magazine. Original-type markings, including caliber, on barrel and elevator and "Kings" patent. From Cimarron Arms Co.
Price: **$695.00**

Cimarron 1873 30″

Dixie 1873

Marlin 336CS

Marlin 1894S

CIMARRON 1873 30″ EXPRESS RIFLE
Caliber: 22 LR, 22 WMR, 357 Mag., 38-40, 44-40, 45 Colt.
Barrel: 30″, octagonal.
Weight: 8½ lbs. **Length:** 48″ overall.
Stock: Walnut.
Sights: Blade front, semi-buckhorn ramp rear. Tang sight optional.
Features: Color case-hardened frame; choice of modern blue-black or charcoal blue for other parts. Barrel marked "Kings improvement." From Cimarron Arms.
Price: $695.00

Cimarron 1873 "Button" Half-Magazine
Similar to the 1873 Express except has 24″ barrel with half-magazine.
Price: $695.00

DIXIE ENGRAVED MODEL 1873 RIFLE
Caliber: 44-40, 11-shot magazine.
Barrel: 20″, round.
Weight: 7¾ lbs. **Length:** 39″ overall.
Stock: Walnut.
Sights: Blade front, adjustable rear.
Features: Engraved and case-hardened frame. Duplicate of Winchester 1873. Made in Italy. From Dixie Gun Works.
Price: $625.00
Price: Plain, blued carbine $495.00

E.M.F. HENRY CARBINE
Caliber: 44-40 or 44 rimfire.
Barrel: 21″.
Weight: About 9 lbs. **Length:** About 39″ overall.
Stock: Oil-stained American walnut.
Sights: Blade front, rear adjustable for elevation.
Features: Reproduction of the original Henry carbine with brass frame and buttplate, rest blued. From E.M.F.
Price: Standard $1,380.00
Price: Engraved $1,598.00

MARLIN 336CS LEVER-ACTION CARBINE
Caliber: 30-30 or 35 Rem., 6-shot tubular magazine.
Barrel: 20″ Micro-Groove®.
Weight: 7 lbs. **Length:** 38½″ overall.
Stock: Select American black walnut, capped p.g. with white line spacers. Mar-Shield® finish; rubber buttpad.
Sights: Ramp front with Wide-Scan™ hood, semi-buckhorn folding rear adjustable for w. and e.
Features: Hammer-block safety. Receiver tapped for scope mount, offset hammer spur; top of receiver sand blasted to prevent glare.
Price: Less scope $357.95

Marlin 30AS Lever-Action Carbine
Same as the Marlin 336CS except has walnut-finished hardwood p.g. stock, 30-30 only, 6-shot. Hammer-block safety.
Price: $304.95

MARLIN 1894S LEVER-ACTION CARBINE
Caliber: 44 Special/44 Magnum, 45 Colt, 10-shot tubular magazine.
Barrel: 20″ Micro-Groove®.
Weight: 6 lbs. **Length:** 37½″ overall.
Stock: American black walnut, straight grip and forend. Mar-Shield® finish. Rubber rifle buttpad.
Sights: Wide-Scan™ hooded ramp front, semi-buckhorn folding rear adjustable for w. and e.
Features: Hammer-block safety. Receiver tapped for scope mount, offset hammer spur, solid top receiver sand blasted to prevent glare.
Price: $401.95

MARLIN 444SS LEVER-ACTION SPORTER
Caliber: 444 Marlin, 5-shot tubular magazine.
Barrel: 22″ Micro-Groove®.
Weight: 7½ lbs. **Length:** 40½″ overall.
Stock: American black walnut, capped p.g. with white line spacers, rubber rifle buttpad. Mar-Shield® finish; swivel studs.
Sights: Hooded ramp front, folding semi-buckhorn rear adjustable for windage and elevation.
Features: Hammer-block safety. Receiver tapped for scope mount; offset hammer spur.
Price: $433.95

Marlin Model 1894CS Carbine
Similar to the standard Model 1894S except chambered for 38 Special/357 Magnum with full-length 9-shot magazine, 18½″ barrel, hammer-block safety, brass bead front sight. Introduced 1983.
Price: $401.95

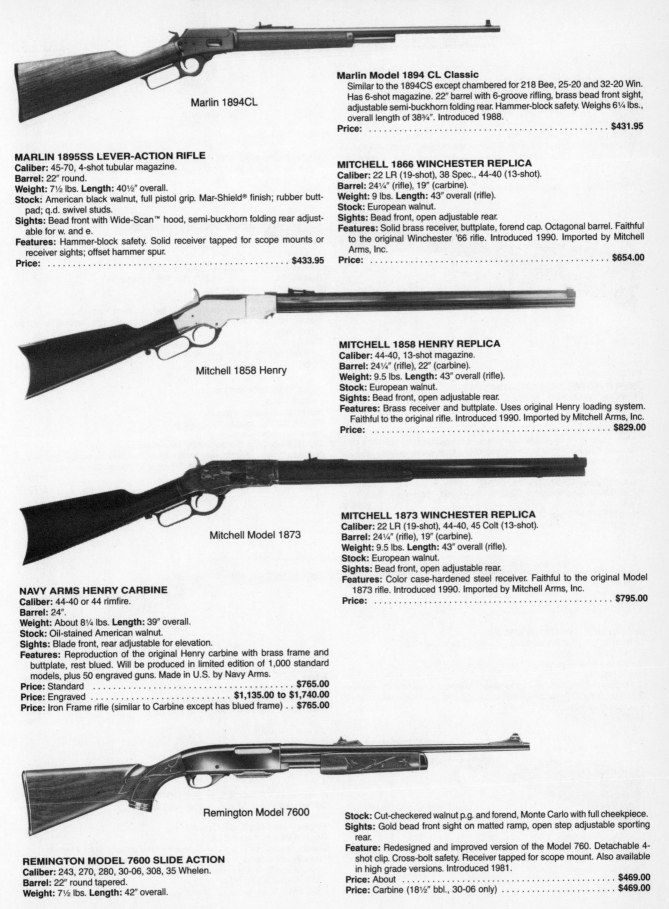

Marlin 1894CL

Marlin Model 1894 CL Classic

Similar to the 1894CS except chambered for 218 Bee, 25-20 and 32-20 Win. Has 6-shot magazine. 22″ barrel with 6-groove rifling, brass bead front sight, adjustable semi-buckhorn folding rear. Hammer-block safety. Weighs 6¼ lbs., overall length of 38¾″. Introduced 1988.

Price: **$431.95**

MARLIN 1895SS LEVER-ACTION RIFLE

Caliber: 45-70, 4-shot tubular magazine.
Barrel: 22″ round.
Weight: 7½ lbs. **Length:** 40½″ overall.
Stock: American black walnut, full pistol grip. Mar-Shield® finish; rubber butt-pad; q.d. swivel studs.
Sights: Bead front with Wide-Scan™ hood, semi-buckhorn folding rear adjustable for w. and e.
Features: Hammer-block safety. Solid receiver tapped for scope mounts or receiver sights; offset hammer spur.
Price: **$433.95**

MITCHELL 1866 WINCHESTER REPLICA

Caliber: 22 LR (19-shot), 38 Spec., 44-40 (13-shot).
Barrel: 24¼″ (rifle), 19″ (carbine).
Weight: 9 lbs. **Length:** 43″ overall (rifle).
Stock: European walnut.
Sights: Bead front, open adjustable rear.
Features: Solid brass receiver, buttplate, forend cap. Octagonal barrel. Faithful to the original Winchester '66 rifle. Introduced 1990. Imported by Mitchell Arms, Inc.
Price: **$654.00**

Mitchell 1858 Henry

MITCHELL 1858 HENRY REPLICA

Caliber: 44-40, 13-shot magazine.
Barrel: 24¼″ (rifle), 22″ (carbine).
Weight: 9.5 lbs. **Length:** 43″ overall (rifle).
Stock: European walnut.
Sights: Bead front, open adjustable rear.
Features: Brass receiver and buttplate. Uses original Henry loading system. Faithful to the original rifle. Introduced 1990. Imported by Mitchell Arms, Inc.
Price: **$829.00**

Mitchell Model 1873

MITCHELL 1873 WINCHESTER REPLICA

Caliber: 22 LR (19-shot), 44-40, 45 Colt (13-shot).
Barrel: 24¼″ (rifle), 19″ (carbine).
Weight: 9.5 lbs. **Length:** 43″ overall (rifle).
Stock: European walnut.
Sights: Bead front, open adjustable rear.
Features: Color case-hardened steel receiver. Faithful to the original Model 1873 rifle. Introduced 1990. Imported by Mitchell Arms, Inc.
Price: **$795.00**

NAVY ARMS HENRY CARBINE

Caliber: 44-40 or 44 rimfire.
Barrel: 24″.
Weight: About 8¼ lbs. **Length:** 39″ overall.
Stock: Oil-stained American walnut.
Sights: Blade front, rear adjustable for elevation.
Features: Reproduction of the original Henry carbine with brass frame and buttplate, rest blued. Will be produced in limited edition of 1,000 standard models, plus 50 engraved guns. Made in U.S. by Navy Arms.
Price: Standard **$765.00**
Price: Engraved .... **$1,135.00 to $1,740.00**
Price: Iron Frame rifle (similar to Carbine except has blued frame) .. **$765.00**

Remington Model 7600

REMINGTON MODEL 7600 SLIDE ACTION

Caliber: 243, 270, 280, 30-06, 308, 35 Whelen.
Barrel: 22″ round tapered.
Weight: 7½ lbs. **Length:** 42″ overall.
Stock: Cut-checkered walnut p.g. and forend, Monte Carlo with full cheekpiece.
Sights: Gold bead front sight on matted ramp, open step adjustable sporting rear.
Feature: Redesigned and improved version of the Model 760. Detachable 4-shot clip. Cross-bolt safety. Receiver tapped for scope mount. Also available in high grade versions. Introduced 1981.
Price: About **$469.00**
Price: Carbine (18½″ bbl., 30-06 only) **$469.00**

CAUTION: PRICES CHANGE, CHECK AT GUNSHOP.

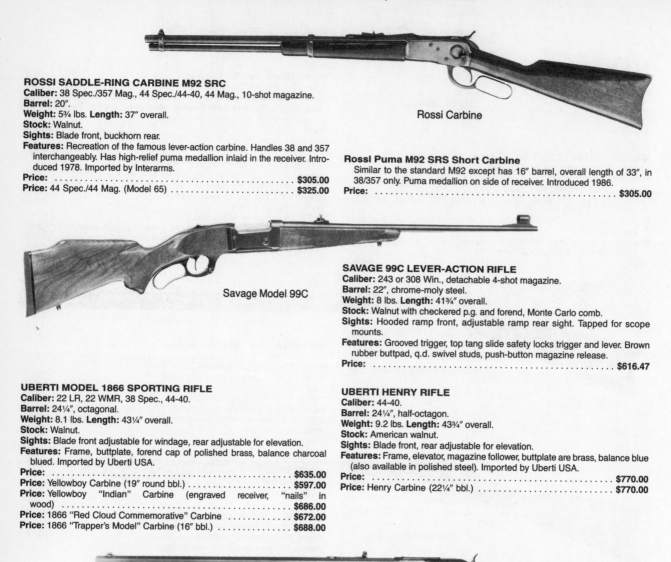

Rossi Carbine

Savage Model 99C

Uberti 1873 Rifle

Winchester Model 94

ROSSI SADDLE-RING CARBINE M92 SRC
Caliber: 38 Spec./357 Mag., 44 Spec./44-40, 44 Mag., 10-shot magazine.
Barrel: 20".
Weight: 5¾ lbs. **Length:** 37" overall.
Stock: Walnut.
Sights: Blade front, buckhorn rear.
Features: Recreation of the famous lever-action carbine. Handles 38 and 357 interchangeably. Has high-relief puma medallion inlaid in the receiver. Introduced 1978. Imported by Interarms.
Price: $305.00
Price: 44 Spec./44 Mag. (Model 65) $325.00

Rossi Puma M92 SRS Short Carbine
Similar to the standard M92 except has 16" barrel, overall length of 33", in 38/357 only. Puma medallion on side of receiver. Introduced 1986.
Price: $305.00

SAVAGE 99C LEVER-ACTION RIFLE
Caliber: 243 or 308 Win., detachable 4-shot magazine.
Barrel: 22", chrome-moly steel.
Weight: 8 lbs. **Length:** 41¾" overall.
Stock: Walnut with checkered p.g. and forend, Monte Carlo comb.
Sights: Hooded ramp front, adjustable ramp rear sight. Tapped for scope mounts.
Features: Grooved trigger, top tang slide safety locks trigger and lever. Brown rubber buttpad, q.d. swivel studs, push-button magazine release.
Price: $616.47

UBERTI MODEL 1866 SPORTING RIFLE
Caliber: 22 LR, 22 WMR, 38 Spec., 44-40.
Barrel: 24¼", octagonal.
Weight: 8.1 lbs. **Length:** 43¼" overall.
Stock: Walnut.
Sights: Blade front adjustable for windage, rear adjustable for elevation.
Features: Frame, buttplate, forend cap of polished brass, balance charcoal blued. Imported by Uberti USA.
Price: $635.00
Price: Yellowboy Carbine (19" round bbl.) $597.00
Price: Yellowboy "Indian" Carbine (engraved receiver, "nails" in wood) $686.00
Price: 1866 "Red Cloud Commemorative" Carbine $672.00
Price: 1866 "Trapper's Model" Carbine (16" bbl.) $688.00

UBERTI HENRY RIFLE
Caliber: 44-40.
Barrel: 24¼", half-octagon.
Weight: 9.2 lbs. **Length:** 43¾" overall.
Stock: American walnut.
Sights: Blade front, rear adjustable for elevation.
Features: Frame, elevator, magazine follower, buttplate are brass, balance blue (also available in polished steel). Imported by Uberti USA.
Price: $770.00
Price: Henry Carbine (22¼" bbl.) $770.00

UBERTI 1873 SPORTING RIFLE
Caliber: 22 LR, 22 WMR, 38 Spec., 357 Mag., 44-40, 45 Colt.
Barrel: 24¼", octagonal.
Weight: 8.1 lbs. **Length:** 43¼" overall.
Stock: Walnut.
Sights: Blade front adjustable for windage, open rear adjustable for elevation.
Features: Color case-hardened frame, blued barrel, hammer, lever, buttplate, brass elevator. Imported by Uberti USA.

Price: $756.00
Price: 1873 Carbine (19" round bbl.) $721.00
Price: 1873 Carbine, nickel-plated $818.00
Price: 1873 "Trapper's Model" Carbine (16" bbl.) $721.00

WINCHESTER MODEL 94 BIG BORE SIDE EJECT
Caliber: 307 Win., 356 Win., 6-shot magazine.
Barrel: 20".
Weight: 7 lbs. **Length:** 38⅝" overall.
Stock: American walnut. Satin finish.
Sights: Hooded ramp front, semi-buckhorn rear adjustable for w. and e.
Features: All external metal parts have Winchester's deep blue finish. Rifling twist 1-in-12". Rubber recoil pad fitted to buttstock. Introduced 1983. From U.S. Repeating Arms Co.
Price: Walnut $319.00

CAUTION: PRICES CHANGE, CHECK AT GUNSHOP.

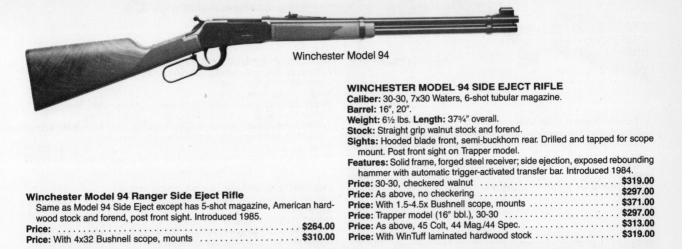

Winchester Model 94

Winchester Model 94 Ranger Side Eject Rifle
Same as Model 94 Side Eject except has 5-shot magazine, American hardwood stock and forend, post front sight. Introduced 1985.
Price: **$264.00**
Price: With 4x32 Bushnell scope, mounts **$310.00**

WINCHESTER MODEL 94 SIDE EJECT RIFLE
Caliber: 30-30, 7x30 Waters, 6-shot tubular magazine.
Barrel: 16″, 20″.
Weight: 6½ lbs. **Length:** 37¾″ overall.
Stock: Straight grip walnut stock and forend.
Sights: Hooded blade front, semi-buckhorn rear. Drilled and tapped for scope mount. Post front sight on Trapper model.
Features: Solid frame, forged steel receiver; side ejection, exposed rebounding hammer with automatic trigger-activated transfer bar. Introduced 1984.
Price: 30-30, checkered walnut **$319.00**
Price: As above, no checkering **$297.00**
Price: With 1.5-4.5x Bushnell scope, mounts **$371.00**
Price: Trapper model (16″ bbl.), 30-30 .... **$297.00**
Price: As above, 45 Colt, 44 Mag./44 Spec. **$313.00**
Price: With WinTuff laminated hardwood stock **$319.00**

CENTERFIRE RIFLES—BOLT ACTIONS

Includes models for a wide variety of sporting and competitive purposes and uses.

Alpine Rifle

ALPINE BOLT-ACTION RIFLE
Caliber: 22-250, 243 Win., 270, 30-06, 308, 7mm Rem. Mag., 8mm, 5-shot magazine (3 for magnum).
Barrel: 23″ (std. cals.), 24″ (mag.).
Weight: 7½ lbs.
Stock: European walnut. Full p.g. and Monte Carlo; checkered p.g. and forend; rubber recoil pad; white line spacers; sling swivels.
Sights: Ramp front, open rear adjustable for w. and e.
Features: Made by Firearms Co. Ltd. in England. Imported by Mandall Shooting Supplies.
Price: Standard Grade **$375.00**
Price: Supreme Grade **$395.00**
Price: Custom Grade **$425.00**

A-Square Hannibal

A-SQUARE HANNIBAL BOLT-ACTION RIFLE
Caliber: 7mm Rem. Mag., 30-06, 300 Win. Mag., 300 H&H, 300 Wea. Mag., 8mm Rem. Mag., 338 Win. Mag., 340 Wea. Mag., 338 A-Square Mag., 9.3x62, 9.3x64, 375 H&H, 375 Wea. Mag., 375 A-Square Mag., 378 Wea. Mag., 416 Taylor, 416 Rem. Mag., 416 Hoffman, 416 Rigby, 416 Wea. Mag., 404 Jeffery, 425 Express, 458 Win. Mag., 458 Lott, 450 Ackley, 460 Short A-Square Mag., 460 Wea. Mag., 495 A-Square Mag., 500 A-Square Mag.
Barrel: 20″ to 26″ (no-cost customer option).
Weight: 8½ to 11 lbs.
Stock: Claro walnut with hand-rubbed oil finish; classic style with A-Square Coll-Chek® features for reduced recoil; flush detachable swivels. Customer choice of length of pull. Available with synthetic stock.
Sights: Choice of three-leaf express, forward or normal-mount scope, or combination (at extra cost).
Features: Matte non-reflective blue, double cross-bolts, steel and fiberglass reinforcement of wood from tang to forend tip; Mauser-style claw extractor; expanded magazine capacity. Right-hand only. Introduced 1983. Made in U.S. by A-Square Co., Inc.
Price: Walnut stock **$1,700.00**
Price: Synthetic stock **$1,900.00**

A-SQUARE CAESAR BOLT-ACTION RIFLE
Caliber: 30-06, 7mm Rem. Mag., 300 Win. Mag., 300 H&H, 300 Wea. Mag., 8mm Rem. Mag., 338 Win. Mag., 340 Wea. Mag., 375 Wea. Mag., 375 H&H, 416 Hoffman, 416 Rem. Mag., 416 Taylor, 425 Express, 450 Ackley, 458 Lott, 458 Win. Mag., 9.3x62, 9.3x64.
Barrel: 20″ to 26″ (no-cost customer option).
Weight: 8½ to 11 lbs.
Stock: Claro walnut with hand-rubbed oil finish; classic style with A-Square Coll-Chek® features for reduced recoil; flush detachable swivels. Customer choice of length of pull.
Sights: Choice of three-leaf express, forward or normal-mount scope, or combination (at extra cost).
Features: Matte non-reflective blue, double cross-bolts, steel and fiberglass reinforcement of wood from tang to forend tip; Mauser-style claw extractor; expanded magazine capacity. Right- or left-hand. Introduced 1984. Made in U.S. by A-Square Co., Inc.
Price: **$1,750.00**

Anschutz Classic 1700

ANSCHUTZ CLASSIC 1700 RIFLES
Caliber: 22 Hornet, 5-shot clip; 222 Rem., 2-shot clip.
Barrel: 23½", ¹³⁄₁₆" dia. heavy.
Weight: 7¾ lbs. **Length:** 42½" overall.
Stock: Select European walnut with checkered pistol grip and forend.
Sights: None furnished, drilled and tapped for scope mounting.
Features: Adjustable single stage trigger. Receiver drilled and tapped for scope mounting. Introduced 1988. Imported from Germany by PSI.
Price: **$1,100.00**
Price: Meistergrade (select stock, gold engraved trigger guard) . . .**$1,265.00**

Anschutz Custom 1700 Rifles
Similar to the Classic models except have roll-over Monte Carlo cheekpiece, slim forend with Schnabel tip, Wundhammer palm swell on pistol grip, rosewood grip cap with white diamond insert. Skip-line checkering on grip and forend. Introduced 1988. Imported from Germany by PSI.
Price: **$1,130.00**
Price: Meistergrade (select stock, gold engraved trigger guard) . . .**$1,295.00**

ANSCHUTZ BAVARIAN BOLT-ACTION RIFLE
Caliber: 22 Hornet, 222 Rem., detachable clip.
Barrel: 24".
Weight: 7¼ lbs. **Length:** 43" overall.
Stock: European walnut with Bavarian cheek rest. Checkered p.g. and forend.
Sights: Hooded ramp front, folding leaf rear.
Features: Uses the improved 1700 Match 54 action with adjustable trigger. Drilled and tapped for scope mounting. Introduced 1988. Imported from Germany by Precision Sales International.
Price: **$1,130.00**
Price: Meistergrade (select stock, gold engraved trigger guard) . . .**$1,295.00**

> Consult our Directory pages for the location of firms mentioned.

BEEMAN/HW 60J BOLT-ACTION RIFLE
Caliber: 222 Rem.
Barrel: 22.8".
Weight: 6.5 lbs. **Length:** 41.7" overall.
Stock: Walnut with cheekpiece; cut checkered p.g. and forend.
Sights: Hooded blade on ramp front, open rear.
Features: Polished blue finish; oil-finished wood. Imported from West Germany by Beeman. Introduced 1988.
Price: **$780.00**

Beeman/HW 60J

BEEMAN/KRICO MODEL 600/700 BIG GAME RIFLE
Caliber: 243 (M600), 30-06 (M700).
Barrel: 23½".
Weight: 7 lbs. **Length:** 43½" overall.
Stock: European classic-style walnut. Wundhammer palm swell. Rosewood schnabel tip; checkered grip and forend; rubber buttpad.
Sights: Hooded ramp front, open rear adjustable for windage.
Features: Silent safety, hammer swaged barrel. Detachable three-shot magazine. Imported from West Germany by Beeman.
Price: Model 600 . . . .**$1,898.00**
Price: Model 700 . . . .**$1,953.00**

Beeman/Krico 720

Beeman/Krico Model 720 Bolt-Action Rifle
Similar to the Model 700 except has 20.75" barrel, weighs 6.8 lbs., and has full-length Mannlicher-style stock with metal schnabel forend tip; double set trigger with optional match trigger available. Receiver drilled and tapped for scope mounting. Imported from West Germany by Beeman.
Price: Model 720 (270 Win.) **$1,820.00**
Price: Model 720 (30-06) **$1,820.00**

Blaser R84

BLASER R84 BOLT-ACTION RIFLE
Caliber: Std. cals.—22-250, 243, 6mm Rem., 25-06, 270, 280, 30-06; magnum cals.—257 Wea., 264 Win. Mag., 7mm Rem. Mag., 300 Win. Mag., 300 Wea., 338 Win. Mag., 375 H&H.
Barrel: 23" (24" in magnum cals.).
Weight: 7-7¼ lbs. **Length:** Std. cals.—41" overall (23" barrel).
Stock: Two-piece Turkish walnut. Solid black buttpad.
Sights: None furnished. Comes with low-profile Blaser scope mounts.
Features: Interchangeable barrels (scope mounts on barrel), and magnum/standard caliber bolt assemblies. Left-hand models available in all calibers. Imported from West Germany by Autumn Sales, Inc.
Price: Right-hand, standard or magnum calibers **$1,595.00**
Price: Left-hand, standard or magnum calibers **$1,645.00**
Price: Interchangeable barrels, standard or magnum calibers **$545.00**

CAUTION: PRICES CHANGE, CHECK AT GUNSHOP.

Beretta Model 500

BRNO ZKK 600, 601, 602 BOLT-ACTION RIFLES
Caliber: 30-06, 270, 7x57, 7x64 (M600); 223, 243, 308 (M601); 8x68S, 375 H&H, 458 Win. Mag. (M602), 5-shot magazine.
Barrel: 23½" (M600, 601), 25" (M602).
Weight: 6 lbs., 3 oz. to 9 lbs., 4 oz. **Length:** 43" overall (M601).
Stock: Walnut.
Sights: Hooded ramp front, open folding leaf adjustable rear.
Features: Adjustable set trigger (standard trigger included); easy-release floor-plate; sling swivels. Imported from Czechoslovakia by TD Arms.
Price: ZKK 600 Standard $599.00
Price: As above, Monte Carlo stock $649.00
Price: ZKK 601 Standard $549.00
Price: As above, Monte Carlo stock $599.00
Price: ZKK 602, Monte Carlo stock $749.00
Price: As above, standard stock $689.00

BERETTA 500 SERIES CUSTOM BOLT-ACTION RIFLES
Caliber: 222, 243, 308 (M501); 30-06.
Barrel: 23" to 24".
Weight: 6.8 to 8.4 lbs. **Length:** NA.
Stock: Close-grained walnut, with oil finish, hand checkering.
Sights: None furnished; drilled and tapped for scope mounting.
Features: Model 500—short action; 501—medium action; 502—long action. All models have rubber buttpad. Imported from Italy by Beretta U.S.A. Corp. Introduced 1984.
Price: Model 500 and 501 . . . . $725.00

BRNO ZKB 680 FOX BOLT-ACTION RIFLE
Caliber: 22 Hornet, 222 Rem., 5-shot magazine.
Barrel: 23½".
Weight: 5 lbs., 12 oz. **Length:** 42½" overall.
Stock: Turkish walnut, with Monte Carlo.
Sights: Hooded front, open adjustable rear.
Features: Detachable box magazine; adjustable double set triggers. Imported from Czechoslovakia by TD Arms.
Price: $499.00

Browning A-Bolt

Browning A-Bolt Gold Medallion
Similar to the standard A-Bolt except has select walnut stock with brass spacers between rubber recoil pad and between the rosewood grip cap and forend tip; gold-filled barrel inscription; palm-swell pistol grip, Monte Carlo comb, 22 lpi checkering with double borders; engraved receiver flats. In 270, 30-06, 7mm Rem. Mag only. Introduced 1988.
Price: $724.95

BROWNING A-BOLT RIFLE
Caliber: 25-06, 270, 30-06, 280, 7mm Rem. Mag., 300 Win. Mag., 338 Win. Mag., 375 H&H Mag.
Barrel: 22" medium sporter weight with recessed muzzle; 26" on mag. cals.
Weight: 6½ to 7½ lbs. **Length:** 44¾" overall (magnum and standard), 41¾" (short action).
Stock: Classic style American walnut; recoil pad standard on magnum calibers.
Features: Short-throw (60°) fluted bolt, three locking lugs, plunger-type ejector; adjustable trigger is grooved and gold-plated. Hinged floorplate, detachable box magazine (4 rounds std. cals., 3 for magnums). Slide tang safety. Medallion has glossy stock finish, rosewood grip and forend caps, high polish blue. Introduced 1985. Imported from Japan by Browning.
Price: Medallion, no sights $554.95
Price: Hunter, no sights $477.95
Price: Hunter, with sights $538.95
Price: Medallion, 375 H&H Mag., with sights $648.95

Browning A-Bolt "Stainless Stalker"
Similar to the Hunter model A-Bolt except receiver is made of stainless steel; the rest of the exposed metal surfaces are finished with a durable matte silver-gray. Graphite-Fiberglass composite textured stock. No sights are furnished. Available in 270, 30-06, 7mm Rem. Mag., 375 H&H. Introduced 1987.
Price: $608.95
Price: Composite Stalker (as above, checkered stock) $477.95
Price: Left-hand, no sights $627.95
Price: 375 H&H, with sights $699.95
Price: 375 H&H, left-hand, with sights $721.95

Browning A-Bolt Stainless Stalker

Browning A-Bolt Left Hand
Same as the Medallion model A-Bolt except has left-hand action and is available only in 270, 30-06, 7mm Rem. Mag. Introduced 1987.
Price: $578.95

Browning Micro Medallion

Browning A-Bolt Micro Medallion
Similar to the standard A-Bolt except is a scaled-down version. Comes with 20" barrel, shortened length of pull (13⅝"); three-shot magazine capacity; weighs 6 lbs., 1 oz. Available in 243, 308, 7mm-08, 257 Roberts, 223, 22-250. Introduced 1988.
Price: No sights $554.95

Browning Short Action A-Bolt
Similar to the standard A-Bolt except has short action for 22 Hornet, 223, 22-250, 243, 257 Roberts, 7mm-08, 284 Win., 308 chamberings. Available in Hunter or Medallion grades. Weighs 6½ lbs. Other specs essentially the same. Introduced 1985.
Price: Medallion, no sights $554.95
Price: Hunter, no sights $477.95
Price: Hunter, with sights $538.95

Century Centurion 14

CENTURY CENTURION 14 SPORTER
Caliber: 303 British, 7mm Rem. Mag., 300 Win. Mag., 5-shot magazine.
Barrel: 24".
Weight: NA. **Length:** 43.3" overall.
Stock: Walnut-finished European hardwood. Checkered p.g. and forend. Monte Carlo comb.
Sights: None furnished.
Features: Uses modified Pattern 14 Enfield action. Drilled and tapped for scope mounting. Blue finish. From Century International Arms.
Price: 303, about **$225.95**
Price: Magnum calibers, about **$251.95**

Century Enfield

CENTURY ENFIELD SPORTER #4
Caliber: 303 British, 10-shot magazine.
Barrel: 25.2".

Weight: NA. **Length:** 44.5" overall.
Stock: Beechwood with checkered p.g. and forend, Monte Carlo comb.
Sights: Blade front, adjustable aperture rear.
Features: Uses Lee-Enfield action; blue finish. Introduced 1987. From Century International Arms.
Price: **$185.95**
Price: Jungle Sporter (20½" bbl.) **$212.95**

Century Swedish

CENTURY SWEDISH SPORTER #38
Caliber: 6.5x55 Swede, 5-shot magazine.
Barrel: 24".

Weight: NA. **Length:** 44.1" overall.
Stock: Walnut-finished European hardwood with checkered p.g. and forend; Monte Carlo comb.
Sights: Blade front, adjustable rear.
Features: Uses M38 Swedish Mauser action; comes with Holden Ironsighter see-through scope mount. Introduced 1987. From Century International Arms.
Price: About **$212.95**

Dakota 76 Classic

Dakota 76 Short Action Rifles
A scaled-down version of the standard Model 76. Standard chamberings are 22-250, 243, 6mm Rem., 250-3000, 7mm-08, 308 and 358; others on special order. Short Classic Grade has 21" barrel; Alpine Grade is lighter (6½ lbs.), has a blind magazine and slimmer stock. Introduced 1989.
Price: Short Classic **$1,950.00**
Price: Alpine **$1,850.00**

DAKOTA 76 CLASSIC BOLT-ACTION RIFLE
Caliber: 257 Roberts, 270, 280, 30-06, 7mm Rem. Mag., 338 Win. Mag., 300 Win. Mag., 375 H&H, 458 Win. Mag.
Barrel: 23".
Weight: 7½ lbs. **Length:** NA.
Stock: Medium fancy grade walnut in classic style. Checkered p.g. and forend; solid buttpad. Composite stock also available.
Sights: None furnished; drilled and tapped for scope mounts.
Features: Has many features of the original Model 70 Winchester. One-piece rail trigger guard assembly; steel grip cap. Adjustable trigger. Many options available. Left-hand rifle available at same price. Introduced 1988. From Dakota Arms, Inc.
Price: Wood or composite stock **$1,950.00**

Dakota 76 Safari

Dakota 416 Rigby African
Similar to the 76 Safari except chambered for 416 Rigby, four-round magazine, select wood, two stock cross-bolts. Has 24" barrel, weight of 9.4 lbs. Ramp front sight, standing leaf rear. Introduced 1989.
Price: **$3,500.00**

DAKOTA 76 SAFARI BOLT-ACTION RIFLE
Caliber: 338 Win. Mag., 300 Win. Mag., 375 H&H, 458 Win. Mag.
Barrel: 23".
Weight: 8½ lbs. **Length:** NA.
Stock: Fancy walnut with ebony forend tip; point-pattern with wraparound forend checkering. Composite stock also available.
Sights: Ramp front, standing leaf rear.
Features: Has many features of the original Model 70 Winchester. Barrel band front swivel, inletted rear. Cheekpiece with shadow line. Steel grip cap. Introduced 1988. From Dakota Arms, Inc.
Price: Wood stock **$2,850.00**
Price: Composite stock **$2,450.00**

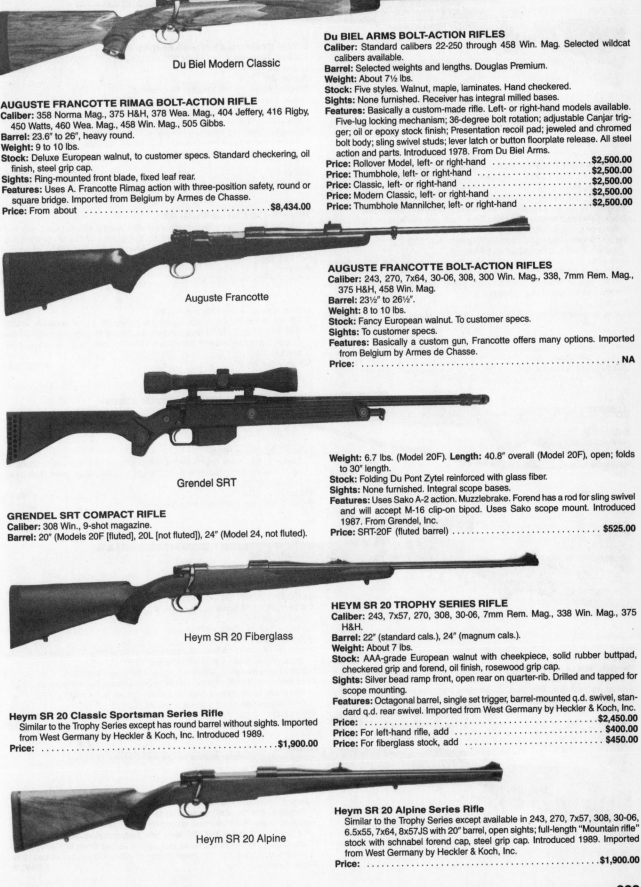

Du Biel Modern Classic

Auguste Francotte

Grendel SRT

Heym SR 20 Fiberglass

Heym SR 20 Alpine

AUGUSTE FRANCOTTE RIMAG BOLT-ACTION RIFLE

Caliber: 358 Norma Mag., 375 H&H, 378 Wea. Mag., 404 Jeffery, 416 Rigby, 450 Watts, 460 Wea. Mag., 458 Win. Mag., 505 Gibbs.
Barrel: 23.6" to 26", heavy round.
Weight: 9 to 10 lbs.
Stock: Deluxe European walnut, to customer specs. Standard checkering, oil finish, steel grip cap.
Sights: Ring-mounted front blade, fixed leaf rear.
Features: Uses A. Francotte Rimag action with three-position safety, round or square bridge. Imported from Belgium by Armes de Chasse.
Price: From about $8,434.00

GRENDEL SRT COMPACT RIFLE

Caliber: 308 Win., 9-shot magazine.
Barrel: 20" (Models 20F [fluted], 20L [not fluted]), 24" (Model 24, not fluted).

Heym SR 20 Classic Sportsman Series Rifle

Similar to the Trophy Series except has round barrel without sights. Imported from West Germany by Heckler & Koch, Inc. Introduced 1989.
Price: $1,900.00

Du BIEL ARMS BOLT-ACTION RIFLES

Caliber: Standard calibers 22-250 through 458 Win. Mag. Selected wildcat calibers available.
Barrel: Selected weights and lengths. Douglas Premium.
Weight: About 7½ lbs.
Stock: Five styles. Walnut, maple, laminates. Hand checkered.
Sights: None furnished. Receiver has integral milled bases.
Features: Basically a custom-made rifle. Left- or right-hand models available. Five-lug locking mechanism; 36-degree bolt rotation; adjustable Canjar trigger; oil or epoxy stock finish; Presentation recoil pad; jeweled and chromed bolt body; sling swivel studs; lever latch or button floorplate release. All steel action and parts. Introduced 1978. From Du Biel Arms.
Price: Rollover Model, left- or right-hand $2,500.00
Price: Thumbhole, left- or right-hand $2,500.00
Price: Classic, left- or right-hand $2,500.00
Price: Modern Classic, left- or right-hand $2,500.00
Price: Thumbhole Mannlicher, left- or right-hand $2,500.00

AUGUSTE FRANCOTTE BOLT-ACTION RIFLES

Caliber: 243, 270, 7x64, 30-06, 308, 300 Win. Mag., 338, 7mm Rem. Mag., 375 H&H, 458 Win. Mag.
Barrel: 23½" to 26½".
Weight: 8 to 10 lbs.
Stock: Fancy European walnut. To customer specs.
Sights: To customer specs.
Features: Basically a custom gun, Francotte offers many options. Imported from Belgium by Armes de Chasse.
Price: . . . . NA

Weight: 6.7 lbs. (Model 20F). **Length:** 40.8" overall (Model 20F), open; folds to 30" length.
Stock: Folding Du Pont Zytel reinforced with glass fiber.
Sights: None furnished. Integral scope bases.
Features: Uses Sako A-2 action. Muzzlebrake. Forend has a rod for sling swivel and will accept M-16 clip-on bipod. Uses Sako scope mount. Introduced 1987. From Grendel, Inc.
Price: SRT-20F (fluted barrel) $525.00

HEYM SR 20 TROPHY SERIES RIFLE

Caliber: 243, 7x57, 270, 308, 30-06, 7mm Rem. Mag., 338 Win. Mag., 375 H&H.
Barrel: 22" (standard cals.), 24" (magnum cals.).
Weight: About 7 lbs.
Stock: AAA-grade European walnut with cheekpiece, solid rubber buttpad, checkered grip and forend, oil finish, rosewood grip cap.
Sights: Silver bead ramp front, open rear on quarter-rib. Drilled and tapped for scope mounting.
Features: Octagonal barrel, single set trigger, barrel-mounted q.d. swivel, standard q.d. rear swivel. Imported from West Germany by Heckler & Koch, Inc.
Price: $2,450.00
Price: For left-hand rifle, add $400.00
Price: For fiberglass stock, add $450.00

Heym SR 20 Alpine Series Rifle

Similar to the Trophy Series except available in 243, 270, 7x57, 308, 30-06, 6.5x55, 7x64, 8x57JS with 20" barrel, open sights; full-length "Mountain rifle" stock with schnabel forend cap, steel grip cap. Introduced 1989. Imported from West Germany by Heckler & Koch, Inc.
Price: $1,900.00

Heym Express

HEYM MAGNUM EXPRESS SERIES RIFLE
Caliber: 404 Jeffery, 416 Rigby, 500 Nitro Express 3", 460 Wea. Mag., 500 A-Square, 450 Ackley.
Barrel: 24".
Weight: About 9.9 lbs. **Length:** 45¼" overall.
Stock: Classic English design of AAA-grade European walnut with cheekpiece, solid rubber buttpad, steel grip cap.
Sights: Post front on ramp, three-leaf express rear.
Features: Modified magnum Mauser action, Timney single trigger; special hinged floorplate; barrel-mounted q.d. swivel, q.d. rear; double recoil lug in stock. Introduced 1989. Imported from West Germany by Heckler & Koch, Inc.
Price: **$3,500.00**
Price: For left-hand rifle, add **$500.00**

Heym SR 20 Classic Safari Rifle
Similar to the Trophy Series except in 404 Jeffery, 425 Express, 458 Win. Mag. 24" barrel; has large post front sight, express rear; barrel-mounted ring-type front q.d. swivel, q.d. rear; double-lug recoil bolt in stock. Introduced 1989. Imported from West Germany by Heckler & Koch, Inc.
Price: **$2,250.00**
Price: For left-hand rifle, add **$350.00**

HOWA M1500 TROPHY BOLT-ACTION RIFLE
Caliber: 223, 22-250, 243, 270, 30-06, 308, 7mm Rem. Mag., 300 Win. Mag., 338 Win. Mag.
Barrel: 22" (24" in magnum calibers).
Weight: 7½-7¾ lbs. **Length:** 42" overall (42½" for 270, 30-06, 7mm).
Stock: American walnut with Monte Carlo comb and cheekpiece; 18 lpi checkering on p.g. and forend.
Sights: Hooded ramp gold bead front, open round-notch rear adjustable for w. and e. Drilled and tapped for scope mounts.
Features: Trigger guard and magazine box are a single unit with a hinged floorplate. Comes with q.d. swivel studs. Composition non-slip buttplate with white spacer. Magnum models have rubber recoil pad. Introduced 1979. Imported from Japan by Interarms.
Price: **$539.00**
Price: 7mm Rem. Mag., 300 Win. Mag., 338 Win. Mag. **$559.00**

Howa Heavy Barrel Varmint Rifle
Similar to the Trophy model except has heavy 24" barrel, available in 223, 308 and 22-250 only, Parkerized finish. No sights furnished; drilled and tapped for scope mounts. Introduced 1989. Imported from Japan by Interarms.
Price: **$579.00**

Howa Lightning

Howa Lightning Rifle
Similar to the Howa Trophy model except comes with lightweight Carbolite stock; weighs 7 lbs. Available in 270, 30-06, 300 Win. Mag., 7mm Rem. Mag. Introduced 1988.
Price: 270, 30-06 . . . . **$539.00**
Price: 7mm Rem. Mag., 300 Win. Mag. **$559.00**

Jaeger Hunter

JAEGER "HUNTER" RIFLE
Caliber: 243, 257 Roberts, 25-06, 7x57, 7mm-08, 308, 280 Rem., 30-06, 4-shot magazine.
Barrel: 22" or 24"; Douglas Premium.
Weight: About 7 lbs.
Stock: Bell & Carlson Kevlar/fiberglass with integral sling, 1" rubber recoil pad, black wrinkle finish. Checkered grip and forend.
Sights: None furnished. Drilled and tapped for scope mounting.
Features: Uses Mauser-type action with claw extractor, hinged floorplate, single stage adjustable trigger. Custom options available. Introduced 1989. From Paul Jaeger, Inc.
Price: From **$595.00**
Price: With laminated stock from **$870.00**

Jaeger "Alaskan" Rifle
Similar to the "Hunter" except chambered for 7mm Rem. Mag., 300 Win. Mag. and 338 Win. Mag. Has Jaeger ramp front sight with silver bead, Williams open rear. Weight is 8 lbs. Bead-blasted blue/black finish. Douglas Premium barrel. Custom options available. Introduced 1989.
Price: From **$749.00**

Jaeger African

Jaeger "African" Rifle
Similar to the "Hunter" except has Deluxe stock with graphite reinforcing, swivel studs. Weight is 9 lbs., magazine holds three rounds. Chambered for 375 H&H, 416 Taylor, 458 Win. Mag. Has Jaeger custom banded front ramp with flip-up night-sight and hood; rear sight is Jaeger single leaf with deep V-notch regulated at 50 yards. Bead-blasted blue/black finish. Introduced 1989.
Price: From **$995.00**

Kimber Big Game

KIMBER BIG GAME RIFLE

Caliber: 257 Roberts, 25-06, 7x57, 270, 280, 30-06, 7mm Rem. Mag., 300 Win. Mag., 300 H&H, 35 Whelen, 338 Win. Mag., 375 H&H.
Barrel: 22" (24" for magnums).
Weight: 7½ lbs. (8½ lbs. for magnum). **Length:** 42" overall.
Stock: Three styles available—Deluxe Grade is of AA Claro walnut with ebony forend tip, in "A" English walnut for magnums; plain butt, no cheekpiece; hand checkered 20 lpi, borderless; rubber recoil pad; fully inletted swivel studs. Hunter Grade is of non-checkered laminate, classic style; rubber recoil pad and swivel studs; available in 270, 30-06, 7mm Rem. Mag., 300 Win. Mag. and 338 Win. Mag. Super America Grade is of AAA Claro walnut with ebony forend tip in standard calibers, AA English walnut in magnums; beaded cheekpiece; borderless hand checkering, wraparound full coverage; rubber recoil pad and fully inletted sling swivel studs.

Sights: None furnished. Drilled and tapped for scope mounting.
Features: Model 70-type override trigger design and pre-'64 Model 70-type ejector. Mauser-type head-locking bolt action, steel trigger guard and floorplate. Fully adjustable trigger, Mauser-type extractor. Three-position Winchester-style safety, Mauser-type bolt stop. Featherweight barrel configurations except in magnum calibers. Introduced 1988. From Kimber of Oregon, Inc.
Price: Hunter Grade, with dovetail receiver, 270, 30-06 . . . . $1,495.00
Price: Hunter Grade, 7mm Rem. Mag., 300 Win. Mag., 338 Win. Mag. $1,595.00
Price: Deluxe Grade, round top receiver, std. cals $1,795.00
Price: Deluxe Grade, magnum cals $1,895.00
Price: Deluxe Grade, 375 H&H $1,995.00
Price: Super Grade, square bridge receiver, std. cals. $1,995.00
Price: Super Grade, dovetail receiver, mag. cals $2,095.00
Price: Super Grade, 375 H&H $2,195.00
Price: Optional barrel quarter-rib with sights $299.95
Price: Optional open sights $89.95

Kimber Ultra Varmint

KIMBER MODEL 84 RIFLE

Caliber: 17 Rem., 222 Rem., 223 Rem., 4-shot magazine.
Barrel: 22" (Sporter), 24" (Varminter). Chromemoly steel except Ultra Varminter which is stainless steel.
Weight: 6½ lbs. (Sporter). **Length:** 40½" overall.
Stock: Deluxe Grade has AA Claro walnut, ebony forend tip, no cheekpiece; 20 lpi hand checkering, Niedner-style buttplate, fully inletted swivel studs, steel grip cap; Hunter Grade has non-checkered classic-style laminate stock with recoil pad, swivel studs; Super America is AAA Claro walnut with ebony forend tip, beaded cheekpiece, 20 lpi borderless checkering, Niedner-style buttplate, steel grip cap, fully inletted swivel studs; Ultra Varminter is laminated birch without cheekpiece, 20 lpi checkering, curved rubber buttpad; Super Varminter is AAA Claro walnut with ebony forend tip, beaded cheekpiece, wrap around 20 lpi checkering, curved buttpad, fully inletted swivel studs.
Sights: None furnished; drilled and tapped for scope mounting.
Features: Mauser-type, head-locking action with Mauser-type extractor. Fully adjustable trigger. Positive rotating disc-type safety. Round top receiver with two-piece screw-on scope mount bases. Introduced 1984. From Kimber of Oregon, Inc.
Price: Hunter Grade, Sporterweight $995.00
Price: Deluxe Grade, Sporterweight, right- or left-hand $1,295.00
Price: Super Grade, Sporterweight $1,495.00
Price: Ultra Varminter, medium heavy stainless bbl. $1,295.00
Price: Super Varminter, medium heavy bbl. $1,495.00
Price: Optional open sights, add $89.95
Price: Barrel quarter-rib with sights, add $299.95

Kimber 89 African

KRICO MODEL 600 BOLT-ACTION RIFLE

Caliber: 222, 223, 22-250, 243, 308, 5.6x50 Mag., 4-shot magazine.
Barrel: 23.6".
Weight: 7.9 lbs. **Length:** 43.7" overall.
Stock: European walnut with Monte Carlo comb.
Sights: None furnished; drilled and tapped for scope mounting.
Features: Rubber recoil pad, sling swivels, checkered grip and forend. Polished blue finish. Imported from West Germany by Mandall Shooting Supplies.
Price: $1,250.00

MARK X AMERICAN FIELD SERIES

Caliber: 22-250, 243, 25-06, 270, 7x57, 7mm Rem. Mag., 308 Win., 30-06, 300 Win. Mag.
Barrel: 24".
Weight: 7 lbs. **Length:** 45" overall.
Stock: Genuine walnut stock, hand checkered with 1" sling swivels.
Sights: Ramp front with removable hood, open rear sight adjustable for windage and elevation.
Features: Mauser-system action. One-piece trigger guard with hinged floorplate, drilled and tapped for scope mounts and receiver sight, hammer-forged chrome vanadium steel barrel. Imported from Yugoslavia by Interarms.
Price: With adj. trigger, sights $619.00
Price: 7mm Rem. Mag., 300 Win. Mag. $639.00

KIMBER MODEL 89 AFRICAN

Caliber: 375 H&H (5-shot); 404 Jeffery, 416 Rigby (4-shot); 460 Wea. Mag., 505 Gibbs (3-shot).
Barrel: 24", six-groove.
Weight: 10-10½ lbs. **Length:** 47" overall.
Stock: AA grade English walnut with ebony forend tip. Beaded English-style cheekpiece, borderless wraparound hand checkering.
Sights: Blade front on ramp, express rear on contoured quarter-rib.
Features: Controlled feed head locking Kimber magnum action with Mauser-style extractor and bolt-stop. Winchester pre-'64-type three-position safety and ejection system. Twin recoil cross pins in stock. Barrel mounted recoil lug in addition to integral receiver lug. Drop box magazine, trapdoor grip cap. Rubber buttpad, barrel-mounted front swivel stud. Announced 1989.
Price: $3,595.00

KRICO MODEL 700 BOLT-ACTION RIFLES

Caliber: 17 Rem., 222, 222 Rem. Mag., 223, 5.6x50 Mag., 243, 308, 5.6x57 RWS, 22-250, 6.5x55, 6.5x57, 7x57, 270, 7x64, 30-06, 9.3x62, 6.5x68, 7mm Rem. Mag., 300 Win. Mag., 8x68S, 7.5 Swiss, 9.3x64, 6x62 Freres.
Barrel: 23.6" (std. cals.), 25.5 (mag. cals.).
Weight: 7 lbs. **Length:** 43.3" overall (23.6" bbl.).
Stock: European walnut, Bavarian cheekpiece.
Sights: Blade on ramp front, open adjustable rear.
Features: Removable box magazine; sliding safety. Drilled and tapped for scope mounting. Imported from West Germany by Mandall Shooting Supplies.
Price: Model 700 . . . . $995.00
Price: Model 700 Deluxe S $1,495.00
Price: Model 700 Deluxe $1,025.00
Price: Model 700 Stutzen (full stock) $1,295.00

Mark X LTW

Mini-Mark X

Mauser Model 99

Mauser Model 66

McMillan Signature Sporter

Mark X Viscount Rifle

Same gun and features as the Mark X American Field except has stock of European hardwood. Imported from Yugoslavia by Interarms. Reintroduced 1987.
Price: $499.00
Price: 7mm Rem. Mag., 300 Win. Mag. $519.00

Mark X LTW Sporter Bolt-Action Rifle

Similar to the standard Mark X except comes with lightweight Carbolite composition stock, 20″ barrel; weighs 7 lbs. Available in 270, 30-06, 300 Win. Mag., 7mm Rem. Mag. Introduced 1988.
Price: 270, 30-06 .... $519.00
Price: 7mm Rem. Mag, 300 Win. Mag. $539.00

Mini-Mark X Rifle

Scaled-down version of the Mark X American Field. Uses miniature M98 Mauser-system action, chambered for 223 Rem.; 20″ barrel with open adjustable sights. Overall length of 39¾″, weight 6.35 lbs. Drilled and tapped for scope mounting. Checkered hardwood stock. Adjustable trigger. Introduced 1987. Imported from Yugoslavia by Interarms.
Price: $429.00

MAUSER MODEL 99 BOLT-ACTION RIFLE

Caliber: 243, 25-06, 270, 308, 30-06, 5.6x57, 6.5x57, 7x57, 7x64 (standard cals.); 7mm Rem. Mag., 257 Wea. Mag., 270 Wea. Mag., 300 Wea. Mag., 300 Win. Mag., 338 Win. Mag., 375 H&H, 8x68S, 9.3x64 (magnum cals.); removable 4-shot magazine (std. cals.), 3-shot (magnum cals.).
Barrel: 24″ (std.), 26″ (mag.).
Weight: About 8 lbs. **Length:** 44″ overall (std. cals.).
Stock: Hand-checkered European walnut with rosewood grip cap.
Sights: None furnished. Drilled and tapped for scope mounting.
Features: Accuracy bedding with free-floated barrel, three front-locking bolt lugs, 60-degree bolt throw. Fastest lock time of any sporting rifle. Adjustable single-stage trigger. Silent safety locks bolt, sear, trigger. Introduced 1989. Imported from West Germany by Precision Imports, Inc.
Price: Classic stock, oil finish, std. cals. $1,195.00
Price: As above, magnum cals. $1,245.00
Price: Classic stock, high luster finish, std. cals. $1,345.00
Price: As above, magnum cals. $1,395.00
Price: Monte Carlo stock, oil finish, std. cals. $1,195.00
Price: As above, magnum cals. $1,245.00
Price: Monte Carlo stock, high luster, std. cals. $1,345.00
Price: As above, magnum cals. $1,395.00

MAUSER MODEL 66 BOLT-ACTION RIFLE

Caliber: 243, 270, 308, 30-06, 5.6x57, 6.5x57, 7x64, 9.3x62, 7mm Rem. Mag., 300 Wea. Mag., 300 Win. Mag., 6.5x68, 8x68S, 9.3x64, 375 H&H, 458 Win. Mag. Three-shot magazine.
Barrel: 21″ (Stutzen), 24″ (standard cals.), 26″ (magnum cals.).
Weight: 7.5 to 9.3 lbs. **Length:** 39″ overall (std. cals.).
Stock: Hand-checkered European walnut, hand-rubbed oil finish. Rosewood forend and grip caps.
Sights: Blade front on ramp, open rear adjustable for windage and elevation.
Features: Telescopic short-stroke action; interchangeable, free-floated, medium-heavy barrels. Mini-claw extractor; adjustable single-stage trigger; internal magazine. Introduced 1989. Imported from West Germany by Precision Imports, Inc.
Price: With Monte Carlo stock $1,885.00
Price: Stutzen (full-length stock) $1,985.00
Price: Safari model $2,200.00

McMILLAN SIGNATURE CLASSIC SPORTER

Caliber: 22-250, 243, 6mm Rem., 7mm-08, 284, 308 (short action); 25-06, 270, 280 Rem., 30-06, 7mm Rem. Mag., 300 Win. Mag., 300 Wea. (long action); 338 Win. Mag., 340 Wea., 375 H&H (magnum action).
Barrel: 22″, 24″, 26″.
Weight: 7 lbs. (short action).
Stock: McMillan fiberglass in green, beige, brown or black. Recoil pad and 1″ swivels installed. Length of pull up to 14¼″.
Sights: None furnished. Comes with 1″ rings and bases.
Features: Uses McMillan right- or left-hand action with matte black finish. Trigger pull set at 3 lbs. Four-round magazine for standard calibers; three for magnums. Aluminum floorplate. Fibergrain and wood stocks optional. Introduced 1987. From G. McMillan & Co.
Price: $1,795.00

CAUTION: PRICES CHANGE, CHECK AT GUNSHOP.

McMillan Classic Stainless

McMillan Signature Super Varminter
Similar to the Classic Sporter except has heavy contoured barrel, adjustable trigger, field bipod and special hand-bedded fiberglass stock (Fibergrain optional). Chambered for 223, 22-250, 220 Swift, 243, 6mm Rem., 25-06, 7mm-08 and 308. Comes with 1″ rings and bases. Introduced 1989.
Price: $1,850.00

McMillan Classic Stainless Sporter
Similar to the Classic Sporter except barrel and action made of stainless steel. Same calibers, in addition to 416 Rem. Mag. Comes with fiberglass stock, right- or left-hand action in natural stainless, glass bead or black chrome sulfide finishes. Introduced 1990. From G. McMillan & Co.
Price: $1,950.00

McMillan Signature Titanium Mountain Rifle
Similar to the Classic Sporter except action made of titanium alloy, barrel of chromemoly steel (titanium match-grade barrel optional). Stock is of graphite reinforced fiberglass. Weight is 5½ lbs. Chambered for 270, 280 Rem., 30-06, 7mm Rem. Mag., 300 Win. Mag. Fibergrain stock optional. Introduced 1989.
Price: $2,495.00
Price: With titanium barrel $2,995.00

McMillan Alaskan

McMillan Signature Alaskan
Similar to the Classic Sporter except has match-grade barrel with single leaf rear sight, barrel band front, 1″ detachable rings and mounts, steel floorplate, electroless nickel finish. Has wood Monte Carlo stock with cheekpiece, palm-swell grip, solid buttpad. Chambered for 270, 280 Rem., 30-06, 7mm Rem. Mag., 300 Win. Mag., 300 Wea., 358 Win., 340 Wea., 375 H&H. Introduced 1989.
Price: $2,495.00

McMillan Safari

McMILLAN SIGNATURE SAFARI RIFLE
Caliber: 300 Win. Mag., 300 Wea., 338 Win. Mag., 340 Wea., 375 H&H, 378 Wea., 416 Taylor, 416 Rem., 416 Rigby, 458 Win. Mag.
Barrel: 24″.
Weight: About 9-10 lbs. **Length:** 43″ overall.
Stock: McMillan fiberglass Safari.
Sights: Barrel band front ramp, multi-leaf express rear.
Features: Uses McMillan Safari action. Has q.d. 1″ scope mounts, positive locking steel floorplate, barrel band sling swivel. Match-grade barrel. Matte black finish standard. Introduced 1989. From G. McMillan & Co.
Price: $3,195.00

Norinco 64/70

NORINCO MODEL 64/70 BOLT-ACTION RIFLE
Caliber: 243, 308, 270, 30-06, 7mm Rem. Mag., 300 Win. Mag., 5-shot (std. cals.), 3-shot (magnum cals.).
Barrel: 22″ (std. cals.), 24″ (magnum cals.).
Weight: 8.5 lbs.
Stock: American walnut.
Sights: Blade front on ramp, open adjustable rear. Drilled and tapped for scope mounting.
Features: Mauser-type extractor; three-position safety; hinged floorplate; blue finish. Introduced 1990. Imported from China by China Sports, Inc.
Price: ....NA

RAHN "DEER SERIES" BOLT-ACTION RIFLE
Caliber: 25-06, 308, 270.
Barrel: 24″.
Weight: NA. **Length:** NA.
Stock: Circassian walnut with rosewood forend and grip caps, Monte Carlo cheekpiece, semi-Schnabel forend; hand checkered.
Sights: Bead front, open adjustable rear. Drilled and tapped for scope mount.
Features: Free-floating barrel; rubber recoil pad; one-piece trigger guard with hinged, engraved floorplate; 22 rimfire conversion insert available. Introduced 1986. From Rahn Gun Works, Inc.
Price: $1,000.00
Price: With custom stock made to customer specs $1,075.00

Rahn "Himalayan Series" Rifle
Similar to the "Deer Series" except chambered for 5.6x57 or 6.5x68S, short stock of walnut or fiberglass, and floorplate engravings of a yak with scroll border. Introduced 1986.
Price: $1,200.00
Price: With walnut stock made to customer specs $1,275.00

Rahn Elk

Rahn "Elk Series" Rifle
Similar to the "Deer Series" except chambered for 6mmx56, 30-06, 7mm Rem. Mag. and has elk head engraving on floorplate. Introduced 1986.
Price: $1,150.00
Price: With stock made to customer specs $1,225.00

Rahn "Safari Series" Rifle
Similar to the "Deer Series" except chambered for 308 Norma Mag., 300 Win. Mag., 8x68S, 9x64. Choice of Cape buffalo, rhino or elephant engraving. Gold oval nameplate with three initials. Introduced 1986.
Price: $1,300.00
Price: With stock made to customer specs $1,375.00

Remington 700 Classic

REMINGTON 700 "CLASSIC" RIFLE
Caliber: 25-06 Rem. only, 4-shot magazine.
Barrel: 24".

Weight: About 7¾ lbs. **Length:** 44½" overall.
Stock: American walnut, 20 lpi checkering on p.g. and forend. Classic styling. Satin finish.
Sights: None furnished. Receiver drilled and tapped for scope mounting.
Features: A "classic" version of the M700ADL with straight comb stock. Fitted with rubber recoil pad. Sling swivel studs installed. Hinged floorplate. Limited production in 1989 only.
Price: About $519.00

Remington 700 ADL

REMINGTON 700 ADL BOLT-ACTION RIFLE
Caliber: 243, 270, 308, 30-06 and 7mm Rem. Mag.
Barrel: 22" or 24" round tapered.

Weight: 7 lbs. **Length:** 41½" to 43½" overall.
Stock: Walnut. RKW finished p.g. stock with impressed checkering, Monte Carlo.
Sights: Gold bead ramp front; removable, step-adj. rear with windage screw.
Features: Side safety, receiver tapped for scope mounts.
Price: About $419.00
Price: 7mm Rem. Mag., about $444.00
Price: Model 700 ADL/LS (laminated stock, 243, 270, 30-06 only) .. $469.00
Price: As above, 7mm Rem. Mag. $491.00

Remington 700 BDL

Remington 700 BDL Bolt-Action Rifle
Same as the 700 ADL except chambered for 222, 223 (short action, 24" barrel), 22-250, 25-06, 6mm Rem. (short action, 22" barrel), 243, 270, 7mm-08, 30-06, 308; skip-line checkering; black forend tip and grip cap with white

line spacers. Matted receiver top, quick-release floorplate. Hooded ramp front sight; q.d. swivels.
Price: About $495.00
Also available in 17 Rem., 7mm Rem. Mag., 300 Win. Mag. (long action, 24" barrel), 338 Win. Mag., 35 Whelen (long action, 22" barrel). Overall length 44½", weight about 7½ lbs.
Price: About $519.00
Price: Custom Grade I, about $1,314.00
Price: Custom Grade II, about $2,335.00
Price: Custom Grade III, about $3,650.00
Price: Custom Grade IV, about $5,695.00

Remington 700 BDL Left Hand
Same as 700 BDL except mirror-image left-hand action, stock. Available in 22-250, 243, 308, 270, 30-06 only.
Price: About $552.00
Price: 7mm Rem. Mag., 338 Win. Mag., about $575.00

Remington Model 700 "Mountain Rifle"
Similar to the 700 BDL except weighs 6¾ lbs., has a 22" tapered barrel. Redesigned pistol grip, straight comb, contoured cheekpiece, satin stock finish, fine checkering, hinged floorplate and magazine follower, two-position thumb safety. Chambered for 243, 270 Win., 7x57, 7mm-08, 280 Rem., 30-06, 308, 4-shot magazine. Over-all length is 42½". Introduced 1986.
Price: About $503.00

Remington 700 BDL Varmint

Remington 700 BDL Varmint Special
Same as 700 BDL, except 24" heavy bbl., 43½" overall, wgt. 9 lbs. Cals. 222, 223, 22-250, 243, 6mm Rem., 7mm-08 Rem. and 308. No sights.
Price: About $527.00

CENTERFIRE RIFLES—BOLT ACTIONS

Remington 700 Safari KS

Remington Model 700 Custom "KS" Mountain Rifle

Similar to the 700 "Mountain Rifle" except has Kevlar reinforced resin synthetic stock. Available in both left- and right-hand versions. Chambered for 270 Win., 280 Rem., 30-06, 300 Win. Mag., 300 Wea. Mag., 35 Whelen, 338 Win. Mag., 8mm Rem. Mag., 375 H&H, all with 24″ barrel only. Weight is 6 lbs., 6 oz. Introduced 1986.
Price: About **$902.00**

Remington 700 Safari

Similar to the 700 BDL except 8mm Rem. Mag., 375 H&H, 416 Rem. Mag. or 458 Win. Magnum calibers only with heavy barrel. Hand checkered, oil-finished stock in classic or Monte Carlo style with recoil pad installed. Delivery time is about 5 months.
Price: About **$906.00**
Price: Safari Custom KS (Kevlar stock) **$1,044.00**

Remington 700 AS

Remington Model 700 "AS" Rifle

Similar to the 700 "Mountain Rifle" except stock is of "Arylon" thermoplastic resin. Same style as the "Mountain Rifle," available in black with lightly textured finish (cheekpiece left smooth). Solid buttpad, grip cap with Remington logo. Right-hand action only with hinged floorplate in 22-250, 243, 270, 280 Rem., 308, 30-06, 7mm Rem. Mag., 300 Wea. Mag., 22″ barrel, weight 6¾ lbs. Introduced 1989.
Price: **$512.00**
Price: 7mm Rem. Mag., 300 Wea. Mag. **$533.00**

Remington Model Seven

REMINGTON MODEL SEVEN BOLT-ACTION RIFLE

Caliber: 223 Rem. (5-shot); 243, 7mm-08, 6mm, 308 (4-shot).
Barrel: 18½″.
Weight: 6¼ lbs. **Length:** 37½″ overall.
Stock: Walnut, with modified Schnabel forend. Cut checkering.
Sights: Ramp front, adjustable open rear.
Features: New short-action design; silent side safety; free-floated barrel except for single pressure point at forend tip. Introduced 1983.
Price: About **$503.00**

Remington Seven KS

Remington Model Seven Custom "KS"

Similar to the standard Model Seven except has a stock of lightweight Kevlar aramid fiber and chambered for 223 Rem., 7mm BR, 7mm-08, 35 Rem. and 350 Rem. Mag. Barrel length is 20″ for 35 Rem., 350 Rem. Mag., 18½″ for the others; weight 5¾ lbs. Same stock features, design as the "FS" rifle. Comes with iron sights and is drilled and tapped for scope mounting. Special order through Remington Custom Shop. Introduced 1987.
Price: **$902.00**

Ruger All-Weather M-77

RUGER M-77 MARK II RIFLE

Caliber: 223, 4-shot magazine.
Barrel: 20″.
Weight: 6 lbs., 7 oz. **Length:** 39¾″ overall.
Stock: American walnut.
Sights: None furnished. Receiver has Ruger integral scope mount base, comes with Ruger 1″ rings.
Features: Short action with new trigger and three-position safety. New trigger guard with redesigned floorplate latch. Introduced 1989.
Price: **$531.25**

Ruger All-Weather Stainless M77 Mark II Rifle

Similar to the wood-stock M77 Mark II except all metal parts are of stainless steel, and has an injection-moulded, glass-fiber-reinforced Du Pont Zytel stock. Chambered for 223 Rem., 243 and 308. Has the fixed-blade-type ejector, three-position safety, and new trigger guard with patented floorplate latch. Comes with Integral Scope Base Receiver and 1″ Ruger scope rings, built-in sling swivel loops. Introduced 1990.
Price: KM77MKIIRP **$531.25**

CAUTION: PRICES CHANGE, CHECK AT GUNSHOP.

Ruger Magnum Rifle

Ruger Model M-77RS Magnum Rifle
Similar to Ruger 77 except magnum-size action. Calibers 270, 30-06, 25-06, 7mm Rem. Mag., 300 Win. Mag., 338 Win. Mag., 35 Whelen, with 24″ barrel. Weight about 7 lbs. Integral-base receiver, Ruger 1″ rings and open sights.
Price: **$587.00**

RUGER M-77 MARK II MAGNUM RIFLE
Caliber: 375 H&H (4-shot magazine); 416 Rigby (3-shot magazine).
Barrel: NA.
Weight: 9.25 lbs. (375), 10.25 lbs. (416). **Length:** NA.
Stock: Circassian walnut.
Sights: Ramp front, three leaf express on serrated rib. Rib also serves as base for front scope ring.
Features: Uses an enlarged Mark II action, safety, trigger mechanism, trigger guard, floorplate. Introduced 1989.
Price: About **$1,550.00**

Ruger Model 77R

Ruger Model M-77RS Tropical Rifle
Similar to the Model 77RS Magnum except chambered only for 458 Win. Mag., 24″ barrel, steel trigger guard and floorplate. Weight about 8¾ lbs. Comes with open sights and Ruger 1″ scope rings.
Price: **$679.75**

RUGER M-77R BOLT-ACTION RIFLE
Caliber: 22-250, 220 Swift (Short Stroke action); 270, 7x57, 257 Roberts, 280 Rem., 30-06, 25-06, 7mm Rem. Mag., 300 Win. Mag., 338 Win. Mag. (Magnum action).
Barrel: 22″ round tapered (24″ in 220 Swift and magnum action calibers).
Weight: 6¾ lbs. **Length:** 42″ overall (22″ barrel).
Stock: Hand checkered American walnut, p.g. cap, sling swivel studs and recoil pad.
Sights: None supplied; comes with scope rings.
Features: Integral scope mount bases, diagonal bedding system, hinged floorplate, adjustable trigger, tang safety.
Price: With Ruger steel scope rings, no sights (M-77R) **$531.25**

Ruger International 77

Ruger Model M-77RL Ultra Light
Similar to the standard Model 77 except weighs only 6 lbs., chambered for 270, 30-06, 257, 22-250; barrel tapped for target scope blocks; has 20″ Ultra Light barrel. Over-all length 40″. Ruger's steel 1″ scope rings supplied. Introduced 1983.
Price: **$564.25**

Ruger International Model M-77RSI Rifle
Same as the standard Model 77 except has 18½″ barrel, full-length Mannlicher-style stock, with steel forend cap, loop-type sling swivel. Integral-base receiver, open sights, Ruger 1″ steel rings. Improved front sight. Available in 22-250, 250-3000, 308, 270, 30-06. Weighs 7 lbs. Length overall is 38⅜″.
Price: **$593.75**

Ruger Model M-77RLS Ultra Light Carbine
Similar to the Model 77RL Ultra Light except has 18½″ barrel, Ruger Integral Scope Mounting System, iron sights, and hinged floorplate. Available in 270, 30-06 (Magnum action); 243, 308 (Short Stroke action). Weight is 6 lbs., overall length 38⅞″. Introduced 1987.
Price: **$564.25**

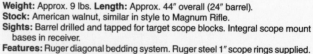

Ruger 77 Varmint

RUGER MODEL 77V VARMINT
Caliber: 22-250, 220 Swift, 243, 6mm, 25-06, 308.
Barrel: 24″ heavy straight tapered, 24″ in 220 Swift.

Weight: Approx. 9 lbs. **Length:** Approx. 44″ overall (24″ barrel).
Stock: American walnut, similar in style to Magnum Rifle.
Sights: Barrel drilled and tapped for target scope blocks. Integral scope mount bases in receiver.
Features: Ruger diagonal bedding system. Ruger steel 1″ scope rings supplied. Fully adjustable trigger. Barreled actions available in any of the standard calibers and barrel lengths.
Price: **$546.25**

Sako Hunter

SAKO HUNTER RIFLE
Caliber: 17 Rem., 222 PPC, 222, 223, 6mm PPC (short action); 22-250, 243, 7mm-08, 308 (medium action); 25-06, 6.5x55, 270, 30-06, 7mm Rem. Mag., 7x64, 300 Win. Mag., 338 Win. Mag., 9.3x62, 375 H&H Mag., 300 Wea. Mag. (long action).
Barrel: 22″ to 24″ depending on caliber.

Weight: 5¾ lbs. (short); 6¼ lbs. (med.); 7¼ lbs. (long).
Stock: Hand-checkered European walnut.
Sights: None furnished. Scope mounts included.
Features: Adj. trigger, hinged floorplate. Imported from Finland by Stoeger.
Price: 17 Rem. **$948.00**
Price: 222, 223, 22-250, 243, 308, 7mm-08 .... **$899.00**
Price: Long action cals. (except magnums) **$931.00**
Price: Magnum cals. **$948.00**
Price: 375 H&H **$963.00**
Price: 300 Wea. **$979.00**
Price: 22 PPC, 6mm PPC, Hunter **$1,133.00**
Price: As above, Deluxe **$1,420.00**

Sako Hunter LS

Sako Hunter Left-Hand Rifle
Same gun as the Sako Hunter except has left-hand action, stock with dull finish. Available in long action and magnum calibers only. Introduced 1987.
Price: Standard calibers $999.00
Price: Magnum calibers $1,033.00
Price: 375 H&H $1,048.00
Price: Deluxe, standard calibers $1,335.00
Price: Deluxe, magnum calibers $1,350.00
Price: Deluxe, 375 H&H $1,365.00

Sako Carbine

Sako Carbine
Similar to the Hunter except with 18½" barrel, same calibers and with conventional oil-finished stock of the Hunter model. Introduced 1986.
Price: 22-250 . . . . $899.00
Price: 25-06 . . . . $931.00
Price: 7mm Rem. Mag., 338 Win. $948.00
Price: As Fiberclass with black fiberglass stock, 25-06, 270, 30-06 $1,275.00
Price: As above, 7mm Rem. Mag., 308 Mag., 338 Win., 375 H&H $1,290.00

Sako Fiberclass

Sako Deluxe Sporter
Same action as Hunter except has select wood, rosewood p.g. cap and forend tip. Fine checkering on top surfaces of integral dovetail bases, bolt sleeve, bolt handle root and bolt knob. Vent. recoil pad, skip-line checkering, mirror finish bluing.
Price: 17 Rem $1,275.00
Price: 222, 223, 22-250, 243, 308, 7mm-08, 25-06, 270, 280 Rem.,
30-06 . . . . $1,265.00
Price: 7mm Rem. Mag., 300 Win. Mag., 338 Win. Mag. $1,275.00
Price: 375 H&H Mag. $1,290.00
Price: 300 Wea. Mag. $1,299.00

Sako Heavy Barrel

Sako Heavy Barrel
Same as std. Super Sporter except has beavertail forend; available in 17 Rem., 222, 223 (short action), 22 PPC, 6mm PPC (single shot), 22-250, 243, 308, 7mm-08 (medium action). Weight from 8¼ to 8½ lbs., 5-shot magazine capacity.
Price: 17 Rem., 222, 223 (short action) $1,030.00
Price: 22-250, 243, 308 (medium action) $1,030.00
Price: 22 PPC, 6mm PPC (single shot) $1,199.00

Sako Hunter LS Rifle
Same gun as the Sako Hunter except has laminated stock with dull finish. Chambered for same calibers. Introduced 1987.
Price: Medium action $1,030.00
Price: Long action $1,069.00
Price: Magnum cals. $1,083.00
Price: 375 H&H $1,099.00

Sako Safari Grade Bolt Action
Similar to the Hunter except available in long action, calibers 300 Win. Mag., 338 Win. Mag. or 375 H&H Mag. only. Stocked in French walnut, checkered 20 lpi, solid rubber buttpad; grip cap and forend tip; quarter-rib "express" rear sight, hooded ramp front. Front sling swivel band-mounted on barrel.
Price: $2,435.00

Sako Mannlicher-Style Carbine
Same as the Hunter except has full "Mannlicher" style stock, 18½" barrel, weighs 7½ lbs., chambered for 243, 25-06, 270, 308 and 30-06, 7mm Rem. Mag., 300 Win. Mag., 338 Win. Mag., 375 H&H. Introduced 1977. From Stoeger.
Price: $1,045.00
Price: Magnum cals. $1,095.00
Price: 375 H&H $1,099.00

Sako Fiberclass Sporter
Similar to the Hunter except has a black fiberglass stock in the classic style, with wrinkle finish, rubber buttpad. Barrel length is 23", weight 7 lbs., 2 oz. Comes with scope mounts. Introduced 1985.
Price: Medium action $1,239.00
Price: Short, medium, long action, std. cals. $1,275.00
Price: Magnum cals. $1,290.00

> Consult our Directory pages for the location of firms mentioned.

Sako Super Deluxe Sporter
Similar to Deluxe Sporter except has select European walnut with high gloss finish and deep cut oak leaf carving. Metal has super high polish, deep blue finish. Special order only.
Price: $2,580.00

SAUER 90 RIFLE
Caliber: 243, 308, 25-06, 270, 30-06, 7mm Rem. Mag., 300 Win., 300 Wea., 375 H&H.
Barrel: 24".
Weight: 7 lbs., 6 oz. to 7 lbs., 12 oz. Length: 42½" overall.
Stock: European walnut. Supreme grade has high gloss; Lux has oil finish.
Sights: Post front on ramp, open rear adjustable for windage.
Features: Detachable 3-4 round box magazine; rear bolt locking lugs; 65° bolt throw; front sling swivel on barrel band. Introduced 1986. Imported from West Germany by Guns Unlimited.
Price: Supreme $1,595.00
Price: Lux $1,495.00

Savage Model 110G

SAVAGE 110G BOLT-ACTION RIFLE

Caliber: 22-250, 223, 270, 308, 30-06, 243, 5-shot; 7mm Rem. Mag., 300 Win. Mag., 4-shot.
Barrel: 22" round tapered, 24" for magnum.
Weight: 6¾ lbs. **Length:** 42⅜" (22" barrel).
Stock: Walnut-finished checkered hardwood with Monte Carlo; hard rubber buttplate.
Sights: Ramp front, step adjustable rear.
Features: Top tang safety, receiver tapped for scope mount. Full floating barrel; adjustable trigger. Introduced 1989.
Price: **$400.00**
Price: Left-hand, 30-06, 270, 7mm Rem. Mag. only, 110 GL **$465.88**
Price: 110 G-X, no sights, Weaver-type integral bases **$392.16**
Price: 110 G-XL, 30-06, 270, 7mm Rem. Mag. only **$458.04**

Savage Model 110F Bolt-Action Rifle

Similar to the Model 110G except has a black Du Pont Rynite® stock with black buttpad, swivel studs, removable open sights. Introduced 1988.
Price: Right-hand only **$489.41**
Price: Model 110-FX (no sights, integral Weaver-type bases) **$481.57**

Savage Model 110B

Savage Model 110B Bolt-Action Rifle

Similar to the Model 110G except has brown laminated Monte Carlo stock with brown buttpad. Cals. 223, 22-250, 243, 308, 270, 30-06, 7mm Rem. Mag., 300 Win. Mag. Weighs 6¾ lbs. Introduced 1989.
Price: **$476.87**

Savage Model 110-GV

Savage 110-GV Varmint Rifle

Similar to the Model 110-G except has medium-weight varmint barrel, no sights, receiver drilled and tapped for scope mounting. Calibers 22-250, 223 only. Introduced 1989.
Price: **$443.92**

Savage 110FP Police

SAVAGE MODEL 110FP POLICE RIFLE

Caliber: 223, 308, 4-shot magazine.
Barrel: 24", heavy.

Weight: 8 lbs. **Length:** 45.5" overall.
Stock: Black Rynite composition.
Sights: None furnished. Receiver drilled and tapped for scope mounting.
Features: Matte finish on all metal parts. Double swivel studs on the forend for sling and/or bipod mount. Introduced 1990. From Savage Arms.
Price: **$564.71**

Steyr Model M

STEYR-MANNLICHER MODEL M

Caliber: 7x64, 7x57, 25-06, 270, 30-06. Left-hand action cals.—7x64, 25-06, 270, 30-06. Optional cals.—6.5x57, 8x57JS, 9.3x62, 6.5x55, 7.5x55.
Barrel: 20" (full-stock); 23.6" (half-stock).
Weight: 6.8 lbs. to 7.5 lbs. **Length:** 39" (full-stock); 43" (half-stock).
Stock: Hand checkered walnut. Full Mannlicher or std. half-stock with M.C. and rubber recoil pad.
Sights: Ramp front, open U-notch rear.
Features: Choice of interchangeable single or double set triggers. Detachable 5-shot rotary magazine. Drilled and tapped for scope mounting. Available as "Professional" model with Parkerized finish and synthetic stock (right-hand action only). Imported by Gun South, Inc.
Price: Full-stock (carbine) **$1,939.00**
Price: Half-stock (rifle) **$1,812.00**
Price: Professional model with iron sights **$1,532.00**

Steyr-Mannlicher "Luxus"

Similar to Steyr-Mannlicher Models L and M except has single set trigger and detachable 3-shot steel magazine. Same calibers as L and M. Oil finish or high gloss lacquer on stock.
Price: Full-stock **$2,495.00**
Price: Half-stock **$2,364.00**

Steyr-Mannlicher L

Steyr-Mannlicher Varmint, Models SL and L
Similar to standard SL and L except chambered only for 222 Rem., 22-250, 243, 308. Has 26" heavy barrel, no sights (drilled and tapped for scope mounts). Choice of single or double set triggers. Five-shot detachable magazine.
Price: $1,939.00

STEYR-MANNLICHER MODELS S & S/T
Caliber: Model S—300 Win. Mag., 7mm Rem. Mag., 300 H&H Mag., 375 H&H Mag. (6.5x68, 8x68S, 9.3x64 optional); S/T—375 H&H Mag., 458 Win. Mag. (9.3x64 optional).
Barrel: 25.6".
Weight: 8.4 lbs. (Model S). **Length:** 45" overall.
Stock: Half-stock with M.C. and rubber recoil pad. Hand checkered walnut.

STEYR-MANNLICHER MODELS SL & L
Caliber: SL—222, 222 Rem. Mag., 223; SL Varmint—222; L—22-250, 6mm, 243, 308 Win.; L Varmint—22-250, 243, 308 Win.
Barrel: 20" (full-stock); 23.6" (half-stock).
Weight: 6 lbs. (full-stock). **Length:** 38¼" (full-stock).
Stock: Hand checkered walnut. Full Mannlicher or standard half-stock with Monte Carlo.
Sights: Ramp front, open U-notch rear.
Features: Choice of interchangeable single or double set triggers. Five-shot detachable "Makrolon" rotary magazine, 6 rear locking lugs. Drilled and tapped for scope mounts. Imported by Gun South, Inc.
Price: Full-stock $1,939.00
Price: Half-stock $1,812.00

Available with optional spare magazine inletted in butt.
Sights: Ramp front, U-notch rear.
Features: Choice of interchangeable single or double set triggers, detachable 4-shot magazine. Drilled and tapped for scope mounts. Imported by Gun South, Inc.
Price: Model S $1,952.00
Price: Model S/T 375 H&H, 458 Win. Mag. $2,176.00

Tikka Rifle

Tikka Premium Grade Rifles
Similar to the standard grade Tikka except has stock with roll-over cheekpiece, select walnut, rosewood grip and forend caps. Hand checkered grip and forend. Highly polished and blued barrel. Introduced 1990. Imported from Finland by Stoeger.
Price: Standard calibers $930.00
Price: Magnum calibers $965.00

TIKKA BOLT-ACTION RIFLE
Caliber: 22-250, 223, 243, 270, 30-06, 7mm Rem. Mag., 300 Win. Mag., 338 Win. Mag.
Barrel: 22" (std. cals.), 24" (magnum cals.).
Weight: 7⅛ lbs. **Length:** 43" overall (std. cals.).
Stock: European walnut with Monte Carlo comb, rubber buttpad, checkered grip and forend.
Sights: None furnished.
Features: Detachable four-shot magazine (standard calibers), three-shot in magnums. Receiver dovetailed for scope mounting. Introduced 1988. Imported from Finland by Stoeger Industries.
Price: Standard calibers $765.00
Price: Magnum calibers $795.00

Ultra Light Model 20

Ultra Light Arms Model 28 Rifle
Similar to the Model 20 except in 264, 7mm Rem. Mag., 300 Win. Mag., 338 Win. Mag. Uses 24" Douglas Premium No. 2 contour barrel. Weighs 5½ lbs., 45" overall length. KDF or U.L.A. recoil arrestor built in. Any custom feature available on any U.L.A. product can be incorporated.
Price: Right hand $2,700.00
Price: Left hand $2,800.00

VOERE 2155, 2165 BOLT-ACTION RIFLE
Caliber: 22-250, 270, 308, 243, 30-06, 7x64, 5.6x57, 6.5x55, 8x57 JRS, 7mm Rem. Mag., 300 Win. Mag., 8x68S, 9.3x62, 9.3x64, 6.5x68.
Stock: European walnut, hog-back style; checkered pistol grip and forend.
Sights: Ramp front, open adjustable rear.
Features: Mauser-type action with 5-shot detachable box magazine; double set or single trigger; drilled and tapped for scope mounting. Imported from Austria by L. Joseph Rahn. Introduced 1984.

ULTRA LIGHT ARMS MODEL 20 RIFLE
Caliber: 17 Rem., 22 Hornet, 222 Rem., 222 Rem. Mag., 223 Rem., 22-250, 6mm Rem., 243, 250-3000, 257 Roberts, 257 Ackley, 7x57, 7x57 Ackley, 7mm-08, 284 Win., 300 Savage, 358 Win.
Barrel: 22" or 24" Douglas Premium No. 1 contour.
Weight: 4½ lbs. **Length:** 41½" overall.
Stock: Composite Kevlar, graphite reinforced. Du Pont Imron paint colors—green, black, brown and camo options. Choice of length of pull.
Sights: None furnished. Scope mount included.
Features: Timney adjustable trigger; two-position three-function safety. Benchrest quality action. Matte or bright stock and metal finish. 3" magazine length. Shipped in a hard case. From Ultra Light Arms, Inc.
Price: Right hand $2,200.00
Price: Model 20 Left Hand (left-hand action and stock) $2,300.00
Price: Model 24 (25-06, 270, 7mm Express Rem., 30-06, 3⅜" magazine length) $2,300.00
Price: Model 24 Left Hand (left-hand action and stock) $2,400.00

Price: M2165, standard calibers, single trigger $885.00
Price: As above, double set triggers $925.00
Price: M2165, magnum calibers, single trigger $915.00
Price: As above, double set triggers $955.00
Price: M2165, full-stock, single trigger $925.00
Price: As above, double set triggers $985.00
Price: M2155 (as above, no jeweling, military safety, single trigger) $700.00
Price: As above, double triggers $750.00

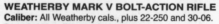

Weatherby Mark V

WEATHERBY MARK V BOLT-ACTION RIFLE
Caliber: All Weatherby cals., plus 22-250 and 30-06.
Barrel: 24″ or 26″ round tapered.
Weight: 6½-10½ lbs. **Length:** 43¼″-46½″ overall.
Stock: Walnut, Monte Carlo with cheekpiece, high luster finish, checkered p.g. and forend, recoil pad.
Sights: Optional (extra).
Features: Cocking indicator, adjustable trigger, hinged floorplate, thumb safety, quick detachable sling swivels.
Price: Cals. 224 and 22-250, std. bbl., right-hand only $1,020.00
Price: With 26″ semi-target bbl., right-hand only $1,045.00
Price: Cals. 240, 257, 270, 7mm, 30-06 and 300 (24″ bbl.) right- or left-hand $1,040.00
Price: With 26″ No. 2 contour bbl., right-hand or 300 W.M. left only $1,065.00
Price: Cal. 340 (26″ bbl.), right- or left-hand $1,065.00
Price: Cal. 378 (26″ bbl.), right- or left-hand $1,225.00
Price: 416 W.M., 24″, right- or left-hand $1,325.00
Price: As above, 26″ $1,360.00
Price: 460 W.M., 24″, right- or left-hand $1,400.00
Price: As above, 26″ $1,425.00

WEATHERBY EUROMARK BOLT-ACTION RIFLE
Caliber: All Weatherby calibers except 224, 22-250.
Barrel: 24″ or 26″ round tapered.
Weight: 6½ to 10½ lbs. **Length:** 44¼″ overall (24″ bbl.).
Stock: Walnut, Monte Carlo with extended tail, fine-line hand checkering, satin oil finish, ebony forend tip and grip cap with maple diamond, solid buttpad.
Sights: Optional (extra).
Features: Cocking indicator; adjustable trigger; hinged floorplate; thumb safety; q.d. sling swivels. Introduced 1986.
Price: With 24″ barrel (240, 257, 270, 7mm, 30-06, 300), right- or left-hand $1,095.00
Price: 26″ No. 2 contour barrel, right- or left-hand (300 only) $1,120.00
Price: 340 W.M., 26″, right- or left-hand $1,120.00
Price: 378 W.M., right- or left-hand $1,275.00
Price: 416 W.M., 24″, right- or left-hand $1,390.00
Price: As above, 26″ $1,415.00
Price: 460 W.M., 24″, right- or left-hand $1,460.00
Price: As above, 26″ $1,485.00

Weatherby Mark V "Safari Grade" Custom Rifles
Uses the Mark V barreled action. Stock is of European walnut with satin oil finish, rounded ebony tip and cap, black presentation recoil pad, no white spacers, and pattern #16 fine-line checkering. Matte finish bluing, floorplate is engraved "Weatherby Safari Grade"; 24″ barrel. Standard rear stock swivel, barrel band front swivel. Has quarter-rib rear sight with a stationary leaf and one folding shallow V leaf. Front sight is a hooded ramp with brass bead. Right- or left-hand. Allow 8-10 months delivery. Introduced 1985.
Price: 300 W.M. $3,064.00
Price: 340 W.M. $3,076.00
Price: 378 W.M. $3,224.00
Price: 416 W.M. $3,308.00
Price: 460 W.M. $3,308.00

Weatherby Mark V "Crown" Custom Rifles
Uses hand-honed, engraved Mark V barreled action with fully-checkered bolt knob, damascened bolt and follower. Floorplate is engraved "Weatherby Custom." Super fancy walnut stock with inlays and stock carving. Gold monogram with name or initials. Right-hand only. Available in 240, 257, 270, 7mm, 300 Wea. Mag. or 30-06. Introduced 1989.
Price: From ....$3,400.00 to $4,534.00
Price: For 340 W.M., add $16.00

Weatherby Weatherguard

Weatherby Mark V Rifle Left Hand
Available in all Weatherby calibers, plus 30-06 with 24″ barrel. Left-hand 26″ barrel available in 300 and 340 calibers. Not available in 224 WM and 22-250 Varmintmaster.

Weatherby Vanguard Weatherguard Rifle
Has a forest green or black wrinkle-finished synthetic stock. All metal is matte blue. Has a 24″ barrel, weighs 7½ lbs., measures 44½″. In 223, 243, and 308; 40½″ in 270, 7mm-08, 7mm Rem. Mag., 30-06. Accepts same scope mount bases as Mark V action. Introduced 1989.
Price: Right-hand only $435.00

Weatherby Ultramark

Weatherby Mark V Ultramark Rifle
Similar to the Mark V except stock is of select Claro walnut with basketweave checkering; hand-honed, jeweled action with a floorplate engraved "Weatherby Ultramark." Available in all Weatherby calibers and 30-06 except 224 Wea. Mag., 460 Wea. Mag. and 22-250. Introduced 1989.
Price: Calibers 240, 257, 270, 7mm, 300 Wea. Mag., 30-06, 24″, right- or left-hand action $1,315.00
Price: As above, 26″ $1,340.00
Price: 340 Wea. Mag., 26″ right- or left-hand $1,340.00

Weatherby Lazermark V Rifle
Same as standard Mark V except stock has extensive laser carving under cheekpiece on butt, p.g. and forend. Introduced 1981.
Price: 22-250, 224 Wea., 24″ bbl., right-hand only $1,140.00
Price: As above, 26″ bbl., right-hand only $1,165.00
Price: 240 Wea. thru 300 Wea., 24″ bbl., right- or left-hand ...$1,160.00
Price: As above, 26″ bbl., right-hand or 300 W.M. left-hand $1,185.00
Price: 340 Wea., right- or left-hand $1,185.00
Price: 378 Wea., right- or left-hand $1,345.00
Price: 416 W.M., 24″, right- or left-hand $1,460.00
Price: As above, 26″ $1,485.00
Price: 460 W.M., 24″ right- or left-hand $1,525.00
Price: As above, 26″ $1,550.00

Weatherby Fibermark

Weatherby Fibermark Rifle
Same as the standard Mark V except the stock is of fiberglass; finished with a non-glare black wrinkle finish and black recoil pad; receiver and floorplate have low luster blue finish; fluted bolt has a satin finish. Available in left- or right-hand, 24″ or 26″ barrel, 240 Weatherby Mag. through 340 Weatherby Mag. calibers. Introduced 1983.
Price: 240 W.M. through 300 W.M., 24″ bbl. **$1,180.00**
Price: 240 W.M. through 340 W.M., 26″ bbl., right-hand or 300, 340, W.M. left-hand only **$1,205.00**

Weatherby Vanguard VGX

WEATHERBY VANGUARD VGX DELUXE RIFLE
Caliber: 22-250, 243, 270, 270 Wea. Mag., 7mm Rem. Mag., 30-06, 300 Win. Mag., 300 Wea. Mag., 338 Win. Mag.; 5-shot magazine (3-shot for magnums).
Barrel: 24″, No. 2 contour.
Weight: 7⅞-8½ lbs. **Length:** 44½″ overall (22-250, 243 are 44″).
Stock: Walnut with high luster finish; rosewood grip cap and forend tip.
Sights: Optional, available at extra cost.
Features: Fully adjustable trigger; side safety; rubber recoil pad. Introduced 1989. Imported from Japan by Weatherby.
Price: **$635.00**

Weatherby Vanguard Classic II Rifle
Similar to the Classic I except has rounded forend with black tip, black grip cap with walnut diamond inlay, 20 lpi checkering. Solid black recoil pad. Oil-finished stock. Available in 22-250, 243, 270, 7mm Rem. Mag., 30-06, 300 Win. Mag., 338 Win. Mag., 270 Wea. Mag., 300 Wea. Mag. Introduced 1989.
Price: **$635.00**

Weatherby Classic I

Weatherby Vanguard Classic I Rifle
Similar to the Vanguard VGX Deluxe except has a "classic" style stock without Monte Carlo comb, no forend tip. Has distinctive Weatherby grip cap. Satin finish on stock. Available in 223, 243, 270, 7mm-08, 7mm Rem. Mag., 30-06, 308; 24″ barrel. Introduced 1989.
Price: **$490.00**

Whitworth Express Rifle

WHITWORTH SAFARI EXPRESS RIFLE
Caliber: 375 H&H, 458 Win. Mag.
Barrel: 24″.
Weight: 7½-8 lbs. **Length:** 44″.
Stock: Classic English Express rifle design of hand checkered, select European walnut.
Sights: Three-leaf open sight calibrated for 100, 200, 300 yards on ¼-rib, ramp front with removable hood.
Features: Solid rubber recoil pad, barrel-mounted sling swivel, adjustable trigger, hinged floorplate, solid steel recoil cross bolt.
Price: 375, 458, with express sights **$789.00**

Wichita Varmint Rifle

WICHITA VARMINT RIFLE
Caliber: 17 Rem. thru 308 Win., including 22 and 6mm PPC.
Barrel: 20⅛″.
Weight: 9 lbs. **Length:** 40⅛″ overall.
Stock: AAA Fancy American walnut. Hand-rubbed finish, hand checkered, 20 lpi pattern. Hand-inletted, glass bedded, steel grip cap. Pachmayr rubber recoil pad.
Sights: None. Drilled and tapped for scope mounts.
Features: Right- or left-hand Wichita action with three locking lugs. Available as a single shot or repeater with 3-shot magazine. Checkered bolt handle. Bolt is hand fitted, lapped and jeweled. Side thumb safety. Firing pin fall is ³⁄₁₆″. Non-glare blue finish. From Wichita Arms.
Price: Single shot **$1,975.00**

Winchester 70 Lightweight

WICHITA CLASSIC RIFLE
Caliber: 17 Rem. thru 308 Win., including 22 and 6mm PPC.
Barrel: 21⅛".
Weight: 8 lbs. **Length:** 41" overall.
Stock: AAA Fancy American walnut. Hand-rubbed and checkered (20 lpi). Hand-inletted, glass bedded, steel grip cap. Pachmayr rubber recoil pad.
Sights: None. Drilled and tapped for scope mounting.
Features: Available as single shot or repeater. Octagonal barrel and Wichita action, right- or left-hand. Checkered bolt handle. Bolt is hand-fitted, lapped and jeweled. Adjustable Canjar trigger is set at 2 lbs. Side thumb safety. Firing pin fall is ³⁄₁₆". Non-glare blue finish. From Wichita Arms.
Price: Single shot $2,950.00

Winchester 70 Super Express

WINCHESTER 70 SUPER EXPRESS MAGNUM
Caliber: 375 H&H Mag., 458 Win. Mag., 3-shot magazine.
Barrel: 24" (375); 22" (458).

Winchester 70 Sporter

WINCHESTER 70 SPORTER
Caliber: 22-250, 223, 243, 25-06, 270, 270 Wea., 30-06, 264 Win. Mag., 7mm Rem. Mag., 300 H&H, 300 Win. Mag., 300 Wea. Mag., 338 Win. Mag., 3-shot magazine.
Barrel: 24".

Winchester 70 Varmint

Winchester Model 70 Heavy Barrel Varmint
Similar to the Model 70 Sporter except has heavy 26" barrel with counter-bored muzzle. Available in 22-250, 223, 243 and 308. Receiver bedded in sporter-style stock. Has rubber buttpad. Receiver drilled and tapped for scope mounting. Weight about 9 lbs., overall length 46". Introduced 1989.
Price: $511.00

Winchester 70 Ranger

WINCHESTER MODEL 70 LIGHTWEIGHT RIFLE
Caliber: 270, 280, 30-06 (standard action); 22-250, 223, 243, 308 (short action), both 5-shot magazine, except 6-shot in 223.
Barrel: 22".
Weight: 6¼ lbs. **Length:** 40½" overall (std.), 40" (short).
Stock: American walnut with satin finish, deep-cut checkering.
Sights: None furnished. Drilled and tapped for scope mounting.
Features: Three position safety; stainless steel magazine follower; hinged floorplate; sling swivel studs. Introduced 1984.
Price: Walnut $447.00
Price: With WinTuff laminated stock, 270, 30-06 only $447.00
Price: With WinCam green laminated stock, 270, 30-06 only $447.00

Weight: 8½ lbs.
Stock: American walnut with Monte Carlo cheekpiece. Wraparound checkering and finish.
Sights: Hooded ramp front, open rear.
Features: Two steel cross bolts in stock for added strength. Front sling swivel stud mounted on barrel. Contoured rubber buttpad. From U.S. Repeating Arms Co.
Price: About $792.00

Weight: 7¾ lbs. **Length:** 44½" overall.
Stock: American walnut with Monte Carlo cheekpiece. Cut checkering and satin finish.
Sights: Optional hooded ramp front, adjustable folding leaf rear. Drilled and tapped for scope mounting.
Features: Three-position safety, stainless steel magazine follower; rubber buttpad, epoxy bedded receiver recoil lug. From U.S. Repeating Arms Co.
Price: With sights $495.00
Price: Without sights $495.00

Winchester Model 70 Winlite Rifle
Similar to the Model 70 Sporter except has McMillan black fiberglass stock. No sights are furnished but receiver is drilled and tapped for scope mounting. Available in 270, 280, 30-06 (22" barrel, 4-shot magazine), 7mm Rem. Mag., 300 Wea., 300 Win. Mag., 338 Win. Mag. (24" barrel, 3-shot magazine). Weight is 6¼-6½ lbs. for 270, 30-06; 6¾-7 lbs. for 7mm Mag., 338. Introduced 1986.
Price: $637.00

Winchester Ranger Rifle
Similar to Model 70 Lightweight except chambered only for 243, 270, 30-06, with 22" barrel. American hardwood stock, no checkering, composition butt-plate. Metal has matte blue finish. Introduced 1985.
Price: About $414.00
Price: Ranger Youth, 243 only, scaled-down stock $406.00

CAUTION: PRICES CHANGE, CHECK AT GUNSHOP.

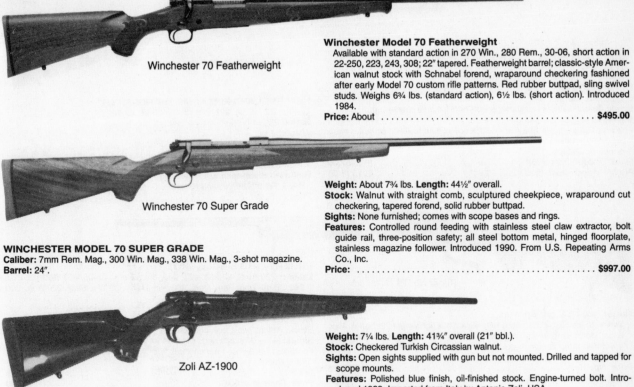

Winchester 70 Featherweight

Winchester Model 70 Featherweight
Available with standard action in 270 Win., 280 Rem., 30-06, short action in 22-250, 223, 243, 308; 22″ tapered. Featherweight barrel; classic-style American walnut stock with Schnabel forend, wraparound checkering fashioned after early Model 70 custom rifle patterns. Red rubber buttpad, sling swivel studs. Weighs 6¾ lbs. (standard action), 6½ lbs. (short action). Introduced 1984.
Price: About **$495.00**

Winchester 70 Super Grade

Weight: About 7¾ lbs. **Length:** 44½″ overall.
Stock: Walnut with straight comb, sculptured cheekpiece, wraparound cut checkering, tapered forend, solid rubber buttpad.
Sights: None furnished; comes with scope bases and rings.
Features: Controlled round feeding with stainless steel claw extractor, bolt guide rail, three-position safety; all steel bottom metal, hinged floorplate, stainless magazine follower. Introduced 1990. From U.S. Repeating Arms Co., Inc.
Price: **$997.00**

WINCHESTER MODEL 70 SUPER GRADE
Caliber: 7mm Rem. Mag., 300 Win. Mag., 338 Win. Mag., 3-shot magazine.
Barrel: 24″.

Zoli AZ-1900

Weight: 7¼ lbs. **Length:** 41¾″ overall (21″ bbl.).
Stock: Checkered Turkish Circassian walnut.
Sights: Open sights supplied with gun but not mounted. Drilled and tapped for scope mounts.
Features: Polished blue finish, oil-finished stock. Engine-turned bolt. Introduced 1989. Imported from Italy by Antonio Zoli, USA.
Price: Model AZ-1900, standard cals. **$1,250.00**
Price: As above, magnum cals. **$1,250.00**
Price: Model AZ-1900 DL (engraved receiver, no sights) **$1,350.00**
Price: As above, magnum cals. **$1,350.00**

ZOLI MODEL AZ-1900 BOLT-ACTION RIFLE
Caliber: 243, 6.5x55, 270, 308, 30-06, 7mm Rem. Mag., 300 Win. Mag.
Barrel: 21″ (24″ on 7mm Rem. Mag., 300 Win. Mag.).

CENTERFIRE RIFLES—SINGLE SHOTS

Classic and modern designs for sporting and competitive use.

Browning Model 1885

BROWNING MODEL 1885 SINGLE SHOT RIFLE
Caliber: 223, 22-250, 30-06, 270, 7mm Rem. Mag., 45-70.
Barrel: 28″.
Weight: About 8½ lbs. **Length:** 43½″ overall.
Stock: Walnut with straight grip, schnabel forend.
Sights: None furnished; drilled and tapped for scope mounting.
Features: Replica of J.M. Browning's high-wall falling block rifle. Octagon barrel with recessed muzzle. Imported from Japan by Browning. Introduced 1985.
Price: **$734.95**

Desert Industries G-90

DESERT INDUSTRIES G-90 SINGLE SHOT RIFLE
Caliber: All popular calibers.
Barrel: 20″ to 26″, interchangeable.
Weight: About 7.5 lbs.
Stock: Walnut.
Sights: None furnished. Drilled and tapped for scope mounting.
Features: Cylindrical falling block action. All steel construction. Blue finish. Introduced 1990. From Desert Industries, Inc.
Price: **$525.00**

New England "Handi-Rifle"

AUGUSTE FRANCOTTE CARPATHE MOUNTAIN RIFLE
Caliber: 243, 270, 308, 30-06, 7x65R, 7x57R, 5.6x52R, 5.6x57R, 6.5x57R, 6.5x68R, 7mm Rem. Mag., 300 Win. Mag.
Barrel: 23.5" to 26".
Weight: NA. **Length:** NA.
Stock: Deluxe walnut to customer specs; oil finish, fine checkering.
Sights: None furnished; scope mount standard.
Features: Single-barrel rifle with sidelock action, third fastener, extractor, manual safety, splinter forend. Many options available. Imported from Belgium by Armes de Chasse.
Price: Boxlock, from about $10,457.00
Price: Sidelock, from about $21,771.00

NEW ENGLAND FIREARMS "HANDI-RIFLE"
Caliber: 22 Hornet, 223, 243, 30-30, 30-06, 45-70.
Barrel: 22".
Weight: 7 lbs.
Stock: Walnut-finished hardwood.
Sights: Ramp front, folding rear. Drilled and tapped for scope mount; 223 Rem. has no open sights, comes with scope mounts.
Features: Break-open action with side-lever release. Blue finish. Introduced 1989. From New England Firearms.
Price: . . . . **NA**

Ruger No. 1B Rifle

Ruger No. 1A Light Sporter
Similar to the No. 1B Standard Rifle except has lightweight 22" barrel, Alexander Henry-style forend, adjustable folding leaf rear sight on quarter-rib, dovetailed ramp front with gold bead. Calibers 243, 30-06, 270 and 7x57. Weight about 7¼ lbs.
Price: No. 1A $603.75
Price: Barreled action $409.00

RUGER NO. 1B SINGLE SHOT
Caliber: 220 Swift, 22-250, 223, 243, 6mm Rem., 25-06, 257 Roberts, 270, 280, 30-06, 7mm Rem. Mag., 300 Win. Mag., 338 Win. Mag., 270 Wea., 300 Wea.
Barrel: 26" round tapered with quarter-rib; with Ruger 1" rings.
Weight: 8 lbs. **Length:** 43⅜" overall.
Stock: Walnut, two-piece, checkered p.g. and semi-beavertail forend.
Sights: None, 1" scope rings supplied for integral mounts.
Features: Under-lever, hammerless falling block design has auto ejector, top tang safety.
Price: $603.75
Price: Barreled action $409.00

Ruger No. 1 International

Ruger No. 1 RSI International
Similar to the No. 1B Standard Rifle except has lightweight 20" barrel, full-length Mannlicher-style forend with loop sling swivel, adjustable folding leaf rear sight on quarter-rib, ramp front with gold bead. Calibers 243, 30-06, 270 and 7x57. Weight is about 7¼ lbs.
Price: No. 1 RSI $624.75
Price: Barreled action $409.00

Ruger No. 1V Special Varminter
Similar to the No. 1B Standard Rifle except has 24" heavy barrel. Semi-beavertail forend, barrel tapped for target scope block, with 1" Ruger scope rings. Calibers 22-250, 220 Swift, 223, 25-06. Weight about 9 lbs.
Price: No. 1V $603.75
Price: Barreled action $409.00

Ruger No. 1H Tropical Rifle
Similar to the No. 1B Standard Rifle except has Alexander Henry forend, adjustable folding leaf rear sight on quarter-rib, ramp front with dovetail gold bead, 24" heavy barrel. Calibers 375 H&H (weight about 8¼ lbs.) and 458 Win. Mag. (weight about 9 lbs.).
Price: No. 1H $603.75
Price: Barreled action $409.00

Ruger No. 1S Medium Sporter
Similar to the No. 1B Standard Rifle except has Alexander Henry-style forend, adjustable folding leaf rear sight on quarter-rib, ramp front sight base and dovetail-type gold bead front sight. Calibers 7mm Rem. Mag., 338 Win. Mag., 300 Win. Mag. with 26" barrel, 45-70 with 22" barrel. Weight about 7½ lbs. in 45-70.
Price: No. 1S $603.75
Price: Barreled action $409.00

NAVY ARMS ROLLING BLOCK RIFLE
Caliber: 45-70.
Barrel: 30".
Stocks: Walnut finished.
Sights: Fixed front, adjustable rear.
Features: Reproduction of classic rolling block action. Available in Buffalo Rifle (octagonal bbl.) and Creedmoor (half-round, half-octagonal bbl.) models. From Navy Arms.
Price: 26", 30" full octagon barrel $485.00
Price: 30", half-round $485.00
Price: 26", half-round $485.00
Price: #2 Creedmoor Target $640.00

C. SHARPS ARMS NEW MODEL 1875 RIFLE
Caliber: 22 LR Stevens, 32-40 & 38-55 Ballard, 38-56 WCF, 40-65 WCF, 40-90 3¼", 40-90 2⅝", 40-70 2⅒", 40-70 2¼", 40-70 2½", 40-50 1¹¹/₁₆", 40-50 1⅞", 45-90 2⁴/₁₀", 45-70 2¹/₁₀".
Barrel: 24", 26", 30", (standard); 32", 34" optional.
Weight: 8-12 lbs.
Stocks: Walnut, straight grip, shotgun butt with checkered steel buttplate.
Sights: Silver blade front, Rocky Mountain buckhorn rear.
Features: Recreation of the 1875 Sharps rifle. Production guns will have case colored receiver. Available in Custom Sporting and Target versions upon request. Announced 1986. From C. Sharps Arms Co.
Price: 1875 Carbine (24" tapered round bbl.) $575.00
Price: 1875 Saddle Rifle (26" tapered oct. bbl.) $685.00
Price: 1875 Sporting Rifle (30" tapered oct. bbl.) $695.00
Price: 1875 Business Rifle (28" tapered round bbl.) $565.00

C. Sharps Arms 1875 Classic Sharps
Similar to the New Model 1875 Sporting Rifle except has 30" full octagon barrel, crescent buttplate with toe plate, Hartford-style forend with cast German silver nose cap. Blade front sight, Rocky Mountain buckhorn rear. Weight is 10 lbs. Introduced 1987. From C. Sharps Arms Co.
Price: $995.00

CENTERFIRE RIFLES—SINGLE SHOTS

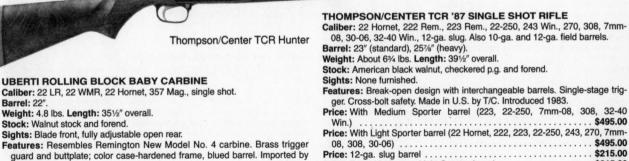

Sharps Long Range Express

Shiloh Sharps 1874 Military Carbine
Has 22" round barrel with blade front sight and full buckhorn ladder-type rear. Military-style buttstock with barrel band on military-style forend. Steel buttplate, saddle bar and ring. Standard supreme grade only. Weight is about 8½ lbs. Calibers 40-70 BN, 45-70, 50-70. Introduced 1989.
Price: $765.00

Shiloh Sharps 1874 Montana Roughrider
Similar to the No. 1 Sporting Rifle except available with half-octagon or full-octagon barrel in 24", 26", 28", 30", 34" lengths; standard supreme or semi-fancy wood, shotgun, pistol grip or military-style butt. Weight about 8½ lbs. Calibers 30-40, 30-30, 40-50x1¹¹⁄₁₆" BN, 40-70x2¹⁄₁₀" BN, 45-70x2¹⁄₁₀" ST. Globe front and tang sight optional.
Price: Standard supreme $725.00
Price: Semi-fancy $810.00

Shiloh Sharps 1874 Military Rifle
Has 30" round barrel. Iron block front sight and Lawrence-style rear ladder sight. Military butt, buttplate, patchbox assembly optional; three barrel bands; single trigger (double set available). Calibers 40-50x1¹¹⁄₁₆" BN, 40-70x2¹⁄₁₀" BN, 40-90 BN, 45-70x2¹⁄₁₀" ST, 50-70 ST.
Price: $845.00

SHILOH SHARPS 1874 LONG RANGE EXPRESS
Caliber: 40-50 BN, 40-70 BN, 40-90 BN, 45-70 ST, 45-90 ST, 45-110 ST, 50-70 ST, 50-90 ST, 50-110 ST, 32-40, 38-55, 40-70 ST, 40-90 ST.
Barrel: 34" tapered octagon.
Weight: 10½ lbs. Length: 51" overall.
Stock: Oil-finished semi-fancy walnut with pistol grip, shotgun-style butt, traditional cheek rest and accent line. Schnabel forend.
Sights: Globe front, sporting tang rear.
Features: Recreation of the Model 1874 Sharps rifle. Double set triggers. Made in U.S. by Shiloh Rifle Mfg. Co.
Price: $850.00
Price: Sporting Rifle No. 1 (similar to above except with 30" bbl., blade front, buckhorn rear sight) $820.00
Price: Sporting Rifle No. 3 (similar to No. 1 except straight-grip stock, standard wood) $725.00
Price: 1874 Hartford model $915.00

Shiloh Sharps 1874 Business Rifle
Similar to No. 3 Rifle except has 28" heavy round barrel, military-style buttstock and steel buttplate. Weight about 9½ lbs. Calibers 40-50 BN, 40-70 BN, 40-90 BN, 45-70 ST, 45-90 ST, 50-70 ST, 50-100 ST, 32-40, 38-55, 40-70 ST, 40-90 ST.
Price: $725.00
Price: 1874 Carbine (similar to above except 24" round bbl., single trigger—double set avail.) $725.00
Price: 1874 Saddle Rifle (similar to Carbine except has 26" octagon barrel, semi-fancy shotgun butt) $790.00

Shiloh Sharps "The Jaeger"
Similar to the Montana Roughrider except has half-octagon 26" lightweight barrel, 30-30 only. Standard supreme black walnut.
Price: $795.00

Thompson/Center Contender

Thompson/Center Youth Model Contender Carbine
Same as the standard Contender Carbine except has 16¼" barrel, shorter buttstock with 12" length of pull. Comes with fully adjustable open sights. Overall length is 29", weight about 4 lbs., 9 oz. Available in 22 LR, 22 WMR, 223 Rem., 7x30 Waters, 30-30, 35 Rem., 44 Mag. Also available with 16¼", rifled vent. rib barrel chambered for 45/410.
Price: $355.00
Price: With 45/410 barrel $380.00
Price: Extra barrels $170.00
Price: Extra 45/410 barrel $195.00
Price: Extra 45-70 barrel $185.00

THOMPSON/CENTER CONTENDER CARBINE
Caliber: 22 LR, 22 Hornet, 223 Rem., 7mm T.C.U., 7x30 Waters, 30-30 Win., 357 Rem. Maximum, 35 Rem., 44 Mag., 410, single shot.
Barrel: 21".
Weight: 5 lbs., 2 oz. Length: 35" overall.
Stock: Checkered American walnut with rubber buttpad. Also with Rynite stock and forend.
Sights: Blade front, open adjustable rear.
Features: Uses the T/C Contender action. Eleven interchangeable barrels available, all with sights, drilled and tapped for scope mounting. Introduced 1985. Offered as a complete Carbine only.
Price: Rifle calibers $385.00
Price: Extra barrels, rifle calibers, each $175.00
Price: 410 shotgun $405.00
Price: Extra 410 barrel $195.00
Price: Rynite stock, forend $355.00
Price: As above, 21" vent rib smoothbore 410 bbl. $375.00

THOMPSON/CENTER TCR '87 SINGLE SHOT RIFLE
Caliber: 22 Hornet, 222 Rem., 223 Rem., 22-250, 243 Win., 270, 308, 7mm-08, 30-06, 32-40 Win., 12-ga. slug. Also 10-ga. and 12-ga. field barrels.
Barrel: 23" (standard), 25⅞" (heavy).
Weight: About 6¾ lbs. Length: 39½" overall.
Stock: American black walnut, checkered p.g. and forend.
Sights: None furnished.
Features: Break-open design with interchangeable barrels. Single-stage trigger. Cross-bolt safety. Made in U.S. by T/C. Introduced 1983.
Price: With Medium Sporter barrel (223, 22-250, 7mm-08, 308, 32-40 Win.) $495.00
Price: With Light Sporter barrel (22 Hornet, 222, 223, 22-250, 243, 270, 7mm-08, 308, 30-06) $495.00
Price: 12-ga. slug barrel $215.00
Price: Extra Medium or Light Sporter barrel $215.00
Price: 10-, 12-ga. field barrels $215.00

Thompson/Center TCR Hunter

UBERTI ROLLING BLOCK BABY CARBINE
Caliber: 22 LR, 22 WMR, 22 Hornet, 357 Mag., single shot.
Barrel: 22".
Weight: 4.8 lbs. Length: 35½" overall.
Stock: Walnut stock and forend.
Sights: Blade front, fully adjustable open rear.
Features: Resembles Remington New Model No. 4 carbine. Brass trigger guard and buttplate; color case-hardened frame, blued barrel. Imported by Uberti USA.
Price: $350.00

Designs for sporting and utility purposes worldwide.

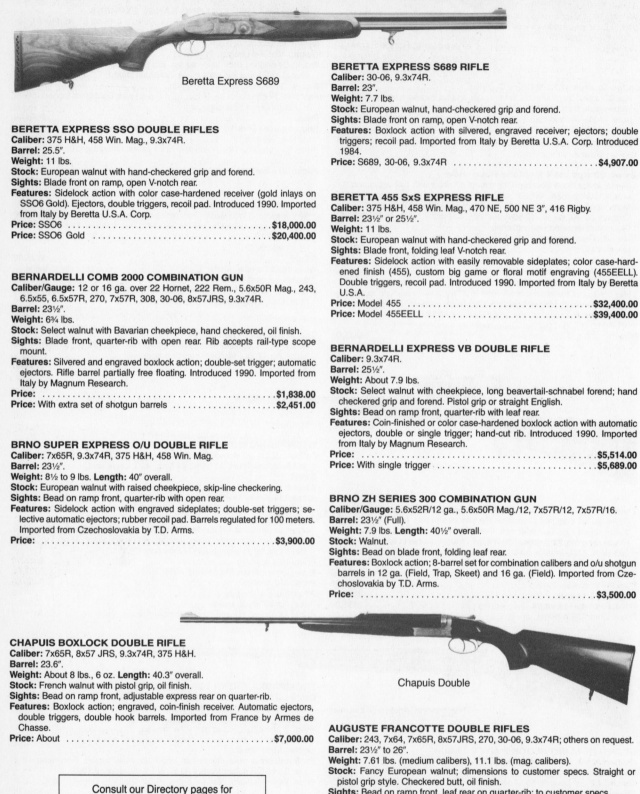

Beretta Express S689

Chapuis Double

BERETTA EXPRESS SSO DOUBLE RIFLES
Caliber: 375 H&H, 458 Win. Mag., 9.3x74R.
Barrel: 25.5″.
Weight: 11 lbs.
Stock: European walnut with hand-checkered grip and forend.
Sights: Blade front on ramp, open V-notch rear.
Features: Sidelock action with color case-hardened receiver (gold inlays on SSO6 Gold). Ejectors, double triggers, recoil pad. Introduced 1990. Imported from Italy by Beretta U.S.A. Corp.
Price: SSO6 ....$18,000.00
Price: SSO6 Gold $20,400.00

BERNARDELLI COMB 2000 COMBINATION GUN
Caliber/Gauge: 12 or 16 ga. over 22 Hornet, 222 Rem., 5.6x50R Mag., 243, 6.5x55, 6.5x57R, 270, 7x57R, 308, 30-06, 8x57JRS, 9.3x74R.
Barrel: 23½″.
Weight: 6¾ lbs.
Stock: Select walnut with Bavarian cheekpiece, hand checkered, oil finish.
Sights: Blade front, quarter-rib with open rear. Rib accepts rail-type scope mount.
Features: Silvered and engraved boxlock action; double-set trigger; automatic ejectors. Rifle barrel partially free floating. Introduced 1990. Imported from Italy by Magnum Research.
Price: $1,838.00
Price: With extra set of shotgun barrels $2,451.00

BRNO SUPER EXPRESS O/U DOUBLE RIFLE
Caliber: 7x65R, 9.3x74R, 375 H&H, 458 Win. Mag.
Barrel: 23½″.
Weight: 8½ to 9 lbs. **Length:** 40″ overall.
Stock: European walnut with raised cheekpiece, skip-line checkering.
Sights: Bead on ramp front, quarter-rib with open rear.
Features: Sidelock action with engraved sideplates; double-set triggers; selective automatic ejectors; rubber recoil pad. Barrels regulated for 100 meters. Imported from Czechoslovakia by T.D. Arms.
Price: $3,900.00

CHAPUIS BOXLOCK DOUBLE RIFLE
Caliber: 7x65R, 8x57 JRS, 9.3x74R, 375 H&H.
Barrel: 23.6″.
Weight: About 8 lbs., 6 oz. **Length:** 40.3″ overall.
Stock: French walnut with pistol grip, oil finish.
Sights: Bead on ramp front, adjustable express rear on quarter-rib.
Features: Boxlock action; engraved, coin-finish receiver. Automatic ejectors, double triggers, double hook barrels. Imported from France by Armes de Chasse.
Price: About $7,000.00

Consult our Directory pages for the location of firms mentioned.

BERETTA EXPRESS S689 RIFLE
Caliber: 30-06, 9.3x74R.
Barrel: 23″.
Weight: 7.7 lbs.
Stock: European walnut, hand-checkered grip and forend.
Sights: Blade front on ramp, open V-notch rear.
Features: Boxlock action with silvered, engraved receiver; ejectors; double triggers; recoil pad. Imported from Italy by Beretta U.S.A. Corp. Introduced 1984.
Price: S689, 30-06, 9.3x74R $4,907.00

BERETTA 455 SxS EXPRESS RIFLE
Caliber: 375 H&H, 458 Win. Mag., 470 NE, 500 NE 3″, 416 Rigby.
Barrel: 23½″ or 25½″.
Weight: 11 lbs.
Stock: European walnut with hand-checkered grip and forend.
Sights: Blade front, folding leaf V-notch rear.
Features: Sidelock action with easily removable sideplates; color case-hardened finish (455), custom big game or floral motif engraving (455EELL). Double triggers, recoil pad. Introduced 1990. Imported from Italy by Beretta U.S.A.
Price: Model 455 ....$32,400.00
Price: Model 455EELL $39,400.00

BERNARDELLI EXPRESS VB DOUBLE RIFLE
Caliber: 9.3x74R.
Barrel: 25½″.
Weight: About 7.9 lbs.
Stock: Select walnut with cheekpiece, long beavertail-schnabel forend; hand checkered grip and forend. Pistol grip or straight English.
Sights: Bead on ramp front, quarter-rib with leaf rear.
Features: Coin-finished or color case-hardened boxlock action with automatic ejectors, double or single trigger; hand-cut rib. Introduced 1990. Imported from Italy by Magnum Research.
Price: $5,514.00
Price: With single trigger $5,689.00

BRNO ZH SERIES 300 COMBINATION GUN
Caliber/Gauge: 5.6x52R/12 ga., 5.6x50R Mag./12, 7x57R/12, 7x57R/16.
Barrel: 23½″ (Full).
Weight: 7.9 lbs. **Length:** 40½″ overall.
Stock: Walnut.
Sights: Bead on blade front, folding leaf rear.
Features: Boxlock action; 8-barrel set for combination calibers and o/u shotgun barrels in 12 ga. (Field, Trap, Skeet) and 16 ga. (Field). Imported from Czechoslovakia by T.D. Arms.
Price: $3,500.00

AUGUSTE FRANCOTTE DOUBLE RIFLES
Caliber: 243, 7x64, 7x65R, 8x57JRS, 270, 30-06, 9.3x74R; others on request.
Barrel: 23½″ to 26″.
Weight: 7.61 lbs. (medium calibers), 11.1 lbs. (mag. calibers).
Stock: Fancy European walnut; dimensions to customer specs. Straight or pistol grip style. Checkered butt, oil finish.
Sights: Bead on ramp front, leaf rear on quarter-rib; to customer specs.
Features: Side-by-side barrels. Chopper lump barrels; special extractor for rimmed cartridges; back-action sidelocks; double trigger with hinged front trigger. Automatic or free safety. Wide range of options available. Imported from Belgium by Armes de Chasse.
Price: ....**NA**

CAUTION: PRICES CHANGE, CHECK AT GUNSHOP.

DRILLINGS, COMBINATION GUNS, DOUBLE RIFLES

AUGUSTE FRANCOTTE BOXLOCK DOUBLE RIFLE
Caliber: 243, 270, 30-06, 7x64, 7x65R, 8x57JRS, 9.3x74R.
Barrel: 23.5″ to 26″.
Weight: NA. **Length:** NA.
Stock: Deluxe European walnut to customer specs; pistol grip or straight grip with Francotte cheekpiece; checkered butt; oil finish.
Sights: Bead front on long ramp, quarter-rib with fixed V rear.
Features: Side-by-side barrels; Anson & Deeley boxlock action with double triggers (front hinged), manual safety, floating firing pins and gas vent safety screws. Splinter or beavertail forend. English scroll engraving; coin finish or color case-hardening. Many options available. Imported from Belgium by Armes de Chasse.
Price: From about $16,457.00

HEYM MODEL 33 BOXLOCK DRILLING
Caliber/Gauge: 5.6x50R Mag., 5.6x52R, 6.5x55, 6.5x57R, 7x57R, 7x65R, 8x57JRS, 9.3x74R, 243, 308, 30-06; 16x16 (2¾″), 20x20 (3″).
Barrel: 25″ (Full & Mod.).
Weight: About 6½ lbs. **Length:** 42″ overall.
Stock: Dark European walnut, checkered p.g. and forend; oil finish.
Sights: Silver bead front, folding leaf rear. Automatic sight positioner. Available with scope and Suhler claw mounts.
Features: Boxlock action with Greener-type cross bolt and safety, double under-lugs. Double set triggers. Plastic or steel trigger guard. Engraving coverage varies with model. Imported from West Germany by Heckler & Koch, Inc.
Price: Model 33 Standard $6,000.00
Price: Model 33 Deluxe (hunting scene engraving) $6,400.00

HEYM MODEL 37B DOUBLE RIFLE DRILLING
Caliber/Gauge: 7x65R, 30-06, 8x57JRS, 9.3x74R; 20 ga. (3″).
Barrel: 25″ (shotgun barrel choked Full or Mod.).
Weight: About 8½ lbs. **Length:** 42″ overall.
Stock: Dark European walnut, hand-checkered p.g. and forend. Oil finish.
Sights: Silver bead front, folding leaf rear. Available with scope and Suhler claw mounts.
Features: Full sidelock construction. Greener-type cross bolt, double under-lugs, cocking indicators. Imported from West Germany by Heckler & Koch, Inc.
Price: Model 37B double rifle drilling $12,000.00
Price: Model 37B Deluxe (hunting scene engraving) $13,900.00

HEYM MODEL 22S SAFETY COMBO GUN
Caliber/Gauge: 16 or 20 ga. (2¾″, 3″), 12 ga. (2¾″) over 22 Hornet, 22 WMR, 222 Rem., 223, 243 Win., 5.6x50R, 5.6x52R, 6.5x55, 6.5x57R, 7x57R, 8x57 JRS.
Barrel: 24″, solid rib.
Weight: About 5½ lbs.
Stock: Dark European walnut, hand-checkered p.g. and forend. Oil finish.
Sights: Silver bead ramp front, folding leaf rear.
Features: Tang-mounted cocking slide, separate barrel selector, single set trigger. Base supplied for quick-detachable scope mounts. Patented rocker-weight system automatically uncocks gun if accidentally dropped or bumped hard. Imported from West Germany by Heckler & Koch, Inc.
Price: Model 22S $2,400.00
Price: Model 22SZ takedown $2,770.00
Price: Model 22SM (rail scope mount, 12 ga.) $2,500.00
Price: 22SMZ (as above except takedown) $2,870.00

Heym Model 37 Sidelock Drilling
Similar to Model 37 Double Rifle Drilling except has 12x12, 16x16 or 20x20 over 5.6x52R, 5.6x50R Mag., 6.5x55, 6.5x57R, 7x57R, 7x65R, 8x57JRS, 9.3x74R, 243, 308 or 30-06. Rifle barrel is manually cocked and uncocked.
Price: Model 37 with border engraving $9,400.00
Price: As above with engraved hunting scenes $11,000.00

HEYM MODEL 55B/55SS O/U DOUBLE RIFLE
Caliber: 7x65R, 308, 30-06, 8x57JRS, 9.3x74R.
Barrel: 25″.
Weight: About 8 lbs., depending upon caliber. **Length:** 42″ overall.
Stock: Dark European walnut, hand-checkered p.g. and forend. Oil finish.
Sights: Silver bead ramp front, open V-type rear.
Features: Boxlock or full sidelock; Kersten double cross bolt, cocking indicators; hand-engraved hunting scenes. Options available include interchangeable barrels, Zeiss scopes in claw mounts, deluxe engravings and stock carving, etc. Imported from West Germany by Heckler & Koch, Inc.
Price: Model 55B boxlock $7,230.00
Price: Model 55SS sidelock $11,230.00
Price: Interchangeable shotgun barrels, add $3,200.00
Price: Interchangeable rifle barrels, add $4,700.00

Heym Model 55BF O/U Combo Gun
Similar to Model 55B o/u rifle except chambered for 12, 16, or 20 ga. (2¾″ or 3″) over 5.6x50R, 222 Rem., 223 Rem., 5.6x52R, 243, 6.5x57R, 270, 7x57R, 7x65R, 308, 30-06, 8x57JRS, 9.3x74R. Has solid rib barrel. Available with interchangeable shotgun and rifle barrels.
Price: Model 55BF boxlock $5,200.00

HEYM MODEL 88B SIDE-BY-SIDE DOUBLE RIFLE
Caliber: 30-06, 8x57JRS, 9.3x74R, 375 H&H.
Barrel: 25″.
Weight: 7½ lbs. (std. cals.), 8½ lbs. (mag.). **Length:** 42″ overall.
Stock: Fancy French walnut, classic North American design.
Sights: Silver bead post on ramp front, fixed or three-leaf express rear.
Features: Action has complete coverage hunting scene engraving. Available as boxlock or with q.d. sidelocks. Imported from West Germany by Heckler & Koch, Inc.
Price: Boxlock, from $9,600.00
Price: Sidelock, Model 88B-SS, from $13,800.00
Price: Disengageable ejectors, add $380.00

Heym Model 88B

Kodiak Mk. IV

KODIAK MK. IV DOUBLE RIFLE
Caliber: 45-70.
Barrel: 24″.
Weight: 10 lbs. **Length:** 42½″ overall.
Stock: European walnut with semi-pistol grip.
Sights: Ramp front with bead, adjustable two-leaf rear.
Features: Exposed hammers, color case-hardened locks. Rubber recoil pad. Comes cased. Introduced 1988. Imported from Italy by Trail Guns Armory.
Price: About $1,495.00

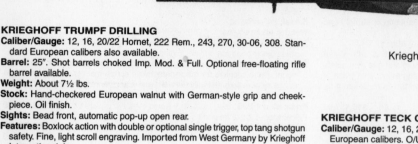

Krieghoff Trumpf

KRIEGHOFF TRUMPF DRILLING
Caliber/Gauge: 12, 16, 20/22 Hornet, 222 Rem., 243, 270, 30-06, 308. Standard European calibers also available.
Barrel: 25″. Shot barrels choked Imp. Mod. & Full. Optional free-floating rifle barrel available.
Weight: About 7½ lbs.
Stock: Hand-checkered European walnut with German-style grip and cheekpiece. Oil finish.
Sights: Bead front, automatic pop-up open rear.
Features: Boxlock action with double or optional single trigger, top tang shotgun safety. Fine, light scroll engraving. Imported from West Germany by Krieghoff International, Inc.
Price: $6,990.00
Price: Neptune (full sidelock drilling), from $11,850.00

Perugini-Visini Victoria Double Rifles
A boxlock double rifle which shares many of the same features of the Selous model. Calibers 7x65R, 30-06, 9.3x74R, 375 H&H Mag., 458 Win. Mag., 470; double triggers; automatic ejectors. Many options available, including an extra 20-ga. barrel set.
Price: Victoria-M (7x65R, 30-06, 9.3x74R), from about $6,800.00
Price: Victoria-D (375, 458, 470), from about $12,500.00

KRIEGHOFF TECK O/U COMBINATION GUN
Caliber/Gauge: 12, 16, 20/22 Hornet, 222, 243, 270, 30-06, 308 and standard European calibers. O/U rifle also available in 458 Win. on special order.
Barrel: 25″ on double rifle combo. 28″ or o/u shotgun. Optional free-floating rifle barrel available.
Weight: 7-7½ lbs.
Stock: Hand-checkered European walnut with German-style grip and cheekpiece.
Sights: White bead front on shotgun, open or folding on rifle or combo.
Features: Boxlock action with non-selective single trigger or optional single/double trigger. Greener cross bolt. Ejectors standard on all but o/u rifle. Top tang safety. Light scroll engraving. Imported from West Germany by Krieghoff International, Inc.
Price: From ....$5,450.00 to $8,750.00
Price: Ulm (full sidelock model) from $13,650.00

Perugini-Visini "Selous"

PERUGINI-VISINI MODEL "SELOUS" SIDELOCK
DOUBLE RIFLE
Caliber: 30-06, 7mm Rem. Mag., 7x65R, 9.3x74R, 270 Win., 300 H&H, 338 Win., 375 H&H, 458 Win. Mag., 470 Nitro.
Barrel: 22″-26″.
Weight: 7¼ to 10½ lbs., depending upon caliber. **Length:** 41″ overall (24″ bbl.).
Stocks: Oil-finished walnut, checkered grip and forend; cheekpiece.
Sights: Bead on ramp front, express rear on quarter-rib.
Features: True sidelock action with ejectors; sideplates are hand detachable; comes with leather trunk case. Introduced 1983. Imported from Italy by Wm. Larkin Moore.
Price: $21,800.00

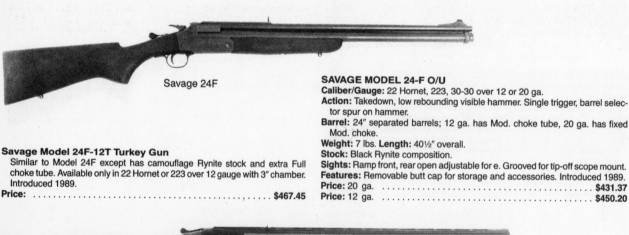

Savage 24F

SAVAGE MODEL 24-F O/U
Caliber/Gauge: 22 Hornet, 223, 30-30 over 12 or 20 ga.
Action: Takedown, low rebounding visible hammer. Single trigger, barrel selector spur on hammer.
Barrel: 24″ separated barrels; 12 ga. has Mod. choke tube, 20 ga. has fixed Mod. choke.
Weight: 7 lbs. **Length:** 40½″ overall.
Stock: Black Rynite composition.
Sights: Ramp front, rear open adjustable for e. Grooved for tip-off scope mount.
Features: Removable butt cap for storage and accessories. Introduced 1989.
Price: 20 ga. $431.37
Price: 12 ga. $450.20

Savage Model 24F-12T Turkey Gun
Similar to Model 24F except has camouflage Rynite stock and extra Full choke tube. Available only in 22 Hornet or 223 over 12 gauge with 3″ chamber. Introduced 1989.
Price: $467.45

Savage Model 389

SAVAGE MODEL 389 O/U COMBINATION
Caliber/Gauge: 12 ga. over 222 or 308.
Barrel: 24″ separated barrels with floating front mount for windage, elevation adjustment. Has choke tubes.
Weight: 8 lbs. **Length:** 43″ overall.
Stock: Oil-finished walnut with recoil pad, cut-checkered grip and forend.
Sights: Blade front, folding leaf rear. Vent. rib milled for scope mount.
Features: Matte finish, extractors, double triggers, q.d. swivel studs. Introduced 1988.
Price: $919.21

Marcel Thys Liege

MARCEL THYS LIEGE DOUBLE RIFLE
Caliber: 22 LR, 22 Hornet, 30-06, 375 H&H, 450 #2, 458 Win. Mag., 470 Nitro, 500 3", 577, 600 Nitro.
Barrel: 24" to 27".
Weight: 6 lbs. to 14 lbs.

Stock: Dark full-grain European walnut with oil finish.
Sights: Bead on ramp front, quarter-rib rear with one standing leaf, two folding leaves.
Features: Sidelock action with hand detachable locks, reinforced Holland-style frame, chopper lump barrels, reinforced top tang extension; full-coverage game scene engraving. Introduced 1990. Imported from Belgium by Cape Outfitters.
Price: Royal LUX (standard game scene engraving, coin finish or color case-hardened action) $18,500.00
Price: King Royal (gold inlaid game scenes) $20,500.00

Valmet 412S Double

TIKKA 412S DOUBLE RIFLE
Caliber: 9.3x74R.
Barrel: 24".
Weight: 8⅝ lbs.
Stock: American walnut with Monte Carlo style.
Sights: Ramp front, adjustable open rear.
Features: Barrel selector mounted in trigger. Cocking indicators in tang. Recoil pad. Valmet scope mounts available. Introduced 1980. Imported from Italy by Stoeger.
Price: With ejectors, 9.3x74R $1,275.00

TIKKA 412S COMBINATION GUN
Caliber/Gauge: 12 over 222, 308.
Barrel: 24" (Imp. Mod.).
Weight: 7⅝ lbs.
Stock: American walnut, with recoil pad. Monte Carlo style. Standard measurements 14"x1⅜"x2"x2⅜".
Sights: Blade front, flip-up-type open rear.
Features: Barrel selector on trigger. Hand-checkered stock and forend. Barrels are screw-adjustable to change bullet point of impact. Barrels are interchangeable. Introduced 1980. Imported from Italy by Stoeger.
Price: $1,135.00
Price: Extra barrels, from $645.00

A. ZOLI RIFLE-SHOTGUN O/U COMBO
Caliber/Gauge: 12 ga. over 222, 308 or 30-06.
Barrel: Combo—24"; shotgun—28" (Mod. & Full).
Weight: About 8 lbs. **Length:** 41" overall (24" bbl.)
Stock: European walnut.
Sights: Blade front, flip-up rear.
Features: Available with German claw scope mounts on rifle/shotgun barrels. Comes with set of 12/12 (Mod. & Full) barrels. Imported from Italy by Mandall Shooting Supplies.
Price: With two barrel sets $1,695.00
Price: As above with claw mounts, scope $2,495.00

RIMFIRE RIFLES—AUTOLOADERS

Designs for hunting, utility and sporting purposes, including training for competition.

AMT Lightning 25/22

AMT Lightning Small-Game Hunting Rifle
Same as the Lightning 25/22 except has conventional stock of black fiberglass-filled nylon, checkered at the grip and forend, and fitted with Uncle Mike's swivel studs. Removable recoil pad provides storage for ammo, cleaning rod and survival knife. No iron sights—receiver grooved for scope mounting. Has a 22" target weight barrel, weighs 6¾ lbs., overall length of 40½". Introduced 1987. From AMT.
Price: $263.00

AMT LIGHTNING 25/22 RIFLE
Caliber: 22 LR, 25-shot magazine.
Barrel: 18", tapered or bull.
Weight: 6 lbs. **Length:** 26½" (folded), 37" (open).
Stock: Folding stainless steel.
Sights: Ramp front, rear adjustable for windage.
Features: Made of stainless steel with matte finish. Receiver dovetailed for scope mounting. Extended magazine release. Standard or "bull" barrel. Youth stock available. Introduced 1984. From AMT.
Price: $278.00

AMERICAN ARMS MINI-MAX 22 RIFLE
Caliber: 22 LR, 10-shot magazine.
Barrel: 18¾".
Weight: 4⅓ lbs. **Length:** 36½" overall.
Stock: Black synthetic.
Sights: Blade front, adjustable open rear.
Features: Receiver grooved for scope mounting; trigger-block safety on trigger guard. Introduced 1990. From American Arms, Inc.
Price: Synthetic stock $99.00
Price: Wood stock $105.00

AMERICAN ARMS EXP-64 AUTO RIFLE
Caliber: 22 LR, 10-shot magazine.
Barrel: 21".
Weight: 7 lbs. **Length:** 40" (22" taken down).
Stock: Synthetic. Rifle takes down for storage in buttstock.
Sights: Blade front, adjustable rear.
Features: Quick takedown for storage, carry. Receiver grooved for scope mounting. Cross-bolt safety. Introduced 1989. Imported from Italy by American Arms, Inc.
Price: $165.00
Price: With hardwood stock, forend (Model SM-64) $149.00

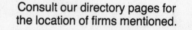

Anschutz Model 525

ANSCHUTZ DELUXE MODEL 525 AUTO
Caliber: 22 LR, 10-shot clip.
Barrel: 24″.
Weight: 6½ lbs. **Length:** 43″ overall.
Stock: European hardwood; checkered pistol grip, Monte Carlo comb, beavertail forend.
Sights: Hooded ramp front, folding leaf rear.
Features: Rotary safety, empty shell deflector, single stage trigger. Receiver grooved for scope mounting. Introduced 1982. Imported from Germany by PSI.
Price: **$435.00**

ARMSCOR MODEL 20P AUTO RIFLE
Caliber: 22 LR, 15-shot magazine.
Barrel: 20½″.
Weight: 6 lbs. **Length:** 40⅝″ overall.
Stock: Walnut-finished mahogany.
Sights: Hooded front, rear adjustable for e.
Features: Receiver grooved for scope mounting. Blued finish. Introduced 1990. Imported from the Philippines by Armscor.
Price: About **$82.95**
Price: Model 20C (carbine-style stock, steel barrel band, butt plate) . **$99.95**
Price: Model 2000 (as above except has checkered stock, fully adjustable sight, rubber buttpad, forend tip), about **$209.95**
Price: Model PPS-50 (similar to Model 20P except has ventilated barrel shroud, 25- and 30-shot magazines) **$124.95**

> Consult our directory pages for
> the location of firms mentioned.

ARMSCOR AK22 AUTO RIFLE
Caliber: 22 LR, 15- and 30-shot magazine.
Barrel: 18¼″.
Weight: 7.4 lbs. **Length:** 37⅞″ overall.
Stock: Plain mahogany.
Sights: Post front, open rear adjustable for w. and e.
Features: Resembles the AK-47. Matte black finish. Introduced 1987. Imported from the Philippines by Armscor.
Price: About **$144.95**
Price: With folding steel stock, about **$184.95**

ARMSCOR MODEL 1600 AUTO RIFLE
Caliber: 22 LR, 15-shot magazine.
Barrel: 20″.
Weight: 7½ lbs. **Length:** 40″ overall.
Stock: Black fiberglass or wood.
Sights: Post front, aperture rear.
Features: Resembles Colt AR-15. Matte black finish. Introduced 1987. Imported from the Philippines by Armscor.
Price: About **$109.95**
Price: M1600R (as above except has retractable buttstock, ventilated forend), about **$119.95**

BERNARDELLI SEMI-AUTOMATIC 22 CARBINE
Caliber: 22 LR, 5- or 10-shot magazine.
Barrel: 20.8″.
Weight: 5 lbs., 6 oz.
Stock: European walnut with Monte Carlo comb, checkered grip and forend.
Sights: Blade front, open adjustable rear.
Features: Push-button safety in rear of trigger guard. Blue/black finish. Imported from Italy by Magnum Research.
Price: **$438.00**
Price: As above, 9mm Flobert shot cartridge, 3- or 4-shot magazine, uncheckered stock **$263.00**

Auto-Ordnance 1927A-3

AUTO-ORDNANCE MODEL 1927A-3
Caliber: 22 LR, 10-, 30- or 50-shot magazine.
Barrel: 16″, finned.
Weight: About 7 lbs.
Stock: Walnut stock and forend.
Sights: Blade front, open rear adjustable for windage and elevation.
Features: Recreation of the Thompson Model 1927, only in 22 Long Rifle. Alloy receiver, finned barrel.
Price: **$487.50**

Browning Auto-22

BROWNING AUTO-22 RIFLE
Caliber: 22 LR, 11-shot.
Barrel: 19¼″.
Weight: 4¾ lbs. **Length:** 37″ overall.
Stock: Checkered select walnut with p.g. and semi-beavertail forend.
Sights: Gold bead front, folding leaf rear.
Features: Engraved receiver with polished blue finish; cross-bolt safety; tubular magazine in buttstock; easy take down for carrying or storage. Imported from Japan by Browning.
Price: Grade I **$344.95**

Browning Auto-22 Grade VI
Same as the Grade I Auto-22 except available with either grayed or blued receiver with extensive engraving with gold-plated animals: right side pictures a fox and squirrel in a woodland scene; left side shows a beagle chasing a rabbit. On top is a portrait of the beagle. Stock and forend are of high-grade walnut with a double-bordered cut checkering design. Introduced 1987.
Price: Grade VI, blue or gray receiver **$708.95**

Calico Model 100

CALICO MODEL M-100 CARBINE
Caliber: 22 LR, 100-shot magazine.
Barrel: 16″.
Weight: 5.7 lbs. (loaded). **Length:** 35.8″ overall (stock extended).
Stock: Folding steel.
Sights: Post front adjustable for elevation, notch rear adjustable for windage.
Features: Uses alloy frame and helical-feed magazine; ambidextrous safety; removable barrel assembly; pistol grip compartment; flash suppressor; bolt stop. Made in U.S. From Calico.
Price: $328.00

Calico Model M-105 Sporter
 Similar to the M-100 except has hand-rubbed wood buttstock and forend. Weight is 4¾ lbs. Introduced 1987.
Price: $356.00

CBC N66 Auto

CBC N66 AUTO RIFLE
Caliber: 22 LR, 14-shot magazine.
Barrel: 19.5″.

Weight: 4 lbs., 2 oz. **Length:** 38.5″ overall.
Stock: Nylon with checkered grip and forend.
Sights: Blade front, fully adjustable rear.
Features: Grooved receiver for scope mounting; top tang safety; tubular magazine housed in buttstock. Made mostly of moulded nylon. Imported from Brazil by Century Arms International, Inc.
Price: $119.95

Charter AR-7 Explorer

CHARTER AR-7 EXPLORER CARBINE
Caliber: 22 LR, 8-shot clip.
Barrel: 16″ alloy (steel-lined).

Weight: 2½ lbs. **Length:** 34½″/16½″ stowed.
Stock: Moulded black Cycolac, snap-on rubber buttpad.
Sights: Square blade front, aperture rear adjustable for elevation.
Features: Takedown design stores barrel and action in hollow stock. Light enough to float.
Price: Black, Silvertone or camouflage finish, about $146.25

Daisy Model 2213

DAISY MODEL 2213 AUTO RIFLE
Caliber: 22 LR, 7-shot clip.
Barrel: 19″.
Weight: 6.5 lbs. **Length:** 34.75″ overall.
Stock: Hardwood.
Sights: Blade on ramp front, removable and fully adjustable notch rear.
Features: Removable trigger assembly; receiver dovetailed for scope mounting. Introduced 1988.
Price: About $139.00

Daisy Model 2203 Auto Rifle
 Similar to the Model 2213 except has a moulded copolymer stock that is adjustable for length of pull. Introduced 1988.
Price: About $99.00

Feather AT-22

FEATHER AT-22 SEMI-AUTO CARBINE
Caliber: 22 LR, 20-shot magazine.
Barrel: 17″.
Weight: 3.25 lbs. **Length:** 34.75″ overall (stock extended).
Stock: Telescoping wire; composition pistol grip.
Sights: Protected post front, adjustable aperture rear.
Features: Removable barrel. Length when folded is 26″. Matte black finish. From Feather Industries. Introduced 1986.
Price: $242.95

KRICO MODEL 260 AUTO RIFLE
Caliber: 22 LR, 5-shot magazine.
Barrel: 19.6″.
Weight: 6.6 lbs. **Length:** 38.9″ overall.
Stock: Beech.
Sights: Blade on ramp front, open adjustable rear.
Features: Receiver grooved for scope mounting. Sliding safety. Imported from West Germany by Mandall Shooting Supplies.
Price: $700.00

Lakefield Model 64B

LAKEFIELD ARMS MODEL 64B AUTO RIFLE
Caliber: 22 LR, 10-shot magazine.
Barrel: 20″.

Weight: 5½ lbs. **Length:** 40″ overall.
Stock: Walnut-finished hardwood with Monte Carlo-type comb, checkered grip and forend.
Sights: Bead front, open adjustable rear. Receiver grooved for scope mounting.
Features: Thumb-operated rotating safety. Blue finish. Side ejection, bolt hold-open device. Introduced 1990. Made in Canada by Lakefield Arms Ltd.
Price: About **$119.95**

Marlin Model 60

MARLIN 60 SEMI-AUTO RIFLE
Caliber: 22 LR, 17-shot tubular magazine.
Barrel: 22″ round tapered.

Weight: About 5½ lbs. **Length:** 40½″ overall.
Stock: Walnut-finished Monte Carlo, full pistol grip; Mar-Shield® finish.
Sights: Ramp front, open adjustable rear.
Features: Matted receiver is grooved for tip-off mounts. Manual bolt hold-open; automatic last-shot bolt hold-open.
Price: **$131.95**

Marlin Model 70 HC

MARLIN MODEL 70 HC AUTO
Caliber: 22 LR, 15-shot clip magazine.
Barrel: 18″ (16-groove rifling).
Weight: 5½ lbs. **Length:** 36½″ overall.
Stock: Walnut-finished hardwood with Monte Carlo, full p.g. Mar-Shield® finish.
Sights: Ramp front, adjustable open rear. Receiver grooved for scope mount.
Features: Receiver top has serrated, non-glare finish; cross-bolt safety; manual bolt hold-open.
Price: **$147.95**

Marlin 70P Papoose

Marlin Model 70P Papoose
Similar to the Model 70 HC except is a takedown model with easily removable barrel—no tools needed. Has 16¼″ Micro-Groove® barrel, walnut-finished hardwood stock, ramp front, adjustable open rear sights, cross-bolt safety. Takedown feature allows removal of barrel without tools. Overall length is 35¼″, weight is 3¾ lbs. Receiver grooved for scope mounting. Comes with zippered case. Introduced 1986.
Price: **$165.95**

Marlin Model 75C

MARLIN MODEL 75C SEMI-AUTO RIFLE
Caliber: 22 LR, 13-shot tubular magazine.
Barrel: 18″.
Weight: 5 lbs. **Length:** 36½″ overall.
Stock: Walnut-finished hardwood; Monte Carlo with full p.g.
Sights: Ramp front, adjustable open rear.
Features: Manual bolt hold-open; automatic last-shot bolt hold-open; cross-bolt safety; receiver grooved for scope mounting.
Price: **$131.95**

Marlin Model 995

MARLIN MODEL 995 SEMI-AUTO RIFLE
Caliber: 22 LR, 7-shot clip magazine.
Barrel: 18″ Micro-Groove®.
Weight: 5 lbs. **Length:** 36¾″ overall.
Stock: American black walnut, Monte Carlo-style, with full pistol grip. Checkered p.g. and forend; white buttplate spacer; Mar-Shield® finish.
Sights: Ramp bead front with Wide-Scan™ hood; adjustable folding semi-buckhorn rear.
Features: Receiver grooved for tip-off scope mount; bolt hold-open device; cross-bolt safety. Introduced 1979.
Price: **$175.95**

RIMFIRE RIFLES—AUTOLOADERS

Mitchell AK-22

MITCHELL AK-22 SEMI-AUTO RIFLE
Caliber: 22 LR, 20-shot magazine; 22 WMR, 10-shot magazine.
Barrel: 18".
Weight: 6½ lbs. **Length:** 36" overall.
Stock: European walnut.
Sights: Post front, open adjustable rear.
Features: Replica of the AK-47 rifle. Wide magazine to maintain appearance. Imported from Italy by Mitchell Arms.
Price: 22 LR $299.95
Price: 22 WMR $324.95

MITCHELL GALIL/22 AUTO RIFLE
Caliber: 22 LR, 20-shot magazine; 22 WMR, 10-shot magazine.
Barrel: 18".
Weight: 6.5 lbs. **Length:** 36" overall.
Stock: European walnut butt, grip, forend.
Sights: Post front adjustable for elevation, rear adjustable for windage.
Features: Replica of the Israeli Galil rifle. Introduced 1987. Imported by Mitchell Arms, Inc.
Price: 22 LR $299.95
Price: 22 WMR $324.95

Mitchell CAR-15/22 Semi-Auto Rifle
Similar to the M-16 A-1/22 rifle except has 16¾" barrel, telescoping butt, giving an overall length of 32" when collapsed. Adjustable post front sight, adjustable aperture rear. Scope mount available. Has 15-shot magazine. Replica of the CAR-15 rifle. Introduced 1990. Imported by Mitchell Arms, Inc.
Price: $329.00

Mitchell M-16A-1/22

MITCHELL M-16A-1/22 RIFLE
Caliber: 22 LR, 15-shot magazine.
Barrel: 20.5".
Weight: 7 lbs. **Length:** 38.5" overall.
Stock: Black composition.
Sights: Adjustable post front, adjustable aperture rear.
Features: Replica of the AR-15 rifle. Full width magazine. Comes with military-type sling. Introduced 1990. Imported by Mitchell Arms, Inc.
Price: 22 LR $299.95

Mitchell PPS/50

MITCHELL PPS/50 RIFLE
Caliber: 22 LR, 30-shot magazine (50-shot drum optional).
Barrel: 16½".
Weight: 5½ lbs. **Length:** 33½" overall.
Stock: Walnut.
Sights: Blade front, adjustable rear.
Features: Full-length perforated barrel shroud. Matte finish. Introduced 1989. Imported by Mitchell Arms.
Price: With 30-shot "banana" magazine $299.95
Price: With 50-shot drum magazine $329.63

Mitchell MAS/22

MITCHELL MAS/22 AUTO RIFLE
Caliber: 22 LR, 20-shot magazine.
Barrel: 18".
Weight: 7½ lbs. **Length:** 28.5" overall.
Stock: Walnut butt, grip and forend.
Sights: Adjustable post front, flip-type aperture rear.
Features: Bullpup design resembles French armed forces rifle. Top cocking lever, flash hider. Introduced 1987. Imported by Mitchell Arms, Inc.
Price: 22 LR $299.95

Norinco 22 ATD

NORINCO MODEL 22 ATD RIFLE
Caliber: 22 LR, 11-shot magazine.
Barrel: 19.4".
Weight: 4.6 lbs. **Length:** 36.6" overall.
Stock: Checkered hardwood.
Sights: Blade front, open adjustable rear.
Features: Browning-design takedown action for storage, transport. Cross-bolt safety. Tube magazine loads through buttplate. Blue finish with engraved receiver. Introduced 1987. Imported from China by Interarms.
Price: $165.00
Price: Camouflage case $16.00

CAUTION: PRICES CHANGE, CHECK AT GUNSHOP.

RIMFIRE RIFLES—AUTOLOADERS

Remington 552 BDL

REMINGTON 552BDL SPEEDMASTER RIFLE
Caliber: 22 S (20), L (17) or LR (15) tubular mag.
Barrel: 21″ round tapered.
Weight: About 5¾ lbs. **Length:** 40″ overall.
Stock: Walnut. Checkered grip and forend.
Sights: Bead front, step open rear adjustable for w. and e.
Features: Positive cross-bolt safety, receiver grooved for tip-off mount.
Price: About **$213.00**

Ruger 10/22 RB

RUGER 10/22 AUTOLOADING CARBINE
Caliber: 22 LR, 10-shot rotary magazine.
Barrel: 18½″ round tapered.
Weight: 5 lbs. **Length:** 37¼″ overall.
Stock: American hardwood with p.g. and bbl. band.
Sights: Gold bead front, folding leaf rear adjustable for e.
Features: Detachable rotary magazine fits flush into stock, cross-bolt safety, receiver tapped and grooved for scope blocks or tip-off mount. Scope base adaptor furnished with each rifle.
Price: Model 10/22 RB (birch stock) **$192.00**

Ruger 10/22 Auto Sporter
Same as 10/22 Carbine except walnut stock with hand checkered p.g. and forend; straight buttplate, no barrel band, has sling swivels.
Price: Model 10/22 DSP **$242.50**

VOERE MODEL 2115 AUTO RIFLE
Caliber: 22 LR, 8- or 15-shot magazine.
Barrel: 18.1″.
Weight: 5.75 lbs. **Length:** 37.7″ overall.
Stock: Walnut-finished beechwood with cheekpiece; checkered pistol grip and forend.
Sights: Post front with hooded ramp, leaf rear.
Features: Clip-fed autoloader with single stage trigger, wing-type safety. Imported from Austria by L. Joseph Rahn. Introduced 1984.
Price: Model 2115 . . . . **$350.00**
Price: Model 2114S (as above except no cheekpiece, checkering or white line spacers at grip, buttplate) **$330.00**

RIMFIRE RIFLES—LEVER & SLIDE ACTIONS

Classic and modern models for sport and utility, including training.

Browning BL-22

BROWNING BL-22 LEVER-ACTION RIFLE
Caliber: 22 S (22), L (17) or LR (15). Tubular magazine.
Barrel: 20″ round tapered.
Weight: 5 lbs. **Length:** 36¾″ overall.
Stock: Walnut, two-piece straight grip Western style.
Sights: Bead post front, folding-leaf rear.
Features: Short throw lever, half-cock safety, receiver grooved for tip-off scope mounts. Imported from Japan by Browning.
Price: Grade I **$286.95**
Price: Grade II (engraved receiver, checkered grip and forend) **$326.95**

Marlin Golden 39AS

MARLIN GOLDEN 39AS LEVER-ACTION RIFLE
Caliber: 22 S (26), L (21), LR (19), tubular magazine.
Barrel: 24″ Micro-Groove®.
Weight: 6¾ lbs. **Length:** 40″ overall.
Stock: American black walnut with white line spacers at p.g. cap and buttplate; Mar-Shield® finish. Swivel studs; rubber buttpad.
Sights: Bead ramp front with detachable Wide-Scan™ hood, folding rear semi-buckhorn adjustable for w. and e.
Features: Hammer-block safety; rebounding hammer. Takedown action, receiver tapped for scope mount (supplied), offset hammer spur; gold-plated steel trigger.
Price: **$358.95**

CAUTION: PRICES CHANGE, CHECK AT GUNSHOP.

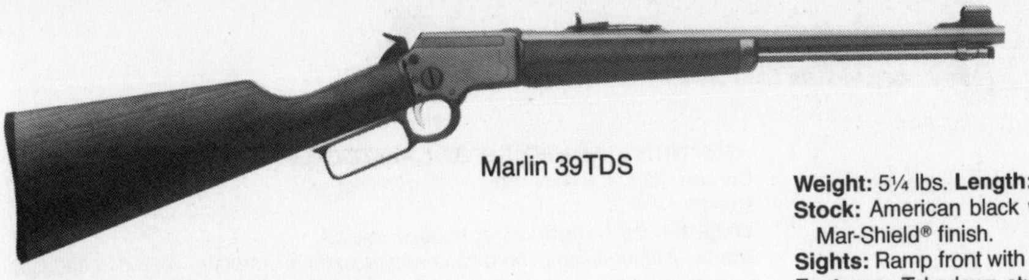

Marlin 39TDS

MARLIN MODEL 39TDS CARBINE
Caliber: 22 S (16), 22 L (12), 22 LR (10).
Barrel: 16½" Micro-Groove®.

Weight: 5¼ lbs. **Length:** 32⅝" overall.
Stock: American black walnut with straight grip; short forend with blued tip. Mar-Shield® finish.
Sights: Ramp front with Wide-Scan™ hood, adjustable semi-buckhorn rear.
Features: Takedown style, comes with carrying case. Hammer-block safety, rebounding hammer; blued metal, gold-plated steel trigger. Introduced 1988.
Price: With case $399.95

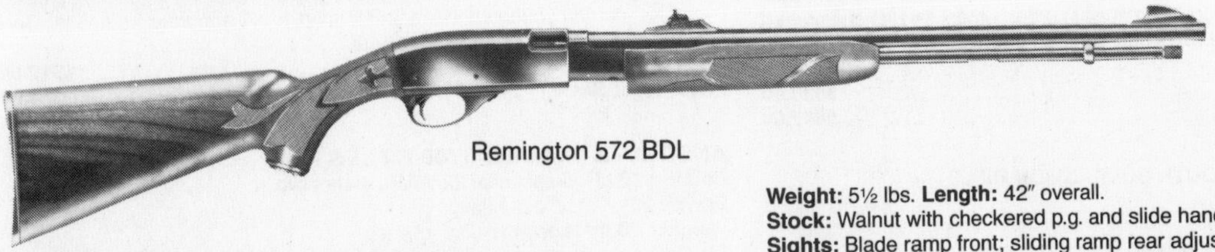

Remington 572 BDL

REMINGTON 572BDL FIELDMASTER PUMP RIFLE
Caliber: 22 S (20), L (17) or LR (14), tubular magazine.
Barrel: 21" round tapered.

Weight: 5½ lbs. **Length:** 42" overall.
Stock: Walnut with checkered p.g. and slide handle.
Sights: Blade ramp front; sliding ramp rear adjustable for w. and e.
Features: Cross-bolt safety; removing inner magazine tube converts rifle to single shot; receiver grooved for tip-off scope mount.
Price: About $223.00

Rossi 62 SA

ROSSI 62 SA PUMP RIFLE
Caliber: 22 LR, 22 WMR.
Barrel: 23", round or octagon.
Weight: 5¾ lbs. **Length:** 39¼" overall.
Stock: Walnut, straight grip, grooved forend.
Sights: Fixed front, adjustable rear.
Features: Capacity 20 Short, 16 Long or 14 Long Rifle. Quick takedown. Imported from Brazil by Interarms.
Price: Blue $195.00
Price: Nickel $210.00
Price: Blue, with octagon barrel $220.00
Price: 22 WMR, as Model 59 .... $240.00

Rossi 62 SAC Carbine
 Same as standard model except 22 LR only, has 16¼" barrel. Magazine holds slightly fewer cartridges.
Price: Blue $195.00
Price: Nickel $210.00

Winchester 9422

WINCHESTER 9422 LEVER-ACTION RIFLE
Caliber: 22 S (21), L (17), LR (15), tubular mag.
Barrel: 20½".
Weight: 6¼ lbs. **Length:** 37⅛" overall.
Stock: American walnut, two-piece, straight grip (no p.g.).
Sights: Hooded ramp front, adjustable semi-buckhorn rear.
Features: Side ejection, receiver grooved for scope mounting, takedown action. From U.S. Repeating Arms Co.
Price: Walnut $323.00
Price: With WinTuff laminated stock, about $338.00

Winchester 9422 Magnum Lever-Action Rifle
 Same as the 9422 except chambered for 22 WMR cartridge, has 11-round mag. capacity.
Price: Walnut $338.00
Price: With WinCam green stock, about $349.00
Price: With WinTuff brown laminated stock, about .. $349.00

RIMFIRE RIFLES—BOLT ACTIONS & SINGLE SHOTS

Includes models for a variety of sports, utility and competitive shooting.

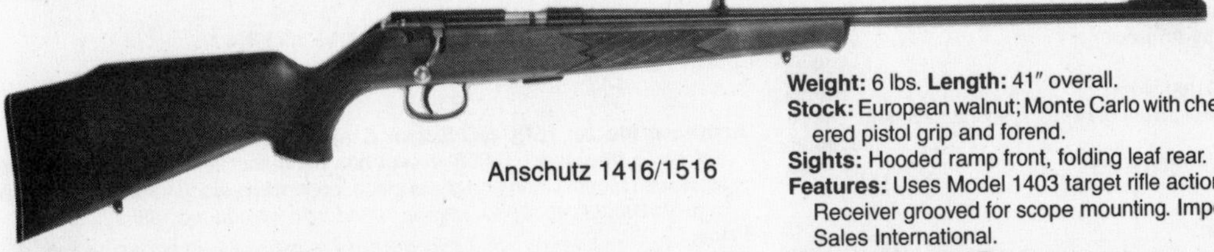

Anschutz 1416/1516

ANSCHUTZ DELUXE 1416/1516 RIFLES
Caliber: 22 LR (1416D), 5-shot clip; 22 WMR (1516D), 4-shot clip.
Barrel: 22½".

Weight: 6 lbs. **Length:** 41" overall.
Stock: European walnut; Monte Carlo with cheekpiece, schnabel forend, checkered pistol grip and forend.
Sights: Hooded ramp front, folding leaf rear.
Features: Uses Model 1403 target rifle action. Adjustable single stage trigger. Receiver grooved for scope mounting. Imported from Germany by Precision Sales International.
Price: 1416D, 22 LR $552.00
Price: 1516D, 22 WMR $589.00
Price: 1416D Classic left-hand $630.00

CAUTION: PRICES CHANGE, CHECK AT GUNSHOP.

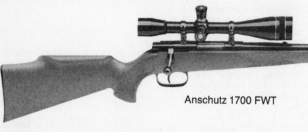

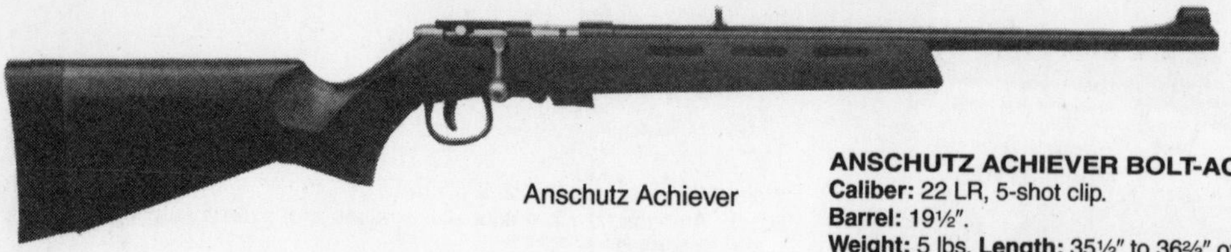

Anschutz Achiever

Anschutz 1418D/1518D Deluxe Rifles

Similar to the 1416D/1516D rifles except has full-length Mannlicher-style stock, shorter 19¾" barrel. Weighs 5½ lbs. Stock has buffalo horn schnabel tip. Double set trigger available on special order. Model 1418D chambered for 22 LR, 1518D for 22 WMR. Imported from Germany by Precision Sales International.

Price: 1418D $830.00
Price: 1518D $847.00

ANSCHUTZ MODEL 1449 YOUTH BOLT-ACTION RIFLE

Caliber: 22 LR, 5-shot clip.
Barrel: 16¼".
Weight: 3½ lbs. **Length:** 32½" overall.
Stock: Walnut-finished European hardwood.
Sights: Hooded ramp front, open adjustable rear.
Features: Uses the Anschutz Mark 2000 action which is grooved for scope mounting. Comes with 5-shot magazine; single shot clip adaptor and 10-shot clip available as accessories. Introduced 1990. Imported from West Germany by Precision Sales International.
Price: $229.90

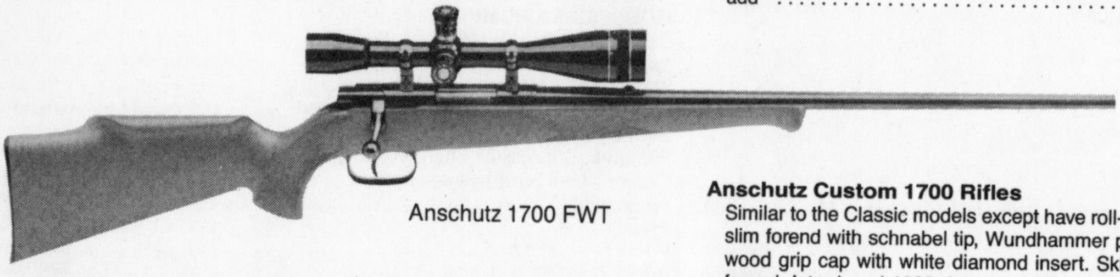

Anschutz 1700 FWT

Anschutz 1700 FWT Bolt-Action Rifle

Similar to the Anschutz Custom except has McMillan fiberglass stock with Monte Carlo, roll-over cheekpiece, Wundhammer swell, and checkering. Comes without sights but the receiver is drilled and tapped for scope mounting. Has 24" barrel, single stage #5095 trigger. Introduced 1989.
Price: $995.00
Price: As above, with Fibergrain stock $1,195.00

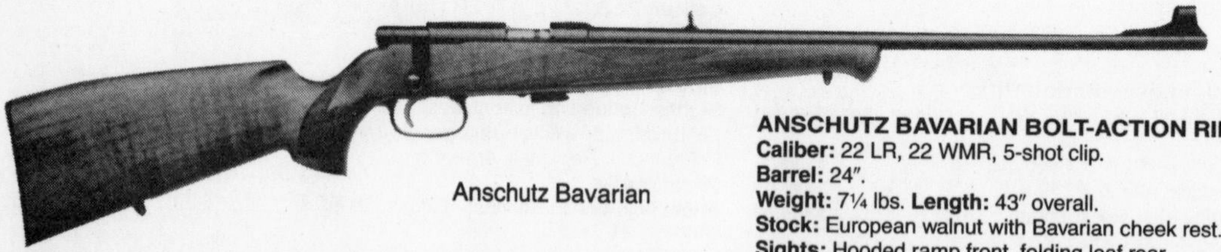

Anschutz Bavarian

ARMSCOR MODEL 14P BOLT-ACTION RIFLE

Caliber: 22 LR, 10-shot magazine.
Barrel: 22⅞".
Weight: 6 lbs. **Length:** 41" overall.
Stock: Walnut-finished mahogany.
Sights: Bead front, rear adjustable for elevation.
Features: Receiver grooved for scope mounting. Blued finish. Introduced 1987. Imported from the Philippines by Armscor.
Price: About $89.95
Price: Model 14D Deluxe (checkered stock) $99.95
Price: Model 14LW Classic Lightweight (straight stock, schnabel forend, checkered walnut) $154.95
Price: As above, 22 WMR (Model 1500 L.W.) . . . . NA

Armscor Model 1500S Rifle

Similar to the Model 14P except chambered for 22 WMR. Has 21.5" barrel, double lug bolt, checkered stock, weighs 6.5 lbs. Introduced 1987.
Price: About $119.95

ANSCHUTZ ACHIEVER BOLT-ACTION RIFLE

Caliber: 22 LR, 5-shot clip.
Barrel: 19½".
Weight: 5 lbs. **Length:** 35½" to 36⅔" overall.
Stock: Walnut-finished hardwood with adjustable buttplate, vented forend, stippled pistol grip. Length of pull adjustable from 11⅞" to 13".
Sights: Hooded front, open rear adjustable for w. and e.
Features: Uses Mark 2000-type action with adjustable two-stage trigger. Receiver grooved for scope mounting. Designed for training in junior rifle clubs and for starting young shooters. Introduced 1987. Imported from West Germany by Precision Sales International.
Price: $319.50
Price: Sight Set #1 . . . . $54.00

ANSCHUTZ CLASSIC 1700 RIFLES

Caliber: 22 LR, 5-shot clip; 22 WMR, 4-shot clip.
Barrel: 23½", ¹³⁄₁₆" dia. heavy.
Weight: 7¾ lbs. **Length:** 42½" overall.
Stock: Select European walnut with checkered pistol grip and forend.
Sights: None furnished, drilled and tapped for scope mounting.
Features: Adjustable single stage trigger. Receiver drilled and tapped for scope mounting. Introduced 1988. Imported from Germany by Precision Sales International.
Price: 22 LR $958.50
Price: 22 WMR $1,015.00
Price: As above, Meistergrade (select walnut, gold engraved trigger guard), add $165.00

Anschutz Custom 1700 Rifles

Similar to the Classic models except have roll-over Monte Carlo cheekpiece, slim forend with schnabel tip, Wundhammer palm swell on pistol grip, rosewood grip cap with white diamond insert. Skip-line checkering on grip and forend. Introduced 1988. Imported from Germany by Precision Sales International.
Price: 22 LR $999.50
Price: 22 WMR $1,029.00
Price: Custom 1700 Meistergrade (select walnut, gold engraved trigger guard), add $165.00

ANSCHUTZ BAVARIAN BOLT-ACTION RIFLE

Caliber: 22 LR, 22 WMR, 5-shot clip.
Barrel: 24".
Weight: 7¼ lbs. **Length:** 43" overall.
Stock: European walnut with Bavarian cheek rest. Checkered p.g. and forend.
Sights: Hooded ramp front, folding leaf rear.
Features: Uses the Improved 1700 Match 54 action with adjustable 5096 trigger. Drilled and tapped for scope mounting. Introduced in 1988. Imported from Germany by Precision Sales International.
Price: 22 LR $999.50
Price: 22 WMR $1,029.00
Price: Custom 1700 Meistergrade (select walnut, gold engraved trigger guard), add $165.00

Armscor Model 1500 SC Super Classic

Similar to the Model 1500S except has hand-checkered American walnut stock with Monte Carlo and cheekpiece, contrasting wood forend tip and grip cap, red rubber recoil pad, engine-turned bolt. Introduced 1990.
Price: $224.95
Price: In 22 LR, as Model 1400 SC $209.95

Beeman/HW 60J-ST

BEEMAN/HW 60J-ST BOLT-ACTION RIFLE
Caliber: 22 LR.
Barrel: 22.8".
Weight: 6.5 lbs. **Length:** 41.7" overall.
Stock: Walnut with cheekpiece, cut checkered p.g. and forend.
Sights: Hooded blade on ramp front, open rear.
Features: Polished blue finish; oil-finished walnut. Imported from West Germany by Beeman. Introduced 1988.
Price: $565.00

BRNO ZKM 452 BOLT-ACTION RIFLE
Caliber: 22 LR, 5- or 10-shot magazine.
Barrel: 25".
Weight: 6 lbs., 10 oz. **Length:** 43½" overall.
Stock: Beechwood.
Sights: Hooded bead front, open rear adjustable for e.
Features: Blue finish; oiled stock with checkered p.g. Imported from Czechoslovakia by TD Arms.
Price: $399.00

Browning A-Bolt 22

Browning A-Bolt Gold Medallion
Similar to the standard A-Bolt except stock is of high-grade walnut with brass spacers between stock and rubber recoil pad and between the rosewood grip cap and forend. Medallion-style engraving covers the receiver flats, and the words "Gold Medallion" are engraved and gold filled on the right side of the barrel. High gloss stock finish. Introduced 1988.
Price: No sights $472.50

BROWNING A-BOLT 22 BOLT-ACTION RIFLE
Caliber: 22 LR, 22 WMR, 5-shot magazines standard.
Barrel: 22".
Weight: 5 lbs., 9 oz. **Length:** 40¼" overall.
Stock: Walnut with cut checkering, rosewood grip cap and forend tip.
Sights: Offered with or without open sights. Open sight model has ramp front and adjustable folding leaf rear.
Features: Short 60-degree bolt throw. Top tang safety. Grooved for 22 scope mount. Drilled and tapped for full-size scope mounts. Detachable magazines. Gold-colored trigger preset at about 4 lbs. Imported from Japan by Browning. Introduced 1986.
Price: A-Bolt 22, no sights $356.50
Price: A-Bolt 22, with open sights $367.50
Price: A-Bolt 22 WMR, no sights $409.50
Price: As above, with sights $419.50

CZ 99 PRECISION 22 BOLT-ACTION RIFLE
Caliber: 22 LR, 5-shot magazine.
Barrel: 20".
Weight: 6.1 lbs. **Length:** 40" overall.
Stock: European hardwood with checkered grip and forend.
Sights: Hooded bead on ramp front, rear adjustable for windage and elevation.
Features: Sliding safety locks trigger and bolt; receiver grooved for scope mounting. Polished blue finish. Introduced 1990. Imported from Yugoslavia by TD Arms.
Price: $269.00

Cabanas Master

Cabanas Leyre Bolt-Action Rifle
Similar to Master model except 44" overall, has sport/target stock.
Price: $134.95
Price: Model R83 (17" barrel, hardwood stock, 40" o.a.l.) $79.95
Price: Mini 82 Youth (16½" barrel, 33" o.a.l., 3½ lbs.) $69.95
Price: Pony Youth (16" barrel, 34" o.a.l., 3.2 lbs.) $79.95
Price: Safari $99.95

CABANAS MASTER BOLT-ACTION RIFLE
Caliber: 177, round ball or pellet; single shot.
Barrel: 19½".
Weight: 8 lbs. **Length:** 45½" overall.
Stocks: Walnut target-type with Monte Carlo.
Sights: Blade front, fully adjustable rear.
Features: Fires round ball or pellet with 22-cal. blank cartridge. Bolt action. Imported from Mexico by Mandall Shooting Supplies. Introduced 1984.
Price: $150.00
Price: Varmint model (has 21½" barrel, 4½ lbs., 41" o.a.l., varmint-type stock) $109.95

Consult our Directory pages for the location of firms mentioned.

CABANAS RIFLE
Caliber: 177.
Barrel: 19".
Weight: 6 lbs., 12 oz. **Length:** 42" overall.
Stock: Target-type thumbhole.
Sights: Blade front, open fully adjustable rear.
Features: Fires round ball or pellets with 22 blank cartridge. Imported from Mexico by Mandall Shooting Supplies.
Price: $159.95

Cabanas Espronceda IV Bolt-Action Rifle
Similar to the Leyre model except has full sporter stock, 18¾" barrel, 40" overall length, weighs 5½ lbs.
Price: $119.95

CAUTION: PRICES CHANGE, CHECK AT GUNSHOP.

Chipmunk Rifle

Daisy Legacy 2202

Kimber 82B

CHIPMUNK SINGLE SHOT RIFLE
Caliber: 22, S, L, LR, single shot.
Barrel: 16⅛".
Weight: About 2½ lbs. **Length:** 30" overall.
Stocks: American walnut, or camouflage.
Sights: Post on ramp front, peep rear adjustable for windage and elevation.
Features: Drilled and tapped for scope mounting using special Chipmunk base ($9.95). Made in U.S.A. Introduced 1982. From Oregon Arms.
Price: **$129.95**

DAISY LEGACY 2201 BOLT-ACTION SINGLE SHOT
Caliber: 22 LR.
Barrel: 19". Octagonal barrel shroud.
Weight: 6.5 lbs. **Length:** 34.75" to 36.75" (variable).
Stock: Moulded copolymer.
Sights: Blade on ramp front, fully adjustable removable notch rear.
Features: Adjustable buttstock length; removable bolt and trigger assembly; adjustable trigger pull; barrel interchanges with smoothbore unit. Receiver dovetailed for scope mounting. Introduced 1988. Made in U.S. by Daisy.
Price: About **$79.00**

Daisy Legacy 2211 Bolt-Action Single Shot
Same gun as the Model 2201 except comes with hardwood stock, fixed length of pull.
Price: About **$119.00**

DAISY LEGACY 2202 BOLT-ACTION REPEATER
Caliber: 22 LR, 10-shot rotary magazine.
Barrel: 19". Octagonal barrel shroud.
Weight: 6.5 lbs. **Length:** 34.75" to 36.75" (variable).
Stock: Moulded lightweight copolymer.
Sights: Blade on ramp front, fully adjustable removable rear.
Features: Adjustable buttstock length; removable bolt and trigger assembly; barrel interchanges with smoothbore unit. Receiver dovetailed for scope mounting. Introduced 1988. Made in U.S. by Daisy.
Price: About **$89.00**

Daisy Legacy 2212 Bolt-Action Repeater
Same as the Model 2202 except has hardwood stock, fixed length of pull.
Price: About **$129.00**

KIMBER MODEL 82B BOLT-ACTION RIFLE
Caliber: 22 LR, 5-shot detachable magazine.
Barrel: 22"; 6-grooves; 1:16" twist.
Weight: About 6¼ lbs. **Length:** 40½" overall (Sporter).
Stock: Three Sporter styles—Hunter Grade has non-checkered classic-style laminated stock with recoil pad, swivel studs; Deluxe Grade is AA Claro walnut with ebony forend tip, no cheekpiece, 20 lpi hand checkering, Niedner-style buttplate, steel grip cap, fully inletted swivel studs; Super America has AAA Claro walnut with ebony forend tip, beaded cheekpiece, 20 lpi hand checkering, Niedner-style buttplate, steel grip cap, fully inletted swivel studs.
Sights: Hooded ramp front with bead, folding leaf rear (optional).
Features: High quality, adult-sized, bolt-action rifle. Barrel screwed into receiver; rocker-type silent safety; twin rear locking lugs. All steel construction. Fully adjustable trigger; round-top receiver with bases for Kimber scope mounts. High polish blue. Barreled actions available. Also available in true left-hand version in selected models. Made in U.S.A. Introduced 1979. Contact Kimber for full details.
Price: Deluxe Grade **$1,195.00**
Price: Super Grade **$1,295.00**
Price: Deluxe Grade, left-hand **$1,195.00**
Price: Hunter Grade **$895.00**

Kimber Model 82, 84 Super Grade
Super-grade version of the Models 82 and 84. Has the Classic stock only of specially selected, high-grade, California Claro walnut, with Continental beaded cheekpiece and ebony forend tip; borderless, full-coverage 20 lpi checkering; Niedner-type checkered steel buttplate. Options include barrel quarter-rib with express rear sight. Available in 22 Long Rifle, 17 Rem., 222 Rem., 223 Rem.
Price: Model 82 22 Long Rifle **$1,295.00**
Price: Model 84, 17, 222, 223 .... **$1,495.00**

Kimber Rimfire Varminter
Similar to the Model 82B except has non-checkered varmint-style laminated stock, 25" target barrel, 5-shot magazine (10-shot clip optional). Introduced 1990. From Kimber of Oregon, Inc.
Price: **$795.00**

KRICO MODEL 300 BOLT-ACTION RIFLES
Caliber: 22 LR, 22 WMR, 22 Hornet.
Barrel: 19.6" (22 RF), 23.6" (Hornet).
Weight: 6.3 lbs. **Length:** 38.5" overall (22 RF).
Stock: Walnut-stained beech.
Sights: Blade on ramp front, open adjustable rear.
Features: Double triggers, sliding safety. Checkered grip and forend. Imported from West Germany by Mandall Shooting Supplies.
Price: Model 300 Standard **$700.00**
Price: Model 300 Deluxe **$795.00**
Price: Model 300 Stutzen (walnut full-length stock) **$825.00**
Price: Model 300 SA (walnut Monte Carlo stock) **$750.00**

LAKEFIELD ARMS MARK I BOLT-ACTION RIFLE
Caliber: 22 LR, single shot.
Barrel: 20½".
Weight: 5½ lbs. **Length:** 39½" overall.
Stock: Walnut-finished hardwood with Monte Carlo-type comb, checkered grip and forend.
Sights: Bead front, open adjustable rear. Receiver grooved for scope mounting.
Features: Thumb-operated rotating safety. Blue finish. Introduced 1990. Made in Canada by Lakefield Arms Ltd.
Price: About **$99.95**

CAUTION: PRICES CHANGE, CHECK AT GUNSHOP.

Lakefield Mark II

Marlin 880

Marlin 25 MN

Marlin 15YN

Mauser Model 201

LAKEFIELD ARMS MARK II BOLT-ACTION RIFLE
Caliber: 22 LR, 10-shot magazine.
Barrel: 20½".

Weight: 5½ lbs. **Length:** 39½" overall.
Stock: Walnut-finished hardwood with Monte Carlo-type comb, checkered grip and forend.
Sights: Bead front, open adjustable rear. Receiver grooved for scope mounting.
Features: Thumb-operated rotating safety. Blue finish. Introduced 1990. Made in Canada by Lakefield Arms Ltd.
Price: About $109.95

MARLIN 880 BOLT-ACTION RIFLE
Caliber: 22 LR; 7-shot clip magazine.
Barrel: 22" Micro-Groove®.
Weight: 5½ lbs. **Length:** 41".
Stock: Monte Carlo American black walnut with checkered p.g. and forend. Rubber buttpad, swivel studs. Mar-Shield® finish.
Sights: Wide-Scan® ramp front, folding semi-buckhorn rear adjustable for w. and e.
Features: Receiver grooved for tip-off scope mount. Introduced 1989.
Price: $192.95

Marlin 881 Bolt-Action Rifle
Same as the Marlin 880 except tubular magazine, holds 17 Long Rifle cartridges. Weight 6 lbs.
Price: $200.95

Marlin 882 Bolt-Action Rifle
Same as the Marlin 880 except 22 WMR cal. only with 7-shot clip magazine, weight about 6 lbs. Comes with swivel studs.
Price: $212.95

Marlin 883 Bolt-Action Rifle
Same as Marlin 882 except tubular magazine holds 12 rounds of 22 WMR ammunition.
Price: $219.95

Marlin 25N Bolt-Action Repeater
Similar to Marlin 880, except walnut-finished p.g. stock, adjustable open rear sight, ramp front.
Price: $139.95

Marlin Model 25MN Bolt-Action Rifle
Similar to the Model 25N except chambered for 22 WMR. Has 7-shot clip magazine, 22" Micro-Groove® barrel, walnut-finished hardwood stock. Introduced 1989.
Price: $159.95

MARLIN 15YN "LITTLE BUCKAROO"
Caliber: 22 LR, single shot.
Barrel: 16¼" Micro-Groove®.
Weight: 4¼ lbs. **Length:** 33¼" overall.
Stock: One-piece walnut-finished hardwood with Monte Carlo; Mar-Shield® finish.
Sights: Ramp front, adjustable open rear.
Features: Beginner's rifle with thumb safety, easy-load feed throat, red cocking indicator. Receiver grooved for scope mounting. Introduced 1989.
Price: $134.95

MAUSER MODEL 201 BOLT-ACTION RIFLE
Caliber: 22 LR, 22 WMR, 5-shot magazine.
Barrel: 21".
Weight: About 6.5 lbs. **Length:** 40" overall.

Stock: Walnut-stained beech with Monte Carlo comb and cheekpiece. Checkered grip and forend.
Sights: Available with or without sights.
Features: Hammer forged medium-heavy, free-floated barrel. Bolt has two front locking lugs, dual extractors. Adjustable trigger. Safety locks bolt, sear and trigger. Receiver accepts rail mounts and is drilled and tapped for scope mounting. Introduced 1989. Imported from West Germany by Precision Imports, Inc.
Price: 22 LR with sights $445.00
Price: As above, no sights $420.00
Price: 22 WMR with sights $490.00
Price: As above, no sights $465.00

CAUTION: PRICES CHANGE, CHECK AT GUNSHOP.

Remington 40XR Custom

NORINCO TYPE EM-332 BOLT-ACTION RIFLE
Caliber: 22 LR, 5-shot magazine.
Barrel: 18.5".
Weight: 4.5 lbs. **Length:** 41.5" overall.
Stock: Hardwood.
Sights: Blade front on ramp, open adjustable rear.
Features: Has magazine holder on side of butt that holds two extra magazines. Blue finish. Introduced 1990. Imported from China by China Sports, Inc.
Price: .... **NA**

REMINGTON 40XR RIMFIRE CUSTOM SPORTER
Caliber: 22 LR.
Barrel: 24".
Weight: 10 lbs. **Length:** 42½" overall.
Stock: Full-sized walnut, checkered p.g. and forend.
Sights: None furnished; drilled and tapped for scope mounting.
Features: Custom Shop gun. Duplicates Model 700 centerfire rifle.
Price: Grade I $1,314.00
Price: Grade II $2,335.00
Price: Grade III $3,650.00
Price: Grade IV $5,695.00

Remington Model 541-T

REMINGTON MODEL 581-S "SPORTSMAN" RIFLE
Caliber: 22 S, L or LR. 5-shot clip magazine.
Barrel: 24" round.
Weight: 4¾ lbs. **Length:** 42⅜" overall.
Stock: Walnut-finished hardwood, Monte Carlo with p.g.
Sights: Bead post front, screw adjustable open rear.
Features: Sliding side safety, wide trigger, receiver grooved for tip-off scope mounts. Comes with single-shot adaptor. Reintroduced 1986.
Price: About $196.00

REMINGTON MODEL 541-T
Caliber: 22 S, L, LR, 5-shot clip.
Barrel: 24".
Weight: 5⅞ lbs. **Length:** 42½" overall.
Stock: Walnut, cut-checkered p.g. and forend. Satin finish.
Sights: None. Drilled and tapped for scope mounts.
Features: Clip repeater. Thumb safety. Reintroduced 1986.
Price: About $355.00

Ruger 77/22

RUGER 77/22 RIMFIRE BOLT-ACTION RIFLE
Caliber: 22 Long Rifle, 10-shot rotary magazine; 22 WMR, 9-shot rotary magazine.
Barrel: 20".
Weight: About 5¾ lbs. **Length:** 39¾" overall.
Stock: Checkered American walnut or Injection-moulded Du Pont Zytel reinforced with nylon.
Sights: Gold bead front, adjustable folding leaf rear or plain barrel with 1" Ruger rings.

Features: Mauser-type action uses Ruger's 10-shot rotary magazine. Three-position safety, simplified bolt stop, patented bolt locking system. Uses the dual screw barrel attachment system of the 10/22 rifle. Integral scope mounting system with 1" Ruger rings. Blued model Introduced in 1983. Stainless steel model and blued model with the synthetic stock Introduced in 1989.
Price: 77/22R (no sights, rings, walnut stock) $382.75
Price: 77/22S (open sights, walnut stock) $382.75
Price: 77/22RS (open sights, rings, walnut stock) $403.75
Price: 77/22RP (no sights, rings, synthetic stock) $315.00
Price: 77/22SP (open sights, synthetic stock) $315.00
Price: 77/22RSP (open sights, rings, synthetic stock) $336.00
Price: K77/22RP (stainless, no sights, rings, synthetic stock) $378.00
Price: K77/22SP (stainless, open sights, synthetic stock) $378.00
Price: K77/22RSP (stainless, open sights, rings, synthetic stock) ... $399.00
Price: 77/22RM (22 WMR, blue, walnut stock) $382.75
Price: 77/22RMP (22 WMR, stainless, synthetic stock) $399.00

VARNER FAVORITE SINGLE SHOT RIFLE
Caliber: 22 LR.
Barrel: 21½"; half-round, half-octagon.
Weight: 5 lbs.
Stock: American walnut.
Sights: Blade front, open step-adjustable rear and peep.
Features: Recreation of the Stevens Favorite rifle with takedown barrel. Target grade barrel. Made in U.S. Introduced 1988. From Varner Sporting Arms, Inc.
Price: Hunter Grade (checkered walnut) $369.00
Price: Hunter Deluxe (AAA Fancy walnut) $499.00
Price: Presentation Grade (AAA Fancy walnut, checkered grip and forend, includes hard custom takedown case) $569.00

Varner Favorite

Varner Favorite Schuetzen
Similar to the Favorite except is a recreation of the Stevens Ladies Favorite Schuetzen (1910-1916). Color case-hardened frame and lever hand engraved with Ulrich-style scrolls. Pistol grip perch belly stock, extended forend of AAA Fancy walnut with extensive checkering. Ladder-style, tang-mounted peep sight adjustable for windage and elevation, globe-type front with six inserts. Has 24" target-grade barrel, half-round, half-octagon. Introduced 1989.
Price: $1,000.00

CAUTION: PRICES CHANGE, CHECK AT GUNSHOP.

Voere Model 1007/1013

VOERE MODEL 1007/1013 BOLT-ACTION RIFLE
Caliber: 22 LR (M1007 Biathlon); 22 WMR (M1013).
Barrel: 18".

Weight: About 5½ lbs. (M1007).
Stock: Oil-finished beechwood.
Sights: Hooded front, open adjustable rear.
Features: Single-stage trigger (M1013 available with double set). Military-look stock; sling swivels. Convertible to single shot. Imported from Austria by L. Joseph Rahn. Introduced 1984.
Price: 1007 Biathlon **$325.00**
Price: 1013, 22 WMR **$350.00**

Weatherby Accumark

WEATHERBY ACCUMARK BOLT-ACTION RIFLE
Caliber: 22 LR, 5-shot magazine.
Barrel: 24".

Weight: 7 lbs.
Stock: Select walnut with hand checkered grip and forend. Deluxe model has high-gloss finish with rosewood grip and forend tips; Classic has oil finish with blackwood grip and forend tips. Both have rubber buttpad, q.d. swivel studs.
Sights: None furnished. Receiver drilled, tapped and grooved for scope mounting.
Features: Fluted bolt body with front double locking lugs, 60-degree bolt lift; fully adjustable trigger for creep and weight of pull. Optional 8-shot magazine available. Introduced 1990. From Weatherby, Inc.
Price: Deluxe or Classic **$635.00**

COMPETITION RIFLES—CENTERFIRE & RIMFIRE

Includes models for classic American and ISU target competition and other sporting and competitive shooting.

Anschutz 1903 D

ANSCHUTZ MODEL 64-MS, 64-MS LEFT SILHOUETTE
Caliber: 22 LR, single shot.
Barrel: 21¾", medium heavy; ⅞" diameter.
Weight: 8 lbs., 1 oz. **Length:** 39½" overall.
Stock: Walnut-finished hardwood, silhouette-type.
Sights: None furnished. Receiver drilled and tapped for scope mounting.
Features: Designed for metallic silhouette competition. Stock has stippled checkering, contoured thumb groove with Wundhammer swell. Two-stage #5091 trigger. Slide safety locks sear and bolt. Introduced 1980. Imported from West Germany by PSI.
Price: Model 64-MS $717.00
Price: Model 64-MS Left $793.00

ANSCHUTZ 1808ED SUPER RUNNING TARGET
Caliber: 22 LR, single shot.
Barrel: 23½"; ⅞" diameter.
Weight: 9¼ lbs. **Length:** 42" overall.
Stock: European hardwood. Heavy beavertail forend, adjustable cheekpiece, buttplate, stippled pistol grip and forend.
Sights: None furnished. Receiver grooved for scope mounting.
Features: Uses Super Match 54 action. Adjustable trigger from 14 oz. to 3.5 lbs. Removable sectioned barrel weights. **Special Order Only.** Introduced 1982. Imported from Germany by PSI.
Price: Right-hand $1,290.00
Price: Left-hand, 1808EDL $1,400.00

ANSCHUTZ 1827B BIATHLON RIFLE
Caliber: 22 LR, 5-shot magazine.
Barrel: 21½".
Weight: 9 lbs. with sights. **Length:** 42½" overall.
Stock: Walnut-finished hardwood; cheekpiece, stippled pistol grip and forend.

ANSHUTZ MODEL 1903 D MATCH RIFLE
Caliber: 22 LR, single shot.
Barrel: 25½", ¾" diameter.
Weight: 8.6 lbs. **Length:** 43¾" overall.
Stock: Walnut-finished hardwood with adjustable cheekpiece; stippled grip and forend.
Sights: None furnished.
Features: Uses Anschutz Match 64 action and #5091 two-stage trigger. A medium weight rifle for Intermediate and advanced Junior Match competition. Introduced 1987. Imported from West Germany by PSI.
Price: Right-hand $831.00
Price: Left-hand $873.00

ANSCHUTZ MODEL 1403D MATCH RIFLE
Caliber: 22 LR only, single shot.
Barrel: 26"; ¹¹⁄₁₆" dia.
Weight: 7¾ lbs. **Length:** 44" overall.
Stock: Walnut-finished hardwood, cheekpiece, checkered p.g., beavertail forend, adjustable buttplate.
Sights: None furnished.
Features: Sliding side safety, adjustable #5053 single stage trigger, receiver grooved for Anschutz sights. Imported from West Germany by PSI.
Price: Without sights $699.50

Sights: Globe front specially designed for Biathlon shooting, micrometer rear with hinged snow cap.
Features: Uses Match 54 action and adjustable trigger; adjustable wooden buttplate, Biathlon butthook, adjustable hand-stop rail. **Special Order Only.** Introduced 1982. Imported from Germany by PSI.
Price: Right-hand $1,744.00
Price: Left-hand $1,863.00

ANSCHUTZ 1911 MATCH RIFLE

Caliber: 22 LR, single shot.
Barrel: 27¼" round (1" dia.).
Weight: 11 lbs. **Length:** 46" overall.
Stock: Walnut-finished European hardwood; American prone style with Monte Carlo, cast-off cheekpiece, checkered p.g., beavertail forend with swivel rail and adjustable swivel, adjustable rubber buttplate.
Sights: None. Receiver grooved for Anschutz sights (extra). Scope blocks.
Features: Two-stage #5018 trigger adjustable from 2.1 to 8.6 oz. Extremely fast lock time. Imported from West Germany by PSI.
Price: Right-hand, no sights **$1,576.00**
Price: M1911-L (true left-hand action and stock) **$1,714.00**

Anschutz 54.18MS REP Deluxe Silhouette Rifle

Same basic action and trigger specifications as the Anschutz 1913 Super Match but with removable 5-shot clip magazine, 22" barrel extendable to 30" using optional extension and weight set. Receiver drilled and tapped for scope mounting. Silhouette stock with thumbhole grip is of fiberglass with walnut wood Fibergrain finish. Introduced 1990. Imported from West Germany by Precision Sales International.
Price: Model 54.18MS REP Deluxe **$1,755.00**
Price: Model 54.18MS Standard with fiberglass stock **$1,395.00**
Price: Model 54. 18MS Standard with wood stock, single shot **$1,212.00**
Price: Model 54. 18MS Left (left-hand bolt and stock) **$1,273.00**

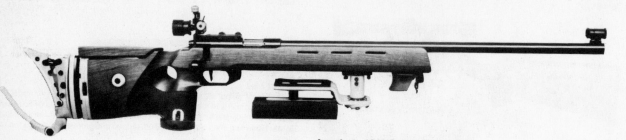

Anschutz Model 1913

Anschutz Model 1910 Super Match II

Similar to the Super Match 1913 rifle except has a stock of European hardwood with tapered forend and deep receiver area. Hand and palm rests not included. Uses Match 54 action. Adjustable hook buttplate and cheekpiece. Sights not included. Introduced 1982. Imported from Germany by PSI.
Price: Right-hand **$2,013.00**
Price: Left-hand **$2,183.00**

Anschutz 1913 Super Match Rifle

Same as the Model 1911 except European walnut International-type stock with adjustable cheekpiece, adjustable aluminum hook buttplate, adjustable hand stop, weight 15½ lbs., 46" overall. Imported from West Germany by PSI.
Price: Right-hand, no sights **$2,255.00**
Price: M1913-L (left-hand action and stock) **$2,440.00**

Anschutz Model 54.18 MS Silhouette Rifle

Same basic features as Anschutz 1913 Super Match but with special metallic silhouette European hardwood stock and two-stage trigger. Has 22" barrel; receiver drilled and tapped.
Price: **$1,212.00**
Price: Model 54.18 MSL (true left-hand version of above) **$1,273.00**

Anschutz Model 1907

Anschutz 1907 Match Rifle

Same action as Model 1913 but with ⅞" diameter 26" barrel. Length is 44½" overall, weight 10 lbs. Blonde wood finish with vented forend. Designed for ISU requirements, suitable for NRA matches.
Price: Right-hand, no sights **$1,344.00**
Price: M1907-L (true left-hand action and stock) **$1,462.00**

Beeman/FWB 2600

BEEMAN/FEINWERKBAU 2600 TARGET RIFLE

Caliber: 22 LR, single shot.
Barrel: 26.3".
Weight: 10.6 lbs. **Length:** 43.7" overall.
Stock: Laminated hardwood and hard rubber.
Sights: Globe front with Interchangeable Inserts; micrometer match aperture rear.
Features: Identical smallbore companion to the Beeman/FWB 600 air rifle. Free floating barrel. Match trigger has fingertip weight adjustment dial. Introduced 1986. Imported from West Germany by Beeman.
Price: Right-hand **$1,450.00**
Price: Left-hand **$1,625.00**

BEEMAN/WEIHRAUCH HW60 TARGET RIFLE

Caliber: 22 LR, single shot.
Barrel: 26.8".
Weight: 10.8 lbs. **Length:** 45.7" overall.
Stock: Walnut with adjustable buttplate. Stippled p.g. and forend. Rail with adjustable swivel.
Sights: Hooded ramp front, match-type aperture rear.
Features: Adjustable match trigger with push-button safety. Left-hand version also available. Introduced 1981. Imported from West Germany by Beeman.
Price: Right-hand $750.00
Price: Left-hand $788.00

CAUTION: PRICES CHANGE, CHECK AT GUNSHOP.

BEEMAN/HW 660 MATCH RIFLE
Caliber: 22 LR.
Barrel: 26".
Weight: 10.7 lbs. **Length:** 45.3" overall.
Stock: Match-type walnut with adjustable cheekpiece and buttplate.
Sights: Globe front, match aperture rear.
Features: Adjustable match trigger; stippled p.g. and forend; forend accessory rail. Imported from West Germany by Beeman. Introduced 1988.
Price: **$798.00**

Beeman/HW 660

Diana 820F Match

DIANA MODEL 820F MATCH RIFLE
Caliber: 22 LR, single shot.
Barrel: 27.1".
Weight: 15.4 lbs. **Length:** 44.4" overall.
Stock: Walnut.
Sights: Tunnel front, fully adjustable match rear.

Features: Designed for free rifle events. Adjustable hook buttplate, adjustable cheekpiece, hand stop. Stock stabilizer and palm rest optional. Trigger adjustable from 1.4 to 8.8 oz. Introduced 1990. Imported from West Germany by Dynamit Nobel-RWS, Inc.
Price: Right-hand only **$1,850.00**

Diana 820L Match

DIANA MODEL 820L MATCH RIFLE
Caliber: 22 LR, single shot.
Barrel: 25.9".
Weight: 10.5 lbs. **Length:** 44.4" overall.
Stock: Walnut.
Sights: Tunnel front, fully adjustable match rear.
Features: Designed for three-position match shooting. Adjustable cheekpiece. Trigger adjustable from 1.4 to 8.8 oz. Accessory buttplate available. Introduced 1990. Imported from West Germany by Dynamit Nobel-RWS, Inc.
Price: Right-hand only **$1,250.00**

F.I.E. 322 Master

F.I.E. MODEL 322 MASTER TARGET RIFLE
Caliber: 22 LR, 6- or 10-shot magazine.
Barrel: 26.2".
Weight: 7 lbs. **Length:** 43.3" overall.
Stock: Match style of Brazilian hardwood. Stippled grip, rubber recoil pad, aluminum forend rail.
Sights: Globe front, match aperture fully adjustable rear.
Features: Adjustable trigger, free-floating barrel, receiver grooved for scope mounting, removable iron sights. Introduced 1990. Imported from Brazil by F.I.E. Firearms.
Price: **$665.00**
Price: Model 422 Match Master (as above except heavy bbl.) **$665.00**

FEDERAL ORDNANCE M14SA TARGET RIFLE
Caliber: 7.62mm NATO (308 Win.).
Barrel: 22".
Weight: 8 lbs., 9 oz. **Length:** 44" overall.
Stock: Fiberglass or wood.
Sights: G.I., fully adjustable for windage and elevation.
Features: Civilian version of the M-14 service rifle. All metal has military blue finish. Comes with G.I.-type manual. Introduced 1988. Made in the U.S. by Federal Ordnance.
Price: With fiberglass stock **$624.95**
Price: With wood stock **$674.95**

Heckler & Koch PSG-1

HECKLER & KOCH PSG-1 MARKSMAN RIFLE
Caliber: 308, 5- and 20-shot magazines.
Barrel: 25.6″, heavy.
Weight: 17.8 lbs. **Length:** 47.5″ overall.
Stock: Matte black high Impact plastic, adjustable for length, pivoting butt cap, vertically-adjustable cheekpiece; target-type pistol grip with adjustable palm shelf.
Sights: Hendsoldt 6x42 scope.
Features: Uses HK-91 action with low-noise bolt closing device; special forend with T-way rail for sling swivel or tripod. Gun comes in special foam-fitted metal transport case with tripod, two 20-shot and two 5-shot magazines, cleaning rod. Imported from West Germany by Heckler & Koch, Inc. Introduced 1986. **Law enforcement sales only.**
Price: $8,859.00

FINNISH LION STANDARD TARGET RIFLE
Caliber: 22 LR, single shot.
Barrel: 27⅝″.
Weight: 10½ lbs. **Length:** 44⁹∕₁₆″ overall.
Stock: French walnut, target style.
Sights: Globe front, International micrometer rear.
Features: Optional accessories: palm rest, hook buttplate, forend stop and swivel assembly, buttplate extension, five front sight aperture inserts, three rear sight apertures, Allen wrench. Adjustable trigger. Imported from Finland by Mandall Shooting Supplies.
Price: $695.00

Kimber Model 82

Kimber Model 82 All American Match
Similar to the Model 82 Government except has target-type stock adjustable for 15 different positions. Pistol grip has palm swell and thumb dent. Barrel is step crowned, air-gauge inspected, free-floating, and is .9″ in diameter. Fully adjustable, single-stage trigger with 1.5 lb. pull weight. Inletted forend accepts optional weights. Introduced 1990. From Kimber of Oregon, Inc.
Price: Less sights $895.00
Price: Front and rear sight package $209.95

KIMBER MODEL 82 GOVERNMENT
Caliber: 22 LR, single shot.
Barrel: 25″, six groove. Match grade.
Weight: 10-10¾ lbs. **Length:** 43½″ overall.
Stock: Target-type of Claro walnut. Length of pull adjustable from 12″ to 13½″. Adjustable handstop.
Sights: Receiver grooved for Kimber scope mounts or optional aperture sight package. Barrel has two rear bases for scope mounting.
Features: Single-stage trigger adjustable for over travel, sear engagement and weight. Super-fast lock time. Meets U.S. Army requirements. Introduced 1988.
Price: Without sights $595.00
Price: Front and rear sight package $209.95

KRICO MODEL 400 MATCH RIFLE
Caliber: 22 LR, 22 Hornet, 5-shot magazine.
Barrel: 23.2″ (22 LR), 23.6″ (22 Hornet).
Weight: 8.8 lbs. **Length:** 42.1″ overall (22 RF).
Stock: European walnut, match type.
Sights: None furnished; receiver grooved for scope mounting.
Features: Heavy match barrel. Double set or match trigger. Imported from West Germany by Mandall Shooting Supplies.
Price: $950.00

KRICO MODEL 500 KRICOTRONIC MATCH RIFLE
Caliber: 22 LR, single shot.
Barrel: 23.6″.
Weight: 9.4 lbs. **Length:** 42.1″ overall.
Stock: European walnut, match type with adjustable butt.
Sights: Globe front, match micrometer aperture rear.
Features: Electronic ignition system for fastest possible lock time. Completely adjustable trigger. Barrel has tapered bore. Imported from West Germany by Mandall Shooting Supplies.
Price: $3,950.00

KRICO MODEL 600 MATCH RIFLE
Caliber: 222, 223, 22-250, 243, 308, 5.6x50 Mag., 4-shot magazine.
Barrel: 23.6″.
Weight: 8.8 lbs. **Length:** 43.3″ overall.
Stock: Match stock of European walnut with cheekpiece.
Sights: None furnished; drilled and tapped for scope mounting.
Features: Match stock with vents in forend for cooling, rubber recoil pad, sling swivels. Imported from West Germany by Mandall Shooting Supplies.
Price: $1,025.00

KRICO MODEL 600 SNIPER RIFLE
Caliber: 222, 223, 22-250, 243, 308, 4-shot magazine.
Barrel: 23.6″.
Weight: 9.2 lbs. **Length:** 45.2″ overall.
Stock: European walnut with adjustable rubber buttplate.
Sights: None supplied; drilled and tapped for scope mounting.
Features: Match barrel with flash hider; large bolt knob; wide trigger shoe. Parkerized finish. Imported from West Germany by Mandall Shooting Supplies.
Price: $2,645.00
Price: As Model 600 Single Shot (match stock) $950.00

MAUSER MODEL 86 SPECIALTY RIFLE
Caliber: 308 Win., 9-shot detachable magazine.
Barrel: 25.6″, fluted, 1:12″ twist.
Weight: About 10.8 lbs. **Length:** 47.7″ overall.
Stock: Laminated wood, fiberglass, or special match thumbhole wood. All have rail in forend and adjustable recoil pad.
Sights: None furnished. Competition metallic sights or scope mount optional.
Features: Match barrel with muzzlebrake. Action has two front bolt locking lugs. Action bedded in stock with free-floated barrel. Match trigger adjustable as

single or two-stage; fully adjustable for weight, slack, and position. Silent safety locks bolt, firing pin. Introduced 1989. Imported from West Germany by Precision Imports, Inc.
Price: With laminated stock $3,875.00
Price: With fiberglass stock $3,990.00
Price: With match thumbhole stock $4,900.00

McMillan Long Range

McMILLAN NATIONAL MATCH RIFLE
Caliber: 308, 5-shot magazine.
Barrel: 24″, stainless steel.
Weight: About 11 lbs. (std. bbl.). **Length:** 43″ overall.
Stock: Modified ISU fiberglass with adjustable buttplate.
Sights: Barrel band and Tompkins front; no rear sight furnished.
Features: McMillan repeating action with clip slot, Canjar trigger. Match-grade barrel. Available in right-hand only. Fibergrain stock, sight Installation, special machining and triggers optional. Introduced 1989. From G. McMillan & Co.
Price: $2,000.00

McMILLAN LONG RANGE RIFLE
Caliber: 300 Win. Mag., single shot.
Barrel: 26″, stainless steel, match grade.
Weight: 14 lbs. **Length:** 46½″ overall.
Stock: Fiberglass with adjustable buttplate and cheekpiece. Adjustable for length of pull, drop, cant and cast-off.
Sights: Barrel band and Tompkins front; no rear sight furnished.
Features: Uses McMillan solid bottom single shot action and Canjar trigger. Barrel twist 1:12″. Introduced 1989. From G. McMillan & Co.
Price: $2,000.00

McMillan M-86

McMILLAN M-86 SNIPER RIFLE
Caliber: 308, 30-06 (4-shot magazine), 300 Win. Mag. (3-shot magazine).
Barrel: 24″, McMillan match-grade in heavy contour.
Weight: 11¼ lbs. (308), 11½ lbs. (30-06, 300). **Length:** 43½″ overall.
Stock: Specially designed McHale fiberglass stock with textured grip and for-end, recoil pad.
Sights: None furnished.
Features: Uses McMillan repeating action. Comes with bipod. Matte black finish. Sling swivels. Introduced 1989. From G. McMillan & Co.
Price: $1,695.00

McMillan M-87

McMILLAN M-87 50-CALIBER RIFLE
Caliber: 50 BMG, single shot.
Barrel: 29″, with muzzlebrake.
Weight: About 21½ lbs. **Length:** 53″ overall.
Stock: McMillan fiberglass.
Sights: None furnished.
Features: Right-handed McMillan stainless steel receiver, chrome-moly barrel with 1:15″ twist. Introduced 1987. From G. McMillan & Co.
Price: $2,995.00
Price: M-87R (5-shot repeater) $3,445.00

McMILLAN M-88 50-CALIBER RIFLE
Similar to the M-87 except has a fully adjustable fiberglass stock, single shot shellholder bolt receiver. Uses McMillan Quick Takedown system. Weight is about 21 lbs. Introduced 1988.
Price: $3,250.00

McMILLAN M-89 SNIPER RIFLE
Caliber: 308 Win., 5-shot magazine.
Barrel: 28″ (with suppressor).
Weight: 15 lbs., 4 oz.
Stock: McMillan fiberglass; adjustable for length; recoil pad.
Sights: None furnished. Drilled and tapped for scope mounting.
Features: Uses McMillan repeating action. Comes with bipod. Introduced 1990. From G. McMillan & Co.
Price: Standard (non-suppressed) $1,950.00

Consult our Directory pages for the location of firms mentioned.

REMINGTON 40-XR KS RIMFIRE POSITION RIFLE
Caliber: 22 LR, single shot.
Barrel: 24″, heavy target.
Weight: 10 lbs. **Length:** 43″ overall.
Stock: Kevlar. Position-style with front swivel block on forend guide rail.
Sights: Drilled and tapped. Furnished with scope blocks.
Features: Meets all I.S.U. specifications. Deep forend, buttplate vertically adjustable, wide adjustable trigger.
Price: About $1,168.00

REMINGTON 40-XC KS NAT'L MATCH COURSE RIFLE
Caliber: 7.62 NATO, 5-shot.
Barrel: 24″, stainless steel.
Weight: 11 lbs. without sights. **Length:** 43½″ overall.
Stock: Kevlar, position-style, with palm swell, handstop.
Sights: None furnished.
Features: Designed to meet the needs of competitive shooters firing the national match courses. Position-style stock, top loading clip slot magazine, anti-bind bolt and receiver, bright stainless steel barrel. Meets all I.S.U. Army Rifle specifications. Adjustable buttplate, adjustable trigger.
Price: About $1,241.00

Remington Model 40-XB

REMINGTON MODEL 40XB-BR KS
Caliber: 22 BR Rem., 222 Rem., 222 Rem. Mag., 223, 6mmx47, 6mm BR Rem., 7.62 NATO (308 Win.).
Barrel: 20″ (light varmint class), 24″ (heavy varmint class).
Weight: Light varmint class, 7¼ lbs.; heavy varmint class, 12 lbs.
Length: 38″ (20″ bbl.), 42″ (24″ bbl.).
Stock: Kevlar.
Sights: None. Supplied with scope blocks.
Features: Unblued stainless steel barrel, trigger adjustable from 1½ lbs. to 3½ lbs. Special 2-oz. trigger at extra cost. Scope and mounts extra.
Price: With Kevlar stock $1,241.00
Price: Extra for 2-oz. trigger, about $146.00

REMINGTON 40-XB RANGEMASTER TARGET Centerfire
Caliber: 222 Rem., 222 Rem. Mag., 223, 220 Swift, 22-250, 6mm Rem., 243, 25-06, 7mm BR Rem., 7mm Rem. Mag., 30-338 (30-7mm Rem. Mag.), 300 Win. Mag., 7.62 NATO (308 Win.), 30-06, single shot.
Barrel: 27¼″.
Weight: 11¼ lbs. **Length:** 47″ overall.
Stock: American walnut with high comb and beavertail forend stop. Rubber non-slip buttplate.
Sights: None. Scope blocks installed.
Features: Adjustable trigger pull. Receiver drilled and tapped for sights.
Price: Standard s.s., stainless steel barrel, about $1,023.00

Remington 40-XB KS

Remington 40-XB KS Varmint Special
Similar to the standard Model 40-XB except has Du Pont Kevlar aramid fiber stock with straight comb, cheekpiece, palm-swell grip, black recoil pad. Swivel studs easily removable. Stock color is satin black with light texture. Single shot or repeater. Chamberings include 220 Swift. Introduced 1987. Custom Shop order.
Price: Single shot $1,168.00
Price: Repeater $1,256.00
Price: Extra for 2-oz. trigger $146.00

Springfield M1A Match

SPRINGFIELD ARMORY M1A SUPER MATCH
Caliber: 308 Win.
Barrel: 22″, heavy Douglas Premium, or Hart stainless steel.
Weight: About 10 lbs. **Length:** 44½″ overall.
Stock: Heavy walnut competition stock with longer pistol grip, contoured area behind the rear sight, thicker butt and forend, glass bedded.
Sights: National Match front and rear.
Features: Has new figure-eight style operating rod guide, new stock design. Introduced 1987. From Springfield Armory, Inc.
Price: About $1,525.00

SPRINGFIELD ARMORY M-21 LAW ENFORCEMENT
Caliber: 308 Win.
Barrel: 22″, Douglas heavy, air-gauged.
Weight: 15.25 lbs. (with bipod, scope mount). **Length:** 44¼″ overall.
Stock: Heavy walnut with adjustable comb, ventilated recoil pad. Glass bedded.
Sights: National Match front and rear.
Features: Refinement of the standard M-1A rifle. Has specially knurled shoulder for new figure-eight operating rod guide. New style folding and removable bipod. Guaranteed to deliver MOA accuracy. Comes with six 20-round magazines, leather military sling, cleaning kit. Introduced 1987. From Springfield Armory.
Price: $2,163.00

Steyr-Mannlicher SSG

STEYR-MANNLICHER SSG MARKSMAN
Caliber: 308 Win.
Barrel: 25.6″.
Weight: 8.6 lbs. **Length:** 44.5″ overall.
Stock: Choice of ABS "Cycolac" synthetic half-stock or walnut. Removable spacers in butt adjusts length of pull from 12¾″ to 14″.
Sights: Hooded blade front, folding leaf rear.
Features: Parkerized finish. Choice of interchangeable single or double set triggers. Detachable 5-shot rotary magazine (10-shot optional). Drilled and tapped for scope mounts. Imported from Austria by Gun South, Inc.
Price: Synthetic half-stock $1,665.00
Price: Walnut half-stock $2,083.00
Price: SSG PII (as above except has large bolt knob, heavy bbl., no sights, forend rail). $1,784.00

Steyr-Mannlicher SSG Match
Same as Model SSG Marksman except has heavy barrel, match bolt, Walther target peep sights and adjustable rail in forend to adjustable sling travel. Weight is 11 lbs.
Price: Synthetic half-stock $2,090.00
Price: Walnut half-stock $2,530.00

CAUTION: PRICES CHANGE, CHECK AT GUNSHOP.

Steyr-Mannlicher Match UIT

STEYR-MANNLICHER MATCH UIT RIFLE
Caliber: 243 Win. or 308 Win., 10-shot magazine.
Barrel: 25.5".
Weight: 10.9 lbs. **Length:** 44.48" overall.

TANNER STANDARD UIT RIFLE
Caliber: 308, 7.5mm Swiss, 10-shot.
Barrel: 25.9".
Weight: 10.5 lbs. **Length:** 40.6" overall.
Stock: Match style of seasoned nutwood with accessory rail; coarsely stippled pistol grip; high cheekpiece; vented forend.
Sights: Globe front with interchangeable inserts, Tanner micrometer-diopter rear with adjustable aperture.
Features: Two locking lug revolving bolt encloses case head. Trigger adjustable from ½ to 6½ lbs.; match trigger optional. Comes with 300-meter test target. Imported from Switzerland by Mandall Shooting Supplies. Introduced 1984.
Price: About $3,695.00

TANNER 300 METER FREE RIFLE
Caliber: 308 Win., 7.5 Swiss, single shot.
Barrel: 27.58".
Weight: 15 lbs. **Length:** 45.3" overall.
Stock: Seasoned walnut, thumbhole style, with accessory rail, palm rest, adjustable hook butt.
Sights: Globe front with interchangeable inserts, Tanner-design micrometer-diopter rear with adjustable aperture.
Features: Three-lug revolving-lock bolt design; adjustable set trigger; short firing pin travel; supplied with 300-meter test target. Imported from Switzerland by Mandall Shooting Supplies. Introduced 1984.
Price: About $4,450.00

Stock: Walnut with stippled grip and forend. Special UIT Match design.
Sights: Walther globe front, Walther peep rear.
Features: Double-pull trigger adjustable for let-off point, slack, weight of first-stage pull, release force and length; buttplate adjustable for height and length. Meets UIT specifications. Introduced 1984. Imported from Austria by Gun South, Inc.
Price: $2,836.00

TANNER 50 METER FREE RIFLE
Caliber: 22 LR, single shot.
Barrel: 27.7".
Weight: 13.9 lbs. **Length:** 44.4" overall.
Stock: Seasoned walnut with palm rest, accessory rail, adjustable hook butt-plate.
Sights: Globe front with interchangeable inserts, Tanner micrometer-diopter rear with adjustable aperture.
Features: Bolt action with externally adjustable set trigger. Supplied with 50-meter test target. Imported from Switzerland by Mandall Shooting Supplies. Introduced 1984.
Price: About $3,450.00

WALTHER KK/MS SILHOUETTE RIFLE
Caliber: 22 LR, single shot.
Barrel: 25.5".
Weight: 8.75 lbs. **Length:** 44.75" overall.
Stock: Walnut with thumbhole, stippled grip and forend.
Sights: None furnished. Receiver grooved for scope mounting.
Features: Over-size bolt knob. Adjustable trigger. Rubber buttpad. Introduced 1989. Imported from Germany by Interarms.
Price: $1,100.00

Walther U.I.T. BV

WALTHER U.I.T. BV UNIVERSAL
Caliber: 22 LR, single shot.
Barrel: 25½".
Weight: 10 lbs., 3 oz. **Length:** 44¾" overall.
Stock: Walnut, adjustable for length and drop; forend guide rail for sling or palm rest.
Sights: Globe-type front, fully adjustable aperture rear.
Features: Conforms to both NRA and U.I.T. requirements. Fully adjustable trigger. Left-hand stock available on special order. Imported from Germany by Interarms.
Price: $1,700.00

Walther GX-1 Match Rifle
Same general specs as U.I.T. except has 25½" barrel, overall length of 44½", weight of 15½ lbs. Stock is designed to provide every conceivable adjustment for individual preference and anatomical compatibility. Left-hand stock available on special order. Imported from Germany by Interarms.
Price: $2,200.00

Walther U.I.T. Match

Walther U.I.T. Match
Same specifications and features as standard U.I.T. Super rifle but has scope mount bases. Forend has new tapered profile, fully stippled. Import from Germany by Interarms.
Price: $1,300.00

Wichita Silhouette

WALTHER RUNNING BOAR MATCH RIFLE
Caliber: 22 LR, single shot.
Barrel: 23.6".
Weight: 8 lbs., 5 oz. **Length:** 42" overall.
Stock: Walnut thumbhole type. Forend and p.g. stippled.
Features: Especially designed for running boar competition. Receiver grooved to accept dovetail scope mounts. Adjustable cheekpiece and buttplate. 1.1 lb. trigger pull. Left-hand stock available on special order. Imported from Germany by Interarms.
Price: $1,300.00

WICHITA SILHOUETTE RIFLE
Caliber: All standard calibers with maximum overall cartridge length of 2.800".
Barrel: 24" free-floated Matchgrade.
Weight: About 9 lbs.
Stock: Metallic gray fiberthane with ventilated rubber recoil pad.
Sights: None furnished. Drilled and tapped for scope mounts.
Features: Legal for all NRA competitions. Single shot action. Fluted bolt, 2-oz. Canjar trigger; glass-bedded stock. Introduced 1983. From Wichita Arms.
Price: $2,150.00
Price: Left-hand $2,325.00

SHOTGUNS—AUTOLOADERS

Includes a wide variety of sporting guns and guns suitable for various competitions.

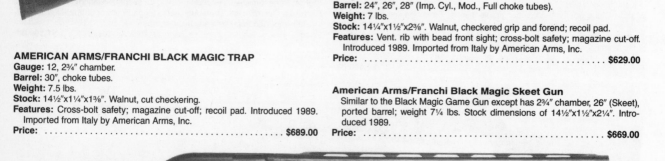

American Arms/Franchi Game

AMERICAN ARMS/FRANCHI BLACK MAGIC TRAP
Gauge: 12, 2¾" chamber.
Barrel: 30", choke tubes.
Weight: 7.5 lbs.
Stock: 14½"x1¼"x1⅜". Walnut, cut checkering.
Features: Cross-bolt safety; magazine cut-off; recoil pad. Introduced 1989. Imported from Italy by American Arms, Inc.
Price: $689.00

AMERICAN ARMS/FRANCHI BLACK MAGIC GAME GUN
Gauge: 12 or 20, 3" chamber.
Barrel: 24", 26", 28" (Imp. Cyl., Mod., Full choke tubes).
Weight: 7 lbs.
Stock: 14¼"x1½"x2⅜". Walnut, checkered grip and forend; recoil pad.
Features: Vent. rib with bead front sight; cross-bolt safety; magazine cut-off. Introduced 1989. Imported from Italy by American Arms, Inc.
Price: $629.00

American Arms/Franchi Black Magic Skeet Gun
Similar to the Black Magic Game Gun except has 2¾" chamber, 26" (Skeet), ported barrel; weight 7¼ lbs. Stock dimensions of 14½"x1½"x2¼". Introduced 1989.
Price: $669.00

Benelli M1 Super 90

BENELLI M1 SUPER 90 FIELD AUTO SHOTGUN
Gauge: 12, 3" chamber.
Barrel: 21", 24", 26", 28" (choke tubes).

Weight: 7 lbs., 4 oz.
Stock: High impact polymer.
Sights: Metal bead front.
Features: Sporting version of the military & police gun. Uses the rotating Montefeltro bolt system. Ventilated rib; blue finish. Extended or hunting magazine tube available with 26", 28" barrels. Comes with set of five choke tubes. Imported from Italy by Heckler & Koch.
Price: $675.00
Price: M1 Super Field with short 3-shot hunting magazine $675.00

Benelli Montefeltro

Benelli Montefeltro Super 90 Shotgun
Similar to the M1 Super 90 except has checkered walnut stock with high-gloss finish. Uses the Montefeltro rotating bolt system with a simple inertia recoil design. Full, Imp. Mod., Mod., Imp. Cyl. choke tubes. Weight is 7-7½ lbs. Finish is matte black. Introduced 1987.
Price: Standard Hunter, 26", 28" $685.00
Price: Left-hand, 26", 28" $745.00
Price: Uplander, 21" or 24" bbl. $685.00
Price: Smoothbore Slug with scope mount, rifle sights $685.00

CAUTION: PRICES CHANGE, CHECK AT GUNSHOP.

Benelli M1 Super 90 Slug

Benelli M1 Super 90 Slug Shotgun
Similar to the M1 Super 90 Field except comes with 19¾" barrel (Cyl. choke) giving 41" overall length and weight of 6 lbs., 13 oz. Has 3" chamber, 7-shot magazine capacity, matte black finish. Standard buttstock of high impact polymer. Rifle sights standard, ghost ring sighting system available. Imported from Italy by Hecker & Koch, Inc.
Price: With rifle sights **$631.00**
Price: With ghost ring sight system **$677.00**

Benelli Black Eagle

Weight: 7.1 to 7.6 lbs. **Length:** 42½" overall (21" barrel).
Stock: European walnut with high gloss finish. Comes with drop adjustment kit.
Features: Uses the Montefeltro rotating bolt inertia recoil operating system with a two-piece steel/aluminum receiver. Drop adjustment kit allows the stock to be custom fitted without modifying the stock. Black lower receiver finish, blued upper. Introduced 1989. Imported from Italy by Heckler & Koch, Inc.
Price: **$807.00**

BENELLI BLACK EAGLE AUTO SHOTGUN
Gauge: 12, 3" chamber.
Barrel: 21", 24", 26", 28" (Full, Mod., Imp. Cyl., Imp. Mod., Skeet choke tubes).

Benelli Black Eagle Slug

BENELLI MONTEFELTRO SUPER 90 SLUG GUN
Gauge: 12, 3" chamber, 4-shot magazine.
Barrel: 24" (Cyl.), smoothbore.
Weight: 7 lbs. **Length:** 45.5" overall.
Stock: European walnut with matte finish; comes with drop adjustment kit.
Sights: Open iron sights and scope mount.
Features: Uses Montefeltro inertia recoil rotating bolt system. Comes with scope mount. Introduced 1990. Imported from Italy by Heckler & Koch, Inc.
Price: **$685.00**

Benelli Black Eagle Slug Gun
Similar to the standard Black Eagle except has 24" (Cyl.) rifled barrel without rib, weighs 7 lbs., 2 oz. Uses the Montefeltro inertia recoil rotating bolt system with two-piece steel and alloy receiver. Top steel receiver drilled and tapped for scope mount (included). Introduced 1990. Imported from Italy by Heckler & Koch, Inc.
Price: With scope mount **$807.00**

Beretta A-303 Skeet

Features: Gas-operated action, alloy receiver, magazine cut-off, push-button safety. Mobilchoke models come with three interchangeable flush-mounted screw-in choke tubes. Imported from Italy by Beretta U.S.A. Introduced 1983.
Price: Mobilchoke, 12 ga. or 20 ga. **$653.00**
Price: 12 ga. trap with Monte Carlo stock **$727.00**
Price: 12 ga. trap with standard trap stock **$673.00**
Price: 12 or 20 ga., Skeet **$673.00**
Price: Slug, 12 or 20 ga. **$680.00**
Price: A-303 Youth Gun, 20 ga., 2¾" chamber, 24" barrel **$733.00**
Price: A-303 Sporting Clays with Mobilchoke **$733.00**

BERETTA A-303 AUTO SHOTGUN
Gauge: 12 or 20, 2¾" or 3" chamber.
Barrel: 12 ga., 3"—24", 26", 28", 30", 32"; 12 ga., 2¾"—26", 28", 30"; 20 ga., 2¾" or 3"—26", 28". All equipped with Mobilchoke choke tubes. Slug model has 22" (Cyl.) barrel.
Weight: About 6½ lbs., 20 gauge; about 7½ lbs., 12 gauge.
Stock: American walnut; hand-checkered grip and forend.

Beretta 1200F

BERETTA 1200F AUTO SHOTGUN
Gauge: 12 ga., 2¾" and 3" chamber.
Barrel: 28" vent. rib with Mobilchoke choke tubes.
Weight: 7.3 lbs.
Stock: Special strengthened technopolymer, matte black finish.
Features: Resists abrasion and adverse effects of water, salt and other damaging materials associated with tough field conditions. Imported from Italy by Beretta U.S.A. Introduced 1988.
Price: **$527.00**

Beretta A-303 Upland Model
Similar to the 12-gauge field A-303 except has 24" vent. rib barrel with Mobilchoke choke tubes, 2¾" chamber, straight English-style stock. Introduced 1989.
Price: **$680.00**

BRI/Benelli

Browning Sweet Sixteen

Browning A-500G

BRI/BENELLI 123-SL-80 RIFLED SHOTGUN
Gauge: 12, 2¾″ chamber.
Barrel: 24⅛″, rifled.
Weight: 9 lbs.
Length: 45½″ overall.
Stock: European walnut with checkered p.g. and forend.
Sights: None furnished. Drilled and tapped for scope mounting.
Features: Rifled bore. Quick interchangeable barrels; cross-bolt safety; engraved receiver; recoil pad. From Ballistic Research Industries.
Price: **$995.00**

BROWNING AUTO-5 LIGHT 12 AND 20, SWEET 16
Gauge: 12, 16, 20, 5-shot; 3-shot plug furnished; 2¾″ or 3″ chamber.
Action: Recoil operated autoloader; takedown.
Barrel: 26″, 28″, 30″ Invector (choke tube) barrel; also available with Light 20 ga. 28″ (Mod.) or 26″ (Imp. Cyl.) barrel.
Weight: 12, 16 ga. 7¼ lbs., 20 ga. 6⅜ lbs.
Stock: French walnut, hand checkered half-p.g. and forend. 14¼″x1⅝″x2½″.
Features: Receiver hand engraved with scroll designs and border. Double extractors, extra bbls. Interchangeable without factory fitting; mag. cut-off; cross-bolt safety. Imported from Japan by Browning.
Price: Light 12, 20, Sweet 16, vent. rib., Invector **$719.95**
Price: Extra Invector barrel **$249.95**
Price: Light 12 Buck Special **$724.95**
Price: 3″ Magnum Buck Special **$747.95**
Price: Extra fixed-choke barrel (Light 20 only) **$194.95**
Price: 12, 16, 20 Buck Special barrel **$254.95**

Browning Auto-5 Magnum 12
Same as standard Auto-5 except chambered for 3″ magnum shells (also handles 2¾″ magnum and 2¾″ HV loads). 28″ Mod., Full; 30″ and 32″ (Full) bbls. Comes with Invector choke tubes. 14″x1⅝″x2½″ stock. Recoil pad. Wgt. 8¾ lbs.
Price: With Invector choke tubes **$742.95**
Price: Extra Invector barrel **$249.95**

Browning Auto-5 Magnum 20
Same as Magnum 12 except 26″ or 28″ barrel with Invector choke tubes. With ventilated rib, 7½ lbs.
Price: Invector only **$742.95**
Price: Extra Invector barrel **$249.95**

BROWNING A-500G AUTO SHOTGUN
Gauge: 12, 3″ chamber.
Barrel: 26″, 28″, 30″, Invector choke tubes. Ventilated rib.
Weight: 7 lbs., 14 oz. (26″ bbl.). **Length:** 47½″ overall.
Stock: 14⅜″x1½″x2″. Select walnut with gloss finish, rounded pistol grip. Recoil pad standard.
Features: Gas-operated action with four-lug rotary bolt, cross-bolt safety. Interchangeable barrels. High-polish blue finish with light engraving on receiver and "A-500G" in gold color. Patented gas metering system to handle all loads. Built-in buffering system to absorb recoil, reduce stress on internal parts. Introduced 1990. Imported by Browning.
Price: **$639.95**
Price: Extra Invector barrels **$249.95**

BROWNING A-500R AUTO SHOTGUN
Gauge: 12 only, 3″ chamber.
Barrel: 24″ Buck Special, 26″, 28″, 30″ with Invector choke tubes.
Weight: 7 lbs., 7 oz. (30″ barrel).
Length: 49½″ overall (30″ bbl.).
Stock: 14¼″x1½″x2½″; select walnut with gloss finish; checkered p.g. and forend; black vent, recoil pad.
Sights: Metal bead front.
Features: Uses a short-recoil action with four-lug rotary bolt and composite and coil spring buffering system. Shoots all loads without adjustment. Has a magazine cut-off, Invector chokes. Introduced 1987. Imported from Belgium by Browning.
Price: **$559.95**
Price: A-500R Buck Special **$559.95**
Price: Extra Invector and Buck Special barrels **$199.95**

> Consult our Directory pages for the location of firms mentioned

CHURCHILL AUTOMATIC SHOTGUN
Gauge: 12, 2¾″ or 3″ chamber, 5-shot magazine.
Barrel: 24″, 25″, 26″, 28″ (choke tubes).
Weight: NA. **Length:** NA.
Stock: Walnut with satin finish, hand checkering.
Features: Gas-operated action, magazine cut-off, non-glare metal finish. Gold-colored trigger. Introduced 1990. Imported by Ellett Bros.
Price: **$549.95**
Price: Turkey, 25″ bbl. **$569.95**

COSMI AUTOMATIC SHOTGUN
Gauge: 12 or 20, 2¾″ or 3″ chamber.
Barrel: 22″ to 34″. Choke (including choke tubes) and length to customer specs. Boehler steel.
Weight: About 6¼ lbs. (20 ga.).
Stock: Length and style to customer specs. Hand-checkered exhibition grade circassian walnut standard.
Features: Hand-made, essentially a custom gun. Recoil-operated auto with tip-up barrel. Made completely of stainless steel (lower receiver polished); magazine tube in buttstock holds 7 rounds. Double ejectors, double safety system. Comes with fitted leather case. Imported from Italy by Incor, Inc.
Price: From **$7,400.00**

CAUTION: PRICES CHANGE, CHECK AT GUNSHOP.

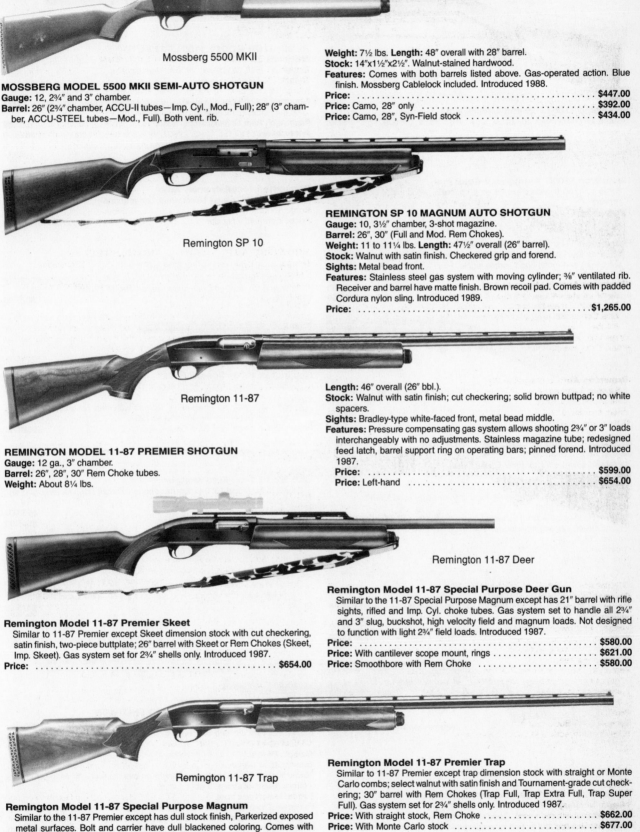

Mossberg 5500 MKII

MOSSBERG MODEL 5500 MKII SEMI-AUTO SHOTGUN
Gauge: 12, 2¾" and 3" chamber.
Barrel: 26" (2¾" chamber, ACCU-II tubes—Imp. Cyl., Mod., Full); 28" (3" chamber, ACCU-STEEL tubes—Mod., Full). Both vent. rib.

Weight: 7½ lbs. **Length:** 48" overall with 28" barrel.
Stock: 14"x1½"x2½". Walnut-stained hardwood.
Features: Comes with both barrels listed above. Gas-operated action. Blue finish. Mossberg Cablelock included. Introduced 1988.
Price: $447.00
Price: Camo, 28" only $392.00
Price: Camo, 28", Syn-Field stock $434.00

Remington SP 10

REMINGTON SP 10 MAGNUM AUTO SHOTGUN
Gauge: 10, 3½" chamber, 3-shot magazine.
Barrel: 26", 30" (Full and Mod. Rem Chokes).
Weight: 11 to 11¼ lbs. **Length:** 47½" overall (26" barrel).
Stock: Walnut with satin finish. Checkered grip and forend.
Sights: Metal bead front.
Features: Stainless steel gas system with moving cylinder; ⅜" ventilated rib. Receiver and barrel have matte finish. Brown recoil pad. Comes with padded Cordura nylon sling. Introduced 1989.
Price: $1,265.00

Remington 11-87

REMINGTON MODEL 11-87 PREMIER SHOTGUN
Gauge: 12 ga., 3" chamber.
Barrel: 26", 28", 30" Rem Choke tubes.
Weight: About 8¼ lbs.

Length: 46" overall (26" bbl.).
Stock: Walnut with satin finish; cut checkering; solid brown buttpad; no white spacers.
Sights: Bradley-type white-faced front, metal bead middle.
Features: Pressure compensating gas system allows shooting 2¾" or 3" loads interchangeably with no adjustments. Stainless magazine tube; redesigned feed latch, barrel support ring on operating bars; pinned forend. Introduced 1987.
Price: $599.00
Price: Left-hand $654.00

Remington 11-87 Deer

Remington Model 11-87 Special Purpose Deer Gun
Similar to the 11-87 Special Purpose Magnum except has 21" barrel with rifle sights, rifled and Imp. Cyl. choke tubes. Gas system set to handle all 2¾" and 3" slug, buckshot, high velocity field and magnum loads. Not designed to function with light 2¾" field loads. Introduced 1987.
Price: $580.00
Price: With cantilever scope mount, rings $621.00
Price: Smoothbore with Rem Choke $580.00

Remington Model 11-87 Premier Skeet
Similar to 11-87 Premier except Skeet dimension stock with cut checkering, satin finish, two-piece buttplate; 26" barrel with Skeet or Rem Chokes (Skeet, Imp. Skeet). Gas system set for 2¾" shells only. Introduced 1987.
Price: $654.00

Remington 11-87 Trap

Remington Model 11-87 Premier Trap
Similar to 11-87 Premier except trap dimension stock with straight or Monte Carlo combs; select walnut with satin finish and Tournament-grade cut checkering; 30" barrel with Rem Chokes (Trap Full, Trap Extra Full, Trap Super Full). Gas system set for 2¾" shells only. Introduced 1987.
Price: With straight stock, Rem Choke $662.00
Price: With Monte Carlo stock $677.00

Remington Model 11-87 Special Purpose Magnum
Similar to the 11-87 Premier except has dull stock finish, Parkerized exposed metal surfaces. Bolt and carrier have dull blackened coloring. Comes with 26" or 28" barrel with Rem Chokes, padded Cordura nylon sling and q.d. swivels. Introduced 1987.
Price: $599.00

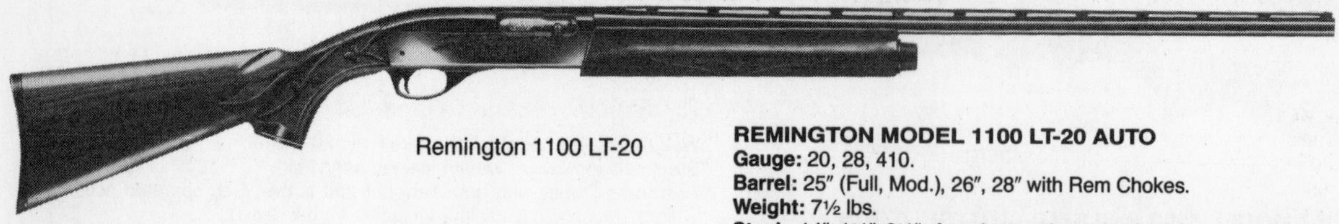

Remington 1100 LT-20

Remington 1100 LT-20 and Small Gauge
Same as 1100 except 20, 28 ga., 2¾", 410 bore, 3" (5-shot). 45½" overall. Available in 25" barrel (Full, Mod., or Imp. Cyl.) only.
Price: With vent rib, about $583.00
Price: 20 ga., 3" Magnum $583.00

Remington 1100D Tournament Auto
Same as 1100 Standard except vent. rib, better wood, more extensive engraving.
Price: About $2,383.00

Remington 1100 LT-20 Tournament Skeet
Same as the 1100 except 26" barrel, special Skeet boring, vent. rib, ivory bead front and metal bead middle sights. 14"x1½"x2½" stock. 20, 28, 410 ga. Wgt. 7½ lbs., cut checkering, walnut, new receiver scroll.
Price: Tournament Skeet (28, 410), about $662.00
Price: Tournament Skeet (20), about $662.00

REMINGTON MODEL 1100 LT-20 AUTO
Gauge: 20, 28, 410.
Barrel: 25" (Full, Mod.), 26", 28" with Rem Chokes.
Weight: 7½ lbs.
Stock: 14"x1½"x2½". American walnut, checkered p.g. and forend.
Features: Quickly interchangeable barrels. Matted receiver top with scroll work on both sides of receiver. Cross-bolt safety.
Price: With Rem Chokes, 20 ga. about $583.00
Price: 28 and 410 . . . . $625.00
Price: Youth Gun LT-20 (21" Rem Choke) $569.00

Remington 1100F Premier Auto
Same as 1100D except select wood, better engraving.
Price: About $4,910.00
Price: With gold inlay, about $7,364.00

Remington 1100 20 Ga. Deer Gun
Same as 1100 except 20 ga. only, 21" barrel (Imp. Cyl.), rifle sights adjustable for w. and e.; recoil pad with white spacer. Weight 7¼ lbs.
Price: About $525.00

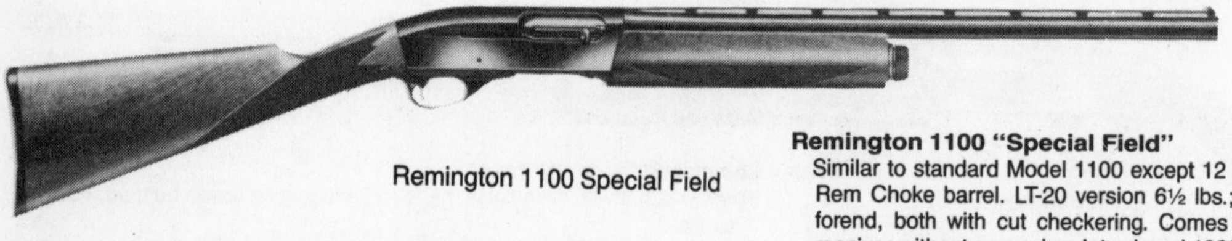

Remington 1100 Special Field

Remington 1100 "Special Field"
Similar to standard Model 1100 except 12 and 20 ga. only, comes with 21" Rem Choke barrel. LT-20 version 6½ lbs.; has straight-grip stock, shorter forend, both with cut checkering. Comes with vent rib only; matte finish receiver without engraving. Introduced 1983.
Price: 12 and 20 ga., 21" Rem Choke, about $583.00

SKB MODEL 1300 UPLAND MAG SHOTGUN
Gauge: 12, 2¾" or 3", 20, 3".
Barrel: 22" (Slug), 26", 28" (Inter Choke tubes).
Weight: 6½ to 7¼ lbs.
Length: 48¼" overall (28" barrel).
Stock: 14½"x1½"x2½". Walnut, with hand checkered grip and forend.
Sights: Metal bead front.
Features: Gas operated with Universal Automatic System. Blued receiver. Magazine cut-off system. Introduced 1988. Imported from Japan by Ernie Simmons Ent.
Price: Field $595.00
Price: 1300 Slug $595.00

SKB Model 3000 Auto Shotgun
Similar to the Model 1900 except has more elaborate engraving, initial plate in buttstock.
Price: Field $599.00
Price: Trap $725.00

SKB Model 1900 Auto Shotgun
Similar to the Model 1300 except has engraved bright-finish receiver, grip cap, gold-plated trigger. Introduced 1988.
Price: Field $655.00
Price: Slug gun (22" barrel, rifle sights) $655.00

SKB Model 1900 Trap
Similar to the Model 1900 Field except in 12 gauge only (2¾" chamber), 30" barrel with Inter Choke tubes and 9.5mm wide rib. Introduced 1988.
Price: $675.00

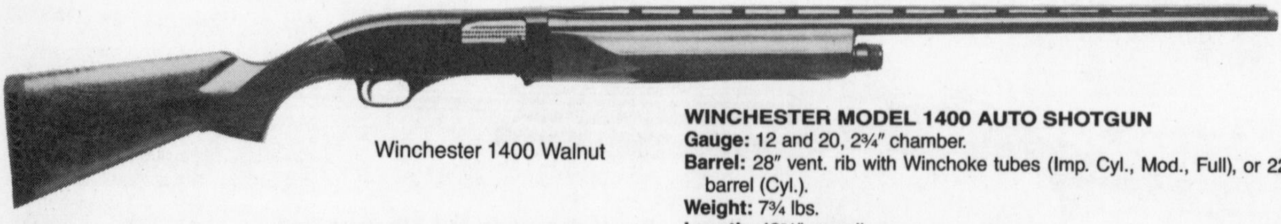

Winchester 1400 Walnut

Winchester Model 1400 Walnut "Slug Hunter"
Similar to the Model 1400 except in 12-ga. only with smooth bore 22" barrel, with adjustable open sights. Comes with Imp. Cyl. and Sabot choke tubes. Receiver is drilled and tapped for scope mounting, has threaded steel inserts and comes with bases. Walnut stock and forend with cut checkering. Introduced 1990. From U.S. Repeating Arms Co., Inc.
Price: $442.00

WINCHESTER MODEL 1400 AUTO SHOTGUN
Gauge: 12 and 20, 2¾" chamber.
Barrel: 28" vent. rib with Winchoke tubes (Imp. Cyl., Mod., Full), or 22" plain barrel (Cyl.).
Weight: 7¾ lbs.
Length: 48⅝" overall.
Stock: Walnut-finished hardwood, finger-grooved forend with deep cut checkering. Also available with walnut stock.
Sights: Metal bead front.
Features: Cross-bolt safety, front-locking rotary bolt, black serrated buttplate, gas-operated action. From U.S. Repeating Arms Co.
Price: Ranger, vent. rib with Winchoke, about $358.00
Price: As above with walnut stock (1400 Walnut) $398.00
Price: Deer barrel combo, about $440.00
Price: Deer gun, about $349.00

Includes a wide variety of sporting guns and guns suitable for competitive shooting.

ARMSCOR MODEL 30 D/IC PUMP SHOTGUN
Gauge: 12, 5-shot magazine.
Barrel: 26″, 30″ (Cyl., Mod., Full tubes).
Weight: 7.4 lbs.
Length: 47″ overall. (28″).
Stock: Plain mahogany.
Sights: Metal bead front.
Features: Double action bars; blue finish; grooved forend. Introduced 1987. Imported from the Philippines by Armscor.
Price: $234.95
Price: With rifle sights (Model 30 DG) $169.95

BRI "SPECIAL" RIFLED PUMP SHOTGUN
Gauge: 12, 3″ chamber.
Barrel: 24″ (Cyl.) rifled.
Weight: 7½ lbs.
Length: 44″ overall.
Stock: Walnut with high straight comb. Rubber recoil pad.
Sights: None. Comes with scope mount on barrel.
Features: Uses Mossberg Model 500 Trophy Slugster action; double slide bars, twin extractors, dual shell latches; top receiver safety. From Ballistic Research Industries. Introduced 1988.
Price: About $695.00

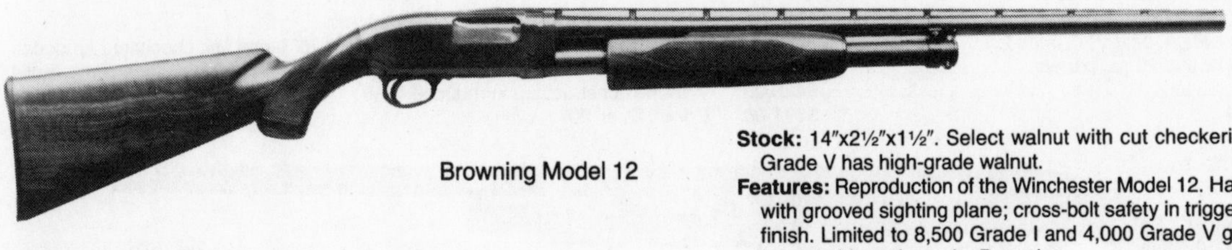

Browning Model 12

Stock: 14″x2½″x1½″. Select walnut with cut checkering, semi-gloss finish; Grade V has high-grade walnut.
Features: Reproduction of the Winchester Model 12. Has high post floating rib with grooved sighting plane; cross-bolt safety in trigger guard; polished blue finish. Limited to 8,500 Grade I and 4,000 Grade V guns. Introduced 1988. Imported from Japan by Browning.
Price: Grade I, 20-ga $734.95
Price: Grade V, 20-ga $1,187.00
Price: Grade I, 28-ga $771.95
Price: Grade V, 28-ga $1,246.00

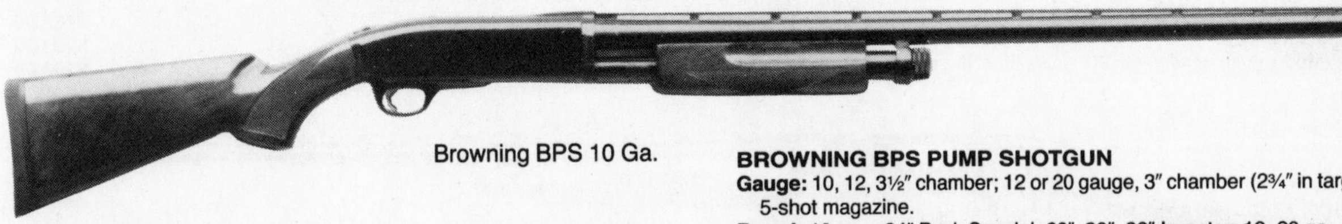

BROWNING MODEL 12 PUMP SHOTGUN
Gauge: 20, 28, 2¾″ chamber.
Barrel: 26″ (Mod.).
Weight: 7 lbs., 1 oz. **Length:** 45″ overall.

Browning BPS 10 Ga.

Browning BPS Pump Shotgun (Ladies and Youth Model)
Same as BPS Upland Special except 20 ga. only, 22″ Invector barrel, stock has pistol grip with recoil pad. Length of pull is 13¼″. Introduced 1986.
Price: $433.50

Browning BPS "Stalker" Pump Shotgun
Same gun as the standard BPS except all exposed metal parts have a matte blued finish and the stock has a durable black finish with a black recoil pad. Available in 10 ga. (3½″) and 12 ga. with 3″ or 3½″ chamber, 22″, 28″, 30″ barrel with Invector choke system. Introduced 1987.
Price: 12 ga., 3″ chamber $433.50
Price: 10, 12 ga., 3½″ chamber $534.95

BROWNING BPS PUMP SHOTGUN
Gauge: 10, 12, 3½″ chamber; 12 or 20 gauge, 3″ chamber (2¾″ in target guns), 5-shot magazine.
Barrel: 10 ga.—24″ Buck Special, 28″, 30″, 32″ Invector; 12, 20 ga.—22″, 24″, 26″, 28″, 30″, 32″ (Imp. Cyl., Mod. or Full). Also available with Invector choke tubes, 12 or 20 ga.; Upland Special has 22″ barrel with Invector tubes. BPS 3½″ has back-bored barrel.
Weight: 7 lbs., 8 oz. (28″ barrel). **Length:** 48¾″ overall (28″ barrel).
Stock: 14¼″x1½″x2½″. Select walnut, semi-beavertail forend, full p.g. stock.
Features: Bottom feeding and ejection, receiver top safety, high post vent. rib. Double action bars eliminate binding. Vent. rib barrels only. Introduced 1977. Imported from Japan by Browning.
Price: 10-ga., Hunting, Invector $534.95
Price: 12-ga., 3½″ Mag., Hunting, Invector PLUS $534.95
Price: 12-ga., Hunting $433.50
Price: 12-, 20-ga., Upland Special, Invector $433.50
Price: 10-ga. and 3½″ 12-ga. Mag., Buck Special $539.95
Price: 12-ga. Buck Special $439.50

Ithaca 87 Supreme

ITHACA MODEL 87 SUPREME PUMP SHOTGUN
Gauge: 12, 20, 3″ chamber, 5-shot magazine.
Barrel: 26″ (Imp. Cyl., Mod., Full tubes), 28″ (Mod.), 30″ (Full). Vent. rib.
Weight: 6¾ to 7 lbs.
Stock: 14″x1½″x2¼″. Full fancy-grade walnut, checkered p.g. and slide handle.
Sights: Raybar front.
Features: Bottom ejection, cross-bolt-safety. Polished and blued engraved receiver. Reintroduced 1988. From Ithaca Acquisition Corp.
Price: $819.00
Price: M87 Camo Vent (28″, Mod. choke tube, camouflage finish) .. $524.00
Price: M87 Field $458.00

Ithaca Model 87 Turkey Gun
Similar to the Model 87 Supreme except comes with 24″ (fixed Full or Full choke tube) barrel, either Camoseal camouflage or matte blue finish, oiled wood, blued trigger.
Price: With fixed choke, blue $409.00
Price: With choke tube, blue $420.00
Price: With fixed choke, Camoseal $514.00
Price: With choke tube, Camoseal $525.00

Ithaca Model 87 Deluxe Pump Shotgun
Similar to the Model 87 Supreme Vent. Rib except comes with choke tubes in 25″, 26″, 28″ (Mod.), 30″ (Full). Standard-grade walnut.
Price: $495.00

Ithaca Model 87 Ultra Field Pump Shotgun
Similar to the Model 87 Supreme except the receiver is made of aircraft-quality aluminum. Available in 12 ga., 2¾" chamber or 20 ga., 2¾" chamber, 25" (Mod.) with choke tube. Weight is 5 lbs. (20 ga.), 6 lbs. (12 ga.). Reintroduced 1988.
Price: **$481.00**
Price: Ultra Deluxe **$514.00**

ITHACA MODEL 87 DEERSLAYER SHOTGUN
Gauge: 12, 20, 3" chamber.
Barrel: 20", 25" (Special Bore), or rifled bore.
Weight: 6 to 6¾ lbs.
Stock: 14"x1½"x2¼". American walnut. Checkered p.g. and slide handle.
Sights: Raybar blade front on ramp, rear adjustable for windage and elevation, and grooved for scope mounting.
Features: Bored for slug shooting. Bottom ejection, cross-bolt safety. Reintroduced 1988. From Ithaca Acquisition Corp.
Price: **$391.00**
Price: Ultra Deerslayer (20 ga. only, 2¾", 5 lbs.) **$444.00**
Price: Deluxe Combo (12 and 20 ga. barrels) **$549.00**
Price: Deluxe **$429.00**
Price: Field Deerslayer **$391.00**

Ithaca Model 87 Basic Field Combo
Similar to the Model 87 Supreme except comes with 28" (choke tubes) and 20" or 25" (Deer, Special Bore) barrels. Oil-finished wood, no checkering, blued trigger.
Price: **$427.00**
Price: As above except with rifled barrel **$459.99**

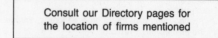

Consult our Directory pages for the location of firms mentioned

Ithaca Deerslayer II Rifled Shotgun
Similar to the Deerslayer except has rifled 25" barrel and checkered American walnut stock and forend with high gloss finish and Monte Carlo comb. Solid frame construction. Introduced 1988.
Price: 12 or 20 .... **$525.00**

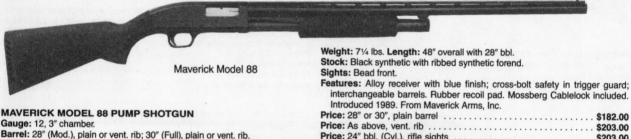

Maverick Model 88

MAVERICK MODEL 88 PUMP SHOTGUN
Gauge: 12, 3" chamber.
Barrel: 28" (Mod.), plain or vent. rib; 30" (Full), plain or vent. rib.

Weight: 7¼ lbs. **Length:** 48" overall with 28" bbl.
Stock: Black synthetic with ribbed synthetic forend.
Sights: Bead front.
Features: Alloy receiver with blue finish; cross-bolt safety in trigger guard; interchangeable barrels. Rubber recoil pad. Mossberg Cablelock included. Introduced 1989. From Maverick Arms, Inc.
Price: 28" or 30", plain barrel **$182.00**
Price: As above, vent. rib **$203.00**
Price: 24" bbl. (Cyl.), rifle sights **$203.00**

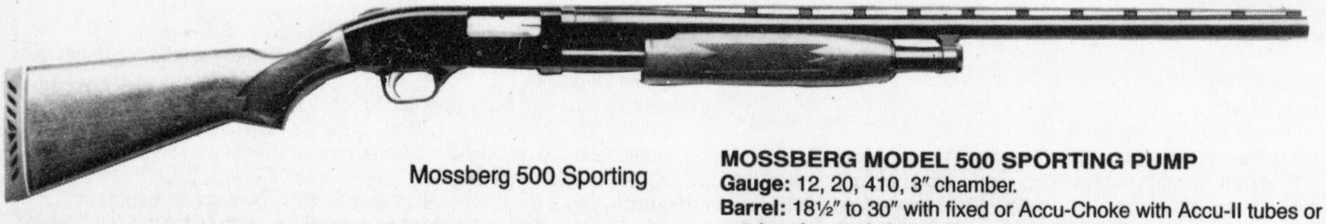

Mossberg 500 Sporting

Mossberg Model 500 Camo Pump
Same as the Model 500 Sporting Pump except entire gun is covered with special camouflage finish. Available with synthetic field or Speedfeed stock. Receiver drilled and tapped for scope mounting. Comes with q.d. swivel studs, swivels, camouflage sling, Mossberg Cablelock. In 12 ga. only.
Price: From about **$322.00**
Price: Camo Combo (as above with extra Slugster barrel), from about **$380.00**
Price: As above with 24" rifled bbl., about **$393.00**

MOSSBERG MODEL 500 SPORTING PUMP
Gauge: 12, 20, 410, 3" chamber.
Barrel: 18½" to 30" with fixed or Accu-Choke with Accu-II tubes or Accu-Steel tubes for steel shot, tubes, plain or vent. rib.
Weight: 6¼ lbs. (410), 7¼ lbs. (12).
Length: 48" overall (28" barrel).
Stock: 14"x1½"x2½". Walnut-stained hardwood. Checkered grip and forend.
Sights: White bead front, brass mid-bead.
Features: Ambidextrous thumb safety, twin extractors, disconnecting safety, dual action bars. Mossberg Cablelock included. From Mossberg.
Price: From about **$275.00**
Price: Sporting Combos (field barrel and Slugster barrel), from **$302.00**

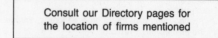

Mossberg 500 Trophy

MOSSBERG MODEL 500 TROPHY SLUGSTER
Gauge: 12, 3" chamber.
Barrel: 24", smooth or rifled bore. Plain (no rib).
Weight: 7¼ lbs. **Length:** 44" overall.
Stock: 14" pull, 1⅜" drop at heel. Walnut-stained hardwood; high comb design with recoil pad and q.d. swivel studs.
Features: Ambidextrous thumb safety, twin extractors, dual slide bars. Comes with scope mount. Mossberg Cablelock included. Introduced 1988.
Price: Smoothbore, about **$322.00**
Price: Rifled bore, about **$342.00**
Price: Smoothbore, rifle sights, about **$293.00**
Price: Rifled bore, rifle sights, about **$316.00**

MOSSBERG MODEL 835 ULTI-MAG PUMP
Gauge: 12, 3½" chamber.
Barrel: 24", 28", Accu-Mag with four choke tubes.
Weight: 7¾ lbs.
Length: 48½" overall.
Stock: 14"x1½"x2½". Walnut-stained hardwood or camo synthetic; both have recoil pad.
Sights: White bead front, brass mid-bead.
Features: Backbored barrel to reduce recoil, improve patterns. Ambidextrous thumb safety, twin extractors, dual slide bars. Mossberg Cablelock included. Introduced 1988.
Price: Blue, wood stock **$428.00**
Price: Camo finish, synthetic stock **$458.00**
Price: Waterfowl Limited Edition (camo.) **$480.00**

CAUTION: PRICES CHANGE, CHECK AT GUNSHOP.

Remington 870 "Wingmaster"

Remington 870 "Special Purpose" Magnum
Similar to the Model 870 except chambered only for 12-ga., 3" shells, vent. rib. 26" or 28" Rem Choke barrel. All exposed metal surfaces are finished in dull, non-reflective black. Wood has an oil finish. Comes with padded Cordura 2" wide sling, quick-detachable swivels. Chrome-lined bores. Dark recoil pad. Introduced 1985.
Price: About **$450.00**

Remington 870 TC Trap
Same as the M870 except 12 ga. only, 30" Rem Choke, vent. rib barrel, Ivory front and white metal middle beads. Special sear, hammer and trigger assy. 14⅜"x1½"x1⅞" stock with recoil pad. Hand fitted action and parts. Wgt. 8 lbs.
Price: Model 870TC Trap, Rem Choke, about **$587.00**
Price: TC Trap with Monte Carlo stock, about **$600.00**

REMINGTON MODEL 870 WINGMASTER
Gauge: 12, 3" chamber.
Barrel: 26", 28", 30" (Rem Chokes).
Weight: 7¼ lbs.
Length: 46½" overall (26" bbl.).
Stock: 14"x2½"x1". American walnut with satin finish, cut-checkered p.g. and forend. Rubber buttpad.
Sights: Ivory bead front, metal mid-bead.
Features: Double action bars; cross-bolt safety; blue finish. Available in right- or left-hand style. Introduced 1986.
Price: **$450.00**
Price: Left-hand (28" only) **$528.00**
Price: Brushmaster Deer Gun (rifle sights, 20" bbl., fixed choke) ... **$424.00**
Price: Deer Gun, left-hand **$485.00**
Price: LW-20 20 ga., vent. rib, 26", 28" (Rem Choke) **$450.00**
Price: As above, Youth Gun (21" Rem Choke, 13" stock) **$434.00**

Remington 870 Small Gauges
Exact copies of the large gauge Model 870, except that guns are offered in 28 ga. and 410 bore, 25" barrel (Full, Mod.). D and F grade prices same as large gauge M870 prices.
Price: With vent. rib barrel, about **$497.00**

Remington 870 Deer

Remington Model 870 Special Purpose Deer Gun
Similar to the 870 Wingmaster except available with 20" barrel with rifled and Imp. Cyl. choke tubes; rifle sights or cantilever scope mount with rings. Metal has black, non-glare finish, satin finish on wood. Recoil pad, detachable sling of camo Cordura nylon. Introduced 1989.
Price: With rifle sights **$424.00**
Price: With scope mount and rings **$496.00**

Remington 870 Special Field

Remington Model 870 "Special Field"
Similar to the standard Model 870 except comes with 21" barrel only, 3" chamber, choked Imp. Cyl., Mod., Full and Rem Choke; 12 ga. weighs 6¾ lbs., LW-20 weighs 6 lbs.; has straight-grip stock, shorter forend, both with cut checkering. Vent. rib barrel only. Introduced 1984.
Price: 12 or 20 ga., Rem Choke, about **$450.00**

Remington Model 870 Express
Similar to the 870 Wingmaster except has a walnut-toned hardwood stock with solid, black recoil pad and pressed checkering on grip and forend. Outside metal surfaces have a black oxide finish. Comes only with 28" vent. rib barrel with a Mod. Rem Choke tube. Introduced 1987.
Price: **$261.00**
Price: Express Combo (with extra 20" Deer barrel) **$358.00**

Remington 870 High Grades
Same as 870 except better walnut, hand checkering. Engraved receiver and barrel. Vent. rib. Stock dimensions to order.
Price: 870D, about **$2,383.00**
Price: 870F, about **$4,910.00**
Price: 870F with gold inlay, about **$7,364.00**

Winchester Model 1300

WINCHESTER MODEL 1300 FEATHERWEIGHT PUMP
Gauge: 12 and 20, 3" chamber, 5-shot capacity.
Barrel: 22", 28", vent. rib, with Full, Mod., Imp. Cyl. Winchoke tubes.
Weight: 6⅜ lbs.
Length: 42⅝" overall.
Stock: American walnut, with deep cut checkering on pistol grip, traditional ribbed forend; high luster finish.
Sights: Metal bead front.
Features: Twin action slide bars; front-locking rotating bolt; roll-engraved receiver; blued, highly polished metal; cross-bolt safety with red indicator. Introduced 1984. From U.S. Repeating Arms Co.
Price: About **$355.00**

SHOTGUNS—SLIDE ACTIONS

Winchester 1300 Rifled Slug

Winchester 1300 Waterfowl Pump
Similar to the 1300 Featherweight except in 3″ 12 ga. only, 28″ vent. rib barrel with Winchoke system; stock and forend of walnut with low-luster finish. All metal surfaces have special non-glare matte finish. Comes with sling. Introduced 1985.

Price: Walnut stock $367.00
Price: With brown laminated stock $367.00

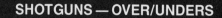

Winchester 1300 Slug Hunter

WINCHESTER RANGER PUMP GUN
Gauge: 12 or 20, 3″ chamber, 5-shot magazine.
Barrel: 28″ vent. rib with Full, Mod., Imp. Cyl. Winchoke tubes.

Winchester Ranger Ladies/Youth Pump Gun
Similar to the standard Ranger except chambered only for 3″ 20 ga., 22″ vent. rib barrel with Winchoke tubes (Full, Mod., Imp. Cyl.) or 22″ plain barrel with fixed Mod. choke. Weighs 6½ lbs., measures 41⅝″ o.a.l. Stock has 13″ pull length and gun comes with discount certificate for full-size stock. Introduced 1983. From U.S. Repeating Arms Co.

Price: Vent. rib barrel, Winchoke, about $294.00
Price: With walnut stock $338.00

Winchester Model 1300 Slug Hunter Deer Gun
Same as the Model 1300 except has rifled 22″ barrel, WinTuff laminated stock or walnut, rifle-type sights. Introduced 1990.

Price: Walnut stock $403.00
Price: Laminated stock $403.00

Winchester Model 1300 Turkey
Similar to the standard Model 1300 Featherweight except 12 ga. only, 30″ barrel with Mod., Full and Extra Full Winchoke tubes, matte finish wood and metal, and comes with recoil pad, Cordura sling and swivels.

Price: With WinCam green-shaded laminated stock, about $384.00
Price: National Wild Turkey Federation edition $403.00

Winchester Model 1300 "Slug Hunter"
Similar to the Model 1300 except in 12-ga. only with smooth bore 22″ barrel, with adjustable open sights. Comes with Imp. Cyl. and Sabot choke tubes. Receiver is drilled and tapped for scope mounting, and comes with bases. Walnut stock and forend with cut checkering. Introduced 1990. From U.S. Repeating Arms Co., Inc.

Price: $403.00

Winchester Ranger

Weight: 7 to 7¼ lbs.
Length: 48⅝″ to 50⅝″ overall.
Stock: Walnut-finished hardwood with ribbed forend.
Sights: Metal bead front.
Features: Cross-bolt safety, black rubber recoil pad, twin action slide bars, front-locking rotating bolt. From U.S. Repeating Arms Co.

Price: Vent. rib barrel, Winchoke, about $268.00

Winchester Ranger Pump Gun Combination
Similar to the standard Ranger except comes with two barrels: 22″ (Cyl.) deer barrel with rifle-type sights and an interchangeable 28″ vent. rib Winchoke barrel with Full, Mod. and Imp. Cyl. choke tubes. Available in 12 and 20 gauge 3″ only, with recoil pad. Introduced 1983.

Price: With two barrels, about $346.00

SHOTGUNS — OVER/UNDERS

Includes a variety of game guns and guns for competitive shooting.

American Arms Silver Sporting

American Arms Silver Lite O/U
Similar to the Silver I except has lightweight alloy receiver with blue finish and engraving. Available in 12- or 20-gauge only. Single selective trigger, automatic selective ejectors. Comes with 26″ barrel with Imp. Cyl., Mod., Full choke tubes. Introduced 1990. Imported by American Arms, Inc.

Price: $679.00

AMERICAN ARMS SILVER SPORTING O/U
Gauge: 12, 2¾″ chambers.
Barrel: 28″ (Skeet, Imp. Cyl., Mod., Full choke tubes).
Weight: 7⅜ lbs. **Length:** 45½″ overall.
Stock: 14⅜″x1½″x2⅜″. Figured walnut, cut checkering; Sporting Clays quick-mount buttpad.
Sights: Target bead front.
Features: Boxlock action with single selective trigger, automatic selective ejectors; special broadway channeled rib; vented barrel rib; chrome bores. Chrome-nickel finish on frame, with engraving. Introduced 1990. Imported from Spain by American Arms, Inc.

Price: $749.00

American Arms Silver II

American Arms Silver II Shotgun

Similar to the Silver I except 26″ barrel (Imp. Cyl., Mod., Full choke tubes, 12 and 20 ga.), 28″ (Imp. Cyl., Mod., Full choke tubes, 12 ga. only), 26″ (Imp. Cyl. & Mod. fixed chokes, 28 and 410), 26″ two-barrel set (Imp. Cyl. & Mod., fixed, 28 and 410); automatic selective ejectors. Weight is about 6 lbs., 15 oz. (12 ga., 26″).
Price: **$599.00**
Price: Two-barrel set (28, 410) **$879.00**

AMERICAN ARMS/FRANCHI SPORTING HUNTER O/U SHOTGUN

Gauge: 12, 3″ chambers.
Barrel: 28″ (Skeet, Imp. Cyl., Mod., Full choke tubes).
Weight: 7 lbs.
Stock: 14¼″x1½″x2⅜″. Figured walnut with cut checkering, semigloss finish; schnabel forend tip. Solid black recoil pad.
Features: Boxlock action with polished blue finish, gold accents. Single selective trigger, automatic selective ejectors, automatic safety. Introduced 1989. Imported from Italy by American Arms, Inc.
Price: **$1,229.99**

AMERICAN ARMS SILVER I O/U

Gauge: 12, 20, 28, 410, 3″ chamber (28 has 2¾″).
Barrel: 26″ (Imp. Cyl. & Mod., all gauges), 28″ (Mod. & Full, 12, 20).
Weight: About 6¾ lbs.
Stock: 14⅛″x1⅜″x2⅜″. Checkered walnut.
Sights: Metal bead front.
Features: Boxlock action with scroll engraving, silver finish. Single selective trigger, extractors. Chrome-lined barrels. Manual safety. Rubber recoil pad. Introduced 1987. Imported from Italy and Spain by American Arms, Inc.
Price: 12 or 20 gauge **$459.00**
Price: 28 or 410 . . . . **$499.00**

American Arms/Franchi Lightweight Hunter

Similar to the Sporting Hunter except comes in 12- or 20-gauge (2¾″ chambers), 26″ barrels with four Franchoke choke tubes. Weighs 6 lbs. Introduced 1989. Imported from Italy by American Arms, Inc.
Price: 12 or 20 . . . . **$1,189.00**

American Arms WT/OU 10 Shotgun

Similar to the WS/OU 12 except chambered for 10-gauge 3½″ shell, 26″ (Full & Full, choke tubes) barrel. Single selective trigger, extractors. Non-reflective finish on wood and metal. Imported by American Arms, Inc.
Price: **$839.00**

American Arms WS/OU 12

AMERICAN ARMS WS/OU 12 SHOTGUN

Gauge: 12, 3½″ chambers.
Barrel: 28″ (Imp. Cyl., Mod., Full choke tubes).
Weight: 6 lbs., 15 oz. **Length:** 46″ overall.
Stock: 14⅛″x1⅛″x2⅜″. European walnut with cut checkering, black vented recoil pad, matte finish.
Features: Boxlock action with single selective trigger, automatic selective ejectors; chrome bores. Matte metal finish. Imported by American Arms, Inc.
Price: **$599.00**

Armsport 2730

ARMSPORT MODEL 2700 O/U GOOSE GUN

Gauge: 10 ga., 3½″ chambers.
Barrel: 32″ (Full & Full).
Weight: About 9.8 lbs.
Stock: European walnut.
Features: Boss-type action; double triggers; extractors. Introduced 1986. Imported from Italy by Armsport.
Price: Fixed chokes **$950.00**

ARMSPORT 2700 SERIES O/U

Gauge: 10, 12, 20, 28, 410.
Barrel: 26″ (Imp. Cyl. & Mod.); 28″ (Mod. & Full); vent. rib.
Weight: 8 lbs.
Stock: European walnut, hand-checkered p.g. and forend.
Features: Single selective trigger, automatic ejectors, engraved receiver. Imported by Armsport. Contact Armsport for complete list of models.
Price: M2733/2735 (Boss-type action, 12, 20, extractors) **$620.00**
Price: M2741/2743 (as above with ejectors) **$675.00**
Price: M2730/2731 (as above with single trigger, screw-in chokes) . . **$775.00**
Price: M2705 (410 ga., 26″ Imp. & Mod., double triggers) **$620.00**

Armsport Tri-Barrel

ARMSPORT 2900 TRI-BARREL SHOTGUN

Gauge: 12, 3″ chambers.
Barrel: 28″ (choke tubes).
Weight: 7¾ lbs.
Stock: European walnut.
Features: Top-tang barrel selector; double triggers; silvered, engraved frame. Introduced 1986. Imported from Italy by Armsport.
Price: **$2,900.00**

SHOTGUNS — OVER/UNDERS

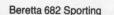

Beretta Onyx

BERETTA MODEL SO5, SO6, SO9 SHOTGUNS
Gauge: 12, 2¾" chambers.
Barrel: To customer's specs.
Stock: To customer's specs.
Features: SO5—Trap, Skeet and Sporting Clays models SO5 and SO5 EELL; SO6—SO6 and SO6 EELL are field models. SO6 has a case-hardened or silver receiver with contour hand engraving. SO6 EELL has hand-engraved receiver in a fine floral or "fine English" pattern or game scene, with bas-relief chisel work and gold inlays. SO6 and SO6 EELL are available, at no extra charge, with sidelocks removable by hand. Imported from Italy by Beretta U.S.A.
Price: SO5 Trap, Skeet, Sporting $11,000.00
Price: SO5 Combo, two-bbl. set $14,600.00
Price: SO6 Trap, Skeet, Sporting $14,400.00
Price: SO6 EELL Field, custom specs $23,600.00
Price: SO9 (12, 20, 28, 410, 26", 28", 30", any choke) $25,200.00

BERETTA OVER/UNDER FIELD SHOTGUNS
Gauge: 12, 20, 28, 2¾" and 3" chambers.
Barrel: 26" and 28" (fixed chokes or Mobilchoke tubes.).
Stock: Close-grained walnut.
Features: Highly-figured, American walnut stocks and forends, and a unique, weather-resistant finish on barrels. Available in two grades: Golden Onyx has individual game scenes of flushing pheasant and rising ducks on the receiver; the 686 Onyx bears a gold P. Beretta signature on each side of the receiver. Imported from Italy by Beretta U.S.A.
Price: 686 Onyx $1,167.00
Price: 686 two bbl. set $1,713.00
Price: 686 Field $1,147.00
Price: 687L Field $1,573.00
Price: 687 Golden Onyx $1,800.00
Price: 687 EL $2,607.00
Price: 687 EELL ....$3,767.00 to $3,820.00

Beretta 682 Sporting

BERETTA SPORTING CLAYS SHOTGUNS
Gauge: 12 and 20, 2¾" chambers.
Barrel: 28", 30", Mobilchoke.
Stock: Close-grained walnut.
Sights: Luminous front sight and center bead.
Features: Equipped with Beretta Mobilchoke flush-mounted screw-in choke tube system. Models vary according to grade, from field-grade Beretta 686 Sporting with its floral engraving pattern, to competition-grade Beretta 682 Sporting with its brushed satin finish and adjustable length of pull to the 687 Sporting with intricately hand-engraved game scenes, fine line, deep-cut checkering. Imported from Italy by Beretta U.S.A. Corp.
Price: 686 Sporting $1,653.00
Price: 682 Sporting, 30" $2,153.00
Price: 682 Super Sport, 28", 30", tapered rib $2,287.00
Price: 687 Sporting $2,173.00
Price: 687 Sporting (20-gauge) $2,173.00
Price: 687 EELL Sporter (hand engraved sideplates, deluxe wood) $4,000.00

BERETTA SERIES 682 COMPETITION OVER/UNDERS
Gauge: 12, 2¾" chambers.
Barrel: Skeet—26" and 28"; trap—30" and 32", Imp. Mod. & Full and Mobilchoke; trap mono shotguns—32" and 34" Mobilchoke; trap top single guns—32" and 34" Full and Mobilchoke; trap combo sets—from 30" o/u, 32" unsingle to 32" o/u, 34" top single.
Stock: Close-grained walnut, hand checkered.
Sights: Luminous front sight and center bead.
Features: Trap Monte Carlo stock has deluxe trap recoil pad. Various grades available; contact Beretta U.S.A. for details. Imported from Italy by Beretta U.S.A. Corp.
Price: 682 Skeet $2,073.00
Price: 682 Trap $2,053.00
Price: 682 Trap Mono shotguns $2,827.00
Price: 682 Trap Top Single shotguns $2,187.00
Price: 682 Trap Combo sets ....$2,773.00 to $2,827.00
Price: 687 EELL Trap ....$3,800.00 to $4,887.00
Price: 687 EELL Skeet (4-bbl. set) $6,767.00

Bernardelli Model 115

Bernardelli Model 115 Over/Under Shotgun
Similar to the Model 192 except designed for competition shooting with thicker barrel walls, specially designed stock with anatomical grip. Leather-faced recoil pad and schnabel forend on Sporting Clays and Skeet guns. Concave top rib, ventilated middle rib. Imported from Italy by Magnum Research.
Price: Model 115 S (inclined-plane locking, ejectors, selective or non-selective trigger, Multichoke standard on Sporting Clays) $2,713.00
Price: Model 115 L (as above with relief engraving) $4,201.00
Price: Model 115 E (as above with engraved sideplates) $6,827.00

BERNARDELLI WATERFOWL CLASSIC O/U SHOTGUN
Gauge: 12, 3½" chambers.
Barrel: 28" (Full, Mod., Imp. choke tubes).
Weight: 7 lbs.
Stock: European walnut with oil finish. Checkered grip and forend.

BERNARDELLI MODEL 192 MS-MC O/U SHOTGUN
Gauge: 12, 2¾" or 3" chambers.
Barrel: 25½" (Imp. Cyl. & Imp. Mod., Cyl. & Mod.), 26¾" (Imp. Cyl. & Imp. Mod., Mod. & Full), 28" (Mod. & Full), 29½" (Imp. Mod. & Full); or with Multichoke tubes.
Weight: About 7 lbs.
Stock: 14"x1⅜"x2⅜". Hand checkered European walnut. English or pistol grip style.
Features: Boxlock action; single selective trigger. Silvered, engraved action. Imported from Italy by Magnum Research.
Price: With Multichokes $1,320.00
Price: Model 192 Waterfowler (3½" chambers, three Multichoke tubes) $1,444.00
Price: Model 192 MS (Sporting Clays, non-selective or selective trigger) $1,698.00
Price: Model 220 MS (similar to M192 except 20 ga., different frame style) $1,334.00

Sights: Front and middle beads.
Features: Boxlock action with single selective trigger, automatic ejectors; rubber recoil pad. Introduced 1989. Imported from Italy by Cabela's.
Price: $899.95

SHOTGUNS — OVER/UNDERS

![BRNO Super over/under shotgun]

BRNO Super

BRNO SUPER OVER/UNDER SHOTGUN
Gauge: 12, 2¾" or 3" chambers.
Barrel: 27½" (Full & Mod.).
Weight: 7 lbs., 4 oz. (Field). **Length:** 44" overall.
Stock: Walnut, with raised cheekpiece.
Features: Sidelock action with double safety interceptor sears; double triggers on Field model; automatic selective ejectors; engraved sideplates. Trap and Skeet models available. Imported from Czechoslovakia by TD Arms.
Price: $899.00

BRNO 500 OVER/UNDER SHOTGUN
Gauge: 12, 2¾" chambers.
Barrel: 27½" (Full & Mod.).
Weight: 7 lbs. **Length:** 44½" overall.
Stock: Walnut, with raised cheekpiece.
Features: Boxlock action with ejectors; double triggers; acid-etched engraving. Imported from Czechoslovakia by TD Arms.
Price: $899.00

Browning Citori PLUS Trap Gun
Similar to the Grade I Citori Trap except comes only with 30" barrels with .745" over-bore, Invector PLUS choke system with Full, Imp. Mod. and Mod. choke tubes; high post, ventilated, tapered, target rib for adjustable impact from 3" to 12" above point of aim. Available with or without ported barrels. Select walnut stock has high-gloss finish, Monte Carlo comb, modified beavertail forend and is fully adjustable for length of pull, drop at comb and drop at Monte Carlo. Has Browning Recoil Reduction System. Introduced 1989.
Price: Grade I, with ported barrel $1,625.00
Price: Grade I, non-ported barrel $1,575.00

BABY BRETTON OVER/UNDER SHOTGUN
Gauge: 12 or 20, 2¾" chambers.
Barrel: 27½" (Cyl., Imp. Cyl., Mod., Full choke tubes).
Weight: About 5 lbs.
Stock: Walnut, checkered pistol grip and forend, oil finish.
Features: Receiver slides open on two guide rods, is locked by a large thumb lever on the right side. Extractors only. Light alloy barrels. Imported from France by Mandall Shooting Supplies.
Price: $895.00

BRNO ZH 301 OVER/UNDER SHOTGUN
Gauge: 12, 2¾" or 3" chambers.
Barrel: 27½" (Full & Mod.).
Weight: 7 lbs. **Length:** 44½" overall.
Stock: Walnut.
Features: Boxlock action with acid-etch engraving; double triggers. Imported from Czechoslovakia by TD Arms.
Price: $599.00

BRNO CZ 581 OVER/UNDER SHOTGUN
Gauge: 12, 2¾" or 3" chambers.
Barrel: 28" (Full & Mod.).
Weight: 7 lbs., 6 oz. **Length:** 45½" overall.
Stock: Turkish walnut with raised cheekpiece.
Features: Boxlock action; automatic selective ejectors; automatic safety; sling swivels; vent. rib; double triggers. Imported from Czechoslovakia by TD Arms.
Price: $649.00

![Browning Citori Gran Lightning]

Browning Citori Gran Lightning

BROWNING CITORI O/U SHOTGUN
Gauge: 12, 20, 28 and 410.
Barrel: 26", 28" (Mod. & Full, Imp. Cyl. & Mod.), in 28 and 410. Also offered with Invector choke tubes. Lightning 3½" has Invector PLUS back-bored barrels.
Weight: 6 lbs., 8 oz. (26" 410) to 7 lbs., 13 oz. (30" 12-ga.).
Length: 43" overall (26" bbl.).
Stock: Dense walnut, hand checkered, full p.g., beavertail forend. Field-type recoil pad on 12 ga. field guns and trap and Skeet models.
Sights: Medium raised beads, German nickel silver.
Features: Barrel selector integral with safety, automatic ejectors, three-piece takedown. Imported from Japan by Browning. Contact Browning for complete list of models and prices.
Price: Grade I Hunting, Invector, 12 and 20 . . . . $1,035.00
Price: Grade III, Invector, 12 and 20 . . . . $1,455.00
Price: Grade VI, Hunting, Invector, 12 and 20 . . . . $2,095.00
Price: Grade I, Hunting, 28 and 410, fixed chokes $1,025.00
Price: Grade III, Lightning, 28 and 410, fixed chokes $1,620.00
Price: Grade VI, 28 and 410, high post rib, fixed chokes $2,265.00
Price: Grade I Lightning, Invector, 12, 16, 20 . . . . $1,045.00
Price: Grade I Lightning, 28", 30" only, 3½", Invector PLUS $1,100.00
Price: Grade III Lightning, Invector, 12, 16, 20 . . . . $1,475.00
Price: Grade VI Lightning, Invector, 12, 16, 20 . . . . $2,125.00
Price: Gran Lightning, 26", 28", Invector $1,380.00

Browning Citori O/U Trap Models
Similar to standard Citori except 12 gauge only; 30", 32" ported or non-ported (Full & Full, Imp. Mod. & Full, Mod. & Full) or Invector PLUS, 34" single barrel in Combo Set (Full, Imp. Mod., Mod.), or Invector model; Monte Carlo cheekpiece (14⅜"x1⅜"x1⅜"x2"); fitted with trap-style recoil pad; conventional target rib and high post target rib.
Price: Grade I, Invector PLUS, ported bbls. $1,625.00
Price: As above, non-ported bbls. $1,575.00
Price: Grade I, Invector, high post target rib $1,160.00
Price: Grade III, Invector, high post target rib $1,600.00
Price: Grade VI, Invector, high post target rib $2,235.00

Browning Citori GTI

Browning Citori GTI Sporting Clays
Similar to the Citori Hunting except has semi-pistol grip with slightly grooved, semi-beavertail forend, satin-finish stock, radiused rubber buttpad. Has three interchangeable trigger shoes, trigger has three length of pull adjustments. Wide 13mm vent. rib, 28" or 30" barrels (ported or non-ported) with Invector PLUS choke tubes. Ventilated side ribs. Introduced 1989.
Price: With ported barrels $1,230.00
Price: With non-ported barrels $1,180.00

Browning Special Sporting Clays

Similar to the GTI except has full pistol grip stock with palm swell, gloss finish, 28″, 30″ or 32″ barrels with back-bored Invector PLUS chokes (ported or non-ported); high post tapered rib. Also available as 28″ and 30″ two-barrel set. Introduced 1989.

Price: With ported barrels $1,240.00
Price: With non-ported barrels $1,190.00
Price: With extra set of ported barrels $2,040.00
Price: With extra set of non-ported barrels $1,990.00

Browning Superlight Citori Over/Under

Similar to the standard Citori except available in 12, 20 with 24″, 26″ or 28″ Invector barrels, 28 or 410 with 26″ barrels choked Imp. Cyl. & Mod. or 28″ choked Mod. & Full. Has straight grip stock, schnabel forend tip. Superlight 12 weighs 6 lbs., 9 oz. (26″ barrels); Superlight 20, 5 lbs., 12 oz. (26″ barrels). Introduced 1982.

Price: Grade I only, 28 or 410 . . . .$1,025.00
Price: Grade III, Invector, 12 or 20 . . . .$1,480.00
Price: Grade III, 28 or 410 . . . .$1,600.00
Price: Grade VI, Invector, 12 or 20 . . . .$2,140.00
Price: Grade VI, 28 or 410 . . . .$2,235.00
Price: Grade I Invector, 12 or 20 . . . .$1,055.00
Price: Grade I Invector, Upland Special (24″ bbls.), 12 or 20 . . . . .$1,055.00

Browning Citori O/U Skeet Models

Similar to standard Citori except 26″, 28″ (Skeet & Skeet) only; stock dimensions of 14⅜″x1½″x2″, fitted with Skeet-style recoil pad; conventional target rib and high post target rib.

Price: Grade I Invector (high post rib) $1,150.00
Price: Grade I, 28 and 410 (high post rib) $1,155.00
Price: Grade III, 12 and 20 (high post rib) $1,600.00
Price: Grade VI, 12 and 20 (high post rib) $2,235.00
Price: Four barrel Skeet set—12, 20, 28, 410 barrels, with case, Grade I only $3,710.00
Price: Grade III, four-barrel set (high post rib) $4,230.00
Price: Grade VI, four-barrel set (high post rib) $4,740.00
Price: Grade I, three-barrel set $2,585.00
Price: Grade III, three-barrel set $2,980.00
Price: Grade VI, three-barrel set $3,640.00

> Consult our Directory pages for
> the location of firms mentioned

Browning Lightning Clays

Browning Lightning Sporting Clays

Similar to the Citori Lightning with rounded pistol grip and classic forend. Has high post tapered rib or lower hunting-style rib with 30″ back-bored Invector PLUS barrels, ported or non-ported. Gloss stock finish, radiused recoil pad. Has "Lightning Sporting Clays Edition" engraved and gold filled on receiver. Introduced 1989.

Price: Low-rib, ported $1,190.00
Price: High-rib, ported $1,240.00
Price: Low-rib, non-ported $1,140.00
Price: High-rib, non-ported $1,190.00

CHAPUIS OVER/UNDER SHOTGUN

Gauge: 12, 16, 20.
Barrel: 22″, 23.6″, 26.8″, 27.6″, 31.5″, chokes to customer specs.
Weight: 5 to 10 lbs. **Length:** NA.
Stock: French walnut, straight English or pistol grip.
Features: Double hook blitz system center sidelock action with notched action zone, automatic ejectors or extractors. Long trigger guard (most models), choice of raised solid rib, vent. rib or ultra light rib. Imported from France by Armes de Chasse.
Price: About $3,500.00

Chapuis Over/Under

CHURCHILL WINDSOR IV OVER/UNDER SHOTGUNS

Gauge: 12, 20, 28, 410, 3″ chambers.
Barrel: 26″ (Skeet & Skeet, Imp. Cyl. & Mod.), 28″ (Mod. & Full), 30″ (Mod. & Full, Full & Full), 12 ga.; 26″ (Skeet & Skeet, Imp. Cyl. & Mod.), 28″ (Mod. & Full), 20 ga.; 25″, 26″ (Imp. Cyl. & Mod.), 28″ (Mod. & Full), 28 ga.; 24″, 26″ (Full & Full), 410 bore; or 27″, 30″ ICT choke tubes.
Stock: European walnut, checkered pistol grip, oil finish.
Features: Boxlock action with silvered, engraved finish; single selective trigger; automatic ejectors. Imported from Italy by Ellett Bros. Introduced 1984.
Price: Windsor IV, 12 and 20 . . . .$851.95
Price: Windsor IV, 28 and 410 . . . .$799.95

Churchill Monarch

CHURCHILL MONARCH OVER/UNDER SHOTGUNS

Gauge: 12 or 20, 28, 410, 3″ chambers.
Barrel: 26″ (410, Mod. & Full), 26″ (Imp. Cyl. & Mod.), 28″ (Mod. & Full). Chrome-lined.
Weight: 12 ga.—7½ lbs., 20 ga.—6½ lbs.
Stock: European walnut with checkered p.g. and forend.
Features: Single selective trigger; blued, engraved receiver; vent. rib. Introduced 1986. Imported by Ellett Bros.
Price: 12-ga., blued receiver $515.95
Price: 20-ga., blued receiver $528.95
Price: 12- or 20-ga., silvered receiver $549.95
Price: 28-ga., silvered receiver $595.95
Price: 410-bore, 26″ (Mod. & Full) $609.95
Price: Turkey Model (12-ga., 24″, Mod. & Full) $779.95

Churchill Regent V Over/Under Shotguns

Similar to the Windsor except better engraving; available only in 12 or 20 gauge (3″ chambers), 28″ barrels, with ICT interchangeable choke tubes (Imp. Cyl., Mod., Full). Dummy sideplates. Introduced 1984.
Price: Regent V, 12 or 20 ga. $921.20

CHARLES DALY FIELD GRADE O/U
Gauge: 12 or 20, 3″ chambers.
Barrel: 12 and 20 ga.—26″ (Imp. Cyl. & Mod.), 12 ga.—28″ (Mod. & Full).
Weight: 6 lbs., 15 oz. (12 ga.), 6 lbs. 10 oz. (20 ga.). **Length:** 43½″ overall (26″ bbl.).
Stock: 14⅛″x1⅜″x2⅜″. Walnut with cut-checkered grip and forend. Black, vent. rubber recoil pad. Semi-gloss finish.
Features: Boxlock action with manual safety; extractors; single selective trigger. Color case-hardened receiver with engraving. Introduced 1989. Imported from Europe by Outdoor Sports Headquarters.
Price: $460.00

Charles Daly Lux Over/Under
Similar to the Field Grade except has automatic selective ejectors, antique silver finish on frame, and has choke tubes for Imp. Cyl., Mod. and Full. Introduced 1989.
Price: $650.00

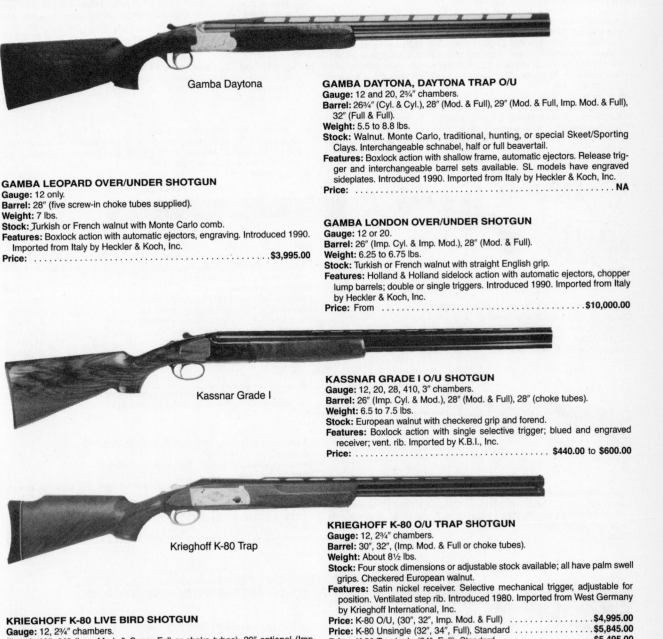

Gamba Daytona

Kassnar Grade I

Krieghoff K-80 Trap

GAMBA DAYTONA, DAYTONA TRAP O/U
Gauge: 12 and 20, 2¾″ chambers.
Barrel: 26¾″ (Cyl. & Cyl.), 28″ (Mod. & Full), 29″ (Mod. & Full, Imp. Mod. & Full), 32″ (Full & Full).
Weight: 5.5 to 8.8 lbs.
Stock: Walnut. Monte Carlo, traditional, hunting, or special Skeet/Sporting Clays. Interchangeable schnabel, half or full beavertail.
Features: Boxlock action with shallow frame, automatic ejectors. Release trigger and interchangeable barrel sets available. SL models have engraved sideplates. Introduced 1990. Imported from Italy by Heckler & Koch, Inc.
Price: .... NA

GAMBA LEOPARD OVER/UNDER SHOTGUN
Gauge: 12 only.
Barrel: 28″ (five screw-in choke tubes supplied).
Weight: 7 lbs.
Stock: Turkish or French walnut with Monte Carlo comb.
Features: Boxlock action with automatic ejectors, engraving. Introduced 1990. Imported from Italy by Heckler & Koch, Inc.
Price: $3,995.00

GAMBA LONDON OVER/UNDER SHOTGUN
Gauge: 12 or 20.
Barrel: 26″ (Imp. Cyl. & Imp. Mod.), 28″ (Mod. & Full).
Weight: 6.25 to 6.75 lbs.
Stock: Turkish or French walnut with straight English grip.
Features: Holland & Holland sidelock action with automatic ejectors, chopper lump barrels; double or single triggers. Introduced 1990. Imported from Italy by Heckler & Koch, Inc.
Price: From $10,000.00

KASSNAR GRADE I O/U SHOTGUN
Gauge: 12, 20, 28, 410, 3″ chambers.
Barrel: 26″ (Imp. Cyl. & Mod.), 28″ (Mod. & Full), 28″ (choke tubes).
Weight: 6.5 to 7.5 lbs.
Stock: European walnut with checkered grip and forend.
Features: Boxlock action with single selective trigger; blued and engraved receiver; vent. rib. Imported by K.B.I., Inc.
Price: .... $440.00 to $600.00

KRIEGHOFF K-80 O/U TRAP SHOTGUN
Gauge: 12, 2¾″ chambers.
Barrel: 30″, 32″, (Imp. Mod. & Full or choke tubes).
Weight: About 8½ lbs.
Stock: Four stock dimensions or adjustable stock available; all have palm swell grips. Checkered European walnut.
Features: Satin nickel receiver. Selective mechanical trigger, adjustable for position. Ventilated step rib. Introduced 1980. Imported from West Germany by Krieghoff International, Inc.
Price: K-80 O/U, (30″, 32″, Imp. Mod. & Full) $4,995.00
Price: K-80 Unsingle (32″, 34″, Full), Standard $5,845.00
Price: K-80 Topsingle (34″, Full), Standard $5,495.00
Price: K-80 Combo (two-barrel set), Standard $7,500.00

KRIEGHOFF K-80 LIVE BIRD SHOTGUN
Gauge: 12, 2¾″ chambers.
Barrel: 28″, 30″ (Imp. Mod. & Super Full or choke tubes), 29″ optional (Imp. Mod. & Special Full).
Weight: About 8 lbs.
Stock: Four stock dimensions available. Checkered walnut.
Features: Steel receiver with satin gray finish, engraving. Selective mechanical trigger adjustable for position. Ventilated step rib. Free-floating barrels. Comes with aluminum case. Introduced 1980. Imported from West Germany by Krieghoff International.
Price: Standard grade $4,995.00

Krieghoff K-80/RT Shotguns
Same as the standard K-80 shotguns except has a removable internally selective trigger mechanism. Can be considered an option on all K-80 guns of any configuration. Introduced 1990.
Price: RT (removable trigger) option on K-80 guns, add $1,200.00
Price: Extra trigger mechanisms $950.00

Krieghoff K-80 Clays

KRIEGHOFF K-80 SPORTING CLAYS O/U
Gauge: 12, 2¾" chambers.
Barrel: 28" or 30" with choke tubes.
Weight: About 8 lbs.
Stock: #3 Sporting stock designed for gun-down shooting.
Features: Choice of standard or lightweight receiver with satin nickel finish and classic scroll engraving. Selective mechanical trigger adjustable for position. Choice of tapered flat, 8mm parallel flat, or step-tapered barrel rib. Free-floating barrels. Aluminum case. Imported from West Germany by Krieghoff International, Inc.
Price: Standard grade with five choke tubes $5,550.00

KRIEGHOFF K-80 SKEET SHOTGUN
Gauge: 12, 2¾" chambers.
Barrel: 28" (Skeet & Skeet, optional Tula or choke tubes).
Weight: About 7¾ lbs.
Stock: American Skeet or straight Skeet stocks, with palm-swell grips. Walnut.
Features: Satin gray receiver finish. Selective mechanical trigger adjustable for position. Choice of ventilated 8mm parallel flat rib or ventilated 8-12mm tapered flat rib. Introduced 1980. Imported from West Germany by Krieghoff International, Inc.
Price: Standard, Skeet chokes $4,890.00
Price: As above, Tula chokes $5,090.00
Price: Lightweight model (weighs 7 lbs.), Standard $4,890.00
Price: Two-Barrel Set (tube concept), 12 ga. Standard $8,700.00
Price: Skeet Special (28", tapered flat rib, Skeet & Skeet choke tubes) $5,250.00

Krieghoff K-80 Four-Barrel Skeet Set
Similar to the Standard Skeet except comes with barrels for 12, 20, 28, 410. Comes with fitted aluminum case.
Price: Standard grade $9,985.00

Krieghoff K-80 International Skeet
Similar to the Standard Skeet except has ½" ventilated Broadway-style rib, special Tula chokes with gas release holes at muzzle. International Skeet stock. Comes in fitted aluminum case.
Price: Standard grade $5,250.00

Laurona Super 85MS

LAURONA SUPER MODEL OVER/UNDERS
Gauge: 12, 20, 2¾" or 3" chambers.
Barrel: 26", 28" (Multichoke), 29" (Multichokes and Full).
Weight: About 7 lbs.
Stock: European walnut. Dimensions vary according to model. Full pistol grip.

Features: Boxlock action, silvered with engraving. Automatic selective ejectors; choke tubes available on most models; single selective or twin single triggers; black chrome barrels. Has 5-year warranty, including metal finish. Imported from Spain by Galaxy Imports.
Price: Model 83 MG, 12 or 20 ga. $1,215.00
Price: Model 84S Super Trap (fixed chokes) $1,340.00
Price: Model 85 Super Game, 12 or 20 ga. $1,215.00
Price: Model 85 MS Super Trap (Full/Multichoke) $1,390.00
Price: Model 85 MS Super Pigeon $1,370.00
Price: Model 85 S Super Skeet, 12 ga. $1,300.00
Price: Model 85 MS Spec. Sporting, 12 ga. $1,325.00

Laurona Sporting Clays

LAURONA SILHOUETTE 300 SPORTING CLAYS
Gauge: 12, 2¾" chambers.
Barrel: 28" (Multichoke tubes, flush-type or knurled).
Weight: 7 lbs., 4 oz.
Stock: 14⅜"x1⅜"x2½". European walnut with full pistol grip, beavertail forend. Rubber buttpad.
Features: Selective single trigger, automatic selective ejectors. Introduced 1988. Imported from Spain by Galaxy Imports.
Price: $1,250.00
Price: Silhouette Ultra-Magnum, 3½" chambers $1,265.00

Laurona Silhouette 300 Trap
Same gun as the Silhouette 300 Sporting Clays except has 29" barrels, trap stock dimensions of 14⅜"x1⅞"x1⅝", weighs 7 lbs., 15 oz. Available with flush or knurled Multichokes.
Price: $1,310.00

Ljutic LM-6

LJUTIC T.C. LM-6 DELUXE O/U SHOTGUN
Gauge: 12 ga.
Barrel: 28" to 34", choked to customer specs for live birds, trap, International Trap.
Weight: To customer specs.
Stock: To customer specs. Oil finish, hand checkered.
Features: Custom-made gun. Hollow-milled rib, pull or release trigger, push-button opener in front of trigger guard. From Ljutic Industries.
Price: Super Deluxe LM-6 o/u $9,984.00
Price: Over/under Combo (interchangeable single barrel, two trigger guards, one for single trigger, one for doubles) $14,995.00
Price: Extra over/under barrel sets, 29"-32" $4,995.00

Ljutic Four-Barrel Skeet Set
LM-6 over/under 12-ga. frame with matched set of four 28" barrels in 12, 20, 28 and 410. Ljutic Paternator chokes and barrel are integral. Stock is to customer specs, of fine American or French walnut with EX (or Extra) Fancy checkering.
Price: Four-barrel set $26,995.00

SHOTGUNS — OVER/UNDERS

Marocchi Avanza

MAROCCHI AVANZA O/U SHOTGUN
Gauge: 12 and 20, 3″ chambers.
Barrel: 26″ (Mod. & Full or Imp. Cyl., Mod., Full Interchokes); 28″ (Mod. & Full or Imp. Cyl. Mod., Full Interchokes).

Weight: 6 lbs., 6 oz. to 6 lbs., 13 oz.
Stock: 14″x2¼″x1½″. Select walnut with cut checkering. Recoil pad.
Features: Single selective trigger, auto-mechanical barrel cycling, automatic selective ejectors, unbreakable firing pins. Ventilated top and middle ribs. Automatic safety. Introduced 1990. Imported from Italy by Precision Sales International.
Price: 12 ga., 26″ or 28″, fixed chokes $879.50
Price: As above, with Interchokes $979.50
Price: 20 ga., 26″ or 28″, fixed chokes $910.00
Price: As above, with Interchokes $1,010.00

Merkel Over/Under

MERKEL OVER/UNDER SHOTGUNS
Gauge: 12, 16, 20, 28, 410, 2¾″, 3″ chambers.
Barrel: 26″, 26¾″, 28″ (standard chokes).
Weight: 6 to 7 lbs.

Stock: European walnut. Straight English or pistol grip.
Features: Models 200E and 201E are boxlocks, 203E and 303E are sidelocks. All have auto. ejectors, articulated front triggers. Auto. safety, selective and non-selective triggers optional. Imported from East Germany by Armes de Chasse.
Price: 200E, about $3,500.00
Price: 201E, about $4,500.00
Price: 203E (sidelock), about $9,000.00
Price: 303E (sidelock), about $10,000.00

Navy Bird Hunter

NAVY ARMS MODEL 83/93 BIRD HUNTER O/U
Gauge: 12, 20, 3″ chambers.
Barrel: 28″ (Imp. Cyl. & Mod., Mod. & Full).
Weight: About 7½ lbs.

Stock: European walnut, checkered grip and forend.
Sights: Metal bead front.
Features: Boxlock action with double triggers; extractors only; silvered, engraved receiver; vented top and middle ribs. Imported from Italy by Navy Arms. Introduced 1984.
Price: Model 83 (extractors) $320.00
Price: Model 93 (ejectors) $380.00

NAVY ARMS MODEL 100 O/U SHOTGUN
Gauge: 12, 20, 28, 2¾″ chambers, 410, 3″ chambers.
Barrel: 12 ga.—28″ (Imp. Cyl. & Mod., Mod. & Full); 20 ga.—28″ (Imp. Cyl. & Mod., Skeet & Skeet); 28 ga.—28″ (Full & Mod., Skeet & Skeet); 410 bore—26″ (Full & Full, Skeet & Skeet).
Weight: 6¼ lbs.
Stock: European walnut; checkered p.g. and forend.
Features: Chrome-lined barrels, hard chrome finished receiver with engraving, vent. rib. Single trigger. Imported from Italy by Navy Arms. Introduced 1986.
Price: $250.00

Navy Arms Model 95/96
Same as the 83/93 Bird Hunter except comes with five interchangeable choke tubes. Model 96 has gold-plated single trigger and ejectors.
Price: Model 95 (extractors) $420.00
Price: Model 96 (ejectors) $530.00

PACHMAYR/PERAZZI MX-20 OVER/UNDER
Gauge: 20, 3″ chambers.
Barrel: 26″ (Cyl., Imp. Cyl., Mod., Imp. Mod., Full choke tubes). Fixed chokes available.
Weight: 6 lbs., 8 oz.
Stock: 14½″x1⅜″x2¼″x1½″; select European walnut with 26 lpl checkering, checkered butt.
Sights: Nickel silver front bead.
Features: Boxlock action, uses special 20-gauge frame. Carved schnabel-type forend. Single selective trigger, automatic selective ejectors, manual safety. Comes with lockable fitted case. Introduced 1986. From Pachmayr, Ltd.
Price: $4,995.00

Pachmayr/Perazzi

PERAZZI MX8/MX8 SPECIAL TRAP, SKEET
Gauge: 12, 2¾″ chambers.
Barrel: Trap—29½″ (Imp. Mod. & Extra Full), 31½″ (Full & Extra Full). Choke tubes optional. Skeet—27⅝″ (Skeet & Skeet).
Weight: About 8½ lbs. (Trap); 7 lbs., 15 oz. (Skeet).
Stock: Interchangeable and custom made to customer specs.
Features: Has detachable and interchangeable trigger group with flat V springs. Flat ⁷⁄₁₆″ ventilated rib. Many options available. Imported from Italy by Perazzi U.S.A., Inc.
Price: From $5,350.00
Price: MX8 Special (adj. four-position trigger), from $5,600.00
Price: MX8 Special Single (32″ or 34″ single barrel, step rib), from $5,350.00
Price: MX8 Special Combo (o/u and single barrel sets), from $7,650.00

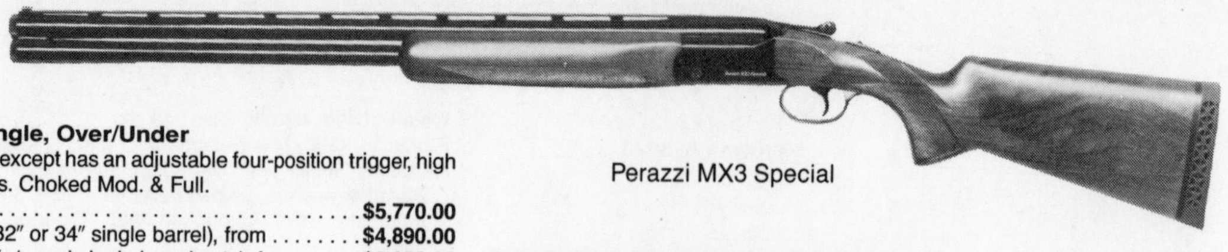

Perazzi MX3 Special

Perazzi MX3 Special Single, Over/Under
Similar to the MX8 Special except has an adjustable four-position trigger, high 7/16"x5/16" rib, weighs 8½ lbs. Choked Mod. & Full.
Price: From $5,770.00
Price: MX3 Special Single (32" or 34" single barrel), from $4,890.00
Price: MX3 Special Combo (o/u and single barrel sets), from $6,850.00

Perazzi Mirage Special Skeet Over/Under
Similar to the MX8 Skeet except has adjustable four-position trigger, Skeet stock dimensions.
Price: From $5,770.00

Perazzi Grand American 88 Special
Similar to the MX8 except has tapered 7/16"x5/16" high ramped rib. Choked Imp. Mod. & Full, 29½" barrels.
Price: From $7,650.00
Price: Special Single (32" or 34" single barrel), from $5,350.00
Price: DB81 Special, from $5,550.00

Perazzi MX1, MX1B Special Over/Under
Similar to the MX8 except has ramped, tapered rib, interchangeable trigger assembly with leaf hammer springs, 27⅝" barrels choked Imp. Mod. & Extra Full. Weight is 7 lbs., 12 oz.
Price: From $5,510.00
Price: MX1B (as above except has flat conventional rib), from $5,510.00

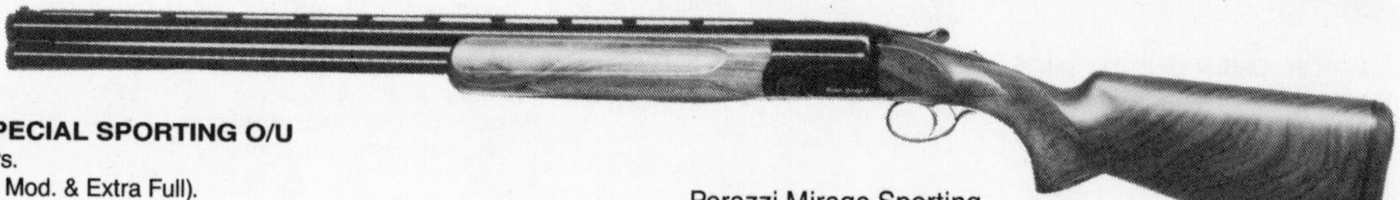

Perazzi Mirage Sporting

PERAZZI MIRAGE SPECIAL SPORTING O/U
Gauge: 12, 2¾" chambers.
Barrel: 27⅝", 28⅜" (Imp. Mod. & Extra Full).
Weight: 7 lbs., 12 oz.
Stock: Special specifications.
Features: Has single selective trigger; flat 7/16"x5/16" vent. rib. Many options available. Imported from Italy by Perazzi U.S.A., Inc.
Price: $6,000.00

Perazzi Mirage Special Four-Gauge Skeet
Similar to the Mirage Sporting model except has Skeet dimensions, interchangeable, adjustable four-position trigger assembly. Comes with four barrel sets in 12, 20, 28, 410, flat 5/16"x5/16" rib.
Price: From $13,400.00
Price: MX3 Special Set, from $12,000.00

Perazzi MX20C

PERAZZI MX12 HUNTING OVER/UNDER
Gauge: 12, 2¾" chambers.
Barrel: 26", 27⅝", 28⅜", 29½" (Mod. & Full); choke tubes available in 27⅝", 29½" only (MX12C).
Weight: 7 lbs., 4 oz.
Stock: To customer specs; Interchangeable.
Features: Single selective trigger; coil springs used in action; schnabel forend tip. Imported from Italy by Perazzi U.S.A., Inc.
Price: From $5,360.00
Price: MX12C (with choke tubes), from $5,670.00

Perazzi MX20 Hunting Over/Under
Similar to the MX12 except 20-ga. frame size. Available in 20, 28, 410 with 2¾" or 3" chambers. 26" standard, and choked Mod. & Full. Weight is 6 lbs., 6 oz.
Price: From $5,870.00
Price: MX20C (as above, 20 ga. only, choke tubes), from $6,180.00

Ruger 12 Ga. Red Label

RUGER "RED LABEL" O/U SHOTGUN
Gauge: 20 and 12, 3" chambers.
Barrel: 12, 20 ga.—26", 28" (Skeet, Imp. Cyl., Full, Mod. Screw-In choke tubes).
Weight: About 7 lbs. (20 ga.), 7½ lbs. (12 ga.). **Length:** 43" overall (26" barrels).
Stock: 14"x1½"x2½". Straight grain American walnut. Checkered p.g. and forend, rubber recoil pad.
Features: Automatic safety/barrel selector, stainless steel trigger and receiver. Patented barrel side spacers may be removed if desired. Available only with stainless receiver. 20 ga. Introduced 1977; 12 ga. Introduced 1982.
Price: 12 or 20 .... $1,102.50

SKB MODEL 505 OVER/UNDER SHOTGUN
Gauge: 12, 2¾" or 3", 20, 3", 28, 2¾", 410, 3".
Barrel: 12 ga.—26", 28", 30" (Imp. Cyl. & Mod., Mod. & Full or Inter Choke tubes); 20 ga.—26", 28" (Imp. Cyl. & Mod., Mod. & Full or Inter Choke tubes); 28 and 410—26", 28" (Imp. Cyl. & Mod., Mod. & Full).
Weight: 6.6 to 7.4 lbs.
Length: 45 3/16" overall.
Stock: 14⅛"x1½"x2 3/16". Hand checkered walnut.
Sights: Metal bead front.
Features: Blued boxlock action; ejectors; single selective trigger. Introduced 1988. Imported from Japan by Ernie Simmons Enterprises.
Price: $1,025.00
Price: Two-barrel Field Set, 12 and 20, choke tubes $1,550.00
Price: Model 505 Trap, Skeet $1,025.00
Price: Model 505 Single Barrel Trap $1,025.00
Price: Skeet set, 20, 28, 410 .... $2,365.00

CAUTION: PRICES CHANGE, CHECK AT GUNSHOP.

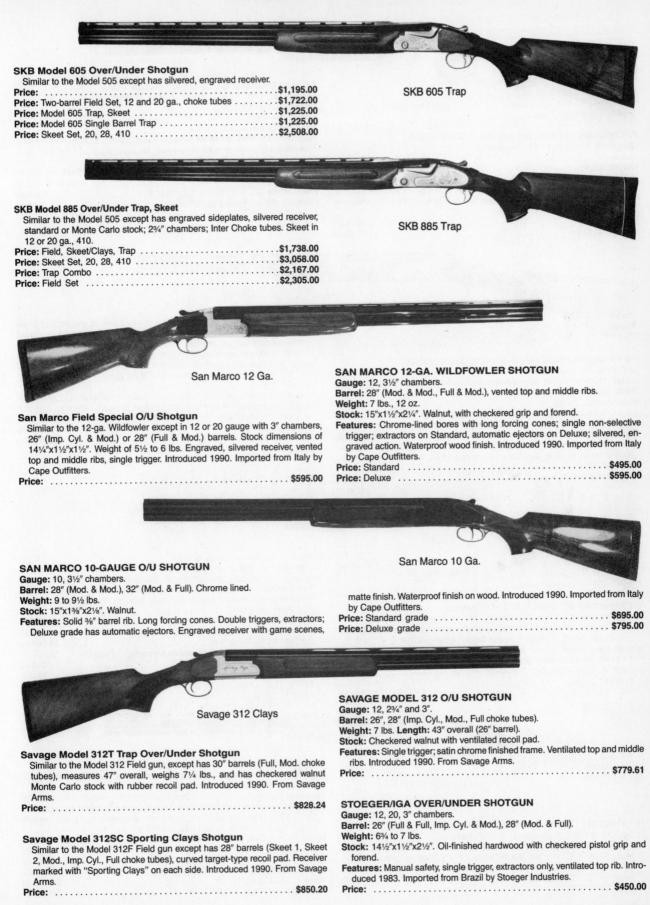

SKB 605 Trap

SKB Model 605 Over/Under Shotgun
Similar to the Model 505 except has silvered, engraved receiver.
Price: $1,195.00
Price: Two-barrel Field Set, 12 and 20 ga., choke tubes $1,722.00
Price: Model 605 Trap, Skeet $1,225.00
Price: Model 605 Single Barrel Trap $1,225.00
Price: Skeet Set, 20, 28, 410 .... $2,508.00

SKB 885 Trap

SKB Model 885 Over/Under Trap, Skeet
Similar to the Model 505 except has engraved sideplates, silvered receiver, standard or Monte Carlo stock; 2¾" chambers; Inter Choke tubes. Skeet in 12 or 20 ga., 410.
Price: Field, Skeet/Clays, Trap $1,738.00
Price: Skeet Set, 20, 28, 410 .... $3,058.00
Price: Trap Combo $2,167.00
Price: Field Set $2,305.00

San Marco 12 Ga.

SAN MARCO 12-GA. WILDFOWLER SHOTGUN
Gauge: 12, 3½" chambers.
Barrel: 28" (Mod. & Mod., Full & Mod.), vented top and middle ribs.
Weight: 7 lbs., 12 oz.
Stock: 15"x1½"x2¼". Walnut, with checkered grip and forend.
Features: Chrome-lined bores with long forcing cones; single non-selective trigger; extractors on Standard, automatic ejectors on Deluxe; silvered, engraved action. Waterproof wood finish. Introduced 1990. Imported from Italy by Cape Outfitters.
Price: Standard $495.00
Price: Deluxe $595.00

San Marco Field Special O/U Shotgun
Similar to the 12-ga. Wildfowler except in 12 or 20 gauge with 3" chambers, 26" (Imp. Cyl. & Mod.) or 28" (Full & Mod.) barrels. Stock dimensions of 14¼"x1½"x1½". Weight of 5½ to 6 lbs. Engraved, silvered receiver, vented top and middle ribs, single trigger. Introduced 1990. Imported from Italy by Cape Outfitters.
Price: $595.00

San Marco 10 Ga.

SAN MARCO 10-GAUGE O/U SHOTGUN
Gauge: 10, 3½" chambers.
Barrel: 28" (Mod. & Mod.), 32" (Mod. & Full). Chrome lined.
Weight: 9 to 9½ lbs.
Stock: 15"x1⅜"x2⅛". Walnut.
Features: Solid ⅜" barrel rib. Long forcing cones. Double triggers, extractors; Deluxe grade has automatic ejectors. Engraved receiver with game scenes,

matte finish. Waterproof finish on wood. Introduced 1990. Imported from Italy by Cape Outfitters.
Price: Standard grade $695.00
Price: Deluxe grade $795.00

Savage 312 Clays

SAVAGE MODEL 312 O/U SHOTGUN
Gauge: 12, 2¾" and 3".
Barrel: 26", 28" (Imp. Cyl., Mod., Full choke tubes).
Weight: 7 lbs. **Length:** 43" overall (26" barrel).
Stock: Checkered walnut with ventilated recoil pad.
Features: Single trigger; satin chrome finished frame. Ventilated top and middle ribs. Introduced 1990. From Savage Arms.
Price: $779.61

Savage Model 312T Trap Over/Under Shotgun
Similar to the Model 312 Field gun, except has 30" barrels (Full, Mod. choke tubes), measures 47" overall, weighs 7¼ lbs., and has checkered walnut Monte Carlo stock with rubber recoil pad. Introduced 1990. From Savage Arms.
Price: $828.24

STOEGER/IGA OVER/UNDER SHOTGUN
Gauge: 12, 20, 3" chambers.
Barrel: 26" (Full & Full, Imp. Cyl. & Mod.), 28" (Mod. & Full).
Weight: 6¾ to 7 lbs.
Stock: 14½"x1½"x2½". Oil-finished hardwood with checkered pistol grip and forend.
Features: Manual safety, single trigger, extractors only, ventilated top rib. Introduced 1983. Imported from Brazil by Stoeger Industries.
Price: $450.00

Savage Model 312SC Sporting Clays Shotgun
Similar to the Model 312F Field gun except has 28" barrels (Skeet 1, Skeet 2, Mod., Imp. Cyl., Full choke tubes), curved target-type recoil pad. Receiver marked with "Sporting Clays" on each side. Introduced 1990. From Savage Arms.
Price: $850.20

Techi-Mec SPL 640

TECHNI-MEC MODEL SR 692 EM OVER/UNDER
Gauge: 12, 16, 20, 2¾″ or 3″ chambers.
Barrel: 26″, 28″, 30″ (Mod., Full, Imp. Cyl., Cyl.).
Weight: 6½ lbs.
Stock: 14½″x1½″x2½″. European walnut with checkered grip and forend.
Features: Boxlock action with dummy sideplates, fine game scene engraving; single selective trigger; automatic ejectors available. Imported from Italy by L. Joseph Rahn. Introduced 1984.
Price: **$956.00**
Price: Slug gun **$780.00**

TECHNI-MEC MODEL SPL 640 FOLDING O/U
Gauge: 12, 16, 20, 28, 2¾″ chambers; 410, 3″ chambers.
Barrel: 26″ (Mod. & Full).
Weight: 5½ lbs.
Stock: European walnut.
Features: Gun folds in half for storage, transportation. Chrome-lined barrels; ventilated rib; photo-engraved silvered receiver. Imported from Italy by L. Joseph Rahn, Mandall. Introduced 1984.
Price: Double triggers .... **$280.00 to 299.95**
Price: Single trigger .... **$300.00 to 350.95**
Price: Model SPL 642, double triggers (Rahn) **$340.00**
Price: As above, single trigger (Rahn) **$355.00**

Tikka 412S Field

TIKKA MODEL 412S FIELD GRADE OVER/UNDER
Gauge: 12, 20, 3″ chambers.
Barrel: 24″, 26″, 28″, 30″ with stainless steel screw-in chokes (Imp. Cyl, Mod., Imp. Mod., Full); 20 ga. 28″ only.
Weight: About 7¼ lbs.
Stock: American walnut. Standard dimensions—13⁹⁄₁₀″x1½″x2⅖″. Checkered p.g. and forend.
Features: Free interchangeability of barrels, stocks and forends into double rifle model, combination gun, etc. Barrel selector in trigger; auto. top tang safety; barrel cocking indicators. Introduced 1980. Imported from Italy by Stoeger.
Price: Model 412S (ejectors) **$995.00**

TIKKA 412 ST Trap and Skeet
Target versions of the 412S gun with hand-honed actions, mechanical single triggers, elongated forcing cones and stainless steel choke tubes. Target safety is locked in "Fire" position (removal of a screw converts it to automatic safety); automatic ejectors; cocking indicators. Walnut stocks with double palm swells are quickly interchangeable. Trap guns have high stepped rib, 30″, 32″ O/U and 32″, 34″ single barrels; Skeet guns in 12, 20 ga. with 28″ barrels.
Grade II guns have semi-fancy wood, matte nickel finished receiver with matte blue locking bolt and lever, gold trigger, pre-drilled stock for insertion of a recoil reducer, more checkering at stock wrist. Introduced 1989.
Price: Grade I **$1,325.00**
Price: Grade II **$1,665.00**

Weatherby Athena V

WEATHERBY ATHENA O/U SHOTGUNS
Gauge: 12, 20, 28, 410 ga. 3″ chambers; 2¾″ on Trap gun.
Action: Boxlock (simulated sidelock) top lever break-open. Selective auto ejectors, single selective trigger (selector inside trigger guard).
Barrel: Fixed choke, 12, 20 ga.—26″, 28″ (Skeet & Skeet); IMC Multi-Choke tubes 12, 20, 410, Field models—26″ (Skeet, Imp. Cyl., Mod.), 28″ (Imp. Cyl., Mod., Full), 30″ (12 ga. only. Full, Mod., Full); o/u trap models—30″, 32″ (Mod., Imp. Mod., Full).
Weight: 12 ga. 7⅜ lbs., 20 ga. 6⅞ lbs.
Stock: American walnut, checkered p.g. and forend (14¼″x1½″x2½″).
Features: Mechanically operated trigger. Top tang safety, Greener cross-bolt, fully engraved receiver, recoil pad installed. IMC models furnished with three interchangeable flush-fitting choke tubes. Imported from Japan by Weatherby. Introduced 1982.
Price: Skeet, fixed choke **$1,690.00**
Price: 12 or 20 ga., IMC Multi-Choke, Field **$1,695.00**
Price: IMC Multi-Choke Trap **$1,695.00**
Price: Athena Grade V (more elaborate engraving) 12 and 20 .... **$2,100.00**
Price: Extra IMC Choke tubes **$18.00**
Price: Master Skeet Tube set (12-ga. gun with six Briley tubes in 20, 28, 410) **$3,360.00**

Weatherby Orion III

WEATHERBY ORION O/U SHOTGUNS
Gauge: 12, 20, 410, 3″ chambers, 28, 2¾″ chambers.
Barrel: Fixed choke, 12, 20, 28, 410—26″, 28″, 30″ (Imp. Cyl. & Mod., Full & Mod., Skeet & Skeet); IMC Multi-Choke, 12, 20, Field models—26″ (Imp. Cyl., Mod., Full, Skeet), 28″ (Imp. Cyl., Mod., Full), 30″ (Mod., Full); O/U Trap models—30″, 32″ (Imp. Mod., Mod., Full); Single bbl. Trap—32″, 34″ (Imp. Mod., Mod., Full).
Weight: 6½ to 9 lbs.
Stock: American walnut, checkered grip and forend. Rubber recoil pad. Dimensions for Field and Skeet models, 14¼″x1½″x2½″.
Features: Selective automatic ejectors, single selective mechanical trigger. Top tang safety, Greener crossbolt. Orion I has plain blued receiver, no engraving; Orion II has engraved, blued receiver; Orion III has silver-gray receiver with engraving. Imported from Japan by Weatherby.
Price: Orion I, Field, 12 or 20, IMC **$900.00**
Price: Orion II, Field, 12 or 20, IMC **$1,055.00**
Price: Orion II, Field, 28 or 410, fixed chokes **$1,055.00**
Price: Orion II, Skeet, 12 or 20, fixed chokes **$1,070.00**
Price: Orion II, Trap, 12, IMC **$1,100.00**
Price: Orion III, Field, 12 or 20, IMC **$1,160.00**

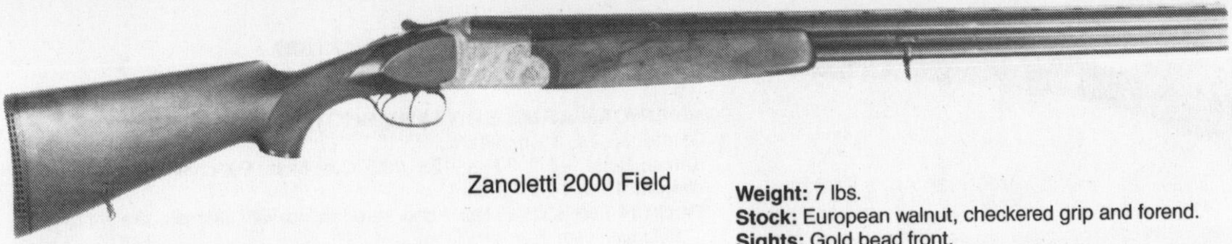

SHOTGUNS — OVER/UNDERS

Zanoletti 2000 Field

PIETRO ZANOLETTI MODEL 2000 FIELD O/U
Gauge: 12 only.
Barrel: 28″ (Mod. & Full).

Weight: 7 lbs.
Stock: European walnut, checkered grip and forend.
Sights: Gold bead front.
Features: Boxlock action with auto ejectors, double triggers; engraved receiver. Imported from Italy by Mandall Shooting Supplies. Introduced 1984.
Price: $895.00

ZOLI SILVER FALCON OVER/UNDER
Gauge: 12 or 20, 3″ chambers.
Barrel: 12 ga.—26″, 28″; 20 ga.—26″; Imp. Cyl., Mod., Imp. Mod., Full choke tubes.
Weight: 6¼ to 7¼ lbs.
Stock: 14¼″x2⅛″x1⁵⁄₁₆″. Turkish circassian walnut.
Features: Boxlock action with silver finish, floral engraving; single selective trigger, automatic ejectors. Introduced 1989. Imported from Italy by Antonio Zoli, USA.
Price: $1,395.00

ZOLI Z90 SPORTING CLAYS SHOTGUN
Gauge: 12, 2¾″ chambers.
Barrel: 28″. Comes with four choke tubes—two Skeet, one each Imp. Cyl. and Mod.
Weight: 7¼ lbs.
Stock: 14¼″x2⅛″x1½″. Turkish circassian walnut with checkered grip and forend.
Features: Sidelock action with silvered and engraved frame, single selective trigger, selective automatic ejectors. Schnabel forend tip; solid rubber buttpad. Introduced 1989. Imported from Italy by Antonio Zoli, USA.
Price: $1,595.00

Zoli Z90 Trap

ZOLI Z90 TRAP GUN
Gauge: 12, 2¾″ chambers.
Barrel: 29½″ or 32″. Comes with Mod., Imp. Mod. and Full choke tubes.
Weight: 8½ lbs.
Stock: 14½″x2⅛″x1½″x1½″. Checkered Turkish circassian walnut with Monte Carlo, recoil pad.
Features: Boxlock action with automatic selective ejectors, single selective trigger adjustable for pull length; step-type vent. rib and vent. center rib. Introduced 1989. Imported from Italy by Antonio Zoli, USA.
Price: $1,795.00

Zoli Z90 Skeet Gun
Similar to the Z90 Trap except has 28″ barrels with Imp. Cyl. & Mod., Skeet & Skeet choke tubes, 14¼″x2¼″x1½″ stock dimensions (drop at heel also available at 2⅛″, 2⅜″ or 2½″). Weighs 7¾ lbs. Available in 12 gauge only. Introduced 1989.
Price: $1,795.00

Zoli Woodsman

ZOLI WOODSMAN OVER/UNDER SHOTGUN
Gauge: 12, 3″ chambers.
Barrel: 23″ (five choke tubes furnished—two each Cyl., plus Imp. Cyl., Mod., Full).

Weight: 6¾ lbs.
Stock: 14½″x2⁵⁄₁₆″x1⅜″. Turkish circassian walnut with skip-line checkering, rubber buttpad; oil finish.
Sights: Rifle-type sights on raised rib. Folding leaf rear, bead front.
Features: Boxlock action with blued and engraved frame, single selective trigger, automatic selective ejectors. Available with or without sling swivels. Introduced 1989. Imported from Italy by Antonio Zoli, USA.
Price: $1,495.00

SHOTGUNS—SIDE-BY-SIDES

Variety of models for utility and sporting use, including some competitive shooting.

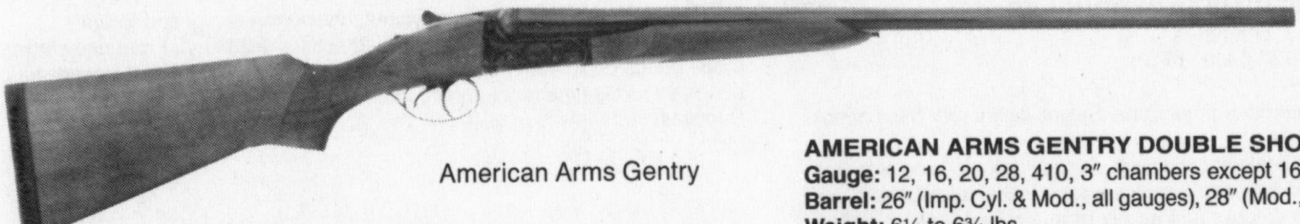

American Arms Gentry

American Arms Derby Side-by-Side
Has sidelock action with English-style engraving on the sideplates. Straight-grip, hand-checkered walnut stock with splinter forend, hand rubbed oil finish. Single non-selective trigger, automatic selective ejectors. Same chokes, rib, barrel lengths as the Gentry. Has 5-year warranty. From American Arms, Inc.
Price: $839.00
Price: 28 and 410 .... $879.00
Price: Two-barrel set, 20/28 ga. $1,069.00

AMERICAN ARMS GENTRY DOUBLE SHOTGUN
Gauge: 12, 16, 20, 28, 410, 3″ chambers except 16, 28, 2¾″.
Barrel: 26″ (Imp. Cyl. & Mod., all gauges), 28″ (Mod., & Full, 12 and 20 gauges).
Weight: 6¼ to 6¾ lbs.
Stock: 14⅛″x1⅜″x2⅜″. Hand-checkered walnut with semi-gloss finish.
Sights: Metal bead front.
Features: Boxlock action with English-style scroll engraving, color case-hardened finish. Double triggers, extractors. Independent floating firing pins. Manual safety. Five-year warranty. Introduced 1987. Imported from Spain by American Arms, Inc.
Price: 12, 16 or 20 gauge $499.00
Price: 28 or 410 .... $549.00

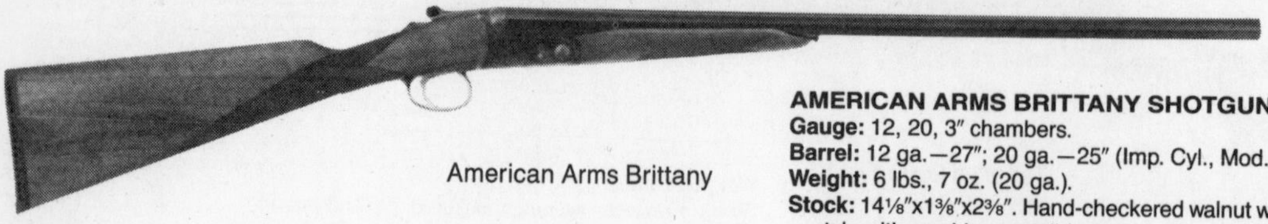

American Arms Brittany

AMERICAN ARMS BRITTANY SHOTGUN
Gauge: 12, 20, 3″ chambers.
Barrel: 12 ga.—27″; 20 ga.—25″ (Imp. Cyl., Mod., Full choke tubes).
Weight: 6 lbs., 7 oz. (20 ga.).
Stock: 14⅛″x1⅜″x2⅜″. Hand-checkered walnut with oil finish, straight English-style with semi-beavertail forend.
Features: Boxlock action with case-color finish, engraving; single selective trigger, automatic selective ejectors; rubber recoil pad. Introduced 1989. Imported from Spain by American Arms, Inc.
Price: **$659.00**

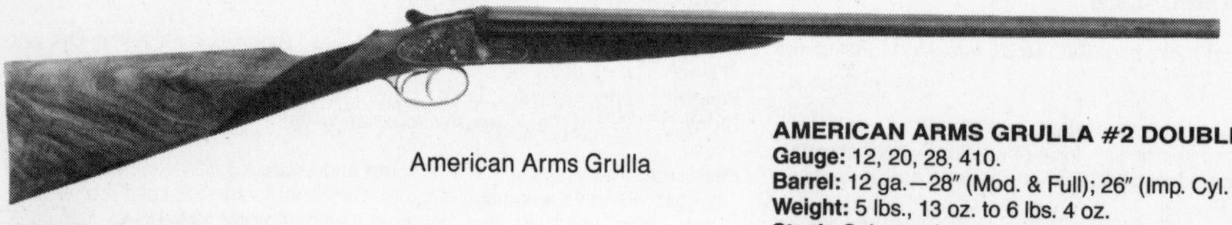

American Arms Grulla

AMERICAN ARMS GRULLA #2 DOUBLE SHOTGUN
Gauge: 12, 20, 28, 410.
Barrel: 12 ga.—28″ (Mod. & Full); 26″ (Imp. Cyl. & Mod.) all gauges.
Weight: 5 lbs., 13 oz. to 6 lbs. 4 oz.
Stock: Select walnut with straight English grip, splinter forend; hand-rubbed oil finish; checkered grip, forend, butt.
Features: True sidelock action with double triggers, detachable locks, automatic selective ejectors, cocking indicators, gas escape valves. Color case-hardened receiver with scroll engraving. English-style concave rib. Introduced 1989. Imported from Spain by American Arms, Inc.
Price: 12, 20, 28, 410 . . . .**$2,279.00**
Price: Two-barrel sets **$3,169.00**

AMERICAN ARMS WS/SS 10
Gauge: 10, 3½″ chambers.
Barrel: 32″ (Full & Full). Flat rib.
Weight: 10 lbs., 13 oz.
Stock: 14⁵⁄₁₆″x1⅜″x2⅜″. Hand-checkered walnut with beavertail forend, full pistol grip, dull finish, rubber recoil pad.
Features: Boxlock action with double triggers and extractors. All metal has Parkerized finish. Comes with camouflaged sling, sling swivels, 5-year warranty. Introduced 1987. Imported from Spain by American Arms, Inc.
Price: **$599.00**

American Arms TS/SS 10 Double Shotgun
Similar to the WS/SS 10 except has 26″ (Full & Full choke tubes) barrels, raised solid rib. Double triggers, extractors. All metal and wood has matte finish. Imported by American Arms, Inc.
Price: **$649.00**

American Arms TS/SS 12 Side-by-Side
Similar to the Waterfowl Special except in 12 ga. with 3½″ chambers, 26″ barrels with Imp. Cyl., Mod., Full choke tubes, single selective trigger, extractors. Comes with camouflage sling, swivels, 5-year warranty. From American Arms, Inc.
Price: **$559.00**

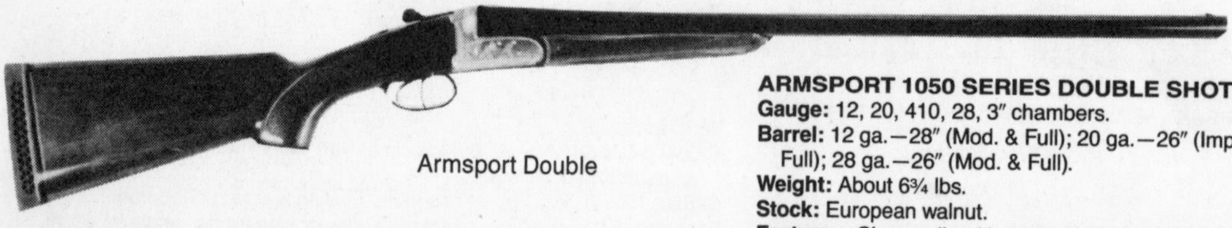

Armsport Double

ARMSPORT 1050 SERIES DOUBLE SHOTGUNS
Gauge: 12, 20, 410, 28, 3″ chambers.
Barrel: 12 ga.—28″ (Mod. & Full); 20 ga.—26″ (Imp. & Mod.); 410—26″ (Full & Full); 28 ga.—26″ (Mod. & Full).
Weight: About 6¾ lbs.
Stock: European walnut.
Features: Chrome-lined barrels. Boxlock action with engraving. Imported from Italy by Armsport.
Price: 12, 20 . . . . **$575.00**
Price: 28, 410 . . . . **$635.00**

ARIZAGA MODEL 31 DOUBLE SHOTGUN
Gauge: 12, 16, 20, 28, 410.
Barrel: 26″, 28″ (standard chokes).
Weight: 6 lbs., 9 oz. **Length:** 45″ overall.
Stock: Straight English style or pistol grip.
Features: Boxlock action with double triggers; blued, engraved receiver. Imported by Mandall Shooting Supplies.
Price: **$425.00**

BGJ 10 GAUGE MAGNUM SHOTGUN
Gauge: 10 ga., 3½″ chambers.
Action: Boxlock.
Barrel: 32″ (Full).
Weight: 11 lbs.
Stock: 14½″x1½″x2⅝″. European walnut, checkered at p.g. and forend.
Features: Double triggers; color hardened action, rest blued. Front and center metal beads on matted rib; ventilated rubber recoil pad. Forend release has positive Purdey-type mechanism. Imported from Spain by Mandall Shooting Supplies.
Price: **$599.95**

BERNARDELLI SERIES S. UBERTO DOUBLES
Gauge: 12, 20, 28, 2¾″ or 3″ chambers.
Barrel: 25⅝″, 26¾″, 28″, 29½″ (Mod. & Full).
Weight: 6 to 6½ lbs.
Stock: 14³⁄₁₆″x2⅜″x1⁹⁄₁₆″ standard dimensions. Select walnut with hand checkering.
Features: Anson & Deeley boxlock action with Purdey locks, choice of extractors or ejectors. Uberto 1 has color case-hardened receiver. Uberto 2 and F.S. silvered and differ in amount and quality of engraving. Custom options available. Imported from Italy by Mandall Shooting Supplies.
Price: S. Uberto 1E **$1,357.00**
Price: As above with ejectors **$1,421.00**
Price: S. Uberto 2E **$1,427.00**
Price: As above with ejectors **$1,491.00**
Price: Model 112EM, single trigger, 12-ga **$1,308.00**
Price: As above, Multichoke, 3″, 12-ga **$1,416.00**
Price: As above, 3½″ Waterfowler, 12-ga **$1,444.00**

Bernardelli System Holland H. Side-by-Side
True sidelock action. Available in 12 gauge only, reinforced breech, three round Purdey locks, automatic ejectors, folding right trigger. Model VB Liscio has color case-hardened receiver and sideplates with light engraving. VB and VB Tipo Lusso are silvered and engraved.
Price: VB Liscio **$8,052.00**
Price: VB Lusso **$11,202.00**
Price: VB Gold **$44,635.00**

CAUTION: PRICES CHANGE, CHECK AT GUNSHOP.

SHOTGUNS—SIDE-BY-SIDES

Bernardelli Series Roma Shotguns

Similar to the Series S. Uberto Models except with dummy sideplates to simulate sidelock action. In 12, 16, 20, 28 gauge, 25½", 26¾", 28", 29" barrels. Straight English or pistol grip stock. Chrome-lined barrels, boxlock action, double triggers, ejectors, automatic safety. Checkered butt. Special choke combinations, barrel lengths optional.

Price: Roma 3E, about $1,479.00
Price: Roma 4E (12, 20, 28), about $1,645.00
Price: Roma 6E (12, 20, 28), about $2,008.00
Price: Roma 3EW with ejectors, about $1,544.00
Price: Roma 4EM with ejectors (12, 20, 28), about $1,710.00
Price: Roma 6EM with ejectors (12, 20, 28), about $1,910.00

BERNARDELLI HEMINGWAY LIGHTWEIGHT DOUBLES

Gauge: 12, 20 (2¾" or 3"), 16 (2¾").
Barrel: 23½" to 28" (Cyl. & Imp. Cyl. to Mod. & Full).
Weight: 6¼ lbs.
Stock: Straight English grip of checkered European walnut.
Features: Silvered and engraved boxlock action. Folding front trigger on double-trigger models. Ejectors. Imported from Italy by Magnum Research.
Price: Hemingway, 12 or 20 .... $1,663.00
Price: With single trigger $1,728.00
Price: Deluxe, with sideplates $1,925.00
Price: As above, single trigger $1,990.00

Bernardelli Brescia

BERNARDELLI SLUG DOUBLE SHOTGUN

Gauge: 12, 2¾" or 3" chambers.
Barrel: 23½" (Cyl. & Cyl.).
Weight: About 7 lbs.
Stock: Checkered European walnut with full pistol grip and cheekpiece. Rubber recoil pad.
Sights: Blade front, folding leaf rear.
Features: Anson & Deeley boxlock action with extractors, Purdey triple locks; one-piece barrel without monobloc. Coin-finish frame with engraving. Double trigger standard, single optional. Introduced 1990. Imported from Italy by Magnum Research.
Price: $1,575.00
Price: With single trigger $1,640.00
Price: Slug Lusso, with sideplates $2,188.00
Price: As above, with single trigger $2,253.00

BERNARDELLI BRESCIA HAMMER DOUBLE SHOTGUN

Gauge: 12, 20 (2¾" or 3"), 16 (2¾").
Barrel: 25½" (Cyl. & Mod., Imp. Cyl. & Imp. Mod.), 26¾" (Imp. Cyl. & Imp. Mod., Mod. & Full), 28" (Mod. & Full), 29½" (Imp. Mod. & Full).
Weight: About 7 lbs.
Stock: Straight English grip. Checkered European walnut.
Features: Color case-hardened boxlock action. Introduced 1990. Imported from Italy by Magnum Research.
Price: $1,838.00
Price: Model Italia, fully engraved $2,135.00
Price: Model Italia Extra $5,776.00

Consult our Directory pages for the location of firms mentioned.

Beretta Model 627 EL

BRNO ZP149, ZP349 SIDE-BY-SIDE

Gauge: 12, 2¾" or 3" chambers.
Barrel: 28½" (Full & Mod.).
Weight: 7 lbs., 3 oz. **Length:** 45" overall.
Stock: Turkish or Yugoslavian walnut with raised cheekpiece.
Features: Sidelock action with double triggers, automatic ejectors, barrel indicators, auto safety. Imported from Czechoslovakia by TD Arms.
Price: ZP149, standard $589.00
Price: As above, engraved $609.00
Price: ZP349, extractors, standard $629.00
Price: As above, engraved $649.00

BERETTA SIDE-BY-SIDE FIELD SHOTGUNS

Gauge: 12 and 20, 2¾" and 3" chambers.
Barrel: 26" and 28" (fixed and Mobilchoke tubes).
Stock: Close-grained American walnut.
Features: Front and center beads on a raised ventilated rib. Has P. Beretta signature on each side of the receiver, while a gold gauge marking is inscribed atop the rib. Imported from Italy by Beretta U.S.A.
Price: 626 Onyx $1,533.00
Price: 627 EL $2,655.00
Price: 627 EELL (pistol grip or straight English stock) $4,453.00

Chapuis Double

CHURCHILL ROYAL SIDE-BY-SIDE SHOTGUN

Gauge: 10 (3½"), 12 (3"), 20, 28, 410 (3").
Barrel: 12 ga.—26" (Imp. Cyl. & Mod.), 28" (Mod. & Full); 20 ga.—26", 28" (Imp. Cyl. & Mod., Mod. & Full); 28, 410—26" (Full & Full).
Weight: 5¾ to 6½ lbs.
Stock: Straight-grip style of checkered European walnut.
Features: Color case-hardened boxlock action with double triggers, extractors; chromed barrels with concave rib. Introduced 1988. Imported by Ellett Bros.
Price: 10-ga. $814.95
Price: 12- and 20-ga. $609.95
Price: 28-ga. $639.95
Price: 410-bore $700.00

CHAPUIS SIDE-BY-SIDE SHOTGUN

Gauge: 12, 16, 20.
Barrel: 22", 23.6", 26.8", 27.6", 31.5", chokes to customer specs.
Weight: 5 to 10 lbs. **Length:** NA.
Stock: French walnut, straight English or pistol grip.
Features: Double hook Blitz system center sidelock action with notched action zone, automatic ejectors or extractors. Long trigger guard (most models), choice of raised solid rib, vent. rib or ultra light rib. Imported from France by Armes de Chasse.
Price: About $3,000.00

Churchill Windsor I

CHURCHILL WINDSOR I SIDE-BY-SIDE SHOTGUNS
Gauge: 12, 16, 20 (2¾" 16 ga., 3" others).
Barrel: 12-ga.—26" (Imp. Cyl. & Mod.), 28" (Mod. & Full); 16-ga.—28" (Mod. & Full); 20-ga.—26" (Imp. Cyl. & Mod.), 28" (Mod. & Full).
Weight: About 8 lbs. (12 ga.).
Stock: Hand-checkered European walnut with rubber buttpad.
Features: Anson & Deeley boxlock action with silvered and engraved finish; automatic top tang safety; double triggers; beavertail forend; extractors only. Imported from Spain by Ellett Bros. Introduced 1984.
Price: 12-ga., 28" bbl. $652.95
Price: 12-ga., (26"), 16-, 20-ga. $659.95

CHARLES DALY MODEL DSS DOUBLE
Gauge: 12, 20, 3" chambers.
Barrel: 27" (12-ga.), 25" (20-ga.); choke tubes.
Weight: 6 lbs., 13 oz. (12-ga.). **Length:** 44.5" overall.
Stock: 14⅛"x1⅜"x2⅜". Figured walnut; pistol grip; cut checkering; black rubber recoil pad; semi-beavertail forend.
Features: Boxlock action with automatic selective ejectors, automatic safety, gold single trigger. Engraved, silvered frame. Introduced 1990. Imported by Outdoor Sports Headquarters.
Price: 12 or 20 . . . . $675.00

CRUCELEGUI HERMANOS MODEL 150 DOUBLE
Gauge: 12, 16 or 20, 2¾" chambers.
Action: Greener triple cross-bolt.
Barrel: 20", 26", 28", 30", 32" (Cyl. & Cyl., Full & Full, Mod. & Full, Mod. & Imp. Cyl., Imp. Cyl. & Full, Mod. & Mod.).
Weight: 5 to 7¼ lbs.
Stock: Hand-checkered walnut, beavertail forend.
Features: Exposed hammers; double triggers; color case-hardened receiver; sling swivels; chrome-lined bores. Imported from Spain by Mandall Shooting Supplies.
Price: $399.95

Ferlib F VII

FERLIB MODEL F VII DOUBLE SHOTGUN
Gauge: 12, 16, 20, 28, 410.
Barrel: 25" to 28".

Weight: 5½ lbs. (20 ga.).
Stock: Oil-finished walnut, checkered straight grip and forend.
Features: Boxlock action with fine scroll engraving, silvered receiver. Double triggers standard. Introduced 1983. Imported from Italy by Wm. Larkin Moore.
Price: F.VI $4,400.00
Price: F.VII $5,200.00
Price: F.VII SC $6,500.00
Price: F.VII SP Sideplate $9,200.00

AUGUSTE FRANCOTTE BOXLOCK SHOTGUN
Gauge: 12, 16, 20, 2¾" or 3" chambers.
Barrel: 26" to 29", chokes to customer specs.
Weight: NA. **Length:** NA.
Stock: Deluxe European walnut to customer specs. Straight or pistol grip; checkered butt; oil finish; splinter or beavertail forend.
Sights: Bead front.
Features: Anson & Deeley boxlock action with double locks, double triggers (front hinged), manual or automatic safety, Holland & Holland ejectors. English

Francotte Boxlock

scroll engraving, coin finish or color case-hardening. Many options available. Imported from Belgium by Armes de Chasse.
Price: From about $12,960.00

AUGUSTE FRANCOTTE SIDELOCK SHOTGUN
Gauge: 12, 16, 20, 2¾" or 3" chambers.
Barrel: 26" to 29", chokes to customer specs.
Weight: NA. **Length:** NA.
Stock: Deluxe European walnut to customer specs. Straight or pistol grip; checkered butt; oil finish; splinter or beavertail forend.

Sights: Bead front.
Features: True Holland & Holland sidelock action with double locks, double triggers (front hinged), manual or automatic safety, Holland & Holland ejectors. English scroll engraving, coin finish or color case-hardening. Many options available. Imported from Belgium by Armes de Chasse.
Price: From about $22,629.00

GAMBA PRINCIPESSA SIDE-BY-SIDE
Gauge: 12 AND 20, 2¾" chamber.
Barrel: 26¾", 28" (Mod. & Full or Imp. Cyl. & Imp. Mod.)
Weight: 6.18 lbs. (20 ga.).
Stock: Walnut, straight English grip with standard forend.
Features: Boxlock action with automatic ejectors; double or single triggers by request. Introduced 1990. Imported from Italy by Heckler & Koch, Inc.
Price: With double triggers $2,450.00
Price: With single trigger $2,850.00

Gamba Principessa

CAUTION: PRICES CHANGE, CHECK AT GUNSHOP.

Gamba Oxford 90

Gamba Oxford 90 Side-by-Side Shotgun
Similar to the Principessa model except has dummy sideplates. Comes with 26" or 28" barrels (Mod. & Full or Imp. Cyl. & Imp. Mod.); weight is 5.5 to 6.8 lbs. depending upon gauge. Introduced 1990. Imported from Italy by Heckler & Koch, Inc.
Price: With double triggers $2,950.00
Price: With single trigger $3,350.00

Garbi Model 100

GARBI MODEL 100 DOUBLE
Gauge: 12, 16, 20, 28.
Barrel: 26", 28", choked to customer specs.
Weight: 5½ to 7½ lbs.
Stock: 14½"x2¼"x1½". European walnut. Straight grip, checkered butt, classic forend.
Features: Sidelock action, automatic ejectors, double triggers standard. Color case-hardened action, coin finish optional. Single trigger; beavertail forend, etc. optional. Five other models are available. Imported from Spain by Wm. Larkin Moore.
Price: From $3,400.00

Garbi Model 101 Side-by-Side
Similar to the Garbi Model 100 except is hand engraved with Continental-style floral and scroll engraving, select walnut stock. Better overall quality than the Model 100. Imported from Spain by Wm. Larkin Moore.
Price: $4,100.00

Garbi Model 103A, B Side-by-Side
Similar to the Garbi Model 100 except has Purdey-type fine scroll and rosette engraving. Better overall quality than the Model 101. Model 103B has nickel-chrome steel barrels, H&H-type easy opening mechanism; other mechanical details remain the same. Imported from Spain by Wm. Larkin Moore.
Price: Model 103A, from $5,500.00
Price: Model 103B, from $7,600.00

Garbi Model 200 Side-by-Side
Similar to the Garbi Model 100 except has heavy-duty locks, magnum proofed. Very fine Continental-style floral and scroll engraving, well figured walnut stock. Other mechanical features remain the same. Imported from Spain by Wm. Larkin Moore.
Price: $7,600.00

HATFIELD UPLANDER SHOTGUN
Gauge: 20, 3" chambers.
Barrel: 26" (Imp. Cyl. & Mod.).
Weight: 5¾ lbs.
Stock: Straight English style, special select XXX fancy walnut. Hand-rubbed oil finish. Splinter forend.
Features: Double locking under-lug boxlock action; color case-hardened frame; single non-selective trigger. Introduced 1988. From Hatfield.

Hatfield Uplander

Price: Grade I $1,295.00
Price: Grade II $2,495.00
Price: Grade III $3,500.00
Price: Grade IV $5,500.00
Price: Grade V $6,900.00
Price: Grade VI $7,900.00
Price: Grade VII $7,900.00
Price: Grade VIII $17,500.00

Kassnar Grade II

KASSNAR GRADE II SIDE-BY-SIDE SHOTGUN
Gauge: 10, 3½", 12, 16, 20, 28, 410, 3" chambers.
Barrel: 10 ga.—32" (Full & Full); 12 and 20 ga.—26" (Imp. Cyl. & Mod.), 28" (Mod. & Full); 16 and 28 ga.—28" (Mod. & Full); 410 bore—26" (Full & Full).
Weight: 5 lbs. (410) to 9 lbs. (10 ga.).
Stock: Checkered European walnut.
Features: Color case-hardened boxlock action with double triggers, automatic top tang safety, extractors, concave rib. Imported by K.B.I., Inc.
Price: . . . . $575.00 to $665.00

MERKEL SIDE-BY-SIDE SHOTGUNS
Gauge: 12, 16, 20, 2¾" or 3" chambers.
Barrel: 26", 26¾", 28" (standard chokes).
Weight: 6 to 7 lbs.
Stock: European walnut. Straight English or pistol grip.
Features: Models 47E, 147E, 76E are boxlocks; others are sidelocks. All have double triggers, double lugs and Greener cross-bolt locking and automatic ejectors. Choking and patterning for steel shot (by importer). Upgraded wood, engraving, etc. optional. Imported from East Germany by Armes de Chasse.

Merkel Double

Price: Model 47E, about $2,000.00
Price: Model 147E, about $2,500.00
Price: Model 76E $3,500.00
Price: Model 47S, about $4,500.00
Price: Model 147S, about $5,000.00
Price: Model 247S about $5,500.00
Price: Model 347S, about $6,000.00
Price: Model 447S, about $6,500.00

SHOTGUNS—SIDE-BY-SIDES

Parker DHE

PARKER DHE SIDE-BY-SIDE SHOTGUN

Gauge: 12, 20, 28, 2¾" or 3" chambers.
Barrel: 26" (Imp. Cyl. & Mod., 2¾" chambers), Skeet & Skeet available, 28" (Mod. & Full, 3" chambers only).

Weight: About 6¾ lbs. (12 ga.), 6½ lbs. (20 ga.), 5½ lbs. (28 ga.), 5 lbs. (410).
Stock: Fancy American walnut, checkered grip and forend. Straight stock or pistol grip, splinter or beavertail forend; 28 lpi checkering.
Features: Reproduction of the original Parker—most parts interchangeable with original. Double or single selective trigger; checkered skeleton buttplate; selective ejectors; bores hard chromed, excluding choke area. Two-barrel sets available. Hand engraved scroll and scenes on case-hardened frame. Fitted leather trunk included. Limited production. Introduced 1984. Made by Winchester in Japan. Imported by Parker Div. of Reagent Chemical.
Price: D Grade, one barrel set $3,370.00
Price: A-1 Special, two-barrel set $11,200.00

Parker-Hale 645E

PIOTTI KING NO. 1 SIDE-BY-SIDE

Gauge: 12, 16, 20, 28, 410.
Barrel: 25" to 30" (12 ga.), 25" to 28" (16, 20, 28, 410). To customer specs. Chokes as specified.
Weight: 6½ lbs. to 8 lbs. (12 ga. to customer specs.).
Stock: Dimensions to customer specs. Finely figured walnut; straight grip with checkered butt with classic splinter forend and hand-rubbed oil finish standard. Pistol grip, beavertail forend, satin luster finish optional.
Features: Holland & Holland pattern sidelock action, automatic ejectors. Double trigger with front trigger hinged standard; non-selective single trigger optional. Coin finish standard; color case-hardened optional. Top rib: level, file cut standard; concave, ventilated optional. Very fine, full coverage scroll engraving with small floral bouquets, gold crown in top lever, name in gold, and gold crest in forend. Imported from Italy by Wm. Larkin Moore.
Price: $14,800.00

Piotti Model King Extra Side-by-Side

Similar to the Piotti King No. 1 except highest quality wood and metal work. Choice of either bulino game scene engraving or game scene engraving with gold inlays. Engraved and signed by a master engraver. Exhibition grade wood. Other mechanical specifications remain the same. Imported from Italy by Wm. Larkin Moore.
Price: $22,500.00

PARKER-HALE MODEL "600" SERIES DOUBLES

Gauge: 12, 16, 20, 2¾" chambers; 28, 410, 3" chambers.
Barrel: 25", 26", 27", 28" (Imp. Cyl. & Mod., Mod. & Full).
Weight: 12 ga., 6¾-7 lbs.; 20 ga., 5¾-6 lbs.
Stock: 14½"x1½"x2½". Hand-checkered walnut with oil finish. "E" (English) models have straight grip, splinter forend, checkered butt. "A" (American) models have p.g. stock, beavertail forend, buttplate.
Features: Boxlock action; silvered, engraved action; automatic safety; ejectors or extractors. E-models have double triggers, concave rib (XXV models have Churchill-type rib); A-models have single, non-selective trigger, raised matted rib. Made in Spain by Ugartechea. Imported by Precision Sports. Introduced 1986.
Price: 640E (12, 16, 20; 26"; 28"), extractors $619.95
Price: 640E (28, 410; 27" only), extractors $699.95
Price: 640A (12, 16, 20; 26"; 28"), extractors $719.95
Price: 640A (28, 410, 27" only), ejectors $799.95
Price: 640M "Big Ten" (10 ga. 26", 30", 32", Full & Full) $748.95
Price: 645E (12, 16, 20; 26"; 28"), with ejectors $784.95
Price: 645E (28, 410; 27"), with ejectors $864.95
Price: 645A (12, 16, 20; 26"; 28"), with ejectors $884.95
Price: 645A (28, 410; 27" only), ejectors $964.95
Price: 645E-XXV (12, 16, 20; 25"), with ejectors $819.95
Price: 645E-XXV (28, 410; 27"), with ejectors $899.95
Price: 645E Bi-Gauge (20/28 or 28/410), ejectors $1,399.95
Price: 645A Bi-Gauge (20/28 or 28/410), ejectors $1,499.95
Price: 670E (12, 16, 20; 26"; 28") sidelock, with ejectors $3,200.00
Price: 670E (28, 410; 27") sidelock, with ejectors $3,400.00
Price: 680E-XXV (12, 16, 20; 25") sidelock, ejectors, case-color action $3,150.00
Price: 680E-XXV (28, 410; 25") sidelock, ejectors, case-color action $3,250.00

Piotti Model Piuma

Piotti Model Lunik Side-by-Side

Similar to the Piotti King No. 1 except better overall quality. Has Renaissance-style large scroll engraving in relief, gold crown in top lever, gold name and gold crest in forend. Best quality Holland & Holland-pattern sidelock ejector double with chopper lump (demi-bloc) barrels. Other mechanical specifications remain the same. Imported from Italy by Wm. Larkin Moore.
Price: $15,400.00

PIOTTI MODEL PIUMA SIDE-BY-SIDE

Gauge: 12, 16, 20, 28, 410.
Barrel: 25" to 30" (12 ga.), 25" to 28" (16, 20, 28, 410).
Weight: 5½ to 6¼ lbs. (20 ga.).
Stock: Dimensions to customer specs. Straight grip stock with checkered butt, classic splinter forend, hand-rubbed oil finish are standard; pistol grip, beavertail forend, satin luster finish optional.
Features: Anson & Deeley boxlock ejector double with chopper lump barrels. Level, file-cut rib, light scroll and rosette engraving, scalloped frame. Double triggers with hinged front standard, single non-selective optional. Coin finish standard, color case-hardened optional. Imported from Italy by Wm. Larkin Moore.
Price: $8,900.00

REMINGTON PARKER AHE SIDE-BY-SIDE

Gauge: 20, 2¾" chambers.
Barrel: 28" (any combination of Skeet, Imp. Cyl., Mod., Full chokes).
Weight: About 6½ lbs.
Stock: Circassian or American walnut; straight or pistol grip; beavertail or splinter forend; rubber recoil pad, Parker buttplate or engraved skeleton steel buttplate. Checkered 28 lpi.
Features: Custom-made gun. Single selective trigger, automatic ejectors;

Remington Parker

scroll-engraved color case-hardened receiver. Automatic ejectors. Limited production. Reintroduced 1988. From Remington.
Price: From $14,100.00

CAUTION: PRICES CHANGE, CHECK AT GUNSHOP.

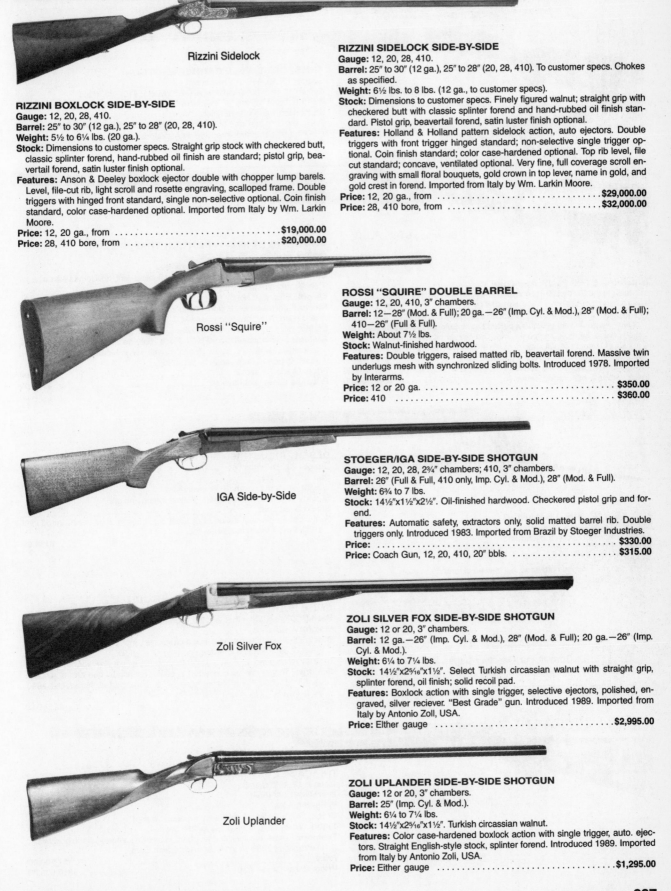

Rizzini Sidelock

RIZZINI BOXLOCK SIDE-BY-SIDE

Gauge: 12, 20, 28, 410.
Barrel: 25″ to 30″ (12 ga.), 25″ to 28″ (20, 28, 410).
Weight: 5½ to 6¼ lbs. (20 ga.).
Stock: Dimensions to customer specs. Straight grip stock with checkered butt, classic splinter forend, hand-rubbed oil finish are standard; pistol grip, beavertail forend, satin luster finish optional.
Features: Anson & Deeley boxlock ejector double with chopper lump barrels. Level, file-cut rib, light scroll and rosette engraving, scalloped frame. Double triggers with hinged front standard, single non-selective optional. Coin finish standard, color case-hardened optional. Imported from Italy by Wm. Larkin Moore.
Price: 12, 20 ga., from **$19,000.00**
Price: 28, 410 bore, from **$20,000.00**

RIZZINI SIDELOCK SIDE-BY-SIDE

Gauge: 12, 20, 28, 410.
Barrel: 25″ to 30″ (12 ga.), 25″ to 28″ (20, 28, 410). To customer specs. Chokes as specified.
Weight: 6½ lbs. to 8 lbs. (12 ga., to customer specs).
Stock: Dimensions to customer specs. Finely figured walnut; straight grip with checkered butt with classic splinter forend and hand-rubbed oil finish standard. Pistol grip, beavertail forend, satin luster finish optional.
Features: Holland & Holland pattern sidelock action, auto ejectors. Double triggers with front trigger hinged standard; non-selective single trigger optional. Coin finish standard; color case-hardened optional. Top rib level, file cut standard; concave, ventilated optional. Very fine, full coverage scroll engraving with small floral bouquets, gold crown in top lever, name in gold, and gold crest in forend. Imported from Italy by Wm. Larkin Moore.
Price: 12, 20 ga., from **$29,000.00**
Price: 28, 410 bore, from **$32,000.00**

Rossi "Squire"

ROSSI "SQUIRE" DOUBLE BARREL

Gauge: 12, 20, 410, 3″ chambers.
Barrel: 12—28″ (Mod. & Full); 20 ga.—26″ (Imp. Cyl. & Mod.), 28″ (Mod. & Full); 410—26″ (Full & Full).
Weight: About 7½ lbs.
Stock: Walnut-finished hardwood.
Features: Double triggers, raised matted rib, beavertail forend. Massive twin underlugs mesh with synchronized sliding bolts. Introduced 1978. Imported by Interarms.
Price: 12 or 20 ga. **$350.00**
Price: 410 . . . .**$360.00**

IGA Side-by-Side

STOEGER/IGA SIDE-BY-SIDE SHOTGUN

Gauge: 12, 20, 28, 2¾″ chambers; 410, 3″ chambers.
Barrel: 26″ (Full & Full, 410 only, Imp. Cyl. & Mod.), 28″ (Mod. & Full).
Weight: 6¾ to 7 lbs.
Stock: 14½″x1½″x2½″. Oil-finished hardwood. Checkered pistol grip and forend.
Features: Automatic safety, extractors only, solid matted barrel rib. Double triggers only. Introduced 1983. Imported from Brazil by Stoeger Industries.
Price: **$330.00**
Price: Coach Gun, 12, 20, 410, 20″ bbls. **$315.00**

Zoli Silver Fox

ZOLI SILVER FOX SIDE-BY-SIDE SHOTGUN

Gauge: 12 or 20, 3″ chambers.
Barrel: 12 ga.—26″ (Imp. Cyl. & Mod.), 28″ (Mod. & Full); 20 ga.—26″ (Imp. Cyl. & Mod.).
Weight: 6¼ to 7¼ lbs.
Stock: 14½″x2⁵⁄₁₆″x1½″. Select Turkish circassian walnut with straight grip, splinter forend, oil finish; solid recoil pad.
Features: Boxlock action with single trigger, selective ejectors, polished, engraved, silver reciever. "Best Grade" gun. Introduced 1989. Imported from Italy by Antonio Zoll, USA.
Price: Either gauge **$2,995.00**

Zoli Uplander

ZOLI UPLANDER SIDE-BY-SIDE SHOTGUN

Gauge: 12 or 20, 3″ chambers.
Barrel: 25″ (Imp. Cyl. & Mod.).
Weight: 6¼ to 7¼ lbs.
Stock: 14½″x2⁵⁄₁₆″x1½″. Turkish circassian walnut.
Features: Color case-hardened boxlock action with single trigger, auto. ejectors. Straight English-style stock, splinter forend. Introduced 1989. Imported from Italy by Antonio Zoli, USA.
Price: Either gauge **$1,295.00**

Variety of designs for utility and sporting purposes, as well as for competitive shooting.

Armsport Single

ARMSPORT SINGLE BARREL SHOTGUN
Gauge: 12, 20, 410; 3″ chamber.
Barrel: 12 ga.—28″ (Full); 20 ga.—26″ (Mod.); 410—26″ (Full).
Weight: About 6½ lbs.
Stock: Hardwood with oil finish.
Features: Chrome-lined barrel, manual safety, cocking indicator. Opening lever behind trigger guard. Imported by Armsport.
Price: **$90.00**

Browning BT-99 PLUS

Browning BT-99 PLUS Trap Gun
Similar to the Grade I BT-99 except comes only with 34″ barrel with .745″ over bore, Invector PLUS choke system with Full, Imp. Mod. and Mod. choke tubes; high post, ventilated, tapered, target rib adjustable from 3″ to 12″ above point of aim. Available with or without ported barrel. Select walnut stock has high-gloss finish, Monte Carlo comb, modified beavertail forend and is fully adjustable for length of pull, drop at comb and drop at Monte Carlo. Has Browning Recoil Reduction System. Introduced 1989.
Price: Grade I, with ported barrel **$1,650.00**
Price: Grade I, non-ported barrel **1,600.00**

BROWNING BT-99 COMPETITION TRAP SPECIAL
Gauge: 12 gauge, 2¾″ chamber.
Action: Top lever break-open, hammerless.
Barrel: 32″ or 34″ with 1¹⁄₃₂″ wide high post floating vent. rib. Comes with Invector choke tubes or fixed Full, Imp. Mod.
Weight: 8 lbs. (32″ bbl.).
Stock: French walnut; hand-checkered, full pistol grip, full beavertail forend; recoil pad. Trap dimensions with M.C. 14⅜″x1⅜″x1⅜″x2″.
Sights: Ivory front and middle beads.
Features: Gold-plated trigger with 3½-lb. pull, deluxe trap-style recoil pad, automatic ejector, no safety. Available with either Monte Carlo or standard stock. Imported from Japan by Browning.
Price: Grade I Invector **$1,005.00**
Price: As above, non-Invector **$981.00**

Desert Industries

DESERT INDUSTRIES BIG TWENTY SHOTGUN
Gauge: 20, 2¾″ chamber.
Barrel: 19″ (Cyl.).
Weight: 4¾ lbs. **Length:** 31¾″ overall.
Stock: Fixed wire, with buttplate. Walnut forend and grip.
Stock: Bead front.
Features: Single shot action of all steel construction. Blue finish. Introduced 1990. From Desert Industries, Inc.
Price: **$189.95**

F.I.E. "S.S.S." SINGLE BARREL
Gauge: 12, 20, 410, 3″ chamber.
Action: Button-break on trigger guard.
Barrel: 18½″ (Cyl.).
Weight: 6½ lbs.
Stock: Walnut-finished hardwood, full beavertail forend.
Features: Exposed hammer. Automatic ejector. Imported from Brazil by F.I.E. Corp.
Price: **$99.95**

HOLMES SUPERTRAP II TRAP SHOTGUN
Gauge: 12, 2¾″ chamber.
Barrel: 30″ standard, other lengths to order. Screw-in chokes.
Weight: About 9 lbs.
Stock: English or Claro walnut. Hand-checkered grip and forend. Standard pull is 14¼″, other lengths to order.
Sights: White bead front on adjustable short rib, adjustable rear rib.
Features: Trigger can be converted to pull or release by one turn of a screw. Very light recoil. Long forcing cone, .750″ bore, ported. Introduced 1990. Made in U.S. by Holmes Firearms Co.
Price: **$2,500.00**

> Consult our Directory pages for the location of firms mentioned

Ithaca Custom Trap

ITHACA 5E CUSTOM TRAP SINGLE BARREL
Gauge: 12, 2¾″ chamber.
Barrel: 32″, 34″ (Full).
Weight: 8½ lbs.
Stock: 14⅜″x1⅜″x1⅜″. AA Fancy American walnut.
Sights: White bead front, brass middle bead.
Features: Frame, top lever, trigger guard extensively engraved and gold inlaid. Reintroduced 1988. From Ithaca Acquisition Corp.
Price: 5E **$7,500.00**
Price: Dollar Grade Trap **$10,000.00**

Krieghoft KS-5 Trap

KRIEGHOFF KS-5 TRAP GUN
Gauge: 12, 2¾" chamber.
Barrel: 32", 34"; Full choke or choke tubes.
Weight: About 8½ lbs.
Stock: Choice of high Monte Carlo (1½"), low Monte Carlo (1⅜") or factory adjustable stock. European walnut.
Features: Ventilated tapered step rib. Adjustable trigger or optional release trigger. Choice of blue or nickeled receiver. Comes with fitted aluminum case. Introduced 1988. Imported from West Germany by Krieghoff International, Inc.
Price: Fixed choke, cased **$2,750.00**

Krieghoff KS-5 Special
Same as the KS-5 except the barrel has a fully adjustable rib and adjustable stock. Rib allows shooter to adjust point of impact from 50%/50% to nearly 90%/10%. Introduced 1990.
Price: **$3,655.00**

KRIEGHOFF K-80 SINGLE BARREL TRAP GUN
Gauge: 12, 2¾" chamber.
Barrel: 32" or 34" Unsingle; 34" Top Single. Fixed Full or choke tubes.
Weight: About 8¾ lbs.
Stock: Four stock dimensions or adjustable stock available. All hand-checkered European walnut.

Features: Satin nickel finish with K-80 logo. Selective mechanical trigger adjustable for finger position. Tapered step vent. rib. Adjustable point of impact on Unsingle.
Price: Standard grade full Unsingle **$5,845.00**
Price: Standard grade full Top Single **$5,495.00**
Price: RT (removable trigger) option, add **$1,200.00**

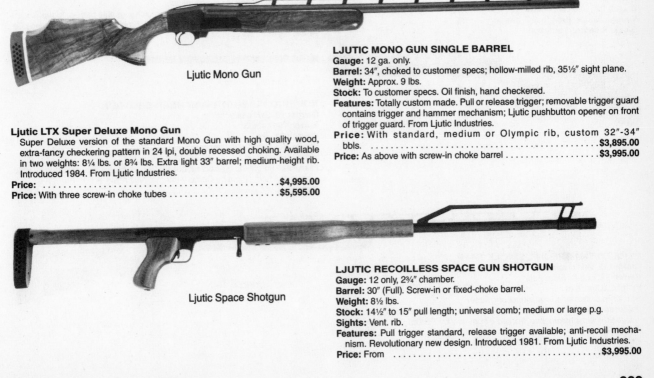

LAURONA GRAND TRAP GTO COMBO
Gauge: 12, 2¾" chamber.
Barrel: 34" (top single barrel), 29" (o/u barrels); Multichokes.
Weight: NA. **Length:** NA.
Stock: European walnut with Monte Carlo comb, orthopedic grip, curved trap recoil pad, full beavertail forend with finger grooves.
Sights: Bead front.
Features: Has 10mm steel rib designed for 40-yard interception. Special elongated forcing cone with flush choke tubes. Bottom chamber area fitted with buffered recoil system. Introduced 1990. Imported from Spain by Galaxy Imports, Ltd.
Price: With both barrel sets **$1,900.00**

Laurona GTU

Laurona Grand Trap GTU Combo
Similar to the GTO except has 34" bottom single barrel and 29" over/under barrels. Has 10mm high steel floating rib with walnut inserts fitted to the forend; screw-in Full choke. Forend is rounded with teardrop cross-section. Butt has straight comb, orthopedic grip, curved trap recoil pad. Comes with both barrel sets. Introduced 1990. Imported from Spain by Galaxy Imports, Ltd.
Price: **$1,980.00**

Ljutic Mono Gun

LJUTIC MONO GUN SINGLE BARREL
Gauge: 12 ga. only.
Barrel: 34", choked to customer specs; hollow-milled rib, 35½" sight plane.
Weight: Approx. 9 lbs.
Stock: To customer specs. Oil finish, hand checkered.
Features: Totally custom made. Pull or release trigger; removable trigger guard contains trigger and hammer mechanism; Ljutic pushbutton opener on front of trigger guard. From Ljutic Industries.
Price: With standard, medium or Olympic rib, custom 32"-34" bbls. **$3,895.00**
Price: As above with screw-in choke barrel **$3,995.00**

Ljutic LTX Super Deluxe Mono Gun
Super Deluxe version of the standard Mono Gun with high quality wood, extra-fancy checkering pattern in 24 lpi, double recessed choking. Available in two weights: 8¼ lbs. or 8¾ lbs. Extra light 33" barrel; medium-height rib. Introduced 1984. From Ljutic Industries.
Price: **$4,995.00**
Price: With three screw-in choke tubes **$5,595.00**

Ljutic Space Shotgun

LJUTIC RECOILLESS SPACE GUN SHOTGUN
Gauge: 12 only, 2¾" chamber.
Barrel: 30" (Full). Screw-in or fixed-choke barrel.
Weight: 8½ lbs.
Stock: 14½" to 15" pull length; universal comb; medium or large p.g.
Sights: Vent. rib.
Features: Pull trigger standard, release trigger available; anti-recoil mechanism. Revolutionary new design. Introduced 1981. From Ljutic Industries.
Price: From **$3,995.00**

Marlin Model 55

NAVY ARMS MODEL 105 FOLDING SHOTGUN
Gauge: 12, 20, 410, 3″ chamber.
Barrel: 28″ (Full); 26″ (Full) in 410 bore.
Stock: Walnut-stained hardwood. Checkered p.g. and forend. Metal bead front.
Features: Folding, hammerless, top-lever action with cross-bar action. Chrome-lined barrel, blued receiver. Deluxe has vent. rib, engraved hard-chrome receiver. Introduced 1987. From Navy Arms.
Price: Model 105S Standard $90.00
Price: Model 105L Deluxe $105.00

MARLIN MODEL 55 GOOSE GUN BOLT ACTION
Gauge: 12 only, 2¾″ or 3″ chamber.
Action: Bolt action, thumb safety, detachable two-shot clip. Red cocking indicator.
Barrel: 36″ (Full).
Weight: 8 lbs. **Length:** 56¾″ overall.
Stock: Walnut-finished hardwood, p.g., ventilated recoil pad. Swivel studs, Mar-Shield® finish.
Features: Brass bead front sight, U-groove rear sight.
Price: $242.95

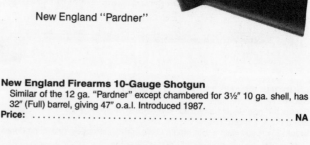

New England "Pardner"

NEW ENGLAND FIREARMS "PARDNER" SHOTGUN
Gauge: 12, 16 (2¾″), 20, 410, 3″ chamber.
Barrel: 12 ga.—24″ (Cyl.), rifle sights, 28″ (Mod., Full); 16 ga.—28″ (Full); 20 ga.—24″ (Cyl.), rifle sights, 26″ (Mod., Full); 410 bore—26″ (Full).
Weight: About 5½ lbs. **Length:** 43″ overall (28″ barrel).
Stock: Walnut-finished hardwood; 13¾″ pull length (12½″ youth).
Features: Transfer-bar ignition; side-lever action release. Blued receiver, blued barrel. Youth model available with 22″ barrel. Introduced 1987. From New England Firearms Co.
Price: .... NA
Price: Deluxe "Pardner" (as above except has Double Back-up buttstock holding two extra shells) .... NA

New England Firearms "Mini-Pardner"
Same as the "Pardner" except has 18½″ barrel, shortened butt, swivel studs; available in 20 or 410, 3″ chamber. Introduced 1989.
Price: .... NA

NEW ENGLAND FIREARMS "HANDI-GUN"
Caliber/Gauge: 22 Hornet, 223, 243, 30-30, 30-06 or 45-70; 12 or 20 ga., 3″ chamber.
Barrel: 22″, Interchangeable.
Weight: 6½ lbs. **Length:** 37″ overall.
Stock: American hardwood.

New England Firearms 10-Gauge Shotgun
Similar of the 12 ga. "Pardner" except chambered for 3½″ 10 ga. shell, has 32″ (Full) barrel, giving 47″ o.a.l. Introduced 1987.
Price: .... NA

New England Firearms Protector, Shark Repeller Shotguns
Similar to the Mini-Pardner except has full buttstock, 18½″ barrel, 12 gauge only. Blue finish with recoil pad. Shark Repeller has nickel finish. Introduced 1990.
Price: .... NA

Sights: Rifle—ramp front, open adjustable rear; shotgun barrel has front bead. Drilled and tapped for scope mounts.
Features: Break-open single shot with interchangeable barrels. Matte electroless nickel or blue finish. Introduced 1987. From New England Firearms Co.
Price: .... NA

Norinco HL-12-101

NORINCO HL12-101 TIGER HEAD SHOTGUN
Gauge: 12, 2¾″ chamber.
Barrel: 29.5″ (Full).
Weight: 5¾ lbs.
Stock: Hardwood with checkered grip and forend.
Sights: Bead front.
Features: Automatic ejector; rubber recoil pad; blue finish. Introduced 1990. Imported from China by Century International Arms, Inc.
Price: $79.95

Perazzi TMX

PERAZZI TM1 SPECIAL SINGLE TRAP
Gauge: 12, 2¾″ chambers.
Barrel: 32″ or 34″ (Extra Full).
Weight: 8 lbs., 6 oz.
Stock: To customer specs; interchangeable.
Features: Tapered and stepped high rib; adjustable four-position trigger. Also available with choke tubes. Imported from Italy by Perazzi U.S.A., Inc.
Price: From $4,380.00
Price: TMX Special Single (as above except special high rib), from $4,380.00

CAUTION: PRICES CHANGE, CHECK AT GUNSHOP.

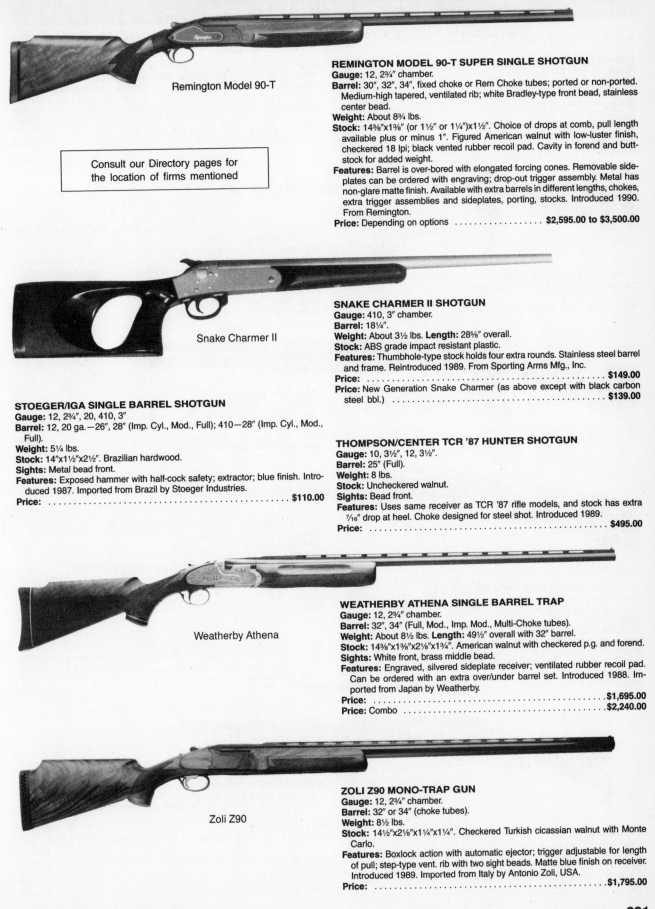

Remington Model 90-T

Consult our Directory pages for the location of firms mentioned

REMINGTON MODEL 90-T SUPER SINGLE SHOTGUN
Gauge: 12, 2¾" chamber.
Barrel: 30", 32", 34", fixed choke or Rem Choke tubes; ported or non-ported. Medium-high tapered, ventilated rib; white Bradley-type front bead, stainless center bead.
Weight: About 8¾ lbs.
Stock: 14⅜"x1⅜" (or 1½" or 1¼")x1½". Choice of drops at comb, pull length available plus or minus 1". Figured American walnut with low-luster finish, checkered 18 lpi; black vented rubber recoil pad. Cavity in forend and buttstock for added weight.
Features: Barrel is over-bored with elongated forcing cones. Removable sideplates can be ordered with engraving; drop-out trigger assembly. Metal has non-glare matte finish. Available with extra barrels in different lengths, chokes, extra trigger assemblies and sideplates, porting, stocks. Introduced 1990. From Remington.
Price: Depending on options . . . . $2,595.00 to $3,500.00

Snake Charmer II

SNAKE CHARMER II SHOTGUN
Gauge: 410, 3" chamber.
Barrel: 18¼".
Weight: About 3½ lbs. **Length:** 28⅝" overall.
Stock: ABS grade impact resistant plastic.
Features: Thumbhole-type stock holds four extra rounds. Stainless steel barrel and frame. Reintroduced 1989. From Sporting Arms Mfg., Inc.
Price: $149.00
Price: New Generation Snake Charmer (as above except with black carbon steel bbl.) $139.00

STOEGER/IGA SINGLE BARREL SHOTGUN
Gauge: 12, 2¾", 20, 410, 3"
Barrel: 12, 20 ga.—26", 28" (Imp. Cyl., Mod., Full); 410—28" (Imp. Cyl., Mod., Full).
Weight: 5¼ lbs.
Stock: 14"x1½"x2½". Brazilian hardwood.
Sights: Metal bead front.
Features: Exposed hammer with half-cock safety; extractor; blue finish. Introduced 1987. Imported from Brazil by Stoeger Industries.
Price: $110.00

THOMPSON/CENTER TCR '87 HUNTER SHOTGUN
Gauge: 10, 3½", 12, 3½".
Barrel: 25" (Full).
Weight: 8 lbs.
Stock: Uncheckered walnut.
Sights: Bead front.
Features: Uses same receiver as TCR '87 rifle models, and stock has extra 7/16" drop at heel. Choke designed for steel shot. Introduced 1989.
Price: $495.00

Weatherby Athena

WEATHERBY ATHENA SINGLE BARREL TRAP
Gauge: 12, 2¾" chamber.
Barrel: 32", 34" (Full, Mod., Imp. Mod., Multi-Choke tubes).
Weight: About 8½ lbs. **Length:** 49½" overall with 32" barrel.
Stock: 14⅜"x1⅜"x2⅛"x1¾". American walnut with checkered p.g. and forend.
Sights: White front, brass middle bead.
Features: Engraved, silvered sideplate receiver; ventilated rubber recoil pad. Can be ordered with an extra over/under barrel set. Introduced 1988. Imported from Japan by Weatherby.
Price: $1,695.00
Price: Combo $2,240.00

Zoli Z90

ZOLI Z90 MONO-TRAP GUN
Gauge: 12, 2¾" chamber.
Barrel: 32" or 34" (choke tubes).
Weight: 8½ lbs.
Stock: 14½"x2⅛"x1¼"x1¼". Checkered Turkish cicassian walnut with Monte Carlo.
Features: Boxlock action with automatic ejector; trigger adjustable for length of pull; step-type vent. rib with two sight beads. Matte blue finish on receiver. Introduced 1989. Imported from Italy by Antonio Zoli, USA.
Price: $1,795.00

Designs for utility, suitable for and adaptable to competitions and other sporting purposes.

ARMSCOR MODEL 30R RIOT GUN
Gauge: 12, 5- or 7-shot capacity.
Barrel: 20" (Cyl.).
Weight: 7.2 lbs. **Length:** 40" overall.
Stock: Plain mahogany.
Sights: Metal bead front.
Features: Double action bars; blue finish; grooved forend. Introduced 1987. Imported from the Philippines by Armscor.

Price: About **$169.95**
Price: Model 30K (21" bbl., 7-shot, olive green butt and forend) **$169.95**
Price: Model 30C (20" bbl., 5-shot, combo black removable butt with pistol grip) **$179.95**
Price: Model 30FS (20" bbl., 5-shot, black folding stock and pistol grip) **$189.95**
Price: Model 30RP (18" bbl., 5-shot, black wood butt and forend with interchangeable pistol grip) **$169.95**

Benelli M3

BENELLI M3 SUPER 90 PUMP/AUTO SHOTGUN
Gauge: 12, 3" chamber, 7-shot magazine.
Barrel: 19¾" (Cyl.).
Weight: 7 lbs., 8 oz. **Length:** 41" overall.

Stock: High-impact polymer with sling loop in side of butt; rubberized pistol grip on optional SWAT stock.
Sights: Post front, buckhorn rear adjustable for w.
Features: Combination pump/auto action. Alloy receiver with inertia recoil rotating locking lug bolt; matte finish; automatic shell release lever. Introduced 1989. Imported by Heckler & Koch, Inc.
Price: **$813.00**
Price: With ghost ring sight system **$860.00**
Price: With folding stock **$880.00**

Benelli M1 Super 90

Benelli M1 Super 90
Similar to the M3 Super 90 Defense except is semi-automatic only, has overall length of 39¾" and weighs 7 lbs., 4 oz. Introduced 1986.
Price: Slug Gun with standard stock **$631.00**
Price: With pistol grip stock (Defense) **$669.00**
Price: With ghost ring sight system **$677.00**

Beretta 1200 FP

BERETTA MODEL 1200 FP AUTO SHOTGUN
Gauge: 12, 2¾" or 3" chamber.
Barrel: 20" (Cyl.).
Weight: 7.3 lbs. **Length:** NA
Stock: Special strengthened technopolymer, matte black finish.
Stock: Fixed rifle type.
Features: Has 6-shot magazine. Introduced 1988. Imported from Italy by Beretta U.S.A.
Price: **$580.00**

ITHACA MODEL 87 M&P DSPS SHOTGUNS
Gauge: 12, 3" chamber, 5- or 8-shot magazine.
Barrel: 20" (Cyl.).
Weight: 7 lbs.
Stock: Walnut.
Sights: Bead front on 5-shot, rifle sights on 8-shot.
Features: Parkerized finish; bottom ejection; cross-bolt safety. Reintroduced 1988. From Ithaca Acquisition Corp.
Price: M&P, 5-shot **$407.00**
Price: DSPS, 8-shot **$407.00**

Ithaca Model 87 Hand Grip Shotgun
Similar to the Model 87 M&P except has black polymer pistol grip and slide handle with nylon sling. In 12 or 20 gauge, 18½" barrel (Cyl.), 5-shot magazine. Reintroduced 1988.
Price: **$391.00**

Mossberg 500

MOSSBERG MODEL 500 SECURITY SHOTGUNS
Gauge: 12, 3" chamber.
Barrel: 18½", 20" (Cyl.).
Weight: 7 lbs.
Stock: Walnut-finished hardwood; synthetic field or Speedfeed.
Sights: Metal bead front.

Features: Available in 6- or 8-shot models. Top-mounted safety, double action slide bars, swivel studs, rubber recoil pad. Blue, Parkerized, nickel finishes. Mossberg Cablelock included. Price list not complete—contact Mossberg for full list.
Price: From about **$276.00**
Price: Mini Combo (as above except also comes with a handguard and pistol grip kit), from about **$284.00**
Price: Maxi Combo (as above except also comes with an extra field barrel), from about **$302.00**
Price: With Ghost-Ring sight, from about **$334.00**
Price: As above, Parkerized, from about **$386.00**

CAUTION: PRICES CHANGE, CHECK AT GUNSHOP.

Mossberg HS 410

Mossberg Model 500, 590 Ghost-Ring Shotguns

Similar to the Model 500 Security except has adjustable blade front, adjustable ghost-ring rear sight with protective "ears." Model 500 has 18.5″ (Cyl.) barrel, 6-shot magazine; Model 590 has 20″ (Cyl.) barrel, 9-shot magazine. Both have synthetic field stock. Mossberg Cablelock included. Introduced 1990. From Mossberg.

Price: Model 500, blue **$334.00**
Price: As above, Parkerized **$386.00**
Price: Model 590, blue **$400.00**
Price: As above, Parkerized **$451.00**

Mossberg Model HS 410 Shotgun

Similar to the Model 500 Security pump except chambered for 410, 3″ shells; has vertical-type pump handle; has special spreader choke attachment on the 18.5″ barrel. Overall length is 37.5″, weight is 6.25 lbs. Blue finish; synthetic field stock. Also available with integral Laser Sight forend. Mossberg Cablelock included. Introduced 1990.

Price: HS 410, about **$380.00**
Price: HS 410 Laser, about **$676.00**

Mossberg 590

Mossberg Model 500 Mariner Pump

Similar to the Model 500 Security except all metal parts finished with MARINECOAT, a Teflon and metal coating to resist rust and corrosion. Choice of synthetic field or Speedfeed stocks or pistol grip. Mossberg Cablelock included.

Price: 6-shot, from about **$373.00**
Price: Mini Combo (as above except includes handguard and pistol grip kit), 6-shot, from about **$380.00**
Price: Mini Combo, 9-shot, from about **$449.00**

Mossberg Model 590 Mariner Shotgun

Same gun as the 590 Military except all metal parts are finished with MARINECOAT, a Teflon and metal coating to resist rust and corrosion. Has 20″ barrel, 9-shot capacity. Mossberg Cablelock included. Introduced 1989.

Price: With synthetic field stock, from about **$441.00**
Price: With Speedfeed stock, from about **$458.00**

Mossberg Model 500, 590 Intimidator Shotguns

Similar to the Model 500 Security with synthetic stock except has integral Laser Sight built into the forend. Mossberg Cablelock included. Introduced 1990.

Price: Model 500, blue, 6-shot, about **$572.00**
Price: Model 500, Parkerized, 6-shot, about **$624.00**
Price: Model 590, blue, 9-shot, about **$638.00**
Price: Model 590, Parkerized, 9-shot, about **$689.00**

> Consult our Directory pages for
> the location of firms mentioned.

Mossberg Bullpup

MOSSBERG 500 BULLPUP

Gauge: 12, 3″ chamber; 6- or 9-shot.
Barrel: 18½″, 20″ (Cyl.).
Weight: 9½ lbs. (6-shot). **Length:** 28½″ overall (18½″ bbl.).
Stock: Bullpup design of high-impact plastics.
Sights: Fixed, mounted in carrying handle.
Features: Uses the M500 pump shotgun action. Cross-bolt and grip safeties. Mossberg Cablelock included. Introduced 1986.

Price: 6-shot **$425.00**
Price: 9-shot **$497.00**

Remington 870P

CROSSFIRE MODEL 88P RIFLE/SHOTGUN

Caliber/Gauge: 243, 308 Win./12 ga., 2¾″ chamber.
Barrel: 20″.
Weight: 9.5 lbs. **Length:** 39.75″ overall.
Stock: Lightweight composite.
Sights: Optional. Adjustable open or optical battle sight.
Features: Combination pump/semi-auto action; each can be independently reloaded while the other is in operation. Has two barrels. Uses 20-shot M-14 magazine for 308, 7-shot box magazine for 12 ga. First round chambered by pump action, fires semi-auto thereafter. Announced 1989. From Sam Inc.

Price: Less sights **$1,399.00**

REMINGTON MODEL 870P POLICE SHOTGUN

Gauge: 12, 3″ chamber.
Barrel: 18″, 20″ (Police Cyl.), 20″ (Imp. Cyl.).
Weight: About 7 lbs.
Stock: Lacquer-finished hardwood or folding stock.
Sights: Metal bead front or rifle sights.
Features: Solid steel receiver, double action slide bars. Blued or Parkerized finish.

Price: Wood stock, 18″ or 20″, bead sight, about **$348.00**
Price: Wood stock, 20″, rifle sights, about **$374.00**

Winchester Defender

WINCHESTER 1300 DEFENDER PUMP GUN
Gauge: 12, 3" chamber, 5- or 8-shot capacity.
Barrel: 18" (Cyl.).
Weight: 6¾ lbs. **Length:** 38⅝" overall.
Stock: Walnut-finished hardwood stock and ribbed forend, or pistol grip.
Sights: Metal bead front.
Features: Cross-bolt safety, front-locking rotary bolt, twin action slide bars. Black rubber buttpad. From U.S. Repeating Arms Co.
Price: 8-shot, wood stock, about $261.00
Price: 5-shot, wood stock, about $256.00
Price: Defender Combo (with p.g. and extra vent. rib 28" bbl.) $346.00

Winchester 8-Shot Pistol Grip Pump Security Shotguns
Same as regular Security Series but with pistol grip and forend of high-impact resistant ABS plastic with non-glare black finish. Introduced 1984.
Price: Pistol Grip Defender, about $261.00

Winchester "Stainless Marine"

Winchester 1300 "Stainless Marine" Pump Gun
Same as the Defender except has bright chrome finish, stainless steel barrel, rifle-type sights only. Phosphate coated receiver for corrosion resistance.
Price: About $423.00

BLACKPOWDER SINGLE SHOT PISTOLS—FLINT & PERCUSSION

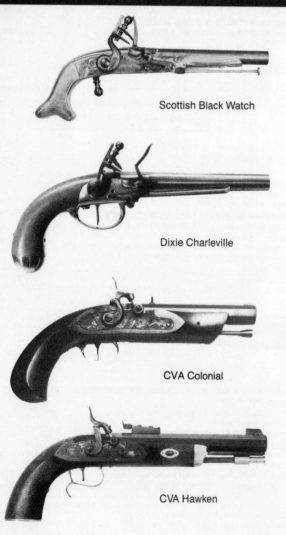

Scottish Black Watch

BLACK WATCH SCOTCH PISTOL
Caliber: 577 (.500" round ball).
Barrel: 7", smoothbore.
Weight: 1½ lbs. **Length:** 12" overall.
Stock: Brass.
Sights: None.
Features: Faithful reproduction of this military flintlock. From Dixie.
Price: $148.00

Dixie Charleville

CHARLEVILLE FLINTLOCK PISTOL
Caliber: 69 (.680" round ball).
Barrel: 7½".
Weight: 48 oz. **Length:** 13½" overall.
Stock: Walnut.
Sights: None.
Features: Brass frame, polished steel barrel, iron belt hook, brass buttcap and backstrap. Replica of original 1777 pistol. Imported by Dixie.
Price: $164.95

CVA Colonial

CVA COLONIAL PISTOL
Caliber: 45.
Barrel: 6¾", octagonal, rifled. **Length:** 12¾" overall.
Stock: Selected hardwood.
Features: Case-hardened lock, brass furniture, fixed sights. Steel ramrod. Available in percussion only. Imported by CVA.
Price: Finished $113.95
Price: Kit $83.95

CVA Hawken

CVA HAWKEN PISTOL
Caliber: 50.
Barrel: 9¾"; 1" flats.
Weight: 50 oz. **Length:** 16½" overall.
Stock: Select hardwood.
Sights: Beaded blade front, fully adjustable open rear.
Features: Color case-hardened lock, polished brass wedge plate, nose cap, ramrod thimbles, trigger guard, grip cap. Hooked breech. Imported by CVA.
Price: $153.95
Price: Kit $111.95

CAUTION: PRICES CHANGE, CHECK AT GUNSHOP.

BLACKPOWDER SINGLE SHOT PISTOLS — FLINT & PERCUSSION

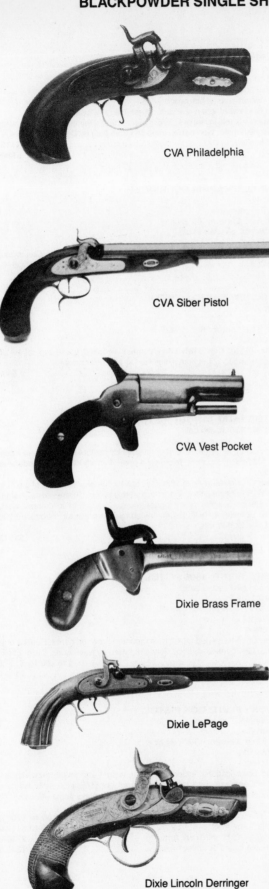

CVA Philadelphia

CVA Siber Pistol

CVA Vest Pocket

Dixie Brass Frame

Dixie LePage

Dixie Lincoln Derringer

CVA PHILADELPHIA DERRINGER PISTOL
Caliber: 45.
Barrel: 3⅛".
Weight: 16 oz. **Length:** 7" overall.
Stock: Select hardwood.
Sights: Fixed.
Features: Engraved wedge holder and barrel. Imported by CVA.
Price: $93.95
Price: Kit form $57.95

CVA SIBER PISTOL
Caliber: 45.
Barrel: 10½".
Weight: 34 oz. **Length:** 15½" overall.
Stock: High-grade French walnut, checkered grip.
Sights: Barleycorn front, micro-adjustable rear.
Features: Reproduction of pistol made by Swiss watchmaker Jean Siber in the 1800s. Precise lock and set trigger give fast lock time. Has engraving, blackened stainless barrel, trigger guard. Imported by CVA.
Price: $414.95

CVA VEST POCKET DERRINGER
Caliber: 44.
Barrel: 2½", brass.
Weight: 7 oz.
Stock: Two-piece walnut.
Features: All brass frame with brass ramrod. A muzzle-loading version of the Colt No. 3 derringer.
Price: Finished $61.95
Price: Kit $53.95

DIXIE ABILENE DERRINGER
Caliber: 41.
Barrel: 2½", six-groove rifling.
Weight: 8 oz. **Length:** 6½" overall.
Stock: Walnut.
Features: All steel version of Dixie's brass-framed derringers. Blued barrel, color case-hardened frame and hammer. Shoots .395" patched ball. Comes with wood presentation case.
Price: $81.50
Price: Kit form $51.95

DIXIE BRASS FRAME DERRINGER
Caliber: 41.
Barrel: 2½".
Weight: 7 oz. **Length:** 5½" overall.
Stock: Walnut.
Features: Brass frame, color case-hardened hammer and trigger. Shoots .395" round ball. Engraved model available. From Dixie Gun Works.
Price: Plain model $49.95
Price: Engraved model $85.95
Price: Kit form, plain model $42.50

DIXIE LE PAGE PERCUSSION DUELING PISTOL
Caliber: 45.
Barrel: 10", rifled.
Weight: 40 oz. **Length:** 16" overall.
Stock: Walnut, fluted butt.
Sights: Blade front, notch rear.
Features: Double set triggers. Blued barrel; trigger guard and butt cap are polished silver. Imported by Dixie Gun Works.
Price: $225.00

DIXIE LINCOLN DERRINGER
Caliber: 41.
Barrel: 2", 8 lands, 8 grooves.
Weight: 7 oz. **Length:** 5½" overall.
Stock: Walnut finish, checkered.
Sights: Fixed.
Features: Authentic copy of the "Lincoln Derringer." Shoots .400" patched ball. German silver furniture includes trigger guard with pineapple finial, wedge plates, nose, wrist, side and teardrop inlays. All furniture, lockplate, hammer, and breech plug engraved. Imported from Italy by Dixie Gun Works.
Price: With wooden case $285.95
Price: Kit (not engraved) $89.95

BLACKPOWDER SINGLE SHOT PISTOLS — FLINT & PERCUSSION

Dixie Queen Anne

DIXIE QUEEN ANNE FLINTLOCK PISTOL
Caliber: 50 (.490″ round ball).
Barrel: 7½″, smoothbore.
Stock: Walnut.
Sights: None.
Features: Browned steel barrel, fluted brass trigger guard, brass mask on butt. Lockplate left in the white. Made by Pedersoli in Itlay. Introduced 1983. Imported by Dixie Gun Works.
Price: **$144.00**
Price: Kit **$119.95**

Dixie Tornado

FRENCH-STYLE DUELING PISTOL
Caliber: 44.
Barrel: 10″.
Weight: 35 oz. **Length:** 15¾″ overall.
Stock: Carved walnut.
Sights: Fixed.
Features: Comes with velvet-lined case and accessories. Imported by Mandall Shooting Supplies.
Price: **$295.00**

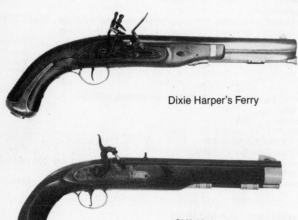

Dixie Harper's Ferry

CVA Kentucky

Kentucky Percussion Pistol
Similar to flint version but percussion lock. Imported by Cabela's, The Armoury, Navy Arms, CVA (50 cal.).
Price: . . . . **$125.00 to $141.95**
Price: In kit form (CVA, Armoury) **$97.95**
Price: Single cased set (Navy Arms) **$205.00**
Price: Double cased set (Navy Arms) **$330.00**

DIXIE PENNSYLVANIA PISTOL
Caliber: 44 (.430″ round ball).
Barrel: 10″ (⅞″ octagon).
Weight: 2½ lbs.
Stock: Walnut-stained hardwood.
Sights: Blade front, open rear drift-adjustable for windage; brass.
Features: Available in flint only. Brass trigger guard, thimbles, nosecap, wedge-plates; high-luster blue barrel. Imported from Italy by Dixie Gun Works.
Price: Finished **$119.95**
Price: Kit **$88.75**

DIXIE PHILADELPHIA DERRINGER
Caliber: 41.
Barrel: 3½″, octagon.
Weight: 8 oz. **Length:** 5½″ overall.
Stock: Walnut, checkered p.g.
Sights: Fixed.
Features: Barrel and lock are blued; brass furniture. From Dixie Gun Works.
Price: **$45.00**

DIXIE SCREW BARREL PISTOL
Caliber: .445″.
Barrel: 2½″.
Weight: 8 oz. **Length:** 6½″ overall.
Stock: Walnut.
Features: Trigger folds down when hammer is cocked. Close copy of the originals once made in Belgium. Uses No. 11 percussion caps.
Price: **$89.00**
Price: Kit **$58.95**

DIXIE TORNADO TARGET PISTOL
Caliber: 44 (.430″ round ball).
Barrel: 10″, octagonal, 1:22″ twist.
Stocks: Walnut, target-style. Left unfinished for custom fitting. Walnut forend.
Sights: Blade on ramp front, micro-type open rear adjustable for windage and elevation.
Features: Grip frame style of 1860 Colt revolver. Improved model of the Tingle and B.W. Southgate pistol. Trigger adjustable for pull. Frame, barrel, hammer and sights in the white, brass trigger guard. Comes with solid brass, walnut-handled cleaning rod with jag and nylon muzzle protector. Introduced 1983. From Dixie Gun Works.
Price: **$151.95**

HARPER'S FERRY 1806 PISTOL
Caliber: 58 (.570″ round ball).
Barrel: 10″.
Weight: 40 oz. **Length:** 16″ overall.
Stock: Walnut.
Sights: Fixed.
Features: Case-hardened lock, brass mounted browned barrel. Replica of the first U.S. Gov't.-made flintlock pistol. Imported by Navy Arms, Dixie, EMF.
Price: . . . . **$165.00 to $195.00**
Price: Kit (Dixie) **$159.00**

KENTUCKY FLINTLOCK PISTOL
Caliber: 44, 45.
Barrel: 10⅛″.
Weight: 32 oz. **Length:** 15½″ overall.
Stock: Walnut.
Sights: Fixed.
Features: Specifications, including caliber, weight and length may vary with importer. Case-hardened lock, blued barrel; available also as brass barrel flint Model 1821. Imported by Cabela's (44, 50), Navy Arms (44 only), The Armoury.
Price: . . . . **$145.00 to $207.00**
Price: In kit form, from . . . . **$90.00 to $112.00**
Price: Single cased set (Navy Arms) **$230.00**
Price: Double cased set (Navy Arms) **$350.00**

CAUTION: PRICES CHANGE, CHECK AT GUNSHOP.

BLACKPOWDER SINGLE SHOT PISTOLS — FLINT & PERCUSSION

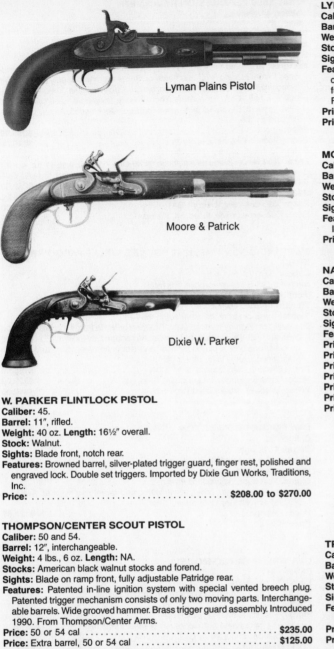

Lyman Plains Pistol

Moore & Patrick

Dixie W. Parker

LYMAN PLAINS PISTOL
Caliber: 50 or 54.
Barrel: 8", 1:30" twist, both calibers.
Weight: 50 oz. **Length:** 15" overall.
Stock: Walnut half-stock.
Sights: Blade front, square notch rear adjustable for windage.
Features: Polished brass trigger guard and ramrod tip, color case-hardened coil spring lock, spring-loaded trigger, stainless steel nipple, blackened iron furniture. Hooked patent breech, detachable belt hook. Introduced 1981. From Lyman Products.
Price: Finished $184.95
Price: Kit $154.95

MOORE & PATRICK FLINT DUELING PISTOL
Caliber: 45.
Barrel: 10", rifled.
Weight: 32 oz. **Length:** 14½" overall.
Stock: European walnut, checkered.
Sights: Fixed.
Features: Engraved, silvered lockplate, blue barrel. German silver furniture. Imported from Italy by Dixie.
Price: $285.00

NAVY ARMS LE PAGE DUELING PISTOL
Caliber: 45.
Barrel: 9", octagon, rifled.
Weight: 34 oz. **Length:** 15" overall.
Stock: European walnut.
Sights: Adjustable rear.
Features: Single set trigger. Polished metal finish. From Navy Arms.
Price: Percussion $355.00
Price: Single cased set, percussion $540.00
Price: Double cased set, percussion $930.00
Price: Flintlock, rifled $435.00
Price: Flintlock, smoothbore $435.00
Price: Flintlock, single cased set $625.00
Price: Flintlock, double cased set $1,100.00

Thompson/Center Scout

W. PARKER FLINTLOCK PISTOL
Caliber: 45.
Barrel: 11", rifled.
Weight: 40 oz. **Length:** 16½" overall.
Stock: Walnut.
Sights: Blade front, notch rear.
Features: Browned barrel, silver-plated trigger guard, finger rest, polished and engraved lock. Double set triggers. Imported by Dixie Gun Works, Traditions, Inc.
Price: . . . . $208.00 to $270.00

THOMPSON/CENTER SCOUT PISTOL
Caliber: 50 and 54.
Barrel: 12", interchangeable.
Weight: 4 lbs., 6 oz. **Length:** NA.
Stocks: American black walnut stocks and forend.
Sights: Blade on ramp front, fully adjustable Patridge rear.
Features: Patented in-line ignition system with special vented breech plug. Patented trigger mechanism consists of only two moving parts. Interchangeable barrels. Wide grooved hammer. Brass trigger guard assembly. Introduced 1990. From Thompson/Center Arms.
Price: 50 or 54 cal $235.00
Price: Extra barrel, 50 or 54 cal $125.00

TRADITIONS TRAPPER PISTOL
Caliber: 45, 50.
Barrel: 9¾", ⅞" flats.
Weight: 2¾ lbs. **Length:** 16⅝" overall.
Stock: Beech.
Sights: Blade front, adjustable rear.
Features: Double set triggers; brass butt cap, trigger guard, wedge plate, forend tip, thimble. From Traditions, Inc.
Price: $140.00
Price: Kit $107.00

BLACKPOWDER REVOLVERS

Army 1851

ARMY 1851 PERCUSSION REVOLVER
Caliber: 44, 6-shot.
Barrel: 7½".
Weight: 45 oz. **Length:** 13" overall.
Stocks: Walnut finish.
Sights: Fixed.
Features: 44-caliber version of the 1851 Navy. Imported by The Armoury, E.M.F.
Price: . . . . $95.00 to $140.00

BLACKPOWDER REVOLVERS

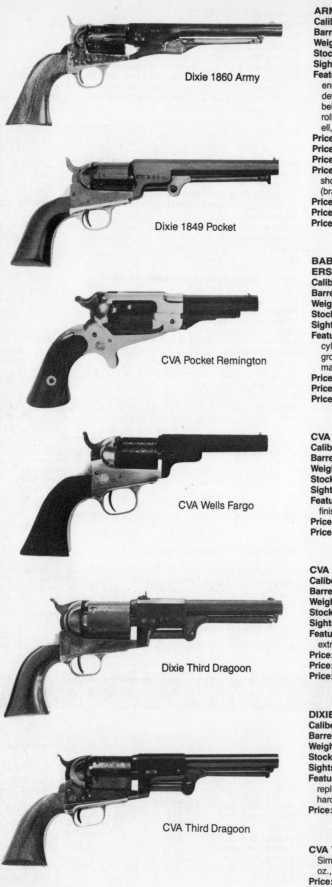

Dixie 1860 Army

Dixie 1849 Pocket

CVA Pocket Remington

CVA Wells Fargo

Dixie Third Dragoon

CVA Third Dragoon

ARMY 1860 PERCUSSION REVOLVER
Caliber: 44, 6-shot.
Barrel: 8".
Weight: 40 oz. **Length:** 13⅝" overall.
Stocks: Walnut.
Sights: Fixed.
Features: Engraved navy scene on cylinder; brass trigger guard; case-hardened frame, loading lever and hammer. Some importers supply pistol cut for detachable shoulder stock, have accessory stock available. Imported by Cabela's, E.M.F., CVA, Navy Arms, The Armoury, Dixie (half-fluted cylinder, not roll engraved), Euroarms of America (brass or steel model), Armsport, Mitchell, Uberti USA.
Price: About . . . . **$92.95 to $235.00**
Price: Single cased set (Navy Arms) **$240.00**
Price: Double cased set (Navy Arms) **$365.00**
Price: 1861 Navy: Same as Army except 36 cal., 7½" bbl., wgt. 41 oz., cut for shoulder stock; round cylinder (fluted avail.), from Armsport, E.M.F., CVA (brass frame), Cabela's, Mitchell . . . . **$99.95 to $249.00**
Price: Steel frame kit (E.M.F., Mitchell, Navy, Euroarms) . . **$125.00- $146.00**
Price: Stainless steel (Uberti USA) **$305.00**
Price: Colt Army Police, fluted cyl. (Cabela's) **$96.95**

BABY DRAGOON 1848, 1849 POCKET, WELLS FARGO REVOLVERS
Caliber: 31.
Barrel: 3", 4", 5"; seven-groove, RH twist.
Weight: About 21 oz.
Stock: Varnished walnut.
Sights: Brass pin front, hammer notch rear.
Features: No loading lever on Baby Dragoon or Wells Fargo models. Unfluted cylinder with stagecoach holdup scene; cupped cylinder pin; no grease grooves; one safety pin on cylinder and slot in hammer face; straight (flat) mainspring. From Dixie, Uberti USA.
Price: 6" barrel, with loading lever (Dixie) **$185.00**
Price: Brass backstrap, trigger guard (Uberti USA) **$229.00**
Price: As above, silver-plated (Uberti USA) **$240.00**

CVA POCKET REMINGTON
Caliber: 31.
Barrel: 4", octagonal.
Weight: 15½ oz. **Length:** 7½" overall.
Stocks: Two-piece walnut.
Sights: Post front, grooved topstrap rear.
Features: Spur trigger, brass frame with blued barrel and cylinder. Available finished or in kit form. Introduced 1984.
Price: Finished **$127.95**
Price: Kit **$95.95**

CVA WELLS FARGO MODEL
Caliber: 31.
Barrel: 4", octagonal.
Weight: 28 oz. (with extra cylinder). **Length:** 9" overall.
Stocks: Walnut.
Sights: Post front, hammer notch rear.
Features: Brass frame and backstrap or steel frame; blue finish. Comes with extra cylinder. Imported by CVA.
Price: Brass frame, finished **$127.95**
Price: As above, kit **$109.95**
Price: Steel frame, finished **$191.95**

DIXIE THIRD MODEL DRAGOON
Caliber: 44 (.454" round ball).
Barrel: 7⅜".
Weight: 4 lbs., 2½ oz.
Stocks: One-piece walnut.
Sights: Brass pin front, hammer notch rear, or adjustable folding leaf rear.
Features: Cylinder engraved with Indian fight scene. This is the only Dragoon replica with folding leaf sight. Brass backstrap and trigger guard; color case-hardened steel frame, blue-black barrel. Imported by Dixie Gun Works.
Price: **$195.00**

CVA Third Model Colt Dragoon
Similar to the Dixie Third Dragoon except has 7½" barrel, weighs 4 lbs., 6 oz., blade front sight. Overall length of 14". 44 caliber, 6-shot.
Price: **$245.00**

CAUTION: PRICES CHANGE, CHECK AT GUNSHOP.

BLACKPOWDER REVOLVERS

DIXIE "WYATT EARP" REVOLVER
Caliber: 44.
Barrel: 12″ octagon.
Weight: 46 oz. **Length:** 18″ overall.
Stocks: Two-piece walnut.
Sights: Fixed.
Features: Highly polished brass frame, backstrap and trigger guard; blued barrel and cylinder; case-hardened hammer, trigger and loading lever. Navy-size shoulder stock ($45.00) will fit with minor fitting. From Dixie Gun Works.
Price: $130.00

Uberti 1851 Squareback

Uberti 1861 Navy Percussion Revolver
Similar to 1851 Navy except has round 7½″ barrel, rounded trigger guard, German silver blade front sight, "creeping" loading lever. Available with fluted or round cylinder. Imported by Uberti USA.
Price: Steel backstrap, trigger guard, cut for stock $245.00
Price: Brass backstrap, trigger guard $229.00
Price: Silver-plated backstrap, trigger guard $249.00
Price: Stainless steel $305.00

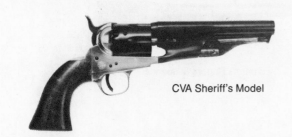

CVA Sheriff's Model

LE MAT CAVALRY MODEL REVOLVER
Caliber: 44/65.
Barrel: 6¾″ (revolver); 4⅞″ (single shot).
Weight: NA.
Stocks: Hand-checkered walnut.
Sights: Post front, hammer notch rear.
Features: Exact reproduction with all-steel construction; 44-cal. 9-shot cylinder, 65-cal. single barrel; color case-hardened hammer with selector; spur trigger guard; ring at butt; lever-type barrel release. From Navy Arms.
Price: Cavalry model (lanyard ring, spur trigger guard) $595.00
Price: Army model (round trigger guard, pin-type barrel release) . . . $595.00
Price: Naval-style (thumb selector on hammer) $595.00

Navy 1858 Remington-Style

GRISWOLD & GUNNISON PERCUSSION REVOLVER
Caliber: 36 or 44, 6-shot.
Barrel: 7½″.
Weight: 44 oz. (36 cal.). **Length:** 13″ overall.
Stocks: Walnut.
Sights: Fixed.
Features: Replica of famous Confederate pistol. Brass frame, backstrap and trigger guard; case-hardened loading lever; rebated cylinder (44 cal. only). Rounded Dragoon-type barrel. Imported by Navy Arms (as Reb Model 1860), E.M.F., Uberti USA
Price: About $229.00
Price: Kit (E.M.F.) $95.00
Price: Single cased set (Navy Arms) $190.00
Price: Double cased set (Navy Arms) $300.00
Price: Reb 1860 (Navy Arms) $100.00
Price: As above, kit $80.00

NAVY MODEL 1851 PERCUSSION REVOLVER
Caliber: 36, 44, 6-shot.
Barrel: 7½″.
Weight: 44 oz. **Length:** 13″ overall.
Stocks: Walnut finish.
Sights: Post front, hammer notch rear.
Features: Brass backstrap and trigger guard; some have 1st Model squareback trigger guard, engraved cylinder with navy battle scene; case-hardened frame, hammer, loading lever. Imported by The Armoury, Cabela's, Mitchell, Navy Arms, E.M.F., Dixie, Euroarms of America, Armsport, CVA (36-cal. only), Uberti USA.
Price: Brass frame . . . . $76.95 to $229.00
Price: Steel frame . . . . $130.00 to $229.00
Price: Stainless (Uberti USA) $295.00
Price: Silver-plated backstrap, trigger guard (Uberti USA) $249.00
Price: Kit form . . . . $110.00 to $123.95
Price: Engraved model (Dixie) $139.95
Price: Single cased set, steel frame (Navy Arms) $215.00
Price: Double cased set, steel frame (Navy Arms) $340.00
Price: London Model with iron backstrap (Uberti USA) $245.00
Price: Confederate Navy (Cabela's) $59.88

CVA Colt Sheriff's Model
Similar to the Uberti 1861 Navy except has 5½″ barrel, brass or steel frame, semi-fluted cylinder. In 36 caliber only.
Price: Brass frame, finished $157.95
Price: As above, kit $137.95
Price: Steel frame, finished $185.95
Price: 1861 Navy, steel frame, 36 cal. $217.95
Price: As above, brass frame, 44 cal. $145.95
Price: As above, kit $127.95

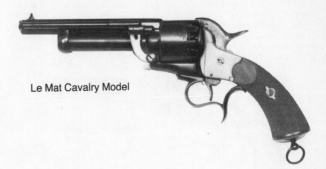

Le Mat Cavalry Model

NAVY DELUXE 1858 REMINGTON-STYLE REVOLVER
Caliber: 44.
Barrel: 8″.
Weight: 2 lbs., 13 oz.
Stocks: Smooth walnut.
Sights: Dovetailed blade front.
Features: First exact reproduction—correct in size and weight to the original, with progressive rifling; highly polished with blue finish, silver-plated trigger guard. From Navy Arms.
Price: Deluxe model $300.00

BLACKPOWDER REVOLVERS

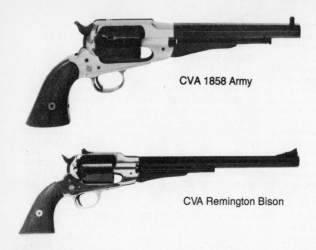

CVA 1858 Army

CVA Remington Bison

POCKET POLICE 1862 PERCUSSION REVOLVER
Caliber: 36, 5-shot.
Barrel: 4½″, 5½″, 6½″, 7½″.
Weight: 26 oz. **Length:** 12″ overall (6½″ bbl.).
Stocks: Walnut.
Sights: Fixed.
Features: Round tapered barrel; half-fluted and rebated cylinder; case-hardened frame, loading lever and hammer; silver or brass trigger guard and backstrap. Imported by CVA (5½″ only), Navy Arms (5½″ only), Uberti USA (5½″, 6½″ only).
Price: About . . . . $143.95 to $200.00
Price: Single cased set with accessories (Navy Arms) $260.00
Price: Stainless steel (Uberti USA) 4½″, 5½″ $289.00
Price: Kit (CVA) $121.95
Price: With silver-plated backstrap, trigger guard (Uberti USA) $245.00

ROGERS & SPENCER PERCUSSION REVOLVER
Caliber: 44.
Barrel: 7½″.
Weight: 47 oz. **Length:** 13¾″ overall.
Stocks: Walnut.
Sights: Cone front, integral groove in frame for rear.
Features: Accurate reproduction of a Civil War design. Solid frame; extra large nipple cut-out on rear of cylinder; loading lever and cylinder easily removed for cleaning. From Euroarms of America (standard blue, engraved, burnished, target models), Navy Arms.
Price: . . . . $160.00 to $240.00
Price: Nickel-plated $215.00
Price: Engraved (Euroarms) $286.00
Price: Kit version $95.00
Price: Target version (Euroarms) $234.00
Price: Brushed satin chrome (Navy Arms) $230.00
Price: Burnished London Gray (Euroarms) $234.00

Ruger Old Army

SHERIFF MODEL 1851 PERCUSSION REVOLVER
Caliber: 36, 44, 6-shot.
Barrel: 5″.
Weight: 40 oz. **Length:** 10½″ overall.
Stocks: Walnut.
Sights: Fixed.
Features: Brass backstrap and trigger guard; engraved navy scene; case-hardened frame, hammer, loading lever. Imported by E.M.F.
Price: Steel frame $170.00
Price: Brass frame . . . . $90.95 to $125.00
Price: Kit, brass or steel frame . . . . $114.00 to $160.00

NEW MODEL 1858 ARMY PERCUSSION REVOLVER
Caliber: 36 or 44, 6-shot.
Barrel: 6½″ or 8″.
Weight: 40 oz. **Length:** 13½″ overall.
Stocks: Walnut.
Sights: Blade front, groove-in-frame rear.
Features: Replica of Remington Model 1858. Also available from some importers as Army Model Belt Revolver in 36 cal., shortened and lightened version of the 44. Target Model (Uberti USA, Navy) has fully adjustable target rear sight, target front, 36 or 44. Imported by Cabela's, CVA (as 1858 Remington Army), Dixie, Navy Arms, The Armoury, E.M.F., Euroarms of America (engraved, stainless and plain), Armsport, Mitchell, Uberti USA.
Price: Steel frame, about . . . . $179.95 to $221.95
Price: Steel frame kit (Euroarms, Navy) . . . . $115.95 to $150.00
Price: Single cased set (Navy Arms) $210.00
Price: Double cased set (Navy Arms) $235.00
Price: Nickel finish (E.M.F.) $152.75
Price: Stainless steel Model 1858 (Euroarms, Uberti, Cabela's, Navy Arms, Armsport) . . . . $140.00 to $220.00
Price: Target Model, adjustable rear sight (Cabela's, Euroarms, Uberti, Navy, E.M.F.) . . . . $95.95 to $239.00
Price: Brass frame (CVA, Cabela's, Navy Arms) . . . . $97.95 to $173.95
Price: As above, kit (CVA, Dixie, Navy Arms) . . . . $94.75 to $151.95
Price: Remington "Texas" (Mitchell) $179.95

CVA 1858 Remington Target
Similar to the New Model 1858 Remington except has ramped blade front sight, adjustable rear.
Price: $239.95

CVA Remington Bison
Similar to the CVA 1858 Remington Target except has 10¼″ octagonal barrel, 44 caliber, brass frame.
Price: Finished $259.95

Euroarms Rogers & Spencer

RUGER 44 OLD ARMY PERCUSSION REVOLVER
Caliber: 44, 6-shot. Uses .457″ dia. lead bullets.
Barrel: 7½″ (6-groove, 16″ twist).
Weight: 46 oz. **Length:** 13¾″ overall.
Stocks: Smooth walnut.
Sights: Ramp front, rear adjustable for w. and e.
Features: Stainless steel standard size nipples, chrome-moly steel cylinder and frame, same lockwork as in original Super Blackhawk. Also available in stainless steel. Made in USA. From Sturm, Ruger & Co.
Price: Stainless steel (Model KBP-7) $407.50
Price: Blued steel (Model BP-7) $319.50

> Consult our Directory pages for
> the location of firms mentioned

NAVY-SHERIFF 1851
Same as 1851 Sheriff model except has 4″ barrel. Imported by E.M.F., Uberti USA, Mitchell.
Price: About . . . . $169.95 to $229.00
Price: Stainless steel (Uberti USA) $295.00

BLACKPOWDER REVOLVERS

Dixie Spiller & Burr

Texas Patterson

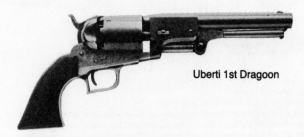

Uberti 1st Dragoon

SPILLER & BURR REVOLVER
Caliber: 36 (.375″ round ball).
Barrel: 7″, octagon.
Weight: 2½ lbs. **Length:** 12½″ overall.
Stocks: Two-piece walnut.
Sights: Fixed.
Features: Reproduction of the C.S.A. revolver. Brass frame and trigger guard. Also available as a kit. From Dixie, Mitchell, Navy Arms.
Price: .... $125.00 to $169.95
Price: Kit form $65.00
Price: Single cased set (Navy Arms) $215.00
Price: Double cased set (Navy Arms) $325.00

TEXAS PATERSON 1836 REVOLVER
Caliber: 36 (.376″ round ball).
Barrel: 7½″.
Weight: 42 oz.
Stocks: One-piece walnut.
Sights: Fixed.
Features: Copy of Sam Colt's first commercially-made revolving pistol. Has no loading lever but comes with loading tool. From Dixie Gun Works, Navy Arms.
Price: About $310.00

UBERTI 1862 POCKET NAVY PERCUSSION REVOLVER
Caliber: 36, 5-shot.
Barrel: 5½″, 6½″, octagonal, 7-groove, LH twist.
Weight: 27 oz. (5½″ barrel). **Length:** 10½″ overall (5½″ bbl.).
Stocks: One-piece varnished walnut.
Sights: Brass pin front, hammer notch rear.
Features: Rebated cylinder, hinged loading lever, brass or silver-plated backstrap and trigger guard, color cased frame, hammer, loading lever, plunger and latch, rest blued. Has original-type markings. From Uberti USA.
Price: With brass backstrap, trigger guard $229.00
Price: With silver-plated backstrap, trigger guard $245.00
Price: Stainless steel (4½″, 5½″ only) $289.00

UBERTI 1st MODEL DRAGOON
Caliber: 44.
Barrel: 7½″, part round, part octagon.
Weight: 64 oz.
Stocks: One-piece walnut.
Sights: German silver blade front, hammer notch rear.
Features: First model has oval bolt cuts in cylinder, square-back flared trigger guard, V-type mainspring, short trigger. Ranger and Indian scene roll-engraved on cylinder. Color case-hardened frame, loading lever, plunger and hammer; blue barrel, cylinder, trigger and wedge. Available with old-time charcoal blue or standard blue-black finish. Polished brass backstrap and trigger guard. From Uberti USA.
Price: $238.00

Uberti 3rd Model Dragoon Revolver
Similar to the 2nd Model except for oval trigger guard, long trigger, modifications to the loading lever and latch. Imported by Uberti USA
Price: Military model (frame cut for shoulder stock, steel backstrap) $259.00
Price: Civilian (brass backstrap, trigger guard) $240.00
Price: Western (silver-plated backstrap, trigger guard) $269.00
Price: Shoulder stock $125.00

Uberti 2nd Model Dragoon Revolver
Similar to the 1st Model except this model is distinguished by its rectangular bolt cuts in the cylinder.
Price: $240.00
Price: As Confederate Tucker & Sherrard, with 3rd Model loading lever and special cylinder engraving. $238.00

WALKER 1847 PERCUSSION REVOLVER
Caliber: 44, 6-shot.
Barrel: 9″.
Weight: 84 oz. **Length:** 15½″ overall.
Stocks: Walnut.
Sights: Fixed.
Features: Case-hardened frame, loading lever and hammer; iron backstrap; brass trigger guard; engraved cylinder. Imported by Cabela's, CVA, Navy Arms, Dixie, Armsport.
Price: About .... $185.00 to $295.00
Price: Single cased set (Navy Arms) $295.00

BLACKPOWDER MUSKETS & RIFLES

ARMOURY R140 HAWKEN RIFLE
Caliber: 45, 50 or 54.
Barrel: 29″.
Weight: 8¾ to 9 lbs. **Length:** 45¾″ overall.
Stock: Walnut, with cheekpiece.
Sights: Dovetail front, fully adjustable rear.
Features: Octagon barrel, removable breech plug; double set triggers; blued barrel, brass stock fittings, color case-hardened percussion lock. From Armsport, The Armoury.
Price: .... $225.00 to $280.00

CVA Apollo 90 Premier Grade Rifle
Similar to the Apollo 90 Standard Grade except has walnut stock, chromed bore. Introduced 1990. Imported by CVA.
Price: Premier Grade $513.95

CVA APOLLO 90 PERCUSSION RIFLE
Caliber: 50.
Barrel: 27″, round, tapered; 1:32″ rifling.
Weight: 7½ lbs. **Length:** 45″ overall.
Stock: Select hardwood. Monte Carlo comb with flutes, beavertail cheekpiece; ventilated rubber recoil pad, sling swivel studs.
Stock: Removable brass bead on ramp front, removable hunting-style open rear adjustable for windage and elevation.
Features: In-line percussion system with push-pull bolt block safety system. One-piece blued barrel and receiver. Receiver drilled and tapped for scope mounting, has loading window and spark protector cover. Vented for gas escape. Introduced 1990. Imported by CVA.
Price: Standard Grade $387.95

CAUTION: PRICES CHANGE, CHECK AT GUNSHOP.

CVA Blazer

CVA BLAZER RIFLE
Caliber: 50 (.490" ball).
Barrel: 28", octagon.

Weight: 6 lbs., 13 oz.
Stock: Hardwood.
Sights: Brass blade front, fixed semi-buckhorn rear.
Features: Straight-line percussion with straight stock of modern design. From CVA.
Price: Finished **$178.95**
Price: Kit **$143.95**

CVA Express

CVA EXPRESS RIFLE
Caliber: 50, 54.
Barrel: 28", round.

Weight: 9 lbs.
Stock: Walnut-stained hardwood.
Sights: Bead and post front, adjustable rear.
Features: Double rifle with twin percussion locks and triggers, adjustable barrels. Hooked breech. Introduced 1989. From CVA.
Price: Finished **$547.95**
Price: Kit, 50 cal. only **$468.95**

CVA Frontier

CVA FRONTIER CARBINE
Caliber: 50.
Barrel: 24" octagon; 15/16" flats.

Weight: 6½ lbs. **Length:** 40" overall.
Stock: Selected hardwood.
Sights: Brass blade front, fixed open rear.
Features: Color case-hardened lockplate, screw-adjustable sear engagement, V-type mainspring. Early style brass trigger with tension spring. Brass buttplate, trigger guard, wedge plate, nose cap, thimble. From CVA.
Price: **$228.95**
Price: Kit **$164.95**

CVA Hunter Hawken

CVA Hunter Hawken Rifle, Carbine
Similar to the CVA Hawken except has select hardwood stock with dark color, non-glare finish, vented rubber recoil pad, sling swivels, and adjustable rear sight. Carbine has 24" barrel, 40" overall length. Black nosecap, trigger guard, thimbles and wedge plates. Available in 50 or 54 caliber. Introduced 1990. Imported by CVA.
Price: Either caliber, rifle or carbine, finished **$267.95**
Price: 50-cal. rifle kit **$219.95**

CVA O/U CARBINE-RIFLE
Caliber: 50.
Barrel: 24".
Weight: 8½ lbs. **Length:** 41¼" overall.
Stock: Checkered walnut.
Sights: Blade front with gold bead, near adjustable for w. and e.
Features: Two-shot over/under with two hammers, two triggers. Adjustable barrels. Polished blue finish. From CVA.
Price: **$579.95**

CVA KENTUCKY RIFLE
Caliber: 50.
Barrel: 33½", rifled, octagon (7/8" flats).
Weight: 7½ lbs. **Length:** 48" overall.
Stock: Select hardwood.
Sights: Brass Kentucky blade-type front, fixed open rear.
Features: Available in percussion only. Stainless steel nipple included. From CVA.
Price: Percussion **$259.95**
Price: Percussion kit **$165.95**
Price: Kentucky Hunter (half-stock) **$274.95**

CVA HAWKEN RIFLE
Caliber: 50, 54.
Barrel: 28", octagon; 1" across flats; 1:66" twist.
Weight: 8 lbs. **Length:** 44" overall.
Stock: Select walnut.
Sights: Beaded blade front, fully adjustable open rear.
Features: Fully adjustable double set triggers; brass patch box, wedge plates, nosecap, thimbles, trigger guard and buttplate; blued barrel; color case-hardened, engraved lockplate. V-type mainspring. Percussion only. Hooked breech, chrome bore. Introduced 1981.
Price: Finished rifle, percussion **$389.95**
Price: St. Louis Hawken (as above, except does not have chrome bore; hardwood stock), finished **$297.95**
Price: As above, combo kit (50, 54-cal. bbls.) **$265.95**
Price: 50-cal./12-ga. combo, finished **$364.95**
Price: As above, kit **$285.95**

> Consult our Directory pages for
> the location of firms mentioned

CVA MOUNTAIN RIFLE
Caliber: 50, 54.
Barrel: 32" octagon, 15/16" flats.
Weight: 9 lbs. **Length:** 48" overall.
Stock: European walnut with cheekpiece.
Sights: German silver blade front, adjustable open rear.
Features: Blued and engraved lockplate; bridle, fly, screw-adjustable sear engagement. Double set triggers. Pewter nose cap, trigger guard, buttplate. From CVA.
Price: Chrome bore **$397.95**
Price: Standard (not chromed) **$306.95**

CAUTION: PRICES CHANGE, CHECK AT GUNSHOP.

BLACKPOWDER MUSKETS & RIFLES

CVA Pennsylvania

Weight: 8 lbs., 3 oz. **Length:** 55¾″ overall.
Stock: Select walnut.
Sights: Brass blade front, fixed semi-buckhorn rear.
Features: Color case-hardened lockplate, brass buttplate, toe plate, patchbox, trigger guard, thimbles, nosecap; blued barrel, double-set triggers; authentic V-type mainspring. Introduced 1983. From CVA.
Price: Finished, percussion $516.95
Price: Finished, flintlock $536.95

CVA PENNSYLVANIA LONG RIFLE
Caliber: 50.
Barrel: 40″, octagonal; ⅞″ flats.

CVA Plainsman

Weight: 6 lbs., 9 oz. **Length:** 40″ overall.
Stock: Select hardwood.
Sights: Brass blade front, fixed semi-buckhorn rear.
Features: Color case-hardened lock plate; screw-adjustable sear engagement, V-type mainspring; single trigger with large guard; black trigger guard, wedge plate and thimble. Introduced 1990. Imported by CVA.
Price: Finished $214.95

CVA PLAINSMAN RIFLE
Caliber: 50.
Barrel: 24″ octagonal, ¹⁵⁄₁₆″ flats; 1:48 rifling.

COOK & BROTHER CONFEDERATE CARBINE
Caliber: 58.
Barrel: 24″.
Weight: 7½ lbs. **Length:** 40½″ overall.
Stock: Select walnut.
Features: Recreation of the 1861 New Orleans-made artillery carbine. Color case-hardened lock, browned barrel. Buttplate, trigger guard, barrel bands, sling swivels and nose cap of polished brass. From Euroarms of America.
Price: $366.00

CVA SQUIRREL RIFLE
Caliber: 36, 36/50 Combo.
Barrel: 25″, octagonal; ⅞″ flats.
Weight: 6 lbs. **Length:** 40¾″ overall.
Stock: Hardwood.
Sights: Beaded blade front, fully adjustable hunting-style rear.
Features: Color case-hardened lockplate, brass buttplate, trigger guard, wedge plates, thimbles; double set triggers; hooked breech; authentic V-type mainspring. From CVA.
Price: Finished, percussion, 36 cal. $249.95
Price: Kit, percussion, 36 cal. $198.95
Price: As above, with 36- and 50-cal. bbls. $252.95

Charles Daly Hawken

CHARLES DALY WILDERNESS HAWKEN
Caliber: 50.
Barrel: 28″ octagonal, ⅞″ flats.
Weight: 7½ lbs. **Length:** 45½″ overall.
Stock: European hardwood.
Sights: Blade front, open fully adjustable rear.
Features: Color case-hardened lock uses coil springs; trigger guard, buttplate, forend cap, ferrules and ramrod fittings are polished brass. Imported by Outdoor Sports Headquarters. Introduced 1984.
Price: Right-hand, percussion $259.95
Price: Left-hand, percussion (50-cal. only) $289.00
Price: Right-hand, flintlock $299.00
Price: Left-hand, flintlock (50-cal. only) $319.00
Price: Wilderness Hawken (50-cal. only) $189.95
Price: Wilderness, Grade II, perc. $269.95
Price: As above, left-hand $299.95
Price: Wilderness, Grade II, flintlock $299.95
Price: Wilderness Hawken Rifle, perc. $189.95
Price: Wilderness Hawken Carbine, perc. (22″ bbl.) $189.95

DIXIE DELUX CUB RIFLE
Caliber: 40.
Barrel: 28″.
Weight: 6½ lbs.
Stock: Walnut.
Sights: Fixed.
Features: Short rifle for small game and beginning shooters. Brass patchbox and furniture. Flint or percussion.
Price: Finished $250.00
Price: Kit $205.00

Dixie Hawken

Weight: 8 lbs. **Length:** 46½″ overall.
Stock: Walnut.
Sights: Blade front, adjustable rear.
Features: Blued barrel, double set triggers, steel crescent buttplate. Imported by Dixie.
Price: Finished $225.00
Price: Kit $185.00

DIXIE HAWKEN RIFLE
Caliber: 45, 50, 54.
Barrel: 30″.

BLACKPOWDER MUSKETS & RIFLES

Dixie Indian Gun

DIXIE INDIAN GUN
Caliber: 75.
Barrel: 31″, round tapered.

Weight: About 9 lbs. **Length:** 47″ overall.
Stock: Hardwood.
Sights: Blade front.
Features: Modified Brown Bess musket; brass furniture, browned lock and barrel. Lock is marked "GRICE 1762" with crown over "GR." Serpent-style sideplate. Introduced 1983.
Price: Complete $410.00
Price: As above, in kit form $395.00

Dixie Tennessee Rifle

DIXIE TENNESSEE MOUNTAIN RIFLE
Caliber: 32 or 50.
Barrel: 41½″, 6-groove rifling, brown finish. **Length:** 56″ overall.
Stock: Walnut, oil finish; Kentucky-style.

Sights: Silver blade front, open buckhorn rear.
Features: Recreation of the original mountain rifles. Early Schultz lock, interchangeable flint or percussion with vent plug or drum and nipple. Tumbler has fly. Double-set triggers. All metal parts browned. From Dixie.
Price: Flint or percussion, finished rifle, 50 cal. $395.00
Price: Kit, 50 cal $335.00
Price: Left-hand model, flint or perc. $395.00
Price: Left-hand kit, flint or perc., 50 cal. $335.00
Price: Squirrel Rifle (as above except in 32 cal. with ¹³⁄₁₆″ barrel flats), flint or percussion $395.00
Price: Kit, 32 cal., flint or percussion $335.00

Dixie 1861

DIXIE 1863 SPRINGFIELD MUSKET
Caliber: 58 (.570″ patched ball or .575″ Minie).
Barrel: 50″, rifled.
Stocks: Walnut stained.
Sights: Blade front, adjustable ladder-type rear.
Features: Bright-finish lock, barrel, furniture. Reproduction of the last of the regulation muzzleloaders. Imported from Japan by Dixie Gun Works.
Price: Finished $475.00
Price: Kit $330.00

DIXIE U.S. MODEL 1861 SPRINGFIELD
Caliber: 58.
Barrel: 40″.
Weight: About 8 lbs. **Length:** 55¹³⁄₁₆″ overall.
Stock: Oil-finished walnut.
Sights: Blade front, step adjustable rear.
Features: Exact recreation of original rifle. Sling swivels attached to trigger guard bow and middle barrel band. Lockplate marked "1861" with eagle motif and "U.S. Springfield" in front of hammer; "U.S." stamped on top of buttplate. From Dixie.
Price: $450.00
Price: Kit $420.00

DIXIE PERCUSSION WESSON RIFLE
Caliber: 50.
Barrel: 28″; 1⅛″ octagon, with false muzzle. **Length:** 45″ overall.
Stock: Hand-checkered walnut.
Sights: Blade front, rear adjustable for elevation.
Features: Adjustable double set triggers, color case-hardened frame. Comes with loading rod and loading accessories. From Dixie Gun Works.
Price: With false muzzle $425.00

Gonic GA-87

EUROARMS BUFFALO CARBINE
Caliber: 58.
Barrel: 26″, round.
Weight: 7¾ lbs. **Length:** 42″ overall.
Stock: Walnut.
Sights: Blade front, open adjustable rear.
Features: Shoots .575″ round ball. Color case-hardened lock, blue hammer, barrel, trigger; brass furniture. Brass patchbox. Imported by Euroarms of America.
Price: $407.00

GONIC GA-87 M/L RIFLE
Caliber: 458 Express, 500 Nitro.
Barrel: 24″ (Carbine), 26″ (Rifle).
Weight: 6 to 6½ lbs. **Length:** 41″ overall (Carbine).
Stock: American walnut with checkered grip and forend, or laminated stock.
Sights: Bead front, open rear adjustable for windage and elevation; drilled and tapped for scope bases.
Features: Closed-breech action with straight-line ignition. Modern trigger mechanism with ambidextrous safety. Satin blue finish on metal, satin stock finish. Introduced 1989. From Gonic Arms, Inc.
Price: Standard Rifle or Carbine, no sights $447.99
Price: As above, with sights $499.23
Price: Deluxe Rifle or Carbine, no sights $478.44
Price: As above, with sights $529.48
Price: For laminated stock, add $27.00
Price: 1 of 1000 Special Edition rifle $702.94

CAUTION: PRICES CHANGE, CHECK AT GUNSHOP.

Hatfield Squirrel Rifle

HATFIELD SQUIRREL RIFLE
Caliber: 36, 45, 50.
Barrel: 39½", octagon, 32" on half-stock.
Weight: 8 lbs. (32 cal.).
Stock: American fancy maple full-stock.
Sights: Silver blade front, buckhorn rear.
Features: Recreation of the traditional squirrel rifle. Available in flint or percussion with brass trigger guard and buttplate. From Hatfield Rifle Works. Introduced 1983.
Price: Full stock, flint or percussion, Grade II $598.00
Price: As above, Grade III $700.00
Price: Mountain Rifle $665.00

HAWKEN RIFLE
Caliber: 45, 50, 54 or 58.
Barrel: 28", blued, 6-groove rifling.
Weight: 8¾ lbs. **Length:** 44" overall.
Stock: Walnut with cheekpiece.
Sights: Blade front, fully adjustable rear.
Features: Coil mainspring, double set triggers, polished brass furniture. From Armsport.
Price: .... $245.00 to $275.00

ITHACA-NAVY HAWKEN RIFLE
Caliber: 50 and 54.
Barrel: 32" octagonal, 1" dia.
Weight: About 9 lbs.
Stocks: Walnut.
Sights: Blade front, rear adjustable for w.
Features: Hooked breech, 1⅞" throw percussion lock. Attached twin thimbles and under-rib. German silver barrel key inlays, Hawken-style toe and buttplates, lock bolt inlays, barrel wedges, entry thimble, trigger guard, ramrod and cleaning jag, nipple and nipple wrench. Introduced 1977. From Navy Arms.
Price: Complete, percussion $355.00
Price: Kit, percussion $315.00

KENTUCKIAN RIFLE & CARBINE
Caliber: 44.
Barrel: 35" (Rifle), 27½" (Carbine).
Weight: 7 lbs. (Rifle), 5½ lbs. (Carbine). **Length:** 51" (Rifle) overall, Carbine 43".
Stock: Walnut stain.
Sights: Brass blade front, steel V-ramp rear.
Features: Octagon bbl., case-hardened and engraved lockplates. Brass furniture. Imported by Dixie, Armsport.
Price: Rifle or carbine, flint, about $225.00
Price: As above, percussion, about $210.00

HARPERS FERRY 1803 FLINTLOCK RIFLE
Caliber: 54 or 58.
Barrel: 35".
Weight: 9 lbs. **Length:** 59½" overall.
Stock: Walnut with cheekpiece.
Sights: Brass blade front, fixed steel rear.
Features: Brass trigger guard, sideplate, buttplate; steel patch box. Imported by Euroarms of America, Navy (54 cal. only).
Price: $512.00
Price: 54 cal. (Navy) $475.00

Consult our Directory pages for the location of firms mentioned.

KENTUCKY FLINTLOCK RIFLE
Caliber: 44, 45, or 50.
Barrel: 35".
Weight: 7 lbs. **Length:** 50" overall.
Stock: Walnut stained, brass fittings.
Sights: Fixed.
Features: Available in Carbine model also, 28" bbl. Some variations in detail, finish. Kits also available from some importers. Imported by Navy Arms, The Armoury, Armsport.
Price: About .... $217.95 to $324.00
Price: Percussion, 45 or 50 cal. (Navy Arms) $240.00

Kentucky Percussion Rifle
Similar to flintlock except percussion lock. Finish and features vary with importer. Imported by Navy Arms (45 cal.), The Armoury, CVA, Armsport (rifle-shotgun combo).
Price: About $259.95
Price: Armsport combo $235.00
Price: 50 cal. (Navy Arms) $240.00
Price: Kit, 50 cal. (CVA) $143.95

Knight MK-85

KNIGHT MK-85 HUNTER RIFLE
Caliber: 45, 50, 54.
Barrel: 20", 22", 24".
Weight: 7 lbs.
Stock: Classic, walnut; recoil pad; swivel studs.
Sights: Hooded blade front on ramp, open adjustable rear.
Features: One-piece in-line bolt assembly with straight through Sure-Fire ignition system. Adjustable Timney Featherweight trigger. Drilled and tapped for scope mounting. Made in U.S. From Modern Muzzleloading, Inc.
Price: $479.95
Price: Stalker (laminated, colored stock) $519.95
Price: Predator (stainless steel, composition stock) $559.95

LONDON ARMORY 2-BAND ENFIELD 1858
Caliber: .577" Minie, .575" round ball.
Barrel: 33".
Weight: 10 lbs. **Length:** 49" overall.
Stock: Walnut.
Sights: Folding leaf rear adjustable for elevation.
Features: Blued barrel, color case-hardened lock and hammer, polished brass buttplate, trigger guard, nosecap. From Navy Arms, Euroarms of America, Dixie.
Price: .... $325.00 to $450.00
Price: Assembled kit (Euroarms) $364.00

BLACKPOWDER MUSKETS & RIFLES

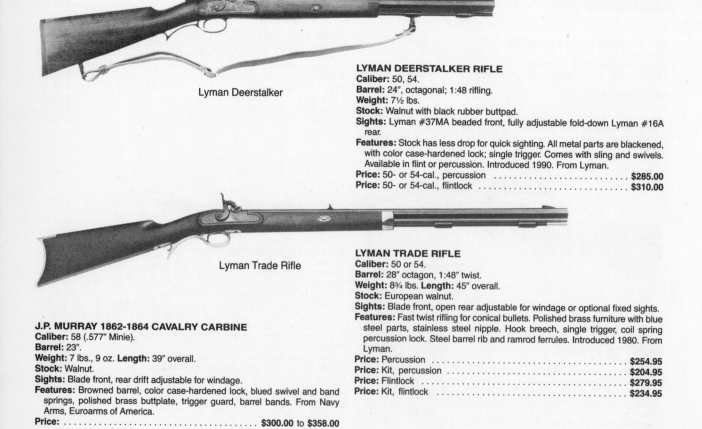

Kodiak MK III

KODIAK MK III DOUBLE RIFLE
Caliber: 54x54, 58x58, 50x50.
Barrel: 28", 5 groove, 1:48" twist.
Weight: 9½ lbs. **Length:** 43¼" overall.
Stock: Czechoslovakian walnut, hand-checkered.
Sights: Adjustable bead front, adjustable open rear.
Features: Hooked breech allows interchangeability of barrels. Comes with sling and swivels, adjustable powder measure, bullet mould and bullet starter. Engraved lockplates, top tang and trigger guard. Locks and top tang polished, rest blued. Introduced 1976. Imported from Italy by Trail Guns Armory, Inc., Navy Arms.
Price: 50, 54, 58 cal. SxS $550.00
Price: Spare barrels, all calibers $294.25
Price: Spare barrels, 12 ga.x12 ga. $195.00

LONDON ARMORY 3-BAND 1853 ENFIELD
Caliber: 58 (.577" Minie, .575" round ball, .580" maxi ball).
Barrel: 39".
Weight: 9½ lbs. **Length:** 54" overall.
Stock: European walnut.
Sights: Inverted "V" front, traditional Enfield folding ladder rear.
Features: Recreation of the famed London Armory Company Pattern 1862 Enfield Musket. One-piece walnut stock, brass buttplate, trigger guard and nose cap. Lockplate marked "London Armoury Co." and with a British crown. Blued Baddeley barrel bands. From Dixie, Euroarms of America, Navy Arms.
Price: About . . . . $350.00 to $427.00
Price: Assembled kit (Euroarms) $380.00

LONDON ARMORY ENFIELD MUSKETOON
Caliber: 58, Minie ball.
Barrel: 24", round.
Weight: 7-7½ lbs. **Length:** 40½" overall.
Stock: Walnut, with sling swivels.
Sights: Blade front, graduated military-leaf rear.
Features: Brass trigger guard, nose cap, buttplate; blued barrel, bands, lockplate, swivels. Imported by Euroarms of America, Navy Arms.
Price: $350.00
Price: Kit $250.00

LYMAN GREAT PLAINS RIFLE
Caliber: 50 or 54 cal.
Barrel: 32", 1:66" twist.
Weight: 9 lbs.
Stock: Walnut.
Sights: Steel blade front, buckhorn rear adjustable for w. and e. and fixed notch primitive sight included.
Features: Blued steel furniture. Stainless steel nipple. Coil spring lock, Hawken-style trigger guard and double set triggers. Round thimbles recessed and sweated into rib. Steel wedge plates and toe plate. Introduced 1979. From Lyman.
Price: Percussion $339.95
Price: Flintlock $359.95
Price: Percussion kit $269.95
Price: Flintlock kit $289.95

Lyman Deerstalker

LYMAN DEERSTALKER RIFLE
Caliber: 50, 54.
Barrel: 24", octagonal; 1:48 rifling.
Weight: 7½ lbs.
Stock: Walnut with black rubber buttpad.
Sights: Lyman #37MA beaded front, fully adjustable fold-down Lyman #16A rear.
Features: Stock has less drop for quick sighting. All metal parts are blackened, with color case-hardened lock; single trigger. Comes with sling and swivels. Available in flint or percussion. Introduced 1990. From Lyman.
Price: 50- or 54-cal., percussion $285.00
Price: 50- or 54-cal., flintlock $310.00

Lyman Trade Rifle

J.P. MURRAY 1862-1864 CAVALRY CARBINE
Caliber: 58 (.577" Minie).
Barrel: 23".
Weight: 7 lbs., 9 oz. **Length:** 39" overall.
Stock: Walnut.
Sights: Blade front, rear drift adjustable for windage.
Features: Browned barrel, color case-hardened lock, blued swivel and band springs, polished brass buttplate, trigger guard, barrel bands. From Navy Arms, Euroarms of America.
Price: . . . . $300.00 to $358.00

LYMAN TRADE RIFLE
Caliber: 50 or 54.
Barrel: 28" octagon, 1:48" twist.
Weight: 8¾ lbs. **Length:** 45" overall.
Stock: European walnut.
Sights: Blade front, open rear adjustable for windage or optional fixed sights.
Features: Fast twist rifling for conical bullets. Polished brass furniture with blue steel parts, stainless steel nipple. Hook breech, single trigger, coil spring percussion lock. Steel barrel rib and ramrod ferrules. Introduced 1980. From Lyman.
Price: Percussion $254.95
Price: Kit, percussion $204.95
Price: Flintlock $279.95
Price: Kit, flintlock $234.95

CAUTION: PRICES CHANGE, CHECK AT GUNSHOP.

BLACKPOWDER MUSKETS & RIFLES

Navy Country Boy

NAVY ARMS CHARLEVILLE MUSKET
Caliber: 69.
Barrel: 44⅝".
Weight: 8¾ lbs. **Length:** 59⅜" overall.
Stock: Walnut.
Sights: Blade front.
Features: Replica of Revolutionary War 1763 musket. Bright metal, walnut stock. From Navy Arms.
Price: Finished $550.00
Price: Kit $450.00
Price: 1777 model $595.00

NAVY ARMS COUNTRY BOY RIFLE
Caliber: 32, 36, 45, 50.
Barrel: 26".
Weight: 6 lbs.
Stock: Walnut.
Sights: Blade front, adjustable rear.
Features: Octagonal rifled barrel; blue finish; hooked breech; Mule Ear lock for fast ignition. From Navy Arms.
Price: $165.00
Price: Kit (50 cal. only) $145.00

NAVY ARMS 1863 SPRINGFIELD
Caliber: 58, uses .575" Minie.
Barrel: 40", rifled.
Weight: 9½ lbs. **Length:** 56" overall.
Stock: Walnut.
Sights: Open rear adjustable for elevation.
Features: Full-size three-band musket. Polished bright metal, including lock. From Navy Arms.
Price: Finished rifle $550.00
Price: Kit $450.00

Parker-Hale 1853

PARKER-HALE ENFIELD PATTERN 1858 NAVAL RIFLE
Caliber: .577".
Barrel: 33".
Weight: 8½ lbs. **Length:** 48½" overall.
Stock: European walnut.
Sights: Blade front, step adjustable rear.
Features: Two-band Enfield percussion rifle with heavy barrel. Five-groove progressive depth rifling, solid brass furniture. All parts made exactly to orignal patterns. Imported from England by Navy Arms.
Price: $550.00

PARKER-HALE ENFIELD 1853 MUSKET
Caliber: .577".
Barrel: 39", 3-groove cold-forged rifling.
Weight: About 9 lbs. **Length:** 55" overall.
Stock: Seasoned walnut.
Sights: Fixed front, rear step adjustable for elevation.
Features: Three-band musket made to original specs from original gauges. Solid brass stock furniture, color hardened lockplate, hammer; blued barrel, trigger. Imported from England by Navy Arms.
Price: $475.00

Parker-Hale 1861

PARKER-HALE ENFIELD 1861 MUSKETOON
Caliber: 58.
Barrel: 24".
Weight: 7 lbs. **Length:** 40½" overall.
Stock: Walnut.
Sights: Fixed front, adjustable rear.
Features: Percussion muzzleloader, made to original 1861 English patterns. Imported from England by Navy Arms.
Price: $450.00

PARKER-HALE VOLUNTEER RIFLE
Caliber: .451".
Barrel: 32".
Weight: 9½ lbs. **Length:** 49" overall.
Stock: Walnut, checkered wrist and forend.
Sights: Globe front, adjustable ladder-type rear.
Features: Recreation of the type of gun issued to volunteer regiments during the 1860s. Rigby-pattern rifling, patent breech, detented lock. Stock is glass bedded for accuracy. Comes with comprehensive accessory/shooting kit. From Navy Arms.
Price: $750.00
Price: Three-band Volunteer $815.00

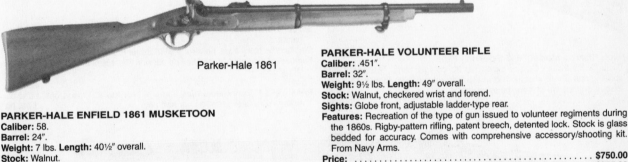

Parker-Hale Whitworth

PARKER-HALE WHITWORTH MILITARY TARGET RIFLE
Caliber: 45.
Barrel: 36".

Weight: 9¼ lbs. **Length:** 52½" overall.
Stock: Walnut. Checkered at wrist and forend.
Sights: Hooded post front, open step-adjustable rear.
Features: Faithful reproduction of the Whitworth rifle, only bored for 45 cal. Trigger has a detented lock, capable of being adjusted very finely without risk of the sear nose catching on the half-cock bent and damaging both parts. Introduced 1978. Imported from England by Navy Arms.
Price: $815.00

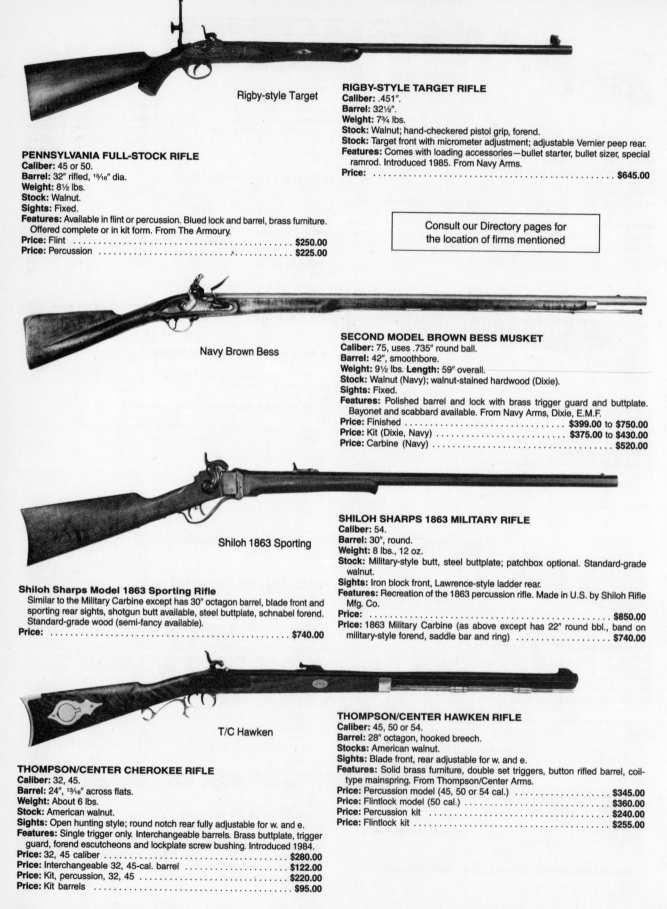

Rigby-style Target

PENNSYLVANIA FULL-STOCK RIFLE
Caliber: 45 or 50.
Barrel: 32" rifled, 15⁄16" dia.
Weight: 8½ lbs.
Stock: Walnut.
Sights: Fixed.
Features: Available in flint or percussion. Blued lock and barrel, brass furniture. Offered complete or in kit form. From The Armoury.
Price: Flint $250.00
Price: Percussion $225.00

RIGBY-STYLE TARGET RIFLE
Caliber: .451".
Barrel: 32½".
Weight: 7¾ lbs.
Stock: Walnut; hand-checkered pistol grip, forend.
Stock: Target front with micrometer adjustment; adjustable Vernier peep rear.
Features: Comes with loading accessories—bullet starter, bullet sizer, special ramrod. Introduced 1985. From Navy Arms.
Price: $645.00

Consult our Directory pages for
the location of firms mentioned

Navy Brown Bess

SECOND MODEL BROWN BESS MUSKET
Caliber: 75, uses .735" round ball.
Barrel: 42", smoothbore.
Weight: 9½ lbs. **Length:** 59" overall.
Stock: Walnut (Navy); walnut-stained hardwood (Dixie).
Sights: Fixed.
Features: Polished barrel and lock with brass trigger guard and buttplate. Bayonet and scabbard available. From Navy Arms, Dixie, E.M.F.
Price: Finished . . . . $399.00 to $750.00
Price: Kit (Dixie, Navy) . . . . $375.00 to $430.00
Price: Carbine (Navy) $520.00

Shiloh 1863 Sporting

Shiloh Sharps Model 1863 Sporting Rifle
Similar to the Military Carbine except has 30" octagon barrel, blade front and sporting rear sights, shotgun butt available, steel buttplate, schnabel forend. Standard-grade wood (semi-fancy available).
Price: $740.00

SHILOH SHARPS 1863 MILITARY RIFLE
Caliber: 54.
Barrel: 30", round.
Weight: 8 lbs., 12 oz.
Stock: Military-style butt, steel buttplate; patchbox optional. Standard-grade walnut.
Sights: Iron block front, Lawrence-style ladder rear.
Features: Recreation of the 1863 percussion rifle. Made in U.S. by Shiloh Rifle Mfg. Co.
Price: $850.00
Price: 1863 Military Carbine (as above except has 22" round bbl., band on military-style forend, saddle bar and ring) $740.00

T/C Hawken

THOMPSON/CENTER HAWKEN RIFLE
Caliber: 45, 50 or 54.
Barrel: 28" octagon, hooked breech.
Stocks: American walnut.
Sights: Blade front, rear adjustable for w. and e.
Features: Solid brass furniture, double set triggers, button rifled barrel, coil-type mainspring. From Thompson/Center Arms.
Price: Percussion model (45, 50 or 54 cal.) $345.00
Price: Flintlock model (50 cal.) $360.00
Price: Percussion kit $240.00
Price: Flintlock kit $255.00

THOMPSON/CENTER CHEROKEE RIFLE
Caliber: 32, 45.
Barrel: 24", 13⁄16" across flats.
Weight: About 6 lbs.
Stock: American walnut.
Sights: Open hunting style; round notch rear fully adjustable for w. and e.
Features: Single trigger only. Interchangeable barrels. Brass buttplate, trigger guard, forend escutcheons and lockplate screw bushing. Introduced 1984.
Price: 32, 45 caliber $280.00
Price: Interchangeable 32, 45-cal. barrel $122.00
Price: Kit, percussion, 32, 45 . . . . $220.00
Price: Kit barrels $95.00

CAUTION: PRICES CHANGE, CHECK AT GUNSHOP.

T/C New Englander

THOMPSON/CENTER PENNSYLVANIA HUNTER RIFLE
Caliber: 50.
Barrel: 31″, half-octagon, half-round.
Weight: About 7½ lbs. **Length:** 48″ overall.
Stock: Black walnut.
Sights: Open, adjustable.
Features: Rifled 1:66″ for round ball shooting. Available in flintlock or percussion.
Price: Percussion $275.00
Price: Flintlock $290.00

THOMPSON/CENTER RENEGADE RIFLE
Caliber: 50 and 54.
Barrel: 26″, 1″ across the flats.
Weight: 8 lbs.
Stock: American walnut.
Sights: Open hunting (Patridge) style, fully adjustable for w. and e.
Features: Coil spring lock, double set triggers, blued steel trim.
Price: Percussion model $295.00
Price: Flintlock model, 50 cal. only $365.00
Price: Percussion kit $210.00
Price: Flintlock kit $225.00
Price: Left-hand percussion, 50 or 54 cal. $305.00

T/C Scout

THOMPSON/CENTER SCOUT RIFLE
Caliber: 50 and 54.
Barrel: 21″, interchangeable, 1:20 twist.

THOMPSON/CENTER NEW ENGLANDER RIFLE
Caliber: 50, 54.
Barrel: 28″, round.
Weight: 7 lbs., 15 oz.
Stock: American walnut or Rynite.
Sights: Open, adjustable.
Features: Color case-hardened percussion lock with engraving, rest blued. Also accepts 12-ga. shotgun barrel. Introduced 1987. From Thompson/Center.
Price: Right-hand model $235.00
Price: As above, Rynite stock $215.00
Price: Left-hand model $250.00
Price: Accessory 12-ga. barrel, right-hand $108.50
Price: As above, left-hand $117.00

Thompson/Center Renegade Hunter
Similar to standard Renegade except has single trigger in a large-bow shotgun-style trigger guard, no brass trim. Available in 50 or 54 caliber. Color case-hardened lock, rest blued. Introduced 1987. From Thompson/Center.
Price: $275.00

Weight: 7 lbs., 4 oz. **Length:** 38⅝″ overall.
Stocks: American black walnut stock and forend.
Sights: Bead front, adjustable semi-buckhorn rear.
Features: Patented in-line ignition system with special vented breech plug. Patented trigger mechanism consists of only two moving parts. Interchangeable barrels. Wide grooved hammer. Brass trigger guard assembly, brass barrel band and buttplate. Ramrod has blued hardware. Comes with q.d. swivels and suede leather carrying sling. Drilled and tapped for standard scope mounts. Introduced 1990. From Thompson/Center Arms.
Price: 50 or 54 cal. $325.00
Price: Extra barrel, 50 or 54 cal. $145.00

T/C White Mountain

TRADITIONS PIONEER RIFLE
Caliber: 50, 54.
Barrel: 27¼″; ¹⁵⁄₁₆″ flats.
Weight: 7 lbs. **Length:** 44″ overall.
Stock: Beech with pistol grip, recoil pad.
Sights: German silver blade front, buckhorn rear with elevation ramp.
Features: V-type mainspring, adjustable single trigger; blackened furniture; color case-hardened lock; large trigger guard. From Traditions, Inc.
Price: Percussion only $175.00

TRADITIONS HAWKEN RIFLE
Caliber: 50, 54.
Barrel: 32¼″; 1″ flats.
Weight: 9 lbs. **Length:** 50″ overall.
Stock: Walnut with cheekpiece.
Sights: Hunting style, click adjustable for windage and elevation.
Features: Fiberglass ramrod, double set triggers, polished brass furniture. From Traditions, Inc.
Price: Percussion $342.00
Price: Kit (54-cal. only) $225.00

THOMPSON/CENTER WHITE MOUNTAIN CARBINE
Caliber: 50.
Barrel: 21″, half-octagon, half-round.
Weight: 6½ lbs. **Length:** 38″ overall.
Stock: American black walnut.
Sights: Open hunting (Patridge) style, fully adjustable rear.
Features: Percussion or flintlock. Single trigger, large trigger guard; rubber buttpad; rear q.d. swivel, front swivel mounted on thimble; comes with sling. Introduced 1989.
Price: Percussion $295.00
Price: Flintlock $310.00

Traditions Hunter Rifle
Similar to the Hawken except has blackened and German silver furniture. Has 28¼″ barrel with 1″ flats.
Price: Percussion only, 50 or 54 cal. $350.00
Price: Hawken Woodsman (50- or 54-cal.) $225.00
Price: As above, kit $173.00
Price: Frontier (beech stock, flintlock) $217.00
Price: As above, percussion $200.00
Price: Frontier Carbine (24″ bbl., 50 cal., percussion) $200.00

BLACKPOWDER MUSKETS & RIFLES

Traditions Pennsylvania

TRADITIONS PENNSYLVANIA RIFLE
Caliber: 45, 50.
Barrel: 40¼", ⅞" flats.

Weight: 9 lbs. **Length:** 57½" overall.
Stock: Walnut.
Sights: Blade front, adjustable rear.
Features: Brass patchbox and ornamentation. Double set triggers. From Traditions Inc.
Price: Flintlock $410.00
Price: Percussion $387.00

Traditions Trapper

TRADITIONS TRAPPER RIFLE
Caliber: 36, 50.
Barrel: 24", ⅞" flats.
Weight: 5 lbs. **Length:** 40½" overall.
Stock: Beech.
Sights: Beaded blade front, adjustable rear.
Features: Metal ramrod, brass furniture. From Traditions Inc.
Price: $200.00
Price: Frontier Scout (similar to above except shorter length of pull, weighs 6 lbs., 26" bbl., 36, 45 or 50 cal.) $187.00

TRADITIONS TROPHY RIFLE
Caliber: 50, 54.
Barrel: 27¼", round.
Weight: 7 lbs. **Length:** 44¾" overall.
Stock: Walnut with full pistol grip and cheekpiece.
Sights: Patridge-style blade front, hunting-style rear click adjustable for windage and elevation.
Features: Engraved, color case-hardened lock with bridle, claw mainspring; single trigger adjustable for weight. Sling swivels; fiberglass ramrod; recoil pad. From Traditions, Inc.
Price: Percussion only $350.00

Dixie Tryon

TRYON RIFLE
Caliber: 50, 54.
Barrel: 34", octagon; 1:63" twist.

Weight: 9 lbs. **Length:** 49" overall.
Stock: European walnut with steel furniture.
Sights: Blade front, fixed rear.
Features: Reproduction of an American plains rifle with double set triggers and back-action lock. Imported from Italy by Dixie.
Price: $340.00
Price: Kit $299.00

Tryon Trailblazer

TRYON TRAILBLAZER RIFLE
Caliber: 50.
Barrel: 32", 1" flats.

Weight: 9 lbs. **Length:** 48" overall.
Stock: European walnut with cheekpiece.
Sights: Blade front, semi-buckhorn rear.
Features: Reproduction of a rifle made by George Tryon about 1820. Double-set triggers, back action lock, hooked breech with long tang. From Armsport, Navy Arms.
Price: $375.00

Uberti Santa Fe

UBERTI SANTA FE HAWKEN RIFLE
Caliber: 50 or 54.
Barrel: 32", octagonal.

Weight: 9.8 lbs. **Length:** 50" overall.
Stock: Walnut, with beavertail cheekpiece.
Sights: German silver blade front, buckhorn rear.
Features: Browned finish, color case-hardened lock, double triggers, German silver ferrule, wedge plates. Imported by Uberti USA.
Price: $385.00
Price: Kit $339.00

CAUTION: PRICES CHANGE, CHECK AT GUNSHOP.

BLACKPOWDER MUSKETS & RIFLES

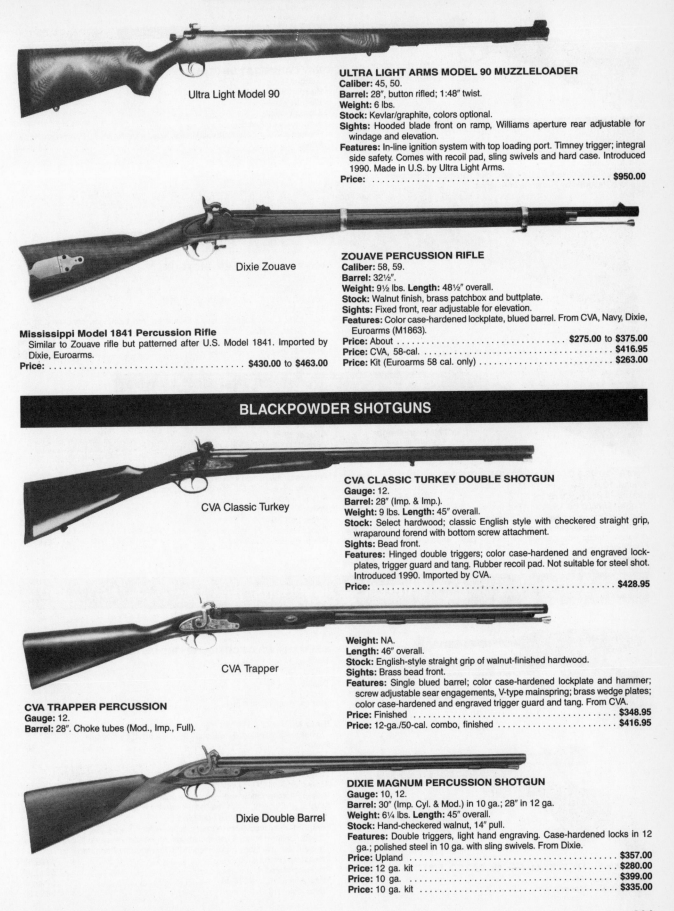

Ultra Light Model 90

ULTRA LIGHT ARMS MODEL 90 MUZZLELOADER
Caliber: 45, 50.
Barrel: 28", button rifled; 1:48" twist.
Weight: 6 lbs.
Stock: Kevlar/graphite, colors optional.
Sights: Hooded blade front on ramp, Williams aperture rear adjustable for windage and elevation.
Features: In-line ignition system with top loading port. Timney trigger; integral side safety. Comes with recoil pad, sling swivels and hard case. Introduced 1990. Made in U.S. by Ultra Light Arms.
Price: **$950.00**

Dixie Zouave

ZOUAVE PERCUSSION RIFLE
Caliber: 58, 59.
Barrel: 32½".
Weight: 9½ lbs. **Length:** 48½" overall.
Stock: Walnut finish, brass patchbox and buttplate.
Sights: Fixed front, rear adjustable for elevation.
Features: Color case-hardened lockplate, blued barrel. From CVA, Navy, Dixie, Euroarms (M1863).
Price: About .... **$275.00** to **$375.00**
Price: CVA, 58-cal. **$416.95**
Price: Kit (Euroarms 58 cal. only) **$263.00**

Mississippi Model 1841 Percussion Rifle
Similar to Zouave rifle but patterned after U.S. Model 1841. Imported by Dixie, Euroarms.
Price: .... **$430.00** to **$463.00**

BLACKPOWDER SHOTGUNS

CVA Classic Turkey

CVA CLASSIC TURKEY DOUBLE SHOTGUN
Gauge: 12.
Barrel: 28" (Imp. & Imp.).
Weight: 9 lbs. **Length:** 45" overall.
Stock: Select hardwood; classic English style with checkered straight grip, wraparound forend with bottom screw attachment.
Sights: Bead front.
Features: Hinged double triggers; color case-hardened and engraved lockplates, trigger guard and tang. Rubber recoil pad. Not suitable for steel shot. Introduced 1990. Imported by CVA.
Price: **$428.95**

CVA Trapper

Weight: NA.
Length: 46" overall.
Stock: English-style straight grip of walnut-finished hardwood.
Sights: Brass bead front.
Features: Single blued barrel; color case-hardened lockplate and hammer; screw adjustable sear engagements, V-type mainspring; brass wedge plates; color case-hardened and engraved trigger guard and tang. From CVA.
Price: Finished **$348.95**
Price: 12-ga./50-cal. combo, finished **$416.95**

CVA TRAPPER PERCUSSION
Gauge: 12.
Barrel: 28". Choke tubes (Mod., Imp., Full).

Dixie Double Barrel

DIXIE MAGNUM PERCUSSION SHOTGUN
Gauge: 10, 12.
Barrel: 30" (Imp. Cyl. & Mod.) in 10 ga.; 28" in 12 ga.
Weight: 6¼ lbs. **Length:** 45" overall.
Stock: Hand-checkered walnut, 14" pull.
Features: Double triggers, light hand engraving. Case-hardened locks in 12 ga.; polished steel in 10 ga. with sling swivels. From Dixie.
Price: Upland **$357.00**
Price: 12 ga. kit **$280.00**
Price: 10 ga. **$399.00**
Price: 10 ga. kit **$335.00**

Navy T&T Shotgun

NAVY ARMS T&T SHOTGUN
Gauge: 12.
Barrel: 28" (Mod. & Full).
Weight: 7½ lbs.
Stock: Walnut.
Sights: Bead front.
Features: Color case-hardened locks, blued steel furniture. From Navy Arms.
Price: $315.00

EUROARMS DUCK SHOTGUN
Gauge: 8, 10, 12.
Barrel: 33".
Weight: 8½ lbs. **Length:** 49" overall.
Stock: Walnut.
Features: Color case-hardened lock; blue hammer, trigger, barrel; brass furniture. Imported by Euroarms of America.
Price: $407.00

Navy Fowler

NAVY ARMS FOWLER SHOTGUN
Gauge: 12.
Barrel: 28".
Weight: 7 lbs., 12 oz. **Length:** 45" overall.
Stock: Walnut.
Features: Color case-hardened lockplates and hammers; checkered stock. Imported by Navy Arms.
Price: Fowler model, 12 ga. only $285.00
Price: Fowler kit, 12 ga. only $190.00

T/C New Englander

THOMPSON/CENTER "NEW ENGLANDER" SHOTGUN
Gauge: 12.
Barrel: 28" (Imp. Cyl.), round.
Weight: 5 lbs., 2 oz.
Stock: Select American black walnut with straight grip.
Features: Percussion lock is color case-hardened, rest blued. Also accepts 26" round 50- and 54-cal. rifle barrel. Introduced 1986.
Price: Right-hand $235.00
Price: Right-hand, Rynite stock $215.00
Price: Left-hand $250.00
Price: Accessory rifle barrel, right-hand, 50 or 54 ...... $108.50
Price: As above, left-hand $117.00

TRAIL GUNS KODIAK 10-GAUGE DOUBLE
Gauge: 10.
Barrel: 20", 30¾" (Cyl. bore).
Weight: About 9 lbs. **Length:** 47⅛" overall.
Stock: Walnut, with cheek rest. Checkered wrist and forend.
Features: Chrome-plated bores; engraved lockplates, brass bead front and middle sights; sling swivels. Introduced 1980. Imported from Italy by Trail Guns Armory.
Price: $425.00

AIRGUNS — HANDGUNS

Beeman/FWB C5

BEEMAN/FWB C5 CO₂ RAPID FIRE PISTOL
Caliber: 177.
Barrel: 7.25".
Weight: 2.42 lbs.
Power: NA.
Stocks: Anatomical match.
Sights: Match.
Features: Velocity 510 fps. Has special trigger shape with swivel action, longitudinal positioning. Introduced 1990. Imported by Beeman.
Price: .... NA

Beeman/Feinwerkbau C10

Weight: 2.5 lbs. **Length:** 16" overall.
Power: Special CO₂ cylinder.
Stock: Stippled walnut with adjustable palm shelf.
Sights: Blade front, open rear adjustable for w. and e. Notch size adjustable for width. Interchangeable front blades.
Features: Fully adjustable trigger; can be set for dry firing. Separate gas chamber for uniform power. Cylinders interchangeable even when full. Short-barrel model also available. Introduced 1988. Imported by Beeman.
Price: Right-hand $798.50
Price: Left-hand $830.00
Price: Mini-C10, right-hand $798.50
Price: Mini-C10, left-hand $830.00

BEEMAN/FEINWERKBAU MODEL C10 CO₂ PISTOL
Caliber: 177, single shot.
Barrel: 10.1", 12-groove rifling.

CAUTION: PRICES CHANGE, CHECK AT GUNSHOP.

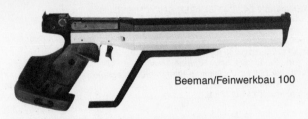

Beeman/Feinwerkbau 100

BEEMAN/FEINWERKBAU FWB-65 MKII AIR PISTOL
Caliber: 177, single shot.
Barrel: 6.1″ or 7.5″, removable bbl. wgt. avail.
Weight: 42 oz. **Length:** 13.3″ or 14.1″ overall.
Power: Spring, sidelever cocking.
Stocks: Walnut, stippled thumbrest; adjustable or fixed.
Sights: Front, Interchangeable post element system, open rear, click adjustable for w. & e. and for sighting notch width. Scope mount avail.
Features: New shorter barrel for better balance and control. Cocking effort 9 lbs. Two-stage trigger, four adjustments. Quiet firing, 525 fps. Programs instantly for recoil or recoilless operation. Permanently lubricated. Steel piston ring. Special switch converts trigger from 17.6 oz. pull to 42 oz. let-off. Imported by Beeman.
Price: Right-hand . . . . **$775.00 to $795.00**
Price: Left-hand, 6.1″ barrel . . . . **$785.00 to $819.50**
Price: Model 65 Mk. I (7.5″ bbl.) . . . . **$765.00 to $799.50**

BEEMAN P1 MAGNUM AIR PISTOL
Caliber: 177, 20, 22, single shot.
Barrel: 8.4″.
Weight: 2.5 lbs. **Length:** 11″ overall.
Power: Top lever cocking; spring piston.
Stocks: Checkered walnut.
Sights: Blade front, square notch rear with click micrometer adjustments for w. and e. Grooved for scope mounting.
Features: Dual power for 177 and 20 cal.: low setting gives 350-400 fps; high setting 500-600 fps. Rearward expanding mainspring simulates firearm recoil. All Colt 45 auto grips fit gun. Dry-firing feature for practice. Optional wooden shoulder stock. Introduced 1985. Imported by Beeman.
Price: 177, 22 cal. **$295.00**
Price: 20 cal. **$299.50**

BEEMAN/WEBLEY HURRICANE PISTOL
Caliber: 177 or 22, single shot.
Barrel: 8″, rifled.
Weight: 2.4 lbs. **Length:** 11½″ overall.
Power: Spring piston.
Stocks: Thumbrest, checkered high-impact synthetic.
Sights: Hooded front; micro-click rear adjustable for w. and e.
Features: Velocity of 470 fps (177 cal.). Single stroke cocking, adjustable trigger pull, manual safety. Rearward recoil like a firearm pistol. Steel piston and cylinder. Scope base included; 1.5x scope **$49.95** extra. Shoulder stock available. Introduced 1977. Imported from England by Beeman.
Price: **$159.95**

BEEMAN/WEBLEY TEMPEST AIR PISTOL
Caliber: 177 or 22, single shot.
Barrel: 6.75″, rifled ordnance steel.
Weight: 32 oz. **Length:** 9″ overall.
Power: Spring piston.
Stocks: Checkered black epoxy with thumbrest.
Sights: Post front; rear has sliding leaf adjustable for w. and e.
Features: Adjustable trigger pull, manual safety. Velocity 470 fps (177 cal.). Steel piston in steel liner for maximum performance and durability. Unique rearward spring simulates firearm recoil. Shoulder stock available. Introduced 1979. Imported from England by Beeman.
Price: **$139.95**

BEEMAN/WEIHRAUCH HW-70 AIR PISTOL
Caliber: 177, single shot.
Barrel: 6¼″, rifled.
Weight: 38 oz. **Length:** 12¾″ overall.
Power: Spring, barrel cocking.
Stocks: Plastic, with thumbrest.
Sights: Hooded post front, square notch rear adjustable for w. and e.
Features: Adjustable trigger, 24-lb. cocking effort, 410 fps MV; automatic barrel safety. Imported by Beeman.
Price: **$149.98**

BEEMAN/FEINWERKBAU MODEL 100 PISTOL
Caliber: 177, single shot.
Barrel: 10.1″, 12-groove rifling.
Weight: 2.5 lbs. **Length:** 16.5″ overall.
Power: Single-stroke pneumatic, sidelever cocking.
Stocks: Stippled walnut with adjustable palm shelf.
Sights: Blade front, open rear adjustable for w. and e. Notch size adjustable for width. Interchangeable front blades.
Features: Velocity 460 fps. Fully adjustable trigger. Cocking effort 12 lbs. Introduced 1988. Imported by Beeman.
Price: Right-hand **$898.50**
Price: Left-hand **$950.00**

Beeman/FWB 65 MKII

Beeman P1 Magnum

Beeman/Webley Hurricane

Beeman/Webley Tempest

Benjamin 242/247

Crosman 357

Crosman SSP 250

CROSMAN MODEL 1322 AIR PISTOL
Caliber: 22, single shot.
Barrel: 8″, button rifled.
Weight: 37 oz. **Length:** 13⅝″.
Power: Hand pumped.
Sights: Blade front, rear adjustable for w. and e.
Features: Moulded plastic grip, hand size pump forearm. Cross-bolt safety. Also available in 177/BB cal. as **Model 1377.**
Price: About $50.00
Price: 1377, about $50.00

Crosman Skanaker

DAISY/POWER LINE MODEL 45 AIR PISTOL
Caliber: 177, 13-shot clip.
Barrel: 5″, rifled steel.
Weight: 1.25 lbs. **Length:** 8.5″ overall.
Power: CO_2.
Stocks: Checkered plastic.
Sights: Fixed.
Features: Velocity 400 fps. Semi-automatic repeater with double-action trigger. Manually operated lever-type trigger block safety; magazine safety. Introduced 1990. From Daisy.
Price: About $69.00

BENJAMIN 242/247 SINGLE SHOT PISTOLS
Caliber: 177 and 22.
Weight: 32 oz. **Length:** 11¾″ overall.
Power: Hand pumped.
Stocks: Walnut pump handle, optional walnut grips.
Sights: Blade front, open adjustable rear.
Features: Bolt action; fingertip safety; adjustable power.
Price: Model 242 (22 cal.) $91.30
Price: Model 247 (177 cal.) $91.30

CROSMAN MODEL 357 AIR PISTOL
Caliber: 177, 6- or 10-shot.
Barrel: 4″ (Model 357-4), 6″ (Model 357-6), rifled steel, 8″ (Model 357-8); rifled brass.
Weight: 32 oz. (6″). **Length:** 11⅜″ overall.
Power: CO_2 Powerlet.
Stocks: Checkered wood-grain plastic.
Sights: Ramp front, fully adjustable rear.
Features: Average 430 fps (Model 357-6). Break-open barrel for easy loading. Single or double action. Vent. rib barrel. Wide, smooth trigger. Two speed loaders come with each gun. Model 357-8 has matte gray finish, black grips.
Price: 4″ or 6″, about $55.00
Price: 8″, about $62.00
Price: Model 1357 (same gun as above, except shoots BBs, 6-shot clip), about $55.00

Crosman Model 3357 Spot Marker
Same specs as 8″ Model 357 but shoots 50-cal. paint balls. Has break-open action for quick loading 6-shot clip of paint balls. CO_2 power allows repeater firing; hammer-block safety; adjustable rear sight, blade front.
Price: About $89.00

CROSMAN MODEL SSP 250 PISTOL
Caliber: 177, 20, 22, single shot.
Barrel: 9⅞″, rifled steel.
Weight: 3 lbs., 1 oz. **Length:** 14″ overall.
Power: CO_2 Powerlet.
Stocks: Composition; black, with checkering.
Sights: Hooded front, fully adjustable rear.
Features: Velocity about 460 fps. Interchangeable accessory barrels. Two-stage trigger. High/low power settings.
Price: About $47.00

Crosman 1322/1377

CROSMAN/SKANAKER MATCH AIR PISTOL
Caliber: 177.
Barrel: 9.94″.
Weight: 37 oz. **Length:** 16.38″ overall.
Power: Refillable CO_2 cylinders.
Stocks: Hardwood, adjustable for thickness; adjustable palm shelf.
Sights: Three-way adjustable post front, open rear with three interchangeable leaves.
Features: Velocity of 550 fps. Angled, adjustable match trigger can be aligned to fit the natural position of the trigger finger. Barrel is hinged near the muzzle for loading. Introduced 1987.
Price: About $650.00

DAISY/POWER LINE MODEL 44 REVOLVER
Caliber: 177 pellets, 6-shot.
Barrel: 6″, rifled steel; interchangeable 4″ and 8″.
Weight: 2.7 lbs.
Power: CO_2.
Stocks: Moulded plastic with checkering.
Sights: Blade on ramp front, fully adjustable notch rear.
Features: Velocity up to 400 fps. Replica of 44 Magnum revolver. Has swingout cylinder and interchangeable barrels. Introduced 1987. From Daisy.
Price: $49.00

AIRGUNS — HANDGUNS

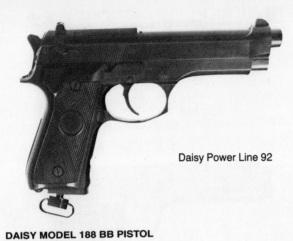

Daisy Power Line 92

DAISY MODEL 188 BB PISTOL
Caliber: BB.
Barrel: 9.9", steel smoothbore.
Weight: 1.67 lbs. **Length:** 11.7" overall.
Stocks: Copolymer; checkered with thumbrest.
Sights: Blade and ramp front, open fixed rear.
Features: 24-shot repeater. Spring action with under-barrel cocking lever. Grip and receiver of Nylafil-copolymer material. Introduced 1979.
Price: About **$25.00**

DAISY/POWER LINE 717 PELLET PISTOL
Caliber: 177, single shot.
Barrel: 9.61".
Weight: 2.8 lbs. **Length:** 13½" overall.
Stocks: Moulded wood-grain plastic, with thumbrest.
Sights: Blade and ramp front, micro-adjustable notch rear.
Features: Single pump pneumatic pistol. Rifled steel barrel. Cross-bolt trigger block. Muzzle velocity 385 fps. From Daisy. Introduced 1979.
Price: About **$68.00**

DAISY/POWER LINE MATCH 777 PELLET PISTOL
Caliber: 177, single shot.
Barrel: 9.61" rifled steel by Lothar Walther.
Weight: 32 oz. **Length:** 13½" overall.
Power: Sidelever, single pump pneumatic.
Stocks: Smooth hardwood, fully contoured with palm and thumbrest.
Sights: Blade and ramp front, match-grade open rear with adjustable width notch, micro. click adjustments.
Features: Adjustable trigger; manual cross-bolt safety. MV of 385 fps. Comes with cleaning kit, adjustment tool and pellets. From Daisy.
Price: About **$236.00**

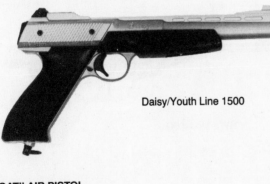

Daisy/Youth Line 1500

"GAT" AIR PISTOL
Caliber: 177, single shot.
Barrel: 7½" cocked, 9½" extended.
Weight: 22 oz.
Power: Spring piston.
Stocks: Cast checkered metal.
Sights: Fixed.
Features: Shoots pellets, corks or darts. Matte black finish. Imported from England by Stone Enterprises, Inc.
Price: **$19.95**

DAISY/POWER LINE MODEL 92 PISTOL
Caliber: 177 pellets, 10-shot magazine.
Barrel: Rifled steel.
Weight: 1.4 lbs. **Length:** 8.5" overall.
Power: CO_2.
Stocks: Cast checkered metal.
Sights: Blade front, adjustable V-slot rear.
Features: Semi-automatic action; 400 fps. Replica of the official 9mm sidearm of the United States armed forces.
Price: About **$64.00**

Daisy Model 188

Daisy/Power Line 747 Pistol
Similar to the 717 pistol except has a 12-groove rifled steel barrel by Lothar Walther. Velocity of 360 fps. Manual cross-bolt safety.
Price: About **$109.00**

Power Line 777

DAISY/POWER LINE CO_2 1200 PISTOL
Caliber: BB, 177.
Barrel: 10½", smooth.
Weight: 1.6 lbs. **Length:** 11.1" overall.
Power: Daisy CO_2 cylinder.
Stocks: Contoured, checkered moulded wood-grain plastic.
Sights: Blade ramp front, fully adjustable square notch rear.
Features: 60-shot BB reservoir, gravity feed. Cross-bolt safety. Velocity of 420-450 fps for more than 100 shots. From Daisy.
Price: About **$39.00**

> Consult our Directory pages for
> the location of firms mentioned.

DAISY/YOUTH LINE MODEL 1500 PISTOL
Caliber: BB, 60-shot reservoir.
Barrel: 1.5", smoothbore.
Weight: 22 oz. **Length:** 11.1" overall.
Power: Daisy CO_2 cylinder.
Stocks: Moulded wood-grain plastic with checkering.
Sights: Blade on ramp front, fully adjustable notch rear.
Features: Velocity of 340 fps. Gravity feed magazine. Cross-bolt safety.
Price: About **$38.00**

CAUTION: PRICES CHANGE, CHECK AT GUNSHOP.

MARKSMAN 17 AIR PISTOL
Caliber: 177, single shot.
Barrel: 7.5".
Weight: 46 oz. **Length:** 14.5" overall.
Power: Spring air, barrel-cocking.
Stocks: Checkered composition with right-hand thumb rest.
Sights: Tunnel front, fully adjustable rear.
Features: Velocity of 360-400 fps. Introduced 1986. Imported from Spain by Marksman Products.
Price: **$85.00**

MARKSMAN #1010 REPEATER PISTOL
Caliber: 177, 18-shot repeater.
Barrel: 2½", smoothbore.
Weight: 24 oz. **Length:** 8¼" overall.
Power: Spring.
Features: Thumb safety. Black finish. Uses BBs, darts or pellets. Repeats with BBs only.
Price: Matte black finish **$23.50**
Price: Model 1010X (as above except nickel-plated) **$31.75**
Price: Model 1015 (brown finish with commemorative medallion) **$26.75**

MARKSMAN PLAINSMAN 1049 CO₂ PISTOL
Caliber: BB, 100-shot repeater.
Barrel: 5⅞", smooth.
Weight: 28 oz. **Length:** 9½" overall.
Stock: Simulated walnut with thumbrest.
Power: 12-gram CO_2 cylinders.
Features: Velocity of 400 fps. Three-position power switch. Automatic ammunition feed. Positive safety.
Price: **$45.00**

Marksman Model 17

Marksman 1010

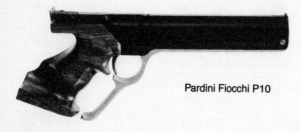

Pardini Fiocchi P10

RWS/DIANA MODEL 5G AIR PISTOL
Caliber: 177, single shot.
Barrel: 7".
Weight: 2¾ lbs. **Length:** 16" overall.
Power: Spring air, barrel cocking.
Stocks: Plastic, thumbrest design.
Sights: Tunnel front, micro-click open rear.
Features: Velocity of 410 fps. Two-stage trigger with automatic safety. Imported from West Germany by Dynamit Nobel-RWS, Inc.
Price: **$160.00**

RWS/Diana Model 5GS Air Pistol
Same as the Model 5G except comes with 1.5x15 pistol scope with ramp-style mount, muzzlebrake/weight. No open sights supplied. Introduced 1983.
Price: **$235.00**

PARDINI FIOCCHI P1O MATCH AIR PISTOL
Caliber: 177.
Barrel: 7.7".
Weight: 37 oz. **Length:** 14" overall.
Power: Single stroke pneumatic.
Stocks: Stippled walnut with palm shelf.
Sights: Post front, fully adjustable open rear.
Features: Muzzle velocity of 425 fps. Cocking lever forms trigger guard. Imported from Italy by Fiocchi of America.
Price: **$400.00**

PARDINI FIOCCHI K58 AIR PISTOL
Caliber: 177, single shot.
Barrel: 9".
Weight: 37.7 oz. **Length:** 15.5" overall.
Power: CO_2.
Stocks: Stippled hardwood; match type.
Sights: Post front, fully adjustable rear; match type.
Features: Has 12.7" sight radius. Introduced 1990. Imported from Italy by Fiocchi of America.
Price: **$550.00**
Price: Model K60 (similar to K58 except made of light alloy, has 9.6" barrel with 36.6-oz. weight, 16" overall length) **$550.00**

RWS Model 5G

RWS Model 10

RWS/Diana Model 10 Match Air Pistol
Refined version of the Model 6M. Has special adjustable match trigger, oil-finished and stippled match grips, barrel weight. Also available in left-hand version, and with fitted case.
Price: Model 10 . . . . **$610.00**
Price: Model 10, left-hand **$655.00**
Price: Model 10, with case **$640.00**
Price: Model 10, left-hand, with case **$685.00**

CAUTION: PRICES CHANGE, CHECK AT GUNSHOP.

RWS/Diana 6G

RWS/DIANA MODEL 6M MATCH AIR PISTOL
Caliber: 177, single shot.
Barrel: 7".
Weight: 3 lbs. **Length:** 16" overall.
Power: Spring air, barrel cocking.
Stocks: Walnut-finished hardwood with thumbrest
Sights: Adjustable front, micro. click open rear.
Features: Velocity of 410 fps. Recoilless double piston system, movable barrel
   shroud to protect from sight during cocking. Imported from West Germany
   by Dynamit Nobel-RWS, Inc.
Price: Right-hand **$345.00**
Price: Left-hand **$360.00**

RWS/Diana Model 6G, 6GS Air Pistols
   Similar to the Model 6M except does not have the movable barrel shroud.
Has click micrometer rear sight, two-stage adjustable trigger, interchangeable
tunnel front sight. Available in right- or left-hand models.
Price: Right-hand **$255.00**
Price: Left-hand **$270.00**
Price: Model 6GS (with 1.5x15 scope, bbl. wgt., right-hand) **$330.00**
Price: As above, left-hand **$345.00**

SHERIDAN MODEL E SILVER CO_2 PISTOL
Caliber: 20 (5mm).
Barrel: 6.5", rifled.
Weight: 27 oz. **Length:** 9" overall.
Power: 12-gram CO_2 cylinder.
Stocks: Walnut.
Sights: Blade front, fully adjustable rear.
Features: Velocity about 400 fps. Turn-bolt single shot action. Gives about 40
   shots per CO_2 cylinder. Introduced 1990. From Sheridan.
Price: **$98.25**

Sheridan Model HB

Sheridan Model E

SHERIDAN MODEL HB PNEUMATIC PISTOL
Caliber: 5mm, single shot.
Barrel: 9⅜", rifled.
Weight: 36 oz. **Length:** 12" overall.
Power: Under-lever pneumatic pump.
Stocks: Checkered simulated walnut; forend is walnut.
Sights: Blade front, fully adjustable rear.
Features: "Controller-Power" feature allows velocity and range control by var-
   ying the number of pumps—3 to 10. Maximum velocity of 400 fps. Introduced
   1982. From Sheridan Products.
Price: **$91.30**

WALTHER CP CO_2 AIR PISTOL
Caliber: 177, single shot.
Barrel: 9".
Weight: 40 oz. **Length:** 14¾" overall.
Power: CO_2.
Stocks: Full target-type stippled wood with adjustable hand shelf.
Sights: Target post front, fully adjustable target rear.
Features: Velocity of 520 fps, CO_2 powered; target-quality trigger; comes with
   adaptor for charging with standard CO_2 air tanks, case, and accessories.
   Introduced 1983. Imported from West Germany by Interarms.
Price: **$850.00**
Price: Junior Model (modified grip, shorter gas cylinder) **$850.00**

AIRGUNS — LONG GUNS

Air Arms Khamsin

AIR ARMS MODEL KHAMSIN
Caliber: 177, 22; single shot.
Barrel: 15", rifled.
Weight: 8 lbs., 2 oz. **Length:** 39¾" overall.
Power: Spring-air, sidelever cocking.
Stock: Oil-finished French walnut thumbhole-style, with cut checkering on p.g.
   and forend. Ventilated rubber buttplate and sling swivels.
Sights: None furnished. Comes with scope anti-slip block.
Features: Velocity up to 852 fps (177 cal.). Polished brass trigger and trigger
   guard. Introduced 1987. Imported from England by Great Lakes Airguns.
Price: Either calliber **$544.50**
Price: With Auto-Load 34-pellet magazine **$579.85**

Air Arms Model Camargue
   Basically the same as the Khamsin model except has a Tyrolean-style stock,
post front sight with protective ears, micrometer-adjustable aperture rear.
Velocity up to 871 fps (177 cal.). From Great Lakes Airguns.
Price: Either caliber **$427.33**
Price: With Auto-Load 34-pellet magazine **$460.85**

Air Arms Model Bora

Similar to the Mistral model except has 11" barrel, weighs 7.7 lbs. and has 35.8" overall length. Velocity up to 872 fps (177 cal.). Imported from England by Great Lakes Airguns.

Price: 177 or 22 .... $293.27
Price: With Auto-Load 34-pellet magazine $328.78

Air Arms Bora

Air Arms Model Mistral

Basically the same as the Model Camargue except has oil-finished beech-wood stock with Monte Carlo. Velocity up to 859 fps (177 cal.). From Great Lakes Alrguns.

Price: Either 177 or 22 caliber $293.27
Price: With Auto-Load 34-pellet magazine $328.78

AIR ARMS SE-90 AIR RIFLE

Caliber: 177, 22, single shot.
Barrel: 15", rifled steel by Walther.
Weight: 8 lbs., 4 oz. **Length:** 42¾" with muzzle weight.
Power: Spring-air, sidelever cocking.
Stock: Hardwood with checkered grip and forend, high cheekpiece.
Sights: None furnished. Comes with anti-slip scope block.
Features: Velocity of 943 fps (177), 730 (22). Uses same action as the Mistral rifle. Blue/black finish on metal parts. Comes with muzzle shroud/weight, brass trigger and trigger guard. Introduced 1990. Imported from England by Great Lakes Airguns.

Price: $364.00

Air Arms SE-90

Anschutz 2001

ANSCHUTZ 2001 MATCH AIR RIFLE

Caliber: 177, single shot.
Barrel: 26".

Weight: 10½ lbs. **Length:** 44½" overall.
Stock: European hardwood; stippled grip and forend.
Sights: Globe front, #6824 Micro Peep rear.
Features: Balance, weight match the 1907 ISU smallbore rifle. Uses #5019 match trigger. Recoil and vibration free. Fully adjustable cheekpiece and buttplate. Introduced 1988. Imported from Germany by Precision Sales International.

Price: Right-hand $1,355.00
Price: Left-hand $1,423.00
Price: Model 2001 DRT (Running Target) $1,445.00

ARS/Farco Shotgun

ARS/FARCO CO₂ AIR SHOTGUN

Caliber: 51 (28 gauge).
Barrel: 30".
Weight: 7 lbs. **Length:** 48½" overall.
Power: 10-oz. refillable CO₂ tank.
Stock: Hardwood.
Sights: Bead front, fixed dovetail rear.
Features: Gives over 100 ft. lbs. energy for taking small game. Imported by Air Rifle Specialists.

Price: $395.00

BEEMAN/FEINWERKBAU 124/127 MAGNUM

Caliber: 177 (FWB-124); 22 (FWB-127); single shot.
Barrel: 18.3", 12-groove rifling.
Weight: 6.8 lbs. **Length:** 43½" overall.
Power: Spring piston air; single stroke barrel cocking.
Stock: Walnut-finished hardwood.
Sights: Tunnel front; click-adjustable rear for w., slide-adj. for e.
Features: Velocity 680-820 fps, cocking effort of 18 lbs. Forged steel receiver; nylon non-drying piston and breech seals. Automatic safety, adjustable trigger. Hand-checkered p.g. and forend, high comb cheekplace, and buttplate with white spacer. Imported by Beeman.

Price: Deluxe model, right-hand $429.98

Beeman/FWB 124

Beeman/FWB 300-S

BEEMAN/FEINWERKBAU 300-S MINI-MATCH
Caliber: 177, single shot.
Barrel: 17⅛".
Weight: 8.8 lbs. **Length:** 40" overall.
Power: Spring piston, single stroke sidelever cocking.
Stock: Walnut. Stippled grip, adjustable buttplate. Scaled-down for youthful or slightly built shooters.
Sights: Globe front with interchangeable inserts, micro. adjustable rear. Front and rear sights move as a single unit.
Features: Recoilless, vibration free. Grooved for scope mounts. Steel piston ring. Cocking effort about 9½ lbs. Barrel sleeve optional. Left-hand model available. Introduced 1978. Imported by Beeman.
Price: Right-hand $879.50
Price: Left-hand $889.00

Beeman/FWB 601 Running Target
Similar to the standard Model 601. Has 16.9" barrel (33.7" with barrel sleeve); special match trigger, short loading gate which allows scope mounting. No sights—built for scope use only. Introduced 1987.
Price: Right-hand $1,125.00
Price: Left-hand $1,255.00
Price: Running target scope mounts $134.95

BEEMAN/FEINWERKBAU 300-S SERIES MATCH RIFLE
Caliber: 177, single shot.
Barrel: 19.9", fixed solid with receiver.
Weight: Approx. 10 lbs. with optional bbl. sleeve. **Length:** 42.8" overall.
Power: Single stroke sidelever, spring piston.
Stock: Match model—walnut, deep forend, adjustable buttplate.
Sights: Globe front with interchangeable inserts. Click micro. adjustable match aperture rear. Front and rear sights move as a single unit.
Features: Recoilless, vibration free. Five-way adjustable match trigger. Grooved for scope mounts. Permanent lubrication, steel piston ring. Cocking effort 9 lbs. Optional 10-oz. barrel sleeve. Available from Beeman.
Price: Right-hand $869.00
Price: Left-hand $950.00

BEEMAN/FEINWERKBAU MODEL 601 AIR RIFLE
Caliber: 177, single shot.
Barrel: 16.6".
Weight: 10.8 lbs. **Length:** 43" overall.
Power: Single stroke pneumatic.
Stock: Special laminated hardwoods and hard rubber for stability.
Sights: Tunnel front with interchangeable inserts, click micrometer match aperture rear.
Features: Recoilless action; double supported barrel; special, short rifled area frees pellet from barrel faster so shooter's motion has minimum effect on accuracy. Fully adjustable match trigger. Trigger and sights blocked when loading latch is open. Imported by Beeman. Introduced 1984.
Price: Right-hand $1,195.00
Price: Left-hand $1,295.00

Beeman/FWB C60

BEEMAN FX-1 AIR RIFLE
Caliber: 177, single shot.
Barrel: 18", rifled.
Weight: 6.6 lbs. **Length:** 43" overall.
Power: Spring-piston, barrel cocking.
Stock: Walnut-stained hardwood.
Sights: Tunnel front with interchangeable inserts; rear with rotating disc to give four sighting notches.
Features: Velocity 680 fps. Match-type adjustable trigger. Receiver grooved for scope mounting. Imported by Beeman.
Price: $149.50

BEEMAN/FWB C60 CO₂ RIFLE
Caliber: 177.
Barrel: 16.9". With barrel sleeve, 25.4".
Weight: 10 lbs. **Length:** 42.6" overall.
Stock: Laminated hardwood and hard rubber.
Sights: Tunnel front with interchangeable inserts, quick release micro. click match aperture rear.
Features: Similar features, performance as Beeman/FWB 601. Virtually no cocking effort. Right- or left-hand. Running target version available. Introduced 1987. Imported from Germany by Beeman.
Price: Right-hand $1,125.00
Price: Left-hand $1,198.00

Beeman FX-2 Air Rifle
Similar to the FX-1 except weighs 5.8 lbs., 41" overall; front sight is hooded post on ramp, rear sight has two-way click adjustments. Adjustable trigger. Imported by Beeman.
Price: $116.50

Beeman HW30

BEEMAN/HW30 AIR RIFLE
Caliber: 177, 22, single shot.
Barrel: 17" (177), 16.9" (20); 12-groove rifling.
Weight: 5.5 lbs.
Power: Spring piston; single-stroke barrel cocking.
Stock: Walnut-finished hardwood.
Sights: Blade front, adjustable rear.
Features: Velocity about 660 fps (177). Double-jointed cocking lever. Cast trigger guard. Synthetic non-drying breech and piston seals. Introduced 1990. Imported by Beeman.
Price: 177 . . . . $165.00
Price: 20 . . . . $175.00

BEEMAN/HW50 LIGHT/SPORTER TARGET RIFLE

Caliber: 177, single shot.
Barrel: 18.4"; 12-groove rifling.
Weight: 6.9 lbs. **Length:** 43.1" overall.
Power: Spring piston; single-stroke barrel cocking.
Stock: Walnut-finished hardwood.
Sights: Blade front, adjustable rear.
Features: Velocity about 705 fps. Synthetic non-drying breech and piston seals. Double-jointed cocking lever. Introduced 1990. Imported by Beeman.
Price: $186.00

Beeman HW50

BEEMAN/HARPER AIRCANE

Caliber: 22 and 25, single shot.
Barrel: 31½", rifled.
Weight: 1 lb. **Length:** 34" overall.
Features: Walking cane also acts as an airgun. Solid walnut handle with polished brass ferrule. Available in various hand-carved models. Intricate deep engraving on the ferrule. Uses rechargeable air "cartridges" loaded with pellets. Kit includes separate pump, extra cartridges and fitted case. Introduced 1987. Imported by Beeman.
Price: Basic set $495.95
Price: Goose, Labrador, Spaniel sets $555.00

BEEMAN/HW 55 TARGET RIFLES

Model	55SM	55MM	55T
Caliber:	177	177	177
Barrel:	18½"	18½"	18½"
Length:	43½"	43½"	43½"
Wgt. lbs.:	7.8	7.8	7.8
Rear sight:	All aperture		
Front sight:	All with globe and four interchangeable inserts.		
Power:	All spring (barrel cocking). 660-700 fps.		
Price:	$389.50	$489.50	$539.50

Features: Trigger fully adj. and removable. Micrometer rear sight adj. for w. and e. in all. Pistol grip high comb stock with beavertail forend, walnut finish stock on 55SM. Walnut stock on 55MM, Tyrolean stock on 55T. Nylon piston seals in all. Model 55MM, left-hand, **$529.50.** Imported by Beeman.

Beeman/HW 55T

BEEMAN/HW77 AIR RIFLE & CARBINE

Caliber: 177, 20 or 22, single shot.
Barrel: 14.5" or 18.5", 12-groove rifling.
Weight: 8.9 lbs. **Length:** 39.7" or 43.7" overall.
Power: Spring-piston; under-lever cocking.
Stocks: Walnut-stained beech; rubber buttplate, cut checkering on grip; cheekpiece.
Sights: Blade front, open adjustable rear.
Features: Velocity 830 fps. Fixed-barrel with fully opening, direct loading breech. Extended under-lever gives good cocking leverage. Adjustable trigger. Grooved for scope mounting. Carbine has 14.5" barrel, weighs 8.7 lbs., and is 39.7" overall. Imported by Beeman.
Price: Right-hand, 177 . . . . $319.98
Price: Left-hand, 177 . . . . $439.98
Price: Right-hand, 20 . . . . $419.98
Price: Left-hand, 20 . . . . $449.98
Price: Right-hand, 22 . . . . $399.98
Price: Left-hand, 22 . . . . $439.98

Beeman HW77

BEEMAN CARBINE MODEL C1

Caliber: 177 or 22, single shot.
Barrel: 14", 12-groove rifling.
Weight: 6¼ lbs. **Length:** 38" overall.
Power: Spring-piston, barrel cocking.
Stock: Walnut-stained beechwood with rubber buttpad.
Sights: Blade front, rear click-adjustable for windage and elevation.
Features: Velocity 830 fps. Adjustable trigger. Receiver grooved for scope mounting. Imported by Beeman.
Price: . . . . $199.95.

BEEMAN RX AIRSPRING MAGNUM AIR RIFLE

Caliber: 177, 20, 22, 25, single shot.
Barrel: 19.6"; 12-groove rifling.
Weight: 8.8 lbs.
Power: Airspring piston air; single stroke barrel cocking.
Stock: Walnut-finished hardwood, hand checkered, with cheekpiece. Adjustable cheekpiece and buttplate.
Sights: Tunnel front, click-adjustable rear.
Features: Velocity adjustable to about 1200 fps. Uses special sealed chamber of air as a mainspring. Airspring cannot take a set. Introduced 1990. Imported by Beeman.
Price: 177 or 22 . . . . $399.50
Price: 20 or 25 . . . . $409.50

Beeman RX

Consult our Directory pages for the location of firms mentioned.

BEEMAN R1 AIR RIFLE
Caliber: 177, 20 or 22, single shot.
Barrel: 19.6″, 12-groove rifling.
Weight: 8.5 lbs. **Length:** 45.2″ overall.
Power: Spring-piston, barrel cocking.
Stock: Walnut-stained beech; cut-checkered pistol grip; Monte Carlo comb and cheekpiece; rubber buttpad.
Sights: Tunnel front with interchangeable inserts, open rear click adjustable for windage and elevation. Grooved for scope mounting.
Features: Velocity of 940-1050 fps (177), 860 fps (20), 800 fps (22). Non-drying nylon piston and breech seals. Adjustable metal trigger. Milled steel safety. Right- or left-hand stock. Available with adjustable cheekpiece and buttplate at extra cost. Custom and Super Laser versions available. Imported by Beeman.
Price: Right-hand, 177 or 22 .... $389.95
Price: Left-hand, 177 or 22 .... $429.95
Price: Right-hand, 20 .... $399.95
Price: Left-hand, 20 .... $439.95

BEEMAN R1 LASER AIR RIFLE
Caliber: 177, 20, 22, 25, single shot.
Barrel: 16.1″ or 19.6″.
Weight: 8.4 lbs. **Length:** 41.7″ overall (16.1″ barrel).
Power: Spring-piston, barrel cocking.
Stock: Laminated wood with Monte Carlo comb and cheekpiece; checkered p.g. and forend; rubber buttpad.
Sights: Tunnel front with interchangeable inserts, open adjustable rear.
Features: Velocity up to 1050 fps (177). Receiver grooved for scope mounting. Imported by Beeman.
Price: 177 or 22 cal. $790.00
Price: 20 cal. $799.00
Price: 25 cal. $799.50

Beeman R7 Air Rifle
Similar to the R8 model except has lighter ambidextrous stock, match-grade trigger block; velocity of 680-700 fps; barrel length 17″; weight 5.8 lbs. Milled steel safety. Imported by Beeman.
Price: 177 .... $229.98
Price: 20 .... $239.98

BEEMAN R8 AIR RIFLE
Caliber: 177, single shot.
Barrel: 18.3″.
Weight: 7.2 lbs. **Length:** 43.1″ overall.
Power: Barrel cocking, spring-piston.
Stock: Walnut with Monte Carlo cheekpiece; checkered pistol grip.
Sights: Globe front, fully adjustable rear; interchangeable inserts.
Features: Velocity of 735 fps. Similar to the R1. Nylon piston and breech seals. Adjustable match-grade, two-stage, grooved metal trigger. Milled steel safety. Rubber buttpad. Imported by Beeman.
Price: $299.98

BEEMAN R1 CARBINE
Caliber: 177, 20, 22, 25, single shot.
Barrel: 16.1″.
Weight: 8.6 lbs. **Length:** 41.7″ overall.
Power: Spring-piston, barrel cocking.
Stock: Stained beech; Monte Carlo comb and checkpiece; cut-checkered p.g.; rubber buttpad.
Sights: Tunnel front with interchangeable inserts, open adjustable rear; receiver grooved for scope mounting.
Features: Velocity up to 1050 fps (177). Non-drying nylon piston and breech seals. Adjustable metal trigger. Right- or left-hand stock. Imported by Beeman.
Price: 177 or 22, right-hand $389.95
Price: As above, left-hand $429.95
Price: 20 or 25 cal., right-hand $399.95
Price: As above, left-hand $439.95

BEEMAN R10 AIR RIFLES
Caliber: 177, 20, 22, single shot.
Barrel: 16.1″ and 19.7″; 12-groove rifling.
Weight: 7.9 lbs. **Length:** 46″ overall.
Power: Spring-piston, barrel cocking.
Stock: Standard—walnut-finished hardwood with Monte Carlo comb, rubber buttplate; Deluxe has white spacers at grip cap, buttplate, checkered grip, cheekpiece, rubber buttplate.
Sights: Tunnel front with interchangeable inserts, open rear click adjustable for w. and e. Receiver grooved for scope mounting.
Features: Over 1000 fps in 177 cal. only; 26-lb. cocking effort; milled steel safety and body tube. Right- and left-hand models. Custom and Super Laser versions available. Introduced 1986. Imported by Beeman.
Price: $419.98

Beeman R8

BEEMAN/WEBLEY ECLIPSE AIR RIFLE
Caliber: 177, 22, single shot.
Barrel: 17.5″.
Weight: 8.25 lbs. **Length:** 44.5″ overall.
Power: Under-lever cocking.
Stock: Lacquer-finished beechwood with high relief cheekpiece, checkered grip with palm swell.
Sights: Blade front, adjustable rear.
Features: Two-stage trigger, ambidextrous safety catch. Receiver grooved for scope mounting, with arrestor grooves. Fitted with Webley's patent mainspring damper to eliminate vibration. Introduced 1990. Imported from England by Beeman.
Price: $399.98

BEEMAN/WEBLEY OMEGA AIR RIFLE
Caliber: 177 or 22, single shot.
Barrel: 19¼″, rifled.
Weight: 7.8 lbs. **Length:** 43½″ overall.
Power: Spring-piston air; barrel cocking.
Stock: Walnut-stained beech with cut-checkered grip; cheekpiece; rubber buttpad.
Features: Special quick-snap barrel latch; self-lubricating piston seal; receiver grooved for scope mounting. Introduced 1985. Imported from England by Beeman.
Price: $349.50

Beeman/Webley Omega

BEEMAN/WEBLEY VULCAN III DELUXE
Caliber: 177 or 22, single shot.
Barrel: 17″, rifled.
Weight: 7.6 lbs. **Length:** 43.7″ overall.
Power: Spring-piston air, barrel cocking.
Stock: Walnut. Cut checkering, rubber buttpad, cheekpiece. Standard version has walnut-stained beech.

Sights: Hooded front, micrometer rear.
Features: Velocity of 830 fps (177), 675 fps (22). Single-stage adjustable trigger; receiver grooved for scope mounting. Self-lubricating piston seal. Introduced 1983. Imported by Beeman.
Price: Standard $199.95
Price: Deluxe $269.95

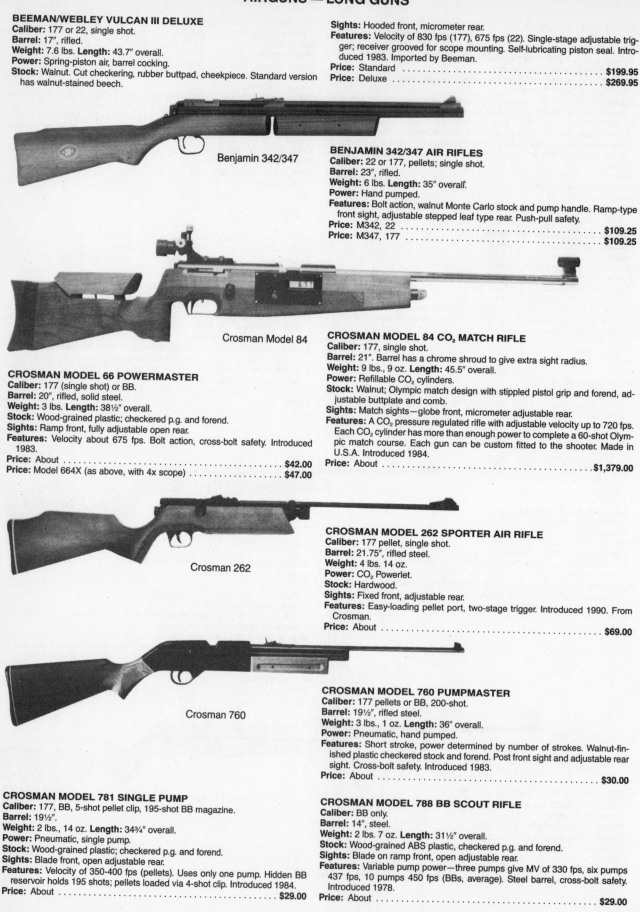

Benjamin 342/347

BENJAMIN 342/347 AIR RIFLES
Caliber: 22 or 177, pellets; single shot.
Barrel: 23″, rifled.
Weight: 6 lbs. **Length:** 35″ overall.
Power: Hand pumped.
Features: Bolt action, walnut Monte Carlo stock and pump handle. Ramp-type front sight, adjustable stepped leaf type rear. Push-pull safety.
Price: M342, 22 .... $109.25
Price: M347, 177 .... $109.25

Crosman Model 84

CROSMAN MODEL 84 CO₂ MATCH RIFLE
Caliber: 177, single shot.
Barrel: 21″. Barrel has a chrome shroud to give extra sight radius.
Weight: 9 lbs., 9 oz. **Length:** 45.5″ overall.
Power: Refillable CO_2 cylinders.
Stock: Walnut; Olympic match design with stippled pistol grip and forend, adjustable buttplate and comb.
Sights: Match sights—globe front, micrometer adjustable rear.
Features: A CO_2 pressure regulated rifle with adjustable velocity up to 720 fps. Each CO_2 cylinder has more than enough power to complete a 60-shot Olympic match course. Each gun can be custom fitted to the shooter. Made in U.S.A. Introduced 1984.
Price: About $1,379.00

CROSMAN MODEL 66 POWERMASTER
Caliber: 177 (single shot) or BB.
Barrel: 20″, rifled, solid steel.
Weight: 3 lbs. **Length:** 38½″ overall.
Stock: Wood-grained plastic; checkered p.g. and forend.
Sights: Ramp front, fully adjustable open rear.
Features: Velocity about 675 fps. Bolt action, cross-bolt safety. Introduced 1983.
Price: About $42.00
Price: Model 664X (as above, with 4x scope) $47.00

Crosman 262

CROSMAN MODEL 262 SPORTER AIR RIFLE
Caliber: 177 pellet, single shot.
Barrel: 21.75″, rifled steel.
Weight: 4 lbs. 14 oz.
Power: CO_2 Powerlet.
Stock: Hardwood.
Sights: Fixed front, adjustable rear.
Features: Easy-loading pellet port, two-stage trigger. Introduced 1990. From Crosman.
Price: About $69.00

Crosman 760

CROSMAN MODEL 760 PUMPMASTER
Caliber: 177 pellets or BB, 200-shot.
Barrel: 19½″, rifled steel.
Weight: 3 lbs., 1 oz. **Length:** 36″ overall.
Power: Pneumatic, hand pumped.
Features: Short stroke, power determined by number of strokes. Walnut-finished plastic checkered stock and forend. Post front sight and adjustable rear sight. Cross-bolt safety. Introduced 1983.
Price: About $30.00

CROSMAN MODEL 781 SINGLE PUMP
Caliber: 177, BB, 5-shot pellet clip, 195-shot BB magazine.
Barrel: 19½″.
Weight: 2 lbs., 14 oz. **Length:** 34¾″ overall.
Power: Pneumatic, single pump.
Stock: Wood-grained plastic; checkered p.g. and forend.
Sights: Blade front, open adjustable rear.
Features: Velocity of 350-400 fps (pellets). Uses only one pump. Hidden BB reservoir holds 195 shots; pellets loaded via 4-shot clip. Introduced 1984.
Price: About $29.00

CROSMAN MODEL 788 BB SCOUT RIFLE
Caliber: BB only.
Barrel: 14″, steel.
Weight: 2 lbs. 7 oz. **Length:** 31½″ overall.
Stock: Wood-grained ABS plastic, checkered p.g. and forend.
Sights: Blade on ramp front, open adjustable rear.
Features: Variable pump power—three pumps give MV of 330 fps, six pumps 437 fps, 10 pumps 450 fps (BBs, average). Steel barrel, cross-bolt safety. Introduced 1978.
Price: About $29.00

CAUTION: PRICES CHANGE, CHECK AT GUNSHOP.

Crosman 782

CROSMAN MODEL 782 BLACK DIAMOND AIR RIFLE
Caliber: 177, 5-shot clip; BB, 195-shot magazine.
Barrel: 18″, rifled steel.

Weight: 2 lbs., 14 oz.
Power: CO_2 Powerlet.
Stock: Wood-grained plastic; checkered grip and forend.
Sights: Blade front, open adjustable rear.
Features: Velocity up to 545 fps (pellets), 590 fps (BB). Black finish with white diamonds. Introduced 1990. From Crosman.
Price: About **$39.95**

Crosman 790

CROSMAN MODEL 2100 CLASSIC AIR RIFLE
Caliber: 177 pellets or BBs, 200-shot BB magazine.
Barrel: 21″, rifled.
Weight: 4 lbs., 13 oz. **Length:** 39¾″ overall.
Power: Pump-up, pneumatic.
Stock: Wood-grained checkered ABS plastic.
Features: Three pumps give about 450 fps, 10 pumps about 795 fps. Crossbolt safety; concealed reservoir holds over 180 BBs.
Price: About **$54.00**

CROSMAN MODEL 790 OUTBACKER AIR RIFLE
Caliber: 177, 5-shot clip; BB, 195-shot magazine.
Barrel: 16³⁄₁₆″, steel, smooth.
Weight: 2 lbs., 14 oz.
Power: Pneumatic, single pump.
Stock: Textured plastic with Alligator grain checkering on grip and forend.
Sights: Pinpoint sight tube looks like real scope, but no magnification.
Features: Velocity up to 400 fps (177), 450 fps (BB). Includes canteen that fits in stock, compass in pistol grip and adventure guide shooting game. Introduced 1990. From Crosman.
Price: About **$40.00**

Crosman 2200

CROSMAN MODEL 2200 MAGNUM AIR RIFLE
Caliber: 22, single shot.
Barrel: 19″, rifled steel.

Weight: 4 lbs., 12 oz. **Length:** 39″ overall.
Stock: Full-size, wood-grained plastic with checkered p.g. and forend.
Sights: Ramp front, open step-adjustable rear.
Features: Variable pump power—three pumps give 395 fps, six pumps 530 fps, 10 pumps 620 fps (average). Full-size adult air rifle. Has white line spacers at pistol grip and buttplate. Introduced 1978.
Price: About **$54.00**

Crosman Backpacker

CROSMAN MODEL 1389 BACKPACKER RIFLE
Caliber: 177, single shot.
Barrel: 14″, rifled steel.

Weight: 3 lbs. 3 oz. **Length:** 31″ overall.
Power: Hand pumped, pneumatic.
Stock: Composition, skeletal type.
Sights: Blade front, rear adjustable for windage and elevation.
Features: Velocity to 560 fps. Detachable stock. Receiver grooved for scope mounting. Metal parts blued.
Price: About **$54.00**

Crosman 3100

DAISY/POWER LINE MODEL 130 AIR RIFLE
Caliber: 177, single shot.
Barrel: 18″, rifled steel.
Weight: 5.9 lbs. **Length:** 41″ overall.
Power: Spring-air, barrel cocking.
Stock: European-style hardwood.
Sights: Hooded front with blade on ramp, micrometer adjustable open rear.
Features: Velocity up to 800 fps. Introduced 1990. Imported from Spain by Daisy.
Price: About **$100.00**

CROSMAN MODEL 3100 RIFLE
Caliber: 177, single shot.
Barrel: 16⁷⁄₁₆″.
Weight: 6 lbs. **Length:** 39¾″ overall.
Power: Spring-air, barrel cocking.
Stock: Hardwood with Monte Carlo.
Sights: Hooded front with three apertures, micro. adjustable rear.
Features: Velocity of 600 fps. Single-stroke cocking; adjustable trigger; thumb safety; rubber buttplate. Introduced 1986. Imported by Crosman.
Price: About **$62.00**

CAUTION: PRICES CHANGE, CHECK AT GUNSHOP.

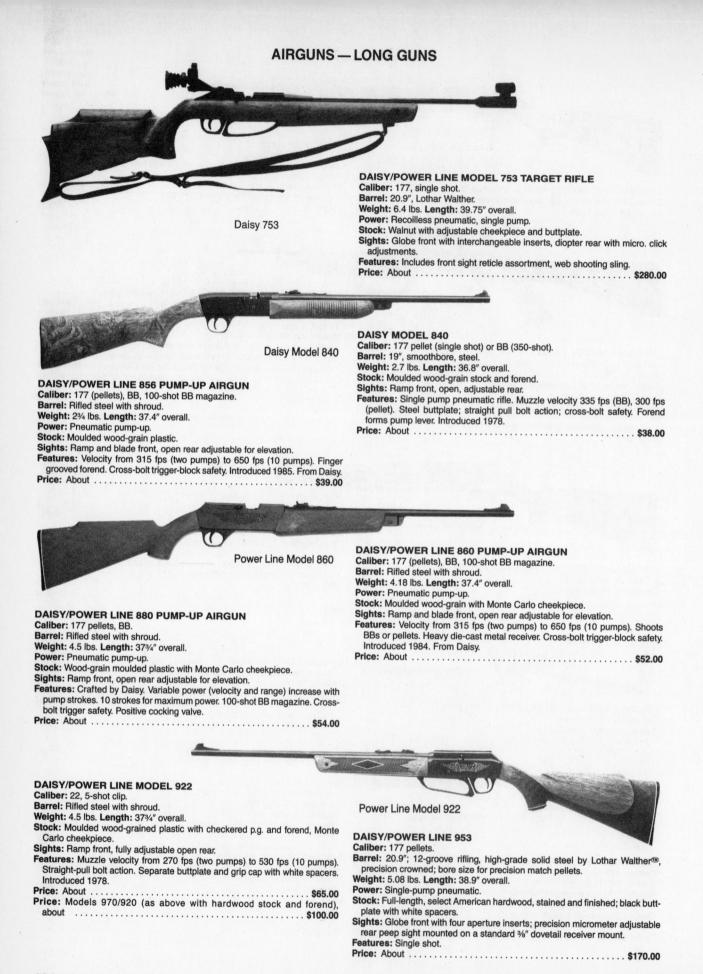

Daisy 753

DAISY/POWER LINE MODEL 753 TARGET RIFLE
Caliber: 177, single shot.
Barrel: 20.9", Lothar Walther.
Weight: 6.4 lbs. **Length:** 39.75" overall.
Power: Recoilless pneumatic, single pump.
Stock: Walnut with adjustable cheekpiece and buttplate.
Sights: Globe front with interchangeable inserts, diopter rear with micro. click adjustments.
Features: Includes front sight reticle assortment, web shooting sling.
Price: About **$280.00**

Daisy Model 840

DAISY MODEL 840
Caliber: 177 pellet (single shot) or BB (350-shot).
Barrel: 19", smoothbore, steel.
Weight: 2.7 lbs. **Length:** 36.8" overall.
Stock: Moulded wood-grain stock and forend.
Sights: Ramp front, open, adjustable rear.
Features: Single pump pneumatic rifle. Muzzle velocity 335 fps (BB), 300 fps (pellet). Steel buttplate; straight pull bolt action; cross-bolt safety. Forend forms pump lever. Introduced 1978.
Price: About **$38.00**

DAISY/POWER LINE 856 PUMP-UP AIRGUN
Caliber: 177 (pellets), BB, 100-shot BB magazine.
Barrel: Rifled steel with shroud.
Weight: 2¾ lbs. **Length:** 37.4" overall.
Power: Pneumatic pump-up.
Stock: Moulded wood-grain plastic.
Sights: Ramp and blade front, open rear adjustable for elevation.
Features: Velocity from 315 fps (two pumps) to 650 fps (10 pumps). Finger grooved forend. Cross-bolt trigger-block safety. Introduced 1985. From Daisy.
Price: About **$39.00**

Power Line Model 860

DAISY/POWER LINE 860 PUMP-UP AIRGUN
Caliber: 177 (pellets), BB, 100-shot BB magazine.
Barrel: Rifled steel with shroud.
Weight: 4.18 lbs. **Length:** 37.4" overall.
Power: Pneumatic pump-up.
Stock: Moulded wood-grain with Monte Carlo cheekpiece.
Sights: Ramp and blade front, open rear adjustable for elevation.
Features: Velocity from 315 fps (two pumps) to 650 fps (10 pumps). Shoots BBs or pellets. Heavy die-cast metal receiver. Cross-bolt trigger-block safety. Introduced 1984. From Daisy.
Price: About **$52.00**

DAISY/POWER LINE 880 PUMP-UP AIRGUN
Caliber: 177 pellets, BB.
Barrel: Rifled steel with shroud.
Weight: 4.5 lbs. **Length:** 37¾" overall.
Power: Pneumatic pump-up.
Stock: Wood-grain moulded plastic with Monte Carlo cheekpiece.
Sights: Ramp front, open rear adjustable for elevation.
Features: Crafted by Daisy. Variable power (velocity and range) increase with pump strokes. 10 strokes for maximum power. 100-shot BB magazine. Cross-bolt trigger safety. Positive cocking valve.
Price: About **$54.00**

DAISY/POWER LINE MODEL 922
Caliber: 22, 5-shot clip.
Barrel: Rifled steel with shroud.
Weight: 4.5 lbs. **Length:** 37¾" overall.
Stock: Moulded wood-grained plastic with checkered p.g. and forend, Monte Carlo cheekpiece.
Sights: Ramp front, fully adjustable open rear.
Features: Muzzle velocity from 270 fps (two pumps) to 530 fps (10 pumps). Straight-pull bolt action. Separate buttplate and grip cap with white spacers. Introduced 1978.
Price: About **$65.00**
Price: Models 970/920 (as above with hardwood stock and forend), about **$100.00**

Power Line Model 922

DAISY/POWER LINE 953
Caliber: 177 pellets.
Barrel: 20.9"; 12-groove rifling, high-grade solid steel by Lothar Walther®, precision crowned; bore size for precision match pellets.
Weight: 5.08 lbs. **Length:** 38.9" overall.
Power: Single-pump pneumatic.
Stock: Full-length, select American hardwood, stained and finished; black buttplate with white spacers.
Sights: Globe front with four aperture inserts; precision micrometer adjustable rear peep sight mounted on a standard ⅜" dovetail receiver mount.
Features: Single shot.
Price: About **$170.00**

CAUTION: PRICES CHANGE, CHECK AT GUNSHOP.

Daisy Model 95

DAISY YOUTHLINE RIFLES

Model:	95	111	105
Caliber:	BB	BB	BB
Barrel:	18″	18″	13½″
Length:	35.2″	34.3″	29.8″
Power:	Spring	Spring	Spring
Capacity:	700	650	400
Price: About	$37.00	$30.00	$25.00

Features: Model 95 stock and forend are wood; 105 and 111 have plastic stocks.

Daisy Red Ryder

DAISY 1938 RED RYDER CLASSIC
Caliber: BB, 650-shot repeating action.
Barrel: Smoothbore steel with shroud.
Weight: 2.2 lbs. **Length:** 35.4″ overall.
Stock: Walnut stock burned with Red Ryder lariat signature.
Sights: Post front, adjustable V-slot rear.
Features: Walnut forend. Saddle ring with leather thong. Lever cocking. Gravity feed. Controlled velocity. One of Daisy's most popular guns.
Price: About $41.00

FAMAS Air Rifle

FAMAS SEMI-AUTO AIR RIFLE
Caliber: 177, 10-shot magazine.
Barrel: 19.2″.
Weight: About 8 lbs. **Length:** 29.8″ overall.
Power: 12 gram CO$_2$.
Stock: Synthetic bullpup design.
Sights: Adjustable front, aperture rear.
Features: Velocity of 425 fps. Duplicates size, weight and feel of the centerfire MAS French military rifle in caliber 223. Introduced 1988. Imported from France by Century International Arms.
Price: $432.95

"GAT" AIR RIFLE
Caliber: 177, single shot.
Barrel: 17¼″ cocked, 23¼″ extended.
Weight: 3 lbs.
Power: Spring piston.
Stock: Composition.
Sights: Fixed.
Features: Velocity about 450 fps. Shoots pellets, darts, corks. Imported from England by Stone Enterprises, Inc.
Price: $34.95

El Gamo 128

EL GAMO 126 SUPER MATCH TARGET RIFLE
Caliber: 177, single shot.
Barrel: Match grade, precision rifled.
Weight: 10.6 lbs. **Length:** 43.8″ overall.
Power: Single pump pneumatic.
Stock: Match-style, hardwood, with stippled grip and forend.
Sights: Hooded front with interchangeable elements, fully adjustable match rear.
Features: Velocity of 590 fps. Adjustable trigger; easy loading pellet port; adjustable buttpad. Introduced 1984. Imported from Spain by Daisy.
Price: About $400.00

MARKSMAN 28 INTERNATIONAL AIR RIFLE
Caliber: 177, single shot.
Barrel: 17″.
Weight: 5¾ lbs.
Power: Spring-air, barrel cocking.
Stock: Hardwood.
Sights: Hooded front, adjustable rear.
Features: Velocity of 580-620 fps. Introduced 1989. Imported from West Germany by Marksman Products.
Price: $170.00

MARKSMAN 29 AIR RIFLE
Caliber: 177 or 22, single shot.
Barrel: 18.5″.
Weight: 6 lbs. **Length:** 41.5″ overall.
Power: Spring air, barrel cocking.
Stock: Stained hardwood.
Sights: Blade front, open adjustable rear.
Features: Velocity of 790-830 fps (177), 610-640 fps (22). Introduced 1986. Imported from England by Marksman Products.
Price: Either caliber $199.00

MARKSMAN 56-FTS FIELD TARGET RIFLE
Caliber: 177, single shot.
Barrel: 19⅝".
Weight: 8.8 lbs.
Power: Spring-air, barrel cocking.
Stock: Hardwood with stippled grip; ambidextrous, with adjustable cheekpiece, adjustable buttplate.
Sights: None furnished.
Features: Velocity of 910-940 fps. Rubber buttpad. Introduced 1989. Imported from West Germany by Marksman Products.
Price: $399.00

MARKSMAN 40 INTERNATIONAL AIR RIFLE
Caliber: 177, single shot.
Barrel: 18⅜".
Weight: 7⅓ lbs.
Power: Spring-air, barrel cocking.
Stock: Hardwood.
Sights: Hooded front, adjustable rear.
Features: Velocity of 700-720 fps. Introduced 1989. Imported from West Germany by Marksman Products.
Price: $199.00

Marksman 58-S

MARKSMAN 58-S SILHOUETTE RIFLE
Caliber: 177, single shot.
Barrel: 16".
Weight: 8.5 lbs.
Power: Spring-air, barrel cocking.
Stock: Hardwood with stippled grip; ambidextrous.
Sights: None furnished.
Features: Velocity 910-940 fps. Adjustable trigger. Introduced 1989. Imported from West Germany by Marksman Products.
Price: $325.00

MARKSMAN MODEL 60 AIR RIFLE
Caliber: 177, single shot.
Barrel: 18.5", rifled.
Weight: 8.9 lbs. **Length:** 44.75" overall.
Power: Spring piston, underlever cocking.
Stock: Walnut-stained beech with Monte Carlo comb, hand-checkered pistol grip, rubber butt pad.
Sights: Blade front, open, micro. adjustable rear.
Features: Velocity of 810-840 fps. Automatic button safety on rear of receiver. Receiver grooved for scope mounting. Fully adjustable Rekord trigger. Introduced 1990. Imported from West Germany by Marksman Products.
Price: $385.00
Price: Model 61 Carbine (14.5" barrel) $385.00

Marksman Model 60

Marksman/Anschutz

MARKSMAN/ANSCHUTZ MODEL 380 MATCH AIR RIFLE
Caliber: 177, single shot.
Barrel: 20.75".

Weight: 10.75 lbs.
Power: Spring piston, sidelever cocking.
Stock: Match-style, walnut, with adjustable cheekpiece, adjustable buttplate.
Sights: Tunnel front with interchangeable inserts, match diopter rear.
Features: Velocity of 600-640 fps. Fully adjustable trigger. Recoilless and vibration free. Introduced 1990. Imported from West Germany by Marksman Products.
Price: Right-hand $1,150.00
Price: Left-hand $1,150.00

Marksman 1790

MARKSMAN 1790 BIATHLON TRAINER
Caliber: 177, single shot.
Barrel: 15", rifled.
Weight: 4.7 lbs.
Power: Spring-air, barrel cocking.
Stock: Synthetic.
Sights: Hooded front, match-style diopter rear.
Features: Velocity of 450 fps. Introduced 1989. From Marksman Products.
Price: $66.75

MARKSMAN 1740 AIR RIFLE
Caliber: 177 or 100-shot BB repeater.
Barrel: 15½", smoothbore.
Weight: 5 lbs., 1 oz. **Length:** 36½" overall.
Power: Spring, barrel cocking.
Stock: Moulded high-impact ABS plastic.
Sights: Ramp front, open rear adjustable for elevation.
Features: Automatic safety; fixed front, adjustable rear sight; shoots 177 cal. BBs, pellets and darts. Velocity about 475-500 fps.
Price: $40.00
Price: Model 1780 (shoots only pellets) $45.00

CAUTION: PRICES CHANGE, CHECK AT GUNSHOP.

MARKSMAN 70T AIR RIFLE
Caliber: 177, 20 or 22, single shot.
Barrel: 19.75″.
Weight: 8 lbs. **Length:** 45.5″ overall.
Power: Spring air, barrel cocking.
Stock: Stained hardwood with Monte Carlo cheekpiece, rubber buttpad, cut checkered p.g.
Sights: Hooded front, open fully adjustable rear.
Features: Velocity of 910-940 fps (177), 810-840 fps (20), 740-780 fps (22); Rekord trigger. Introduced 1988. Imported from West Germany by Marksman Products.
Price: 177 (Model 70T) **$270.00**
Price: 20 (Model 72) **$270.00**
Price: (Model 71) **$270.00**

Marksman 55T Air Rifle
Similar to the Model 70 except has uncheckered hardwood stock, no cheekpiece, plastic buttplate. Overall length is 45.25″, weight is 7½ lbs. Available in 177 caliber only.
Price: **$235.00**
Price: Model 59T (as above, carbine) **$235.00**

MARKSMAN 1750 BB BIATHLON REPEATER RIFLE
Caliber: BB, 18-shot magazine.
Barrel: 15″, smoothbore.
Weight: 4.7 lbs.
Power: Spring piston, barrel cocking.
Stock: Moulded composition.
Sights: Tunnel front, open adjustable rear.
Features: Velocity of 450 fps. Automatic safety. Positive Feed System loads a BB each time gun is cocked. Introduced 1990. From Marksman Products.
Price: **$48.50**

MAUSER MODEL 300 SL AIR RIFLE
Caliber: 177, single shot.
Barrel: 18.9″.
Weight: 8 lbs., 8 oz. **Length:** 43.7″ overall.
Power: Spring air, under-lever cocking.
Stock: Match style, hardwood, with stippled p.g., rubber buttpad.
Sights: Tunnel front, open adjustable rear.
Features: Velocity of 550-600 fps. Dovetail mount for diopter or scope. Automatic safety. Imported from West Germany by Marksman Products.
Price: **$285.00**
Price: With diopter sight **$378.00**

Mauser 300 SL

RWS/Diana Model 26 Air Rifle
Similar to the Model 24 except weighs 6.25 lbs., gives velocity of 750 fps (177), 500 fps (22). Automatic safety, scope rail, synthetic seals.
Price: 177 or 22 . . . . **$160.00**

RWS/DIANA MODEL 24 AIR RIFLE
Caliber: 177, 22, single shot.
Barrel: 17″, rifled.
Weight: 6 lbs. **Length:** 42″ overall.
Power: Spring air, barrel cocking.
Stock: Beech.
Sights: Hooded front, adjustable rear.
Features: Velocity of 700 fps (177). Easy cocking effort; blue finish. Imported from West Germany by Dynamit Nobel-RWS, Inc.
Price: **$120.00**
Price: Model 24J (13.5″ bbl., 177 only) **$110.00**

RWS/Diana Model 28 Air Rifle
Similar to the Model 26 except has Monte Carlo stock with cheekpiece, rubber recoil pad and two-stage trigger. Velocity of 750 fps (177), 500 fps (22).
Price: 177 or 22 . . . . **$170.00**

RWS/Diana Model 34 Air Rifle
Similar to the Model 24 except has 19″ barrel, weighs 7.5 lbs. Gives velocity of 1000 fps (177), 800 fps (22). Adjustable trigger, synthetic seals. Comes with scope rail.
Price: 177 or 22 . . . . **$180.00**
Price: Diana Commemorative Model 34 (as above except different stock with commemorative plaque on right side, 177 only). **$190.00**

RWS/DIANA MODEL 36 AIR RIFLE
Caliber: 177, 22, single shot.
Barrel: 19″, rifled.
Weight: 8 lbs. **Length:** 45″ overall.
Power: Spring air, barrel cocking.
Stock: Beech.
Sights: Hooded front (interchangeable inserts avail.), adjustable rear.
Features: Velocity of 1000 fps (177 cal.). Comes with scope mount; two-stage adjustable trigger. Imported from West Germnay by Dynamit Nobel-RWS, Inc.
Price: **$265.00**
Price: Model 38 (as above, walnut stock) **$300.00**
Price: Model 36S (as above except comes with sling, swivels, barrel weight, 4x20 scope) **$300.00**
Price: Model 36 Muzzlebrake (same as Model 36 except no sights, has muzzlebrake/barrel weight) **$250.00**
Price: Model 36 Carbine (same as Model 36 except has 15″ barrel) **$265.00**

RWS/Diana 38

RWS/DIANA MODEL 45 AIR RIFLE
Caliber: 177, single shot.
Weight: 7¾ lbs. **Length:** 46″ overall.
Power: Spring air, barrel cocking.
Stock: Walnut-finished hardwood with rubber recoil pad.
Sights: Globe front with interchangeable inserts, micro. click open rear with four-way blade.
Features: Velocity of 820 fps. Dovetail base for either micrometer peep sight or scope mounting. Automatic safety. Imported from West Germany by Dynamit Nobel-RWS, Inc.
Price: **$200.00**

RWS/Diana 52

RWS/DIANA MODEL 52 AIR RIFLE
Caliber: 177, 22, single shot.
Barrel: 17", rifled.

Weight: 8½ lbs. **Length:** 43" overall.
Power: Spring air, sidelever cocking.
Stock: Beech, with Monte Carlo, cheekpiece, checkered grip and forend.
Sights: Ramp front, adjustable rear.
Features: Velocity of 1100 fps (177). Blue finish. Solid rubber buttpad. Imported from West Germnay by Dynamit Nobel-RWS, Inc.
Price: $330.00
Price: Model 48 (as above except no Monte Carlo, cheekpiece or checkering) $300.00

RWS/Diana 75 T01

RWS/DIANA MODEL 75 T01 MATCH AIR RIFLE
Caliber: 177, single shot.
Barrel: 19".

RWS/Diana Model 75S T01 Air Rifle
Similar to the Model 75 T01 except has beech stock specially shaped for standing and three-position shooting. Buttplate is vertically adjustable with curved and straight spacers for individual fit, adjustable cheekpiece. Introduced 1990.
Price: Right-hand $840.00
Price: Left-hand $880.00

RWS/Diana Model 72 Air Rifle
Similar to the Model 70 except has recoilless action. Introduced 1990.
Price: $310.00

Weight: 11 lbs. **Length:** 43.7" overall.
Power: Spring air, sidelever cocking.
Stock: Oil-finished walnut with stippled grip, adjustable buttplate, accessory rail. Conforms to I.S.U. rules.
Sights: Globe front with five inserts, fully adjustable match peep rear.
Features: Velocity of 574 fps. Fully adjustable trigger. Model 75 HV has stippled forend, adjustable cheekpiece. Uses double opposing piston system for recoilless operation. Imported from West Germany by Dynamit Nobel-RWS, Inc.
Price: Model 75 T01 .... $760.00

RWS/DIANA MODEL 70 MATCH AIR RIFLE
Caliber: 177, single shot.
Barrel: 13.5".
Weight: 4.5 lbs. **Length:** 33" overall.
Power: Spring air, barrel cocking.
Stock: Beech, match-type.
Sights: Tunnel front with interchangeable inserts, fully adjustable peep rear.
Features: Velocity of 450 fps. Adjustable trigger. Designed and scaled for junior shooters. Introduced 1990. Imported from West Germany by Dynamit Nobel-RWS, Inc.
Price: $170.00

RWS/Diana 100

RWS/DIANA MODEL 100 MATCH AIR RIFLE
Caliber: 177, single shot.
Barrel: 19".

Weight: 11 lbs. **Length:** 43" overall.
Power: Spring air, sidelever cocking.
Stock: Walnut.
Sights: Tunnel front, fully adjustable match rear.
Features: Velocity of 580 fps. Single-stroke cocking; cheekpiece adjustable for height and length; recoilless operation. Cocking lever secured against rebound. Introduced 1990. Imported from West Germany by Dynamit Nobel-RWS, Inc.
Price: Right-hand only $760.00

Sheridan CO₂

SHERIDAN BLUE AND SILVER STREAK RIFLES
Caliber: 5mm (20 cal.), single shot.
Barrel: 18½", rifled.
Weight: 5 lbs. **Length:** 37" overall.
Power: Hand pumped (swinging forend).
Features: Rustproof barrel and piston tube. Takedown. Thumb safety. Mannlicher-type walnut stock.
Price: Blue Streak $115.35
Price: Silver Streak $119.65

SHERIDAN CO₂ AIR RIFLES
Caliber: 5mm (20 cal.), single shot.
Barrel: 18½", rifled.
Weight: 6 lbs. **Length:** 37" overall.
Power: Standard 12-gram CO_2 cylinder.
Stock: Walnut sporter.
Sights: Open, adjustable for w. and e. Optional Sheridan-Williams 5D-SH receiver sight or Weaver D4 scope.
Features: Bolt action single shot, CO_2 powered. Velocity approx. 514 fps, manual thumb safety. Blue or Silver finish.
Price: CO_2 Blue Streak $101.05
Price: CO_2 Silver Streak $105.60
Price: CO_2 Blue Streak with receiver sight $120.15
Price: CO_2 Blue Streak with scope $138.50

CAUTION: PRICES CHANGE, CHECK AT GUNSHOP.

Sterling HR-83

Stock: Stained hardwood, with cheekpiece, checkered pistol grip.
Sights: Tunnel-type front with four interchangeable elements, open adjustable V-type rear.
Features: Velocity of 700 fps (177), 600 fps (22). Bolt action with easily accessible loading port; adjustable single-stage match trigger; rubber recoil pad. Integral scope mount rails. Scope and mount optional. Introduced 1983. Made in U.S.A. by Benjamin Air Rifle Co.

STERLING HR-81/HR-83 AIR RIFLE
Caliber: 177 or 22, single shot.
Barrel: 18½".
Weight: 8½ lbs. **Length:** 42½" overall.
Power: Spring air (barrel cocking).

Price: HR 81-7 (177 cal., standard walnut stock) $286.10
Price: HR 81-2 (as above, 22 cal.) $297.30
Price: HR 83-7 (177 cal., deluxe walnut stock) $406.00
Price: HR 83-2 (as above, 22 cal.) $411.00
Price: For 4x40 wide angle scope, add $125.00
Price: Scope mount and rings $48.15

Steyr CO₂ Match

Weight: 10½ lbs. **Length:** 44½" overall.
Power: CO₂.
Stock: Match. Laminated wood. Adjustable buttplate and cheekpiece.
Sights: Match. Globe front, aperture rear.
Features: Velocity 577 fps. CO₂ cylinders are refillable; about 250 shots per cylinder. Designed for 10-meter shooting. Introduced 1990. Imported from Austria by Gun South, Inc.
Price: $1,375.00

STEYR CO₂ MATCH AIR RIFLE
Caliber: 177, single shot.
Barrel: 23¾", (13¾" rifled).

THEOBEN SIROCCO CLASSIC AIR RIFLE
Caliber: 177 or 22.
Barrel: 15½", Anschutz.
Weight: 7¾ lbs. **Length:** 44" overall.
Power: Gas-ram piston. Variable power.
Stock: Hand-checkered walnut.
Sights: None supplied. Comes with scope mount.
Features: Velocity 1100 fps (177), 900 fps (22). Adjustable recoil pad, barrel weight. Choked or unchoked barrel. Imported from England by Air Rifle Specialists.
Price: $860.00
Price: Grand Prix model (as above except thumbhole stock) $940.00

Theoben Sirocco Eliminator Air Rifle
Similar to the Sirocco Grand Prix except more powerful. Gives 1400 fps in 177 cal., 1100 fps in 22. Walnut thumbhole stock, adjustable recoil pad, scope mount. Variable power. Barrel weight, leather cobra sling, swivels. Choked barrel only.
Price: $1,450.00

THEOBEN-PROMETHEUS SUPER SIROCCO
Caliber: 177 or 22, single shot.
Barrel: 15¾".
Weight: NA. **Length:** 44" overall.
Power: Gas-ram piston.
Stock: English walnut, checkered p.g. and forend.
Sights: None furnished; scope base and rings provided.
Features: Velocity 950-1200 fps. One-stroke cocking mechanism with captive gas-ram piston. Designed to shoot Prometheus and Titan Black pellets. Imported from England by Fisher Enterprises.
Price: Deluxe Super Sirocco $870.00
Price: Grand Prix $925.00
Price: Eliminator (thumbhole stock) $1,475.00

Theoben Prometheus

WALTHER LGR UNIVERSAL MATCH AIR RIFLE
Caliber: 177, single shot.
Barrel: 25.5".
Weight: 13 lbs. **Length:** 44¾" overall.
Power: Spring air, barrel cocking.
Stock: Walnut match design with stippled grip and forend, adjustable cheekpiece, rubber buttpad.
Features: Has the same weight and contours as the Walther U.I.T. rimfire target rifle. Comes complete with sights, accessories and muzzle weight. Imported from West Germany by Interarms.
Price: $1,175.00

WALTHER CG90 AIR RIFLE
Caliber: 177, single shot.
Barrel: 18.9".
Weight: 10.2 lbs. **Length:** 44" overall.
Power: CO₂ cartridge.
Stock: Match type of European walnut; stippled grip.
Sights: Globe front, fully adjustable match rear.
Features: Uses tilting-block action. Introduced 1989. Imported from Germany by Interarms.
Price: $1,225.00

Walther LGR Running Boar Air Rifle
Same basic specifications as standard LGR except has a high comb thumbhole stock. Has adjustable cheekpiece and buttplate, no sights. Introduced 1977.
Price: $1,050.00
Price: LGR Match $850.00

Model 85

PMI 68 Magnum

MODEL 85 PAINT BALL MACHINE PISTOL
Caliber: 9.5mm, 24-shot removable magainze.
Barrel: 5", rifled.
Weight: 25 oz. **Length:** 9⅜" overall.
Stocks: Resin.
Sights: Blade front, notch rear.
Features: Velocity of 440 fps, muzzle energy of 3.4 ft. lbs. Stainless steel impregnated in fiber-filled resin construction. Has a cyclic rate of 1200 rounds per minute; fires from open bolt; reloadable cartridges. Not a firearm by B.A.T.F. standards. Introduced 1987. Made in Canada. From Para-Ordnance, Inc.
Price: $299.95

PURSUIT PMI I PAINT PISTOL
Caliber: 68 (paint balls), 10-shot magazine.
Barrel: 10¼".
Weight: 36 oz. **Length:** 14⅜" overall.
Power: 12-gram CO_2.
Stocks: Checkered, with thumbrest.
Sights: Bead front, open rear.
Features: Rapid-fire, pump-action long-barrel pistol uses factory centerfire bolt. Uses gravity or direct-feed magazine. Introduced 1988. From Pursuit Marketing, Inc.
Price: $169.00

Pursuit PMI II

Pursuit PMI II Paint Pistol
Similar to the PMI I pistol except comes only with 7-oz. Constant Air system, new factory 6-inch aluminum pump handle. Weight, including air tank, is 3¾ lbs. Introduced 1988.
Price: $280.00

PURSUIT PIRANHA PAINT BALL PISTOL
Caliber: 68, 50-shot magazine.
Barrel: 7½".
Weight: 3.7 lbs. (with 3.5-oz. tank).
Power: 3.5-oz. refillable CO_2.
Stocks: Oiled walnut with finger grooves and thumbrest, right- or left-hand.
Sights: Open, fixed.
Features: Velocity of 275 fps. Has Speed Demon centerfire bolt, brass barrel. Gives 150-200 shots per tank. Can be converted to 12-gram CO_2 cartridge. Introduced 1989. From Pursuit Marketing, Inc.
Price: $290.00
Price: With 10¼" barrel $325.00

Pursuit PGP

PURSUIT PGP PAINT PISTOL
Caliber: 68 (paint balls), 10-shot magazine.
Barrel: 6½".
Weight: 36 oz. **Length:** 9" overall.
Power: 12-gram CO_2.
Stocks: Smooth wood with thumbrest.
Sights: Bead front, adjustable rear.
Features: Shoots 68-cal. paint balls; uses gravity-feed magazine. Comes with Rapid Fire Pump Kit. From Pursuit Marketing, Inc.
Price: $135.00

SPLATMASTER® 102 MARKING PISTOL
Caliber: 68 (paint balls), 10- to 15-shot magazine.
Barrel: 6½".
Weight: 1.9 lbs. **Length:** 13⅛" overall.
Power: 12.5-gram CO_2 cylinder.
Stocks: Checkered fiber reinforced plastic.
Sights: Open, fixed.
Features: Velocity about 260 fps. Shoots 68-cal. paint balls. Made of fiber reinforced plastic with an aluminum valve system. Moulded in green. Gives about 30 shots per CO_2 cylinder. Introduced 1983. From National Survival Game, Inc.
Price: $89.95

Splatmaster

SPLATMASTER® RAPIDE™ SEMI-AUTO PISTOL
Caliber: 68, 20-shot spindle magazine.
Barrel: 6½".
Weight: 1.6 lbs. **Length:** 13" overall.
Power: 12-gram CO$_2$.
Stocks: Checkered fiber reinforced plastic.
Sights: Open, fixed.
Features: Velocity about 270 fps. New semi-automatic brass valve system. No cocking necessary. Made of fiber reinforced plastic moulded in green or blue. Gives about 20 shots per CO$_2$ capsule. Introduced 1988. From National Survival Game, Inc.
Price: **$125.00**

Splatmaster Rapide

SPLATMASTER® RAPIDE™ COMP SEMI-AUTO PISTOL
Caliber: 68, 40-shot spindle magazine.
Barrel: 8½".
Weight: 4 lbs., 6 oz. **Length:** 26½" overall.
Power: 7-oz. refillable CO$_2$ cannister.
Stock: Checkered fiber reinforced plastic p.g. and foregrip.
Sights: Open, fixed.
Features: Velocity about 275 fps. Semi-automatic action. Gives about 350 shots per cannister. Barrel lined with brass for better accuracy. Brass valve system. Introduced 1989. From National Survival Game, Inc.
Price: **$280.00**

Splatmaster Rapide Comp

Uzi Mk. I

UZI MKI PUMP ACTION PAINT BALL GUN
Caliber: 68, 38-shot magazine.
Barrel: 7".
Weight: 2 lbs., 8 oz. **Length:** 16" overall.
Power: 12-gram CO$_2$.
Stocks: Grooved plastic.
Sights: Blade front, notch rear.
Features: Velocity of 210 fps, muzzle energy of 4.7 ft. lbs. Gives 30+ shots per CO$_2$; rapid-load magazine. Introduced 1987. Imported from Canada by The Command Post, Inc.
Price: **$119.98**

007 PUMP ACTION PAINT BALL PISTOL
Caliber: 68, 16-shot magazine.
Barrel: 4½".
Weight: 2 lbs., 10 oz. **Length:** 10¼" overall.
Power: 12-gram CO$_2$.
Stocks: Checkered plastic.
Sights: Blade front, notch rear.
Features: Velocity of 205 fps, muzzle energy of 4.5 ft. lbs. Gives 20+ shots per CO$_2$. Rapid loading. Introduced 1987. From The Command Post, Inc.
Price: **$119.98**

007 Sport Paint Ball Pistol
Similar to the 007 Pump except has 25-shot magazine, 6" barrel, wire stock, combat pump handle. Custom built by The Command Post, Inc.
Price: **$179.98**

007 Pump

007 Tournament Paint Ball Pistol
Similar to the 007 Pump except has 25-shot gravity magazine, 2" barrel extension. Custom built by The Command Post, Inc.
Price: **$199.98**

3357 D/A PAINT BALL REVOLVER
Caliber: 50, 6-shot cylinder.
Barrel: 6".
Weight: 2 lbs., 12 oz. **Length:** 12½" overall.
Power: 12-gram CO$_2$.
Stocks: Checkered plastic.
Sights: Ramped blade front, adjustable notch rear.
Features: Velocity of 230 fps, muzzle energy of 2.1 ft. lbs. Gives 30-70 shots per CO$_2$; metal construction; single or double action. Introduced 1987. From The Command Post, Inc.
Price: **$89.98**

Model 3357

CUSTOM GRAVITY-FEED PAINT RIFLE
Caliber: 68, 25-shot magazine.
Barrel: NA.
Weight: 7 lbs. **Length:** 28″ overall.
Power: 12-gram CO_2.
Stock: Wood.
Sights: Optic Point sighting device.
Features: Gravity feed; over-size Deiron pump. Custom built by The Command Post, Inc.
Price: $259.98

PMI Custom

PURSUIT PIRANHA RIFLE
Caliber: 68, 50-shot magazine.
Barrel: 12″.
Weight: 5 lbs., 8 oz.
Power: 7-oz. CO_2 tank.
Stock: Smooth maple.
Sights: Notch and bead with scope rail collar.
Features: Has direct-feed ammo box; Speed Demon centerfire bolt allows field stripping without tools. Honed brass barrel. Cross-bolt safety. Introduced 1990. From Pursuit Marketing, Inc.
Price: $335.00

SNIPER PUMP MK II PAINT BALL GUN
Caliber: 68, 25-shot magazine.
Barrel: NA.
Weight: 6 lbs. **Length:** 26″ overall.
Power: 12-gram CO_2 or 7-oz. bulk CO_2 tank.
Stock: Wire.
Sights: 1.5x scope.
Features: Velocity of about 240 fps. Up to 350 shots per tank. Custom built by The Command Post, Inc.
Price: $299.98

Tippmann SMG-60

007 ASSAULT PUMP PAINT BALL GUN
Caliber: 68, 15-shot magazine.
Barrel: 16″.
Weight: 6 lbs., 5 oz. **Length:** 35″ overall (stock extended).
Power: 12-gram CO_2 or 10-oz. bulk CO_2 tank.
Stock: Folding, plastic and hard rubber over steel.
Sights: Adjustable Optic Point Site.
Features: Velocity of 240 fps, muzzle energy of 6.1 ft. lbs. Convertible power source—20 shots per CO_2 or 500 + shots from remotely mounted bulk tank. Steel construction. Introduced 1987. Custom built by The Command Post, Inc.
Price: $359.98

NINJA PAINT BALL GUN
Caliber: 68, 20-shot magazine.
Barrel: 11″.
Weight: 9 lbs. **Length:** 28″ overall.
Power: 10-oz. bulk CO_2 system.
Stock: Moulded composition.
Sights: 1.5x scope.
Features: Velocity about 225 fps. Gives up to 500 shots per charge. Converts to pistol. Gravity-feed magazine. Available from The Command Post, Inc.
Price: $379.98

PMI CUSTOM PAINT BALL GUN
Caliber: 68, 20-shot magazine.
Barrel: NA.
Weight: 6 lbs. **Length:** 26″ overall.
Power: 10-oz. bulk CO_2.
Stock: Moulded black plastic.
Sights: Post front, notch rear.
Features: Velocity about 290 fps. Easily converted to 12-gram CO_2. Custom built by The Command Post, Inc.
Price: $289.98

Sniper Mk. II

Consult our Directory pages for
the location of firms mentioned.

TIPPMANN SMG-60 AUTOMATIC
Caliber: 60 (paint balls), 15-shot magazine.
Barrel: 11″.
Weight: 5 lbs. **Length:** 29″ overall.
Power: CO_2 cylinder.
Stock: 8-oz. CO_2 cylinder forms stock.
Sights: Fixed.
Features: Velocity of 290-300 fps. Selective-fire paint ball gun (semi- or full-auto). Full-auto rate of fire is 600 r.p.m. Open bolt, blowback action. Introduced 1987. From Tippmann Arms Co.
Price: $349.00

007 Assault

Sporting Leaf and Open Sights

BURRIS SPORTING REAR SIGHT
Made of spring steel, supplied with multi-step elevator for coarse adjustments and notch plate with lock screw for finer adjustments.
Price $14.95

LYMAN No. 16
Middle sight for barrel dovetail slot mounting. Folds flat when scope or peep sight is used. Sight notch plate adjustable for e. White triangle for quick aiming. 3 heights: A — .400″ to .500″, B — .345″ to .445″, C — .500″ to .600″. Price $11.95

MARBLE FALSE BASE #72, #73, #74
New screw-on base for most rifles replaces factory base. ⅜″ dovetail slot permits installation of any folding rear sight. Can be had in sweat-on models also. Price $6.25

MARBLE CONTOUR RAMP #14R
For late model Rem. 725, 740, 760, 742 rear sight mounting. ⁹⁄₁₆″ between mounting screws. Accepts all sporting rear sights. Price $12.75

MARBLE FOLDING LEAF
Flat-top or semi-buckhorn style. Folds down when scope or peep sights are used. Reversible plate gives choice of "U" or "V" notch. Adjustable for elevation. Price $11.75
Also available with both w. and e. adjustment $13.50

MARBLE SPORTING REAR
With white enamel diamond, gives choice of two "U" and two "V" notches or different sizes. Adjustment in height by means of double step elevator and sliding notch piece. For all rifles; screw or dovetail installation.
Price ....$11.95-$13.50

MARBLE #20 UNIVERSAL
New screw or sweat-on base. Both have .100″ elevation adjustment. In five base sizes. Three styles of U-notch, square notch, peep. Adjustable for w. and e.
Price: Screw-on $19.25
Price: Sweat-on $17.65

MILLETT RIFLE SIGHT
Open, fully adjustable rear sight fits standard ⅜″ dovetail cut in barrel. Choice of white outline or target rear blades, .360″. Front with white or orange bar, .343″, .400″, .430″, .460″, .500″, .540″.
Price: Rear sight $52.95
Price: Front sight $11.75

MILLETT SCOPE-SITE
Open, adjustable or fixed rear sights dovetail into a base integral with the top scope-mounting ring. Blaze orange front ramp sight is integral with the front ring half. Rear sights have white outline aperture. Provides fast, short radius, Patridge-type open sights on the top of the scope. Can be used with all Millett rings.
Price: Scope-Site ring set, adjustable $77.95
Price: As above, fixed $44.95
Price: Convertible Top Cap set, adjustable $62.95
Price: As above, fixed $29.65

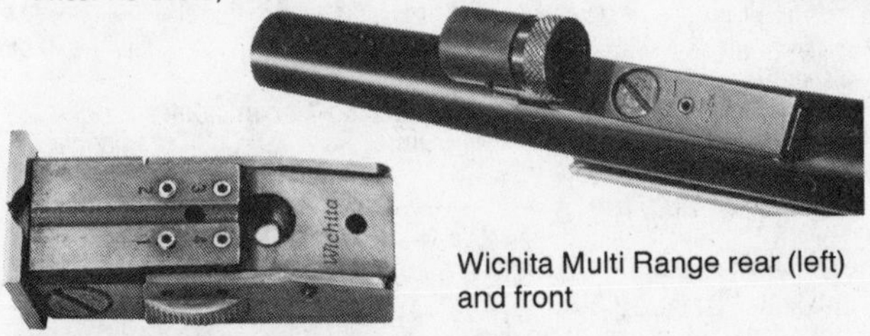

Wichita Multi Range rear (left) and front

WICHITA MULTI RANGE SIGHT SYSTEM
Designed for silhouette shooting. System allows you to adjust the rear sight to four repeatable range settings, once it is pre-set. Sight clicks to any of the settings by turning a serrated wheel. Front sight is adjustable for weather and light conditions with one adjustment. Specify gun when ordering.
Price: Rear sight $88.00
Price: Front sight $66.00

WILLIAMS DOVETAIL OPEN SIGHT
Open rear sight with w. and e. adjustment. Furnished with "U" notch or choice of blades. Slips into dovetail and locks with gib lock. Heights from .281″ to .531″. Price with blade $13.00
Price: Less Blade $8.55

WILLIAMS GUIDE OPEN SIGHT
Open rear sight with w. and e. adjustment. Bases to fit most military and commercial barrels. Choice of square "U" or "V" notch blade, ³⁄₁₆″, ¼″, ⁵⁄₁₆″, or ⅜″ high. Price with blade $15.70
Price: Extra blades, each $4.45
Price: Less blade $11.25

Micrometer Receiver Sights

BEEMAN/WEIHRAUCH MATCH APERTURE SIGHT
Micrometer ¼-minute click adjustment knobs with settings indicated on scales. Price $79.95

BEEMAN/FEINWERKBAU MATCH APERTURE SIGHTS
Locks into one of four eye-relief positions. Micrometer ¼-minute click adjustments; may be set to zero at any range. Extra windage scale visible beside eyeshade. Primarily for use at 5 to 20 meters. Price $159.95

BEEMAN SPORT APERTURE SIGHT
Positive click micrometer adjustments. Standard units with flush surface screwdriver adjustments. Deluxe version has target knobs. For air rifles with grooved receivers.
Price: Standard $36.98
Price: Deluxe $46.98

FREELAND TUBE SIGHT
Uses Unertl 1″ micrometer mounts. For 22-cal. target rifles, including 52 Win., 37, 40X Rem. and BSA Martini. Price $150.00

LYMAN No. 57
¼-min. clicks. Stayset knobs. Quick release slide, adjustable zero scales. Made for almost all modern rifles. Price $59.95

LYMAN No. 66
Fits close to the rear of flat-sided receivers, furnished with Stayset knobs. Quick release slide, ¼-min. adj. For most lever or slide action or flat-sided automatic rifles. Price $59.95

LYMAN No. 66U
Light weight, designed for most modern shotguns with a flat-sided, round-top receiver. ¼-minute clicks. Requires drilling, taping. Not for Browning A-5, Rem. M11. Price $59.95

Millett Ruger Mini-14

Lyman No. 57

MILLETT ASSAULT RIFLE SIGHTS
Fully adjustable, heat-treated nickel steel peep aperture receiver sights for AR-15, Mini-14. AR-15 rear sight has w. & e. adjustments; non-glare replacement ramp-style front also available. Mini-14 sight has fine w. & e. adjustments; replaces original.
Price: Rear sight for above guns $51.45
Price: Front and rear combo for AR-15 ....$62.65
Price: Front sight for AR-15 ....$12.25
Price: Front and rear combo for Mini-14 ....$68.25
Price: Front sight for Mini-14 ....$17.85

WILLIAMS FP
Internal click adjustments. Positive locks. For virtually all rifles, T/C Contender, Heckler & Koch HK-91, Ruger Mini-14, plus Win., Rem. and Ithaca shotguns. Price, from $47.90
Price: With Twilight Aperture $49.37
Price: With Target Knobs $56.90
Price: With Target Knobs & Twilight Aperture $58.37
Price: With Square Notched Blade $50.42
Price: With Target Knobs & Square Notched Blade $59.53
Price: FP-GR (for dovetail-grooved receivers, 22s and air guns) . $47.90

WILLIAMS 5-D SIGHT
Low cost sight for shotguns, 22s and the more popular big game rifles. Adjustment for w. and e. Fits most guns without drilling or tapping. Also for Br. SMLE. Price $27.16
Price: With Twilight Aperture $28.63
Price: With Shotgun Aperture $27.16

WILLIAMS GUIDE
Receiver sight for 30 M1 Car., M1903A3 Springfield, Savage 24s, Savage-Anschutz rifles and Wby. XXII. Utilizes military dovetail; no drilling. Double-dovetail w. adj., sliding dovetail adj. for e. Price $25.79
Price: With Twilight Aperture $27.26
Price: With Open Sight Blade $23.69

Lyman 17A

Lyman Hunting Front

Fire Fly Combat

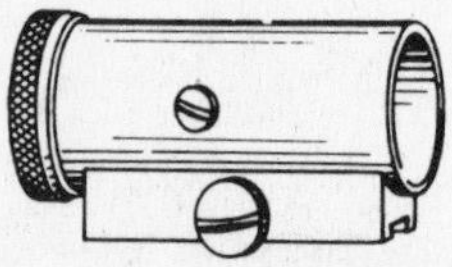

Lyman Screw-On Ramp

Freeland Military

C-More Sights

Front Sights

LYMAN HUNTING SIGHTS
Made with gold or white beads 1/16″ to 3/32″ wide and in varying heights for most military and commercial rifles. Dovetail bases. Price **$8.50**

MARBLE STANDARD
Ivory, red, or gold bead. For all American-made rifles, 1/16″ wide bead with semi-flat face which does not reflect light. Specify type of rifle when ordering. Price **$7.25**

MARBLE-SHEARD "GOLD"
Shows up well even in darkest timber. Shows same color on different colored objects; sturdily built. Medium bead. Various models for different makes of rifles so specify type of rifle when ordering. Price **$9.00**

MARBLE CONTOURED
Same contour and shape as Marble-Sheard but uses standard 1/16″ or 3/32″ bead, ivory, red or gold. Specify rifle type. Price **$8.25**

MARBLE PATRIDGE
Gold-faced Patridge front sight is available in .250″ or .34″ widths and heights from .260″ to .538″. Price **$9.00**

POLY-CHOKE
Rifle front sights available in six heights and two widths. Model A designed to be inserted into the barrel dovetail; Model B is for use with standard .350″ ramp; both have standard 3/8″ dovetails. Gold or ivory color 1/16″ bead. From Marble Arms. Price **$6.00**

Globe Target Front Sights

FREELAND SUPERIOR
Furnished with six 1″ plastic apertures. Available in 4½″-6½″ lengths. Made for any target rifle. Price **$48.50**
Price: With six metal insert apertures **$51.60**
Price: Front base **$12.50**

FREELAND TWIN SET
Two Freeland Superior Front Sights, long or short, allow switching from 50 yd. to 100 yd. ranges and back again without changing rear sight adjustment. Sight adjustment compensation is built into the set; just interchange and you're "on" at either range. Set includes six plastic apertures.
Price: **$67.00**
Price: With six metal apertures **$70.00**

FREELAND MILITARY
Short model for use with high-powered rifles where sight must not extend beyond muzzle. Screw-on base; six plastic apertures. Price **$48.50**
Price: With six metal apertures **$51.60**
Price: Front base **$12.50**

LYMAN No. 17A TARGET
Includes seven interchangeable inserts: four apertures, one transparent amber and two posts .50″ and .100″ in width. Price **$24.95**

Ramp Sights

LYMAN SCREW-ON RAMP
Used with 8-40 screws but may also be brazed on. Heights from .10″ to .350″. Ramp without sight. Price **$15.50**

MARBLE FRONT RAMPS
Available in either screw-on or sweat-on style, five heights; 3/16″, 5/16″, 3/8″, 7/16″, 9/16″. Standard 3/8″ dovetail slot. Price **$14.50**
Hoods for above ramps **$3.15**

WILLIAMS SHORTY RAMP
Companion to "Streamlined" ramp, about ½″ shorter. Screw-on or sweat-on. It is furnished in 1/8″, 3/16″, 9/32″, and 3/8″ heights without hood only. Price **$9.95**

WILLIAMS STREAMLINED RAMP
Hooded style in screw-on or sweat-on models. Furnished in 9/16″, 7/16″, 3/8″, 5/16″, 3/16″ heights. Price with hood **$17.80**
Price: Without hood **$14.70**

Handgun Sights

BO-MAR DE LUXE BMCS
Gives 3/8″ w. and e. adjustment at 50 yards on Colt Gov't 45, sight radius under 7″. For GM and Commander models only. Uses existing dovetail slot. Has shield-type rear blade. Price **$54.75**

BO-MAR LOW PROFILE RIB & ACCURACY TUNER
Streamlined rib with front and rear sights; 7⅛″ sight radius. Brings sight line closer to the bore than standard or extended sight and ramp. Weighs 5 oz. Made for Colt Gov't 45, Super 38, and Gold Cup 45 and 38. Price **$89.00**

BO-MAR COMBAT RIB
For S&W Model 19 revolver with 4″ barrel. Sight radius 5¾″, weight 5½ oz. Price **$79.00**

BO-MAR FAST DRAW RIB
Streamlined full length rib with integral Bo-Mar micrometer sight and serrated fast draw sight. For Browning 9mm, S&W 39, Colt Commander 45, Super Auto and 9mm. Price **$79.00**

BO-MAR WINGED RIB
For S&W 4″ and 6″ length barrels—K-38, M10, HB 14 and 19. Weight for the 6″ model is about 7¼ oz. Price **$89.00**

BO-MAR COVER-UP RIB
Adj. rear sight, winged front guards. Fits right over revolver's original front sight. For S&W 4″ M-10HB, M-13, M-58, M-64 & 65, Ruger 4″ models SDA-34, SDA-84, SS-34, SS-84, GF-34, GF-84. Price **$85.00**

C-MORE SIGHTS
Replacement front sight blades offered in two types and five styles. Made of DuPont Acetal, they come in a set of five high-contrast colors: blue, green, pink, red and yellow. Easy to install. Patridge style for Colt Python (all barrels), Ruger Super Blackhawk (7½″), Ruger Blackhawk (4⅝″); ramp style for Python (all barrels), Blackhawk (4⅝″), Super Blackhawk (7½″ and 10½″). From Magna-port Int'l. Price, per set **$14.95**

FIRE FLY COMBAT HANDGUN SIGHT
Made of aircraft-grade aluminum, this ¼-oz. "channel" sight has a thick, sturdy hollowed post between the side rails to give a Patridge sight picture. All shooting is done with both eyes open, allowing the shooter to concentrate on the target, not the sights. The hole in the sight post gives reduced-light shooting capability and allows for fast, precise aiming. For auto pistols only. Installation must be done by a competent gunsmith. From JAS, Inc. Add $3 postage.
Price: **$39.95**

CAUTION: PRICES CHANGE, CHECK AT GUNSHOP.

Millett 3-Dot

Wichita Series 70/80

MMC M/85

MMC COMBAT FIXED REAR SIGHT (Colt 1911-Type Pistols)
This veteran MMC sight is well known to those who prefer a true combat sight for "carry" guns. Steel construction for long service. Choose from a wide variety of front sights.
Price: Combat Fixed Rear, plain **$18.45**
Price: As above, white outline **$23.65**
Price: Combat Front Sight for above, six styles, from **$5.15**

MMC M/85 ADJUSTABLE REAR SIGHT
Designed to be compatible with the Ruger P-85 front sight. Fully adjustable for windage and elevation.
Price: M/85 Adjustable Rear Sight, plain **$52.45**
Price: As above, white outline **$57.70**

MMC STANDARD ADJUSTABLE REAR SIGHT
Available for Colt 1911 type, Ruger Standard Auto, and now for S&W 469, and 659 pistols. No front sight change is necessary, as this sight will work with the original factory front sight.
Price: Standard Adjustable Rear Sight, plain leaf **$46.05**
Price: Standard Adjustable Rear Sight, white outline **$51.15**

MMC MINI-SIGHT
Miniature size for carrying, fully adjustable, for maximum accuracy with your pocket auto. MMC's Mini-Sight will work with the factory front sight. No machining is necessary, easy installation. Available for Walther PP, PPK, and PPK/S pistols. Will also fit fixed sight Browning Hi-Power (P-35).
Price: Mini-Sight, plain **$58.45**
Price: Mini-Sight, white bar **$63.45**

MEPROLIGHT SIGHTS
Replacement open sights for popular handguns and Uzi carbine, AR-15/M-16 rifles. Both front and rear sights have tritium inserts for illumination in low-light conditions. Inserts give constant non-glare green light for 5 years, even in cold weather. Handguns: S&W 459, 659 (adjustable and non-adjustable), S&W 645, Beretta 92, Colt Gov't 45, Browning Hi-Power, Uzi carbine and mini, SIG Sauer P226, Glock 17, Ruger P-85, universal front sight for revolvers. Also shotgun bead.
Price: Universal front for revolvers **$39.95**
Price: Front and rear sights **$89.95**
Price: Shotgun bead **$29.95**

MILLETT 3-DOT SYSTEM SIGHTS
The 3-Dot System sights use a single white dot on the front blade and two dots flanking the rear notch. Fronts available in Dual-Crimp and Wide Stake-On styles, as well as special applications. Adjustable rear sight available for most popular auto pistols, fixed for Colt only.
Price: Fixed, Colt **$32.95**
Price: Adjustable .... **$46.96 to $52.95**

MILLETT SERIES 100 ADJUSTABLE SIGHTS
Replacement sights for revolvers and auto pistols. Positive click adjustments for windage and elevation. Designed for accuracy and ruggedness. Made to fit S&W, Colt, Beretta, SIG Sauer P220, P225, P226, Ruger P-85, Ruger GP-100 (and others), Glock 17, CZ-75, TZ-75, Dan Wesson, Browning, AMT Hardballer. Rear blades are available in white outline or positive black target. All steel construction and easy to install.
Price .... **$46.95 to $75.35**

MILLETT MARK SERIES PISTOL SIGHTS
Mark I and Mark II replacement combat sights for government-type auto pistols, including H&K P7. Mark I is high profile, Mark II low profile. Both have horizontal light deflectors.
Price: Mark I, front and rear **$32.95**
Price: Mark II, front and rear **$46.95**
Price: For H&K P7 .... **$46.95**

MILLETT REVOLVER FRONT SIGHTS
All-steel replacement front sights with either white or orange bar. Easy to install. For Ruger GP-100, Redhawk, Security-Six, Police-Six, Speed-Six, Colt Trooper, Diamondback, King Cobra, Peacemaker, Python, Dan Wesson 22 and 15-2. Price **$15.25**

MILLETT DUAL-CRIMP FRONT SIGHT
Replacement front sight for automatic pistols. Dual-Crimp uses an all-steel two-point hollow rivet system. Available in eight heights and four styles. Has a skirted base that covers the front sight pad. Easily installed with the Millett Installation Tool Set. Available in Blaze Orange Bar, White Bar, Serrated Ramp, Plain Post. Price **$15.25**

MILLETT STAKE-ON FRONT SIGHT
Replacement front sight for automatic pistols. Stake-On sights have skirted base that covers the front sight pad. Easily installed with the Millet Installation Tool Set. Available in seven heights and four styles—Blaze Orange Bar, White Bar, Serrated Ramp, Plain Post. Price **$15.25**

OMEGA OUTLINE SIGHT BLADES
Replacement rear sight blades for Colt and Ruger single action guns and the Interarms Virginian Dragoon. Standard Outline available in gold or white notch outline on blue metal. From Mag-na-port Int'l. Price **$8.95**

OMEGA MAVERICK SIGHT BLADES
Replacement "peep-sight" blades for Colt, Ruger SAs, Virginian Dragoon. Three models available—No. 1, Plain, No. 2, Single Bar, No. 3 Double Bar Rangefinder. From Mag-na-port Int'l. Price, each **$6.95**

TRIJICON SELF-LUMINOUS SIGHTS
Three-dot sighting system uses self luminous inserts in the sight blade and leaf. Tritium "lamps" are mounted in a metal cylinder and protected by a polished crystal sapphire. For most popular handguns, fixed or adjustable sights, and some rifles. From Trijicon, Inc.
Price: .... **$28.95 to $175.00**

THOMPSON/CENTER "ULTIMATE" SIGHTS
Replacement front and rear sights for the T/C Contender. Front sight has four interchangeable blades (.060", .080", .100", .120"), rear sight has four notch widths of the same measurements for a possible 16 combinations. Rear sight can be used with existing soldered front sights.
Price: Front sight **$35.00**
Price: Rear sight **$65.00**

WICHITA SERIES 70/80 SIGHT
Provides click windage and elevation adjustments with precise repeatability of settings. Sight blade is grooved and angled back at the top to reduce glare. Available in Low Mount Combat or Low Mount Target styles for Colt 45s and their copies, S&W 645, Hi-Power, CZ 75 and others.
Price: **$62.50**

WICHITA SIGHT SYSTEMS
For 45 auto pistols. Target and Combat styles available. Designed by Ron Power. All-steel construction, click adjustable. Each sight has two traverse pins, a large hinge pin and two elevation return springs. Sight blade is serrated and mounted on an angle to deflect light. Patridge front for target, ramp front for combat. Both are legal for ISPC and NRA competitions.
Price: Rear sight, target or combat **$62.50**
Price: Front sight, Patridge or ramp **$9.85**

WICHITA GRAND MASTER DELUXE RIBS
Ventilated rib has wings machined into it for better sight acquisition. Made of stainless steel, sights blued. Uses Wichita Multi-Range rear sight, adjustable front sight. Made for revolvers with 6" barrel.
Price: Model 301 (adj. sight K-frames with custom bbl. of 1.000"-1.032" dia., L and N frames with 1.062"-1.100" bbl.) **$143.00**
Price: Model 302 (fixed sight K-frames; M10, 65, 13 with 1.000" bbl., N-frame with 1.062" bbl.) **$143.00**
Price: Model 303 (Model 29, 629 with factory bbl., adj. sight K, L, N frames) **$143.00**

WICHITA DOUBLE MASTER RIB
Ventilated rib has wings machined on either side of fixed front post sight for better acquisition and is relieved for Mag-na-ports. Milled to accept Weaver See-Thru-style rings. Made of blued steel. Has Wichita Multi-Range rear sight system. Made for Model 29/629 with factory barrel, and all adjustable-sight K, L and N frames.
Price: Model 403 .... **$128.95**

Fire Fly EM-109

MMC Combat

Merit Optical Attachment

Millett Shur-Shot

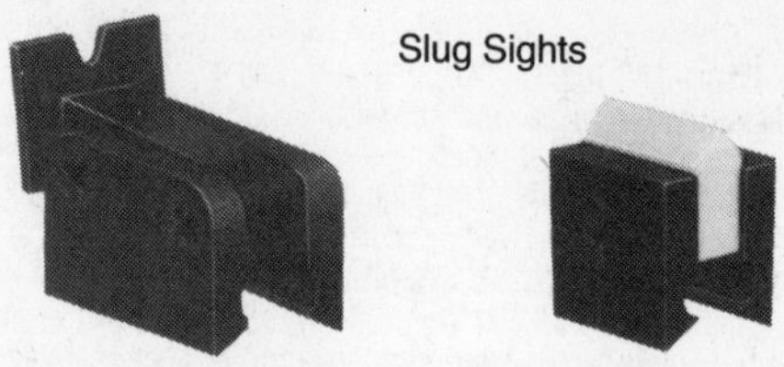

Slug Sights

Shotgun Sights

ACCURA-SITE
For shooting shotgun slugs. Three models to fit most shotguns—"A" for vent. rib barrels, "B" for solid ribs, "C" for plain barrels. Rear sight has windage and elevation provisions. Easily removed and replaced. Includes front and rear sights. Price . . . . **$27.95 to $34.95**

FIRE FLY EM-109 SL SHOTGUN SIGHT
Made of aircraft-grade aluminum, this ¼-oz. "channel" sight has a thick, sturdy hollowed post between the side rails to give a Patridge sight picture. All shooting is done with both eyes open, allowing the shooter to concentrate on the target, not the sights. The hole in the sight post gives reduced-light shooting capability and allows for fast, precise aiming. For sport or combat shooting. For all shotguns with or without vent. rib. From JAS, Inc. Add $3 postage.
Price: **$39.95**

LYMAN
Three sights of over-sized ivory beads. No. 10 Front (press fit) for double barrel or ribbed single barrel guns . . . **$4.25**; No. 10D Front (screw fit) for non-ribbed single barrel guns (comes with wrench) . . . **$5.25**; No. 11 Middle (press fit) for double and ribbed single barrel guns. Price **$4.25**

MMC M&P COMBAT SHOTGUN SIGHT SET
A durable, protected ghost ring aperture, combat sight made of steel. Fully adjustable for windage and elevation.
Price: M&P Sight Set (front and rear) **$73.45**
Price: As above, installed **$83.95**

MARBLE SHOTGUN BEAD SIGHTS
No. 214—Ivory front bead, ¹¹⁄₆₄", tapered shank . . . **$3.70**; No. 223—Ivory rear bead, .080", tapered shank . . . **$3.65**; No. 217—Ivory front bead, ¹¹⁄₆₄", threaded shank . . . **$4.00**; No. 223-T—Ivory rear bead, .080", threaded shank . . . **$5.30**; Reamers, taps and wrenches available from Marbles.

MILLET SHURSHOT SHOTGUN SIGHT
A sight system for shotguns with ventilated rib. Rear sight attaches to the rib, front sight replaces the front bead. Front has an orange face, rear has two orange bars. For 870, 1100 or other models.
Price: Front and rear **$20.95**
Price: Adjustable front and rear **$27.40**

POLY-CHOKE
Replacement front shotgun sights in four styles—Xpert, Poly Bead, Xpert Mid Rib sights, and Bev-L-Block. Xpert Front available in 3x56, 6x48 thread, ³⁄₃₂" or ⁵⁄₃₂" shank length, gold, ivory (**$4.50**); or Sun Spot orange bead (**$4.50**); Poly Bead is standard replacement ⅛" bead, 6x48 (**$2.40**); Xpert Mid Rib in tapered carrier (ivory only) or 3x56 threaded shank (gold only), **$3.50**; Hi and Lo Blok sights with 6x48 thread, gold or ivory (**$3.50**) or Sun Spot Orange (**$4.50**). From Marble Arms.

REDFIELD SLUG SIGHTS
Easy clamp-on rifle-type sights attach to the ventilated rib. Three models available to fit most popular rib sizes, from ¼" to ⅜". Price **$36.95**

SLUG SIGHTS
Made of non-marring black nylon, front and rear sights stretch over and lock onto the barrel. Sights are low profile with blaze orange front blade. Adjustable for windage and elevation. For plain-barrel (non-ribbed) guns in 12, 16 and 20 gauge, and for shotguns with ⁵⁄₁₆" and ⅜" ventilated ribs. From Innovision Ent.
Price: **$9.95**

WILLIAMS GUIDE BEAD SIGHT
Fits all shotguns, ⅛" ivory, red or gold bead. Screws into existing sight hole. Various thread sizes and shank lengths. Price **$4.50**

Sight Attachments

FREELAND LENS ADAPTER
Fits 1⅛" O.D. prescription ground lens to all standard tube and receiver sights for shooting without glasses. Price without lens **$66.50**
Clear lens ground to prescription **$24.00**
Yellow or green prescription lens **$24.00**

MERIT IRIS SHUTTER DISC
Eleven clicks gives 12 different apertures. No. 3 Disc (**$50.00**) and Master, primarily target types, 0.22" to .125"; No. 4, ½" dia. hunting type, .025" to .155". Available for all popular sights. The Master Disc, with flexible rubber light shield, is particularly adapted to extension, scope height, and tang sights. All Merit Deluxe models have internal click springs; are hand fitted to minimum tolerance.
Master Deluxe **$60.00**
No. 4 Hunting Disc **$40.00**

MERIT LENS DISC
Similar to Merit Iris Shutter (Model 3 or Master) but incorporates provision for mounting prescription lens integrally. Lens may be obtained locally from your optician. Sight disc is ⁷⁄₁₆" wide (Mod. 3), or ¾" wide (Master). Model 3 Deluxe. Price **$63.00**
Master Deluxe **$74.00**

MERIT OPTICAL ATTACHMENT
For revolver and pistol shooters, instantly attached by rubber suction cup to regular or shooting glasses. Any aperture .020" to .156". Price, Deluxe (swings aside) **$60.00**

WILLIAMS APERTURES
Standard thread, fits most sights. Regular series ⅜" to ½" O.D., .050" to .125" hole. "Twilight" series has white reflector ring. .093" to .125" inner hole. Price, regular series . . . **$4.05**. Twilight series **$5.55**
Wide open ⁵⁄₁₆" aperture for shotguns fits 5-D and Foolproof sights. Price **$7.15**

CAUTION: PRICES CHANGE, CHECK AT GUNSHOP.

Chokes & Brakes

Briley Screw-In Chokes

Installation of these choke tubes requires that all traces of the original choking be removed, the barrel threaded internally with square threads and then the tubes are custom fitted to the specific barrel diameter. The tubes are thin and, therefore, made of stainless steel. Cost of installation for single-barrel guns (pumps, autos) runs **$75.00**; un-single target guns run **$150.00**; over/unders and side-by-sides cost **$150.00** per barrel. Steel shot, add **$10.00**. Prices include one choke tube and a wrench for disassembly.

Cellini Stabilizer System

Designed for handgun, rifle and shotgun applications, the Cellini Stabilizer System is available as a removable factory-installed accessory. Overall length is 1¾″, weight is 2 oz., and is said to reduce muzzle jump to nearly zero, even for automatic weapons. If installed by the maker, cost starts at **$185** for rifles; double shotguns, **$180**; handguns **$165**; single barrel shotguns start at **$75**. From Vito Cellini.

Cutts Compensator

The Cutts compensator is one of the oldest variable choke devices available. Manufactured by Lyman Gunsight Corporation, it is available with a steel body. A series of vents allows gas to escape upward and downward. For the 12-ga. Comp body, six fixed-choke tubes are available: the Spreader—popular with Skeet shooters; Improved Cylinder; Modified; Full; Superfull, and Magnum Full. Full, Modified and Spreader tubes are available for 12 or 20, and an Adjustable Tube, giving Full through Improved Cylinder chokes, is offered in 12 and 20 gauges. Cutts Compensator, complete with wrench, adaptor and any single tube **$68.80**; with adjustable tube **$89.80**. All single choke tubes **$18.95** each. No factory installation available.

Emsco Choke

E.M. Schacht of Waseca, Minn., offers the Emsco, a small diameter choke which features a precision curve rather than a taper behind the 1½″ choking area. Nine settings are available in this 5 oz. attachment. Its removable recoil sleeve can be furnished in dural if desired. Choice of three sight heights. For 12, 16 or 20 gauge. Price installed, **$35.50, plus postage**. Not installed, **$27.50**.

Fabian Bros. Muzzle Stabilizer

A muzzlebrake/flash hider system that installs without gunsmithing on most military-type rifles, except Ruger Mini-14 and the Uzi Carbine. Adjustable for right- or left-handed shooters to eliminate muzzle rise and sideswing. No increase in sound level. Fabian Bros. offers a low-cost barrel threading service for the Mini-14 and Uzi Carbine. Available for most popular military-type rifles and carbines. Standard model, **$34.95**; Semi-Custom model (Cobray M11, MAC-10, Valmet), **$69.95**; Deluxe (M1A/M-14, M-60), **$79.95**; stainless steel, **$39.95**. All prices do not include shipping.

Gentry Quiet Muzzle Brake

Developed by gunmaker David Gentry, the "Quiet Muzzle Brake" is said to reduce recoil by 65 to 80 percent with no loss of accuracy or velocity. There is no increase in noise level because the noise and gasses are directed away from the shooter. The barrel is threaded for installation and the unit is blued to match the barrel finish. Price, installed, is **$150.00**. Add **$15.00** for stainless steel, **$25.00** for knurled cap to protect threads.

Gunners Choice Recoil Reducer

This screw-on muzzlebrake is said to reduce up to 80 percent of muzzle blast, neutralizing gas-induced recoil on rifles and pistols. There is no loss of accuracy or velocity and no increased noise level to the shooter. Overall length is 2″, adding 1½″ to the barrel length. Weight is 1 to 2 ozs., depending on model. Has hard anodized black finish. Blank caliber finished units with .250″ center hole available to qualified gunsmiths. Price, including installation is **$159.95**, plus **$4.00** shipping. From Intermountain Arms.

KDF Recoil Arrestor

This threaded muzzlebrake has 24 pressure ports that direct combustion gases in all directions to reduce felt recoil up to a claimed 80 percent without affecting accuracy or ballistics. It is said to reduce felt recoil of a 30-06 to that of a 243. Price is from **$150.00** to **$180.00** installed. From KDF Inc.

Lyman CHOKE

The Lyman CHOKE is similar to the Cutts Comp in that it comes with fixed-choke tubes or an adjustable tube, with or without recoil chamber. The adjustable tube version sells for **$39.95** with recoil chamber, in 12 or 20 gauge. Lyman also offers Single-Choke tubes at **$18.95**. This device may be used with or without a recoil-reduction chamber; cost of the latter is **$8.95** extra. Available in 12 or 20 gauge only. No factory installation offered.

Mag-na-port

Electrical Discharge Machining works on any firearm except those having non-conductive shrouded barrels. EDM is a metal erosion technique using carbon electrodes that control the area to be processed. The Mag-na-port venting process utilizes small trapezoidal openings to direct powder gases upward and outward to reduce recoil.

No effect is had on bluing or nickeling outside the Magna-port area so no refinishing is needed. Cost for the Mag-na-port treatment is **$65.00** for revolvers, **$90.00** for auto pistols, **$85.00** for rifles, plus transportation both ways, and **$2.50** for handling.

Poly-Choke

Marble Arms Corp., manufacturer of the Poly-Choke adjustable shotgun choke, now offers two models in 12, 16, 20, and 28 gauge—the Ventilated and Standard style chokes. Each provides nine choke settings including Xtra-Full and Slug. The Ventilated model reduces 20 percent of a shotgun's recoil, the company claims, and is priced at **$83.00**. The Standard Model is **$75.00**. Postage not included. Contact Marble Arms for more data.

Reed-Choke

Reed-Choke is a system of interchangeable choke tubes that can be installed in any single or double-barreled shotgun, including over/unders. The existing chokes are bored out, the muzzles over-bored and threaded for the tubes. A choice of three Reed-Choke tubes are supplied—Skeet, Imp. Cyl., Mod., Imp. Mod., or Full. Flush fitting, no notches exposed. Designed for thin-walled barrels. Made from 174 stainless steel. Cost of the installation is **$179.95** for single-barrel guns, **$229.95** for doubles. Extra tubes cost **$40** each. Postage and handling charges are **$8.50**.

Pro-port

A compound ellipsoid muzzle venting process similar to Mag-na-porting, only exclusively applied to shotguns. Like Mag-na-porting, this system reduces felt recoil, muzzle jump, and shooter fatigue. Very helpful for trap doubles shooters. Pro-Port is a patented process and installation is available in both the U.S. and Canada. Cost for the Pro-Port process is **$110.00** for over/unders (both barrels); **$80.00** for only the top or bottom barrel; and **$69.00** for single-barrel shotguns. Prices do not include shipping and handling. From Pro-port Ltd.

SSK Arrestor Brake

This is a true muzzlebrake with an expansion chamber. It takes up about 1 inch of barrel and reduces velocity accordingly. Some Arrestors are added to a barrel, increasing its length. Said to reduce the felt recoil of a 458 to that approaching a 30-06. Can be set up to give zero muzzle rise in any caliber, and can be added to most guns. For handgun or rifle. Prices start at **$75.00**. Contact SSK Industries for full data.

Techni-Port

The Techni-Port recoil compensation system is intended for revolvers, single shot pistols and rifles. This is a machined process which involves back-boring the muzzle (with a 30° internal crown) and cutting an oval port on each side of the barrel. The process is said to reduce muzzle jump up to 60 percent and felt recoil up to 50 percent, with no reduction in velocity or accuracy. Cost of the Techni-Port process is **$99.95**, plus **$6.00** for return freight and insurance. Available from Delta Vectors, Inc.

Walker Choke Tubes

This interchangeable choke tube system uses an adaptor fitted to the barrel without swaging. Therefore, it can be fitted to any single-barreled gun. The choke tubes use the conical-parallel system as used on all factory-choked barrels. These tubes can be used in Winchester, Mossberg, Smith & Wesson, Weatherby, or similar barrels made for the standard screw-in choke system. Available for 10 gauge, 12, 16 and 20. Factory installation (single barrel) with standard Walker choke tube is **$95.00**, **$190.00** for double barrels with two choke tubes. A full range of constriction is available. Contact Walker Arms for more data.

Walker Full Thread Choke Tubes

An interchangeable choke tube system using fully threaded inserts. Designed specifically for over/under or side-by-side shotgun barrels, but can be installed in single barrels, and is nearly invisible. No swaging, adaptor or change in barrel exterior dimensions. Available in 12 or 20 gauge. Factory installation cost: **$100.00**, single barrel with one choke tube; **$200.00** for double barrels with two choke tubes. Contact Walker Arms Co. for more data.

HUNTING, TARGET ■ & VARMINT ■ SCOPES

Maker and Model	Magn.	Field at 100 Yds. (feet)	Relative Bright-ness	Eye Relief (in.)	Length (in.)	Tube Diam. (in.)	W&E Adjust-ments	Weight (ozs.)	Price	Other Data
Action Arms										
Micro-Dot										
1.5-4.5x LER Pistol	1.5-4.5	80-26	—	12-24	8.8	1	Int.	9.5	**$265.00**	[1]60mm objective. [2]56mm objective. Variable intensity LED red aiming dot. Average battery life 20 to 4500 hours. Waterproof, nitrogen filled aluminum tube. Fits most standard 1" rings. Imported by Action Arms Ltd.
1.5-4.5x Rifle	1.5-4.5	80-26	—	3	9.8	1	Int.	10.5	**270.00**	
2-7x32	2-7	54-18	—	3	11	1	Int.	12.1	**290.00**	
3-9x40	3-9	40-14	—	3	12.2	1	Int.	13.3	**295.00**	
4x-12x[2]	4-12	—	—	3	14.3	1	Int.	18.3	**450.00**	
24x[1]	24	—	—	3	15	1	Int.	18.8	**450.00**	
Ultra-Dot 1x	—	—	—	—	5.1	1	Int.	4.0	**195.00**	
ADCO										
Mirage[1]	0	—	—	—	5	1	Int.	4	**189.00**	[1]Black finish; nickel finish **$199.00.** Uses long-life lithium wafer battery that fits into the sight body—no battery appendage. From ADCO.
Aimpoint										
AP 1000[1]	0	—	—	—	6	—	Int.	7.8	**189.95**	Illuminates red dot in field of view. No parallax (dot does not need to be centered). Unlimited field of view and eye relief. On/off, adj. intensity. Dot covers 3" @ 100 yds. Mounts avail. for all sights and scopes. [1]Clamps to Weaver-type bases. Available in blue (AP1000-B) or stainless (AP1000-S) finish. 3x scope attachment (for rifles only), **$106.95.** [2]Requires 1" rings. Black or stainless finish. 3x scope attachment (for rifles only) **$129.95.** [3]Projects intense red dot of visible laser light; ¼" click adj. @ 50 yards; uses three AAA Alkaline batteries for up to 9 hours continuous use. Comes with 1" rings. From Aimpoint. Made in Sweden.
Series 3000 Short[2]	0	—	—	—	5.5	1	Int.	5.5	**249.95**	
Series 3000 Long[2]	0	—	—	—	6⅞	1	Int.	5.8	**259.95**	
Laserpoint[3]	—	—	—	—	7	1	Int.	5.9	**399.95**	
Armson										
O.E.G.	0	—	—	—	5⅛	1	Int.	4.3	**183.90**	Shows red dot aiming point. No batteries needed. Standard model fits 1" ring mounts (not incl.). Other models available for many popular shotguns, para-military rifles and carbines. [1]Daylight Only Sight with ⅜" dovetail mount for 22s. Does not contain tritium. Also avail. as 22 D/N (Day-Night) with tritium, **$144.90.** From Trijicon, Inc.
22 DOS[1]	0	—	—	—	3¾	—	Int.	3.0	**105.90**	
Bausch & Lomb										
2x Handgun	2	22.5	—	10-24	8.4	1	Int.	6.7	**329.95**	All except Target scopes have ¼-minute click adjustments; Target scopes have ⅛-minute adjustments with standard turrets and expanded turret knobs. Target scopes come with sunshades, screw-on lens caps. Contact Bushnell for details.
4x Handgun	4	25	—	10-20	8.4	1	Int.	7.0	**340.95**	
4x Balfor Compact	4	25	—	3.3	10.0	1	Int.	10.0	**356.95**	
1.5-6x	1.5-6	75-18	294-18.4	3.3	10.6	1	Int.	10.5	**549.95**	
2-8x Balvar Compact	2-8	51-13	—	3.5	10.0	1	Int.	11.5	**471.95**	
3-9x40	3-9	36-12	—	3.2	13.0	1	Int.	16.2	**523.95**	
2.5-10x Balvar	2.5-10	43.5-11	—	3.3	13.8	1	Int.	13	**601.95**	
6-24x Varmint	6-24	18-4.5	66.1-4.2	3.1	16.6	1	Int.	20.1	**654.95**	
■ 12x-32x40	12-32	—	—	3.2	13.5	1	Int.	18.9	**778.95**	
■ 24x Target	24	4.7	—	3.2	15.2	1	Int.	15.7	**732.95**	
■ 36x Target	36	3.5	—	3.2	15.2	1	Int.	15.7	**758.95**	
Scope Chief VI	4	29	96	3½	12	1	Int.	9.3	**293.95**	
Scope Chief VI	3-9	35-12.6	267-30	3.3	12.6	1	Int.	14.3	**327.95**	
Scope Chief VI	1½-4½	73.7-24.5	267-30	3.5-3.5	9.6	1	Int.	9.5	**314.95**	
Scope Chief VI	4-12	29-10	150-17	3.2	13.5	1	Int.	17	**366.95**	
Beeman										
Blue Ring 20[1]	1.5	14	150	11-16	8.3	¾	Int.	3.6	**49.95**	All scopes have 5-pt. reticle, all glass, fully coated lenses. [1]Pistol scope; cast mounts included. [2]Pistol scope; silhouette knobs. [3]Rubber armor coating; built-in double adj. mount, parallax-free setting. [4]Objective focus, built-in double-adj. mount; matte finish. [5]Objective focus. [6]Has 8 lenses; objective focus; milled mounts included. [7]Includes cast mounts. [8]Objective focus; silhouette knobs; matte finish. [9]Has 9 lenses; objective focus. [10]Also in "L" models with reticle lighted by ambient light or tiny add-on illuminator. Lighted models slightly higher priced. Imported by Beeman.
Blue Ribbon 25[2]	2	19	150	10-24	9¹⁄₁₆	1	Int.	7.4	**129.95**	
SS-1[3]	2.5	30	61	3.25	5½	1	Int.	7	**179.95**	
SS-2[4,10]	3	34.5	74	3.5	6.8	1.38	Int.	13.6	**225.00**	
Blue Ribbon 50R[5]	2.5	33	245	3.5	12	1	Int.	11.8	**169.98**	
Blue Ring 35R[6]	3	25	67	2.5	11¼	¾	Int.	5.1	**69.98**	
30A[7]	4	21	21	2	10.2	¾	Int.	4.5	**36.95**	
Blue Ribbon 66R[8]	2-7	62-16	384-31	3	11.4	1	Int.	14.9	**239.95**	
Blue Ring 45R[9]	3-7	26-12	67-9	2.5	10⅝	¾	Int.	6	**99.95**	
Blue Ring 49R[5]	4	30	64	3	11.8	1	Int.	11.3	**69.95**	
MS-1	4	23	30	3.5	7.5	1	Int.	8	**199.95**	
SS-3[4]	1.5-4	44.6-24.6	172-24	3	5.75	⅞	Int.	8.5	**250.00**	
Blue Ribbon 67R[8]	3-9	435-15	265-29	3	14.4	1	Int.	15.2	**349.00**	
Blue Ribbon 68R[8]	4-12	30.5-11	150-13.5	3	14.4	1	Int.	15.2	**379.95**	
Blue Ribbon 54R[5]	4	29	96	3.5	12	1	Int.	12.3	**169.98**	
SS-2[4,10]	4	24.6	41	5	7	1.38	Int.	13.7	**250.00**	
Burris										
Fullfield										All scopes avail. in Plex reticle. Steel-on-steel click adjustments. [1]Dot reticle $13 extra. [2]Post crosshair reticle $13 extra. [3]Matte satin finish $20 extra. [4]Available with parallax adjustment $28 extra (standard on 10x, 12x, 4-12x, 6-12x, 6-18x and 3-12x Signature). [5]Silver Safari finish $30 extra. [6]Target knobs $20 extra. [7]Sunshade avail. [8]Avail. with Fine Plex reticle. [9]Available with German three-post reticle.
1½x	1.6	62	—	3¼	10¼	1	Int.	9.0	**200.00**	
2½x	2.5	55	—	3¼	10¼	1	Int.	9.0	**211.95**	
4x[1,2,3]	3.75	36	—	3¼	11¼	1	Int.	11.5	**224.95**	
6x[1,3]	5.8	23	—	3¼	13	1	Int.	12.0	**242.95**	
10x[1,4,6,7,8]	9.8	12	—	3¼	15	1	Int.	15	**296.95**	
12x[1,4,6,7,8]	11.8	10.5	—	3¼	15	1	Int.	15	**305.95**	
1¾-5x[1,2]	1.7-4.6	66-25	—	3¼	10⅞	1	Int.	13	**269.95**	
2-7x[1,2,3]	2.5-6.8	47-18	—	3¼	12	1	Int.	14	**298.95**	LER = Long Eye Relief; IER = Intermediate Eye Relief; XER = Extra Eye Relief. From Burris.
3-9x[1,2,3]	3.3-8.7	38-15	—	3¼	12⅝	1	Int.	15	**314.95**	
4-12x[1,4,8]	4.4-11.8	27-10	—	3¼	15	1	Int.	18	**382.95**	
6-18x[1,4,6,7,8]	6.5-17.6	16-7	—	3¼	15.8	1	Int.	18.5	**382.95**	
Mini Scopes										
4x[4,5]	3.6	24	—	3¾-5	8¼	1	Int.	7.8	**182.95**	
6x[1,4]	5.5	17	—	3¾-5	9	1	Int.	8.2	**200.95**	
2-7x	2.5-6.9	32-14	—	3¾-5	12	1	Int.	10.5	**249.95**	
3-9x[5]	3.6-8.8	25-11	—	3¾-5	12⅝	1	Int.	11.5	**254.95**	

CAUTION: PRICES CHANGE, CHECK AT GUNSHOP.

Maker and Model	Magn.	Field at 100 Yds. (feet)	Relative Brightness	Eye Relief (in.)	Length (in.)	Tube Diam. (in.)	W&E Adjustments	Weight (ozs.)	Price	Other Data
Burris (cont'd.) 4-12x[1,4,6]	4.5-11.6	19-8	—	3¾-4	15	1	Int.	15	337.95	
Signature Series 1.5-6x[2,3,5,9]	1.7-5.8	70-20	—	3½-4	10.8	1	Int.	13.0	346.95	
4x	4.0	30	—	3	12⅛	1	Int.	14	325.95	
6x	6.0	20	—	3	12⅛	1	Int.	14	340.95	
3-9x	3.3-8.8	36-14	—	3	12⅞	1	Int.	15.5	412.95	
3-12x	3.3-11.7	34-9	—	3	14¼	1	Int.	21	517.95	
6-24x[1,3,5,6,8]	6.6-23.8	17-6	—	3-2½	16.0	1	Int.	22.7	571.95	
Handgun 1½-4x LER[1,5]	1.6-3.8	16-11	—	11-25	10¼	1	Int.	11	278.95	
2½-7x LER[4,5]	2.7-6.7	12-7.5	—	11-28	12	1	Int.	12.5	289.95	
1x LER[1]	1.1	27	—	10-24	8¾	1	Int.	6.8	170.95	
2x LER[4,5,6]	1.7	21	—	10-24	8¾	1	Int.	6.8	175.95	
3x LER[4,6]	2.7	17	—	10-20	8⅞	1	Int.	6.8	192.95	
4x LER[1,4,5,6]	3.7	11	—	10-22	9⅝	1	Int.	9.0	199.95	
5x LER[1,4,6]	4.5	8.7	—	12-22	10⅞	1	Int.	9.2	215.95	
7x IER[1,4,5,6]	6.5	6.5	—	10-16	11¼	1	Int.	10	233.95	
10x IER[1,4,6]	9.5	4	—	8-12	13½	1	Int.	14	287.95	
Scout Scope 1½x XER[3,9]	1.5	22	—	7-18	9	1	Int.	7.3	175.95	
2¾x XER[3,9]	2.7	15	—	7-14	9⅜	1	Int.	7.5	182.95	
Bushnell Armor Site 3-9x40	3-9	39-13	—	3.3	12	1	Int.	12.5	523.95	All Scope Chief, Banner and Custom models come with Multi-X reticle. [1]Also in 40mm. **Only selected models shown.** Contact Bushnell for complete details.
■ **Sportview Rangemaster** 4-12x	4-12	27-9	—	3.2	13.5	1	Int.	14	154.95	
Sportview Standard 4x	4	28	—	4	11.75	1	Int.	9.5	69.95	
Sportview Standard 3-9x	3-9	38-12	—	3.5	11.75	1	Int.	10	84.95	
Banner 22 Rimfire 4x	4	28	—	3	11.9	1	Int.	8	78.95	
Banner 22 Rimfire 3-7x	3-7	29-13	—	2.5	10	¾	Int.	6.5	89.95	
Banner 3-9x56	3-9	39-12.5	—	3.5	14.4	1	Int.	18.4	274.95	
Banner 10x[3]	10	12	—	3	14.7	1	Int.	14.3	289.95	
Banner Lite-Site 3-9x[1]	3-9	36-12	—	3.3	13.6	1	Int.	14	346.95	
Banner Shotgun 2.5x	2.5	45	—	3.5	10.9	1	Int.	8	100.95	
Banner Standard 4x	4	29	—	3.5	12	1	Int.	10	128.95	
Banner Standard 6x[1]	6	19.5	—	3	13.5	1	Int.	11.5	189.95	
Banner Standard 3-9x	3-9	43-14	—	3	12.1	1	Int.	14	167.95	
Trophy WA 1.75-5x	1.75-5	68.5-24.5	—	3.2	10.4	1	Int.	10.2	196.95	
Trophy WA 4x	4	34.2	—	3.4	12.4	1	Int.	11.9	165.95	
Trophy WA 3-9x	3-9	39-13	—	3.3	11.8	1	Int.	12.9	209.95	
Charles Daly 4x32	4	28	—	3.25	11.75	1	Int.	9.5	70.00	[1]Pistol scope. [2]Adj. obj. From Outdoor Sports Headquarters.
4x32[2]	4	28	—	3	9	1	Int.	8.5	129.00	
4x40 WA	4	36	—	3.25	13	1	Int.	11.5	98.00	
2.5x20[1]	2.5	17	—	3	7.3	1	Int.	7.25	80.00	
2.5x32	2.5	47	—	3	12.25	1	Int.	10	80.00	
2-7x32 WA	2-7	56-17	—	3	11.5	1	Int.	12	125.00	
3-9x40	3-9	35-14	—	3	12.5	1	Int.	11.25	77.00	
3-9x40 WA	3-9	36-13	—	3	12.75	1	Int.	12.5	125.00	
4-12x40 WA	4-12	30-11	—	3	13.75	1	Int.	14.5	133.00	
2x20[1]	2	16	—	16-25	8.75	1	Int.	6.5	107.00	
Interaims Mark V	0	—	—	—	5	1	Int.	6	174.95	Mark V for rifles, handguns, shotguns. Projects red dot aiming point. Dot size 1½" @ 100 yds. Pro V intended for handguns. Dot size less than 1½" @ 100 yds. Both waterproof. Battery life 50-10,000 hours. Black or nickel finish on Pro V. Imported by Stoeger.
Pro V	0	—	—	—	4.5	1	Int.	4	204.95	
aus Jena ZF4x32-M	4	32	—	3.5	10.8	26mm	Int.	10	350.00	Fixed power scopes have 26mm alloy tubes, variables, 30mm alloy; rings avail. from importer. Also avail. with rail mount. Multi-coated lenses. Waterproof and fogproof. ⅓-min. clicks. Choice of nine reticles. Imported from E. Germany by Europtik, Ltd.
ZF6x42-M	6	22	—	3.5	12.6	26mm	Int.	13	410.00	
ZF8x56-M	8	17	—	3.5	14	26mm	Int.	17	470.00	
VZF1.5-6x42-M	1.5-6	67.8-22	—	3.5	12.6	30mm	Int.	14	595.00	
UZF3-12x56-M	3-12	30-11	—	3.5	15	30mm	Int.	18	665.00	
Kahles 2.5x20[1]	2.5	61	—	3.25	9.6	1	Int.	12.7	460.00	[1]Steel only. [2]Lightweight model weighs 11 oz. [3]Aluminum only. [4]Lightweight model weighs 16 oz. [5]Lightweight model weighs 12.7 oz. [6]Lightweight model weighs 16 oz. [7]Lightweight model weighs 15.5 oz. [8]Lightweight model weighs 18 oz. Lightweight models priced slightly higher. Imported by Swarovski America, Ltd.
4x32[2]	4	33	—	3.25	11.3	1	Int.	15	490.00	
7x56[3]	7	20	—	3.25	14.4	1	Int.	16	630.00	
8x56[4]	8	17.1	—	3.25	14.4	1	Int.	23	640.00	
1.4-4.5x20[5]	1.1-4.5	79-29.5	—	3.25	10.5	30mm	Int.	15	600.00	
1.5-6x42[6]	1.5-6	61-21	—	3.25	12.6	30mm	Int.	20	686.00	
2.2-9x42[7]	2.2-9	39.5-15	—	3.25	13.3	30mm	Int.	20.4	820.00	
3-12x56[8]	3-12	30-11	—	3.25	15.25	30mm	Int.	25	900.00	
K-ZF84 (6x42)	6	23	—	3.25	15.5	1	Int.	17.5	855.00	
K-ZF10x42	10	13	—	3.25	13.25	1	Int.	18	885.00	
Kilham Hutson Handgunner II	1.7	8	—	—	5½	⅞	Int.	5.1	119.95	Unlimited eye relief; internal click adjustments; crosshair reticle. Fits Thompson/Center rail mounts, for S&W K, N, Ruger Blackhawk, Super, Super Single-Six, Contender.
Hutson Handgunner	3	8	—	10-12	6	⅞	Int.	5.3	119.95	
Laser Aim LA1	—	—	—	—	3.93	.812	Int.	4	298.00	Projects high intensity beam of laser light up to 300 yards. Dot size at 100 yards is 1". Adjustable for w. & e. Includes rings to mount on scope rail, battery charger plugs into cigarette lighter. Optional 110V charger, $19.95. From Emerging Technologies, Inc.

HUNTING, TARGET ■ VARMINT ■ SCOPES

Maker and Model	Magn.	Field at 100 Yds. (feet)	Relative Bright-ness	Eye Relief (in.)	Length (in.)	Tube Diam. (in.)	W&E Adjust-ments	Weight (ozs.)	Price	Other Data
Laser Devices										
He Ne FA-6	—	—	—	—	6.2	—	Int.	11	229.50	Projects high intensity beam of laser light onto target as an aiming point. Adj. for w. & e. FA-6 uses two 9V, others use eight AA batteries. [1]Diode laser sight system. Dot less than 1" wide at 100 yds. Built-in rings fit Weaver base. Comes with lithium batteries. Rear mounted, detachable pressure-activated switch. Black or stainless. From Laser Devices, Inc.
He Ne FA-9	—	—	—	—	12	—	Int.	16	299.00	
He Ne FA-9P	—	—	—	—	9	—	Int.	14	299.00	
FA-4[1]	—	—	—	—	4.5	—	Int.	3.5	299.00	
Lasersight										
LS45	0	—	—	—	7.5	—	Int.	8.5	245.95	Projects a highly visible beam of concentrated laser light onto the target. Adjustable for w. & e. Visible up to 500 yds. at night. For handguns, rifles, shotguns. Uses two standard 9V batteries. LS25 uses two AAA alkaline batteries, 8-hr. life; size of small tactical flashlight, uses Mini-Mag mount. LS55 uses three AAA batteries, 9-hr. life (continuous beam), 16-hr. life (pulsed beam). From Imatronic Lasersight.
LS25	0	—	—	—	6	¾	Int.	3.5	299.95	
LS55	0	—	—	—	7	1	Int.	7	349.95	
Leatherwood										
ART II	3.0-8.8	31-12	—	3.5	13.9	1	Int.	42	750.00	Compensates for bullet drop via external circular cam. Matte gray finish. Designed specifically for the M1A/M-14 rifle. Quick Detachable model for rifles with Weaver-type bases. From North American Specialties.
Leupold										
Alaskan 2.5x	2.5	34.4	—	4.2	10.1	⅞	Int.	9.9	241.10	Constantly centered reticles, choice of Duplex, tapered CPC, Leupold Dot, Crosshair and Dot. CPC and Dot reticles extra. [1]2x and 4x scopes have from 12"-24" of eye relief and are suitable for handguns, top ejection arms and muzzleloaders [2]3x9 Compact, 6x Compact, 12x, 3x9, 3.5x10 and 6.5x20 come with Adjustable Objective. [3]Target scopes have 1-min. divisions with ¼-min. clicks, and Adjustable Objectives. 50-ft. Focus Adaptor available for indoor target ranges, **$44.80.** Sunshade available for all Adjustable Objective scopes, **$13.05.** [4]Also available in matte finish for about **$20.00** extra. [5]Dot or Duplex; focused at 300 yds. with A.O. **$368.40.** [6]Compact Silver **$366.80.** [7]Also 50mm with Multi-coat 4 **$535.70.** [8]With CPC, **$275.40;** with Leupold Dot, **$275.40.** [9]With Multicoat 4, Leupold Dot, **$637.90.** [10]Add **$37.50** for A.O. [11]Matte finish.
Alaskan 4x	3.7	24	—	3.9	9.9	⅞	Int.	10.7	258.90	
Alaskan 6x	5.8	15.2	—	3.8	10.8	⅞	Int.	11.4	276.80	
Vari-X III 3.5x10 STD Police[11]	3.5-10	29.5-10.7	—	3.6-4.6	12.5	1	Int.	13.5	548.90	
M8-2X EER[1]	1.7	21.2	—	12-24	7.9	1	Int.	6.0	198.00	
M8-2X EER Silver[1]	1.7	21.2	—	12-24	7.9	1	Int.	6.0	219.50	
M8-4X EER[1]	3.7	9	—	12-24	8.4	1	Int.	7.0	241.80	
M8-4X EER Silver[1]	3.7	9	—	12-24	8.4	1	Int.	7.0	263.20	
M8-2.5X Compact	2.3	39.5	—	4.9	8.0	1	Int.	6.5	226.80	
M8-4X Compact	3.6	25.5	—	4.5	9.2	1	Int.	7.5	253.90	
2-7x Compact	2.5-6.6	41.7-16.5	—	5-3.7	9.9	1	Int.	8.5	320.40	
6x Compact & A.O.	5.7	16.2	—	3.9	10.7-11.0	1	Int.	10.0	345.40	
3-9x Compact & A.O.[7]	3.2-8.6	34-13.5	—	4.0-3.0	11-11.3	1	Int.	11.0	382.90	
M8-4X[4]	4.0	24	—	4.0	10.7	1	Int.	9.3	253.90	
M8-6X	5.9	17.7	—	4.3	11.4	1	Int.	10.0	271.10	
M8-6x 42mm	6.0	17	—	4.5	12	1	Int.	11.3	316.80	
M8-8X[2]	7.8	14.3	—	3.9	12.4	1	Int.	13.0	361.40	
M8-8x36[5]	7.7	14	—	3.7	11.8	1	Int.	10	361.40	
M8-12X[2]	11.6	9.1	—	4.2	13.0	1	Int.	13.5	373.40	
6.5x20 Target AO[9]	6.5-19.2	14.2-5.5	—	5.3-3.6	14.2	1	Int.	17.5	616.40	
M8-12X Target[3]	11.6	9.1	—	4.2	13.0	1	Int.	15.0	445.50	
BR-24X[3]	24.0	4.7	—	3.2	13.8	1	Int.	15.3	648.20	
BR-36X[3]	36.0	3.2	—	3.4	14.1	1	Int.	15.6	648.20	
Vari-X II 1x4	1.6-4.2	70.5-28.5	—	4.3-3.8	9.2	1	Int.	9.0	282.10	
Vari-X-II 2x7	2.5-6.6	42.5-17.8	—	4.9-3.8	11.0	1	Int.	10.5	329.80	
Vari-X-II 3x9[1,4]	3.3-8.6	32.3-14.0	—	4.1-3.7	12.3	1	Int.	13.5	354.30	
Vari-X-III 1.5x5	1.5-4.5	66.0-23.0	—	5.3-3.7	9.4	1	Int.	9.5	390.70	
Vari-X-III 2.5x8[4]	2.6-7.8	37.0-13.5	—	4.7-3.7	11.3	1	Int.	11.5	440.70	
Vari-X-III 3.5x10	3.3-9.7	29.5-10.7	—	4.6-3.6	12.4	1	Int.	13.0	461.10	
Vari-X-III 3.5x10[2]	3.3-9.7	29.5-10.7	—	4.6-3.6	12.4	1	Int.	14.4	498.60	
Mark 4 M1-10x[11]	10	11.1	—	3.6	13⅛	1	Int.	21	1,339.30	
Mark 4 M1-16x[11]	16	6.6	—	4.1	12⅞	1	Int.	22	1,339.30	
Mark 4 M3-10x[11]	10	11.1	—	3.6	13⅛	1	Int.	21	1,339.30	
Vari-X-III 6.5x20[3]	6.5-19.2	14.2-5.5	—	5.3-3.6	14.2	1	Int.	16.0	546.30	
Mirador										
RXW 4x40[1]	4	37	—	3.8	12.4	1	Int.	12	179.95	[1]Wide Angle scope. Multi-coated objective lens. Nitrogen filled; waterproof; shockproof. From Mirador Optical Corp.
RXW 1.5-5x20[1]	1.5-5	46-17.4	—	4.3	11.1	1	Int.	10	188.95	
RXW 3-9x40	3-9	43-14.5	—	3.1	12.9	1	Int.	13.4	251.95	
Nichols										
"Grand Slam"										
6x46 W.A.	6	22.5	—	3.5	13.0	1	Int.	13.7	175.00	[1]Matte finish; also avail. with high gloss. [2]Adj. obj. [3]Stainless; also 3-9x40, blue, **$120.00.** [4]50-yd. parallax, with 22 rings; also with adj. obj., **$108.50.** [5]Also in stainless. [6]50-yd. parallax, with 22 rings, **$74.50.** [7]Also 3-9x40, **$103.50.** Imported by Ernie Simmons Ent.
2.5-10x46 W.A.[1]	2.5-10	24.0-10.5	—	3.7-3.6	13.1	1	Int.	15.3	189.00	
4-12x46 W.A.[2]	4-12	21.0-10.0	—	3.6-3.5	13.7	1	Int.	15.8	272.00	
6-20x46 W.A.[2]	6-20	18.3-7.0	—	3.6-3.5	15.4	1	Int.	17.6	324.00	
"Magnum Target"										
12x44[2]	12	8.7	—	3.1	14.3	1	Int.	19.1	437.50	
24x44[2]	24	4.3	—	2.9	14.3	1	Int.	18.4	437.50	
6-20x44[2]	6-20	17.4-5.4	—	3.1-3.0	14.4	1	Int.	19.8	481.00	
"Classic"										
4x40 W.A.	4	37.0	—	3.8	13.0	1	Int.	11.6	116.50	
6x40 W.A.	6	24.5	—	3.3	13.0	1	Int.	11.6	118.50	
1.5-4.5x W.A.	1.5-4.5	54.0-22.0	—	3.4-3.3	11.5	1	Int.	10.9	135.50	
2-7x32 W.A.	2-7	36.7-15.8	—	2.8-2.6	11.7	1	Int.	10.9	135.50	
3-9x32 W.A.[3]	3-9	39.3-13.1	—	3.4-2.9	11.4	1	Int.	10.5	135.50	
4-12x40	4-12	30.0-11.0	—	3.9-3.2	12.3	1	Int.	12.3	142.00	
"Air Gun/Rimfire"										
4x32[4]	4	28.5	—	3.1	12.2	1	Int.	10.7	87.50	
2-7x32 W.A.	2-7	36.7-15.7	—	2.8-2.6	11.8	1	Int.	10.5	155.50	
"Classic Handgun"										
2x20[5]	2	17.0	—	8.6-19.5	7.4	1	Int.	7.5	112.00	
2-7x28[5]	2-7	40.0-9.7	—	8.9-19.5	9.0	1	Int.	9.0	216.50	
"Bullet"										
4x32[6]	4	28.5	—	3.1	12.2	1	Int.	10.7	68.50	
3-9x32[7]	3-9	34.5-23.6	—	3.1-3.0	12.6	1	Int.	11.2	98.00	

CAUTION: PRICES CHANGE, CHECK AT GUNSHOP.

Maker and Model	Magn.	Field at 100 Yds. (feet)	Relative Bright-ness	Eye Relief (in.)	Length (in.)	Tube Diam. (in.)	W&E Adjust-ments	Weight (ozs.)	Price	Other Data
Nikon										Super multi-coated lenses and blackening of all internal metal parts for maximum light gathering capability; positive ¼ MOA; fogproof; waterproof; shockproof; luster and matte finish. From Nikon Inc.
4x40	4	26.7	—	3.5	11.7	1	Int.	11.7	263.00	
1.5-4.5x20	1.5-4.5	67.8-22.5	—	3.7-3.2	10.1	1	Int.	9.5	327.00	
1.5-4.5x24EER	1.5-4.4	13.7-5.8	—	24-18	8.9	1	Int.	9.3	332.00	
2-7x32	2-7	46.7-13.7	—	3.9-3.3	11.3	1	Int.	11.3	374.00	
3-9x40	3-9	33.8-11.3	—	3.6-3.2	12.5	1	Int.	12.5	411.00	
4-12x40	4-12	25.7-8.6	—	3.6-3.2	14	1	Int.	16.6	512.00	
6.5-20x44	6.5-19.4	16.2-5.4	—	3.5-3.1	14.8	1	Int.	19.6	599.00	
2x20 P	2	22	—	26.4	8.1	1	Int.	6.3	207.00	
Pentax										Multi-coated lenses, fogproof, waterproof, nitrogen filled. Penta-Plex reticle. Click ¼-MOA adjustments. Matte finish $20.00 extra. [1]Also in matte chrome $260.00. [2]Also in matte chrome $390.00. [3]Gloss finish only. Imported by Pentax Corp.
1.5-5x	1.5-5	66-25	—	3-3¼	11	1	Int.	13	330.00	
4x	4	35	—	3¼	11.6	1	Int.	12.2	280.00	
6x	6	20	—	3¼	13.4	1	Int.	13.5	310.00	
2-7x	2-7	42.5-17	—	3-3¼	12	1	Int.	14	360.00	
3-9x	3-9	33-13.5	—	3-3¼	13	1	Int.	15	380.00	
3-9x Mini	3-9	26.5-10.5	—	3¾	10.4	1	Int.	13	320.00	
4-12x Mini[3]	4-12	19-8	—	3.75-4	11.3	1	Int.	11.3	410.00	
6-18x[3]	6-18	16-7	—	3-3.25	15.8	1	Int.	15.8	460.00	
Pistol										
2x LER[1]	2	21	—	10-24	8¾	1	Int.	6.8	240.00	
1.5-4x LER[2]	1.5-4	16-11	—	11-25	10	1	Int.	11	360.00	
RWS										Air gun scopes. All have Dyna-Plex reticle. Model 800 is for air pistols. Imported from Japan by Dynamit Nobel of America.
100	4	—	—	8	10½	¾	Int.	7	54.00	
300	4	—	—	8	12¾	1	Int.	11	120.00	
350	4	—	—	8	10	1	Int.	10	100.00	
400	2-7	—	—	8	12¾	1	Int.	12	125.00	
800	1.5	—	—	28	8¾	1	Int.	6	100.00	
CS-10	2.5	—	—	8	5¾	1	Int.	7	110.00	
Redfield										*Accutrac feature avail. on these scopes at extra cost. Traditionals have round lenses. 4-Plex reticle is standard. [1]"Magnum Proof." Specially designed for magnum and auto pistols. Uses "Double Dovetail" mounts. Also in brushed aluminum finish. 2½x $211.95, 4x $222.95. [2]With matte finish $468.95. [3]Also available with matte finish at extra cost. [4]All Golden Five Star scopes come with Butler Creek flip-up lens covers. [5]Black anodized finish. Also in nickel finish. [6]56mm adj. objective; European #4 reticle; comes with 30mm steel rings with Rotary Dovetail System, hardwood box. ¼-min. click adj. Also in matte finish, $723.95. [7]Also available nickel-plated, $299.95.
Ultimate Illuminator 3-9x	3.4-9.1	27-9	—	3-3.5	15.1	1	Int.	20.5	625.95	
Ultimate Illuminator 3-12x[6]	2.9-11.7	27-10.5	—	3-3½	15.4	30mm	Int.	23	714.95	
Illuminator Trad. 3-9x	2.9-8.7	33-11	—	3½	12¾	1	Int.	17	444.95	
Illuminator Widefield 4x	4.2	28	—	3-3.5	11.7	1	Int.	13.5	382.95	
Illuminator Widefield 2-7x	2.0-6.8	56-17	—	3-3.5	11.7	1	Int.	13.5	437.95	
Illuminator Widefield 3-9x[2]	2.9-8.7	38-13	—	3½	12¾	1	Int.	17	493.95	
Tracker 4x[3]	3.9	28.9	—	3½	11.02	1	Int.	9.8	147.95	
Tracker 2-7x[3]	2.3-6.9	36.6-12.2	—	3½	12.20	1	Int.	11.6	189.95	
Tracker 3-9x[3]	3.0-9.0	34.4-11.3	—	3½	14.96	1	Int.	13.4	212.95	
Traditional 4x ¾"	4	24½	27	3½	9⅜	¾	Int.	—	135.95	
Traditional 2½x	2½	43	64	3½	10¼	1	Int.	8½	169.95	
Golden Five Star 4x[4]	4	28.5	58	3.75	11.3	1	Int.	9.75	204.95	
Golden Five Star 6x[4]	6	18	40	3.75	12.2	1	Int.	11.5	232.95	
Golden Five Star 2-7x[4]	2.4-7.4	42-14	207-23	3-3.75	11.25	1	Int.	12	264.95	
Golden Five Star 3-9x[4,7]	3.0-9.1	34-11	163-18	3-3.75	12.50	1	Int.	13	282.95	
Golden Five Star 4-12x A.O.[4]	3.9-11.4	27-9	112-14	3-3.75	13.8	1	Int.	16	362.95	
Golden Five Star 6-18x A.O.[4]	6.1-18.1	18.6	50-6	3-3.75	14.3	1	Int.	18	382.95	
Compact Scopes										
Golden Five Star Compact 4x	3.8	28	—	3.5	9.75	1	Int.	8.8	198.95	
Golden Five Star Compact 6x	6.3	17.6	—	3.5	10.70	1	Int.	9.5	221.95	
Golden Five Star Compact 2-7x	2.4-7.1	40-16	—	3-3.5	9.75	1	Int.	9.8	262.95	
Golden Five Star Compact 3-9x	3.3-9.1	32-11.25	—	3-3.5	10.7	1	Int.	10.5	280.95	
Golden Five Star Compact 4-12x	4.1-12.4	22.4-8.3	—	3-3.5	12	1	Int.	13	354.95	
Pistol Scopes										
2½xMP[1]	2.5	9	64	14-19	9.8	1	Int.	10.5	208.95	
4xMP[1]	3.6	9	—	12-22	9¹¹⁄₁₆	1	Int.	11.1	221.95	
1-4x	1.3-4.0	80-26	—	3-3.75	9.50	1	Int.	10.25	251.95	
2-6x[5]	2-5.5	25-7	—	10-18	10.4	1	Int.	11	264.95	
Widefield Low Profile Compact										
Widefield 4xLP Compact	3.7	33	—	3.5	9.35	1	Int.	10	244.95	
Widefield 3-9x LP Compact	3.3-9	37.0-13.7	—	3-3.5	10.20	1	Int.	13	312.95	
Low Profile Scopes										
Widefield 2¾xLP	2¾	55½	69	3½	10½	1	Int.	8	228.95	
Widefield 4xLP	3.6	37½	84	3½	11½	1	Int.	10	255.95	
Widefield 6xLP	5.5	23	—	3½	12¾	1	Int.	11	277.95	
Widefield 1¾x-5xLP	1¾-5	70-27	136-21	3½	10¾	1	Int.	11½	314.95	
Widefield 2x-7xLP*	2-7	49-19	144-21	3½	11¾	1	Int.	13	322.95	
Widefield 3x-9xLP*	3-9	39-15	112-18	3½	12½	1	Int.	14	357.95	
Schmidt & Bender										[1]All steel. [2]Black chrome finish. [3]For silhouette and varmint shooting. Choice of nine reticles. 30-year warranty. All have ⅓-min. click adjustments, centered reticles, nitrogen filling. Most models avail. in aluminum with mounting rail. Imported from West Germany by Paul Jaeger, Inc.
Vari-M 1¼-4x20[1]	1¼-4	96-16	—	3¼	10.4	30mm	Int.	12.3	550.00	
Vari-M 1½-6x42	1½-6	60-19.5	—	3¼	12.2	30mm	Int.	17.5	595.00	
Vari-M 2½-10x56	2½-10	37.5-12	—	3¼	14.6	30mm	Int.	21.9	695.00	
All Steel 1½x15[2]	1½	90	—	3¼	10	1	Int.	11.8	395.00	
All Steel 4x36[2]	4	30	—	3¼	11.4	1	Int.	14	450.00	
All Steel 6x42[2]	6	21	—	3¼	13.2	1	Int.	17.3	495.00	

Maker and Model	Magn.	Field at 100 Yds. (feet)	Relative Brightness	Eye Relief (In.)	Length (In.)	Tube Diam. (In.)	W&E Adjustments	Weight (ozs.)	Price	Other Data
Schmidt & Bender (cont'd.)										
All Steel 8x56[2]	8	16.5	—	3¼	14.8	1	Int.	21.9	525.00	
■ All Steel 12x42[3]	12	16.5	—	3¼	13	1	Int.	17.9	565.00	
All Steel 4-12x42	4-12	34.7-12	—	3¼	13.25	30mm	Int.	23	650.00	
Shepherd										
3940-E	3-9	43.5-15	178-20	3.3	13	1	Int.	17	497.28	[1]Also avail. as 310-MOA, 310-1, 310-E. **$413.60** with ultra fine crosshair. [2]Also avail. as 310-P2, 310-P3 (**$413.60**) with matte finish, click adj. [3]Also avail. as 310-M2, 310-M3 (**$403.60**). [4]Matte finish, click adj. **$409.75**. Dual reticle system with instant range finder, bullet drop compensator. Waterproof, nitrogen filled, shockproof. From Shepherd Scope Ltd.
310-2[1,2,3]	3-10	35.3-11.6	178-16	3-3.75	12.8	1	Int.	18	413.60	
27-2[4]	2.5-7.5	42-14	164-18	2.5-3	11.6	1	Int.	16.3	349.00	
CBS[4]	1.5-5	82.5-27.5	45.5-40.9	2.5-3.25	11	1	Int.	14.9	409.75	
Simmons										
1001[3]	4	15	—	3.4	8.1	¾	Int.	3.5	31.95	[1]With ring mount. [2]With ring mount. [3]With rings. [4]½-min. dot or Truplex; Truplex reticle also avail. with dot. Sunshade, screw-in lens covers. Parallax adj.; Silhouette knobs; graduated drums. Truplex reticle in all models. All scopes sealed, fogproof, with constantly centered reticles. Imported from Japan by Simmons Outdoor Corp. **Partial listing.** Contact Simmons for complete details. Prices are approximate.
1002 Rimfire[1]	4	23	—	3	11.5	¾	Int.	6	13.95	
1004 Rimfire[2]	3-7	22.5-9.5	—	3	11	¾	Int.	8.4	43.95	
1022	4	36	—	3.5	11.6	1	Int.	10.0	82.95	
1025 W.A.	6	24.5	—	3	12.4	1	Int.	12	153.95	
1027 W.A.	2-7	54.6-18.3	—	3-3¼	12	1	Int.	12.8	148.95	
1029	3-9	42-14	—	3.1-2.5	13.1	1	Int.	14.3	170.95	
1044 W.A.	3-10	36.2-10.5	—	3.9-3.3	13.1	1	Int.	16.3	273.95	
1038 Mono Tube	3-9	42-14	—	3-3¼	13.3	1	Int.	13	227.95	
1040 Mono Tube	2-7	54-18	—	3-3¼	13.1	1	Int.	12.9	223.95	
1067	3-9	42-14	216-54	3.3	13	1	Int.	16.2	360.95	
1068	4-12	31-11	121-14	3.9-3.2	14.2	1	Int.	19.1	368.95	
1080 Handgun	2	18	—	10-20	7.1	1	Int.	8.1	135.95	
1084 Handgun[4]	4	9	—	10-20	8.7	1	Int.	9.5	190.95	
1090 Shotgun	1.5	49.9	—	5	6.8	1	Int.	7.0	145.95	
21005 Shotgun	2.5	29	—	4.6	7.1	1	Int.	7.1	81.95	
22000	1.5-4	13.6-6.3	—	10-25.7	8.6	1	Int.	8.75	287.95	
22001	2.5-7	9.7-4	—	8.9-19.4	9.2	1	Int.	9	303.95	
23000	12	8.7	—	3.1	14.5	1	Int.	18.3	586.95	
23002	6-20	17.4-5.4	—	3.1-2.5	14.6	1	Int.	19.7	646.95	
WTC12	2.5-8	46.5-14.5	—	3.2-3.0	11.3	1	Int.	11.8	159.95	
WTC13	3.5-10	34-11.5	—	3.2	12.4	1	Int.	12.8	173.95	
WT01	4	29	—	3.7	12	1	Int.	9.1	89.95	
WT02	3-9	37-12.7	—	3.1-2.9	12.8	1	Int.	12.8	112.95	
Swarovski Habicht										
4x32	4	33	—	3¼	11.3	1	Int.	15	515.00	All models offered in either steel or lightweight alloy tubes except 1.5x20, ZFM 6x42 and Cobras. Weights shown are for lightweight versions. Choice of nine constantly centered reticles. Eyepiece recoil mechanism and rubber ring shield to protect face. Cobra and ZFM also available in NATO Stanag 2324 mounts. Imported by Swarovski America Ltd.
6x42	6	23	—	3¼	12.6	1	Int.	17.9	565.00	
8x56	8	17	—	3¼	14.4	1	Int.	23	665.00	
1.5-4.5x20	1.4-4.5	74-25.5	—	3.5	9.5	1	Int.	11.3	525.00	
1.5-6x42	1.5-6	61-21	—	3¼	12.6	30mm	Int.	16	720.00	
2.2-9x42	2.2-9	39.5-15	—	3¼	13.3	30mm	Int.	15.5	875.00	
3-12x56	3-12	30-11	—	3¼	15.25	1	Int.	18	950.00	
Cobra 1.5-14	1.5	50	—	3.9	7.87	1	Int.	10	550.00	
AL Scopes										
4x32A	4	30	—	3.2	11.5	1	Int.	10.8	420.00	
6x36A	6	21	—	3.2	11.9	1	Int.	11.5	450.00	
3-9x36	3-9	39-13.5	—	3.3	11.9	1	Int.	13	565.00	
Swift										
600 4x15	4	16.2	—	2.4	11	¾	Int.	4.7	19.75	All Swift scopes, with the exception of the 4x15, have Quadraplex reticles and are fogproof and waterproof. The 4x15 has crosshair reticle and is non-waterproof. [1]Available in black or silver finish—same price.
601 3-7x20	3-7	25-12	—	3-2.9	11	1	Int.	5.6	48.50	
650 4x32	4	29	—	3.5	12	1	Int.	9	74.00	
653 4x40WA	4	35.5	—	3.75	12.25	1	Int.	12	96.50	
654 3-9x32	3-9	35.75-12.75	—	3	12.75	1	Int.	13.75	94.50	
656 3-9x40WA	3-9	42.5-13.5	—	2.75	12.75	1	Int.	14	103.50	
657 6x40	6	18	—	3.75	13	1	Int.	10	100.00	
660 4x20	4	25	—	4	11.8	1	Int.	9	79.50	
664 4-12x40	4-12	27-9	—	3-2.8	13.3	1	Int.	14.8	140.00	
665 1.5-4.5x21	1.5-4.5	69-24.5	—	3.5-3	10.9	1	Int.	9.6	102.75	
Pistol Scopes										
661 4x32	4	90	—	10-22	9.2	1	Int.	9.5	108.50	
662 2.5x32	2.5	14.3	—	9-22	8.9	1	Int.	9.3	102.50	
663 2x20[1]	2	18.3	—	9-21	7.2	1	Int.	8.4	103.50	
Tasco										
WA 1-3.5x20 Wide Angle[1,3,10]	1-3.5	115-31	400.0-32.4	3½	9¾	1	Int.	10.2	196.00	[1]Water, fog & shockproof; fully coated optics; ¼-min. click stops; haze filter caps; lifetime warranty. [3]World Class Wide Angle; Supercon multi-coated optics; Opti-Centered® 30/30 range finding reticle; lifetime warranty. [4]Shock-absorbing 30mm tubes; 44 and 52mm objective lenses; Opti-Centered® 30/30 range finding reticle. [5]Selective Bi-reticle display—converts from 30/30 to lighted post reticle. [6]Illuminated Opti-Centered Post Reticle. [7]⅓ greater zoom range. [8]Trajectory compensating scopes, Opti-Centered stadia reticle. [9]Anodized finish. [10]True one-power scope. [11]Coated optics; crosshair reticle; ring mounts included to fit most 22, 10mm receivers. [12]Fits Remington 870,1100. [13]Electronic dot reticle with rheostat. Coated optics. Adj. for windage and elevation. Waterproof, shockproof, fogproof. Lithium battery. 3x power booster avail. Matte black or matte alum. finish. Dot or T-3 reticle. **Contact Tasco for details on complete line.**
TT156x42	1.5-6	59-20	784-49	3.5-4	12.0	30mm	Int.	16.4	528.00	
DWC2510x44	2.5-10	41-11	309.7-19.3	4	12.5	1	Int.	14.4	224.00	
WA 4x40 Wide Angle[1,3]	4	36	100.0	3¼	13	1	Int.	11.5	144.00	
WA 3-9x40 Wide Angle[1,3]	3-9	43½-15	176.8-19.3	3⅛	12¾	1	Int.	12.5	176.00	
WA 2-7x32 Wide Angle[1,3]	2-7	56-17	256.0-20.2	3¼	11½	1	Int.	12	188.00	
DWA27x32	2-7	56-17	256-20.3	3.25	11.5	1	Int.	12.0	188.00	
WA 1.75-5x20 Wide Angle[1,3]	1.75-5	72-24	129.9-16.0	3	10⅝	1	Int.	9.8	205.00	
ER39x40WA	3-9	41-14	176.8-19.3	3	12.75	1	Int.	16	344.00	
TT39x42DS	3-9	37-13	196-21.6	3.5-4	12.5	30mm	Int.	16.8	480.00	
DWA39x40	3-9	41-15	176.8-19.3	3	13.0	1	Int.	14.0	176.00	
W 3-12x40 MAG-IV[1,2,7]	3-12	33-11	176.8-10.8	3	12⅛	1	Int.	12	136.00	
W 4-16x40 MAG-IV[1,2,7]	4-16	25½-7	100.0-6.2	3	14¼	1	Int.	16.75	176.00	
TR 4-16x40[1,2,7]	4-16	25½-7	100.0-6.2	3	14¼	1	Int.	16.75	224.00	
CW4x32LE	4	25	64	5	10.0	1	Int.	9.5	159.20	
DWA4x40	4	36	100	3	13.0	1	Int.	11.5	144.00	

Maker and Model	Magn.	Field at 100 Yds. (feet)	Relative Brightness	Eye Relief (in.)	Length (in.)	Tube Diam. (in.)	W&E Adjustments	Weight (ozs.)	Price	Other Data
Tasco (cont'd.)										
W 4x32[1,2,9]	4	28	64.0	3	11¾	1	Int.	9.5	67.20	[1]Also in silver finish, $220.00 (#8316); also avail. with rail mount, black finish, $215.00 (#8317); with lighted reticle, black finish, $245.00 (#8326); with rail, lighted reticle, black finish, $250.00 (#8327). [2]With lighted reticle, $190.00 (#8322); silver finish, $195.00 (#8323); with lighted reticle, rail mount, black only, $195.00 (#8320). [3]With lighted reticle, $245.00 (#8626). [4]With lighted reticle, $135.00 (#8630); with rail mount, lighted reticle, $140.00 (#8640). From Thompson/Center.
W 3-9x32[1,2,9]	3-9	35.14	112.3-12.2	3¼	12¾	1	Int.	12.3	86.40	
P1x22	1	65-24	—	8-28	7¾	1	Int.	8	160.00	
P2x22	2	26-18	—	10-24	7¾	1	Int.	7.6	160.00	
P4x30	4	7-6	—	12-24	9¾	1	Int.	12.1	216.00	
P6x40	6	5-5½	—	12-23	11	1	Int.	14.2	216.00	
RF 4x15[11]	4	21	13.6	2½	11	¾	Int.	4	14.80	
RF 4x20DS[11]	4	20	25.0	2½	10½	¾	Int.	3.8	23.20	
SG 2.5x32 with Shotgun Mount[1,12]	2.5	42	163.8	3¼	11¾	1	Int.	15.7	104.00	
Propoint II										
PDP2[13]	1	25-12	—	—	5	30mm	Int.	5.5	280.00	
Thompson/Center Recoil Proof Pistol Scopes										
8312 Compact Rail[2]	2.5	15	64	9-21	7.25	1	Int.	6.6	135.00	
8315 Compact[1]	2.5-7	15-5	125-16	8-21	9.25	1	Int.	9.2	210.00	
Rifle Scopes										
8261 Compact	1.5-5	61-20	177-16	3	10	1	Int.	8.5	160.00	
8623 Compact W.A.	3-9	33-11	113-13	3	10.75	1	Int.	9.9	175.00	
8624 Compact	4	26	64	3	10	1	Int.	8.2	130.00	
Trijicon Spectrum										
4x40[1]	4	38	—	3.0	12.2	1	Int.	15.0	467.00	[1]Self-luminous low-light reticle glows in poor light; allows choice of red, amber or green via a selector ring on objective end. [2]Advanced Combat Optical Gunsight for AR-15, M-16, with integral mount. [3]Reticle glows only red in poor light. From Trijicon, Inc.
6x56[1]	6	24	—	3.0	14.1	1	Int.	20.3	527.00	
1-3x20[1]	1-3	94-33	—	3.7-4.9	9.6	1	Int.	13.2	499.00	
3-9x40[1]	3-9	35-14	—	3.3-3.0	13.1	1	Int.	16.0	515.00	
3-9x56[1]	3-9	35-14	—	3.3-3.0	14.2	1	Int.	21.5	598.00	
ACOG[2]	4	37	—	1.5	5.8	—	Int.	9.7	695.00	
4x32 Red[3]	4	29	—	3.3	11.6	1	Int.	10.2	298.00	
Unertl										
■ 1" Target	6,8,10	16-10	17.6-6.25	2	21½	¾	Ext.	21	217.00	[1]Dural ¼ MOA click mounts. Hard coated lenses. Non-rotating objective lens focusing. [2]¼ MOA click mounts. [3]With target mounts. [4]With calibrated head. [5]Same as 1" Target but without objective lens focusing. [6]Price with ¼ MOA click mounts. [7]With new Posa mounts. [8]Range focus unit near rear of tube. Price is with Posa mounts. Magnum clamp. With standard mounts and clamp ring $363.
■ 1¼" Target[1]	8,10,12,14	12-16	15.2-5	2	25	¾	Ext.	21	281.00	
■ 1½" Target	8,10,12,14, 16,18,20	11.5-3.2	—	2¼	25½	¾	Ext.	31	303.00	
■ 2" Target[2]	8,10,12, 14,16,18, 24,30,36	8	22.6-2.5	2¼	26¼	1	Ext.	44	401.00	
■ Varmint, 1¼[3]	6,8,10,12	1-7	28-7.1	2½	19½	⅞	Ext.	26	275.00	
■ Ultra Varmint, 2"[4]	8,10,12,15	12.6-7	39.7-11	2½	24	1	Ext.	34	390.00	
■ Small Game[5]	4,6	25-17	19.4-8.4	2¼	18	¾	Ext.	16	163.00	
■ Vulture[6]	8	11.2	29	3-4	15⅝	1	Ext.	15½	310.00	
	10	10.9	18½	—	16⅛					
■ Programmer 200[7]	8,10,12, 14,16,18, 20,24,30,36	11.3-4	39-1.9		26½	1	Ext.	45	495.00	
■ BV-20[8]	20	8	4.4	4.4	17⅞	1	Ext.	21¼	363.00	
Weatherby										
Mark XXII	4	25	50	2.5-3.5	11¾	⅞	Int.	9.25	135.00	Lumiplex reticle in all models. Blue-black, nonglare finish.
Supreme 1¾-5x20	1.7-5	66.6-21.4	—	3.4	10.7	1	Int.	11	240.00	
Supreme 2-7x34	2.1-6.8	59-16	—	3.4	11¼	1	Int.	10.4	300.00	
Supreme 4x44	3.9	32	—	3	12½	1	Int.	11.6	300.00	
Supreme 3-9x44	3.1-8.9	36-13	—	3.5	12.7	1	Int.	11.6	350.00	
Weaver										
K2.5	2.5	35	—	3.7	10.2	1	Int.	8.5	118.31	Micro-Trac adjustment system with ¼-min. clicks on all models. All have Dual-X reticle. One-piece aluminum tube, satin finish, nitrogen filled, multi-coated lenses, waterproof. From Weaver.
K4	3.7	26.5	—	3.3	11.3	1	Int.	10	128.33	
K6	5.7	18.5	—	3.3	11.4	1	Int.	11.2	139.78	
V3	1.1-2.8	88-32	—	3.9-3.7	9.2	1	Int.	8.5	155.18	
V9	2.8-8.7	33-11	—	3.5-3.4	11.3	1	Int.	11.1	167.42	
V10	2.2-9.6	38.5-7.5	—	3.4-3.3	12.2	1	Int.	12.8	177.80	
KT15	14.6	7.5	—	3.2	12.9	1	Int.	14.6	280.00	
RK4	3.8	25	—	3	10.8	⅞	Int.	7.7	108.62	
RV7	2.2-6.5	43-15	—	2.9-2.6	11.5	⅞	Int.	8.5	131.96	
Williams										
Twilight Crosshair TNT	1½-5	57¾-21	177-16	3½	10¾	1	Int.	10	196.30	TNT models
Twilight Crosshair TNT	2½	32	64	3¾	11¼	1	Int.	8½	138.95	
Twilight Crosshair TNT	4	29	64	3½	11¾	1	Int.	9½	145.25	
Twilight Crosshair TNT	2-6	45-17	256-28	3	11½	1	Int.	11½	196.30	
Twilight Crosshair TNT	3-9	36-13	161-18	3	12¾	1	Int.	13½	206.30	
Pistol Scopes										
Twilight 1.5x TNT	1.5	19	177	18-25	8.2	1	Int.	6.4	143.70	
Twilight 2x TNT	2	17.5	100	18-25	8.5	1	Int.	6.4	145.80	
Zeiss										
Diatal C 4x32	4	30	—	3.5	10.6	1	Int.	11.3	525.00	All scopes have ¼-minute click-stop adjustments. Choice of Z-Plex or fine crosshair reticles. Rubber armored objective bell, rubber eyepiece ring. Lenses have T-Star coating for highest light transmission. Z-Series scopes offered in non-rail tubes with duplex reticles only. Imported from West Germany by Carl Zeiss Optical, Inc.
Diatal C 6x32	6	20	—	3.5	10.6	1	Int.	11.3	565.00	
Diatal C 10x36	10	12	—	3.5	12.7	1	Int.	14.1	675.00	
Diatal ZA 4x32	4	34.5	—	3.5	10.8	1.02 (26mm)	Int.	10.6	525.00	
Diatal ZA 6x42	6	22.9	—	3.5	12.7	1.02 (26mm)	Int.	13.4	620.00	
Diatal ZA 8x56	8	18	—	3.5	13.8	1.02 (26mm)	Int.	17.6	710.00	
Diavari C 1.5-4.5	1.5-4.5	72-27	—	3.5	11.8	1	Int.	13.4	725.00	
Diavari C 3-9x36	3-9	36-13	—	3.5	11.2	1	Int.	15.2	755.00	

CAUTION: PRICES CHANGE, CHECK AT GUNSHOP.

Maker and Model	Magn.	Field at 100 Yds. (feet)	Relative Brightness	Eye Relief (in.)	Length (in.)	Tube Diam. (in.)	W&E Adjustments	Weight (ozs.)	Price	Other Data
Zeiss (cont'd.)										
Diavari ZA 1.5-6	1.5-6	65.5-22.9	—	3.5	12.4	1.18 (30mm)	Int.	18.5	870.00	
Diavari ZA 2.5-10	2.5-10	41-13.7	—	3.5	14.4	1.18 (30mm)	Int.	22.8	1,030.00	
Zeitz										
30mm Superb Series W.A.										
1.5x20	1.5	78.73	69.64	3.9	9.4	1.18	Int.	12.3	300.53	30mm Superb Series: All models can be ordered with target or external knobs, magnifying reticle (European style), objective adjustment (O.A.), and choice of six reticles. Variables—IPC, extra-heavy construction of 6061 T-6 alloy. Fog-proof, recoil-proof coated optics.
4x42	4	31.16	43.40	4.5	12.2	1.18	Int.	14.6	374.78	
6x42	6	19	19.29	3.7	12.2	1.18	Int.	14.6	385.39	
8x56	8	13.12	19.29	3.7	13.5	1.18	Int.	19.0	424.28	
15x56[1]	15	8.5	5.38	3.3	15.9	1.18	Int.	25.7	601.07	
30mm Variables										
1-4x20	1-4	101-30.1	157-9.8	4.3-3.3	9.4	1.18	Int.	11.1	434.89	
2-8x42	2-8	46.9-16	173-11	4.5-3.5	13.3	1.18	Int.	17.4	493.23	
2.5-10	2.5-10	42.6-13	111.1-69	4.3-3.3	13.3	1.18	Int.	17.4	510.91	
3-12x56	3-12	37.7-10.8	137-16	3.9-3.3	14.3	1.18	Int.	25.7	601.07	
4-20x42	4-20	26-6	40-4	3.3-3.0	17.7	1.18	Int.	23.8	664.71	
American 1" Series W.A.										
Adirondack 1x20	1	NA	NA	NA	NA	1	Int.	NA	159.10	American Series: Special reticles (12), target knobs, BDC objective lens adjustment feature can be added to any scope at extra cost. Sunshades also avail. 12x thru 24x can be made on special order. German-type speed focus avail. as option on all American Series scopes. Waterproof, fog-proof, recoil-proof, fully coated.
Raton 2.5x32	2.5	33.0	161	3.5	11.7	1	Int.	9.2	160.00	
Las Vegas 4x32[2]	4	29.0	64	3.3	11.7	1	Int.	9.2	162.64	
Kalispell 6x40[3]	6	18.5	45	3.2	13.0	1	Int.	10.2	187.07	
Pecos 8x40 O.A.	8	13.5	25	3.0	13.0	1	Int.	10.2	239.46	
San Antonio 10x40 O.A.	10	12.5	16	3.0	13.0	1	Int.	10.4	242.67	
Variables										
Abeline 1-3x20	1-3	NA	NA	NA	NA	1	Int.	NA	224.51	
Shiloh 1.5-4.5x20	1.5-4.5	NA	NA	NA	NA	1	Int.	NA	228.05	
Denver 2-7x32[4]	2-7	NA	NA	NA	NA	1	Int.	NA	213.91	
Santa Fe 3-9x32[5]	3-9	43.5-15	114-13	3.3-3.0	12.2	1	Int.	12.0	210.37	
Sutter's Creek 4-12x40 O.A.	4-12	30.5-11	100-12.3	3.0	15.8	1	Int.	15.0	284.63	
European 1" Series										
Jutland 4x20[6]	4	33	25	3.2	11.0	1	Int.	10.5	197.00	European 1": All wide angle with choice of 12 reticles, obj. adj. avail. on some models. BDC and target knobs avail. on all as options. Sunshades, locking lens covers, speed focus also optional. **Partial listing of models shown.** Contact Zeitz Optics U.S.A. for full details.
Grenoble 6x40	6	26	43.56	3	13.2	1	Int.	13.7	230.46	
Rhineland 8x56	8	20	49	3.2	13.5	1	Int.	17.2	292.50	
Hamburg 10x56[7] O.A.	10	NA	NA	3.2	13.5	1	Int.	17.2	354.21	
Brunswick 15x56 O.A.	15	NA	NA	3.1	13.5	1	Int.	17.6	390.85	[1]With adj. obj.; [2]Also 4x40, 4x40 with adj. obj.; [3]Also with adj. obj.; [4]Also 2-7x40, 2-7x40 with adj. obj.; [5]Also 3-9x40, 3-9x40 with adj. obj.; [6]Also 4x30, 4x40; [7]Also 10x40.
Zero Mag										
Zero Mag	0	—	—	—	5	—	Int.	7	59.95	Has optional indirect lighting element to illuminate crosshairs ($79.95). For vent. rib, Rem. slug barrel, std. Weaver base, std. 22 dovetail, Hastings slug barrel mounts. From Autumn Tracker Design.

■ Signifies target and/or varmint scope. Hunting scopes in general are furnished with a choice of reticle—crosshairs, post with crosshairs, tapered or blunt post, or dot crosshairs, etc. The great majority of target and varmint scopes have medium or fine crosshairs but post or dot reticles may be ordered. W—Windage E-Elevation MOA-Minute of angle or 1" (approx.) at 100 yards, etc.

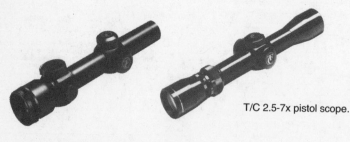

T/C 4x Electra-Dot rifle scope.

T/C 2.5-7x pistol scope.

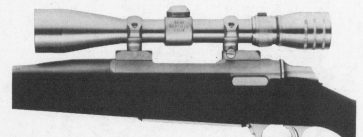

Redfield Golden Five Star 3x-9x variable with nickel-plated finish.

Beeman P1 pistol with Beeman Blue Ribbon 25 scope.

CAUTION: PRICES CHANGE, CHECK AT GUNSHOP.

SCOPE MOUNTS

Maker, Model, Type	Adjust.	Scopes	Price	Suitable for
Action Arms	No	1″ split rings.	**From $16.00**	For UZI, Ruger Mk. II, Mini-14, Win. 94, AR-15, Rem. 870, Ithaca 37, and many other popular rifles, handguns. From Action Arms.
Aimpoint	No	1″	**39.95-79.95**	Mounts/rings for all Aimpoint sights and 1″ scopes. For many popular revolvers, auto pistols, shotguns, military-style rifles/carbines, sporting rifles. Most require no gunsmithing. Contact Aimpoint for details.
Aimtech				Mount scopes, lasers, electronic sights using Weaver-style base. All mounts allow use of iron sights; no gunsmithing. Available in satin black or satin stainless finish. From L&S Technologies, Inc.
S&W K,L,N frame	No	1″	59.95	
Taurus revolvers	No	1″	59.95	
Rossi revolvers	No	1″	59.95	
Astra revolvers	No	1″	59.95	
Glock 17, 17L, 19	No	1″	59.95	
S&W 45, 9mm autos	No	1″	49.95	
Ruger Mk I, Mk II	No	1″	39.95	
AMT Auto Mag II, III	No	1″	49.95	
Govt. 45 Auto	No	1″	49.95	
Browning Hi-Power	No	1″	49.95	
Browning Buck Mark/Challenger II	No	1″	49.95	
Beretta/Taurus auto	No	1″	49.95	
S&W 422	No	1″	49.95	
A.R.M.S.				¹See-through mount. ²Also FNC—$89.00 From A.R.M.S., Inc.
Swan G-3	No	Weaver-type	145.00	
M16A1/A2/AR-15¹	No	Weaver-type rail	37.90	
FN FAL LAR	No	Weaver-type rail	95.00	
FN FAL LAR Para.²	No	—	120.00	
Beretta AR-70	No	—	59.00	
Armson				¹Fastens with one nut. ²Models 181, 182, 183, 184, etc. ³Claw mount. ⁴Claw mount, bolt cover still easily removable. From Trijicon, Inc.
AR-15¹	No	O.E.G.	35.95	
Mini-14²	No	O.E.G.	49.95	
H&K³	No	O.E.G.	67.95	
UZI⁴	No	O.E.G.	67.95	
Armsport				¹Weaver-type rings. ²Weaver-type base; most poular rifles. Made in U.S. From Armsport.
100 Series¹	No	1″ rings. Low, med., high	12.50	
104 22-cal.	No	1″	12.50	
201 See-Thru	No	1″	16.00	
1-Piece Base²	No		6.30	
2-Piece Base²	No		3.15	
B-Square				¹Clamp-on, blue finish. Stainless finish $59.95. ²For Bushnell Phantom only. ³Blue finish; stainless finish $59.95. ⁴Clamp-on, for Bushnell Phantom only, blue; stainless finish $49.95. ⁵Requires drilling & tapping. ⁶No gunsmithing, no sight removal; blue; stainless finish $79.95. ⁷Weaver-style rings. Rings not included with Weaver-type bases. ⁸NATO Stanag dovetail model, $99.50. ⁹Blue; stainless $69.95. ¹⁰Blue; stainless $49.95. ¹¹Handguard mounts. ¹²Receiver mounts. **Partial listing of mounts shown here. Contact B-Square for more data.**
Pistols			69.95	
Beretta/Taurus 92/99⁷	—	1″	39.95	
Browning Buck Mark⁷	No	1″	69.95	
Colt 45 Auto	E only	1″	49.95	
Colt Python, King Cobra¹,⁷	E	1″	19.95	
Daisy 717/722 Champion²	No	1″	49.95	
Dan Wesson Clap-On³,⁷	E	1″	39.95	
Ruger 22 Auto Mono-Mount⁴	No	1″	39.95	
Ruger Single-Six⁵	No	1″	59.95	
Ruger Blackhawk, Super B'hwk⁹	W&E	1″	39.95	
Ruger GP-100¹⁰	No	1″	59.95	
Ruger Redhawk⁹	W&E	1″	39.95	
S&W 422¹⁰	No	1″	39.95	
Taurus 66¹⁰	No	1″	49.95	
S&W K, L, N frame³,⁷	No	1″	49.95	
T/C Contender	W&E	1″		
Rifles				
Charter AR-7	No	1″	19.95	B-Square makes mounts for the following military rifles: AK47/AKS, Egyptian Hakim, French MAS 1936, M91 Argentine Mauser, Model 98 Brazilian and German Mausers, Model 93, Spanish Mauser (long and short), Model 1916 Mauser, Model 38 and 96 Swedish Mausers, Model 91 Russian (round and octagon receivers), Chinese SKS 56, SMLE No. 1, Mk. III, 1903 Springfield, U.S. 30-cal. Carbine. Those following replace gun's rear sight: AK47/AKS, P14/1917 Enfield, FN49, M1 Garand, M1-A/M14 (no sight removal), SMLE No. 1, MK III/No. 4 & 5, MK 1, 1903/1903-A3 Springfield, Beretta AR 70 (no sight removal).
Mini-14⁶,⁷	W&E	1″	49.95	
M-94 Side Mount	W&E	1″	49.95	
RWS, Beeman/FWB Air Rifles	E only	—	49.95	
Ruger 77⁷	W&E	1″	49.95	
Ruger Ranch/Mini Thirty⁷	W&E	1″	49.95	
SMLE Side Mount	W&E	1″	49.95	
Rem. Model Seven, 600, 660, etc.⁷	No	1″ One piece base	9.95	
Military				
AK-47/AKM/AKS/SKS-56¹¹	No	1″	49.95	
AK-47, SKS-56¹²	No	1″	59.95	
M1-A⁸	W&E	1″	99.50	
AR-15/16⁸	W&E	1″	39.95	
FN-LAR/FAL⁷,⁸	E only	1″	149.50	
HK-91/93/94⁷,⁸	E only	1″	99.50	
Shotguns⁷				
Browning A-5⁷	No	1″	49.95	
Franchi 48/AL⁷	No	1″	49.95	
Franchi Elite, Prestige, SPAS⁷	No	1″	49.95	
Ithaca 37⁷	No	1″	39.95	
Mossberg 500, 712, 5500⁷	No	1″	39.95	
Rem. 870/1100⁷ (12 & 20 ga.)	No	1″	39.95	
Remington 870, 1100 (and L.H.)⁷	No	1″	39.95	

SCOPE MOUNTS

Maker, Model, Type	Adjust.	Scopes	Price	Suitable for
Bausch & Lomb	No	1″	62.95	Rem. 700, 7400/7600, Ruger 77, Browning A-Bolt, Browning BBR, Savage 110, Win. 70, Marlin 336. Contact Bushnell for details.
Beeman				
Double Adjustable	W&E	1″	29.98	All grooved receivers and scope bases on all known air rifles and 22-cal. rimfire rifles (½″ to ⅝″—6mm to 15mm). [1]Centerfire rifles. Scope detaches easily, returns to zero.
Deluxe Ring Mounts	No	1″	28.98	
Professional Mounts	W&E	1″	98.95	
Professional Pivot[1]	W	1″	269.50	
Bock				
Swing ALK[1]	W&E[1]	1″, 26mm, 30mm	224.00	[1]Q.D.; pivots right for removal. For Steyr-Mannlicher, Win. 70, Rem. 700, Mauser 98, Dakota, Sako, Sauer 80, 90. Magnum has extra-wide rings, same price. [2]Heavy duty claw-type; reversible for front or rear removal. For Steyr-Mannlicher rifles. [3]True claw mount for bolt-action rifles. Also in extended model. For Steyr-Mannlicher, Win. 70, Rem. 700. Also avail. as Gunsmith Bases—bases not drilled or contoured—same price. [4]Extra-wide rings. [5]Fit most 22 rimfires with dovetail receivers. Imported from West Germany by Gun South, Inc.
Safari KEMEL[2]	W&E	1″, 26mm, 30mm	149.00	
Claw KEMKA[3]	W&E	1″, 26mm, 30mm	224.00	
ProHunter Fixed[4]	No	1″, 26mm, 30mm	94.00	
Dovetail 22[5]	No	1″, 26mm	62.00	
Buehler				
One Piece (T)[1]	W only	1″ split rings, 3 heights. 1″ split rings, engraved 26mm split rings, 2 heights 30mm split rings, 1 height	Complete—78.50 Rings only—107.00 Rings only—56.00 Rings only—67.75	[1]Most popular models. [2]Sako dovetail receivers. [3]15 models. [4]No drilling & tapping. [5]Aircraft alloy, dyed blue or to match stainless; for Colt Diamondback, Python, Trooper, Ruger Blackhawk, Single-Six, Security-Six, S&W K-frame, Dan Wesson.
One Piece Micro Dial (T)[1]	W&E	1″ split rings.	Complete—100.50	
Two Piece (T)[1]	W only	1″ split rings.	Complete—78.50	
Two Piece Dovetail (T)[2]	W only	1″ split rings.	Complete—96.50	
One Piece Pistol (T)[3]	W only	1″ split rings.	Complete—78.50	
One Piece Pistol Stainless (T)[1]	W only	1″ stainless rings.	Complete—101.50	
One Piece Ruger Mini-14 (T)[4]	W only	1″ split rings.	Complete—96.50	
One Piece Pistol M83 Blue[4,5]	W only	1″ split rings.	Complete—89.50	
One Piece Pistol M83 Silver[4,5]	W only	1″ stainless rings.	Complete—104.00	
Burris				
Supreme One Piece (T)[1]	W only	1″ split rings, 3 heights.	1 piece base—24.95	[1]Most popular rifles. Universal rings, mounts fit Burris, Universal, Redfield, Leupold and Browning bases. Comparable prices. [2]Browning Standard 22 Auto rifle. [3]Grooved receivers. [4]Universal dovetail; accept Burris, Universal, Redfield, Leupold rings. For Dan Wesson, S&W, Virginian, Ruger Blackhawk, Win. 94. [5]Medium standard front, extension rear, per pair. Low standard front, extension rear, per pair. [6]Mini scopes, scopes with 2″ bell, for M77R. [7]Selected rings and bases available with matte Safari or silver finish. [8]For S&W K,L,N frames, Colt Python, Dan Wesson with 6″ or longer barrels.
Trumount Two Piece (T)	W only	1″ split rings, 3 heights.	2 piece base—22.95	
Browning Auto Mount[2]	No	1″, split rings.	18.95	
Rings Mounts[3]	No	1″, split rings.	1″ rings—17.95	
L.E.R. Mount Bases[4]	W only	1″ split rings.	22.95	
L.E.R. No Drill-No Tap Bases[4,7,8]	W only	1″ split rings.	37.00–41.75	
Extension Rings[5]	No	1″ scopes.	38.95	
Ruger Ring Mount[6]	W only	1″ split rings.	43.95	
Std. 1″ Rings	—	Low, medium, high heights.	31.95	
Zee Rings	—	Fit Weaver bases; medium and high heights	26.95	
Bushnell				
Detachable (T) mounts only[1]	W only	1″ split rings, uses Weaver base.	Rings—20.95	[1]Most popular rifles. Includes windage adj.
22 mount	No	1″ only.	Rings— 9.95	
Cape Outfitters				
Quick Detachable	No	1″ split rings, lever quick detachable	89.95	Double rifles; SIG Sauer, Win. Model 70, Rem. 700, Browning Safari, Mauser 98, grooved receiver 22s. All steel; returns to zero. From Cape Outfitters.
Clearview				
Universal Rings (T)[1]	No	1″ split rings.	19.95	[1]All popular rifles including Sav. 99. Uses Weaver bases. [2]Allows use of open sights. [3]For 22 rimfire rifles, with grooved receivers or bases. [4]Fits 13 models. Broadest view area of the type. [5]Side mount for both M94 and M94-375 Big Bore.
Mod. 101, & 336[2]	No	1″ split rings.	19.95	
Broad-View[4]	No	1″	19.95	
Model 22[3]	No	¾″, ⅞″, 1″	11.95	
94 Winchester[5]	No	1″	19.95	
Conetrol				
Huntur[1]	W only	1″, 26mm, 26.5mm solid or split rings, 3 heights.	59.91	[1]All popular rifles, including metric-drilled foreign guns. Price shown for base, two rings. Matte finish. [2]Gunnur grade has mirror-finished rings, satin-finish base. Price shown for base, two rings. [3]Custum grade has mirror-finished rings and mirror-finished, streamlined base. Price shown for base, 2 rings. [4]Win. 94, Krag, older split-bridge Mannlicher-Schoenauer, Mini-14, etc. Prices same as above. [5]For all popular guns with integral mounting provision, including Sako, BSA, Ithacagun, Ruger, H&K, BRNO—$29.37-$44.37—and many others. Also for grooved-receiver rimfires and air rifles. Prices same as above. [6]For XP-100, T/C Contender, Colt SAA, Ruger Blackhawk, S&W. [7]Sculptured 2-piece bases as found on fine custom rifles. Price shown is for base alone. Also available unfinished—$74.91. [8]30mm rings made in projectionless style, medium height only. Three-ring mount available for T/C Contender pistol, in Conetrol's three grades.
Gunnur[2]	W only	1″, 26mm, 26.5mm solid or split rings, 3 heights.	74.91	
Custum[3]	W only	1″, 26mm, 26.5mm solid or split rings, 3 heights.	89.91	
One Piece Side Mount Base[4]	W only	1″, 26mm, 26.5mm solid or split rings, 3 heights.	—	
Daptar Bases[5]	W only	1″, 26mm, 26.5mm solid or split rings, 3 heights.	—	
Pistol Bases, 2 or 3-ring[6]	W only	1″ scopes.	—	
Fluted Bases[7]	W only	Standard Conetrol rings	99.99	
30mm Rings[8]	W only	30mm	49.98-69.96	

CAUTION: PRICES CHANGE, CHECK AT GUNSHOP.

SCOPE MOUNTS

Maker, Model, Type	Adjust.	Scopes	Price	Suitable for
EAW				[1]Also 30mm rings to fit Redfield or Leupold-type bases, low and high, **$104**; 1" or 26mm rings only, **$89**. Most popular rifles. Elevation adjusted with variable-height sub-bases for rear ring. Imported by Del Sports, Inc., Paul Jaeger, Inc.
Quick Detachable Top Mount[1]	W&E	1"/26mm	224.95	
	W&E	1"/26mm with front extension ring.	224.95	
	W&E	30mm	224.95	
	W&E	30mm with front extension ring.	224.95	
Griffin & Howe				All popular models (Garand **$215**). All rings **$75**. Top ejection rings available. Price installed for side mount.
Standard Double Lever (S)	No	1" or 26mm split rings.	305.00	
Holden				[1]Most popular rifles including Ruger Mini-14, H&R M700, and muzzleloaders. Rings have oval holes to permit use of iron sights. [2]For 1" dia. scopes. [3]For ¾" or ⅞" dia. scopes. [4]For 1" dia. extended eye relief scopes. [5]702—Browning A-Bolt; 709—Marlin 39A. [6]732—Ruger 77/22 R&RS, No. 1 Ranch Rifle; 777 fits Ruger 77R, RS. Both 732, 777 fit Ruger integral bases. [7]Fits most popular blackpowder rifles; one model for Holden Ironsighter mounts, one for Weaver rings. Adj. rear sight is integral.
Wide Ironsighter®	No	1" split rings.	26.95	
Ironsighter Center Fire[1]	No	1" split rings.	26.95	
Ironsighter S-94	No	1" split rings.	31.95	
Ironsighter 22 cal. rimfire				
Model #550[2]	No	1" split rings.	14.95	
Model #600[3]	No	⅞" split rings also fits ¾".	14.95	
Series #700[5]	No	1" split rings.	26.95	
Model 732, 777[6]	No	1" split rings.	56.95	
Ironsighter Handguns[4]	No	1" split rings.	31.95	
Blackpowder Mount[7]	No	1"	29.95	
Jaeger				All popular models. From Paul Jaeger, Inc.
QD, with windage (S)	W only	1", 3 heights.	250.00	
Kimber				[1]High rings and low rings. For either Kimber grooved receivers or other popular rifles using Kimber two-piece screw-on bases. Non-detachable. Vertically split rings. [2]One height for Kimber grooved receiver or other rifles using Kimber screw-on bases. Vertically split. Quick detachable.
Deluxe[1]	No	1" split rings.	79.95	
Double Lever Q.D.	No	1" split rings.	109.95	
Kris Mounts				[1]One-piece mount for Win. 94. [2]Most popular rifles and Ruger. [3]Blackhawk revolver. Mounts have oval hole to permit use of iron sights.
Side-Saddle[1]	No	1", 26mm split rings.	12.98	
Two Piece (T)[2]	No	1", 26mm split rings.	8.98	
One Piece (T)[3]	No	1", 26mm split rings.	12.98	
KWIK MOUNT				Wrap-around design; no gunsmithing required. Models for Browning BPS, A-5 12 ga., Sweet 16, 20, Rem. 870/1100 (LTW and L.H.), S&W 916, Mossberg 500, Ithaca 37 & 51 12 ga., S&W 1000/3000, Win. 1400. From KenPatable Ent.
Shotgun Mount	No	1", laser on red dot device.	49.95	
Kwik-Site				[1]Most rifles. Allows use of iron sights. [2]22-cal. rifles with grooved receivers. Allows use of iron sights. [3]Model 94, 94 Big Bore. No drilling or tapping. Also in adjustble model **$49.95**. [4]Most rifles. One-piece solid construction. Use on Weaver bases. 32mm obj. lens or larger. [5]Non-see-through model; for grooved receivers. [6]Allows Mag Lite or C or D, Mini Mag Lites to be mounted atop See-Thru mounts. [7]Fits any Redfield, Tasco, Weaver or universal-style dovetail base. Bright blue, black matte or satin finish. Standard, high heights. [8]Integral one-piece base and ring. [9]Detachable.
KS-See-Thru[1]	No	1"	21.95	
KS-22 See-Thru[2]	No	1"	18.95	
KS-W94[3]	No	1"	30.95	
KSM Bench Rest[4]	No	1"	30.95	
KS-WEV	No	1"	21.95	
KS-WEV-HIGH	No	1"	21.95	
KS-T22 1"[5]	No	1"	18.95	
KS-FLM Flashlite[6]	No	Mini or C cell flashlight	49.95	
KS-T88[7]	No	1", 30mm	9.75	
Imperial[8]	No	1"	30.95	
Combo Bases & Rings[9]	—	1"	26.75	
Laserscope	No	Laserscope	37.95 to 99.50	Mounts Laserscope above or below barrel. For most popular military-type rifles, UZI, H&K submachine guns, Desert Eagle pistols. From Laser Devices, Inc.
Laser Aim	No	Laser Aim	37.00 to 133.35	Mounts Laser Aim above or below barrel. Avail. for most popular handguns, rifles, shotguns, including militaries. From Emerging Technologies, Inc.
Lasersight	No	LS45 only	29.95 to 149.00	For the LS45 Lasersight. Allows LS45 to be mounted alongside any 1" scope. Universal adapter attaches to any full-length Weaver-type base. For most popular military-type rifles, Mossberg, Rem. shotguns, Python, Desert Eagle, S&W N frame, Colt 45ACP. From Imatronic Lasersight.
Leupold				[1]Rev. front and rear combinations. [2]Avail. polished, matte or silver (low, med. only) finish. [3]Base and two rings; Casull, Ruger, S&W, T/C; add **$5.00** for silver finish. [4]Rem. 700, Win. 70-type actions. [5]For Ruger No. 1, 77/22; interchangeable with Ruger units. [6]For dovetailed rimfire rifles. [7]Sako; high, medium, low. [8]Must be drilled, tapped for each action. [9]Unfinished bottom, top completed; sold singly. [10]Fit all Leupold STD one-, two-piece bases.
Alaskan Rings[10]		⅞"	32.00	
STD Bases[1]	W only	One- or two-piece bases	22.10	
STD Rings[2]		1" Super low, low, medium, high	32.00	
STD Handgun mounts[3]	No		56.40	
Dual Dovetail Bases[1,4]	No		22.10	
Dual Dovetail Rings		1", Super low, low	32.00	
Ring Mounts[5,6,7]	No	1"	81.10	
Gunmaker Base[8]	W only	1"	14.60	
Gunmaker Ring Blanks[9]		1"	21.10	

SCOPE MOUNTS

Maker, Model, Type	Adjust.	Scopes	Price	Suitable for
Leatherwood				
Bridge Bases[1]	No	ART II or all dovetail rings	15.00	[1]Many popular bolt actions. Mounts accept Weaver or dovetail-type rings. From North American Specialties.
M1A/M-14 Q.D.	No	ART II or all dovetail rings.	105.00	
AR-15/M-16 Base	No	ART II or all dovetail rings.	25.00	
FN-FAL Base	No	ART II or all dovetail rings.	100.00	
FN Para. Base	No	ART II or all dovetail rings.	110.00	
Steyr SSG Base	No	ART II or all dovetail rings.	55.00	
Marlin				
One Piece QD (T)	No	1" split rings	14.95	Most Marlin lever actions.
Millett				
Black Onyx Smooth		1", low, medium, high	29.65	Rem. 40X, 700, 722, 725, Ruger 77 (round top), Weatherby, FN Mauser, FN Brownings, Colt 57, Interarms MkX, Parker-Hale, Sako (round receiver), many others. [1]Fits Win. M70, 70XTR, 670, Browning BBR, BAR, BLR, A-Bolt, Rem. 7400/7600, Four, Six, Marlin 336, Win. 94 A.E., Sav. 110. [2]To fit Weaver-type bases. Also for Colt, Dan Wesson, Ruger handguns—$44.95-$77.95. Avail. for Scope-Site (fixed, $44.95, or adjustable, $77.95.) Universal Bases also for Browning BAR, BLR, A-Bolt, Rem. 7400, 7600, Marlin 336, Win. 94 AE, Savage 110. [3]Engraved. Smooth $30.65. [4]For Rem. 870, 1100; smooth. [5]Two and three-ring sets for Colt Python, Trooper, Diamondback, Peacekeeper, Dan Wesson, Ruger Redhawk, Super Redhawk.
Chaparral Engraved		Engraved	43.95	
Universal Two Piece Bases				
700 Series	W only	Two-piece bases	23.95	
FN Series	W only	Two-piece bases	23.95	
70 Series[1]	W only	1", two-piece bases	23.95	
Angle-Loc[2] Rings	W only	1", low, medium, high	44.95-77.95	
Ruger 77 Rings[3]	—	1"	44.95	
Shotgun Rings[4]	—	1"	29.65	
Handgun Bases, Rings[5]	—	1"	32.95-61.35	
R.A.T.	No.	1"	14.95	Allow mounting scopes, dot sights on vent. rib shotguns. Also for Rem. and Hastings slug barrels ($19.95). From Autumn Tracker Design.
Ram-Line				
Mini-14 Mount	Yes	1"	$24.97	No drilling or tapping. Use std. dovetail rings. Has built-in shell deflector. Made of solid black polymer. From Ram-Line, Inc.
Redfield				
JR-SR (T)[1]	W only	¾", 1", 26mm, 30mm	JR—20.95-52.95 SR—20.95-39.95	[1]Low, med & high, split rings. Reversible extension front rings for 1". 2-piece bases for Sako. Colt Sauer bases $39.85. Med. Top Access JR rings nickel-plated, $29.95. SR two-piece ABN mount nickel-plated, $23.95. [2]Split rings for grooved 22s. See-Thru mounts $16.95. [3]Used with MP scopes for: S&W K or N frame, XP-100, Colt J or I frame, T/C Contender, Colt autos, blackpowder rifles. [4]One- and two-piece aluminum base; three ring heights. [5]For Ruger Model 77 rifles, medium and high; medium only for M77/22. [6]For Model 77. Also in matte finish, $44.95. [7]Nickel-plated, $30.95. Shotgun MAGMOUNT—Any Weaver-style mount system. Fits most vent. rib shotguns, incl. SxS and O/U. Pumps, autos use extended eye relief scopes; SxS, O/Us use std. rifle scopes. Pistol MAGMOUNT—Clamps onto most handguns; no gunsmithing; uses Weaver-style bases. M/L MAGMOUNT—Fits T/C, Lyman, CVA rifles, others with 1", 15/16" or 7/8" octagon bbl. flats; no gunsmithing.
Ring (T)[2]	No	¾" and 1"	27.95	
Double Dovetail MP[3]	No	1" split rings	58.95	
Midline Base & Rings[4]	No	1"	13.95	
Widefield See-Thru Mounts[4]	No	1"	16.95	
Ruger Rings[5]	No	1", med., high	32.95	
Ruger 30mm[6]	No	1"	43.95	
Midline Ext. Rings	No	1"	18.95	
Steel "WS" Rings[7]	W	1"	24.95	
MAGMOUNT				
Shotgun	No	1"	36.95	
Pistol	No	1"	50.95	
Muzzleloader	No	1"	39.95	
S&K				
Insta-Mount (T) bases and rings[1]	W only	Use S&K rings only	25.00-99.00	[1]1903, A3, M1 Carbine, Lee Enfield #1, MK. III, #4, #5, M1917, M98 Mauser, FN Auto, AR-15, AR-180, M-14, M-1, Ger. K-43, Mini-14, M1-A, Krag, AKM, AK-47, Win. 94, SKS Type 56, Daewoo, H&K. [2]Most popular rifles already drilled and tapped. Horizontally and vertically split rings, matte or high gloss.
Conventional rings and bases[2]	W only	1" split rings	From 50.00	
Skulptured Bases, Rings[2]	W only	1", 26mm, 30mm	From 50.00	
SSK Industries				
T'SOB	No	1"	55.00-145.00	Custom installation using from two to four rings (included). For T/C Contender, most 22 auto pistols, Ruger and other S.A. revolvers, Ruger, Dan Wesson, S&W, Colt DA revolvers. Black or white finish. Uses Kimber rings in two- or three-ring sets. In blue or SSK Khrome. For T/C Contender or most popular revolvers. Standard, non-detachable model also available, from $125.00.
Quick Detachable	No	1"	From 160.00	
Sako				
QD Dovetail	W only	1" only	41.50-49.00	Sako, or any rifle using Sako action, 3 heights available. Stoeger, importer.
Simmons				
1460[1]	No	1"	17.95	[1]Browning Auto. [2]Marlin 336, 444, 36, 62, Glenfield 30. [3]Rem. 700 SA/Seven. [4]Rem. 700 L.A. [5]Win. 70A. [6]Sav. 110. [7]Rem. 870, 1100, 11-87. [8]Rem. Seven, 700 LA/SA; two-piece, med. rings. [9]Rem. Four, Six, 7400/7600, two-piece, med. rings. [10]Win. 70A LA/SA, two-piece, med. rings. [11]Sav. 110, two-piece, med. rings. From Simmons.
1462[2]	No	1"	17.95	
1465[3]	No	1"	17.95	
1466[4]	No	1"	17.95	
1469[5]	No	1"	17.95	
1471[6]	No	1"	17.95	
21000[7]	No	1"	36.95	
SRB01[8]	No	1"	41.95	
SRB02[9]	No	1"	41.95	
SRB04[10]	No	1"	41.95	
SRB08[11]	No	1"	41.95	

CAUTION: PRICES CHANGE, CHECK AT GUNSHOP.

Maker, Model, Type	Adjust.	Scopes	Price	Suitable for
Tasco				[1]Many popular rifles. [2]For 22s with grooved receivers. [3]Most popular rifles. [4]"Quick Peep" 1" ring mount; fits all 22-cal. rifles with grooved receivers. [5]For Ruger Mini-14; also in brushed aluminum. [6]Side mount for Win. 94. [7]Side mount rings and base for Win. 94 in 30-30, 375 Win. [8]Avail. for most rifles. Steel or aluminum rings. Contact Tasco for details on complete line.
791 and 793 series[1]	No	1", regular or high	9.75	
797[2]	No	Split rings	9.75	
799[4]	No	1" only	9.75	
885 BK[7]	No	1" only	16.00	
895[6]	No	1" only	9.60	
896[5]	No	1" only	44.00	
800L Series (with base)[3]	No	1" only. Rings and base	12.40	
World Class[8]				
Steel Bases	Yes	1", 26mm, 30mm	20.00-35.20	
Steel Rings	Yes	1", 26mm	49.95	
Steel 30mm Rings	Yes	30mm	65.95	
Thompson/Center				[1]All Contenders except vent. rib. [2]T/C rail mount scopes; all Contenders except vent. rib. [3]All S&W K and Combat Masterpiece, Hi-Way Patrolman, Outdoorsman, 22 Jet, 45 Target 1955. Requires drilling, tapping. [4]Blackhawk, Super Blackhawk, Super Single-Six. Requires drilling, tapping. [5]45 or 50 cal.; replaces rear sight. [6]Rail mount scopes; 54-cal. Hawken, 50, 54, 56-cal. Renegade. Replaces rear sight. [7]Cherokee 32 or 45 cal., Seneca 36 or 45 cal. Replaces rear sight. Carbine mount #9743 for Short Tube scope #8640, $11.50. [8]For T/C "Short Tube" scope #8630; matte blue; also #9710 base for std. scope; no gunsmithing. [9]Also silver finish, $45.00. [10]For Contender Carbine, pistol, Scout; silver finish, $38.00. [11]For Contender pistol, Carbine, Scout, all M/L long guns.
Contender 9746[1]	No	T/C Lobo	15.50	
Contender 9741[2]	No	2½, 4 RP	15.50	
Contender 7410	No	Bushnell Phantom, 1.3x2.5x	15.50	
S&W 9747[3]	No	Lobo or RP	15.50	
Ruger 9748[4]	No	Lobo or RP	15.50	
Hawken 9749[5]	No	Lobo or RP	15.50	
Hawken/Renegade 9754[6]	No	Lobo or RP	15.50	
Cherokee/Seneca 9756[7]	No	Lobo or RP	15.50	
New Englander 9757	No	Lobo or RP	33.95	
TCR '87 Base 9760[8]	Yes	1"	41.50	
Detachable Rings[9]	No	1"	33.95	
T/C Base[10]	Yes	1"	Rings 42.00 Base 18.50	
Quick Release System[11]	No	1"		
Unertl				[1]Unertl target or varmint scopes. Posa or standard mounts, less bases.
¼ Click[1]	Yes	¾", 1" target scopes	Per set 100.00	
Weaver				[1]Nearly all modern rifles. Low, med., high. 1" extension $29.49. 1" med. stainless steel $38.60. [2]Nearly all modern rifles, shotguns. [3]Most modern big-bore rifles; std., high. [4]22s with ⅜" grooved receivers. [5]Nearly all modern rifles. 1" See-Thru extension $28.06. [6]Most modern big bore rifles. [7]No drilling, tapping. For Colt Python, Trooper, 357, Officer's Model, Ruger Blackhawk & Super, Mini-14, Security-Six, 22 auto pistols, Redhawk, Blackhawk SRM 357, S&W current K, L with adj. sights. [8]For Rem. 870/1100, Mossberg 500. No gunsmithing. [9]For some popular sporting rifles. [10]Dovetail design mount for Rem. 700, Win. 70, FN Mauser, low, med., high rings; std., extension bases. From Weaver.
Detachable Mounts				
Top Mount[1]	No	1"	26.42	
		⅞"	25.39	
Side Mount[2]	No	1"	27.94	
		1"	33.01	
		1" Long	35.80	
Pivot Mount[3]	No	1"	20.31	
Tip-Off Mount[4]	No	⅞"	25.90	
		1"		
See-Thru Mount				
Traditional[6]	No	1"	NA	
Symmetrical[6]	No	1"	NA	
Detachable[5]	No	1"	26.42	
Tip-Off[4]	No	1", ⅞"	19.05	
Pro View[6]	No	1"	NA	
Mount Base System[7]				
Blue Finish	No	1"	68.69	
Stainless Finish	No	1"	96.11	
Shotgun Mount System[8]	No	1"	68.69	
Rifle Mount System[9]	No	1"	30.48	
Imperial Mount Systems[10]				
Bases, pair	Yes	1"	23.61	
Rings, pair	No	1"	30.64	
Wideview				Models for many popular rifles—$14.95. Low ring, high ring and grooved receiver types. From Wideview Scope Mount Corp.
WSM-22	No	1"	14.95	
WSM-94	No	1"	24.95	
WSM-94AE	No	1"	22.95	
Premium See-Thru	No	1"	20.95	
22 Premium See-Thru	No	¾", 1"	14.95	
Universal Ring Angle Cut	No	1"	22.95	
Universal Ring Straight Cut	No	1"	20.95	
Solid Mounts				
Lo Ring Solid	No	1"	14.95	
Hi Ring Solid	No	1"	14.95	
Williams				[1]Most rifles, Br. S.M.L.E. (round rec.) $3.85 extra. [2]Same. [3]Most rifles including Win. 94 Big Bore. [4]Many modern rifles. [5]Most popular rifles.
Offset (S)[1]	No	⅞", 1", 26mm solid, split or extension rings	62.40	
QC (T)[2]	No	Same	45.00	
QC (S)[3]	No	Same	51.40	
Sight-Thru[4]	No	1", ⅞" sleeves $3.20.	21.00	
Streamline[5]	No	1" (bases form rings).	21.00	
York				Centers scope over the action. No drilling, tapping or gunsmithing. Uses standard dovetail rings. From York M-1 Conversions.
M-1 Garand	Yes	1"	39.95	

(S)—Side Mount   (T)—Top Mount   22mm = .866"   25.4mm = 1.024"   26.5mm = 1.045"   30mm = 1.81"

CAUTION: PRICES CHANGE, CHECK AT GUNSHOP.

SPOTTING SCOPES

Kowa TSN-1 45°.

Mirador TTB Draw Tube scopes.

Redfield Waterproof Spotter.

BAUSCH & LOMB DISCOVERER—15x to 60x zoom, 60mm objective. Constant focus throughout range. Field at 1000 yds. 40 ft (60x), 156 ft. (15x). Comes with lens caps. Length 17½", wgt. 47¼ oz.
  Price: **$422.95**
BAUSCH & LOMB ELITE—22x fixed or 15x to 45x zoom, 60mm objective. Field at 1000 yds. 120 ft. (fixed), 119-62 ft. (zoom). Length is 11.8" (fixed), 12.1" (zoom); weight 21.5 oz. (fixed), 22.5 oz. (zoom). Tripod mount. Comes with black case.
  Price: Fixed **$575.95**
  Price: Zoom **$719.95**
BUSHNELL SPACEMASTER II—70mm objective. Field at 1000 yds., 158-37 ft. Relative brightness, 5.76. Wgt., 50 oz. Length closed, 13", prism focusing.
  Price: Without eyepiece **$384.95**
  Price: 15x, 20x, 40x and 60x eyepieces, each **$68.95**
  Price: 22x wide angle eyepiece **$89.95**
BUSHNELL ZOOM SPACEMASTER II—15x-45x zoom. 70mm objective. Field at 1000 yards 130-65 ft. Relative brightness 9-1.7. Wgt. 53 oz., length 14". Shooter's stand tripod, carrying case.
  Price: **$586.95**
BUSHNELL COMPETITOR—40mm objective, 20x. Prismatic. Field at 1000 yards 140 ft. Minimum focus 33 ft. Length 10", weight 14.5 oz.
  Price: **$133.95**
BUSHNELL COMPACT COMPETITOR—20x, 40mm objective. Field at 1000 yds. 141 ft. Focuses down to 33 ft. for indoor use. Tripod mount. Length 10.5"; weight 14.5 oz.
  Price: **$133.95**
BUSHNELL SPACEMASTER—15x-45x zoom. Rubber armored, prismatic. 60mm objective. Field at 1000 yards 110-65 ft. Minimum focus 20 ft. Length with caps 11.6", weight 36 oz.
  Price: With tripod and carrying case. **$533.95**
  Price: Interchangeable eyepieces—15x, 20x, 22x, 25x, 60x, each **$68.95**
  Price: 15-36x zoom eyepiece **$178.95**
  Price: Fogproof, waterproof model, 15x-45x zoom; wgt. 38 oz. .. **$900.95**
BUSHNELL STALKER—10x to 30x zoom, 50mm objective. Field at 1000 yds. 142 ft. (10x) to 86 ft. (30x). Length 10.5"; weight 18 oz. Camo armored. Comes with tripod.
  Price: **$422.95**
KOWA TSN-1-45°—Off-set-type. 77mm objective, 25x, fixed and zoom eyepieces; field at 1000 yds. 94 ft.; relative brightness 9.6; length 15.4"; wgt. 48.8 oz. Lens shade and caps. Straight-type (TSN-2) also available with similar specs and prices.
  Price: **$699.90**
  Price: 20x-60x zoom eyepiece **$199.95**
  Price: 20x eyepiece (wide angle) **$169.95**
  Price: 25x, 40x eyepiece **$99.95, $119.95**
  Price: 25x LER eyepiece **$159.95**

KOWA TS-6—Compact straight-type. 60mm objective, 25x fixed power eyepiece; field at 1000 yards 93 ft.; relative brightness 5.8; length 12.5"; weight 25 oz. Lens shade and caps included. Off-set type also available (TS-7).
  Price: **$413.90**
  Price: 25x eyepiece **$75.95**
  Price: 20x eyepiece (wide angle) **$85.95**
  Price: 40x eyepiece **$75.95**
  Price: 25x LER eyepiece **$139.95**
KOWA TS-601—45° off-set type. 60mm multi-coated objective, 25x fixed and zoom eyepieces; field at 1000 yards 93 ft.; relative brightness 5.8; length 14.8"; weight 37 oz. Comes with lens shade and caps. Straight-type also available (TS-602).
  Price: **$479.90**
  Price: 25x eyepiece **$83.95**
  Price: 20x eyepiece (wide angle) **$97.95**
  Price: 40x eyepiece **$87.95**
  Price: 25x-60x zoom eyepiece **$179.95**
  Price: 25x LER eyepiece **$159.95**
KOWA TS-9C—Straight-type. 50mm objective, 20x compact model; fixed power eyepieces; objective focusing down to 17 ft.; field at 1000 yds. 157 ft.; relative brightness 6.3; length 9.65"; wgt. 22.9 oz. Lens caps.
  Price: **$169.95**
  Price: 15x, 20x eyepieces, each **$28.95**
  Price: 11x-33x zoom eyepiece **$102.95**
  Price: As above, rubber armored (TS-9R) **$269.95**
LEUPOLD 20x50 COMPACT—50mm objective, 20x. Field at 100 yards 11.5 ft.; eye relief 1"; length 9.4"; weight 20.5 oz.
  Price: Armored model **$515.50**
  Price: Packer Tripod **$73.60**
LEUPOLD 25x50 COMPACT—50mm objective, 25x. Field at 100 yds. 8.3 ft.; eye relief 1"; length overall 9.4"; weight 20.5 oz.
  Price: Armored model **$544.50**
  Price: Armored, with reticle **$573.40**
  Price: Packer Tripod **$73.60**
LEUPOLD 30x60 COMPACT—60mm objective, 30x. Field at 100 yds. 6.4 ft.; eye relief 1"; length over-all 12.9"; weight 26 oz.
  Price: Armored model **$573.40**
  Price: Packer Tripod **$73.60**
MIRADOR TTB SERIES—Draw tube armored spotting scopes. Available with 75mm or 80mm objective. Zoom model (28x-62x, 80mm) is 11⅞" (closed), weighs 50 oz. Field at 1000 yds. 70-42 ft. Comes with lens covers.
  Price: 28-62x80mm **$908.95**
  Price: 32x80mm **$773.95**
  Price: 26-58x75mm **$791.95**
  Price: 30x75mm **$656.95**

CAUTION: PRICES CHANGE, CHECK AT GUNSHOP.

MIRADOR SSD SPOTTING SCOPES—60mm objective, 15x, 20x, 22x, 25x, 40x, 60x, 20-60x; field at 1000 yds. 37 ft.; length 10¼"; weight 33 oz.

Price: 25x $512.95
Price: 22x Wide Angle $521.95
Price: 20-60x Zoom $656.95
Price: As above, with tripod, case $845.95

MIRADOR SIA SPOTTING SCOPES—Similar to the SSD scopes except with 45° eyepiece. Length of 12¼", weight 39 oz.

Price: 25x $647.95
Price: 22x Wide Angle $656.95
Price: 20-60x Zoom $791.95

MIRADOR SSA SPOTTING SCOPES—Lightweight, slender version of the SSD series with 50mm objective. Length 11⅛", weight 28 oz.

Price: 20x $368.95
Price: 18x Wide Angle $377.95
Price: 16-48x Zoom $512.95

MIRADOR SSR SPOTTING SCOPES—50mm objective. Similar to SSD except rubber armored in black or camouflage. Length 11⅛", weight 31 oz.

Price: Black, 20x $413.95
Price: Black, 18x Wide Angle $422.95
Price: Black, 16-48x Zoom $557.95
Price: Camouflage, 20x $422.95
Price: Camouflage, 18x Wide Angle $431.95
Price: Camouflage, 16-48x Zoom $566.95

MIRADOR SSF FIELD SCOPES—Fixed or variable power, choice of 50mm, 60mm, 75mm objective lens. Length 9¾", weight 20 oz. (15-32x50).

Price: 20x50mm $269.95
Price: 25x60mm $323.95
Price: 30x75mm $377.95
Price: 15-32x50mm Zoom $422.95
Price: 18-40x60mm Zoom $476.95
Price: 22-50x75mm Zoom $530.95

MIRADOR SRA MULTI ANGLE SCOPES—Similar to SSF Series except eyepiece head rotates for viewing from any angle.

Price: 20x50mm $422.95
Price: 25x60mm $476.95
Price: 30x75mm $530.95
Price: 15-32x50mm Zoom $575.95
Price: 18-40x60mm Zoom $629.95
Price: 22-50x75mm Zoom $683.95

MIRADOR SIB FIELD SCOPES—Short-tube, 45° scopes with porro-prism design. 50mm and 60mm objective. Length 10¼", weight 18.5 oz. (15-32x50mm); field at 1000 yds. 129-81 ft.

Price: 20x50mm $341.95
Price: 25x60mm $395.95
Price: 15-32x50mm Zoom $494.95
Price: 18-40x60mm Zoom $548.95

NICHOLS "BACKPACKER" COMPACT—25x, 50mm objective. Field at 1000 yds. 101.2 ft. Overall length 8.76", weight 20.6 oz. Gray finish. Comes with tripod.

Price: $130.50

NICHOLS "GRANDSLAM"—25x, 50mm objective. Field at 1000 yds. 91.6 ft. Overall length 12.2", weight 24.7 oz. Gray finish. Comes with tripod.

Price: $212.00
Price: 17x-52x Zoom, with 25x lens, tripod $369.00

REDFIELD 25x WATERPROOF SPOTTER—60mm objective, 25x fixed power. Black rubber armor coat. Field at 1000 yds. 100 ft. Length 12.5", weight 24 oz. Comes with lens covers, vinyl carrying case.

Price: $414.95

REDFIELD 30x CAT SPOTTER—60mm objective, 30x. Field of view 9.5 ft. at 100 yds. Uses catadioptric lens system. Length overall is 7.5", weight is 11.5 oz. Eye relief 0.5".

Price: With Armor Camouflage $465.95

REDFIELD REGAL II—Regal II has 60mm objective, interchangeable 25x and 18x-40x zoom eyepieces. Field at 1000 yds.—125 ft. @ 25x. Dual rotation of eyepiece and scope body. With aluminum carrying case, tripod.

Price: $716.95

REDFIELD REGAL IV—Conventional straight thru viewing. Regal IV has 60mm objective and interchangeable 25x and 20x-60x zoom eyepieces. Field at 1000 yds.—94 ft. @ 25x. With tripod and aluminum carrying case.

Price: Regal IV with black rubber Armorcoat $753.95

REDFIELD REGAL VI—60mm objective, 25x fixed and 20x-60x interchangeable eyepieces. Has 45° angled eyepiece, front-mounted focus ring, 180° tube rotation. Field at 1000 yds., 94 ft. @ 25x; length, 12¼"; weight, 40 oz. Comes with tripod, aluminum carrying case.

Price: Regal VI $791.95

SIMMONS 1210—50mm objective, 25x standard, 17x, 35x, 52x, 17-52x zoom eyepieces available. Field at 1000 yds. 22 ft. Length 12.2", weight 32 oz. Comes with tripod, 3x finder scope with crosshair.

Price: About $246.95
Price: Fixed eyepieces $75.95
Price: Zoom eyepieces $187.95

SIMMONS 1215—50mm objective, 25x standard, 17x, 35x, 52x, 17-52x zoom eyepieces available. Field at 1000 yds. 22 ft. Length 12.2", weight 48 oz. Comes with tripod, 3x finder scope with crosshair. Green camo rubber.

Price: About $394.95
Price: Fixed eyepieces $75.95
Price: Zoom eyepiece $187.95

SIMMONS 1220—60mm objective, 25x standard, 17x, 35x, 52x, 17-52x zoom eyepieces available. Field at 1000 yds. 22 ft. Length 13.8", weight 44 oz. with tripod (included). Has 3x finder scope with crosshairs.

Price: About $474.95
Price: Fixed eyepieces $75.95
Price: Zoom eyepiece $187.95

SIMMONS 1221—56.5mm objective, 20x. Has built-in electronic finder scope that requires two AAA batteries. Field at 1000 yds. is 150 ft. Length 11½"; weight 33 oz.

Price: $524.95

SIMMONS 1299 15-60x ZOOM—60mm objective, 15-60x zoom. Field at 1000 yds. 156-40 ft. Slide-out sunshade. Has 3x finder scope. Photo adaptable and comes with a photo adapter tube for T-mount cameras. Black finish. Tripod not included.

Price: $524.95

SWAROVSKI HABICHT HAWK 30x75S TELESCOPE—75mm objective, 30x. Field at 1000 yds. 90 ft. Minimum focusing distance 90 ft. Length: closed 13", extended 20½". Weight 47 oz. Precise recognition of smallest details even at dusk. Leather or rubber covered, with caps and carrying case.

Price: $725.00

SWAROVSKI 25-40x75 TELESCOPE—75mm objective, variable power from 25x to 40x with a field of 98 ft. (25x) and 72 ft. (40x). Minimum focusing distance 66 ft. Length closed is 14.3", extended 21.7"; weight 46.8 oz. Rubber covered.

Price: Standard $1,000.00

SWIFT STALKER M838—40mm objective, 25x. Eye relief of 15mm. Field at 1000 yds. is 80 ft. Length is 10.25", weight with tripod 26.2 oz. Comes with low-level tripod, lens covers.

Price: $115.00

SWIFT TELEMASTER M841—60mm objective. 15x to 60x variable power. Field at 1000 yards 160 feet (15x) to 40 feet (60x). Wgt. 3.4 lbs. 17.6" overall.

Price: $399.50

SWIFT M700 SCOUT—9x-30x, 30mm spotting scope. Length 15½", weighs 2.1 lbs. Field of 204 ft. (9x), 60 ft. (30x).

Price: $145.00

SWIFT SEARCHER M839—60mm objective, 20x, 40x. Field at 1000 yds. 118 ft. (30x), 59 ft. (40x). Length 12.6", weight 3 lbs. Rotating eyepiece head for straight or 45-degree viewing.

Price: $398.00
Price: 30x, 50x eyepieces, each $45.00
Price: Tripod $38.00

TASCO 17EB SPOTTING SCOPE—60mm objective lens, 20-60x zoom with black metal tripod, micro-adjustable elevation control. Built-in sights.

Price: $219.95

TASCO 20EB SPOTTING SCOPE—50mm objective lens, 15-45x zoom. Field at 1000 yds. 95-42 ft.; includes tripod with pan-head lever. Built-in sights.

Price: $129.95

TASCO 34TZB RUBBER COVERED—50mm objective lens, 15-40x zoom. Field at 100 yards 12.6 to 7.9 ft. With tripod, weight 29.9 oz., length 13¾".

Price: $359.95

TASCO 9002T WORLD CLASS SPOTTING SCOPE—60mm objective lens, 15-60x zoom. Field at 1000 yds. 160 ft. @ 15x. Fully multi-coated optics, includes camera adaptor, camera case, tripod with pan-head lever.

Price: $549.95

UNERTL "FORTY-FIVE"—54mm objective. 20x (single fixed power). Field at 100 yds. 10'10"; eye relief 1"; focusing range infinity to 33 ft. Wgt. about 32 oz.; overall length 15¾". With lens covers.

Price: With multi-layer lens coating $370.00
Price: With mono-layer magnesium coating $290.00

UNERTL RIGHT ANGLE—63.5mm objective, 24x. Field at 100 yds., 7 ft. Relative brightness, 6.96. Eye relief, ½". Wgt., 41 oz. Length closed, 19". Push-pull and screw-focus eyepiece. 16x and 32x eyepieces **$50.00** each.

Price: $325.00

UNERTL STRAIGHT PRISMATIC—Same as Unertl Right Angle except straight eyepiece and wgt. of 40 oz.

Price: $280.00

UNERTL 20x STRAIGHT PRISMATIC—54mm objective, 20x. Field at 100 yds., 8.5 ft. Relative brightness, 6.1. Eye relief, ½". Wgt. 36 oz. Length closed, 13½". Complete with lens covers.

Price: $242.00

UNERTL TEAM SCOPE—100mm objective. 15x, 24x, 32x eyepieces. Field at 100 yds. 13 to 7.5 ft. Relative brightness, 39.06 to 9.79. Eye relief, 2" to 1½". Weight 13 lbs.; 29⅞" overall. Metal tripod, yoke and wood carrying case furnished (total weight, 80 lbs.)

Price: $1,400.00

PERIODICAL PUBLICATIONS

Action Digest (Q)
J. Fores Publications, P.O. Box 163001, Miami, FL 33116. $12 yr. Articles on shooting, self-defense, military history, survival, exotic weapons.

Action Pursuit Games Magazine (M)
CFW Enterprises, Inc., 4201 W. Vanowen Pl., Burbank, CA 91505. $2.95 single copy U.S., $3.50 Canada. World's leading magazine of paintball sports.

Airgun World
10 Sheet St., Windsor, Berks., SL4 1BG, England. £14.40 (£19.50 overseas) for 12 issues. Monthly magazine catering exclusively to the airgun enthusiast.

Airgunners Forum*
1804 E. Sprague St., Winston-Salem, NC 27107. $10.00 for 6 issues pr. year, $18.00 f. 2 yrs; outside U.S.A. $18.00 per yr. Newspaper-style with material for airgun enthusiasts, whether collectors, competitors or technicians.

Alaska Magazine
Alaska Publishing Properties Inc., 808 E St., Anchorage, AK 99501. $24.00 yr. Hunting, Fishing and Life on the Last Frontier articles of Alaska and western Canada.

American Airgunner (Q)
P.O. Box 711, Comanche, TX 76442. $15 yr. Anything and everything about airguns.

American Field†
222 W. Adams St., Chicago, IL 60606. $25.00 yr. Field dogs and trials, occasional gun and hunting articles.

American Firearms Industry
Nat'l. Assn. of Federally Licensed Firearms Dealers, 2801 E. Oakland Park Blvd., Ft. Lauderdale, FL 33306. $25.00 yr. For firearms retailers, distributors and manufacturers.

American Handgunner*
591 Camino de la Reina, Suite 200, San Diego, CA 92108. $14.75 yr. Articles for handgun enthusiasts, competitors, police and hunters.

American Hunter (M)
National Rifle Assn., 1600 Rhode Island Ave., N.W., Washington, DC 20036. $25.00 yr. Wide scope of hunting articles.

American Rifleman (M)
National Rifle Assn., 1600 Rhode Island Ave., N.W., Washington, DC 20036. Publications Div., 470 Spring Park Pl., Suite 1000, Herndon, VA 22070. $25.00 yr. Firearms articles of all kinds.

American Survival Guide
McMullen Publishing, Inc., 2145 West La Palma Ave., Anaheim, CA 92801. 12 issues $23.95/714-778-5773.

American West*
Amer. West Management Corp., 7000 E. Tanque Verde Rd., Suite #30, Tucson, AZ 85715. $15.00 yr.

Angler & Hunter
Ontario's Wildlife Magazine, P.O. Box 1541, Peterborough, Ont. K9J 7H7, Canada. $19.95 yr. Canada; all others $24.95 yr. for 10 issues (includes Canadian Hunting annual and Canadian Fishing annual).

Arms Collecting (Q)
Museum Restoration Service, P.O. Drawer 390, Bloomfield, Ont., Canada K0K 1G0 and P.O. Box 70, Alexandria Bay, NY 13607. $12.50 yr. $35.00 3 yrs. $60.00 5 yrs.

Australian Gunsports (Q)
Action Publishing Pty Ltd, P.O. Box 16, Alexandria, NSW 2015, Australia. $3.95 Aust. p. issue. Hunting, shooting articles.

Australian Shooters' Journal
Sporting Shooter's Assn. of Australia, P.O. Box 2066, Kent Town SA 5071, Australia. $40.00 yr. locally; $50.00 yr. overseas surface mail only. Hunting and shooting articles.

The Backwoodsman Magazine
P.O. Box 627, Westcliffe, CO 81252. $13.50 for 6 issues per yr., $25.00 for 2 yrs.; sample copy $2.50. Subject incl. muzzle-loading, woodslore, primitive survival, trapping, homesteading, blackpowder cartridge guns, 19th century how-to.

Black Powder Times
P.O. Box 842, Mount Vernon, WA 98273. $15.00 yr. Tabloid newspaper for blackpowder activities; test reports.

The Blade Magazine*
P.O. Box 22007, Chattanooga, TN 37422. $15.99 yr. Add $13.00 for foreign subscription. A magazine for all enthusiasts of the edged blade.

The Caller (Q) (M)
National Wild Turkey Federation, P.O. Box 530, Edgefield, SC 29824. Tabloid newsletter for members.

Combat Handguns*
Harris Publications, Inc., 1115 Broadway, New York, NY 10010. Single copy $2.95 U.S.A.; $3.25 Canada.

Deer Unlimited*
P.O. Box 1129, Abbeville, SC 29620. $12.00 yr.

Deutsches Waffen Journal
Journal-Verlag Schwend GmbH, Postfach 100340, D7170 Schwäbisch Hall, Germany. DM85.00 yr. plus DM16.80 for postage. Antique and modern arms. German text.

Ducks Unlimited, Inc. (M)
1 Waterfowl Way, Long Grove, IL 60047

The Field
6 Sheet Street, Windsor, Berkshire, SL4 1BG, England. £25.00 sterling U.S. (approx. $45.00) yr. Hunting and shooting articles, and all country sports.

Field & Stream
Times Mirror Magazines, Two Park Ave., New York, NY 10016. $11.94 yr. Articles on firearms plus hunting and fishing.

FIRE
Euro-Editions, Boulevard Du Triomphe 132, B1160 Brussels, Belgium. Belg. Franc 3000 for 11 issues. Arms, shooting, ammunition. French text.

The Fouling Shot*
Ralland J. Fortier, Director of Membership, 4103 Foxcraft Dr., Traverse City, MI 49684. Annual dues $12 include 6 issues. Official journal of the association.

Fur-Fish-Game
A.R. Harding Pub. Co., 2878 E. Main St., Columbus, OH 43209. $12.00 yr. "Gun Rack" column by Don Zutz.

Gray's Sporting Journal
Gray's Sporting Journal, Inc., On The Common, P.O. Box 130, Lyme, NH 03768. $34.95 per yr. for 6 consecutive issues. Hunting and fishing journals.

The Gun Report
World Wide Gun Report, Inc., Box 111, Aledo, IL 61231. $29.00 yr. For the antique and collectable gun dealer and collector.

The Gunrunner
Div. of Kexco Publ. Co. Ltd., Box 565G, Lethbridge, Alb., Canada T1J 3Z4. $20.00 yr. Monthly newspaper, listing everything from antiques to artillery.

Gun List
700 E. State St., Iola, WI 54990. $17.95 yr. (12 issues); $33.50 2 yrs.

Gun Show Calendar (Q)
700 E. State St., Iola, WI 54990. $12.95 yr. Gun shows listed chronologically by date, and alphabetically by state.

Gun Week†
Second Amendment Foundation, P.O. Box 488, Station C, Buffalo, NY 14209. $27.00 yr. U.S. and possessions; $33.00 yr. other countries. Tabloid paper on guns, hunting, shooting and collecting.

Gun World
Gallant Publishing Co., 34249 Camino Capistrano, Capistrano Beach, CA 92624. $20.00 yr. For the hunting, reloading and shooting enthusiast.

Guns & Ammo
Petersen Pub. Co., 8490 Sunset Blvd., Los Angeles, CA 90069. $19.94 yr. Guns, shooting, and technical articles.

Guns
Guns Magazine, P.O. Box 85201, San Diego, CA 92138. $19.95 yr. In-depth articles on a wide range of guns, shooting equipment and related accessories for gun collectors, hunters and shooters.

Guns Review
Ravenhill Pub. Co. Ltd., Box 35, Standard House, Bonhill St., London EC 2A 4DA, England. £15.60 sterling (approx. U.S. $33 USA & Canada) yr. For collectors and shooters.

Guns & Weapons*
Ink on Paper Publications, Suite A, Hill House, Hill Ave., Amersham, Bucks, England. UK shooting bi-monthly, write for info.

Handgun Quarterly (Q)
PJS Publications, News Plaza, P.O. Box 1790, Peoria, IL 61656. Cover price $3.95; subscriptions $17.95 for 6 issues. Various recreational uses of handguns; hunting, silhouette, practical pistol and target shooting.

Handloader*
Wolfe Pub. Co., 6471 Airpark Dr., Prescott, AZ 86301. $19.00 yr. The journal of ammunition reloading.

HUNT Magazine*
TimberLine-B, Inc., P.O. Box 58069, Renton, WA 98058. $11.97 yr.; Canadian and foreign countries add U.S. $8 for postage. Geared to the serious hunter, with action hunting articles.

The Insider Gun News
The Gunpress Publishing Co., 1347 Webster St. NE, Washington, DC 20017. Editor John D. Aquilino. $50.00 yr. (12 issues). Newsletter by former NRA communications director.

INSIGHTS*
NRA, 1600 Rhode Island Ave., N.W., Washington, DC 20036. Editor John E. Robbins. $10.00 yr., which includes NRA junior membership, $9.00 for adult subscriptions (12 issues). Plenty of details for the young hunter and target shooter; emphasizes gun safety.

International Shooting Sport*/UIT Journal
International Shooting Union (UIT), Bavariaring 21, D-8000 Munich 2, Fed. Rep. of Germany. Europe: (Deutsche Mark) DM44.00 yr.; outside Europe: DM50.00 yr. For international sport shooting.

The Journal of the Arms & Armour Society (M)
ARE North (Secy.), Dept. of Metalwork, Victoria and Albert Museum, London, England. $20.00 yr. Articles for the historian and collector.

Journal of the Historical Breechloading Smallarms Assn.
Publ. annually. Imperial War Museum, Lambeth Road, London SE1 6HZ, England. $8.00 yr. Articles for the collector plus mailings of lecture transcripts, short articles on specific arms, reprints, newsletters, etc.; a surcharge is made for airmail.

Knife World
Knife World Publications, P.O. Box 3395, Knoxville, TN 37927. $12.50 yr., $21.00 2 yrs. Published monthly for knife enthusiasts and collectors. Articles on custom and factory knives; other knife related interests.

Law and Order
Law and Order Magazine, 1000 Skokie Blvd., Wilmette, IL 60091. $17.00 yr. Articles for law enforcement professionals.

Man At Arms*
P.O. Box 460, Lincoln, RI 02865. $22.00 yr., plus $8.00 for foreign subscribers. The magazine of arms collecting-investing, with excellent brief articles for the collector of antique arms and militaria.

MAN/MAGNUM
S.A. Man (1982) (Pty) Ltd., P.O. Box 35204, Northway, Durban 4065, Rep. of South Africa. SA Rand 44.00 for 12 issues. Africa's only publication on hunting, shooting, firearms, bushcraft, knives, etc.

The Marlin Collector (M)
R.W. Paterson, 407 Lincoln Bldg., 44 Main St., Champaign, IL 61820.

Muzzle Blasts (M)
National Muzzle Loading Rifle Assn., P.O. Box 67, Friendship, IN 47021. $25.00 yr. For the blackpowder shooter.

Muzzleloader Magazine*
Rebel Publishing Co., Inc., Dept. Gun, Route 5, Box 347-M, Texarkana, TX 75501. $12.00 U.S., $15.00 U.S. for foreign subscribers a yr. The publication for blackpowder shooters.

National Defense (M)*
American Defense Preparedness Assn., Rosslyn Center, Suite 900, 1700 North Moore St., Arlington, VA 22209. $30.00 yr. Articles on military-related topics, including weapons, materials technology, management.

National Knife Magazine (M)
Natl. Knife Coll. Assn., 7201 Shallowford Rd., P.O. Box 21070, Chattanooga, TN 37421. Membership $24 yr, $64.00 International yr.

National Rifle Assn. Journal (British) (Q)
Natl. Rifle Assn. (BR.), Bisley Camp, Brookwood, Woking, Surrey, England. GU24, OPB. $25.00 including air postage.

National Wildlife*
Natl. Wildlife Fed., 1400 16th St. N.W., Washington, DC 20036, $15.00 yr. (6 issues); *International Wildlife*, 6 issues, $15.00 yr. Both, $20.00 yr., includes all membership benefits. Write attn.: Membership Services Dept., for more information.

New Zealand Wildlife (Q)
New Zealand Deerstalkers Assoc., Inc., P.O. Box 6514, Wellington, N.Z. $30.00 (N.Z.). Hunting, shooting and firearms/game research articles.

North American Hunter* (M)
P.O. Box 3401, Minnetonka, MN 55343. $18.00 yr. (6 issues). Articles on North American game hunting.

Outdoor Life
Times Mirror Magazines, Two Park Ave., New York, NY 10016. Special 1-yr. subscription, $9.97. Extensive coverage of hunting and shooting. Shooting column by Jim Carmichel.

PaintBall Magazine*
CFW Enterprises, Inc., 4201 W. Vanowen Place, Burbank, CA 91505. $3.00 single copy U.S., $3.50 Canada. The complete guide to airgun pursuit games.

Petersen's HUNTING Magazine
Petersen Publishing Co., 8490 Sunset Blvd., Los Angeles, CA 90069. $17.94 yr.; foreign countries $27.94 yr. Hunting articles for all game; test reports.

Point Blank
Citizens Committee for the Right to Keep and Bear Arms (sent to contributors), Liberty Park, 12500 NE 10th Pl., Bellevue, WA 98005

POINTBLANK
Natl. Firearms Assn., Box 1779, Edmonton, AB T5J 2P1, Canada. Official publication of the NFA.

The Police Marksman*
6000 E. Shirley Lane, Montgomery, AL 36117. $16.95 yr. For law enforcement personnel.

Police Times (M)
Membership Records, 1100 NE 125th St., No. Miami, FL 33161.

Popular Mechanics
Hearst Corp., 224 W. 57th St., New York, NY 10019. $15.94 yr. Firearms, camping, outdoors oriented articles.

Precision Shooting
Precision Shooting, Inc., 37 Burnham St., East Hartford, CT 06108. $20.00 yr. Journal of the International Benchrest Shooters, and target shooting in general. Also considerable coverage of varmint shooting.

Rifle*
Wolfe Publishing Co., 6471 Airpark Dr., Prescott, AZ 86301. $19.00 yr. The sporting firearms journal.

Rod & Rifle Magazine
Lithographic Serv. Ltd., P.O. Box 38-138, Petone, New Zealand. $50.00 yr. (6 issues). Hunting, shooting and fishing articles.

Safari* (M)
Safari Magazine, 4800 W. Gates Pass Rd., Tucson, AZ 85745/602-620-1220. $25.00 (6 times). The journal of big game hunting, published by Safari Club International.

Schweizer Waffen-Magazin
Orell Füssli Zeitschriften, Postfach, CH-8036 Zürich, Switzerland. SF 114.50 (approx. U.S. $73.90 air mail) for 10 issues. Modern and antique arms. German text.

Second Amendment Reporter
Second Amendment Fdn., James Madison Bldg., 12500 NE 10th Pl., Bellevue, WA 98005. $15.00 yr. (non-contributors).

Shooting Industry
Publisher's Dev. Corp., 591 Camino de la Reina, Suite 200, San Diego, CA 92108. $50.00 yr. To the trade $25.00.

Shooting Magazine
10 Sheet St., Windsor, Berks. SL4 1BG England. £16.80, or £22.50 overseas for 12 issues. Monthly journal for all shooters, with informed articles covering the whole shooting spectrum.

Shooting Sports Retailer*
SSR Publishing, Inc., P.O. Box 129, Chester, CT 06412/203-526-4770. 6 issues yr. Free to qualifying retailers, wholesalers, manufacturers, distributors; $24 annually for all other subscribers; $35 for foreign subscriptions; single copy $4.

The Shooting Times & Country Magazine (England)†
10 Sheet St., Windsor, Berkshire SL4 1BG, England. £54 (approx. $98.00) yr. (52 issues). Game shooting, wild fowling, hunting, game fishing and firearms articles.

Shooting Times
PJS Publications, News Plaza, P.O. Box 1790, Peoria, IL 61656. $15.97 yr. Guns, shooting, reloading; articles on every gun activity.

The Shotgun News‡
Snell Publishing Co., Box 669, Hastings, NE 68902. $18.00 yr.; all other countries $100.00 yr. Sample copy $3.00. Gun ads of all kinds.

Shotgun Sports
P.O. Box 6810, Auburn, CA 95603/916-889-2220.

Shotgun West
1253 7th St. #101, Santa Monica, CA 90401. $8.50 yr. Trap, Skeet and international shooting, scores; articles, schedules.

The Sixgunner (M)
Handgun Hunters International, P.O. Box 357, MAG, Bloomingdale, OH 43910

The Skeet Shooting Review
National Skeet Shooting Assn., P.O. Box 680007, San Antonio, TX 78268. $15.00 yr. (Assn. membership of $20.00 includes mag.) Competition results, personality profiles of top Skeet shooters, how-to articles, technical, reloading information.

Soldier of Fortune
Subscription Dept., P.O. Box 348, Mt. Morris, IL 61054. $26.00 yr.; $33.00 foreign.

Sporting Clays Magazine*
21 Airport Rd., Suite 21-J, Hilton Head Island, SC 29926. $24.00 yr. (6 issues).

Sporting Goods Business
Gralla Pub., 1515 Broadway, New York, NY 10036. Trade journal.

The Sporting Goods Dealer
1212 No. Lindbergh Blvd., St. Louis, MO 63132. $50.00 yr. Full-line sporting goods trade journal.

Sporting Gun
Bretton Court, Bretton, Peterborough PE3 8DZ, England. £20.00 (approx. U.S. $36.00), airmail £30.50 yr. For the game and clay enthusiasts.

Sports Afield
The Hearst Corp., 250 W. 55th St., New York, NY 10019. $13.97 yr. Grits Gresham on firearms, ammunition and Thomas McIntyre, Gerald Almy on hunting.

The Squirrel Hunter
P.O. Box 254, Hoskinston, KY 40844. $12.00 yr. Articles about squirrel hunting.

TACARMI
Via E. De Amicis, 25; 20123 Milano, Italy. $75.00 yr. approx. Antique and modern guns. (Italian text.)

Trap & Field
1000 Waterway Blvd., Indianapolis, IN 46202. $20.00 yr. Official publ. Amateur Trapshooting Assn. Scores, averages, trapshooting articles.

Turkey Call* (M)
Natl. Wild Turkey Federation, Inc., P.O. Box 530, Edgefield, SC 29824. $20.00 with membership (6 issues per yr.)

The U.S. Handgunner* (M)
U.S. Revolver Assn., 96 West Union St., Ashland, MA 01721. $6.00 yr. General handgun and competition articles. Bi-monthly sent to members.

VDB-Aktuell (Q)
GFI-Verlag, Theodor-Heuss-Ring 62, 5000 Köln 1, West Germany. For hunters, target shooters and outdoor people. (German text.)

Waterfowler's World*
P.O. Box 38306, Germantown, TN 38183. $14.00 yr.

Wild Sheep (M) (Q)
Foundation For North American Wild Sheep, 720 Allen Ave., Cody, WY 82414. Official journal of the foundation.

Women & Guns
P.O. Box 488, Sta. C, Buffalo, NY 14209. $24.95 yr. U.S.; $28.95 yr. Canada (12 issues). For women shooters.

---

*Published bi-monthly †Published weekly ‡Published three times per month. All others are published monthly.
M = Membership requirements; write for details. Q = Published Quarterly.

The Arms Library for

COLLECTOR · HUNTER · SHOOTER · OUTDOORSMAN

A selection of books—old, new and forthcoming—for everyone in the arms field, with a brief description by . . . JOE RILING

IMPORTANT NOTICE TO BOOK BUYERS

Books listed here may be bought from Ray Riling Arms Books Co., 6844 Gorsten St., P.O. Box 18925, Philadelphia, PA 19119, phone 215/438-2456. Joe Riling is the researcher and compiler of "The Arms Library" and a seller of gun books for over 30 years.

The Riling stock includes books classic and modern, many hard-to-find items, and many not obtainable elsewhere. These pages list a portion of the current stock. They offer prompt, complete service, with delayed shipments occurring only on out-of-print or out-of-stock books.

NOTICE FOR ALL CUSTOMERS: Remittance in U.S. funds must accompany all orders. For U.S. add $2.00 per book for postage and insurance. Minimum order $10.00. For

UPS add 50% to mailing costs.

All foreign countries add $5.00 per book. All foreign orders are shipped at the buyer's risk unless an additional $5 for insurance is included.

Payments in excess of order or for "Backorders" are credited or fully refunded at request. Books "As-Ordered" are not returnable except by permission and a handling charge on these of $2.00 per book is deducted from refund or credit. Only Pennsylvania customers must include current sales tax.

All full variety of arms books also available from Rutgers Book Center, 127 Raritan Ave., Highland Park, NJ 08904.

*New Book

ballistics and handloading

ABC's of Reloading, 4th Edition, by Dean A. Grennell, DBI Books, Inc., Northbrook, IL, 1988. 288 pp., illus. Paper covers. $15.95.

An all-new book with everything from a discussion of the basics up through and including advanced techniques and procedures.

The Art of Bullet Casting from Handloader & Rifle Magazines 1966-1981, compiled by Dave Wolfe, Wolfe Publishing Co., Prescott, AZ, 1981. 258 pp., illus. Paper covers. $12.95. Deluxe hardbound. $19.50.

Articles from "Handloader" and "Rifle" magazines by authors such as Jim Carmichel, John Wootters, and the late George Nonte.

Ballistic Science for the Law Enforcement Officer, by Charles G. Wilber, Ph.D., Charles C. Thomas, Springfield, IL, 1977. 309 pp., illus. $80.00.

A scientific study of the ballistics of civilian firearms.

Basic Handloading, by George C. Nonte, Jr., Outdoor Life Books, New York, NY, 1982. 192 pp., illus. Paper covers. $4.50.

How to produce high-quality ammunition using the safest, most efficient methods known.

The Bullet's Flight, by Franklin Mann, Wolfe Publishing Co., Inc., Prescott, AZ, 1980. 391 pp., illus. $40.00.

The ballistics of small arms. A reproduction of Harry Pope's personal copy of this classic with his marginal notes.

The Bullet Swage Manual. MDSU/I, by Ted Smith, Corbin Manufacturing and Supply Co., White City, OR, 1988. 45 pp., illus. Paper covers. $10.00.

A book that fills the need for information on bullet swaging.

Cartridges of the World, 6th Edition, by Frank C. Barnes, DBI Books, Inc., Northbrook, IL, 1989. 448 pp., illus. Paper covers. $18.95.

Completely revised edition of the general purpose reference work for which collectors, police, scientists and laymen reach first for answers to cartridge identification questions.

Cast Bullets, by Col. E. H. Harrison, A publication of the National Rifle Association of America, Washington, DC, 1979. 144 pp., illus. Paper covers. $12.95.

An authoritative guide to bullet casting techniques and ballistics.

Complete Guide to Handloading, by Philip B. Sharpe, Wolfe Publishing Co., Prescott, AZ, 1988. 465;229 pp., illus. $60.00.

A limited edition reprint of Sharpe's most sought-after classic. Includes the supplement.

*The Complete Handloader, by John Wootters, Stackpole Books, Harrisburg, PA, 1989. 224 pp., illus. $29.95.

One of the deans of gun writers shares a lifetime of experience and recommended procedures on handloading for rifles, handguns, and shotguns.

The Complete Handloader for Rifles, Handguns and Shotguns, by John Wootters, Stackpole Books, Harrisburg, PA, 1988. 214 pp., illus. $29.95.

Loading-bench know-how.

Computer for Handloaders, by Homer Powley. A slide rule plus 12-page instruction book for use in finding charge, most efficient powder and velocity for any modern centerfire rifle. $10.00.

Discover Swaging, by David R. Corbin, Stackpole Books, Harrisburg, PA, 1979. 283 pp., illus. $18.95.

A guide to custom bullet design and performance.

Extended Ballistics for the Advanced Rifleman, by Art Blatt, Pachmayr, Inc., Los Angeles, CA, 1986. 379 pp. Spiral bound. $12.95.

Enhanced data on all factory centerfire rifle loads from Federal, Hornady, Norma, Remington, Weatherby, and Winchester.

*Firearms Pressure Factors, by Dr. Lloyd Brownell, Wolfe Publishing Co., Prescott, AZ, 1990. 200 pp., illus. $14.00.

The only book available devoted entirely to firearms and pressure. Contains chapters on secondary explosion effect, modern pressure measuring techniques in revolvers and rifles, and Dr. Brownell's series on pressure factors.

The Gun Digest Black Powder Loading Manual, by Sam Fadala, DBI Books, Inc., Northbrook, IL, 1982. 244 pp., illus. Paper covers. $13.95.

Covers 450 loads for 86 of the most popular blackpowder rifles, handguns and shotguns.

Gun Digest Book of Handgun Reloading, by Dean A. Grennell and Wiley M. Clapp, DBI Books, Inc., Northbrook, IL, 1987. 256 pp., illus. Paper covers. $13.95.

Detailed discussions of all aspects of reloading for handguns, from basic to complex. New loading data.

Handbook of Bullet Swaging No. 7, by David R. Corbin, Corbin Manufacturing and Supply Co., White City, OR, 1986. 199 pp., illus. Paper covers. $10.00.

This handbook explains the most precise method of making quality bullets.

Handbook for Shooters and Reloaders, by P.O. Ackley, Salt Lake City, UT, 1970, (Vol. I), illus. (Vol. II), a new printing with specific new material. 495 pp., illus. $15.95 each.

Handbook of Metallic Cartridge Reloading, by Edward Matunas, Winchester Press, Piscataway, NJ, 1981. 272 pp., illus. $19.95.

Up-to-date, comprehensive loading tables prepared by four major powder manufacturers.

*Handloader's Bullet Making Annual, various contributors, Wolfe Publishing Co., Prescott, AZ, 1990. 122 pp., illus. Soft covers. $6.95.

Directed to those handloaders and shooters who wish to further their knowledge about techniques and tools employed to cast and swage bullets.

*Handloader's Digest, 12th Edition, edited by Ken Warner, DBI Books, Inc., Northbrook, IL, 1990. 384 pp., illus. Soft covers. $18.95.

This expanded edition offers something for any shooter. Includes over 200 pages of catalog covering all currently available loading tools, components, chronographs and accessories.

Handloader's Guide, by Stanley W. Trzoniec, Stoeger Publishing Co., So. Hackensack, NJ, 1985. 256 pp., illus. Paper covers. $11.95.

The complete step-by-step fully illustrated guide to handloading ammunition.

Handloader's Manual of Cartridge Conversions, by John J. Donnelly, Stoeger Publishing Co., So. Hackensack, NJ, 1986. Unpaginated. $34.95.

From 14 Jones to 70-150 Winchester in English and American cartridges, and from 4.85 U.K. to 15.2x28R Gevelot in metric cartridges. Over 900 cartridges described in detail.

Handloading, by Bill Davis, Jr., NRA Books, Wash., D.C., 1980. 400 pp., illus. Paper covers. $15.95.

A complete update and expansion of the NRA Handloader's Guide.

Handloading Ammunition, by J.R. Mattern, Wolfe Publishing Co., Prescott, AZ, 1988. 380 pp., illus. $39.00.

A limited edition reprint. The handloader's classic handbook covering all phases of loading metallic ammunition.

Hodgdon Powder Data Manual No. 25, Hodgdon Powder Co., Inc., Shawnee Mission, KS, 1986. 544 pp., illus. $16.95.

For the first time includes data for Hercules, Winchester, and DuPont powders.

Handloading for Hunters, by Don Zutz, Winchester Press, Piscataway, NJ, 1977. 288 pp., illus. $30.00.

Precise mixes and loads for different types of game and for various hunting situations with rifle and shotgun.

The Home Guide to Cartridge Conversions, by Maj. George C. Nonte Jr., The Gun Room Press, Highland Park, NJ, 1976. 404 pp., illus. $22.95.

Revised and updated version of Nonte's definitive work on the alteration of cartridge cases for use in guns for which they were not intended.

Hornady Handbook of Cartridge Reloading, Hornady Mfg. Co., Grand Island, NE, 1981. 650 pp., illus. $15.95.

New edition of this famous reloading handbook. Latest loads, ballistic information, etc.

Lyman Cast Bullet Handbook, 3rd Edition, edited by C. Kenneth Ramage, Lyman Publications, Middlefield, CT, 1980. 416 pp., illus. Paper covers. $18.95.

Information on more than 5,000 tested cast bullet loads and 19 pages of trajectory and wind drift tables for cast bullets.

Lyman Black Powder Handbook, ed. by C. Kenneth Ramage, Lyman Products for Shooters, Middlefield, CT, 1975. 239 pp., illus. Paper covers. $14.95.

The most comprehensive load information ever published for the modern black powder shooter.

Lyman Pistol & Revolver Handbook, edited by C. Kenneth Ramage, Lyman Publications, Middlefield, CT, 1978. 280 pp., illus. Paper covers. $14.95.

An extensive reference of load and trajectory data for the handgun.

Lyman Reloading Handbook No. 46, edited by C. Kenneth Ramage, Lyman Publications, Middlefield, CT, 1982. 300 pp., illus. $18.95.

A large and comprehensive book on reloading. Extensive list of loads for jacketed and cast bullets.

Lyman Shotshell Handbook, 3rd Edition, edited by C. Kenneth Ramage, Lyman Publications, Middlefield, CT, 1984. 312 pp., illus. Paper covers. $18.95.

Has 2,000 loads, including slugs and buckshot, plus feature articles and a full color I.D. section.

Manual of Pistol and Revolver Cartridges, Volume 1, Centerfire and Metric Calibers, by Hans A. Erlmeier and Jakob H. Brandt, Journal-Verlag, Wiesbaden, Germany, 1967. 271 pp., illus. $34.95.

Specifications for each cartridge cataloged; tells bullet and case type with important case dimensions.

Manual of Pistol and Revolver Cartridges, Volume 2, Centerfire U.S. and British Calibers, by Hans A. Erlmeier and Jakob H. Brandt, Journal-Verlag, Wiesbaden, Germany, 1981. 270 pp., illus. $34.95.

Catalog system allows cartridges to be traced by caliber or alphabetically.

Metallic Cartridge Reloading, 2nd Edition, by Edward A. Matunas, DBI Books, Inc., Northbrook, IL., 1988. 320 pp., illus. Paper covers. $16.95.

A true reloading manual with a wealth of invaluable technical data provided by a recognized expert.

The Military Cartridges Caliber 7.62x51mm NATO, Their Development and Variants, by Jakob H. Brandt et al, Journal-Verlag, Schwabish Hall, W. Germany, N.D. 314 pp., illus. $65.00.

This encyclopedia reference book is the complete work on the 7.9mm cartridge. Text is in both German and English. Lengths and weights as well as markings, powders and more are listed for over 350 variants.

Modern Handloading, by Maj. Geo. C. Nonte, Winchester Press, Piscataway, NJ, 1972. 416 pp., illus. $15.00.

Covers all aspects of metallic and shotshell ammunition loading, plus more loads than any book in print.

Pet Loads, by Ken Waters, Wolfe Publishing Co., Prescott, AZ, 3rd edition, 1986. 2 volumes of 636 pp. Limp fabricoid covers. $27.50.

Ken Water's favorite loads that have appeared in "Handloader" magazine.

Practical Dope on the .22, by F.C. Ness, Wolfe Publishing Co., Prescott, AZ, 1989. 313 pp., illus. $39.00.

A limited edition reprint. Much information on 22 rifles, actions, loads, test firing, etc.

Practical Handgun Ballistics, by Mason Williams, Charles C. Thomas, Publisher, Springfield, IL, 1980. 215 pp., illus. $55.00.

Factual information on the practical aspects of ammunition performance in revolvers and pistols.

Precision Handloading, by John Withers, Stoeger Publishing Co., So. Hackensack, NJ, 1985. 224 pp., illus. Paper covers. $11.95.

An entirely new approach to handloading ammunition.

Rediscover Swaging, by David R. Corbin, Corbin Manufacturing and Supply, Inc., Phoenix, OR, 1983. 240 pp., illus. $18.50.

A new textbook on the subject of bullet swaging.

Reloader's Guide, 3rd Edition, by R.A. Steindler, Stoeger Publishing Co., So. Hackensack, NJ, 1984. 224 pp., illus. Paper covers. $9.95.

Complete, fully illustrated step-by-step guide to handloading ammunition.

Reloading for Shotgunners, 2nd Edition, edited by Robert S.L. Anderson, DBI Books, Inc., Northbrook, IL, 1985. 256 pp., illus. Paper covers. $13.95.

The very latest in reloading information for the shotgunner.

***Sierra Handgun Manual, 3rd Edition,** edited by Kenneth Ramage, Sierra Bullets, Santa Fe Springs, CA, 1990. 704 pp., illus. 3-ring binder. $19.95.

New listings for XP-100 and Contender pistols and TCU cartridges . . . part of a new single shot section. Covers the latest loads for 10mm Auto, 455 Super Mag, and Accurate powders.

***Sierra Rifle Manual, 3rd Edition,** edited by Kenneth Ramage, Sierra Bullets, Santa Fe Springs, CA, 1990. 856 pp., illus. 3-ring binder. $24.95.

Updated load information with new powder listings and a wealth of inside tips.

Sixgun Cartridges and Loads, by Elmer Keith, The Gun Room Press, Highland Park, NJ, 1986. 151 pp., illus. $19.95.

A manual covering the selection, uses and loading of the most suitable and popular revolver cartridges. Originally published in 1936. Reprint.

Speer Reloading Manual Number 11, edited by members of the Speer research staff, Omark Industries, Lewiston, ID, 1987. 621 pp., illus. $13.95.

Reloading manual for rifles and pistols.

Why Not Load Your Own? by Col. T. Whelen, A. S. Barnes, New York, 1957, 4th ed., rev. 237 pp., illus. $10.95.

A basic reference on handloading, describing each step, materials and equipment. Loads for popular cartridges are given.

Yours Truly, Harvey Donaldson, by Harvey Donaldson, Wolfe Publ. Co., Inc., Prescott, AZ, 1980. 288 pp., illus. $19.50.

Reprint of the famous columns by Harvey Donaldson which appeared in "Handloader" from May 1966 through December 1972.

COLLECTORS

The American Cartridge, by Charles R. Suydam, Borden Publishing Co., Alhambra, CA, 1986. 184 pp., illus. $12.50.

An illustrated study of the rimfire cartridge in the United States.

American Percussion Revolvers, by Frank M. Sellers and Samuel E. Smith, Museum Restoration Service, Ottawa, Canada, 1971. 231 pp., illus. $29.95.

The ultimate reference book on American percussion revolvers.

***America's Premier Gunmakers: Browning,** by K.D. Kirkland, W.H. Smith Publishers, Inc., New York, NY, 1989. 112 pp., illus. $9.98.

Traces the history of the firm and the arms invented by John Browning.

America's Premier Gunmakers: Colt, by K.D. Kirkland, Exeter Books, New York, NY, 1988. 112 pp., illus. $9.98.

Traces the history of Colt from its 19th century origins, through the turbulent years that followed.

America's Premier Gunmakers: Remington, by K.D. Kirkland, Exeter Books, New York, NY, 1988. 112 pp., illus. $9.98.

With the aid of beautiful color photographs, this volume tells the fascinating story of Remington.

***America's Premier Gunmakers: Winchester,** by K.D. Kirkland, W.H. Smith Publishers, Inc., New York, NY, 1989, 112 pp., illustrated. $9.98.

Traces the history of the Winchester Company and it's products.

". . . And Now Stainless", by Dave Ecker with Bob Zwirz, Charter Arms Corp., Bridgeport, CT, 1981. 165 pp., illus. $25.00.

The Charter Arms story. Covers all models to date.

Antique Guns: The Collector's Guide, by John E. Traister, Stoeger Publishing Co., So. Hackensack, NJ, 1988. 320 pp., illus. Paper covers. $14.95.

Covers all categories, history, craftsmanship, firearms components, gunmakers and values on the gun-trading market.

Arms & Accoutrements of the Mounted Police 1873-1973, by Roger F. Phillips and Donald J. Klancher, Museum Restoration Service, Ont., Canada, 1982. 224 pp., illus. $49.95.

A definitive history of the revolvers, rifles, machine guns, cannons, ammunition, swords, etc. used by the NWMP, the RNWMP and the RCMP during the first 100 years of the Force.

Arms Makers of Eastern Pennsylvania: The Colonial Years to 1790, by James B. Whisker and Roy F. Chandler, Acorn Press, Bedford, PA, 1984. Unpaginated. $10.00.

Definitive work on Eastern Pennsylvania gunmakers.

Arms Makers of Maryland, by Daniel D. Hartzler, George Shumway, York, PA, 1975. 200 pp., illus. $40.00.

A thorough study of the gunsmiths of Maryland who worked during the late 18th and early 19th centuries.

***Astra Automatic Pistols,** by Leonardo M. Antaris, FIRAC Publishing Co., Sterling, CO, 1989. 248 pp., illus. $43.00.

Charts, tables, serial ranges, etc. The definitive work on Astra pistols.

Basic Documents on U.S. Marital Arms, commentary by Col. B. R. Lewis, reissue by Ray Riling, Phila., PA, 1956 and 1960. *Rifle Musket Model 1855.* The first issue rifle of musket caliber, a muzzle loader equipped with the Maynard Primer, 32 pp. $2.50. *Rifle Musket Model 1863.* The typical Union muzzle-loader of the Civil War, 26 pp. $1.75. *Breech-Loading Rifle Musket Model 1866.* The first of our 50-caliber breechloading rifles, 12 pp. $1.75. *Remington Navy Rifle Model 1870.* A commercial type breech-loader made at Springfield, 16 pp. $1.75. *Lee Straight Pull Navy Rifle Model 1895.* A magazine cartridge arm of 6mm caliber. 23 pp. $3.00. *Breech-Loading Arms* (five models) 27 pp. $2.75. *Ward-Burton Rifle Musket 1871-16* pp. $2.50. *U.S. Magazine Rifle and Carbine (cal. 30) Model 1892* (the Krag rifle) 36 pp. $3.00.

The Belton Systems, 1758 and 1784-86: America's First Repeating Firearms, by Robert Held, Andrew Mowbray, Inc., Lincoln, RI, 1986. 93 pp., illus. Limited, numbered edition. Stiff paper covers. $40.00.

This monograph examines the first repeating firearms to be made in America, their history, their functions, their position in relation to analogous arms in America and Europe.

Beretta Automatic Pistols, by J.B. Wood, Stackpole Books, Harrisburg, PA, 1985. 192 pp., illus. $19.95.

Only English-language book devoted entirely to the Beretta line. Includes all important models.

***Blue Book of Gun Values, 11th edition,** compiled by S.P. Fjestad, Investment Rarities, Inc., Minneapolis, MN, 1990. 621 pp., illus. Soft covers. $18.95.

Uses percentage grading system to determine each gun's value based on its unique condition.

Breech-Loading Carbines of the United States Civil War Period, by Brig. Gen. John Pitman, Armory Publications, Tacoma, WA, 1987. 94 pp., illus. $34.95.

The first in a series of previously unpublished manuscripts originated by the late Brigadier General John Putnam. Exploded drawings showing parts actual size follow each sectioned illustration.

The Bren Gun Saga, by Thomas B. Dugelby, Collector Grade Publications, Toronto, Canada, 1986. 300 pp., illus. $50.00.

Contains information on all models of Bren guns used by all nations.

COLLECTORS (cont.)

British Military Longarms 1715-1865, by D. W. Bailey, Arms & Armour Press, London, England, 1986. 160 pp., illus. $19.95.
166 different guns photographed in full-length views plus detailed close-ups of locks, markings and structural variations.
The British Service Lee, by Ian Skennerton, Ian Skennerton, Margate, Australia, 1987. 410 pp., illus. $45.00
Lee-Metford and Lee-Enfield rifles and carbines, 1880-1980.
The Browning Connection, by Richard Rattenbury, Buffalo Bill Historical Center, Cody, WY, 1982. 71 pp., illus. Paper covers. $10.00.
Patent prototypes in the Winchester Museum.
Browning Dates of Manufacture, compiled by George Madis, Art and Reference House, Brownsboro, TX, 1989. 48 pp. $5.00.
Gives the date codes and product codes for all models from 1824 to the present.
Bullard Arms, by G. Scott Jamieson, The Boston Mills Press, Ontario, Canada, 1989. 244 pp., illus. $35.00.
The story of a mechanical genius whose rifles and cartridges were the equal to any made in America in the 1880s.
The Burnside Breech Loading Carbines, by Edward A. Hull, Andrew Mowbray, Inc., Lincoln, RI, 1986. 95 pp., illus. $16.00.
No. 1 in the "Man at Arms Monograph Series." A model-by-model historical/technical examination of one of the most widely used cavalry weapons of the American Civil War based upon important and previously unpublished research.
California Gunsmiths 1846-1900, by Lawrence P. Sheldon, Far Far West Publ., Fair Oaks, CA, 1977. 289 pp., illus. $29.65.
A study of early California gunsmiths and the firearms they made.
Carbines of the Civil War, by John D. McAulay, Pioneer Press, Union City, TN, 1981. 123 pp., illus. Paper covers. $7.95.
A guide for the student and collector of the colorful arms used by the Federal cavalry.
Cartology Savalog, by Gerald Bernstein, Gerald Bernstein, St. Louis, MO, 1976. 177 pp., illus. Paper covers. $8.95.
An infinite variations catalog of small arms ammunition stamps.
***Cartridges for Breechloading Rifles,** by A. Mattenheimer, Armory Publications, Oceanside, CA, 1989. 90 pp. with two 15"x19" color lithos containing 163 drawings of cartridges and firearms mechanisms. $29.95.
Reprinting of this German work on cartridges. Text in German and English.
Cartridges of the World, 6th Edition, by Frank C. Barnes, DBI Books, Inc., Northbrook, IL, 1989. 448 pp., illus. Paper covers. $18.95.
Completely revised edition of the general purpose reference work for which collectors, police, scientists and laymen reach first for answers to cartridge identification questions.
A Catalog Collection of 20th Century Winchester Repeating Arms Co., compiled by Roger Rule, Alliance Books, Inc., Northridge, CA, 1985. 396 pp., illus. $29.95.
Reflects the full line of Winchester products from 1901-1931 with emphasis on Winchester firearms.
Civil War Breechloading Rifles, by John D. McAulay, Andrew Mowbray, Inc., Lincoln, RI, 1987. 128 pp., illus. Paper covers. $12.00.
A survey of the innovative infantry arms of the American Civil War.
Civil War Carbines, by A.F. Lustyik, World Wide Gun Report, Inc., Aledo, IL, 1962. 63 pp., illus. Paper covers. $3.50.
Accurate, interesting summary of most carbines of the Civil War period, in booklet form, with numerous good illus.
Collecting Antique Firearms, by Dr. Martin Kelvin, Stanley Paul, London, 1987. 181 pp., illus. $55.00.
A book to add to the treasure store of any antique gun collector.
Collecting Shotgun Cartridges, by Ken Rutherford, Stanley Paul, London, 1987. 139 pp., illus. $45.00.
An illustrated catalog of all the major known suppliers and designs in Britain and Ireland.
A Collector's Guide to Colt's .38 Automatic Pistols, by Douglas G. Sheldon, Douglas Sheldon, Willernie, MN, 1987. 185 pp., illus. Paper covers. $19.95.
The production history of the .38 caliber Colt automatic pistols.
A Collector's Guide to the M1 Garand and the M1 Carbine, by Bruce N. Canfield, Andrew Mowbray, Inc., Publisher, Lincoln, RI, 1988. 144 pp., illus. $35.00.
A comprehensive guide to the most important and ubiquitous American arms of WWII and Korea.
***A Collector's Guide to the '03 Springfield,** by Bruce N. Canfield, Andrew Mowbray Inc, Lincoln, RI, 1989. 160 pp., illus. $35.00.
A comprehensive guide follows the '03 through its unparalleled tenure of service. Covers all of the interesting variations, modifications and accessories of this highly collectible military rifle.
A Collector's Guide to Tokarev Pistols, by John Remling, Collector's Services, East Stroudsburg, PA, 1985. 81 pp., illus. $12.95.
Covers all models and variations of this firearm.
Colonial Frontier Guns, by T.M. Hamilton, Pioneer Press, Union City, TN, 1988. 176 pp., illus. Paper covers. $13.95.
A complete study of early flint muskets of this country.
Colt, An American Legend, by R.L. Wilson, Abbeville Press, New York, NY, 1985. 310 pp., illus. $29.95.
Every model Colt ever produced is shown in magnificent color.
The Colt-Burgess Magazine Rifle, by Samuel L. Maxwell Sr., Samuel L. Maxwell, Bellvue, WA, 1985. 176 pp., illus. $35.00.
Serial numbers, engraved arms, newly discovered experimental models, etc.
Colt Cavalry, Artillery and Militia Revolvers 1873-1903, by Keith Cochran, Cochran Publishing Co., Rapid City, SD, 1988. 288 pp., illus. $45.00.
A history and text book of the Colt Cavalry Model revolver with a complete analysis, nearly every variation and mark illustrated.
Colt Firearms from 1836, by James E. Serven, new 8th edition, Stackpole Books, Harrisburg, PA, 1979. 398 pp., illus. Deluxe ed. $49.95.
Excellent survey of the Colt company and its products. Updated with new SAA production chart and commemorative list.

The Colt Heritage, by R.L. Wilson, Simon & Schuster, 1979. 358 pp., illus. $75.00.
The official history of Colt firearms 1836 to the present.
***Colt Peacemaker British Model,** by Keith Cochran, Cochran Publishing Co., Rapid City, SD, 1989. 160 pp., illus. $35.00.
Covers those revolvers Colt squeezed in while completing a large order of revolvers for the U.S. Cavalry in early 1874, to those magnificent cased target revolvers used in the pistol competitions at Bisley Commons in the 1890s.
Colt Peacemaker Encyclopedia, by Keith Cochran, Keith Cochran, Rapid City, SD, 1986. 434 pp., illus. $59.95.
A must book for the Peacemaker collector.
Colt Peacemaker Ready-Reference Handbook, by Keith Cochran, Cochran Publishing Co., Rapid City, SD, 1985. 76 pp., illus. Paper covers. $12.95.
A must book for the SAA collector.
Colt Peacemaker Yearly Variations, by Keith Cochran, Keith Cochran, Rapid City, SD, 1987. 96 pp., illus. $17.95.
A definitive, precise listing for each year the Peacemaker was manufactured from 1873-1940.
Colt Pistols 1836-1976, by R.L. Wilson in association with R.E. Hable, Jackson Arms, Dallas, TX, 1976. 380 pp., illus. $125.00.
A magnificently illustrated book in full color featuring Colt firearms from the famous Hable collection.
***Colt Revolvers and the Tower of London,** by Joseph G. Rosa, Royal Armouries of the Tower of London, London, England, 1988. 72 pp., illus. Soft covers. $15.00.
Details the story of Colt in London through the early cartridge period.
***The Colt U.S. General Officers' Pistols,** by Horace Greeley IV, Andrew Mowbray Inc., Lincoln, RI, 1990. 199 pp., illus. $38.00.
These unique weapons, issued as a badge of rank to General Officers in the U.S. Army from WWII onward, remain highly personal artifacts of the military leaders who carried them. Includes serial numbers and dates of issue.
Colt Revolvers and the U.S. Navy 1865-1889, by C. Kenneth Moore, Dorrance and Co., Bryn Mawr, PA, 1987. 140 pp., illus. $29.95.
The Navy's use of all Colt handguns and other revolvers during this era of change.
The Colt Rifle 1884-1902, by Ted Tivey, Ted Tivey, N.S.W., Australia, 1984. 119 pp., illus. $30.00.
Covers the production era of the Colt slide action "Lightning" models made for the sporting world.
Colt's Dates of Manufacture 1837-1978, by R.L. Wilson, published by Maurie Albert, Coburg, Australia; N.A. distributor I.D.S.A. Books, Hamilton, OH, 1983. 61 pp. $10.00.
An invaluable pocket guide to the dates of manufacture of Colt firearms up to 1978.
Colt's SAA Post War Models, George Garton, revised edition, Gun Room Press, Highland Park, NJ, 1987. 166 pp., illus. $29.95.
The complete facts on Colt's famous post war single action army revolver using factory records to cover types, calibers, production numbers and many variations of this popular firearm.
The Colt Whitneyville-Walker Pistol, by Lt. Col. Robert D. Whittington, Brownlee Books, Hooks, TX, 1984. 96 pp., illus. Limited edition. $20.00.
A study of the pistol and associated characters 1846-1851.
***The Complete Kalashnikov Family of Assault Rifles,** by Duncan Long, Paladin Press, Boulder, CO, 1989. 192 pp., illus. Soft covers. $14.00.
The scoop on this international collection of rifles from one of America's most trusted firearms writers.
Confederate Revolvers, by William A. Gary, Taylor Publishing Co., Dallas, TX, 1987. 174 pp., illus. $45.00.
Comprehensive work on the rarest of Confederate weapons.
Contemporary Makers of Muzzleloading Firearms, by Robert Weil, Screenland Press, Burbank, CA, 1981. 300 pp., illus. $39.95.
Illustrates the work of over 30 different contemporary makers.
Dance & Brothers; Texas Gunmakers of the Confederacy, by Gary Wiggins, Moss Publications, Orange, VA, 1986. 151 pp., illus. $29.95.
Presents a thorough and detailed study of the legendary Texas gunmakers, Dance & Brothers.
The Deringer in America, Volume 1, The Percussion Period, by R.L. Wilson and L.D. Eberhart, Andrew Mowbray Inc., Lincoln, RI, 1985. 271 pp., illus. $48.00.
A long awaited book on the American percussion deringer.
Development of the Henry Cartridge and Self-Contained Cartridges for the Toggle-Link Winchesters, by R. Bruce McDowell, A.M.B., Metuchen, NJ, 1984. 69 pp., illus. Paper covers. $10.00.
From powder and ball to the self-contained metallic cartridge.
***Dominion Ammunition Catalog No. 15,** Reprinted by Robert Roe, Prince Rupert, Canada, 1990. 52 pp., illus. Soft covers. $25.00.
A reprint of the 1916 ammunition catalog of the Dominion Cartridge Co., Ltd, of Montreal, Canada.
Early Indian Trade Guns: 1625-1775, by T.M. Hamilton, Museum of the Great Plains, Lawton, OK, 1968. 34 pp., illus. Paper covers. $7.95.
Detailed descriptions of subject arms, compiled from early records and from the study of remnants found in Indian country.
Eley Brothers Cartridge Catalog and Price List 1910-11, reprinted by Armory Publications, Tacoma, WA, 1984, 92 pp., illus. Paper covers. $25.00.
Fascimile reprint gives specifications for every cartridge manufactured by Eley Brothers during this period. Lots of ballistic data.
English Pistols: The Armories of H.M. Tower of London Collection, by Howard L. Blackmore, Arms and Armour Press, London, England, 1985. 64 pp., illus. Soft covers. $14.95.
All the pistols described and pictured are from this famed collection.
European Firearms in Swedish Castles, by Kaa Wennberg, Bohuslaningens Boktryckeri AB, Uddevalla, Sweden, 1986. 156 pp., illus. $45.00.
The famous collection of Count Keller, the Ettersburg Castle collection, and others. English text.
Evolution of the Winchester, by R. Bruce McDowell, Armory Publications, Tacoma, WA, 1986. 200 pp., illus. $37.50.
Historic lever-action, tubular-magazine firearms.

COLLECTORS (cont.)

Fifteen Years in the Hawken Lode, by John D. Baird, The Gun Room Press, Highland Park, NJ, 1976. 120 pp., illus. $19.95.

A collection of thoughts and observations gained from many years of intensive study of the guns from the shop of the Hawken brothers.

Firearms of the American West, 1803-1865, by Louis A. Garavaglia and Charles G. Worman, University of New Mexico Press, Albuquerque, NM, 1985. 300 pp., illus. $35.00.

An encyclopedic study tracing the development and uses of firearms on the frontier during this period.

Firearms of the American West, 1866-1894, by Louis A. Garavaglia, and Charles G. Wormer, University of New Mexico Press, Albuquerque, NM, 1985. 448 pp., illus. $40.00.

The second volume in this study examines guns as an integral part of the frontier experience in a society where peace officers and judges were few.

Firepower from Abroad: The Confederate Enfield and the LeMat Revolver, by Wiley Sword, Andrew Mowbray, Inc., Lincoln, RI, 1986. 119 pp., illus. $16.00.

No. two in the "Man at Arms Monograph Series." With new data on a variety of Confederate small arms.

***Flayderman's Guide to Antique American Firearms . . . and Their Values, 5th Edition,** by Norm Flayderman, DBI Books, Inc., Northbrook, IL, 1990. 624 pp., illus. Soft covers. $24.95.

Updated edition of this bible of the antique gun field.

Frank and George Freund and the Sharps Rifle, by Gerald O. Kelver, Gerald O. Kelver, Brighton, CO, 1986. 60 pp., illus. Paper covers. $12.00.

Pioneer gunmakers of Wyoming Territory and Colorado.

The 45/70 Trapdoor Springfield Dixie Collection, compiled by Walter Crutcher and Paul Oglesby, Pioneer Press, Union City, TN, 1975. 600 pp., illus. Paper covers. $9.95.

An illustrated listing of the 45-70 Springfields in the Dixie Gun Works Collection. Little known details and technical information is given, plus current values.

French Military Weapons, 1717-1938, Major James E. Hicks, N. Flayderman & Co., Publishers, New Milford, CT, 1973. 281 pp., illus. $22.50.

Firearms, swords, bayonets, ammunition, artillery, ordnance equipment of the French army.

Game Guns and Rifles, by Richard Akehurst, Arms and Armour Press, London, England, 1985. 176 pp., illus. $35.00.

Reprint of a classic account on sporting arms.

***German Pistols and Holsters 1934-1945, Vol. 2,** by Robert Whittington, Brownlee Books, Hooks, TX, 1990. 312 pp., illus. $45.00.

This volume addresses pistols only: military (Heer, Luftwaffe, Kriegsmarine & Waffen-SS), captured, commercial, police, NSDAP and government.

The German Assault Rifle 1935-1945, by Peter R. Senich, Paladin Press, Boulder, CO, 1987. 328 pp., illus. $39.95.

A complete review of machine carbines, machine pistols and assault rifles employed by Hitler's Wehrmacht during WWII.

The Government Models: The Development of the Colt Model of 1911, by William H.D. Goddard, Andrew Mowbray, Inc., Publishers, Lincoln, RI, 1988. 223 pp., illus. $58.50.

An authoritative source on the world's most popular military sidearm.

Great British Gunmakers 1540-1740, by W. Keith Neal and D.H.L. Back, Historical Firearms, London, England, 1984. 479 pp., illus. $135.00.

A limited, numbered edition covering a total of 159 English gunmakers.

Gun Collecting, by Geoffrey Boothroyd, Sportsman's Press, London, 1989. 208 pp., illus. $24.95.

The most comprehensive list of 19th century British gunmakers and gunsmiths ever published.

Gun Collector's Digest, 5th Edition, edited by Joseph J. Schroeder, DBI Books, Inc., Northbrook, IL, 1989. 224 pp., illus. Paper covers. $14.95.

The latest edition of this sought-after series.

The Gun Digest Book of Modern Gun Values, 7th Edition, by Jack Lewis, DBI Books, Inc., Northbrook, IL, 1989. 496 pp., illus. Paper covers. $17.95.

Updated and expanded edition of the book that's become the standard for valuing modern firearms.

Gunmakers of London 1350-1850, by Howard L. Blackmore, George Shumway Publisher, York, PA, 1986. 222 pp., illus. $85.00.

A listing of all the known workmen of gun making in the first 500 years, plus a history of the guilds, cutlers, armourers, founders, blacksmiths, etc. 260 gunmarks are illustrated.

The Gunsmiths and Gunmakers of Eastern Pennsylvania, by James B. Whisker and Roy Chandler, Old Bedford Village Press, Bedford, PA, 1982. 130 pp., illus. Limited, numbered edition. Paper covers. $17.50.

Locates over 2,000 gunsmiths practicing before 1900, with references and documentation.

The Gunsmiths and Gunmakers of Western Pennsylvania, by James B. Whisker and Vaughn E. Whisker, Old Bedford Village Press, Bedford, PA, 1982. 103 pp., illus. Limited, numbered and signed edition. Paper covers. $17.50.

Lists over 650 names of gunsmiths practicing before 1900.

Gunsmiths of Ohio—18th & 19th Centuries: Vol. I, Biographical Data, by Donald A. Hutslar, George Shumway, York, PA, 1973. 444 pp., illus. $35.00.

An important source book, full of information about the old-time gunsmiths of Ohio.

Gun Traders Guide, 13th Edition, compiled by the editors of Stoeger Publishing Co., illus. Paper covers. $14.95.

Fully illustrated guide to identification of modern firearms with current market values.

Handbook of the Pedersen Self-Loading Rifles Model P.A., a facsimile reprint of this Vickers-Armstrong Ltd. manual, ca. 1930s by Robert T. Sweeney, San Francisco, CA, 1985. 32 pp., illus. Paper covers. $9.50.

Reprint of an original operator's manual for the British version of a semi-automatic military arm that was a major contender of the Garand rifle.

***The Handgun,** by Geoffrey Boothroyd, David and Charles, North Pomfret, VT, 1989. 566 pp., illus. $55.00.

Every chapter deals with an important period in handgun history from the 14th century to the present.

The Hawken Rifle: Its Place in History, by Charles E. Hanson, Jr., The Fur Press, Chadron, NE, 1979. 104 pp., illus. Paper covers. $6.00.

A definitive work on this famous rifle.

Hawken Rifles, The Mountain Man's Choice, by John D. Baird, The Gun Room Press, Highland Park, NJ, 1976. 95 pp., illus. $19.95.

Covers the rifles developed for the Western fur trade. Numerous specimens are described and shown in photographs.

Historic Pistols: The American Martial Flintlock 1760-1845, by Samuel E. Smith and Edwin W. Bitter, The Gun Room Press, Highland Park, NJ, 1986. 353 pp., illus. $64.50.

Covers over 70 makers and 163 models of American martial arms.

Historical Hartford Hardware, by William W. Dalrymple, Colt Collector Press, Rapid City, SD, 1976. 42 pp., illus. Paper covers. $5.50.

Historically associated Colt revolvers.

The History of Smith and Wesson, by Roy G. Jinks, Willowbrook Enterprises, Springfield, MA, 1988. 290 pp., illus. $21.95.

Revised 10th Anniversary edition of the definite book on S&W firearms.

History of Winchester Firearms 1866-1980, by Duncan Barnes, et al, Winchester Press, Piscataway, NJ, 1985. 256 pp., illus. $18.95.

A most complete and authoritative account of Winchester firearms.

How to Buy and Sell Used Guns, by John Traister, Stoeger Publishing Co., So. Hackensack, NJ, 1984. 192 pp., illus. Paper covers. $9.95.

A new guide to buying and selling guns.

Illustrations of United States Military Arms 1776-1903 and Their Inspector's Marks, compiled by Turner Kirkland, Pioneer Press, Union City, TN, 1988. 37 pp., illus. Paper covers. $4.95.

Reprinted from the 1949 Bannerman catalog. Valuable information for both the advanced and beginning collector.

Japanese Handguns, by Frederick E. Leithe, Borden Publishing Co., Alhambra, CA, 1985. 160 pp., illus. $19.95.

An identification guide to all models and variations of Japanese handguns.

The Kentucky Rifle: A True American Heritage in Picture, by The Kentucky Rifle Association, The Forte Group of Creative Companies, Inc., Alexandria, VA, second edition, 1985. 110 pp., illus. $27.50.

This classic essay reveals both the beauty and the decorative nature of the Kentucky by providing detailed photographs of some of the most significant examples of American rifles, pistols, and accoutrements.

Kentucky Rifles and Pistols 1756-1850, compiled by members of the Kentucky Rifle Association, Wash., DC, Golden Age Arms Co., Delaware, OH, 1976. 275 pp., illus. $35.00.

Profusely illustrated with more than 300 examples of rifles and pistols never before published.

Know Your Broomhandle Mausers, by R.J. Berger, Blacksmith Corp., Southport, CT, 1985. 96 pp., illus. Paper covers. $6.95.

An interesting story on the big Mauser pistol and its variations.

Know Your Ruger Single Action Revolvers 1953-1963, by John C. Dougan, edited by John T. Amber, Blacksmith Corp., Southport, CT, 1981. 199 pp., illus. $35.00.

A definitive reference work for the Ruger revolvers produced in the period 1953-1963.

Krag Rifles, by William S. Brophy, The Gun Room Press, Highland Park, NJ, 1980. 200 pp., illus. $35.00.

The first comprehensive work detailing the evolution and various models, both military and civilian.

The Krieghoff Parabellum, by Randall Gibson, Midland, TX, 1988. 279 pp., illus. $40.00.

A comprehensive text pertaining to the Lugers manufactured by H. Krieghoff Waffenfabrik.

Lever Action Magazine Rifles Derived from the Patents of Andrew Burgess, by Samuel L. Maxwell Sr., Samuel L. Maxwell, Bellevue, WA, 1976. 368 pp., illus. $29.95.

The complete story of a group of lever action magazine rifles collectively referred to as the Burgess/Morse, the Kennedy or the Whitney.

Longrifles of North Carolina, by John Bivens, George Shumway Publisher, York, PA, 1988. 256 pp., illus. $40.00.

Covers art and evolution of the rifle, immigration and trade movements. Committee of Safety gunsmiths, characteristics of the North Carolina rifle.

Longrifles of Pennsylvania, Volume 1, Jefferson, Clarion & Elk Counties, by Russel H. Harringer, George Shumway Publisher, York, PA, 1984. 200 pp., illus. $40.00.

First in series that will treat in great detail the longrifles and gunsmiths of Pennsylvania.

The Luger Book, by John Walter, Arms & Armour Press, London, England, 1987. 288 pp., illus. $45.00.

The encyclopedia of the Borchardt and the Borchardt-Luger handguns, 1885-1985.

***Lugers at Random,** by Charles Kenyon, Jr., Handgun Press, Glenview, IL, 1990. 420 pp., illus. $39.95.

A new printing of this classic and sought-after work on the Luger pistol. A boon to the Luger collector/shooter.

Marlin Firearms: A History of the Guns and the Company That Made Them, by Lt. Col. William S. Brophy, USAR, Ret., Stackpole Books, Harrisburg, PA, 1989. 672 pp., illus. $59.95.

The definitive book on the Marlin Firearms Co. and their products.

Massachusetts Military Shoulder Arms 1784-1877, by George D. Moller, Andrew Mowbray Publisher, Lincoln, RI, 1989. 250 pp., illus. $24.00.

A scholarly and heavily researched study of the military shoulder arms used by Massachusetts during the 90-year period following the Revolutionary War.

Mauser Bolt Rifles, by Ludwig Olson, F. Brownell & Son, Inc., Montezuma, IA, 1976. 364 pp., illus. $45.00.

The most complete, detailed, authoritative and comprehensive work ever done on Mauser bolt rifles.

COLLECTORS (cont.)

Military Pistols of Japan, by Fred L. Honeycutt, Jr., Julin Books, Lake Park, FL. 1982. 167 pp., illus. $29.00.
Covers every aspect of military pistol production in Japan through WWII.

***Military Rifles of Japan, 3rd Edition,** by F.L. Honeycutt, Julin Books, Lake Park, FL, 1989. 208 pp., illus. $37.00.
A new revised and updated edition. Includes the early Murata-period markings, etc.

M1 Carbine, by Larry Ruth, Gunroom Press, Highland Park, NJ, 1987. 291 pp., illus. Cloth $24.95; Paper $17.95.
The origin, development, manufacture and use of this famous carbine of World War II.

***The M1 Garand: Post World War,** by Scott A. Duff, Scott A. Duff, Export, PA, 1990. 139 pp., illus. Soft covers. $17.95.
A detailed account of the activities at Springfield Armory through this period. International Harvester, H&R, Korean War production and quantities delivered. Serial numbers.

Military Holsters of World War 2, by Eugene J. Bender, Taylor Publishing Co., Dallas, TX, 1984. 205 pp., illus. $35.00.
Covers 24 nations which produced holsters for their military weapons.

More Single Shot Rifles, by James C. Grant, The Gun Room Press, Highland Park, NJ, 1976. 324 pp., illus. $25.00.
Details the guns made by Frank Wesson, Milt Farrow, Holden, Borchardt, Stevens, Remington, Winchester, Ballard and Peabody-Martini.

The Navy Luger, by Joachim Gortz and John Walter, Handgun Press, Glenview, IL, 1988. 128 pp., illus. $24.95.
The 9mm Pistole 1904 and the Imperial German Navy. A concise illustrated history.

The Northwest Gun, by Charles E. Hanson, Jr., Nebraska State Historical Society, Lincoln, NE, 1976. 85 pp., illus., paper covers. $6.00.
Number 2 in the Society's "Publications in Anthropology." Historical survey of rifles which figured in the fur trade and settlement of the Northwest.

The P-08 Parabellum Luger Automatic Pistol, edited by J. David McFarland, Desert Publications, Cornville, AZ, 1982. 20 pp., illus. Paper covers. $6.00.
Covers every facet of the Luger, plus a listing of all known Luger models.

Paterson Colt Pistol Variations, by R.L. Wilson and R. Phillips, Jackson Arms Co., Dallas, TX, 1979. 250 pp., illus. $35.00.
A tremendous book about the different models and barrel lengths in the Paterson Colt story.

Pennsylvania Longrifles of Note, by George Shumway, George Shumway, Publisher, York, PA, 1977. 63 pp., illus. Paper covers. $6.95.
Illustrates and describes samples of guns from a number of Pennsylvania rifle-making schools.

The Pinfire System, by Gene P. Smith and Chris C. Curtis, The Pinfire System, San Francisco, CA, 1983. 216 pp., illus. $50.00.
The first attempt to record the invention, development and use of pinfire cartridge arms and ammunition.

***The Plains Rifle,** by Charles Hanson, Gun Room Press, Highland Park, NJ, 1989. 169 pp., illus. $24.95.
All rifles that were made with the plainsman in mind, including pistols.

Pollard's History of Firearms, edited by Claude Blair, Macmillan Publishing Co., N.Y., NY, 1983, 559 pp., illus. $40.00.
The most comprehensive survey of the origins and development of world firearms from the Middle Ages to the present day.

The Rare and Valuable Antique Arms, by James E. Serven, Pioneer Press, Union City, TN, 1976. 106 pp., illus. Paper covers. $4.95.
A guide to the collector in deciding which direction his collecting should go, investment value, historic interest, mechanical ingenuity, high art or personal preference.

Reloading Tools, Sights and Telescopes for Single Shot Rifles, by Gerald O. Kelver, Brighton, CO, 1982. 163 pp., illus. Paper covers. $12.00.
A listing of most of the famous makers of reloading tools, sights and telescopes with a brief description of the products they manufactured.

***Revolvers of the British Services 1854-1954,** by W.H.J. Chamberlain and A.W.F. Taylerson, Museum Restoration Service, Ottawa, Canada, 1989. 80 pp., illus. $27.50.
Covers the types issued among one or more of the United Kingdom's naval, land or air services.

Rifles in Colonial America, Vol. I, by George Shumway, George Shumway, Publisher, York, PA, 1980. 353 pp., illus. $49.50.
An extensive photographic study of American longrifles made in the late Colonial, Revolutionary, and post-Revolutionary periods.

Rifles in Colonial America, Vol. II, by George Shumway, George Shumway, Publisher, York, PA, 1980. 302 pp., illus. $49.50.
Final volume of this study of the early evolution of the rifle in America.

The Rimfire Cartridge in the United States and Canada 1857-1984, by John L. Barber, Armory Publications, Tacoma, WA, 1987. 221 pp., illus. $39.95.
An illustrated history of its manufacturers and their patents.

***The Royal Gunroom at Sandringham,** by David Baker, Paidon, Christie's Ltd., Oxford, England, 1989. 160 pp., illus. $150.00.
The British Royal Family's collection of rifles, shotguns and pistols housed at Sandringham is of unique historical importance. Includes the finest items in this collection.

Ruger Rimfire Handguns 1949-1982, by J.C. Munnell, G.D.G.S. Inc., McKeesport, PA, 1982. 189 pp., illus. Paper covers. $13.50.
Updated edition with additional material on the semi-automatic pistols and the New Model revolvers.

Samuel Colt's New Model Pocket Pistols; The Story of the 1855 Root Model Revolver, by S. Gerald Keogh, S.G. Keogh, Ogden, UT, 1974. 31 pp., illus., paper covers. $10.00.
Collector's reference on various types of the titled arms, with descriptions, illustrations, and historical data.

Scottish Arms Makers, by Charles E. Whitelaw, Arms and Armour Press, London, England, 1982. 363 pp., illus. $29.95.
An important and basic addition to weapons reference literature.

***Service Handguns: A Collector's Guide,** by Klaus-Peter Konig and Martin Hugo, David and Charles, N. Pomfret, NH, 1989. 264 pp., illus. $45.00.
Over 200 pistols and revolvers are detailed, most of which have been introduced into the military and police service in Europe since 1850.

Shotshell Boxes; Prices Realized at Auction, 1985,86,87, compiled by Bob Strauss, Circus Promotions, Jefferson, ME, 1988. 19 pp., illus. Paper covers. $10.00.
An illustrated price guide to values of old shotshell boxes.

The Shotshell in the United States, by Richard J. Iverson, Circus Promotions Corp., Jefferson, ME, 1988. 193 pp., illus. Paper covers. $35.00.
Lists manufacturers, distributors, trade brands, headstamps, gauges, shot sizes, colors and configurations.

Simeon North: First Official Pistol Maker of the United States, by S. North and R. North, The Gun Room Press, Highland Park, NJ, 1972. 207 pp., illus. $9.95.
Reprint of the rare first edition.

The Story of Merwin Hulbert & Co. Firearms, by Art Phelps, Rough & Ready Press, Rough & Ready, CA, 1989. 250 pp., illus. $44.95.
The new standard reference work for guns made by Merwin Hulbert & Co.

Research Service, Silver Spring, MD, 1986. 209 pp., illus. Paper covers. $15.00.
Contains information on about 33,800 individual U.S. military weapons, rifles and handguns.

Sharps Firearms, by Frank Seller, Frank M. Seller, Denver, CO, 1982. 358 pp., illus. $39.95.
Traces the development of Sharps firearms with full range of guns made including all martial variations.

Simonov SKS-45 Type Carbines, by Wyant LaMont and Stephen Fuller, Pantera Groups, Burbank, CA, 1988. 218 pp., illus. $21.95.
Covers the history of the development of the Simonov SKS-45 type carbine, numerous combat photographs and detailed directions for maintenance and repair.

Southern Derringers of the Mississippi Valley, by Turner Kirkland, Pioneer Press, Tenn., 1971. 80 pp., illus., paper covers. $5.00.
A guide for the collector, and a much-needed study.

Soviet Russian Postwar Military Pistols and Cartridges, by Fred A. Datig, Handgun Press, Glenview, IL, 1988. 152 pp., illus. $29.95.
Thoroughly researched, this definitive sourcebook covers the development and adoption of the Makarov, Stechkin and the new PSM pistols. Also included in this source book is coverage on Russian clandestine weapons and pistol cartridges.

***Spencer Repeating Firearms,** by Roy M. Marcot, Revised edition, Northwood Heritage Press, Irvine, CA, 1989. 300 pp., illus. $45.00.
A detailed, reliable, exhaustive study on the Spencer repeating rifle and carbine 1858-1862; Roper repeating rifle and shotgun 1866-1876; Spencer slide-action shotgun 1871-1907; plus related ammo and accoutrements.

The Springfield 1903 Rifles, by Lt. Col. William S. Brophy, USAR, Ret., Stackpole Books Inc., Harrisburg, PA, 1985. 608 pp., illus. $49.95.
The illustrated, documented story of the design, development, and production of all the models, appendages, and accessories.

Springfield Shoulder Arms 1795-1865, by Claud E. Fuller, S. & S. Firearms, Glendale, NY, 1986. 76 pp., illus. Paper covers. $15.00.
Exact reprint of the scarce 1930 edition of one of the most definitive works on Springfield flintlock and percussion muskets ever published.

Still More Single Shot Rifles, by James J. Grant, Pioneer Press, Union City, TN, 1979. 211 pp., illus. $17.50.
A sequel to the author's classic works on single shot rifles.

***The Sumptuous Flaske,** by Herbert G. Houze, Andrew Mowbray, Inc., Lincoln, RI, 1989. 158 pp., illus. Soft covers. $35.00.
Catalog of a recent show at the Buffalo Bill Historical Center bringing together some of the finest European and American powder flasks of the 16th to 19th centuries.

System Mauser: A Pictorial History of the 1896 Self-Loading Pistol, by John W. Breathed, Jr. and Joseph J. Schroeder, Jr., Handgun Press, Glenview, IL, 1987. 273 pp., illus. $29.95.
The definitive work on this famous German handgun.

The 36 Calibers of the Colt Single Action Army, by David M. Brown, Publ. by the author at Albuquerque, NM, new reprint 1971. 222 pp., well-illus. $65.00.
Edited by Bev Mann of "Guns" Magazine. This is an unusual approach to the many details of the Colt S.A. Army revolver. Halftone and line drawings of the same models make this of especial interest.

Thoughts on the Kentucky Rifle in its Golden Age, by Joe Kindig, George Shumway, Publisher, York, PA, 1984. 561 pp., illus. $75.00.
A new printing of the classic work on Kentucky rifles.

The Trapdoor Springfield, by M.D. Waite and B.D. Ernst, The Gun Room Press, Highland Park, NJ, 1983. 250 pp., illus. $35.00.
The first comprehensive book on the famous standard military rifle of the 1873-92 period.

Underhammer Guns, by H.C. Logan, Stackpole Books, Harrisburg, PA, 1965. 250 pp., illus. $10.00.
A full account of an unusual form of firearm dating back to flintlock days. Both American and foreign specimens are included.

UK and Commonwealth FALS, by R. Blake Stevens, Collector Grade Publications, Toronto, Canada, 1987. 260 pp., illus. $36.00.
The complete story of the L1A1 in the UK, Australia and India.

United States Martial Flintlocks, by Robert M. Reilly, Andrew Mowbray, Inc., Lincoln, RI, 1986. 263 pp., illus. $39.50.
A comprehensive illustrated history of the flintlock in America from the Revolution to the demise of the system.

***U.S. Military Arms Dates of Manufacture from 1795,** by George Madis, David Madis, Dallas, TX, 1989. 64 pp. Soft covers. $5.00.
Lists all U.S. military arms of collector interest alphabetically, covering about 250 models.

U.S. Military Small Arms 1816-1865, by Robert M. Reilly, The Gun Room Press, Highland Park, NJ, 1983. 270 pp., illus. $35.00.
Covers every known type of primary and secondary martial firearms used by Federal forces.

COLLECTORS (cont.)

Walther P-38 Pistol, by Maj. George Nonte, Desert Publications, Cornville, AZ, 1982. 100 pp., illus. Paper covers. $7.50.

Complete volume on one of the most famous handguns to come out of WWII. All models covered.

Walther Models PP and PPK, 1929-1945, by James L. Rankin, assisted by Gary Green, James L. Rankin, Coral Gables, FL, 1974. 142 pp., illus. $30.00.

Complete coverage on the subject as to finish, proofmarks and Nazi Party inscriptions.

Walther Volume II, Engraved, Presentation and Standard Models, by James L. Rankin, J.L. Rankin, Coral Gables, FL, 1977. 112 pp., illus. $30.00.

The new Walther book on embellished versions and standard models. Has 88 photographs, including many color plates.

Walther, Volume III, 1908-1980, by James L. Rankin, Coral Gables, FL, 1981. 226 pp., illus. $30.00.

Covers all models of Walther handguns from 1908 to date, includes holsters, grips and magazines.

Weapons of the American Civil War, by Ian Hogg, Outlet Books, Inc., Secaucus, NJ, 1987. 176 pp., illus. $9.98.

Civil War weaponry and its effectiveness upon the battlefield. Weapons of all caliber are fully described and examined within their historic context.

Webley Revolvers, by Gordon Bruce and Christien Reinhart, Stocker-Schmid, Zurich, Switzerland, 1988. 256 pp., illus. $49.50.

A revised edition of Dowell's "Webley Story."

Westley Richards Guns and Rifles, a reprint of the Westley Richards firm's centennial catalog of 1912, by Armory Publications, Oceanside, CA, 1988. 211 pp., illus. $34.95.

A century of gun and rifle manufacture, 1812-1912.

The Whitney Firearms, by Claud Fuller, Standard Publications, Huntington, WV, 1946, 334 pp., many plates and drawings, $40.00.

An authoritative history of all Whitney arms and their maker. Highly recommended. An exclusive with Ray Riling Arms Books Co.

The Winchester Book, by George Madis, David Madis Gun Book Distributor, Dallas, TX, 1986. 650 pp., illus. $45.50.

A new, revised 25th anniversary edition of this classic book on Winchester firearms. Complete serial ranges have been added.

Winchester Dates of Manufacture 1849-1984, by George Madis, Art & Reference House, Brownsboro, TX, 1984. 59 pp. $5.95.

A most useful work, compiled from records of the Winchester factory.

The Winchester Handbook, by George Madis, Art & Reference House, Lancaster, TX, 1982. 287 pp., illus. $19.95.

The complete line of Winchester guns, with dates of manufacture, serial numbers, etc.

The Winchester Lever Legacy, by Clyde "Snooky" Williamson, Buffalo Press, Zachary, LA. 684 pp., illus. $59.95.

The most comprehensive book ever written about shooting and hunting with the old Winchester lever action.

Winchester: The Golden Age of American Gunmaking and the Winchester 1 of 1000, by R.L. Wilson, Winchester Arms Museum, Cody, WY, 1983. 144 pp., illus. $45.00.

The author traces the evolution of the firm; against this background he then examines the Winchester Model 1873 and 1876, 1 of 100 and 1000 series rifles.

Winchester's 30-30, Model 94, by Sam Fadala, Stackpole Books, Inc., Harrisburg, PA, 1986. 223 pp., illus. $24.95.

The story of the rifle America loves.

*World War 2 Small Arms, by John Weeks, Chartwell Books, Inc., Secaucus, NJ, 1989. 144 pp., illus. $10.95.

Assesses the weapons of each of the major combatant nations, their production, history, design and features.

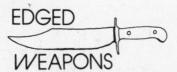
EDGED WEAPONS

The American Eagle Pommel Sword: The Early Years 1793-1830, by Andrew Mowbray, Publisher, Lincoln, RI, 1988. 224 pp., illus. $45.00.

Provides an historical outline, a collecting structure and a vast new source of information for this rapidly growing field.

American Knives; The First History and Collector's Guide, by Harold L. Peterson, The Gun Room Press, Highland Park, NJ, 1980. 178 pp., illus. $19.95.

A reprint of this 1958 classic. Covers all types of American knives.

American Primitive Knives 1770-1870, by G.B. Minnes, Museum Restoration Service, Ottawa, Canada, 1983. 112 pp., illus. $19.95.

Origins of the knives, outstanding specimens, structural details, etc.

The Ames Sword Co., 1829-1935, by John D. Hamilton, Mowbray Co., Providence, RI, 1983. 255 pp., illus. $45.00.

The story of the most prolific American sword makers over the longest period of time.

The American Sword, 1775-1945, by Harold L. Peterson, Ray Riling Arms Books, Co., Phila., PA, 1980. 286 pp. plus 60 pp. of illus. $45.00.

1977 reprint of a survey of swords worn by U.S. uniformed forces, plus the rare "American Silver Mounted Swords, (1700-1815)."

Blacksmithing for the Home Craftsman, by Joe Pehoski, Joe Pehoski, Washington, TX, 1973. 44 pp., illus. Paper covers $5.00.

This informative book is chock-full of drawings and explains how to make your own forge.

Blades and Barrels, by H. Gordon Frost, Wallon Press, El Paso, TX, 1972. 298 pp., illus. $19.95.

The first full scale study about man's attempts to combine an edged weapon with a firearm.

The Book of the Sword, by Richard F. Burton, Dover Publications, New York, NY, 1987. 199 pp., illus. Paper covers.

Traces the swords origin from its birth as a charged and sharpened stick through diverse stages of development.

Bowie Knives, by Robert Abels, Sherwood International Corp., Northridge, CA, 1988. 30 pp., illus. Paper covers. $14.95.

Reprint of the classic work on Bowie knives.

Collecting the Edged Weapons of Imperial Germany, by Thomas M. Johnson and Thomas T. Wittmann, Johnson Reference Books, Fredricksburg, VA, 1989. 363 pp., illus. $39.50.

An in-depth study of the many ornate military, civilian, and government daggers and swords of the Imperial era.

*Collector's Handbook of World War 2 German Daggers, by LTC (Ret.) Thomas M. Johnson, Johnson Reference Books, Fredricksburg, VA, 1990. Soft covers. $15.00.

A guide to German daggers and accoutrements in a convenient format. Includes historical background, documentation, tables, index.

Commando Dagger, by Leroy Thompson, Paladin Press, Boulder, CO, 1984. 176 pp., illus. $29.95.

The complete illustrated history of the Fairbairn-Sykes fighting knife.

The Complete Bladesmith: Forging Your Way to Perfection, by Jim Hrisoulas, Paladin Press, Boulder, CO, 1987. 192 pp., illus. $25.00.

Novice as well as experienced bladesmith will benefit from this definitive guide to smithing world-class blades.

Custom Knifemaking, by Tim McCreight, Stackpole Books, Inc., Harrisburg, PA, 1985. 224 pp., illus. $14.95.

Ten projects from a master craftsman.

The Gun Digest Book of Knifemaking, by Jack Lewis and Roger Combs, DBI Books, Inc., Northbrook, IL, 1989. 256 pp., illus. Paper covers. $13.95.

All the ins and outs from the world of knifemaking in a brand new book.

Gun Digest Book of Knives, 3rd Edition, by Jack Lewis and Roger Combs, DBI Books, Inc., Northbrook, IL, 1988. 256 pp., illus. Paper covers. $13.95.

All new edition covers practically every aspect of the knife world.

How to Make Knives, by Richard W. Barney & Robert W. Loveless, Beinfeld Publ., Inc., No. Hollywood, CA, 1977. 178 pp., illus. $17.95.

A book filled with drawings, illustrations, diagrams, and 500 how-to-do-it photos.

The Japanese Sword, by Kanzan Sato, Kodansha International Ltd. and Shibundo, Tokyo, Japan, 1983. 210 pp., illus. $27.95.

The history and appreciation of the Japanese sword, with a detailed examination of over a dozen of Japan's most revered blades.

Japanese Swordsmanship, by Gordon Warner and Don. F. Draeger, Weatherhill, New York, NY, 1984. 296 pp., illus. $29.95.

Technique and practice of Japanese swordsmanship.

Kentucky Knife Traders Manual No. 6, by R.B. Ritchie, Hindman, KY, 1980. 217 pp., illus. Paper covers. $10.00.

Guide for dealers, collectors and traders listing pocket knives and razor values.

*Knife and Tomakawk Throwing: The Art of the Experts, by Harry K. McEvoy, Charles E. Tuttle, Rutland, VT, 1989. 150 pp., illus. Soft covers. $7.95.

The first book to employ side-by-side the fascinating art and science of knives and tomahawks.

*Knives '91, 11th Edition, edited by Ken Warner, DBI Books, Inc., Northbrook, IL, 1990. 288 pp., illus. Soft covers. $14.95.

Covers trends and technology for both custom and factory knives.

Knife Throwing a Practical Guide, by Harry K. McEvoy, Charles E. Tuttle Co., Rutland, VT, 1973. 108 pp., illus. Paper covers. $5.00.

If you want to learn to throw a knife this is the "bible."

Levine's Guide to Knives And Their Values, 2nd Edition, by Bernard Levine, DBI Books, Inc., Northbrook, IL, 1985. 480 pp., illus. Paper covers. $21.95.

An important guide to today's knife values and collecting them.

Military Swords of Japan 1868-1945, by Richard Fuller and Ron Gregory, Arms and Armour Press, London, England, 1986. 127 pp., illus. $24.95.

A wide-ranging survey of the swords and dirks worn by the armed forces of Japan until the end of World War II.

Rice's Trowel Bayonet, reprinted by Ray Riling Arms Books, Co., Phila., PA, 1968. 8 pp., illus. Paper covers. $3.00.

A facsimile reprint of a rare circular originally published by the U.S. government in 1875 for the information of U.S. troops.

The Samurai Sword, by John M. Yumoto, Charles E. Tuttle Co., Rutland, VT, 1958. 191 pp., illus. $12.50.

A must for anyone interested in Japanese blades, and the first book on this subject written in English.

Scottish Swords from the Battlefield at Culloden, by Lord Archibald Campbell, The Mowbray Co., Providence, RI, 1973. 63 pp., illus. $12.00.

A modern reprint of an exceedingly rare 1894 privately printed edition.

Secrets of the Samurai, by Oscar Ratti and Adele Westbrook, Charles E. Tuttle Co., Rutland, VT, 1983. 483 pp., illus. $35.00.

A survey of the martial arts of feudal Japan.

Survival/Fighting Knives, by Leroy Thompson, Paladin Press, Boulder, CO, 1986. 104 pp., illus. Paper covers. $14.00.

Covers utility blades, hollow-handled survival knives—both commercial and custom-made—survival kits, folders, combat and street-fighting knives, and knife specs and evaluations.

*Switchblade: The Ace of Blades, by Ragnar Benson, Paladin Press, Boulder, Co, 1989. 104 pp., illus. Soft covers. $10.00.

Types of switchblades and their operating mechanisms; how to use switchblade, butterfly, and gravity knives; unusual collector's models; federal and state laws.

Swords for the Highland Regiments 1757-1784, by Anthony D. Darling, Andrew Mowbray, Inc., Publisher, Lincoln, RI, 1988. 62 pp., illus. $18.00.

The basket-hilted swords used by private highland regiments in the 18th century British army.

*Swords of Germany 1900/1945, by John R. Angolia, Johnson Reference Books, Fredricksburg, VA, 1990. 460 pp., illus. $37.95.

If you have an interest in edged weapons of Imperial and Nazi Germany, this is a highly recommended book

EDGED WEAPONS (cont.)

Sword of the Samurai, by George R. Parulski, Jr., Paladin Press, Boulder, CO, 1985. 144 pp., illus. $24.95.

The classical art of Japanese swordsmanship.

Swords from Public Collections in the Commonwealth of Pennsylvania, edited by Bruce S. Bazelon, Andrew Mowbray Inc., Lincoln, RI, 1987. 127 pp., illus. Paper covers. $12.00.

Contains new information regarding swordmakers of the Philadelphia area.

Tomahawks Illustrated, by Robert Kuck, Robert Kuck, New Knoxville, OH, 1977. 112 pp., illus. Paper covers. $12.00.

A pictorial record to provide a reference in selecting and evaluating tomahawks.

GENERAL

Advanced Muzzleloader's Guide, by Toby Bridges, Stoeger Publishing Co., So. Hackensack, NJ, 1985. 256 pp., illus. Paper covers. $11.95.

The complete guide to muzzle-loading rifles, pistols and shotguns—flintlock and percussion.

Air Gun Digest, 2nd Edition, by J.I. Galan, DBI Books, Inc., Northbrook, IL, 1988. 256 pp., illus. Paper covers. $14.95.

Everything from A to Z on air gun history, trends and technology

The AK47 Story, by Edward Ezell, Stackpole Books, Harrisburg, PA, 1988. 256 pp., illus. $12.95.

Evolution of the Kalashnikov weapons.

American Gunsmiths, by Frank M. Sellers, The Gun Room Press, Highland Park, NJ, 1983. 349 pp. $39.95.

A comprehensive listing of the American gun maker, patentee, gunsmith and entrepreneur.

American and Imported Arms, Ammunition and Shooting Accessories, Catalog No. 18 of the Shooter's Bible, Stoeger, Inc., reprinted by Fayette Arsenal, Fayetteville, NC, 1988. 142 pp., illus. Paper covers. $10.95.

A facsimile reprint of the 1932 Stoeger's Shooter's Bible.

American Tools of Intrigue, by John Minnery & Jose Ramos, Desert Publications, Cornville, AZ, 1981. 128 pp., illus. Paper covers. $10.00.

Clandestine weapons which the Allies supplied to resistance fighters.

Archer's Digest, 4th Edition, edited by Roger Combs, DBI Books, Inc., Northbrook, IL, 1986. 256 pp., illus. Paper covers. $13.95.

Authoritative information on all facets of the archer's sport.

Assault Pistols, Rifles and Submachine Guns, by Duncan Long, Paladin Press, Boulder, CO, 1986. 152 pp., illus. Paper covers. $19.95.

A detailed guide to modern military, police and civilian combat weapons, both foreign and domestic.

The Australian Guerilla: Sniping, by Ion L. Idriess, Paladin Press, Boulder, CO, 1989. 104 pp. Paper covers. $8.00.

This classic reprint by Ion Idriess, one of Australia's greatest snipers, covers the art of sniping down to its most esoteric detail.

Be an Expert Shot with Rifle or Shotgun, by Clair Rees, Winchester Press, Piscataway, NJ, 1984. 192 pp., illus. $19.95.

The illustrated self-coaching method that turns shooters into fine marksmen.

Beginner's Guide to Guns and Shooting, Revised Edition, by Clair F. Rees, DBI Books, Inc., Northbrook, IL, 1988. 224 pp., illus. Paper covers. $13.95.

The "how to" book for beginning shooters. The perfect teaching tool for America's youth, the future of our sport, for novices of any age.

Benchrest Actions and Triggers, by Stuart Otteson, Wolfe Publishing Co., Inc., Prescott, AZ, 1983. 61 pp., illus. Paper covers. $9.50.

A combined reprinting of the author's "Custom Benchrest Actions" articles which appeared in "Rifle" Magazine.

Buckskins and Black Powder, by Ken Grissom, Winchester Press, Piscataway, NJ, 1983. 224 pp., illus. $15.95.

A mountain man's guide to muzzleloading.

Carbine; The Story of David Marshall "Carbine" Williams, by Ross E. Beard, Jr., The Sandlapper Store, Inc., Lexington, SC, 1977. 315 pp., illus. $25.00.

The story of the man who invented the M1 Carbine and holds 52 other firearms patents.

Cartridges of the World, 6th Edition, by Frank C. Barnes, DBI Books, Inc., Northbrook, IL, 1989. 448 pp., illus. Paper covers. $18.95.

Completely revised edition of the general purpose reference work for which collectors, police, scientists and laymen reach first for answers to cartridge identification questions.

*Civil War Chief of Sharpshooters Hiram Berdan, Military Commander and Firearms Inventor, by Roy M. Marcot, Northwood Heritage Press, Irvine, CA, 1990. 400 pp., illus. $59.95.

Details the life and career of Col. Hiram Berdan and his U.S. Sharpshooters.

Colonial Riflemen in the American Revolution, by Joe D. Huddleston, George Shumway Publisher, York, PA, 1978. 70 pp., illus. $18.00.

This study traces the use of the longrifle in the Revolution for the purpose of evaluating what effects it had on the outcome.

Competitive Shooting, by A.A. Yuryev, introduction by Gary L. Anderson, NRA Books, The National Rifle Assoc. of America, Wash., DC, 1985. 399 pp., illus. $29.95.

A unique encyclopedia of competitive rifle and pistol shooting.

*The Complete Black Powder Handbook, Revised Edition, by Sam Fadala, DBI Books, Inc., Northbrook, IL, 1990. 320 pp., illus. Soft covers. $15.95.

Expanded and refreshed edition of the definitive book on the subject of blackpowder.

Complete Book of Shooting: Rifles, Shotguns, Handguns, by Jack O'Connor, Stackpole Books, Harrisburg, PA, 1983. 392 pp., illus. $24.95.

A thorough guide to each area of the sport, appealing to those with a new or ongoing interest in shooting

The Complete Book of U.S. Sniping, by P.R. Senich, Paladin Press, Boulder, CO, 1988. 280 pp., illus. $34.95.

U.S. sniping material from its infancy to the current sophisticated systems in use today.

The Complete Guide to Game Care and Cookery, Revised Edition, by Sam Fadala, DBI Books, Inc., Northbrook, IL, 1989. 320 pp., illus. Paper covers. $14.95.

Over 500 detailed photos and hundreds of tested recipes anyone can master.

Crossbows, Edited by Roger Combs, DBI Books, Inc., Northbrook, IL, 1986. 192 pp., illus. Paper covers. $12.95.

Complete, up-to-date coverage of the hottest bow going—and the most controversial.

Custer Battle Guns, by John S. DuMont, Phoenix Publisher, Sugar Hill, NH, 1988. 120 pp., illus. $35.00.

Revised and expanded edition of this definitive work on the guns used by General Custer and his men at the Battle of Little Big Horn.

*The Devil's Paintbrush, by Dolf L. Goldsmith, Collector Grade Publications, Toronto, Canada, 1989. 367 pp., illus. $60.00.

A comprehensive and long overdue treatise on the world's first machine gun and Sir Hiram Maxim's gun.

The Emma Gees, by Herbert W. McBride, Lancer Publications, Mt. Ida, AR, 1988. 218 pp., illus. $18.95.

The author's service with the Machine Gun Section of the 21st Battalion Canadian Expeditionary Force in World War I.

The Encyclopedia of Infantry Weapons of World War II, by Ian V. Hogg, Harper & Row, New York, NY, 1977. 192 pp., illus. $15.95.

A fully comprehensive and illustrated reference work that includes every major type of weapon used by every army in the world during World War II.

Encyclopedia of Modern Firearms, Vol. 1, compiled and publ. by Bob Brownell, Montezuma, IA, 1959. 1057 pp. plus index, illus. $50.00. Dist. By Bob Brownell, Montezuma, IA 50171.

Massive accumulation of basic information of nearly all modern arms pertaining to "parts and assembly." Replete with arms photographs, exploded drawings, manufacturers' lists of parts, etc.

*Firearms Engraving as Decorative Art, by Dr. Fredric A. Harris, Taylor Publishing Co., Dallas, TX, 1990. 172 pp., illus. $60.00.

Specific detail on the styles of such well-known engravers as L.D. Nimschke, J. Ulrich, Conrad F., John and Herman Ulrich, Gustave Young, as well as others.

Firearms for Survival, by Duncan Long, Paladin Press, Boulder, CO, 1988. 144 pp., illus. Paper covers. $16.95.

First complete work on survival firearms for self-defense, hunting, and all-out combat.

*Flayderman's Guide to Antique American Firearms . . . and Their Values, 5th Edition, by Norm Flayderman, DBI Books, Inc., Northbrook, IL, 1990. 624 pp., illus. Soft covers. $24.95.

Updated edition of this bible of the antique gun field.

*The Frontier Rifleman, by H.B. LaCrosse Jr., Pioneer Press, Union City, TN, 1989. 183 pp., illus. Soft covers. $14.95.

The Frontier rifleman's clothing and equipment during the era of the American Revolution, 1760-1800.

The German Sniper, 1914-45, by Peter R. Senich, Paladin Press, Boulder, CO, 1982. 468 pp., illus. $49.95.

The development and application of Germany's sniping weapons systems and tactics traced from WW I through WW II.

*Good Friends, Good Guns, Good Whiskey: The Selected Works of Skeeter Skelton, by Skeeter Skelton, PJS Publications, Peoria, IL, 1989. 347 pp. $21.95.

A guidebook to the world of Skeeter Skelton.

Good Guns, by Stephen Bodio, Nick Lyons Books, New York, NY, 1986. 128 pp., illus. $14.95.

A celebration of fine sporting guns.

Great Sporting Posters, by Sid Latham, Stackpole Books, Harrisburg, PA, 1980. 48 pp., illus. Paper covers. $19.95.

Twenty-three full-color reproductions of beautiful hunting and fishing poster art, mostly of the early 1900s.

The Gun and Its Development, by W.W. Greener, Chartwell Books, Inc., Secaucus, NJ, 1988. 804 pp., illus. $15.95.

Reprint of the scarce 9th edition of this classic work on firearms.

*Gun Digest, 1991, 45th Edition, edited by Ken Warner, DBI Books, Inc., Northbrook, IL, 1990. 496 pp., illus. Soft covers. $18.95.

The latest edition of "The World's Greatest Gunbook."

The Gun Digest Book of Assault Weapons, 2nd Edition, edited by Jack Lewis, DBI Books, Inc., Northbrook, IL, 1989. 256 pp., illus. Paper covers. $14.95.

An in-depth look at the history and uses of these arms.

Gun Digest Book of Metallic Silhouette Shooting, 2nd Edition, by Elgin Gates, DBI Books, Inc., Northbrook, IL, 1979. 256 pp., illus. Paper covers. $14.95.

Examines all aspects of this fast growing sport including history, rules and meets.

The Gun Digest Book of Modern Gun Values, 7th Edition, by Jack Lewis, DBI Books, Inc., Northbrook, IL, 1989. 496 pp., illus. Paper covers. $17.95.

Updated and expanded edition of the book that's become the standard for valuing modern firearms.

Gun Digest Treasury, 6th Edition, edited by Ken Warner, DBI Books, Inc., Northbrook, IL, 1987. 320 pp., illus. Paper covers. $15.95.

The best articles from the first 40 years of "Gun Digest" are compiled here in one book. Complete indexes for all "Gun Digest," "Guns Illustrated," "Gun Digest Hunting Annual" and "Handloader's Digest" through 1987 editions.

*Gunproof Your Children/Handgun Primer, by Massad Ayoob, Police Bookshelf, Concord, NH, 1989. Soft covers. $4.95.

Two books in one. The first, keeping children safe from unauthorized guns in their hands; the second, a compact introduction to handgun safety.

GENERAL (cont.)

Guns and Shooting Yearbook 1989, edited by Jim Carmichel, Stackpole Books, Harrisburg, PA, 1989. 190 pp., illus. $19.95.

A prime collection of the finest articles of the year by many of the major gun/hunting writers of the world.

Guns at the Little Big Horn, by Dick Harmon et al., Andrew Mowbray, Publisher, Lincoln, RI, 1988. 48 pp., illus. Paper covers. $6.50.

The weapons of Custer's last stand.

***Guns Illustrated, 1991, 23rd Edition,** edited by Harold A. Murtz, DBI Books, Inc., Northbrook, IL, 1990. 320 pp., illus. Soft covers. $16.95.

The latest edition of this much acclaimed annual.

Guns, Loads, and Hunting Tips, by Bob Hagel, Wolfe Publishing Co., Prescott, AZ, 1986. 509 pp., illus. $19.95.

A large hardcover book literally packed with shooting, hunting and handloading wisdom.

Guns of the Elite, by George Markham, Arms and Armour Press, Poole, England, 1987. 184 pp., illus. $24.95.

Special Forces firearms, 1940 to the present.

Gunshot Wounds, by Vincent J.M. DiMaio, M.D., Elsevier Science Publishing Co., New York, NY, 1985. 331 pp., illus. $65.00.

Practical aspects of firearms, ballistics, and forensic techniques.

Gun Talk, edited by Dave Moreton, Winchester Press, Piscataway, NJ, 1973. 256 pp., illus. $9.95.

A treasury of original writing by the top gun writers and editors in America. Practical advice about every aspect of the shooting sports.

The Gun That Made the Twenties Roar, by Wm. J. Helmer, rev. and enlarged by George C. Nonte, Jr., The Gun Room Press, Highland Park, NJ, 1977. Over 300 pp., illus. $21.95.

Historical account of John T. Thompson and his invention, the infamous "Tommy Gun."

The Gunfighter, Man or Myth? by Joseph G. Rosa, Oklahoma Press, Norman, OK, 1969. 229 pp., illus. (including weapons). Paper covers. $9.95.

A well-documented work on gunfights and gunfighters of the West and elsewhere. Great treat for all gunfighter buffs.

The Gunfighters, by Dale T. Schoenberger, The Caxton Printers, Ltd., Caldwell, ID, 1971. 207 pp., illus. $18.95.

Startling expose of our foremost Western folk heroes.

Guns of the American West, by Joseph G. Rosa, Crown Publishers, New York, NY, 1985. 192 pp., illus. $24.95.

More than 300 photos, line drawings and engravings complement this lively account of the taming of the West.

Guns & Shooting: A Selected Bibliography, by Ray Riling, Ray Riling Arms Books Co., Phila., PA, 1982. 434 pp., illus. Limited, numbered edition. $75.00.

A limited edition of this superb bibliographical work, the only modern listing of books devoted to guns and shooting.

"Hell, I Was There!," by Elmer Keith, Petersen Publishing Co., Los Angeles, CA, 1979. 308 pp., illus. $24.95.

Adventures of a Montana cowboy who gained world fame as a big game hunter.

***Hidden Threat, a Guide to Covert Weapons,** by Mark Smith, Paladin Press, Boulder, CO, 1989. 168 pp., illus. Soft covers. $12.00.

Intended for use by law enforcement personnel to enhance their knowledge and security when searching subjects, vehicles or premises; provides a fascinating glimpse into the darker side of police work.

Hit the White Part, by Massad Ayoob, Concord, NH, 1982. 107 pp., illus. Paper covers. $7.95.

Second Chance, the art of bowling pin shooting.

How to Make Practical Pistol Leather, by J. David McFarland, Desert Publications, Cornville, AZ, 1982. 68 pp., illus. Paper covers. $8.00.

A guide for designing and making holsters and accessories for law enforcement, security, survival and sporting use.

Kill or Get Killed, by Col. Rex Applegate, new rev. and enlarged ed. Paladin Press, Boulder, CO, 1976. 421 pp., illus. $24.95.

For police and military forces. Last word on mob control.

The Last Book: Confessions of a Gun Editor, by Jack O'Connor, Amwell Press, Clinton, NJ, 1984. 247 pp., illus. $30.00.

Jack's last book. Semi-autobiographical.

The Law Enforcement Book of Weapons, Ammunition and Training Procedures, Handguns, Rifles and Shotguns, by Mason Williams, Charles C. Thomas, Publisher, Springfield, IL, 1977. 496 pp., illus. $135.00.

Data on firearms, firearm training, and ballistics.

The Lewis Gun, by J. David Truby, Paladin Press, Boulder, CO, 1988. 206 pp., illus. $29.95.

The development and employment of this much loved and trusted weapon throughout the early decades of this century.

***Machine Guns, a Pictorial, Tactical & Practical History,** by Jim Thompson, Paladin Press, Boulder, CO, 1989. 248 pp., illus. $39.95.

The historical development of each weapon, useful information on how it shoots and exhaustive advice on ammunition, combined with the rules and regulations governing machinegun ownership in this country.

The Manufacture of Gunflints, by Sydney B.J. Skertchly, facsimile reprint with new introduction by Seymour de Lotbiniere, Museum Restoration Service, Ontario, Canada, 1984. 90 pp., illus. $24.50.

Limited edition reprinting of the very scarce London edition of 1879.

Master Tips, by J. Winokur, Potshot Press, Pacific Palisades, CA, 1985. 96 pp., illus. Paper covers. $11.95.

Basics of practical shooting.

Meditations on Hunting, by Jose Ortega y Gasset, Charles Scribner's Sons, New York, NY, 1985. 132 pp. Paper covers $7.95.

Anticipates with profound accuracy the direction and basic formations of discipline which does not yet exist, a true ecology of men. A new printing of this 1942 classic.

Military Small Arms of the 20th Century, 5th Edition, by Ian V. Hogg and John Weeks, DBI Books, Inc., Northbrook, IL, 1985. 304 pp., illus. Paper covers. $16.95.

Fully revised and updated edition of the standard reference in its field.

Modern Airweapon Shooting, by Bob Churchill and Granville Davis, David & Charles, London, England, 1981. 196 pp., illus. $27.95.

A comprehensive, illustrated study of all the relevant topics, from beginnings to world championship shooting.

Modern Law Enforcement Weapons and Tactics, by Wiley M. Clapp, DBI Books, Inc., Northbrook, IL, 1986. 256 pp., illus. Paper covers. $14.95.

An in-depth look at weapons and equipment used by law enforcement agencies of today.

Modern Sporting Guns, by Jan Stevensen, Outlet Books, New York, NY, 1988. 208 pp., illus. $14.98.

Complete guide to target and sporting weapons. Illustrated with cutaway drawings, detailed diagrams and full-color plates.

No Second Place Winner, by Wm. H. Jordan, publ. by the author, Shreveport, LA (Box 4072), 1962. 114 pp., illus. $15.95.

Guns and gear of the peace officer, ably discussed by a U.S. Border Patrolman for over 30 years, and a first-class shooter with handgun, rifle, etc.

Outdoor Life Gun Data Book, by F. Philip Rice, Outdoor Life Books, New York, NY, 1987. 412 pp., illus. $27.95.

All the facts and figures that hunters, marksmen, handloaders and other gun enthusiasts need to know.

The Police Sniper, by Burt Rapp, Paladin Press, Boulder, CO, 1989. 200 pp., illus. Paper covers. $12.95.

An all-new work that covers this specialized topic unlike any other book.

E.C. Prudhomme, Master Gun Engraver, A Retrospective Exhibition: 1946-1973, intro. by John T. Amber, The R. W. Norton Art Gallery, Shreveport, LA, 1973. 32 pp., illus. Paper covers. $5.00.

Examples of master gun engravings by Jack Prudhomme.

The Quiet Killers II: Silencer Update, by J. David Truby, Paladin Press, Boulder, CO, 1979. 92 pp., illus. Paper covers. $8.00.

A unique and up-to-date addition to your silencer bookshelf.

A Rifleman Went to War, by H. W. McBride, Lancer Militaria, Mt. Ida, AR, 1987. 398 pp., illus. $19.95.

The classic account of practical marksmanship on the battlefields of World War I.

Sharpshooter: Hiram Berdan, His Famous Sharpshooters and Their Sharps Rifles, by Wiley Sword, Andrew Mowbray, Inc., Lincoln, RI, 1988. 96 pp., illus. $16.00.

The story of the U.S. Sharpshooters from beginning to end. No. 3 in "Man at Arms Monogram Series."

***Shooter's Bible, 1940, Stoeger Arms Corp.,** Stoeger, Inc., So. Hackensack, NJ, 1990. 512 pp., illus. Soft covers. $16.95.

Reprint of the Stoeger Arms Corp. catalog No. 33 of 1940.

***Shooter's Bible, 1990, 81st Edition,** Edited by William S. Jarrett, Stoeger Publishing Co., S. Hackensack, NJ, 1990. 576 pp., illus. Soft covers. $16.95.

New and completely revised with 25,000 different items and 8000 illustrations.

Shooting, by Edward A. Matunas, Stackpole Books, Harrisburg, PA, 1986. 416 pp., illus. $31.95.

How to become an expert marksman with rifle, shotgun, handgun, muzzleloader and bow.

Small Arms of the World, 12th Edition, by W.H.B. Smith, revised by Edward C. Ezell, Stackpole Books, Harrisburg, PA, 1983. 1,024 pp., illus. $49.95.

An encyclopedia of global weapons—over 3,500 entries.

Small Arms Today, 2nd Edition, by Edward C. Ezell, Stackpole Books, Harrisburg, PA, 1988. 479 pp., illus. Paper covers. $19.95.

Latest reports on the world's weapons and ammunition.

The SPIW: Deadliest Weapon that Never Was, by R. Blake Stevens, and Edward C. Ezell, Collector Grade Publications, Inc., Toronto, Canada, 1985. 138 pp., illus. $29.95.

The complete saga of the fantastic flechette-firing Special Purpose Individual Weapon.

Steindler's New Firearms Dictionary, by R.A. Steindler, Stackpole Books, Inc., Harrisburg, PA, 1985. 320 pp., illus. $24.95.

Completely revised and updated edition of this standard work.

The Street Smart Gun Book, by John Farnam, Police Bookshelf, Concord, NH, 1986. 45 pp., illus. Paper covers. $11.95.

Weapon selection, defensive shooting techniques, and gunfight-winning tactics from one of the world's leading authorities.

Stress Fire, Vol. 1: Stress Fighting for Police, by Massad Ayoob, Police Bookshelf, Concord, NH, 1984. 149 pp., illus. Paper covers. $9.95.

Gunfighting for police, advanced tactics and techniques.

Survival Guns, by Mel Tappan, the Janus Press, Rouge River, OR, 1987. 458 pp., illus. Paper covers. $14.95.

A guide to the selection, modification and use of firearms and related devices for defense, food gathering, predator and pest control under conditions of long term survival.

***The Terrifying Three-Uzi, Ingram and Intratec Weapons Families,** by Duncan Long, Paladin Press, Boulder, CO, 1989. 136 pp., illus. Soft covers. $20.00.

Discover everything you wanted to know about submachine guns in general, and the "terrifying three" in particular, including specifications for the various models and their variants.

Thompson Guns 1921-1945, Anubis Press, Houston, TX, 1980. 215 pp., illus. Paper covers. $11.95.

Facsimile reprinting of five complete manuals on the Thompson submachine gun.

To Ride, Shoot Straight, and Speak the Truth, by Jeff Cooper, Paladin Press, Boulder, CO, 1988. 384 pp., illus. $26.00.

Cooper, a combat pistol shooting master and the nation's foremost instructor of defensive weaponcraft, squarely faces the facts of modern life and concludes that the armed citizen is the correct answer to the armed sociopath.

The Trappers Handbook, by Rick Jamison, DBI Books, Inc., Northbrook, IL, 1983. 224 pp., illus. Paper covers. $13.95.

Gives the ins and outs of successful trapping from making scent to marketing the pelts. Tips and solutions to trapping problems.

A Treasury of Modern Small Arms, by Jacob Burk, Gallery Books, New York, NY, 1988. 192 pp., illus. $17.95.

A carefully detailed volume with over 200 clear, close-up photos of the best-loved small arms in the world today.

GENERAL (cont.)

A Treasury of Outdoor Life, edited by William E. Rae, Stackpole Books, Harrisburg, PA, 1983. 520 pp., illus. $24.95.

The greatest hunting, fishing, and survival stories from America's favorite sportsman's magazine.

Triggernometry, by Eugene Cunningham, Caxton Printers Ltd., Caldwell, ID, 1970. 441 pp., illus. $17.95.

A classic study of famous outlaws and lawmen of the West—their stature as human beings, their exploits and skills in handling firearms. A reprint.

*U.S. Marine Corps Scout/Sniper Training Manual, Lancer Militaria, Mt. Ida, AR, 1989. Soft covers. $14.95.

Reprint of the original sniper training manual used by the Marksmanship Training Unit of the Marine Corps Development and Education Command in Quantico, Virginia.

*U.S. Marine Corps Sniping, Lancer Militaria, Mt. Ida, AR, 1989. Irregular pagination. Soft covers. $14.95.

A reprint of the official Marine Corps FMFM1-3B.

*Unrepentant Sinner, by Charles Askins, Tejano Publications, San Antonio, TX, 1985. 322 pp., illus. Soft covers. $17.95.

The autobiography of Colonel Charles Askins.

Vietnam Weapons Handbook, by David Rosser-Owen, Patrick Stephens, Wellingborough, England, 1986. 136 pp., illus. Paper covers. $9.95.

Covers every weapon used by both sides.

*Warsaw Pact Weapons Handbook, by Jacques F. Baud, Paladin Press, Boulder, CO, 1989. 168 pp., illus. Soft covers. $15.00.

The most complete handbook on weapons found behind the Iron Curtain.

The Winchester Era, by David Madis, Art & Reference House, Brownsville, TX, 1984. 100 pp., illus. $14.95.

Story of the Winchester company, management, employees, etc.

With British Snipers to the Reich, by Capt. C. Shore, Lander Militaria, Mt. Ida, AR, 1988. 420 pp., illus. $24.95.

One of the greatest books ever written on the art of combat sniping.

You Can't Miss, by John Shaw and Michael Bane, John Shaw, Memphis, TN, 1983. 152 pp., illus. Paper covers. $9.95.

The secrets of a successful combat shooter; tells how to better your defensive shooting skills.

Gunsmithing

Advanced Gunsmithing, by W.F. Vickery, Wolfe Publishing Co., Prescott, AZ, 1988. 429 pp., illus. $42.00.

A limited edition reprint. No modern-day equivalent to this classic on the subject and no other source for tuning some old guns.

The Art of Engraving, by James B. Meek, F. Brownell & Son, Montezuma, IA, 1973. 196 pp., illus. $33.95.

A complete, authoritative, imaginative and detailed study in training for gun engraving. The first book of its kind—and a great one.

Artistry in Arms, The R. W. Norton Gallery, Shreveport, LA, 1970. 42 pp., illus. Paper covers. $5.00.

The art of gunsmithing and engraving.

Building the Kentucky Pistol, by James R. Johnston, Golden Age Arms Co., Worthington, OH, 1974. 36 pp., illus. Paper covers. $4.00.

A step-by-step guide for building the Kentucky pistol. Illus. with full page line drawings.

Building the Kentucky Rifle, by J.R. Johnston. Golden Age Arms Co., Worthington, OH, 1972. 44 pp., illus. Paper covers. $5.00.

How to go about it, with text and drawings.

Checkering and Carving of Gun Stocks, by Monte Kennedy, Stackpole Books, Harrisburg, PA, 1962. 175 pp., illus. $29.95.

Revised, enlarged cloth-bound edition of a much sought-after, dependable work.

The Colt .45 Automatic Shop Manual, by Jerry Kuhnhausen, VSP Publishers, McCall, ID, 1987. 200 pp., illus. Paper covers. $17.95.

Covers repairing, accurizing, trigger/sear work, action tuning, springs, bushings, rebarreling, and custom .45 modification.

The Colt Double Action Revolvers: A Shop Manual, Volume 1, by Jerry Kuhnhausen, VSP Publishers, McCall, ID, 1988. 224 pp., illus. Paper covers. $19.95.

Covers D, E, and I frames.

The Colt Double Action Revolvers: A Shop Manual, Volume 2, by Jerry Kuhnhausen, VSP Publishers, McCall, ID, 1988. 156 pp., illus. Paper covers. $15.95.

Covers J, V, and AA models.

The Complete Rehabilitation of the Flintlock Rifle and Other Works, by T.B. Tyron, Limbo Library, Taos, NM, 1972. 112 pp., illus. Paper covers. $6.95.

A series of articles which first appeared in various issues of the "American Rifleman" in the 1930s.

Do-It-Yourself Gunsmithing, by Jim Carmichel, Outdoor Life-Harper & Row, New York, NY, 1977. 371 pp., illus. $16.95.

The author proves that home gunsmithing is relatively easy and highly satisfying.

Firearms Assembly 3: The NRA Guide to Rifle and Shotguns, NRA Books, Wash., DC, 1980. 264 pp., illus. Paper covers. $11.50.

Text and illustrations explaining the takedown of 125 rifles and shotguns, domestic and foreign.

Firearms Assembly 4: The NRA Guide to Pistols and Revolvers, NRA Books, Wash., DC, 1980. 253 pp., illus. Paper covers. $11.50.

Text and illustrations explaining the takedown of 124 pistol and revolver models, domestic and foreign.

Firearms Blueing and Browning, By R.H. Angier, Stackpole Books, Harrisburg, PA. 151 pp., illus. $14.95.

A world master gunsmith reveals his secrets of building, repairing and renewing a gun, quite literally, lock, stock and barrel. A useful, concise text on chemical coloring methods for the gunsmith and mechanic.

First Book of Gunsmithing, by John E. Traister, Stackpole Books, Harrisburg, PA, 1981. 192 pp., illus. $18.95.

Beginner's guide to gun care, repair and modification.

*The Gun Digest Book of Firearms Assembly/Disassembly, Part 1: Automatic Pistols, Revised Edition, by J.B. Wood, DBI Books, Inc., Northbrook, IL, 1990. 480 pp., illus. Soft covers. $16.95.

Covers 58 popular autoloading pistols plus nearly 200 variants of those models integrated into the text and completely cross-referenced in the index.

*The Gun Digest Book of Firearms Assembly/Disassembly Part 2: Revolvers, Revised Edition, by J.B. Wood, DBI Books, Inc., Northbrook, IL, 1990. 480 pp., illus. Soft covers. $16.95.

Covers 49 popular revolvers plus 130 variants. The most comprehensive and professional presentation available to either hobbyist or gunsmith.

The Gun Digest Book of Firearms Assembly/Disassembly Part III: Rimfire Rifles, by J. B. Wood, DBI Books, Inc., Northbrook, IL, 1980. 288 pp., illus. Paper covers. $13.95.

A most comprehensive, uniform, and professional presentation available for disassembling and reassembling most rimfire rifles.

The Gun Digest Book of Firearms Assembly/Disassembly Part IV: Centerfire Rifles, by J. B. Wood, DBI Books, Inc., Northbrook, IL, 1980. 288 pp., illus. Paper covers. $13.95.

A professional presentation on the disassembly and reassembly of centerfire rifles.

The Gun Digest Book of Firearms Assembly/Disassembly Part V: Shotguns, by J.B. Wood, DBI Books, Inc., Northbrook, IL, 1980. 288 pp., illus. Paper covers. $13.95.

A professional presentation on the complete disassembly and assembly of 26 of the most popular shotguns, new and old.

The Gun Digest Book of Firearms Assembly/Disassembly Part VI: Law Enforcement Weapons, by J.B. Wood, DBI Books, Inc., Northbrook, IL, 1981. 288 pp., illus. Paper covers. $13.95.

Step-by-step instructions on how to completely dismantle and reassemble the most commonly used firearms found in law enforcement arsenals.

The Gun Digest Book of Pistolsmithing, by Jack Mitchell, DBI Books, Inc., Northbrook, IL, 1980. 288 pp., illus. Paper covers. $13.95.

An expert's guide to the operation of each of the handgun actions with all the major functions of pistolsmithing explained.

Gun Digest Book of Riflesmithing, by Jack Mitchell, DBI Books, Inc., Northbrook, IL, 1982. 256 pp., illus. Paper covers. $13.95.

The art and science of rifle gunsmithing. Covers tools, techniques, designs, finishing wood and metal, custom alterations.

Gun Digest Book of Shotgun Gunsmithing, by Ralph Walker, DBI Books, Inc., Northbrook, IL, 1983. 256 pp., illus. Paper covers. $13.95.

The principles and practices of repairing, individualizing and accurizing modern shotguns by one of the world's premier shotgun gunsmiths.

Gun Owner's Book of Care, Repair & Improvement, by Roy Dunlap, Outdoor Life-Harper & Row, NY, 1977. 336 pp., illus. $12.95.

A basic guide to repair and maintenance of guns, written for the average firearms owner.

Guns and Gunmaking Tools of Southern Appalachia, by John Rice Irwin, Schiffer Publishing Ltd., 1983. 118 pp., illus. Paper covers. $9.95.

The story of the Kentucky rifle.

Gunsmith Kinks, by F.R. (Bob) Brownell, F. Brownell & Son, Montezuma, IA, 1st ed., 1969. 496 pp., well illus. $18.95.

A widely useful accumulation of shop kinks, short cuts, techniques and pertinent comments by practicing gunsmiths from all over the world.

Gunsmith Kinks 2, by Bob Brownell, F. Brownell & Son, Publishers, Montezuma, IA, 1983. 496 pp., illus. $18.95.

An incredible collection of gunsmithing knowledge, shop kinks, new and old techniques, shortcuts and general know-how straight from those who do them best—the gunsmiths.

Gunsmithing at Home, by John E. Traister, Stoeger Publishing Co., So. Hackensack, NJ, 1985. 256 pp., illus. Paper covers. $11.95.

Over 25 chapters of explicit information on every aspect of gunsmithing.

Gunsmithing With Simple Hand Tools, by Andrew Dubino, Stackpole Books, Harrisburg, PA, 1987. 205 pp., illus. $19.95.

How to repair, improve, and add a touch of class to the guns you own.

The Gunsmith's Manual, by J.P. Stelle and Wm. B. Harrison, The Gun Room Press, Highland Park, NJ, 1982. 376 pp., illus. $19.95.

For the gunsmith in all branches of the trade.

How to Build Your Own Wheellock Rifle or Pistol, by George Lauber, The John Olson Co., Paramus, NJ, 1976. Paper covers. $12.50.

Complete instructions on building these arms.

How to Build Your Own Flintlock Rifle or Pistol, by George Lauber, The John Olson Co., Paramus, NJ, 1976. Paper covers. $12.50.

The second in Mr. Lauber's three-volume series on the art and science of building muzzle-loading blackpowder firearms.

"How to Build Your Own Percussion Rifle or Pistol," by George Lauber, The John Olson Co., Paramus, NJ, 1976. Paper covers. $12.50.

The third and final volume of Lauber's set of books on the building of muzzle-loaders.

Learn Gunsmithing, by John Traister, Winchester Press, Piscataway, NJ, 1980. 202 pp., illus. $16.95.

The troubleshooting method of gunsmithing for the home gunsmith and professional alike.

The Modern Kentucky Rifle, How to Build Your Own, by R.H. McCrory. McCrory, Wantagh, NY, 1961. 68 pp., illus. Paper bound. $6.00.

A workshop manual on how to fabricate a flintlock rifle. Also some information on pistols and percussion locks.

The Modern Rifle Barrel, by Harold Hoffman, H&P Publishing, San Angelo, TX, 1988. 132 pp., illus. Paper covers. $24.95.

Practical details of the drilling and reaming of rifle and shotgun barrels and of button rifling for long guns and handguns.

GUNSMITHING (cont.)

The NRA Gunsmithing Guide—Updated, by Ken Raynor and Brad Fenton, National Rifle Association, Wash., DC, 1984. 336 pp., illus. Paper covers. $15.95.

Material includes chapters and articles on all facets of the gunsmithing art.

Pistolsmithing, by George C. Nonte, Jr., Stackpole Books, Harrisburg, PA, 1974. 560 pp., illus. $27.95.

A single source reference to handgun maintenance, repair, and modification at home, unequaled in value.

Practical Gunsmithing, by Edward A. Matunas, Stackpole Books, Harrisburg, PA, 1989. 352 pp., illus. $31.95.

A complete guide to maintaining, repairing, and improving firearms.

Recreating the American Longrifle, by William Buchele, et al., George Shumway, Publisher, York, PA, 1983. 175 pp., illus. Paper covers. $20.00; cloth $27.50.

Includes full-scale plans for building a Kentucky rifle.

Respectfully Yours H.M. Pope, compiled and edited by G.O. Kelver, Brighton, CO, 1976. 266 pp., illus. $19.00.

A compilation of letters from the files of the famous barrelmaker, Harry M. Pope.

*Ruger Double Action Revolvers, Vol. 1, Shop Manual, by Jerry Kuhnhausen, VSP Publishers, McCall, ID, 1989. 176 pp., illus. Soft covers. $16.95.

Covers the Ruger Six series of revolvers: Security-Six, Service-Six, and Speed-Six. Includes step-by-step function checks, disassembly, inspection, repairs, rebuilding, reassembly, and custom work.

The S&W Revolver: A Shop Manual, by Jerry Kuhnhausen, VSP Publishers, McCall, ID, 1987. 152 pp., illus. Paper covers. $17.95.

Covers accurizing, trigger jobs, action tuning, rebarreling, barrel setback, forcing cone angles, polishing and rebluing.

Survival Gunsmithing, by J.B. Wood, Desert Publications, Cornville, AZ, 1986. 92 pp., illus. Paper covers. $9.95.

A guide to repair and maintenance of many of the most popular rifles, shotguns and handguns.

The Trade Gun Sketchbook, by Charles E. Hanson, The Fur Press, Chadron, NE, 1979. 48 pp., illus. Paper covers. $4.00.

Complete full-size plans to build seven different trade guns from the Revolution to the Indian Wars and a two-thirds size for your son.

The Trade Rifle Sketchbook, by Charles E. Hanson, The Fur Press, Chadron, NE, 1979. 48 pp., illus. Paper covers. $4.00.

Includes full-scale plans for 10 rifles made for Indian and mountain men; from 1790 to 1860, plus plans for building three pistols.

American Pistol and Revolver Design and Performance, by L. R. Wallack, Winchester Press, Piscataway, NJ, 1978. 224 pp., illus. $19.95.

How different types and models of pistols and revolvers work, from trigger pull to bullet impact.

American Police Handgun Training, by Charles R. Skillen and Mason Williams, Charles C. Thomas, Springfield, IL, 1980. 216 pp., illus. $50.00.

Deals comprehensively with all phases of current handgun training procedures in America.

Askins on Pistols and Revolvers, by Col. Charles Askins, NRA Books, Wash., DC, 1980. 144 pp., illus. Paper covers. $14.95.

A book full of practical advice, shooting tips, technical analysis and stories of guns in action.

Automatics, Fast Firepower, Tactical Superiority, by Duncan Long, Paladin Press, Boulder, CO, 1986. 136 pp., illus. Paper covers. $16.00.

The pluses and minuses of dozens of automatic pistols are presented. Field stripping procedures for various pistol models are given.

Blue Steel and Gun Leather, by John Bianchi, Beinfeld Publishing, Inc., No. Hollywood, CA, 1978. 200 pp., illus. $12.95.

A complete and comprehensive review of holster uses plus an examination of available products on today's market.

Browning Hi-Power Pistols, Desert Publications, Cornville, AZ, 1982. 20 pp., illus. Paper covers. $8.00.

Covers all facets of the various military and civilian models of the Browning Hi-Power pistol.

Colt Automatic Pistols, by Donald B. Bady, Borden Publ. Co., Alhambra, CA, 1974, 368 pp., illus. $19.95.

The rev. and enlarged ed. of a key work on a fascinating subject. Complete information on every automatic marked with Colt's name.

The Colt .45 Auto Pistol, compiled from U.S. War Dept. Technical Manuals, and reprinted by Desert Publications, Cornville, AZ, 1978. 80 pp., illus. Paper covers. $9.95.

Covers every facet of this famous pistol from mechanical training, manual of arms, disassembly, repair and replacement of parts.

Combat Guns, edited by Chris Bishop and Ian Drury, Chartwell Books, Inc., Secaucus, NJ, 1987. 286 pp., illus. $22.95.

An illustrated encyclopedia of 20th century firearms.

*Combat Revolvers: The Best (and Worst) Modern Wheelguns, by Duncan Long, Paladin Press, Boulder, CO, 1989. 115 pp., illus. Soft covers. $16.95.

A no-holds-barred look at the best and worst combat revolvers available today.

Combat Shooting for Police, by Paul B. Weston, Charles C. Thomas, Springfield, IL, 1967. A reprint. 194 pp., illus. $40.00.

First publ. in 1960, this popular self-teaching manual gives basic concepts of defensive fire in every position.

The Complete Book of Combat Handgunning, by Chuck Taylor, Desert Publications, Cornville, AZ, 1982. 168 pp., illus. Paper covers. $16.95.

Covers virtually every aspect of combat handgunning.

*Competitive Pistol Shooting, by Laslo Antal, A&C Black, Cambs, England, 1989. 176 pp., illus. Soft covers. $17.50.

Covers free pistol, air pistol, rapid fire, etc.

The Defensive Use of the Handgun for the Novice, by Mason Williams, Charles C. Thomas, Publisher, Springfield, IL, 1980. 226 pp., illus. Paper covers. $20.00.

This book was developed for the homeowner, housewife, elderly couple, and the woman who lives alone. Basic instruction for purchasing, loading and firing pistols and revolvers.

Experiments of a Handgunner, by Walter Roper, Wolfe Publishing Co., Prescott, AZ, 1989. 202 pp., illus. $37.00.

A limited edition reprint. A listing of experiments with functioning parts of handguns, with targets, stocks, rests, handloading, etc.

Fast and Fancy Revolver Shooting, by Ed. McGivern, Anniversary Edition, Winchester Press, Piscataway, NJ, 1984. 484 pp., illus. $15.95.

A fascinating volume, packed with handgun lore and solid information by the acknowledged dean of revolver shooters.

The Gun Digest Book of Combat Handgunnery, 2nd Edition, by Chuck Karwan, DBI Books, Inc., Northbrook, IL, 1989. 256 pp., illus. Paper covers. $14.95.

This all-new edition looks at real world combat handgunnery from three different perspectives—military, police and civilian.

*The Gun Digest Book of Firearms Assembly/Disassembly, Part 1: Automatic Pistols, Revised Edition, by J.B. Wood, DBI Books, Inc., Northbrook, IL, 1990. 480 pp., illus. Soft covers. $16.95.

Coves 58 popular autoloading pistols plus nearly 200 variants of those models integrated into the text and completely cross-referenced in the index.

*The Gun Digest Book of Firearms Assembly/Disassembly Part 2: Revolvers, Revised Edition, by J.B. Wood, DBI Books, Inc., Northbrook, IL, 1990. 480 pp., illus. Soft covers. $16.95.

Covers 49 popular revolvers plus 130 variants. The most comprehensive and professional presentation available to either hobbyist or gunsmith.

Gun Digest Book of Handgun Reloading, by Dean A. Grennell and Wiley M. Clapp, DBI Books, Inc., Northbrook, IL, 1987. 256 pp., illus. Paper covers. $13.95.

Detailed discussions of all aspects of reloading for handguns, from basic to complex. New loading data.

Gun Digest Book of Metallic Silhouette Shooting, 2nd Edition, by Elgin Gates, DBI Books, Inc., Northbrook, IL, 1988. 256 pp., illus. Paper covers. $14.95.

All about the rapidly growing sport. With a history and rules of the International Handgun Metallic Silhouette Association.

The Gun Digest Book of 9mm Handguns, by Dean A. Grennell and Wiley Clapp, DBI Books, Inc., Northbrook, IL, 1986. 256 pp., illus. Paper covers. $13.95.

The definitive book on the 9mmP pistol.

The Gun Digest Book of Pistolsmithing, by Jack Mitchell, DBI Books, Inc., Northbrook, IL, 1980. 288 pp., illus. Paper covers. $13.95.

An expert's guide to the operation of each of the handgun actions with all the major functions of pistolsmithing explained.

Gun Digest Book of the .45, by Dean A. Grennell, DBI Books, Inc., Northbrook, IL, 1989. 256 pp., illus. Paper covers. $14.95.

Definitive work on one of America's favorite calibers.

Hallock's .45 Auto Handbook, by Ken Hallock, The Mihan Co., Oklahoma City, OK, 1981. 178 pp., illus. Paper covers. $11.95.

For gunsmiths, dealers, collectors and serious hobbyists.

Handgun Digest, 1st Edition, by Dean A. Grennell, DBI Books, Inc., Northbrook, IL, 1987. 256 pp., illus. Paper covers. $13.95.

Full coverage of all aspects of handguns and handgunning from a highly readable, knowledgeable author.

*Handguns '91, 3rd Edition, edited by Jack Lewis, DBI Books, Inc., Northbrook, IL, 1990. 256 pp., illus. Soft covers. $15.95.

An informative annual giving a complete overview of handguns.

Handguns: From Matchlock to Laser-Sighted Weapon, by John Batchlor and John Walter, David and Charles, Devon, England, 1988. 160 pp., illus. $19.95.

The story of the handgun dating from medieval times.

Handguns of the World, by Edward C. Ezell, Stackpole Books, Harrisburg, PA, 1981. 704 pp., illus. $39.95.

Encyclopedia for identification and historical reference that will be appreciated by gun enthusiasts, collectors, hobbyists or professionals.

*High Standard Automatic Pistols 1932-1950, by Charles E. Petty, The Gunroom Press, Highland Park, NJ, 1989. 124 pp., illus. $20.00.

A definitive source of information for the collector of High Standard arms.

*Hunting for Handgunners, by Larry Kelly and J.D. Jones, DBI Books, Inc., Northbrook, IL, 1990. 256 pp., illus. Soft covers. $14.95.

A definitive work on an increasingly popular sport.

The Illustrated Encyclopedia of Pistols and Revolvers, by Major Frederick Myatt, Crescent Books, New York, NY, 1980. 208 pp., illus. $14.95.

An illustrated history of handguns from the 16th century to the present.

Know Your 45 Auto Pistols—Models 1911 & A1, by E.J. Hoffschmidt, Blacksmith Corp., Southport, CT, 1974. 58 pp., illus. Paper covers. $6.95.

A concise history of the gun with a wide variety of types and copies.

*Know Your Czechoslovakian Pistols, by R.J. Berger, Blacksmith Corp., Chino Valley, AZ, 1989. 96 pp., illus. Soft covers. $9.95.

A comprehensive reference which presents the fascinating story of Czech pistols.

Know Your Walther P.38 Pistols, by E.J. Hoffschmidt, Blacksmith Corp., Southport, CT, 1974. 77 pp., illus. Paper covers. $6.95.

Covers the Walther models Armee, M.P., H.P., P.38—history and variations.

Know Your Walther PP & PPK Pistols, by E.J. Hoffschmidt, Blacksmith Corp., Southport, CT, 1975. 87 pp., illus. Paper covers. $6.95.

A concise history of the guns with a guide to the variety and types.

The Luger Pistol (Pistole Parabellum), by F.A. Datig, Borden Publ. Co., Alhambra, CA, 1962. 328 pp., well illus. $19.95.

An enlarged, rev. ed. of an important reference on the arm, its history and development from 1893 to 1945.

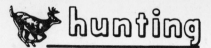

Luger Variations, by Harry E. Jones, Harry E. Jones, Torrance, CA, 1975. 328 pp., 160 full page illus., many in color. $35.00.

A rev. ed. of the book known as "The Luger Collector's Bible."

The M1911A1 Automatic Pistol: Proud American Legend, edited by the American Historical Foundation, Richmond, VA, 1985. 240 pp., illus. Paper covers. $8.95.

Contains reprints of rare governmental manuals, combat photographs and original works by the foundation staff.

The Mauser Self-Loading Pistol, by Belford & Dunlap, Borden Publ. Co., Alhambra, CA. Over 200 pp., 300 illus., large format. $18.95.

The long-awaited book on the "Broom Handles," covering their inception in 1894 to the end of production. Complete and in detail: pocket pistols, Chinese and Spanish copies, etc.

Military Pistols and Revolvers, by Ian V. Hogg, Arms & Armour Press, Dorset, England, 1987. 128 pp., illus. $24.95.

This superbly illustrated book tells the story of the handguns used by the world's armies from the 19th century to the present.

Modern American Pistols and Revolvers, by A.C. Gould, Wolfe Publishing Co., Prescott, AZ, 1988. 222 pp., illus. $37.00.

A limited edition reprint. An account of the development of those arms as well as the manner of shooting them.

Modern Handguns, by Robert Adams, Book Sales, Secaucus, NJ, 1989. 128 pp., illus. $10.98.

History and technical discussion of collectible pistols.

The New Handbook of Handgunning, by Paul B. Weston, Charles C. Thomas, Publisher, Springfield, IL, 1980. 102 pp., illus. $35.00.

A step-by-step, how-to manual of handgun shooting.

The Pistol Guide, by George C. Nonte, Stoeger Publ. Co., So. Hackensack, NJ, 1980. 256 pp., illus. Paper covers. $10.95.

A unique and detailed examination of a very specialized type of gun: the autoloading pistol.

Pistol & Revolver Guide, 3rd Ed., by George C. Nonte, Stoeger Publ. Co., So. Hackensack, NJ, 1975. 224 pp., illus. Paper covers. $6.95.

The standard reference work on military and sporting handguns.

Police Handgun Manual, by Bill Clede, Stackpole Books, Inc., Harrisburg, PA, 1985. 128 pp., illus. $15.95.

How to get street-smart survival habits.

*Powerhouse Pistols—The Colt 1911 and Browning Hi-Power Sourcebook, by Duncan Long, Paladin Press, Boulder, CO, 1989. 152 pp., illus. Soft covers. $19.95.

The author discusses internal mechanisms, outward design, test-firing results, maintenance and accessories.

Report of Board on Tests of Revolvers and Automatic Pistols. From the Annual Report of the Chief of Ordnance, 1907. Reprinted by J.C. Tillinghast, Marlow, NH, 1969. 34 pp., 7 plates, paper covers. $5.00.

A comparison of handguns, including Luger, Savage, Colt, Webley-Fosbery and other makes.

Revolvers, by Ian V. Hogg, Arms & Armour Press, London, England, 1984. 72 pp., illus. $14.95.

An illustrated guide with prices based on recent auction records.

Revolver Guide, by George C. Nonte, Jr., Stoeger Publishing Co., So. Hackensack, NJ, 1980. 288 pp., illus. Paper covers. $10.95.

Fully illustrated guide to selecting, shooting, caring for and collecting revolvers of all types.

The Ruger .22 Automatic Pistol, Standard/Mark I/Mark II Series, by Duncan Long, Paladin Press, Boulder, CO, 1989. 168 pp., illus. Paper covers. $12.00.

The definitive book about the pistol that has served more than 1 million owners so well.

*The Semiautomatic Pistols in Police Service and Self Defense, by Massad Ayoob, Police Bookshelf, Concord, NH, 1990. 25 pp., illus. Soft covers. $9.95.

First quantitative, documented look at actual police experience with 9mm and 45 police service automatics.

Shoot a Handgun, by Dave Arnold, PVA Books, Canyon County, CA, 1983. 144 pp., illus. Paper covers. $8.95.

A complete manual of simplified handgun instruction.

Shoot to Win, by John Shaw, Blacksmith Corp., Southport, CT, 1985. 160 pp., illus. Paper covers. $9.95.

The lessons taught here are of interest and value to all handgun shooters.

Sixgun Cartridges and Loads, by Elmer Keith, reprint edition by The Gun Room Press, Highland Park, NJ, 1984. 151 pp., illus. $19.95.

A manual covering the selection, use and loading of the most suitable and popular revolver cartridges.

*Skeeter Skelton on Handguns, by Skeeter Skelton, PJS Publications, Peoria, IL, 1980. 122 pp., illus. Soft covers. $5.00.

A treasury of facts, fiction, and fables.

*Successful Pistol Shooting, by Frank and Paul Leatherdale, The Crowood Press, Ramsbury, England, 1988. 144 pp., illus. $24.95.

Easy-to-follow instructions to help you achieve better results and gain more enjoyment from both leisure and competitive shooting.

Textbook of Pistols & Revolvers, by Julian Hatcher, Wolfe Publishing Co., Prescott, AZ, 1988. 533 pp., illus. $54.00.

A limited edition reprint. Hatcher wrote this shooters' bible in 1935 and it remains a classic full of invaluable information.

The Walther P-38 Pistol, by Maj. Geo. C. Nonte, Paladin Press, Boulder, CO, 1975. 90 pp., illus. Paper covers. $7.50.

Covers all facets of the gun—development, history, variations, technical data, practical use, rebuilding, repair and conversion.

NORTH AMERICA

Advanced Deer Hunting, by John Weiss, Stackpole Books, Harrisburg, PA, 1988. 352 pp., illus. $28.95.

New strategies based on the latest studies of whitetail behavior.

Advanced Wild Turkey Hunting & World Records, by Dave Harbour, Winchester Press, Piscataway, NJ, 1983. 264 pp., illus. $19.95.

The definitive book, written by an authority who has studied turkeys and turkey calling for over 40 years.

After Your Deer is Down, by Josef Fischl and Leonard Lee Rue, III, Winchester Press, Piscataway, NJ, 1981. 160 pp., illus. Paper covers. $10.95.

The care and handling of big game, with a bonus of venison recipes.

Alaska Game Trails with a Master Guide, by Charles J. Keim, Alaska Northwest Publishing Co., Anchorage, AK, 1984. 310 pp., illus. Paper covers. $8.95.

High adventure tales of fair chase with Alaska's first master guide, Hal Waugh.

*Alaska Safari, by Harold Schetzle, Great Northwest Publishing and Distributing Co., Inc., Anchorage, AK, 1990. 366 pp., illus. $29.50.

The most comprehensive and up-to-date guide to Alaska big game hunting available anywhere.

Alaska Wilderness Hunter, by Harold Schetzle, Great Northwest Publishing and Distributing Co., Anchorage, AK, 1987. 224 pp., illus. $19.95.

A superb collection of Alaska hunting adventures by master guide Harold Schetzle.

*Alaskan Yukon Trophies Won and Lost, by G.O. Young, Wolfe Publishing Co., Prescott, AZ, 1989. 273 pp., illus. $35.00.

A new printing of the classic book on Alaskan big game hunting.

*All About Bears, by Duncan Gilchrist, Stoneydale Press Publishing Co., Stevensville, MT, 1989. 176 pp., illus. $19.95.

Covers all kinds of bears—black, grizzly, Alaskan brown, polar and leans on a lifetime of hunting and guiding experiences to explore proper hunting techniques.

All About Deer in America, edited by Robert Elman, Winchester Press, Piscataway, NJ, 1976. 256 pp., illus. $15.95.

Twenty of America's great hunters share the secrets of their hunting success.

All About Varmint Hunting, by Nick Sisley, The Stone Wall Press, Inc., Wash., DC, 1982. 182 pp., illus. Paper covers. $10.95.

The most comprehensive up-to-date book on hunting common varmints found throughout North America.

All-American Deer Hunter's Guide, edited by Jim Zumbo and Robert Elman, Winchester Press, Piscataway, NJ, 1983. 320 pp., illus. $29.95.

The most comprehensive, thorough book yet published on American deer hunting.

All Season Hunting, by Bob Gilsvik, Winchester Press, Piscataway, NJ, 1976. 256 pp., illus. $14.95.

A guide to early-season, late-season and winter hunting in America.

*The Bear Hunter's Century, by Paul Schullery, Stackpole Books, Harrisburg, PA, 1989. 240 pp., illus. $19.95.

Thrilling tales of the bygone days of wilderness hunting.

Bear Hunting, by Jerry Meyer, Stackpole Books, Harrisburg, PA, 1983. 224 pp., illus. $16.95.

First complete guide on the how-to's of bear hunting. Information on every type of bear found in the U.S. and Canada.

Bear in Their World, by Erwin Bauer, an Outdoor Life Book, New York, NY, 1985. 254 pp., illus. $32.95.

Covers all North American bears; including grizzlies, browns, blacks, and polars.

The Best of Babcock, by Havilah Babcock, selected and with an introduction by Hugh Grey, The Gunnerman Press, Auburn Hills, MI, 1985. 262 pp., illus. $19.95.

A treasury of memorable pieces, 21 of which have never before appeared in book form.

The Best of Nash Buckingham, by Nash Buckingham, selected, edited and annotated by George Bird Evans, Winchester Press, Piscataway, NJ, 1973. 320 pp., illus. $17.95.

Thirty pieces that represent the very cream of Nash's output on his whole range of outdoor interests—upland shooting, duck hunting, even fishing.

Big Game, Big Country, by Dr. Chauncey Guy Suits, Great Northwest Publishing and Distributing Co., Anchorage, AK, 1987. 224 pp., illus. $19.95.

Chronicals more than a decade of high-quality wilderness hunting by one of this country's more distinguished big game hunters.

Big Game of North America, Ecology and Management, by Wildlife Management Institute, Stackpole Books, Harrisburg, PA, 1983. 512 pp., illus. $34.95.

An outstanding reference for professionals and students of wildlife management.

Big Game Record of British Columbia, compiled by the Trophy Wildlife Records Club of British Columbia, Nanoose, British Columbia, 1983. 216 pp., illus. $35.00.

The official record book for native big game trophies taken in British Columbia.

*Big Game Trails in the Far North, by Col. Philip Neuweiler, Great Northwest Publishing and Distributing Co., Inc., Anchorage, AK, 1990. 320 pp., illus. $35.00.

This book is the result of 50 years hunting big game in the Far North.

Bird Hunting with Dalrymple, by Byron W. Dalrymple, Stackpole Books, Harrisburg, PA, 1987. 256 pp., illus. $24.95.

The rewards of shotgunning across North America.

The Bobwhite Quail Book, Compiled by Lamar Underwood, Amwell Press, Clinton, NJ, 1981. 442 pp., illus. $25.00.

An anthology of the finest stories on Bobwhite quail ever assembled under one cover.

Bobwhite Quail Hunting, by Charley Dickey, printed for Stoeger Publ. Co., So. Hackensack, NJ, 1974. 112 pp., illus. Paper covers. $3.95.
Habits and habitats, techniques, gear, guns and dogs.

The Book Shop Moose Book, by James MacNeil, Highway Book Shop, Cobalt, Ontario, Canada, 1986. 112 pp., illus. Paper covers. $6.50.
A most useful guide for the prospective moose hunter.

The Bottoms, by David Hagerbaumer and Dwight Schuh, Amwell Press, Clinton, NJ, 1988. 128 pp., illus. $37.50.
The Bottoms comprise a geographic area in the Midwest, along the Mississippi River. It tells the story that lives in dreams, if not the memory, of every serious waterfowler.

*Bowhunter's Digest, 3rd Edition, by Chuck Adams, DBI Books, Inc., Northbrook, IL, 1990. 288 pp., illus. Soft covers. $14.95.
All-new edition covers all the necessary equipment and how to use it, plus the fine points on how to improve your skill.

Brown Feathers, by Steven J. Julak, Stackpole Books, Harrisburg, PA, 1988. 224 pp., illus. $16.95.
Waterfowling tales and upland dreams.

*Bucks I Have Taken, by Jay M. Gates, Jay M. Gates, Deer Hunter Enterprises, Kingman, AZ, 1989. 200 pp., illus. $20.95.
Learn the techniques that got Gates eight consecutive North American Slams, Boone & Crockett records and trophy deer every year since he was 12. How to hunt all five North American species.

Bugling for Elk, by Dwight Schuh, Stoneydale Press Publishing Co., Stevensville, MT, 1983. 162 pp., illus. $17.95.
A complete guide to early season elk hunting.

*Call of the Quail: A Tribute to the Gentleman Game Bird, by Michael McIntosh, et al., Countrysport, Inc., Traverse City, MI, 1989. 175 pp., illus. $39.50.
An original anthology on quail hunting by Michael McIntosh, Dr. James Nelson, Charles Waterman, Charley Dickey, Tom Huggler, David Simpson and Rocky Evans.

Campfires and Game Trails: Hunting North American Big Game, by Craig Boddington, Winchester Press, Piscataway, NJ, 1985. 295 pp., illus. $19.95.
How to hunt North America's big game species.

The Complete Book of Hunting, by Robert Elman, Abbeville Press, New York, NY, 1982. 320 pp., illus. $29.95.
A compendium of the world's game birds and animals, handloading, international hunting, etc.

The Complete Book of Hunting: A Guide to Game Hunting, Wildfowling and Competition Shooting, edited by David Petzal, W.H. Smith, Publishers, New York, NY, 1988. 192 pp., illus. $14.98.
Equipment, game and dogs, plus techniques and reading the land.

The Complete Book of the Wild Turkey, by Roger M. Latham, Stackpole Books, Harrisburg, PA, 1978. 228 pp., illus. $14.95.
A new revised edition of the classic on American wild turkey hunting.

The Complete Guide to Bird Dog Training, by John R. Falk, Winchester Press, Piscataway, NJ, 1976. 256 pp., illus. $16.95.
How to choose, raise, train, and care for a bird dog.

The Complete Guide to Bowhunting Deer, by Chuck Adams, DBI Books, Inc., Northbrook, IL, 1984. 256 pp., illus. Paper covers. $13.95.
Plenty on equipment, bows, sights, quivers, arrows, clothes, lures and scents, stands and blinds, etc.

The Complete Guide to Game Care and Cookery, Revised Edition, by Sam Fadala, DBI Books, Inc., Northbrook, IL, 1989. 320 pp., illus. Paper covers. $14.95.
Over 500 detailed photos and hundreds of tested recipes anyone can master.

The Complete Smoothbore Hunter, by Brook Elliot, Winchester Press, Piscataway, NJ, 1986. 240 pp., illus. $16.95.
Advice and information on guns and gunning for all varieties of game.

The Complete Turkey Hunt, by William Morris Daskal, El-Bar Enterprises Publishers, New York, NY, 1982. 129 pp., illus. Paper covers. $7.95.
Covers every aspect of turkeys and turkey hunting, by an expert.

Complete Turkey Hunting, by John Phillips, Stackpole Books, Harrisburg, PA, 1988. 320 pp., illus. $24.95.
The definitive work on hunting America's largest game bird.

Confessions of an Outdoor Maladroit, by Joel M. Vance, Amwell Press, Clinton, NJ, 1983. $20.00.
Anthology of some of the wildest, irreverent, and zany hunting tales ever.

The Corey Ford Sporting Treasury, by Corey Ford, Willow Creek Press, Wautoma, WI, 1987. 351 pp. $25.00.
Minutes of the "Lower Forty" and other treasured Corey Ford stories return to print.

Covey Rises and Other Pleasures, by David H. Henderson, Amwell Press, Clinton, NJ, 1983. 155 pp., illus. $17.50.
A collection of essays and stories concerned with field sports.

Coveys and Singles: The Handbook of Quail Hunting, by Robert Gooch, A.S. Barnes, San Diego, CA, 1981. 196 pp., illus. $11.95.
The story of the quail in North America.

*Death in a Lonely Land, by Peter Capstick, St. Martin's Press, New York, NY, 1990. 284 pp., illus. $19.95, Pieces culled from magazine articles written by this very readable author.

Deer and Deer Hunting: The Serious Hunter's Guide, by Dr. Rob Wegner, Stackpole Books, Harrisburg, PA, 1984. 384 pp., illus. $24.95.
In-depth information from the editor of "Deer & Deer Hunting" magazine. Major bibliography of English language books on deer and deer hunting from 1838-1984.

Deer and Deer Hunting Book 2, by Robert Wegner, Stackpole Books, Harrisburg, PA, 1987. 400 pp., illus. $29.95.
Strategies and tactics for the advanced hunter.

The Deer Book, edited by Lamar Underwood, Amwell Press, Clinton, NJ, 1982. 480 pp., illus. $25.00.
An anthology of the finest stories on North American deer ever assembled under one cover.

*Deer Hunting Coast to Coast, by C. Boddington and R. Robb, Safari Press, Long Beach, CA, 1989. 248 pp., illus. $24.95.
Join the authors as they hunt whitetail deer in eastern woodlot, southern swamps, midwestern prairies, and western river bottom; mule deer in badland, deserts, and high alpine basins; blacktails in oak grasslands and coastal jungles.

Deer Hunting, by R. Smith, Stackpole Books, Harrisburg, PA, 1978. 224 pp., illus. Paper covers. $11.95.
A professional guide leads the hunt for North America's most popular big game animal.

Deer Hunter's Guide to Guns, Ammunition, and Equipment, by Edward A. Matunas, an Outdoor Life Book, distributed by Stackpole Books, Harrisburg, PA, 1983. 352 pp., illus. $24.95.
Where to hunt for North American deer. An authoritative guide that will help every deer hunter get maximum enjoyment and satisfaction from his sport.

Deer Hunter's Yearbook 1988, by Outdoor Life Magazine editors, Stackpole Books, Harrisburg, PA, 1988. 192 pp., illus. $19.95.
A collection of articles from "Outdoor Life" Magazine on hunting deer.

Deer in Their World, by Erwin Bauer, Stackpole Books, Harrisburg, PA, 1984. 256 pp., illus. $29.95.
A showcase of more than 250 natural habitat deer photographs. Substantial natural history of North American deer.

*The Deer of North America, edited by Leonard Lee Rue, Stackpole Books, Harrisburg, PA, 1989. 544 pp., illus. $32.95.
Updated and expanded edition of this definitive work on North American deer.

The Desert Bighorn, its Life History, Ecology, and Management, edited by Gale Monson and Lowel Sumner, University of Arizona Press, Tucson, AZ, 1985. 370 pp., illus. Paper covers. $14.95.
There is nothing else around that can tell you anywhere near as much about desert sheep.

Dove Hunting, by Charley Dickey, Galahad Books, NY, 1976. 112 pp., illus. $10.00.
This indispensable guide for hunters deals with equipment, techniques, types of dove shooting, hunting dogs, etc.

Drummer in the Woods, by Burton L. Spiller, Stackpole Books, Harrisburg, PA, 1990. 240 pp., illus. Soft covers. $16.95.
Twenty-one wonderful stories on grouse shooting by "the Poet Laureate of Grouse."

The Duck Hunter's Handbook, by Bob Hinman, revised, expanded, updated edition, Winchester Press, Piscataway, NJ, 1985. 288 pp., illus. $15.95.
The duck hunting book that has it all.

The Duck-Huntingest Gentlemen, by Keith C. Russell et al., Winchester Press, Piscataway, NJ, 1980. 284 pp., illus. $17.95.
A collection of stories on waterfowl hunting.

Ducks of the Mississippi Flyway, ed. by John McKane, North Star Press, St. Cloud, MN, 1969. 54 pp., illus. Paper covers. $10.00.
A duck hunter's reference. Full color paintings of some 30 species, plus descriptive text.

Early American Waterfowling, 1700's-1930, by Stephen Miller, Winchester Press, Piscataway, NJ, 1986. 256 pp., illus. $27.95.
Two centuries of literature and art devoted to the nation's favorite hunting sport.

*Eastern Upland Shooting, by Dr. Charles C. Norris, Countrysport Press, Traverse City, MI, 1989. 408 pp., illus. $29.50.
The authors' observations and experiences on a shooting career of over 50 years. With special reference to bird dogs and their handlers.

The Education of Pretty Boy, by Havilah Babcock, The Gunnerman Press, Auburn Hills, MI, 1985. 160 pp., illus. $19.95.
Babcock's only novel, a heartwarming story of an orphan boy and a gun-shy setter.

Elk and Elk Hunting, by Hart Wixom, Stackpole Books, Harrisburg, PA, 1986. 288 pp., illus. $29.95.
Your practical guide to fundamentals and fine points of elk hunting.

Elk Hunting in the Northern Rockies, by Ed. Wolff, Stoneydale Press, Stevensville, MT, 1984. 162 pp., illus. $17.95.
Helpful information about hunting the premier elk country of the northern Rocky Mountain states—Wyoming, Montana and Idaho.

Fair Chase, by Jim Rikhoff, Amwell Press, Clinton, NJ, 1984. 323 pp., illus. $25.00.
A collection of hunting experiences from the Arctic to Africa, Mongolia to Montana, taken from over 25 years of writing.

*Field Dressing Big Game, by James Churchill, Stackpole Books, Harrisburg, PA, 1989. 88 pp., illus. Soft covers. $10.95.
Dressing, caping, skinning and butchering instructions.

Field Dressing Small Game and Fowl, by James Churchill, Stackpole Books, Harrisburg, PA, 1987. 112 pp., illus. Paper covers. $10.95.
The illustrated guide to dressing 20 birds and animals.

Field Judging Trophy Animals, by William Shuster, Stackpole Books, Harrisburg, PA, 1987. 132 pp., illus. Paper covers. $8.95.
Expert advice and practical suggestions.

Fireside Waterfowler, edited by David E. Wesley and William G. Leitch, A Ducks Unlimited Book, Stackpole Books, Harrisburg, PA, 1987. 357 pp., illus. $29.95.
Fundamentals of duck and goose hunting.

Fireworks in the Peafield Corner, by Archibald Rutledge, Amwell Press, Clinton, NJ, 1986. 357 pp., illus. In slipcase. $30.00.
A treasury of the best of the sage of Hampton plantation, Archibald Rutledge, the first poet laureate of South Carolina.

For Whom the Ducks Toll, by Keith C. Russell, et al., Winchester Press, Piscataway, NJ, 1984. 288 pp., illus. Slipcased, limited and signed edition. $30.00. Trade edition, $16.95.
A select gathering of memorable waterfowling tales by the author and 68 of his closest friends.

The Formidable Game, by John H. Batten, Amwell Press, Clinton, NJ. 1983. 264 pp., illus. $175.00.

Deluxe, limited, signed and numbered edition. Big game hunting in India, Africa and North America by a world famous hunter.

Fur Trapping In North America, by Steven Geary, Winchester Press, Piscataway, NJ, 1985. 160 pp., illus. Paper covers. $10.95.

A comprehensive guide to techniques and equipment, together with fascinating facts about fur bearers.

A Gallery of Waterfowl and Upland Birds, by Gene Hill, with illustrations by David Maass, Petersen Prints, Los Angeles, CA, 1978. 132 pp., illus. $44.95.

Gene Hill at his best. Liberally illustrated with 51 full-color reproductions of David Maass' finest paintings.

Game in the Desert Revisited, by Jack O'Connor, Amwell Press, Clinton, NJ, 1984. 306 pp., illus. $27.50.

Reprint of a Derrydale Press classic on hunting in the Southwest

Getting the Most Out of Modern Waterfowling, by John O. Cartier, St. Martin's Press, NY, 1974. 396 pp., illus. $22.50.

The most comprehensive, up-to-date book on waterfowling imaginable.

Georgia's Greatest Whitetails, by Duncan Dobie, Bucksnort Publishing, Marietta, GA, 1986. 476 pp., illus. $24.00.

Georgia's greatest whitetails, featuring all of the spine-tingling stories behind these record-breaking bucks, 42 in all.

The Gordon MacQuarrie Trilogy, by Gordon MacQuarrie, compiled and edited by Zack Taylor, Willow Creek Press, Oshkosh, WI, 1985. A three book, slip-cased set. $45.00.

Three-volume set comprising: **Stories of the Old Duck Hunters and Other Drivel, More Stories of the Old Duck Hunters, Last Stories of the Old Duck Hunters.**

The Grand Spring Hunt for America's Wild Turkey Gobbler, by Bart Jacob with Ben Conger, Winchester Press, Piscataway, NJ, 1985. 176 pp., illus. $15.95.

The turkey book for novice and expert alike.

Grizzly Country, by Andy Russell, A.A. Knopf, NYC, 1973, 302 pp., illus. $15.95.

Many-sided view of the grizzly bear and his world, by a noted guide, hunter and naturalist.

Grizzlies Don't Come Easy, by Ralph Young, Winchester Press, Piscataway, NJ, 1981. 200 pp., illus. $15.95.

The life story of a great woodsman who guided famous hunters such as O'Connor, Keith, Fitz, Page and others.

Grouse and Grouse Hunting, by Frank Woolner, Nick Lyons Books, N.Y., NY, 1987. 192 pp., illus. $18.95.

An authoritative and affectionate portrait of one of America's greatest game birds.

Grouse Hunter's Guide, by Dennis Walrod, Stackpole Books, Harrisburg, PA, 1985. 192 pp., illus. $16.95.

Solid facts, observations, and insights on how to hunt the ruffed grouse.

Gunning for Sea Ducks, by George Howard Gillelan, Tidewater Publishers, Centreville, MD, 1988. 144 pp., illus. $14.95.

A book that introduces you to a practically untouched arena of waterfowling.

*History of Wild Sheep Hunting in North America: Wild Sheep and Wild Sheep Hunters of the New World, by Raul Valdez, Wild Sheep International, Mesilla, NM, 1989. 250 pp., illus. $75.00.

Traces the history of wild sheep hunting in North America from the pre-Columbian period to the present.

Horned and Antlered Game, by Erwin Bauer, Stackpole Books, Harrisburg, PA, 1987. 256 pp., illus. $32.95.

This book features spectacular color photographs and text brimming with animal lore.

Horns in the High Country, by Andy Russell, Alfred A. Knopf, NY, 1973. 259 pp., illus. Paper covers. $12.95.

A many-sided view of wild sheep and their natural world.

How to Get Your Deer, by John O. Cartier, Stackpole Books, Harrisburg, PA, 1986. 320 pp., illus. $24.95.

An authoritative guide to deer hunting that shows you how to match wits with your quarry and win.

How to Hunt, by Dave Bowring, Winchester Press, Piscataway, NJ, 1982. 208 pp., illus. Paper covers. $10.95; cloth, $15.00.

A basic guide to hunting big game, small game, upland birds, and waterfowl.

A Hunter's Fireside Book, by Gene Hill, Winchester Press, Piscataway, NJ, 1972. 192 pp., illus. $15.95.

An outdoor book that will appeal to every person who spends time in the field—or who wishes he could.

The Hunter's Rifle, by Col. Charles Askins, The National Rifle Association, Wash., DC, 1984. 176 pp., illus. Paper covers. $17.95.

A book on the hunting rifle and cartridges for killing big game.

The Hunter's Shooting Guide, by Jack O'Connor, Outdoor Life Books, New York, NY, 1982. 176 pp., illus. Paper covers. $5.95.

A classic covering rifles, cartridges, shooting techniques for shotguns/rifles/handguns.

The Hunter's World, by Charles F. Waterman, Winchester Press, Piscataway, NJ, 1983. 250 pp., illus. $29.95.

A classic. One of the most beautiful hunting books that has ever been produced.

Hunting the Alaskan Brown Bear, by John Eddy, Wolfe Publishing Co., Prescott, AZ, 1988. 253 pp., illus. $47.00.

A limited edition reprint of the best book on the big brown bear of the North.

Hunting the American Wild Turkey, by Dave Harbour, Stackpole Books, Harrisburg, PA, 1975. 256 pp., illus. $14.95.

The techniques and tactics of hunting North America's largest, and most popular, woodland game bird.

Hunting America's Game Animals and Birds, by Robert Elman and George Peper, Winchester Press, Piscataway, NJ, 1975. 368 pp., illus. $16.95.

A how-to, where-to, when-to guide—by 40 top experts—covering the continent's big, small, upland game and waterfowl.

Hunting Ducks and Geese, by Steven Smith, Stackpole Books, Harrisburg, PA, 1984. 160 pp., illus. $15.95.

Hard facts, good bets, and serious advice from a duck hunter you can trust.

*Hunting for Handgunners, by Larry Kelly and J.D. Jones, DBI Books, Inc., Northbrook, IL, 1990. 256 pp., illus. Soft covers. $14.95.

A definitive work on an increasingly popular sport.

Hunting Fringeland Deer, by David Richey, Stackpole Books, Harrisburg, PA, 1987. 208 pp., illus. $24.95.

Tactics for trail watching, stillhunting and driving whitetails in farmlands, edge country and populated areas.

Hunting in the Rockies, by Jack O'Connor, Safari Press, Long Beach, CA, 1988. 297 pp., illus. $29.95.

This new revised edition of Jack O'Connor's hard-to-find book on the game animals of the Rockies includes tips for hunting throughout the entire Rocky Mountain region.

Hunting in the Southlands, edited by Lamar Underwood, Amwell Press, Clinton, NJ, 1987. 565 pp., illus. $35.00.

An anthology of the best stories of southern hunts including dove, turkey, waterfowl, deer, quail and more.

Hunting North America's Big Game, by Bob Hagel, Stackpole Books, Harrisburg, PA, 1987. 220 pp., illus. $27.95.

Complete and reliable coverage on how to approach, track, and shoot game in different terrains.

Hunting on Horseback, by Jim Ottman, Paladin Press, Boulder, CO, 1987. 151 pp., illus. $16.95.

Advice on how to get into shape for a horseback hunt, in addition to providing tips about weapons, ammunition, equipment, setting up a base camp and packing with a horse.

Hunting on Three Continents with Jack O'Connor, by Jack O'Connor with an introduction by John Batten, Safari Press, Long Beach, CA, 1987. 303 pp., illus. $35.00.

A collection of the author's best material written for Petersen's "Hunting" Magazine during the years 1973-1977.

Hunting Open-Country Mule Deer, by Dwight Schuh, Sage Press, Nampa, ID, 1989. 180 pp., illus. $17.95.

A guide taking Western bucks with rifle and bow.

Hunting Predators for Hides and Profits, by Wilf E. Pyle, Stoeger Publishing Co., So. Hackensack, NJ, 1985. 224 pp., illus. Paper covers. $11.95.

The author takes the hunter through every step of the hunting/marketing process.

Hunting Rabbits and Hares, by Richard P. Smith, Stackpole Books, Harrisburg, PA, 1986. 160 pp., illus. Paper covers. $12.95.

The complete guide to North America's favorite small game.

Hunting the Rocky Mountain Goat, by Duncan Gilchrist, Duncan Gilchrist, Hamilton, MT, 1983. 175 pp., illus. Paper covers. $10.95.

Hunting techniques for mountain goats and other alpine game. Tips on rifles for the high country.

Hunting and Stalking Deer Throughout the World, by Kenneth G. Whitehead, Batsford Books, London, 1982. 336 pp., illus. $35.00.

Comprehensive coverage of deer hunting areas on a country-by-country basis, dealing with every species in any given country.

Hunting the Southwest, by Jack Samson, The Amwell Press, Clinton, NJ, 1985. 172 pp., illus. In slipcase $27.50.

The most up-to-date look at one of the most difficult and diverse hunting areas in the world today.

*Hunting Superbucks, by Kathy Etling, Grolier Book Clubs, Danbury, CT, 1989. 444 pp., illus. $32.95.

How to find and hunt today's trophy mule and whitetail deer.

Hunting Trips in North America, by F.C. Selous, Wolfe Publishing Co., Prescott, AZ, 1988. 395 pp., illus. $52.00.

A limited edition reprint. Coverage of caribou, moose and other big game hunting in virgin wilds.

Hunting Trophy Deer, by John Wootters, Winchester Press, Piscataway, NJ, 1983. 265 pp., illus. $15.95.

All the advice you need to succeed at bagging trophy deer.

Hunting Upland Gamebirds, by Steve Smith, Stackpole Books, Harrisburg, PA, 1987. 176 pp., illus. $16.95.

What the wingshooter needs to know about the birds, the game, and the new clay games.

Hunting Wild Turkeys in the Everglades, by Frank P. Harben, Harben Publishing Co., Safety Harbor, FL, 1983. 341 pp., illus. Paper covers. $8.95.

Describes techniques, ways and means of hunting this wary bird.

*Hunting Wild Turkeys with Ray Eye, by Michael Pearce and Ray Eye, Stackpole Books, Harrisburg, PA, 1990. 208 pp., illus. $22.95.

Whether you hunt in spring or fall, with a gun or bow and arrow, alone or with a partner, you will find in this book a wealth of practical information.

*Indian Hunts and Indian Hunters of the Old West, by Dr. Frank C. Hibben, Safari Press, Long Beach, CA, 1989. 228 pp., illus. $24.95.

Tales of some of the most famous American Indian hunters of the Old West as told to the author by an old Navajo hunter.

I Don't Want to Shoot an Elephant, by Havilah Babcock, The Gunnerman Press, Auburn Hills, MI, 1985. 184 pp., illus. $19.95.

Eighteen delightful stories that will enthrall the upland gunner for many pleasurable hours.

In Search of the Wild Turkey, by Bob Gooch, Greatlakes Living Press, Ltd., Waukegan, IL, 1978. 182 pp., illus. $9.95.

A state-by-state guide to wild turkey hot spots, with tips on gear and methods for bagging your bird.

Instinctive Shooting, by G. Fred Asbell, Stackpole Books, Harrisburg, PA, 1988. 132 pp., illus. Paper covers. $13.95.

Expert advice on applying instinctive shooting to bowhunting. Written by the president of the Pope & Young Club.

Jaybirds Go to Hell on Friday, by Havilah Babcock, The Gunnerman Press, Auburn Hills, MI, 1985. 149 pp., illus. $19.95.

Sixteen jewels that reestablish the lost art of good old-fashioned yarn telling.

A Listening Walk . . . and Other Stories, by Gene Hill, Winchester Press, Piscataway, NJ, 1985. 208 pp., illus. $15.95.

Vintage Hill. Over 60 stories.

HUNTING (cont.)

Making Game: An Essay on Woodcock, by Guy De La Valdene, Willow Creek Press, Oshkosh, WI, 1985. 202 pp., illus. $20.00.
The most delightful book on woodcock yet published.

Marsh Tales, by William N. Smith, Tidewater Publishers, Centreville, MD, 1985. 228 pp., illus. $15.95.
Market hunting, duck trapping, and gunning.

Matching the Gun to the Game, by Clair Rees, Winchester Press, Piscataway, NJ, 1982. 272 pp., illus. $17.95.
Covers selection and use of handguns, blackpowder firearms for hunting, matching rifle type to the hunter, calibers for multiple use, tailoring factory loads to the game.

Measuring and Scoring North American Big Game Trophies, by Wm. H. Nesbitt and Philip L. Wright, The Boone and Crockett Club, Alexandria, VA, 1986. 176 pp., illus. $15.00.
The Boone and Crockett Club official scoring system, with tips for field evaluation of trophies.

Meat on the Table: Modern Small-Game Hunting, by Galen Geer, Paladin Press, Boulder, CO, 1985. 216 pp., illus. $16.95.
All you need to know to put meat on your table from this comprehensive course in modern small-game hunting.

Mixed Bag, by Jim Rikhoff, National Rifle Association of America, Wash., DC, 1981. 284 pp., illus. Paper covers. $9.95.
Reminiscences of a master raconteur.

Modern Pheasant Hunting, by Steve Grooms, Stackpole Books, Harrisburg, PA, 1982. 224 pp., illus. Paper covers. $10.95.
New look at pheasants and hunters from an experienced hunter who respects this splendid gamebird.

Modern Waterfowl Guns and Gunning, by Don Zutz, Stoeger Publishing Co., So. Hackensack, NJ, 1985. 224 pp., illus. Paper covers. $11.95.
Up-to-date information on the fast-changing world of waterfowl guns and loads.

*Montana: Land of Giant Rams, by Duncan Gilchrist, Stoneydale Press Publishing Co., Stevensville, MT, 1990. 208 pp., illus. $19.95.
Latest information on Montana bighorn sheep and why so many Montana bighorn rams are growing to trophy size.

More and Better Pheasant Hunting, by Steve Smith, Winchester Press, Piscataway, NJ, 1986. 192 pp., illus. $15.95.
Complete, fully illustrated, expert coverage of the bird itself, the dogs, the hunt, the guns, and the best places to hunt.

More Grouse Feathers, by Burton L. Spiller, Crown Publ., NY, 1972. 238 pp., illus. $15.00.
Facsimile of the original Derrydale Press issue of 1938. Guns and dogs, the habits and shooting of grouse, woodcock, ducks, etc. Illus. by Lynn Bogue Hunt.

More Than a Trophy, by Dennis Walrod, Stackpole Books, Harrisburg, PA, 1983. 256 pp., illus. Paper covers. $12.95.
Field dressing, skinning, quartering, and butchering to make the most of your valuable whitetail, blacktail or mule deer.

More Stories of the Old Duck Hunter, by Gordon MacQuarrie, Willow Creek Press, Oshkosh, WI, 1983. 200 pp., illus. $15.00.
Collection of 18 treasured stories of The Old Duck Hunters originally published in major magazines of the 1930s and '40s.

Mostly Tailfeathers, by Gene Hill, Winchester Press, Piscataway, NJ, 1975. 192 pp., illus. $14.95.
An interesting, general book about bird hunting.

Mostly Huntin', by Bill Jordan, Everett Publishing Co., Bossier City, LA, 1987. 254 pp., illus. $21.95.
Jordan's hunting adventures in North America, Africa, Australia, South America and Mexico.

Movin' Along with Charley Dickey, by Charlie Dickey, Winchester Press, Piscataway, NJ, 1985. 224 pp., illus. $14.95.
More wisdom, wild tales, and wacky wit from the Sage of Tallahassee.

Murry Burnham's Hunting Secrets, by Murry Burnham with Russell Tinsley, Winchester Press, Piscataway, NJ, 1984. 244 pp., illus. $17.95.
One of the great hunters of our time gives the reasons for his success in the field.

The Muzzleloading Hunter, by Rick Hacker, Stackpole Books, Harrisburg, PA, 1989. 295 pp., illus. $19.95.
The book for anyone interested in the rapidly growing sport of hunting with a muzzleloader.

*My Friend the Partridge, Memories of New England Shooting, by S.T. Hammond, The Gunnerman Press, Auburn Hills, MI, 1989. 148 pp.
A limited, numbered reprint of this scarce work on ruffed grouse hunting. The author's experience spanned 60 years from the 1840s into the present century.

My Health is Better in November, by Havilah Babcock, University of S. Carolina Press, Columbia, SC, 1985. 284 pp., illus. $19.95.
Adventures in the field set in the plantation country and backwater streams of South Carolina.

My Lost Wilderness: Tales of an Alaskan Woodsman, by Ralph Young, Winchester Press, Piscataway, NJ, 1983. 193 pp., illus. $22.50.
True tales of an Alaskan hunter, guide, fisherman, prospector, and backwoodsman.

New England Grouse Shooting, by William Harnden Foster, Willow Creek Press, Oshkosh, WI, 1983. 213 pp., illus. $45.00.
A new release of a classic book on grouse shooting.

North American Big Game Animals, by Byron W. Dalrymple and Erwin Bauer, Outdoor Life Books/Stackpole Books, Harrisburg, PA, 1985. 258 pp., illus. $29.95.
Complete illustrated natural histories. Habitat, movements, breeding, birth and development, signs, and hunting.

North American Elk: Ecology and Management, edited by Jack Ward Thomas and Dale E. Toweill, Stackpole Books, Harrisburg, PA, 1982. 576 pp., illus. $39.95.
The definitive, exhaustive, classic work on the North American elk.

The North American Waterfowler, by Paul S. Bernsen, Superior Publ. Co., Seattle, WA, 1972. 206 pp. Paper covers. $4.95.
The complete inside and outside story of duck and goose shooting. Big and colorful, illus. by Les Kouba.

Of Bears and Man, by Mike Cramond, University of Oklahoma Press, Norman, OK, 1986. 433 pp., illus. $29.95.
The author's lifetime association with bears of North America. Interviews with survivors of bear attacks.

Of Bench and Bears; Alaska's Bear Hunting Judge, by Richard C. Folta, Great Northwest Publishing and Distributing Co., Anchorage, AK, 1986. 224 pp., illus. $20.00.
Alaska's bear hunting judge who personally bagged some 200 bears during his half century of Alaskan hunting.

*The Old Man and the Boy and The Old Man Grows Older, by Robert Ruark, Stackpole Books, Harrisburg, PA, 1989. 620 pp., illus. Soft covers. $17.95.
Two novels in one volume. Classic tales of the coming of age of a boy and young man as he is nurtured and educated by his remarkable sportsman grandfather.

The Old Pro Turkey Hunter, by Gene Nunnery, Gene Nunnery, Meridian, MS, 1980. 144 pp., illus. $12.95.
True facts and old tales of turkey hunters.

1001 Hunting Tips, by Robert Elman, Winchester Press, Piscataway, NJ, 1983. 544 pp., illus. $22.95.
New edition, updated and expanded. A complete course in big and small game hunting, wildfowling and hunting upland birds.

The Only Good Bear is a Dead Bear, by Jeanette Hortick Prodgers, Falcon Press, Helena, MT, 1986. 204 pp. Paper covers. $7.95.
A collection of the West's best bear stories.

Opening Shots and Parting Lines: The Best of Dickey's Wit, Wisdom, and Wild Tales for Sportsmen, by Charley Dickey, Winchester Press, Piscataway, NJ, 1983. 208 pp., illus. $14.95.
Selected by the writer who has entertained millions of readers in America's top sporting publications—49 of his best pieces.

The Orvis Book of Upland Bird Shooting, by Geoffrey Norman, Winchester Press, Piscataway, NJ, 1985. 155 pp., illus. $15.95.
A marvelously full and helpful look at the world of upland bird shooting.

The Outdoor Life Bear Book, edited by Chet Fish, an Outdoor Life book, distributed by Stackpole Books, Harrisburg, PA, 1983. 352 pp., illus. $26.95.
All-time best personal accounts of terrifying attacks, exciting hunts, and intriguing natural history.

The Outdoor Life Deer Hunter's Encyclopedia, by John Madson, et al., Stackpole Books, Harrisburg, PA, 1985. 800 pp., illus. $49.95.
The largest, most comprehensive volume of its kind ever published.

Outdoor Life Deer Hunter's Yearbook 1989, edited by George H. Haas, Stackpole Books, Harrisburg, PA, 1989. 190 pp., illus. $19.95.
Thirty-eight of the best articles on deer and elk hunting are presented here, most with color illustrations.

Outdoor Yarns & Outright Lies, by Gene Hill and Steve Smith, Stackpole Books, Harrisburg, PA, 1984. 168 pp., illus. $16.95.
Fifty or so stories by two good sports.

The Outlaw Gunner, by Harry M. Walsh, Tidewater Publishers, Cambridge, MD, 1973. 178 pp., illus. $12.50.
A colorful story of market gunning in both its legal and illegal phases.

Picking Your Shots, by Steve Smith, Stackpole Books, Harrisburg, PA, 1986. 160 pp., illus. $16.95.
Stories of dogs and birds, and guns and days afield.

Pinnell and Talifson: Last of the Great Brown Bear Men, by Marvin H. Clark, Jr., Great Northwest Publishing and Distributing Co., Spokane, WA, 1980. 224 pp., illus. $20.00.
The story of these famous Alaskan guides and some of the record bears taken by them.

The Practical Hunter's Handbook, by Anthony J. Acerrano, Winchester Press, Piscataway, NJ, 1978. 224 pp., illus. Paper covers. $12.95.
How the time-pressed hunter can take advantage of every edge his hunting situation affords him.

Predator Caller's Companion, by Gerry Blair, Winchester Press, Piscataway, NJ, 1981. 280 pp., illus. $18.95.
Predator calling techniques and equipment for the hunter and trapper.

Predators of North America, by Erwin Bauer, Stackpole Books, Harrisburg, PA, 1988. 256 pp., illus. $34.95.

Pronghorn, North America's Unique Antelope, by Charles L. Cadieux, Stackpole Books, Harrisburg, PA, 1986. 256 pp., illus. $24.95.
The practical guide for hunters.

Quail Hunting in America, by Tom Huggler, Stackpole Books, Harrisburg, PA, 1987. 288 pp., illus. $19.95.
Tactics for finding and taking bobwhite, valleys, Gambel's Mountain, scaled-blue, and Mearn's quail by season and habitat.

Radical Elk Hunting Strategies, by Mike Lapinski, Stoneydale Press Publishing Co., Stevensville, MT, 1988. 161 pp., illus. $17.95.
Secrets of calling elk in close.

Ralf Coykendall's Duck Decoys and How to Rig Them, revised by Ralf Coykendall, Jr., Winchester Press, Piscataway, NJ, 1983. 128 pp., illus. Slipcased. $21.95.
For every discriminating book collector and sportsman, a superb new edition of a long out-of-print classic.

Ranch Life and the Hunting Trail, by Theodore Roosevelt, Readex Microprint Corp., Dearborn, MI, 1966. 186 pp. With drawings by Frederic Remington. $22.50.
A facsimile reprint of the original 1899 Century Co. edition. One of the most fascinating books of the West of that day.

Records of Alaska Big Game, edited by Norman B. Grant, Alaska Big Game Trophy Club, Anchorage, AK, 1971. 111 pp., illus. $95.00.
Contains the recorded and tabulated trophies of Alaskan big game, including the name of the hunter, date and place, and measurement.

*Records of North American Big Game 1932, by Prentis N. Grey, Boone and Crockett Club, Dumfries, VA, 1988. 178 pp., illus. $79.95.
A reprint of the book that started the Club's record keeping for native North American big game.

Records of North American Big Game, 9th Edition, 1988, edited by William H. Nesbitt and Jack Reneau, Boone and Crockett Club, Dumfries, VA, 1989. 512 pp., illus. $49.95.

A special Centennial Year edition of useful statistics and good reading about our native big game animals. With a special full-color section.

Records of North American Whitetailed Deer, by the editors of the Boone and Crockett Club, Dumfries, VA, 1987. 256 pp., illus. Flexible covers. $15.00.

Contains data on 1,293 whitetail trophies over the all-time record book minimum, listed and ranked by state or province and divided into typical and non-typical categories.

Ridge Runners & Swamp Rats, by Charles F. Waterman, Amwell Press, Clinton, NJ, 1983. 347 pp., illus. $25.00.

Tales of hunting and fishing.

Ringneck! Pheasants & Pheasant Hunting, by Ted Janes, Crown Publ., NY, 1975. 120 pp., illus. $15.95.

A thorough study of one of our more popular game birds.

*Ruffed Grouse, edited by Sally Atwater and Judith Schnell, Stackpole Books, Harrisburg, PA, 1989. 370 pp., illus. $59.95.

Everything you ever wanted to know about the ruffed grouse. More than 25 wildlife professionals provided in-depth information on every aspect of this popular game bird's life. Lavishly illustrated with over 300 full-color photos.

*Shadows of the Tundra, by Tom Walker, Stackpole Books, Harrisburg, PA, 1990. 192 pp., illus. $19.95.

Alaskan tales of predator, prey, and man.

Charles Sheldon Trilogy, by Charles Sheldon, Amwell Press, Clinton, NJ, 1983. 3 volumes in slipcase. **The Wilderness of the Upper Yukon,** 363 pp., illus.; **The Wilderness of the North Pacific Coast Islands,** 246 pp., illus.; **The Wilderness of Denali,** 412 pp., illus. Deluxe edition. $205.00.

Custom-bound reprinting of Sheldon's classics, each signed and numbered by the author's son, William G. Sheldon.

*Shots at Big Game, by Craig Boddington, Stackpole Books, Harrisburg, PA, 1989. 198 pp., illus. $24.95.

How to shoot a rifle accurately under hunting conditions.

*Small Game & Varmint Hunting, by Wilf E. Pyle, Stoeger Publishing Co., So. Hackensack, NJ, 1989. 288 pp., illus. Soft covers. $14.95.

Provides information on modern techniques and methods needed for successful hunting of small game.

Sport and Travel; East and West, by Frederick Courteney Selous, Wolfe Publishing Co., Prescott, AZ, 1988. 311 pp., illus. $29.00.

A limited edition reprint. One of the few books Selous wrote covering North American hunting. His daring in Africa is equalled here as he treks after unknown trails and wild game.

Spring Turkey Hunting, by John M. McDaniel, Stackpole Books, Harrisburg, PA, 1986. 224 pp., illus. $21.95.

The serious hunter's guide.

Squirrels and Squirrel Hunting, by Bob Gooch. Tidewater Publ., Cambridge, MD, 1973. 148 pp., illus. $8.95.

A complete book for the squirrel hunter, beginner or old hand. Details methods of hunting, squirrel habitat, management, proper clothing, care of the kill, cleaning and cooking.

The Still-Hunter, by Theodore S. Van Dyke, reprinted by the Gunnerman Press, Auburn Hills, MI, 1988. 390 pp., illus. $21.95.

Covers each aspect of this fine sport in such complete detail that both the novice and the experienced hunter will profit from its reading.

Strayed Shots and Frayed Lines, edited by John E. Howard, Amwell Press, Clinton, NJ, 1982. 425 pp., illus. $25.00.

Anthology of some of the finest, funniest stories on hunting and fishing ever assembled.

Successful Big Game Hunting, by Duncan Gilchrist, Stoneydale Publishing Co., Stevensville, MT, 1987. 176 pp., illus. $17.95.

Secrets of a big game hunter-guide.

Successful Goose Hunting, by Charles L. Cadieux, Stone Wall Press, Inc., Washington, DC, 1986. 223 pp., illus. $24.95.

Here is a complete book on modern goose hunting by a lifetime waterfowler and professional wildlifer.

Successful Handgun Hunting, by Phil W. Johnson. The Shooting Sports Press, Minneapolis, MN, 1988. 216 pp., illus. $19.95.

The definitive work on the most exciting sport in America.

Successful Waterfowling, by Zack Taylor, Crown, Publ., NY, 1974. 276 pp., illus. Paper covers. $15.95.

The definitive guide to new ways of hunting ducks and geese.

*Supreme Duck Shooting Stories, by William Hazelton, The Gunnerman Press, Auburn Hills, MI, 1989. 160 pp. illus. $19.95.

Originally published in 1931, this is about duck hunting as it was.

Taking Big Bucks, by Ed Wolff, Stoneydale Press, Stevensville, MT, 1987. 169 pp., illus. $17.95.

Solving the whitetail riddle.

*Tales of Alaska's Big Bears, by Jim Rearden, Wolfe Publishing Co., Prescott, AZ, 1989. 125 pp., illus. Soft covers. $12.95.

A collection of bear yarns covering nearly three-quarters of a century.

Tales of Quails 'n Such, by Havilah Babcock, University of S. Carolina Press, Columbia, SC, 1985. 237 pp. illus. $19.95.

A group of hunting stories, told in informal style, on field experiences in the South in quest of small game.

*They Left Their Tracks, by Howard Copenhaver, Stoneydale Press Publishing Co., Stevensville, MT, 1990. 190 pp., illus. $18.95.

Recollections of 60 years as an outfitter in the Bob Marshall Wilderness.

Timberdoodle, by Frank Woolner, Nick Lyons Books, N. Y., NY, 1987. 168 pp., illus. $18.95.

The classic guide to woodcock and woodcock hunting.

Topflight; A Speed Index to Waterfowl, by J.A. Ruthven & Wm. Zimmerman, Moebius Prtg. Co., Milwaukee, WI, 1968. 112 pp. $10.00.

Rapid reference for specie identification. Marginal color band of book directs reader to proper section. 263 full-color illustrations of body and feather configurations.

Track of the Kodiak, by Marvin H. Clark, Great Northwest Publishing and Distributing Co., Anchorage, AK, 1984. 224 pp., illus. $20.00.

A full perspective on Kodiak Island bear hunting.

Tracking Wounded Deer, by Richard P. Smith, Stackpole Books, Harrisburg, PA, 1988. 159 pp., illus. Paper covers. $15.95.

How to find and tag deer shot with bow or gun.

Trail and Campfire, edited by George Bird Grinnel and Theodore Roosevelt, The Boone and Crockett Club, Dumfries, VA, 1989. 357 pp., illus. $39.50.

Reprint of the Boone and Crockett Club's 3rd book published in 1897.

Tranquillity, by Col. H.P. Sheldon, Willow Creek Press, Oshkosh, WI, 1986. In slipcase with its acclaimed companion volumes. **Tranquillity Revisited** and **Tranquillity Regained.** The 3 volume set. $45.00.

A reprint of this 1936 Derrydale Press classic set.

The Trophy Hunter, by Col. Allison, Stackpole Books, Harrisburg, PA, 1981. 240 pp., illus. $24.95.

Action-packed tales of hunting big game trophies around the world—1860 to today.

Trophy Hunter in Asia, by Elgin T. Gates, Charger Productions Inc., Capistrano Beach, CA, 1982. 272 pp., illus. $19.95.

Fascinating high adventure with Elgin Gates, one of America's top trophy hunters.

Trophy Rams of the Brooks Range Plus Secrets of a Sheep and Mountain Goat Guide, by Duncan Gilchrist, Pictorial Histories Publishing Co., Missoula, MT, 1984. 176 pp., illus. $19.95.

Covers hunting a remote corner of the Brooks Range for virgin herds of dall rams.

The Turkey Hunter's Book, by John M. McDaniel, Amwell Press, Clinton, NJ, 1980. 147 pp., illus. Paper covers. $9.95.

One of the most original turkey hunting books to be published in many years.

Turkey Hunter's Digest, by Dwain Bland, DBI Books, Inc., Northbrook, IL, 1986. 256 pp., illus. Paper covers. $13.95.

Describes and pictures all varieties of turkey. Offers complete coverage on calls, calling techniques, appropriate guns, bows, cameras and other equipment.

Turkey Hunting, Spring and Fall, by Doug Camp, Outdoor Skills Bookshelf, Nashville, TN, 1983. 165 pp., illus. Paper covers. $12.95.

Practical turkey hunting, calling, dressing and cooking, by a professional turkey hunting guide.

Turkey Hunter's Guide, by Byron W. Dalrymple, et al., a publication of The National Rifle Association, Washington, DC, 1979. 96 pp., illus. Paper covers. $9.95.

Expert advice on turkey hunting hotspots, guns, guides, and calls.

The Upland Gunner's Book, edited by George Bird Evans, The Amwell Press, Clinton, NJ, 1985. 263 pp., illus. In slipcase. $27.50.

An anthology of the finest stories ever written on the sport of upland game hunting.

The Waterfowl Gunner's Book, edited by F. Phillips Williamson, The Amwell Press, Clinton, NJ, 1986. 282 pp., illus. In slipcase. $27.50. An anthology of the finest duck hunting stories ever gathered under one cover.

*Western Hunting Guide, by Mike Lapinski, Stoneydale Press Publishing Co., Stevensville, MT, 1989. 168 pp., illus. $17.95.

A complete where-to-go and how-to-do-it guide to Western hunting.

The Whispering Wings of Autumn, by Gene Hill and Steve Smith, Amwell Press, Clinton, NJ, 1982. 192 pp., illus. $17.50.

A collection of both fact and fiction on two of North America's most famous game birds, the ruffed grouse and the woodcock.

White-Tailed Deer: Ecology and Management, by Lowell K. Halls, Stackpole Books, Harrisburg, PA, 1984. 864 pp., illus. $39.95.

The definitive work on the world's most popular big game animal.

The Wild Bears, by George Laycock, Outdoor Life Books, N. Y., NY, 1987. 272 pp., illus. Soft covers. $19.95.

The story of the grizzly, brown and black bears, their conflicts with man, and their chances of survival in the future.

The Wilderness Hunter, by Theodore Roosevelt, Wolfe Publishing Co., Prescott, AZ, 1989. 280 pp., illus. $49.00.

A limited edition reprint. An account of the big game of the United States, and its chase with horse, hound, or rifle.

Wilderness Hunting and Wildcraft by Townsend Whelen, Wolfe Publishing Co., Prescott, AZ, 1988. 338 pp., illus. $39.00.

A limited edition reprint. Plentiful information on sheep and mountain hunting with horses and on life histories of big game animals.

*The Wildfowler's Quest, by George Reiger, Lyons & Burford, Publishers, New York, NY, 1989. 320 pp., illus. $24.95.

A richly evocative look into one man's passionate pursuit of ducks, geese, turkey, woodcock, and other wildfowl all over the world.

Wild Sheep and Wild Sheep Hunters of the Old World, by Raul Valdez, Wild Sheep & Goat International, Mesilla, NM, 1983. 207 pp., illus. Limited, signed and numbered edition. $65.00.

A definitive work on Old World sheep hunting.

The Wild Sheep of the World, by Raul Valdez, Wild Sheep and Goat International, Mesilla, NM, 1983. 150 pp., illus. $45.00.

The first comprehensive survey of the world's wild sheep written by a zoologist.

The Wild Turkey Book, edited and with special commentary by J. Wayne Fears, Amwell Press, Clinton, NJ, 1982. 303 pp., illus. $22.50.

An anthology of the finest stories on wild turkey ever assembled under one cover.

*The Wings of Dawn, by George Reiger, Lyons & Burford, Publishers, New York, NY, 1989. 320 pp., illus. Soft covers. $15.95.

This memorable and rich portrait of the waterfowler's world includes the history of the sport, natural history of all types of ducks and geese, useful hunting advice, and more.

Woodchucks and Woodchuck Rifles, by Charles Landis, Wolfe Publishing Co., Prescott, AZ, 1988. 402 pp., illus. $42.00.

A limited edition reprint of the most complete text on the subject.

Woodcock Shooting, by Steve Smith, Stackpole Books, Inc., Harrisburg, PA, 1988. 142 pp., illus. $14.95.

A definitive book on woodcock hunting and the characteristics of a good woodcock dog.

HUNTING (cont.)

AFRICA/ASIA

The African Elephant and Its Hunters, by Dennis D. Lyell, Trophy Room Books, Agoura, CA, 1987. 200 pp., illus. $75.00.
Limited, numbered facsimile edition of this scarce 1924 book.

African Game Trails, by Theodore Roosevelt, St. Martin's Press, New York, NY, 1988. 583 pp., illus. $19.95.
The 1908 safari of President Teddy Roosevelt and his son Kermit to East Africa.

African Hunter, by James Mellon, Safari Press, Long Beach, CA, 1988. 522 pp., illus. $100.00.
The most ardent and intricately detailed book on African game hunting to appear in 50 years.

African Hunter, by Baron Bror von Blixen-Finecke, St. Martin's Press, New York, NY, 1986. 284 pp., illus. $14.95.
Reprint of the scarce 1938 edition. An African hunting classic.

African Hunting and Adventure, by William Charles Baldwin, Books of Zimbabwe, Bulawayo, 1981. 451 pp., illus. $75.00.
Facsimile reprint of the scarce 1863 London edition. African hunting and adventure from Natal to the Zambezi

African Nature Notes and Reminiscences, by F. Courteney Selous, Galago Publishing Ltd., Alberton, RSA, 1986. 356 pp., illus. $40.00.
Reprint of the very scarce 1910 edition and the hardest to find of all of this author's works.

African Rifles & Cartridges, by John Taylor, The Gun Room Press, Highland Park, NJ, 1977. 431 pp., illus. $29.95.
Experiences and opinions of a professional ivory hunter in Africa describing his knowledge of numerous arms and cartridges for big game. A reprint.

The African Safari, by P. Jay Fetner, St. Martin's Press, Inc., N. Y., NY, 1987. 700 pp., illus. $60.00.
A lavish, superbly illustrated, definitive work that brings together the practical elements of planning a safari with a proper appreciation for the animals and their environment.

*After Big Game in Central Africa, by Edouard Foa, St. Martin's Press, New York, NY, 1989. 400 pp., illus. $16.95.
Reprint of the scarce 1899 edition. This sportsman covered 7200 miles, mostly on foot—from Zambezi delta on the east coast to the mouth of the Congo on the west.

Bell of Africa, by Walter (Karamojo) D. M. Bell, Neville Spearman, Suffolk, England, 1983. 236 pp., illus. $24.95.
Autobiography of the greatest elephant hunter of them all.

The Big Game Hunters, by Michael Brander, St. Martin's Press, New York, NY, 1989. 192 pp., illus. $24.95.
The adventures of 19 sportsmen of yore in Asia, Africa, and America.

*Big Game Hunting and Collecting in East Africa 1903-1926, by Kalman Kittenberger, St. Martin's Press, New York, NY, 1989. 496 pp., illus. $16.95.
One of the most heartstopping, charming and funny accounts of adventure in the Kenya Colony ever penned.

Big Game Hunting Around the World, by Bert Klineburger and Vernon W. Hurst, Exposition Press, Jericho, NY, 1969. 376 pp., illus. $30.00.
The first book that takes you on a safari all over the world.

Big Game Hunting in North-Eastern Rhodesia, by Owen Letcher, St. Martin's Press, New York, NY, 1986. 272 pp., illus. $15.95.
A classic reprint and one of the very few books to concentrate on this fascinating area, a region that today is still very much safari country.

The Book of the Lion, by Sir Alfred E. Pease, St. Martin's Press, New York, NY, 1986. 305 pp., illus. $15.95.
Reprint of the finest book ever published on the subject. The author describes all aspects of lion history and lion hunting, drawing heavily on his own experiences in British East Africa.

Bror Blixen: The African Letters, edited by G.F.V. Kleen, St. Martin's Press, New York, NY, 1988. 197 pp., illus. $18.95.
The letters of Bror Blixen, one of the truly great big game hunters of his generation and husband to Isak Dinesen, author of "Out of Africa".

Chronicles of a Second African Trip, by George Eastman, The Friends of the University of Rochester Libraries, Rochester, NY, 1987. 89 pp., illus. In slipcase, $35.00.
Eastman's exciting story of his pursuit of elephant and white rhino. Beautifully illustrated with photographs by Martin Johnson.

Death in the Dark Continent, by Peter Capstick, St. Martin's Press, New York, NY, 1983. 238 pp., illus. $15.95.
A book that brings to life the suspense, fear and exhilaration of stalking ferocious killers under primitive, savage conditions, with the ever present threat of death.

Death in the Long Grass, by Peter Hathaway Capstick, St. Martin's Press, New York, NY, 1977. 297 pp., illus. $15.95.
A big game hunter's adventures in the African bush.

Death in the Silent Places, by Peter Capstick, St. Martin's Press, New York, NY, 1981. 243 pp., illus. $15.95.
The author recalls the extraordinary careers of legendary hunters such as Corbett, Karamojo Bell, Stigand and others.

Dusty Days and Distant Drums, by William R. Rindome, Game Fields Press, Lake Oswego, OR, 1984. 258 pp., illus. $37.50.
An African hunting chronicle.

East of the Sun and West of the Moon, by Theodore and Kermit Roosevelt, Wolfe Publishing Co., Prescott, AZ, 1988. 284 pp., illus. $25.00.
A limited edition reprint. A classic on Marco Polo sheep hunting. A life experience unique to hunters of big game.

Elephant, by Commander David Enderby Blunt, The Holland Press, London, England, 1985. 260 pp., illus. $35.00.
A study of this phenomenal beast by a world-leading authority.

Elephant Hunting in East Equatorial Africa, by Arthur H. Neumann, Books of Zimbabwe, Bulawayo, 1982. 455 pp., illus. $85.00.
Facsimile reprint of the scarce 1898 London edition. An account of three years ivory hunting under Mount Kenya.

Elephants of Africa, by Dr. Anthony Hall-Martin, New Holland Publishers, London, England, 1987. 120 pp., illus. $75.00.
A superbly illustrated overview of the African elephant with reproductions of paintings by the internationally acclaimed wildlife artist Paul Bosman.

Ends of the Earth, by Roy Chapman Andrews, Wolfe Publishing Co., Prescott, AZ, 1988. 230 pp., illus. $27.00.
A limited edition reprint. Includes adventures in China and hunting in Mongolia. Andrews was a distinguished hunter and scout.

First Wheel, by Bunny Allen, Amwell Press, Clinton, NJ, 1984. Limited, signed and numbered edition in the NSFL "African Hunting Heritage Series." 292 pp., illus. $100.00.
A white hunter's diary, 1927-47.

From Mt. Kenya to the Cape, by Craig Boddington, Safari Press, Long Beach, CA, 1987. 274 pp., illus. $45.00.
Ten years of African hunting adventures.

Green Hills of Africa, by Ernest Hemingway. Charles Scribner's Sons, NY, 1963. 285 pp., illus. Paper covers. $11.95.
A famous narrative of African big game hunting, that was first published in 1935.

Gun and Camera in Southern Africa, by H. Anderson Bryden, Wolfe Publishing Co., Prescott, AZ, 1989. 201 pp., illus. $37.00.
A limited edition reprint. The year was 1893 and author Bryden wandered for a year in Bechuanaland and the Kalahari Desert hunting the white rhino, lechwe, eland, and other animals.

Horn of the Hunter, by Robert Ruark, Safari Press, Long Beach, CA, 1987. 315 pp., illus. $35.00.
Ruark's most sought-after title on African hunting, here in reprint.

The Hunter is Death, by T. V. Bulpin, Safari Press, Long Beach, CA, 1987. 348 pp., illus. $30.00.
This is the life story of George Rushby, professional ivory hunter who killed the man-eating lions of the Njombe district.

A Hunter's Wanderings in Africa, by F. C. Selous, Books of Zimbabwe, Bulawayo, 1981. 455 pp., illus. $85.00.
A facsimile reprint of the 1881 London edition. A narrative of nine years spent among the game of the interior of South Africa.

Hunting Big Game, 2 volumes, by Townsend Whelen, Wolfe Publishing Co., Prescott, AZ, 1989. Volume I, Africa and Asia, 339 pp., illus.; Volume 2, The America's, 282 pp., illus. $90.00.
A limited edition reprint. Articles and stories by F.C. Selous, Sir Samuel Baker, Arthur H. Neumann, Theodore Roosevelt and others.

Hunting the Elephant in Africa, by Captain C.H. Stigand, St. Martin's Press, New York, NY, 1986. 379 pp., illus. $14.95.
A reprint of the scarce 1913 edition; vintage Africana at its best.

Hunting in Many Lands, by Theodore Roosevelt and George Bird Grinnel, The Boone and Crockett Club, Dumfries, VA, 1987. 447 pp., illus. $40.00.
Limited edition reprint of this 1895 classic work on hunting in Africa, India, Mongolia, etc.

Jim Corbett's India, selected by R.E. Hawkins, Oxford University Press, Oxford, NY, 1986. 250 pp., illus. Paper covers. $9.95.
Stories from "Maneaters of Kumaon," "My India," "Jungle Lore" and other books by Jim Corbett.

*The Ivory Trail, by Tom Bulpin, Safari Press, Long Beach, CA, 1988. 235 pp., illus. $27.50.
The uproarious adventures of "Bvekenya," the greatest of all ivory poachers and a legend of the South African bush.

*Jaguar Hunting in the Mato Grosso and Bolivia, by T. Almedia, Safari Press, Long Beach, CA, 1989. 256 pp., illus. $35.00.
Not since Sacha Siemel has there been a book on jaguar hunting like this one.

Karamojo Safari, by W.D.M. Bell, Neville Spearman, Suffolk, England, 1984. 288 pp., illus. $24.95.
The true story of Bell's life in Karamojo.

Lake Ngami, by Charles Anderson, New Holland Press, London, England, 1987. 576 pp., illus. $35.00.
Originally published in 1856. Describes two expeditions into what is now Botswana, depicting every detail of landscape and wildlife.

Last Horizons: Hunting, Fishing and Shooting on Five Continents, by Peter Capstick, St. Martin's Press, New York, NY, 1989. 288 pp., illus. $19.95.
The first in a two volume collection of hunting, fishing and shooting tales from the selected pages of The American Hunter, Guns & Ammo and Outdoor Life.

The Last Ivory Hunter: The Saga of Wally Johnson, by Peter Capstick, St. Martin's Press, New York, NY, 1988. 220 pp., illus. $18.95.
A grand tale of African adventure by the foremost hunting author of our time. Wally Johnson spent half a century in Mozambique hunting white gold—ivory.

*Last of the Ivory Hunters, by John Taylor, Safari Press, Long Beach, CA, 1990. 354 pp., illus. $29.95.
Reprint of the classic book "Pondoro" by one of the most famous elephant hunters of all time.

The Man-Eaters of Tsavo, by Lt. Col. J.H. Patterson, St. Martin's Press, New York, NY, 1986. 346 pp., illus. $14.95.
A reprint of the scarce original book on the man-eating lions of Tsavo.

Memories of an African Hunter, by Denis D. Lyell, St. Martin's Press, New York, NY, 1986. 288 pp., illus. $15.95.
A reprint of one of the truly great writers on African hunting. A gripping and highly readable account of Lyell's many years in the African bush.

No More the Tusker, by G.G. Rushby, Trophy Room Books, Agoura, CA, 1989. 211 pp., illus. Limited, numbered edition. $60.00.
In this book the author describes the techniques of elephant hunting.

On the Trail of the African Elephant, by Tony Sanchez-Arino, Roland World, London, 1987. 247 pp., illus. Limited signed edition. $75.00.
The author describes the three types of elephant and their distribution, making a comprehensive survey country by country of their status throughout Africa.

Persia: Safari on the Summits, by Richardo Medem Sanjuan, Trophy Room Press, Aguoura, CA, 1987. 200 pp., illus. Limited, numbered edition. $90.00.
Finest book on Persian hunting written by a Western world author.
Peter Capstick's Africa: A Return to the Long Grass, by Peter Hathaway Capstick, St. Martin's Press, N. Y., NY, 1987. 213 pp., illus. $29.95.
A first-person adventure in which the author returns to the long grass for his own dangerous and very personal excursion.
The Recollections of an Elephant Hunter 1864-1875, by William Finaughty, Books of Zimbabwe, Bulawayo, Zimbabwe, 1980. 244 pp., illus. $85.00.
Reprint of the scarce 1916 privately published edition. The early game hunting exploits of William Finaughty in Matabeleland and Nashonaland.
*Round the Campfire, by A.M.H. Henley, Amwell Press, Clinton, NJ, 1989. 250 pp., illus. Limited, signed and numbered edition. In slipcase. $50.00.
Tales of a professional white hunter. Number 25 in the African Heritage Hunting book series by the National Sporting Fraternity.
*Safari: A Chronicle of Adventure, by Bartle Bull, Viking/Penguin, London, England, 1989. 383 pp., illus. $40.00.
The thrilling history of the African safari, highlighting some of Africa's best-known personalities
Safari: The Last Adventure, by Peter Capstick, St. Martin's Press, New York, NY, 1984. 291 pp., illus. $15.95.
A modern comprehensive guide to the African Safari.
The Shamba Raiders: Memories of a Game Warden, by Bruce Kinlock, Safari Press, Long Beach, CA, 1988. 405 pp., illus. $35.00.
Thrilling stories of encounters with rogue elephants, buffalo and other dangerous animals.
South Pacific Trophy Hunter, by Murray Thomas, Safari Press, Long Beach, CA, 1988. 181 pp., illus. $37.50.
A record of a hunter's search for a trophy of each of the 15 major game species in the South Pacific region.
Tales of the Big Game Hunters, selected and introduced by Kenneth Kemp, The Sportsman's Press, London, 1986. 209 pp., illus. $15.00.
Writings by some of the best known hunters and explorers, among them: Frederick Courteney Selous, R.G. Gordon Cumming, Sir Samuel Baker, and elephant hunters Neumann and Sutherland.
Tanzania Safari, by Brian Herne, Amwell Press, Clifton, NJ, 1982. 259 pp., illus. Limited, signed and numbered edition. $125.00.
The story of Tanzania and hunting safaris, professional hunters, and a little history, too.
The Trophy Hunter in Africa, by Elgin T. Gates, Amwell Press, Clinton, NJ, 1989. 315 pp., illus. A limited, signed and numbered deluxe edition, in a slipcase. $85.00.
The late Elgin T. Gates was considered by many authorities the greatest hunter of them all. Here he describes his trophy hunts in Africa.
Uganda Safaris, by Brian Herne, Winchester Press, Piscataway, NJ, 1979. 236 pp., illus. $12.95.
The chronicle of a professional hunter's adventures in Africa.
Use Enough Gun, by Robert Ruark, Safari Press, Long Beach, CA, 1988. 330 pp., illus. $35.00.
A record of a lifetime's bag, the story of a man's education as a hunter.
The Wanderings of an Elephant Hunter, by W.D.M. Bell, Neville Spearman, Suffolk, England, 1981. 187 pp., illus. $24.95.
The greatest of elephant books by perhaps the greatest elephant hunter of all times, "Karamojo" Bell.
A White Hunters Life, by Angus MacLagan, an African Heritage Book, published by Amwell Press, Clinton, NJ, 1983. 283 pp., illus. Limited, signed, and numbered deluxe edition, in slipcase. $100.00.
True to life, a sometimes harsh yet intriguing story.
Wild Ivory, by Horace S. Mazet, Nautulus Books, No. Plainfield, NJ, 1971. 280 pp., illus. $30.00.
The true story of the last of the old elephant hunters.
Wild Sports of Southern Africa, by William Cornwallis Harris, New Holland Press, London, England, 1987. 376 pp., illus. $35.00.
Originally published in 1863, describes the author's travels in Southern Africa.
With a Rifle in Mongolia, by Count Hoyos-Sprizenstein, Safari Press, Long Beach, CA, 1987. 144 pp., illus. In slipcase. $85.00.
First English edition of the author's 1911 expedition to Mongolia and China.

The Accurate Rifle, by Warren Page, Winchester Press, Piscataway, NJ, 1973. 256 pp., illus. Paper covers. $9.95.
A masterly discussion. A must for the competitive shooter hoping to win, and highly useful to the practical hunter.
The AK-47 Assault Rifle, Desert Publications, Cornville, AZ, 1981. 150 pp., illus. Paper covers. $8.95.
Complete and practical technical information on the only weapon in history to be produced in an estimated 30,000,000 units.
*AR-15/M16 Super Systems, by Duncan Long, Paladin Press, Boulder, CO, 1989. 144 pp., illus. Soft covers. $19.95.
Taking up where other AR-15 books leave off, this book shows you how to customize this reliable firearm into a super system suited to your needs.
The AR-15/M16, A Practical Guide, by Duncan Long. Paladin Press, Boulder, CO, 1985. 168 pp., illus. Paper covers. $16.95.
The definitive book on the rifle that has been the inspiration for so many modern assault rifles.
American Rifle Design and Performance, by L.R. Wallack, Winchester Press, Piscataway, NJ, 1977. 288 pp., illus. $20.00.
An authoritative, comprehensive guide to how and why every kind of sporting rifle works.

Big Game Rifles and Cartridges, by Elmer Keith, reprint edition by The Gun Room Press, Highland Park, NJ, 1984. 161 pp., illus. $24.95.
Reprint of Elmer Keith's first book, a most original and accurate work on big game rifles and cartridges.
The Black Rifle, M16 Retrospective, R. Blake Stevens and Edward C. Ezell, Collector Grade Publications, Toronto, Canada, 1987. 400 pp., illus. $47.50.
The complete story of the M16 rifle and its development.
The Bolt Action, Volume 2, by Stuart Otteson, Wolfe Publishing Co., Inc. Prescott, AZ, 1985. 289 pp., illus. $22.50.
Covers 17 bolt actions from Newton to Ruger.
Bolt Action Rifles, revised edition, by Frank de Haas, DBI Books, Inc., Northbrook, IL, 1984. 448 pp., illus. Paper covers. $15.95.
A revised edition of the most definitive work on all major bolt-action rifle designs. Detailed coverage of over 110 turnbolt actions, including how they function, takedown and assembly, strengths and weaknesses, dimensional specifications.
The Book of the Garand, by Maj.-Gen. J.S. Hatcher, The Gun Room Press, Highland Park, NJ, 1977. 292 pp., illus. $24.95.
A new printing of the standard reference work on the U.S. Army M1 rifle.
The Book of the Rifle, by T.F. Fremantle, Wolfe Publishing Co., Prescott, AZ, 1988. 558 pp., illus. $54.00.
A limited edition reprint. This book records the point of the rifle's evolution at the opening of the 19th century.
*The Book of the Twenty-Two: The All American Caliber, by Sam Fadala, Stoeger Publishing Co., So. Hackensack, NJ, 1989. 288 pp., illus. Soft covers. $14.95.
The All American Caliber from BB caps up to the powerful 226 Barnes. It's about ammo history, plinking, target shooting, and the quest for the one-hole group.
The Breech-Loading Single-Shot Rifle, by Major Ned H. Roberts and Kenneth L. Waters, Wolfe Publishing Co., Prescott, AZ, 1987. 333 pp., illus. $28.50.
A comprehensive history of the evolution of Scheutzen and single shot rifles.
Custom Muzzleloading Rifles, by Toby Bridges, Stackpole Books, Harrisburg, PA, 1986. 224 pp., illus. Paper covers. $16.95.
An illustrated guide to building or buying a handcrafted muzzleloader.
F.N.-F.A.L. Auto Rifles, Desert Publications, Cornville, AZ, 1981. 130 pp., illus. Paper covers. $7.50.
A definitive study of one of the free world's finest combat rifles.
The Fighting Rifle, by Chuck Taylor, Paladin Press, Boulder, CO, 1983. 184 pp., illus. Paper covers. $16.95.
The difference between assault and battle rifles and auto and light machine guns.
A Forgotten Heritage; The Story of a People and the Early American Rifle, by Harry P. Davis, The Gun Room Press, Highland Park, NJ, 1976. 199 pp., illus. $9.95.
Reprint of a very scarce history, originally published in 1941, the Kentucky rifle and the people who used it.
*Forty Years With the .45-70, by Paul A. Matthews, Wolfe Publishing Co., Prescott, AZ, 1989. 147 pp., illus. $11.50.
The author relates his personal experiences of over 40 years with a number of different 45-70 rifles.
The Golden Age of Single-Shot Rifles, by Edsall James, Pioneer Press, Union City, TN, 1975. 33 pp., illus. Paper covers. $2.75.
A detailed look at all of the fine, high quality sporting single shot rifles that were once the favorite of target shooters.
The Great Rifle Controversy, by Edward Ezell, Stackpole Books, Harrisburg, PA, 1984. 352 pp., illus. $29.95.
Search for the ultimate infantry weapon from WW II through Vietnam and beyond.
The Gun Digest Book of Firearms Assembly/Disassembly Part III: Rimfire Rifles, by J.B. Wood, DBI Books, Inc., Northbrook, IL, 1980. 288 pp., illus. Paper covers. $13.95.
A most comprehensive, uniform, and professional presentation available for disassembling and reassembling most rimfire rifles.
The Gun Digest Book of Firearms Assembly/Disassembly Part IV: Centerfire Rifles, by J.B. Wood, DBI Books, Inc., Northbrook, IL, 1980. 288 pp., illus. Paper covers. $13.95.
A professional presentation on the disassembly and reassembly of centerfire rifles.
Gun Digest Book of Riflesmithing, by Jack Mitchell, DBI Books, Inc., Northbrook, IL, 1982. 256 pp., illus. Paper covers. $11.95.
Covers major and minor gunsmithing operations for rifles—locking systems, triggers, safeties, rifling, crowning, scope mounting, and more.
Jim Carmichel's Book of the Rifle, by Jim Carmichel, an Outdoor Life Book, New York, NY, 1985. 564 pp., illus. $34.95.
The most important book of the author's career, and the most comprehensive ever published on the subject.
Keith's Rifles for Large Game, by Elmer Keith, The Gun Room Press, Highland Park, NJ, 1986. 406 pp., illus. $39.95.
Covers all aspects of selecting, equipping, use and care of high power rifles for hunting big game, especially African.
Know Your M1 Garand, by E. J. Hoffschmidt, Blacksmith Corp., Southport, CT, 1975, 84 pp., illus. Paper covers. $6.95.
Facts about America's most famous infantry weapon. Covers test and experimental models, Japanese and Italian copies, National Match models.
Managing & Mastering the Set Triggered Rifle, by Frank de Haas, Frank de Haas, Orange City, IA, 1986. 56 pp., illus. Paper covers. $5.95.
A manual on how to get the most out of a set-triggered rifle for the sport of target shooting and hunting, and doing it safely.
Manufacture of the Model 1903 Springfield Service Rifle, by Fred H. Colvin and Ethan Viall, et al., Wolfe Publishing Co., Inc., Prescott, AZ, 1985. 450 pp., illus. $29.95.
In three parts. Part 1 is a reprint of Colvin and Viall's 1917 work **U.S. Rifles and Machine Guns;** Part 2 is G.P.O. 1911 **Instructions to Bidders . . . Model 1903;** Part 3 is a reprint of two articles on the Springfield from 1928 issues of "Army Ordnance" magazine.

RIFLES (cont.)

The M-14 Rifle, facsimile reprint of FM 23-8, Desert Publications, Cornville, AZ, 50 pp., illus. Paper $7.95.

In this well illustrated and informative reprint, the M-14 and M-14E2 are covered thoroughly.

M1 Carbine Owner's Manual, M1, M2 & M3 .30 Caliber Carbines, Firepower Publications, Cornville, AZ, 1984. 102 pp., illus. Paper covers. $9.95.

The complete book for the owner of an M1 Carbine.

Military and Sporting Rifle Shooting, by Captain E.C. Crossman, Wolfe Publishing Co., Prescott, AZ, 1988. 449 pp., illus. $45.00.

A limited edition reprint. A complete and practical treatise covering the use of rifles.

The Mini-14, by Duncan Long, Paladin Press, Boulder, CO, 1987. 120 pp., illus. Paper covers. $10.00.

History of the Mini-14, the factory-produced models, specifications, accessories, suppliers, and much more.

Modern Military Bullpup Rifles, by T.B. Dugelby, Collector Grade Publications, Toronto, Canada, 1984. 97 pp., illus. $20.00.

The EM-2 concept comes to age.

Modern Sniper Rifles, by Duncan Long, Paladin Press, Boulder, CO, 1988. 120 pp., illus. Paper covers. $16.95.

An in-depth look at the variety of rifles currently on the market that are suitable for long-distance precision shooting.

Modern Sportsman's Gun and Rifle, by J.H. Walsh ("Stonehenge"), Wolfe Publishing Co., Prescott, AZ, 1988. In two volumes, Vol. 1, 459 pp., Vol. 2, 546 pp., illus. $110.00.

A limited edition reprint. An extremely rare set of books first published in 1880s. Covers game, sporting and match rifles, and revolvers.

***More Single Shot Rifles and Actions,** by Frank de Haas, Frank de Haas, Orange City, IA, 1989. 146 pp., illus. Soft covers. $22.50.

A definitive book with in-depth studies, illustrations, drawings and descriptions of over 45 obsolete single shot rifles and actions.

North American FALS, by R. Blake Stevens, Collector Grade Publications, Toronto, Canada, 1979. 166 pp., illus. $24.00.

NATO's search for a standard rifle.

100 Years of Shooters and Gunmakers of Single Shot Rifles, by Gerald O. Kelver, Brighton, CO, 1975. 212 pp., illus. Paper covers. $15.00.

The Schuetzen rifle, targets and shooters, primers, match rifles, original loadings and much more. With chapters on famous gunsmiths like Harry Pope, Morgan L. Rood and others.

The Pennsylvania Rifle, by Samuel E. Dyke, Sutter House, Lititz, PA, 1975. 61 pp., illus. Paper covers. $5.00.

History and development, from the hunting rifle of the Germans who settled the area. Contains a full listing of all known Lancaster, PA, gunsmiths from 1729 through 1815.

***The Remington 700,** by John F. Lacy, Taylor Publishing Co., Dallas, TX, 1990. 208 pp., illus. $44.95.

Covers the different models, limited editions, chamberings, proofmarks, serial numbers, military models, and much more.

The Revolving Rifles, by Edsall James, Pioneer Press, Union City, TN, 1975. 23 pp., illus. Paper covers. $2.50.

Valuable information on revolving cylinder rifles, from the earliest matchlock forms to the latest models of Colt and Remington.

Rifle Guide, by Robert A. Steindler, Stoeger Publishing Co., South Hackensack, NJ, 1978. 304 pp., illus. Paper covers. $9.95.

Complete, fully illustrated guide to selecting, shooting, caring for, and collecting rifles of all types.

The Rifle in America, by Philip B. Sharpe, Wolfe Publishing Co., Prescott, AZ, 1988. 641 pp., illus. $59.00.

A limited edition reprint. A marvelous volume packed with information for the man who is interested in rifles, from the man whose life was guns.

Rifle and Marksmanship, by Judge H.A. Gildersleeve, reprinted by W.S. Curtis, Buckinghamshire, England, 1986. 131 pp., illus. $25.00.

Reprint of a book first published in 1878 in New York, catering to the shooter of early breechloaders and late muzzleloaders.

Rifle Shooting as a Sport, by Bernd Klingner, A.S. Barnes and Co., Inc., San Diego, CA, 1980. 186 pp., illus. Paper covers. $15.00.

Basic principles, positions and techniques by an international expert.

The Rifleman's Rifle: Winchester's Model 70, 1936-63, by Roger D. Rule, Alliance Books, Inc., Northridge, CA, 1982. 368 pp., illus. $59.95.

The most complete reference book on the Model 70, with much fresh information on the Model 54 and the new Model 70s.

Ned H. Roberts and the Schuetzen Rifle, edited by Gerald O. Kelver, Brighton, CO, 1982. 99 pp., illus. $12.00.

A compilation of the writings of Major Ned H. Roberts which appeared in various gun magazines.

The Ruger No. 1, by J.D. Clayton, edited by John T. Amber, Blacksmith Corp., Southport, CT, 1983. 200 pp., illus. $39.50.

Covers this famous rifle from original conception to current production.

Schuetzen Rifles, History and Loading, by Gerald O. Kelver, Gerald O. Kelver, Publisher, Brighton, CO, 1972. Illus. $12.00.

Reference work on these rifles, their bullets, loading, telescopic sights, accuracy, etc. A limited, numbered ed.

Semi-Auto Rifles: Data and Comment, edited by Robert W. Hunnicutt, The National Rifle Association, Washington, DC, 1988. 156 pp., illus. Paper covers. $12.95.

A book for those who find military-style self-loading rifles interesting for their history, intriguing for the engineering that goes into their design, and a pleasure to shoot.

Single Shot Actions—Their Design and Construction, by Frank de Haas, Orange City, IA, 1990. $35.95.

***Single Shot Rifles and Actions,** by Frank de Haas, Frank de Haas, Orange City, IA, 1990. 352 pp., illus. Soft covers. $25.00.

The definitive book on over 60 single shot rifles and actions. Covers history, parts, design and construction.

Single Shot Rifle Notes, Yesterday and Today, by Gerald O. Kelver, Brighton, CO, 1988. 254 pp., illus. Paper covers. $16.00.

A mixing of old traditions and those of today with regard to single shot rifle shooting.

The Springfield Rifle M1903, M1903A1, M1903A3, M1903A4, Desert Publications, Cornville, AZ, 1982. 100 pp., illus. Paper covers. $7.95.

Covers every aspect of disassembly and assembly, inspection, repair and maintenance.

The Sturm, Ruger 10/22 Rifle and .44 Magnum Carbine, by Duncan Long, Paladin Press, Boulder, CO, 1988. 108 pp., illus. Paper covers. $10.00.

An in-depth look at both weapons detailing the elegant simplicity of the Ruger design. Offers specifications, troubleshooting procedures and ammunition recommendations.

***Successful Rifle Shooting with Small-Bore and Air Rifle,** by David Parish, The Crowood Press, Wiltshire, England, 1989. 128 pp., illus. $24.95.

Offers expert, easy-to-follow instructions to help you achieve better results and gain more enjoyment from both leisure and competitive shooting.

***The Ultimate in Rifle Accuracy,** by Glenn Newick, Benchrest and Bucks, Houston, TX, 1989. 200 pp., illus. $34.95.

Getting the most out of your equipment and yourself.

Henry Wilkinson's Observations on Muskets, Rifles and Projectiles, a facsimile reprint of the scarce 1852 London edition. Reprinted by W.S. Curtis, Bucks, England, 1983. 63 pp., illus. Paper covers. $12.95.

Includes the author's scarce work "Treatise on Elastic Concave Wadding."

The American Shotgun, by Charles Askins, Wolfe Publishing Co., Prescott, AZ, 1988. 321 pp., illus. $39.00.

A limited edition reprint. Askins covers shotguns and patterning extremely well.

The American Shotgun, by David F. Butler, edited by C. Kenneth Ramage, Lyman Publications, Middlefield, CT, 1973. 243 pp., illus. Paper covers. $14.95.

A comprehensive history of the American smoothbore's evolution from Colonial times to the present day.

American Shotgun Design and Performance, by L.R. Wallack, Winchester Press, Piscataway, NJ, 1977. 184 pp., illus. $16.95.

An expert lucidly recounts the history and development of American shotguns and explains how they work.

***Best Guns,** by Michael McIntosh, Countrysport, Inc., Traverse City, MI, 1989. 288 pp., illus. $39.50.

Devoted to the best shotguns ever made in the United States and the best presently being made in the world.

The British Shotgun, Volume 1, 1850-1870, by I.M. Crudington and D.J. Baker, Barrie & Jenkins, London, England, 1979. 256 pp., illus. $29.95.

An attempt to trace, as accurately as is now possible, the evolution of the shotgun during its formative years in Great Britain.

Clay Target Shooting, by Paul Bentley, A&C Black, London, England, 1987. 144 pp., illus. $25.00.

Practical book on clay target shooting written by a very successful international competitor, providing valuable professional advice and instruction for shooters of all disciplines.

Combat Shotgun Training, by Charles R. Skillen, Charles C. Thomas, Publisher, Springfield, IL, 1982. 201 pp., illus. $60.00.

Complete, authoritative information on the use of the shotgun in law enforcement.

***Cradock on Shotguns,** by Chris Cradock, Banford Press, London, England, 1989. 200 pp., illus. $39.95.

A definitive work on the shotgun by a British expert on shotguns.

***The Defensive Shotgun,** by Louis Awerbuck, S.W.A.T. Publications, Cornville, AZ, 1989. 77 pp., illus. Soft covers. $10.95.

This book cuts through the maze of myths concerning the shotgun and its attendant ballistic effects.

The Double Shotgun, by Don Zutz, Winchester Press, Piscataway, NJ, 1985. 304 pp., illus. $19.95.

Revised, updated, expanded edition of the history and development of the world's classic sporting firearms.

Field, Cover and Trap Shooting, by Adam H. Bogardus, Wolfe Publishing Co., Prescott, AZ, 1988. 446 pp., illus. $43.00.

A limited edition reprint. Hints for skilled marksmen as well as young sportsmen. Includes haunts and habits of game birds and waterfowl.

Game Gun, by Richard S. Grozik, Willow Creek Press, Oshkosh, WI, 1986. 150 pp., illus. $39.00.

Transports you to the workshops of the finest gunmakers in England, Europe, Canada, and the U.S. through picture and text.

The Golden Age of Shotgunning, by Bob Hinman, Wolfe Publishing Co., Inc., Prescott, AZ, 1982. $17.95.

A valuable history of the late 1800s detailing that fabulous period of development in shotguns, shotshells and shotgunning.

The Gun Digest Book of Firearms Assembly/Disassembly, Part V: Shotguns, by J.B. Wood, DBI Books, Inc., Northbrook, IL, 1980. 288 pp., illus. Paper covers. $13.95.

A professional presentation on the complete disassembly and assembly of 26 of the most popular shotguns, new and old.

Gun Digest Book of Shotgun Gunsmithing, by Ralph Walker, DBI Books, Inc., Northbrook, IL, 1983. 256 pp., illus. Paper covers. $13.95.

The principles and practices of repairing, individualizing and accurizing modern shotguns by one of the world's premier shotgun gunsmiths.

The Gun Digest Book of Trap & Skeet Shooting, 2nd Edition, by Art Blatt, DBI Books, Inc., Northbrook, IL, 1989. 288 pp., illus. Paper covers. $14.95.

This new edition contains lots of valuable information for the intermediate and advanced competition shooter.

Hartman on Skeet, By Barney Hartman, Stackpole Books, Harrisburg, PA, 1973. 143 pp., illus. $10.00.

A definitive book on Skeet shooting by a pro.

The History of W. & C. Scott Gunmakers, by J.A. Crawford and P.G. Whatley, second edition, Rowland Ward's at Holland & Holland, Ltd., London, England, 1986. 92 pp., illus. $22.50.

The guns, gunmaking operations, tables of serial numbers for W. & C. Scott and Webley & Scott guns and rifles from 1865-1980.

*How to Shoot, by Robert Churchill, Sportsman's Press, London, England, 1988. 110 pp., illus. $15.00.

Lessons in the science of shotgun shooting.

How to be a Winner Shooting Skeet & Trap, by Tom Morton, Tom Morton, Knoxville, MD, 1974. 144 pp., illus. Paper covers. $10.95.

The author explains why championship shooting is more than a physical process.

L.C. Smith Shotguns, by Lt. Col. William S. Brophy, The Gun Room Press, Highland Park, NJ, 1979. 244 pp., illus. $35.00.

The first work on this very important American gun and manufacturing company.

Lefever: Guns of Lasting Fame, by Robert W. (Bob) Elliot and Jim Cobb, Robert W. (Bob) Elliot, Lindale, TX, 1986. 174 pp., illus. $29.95.

Hundreds of photographs, patent drawings and production figures are given on this famous maker's shotguns.

A Manual of Clayshooting, by Chris Cradock, Hippocrene Books, Inc., New York, NY, 1983. 192 pp., illus. $34.95.

Covers everything from building a range to buying a shotgun, with lots of illustrations and diagrams.

Matt Eastman's Guide to Browning Sporting Firearms' Serial Numbers, 1924 to Present, together with, **Matt Eastman's Guide to Browning Sporting Firearms 1924-1985,** compiled by Matt Eastman, Fitzgerald, GA, 1986. 32; 11 pp. The two booklets. Paper covers. $15.95.

Covers all the Belgian and Japanese guns from 1924 to present.

The Modern Shotgun, by Major Sir Charles Burrard, Ashford Press, Southampton, England, 1986 reprint of this 3-volume set. The set, $89.95.

Reprinting of the most classic and informative work on the shotgun.

The Mysteries of Shotgun Patterns, by George G. Oberfell and Charles E. Thompson, Oklahoma State University Press, Stillwater, OK, 1982. 164 pp., illus. Paper covers. $25.00.

Shotgun ballistics for the hunter in non-technical language, with information on improving effectiveness in the field.

The Orvis Wing-Shooting Handbook, by Bruce Bowlen, Nick Lyons Books, New York, NY, 1985. 83 pp., illus. Paper covers. $8.95.

Proven techniques for better shotgunning.

Parker, America's Finest Shotgun, by Peter H. Johnson, Stackpole Books, Inc., Harrisburg, PA, 1985. 272 pp., illus. $17.95.

A look at one of the rarest and finest shotguns in history.

Plans and Specifications of the L.C. Smith Shotgun, by Lt. Col. William S. Brophy, USAR Ret., F. Brownell & Son, Montezuma, IA, 1982. 247 pp., illus. $19.95.

The only collection ever assembled of all the drawings and engineering specifications on the incomparable and very collectable L.C. Smith shotgun.

Police Shotgun Manual, by Bill Clede, Stackpole Books, Harrisburg, PA, 1986. 128 pp., illus. $15.95.

How to survive against all odds. Latest shotgun techniques for tough situations.

The Police Shotgun Manual, by Robert H. Robinson, Charles C. Thomas, Springfield, IL, 1973. 153 pp., illus. $48.00.

A complete study and analysis of the most versatile and effective weapon in the police arsenal.

Purdey's, the Guns and the Family, by Richard Beaumont, David and Charles, Pomfret, VT, 1984. 248 pp., illus. $34.95.

Records the history of the Purdey family from 1814 to today, how the guns were and are built and daily functioning of the factory.

Recreating the Double Barrel Muzzle-Loading Shotgun, by William R. Brockway, George Shumway Publisher, York, PA, 1985. 198 pp., illus. Paper covers. $20.00; cloth, $27.50.

Treats the making of double guns of classic type.

Reloading for Shotgunners, 2nd Edition, edited by Robert S.L. Anderson, DBI Books, Inc., Northbrook, IL, 1985. 256 pp., illus. Paper covers. $13.95.

The very latest in reloading information for the shotgunner.

75 Years with the Shotgun, by C.T. (Buck) Buckman, Valley, Publ., Fresno, CA, 1974. 141 pp., illus. $10.00.

An expert hunter and trapshooter shares experiences of a lifetime.

The Shotgun, by Macdonald Hastings, David & Charles, London, England, 1983. 240 pp., illus. $34.95.

The story of the shotgun's development since Lt. Col. Peter Hawker made gunning a gentleman's recreation up to the present day.

The Shotgun in Combat, by Tony Lesce, Desert Publications, Cornville, AZ, 1979. 148 pp., illus. Paper covers. $10.00.

A history of the shotgun and its use in combat.

Shotgun Digest, 3rd Edition, edited by Jack Lewis, DBI Books, Inc., Northbrook, IL, 1986. 256 pp., illus. Paper covers. $13.95.

A new look at shotguns.

The Shotgun: History and Development, by Geoffrey Boothroyd, A & C Black Publisher, Ltd. London, England, 1986. 256 pp., illus. $29.95.

From the days of the flintlock, through the percussion era to the early pinfire breechloaders, and the later hammer centerfire breechloaders.

Shotgunners Guide, by Monte Burch, Winchester Press, Piscataway, NJ, 1980. 208 pp., illus. $18.95.

A basic book for the young and old who want to try shotgunning or who want to improve their skill.

Shotgunning: The Art and the Science, by Bob Brister, Winchester Press, Piscataway, NJ, 1976. 321 pp., illus. $17.95.

Hundreds of specific tips and truly novel techniques to improve the field and target shooting of every shotgunner.

*Shotgunning Trends in Transition, by Don Zutz, Wolfe Publishing Co., Prescott, AZ, 1990. 314 pp., illus. $29.50.

This book updates American shotgunning from those post WWII transitional years to the high-tech present.

*Shotguns and Cartridges for Game and Clays, by Gough Thomas, edited by Nigel Brown, A & C Black, Ltd., Cambs, England, 1989. 256 pp., illus. Soft covers. $24.95.

Gough Thomas' well-known and respected book for game and clay pigeon shooters in a thoroughly up-dated edition.

Shotguns by Keith, by Elmer Keith, Wolfe Publishing Co., Prescott, AZ, 1988. 305 pp., illus. $39.00.

A limited edition reprint. The master reveals his knowledge again.

Shotguns and Gunsmiths, The Vintage Years, by Geoffrey Boothroyd, A & C Black, London, England, 1986. 240 pp., illus. $32.50.

The guns made by Boswell, Purdey, Lang, Scott, Grant, Greener, and Westley Richards and others.

The Side-by-Side, a History and Digest of Double Barrel Breech Loading Shotguns, by Charles E. Carder, Kopp Publishing Co., Lexington, MO, 1989. 230 pp., illus. $19.95.

If you own, collect, sell, or repair side-by-sides, this is the book for you. Lists manufacturers, models, options, dates, trademarks, tradenames, photos, sketches, values, and history.

Sporting Clays, by A.J. "Smoker" Smith, Willowcreek Press, Wautoma, WI, 1989. 150 pp., illus. $19.50.

The author reveals techniques that led him to win almost every major sporting clays competition in England, where the sport originated.

*The Sporting Clay Handbook, by Jerry Meyer, Lyons and Burford Publishers, New York, NY, 1990. 140 pp., illus. Soft covers. $14.95.

A superb introduction to the fastest growing, and most exciting, gun game in America.

Sporting Pigeon Shooting, by Michael Brander, London, England, 1986. 122 pp., illus. $19.95.

In this book the author argues for a new appreciation of sporting pigeon shooting. In addition to practical advice on the all-important preparations, and on decoying and shooting, the book also gives a brief background to the sport and species.

Skeet Shooting with D. Lee Braun, edited by R. Campbell, Grosset & Dunlap, NY, 1967. 160 pp., illus. Paper covers. $5.95.

Thorough instructions on the fine points of Skeet shooting.

U.S. Shotguns, All Types, reprint of TM9-285, Desert Publications, Cornville, AZ, 1987. 257 pp., illus. Paper covers. $9.95.

Covers operation, assembly and disassembly of nine shotguns used by the U.S. armed forces.

The Winchester Model Twelve, by George Madis, David Madis, Dallas, TX, 1984. 176 pp., illus. $19.95.

A definitive work on this famous American shotgun.

*Winchester Shotguns and Shotshells, by Ronald W. Stadt, Armory Publications, Tacoma, WA, 1984. 184 pp., illus. $34.95.

From the hammer and double guns to the Model 59.

Wing & Shot, by R.G. Wehle, Country Press, Scottsville, NY, 1967. 190 pp., illus. $24.95.

Step-by-step account on how to train a fine shooting dog.

The World's Fighting Shotguns, by Thomas F. Swearengen, T. B. N. Enterprises, Alexandria, VA, 1979. 500 pp., illus. $34.95.

The complete military and police reference work from the shotgun's inception to date, with up-to-date developments.

ARMS ASSOCIATIONS IN AMERICA AND ABROAD

UNITED STATES

ALABAMA

Alabama Gun Collectors Assn.
Secretary, P.O. Box 6080, Tuscaloosa, AL 35405

ALASKA

Alaska Gun Collectors Assn. Inc.
Wayne Anthony Ross, P.O. Box 101522, Anchorage, AK 99510

ARIZONA

Arizona Arms Assn.
Don DeBusk, Pres., 3340 W. Frier, Phoenix, AZ 85021/602-841-2337

CALIFORNIA

California Gun Rights Projects of CCRKBA
225 Chester Ave., Third Floor, Sacramento, CA 93301
California Waterfowl Assn.
3840 Rosin Ct., #200, Sacramento, CA 95834
Greater Calif. Arms & Collectors Assn.
Donald L. Bullock, 8291 Carburton St., Long Beach, CA 90808
Los Angeles Gun & Ctg. Collectors Assn.
F.H. Ruffra, 20810 Amie Ave., Apt. #9, Torrance, CA 90503

COLORADO

Colorado Gun Collectors Assn.
L.E.(Bud) Greenwald, 2553 So. Quitman St., Denver, CO 80219/303-935-3850

CONNECTICUT

Ye Conn. Gun Guild, Inc.
Dick Fraser, P.O. Box 425, Windsor, CT 06095

FLORIDA

Tampa Bay Arms Collectors' Assn.
John Tuvell, 2461 - 67th Ave., S., St. Petersburg, FL 33712
Unified Sportsmen of Florida
P.O. Box 6565, Tallahassee, FL 32314

GEORGIA

Georgia Arms Collectors
Michael Kindberg, Pres., P.O. Box 277, Alpharetta, GA 30239

ILLINOIS

Illinois State Rifle Assn.
P.O. Box 27, Kankakee, IL 60901
Illinois Gun Collectors Assn.
T.J. Curl, Jr., P.O. Box 971, Kankakee, IL 60901
Mississippi Valley Gun & Cartridge Coll. Assn.
Jerry W. Bates, 4320 - 8th St., East Moline, IL 61244/309-796-0616
Sauk Trail Gun Collectors
Gordell M. Matson, P.O. Box 1113, Milan, IL 61264
Wabash Valley Gun Collectors Assn., Inc.
Jerry D. Holycross, RR #6 Box 341, Danville, IL 61832

INDIANA

Indiana Sportsmen's Council-Legislative
Maurice Latimer, P.O. Box 93, Bloomington, IN 47402
Indiana State Rifle & Pistol Assn.
Thos. Glancy, P.O. Box 552, Chesterton, IN 46304
Southern Indiana Gun Collectors Assn., Inc.
Sheila McClary, 309 W. Monroe St., Boonville, IN 47601/812-897-3742

IOWA

Central States Gun Collectors Assn.
Avery Giles, 1104 S. 1st Ave., Marshtown, IA 50158

KANSAS

Kansas Cartridge Coll. Assn.
Bob Linder, Box 84, Plainville, KS 67663

KENTUCKY

Kentuckiana Arms Coll. Assn.
Tony Wilson, Pres., Box 1776, Louisville, KY 40201
Kentucky Gun Collectors Assn., Inc.
Ruth Johnson, Box 64, Owensboro, KY 42302

LOUISIANA

Washitaw River Renegades
Sandra Rushing, P.O. Box 256, Main St., Grayson, LA 71435

MARYLAND

Baltimore Antique Arms Assn.
Stanley I. Kellert, 8340 Dubbs Dr., Severn, MD 21144

MASSACHUSETTS

Bay Colony Weapons Collectors, Inc.
John Brandt, Box 111, Hingham, MA 02043
Massachusetts Arms Collectors
John J. Callan, Jr., P.O. Box 1001, Worcester, MA 01613/508-892-3837

MISSISSIPPI

Mississippi Gun Collectors Assn.
Jack E. Swinney, P.O. Box 16323, Hattiesburg, MS 39404

MISSOURI

Mineral Belt Gun Coll. Assn.
D.F. Saunders, 1110 Cleveland Ave., Monett, MO 65708
Missouri Valley Arms Collectors Assn., Inc.
L.P. Brammer II, Membership Secy., P.O. Box 33033, Kansas City, MO 64114

MONTANA

Montana Arms Collectors Assn.
Lewis E. Yearout, 308 Riverview Dr. East, Great Falls, MT 59404
The Winchester Arms Coll. Assn.
Richard Berg, P.O. Box 6754, Great Falls, MT 59406

NEW HAMPSHIRE

New Hampshire Arms Collectors, Inc.
Frank H. Galeucia, Rte. 28, Box 44, Windham, NH 03087

NEW JERSEY

Englishtown Benchrest Shooters Assn.
Michael Toth, 64 Cooke Ave., Carteret, NJ 07008
Jersey Shores Antique Arms Collectors
Joe Sisia, P.O. Box 100, Bayville, NJ 08721
New Jersey Arms Collectors Club, Inc.
Angus Laidlaw, 230 Valley Rd., Montclair, NJ 07042

NEW YORK

Empire State Arms Coll. Assn.
P.O. Box 2328, Rochester, NY 14623

Iroquois Arms Collectors Assn.
Kenneth Keller, club secy., (Susann Keller, show secy.) 214 - 70th St., Niagara Falls, NY 14304
Mid-State Arms Coll. & Shooters Club
Jack Ackerman, 24 S. Mountain Terr., Binghamton, NY 13903

NORTH CAROLINA

North Carolina Gun Collectors Assn.
Jerry Ledford, 3231 - 7th St. Dr. NE, Hickory, NC 28601

OHIO

Ohio Gun Collectors, Assn.
P.O. Box 24 F, Cincinnati, OH 45224
The Stark Gun Collectors, Inc.
William I. Gann, 5666 Waynesburg Dr., Waynesburg, OH 44688

OKLAHOMA

Indian Territory Gun Collector's Assn.
P.O. Box 4491, Tulsa, OK 74159

OREGON

Oregon Cartridge Coll. Assn.
Terry A. White, 9480 S. Gribble Rd., Canby, OR 97013
Oregon Arms Coll. Assn., Inc.
Ted Dowd, P.O. Box 25103, Portland, OR 97225

PENNSYLVANIA

Presque Isle Gun Coll. Assn.
James Welch, 156 E. 37 St., Erie, PA 16504

SOUTH CAROLINA

Belton Gun Club, Inc.
J.K. Phillips, 195 Phillips Dr., Belton, SC 29627
South Carolina Shooting Assn.
P.O. Box 210133, Columbia, SC 29221

SOUTH DAKOTA

Dakota Territory Gun Coll. Assn., Inc.
Curt Carter, Castlewood, SD 57223

TENNESSEE

Smoky Mountain Gun Coll. Assn., Inc.
Hugh W. Yabro, Pres., P.O. Box 23225, Knoxville, TN 37933
Tennessee Gun Collectors Assn., Inc.
M.H. Parks, 3556 Pleasant Valley Rd., Nashville, TN 37204

TEXAS

Houston Gun Collectors Assn., Inc.
P.O. Box 741429, Houston, TX 77274
Texas Cartridge Coll. Assn., Inc.
Dan LeClaire, 5422 Fayette, Houston, TX 77056
Texas Gun Collectors Assn.
85 Wells Fargo Trail, Austin, TX 78737
Texas State Rifle Assn.
P.O. Drawer 710549, Dallas, TX 75371

WASHINGTON

Washington Arms Collectors, Inc.
J. Dennis Cook, P.O. Box 7335, Tacoma, WA 98407

WISCONSIN

Great Lakes Arms Coll. Assn., Inc.
Edward C. Warnke, 2913 Woodridge Lane, Waukesha, WI 53188
Wisconsin Gun Collectors Assn., Inc.
Lulita Zellmer, P.O. Box 181, Sussex, WI 53089

WYOMING

Wyoming Gun Collectors
Bob Funk, Box 1805, Riverton, WY 82501

NATIONAL ORGANIZATIONS

Amateur Trapshooting Assn.
601 W. National Rd., Vandalia, OH 45377
American Coon Hunters Assn.
Opal Johnston, P.O. Cadet, Route 1 Box 492, Old Mines, MO 63630
American Custom Gunmakers Guild
Jan Melchert, Exec. Director, 220 Division St., Northfield, MN 55057
American Defense Preparedness Assn.
Two Colonial Place, 2101 Wilson Blvd., Suite 400, Arlington, VA 22209-3061
American Pistolsmiths Guild
Al Marvel, Pres., 3922 Madonna Rd., Jarrettsville, MD 21084
American Police Pistol & Rifle Assn.
1100 N.E. 125th St., No. Miami, FL 33161
American Shooting Sports Coalition, Inc.
P.O. Box 1447, Fort Washington, PA 19034 (industry)
American Single Shot Rifle Assn.
L.B. Thompson, 987 Jefferson Ave., Salem, OH 44460
American Society of Arms Collectors, Inc.
George E. Weatherly, P.O. Box 2567, Waxahatchie, TX 75165
Association of Firearm and Toolmark Examiners
Eugenia A. Bell, Secy., 7857 Esterel Dr., LaJolla, CA 92037; membership sec'y.: Andrew B. Hart, 80 Mountain View Ave., Rensselaer, NY 12144
Boone & Crockett Club
241 South Fraley Blvd., P.O. Box 547, Dumfries, VA 22026
Browning Collectors Assn.
Mrs. Judy A. Rogers, 4928 Merrick Ave., Grand Island, NE 68801
The Cast Bullet Assn., Inc.
Ralland J. Fortier, Membership Director, 4103 Foxcraft Dr., Traverse City, MI 49684
Citizens Committee for the Right to Keep and Bear Arms
Natl. Hq.: Liberty Park, 12500 N.E. Tenth Pl., Bellevue, WA 98005
Colt Collectors Assn.
3200 Westminster, Dallas, TX 75205
Deer Unlimited of America, Inc.
P.O. Box 1129, Abbeville, SC 29620
Ducks Unlimited, Inc.
One Waterfowl Way, Long Grove, IL 60047
Experimental Ballistics Associates
Homer Powley, 27131-183rd Ave., Eldridge, IA 52748
Firearms Coalition
Box 6537, Silver Spring, MD 20906/301-871-3006
Firearms Engravers Guild of America
Robert Evans, Secy., 332 Vine St., Oregon City, OR 97045
Foundation For North American Wild Sheep
720 Allen Ave., Cody, WY 82414
Garand Collectors Assn.
P.O. Box 181, Richmond, KY 40475
Golden Eagle Collectors Assn.
Chris Showler, P.O. Box 62213, Sunnyvale, CA 94086-2213
Gun Owners of America
8001 Forbes Place, Suite 102, Springfield, VA 22151/703-321-8585
Handgun Hunters International
J.D. Jones, Dir., P.O. Box 357 MAG, Bloomingdale, OH 43910
Harrington & Richardson Gun Coll. Assn.
George L. Cardet, 525 N.W. 27th Ave., Suite 201, Miami, FL 33125
International Benchrest Shooters
Joan Borden, RD 1, Box 244A, Tunkhannock, PA 18657
International Cartridge Coll. Assn., Inc.
Charles Spano, 570 Memorial Circle, Suite D, Ormond Beach, FL 32074
IHMSA
(Intl. Handgun Metallic Silhouette Assn.)
Frank Scotto, 127 Winthrop Terr., Meriden, CT 06450

IPPA
(International Paintball Players Assn.)
P.O. Box 90051, Los Angeles, CA 90009/213-322-3107
Jews For The Preservation of Firearms Ownership (JPFO)
2872 So. Wentworth Ave., Milwaukee, WI 53207
The Mannlicher Collectors Assn.
Rev. Don L. Henry, Secy., P.O. Box 7144, Salem, OR 97303
Marlin Firearms Coll. Assn., Ltd.
Dick Paterson, Secy., 407 Lincoln Bldg., 44 Main St., Champaign, IL 61820
Miniature Arms Collectors/Makers Society Ltd.
Joseph J. Macewicz, Exec. Secy., 104 White Sand Lane, Racine, WI 53402
National Association of Buckskinners
Barbara Pray, 1981 E. 94th Ave., Thornton, CO 80229
National Assn. of Federally Licd. Firearms Dealers
Andrew Molchan, 2801 E. Oakland Park Blvd., Ft. Lauderdale, FL 33306
National Association to Keep and Bear Arms
P.O. Box 78336, Seattle, WA 98178
National Automatic Pistol Collectors Assn.
Tom Knox, P.O. Box 15738, Tower Grove Station, St. Louis, MO 63163
National Bench Rest Shooters Assn., Inc.,
Pat Baggett, 2027 Buffalo, Levelland, TX 79336
National Firearms Assn.
Terry Williams, President, P.O. Box 160038, Austin, TX 78716
National Muzzle Loading Rifle Assn.
Box 67, Friendship, IN 47021
National Reloading Mfrs. Assn.
4905 S.W. Griffith Dr., Suite 101, Beaverton, OR 97005
National Rifle Assn. of America
1600 Rhode Island Ave., N.W., Washington, DC 20036
(Contact the NRA for info on their silhouette program.)
National Shooting Sports Fdtn., Inc.
Robert T. Delfay, Exec. Director, 555 Danbury Rd., Wilton, CT 06897/203-762-1320
National Skeet Shooting Assn.
Mike Hampton, Exec. Director, P.O. Box 680007, San Antonio, TX 78268-0007
National Wild Turkey Federation, Inc.
P.O. Box 530, Edgefield, SC 29824
North American Airgunners Assn.
1804 E. Sprague St., Winston-Salem, NC 27107
North American Hunting Club
P.O. Box 3401, Minnetonka, MN 55343
North-South Skirmish Assn., Inc.
T.E. Johnson, Jr., P.O. Box 12122, Richmond, VA 23241
Professional Gunsmiths of America
13 Highway Route 1, Box 224 E, Lexington, MO 64067
Remington Society of America
Gordon Stanley, P.O. Box 40, Fulton, TX 78358
Ruger Collector's Assn., Inc.
P.O. Box 1778, Chino Valley, AZ 86323
Safari Club International
Jim Morehouse, 4800 W. Gates Pass Rd., Tucson, AZ 85745/602-620-1220
Sako Collectors Assn., Inc.
Karen Reed, 1725 Woodhill Ln., Bedford, TX 76021
Second Amendment Foundation
James Madison Building, 12500 N.E. 10th Pl., Bellevue, WA 98005
Smith & Wesson Coll. Assn.
George Linne, 133 So. 11th St., Chouteau Ctr., Suite 400, St. Louis, MO 63102
The Society of American Bayonet Collectors
P.O. Box 44021, Baton Rouge, LA 70804
Southern California Schuetzen Society
Dean Lillard, 34657 Ave. E., Yucaipa, CA 92399
Sporting Arms & Ammunition Manufacturers Institute (SAAMI)
555 Danbury Rd., Wilton, CT 06897
The Thompson/Center Assn.
Joe Wright, Pres., Box 792, Northboro, MA 01532/508-393-3834
USPSA/IPSC
Dave Stanford, P.O. Box 811, Sedro Woolley, WA 98284/206-855-2245
U.S. Revolver Assn.
Chick Shuter, 96 West Union St., Ashland, MA 01721

U.S. Sporting Clays Assn.
50 Briar Hollow, Suite 490 East, Houston, TX 77027
Winchester Arms Collectors Assoc.
Richard Berg, Secy., P.O. Box 6754, Great Falls, MT 59406
World Fast Draw Assn.
Dick Plum, 16421 McFadden, Apt. 350, Tustin, CA 92680

AUSTRALIA

Sporting Shooters' Assn. of Australia Inc.
P.O. Box 2066, Kent Town SA 5071, Australia

CANADA

ALBERTA

Canadian Historical Arms Society
P.O. Box 901, Edmonton, Alb., Canada T5J 2L8
National Firearms Assn.
Natl. HQ: P.O. Box 1779, Edmonton, Alta. T5J 2P1, Canada

BRITISH COLUMBIA

Historical Arms Collectors Society of B.C.
P.O. Box 86166, North Vancouver, B.C. V7L 4J8 Canada

MANITOBA

The Association of Automatic Firearms Collectors and Shooters
131 Nemy Cresent, Winnipeg, MB R2Y 0K6, Canada

ONTARIO

Tri-County Antique Arms Fair
P.O. Box 122, RR # 1, North Lancaster, Ont., K0C 1Z0, Canada

EUROPE

ENGLAND

Arms and Armour Society of London
A.R.E. North, Dept. of Metalwork, Victoria & Albert Museum, South Kensington, London SW7 2RL
Historical Breechloading Smallarms Assn.
D.J. Penn, M.A., Imperial War Museum, Lambeth Rd., London SE 1 6HZ, England. Journal and newsletter are $8 a yr., plus surcharge for airmail
National Rifle Assn.
(Great Britain)
Bisley Camp, Brookwood, Woking, Surrey, GU24 OPB, England/0483.797777

FRANCE

Syndicat National de l'Arquebuserie du Commerce de l'Arme Historique
B.P. No. 3, 78110 Le Vesinet, France

GERMANY (WEST)

Deutscher Schützenbund
Lahnstrasse 120,6200 Wiesbaden-Klarenthal, West Germany

NEW ZEALAND

New Zealand Deerstalkers Assn.
Michael Watt, P.O. Box 6514, Wellington, New Zealand

SOUTH AFRICA

Historical Firearms Soc. of South Africa
P.O. Box 145, 7725 Newlands, Republic of South Africa

DIRECTORY OF THE ARMS TRADE

This year we've changed the format of the Directory of the Arms Trade to help you, the reader, find more easily the manufacturer that carries the product you are seeking. We've created a Product Directory and a Manufacturers' Directory.

The **Product Directory** contains the same product categories as in past editions of Gun Digest. However, this time around we're listing only the manufacturers' names in alphabetical order.

The **Manufacturers' Directory** lists alphabetically the manufacturers, their addresses and phone numbers.

PRODUCT DIRECTORY

AMMUNITION (Commercial)

Action Ammo Ltd.
ACTIV Industries, Inc.
AFSCO Ammunition
A&M Waterfowl, Inc.
A-Square Co., Inc.
Atlanta Discount Ammo
Ballistic Research Industries (BRI)
Black Hills Ammunition
Blount Sporting Equipment Division
Cascade Cartridge, Inc. (See Blount Sporting Equipment Division)
Dynamit Nobel-RWS, Inc.
Eldorado Cartridge Corp.
Elite Ammunition
Estate Cartridge, Inc.
Federal Cartridge Co.
Fisher Enterprises (Prometheus airgun pellets)
Frontier Cartridge Division
Hansen Cartridge Co.
ICI-America
M&D Munitions Ltd.
Omark Industries (See Blount Sporting Equipment Division)
Palcher Ammunition
P.P.C. Corp.
Precision Prods. of Wash., Inc.
Pro Load Ammunition, Inc.
Prometheus/Titan Black (See Fisher Enterprises)
Remington Arms Co.
RWS (See Dynamit Nobel)
Southern Ammunition Co., Inc.
3-D Ammunition & Bullets
United States Ammunition Co., Inc.
Weatherby, Inc.
Winchester Div., Olin Corp.
Zero Ammunition Co., Inc.

AMMUNITION (Custom)

Accuracy Systems, Inc.
AFSCO Ammunition
Allred Bullet Co.
Apex Rifle Co.
A-Square Co., Inc.
Atlanta Discount Ammo
Beal's Bullets (Automag specialists)
B.E.L.L. (See Eldorado Cartridge Corp.)
Black Mountain Bullets
Buffalo Bullet Co., Inc. (muzzle-loading bullets)
Cartridges Unlimited (British Express; metric; U.S.)
Cor-Bon, Inc. (bullets)
Country Armourer, The
Cumberland Arms
Custom Hunting Ammo & Arms
Custom Tackle & Ammo
Eldorado Cartridge Corp.
Elite Ammunition
Elko Arms
Ellis Sport Shop, E.W.
Epps (Orillia) Northern Ltd., Ellwood
Estate Cartridge, Inc. (shotshell)
First Distributors, Inc., Jack
Freedom Arms, Inc.
Gammog, Gregory B. Gally
Gonzalez, Ramon B.
"Gramps" Antique Cartridges
Hardin Specialty Distributors
Hindman, Ace
Jensen's Custom Ammunition
Jett & Co., Inc.
Keeler, R.H. (armor piercing for police and military only)
Lindsley Arms Cartridge Co., Inc.
Lomont Precision Bullets (custom cast bullets only)
Mack's Sport Shop
MagSafe Ammo Co.
McConnellstown Reloading & Cast Bullets, Inc.
McMurdo, Lynn (custom 50-cal. bullets)
M&D Munitions Ltd.
NAI/Ballistek (cases for 25-20 Win. single shot)
North American Arms
Palcher Ammunition
Patriot Mfg. & Sales
Personal Protection Systems, Ltd. (high-performance handgun loads)
Precision Munitions, Inc. (reloaded ammo)
Sailer, Anthony F. (See AFSCO)
Sanders Custom Gun Service
Spence, George W. (boxer-primed cartridges)
State Arms Gun Co.
3-D Ammunition & Bullets (reloaded police ammo)
3-Ten Corp. (44 magnum bulleted shot loads; handgun)
Thunderbird Cartridge Co., Inc.
Trophy Bonded Bullets, Inc.
Vitt/Boos
Wardrop, R.A.
Widener's Reloading & Shooting Supply, Inc.
Worthy Products, Inc.
Zero Ammunition Co., Inc.

AMMUNITION (Foreign)

Action Arms Ltd.
AFSCO Ammunition
Atlanta Discount Ammo
Beeman Precision Arms, Inc.
Champion's Choice, Inc. (Lapua ammo)
Chinasports, Inc.
Dynamit Nobel-RWS, Inc. (RWS, Geco, Rottweil)
Fiocchi of America, Inc.
Hansen Cartridge Co.
Hirtenberger Patronen-, Zundhutchen- & Metallwarenfabrik
Hunters Specialty, Inc. (Hirtenberger)
Jager, Inc., Paul (RWS centerfire ammo)
PMC-Eldorado Cartridge Co.
PTK International
RWS (See Dynamit Nobel-RWS, Inc.)

AMMUNITION COMPONENTS—BULLETS, POWDER, PRIMERS

Accurate Arms Co., Inc. (powders)
Acme Custom Bullets
Alaska Bullet Works (Alaska copper-bond; Kodiak bonded core bullets)
Allred Bullet Co. (custom bullets)
American Bullets
American Products Co. (12-ga. shot wad)
Ammo-O-Mart Ltd. (Nobel powder)
A-Square Co., Inc. (custom bullets; brass)
Atlanta Discount Ammo
Ballistic Prods., Inc. (shotgun powders, primers)
Ballistic Research Industries (BRI), (Sabo shotgun slug; Gualandi slug)
Barnes Bullets, Inc.
B.E.L.L. (See Eldorado Cartridge Corp.)
Bell's Custom Shop
Berger Bullets (custom 22, 6mm benchrest bullets)
Bergman and Williams (copper tube 308 custom bullets; lead wire in all sizes)
Bertram Bullet Co. (See Huntington Die Specialties)
Bitterroot Bullet Co.
Black Mountain Bullets (custom Fluid King match bullets)
Blount Sporting Equipment Division
Bruno Bullets Shooters Supply (22, 6mm benchrest bullets)
Buffalo Bullet Co., Inc.
Buffalo Rock Shooters Supply
Cartridges Unlimited (obsolete cast bullets)
CCI (See Blount Sporting Equipment Division)
CheVron Bullets
Colorado Sutlers Arsenal
Competition Bullets, Inc.
Cooper-Woodward
Corbin Mfg. & Supply, Inc. (bullets)
Cor-Bon, Inc. (375, 44, 45 solid brass partition bullets)
Creative Cartridge Co.
DuPont (See IMR Powder Co.)
Dynamit Nobel-RWS, Inc. (RWS percussion caps)
Eldorado Cartridge Corp.,
Excaliber Wax, Inc. (wax bullets)
Federal Cartridge Co. (primers)
Fiocchi of America, Inc. (primers; shotshell cases)
Fisher Enterprises
Fowler Bullets (benchrest bullets)
Freedom Arms, Inc.
Glaser Safety Slug, Inc.
GOEX, Inc. (blackpowder)
Golden Powder International Sales, Inc. (Golden Powder/blackpowder)
Green Bay Bullets (cast lead bullets)
Grizzly Bullets (custom)
Gun City
Hardin Specialty Distr. (casings, 7.63mm/44 Automag)
Harrison Bullet Works, (custom swaged 41 magnum bullets)
Hart & Son, Inc., Robert W.
Hercules, Inc. (smokeless powder)
Hodgdon Powder Co., Inc. (smokeless, Pyrodex and blackpowder)
Hornady Mfg. Co.
Hunters Specialty, Inc. (Hirtenberger bullets)
Huntington Die Specialties
IMR Powder Co. (smokeless powders only)
Jaro Manuf. (bullets)
Jensen's Custom Ammunition
Kodiak Custom Bullets
Lage Uniwad, Inc.
Lane Bullets (custom cast handgun bullets)
Lindsley Arms Cartridge Co., Inc. (brass)
Ljutic Industries, Inc. (Mono-wads)
Lomont Precision Bullets (custom cast bullets)
Low, Paul E., Jr. (jacketed 44- & 45-cal.)
Mack's Sport Shop (custom bullets)
Magnus Bullet Co., Inc.
MagSafe Ammo Co. (controlled core bullets for reloading)
Mayville Engineering Co. (non-toxic steel shot kits)
McConnellstown Reloading & Cast Bullets, Inc.
McMurdo, Lynn (50-cal. custom bullets)
M&D Munitions Ltd.
Metallic Casting & Copper Corp. (MCC) (cast bullets)
Michael's Antiques (Balle Blondeau)
Midway Arms, Inc.
Miller Trading Co. (bullets)
Mushroom Express Bullet Co. (ML bullets only)
Necromancer Industries, Inc.
NORMA (See Federal Cartridge Co.)
Nosler Bullets, Inc.
Old Western Scrounger, Inc.
Omark (See Blount Sporting Equipment Division)
Orion Bullets (partitioned, bonded bullets)
Patriot Manufacturing & Sales (custom bullets)
Pattern Control (plastic wads)
PMC-Eldorado Cartridge Co.
Polywad, Inc. (Spred-Rs for shotshells)
Pomeroy, Robert (formed cases, obsolete cases, bullets)
Power Plus Enterprises, Inc. (12-ga. slugs; 308, 45 ACP, 357 custom bullets)
Precision Munitions, Inc. (cast bullets)
Professional Hunter Supplies (408, 375, 308, 510 custom bullets)
Prometheus/Titan Black (See Fisher Enterprises)
Pyrodex (See Hodgdon Powder Co., Inc.) (blackpowder substitute)
Reardon Products (dry-lube powder)
Redwood Bullet Works (custom bullets)
Remington Arms Co.
Renner Co., R.J. (rubber bullets)
Rolston, Fred, Jr. (cast bullets only)
Rubright Bullets (custom 22 & 6mm benchrest bullets)
Sierra Bullets, Inc. (jacketed rifle and handgun bullets)
Southern Ammunition Co., Inc.
Speer Products (See Blount Sporting Equipment Division)
Sport Flite Mfg., Inc. (zinc bases, lead wire)
Swift Bullet Co. (375 big game, 224 custom)
Taracorp Industries (Lawrence Brand lead shot)
3-D Ammunition & Bullets
Thunderbird Cartridge Co., Inc. (powder)
Trophy Bonded Bullets, Inc. (big game 458, 308, 375 bonded cust. bullets only)
True Flite Bullet Co. (Tru Flite bullets)
United States Ammunition Co. (bullets)
Vitt/Boos (Aerodynamic shotgun slug, 12-ga. only)
Warren Muzzleloading Co., Inc.
Watson Trophy Match Bullets, Ed (22, 6mm custom benchrest bullets)
Widener's Reloading & Shooting
Winchester Div., Olin Corp.
Woodland Bullets (bullets)
Worthy Products, Inc. (slug loads)
Zero Ammunition, Inc.

ANTIQUE ARMS DEALERS

Ad Hominem
Ammunition Consulting Services, Inc.
Antique Arms Co.
Antique Gun Parts, Inc.
Aplan, James O.
Beeman Precision Arms, Inc. (airguns only)
Boggs, Wm.
Can Am Enterprises
Cape Outfitters
Century Intl. Arms, Inc.
Clements Handicrafts Unltd., Chas
Condon, Inc., David
Continental Kite & Key Co. (CONKKO)
Corry, John (English guns)
Dixie Gun Works, Inc.
Dyson & Son Ltd., Peter (accoutrements for ant. gun coll.; custom- and machine-made)
Ed's Gun House
Epps (Orillia) Nothern Ltd., Ellwood
Fagan & Co., William
First Distributors, Inc., Jack
Flayderman & Co., N.
Flintlock Muzzle Loading Gun Shop, The
Frielich, Robert S.
Fulmer Antique Firearms, Chet
Glass, Herb
Goergen, James
Griffin's Guns & Antiques
Guncraft Sports, Inc.
Hallowell & Co.
Hansen Cartridge Company
Kelley's
Lever Arms Serv. Ltd.
Liberty Antique Gunworks
Log Cabin Sport Shop
Lone Pine Trading Post
McKee, Arthur (Rem. double shotguns)
Michael's Antiques
Museum of Historical Arms
Muzzleloaders Etc., Inc.
Navy Arms Co.
New Orleans Arms Co.
Old Western Scrounger, Inc.
Pioneer Guns
Pony Express Sport Shop, Inc.
Retting, Inc., Martin B.

Rutgers Gun & Boat Center
San Francisco Gun Exch.
Semmer, Charles
Sherwood Intl. Export Corp.
S&S Firearms
Steves House of Guns

Stott's Creek Armory, Inc.
Ward & Van Valkenburg
Wayne, James
Wiest, M.C.
Yearout, Lewis

APPRAISERS, GUNS, ETC.

Ad Hominem
Ahlman's, Inc.
Ammunition Consulting Serv., Inc.
Antique Gun Parts, Inc.
Aplan, James O.
The Armoury, Inc.
Beeman Precision Arms, Inc. (airguns only)
Bess, Gordon
Butterfield & Butterfield
Camilli, Lou
Cape Outfitters
Christie's East
Christopher Firearms Co., Inc., E.
Clements, Chas
Condon, Inc., David
Custom Tackle & Ammo
Dilliott Gunsmithing, Inc.
D.O.C. Specialists
Ed's Gun House
Ellis Sport Shop, E.W.
Epps (Orillia) Northern Ltd., Ellwood
Flayderman & Co., Inc., N.
Forgett, Valmore J., Jr.
Frederick Gun Shop
Goergen, James
"Gramps" Antique Cartridges
Greenwald, Leon E."Bud"
Griffin & Howe
Guncraft Sports, Inc.

Hallowell & Co.
Hansen Cartridge Company
Idaho Ammunition Service (ammunition)
Irwin, Campbell H.
Kelley's
Liberty Antique Gunworks
Lone Pine Trading Post
Martin, Elwyn H.
Mazur Restoration, Pete
Miller Trading Co.
Museum of Historical Arms, Inc., The
New England Arms Co.
Orvis Co., Inc., The
Paragon Sales, Inc.
Pioneer Guns
Pony Express Sport Shop, Inc.
Rahn Gun Works, Inc.
Richards, John
Sarco, Inc.
Storey, Dale
Ten-Ring Precision, Inc.
Tillinghast, James C.
Unick's Gunsmithing
Wayne, James
Wells Ltd., R.A.
Wiest, M.C.
Winchester Sutler, Inc.
Wisner's Gun Shop, Inc.
Yearout, Lewis

AUCTIONEERS, GUNS, ETC.

Ammunition Consulting Serv., Inc.
Bourne Co., Inc., Richard A.
Butterfield & Butterfield
Christie's East
Fagan & Co., William

Kelley's
"Little John's" Antique Arms
Parke-Bernet (See Sotheby's)
Sotheby's
Tillinghast, James C.

BOOKS (ARMS), Publishers and Dealers

Armory Publications
Arms & Armour Press Ltd.
Beeman Precision Arms, Inc. (airguns only)
Blacksmith Corp.
Blacktail Mountain Books
DBI Books, Inc.
DeHaas, Frank
Fortress Publications, Inc.
Guncraft Books
Gun Hunter Books
Gun Room Press, The
Gunnerman Books
Handgun Press
Kopp Publishing Co.

Lyman Products, Corp.
Madis, David
McKee Publications
Outdoorsman's Bookstore, The
Paladin Press
Pettinger Arms Books, Gerald
Riling Arms Books Co., Ray
Rutgers Book Center (bookseller)
Stackpole Books
Stoeger Publishing Co.
Trotman, Ltd., Ken
Wahl Corp., Paul
Winchester Press
Wolfe Publishing Co.

BULLET AND CASE LUBRICANTS

American Gas & Chemical Co., Ltd.
Blount Sporting Equipment Division
C-H Tool & Die Corp.
Clenzoil Corp.
Cooper-Woodward (Perfect Lube)
Corbin Mfg. & Supply, Inc.
Dillon Precision Prods., Inc.
Green Bay Bullets (EZE-Size case lube)
Javelina Products (Alox beeswax; bullet lubricant)
LeClear Industries
Lee Precision, Inc.
Lyman Products Corp. (Size-Ezy)
Magma Engineering Co.
Micro-Lube

Midway Arms, Inc.
M&M Engineering (case lubes)
M&N Bullet Lube
NEI (Ten X-Lube; mould prep.)
Northeast Industrial, Inc. (See NEI)
Pacific Tool Co.
Redding, Inc.
Rooster Laboratories (Zambini and HVR bullet lubes; case lubes & polish)
SAECO (See Redding, Inc.)
Sandia Die & Cartridge Co.
Shooters Accessory Supply (See Corbin Mfg. & Supply, Inc.)
Tamarack Prods., Inc. (bullet lube)
TDP Industries, Inc.

BULLET SWAGE DIES AND TOOLS

Bullet Swaging Supply, Inc.
C-H Tool & Die Corp.
Clerke Co., J.A. (moulds)
Coats, Mrs. Lester (lead wire core cutter)
Corbin Mfg. & Supply, Inc.
Hanned Precision (cast bullet tools)
Hollywood Loading Tools (See M&M Engineering)

Huntington Die Specialties
M&M Engineering
Necromancer Industries, Inc.
Rorschach Precision Products
SAS Dies (See Corbin Mfg. & Supply)
Seneca Run Iron Works, Inc. (muzzle-loading round ball)
Sport Flite Mfg., Inc.

CARTRIDGES FOR COLLECTORS

Ad Hominem
Ammo-Mart Ltd.
Ammunition Consulting Serv., Inc.
Burgess, Ida I.

Cameron's
Cape Outfitters
Duffy, Chas. E.
Dunn, Tom M.

Eldorado Custom Shop (antique brass)
Epps (Orillia) Northern Ltd., Ellwood
Excaliber Wax, Inc.
Fiocchi of America
First Distributors, Inc., Jack
Furr Arms
Glaser Safety Slug, Inc.
"Gramps" Antique Cartridges
Griffin's Guns & Antiques
Hansen Cartridge Company
Idaho Ammunition Service (ammunition)

Kelley's
Metallic Casting & Copper Corp. (MCC)
Old Western Scrounger, Inc.
PMC-Eldorado Cartridge Co.
Ramos, Jesse
San Francisco Gun Exchange
Spence, George W.
Tillinghast, James C.
Ward & Van Valkenburg
Yearout, Lewis

CASES, CABINETS AND RACKS—GUN

A&B Industries, Inc. (cases: Top-Line Prods.)
Abel Safe & File Co.
Alco Carrying Cases (aluminum)
Allen Co., Bob (carrying cases)
American Import Co., The
API Outdoors, Inc. (racks)
Arkfield Mfg. & Dist. Co., Inc. (security steel cabinets)
Art Jewel Enterprises Ltd. (cases)
Beeman Precision Arms, Inc.
Big Spring Enterprise "Bore Stores" (synthetic cases)
Boyt Co., Div. of Welsh Sporting Goods
Browning, (Gen. Off.)
Cascade Fabrication (aluminum cases)
Chipmunk (See Oregon Arms, Inc.)
Dara-Nes, Inc. (See Nesci)
Dart Mfg. Co.
Detroit-Armor Corp. (Saf-Gard steel gun safe)
Doskocil Mfg. Co., Inc. (Gun Guard carrying)
East Enterprises, Inc.
Epps (Orillia) Northern Ltd., Ellwood (custom gun cases)
Eversull & Co., Inc., K
Flambeau Products Corp.
Fort Knox Security Products (safes)
Galati International (cases)
Gun-Ho Sports Cases
Gun Parts Corp. (cases)
Gusdorf Corp. (gun cabinets)

Hall Plastics, Inc., John (cases)
Hansen Cartridge Co.
Hogue Grips
Huey Gun Cases, Marvin (handbuilt leather cases)
Hugger Hooks Co.
Jumbo Sports Prods.
Kalispel Metal Prods. (aluminum boxes)
Kane Products, Inc.
KLP Mfg. (Cordura nylon carry cases)
Knock on Wood Antiques (gun & security cabinets)
Kolpin Mfg., Inc.
McGuire, Bill (custom)
Nesci Enterprises, Inc. (firearms security chests)
Oregon Arms, Inc. (soft cases)
Penguin Industries, Inc.
Protecto Plastics (carrying cases)
Rahn Gun Works, Inc. (leather trunk cases)
Red Head, Inc.
San Angelo Mfg. Co.
Schulz Industries (carrying cases)
Security Gun Chest (See Tread Corp.)
Sports Support Systems, Inc.
SSK Co. (wooden cases)
Sweet Home Inc.
Tread Corp. (security gun chest)
Unick's Gunsmithing
WAMCO, Inc. (wooden display cases)
Weather Shield Sports Equipment, Inc.
Wilson Case Co. (cases)

CHOKE DEVICES, RECOIL ABSORBERS & RECOIL PADS

Action Products, Inc. (recoil shock eliminator)
Apex Rifle Co.
Arms Ingenuity Co. (Jet-Away)
Armsport, Inc. (choke devices)
Baker, Stan (shotgun specialist)
Briley Mfg. Co. (choke tubes)
C&H Research (Mercury recoil suppressor)
Cellini Vito Francesca, Inc. (recoil reducer; muzzlebrake)
Clinton River Gun Serv., Inc. (Reed Choke)
Cubriel, Reggie (leather recoil pads)
Delta Vectors, Inc. (Techni-Port recoil compensation)
Edwards Recoil Reducer
E&L Mfg., Inc.
Emsco Variable Shotgun Chokes
Fabian Bros. Sptg. Goods, Inc. (DTA Muzzle Mizer rec. abs.; MIL/brake)
Freshour Mfg. (muzzlebrakes)
Gentry Custom Gunmaker, David (muzzlebrakes)
Griggs Products (recoil director)

Gun Parts Corp.
Harper, William E.
Hastings
I.N.C., Inc. (Sorbothane Kick-Eez recoil pad)
Intermountain Arms (Gunner's Choice muzzlebrake)
KDF, Inc. (muzzlebrake)
Lyman Products Corp. (Cutts Comp.)
Mag-na-port International, Inc. (muzzlebrake system)
Mag-Na-Port of Canada
Marble Arms Corp. (Poly Choke)
Pachmayr Ltd. (recoil pads)
P.A.S.T. Corp. (recoil reducer shield)
Poly Choke (See Marble Arms)
Pro-Port Ltd.
Protektor Model Co. (shoulder recoil pad)
Reed Choke (See Clinton River Gun Svc.)
Sipes Gun Shop
Upper Missouri Trading Co.
Walker Arms Co., Inc.

CHRONOGRAPHS AND PRESSURE TOOLS

Competition Electronics, Inc.
Custom Chronograph, Inc.
D&H Precision Tooling (pressure testing receiver)
H-S Precision, Inc. (pressure barrels)

Jaeger, Inc., Paul
Oehler Research, Inc.
P.A.C.T., Inc. (Precision chronogr.)
Quartz-Lok
Tepeco (Tepeco Speed-Meter)

CLEANING AND REFINISHING SUPPLIES

Acculube II, Inc. (lubricants/cleaners)
Accupro Gun Care (chemical bore cleaner)
Adco International
All's
Alsa Corp., The (ALLGUN Universal gun care kit)
American Gas & Chemical Co., Ltd. (TSI gun lube)
Anderson Mfg. Co. (stock finishes)
Armite Labs. (pen oiler)
Armoloy Co. of Ft. Worth (refinishing)
Beeman Precision Arms, Inc. (airguns only)
Belltown, Ltd. (gun cleaning cloth kit)
Birchwood-Casey

Blount Sporting Equipment Division
Blue and Gray Prods., Inc.
Break-Free (lubricants)
Brobst, Jim (J-B Cleaning Compound)
Brownells, Inc.
Browning (Gen. Off.)
Chopie Mfg., Inc. (Black Solve gun cleaner)
Clenzoil Corp.
Crouse's Country Cover (Masking Gun Oil)
Dewey Mfg. Co., J. (one-piece gun cleaning rod)
Dri-Slide, Inc.
Dutchman's Firearms, Inc., The
Eezox, Inc. (cleaner, rust preventative)

E&L Mfg., Inc.
Flouramics, Inc. (lubricant-gun coat)
Force 10, Inc. (anti-rust protectant)
Forster Products, Inc.
Fountain Products
Forty-Five Ranch Enterprises
Grace Metal Products, Inc.
Gun Parts Corp. (gun blue)
Heller & Levin Associates, Inc.
Hoppe's Division, Penguin Ind., Inc.,
Hydrosorbent Products (silica gel
    dehumidifier)
Jantz Supply, Ken
J-B Bore Cleaner
Johnston Brothers
Kellog's Professional Prods., Inc.
Kleen-Bore, Inc.
Kleinendorst, K.W. (rifle cleaning cables)
Kopp, Terry K. (stock rubbing compound;
    rust preventative grease)
Lee, Mark (rust blue solution)
LEM Gun Specialties (Lewis Lead
    Remover)
Lortone, Inc.
LPS Chemical Prods.
LT Industries, Inc. (airguns—flexible
    cleaning rods/felt cleaning pellets)
Lynx-Line (See Williams Shootin' Iron
    Service)
Marble Arms Co.
Marsh, Mike (gun accessories)
Micro Sight Co. (stock bedding compound)
Nesci Enterprises, Inc.
Old World Oil Products (gun stock finish)
Omark (See Blount Sporting Equipment
    Division)
Original Mink Oil, Inc.
Outers Laboratories, Div. of Blount
Ox-Yoke Originals, Inc. (dry lubrication
    patches)
Parker-Hale/Precision Sports

Pease Accuracy, Bob
P&M Sales and Service
Precision Sports (Parker Hale)
R&S Industries Corp. (Miracle All Purpose
    polishing cloth)
Reardon Products (Dry-Lube)
Red Star Target Co.
Rice Protective Gun Coatings
Richards Classic Oil Finish (gunstock oils,
    wax)
RIG Products
Rooster Laboratories (cartridge/case
    cleaner, polish, protectant)
Rusteprufe Labs.
Rust Guardit (See Kleen-Bore, Inc.)
Scott, Inc., Tyler (muzzle-loading black
    solvent; patch lube)
Seacliff International, Inc. (portable parts
    washer)
Shooter's Choice (See Venco Industries)
Sports Suppot Systems, Inc.
Taylor & Robbins (Throat Saver, cleaning
    rod guide)
TDP Industries, Inc.
Texas Platers Supply Co.
Totally Dependable Products (See TDP
    Industries, Inc.)
Treso, Inc. (Durango Gun Rod)
United States Products Co. (Gold
    Medallion bore cleaner/conditioner)
Van Gorden, C.S. (Van's Instant Blue)
Venco Industries, Inc. (Shooter's Choice
    bore cleaner and conditioner)
WD-40 Co.
Williams Gun Sight Co. (finish kit)
Williams Shootin' Iron Service (Lynx Line)
Wisconsin Platers Supply Co. (See Texas
    Platers Supply Co.)
Z-Coat Co.
Zip Aerosol Prods. (See RIG Products)

CUSTOM GUNSMITHS

Accuracy Gun Shop
Accuracy Unlimited
Accurate Plating & Weaponry, Inc.
Ahlman's, Inc.
Aldis, Richard L.
Allen, Inc., Don
Alpine's Precision Gunsmithing
American Custom Gunmakers Guild
Amrine's Gun Shop
Ann Arbor Rod and Gun Co.
Antique Arms Co.
Apel, Dietrich
Armament Gunsmithing Co., Inc.
Arms Craft Gunsmithing (rebluing,
    restorations)
Arms Ingenuity Co.
Arms Services Corp.
Armurier, Hiptmayer
Atzigen, Ed von
A&W Repair (stock restoration)
Baer Custom Guns (rifles)
Bain and Davis, Inc.
Balickie Custom Stocks, Joe J.
Barnes Custom Shop
Barta's Gunsmithing
Bartlett, Donald
Beal, R.S., Jr.
Behlert Precision (custom)
Beitzinger, George
Belding's Custom Gun Shop
Bell's Custom Shop (handguns)
Bellm Contenders
Benchmark Guns
Bergmann & Williams
Bess, Gordon
Betz, Harold A.
Biesen, Al
Biesen, Roger
Billeb, Stephen L.
Billings Gunsmiths, Inc.
Billingsley, Ross (custom rifles)
Bill's Gun Repair
Bishop & Son, Inc., E.C.
Bolden, Duane (rust bluing)
Boswell, Charles (gunmakers)
Bowen Classic Arms Corp.
Bowerly, Kent
Brace, Larry D.
Brazos Arms Co. (gunsmithing)
Brgoch, Frank
Briganti Custom Gunsmith
Brown Precision, Inc. (rifles)

Bruno Bullets/Shooters Supply
Budin, Dave
Burgess, Ida I. (bluing repairs)
Burkhart, Don
Bustani, Leo
Cache La Poudre Rifleworks
    (muzzleloaders)
Camilli, Lou (muzzleloaders)
Campbell, Dick
Carter, Ralph L.
Caudill, Larry T.
Caywood, Shane
Champlin Firearms, Inc.
Champlin, R. MacDonald (muzzle-loading
    rifles and pistols)
Christopher Firearms Co., Inc., E.
Chuck's Gun Shop
Classic Arms Corp.
Clinton River Gun Serv., Inc.
Coffin, Charles H.
Coffin, Jim
Conrad, C.A.
Corkys Gun Clinic
Costa, David
Cox, C. Ed
Crocker, Gordon D. (rifles)
Cumberland Arms
Cumberland Knife & Gun Works
    (muzzleloaders)
Custom Gun Guild
Dangler, Homer L. (Kentucky rifles)
Davenport, Sterling
Davis Service Center, Bill
D&D Gunsmiths, Ltd.
Delorge, Ed
Dever, Jack
Devereaux, R.H.
Dilliott Gunsmithing, Inc.
DiStefano, Dominic
Dixon, William
Donnelly-Siskiyou Gun Works, C.P.
Dowtin Gunworks (DGW)
Dressel, Paul G., Jr.
Duffy, Charles E.
Duncan's Gunworks, Inc.
Echols, D'Arcy A.
Eggleston, Jere
Elko Arms
Emmons, Bob
Englishtown Sporting Goods Co., Inc.
Erhardt, Dennis
Eversull & Co., Inc., K.

Eyster, Ken
Farmer-Dressel, Sharon
Fautheree, Andy
Fellowes, Ted (muzzleloaders)
FERLIB, Armi di Ferraglio Libero
Ferris Firearms
Fiberpro, Inc. (rifles)
First Distributors, Inc., Jack
Fish, Marshall F.
Fisher, Jerry A.
Flaig's
Flint Creek Arms Co. (bluing, repairs)
Flynn's Cust. Guns
Fogle, James W.
Forster, Larry L.
Forthofer's Gunsmithing, Pete
Forty-Niner Trading Co.
Fountain Products
Frank Custom Guns, Ron
Frazier Brothers Sporting Goods
Fredrick Gun Shop
Freeland's Scope Stands, Inc.
Frontier Arms Co.
Furr, Karl J.
Gander Mountain, Inc.
Garrett Accur-Lt. D.F.S. Co.
Gator Guns & Repair
Genecco Gun Works, K.
Gentry Custom Gunmaker, David (custom
    Montana Mtn. Rifle)
Gillman, Edwin
Gilman-Mayfield
Giron, Robert E.
Goens, Dale W.
Gonzalez, Ramon B.
Goode, A.R.
Goodling's Gunsmithing
Goodwin, Fred, Goodwin's Gunshop
Gordie's Gun Shop
Grace, Charles E.
Granger, Georges
Graybill, Gene
Green, Roger M.
Greg Gunsmithing Repair
Griffin & Howe
Guncraft, Inc.
Guncraft Sports, Inc.
Gun Doctor, The
Guns
Gunsite Gunsmithy
Gun Works, The (muzzleloaders)
Hagn Rifles & Actions (s.s. actions & rifles)
Hallberg, Fritz
Hammans, Charles E.
Hanson's Gun Center, Dick
Harkrader's Cust. Gun Shop
Hart & Son, Inc., Robert W. (actions,
    stocks)
Hartmann & Weiss GmbH
Hecht, Hubert J., Waffen-Hecht
Heilmann, Stephen
Henriksen, Iver (rifles)
High Bridge Arms, Inc.
Hiptmayer, Klaus
Hoag, James W.
Hobaugh, Wm.
Hobbie Gunsmithing, Duane A.
Hodgson, Richard
Hoenig & Rodman
Hofer, Peter
Holland, Dick
Hollis Gun Shop
Holmes Firearms Corp.
Horst, Alan K. (custom)
H-S Precision, Inc.
Huebner, Corey O.
Hughes, Steven Dodd (muzzleloaders)
Hunkeler, Al (muzzleloaders)
Hyper-Single, Inc.,(precision single shot
    rifles)
Intermountain Arms
Iron Sight Gunworks, Inc.
Irwin, Campbell H.
Jackalope Gun Shop
Jaeger, Inc., Paul
Jamison, R.L., Jr.
Jarrett Rifles, Inc. (rifles)
Jim's Gun Shop
Johnson, Neal G.
Johnson, Peter S., c/o Orvis Co.
Juenke, Vern
Jurras, L.E.
Kartak Gun Works
Ken's Gun Specialties

Kesselring Gun Shop
Kilham, Benjamin
Klein, Don
Kleinendorst, K.W.
KOGOT
Kopp, Terry K.
Korzinek, J. (riflesmith)
LaFrance Specialties
Lair, Sam (single shots)
Lampert, Ron L.
Lawson Co., Harry
Lawson, John G.
Lee, Mark
LeFever & Sons, Inc., Frank
Liberty Antique Gunworks
Lilja Precision Rifle Barrels, Inc.
Lind, Al
Ljutic Industries, Inc. (shotguns)
Lofland, James W. (single shot rifles)
Logan, Harry M.
London Guns Ltd.
Long Island Gunsmith, Ltd. (Carriage
    Trade Shotgun)
MacDonald, R. Champlin
Mag-na-port International, Inc.
Makinson, Nick (English guns; repairs &
    renovations)
Mandarino, Monte (Penn. rifles)
Manley Shooting Supplies, Lowell
Marquart Precision Co.
Martin, Elwyn H.
Maryland Gun Works, Ltd.
Masker, Seely, Custom Rifles (benchrest)
Mathews & Son, Inc., Geo. E.
Matthews, Larry
Mazur Restoration, Pete (double-barrel
    rifles & shotguns)
McCann's Muzzle-Gun Works (ML)
McCormick's Custom Gun Bluing
McFarland, Stan (custom rifles)
McGowen Rifle Barrels
McGuire, Bill
McMurdo, Lynn
Mercer, R.M.
Miller Arms, Inc.
Miller Co., David
Miller, S.A., Point Roberts Sports Ltd.
Miller, Tom
Milliron Custom Guns & Stocks, Earl
Mills, Hugh B., Jr.
Monell Custom Guns
Larkin Moore & Co., Wm.
Morrison Custom Rifles, J.W.
Moschetti, Mitch
Mountain Bear Rifle Works, Inc.
MPI Stocks
Mrock, Larry
Neighbor, William (See Bill's Gun Repair)
Nelson, Stephen E.
Nettestad, Bruce A.
New England Arms Co.
New England Custom Gun Service (See
    Apel, Dietrich)
Newman Gunshop (muzzleloaders)
Nickels, Paul R.
Nicklas, Ted
Nittler, William J. (shotgun barrels and
    actions; repairs)
Noreen, Peter H.
Norman, Jim
North Fork Custom Gunsmithing
Nu-Line Guns
Oakland Custom Arms, Inc.
Olson, Eric
Olson, Vic
Oregon Trail Riflesmiths, Inc.
Orvis Co., Inc., The
Ottmar, Maurice
Pachmayr Ltd.
Pagel Gun Works (custom gunmaking and
    refinishing)
Pasadena Gun Center
Paterson Gunsmithing
Pence Precision Barrels
Penrod Precision
Peterson Gun Shop, A.W. (muzzleloaders)
Plante, Eugene T.
Power Custom, Inc.
Precision Specialties
Professional Gunsmiths of America
R&J Gunshop
Rifle Shop
Roberts, J.J.
Roberts, Wm. A., Jr. (muzzleloaders)

Robinson, Don (airrifle stocks)
Rocky Mountain Rifle Works, Ltd.
Rogers Gunsmithing, Bob
Royal Arms
Russell's Rifle Shop
Ryan, Chad
Sanders Custom Gun Serv.
Sandy's Custom Gunshop
Schaefer, Roy V.
Schumakers Gun Shop
Schwartz Custom Guns, Wayne E.
Schwartz Custom Guns, David W.
Scott Fine Guns, Inc., Thad
Shane's Gunsmithing
Shaw, Inc., E.R.
Shaw's
Shell Shack (muzzleloaders)
Sherk, Dan A.
Shilen Rifles, Inc.
Shiloh Rifle Mfg. Co., Inc.
Shockley, Harold H. (hot bluing & plating)
Shootin' Shack ('smithing services)
Shootist Supply
Silver Shields, Inc.
Sipes Gun Shop
Skinner, John R.
Sklany, Steve (Ferguson rifle)
Slezak, Jerome F.
Smith, Art
Smith, John
Snapp's Gunshop
Speiser, Fred D.
Spencer Reblue Service (electroless nickel plating)
Sportsmen's Equip. Co.
Sportsmen's Exchange & Western Gun Traders, Inc.
SSK Industries
Starnes, Ken
Steelman's Gun Shop
Steffens, Ron
Stegall, Keith
Storey, Dale A.
Stott's Creek Armory, Inc. (single shot and muzzle-loading work/restoration only)
Strawbridge, Victor W.
Stroup, Earl R. (rifles)

Strutz, W.C.
Sunora Gun Shop
Swann, D.J. (makers of falling block rifle)
Swenson's 45 Shop, A.D.
Talmage, William G.
Taylor & Robbins
Tennessee Valley Mfg.
Tertin, James A.
Thompson, Larry R.
Titus Shooting Specialties, Daniel
Tom's Gunshop
Trapper Gun, Inc.
Trevallion Gunstocks, David
Trinko's Gun Serv.
Tucker, James C.
Ulrich, Dennis A.
Unick's Gunsmithing
Upper Missouri Trading Co.
Vais Arms
Van Epps, Milton
Van Horn, Gil
Van Patten, J.W.
Vest, John
Vic's Gun Refinishing
Walker Arms Co., Inc.
Wallace, R.D.
Wardrop, R.A.
Weatherby, Inc.
Weaver Arms Corp.
Weber, Chris/Waffen-Weber
Weems, Cecil
Wells, Fred
Wells Ltd., R.A.
West, Robert G.
Western Gunstock Mfg. Co.
Wiebe, Duane
Wiest, M.C.
Williams Gun Sight Co.
Williams Shootin' Iron Service
Williamson-Pate Gunsmith Service
Wills, David W.
Wilson's Gun Shop
Winter, Robert M.
Wisner's Gun Shop, Inc.
Womack, Lester
Yee, Mike
Zeeryp, Russ

Penrod Precision
Precise Chambering Co.
Precise Metalsmithing Enterprises
Precision Specialties, Ltd.
Rogers Gunsmithing, Bob
Shirley & Co. Riflemakers, J.A.
Shockley, Harold H.
Silver Shields, Inc.
Sipes Gun Shop
Snapp's Gunshop
Steffens, Ron (bluing barrels w/o bluing bore)

Storey, Dale A.
Talley, Dave
Unick's Gunsmithing
Van Patten, J.W.
Vic's Gun Refinishing
Waldron, Herman
Wallace, R.D.
Wardell Precision Handguns Ltd.
Wells, Fred
Werth, Terry
West, Robert G.
Westrom, John

DECOYS

Advance Scouts, Inc. (goose getters)
A&M Waterfowl, Inc. (motorized ducks, geese)
Carry-Lite, Inc.
Deer Me Products Co. (anchors)
Farm Form, Inc. (goose)
Flambeau Prods. Corp.

Klingler, Kenneth J.
North Wind Decoys Co. (goose, duck windsock)
Penn's Woods Products, Inc.
Quack Decoy Corp.
Royal Arms (wooden, duck)
Skaggs, Ron E.

ENGRAVERS, ENGRAVING TOOLS

Adams, John J.
Alfano, Sam
Allard, Gary
Baron Technology
Bates, Billy R.
Bell Originals, Inc., Sid
Bledsoe, Weldon
Bleile, C. Roger
Bochenski, Rudolph V.
Boessler, Erich
Bone, Ralph P.
Bonham, Henry "Hank"
Bratcher, Dan
Brgoch, Frank
Brooker, Dennis B.
Brownells, Inc. (engraving tools)
Burgess, Byron
Burt, Robert B.
Cannavaro, Brian V.
Christopher Firearms Co., Inc., E.
Churchill, Winston
Clark Firearms Engraving
Clark, Frank
Crocker Engraving
Delorge, Ed
Dilling Engravers, W.R.
Drain, Mark
Dubber, Michael W.
Evans, Robert
Eyster Heritage Gunsmiths, Inc., Ken
Fanzoj, John
Favre, Jacqueline
FERLIB, Armi di Ferraglio Libero
Firearms Engravers Guild of America
Flannery Engraving Co., Jeff W.
Floatstone Mfg. Co.
Fogle, James W.
Fountain Products
Frank, Henry
Francolini, Leonard
Glimm, Jerome C.
Gournet, Geoffroy R.
Grant, Howard V.
Griffin & Howe
GRS Corp. (Gravermeister tool)
Gurney Engraving Method
Gwinnell, Bryson J.
Hand Engravers Supply Co.
Harris Hand Engraving, Paul A.
Harwood, Jack O.
Hendricks, Frank E.
Hiptmayer, Heidemarie
Horst, Alan K.
Ingle, Ralph W., Master Engraver
Jaeger, Inc., Paul
Jantz Supply, Ken (tools)
Johns, Bill
Kamyk, Steven
Kehr, Roger
Kelly, Lance
Koevenig Engraving Service, E.J.
Kudlas, John
Largent, Nelson H.

Leibowitz, Leonard (etcher)
Letschnig, Franz, Master-Engraver
Lindsay, Steve
London Guns Ltd.
Mains, Wm. H.
Maki, Robert E.
Mandarino, Laura
Marek, George
McDonald, Dennis
McKenzie, Lynton S.M.
Mele, Frank
Miller, S.A.
Mittermeier, Frank (tool)
Moschetti, Mitch
Nelson, Gary K.
New Orleans Arms Co.
New Orleans Jewelers Supply (engraving tool)
NgraveR Co. (MagnaGraver tool)
Oker's Engraving
Old Dominion Engravers
Pachmayr Ltd.
Pedersen & Son, C.R.
Peters, E. Larry
Pilkington, Scott
Piquette, Paul R.
Plante, Eugene T.
Potts, Wayne E.
Pranger, Ed
Puccinelli Design, Leonard
Rabeno, Martin
Riggs, Jim (handguns)
Roberts, J.J.
Rohner, John R. and Hans
Rosser, Bob
Rundell, Joe
Runge, Robert P.
Sampson, Roger
Shaw's
Sherwood, George
Shostle, Ben
Sinclair, W.P.
Skaggs, Ron E.
Smith, Mark A.
Smith, Ron
Theis, Terry
Thiewes, George W.
Thirion, Denise
Valade, Robert B.
Vest, John
Viramontez, Ray
Wagoner, Vernon G.
Wallace, R.D.
Wallace, Terry
Warren, Floyd E.
Warren, Kenneth W.
Welch, Sam
Wells, Rachel
Willig, Claus
Wolfe, Bernie (engraving, plating, scrimshawing)
Wood, Mel

CUSTOM METALSMITHS

Accuracy Unlimited
Ahlman's, Inc.
Alley Supply Co.
Apel, Dietrich
Armament Gunsmithing Co., Inc.
Baer Custom Guns
Barta's Gunsmithing
Behlert Precision
Beitzinger, George
Bellm Contenders
Benchmark Guns
Billingsley, Ross (rifle)
Bishop & Son, Inc., E.C.
Boeke, Gregg
Brace, Larry D.
Briganti Custom Gunsmith
Bustani, Leo
Campbell, Dick
Carter, Ralph L.
Champlin Firearms, Inc.
Clinton River Gun Serv., Inc.
Condor Mfg. Co.
Cook, Dave
Costa, David
Crandall Tool & Machine Co.
Crocker, Gordon D.
Cullity Restoration, Daniel
Custom Gun Guild
D&D Gunsmiths, Ltd.
Dever, Jack
D&H Precision Tooling
Dilliott Gunsmithing, Inc.
DiStefano, Dominic
Duncan's Gunworks, Inc.
Echols, D'Arcy A.
Eyster Heritage Gunsmiths, Inc., Ken
Farmer-Dressel, Sharon
Fish, Marshall F.
Flaig's
Fountain Products
Fredrick Gun Shop (engine turning)
Fullmer, Geo. M. (precise chambering—300 cals.)
Genecco Gun Works, K.
Gentry Custom Gunmaker, David
Giron, Robert E.

Goens, Dale W.
Goodwin, Fred
Gordie's Gun Shop
Green, Roger M.
Griffin & Howe
Gun Doctor, The
Guns
Hagn Rifles & Actions
Harkrader's Custom Gun Shop
Hart & Son, Inc., Robert W.
Hecht, Hubert J., Waffen-Hecht
Heilmann, Stephen
Heppler's Machining
Hiptmayer, Klaus
Hobaugh, Wm. H.
Hollis Gun Shop
Hyper-Single, Inc.
Intermountain Arms
Jaeger, Inc., Paul
Jamison, R.L., Jr.
Jantz Supply, Ken
Jones Custom Products, Neil A.
Jurras, L.E.
Kartak Gun Works
Kilham, Benjamin
Klein, Don
Kleinendorst, K.W.
Kopp, Terry K.
Lampert, Ron L.
Lee Supplies, Mark
Lilja Precision Rifle Barrels, Inc.
Logan, Harry M.
Matthews, Larry
Mazur Restoration, Pete (traditional metal finishing)
McFarland, Stan
Miller Arms, Inc.
Morrison Custom Rifles, J.W.
Mullis Guncraft
Nettestad, Bruce A.
New England Custom Gun Service (See Apel, Dietrich)
Noreen, Peter H.
Olson, Vic
Pagel Gun Works
Pasadena Gun Center

GAME CALLS

Burnham Bros.
Carter's Wildlife Calls, Inc., Garth
Cedar Hill Game Call Co.
Dr. O's Products, Ltd.
Green Head Corp.
Hall's Shooting Products, Inc., Joe
Haydel's Game Calls, Inc.

Hunter's Specialties, Inc.
Keowee Game Calls
Kingyon, Paul L.
Knight & Hale Game Calls
Lohman Mfg. Co.
Mallardtone Game Calls
Marsh, Johnny (duck & goose calls)

Mountain Hollow Game Calls
Oakman Turkey Calls
Olt Co., Phil S.
Penn's Woods Products, Inc.
Preston Pittman Game Calls, Inc.
   (diaphragm turkey calls)
Primos Wild Game Calls, Inc.

Quaker Boy, Inc.
Rickard, Inc., Pete
Salter Calls, Inc., Eddie
Scotch Hunting Products Co., Inc.
Stewart Game Calls, Inc., Johnny
Tink's Safariland Hunting Corp.

GUN PARTS, U.S. AND FOREIGN

AMT (Ardacia Machine & Tool, Inc.)
Action Ammo, Ltd.
American Industries, Inc.
Amherst Arms (U.S. Military)
Armes de Chasse
Armsport, Inc.
Aztec International Ltd.
Badger Shooter's Supply
Behlert Custom Guns, Inc. (handgun parts)
Can Am Enterprises
Caspian Arms
Cherokee Gun Accessories
D&E Magazines Mfg.
Duffy, Charles E.
Eagle International, Inc.
Essex Arms (45 1911A1 frames & slides)
Fabian Bros. Sporting Goods, Inc.
Federal Ordnance, Inc.
Jack First Distributors, Inc.
Galati International
Gun Parts Corp.
Gun-Tec (Win. mag. tubing; Win. 92
   conversion parts)
Hansen Cartridge Company

Hastings
Heller & Levin Associates, Inc.
Liberty Antique Gunworks (S&W only)
Lodewick, Walter H. (Winchester parts)
Martz, John V. (parts for Luger and P-38s)
McKee, Arthur (micrometer receiver sights)
Olympic Arms, Inc.
Pacific Intl. Merch. Corp. (Vega 45 Colt
   mag.)
Para-Ordnance Mfg., Inc. (frames only)
Pre-64 Winchester Parts Co.
Quality Parts Co.
Ranch Products
Retting, Inc., Martin B.
Royal Ordnance Works Ltd.
Sarco, Inc.
Sherwood Intl. Export Corp.
Smires, Clifford L. (Mauser rifle parts)
Springfield Sporters, Inc.
Triple-K Mfg. Co. (magazines, gun parts)
T&S Industries, Inc.
Weisz Antique Gun Parts
W.C. Wolff Co.
Zoli U.S.A., Inc., Antonio

GUNS (Air)

Air Rifle Specialists
Beeman Precision Arms, Inc.
   (Feinwerkbau, Weihrauch, Webley)
Benjamin Air Rifle Co.
Brass Eagle, Inc. (paintball guns)
Chinasports, Inc.
Command Post, Inc., The (airsoft, paintball
   marking guns)
Component Concepts, Inc. (paintball)
Crosman Airguns (a Coleman Co.)
Daisy Mfg. Co.
Dynamit Nobel-RWS, Inc. (Dianawerk)
Fiocchi of America, Inc.
Fisher Enterprises
Great Lakes Airguns
Hebard Guns, Gil

Interarms (Walther)
Mac-1 Airgun Distributors
Marksman Products
McMurray & Son (See Mac-1 Airgun
   Distributors)
National Survival Game, Inc. (paintball
   guns)
N.S.G., Inc. (See National Survival Game,
   Inc.)
Phoenix Arms Co., Ltd. (Jackal)
Precision Sales International, Inc.
Pursuit Marketing, Inc. (PMI) (paintball)
Sheridan Products, Inc.
Stone Enterprises Ltd.
Tippman Pneumatics, Inc.

GUNS (Foreign)

Action Arms Ltd.
American Arms, Inc.
Anschutz (See Preciison Sales—PSI)
Armes de Chasse (Merkel)
Armscor Precision
Arms Corp. of America, Inc.
Arms Corp. of the Philippines (See
   Armscor Precision)
Armsport, Inc.
Autumn Sales, Inc.
Ballistic Research Industries (BRI)
Beeman Precision Arms, Inc. (FWB,
   Weihrauch, FAS, Unique, Korth,
   Hammerli firearms)
Benelli Armi, S.p.A. (See Sile
   Distributors—handguns; Heckler &
   Koch—shotguns)
Beretta U.S.A.
Boswell, Charles (gunmakers)
Bretton
BRI (See Ballistic Research Industries)
BRNO (See T.D. Arms)
Browning (Gen. offices)
Browning (Parts & Service)
Cape Outfitters
Century Intl. Arms, Inc.
Chapuis Armes
Chinasports, Inc.
Cimarron Arms (Uberti)
Classic Doubles International, Inc.
   (shotguns)
Connecticut Valley Arms Co.
CVA (See Connecticut Valley Arms Co.)
Daly, Charles (See Outdoor Sports HQ)
Dixie Gun Works, Inc. (ML guns)
Dynamit Nobel-RWS, Inc. (Rottweil)
Eagle Imports, Inc.
Elko Arms
Elett Bros. (Churchill shotguns)
EMF Co., Inc. (early and modern firearms)
Euroarms of America, Inc. (ML)
Excam, Inc.

Fanzoj, John
FERLIB, Armi di Ferraglio Libero
F.I.E. Corp. (See Firearms Import &
   Export Corp.)
Fiocchi of America, Inc.
Francotte, Auguste & Cie, S.A.
Frankonia Jagd, Hofmann & Co.
Frigon Guns (custom-made)
Galaxy Imports, Ltd., Inc.
Gamba, Renato, S.p.A.
Garbi, Armas (See Moore & Co., Wm.
   Larkin) (shotguns)
Gilbert Equipment Co.
Glock, Inc.
Griffin & Howe (Purdey, Holland & Holland)
Gun South, Inc. (See GSI) (Steyr, FN,
   Mannlicher)
Hallowell & Co. (agents for John Rigby &
   Co.)
Heckler & Koch, Inc.
Heym, Friedrich Wilh. (See Heckler &
   Koch)
Incor, Inc. (Cosmi auto shotgun)
Interarmco (See Interarms/Walther)
Interarms Ltd.
Jaeger, Inc., Paul
K.B.I., Inc. (Baikal shotguns)
KDF, Inc. (Mauser rifles)
Kimel Industries
Krieghoff International, Inc.
Lakefield Arms Ltd.
Laurona Shotguns (See Galaxy Imports)
Llama (See Stoeger Industries)
Magnum Research, Inc. (Desert Eagle)
Mandall Shooting Supplies
Mannlicher (See Gun South)
Mauser-Werke Oberndorf
Merkuria, FTC (BRNO)
Midwest Gun Sport (E. Dumoulin)
Mitchell Arms, Inc.
Moore & Co., Wm. Larkin (Garbi, Ferlib,
   Piotti, Perugini Visini)

Navy Arms Co.
Norinco (See Chinasports, Inc.)
Outdoor Sports Headquarters, Inc.
   (Charles Daly shotguns)
Pachmayr Ltd.
Pacific Intl. Merch. Corp.
Parker Reproductions
Parker-Hale, Bisleyworks
Perazzi U.S.A., Inc.
Perugini Visini & Co.
Poly Technologies, Inc. (See PTK
   International, Inc.)
Precision Imports, Inc. (Mauser)
Precision Sales Intl., Inc., PSI (Anschutz)
Precision Sports (Parker-Hale)
PTK International, Inc.
Quality Arms, Inc. (Bernardelli; Ferlib;
   Bretton shotguns)
Rahn Gun Works, Inc.
Rottweil (See Dynamit Nobel/RWS, Inc.)
Samco Global Arms
Sauer (See Sigarms)

Scott Fine Guns, Inc., Thad (Perugini
   Visini; Bertuzzi; Mario Beschi shotguns)
Sigarms, Inc.
Sile Distributors
Simmons Enterprises, Ernie (Sauer rifles;
   SKB shotguns)
Sodia Jagdgewehrfabrik, Franz
Sportarms of Florida
Springfield Armory, Inc.
State Arms Gun Co. (.50 bolt-action rifle)
Steyr-Daimler-Puch (See GSI) (rifles)
Stoeger Industries
Taurus International Mfg., Inc.
T.D. Arms
Tradewinds, Inc.
Uberti USA, Inc.
Ugartechea, Ignacio
Valmet (See Stoeger)
Verney-Carron
Waffen-Frankonia (See Frankonia Jagd)
Weatherby, Inc.
Zavodi Crvena Zastava (See Interarms)
Zoli USA, Inc., Antonio

GUNS (U.S.-made)

A.A. Arms, Inc.
Accuracy Systems, Inc.
Accu-Tek
AMAC
American Arms, Inc.
American Derringer Corp.
American Industries, Inc.
AMT
Armament Systems and Procedures, Inc.
   (ASP pistol)
Armitage International, Ltd. (Scarab
   Skorpion 9mm pistol)
A-Square Co., Inc.
Auto-Ordnance Corp.
Ballistic Reasearch Industries (BRI)
Barrett Firearms Mfg., Inc. (Light Fifty)
Beretta U.S.A.
BF Arms (single shot pistol)
Browning (Gen. Offices)
Browning (Parts & Service)
Bryco Arms (Distributed by Jennings
   Firearms)
Bushmaster Firearms Co. (police handgun)
Calico Hardwoods, Inc.
Century Gun Dist., Inc. (Century Model
   100 SA rev.)
Charter Arms Corp.
Chipmunk (See Oregon Arms, Inc.)
Colt Firearms
Competition Limited
Coonan Arms, Inc. (357 Mag. autom.)
Daisy Mfg. Co., Inc.
Dakota Arms, Inc. (bolt-action rifles)
Davis Industries (derringers; 32 auto pistol)
Desert Industries, Inc.
Detonics (See New Detonics Mfg. Corp.)
   (auto pistol)
DuBiel Arms Co.
EMF Co., Inc.
Encom America, Inc.
Excam, Inc.
Falling Block Works
Feather Industries, Inc.
Federal Eng. Corp.
F.I.E. Corp. (See Firearms Import & Export
   Corp.)
Freedom Arms, Inc. (mini and Casull
   revolvers)
Gilbert Equipment Co.
Göncz Armament, Inc.
Gonic Arms, Inc.
Grendel, Inc.
Hatfield International, Inc. (squirrel rifle)
Holmes Firearms Corp.
Horton Dist. Co., Inc., Lew (sporting
   firearms wholesaler)
IAI (Irwindale Arms, Inc.)
Intratec
Ithaca Aquisition Corp./Ithaca Gun Co.
Jennings Firearms, Inc.
Johnson, Iver (See AMAC)
Kimber of Oregon, Inc.
Kimel Industries
Ljutic Industries, Inc. (Mono-Gun)

Lorcin Engineering Co., Inc. (L-25 pistol)
Magnum Research, Inc.
Marlin Firearms Co.
Maverick Arms, Inc.
Merrill Pistol (See RPM)
MK Arms, Inc. (semi-auto carbines)
M.O.A. Corp. (Maximum pistol)
Modern Muzzleloading, Inc.
Mossberg & Sons, O.F.
Navy Arms Co.
New England Firearms Co., Inc.
North American Arms
North American Specialties
Olympic Arms (See Safari Arms/SGW)
Oregon Arms, Inc.
Oregon Trail Riflesmiths, Inc.
   (muzzleloaders)
Pachmayr Ltd.
Parker-Hale/Precision Sports
Patriot Distribution Co. (Avenger pistol)
Phelps Mfg. Co. (Heritage I in 45-70)
Precision Small Parts, Inc.
Rahn Gun Works, Inc.
Ram-Line, Inc.
Raven Arms (P-25 pistols)
Remington Arms Co.
RPM (R&R Sporting Arms, Inc.) (XL pistol;
   formerly Merrill)
Ruger (See Sturm, Ruger & Co.)
Safari Arms/SGW
SAM, Inc. (See Special Service Arms
   Mfg., Inc.)
Savage Industries, Inc.
Sedco Industries, Inc. (SP-22 pistols)
Seecamp Co., Inc., L.W.
Sharps Arms Co., Inc., C.
Shiloh Rifle Mfg. Co., Inc.
Smith & Wesson
Sokolovsky Corp. (45 Automaster pistol)
Special Service Arms Mfg., Inc.
Sporting Arms, Mfg. (Night
   Charmer/Snake Charmer II)
Springfield Armory, Inc.
Sturm, Ruger & Co., Inc.
Sundance Industries, Inc. (Model A-25
   pistol)
Super Six Limited
Taurus International, Inc.
Texas Longhorn Arms, Inc. (single-action
   sixgun)
Thompson/Center Arms
TMI Products
Trail Guns Armoury (muzzleloaders)
Ultra Light Arms, Inc.
U.S. Repeating Arms Co.
Varner Sporting Arms, Inc.
Weatherby, Inc.
Wesson Arms, Dan
Wichita Arms, Inc.
Wildey, Inc.
Wilkinson Arms
Winchester (See U.S. Repeating Arms
   Co.)
Wyoming Armory, Inc.

GUNS AND GUN PARTS, REPLICA AND ANTIQUE

Antique Arms Co.
Antique Gun Parts, Inc. (muzzleloaders)
Armsport, Inc.
Beeman Precision Arms, Inc.

Border Guns & Leather
Cache La Poudre Rifleworks
Day & Sons, Inc., Leonard
Dixie Gun Works, Inc.

Dwyer, Dan (manufacturer of obsolete and antique parts)
Federal Ordnance, Inc.
First Distributors, Inc., Jack
Goodwin, Fred (Win. rings & studs)
Gun Parts Corp.
Hansen Cartridge Company
Hopkins & Allen Arms (parts only)
House of Muskets, Inc., The (ML supplies)
Kopp, Terry K. (restoration and parts 1890 and 1906 Win.)
Liberty Antique Gunworks (S&W only)
Log Cabin Sport Shop
Lucas, Edw. E. (45/70 Springfield parts; some Sharps, Spencer parts)
Lyman Products Corp.

McKee, Arthur
Munsch Gunsmithing, Tommy (Win. obsolete and Marlin parts only)
October Country
Ram-Line, Inc.
Sarco, Inc.
Shiloh Rifle Mfg. Co., Inc. (Sharps)
Sklany, Steve
South Bend Replicas, Inc.
S&S Firearms
Taylor's & Co., Inc.
Traditions, Inc.
Upper Missouri Trading Co.
Weisz Antique Gun Parts
Wescombe (Rem. rolling block parts)
Winchester Sutler, Inc.

GUNS, SURPLUS—PARTS AND AMMUNITION

Aztec International Ltd.
Braun, M.
Can Am Enterprises (Enfield rifles)
Century Intl. Arms, Inc.
Federal Ordnance, Inc.
Garcia National Gun Traders, Inc.
Gun Parts Corp.
Hansen Cartridge Company
Kimel Industries

Lever Arms Service Ltd.
Paragon Sales, Inc. (ammunition)
Raida Intertraders S.A. (surplus guns)
Sarco, Inc. (military surplus ammo)
Sherwood Intl. Export Corp.
Southern Ammunition Co., Inc.
Southern Armory (modern military parts)
Springfield Sporters, Inc.

GUNSMITHS, CUSTOM (see Custom Gunsmiths)

GUNSMITHS, HANDGUN (see Pistolsmiths)

GUNSMITH SCHOOLS

Colorado School of Trades
Lassen Community College
Modern Gun Repair School (correspondence school only)
Montgomery Technical College (also 1-yr. engraving school)
Murray State College
North American Correspondence Schools
Pennsylvania Gunsmith School

Piedmont Community College
Pine Technical Institute
Professional Gunsmiths of America (Technical training ctr.)
Shenandoah School of Gunsmithing
Southeastern Community College
Trinidad State Junior College
Yavapai College

GUNSMITH SUPPLIES, TOOLS, SERVICES

Allen, Inc., Don (stock duplicating machine)
Alley Supply Co. (JET line lathes, mills, etc.; Sweany Site-A-Line Optical bore collimator)
All's, The Jim J. Tembilis Co., Inc.
Armite Labs. (pen oiler)
Atlantic Mills, Inc. (gun cleaners, patches, shop wipes)
Baiar, Jim (hex screws)
Baron Technology (chemical etching, plating)
Behlert Precision
Bell Design Gun Services (Accusorb bedding system)
Bell Originals, Inc., Sid (floorplate decoration)
Bellm Contenders (rifles only)
Biesen, Al (grip caps, buttplates)
Biesen, Roger
Birchwood-Casey
Blue Ridge Machinery and Tools, Inc. (gunsmithing lathe, mills and shop supplies)
Briganti Custom Gunsmith (cold rust bluing, hand polishing, metal work)
Brownells, Inc.
Brownell Checkering Tools, W.E.
B-Square Co.
Buehler Scope Mounts
Canjar Co., M.H. (triggers, etc.)
Chapman Mfg. Co.
Chopie Mfg., Inc.
Classic Arms Corp. (floorplates, grip caps)
Clymer Mfg. Co., Inc. (reamers)
Cook, Dave (metalsmithing only)
Crouse's Country Cover (Masking Gun Oil)
Davidson Products For Shooters
Dayton Traister Co. (triggers; safeties)
Decker Shooting Products
Defense Moulding Enterprises (magazines)
Dem-Bart Hand Checkering Tools, Inc.
Dremel Mfg. Co. (grinders)
Duffy, Charles E.
The Dutchman's Firearms, Inc.
Dyson & Son Ltd., Peter (accessories for antique gun collectors)
Edmund Scientific Co.
First, Distributors, Inc., Jack
Fisher, Jerry

Flashette Co. (bore illuminator gun cleaning aid)
Forster Products, Inc.
Garrett Accur-Lt. D.F.S. Co.
Grace Metal Products (screwdrivers, drifts)
GRS Corp. (Gravermeister; Grave Max tools)
Gunline Tools
Gun Parts Corp.
Gun-Tec (files)
Half Moon Rifle Shop (hex screws)
Henriksen Tool Co., Inc. (reamers)
High-Tech Specialty Lubricants
Huey Gun Cases, Marvin (high-grade English ebony tools)
Jantz Supply, Ken
JGS Precion Tool Mfg.
Jim's Gun Shop ("Belgian Blue" rust blues; stock fillers)
Kasenit Co., Inc. (surface hardening compound)
Kopp, Terry K. (stock rubbing compound; rust preventive grease)
Korzinek, J. (stainless steel bluing)
Lawson, John G.
Lea Mfg. Co.
Lee Supplies, Mark
Liberty Antique Gunworks (spl. S&W tools)
Lock's Phila. Gun Exch.
Lortone, Inc.
Marsh, Mike (gun accessories)
McMillan Rifle Barrels (services)
MDS, Inc. (bore lights)
Meier Works (European accessories)
Metalife Industries (Metalife refinishing services)
Michaels of Oregon Co.
Miller Single Trigger Mfg. Co. (selective or non-selective for shotguns)
Miniature Machine Co. (MMC) (screwdriver grinding fixtures)
Mittermeier, Frank
Nitex, Inc. (custom metal finish)
N&J Sales Co. (screwdrivers)
Palmgren Steel Prods. (vises, etc.)
Panavise Prods., Inc.
Parker-Hale (See Precision Sports)
Pilkington Gun Co. (Q.D. scope mount)
Redman's Rifling & Reboring (22 rimfire liners)

Roto/Carve (tool)
Russell Co., A.G. (Arkansas oilstones)
Rusteprufe Laboratories
Scott/McDougall Custom Gunsmiths
Seacliff International Inc. (portable parts washer)
Shaw's
Sports Support Systems, Inc. (Present Arms trade name)
Starrett Co., L.S.
Stuart Products, Inc. (Sight-Vise)
Texas Platers Supply Co. (plating kit)

Timney Mfg., Inc. (triggers)
Treville, Stan de (checkering patterns)
Walker Arms Co., Inc. (tools)
Washita Mountain Whetstone Co.
Weaver Arms Corp. (action wrenches & transfer punches)
Will-Burt Co. (vises)
Williams Gun Sight Co.
Williams Shootin' Iron Service
Wilson Arms Co.
Wolff Co., W.C. (springs)

HANDGUN ACCESSORIES

AA Arms, Inc.
Action Ammo Ltd.
Adco International
Ajax Custom Grips, Inc.
Allen Companies, Bob
American Gas & Chemical Co. Ltd. (cleaning lube)
American Gripcraft (exotic wood)
AMT (Arcadia Machine & Tool, Inc.)
Answer Products Co. (Accu-Comfort Magnum Pistol Glove)
Armsport, Inc.
Baramie Corp. (Hip-Grip)
Bar-Sto Precision Machine (barrels)
Behlert Precision
Brauer Bros. Mfg. Co.
Brown Products, Ed
Centaur Systems, Inc. (Quadra-Lok barrels)
Central Specialties Co. (trigger locks only)
D&E Magazines Mfg. (clips)
Detonics (See New Detonics Mfg. Corp.)
Dibble, Derek A. (magazines)
Doskocil Mfg. Co., Inc (Gun Guard cases)
Eagle International, Inc.
Essex Arms (45 Auto frames)
Frielich Police Equipment (cases)
Frielich, R.S. (cases)
Galati International
Glock, Inc.
Gremmel Enterprises (conversion units)
Gun-Ho Sports Cases
Gun Parts Corp.
Hebard Guns, Gil
Hill Speed Leather, Ernie
H.K.S. Products (revolver speed loaders)
Intratec
Jett & Co., Inc.
King's Gun Works
K&K Ammo Wrist Band
Kopp, Terry K.

Lee's Red Ramps (ramp insert, spring kits)
Lee Precision, Inc. (pistol rest holders)
Liberty Antique Gunworks (shims for S&W revolvers)
Lomont Precision Bullets, Kent (Auto Mag only)
Lone Star Gunleather
Magnum Research, Inc.
Mag-Pack
M.A.M. Products, Inc. (free standing brass catcher for all auto pistols and/or semi-auto rifles)
Millett Industries
MTM Molded Prods. Co.
Noble Co., Jim
No-Sho Mfg. Co.
Owen, Harry (See Sport Specialties)
Pachmayr Ltd.(cases)
Pacific Intl. Merch. Corp. (Vega 45 Colt combination magazine)
Pflumm Gun Mfg. Co. (pistol cases)
Poly Choke Div. (See Marble Arms Corp.) (handgun ribs)
Ranch Products (third-moon clips)
Ransom Intl. Corp.
Rupert's Gun Shop
Safariland Leather Products
Sile Distributors
Sonderman, Robert (solid walnut fitted handgun cases; other woods)
Southwind Sancions
Sport Specialties (22 rimfire adapters; 22 insert barrels for T/C Contender, automatic pistols)
Sportsmen's Equipment Co.
SSK Industries
Tyler Mfg.-Dist., Melvin (grip adaptor)
Wardell Precision Handguns Ltd. (grip adaptor)
Wilson's Gun Shop

HANDGUN GRIPS

Action Products, Inc.
Ajax Custom Grips, Inc.
Altamont Mfg. Co.
Armitage International Ltd.
Art Jewel Enterprises Ltd. (Eagle Grips)
Barami Corp.
Bear Hug Grips, Inc. (custom)
Beeman Precision Arms, Inc. (airguns only)
Behlert Precision
Boone's Custom Ivory Grips, Inc.
Boyd's Gunstock Industries, Inc.
Davis Service Center, Bill
Fishpaw, Roy C. (custom wood & ivory)
Fitz Pistol Grip Co.
Gun Parts Corp.
Herrett's Stocks, Inc.
Hogue Grips (Monogrip)
Jones Munitions Systems, Paul (See Fitz Co.)
Logan Security Products Co. ("Streetloader" for K&L frame S&Ws)

Maloni, Russ (See Russwood)
Monogrip (See Hogue)
Monte Kristo Pistol Grip Co.
Mustang Custom Pistol Grips (See R.J. Renner Co.)
Newell, Robert H. (custom stocks)
Nygord Precision Products
Olympic Arms, Inc. (See Safari Arms/SGW)
Pachmayr Ltd.
Renner Co., R.J.
Rosenberg & Sons, A. Jack
Royal Ordnance Works Ltd.
Russwood Custom Pistol Grips (custom exotic woods)
St. Henri, Jean (custom)
Sile Distributors
Spegel, Craig
Wallace, R.D. (custom only)
Wayland Prec. Wood Prods. ("Classic" & "Double Diamond" grips)
Wilson's Gun Shop

HEARING PROTECTORS

AO Safety Prods. (ear valves, muffs)
Bausch & Lomb, Inc.
Bilsom Interntl., Inc. (ear plugs, muffs)
Clark Co., Inc., David
E-A-R Div., Cabot Corp.
Flents Products Co., Inc.

Marble Arms Corp.
North Consumer Prods. Div. (Lee Sonic ear valves)
Safety Direct (Silencio)
Smith & Wesson
Willson Safety Prods. Div. (Ray-O-Vac)

HOLSTERS AND LEATHER GOODS

A.A. Arms, Inc.
A&B Industries, Inc.
Alessi Holsters, Inc.
Allen Co., Bob
American Sales & Mfg. Co.
Armament Systems and Procedures, Inc.

Arratoonian, Andy
Bachman, Rick M. (See Old West Reproductions)
Bandcor Industries
Bang-Bang Boutique
Barami Corp.

Beeman Precision Arms, Inc. (airguns only)
Behlert Precision
Bianchi International, Inc.
Blocker's Custom Holsters, Ted
Border Guns & Leather (Old West custom)
Boyt Co., Div. of Welsh Sporting Goods
Brauer Bros. Mfg. Co.
Browning (Gen. Off.)
Bucheimer Co., J.M.
Cathey Enterprises, Inc.
Cattle Baron Leather Co.
Chace Leather Prods.
Cherokee Gun Accessories
Clements, Chas
Dart Manufacturing Co.
Davis Leather Co., G. Wm.
DeSantis Holster & Leather Co.
El Paso Saddlery
Epps (Orillia) Northern Ltd., Ellwood (custom made)
Eutaw Company, Inc.
Galati International
GALCO International, Ltd.
Glock, Inc. (holsters)
GML Products, Inc.
Gould & Goodrich Leather, Inc. (licensed mfgs. of S&W leather products)
Gunfitters, The (custom holsters)
Gun Parts Corp.
Henigson & Associates, Steve
High North Products (1-oz. Mongoose gun sling)
Hill Speed Leather, Ernie
Holster Outpost
Horsehoe Leather Prods. (See Andy Arratoonian)
Hoyt Holster Co., Inc.
Hume, Don
Hunter Co., Inc.
John's Custom Leather
Jumbo Sports Prods.
Kane Products, Inc. (GunChaps)

Kirkpatrick Leather Co.
Kolpin Mfg., Inc.
Lawrence Leather Co.
Lone Star Gunleather
Magnolia Sports, Inc.
Michael's of Oregon, Co. (Uncle Mike's)
Nelson Combat Leather, Bruce
Noble Co., Jim (Supreme quick-draw shoulder holster, etc.)
No-Sho Mfg. Co.
Null Holsters Ltd., K.L.
Oklahoma Leather Products, Inc.
Old West Reproductions
Orient-Western
Pathfinder Sports Leather
Pony Express Sport Shop, Inc.
Proline Handgun Leather, Greg Kramer (concealment and duty rigs)
Red Head, Inc.
Renegade
Roy's Custom Leather Goods
Rybka Custom Leather Equipment, Thad
Safariland Leather Products
Safety Speed Holster
Schulz Industries
Shurkatch Corp.
Sile Distr.
Silhouette Leathers (custom holsters)
Smith Saddlery, Jesse W.
Smith & Wesson Leather (See Gould & Goodrich Leather, Inc.)
Southwind Sanctions
Sparks, Milt
Stalker, Inc.
Strong Holster Co.
Torel, Inc. (gun slings)
Triple-K Mfg. Co.
Uncle Mike's (See Michaels of Oregon)
Viking Leathercraft, Inc.
Whinnery, Walt
Wild Bill Cleaver (antique holstermaker)
Zeus International (all leather shotshell belt)

HUNTING AND CAMP GEAR, CLOTHING, ETC.

API Outdoors, Inc.
Allen Co., Bob
Barbour, Inc.
Bauer, Eddie
Bean, L.L.
Bear Archery (Himalayan backpack)
Big Beam (See Teledyne Co.) (lamp)
Browning (Gen. Off.)
Brunton USA (compasses)
Cabela's (mail order)
Chippewa Shoe Co. (boots)
Coleman Co., Inc.
Danner Shoe Mfg. Co. (boots)
Deer-Me Prod. Co. (tree steps)
Dr. O's Products, Ltd.
Dunham Co. (boots)
Durango Boot (See Northlake Boot Co.)
Eutaw Company, Inc.
Frankonia Jagd, Hofmann & Co.
Game-Winner, Inc. (camouflage suits; orange vests)
Gander Mountain, Inc.
Glacier Glove (neoprene gloves for hunting)
Gun Club Sportswear
Hinman Outfitters, Bob
Hunter's Specialties, Inc.
Kenko Intl., Inc. (footwear & socks)
LaCrosse Footwear, Inc.
Langenberg Hat Co.
Liberty Trouser Co.
Marathon Rubber Prods. Co., Inc. (rain gear)

Marble Arms Corp.
Newbern Glove (hunting/shooting gloves)
Northlake Boot Co. (Durango)
Orvis Co., The (fishing gear; clothing)
P.A.S.T. Corp. (shooting shirts)
Pendleton Woolen Mills (OutdoorsMan cloth)
Precise International
Pro-Mark (shooting/hunting gloves)
Pyramid, Inc. (portable camp stove)
Ranger Mfg. Co., Inc. (camouflage suits)
Red Ball (boots)
Red Head, Inc.
Refrigiwear, Inc.
Re-Heater, Inc. (re-usable portable heat pack)
Remington Footwear Co.
Safari Gun Co.
Scansport, Inc. (wool hunting packs)
Servus Rubber Co. (footwear)
Teledyne Co.
10-X Mfg. Products Group
Thermos Div., KST Co. (Pop Tent)
Thompson, Norm
Tink's Safariland Hunting Corp. (camouflage rain gear)
Waffen-Frankonia (See Frankonia Jagd)
Walker Shoe Co. (boots)
Warner, Glenn, Endicott Johnson (boots)
Wolverine Boots & Shoes Div. (footwear)
Woolrich Woolen Mills
Wyoming Knife Co. (saw)

KNIVES AND KNIFEMAKER'S SUPPLIES—FACTORY AND MAIL ORDER

Alcas Cutlery Corp. (Cutco)
Atlanta Cutlery (mail order, supplies)
Bean, L.L. (mail order)
Benchmark Knives (See Gerber)
Blackjack Knives
Boker USA, Inc.
Bowen Knife Co.
Browning (Gen. Off.)
Brunton USA
Buck Knives, Inc.
Camillus Cutlery Co. (Sword Brand)
Case & Sons Cutlery Co., W.R.
Cattle Baron Leather Co.
Charter Arms Corp. (Skatchet)

Chicago Cutlery Co.
Christopher Firearms Co., Inc., E. (supplies)
Clements, Chas (exotic sheaths)
Coleman Co., Inc.
Collins Brothers Div. (See Bowen Knife Co.) (belt-buckle knife)
Colonial Knife Co. (Master Brand)
Compass Industries, Inc.
Crosman Blades
Custom Knifemaker's Supply
Damascus-U.S.A.
Dixie Gun Works, Inc. (supplies)
Ek Commando Knife Co.

Eze-Lap Diamond Prods. (knife sharpeners)
Fiskars (See Gerber)
Gerber Legendary Blades
G96 Designtech, Inc.
Green Head Corp.
Gutmann Cutlery Co., Inc.
H&B Forge Co. (throwing knives, tomahawks)
Harrington Cutlery, Inc., Russell (Dexter, Green River Works)
Henckels Zwillingswerk, Inc., J.A.
Indian Ridge Traders (See Koval Knives)
J.A. Blades, Inc. (supplies)
Jewel Ent., Art
KA-BAR Cutlery
KA-BAR Knives
Kershaw Knives/Kai Cutlery USA Ltd.
Koval Knives/IRT (supplies)
Lamson & Goodnow Mfg. Co.
Lansky Sharpeners (sharpening devices)
Linder Solingen Knives
Mar Knives, Inc., Al
Matthews Cutlery (mail order)
Murphy Co., Inc., R. (StaySharp)
Normark Corp.

Ontario Knife (Old Hickory)
Outdoor Edge Cutlery Corp.
Parker-Case
Phoenix Arms Co. Ltd., Hy-Score Works
Plaza Cutlery, Inc. (mail order)
Precise International
Queen Cutlery Co.
Randall-Made Knives
R&C Knives and Such (mail order)
Russell Co., A.G.
Scansport, Inc.
Schrade Cutlery Corp.
Sheffield Knifemakers Supply
Smith & Wesson
Smith Saddlery, Jesse W. (sheathmakers)
Swiss Army Knives, Inc.
Tekna
Thompson/Center Arms
Tru-Balance Knife Co.
Utica Cutlery Co. (Kutmaster)
Valor Corp.
Washita Mountain Whetstone Co.
Wenoka/Seastyle
Western Cutlery (See Coleman Co., Inc.)
Whinnery, Walt (sheathmaker)
Wyoming Knife Co.

LABELS, BOXES, CARTRIDGE HOLDERS

Barbour, Inc.
Cabinet Mtn. Outfitter (cartridge holders)
Corbin Mfg. & Supply, Inc.
Del Rey Products
Flambeau Prods. Corp.

Hunter Co., Inc.
Peterson Instant Targets Co. (See Lyman Products Corp.) (cartridge box labels; Targ-Dots)

LOAD TESTING AND PRODUCT TESTING, (CHRONOGRAPHING, BALLISTIC STUDIES)

Accuracy Systems, Inc.
Apex Rifle Co.
Ballistic Research (ballistic studies, pressure and velocity)
Blackwell, W.W. (internal ball. computer program for rifle cartridges)
Corbin Applied Technology
D&H Precision Tooling (pressure testing equipment)
H-S Precision, Inc.
Hutton Rifle Ranch (ballistic studies)

Lomont Precision Bullets (handguns, handgun ammunition)
Plum City Ballistics Range
Quartz-Lok
Rupert's Gun Shop
Russell's Rifle Shop (load testing and chronographing to 300 yds.)
Shooting Chrony, Inc.
Sierra Bullets (chronographing, ballistic studies)
Thunderbird Cartridge Co., Inc.
White Laboratory, Inc., H.P.

MISCELLANEOUS

Action, left-hand (Gentry Custom Gunmaker, David)
Action, Mauser-style only (Crandall Tool & Machine Co.)
Action, single shot (Miller Arms, Inc.)
Actions, rifle, stainless steel (Hall Manufacturing)
Activator (B.M.F. Activator, Inc.)
Adapters for subcalibers (See Sport Specialties)
Airgun accessories, Beeman Pell seat, Pell Size, etc. (Beeman Precision Arms, Inc.)
Archery (Bear Archery)
Arms restoration (Mazur Restoration, Pete)
Assault rifle accessories (Cherokee Gun Accessories)
Assault rifle accessories (Feather Industries, Inc.)
Assault rifle accessories, folding stock (Ram-Line, Inc.)
Bedding kit, Tru-Set (Fenwal, Inc.)
Belt buckles, laser engr. hardwood (Herrett's Stocks, Inc.)
Belt buckles (Just Brass, Inc.)
Belt buckles (Pilgrim Pewter, Inc.)
Benchrest accessories (Davidson Products for Shooters)
Benchrest & accuracy shooters equipment (Bob Pease Accuracy)
Benchrest rifles & accessories (Hart & Son, Inc., Robert W.)
Bore collimator, Sweany Site-A-Line optical collimator (Alley Supply Co.)
Bore illuminator, gun cleaning aid (Flashette Co.)
Bore lights (MDS, Inc.)
Brass catcher, free standing for all auto pistols and/or semi-auto rifles (M.A.M. Products, Inc.)
Bull-Pup conversion kits (Bull-Pup Industries, Inc.)
Cannons (South Bend Replicas, Inc.)
Cartridge adapters (Sport Specialties)
Case gauge (Plum City Ballistics Range)

Cased, high-grade English tools, ebony, horn, ivory handles (Huey Gun Cases, Marvin)
Clips, handgun and rifle (D&E Magazines Mfg.)
Compasses (Brunton USA)
Computer & PSI calculator (Hutton Rifle Ranch)
Computer software, ArmsLoad, ArmsCalc, ArmsInv (Arms)
Computer systems, software, books for ballistic research (Corbin Applied Technology)
Convert-A-Pell (Jett & Co., Inc.)
Crossbows (Barnett International)
Damascus steel (Damascus-USA)
Deer Drag (D&H Prods. Co., Inc.)
Dehumidifiers (Buenger Enterprises)
Dehumidifiers, silica gel dehumidifier (Hydrosorbent Products)
Dryer, thermo-electric, Golden-Rod (Buenger Enterprises)
Dummy rounds (Duds Ammo & Supply Co.)
E-Z Loader, for 22-cal. rifles (Del Rey Products)
Ear-valve, Lee-Sonic (North Consumer Prods. Div.)
Farrsight, sighting aids for handgunners—clip on aperture (Farr Studio)
Firearms training (Ballistics Software Intl.)
Firearms training (Scott/McDougall Custom Gunsmiths)
Flares (Aztec International Ltd.)
Flashlights (Tekna)
Game scent (Buck Stop Lure Co., Inc.)
Game scent, CMO scents and lures (Cabinet Mtn. Outfitter)
Game scent, scents and lures (Dr. O's Products Ltd.)
Game scent, Indian Buck lure (Rickard, Inc., Pete)
Game Scent, buck lure (Tink's Safariland Hunting Corp.)

Gas pistol (Penguin Industries, Inc.)
Grip caps (Classic Arms Corp.)
Gun bedding kit (Fenwal, Inc., Resins System Div.)
Gun jewelry (Bilal, Mustafa)
Gun photographer (Bilal, Mustafa)
Gun photographer (Hanusin, John)
Gun photographer (Intl. Photographic Assoc., Inc.)
Gun photographer (Semmer, Charles)
Gun photographer (Weyer International)
Gun safes (Abel Safe & File Co.)
Gun safety, Gun Alert covers (Master Products, Inc.)
Gun slings (Torel, Inc.)
Gun vise (Pflumm Gun Mfg. Co.)
Hand exerciser (Action Products, Inc.)
Hearing protector (Clark Co., Inc., David)
Horsepac (Yellowstone Wilderness Supply)
Hooks for pegboards (Hugger Hooks Co.)
Insect repellent (Armor, Div. of Buck Stop, Inc.)
Insert barrels and cartridge adapters (Sport Specialties)
Insert barrels (Gremmel Enterprises)
IR detection systems (GTS Enterprises, Inc.)
Knife sharpeners (Lansky Sharpeners)
Laser aim (Laser Aim, Inc.)
Laser aim (Laser Devices, Inc.)
Locks, gun (Master Lock Co.)
Lubricant/Gun Coat (Flouramics, Inc.)
Lugheads, floorplate overlays (Bell Originals, Inc., Sid)
Lug recess insert (P.P.C. Corp.)
Magazines, plastic cartridge—high impact (Defense Moulding Enterprises)
Magazines (Dibble, Derek A.)
Magazines, stainless steel (Mitchell Arms, Inc.)
Magazines (Ram-Line, Inc.)
Miniature cannons, replicas; Gatling guns (Furr Arms)
Monte Carlo pad (Hoppe's Division, Penguin Ind., Inc.)
Old Gun Industry Art (Hansen Cartridge Company)
Police batons & accessories (Armament Systems and Procedures, Inc.)
Powderhorns (Frontier)
Powderhorns (Tennessee Valley Mfg.)
Practice wax bullets (Brazos Arms Co.)
Ransom handgun rests (Ransom Intl. Corp.)
Record books, for dealers and collectors (PFRB Company)
Reload-A-Stand, portable (Engineered Accessories)
Rifle magazines, 30-rd. Mini-14 (Butler Creek Corp.)
Rifle magazines, 25-rd. 22-cal. (Condor Mfg.)
Rifle magazines, 30-cal. M1 15 & 30-round (Miller, S.A.)
Rifle slings (Bianchi International, Inc.)
Rifle slings (Butler Creek Corp.)
Rifle slings (Chace Leather Prods.)
Rifle slings, 1-oz. Mongoose gun sling (High North Products)
Rifle slings (John's Custom Leather)
Rifle slings (Kirkpatrick Leather Co.)

Rifle slings (Kolpin Mfg., Inc.)
Rifle slings (Pathfinder Sports Leather)
Rifle slings (Schulz Industries)
RIG, NRA scoring plug (RIG Products)
Rubber cheekpiece (Lodewick, W.H.)
Rust prevention (Rusteprufe Laboratories)
Saddle rings, studs (Goodwin, Fred)
Safaris (Africa) (Professional Hunter Specialties)
Safeties, for Rem. 870P (Harper, William E.)
Safeties (Williams Gun Sight Co.)
Safety devices (P&M Sales and Service)
Safety slug (Glaser Safety Slug)
Sav-Bore (Saunders Sptg. Gds.)
Scrimshaw (Bonham, Henry "Hank")
Scrimshaw (Boone's Custom Ivory Grips, Inc.)
Scrimshaw (Marek, George)
Scrimshaw (Sherwood, George)
Scrimshaw, handgun grips—ivory or Micarta (Taylor, Twyla)
Sharpening stones, Arkansas oilstones (Russell Co., A.G.)
Shell catcher (Condor Mfg.)
Shell catchers (T&S Industries, Inc.)
Shellholders (Kolpin Mfg., Inc.)
Shooting coats (10-X Products Group)
Shooting glasses (American Optical Corp.)
Shooting glasses, Ray Ban (Bausch & Lomb, Inc.)
Shooting glasses (Bilsom Interntl, Inc.)
Shooting glasses (Willson Safety Prods. Division)
Shooting gloves, singles only, right or left (Churchill Glove Co., James)
Shooting range equipment (Caswell Internatl. Corp.)
Shotgun bore (Custom Shooting Prods.)
Shotgun ribs (Poly Choke Div., Marble Arms Corp.)
Shotgun sight, binocular (Trius Products, Inc.)
Shotgun specialist, ventilated, free-floating ribs (Moneymaker Guncraft)
Shotgun speedloader (Armstec, Inc.)
Shotshell adapter, Plummer 410 converter (PC Co.)
Shotshell adapter, 12 ga./410 converter (Ramos, Jesse)
Sight-vise (Stuart Products, Inc.)
Snap caps (Armsport, Inc.)
Snap caps (Edwards Recoil Reducer)
Sportsmen's jewelry (Bell Originals, Inc., Sid)
Springs (Wolff Co., W.C.)
Stock duplicating machine (Allen, Inc., Don)
Supersound, safety device (Edmund Scientific Co.)
Swivels (Michaels of Oregon)
Swivels (Sile Distributors)
Swivels (Williams Gun Sight Co.)
Tomahawks (H&B Forge Co.)
Tree Stand, climbing (API Outdoors, Inc.)
Treestands (East Enterprises, Inc.)
Treestands (Summit Specialties, Inc.)
Tree Steps (Deer Me Products Co.)
Trophies (Blackinton & Co., V.H.)
Warning signs (Delta Ltd.)
World hunting information (J/B Adventures & Safaris, Inc.)

MUZZLE-LOADING GUNS, BARRELS OR EQUIPMENT

Adkins, Luther (breech plugs)
Anderson Mfg. Co. (Accra-Shot)
Antique Gun Parts, Inc. (parts)
Armoury, Inc., The
Armsport, Inc.
B-Square Co.
Beaver Lodge (custom ML)
Beeman Precision Arms, Inc.
Blackhawk East (blackpowder)
Blackhawk Mtn. (blackpowder)
Blackhawk West (blackpowder)
Blue and Gray Prods., Inc. (equipment)
Brazos Arms Co.
Butler Creek Corp. (poly & maxi patch)
Cache La Poudre Rifleworks (custom muzzleloaders)
Champlin, R. MacDonald (custom muzzleloaders)
Cheney Firearms Co. (rifles)
Chopie Mfg., Inc. (nipple wrenches)

Connecticut Valley Arms Co. (muzzleloaders, kits)
Cumberland Knife & Gun Works
Cureton, Earl T. (powder horns)
CVA (See Connecticut Valley Arms Co.)
Dangler, Homer L.
Day & Sons, Inc., Leonard
DeHaas Barrels
Denver Arms, Ltd.
Dixie Gun Works, Inc.
Dixon Muzzleloading Shop, Inc.
Dyson & Son Ltd., Peter (accoutrements for ML shooter replicas)
EMF Co., Inc.
Euroarms of America, Inc.
Eutaw Company, Inc.
Fautheree, Andy (custom ML guns)
Fellowes, Ted (custom ML)
Fish, Marshall F. (antique ML repairs)
Flintlock Muzzle Loading Gun Shop, The

Forster Products, Inc.
Frontier (powderhorns)
Getz Barrel Co. (barrels)
GOEX, Inc. (blackpowder)
Gonic Arms, Inc.
Goode, A.R. (ML rifle barrels)
Guncraft, Inc.
Gun Parts Corp.
Gun Works, The (supplies)
Hatfield International, Inc. (squirrel rifle)
Hopkins & Allen (parts only)
House of Muskets, Inc., The (ML barrels and supplies)
Hughes, Steven Dodd (custom guns)
Hunkeler, A. (muzzle-loading guns)
Large Gun & Mach. Shop, Wm.
Lever Arms Serv. Ltd.
Log Cabin Sport Shop
Lyman Products Corp.
MacDonald, R. Champlin
McCann's Muzzle-Gun Works
Modern Muzzleloading, Inc.
Mountain State Muzzleloading Supplies
Muzzleload Magnum Products (MMP)
Muzzleloaders Etc., Inc.
Navy Arms Co.
Newman Gunshop (custom ML rifles)
October Country
Oregon Trail Riflesmiths, Inc.
Ox-Yoke Originals, Inc. (dry lube patches)
Peterson Gun Shop, A.W.

Phyl-Mac
Rooster Laboratories (patch and ball bullet lubricants)
R.V.I. (high grade BP accoutrements)
Scott, Inc., Tyler (Shooter's Choice black solvent; patch lube)
Sharps Arms Co., Inc., C.
Shaw, Inc., E.R. (barrels)
Sile Distributors
Siler Locks, C.E. (flintlocks)
South Bend Replicas, Inc.
Swampfire Shop, The
Taylor's & Co., Inc.
TDP Industries, Inc.
Tennessee Valley Mfg. (powderhorns)
Ten-Ring Precision, Inc.
Traditions, Inc. (guns, kits, accessories)
Trail Guns Armory
Uberti USA, Inc.
Ultra Light Arms, Inc.
Upper Missouri Trading Co.
Vibra-Tek Co.
Warren Muzzle Loading Co., Inc. (blackpowder accessories)
Wells, Fred
Wescombe (parts)
Williamson-Pate Gunsmith Serv.
Winchester Sutler, Inc. (haversacks)
Winter & Associates (Olde Pennsylvania ML accessories)

PISTOLSMITHS

Accuracy Gun Shop
Accuracy Systems, Inc.
Accuracy Unlimited
Ahlman's, Inc.
Alpha Precision, Inc.
American Pistolsmiths Guild
Ann Arbor Rod and Gun Co.
Armament Gunsmithing Co., Inc.
Baer Custom Guns (accurizing 45 autos and Comp II Syst.; custom XP100s, PPC revolver)
Bain and Davis, Inc.
Bar-Sto Precision Machine (single-shot barrels for 45 ACP)
Barta's Gunsmithing
Beal, R.S., Jr. (conversions)
Behlert Precision (short actions)
Bell's Custom Shop
Bill's Gun Repair
Border Guns & Leather
Bowen Classic Arms Corp.
Brian, C.T.
Brown Products, Ed
Bustani, Leo
Campbell, Dick (PPC guns; custom)
Cellini, Vito
Clark Custom Guns, Inc.
Competitive Pistol Shop, The
Corkys Gun Clinic
Costa, David
Custom Gun Guild
Davis Service Center, Bill
Day & Sons, Inc., Leonard
D&D Gunsmiths, Ltd.
Dilliot Gunsmithing, Inc.
Giron, Robert E.
DiStefano, Dominic (accurizing)
Duncan's Gunworks, Inc.
Dwyer, Dan
Dyson & Son Ltd., Peter
Englishtown Sporting Gds. Co., Inc.
First Distributors, Inc., Jack
Fountain Products
Frielich Police Equipment
Genecco Gun Works, K.
Gilman-Mayfield
Gunsite Gunsmithy
Hallberg, Fritz
Hamilton, Keith
Hammond, Guy
Hanson's Gun Center
Hebard Guns, Gil
Heinie, Richard
High Bridge Arms, Inc.
Hoag, James W.
Irwin, Campbell H.
Jaeger, Inc., Paul
Jones, J.D.
Jungkind, Reeves C.
Jurras, L.E.

Ken's Gun Specialties
Kilham, Benjamin
Kopp, Terry K. (rebarreling, conversions)
LaFrance Specialties
Largent, Nelson H.
Laughridge, William R.
Lawson, John G.
Lomont Precision Bullets (Auto Mag only)
Long, George F.
Mac's .45 Shop
Mag-na-port International, Inc.
Mahony, Phillip Bruce
Marent, Rudolf (Hammerli)
Martin, Elwyn H.
Martz, John V. (custom German Lugers & P-38s)
Marvel, Alan
Maryland Gun Works, Ltd.
McMurdo, Lynn
Mountain Bear Rifle Works, Inc.
Mullis Guncraft
Nastoff's 45 Shop (1911 conversions)
Neighbor, William
Novak, Wayne
Nu-Line Guns
Nygord Precision Products
Pachmayr Ltd.
Paris, Frank J.
Paterson Gunsmithing
Phillips & Bailey, Inc.
Plaxco, J. Michael
Power Custom, Inc.
Precision Specialties
Roberts Custom Guns
Rogers Gunsmithing, Bob (custom)
Scott/McDougall Custom Gunsmiths
Seecamp Co., Inc., L.W.
Shockley, Harold H.
Shows, Hank
Sipes Gun Shop
Spokhandguns, Inc.
Sportsmen's Equipmt. Co. (specialty limiting trigger motion in autos)
SSK Industries
Steger, James R.
Strawbridge, Victor W.
Stroup, Earl R.
Swenson's 45 Shop, A.D.
Ten-Ring Precision, Inc.
Thompson, Randall
Timney Mfg., Inc.
Trapper Gun, Inc.
Ulrich, Dennis A.
Unick's Gunsmithing
Vic's Gun Refinishing
Wallace, R.D.
Walters Industries
Wilson's Gun Shop
Wisner's Gun Shop, Inc.

REBORING AND RERIFLING

Ackley, P.O. (See Bellm Contenders)
Apex Rifle Co.
Barnes Custom Shop
Bellm Contenders (rifle only)
Goode, A.R.
Kopp, Terry K. (Invis-A-Line bbl.; relining)
LaBounty Precision Reboring
Large Gun & Mach. Shop, Wm.

Matco, Inc.
Nu-Line Guns
Redman's Reboring & Rerifling
Ridgetop Sporting Goods
Silver Shields, Inc.
Snapp's Gunshop
Van Patten, J.W.
West, Robt. G. (barrel relining)

RELOADING TOOLS AND ACCESSORIES

ACTIV Industries, Inc. (plastic hulls, wads)
Advance Car Mover Co., Inc. (bottom pour lead casting ladles)
Alpine's Precision Gunsmithing
American Products Co. (12-ga. shot wad)
Ammo Load, Inc.
AMT (Arcadia Machine & Tool, Inc.)
ASI (Autoscale)
Balaance Co. (Adjustable bar for Lee Auto-Disk measure)
Ballistic Products, Inc. (for shotguns)
Ballistic Research Industries (BRI) (shotgun slugs)
Belding & Mull, Inc.
Berdon Machine Co. (metallic press)
Blackwell, W.W. (Load from a Disk)
Blount Sporting Equipment Division
Bonanza (See Forster Products)
B-Square Co.
Bullet Swaging Supply, Inc.
Camdex, Inc.
Carbide Die & Mfg. Co., Inc.
Carter Gun Works
Cascade Cartridge, Inc. (See Blount Sporting Equipment Division)
Chevron Case Master
C-H Tool & Die Corp.
Chu Tani Industries, Inc. (lube-sizer adapter mts. on C- or O-type press)
Clift Mfg., L.R. (reloading bench)
Coats, Mrs. Lester (lead wire core cutter)
Colorado Shooter's Supply
Colorado Sutlers Arsenal
Container Development Corp.
Continental Kite & Key Co. (CONKKO) (primer pocket cleaner)
Cooper-Woodward (Perfect Lube)
Corbin Mfg. & Supply, Inc.
Custom Products (decapping tool, dies)
Dewey Mfg. Co., J.
Dillon Precision Prods., Inc.
Efemes Enterprises (Berdan decapper)
Engineered Accessories (Reload-A-Stand, portable)
Fitz Pistol Grip Co. (Fitz Flipper)
Flambeau Prods. Corp.
Forster Products, Inc.
Francis Tool Co. (powder measure)
Fullmer, Geo. M. (seating die)
Green, Arthur S. (metals, fluxes, ladles for bullet casting)
Hanned Precision (22-SGB tool)
Hart & Son, Inc., Robert W.
Hensley & Gibbs (bullet moulds)
Hindman, Ace (Reloader's Logbook)
Hollywood Loading Tools (See M&M Engineering)
Hornady Mfg. Co.
Huntington Die Specialties (Compact Press)
Javelina Products (Alox beeswax)
Jones Munitions Systems, Paul (See Fitz Pistol Grip Co.)
Jones Custom Products, Neil A. (decapping tool, dies)
King & Co.
Lage Uniwad, Inc. (Universal Shotshell Wad)
Lee Precision, Inc.
Littleton, J.F.
Ljutic Industries, Inc. (plastic wads)
Lock's Phila. Gun Exch.
Lortone, Inc. (tumblers, metal polishing media arbors)
Lyman Products Corp.
Magma Eng. Co.

Marquart Precision Co. (precision case-neck turning tool)
Mayville Eng. Co. (shotshell loader; steel shot kits)
McKillen & Heyer, Inc. (case gauge)
MCS, Inc. (See Mo's Competitor Supplies)
MEC, Inc. (See Mayville Eng. Co.)
Metallic Casting & Copper Corp. (MCC)
Midway Arms, Inc. (cartridge boxes)
M&M Engineering
MMP (Tri-Cut trimmer; power powder trickler)
Mo's Competitor Supplies (neck turning tool)
MTM Molded Products
Multi-Scale Charge Ltd.
Muzzleload Magnum Products (MMP)
Necromancer Industries, Inc. (Compucaster automated bullet casting machine)
NEI (bullet mould)
Northeast Industrial, Inc. (See NEI)
Ohaus Scale (See RCBS)
Old Western Scrounger Inc. (press for 50-cal. B.M.G round)
Omark (See Blount Sporting Equipment Division)
Pacific Tool Co.
Pattern Control (shotshell wads)
Pflumm Gun Mfg. Co. (Drawer Vise)
Pitzer Gun Tool Co. (bullet lube/sizer)
Plum City Ballistics Range
Ponsness-Warren
P&P Tool Co. (12-ga. shot wad)
Precision Castings & Equipment, Inc. (commercial casting machine; case roller; lube/sizer)
Quinetics Corp. (kinetic bullet puller)
Ransom Intl. Corp. (Grandmaster program loader)
Rapine Bullet Mfg. Co.
RCBS (See Blount Sporting Equipment Division)
R.D.P. Tool Co., Inc. (progressive loader)
Redding, Inc.
Rhino Replacement Parts (shotgun flechette rounds)
Roberts Products (Pak-Tool)
Rochester Lead Works (lead wire)
Rooster Laboratories (Universal Heater for lubricator-sizers)
Rorschach Precision Products (carboloy bullet dies)
SAECO (See Redding)
Sandia Die & Cartridge Co.
Shooters Accessory Supply (SAS) (See Corbin Mfg. & Supply)
Simmons, Jerry (Pope de- and recapper)
Sport Flite Mfg., Inc. (swaging dies)
SSK Industries
Star Machine Works
Stuart Products, Inc. (sight vise)
Sunora Gun Shop
Trammco, Inc. (Electra-Jacket bullet plater)
Tru-Square Metal Products (Thumbler's tumbler case polishers; Ultra Vibe 18)
T&S Industries, Inc.
Vibra-Tek Co. (brass polisher; Brite Rouge)
Weatherby, Inc.
Webster Scale Mfg. Co.
Whitetail Design & Engineering Ltd. (Match Prep primer pocket tool)
Widener's Reloading & Shooting Supply
Wilson, Inc., L.E.

RESTS—BENCH, PORTABLE, ETC.

Armor Metal Products (port. shoot. bench)
B-Square Co. (handgun)
Butler Creek Corp.
Cravener's Gun Shop
Decker Shooting Products (rifle rests)

Hall's Shooting Products, Inc., Joe (adjustable portable)
Harris Engineering, Inc. (bipods)
Hart & Son, Inc., Robert W.
Hidalgo, Tony (adjustable shooting seat)

Holden Co., J.B.
Hoppe's Div., Penguin Industries, Inc. (benchrests and bags)
Protektor Model Co. (sandbags)
Ransom Intl. Corp. (handgun rest)
San Angelo Mfg. Co.

Sinclair International, Inc.
Sports Support Systems, Inc.
Ultra Light Arms, Inc.
Wichita Arms, Inc.
World of Targets (shooting bench—Porta Bench)

RIFLE BARREL MAKERS (See also Muzzle-Loading Guns, Barrels or Equipment)

Ackley, P.O. (See Bellm Contenders)
Apex Rifle Co.
Baiar, Jim
Bellm Contenders (new rifle barrels, including special and obsolete)
Bustani, Leo (Win.92 take-down; Trapper 357-44 magnum barrels)
Carter, Ralph L.
Clerke Co., J.A.
Competition Limited
Donnelly Siskiyou Gun Works, P.
Douglas Barrels, Inc.
Gentry Custom Gunmaker, David
Getz Barrel Co.
Goode, A.R.
H-S Precision, Inc.
Half Moon Rifle Shop
Hart Rifle Barrels, Inc.
Hart & Son, Inc., Robert W.
Hastings (shotguns only)
Jackalope Gun Shop
KOGOT Octagon Barrels

Kopp, Terry K. (22-cal. blanks)
Krieger Barrels, Inc.
Lilja Precision Rifle Barrels, Inc.
Marquart Precision Co.
Matco, Inc.
McGowen Rifle Barrels
McMillan Rifle Barrels U.S. International
Nu-Line Guns
Oakland Custom Arms, Inc.
Obermeyer Rifled Barrels
Olympic Arms, Inc.
Pence Precision Barrels
Redman's Rifling & Reboring
Rocky Mountain Rifle Works, Ltd.
Sanders Cust. Gun Serv.
Schneider, Gary
Shaw, Inc., E.R. (also shotgun barrels)
Shilen Rifles, Inc.
Shiloh Rifle Mfg. Co., Inc.
Strutz Rifle Barrels, Inc., W.C.
Wells, Fred
Wilson Arms Co.

SCOPES, MOUNTS, ACCESSORIES, OPTICAL EQUIPMENT

Action Arms Ltd.
Adco International (Inter-Aims Mark V sight)
Aimpoint U.S.A. (electronic sight)
Aimtech Mount Systems
Alley Supply Co.
American Import Co., The
Anderson Mfg. Co. (lens caps: Storm King, Storm Queen)
A.R.M.S., Inc. (mounts)
Armsport, Inc.
Armson, Inc. (See Trijicon, Inc.)
Bausch & Lomb, Inc.
Beeman Precision Arms, Inc. (airguns only)
B-Square Co. (Mini-14 mount)
Buehler Scope Mounts
Burris Co., Inc.
Bushnell
Butler Creek Corp. (lens caps)
Cape Outfitters (mount)
Celestron International (spotting scope)
Clear View Mfg. Co., Inc. (See-Thru mounts)
Compass Industries, Inc.
Conetrol Scope Mounts
Del-Sports, Inc. (EAW mounts)
D&H Prods. Co., Inc. (lens covers)
Dickson (See American Import Co.)
Dynamit Nobel-RWS, Inc. (Laser sight & mounts)
Emerging Technologies, Inc. (Laser sight & mounts)
Europtik, Ltd.
Flaig's
Freeland's Scope Stands, Inc.
GSI, Inc. (Bock mounts)
Griffin & Howe, Inc.
Gun Parts Corp.
Gun South, Inc. (See GSI, Inc.) (KSM mounts)
Heckler & Koch, Inc.
Hermann Leather Co., H.J. (lens caps)
Holden Co., J.B. (mounts)
Imatronic, Inc. (Laser Sights)
Jaeger, Inc., Paul (Schmidt & Bender; EAW mounts, Noble)
Jason Empire, Inc.
Kenko Intl., Inc. (optical equipment)
KenPatable Ent., Inc.
Kilham, Benjamin (Hutson handgun scopes)
Kowa Optimed, Inc.
Kris Mounts
Kwik Mount Corp.
Kwik-Site
L&S Technologies, Inc. (See Aimtech Mount Systems)
Laser Devices, Inc. (Laser Sight)
Leica USA (binoculars)
Leitz (See Leica USA)
Leupold & Stevens, Inc.

Lodewick, W.H. (scope safeties)
Marble Arms Corp.
Marlin Firearms Co.
Michaels of Oregon (QD scope covers)
Military Armament Corp. (Leatherwood)
Millett Industries (mounts)
Mirador Optical Corp.
Nikon, Inc.
North American Specialties
Olympic Arms, Inc.
Orchard Park Enterprise (Saddleproof mounts only)
Pachmayr Ltd.
Pentax Corp. (riflescopes)
Pilkington Gun Co. (QD mount)
Pioneer Marketing & Research, Inc. (German Steiner binoculars; scopes)
Precision Sport Optics
Ram-Line, Inc. (see-thru mount for Mini-14)
Ranging, Inc.
Redfield, Inc.
Sanders Cust. Gun Serv. (MSW)
Schmidt & Bender (See Paul Jaeger, Inc.)
Seattle Binocular & Scope Repair Co.
Shepherd Scope Ltd.
Sherwood Intl. Export Corp. (mounts)
Shooters Supply (mount for M14/M1A rifles)
Simmons Enterprises, Ernie (Nichols sport optics)
Simmons Outdoor Corp.
S&K Mfg. Co. (Insta-Mount)
Sports Support Systems, Inc.
Springfield Armory, Inc.
SSK Industries (bases)
Steiner Binoculars (See Pioneer Marketing & Research)
Stoeger Industries
Supreme Lens Covers (See Butler Creek) (lens caps)
Swarovski Optik
Swift Instruments, Inc.
Tasco Sales, Inc.
Tele-Optics (optical equipment repair services only)
Tele-Optics, Inc. (spotting scopes)
Thompson/Center Arms (handgun scope)
Trijicon, Inc. (rifle scopes)
Unertl Optical Co., John
United Binocular Co.
Wasp Shooting Systems (mounting system for Ruger Mini-14 only)
Weatherby, Inc.
Weaver, Div. of Blount Sporting Eqip.
Weaver Scope Repair Service
Wide View Scope Mount Corp.
Williams Gun Sight Co.
Williams, Inc., Boyd (BR)
York M-1 Conversions
Zeiss Optical, Inc., Carl
Zeitz Optics, U.S.A.

SIGHTS, METALLIC

Alley Supply Co.
All's, The Jim J. Tembelis Co., Inc.
 (shotgun Accura-Sites)
Armson, Inc. (See Trijicon, Inc.)
Beeman Precision Arms, Inc.
Behlert Precision
Bo-Mar Tool & Mfg. Co.
Burris Co., Inc.
Cherokee Gun Accessories (Tritium
 Tacsight)
Clerke Co., J.A.
Farr Studio (sighting aids—clip-on
 aperture; the Farr Sight; the
 Concentrator)
Fautheree, Andy ("Calif. Sight" for ML)
Freeland's Scope Stands, Inc.
Gun Parts Corp.
Innovision Enterprises (Slug Sights)
Iron Sight Gunworks, Inc.

Jaeger, Inc., Paul
Kiss Sights
Lofland, James W. (single shot replica)
Lyman Products Corp.
Marble Arms Corp.
Meier Works (Express sights)
Meprolight
Merit Corp.
Millett Industries
Miniature Machine Co. (MMC)
MMC Co., Inc. (See Miniature Mach. Co.)
Omega Sales, Inc.
Pachmayr Ltd.
Poly Choke Div. (See Marble Arms Corp.)
Slug Site Co.
Tradewinds, Inc.
Trijicon, Inc.
Wichita Arms, Inc.
Williams Gun Sight Co.

STOCKS (Commercial and Custom)

Ahlman's, Inc.
Allen, Inc., Don
Angelo & Little Custom Gun Stock Blanks
 (blanks only)
Ann Arbor Rod and Gun Co.
Apel, Dietrich
Arms Ingenuity
Bain & Davis, Inc. (custom)
Balickie, Joe J.
Bartas Gunsmithing
Bartlett, Donald
Beeman Precision Arms, Inc. (airguns
 only)
Belding's Custom Gun Shop
Bell & Carlson, Inc. (commercial)
Bellm Contenders
Benchmark Guns
Biesen, Al
Biesen, Roger
Billeb, Stephen L.
Billings Gunsmiths, Inc.
Bishop & Son, Inc., E.C.
Boeke, Gregg (custom)
Boltin, John M.
Bone, Ralph P.
Bowerly, Kent (custom)
Boyd's Gunstock Industries, Inc.
 (commercial)
Brace, Larry D.
Brgoch, Frank
Briganti Custom Gunsmith
Brown Precision, Inc.
Burres, Jack (English, Claro, Bastogne
 Paradox walnut blanks only)
Calico Hardwoods, Inc. (blanks)
Camilli, Lou
Campbell, Dick (custom)
Cape Outfitters
Caudill, Larry T. (custom)
Caywood, Shane (custom)
Champlin Firearms, Inc.
Churchill, Winston
Clerke Co., J.A.
Clifton Arms, Inc.
Clinton River Gun Serv., Inc.
Coffin, Charles H.
Coffin, Jim
Conrad, C.A. (custom)
Costa, David (custom)
Cubriel, Reggie (custom stockmaker)
Custom Gun Guild
Dahl's Custom Stocks
Dakota Arms, Inc.
Dangler, Homer L.
Davenport, Sterling
D&D Gunsmiths, Ltd. (custom)
Dever, Jack
Devereaux, R.H. "Dick"
Dixon, William
Dowtin Gunworks (DGW) (custom; blanks)
Dressel, Paul G., Jr. (custom)
Duncan's Gunworks, Inc. (custom)
Echols, D'Arcy A. (custom)
Eggleston, Jere (custom)
Emmons, Bob (custom)
Englishtown Sporting Goods Co., Inc.
 (custom)
Erhardt, Dennis
Eversull & Co., Inc., K.
Eyster Heritage Gunsmiths, Inc., Ken
 (custom)
Fajen, Inc., Reinhart

Farmer-Dressel, Sharon (custom)
Fellowes, Ted, Beaver Lodge (custom ML)
Fiberpro, Inc. (blanks; fiberglass; Kevlar)
Fisher, Jerry A.
Flaig's
Flynn's Custom Guns
Folks, Donald E. (custom trap, Skeet,
 livebird stocks)
Forster, Larry L.
Fountain Products (custom)
Frank Custom Guns, Ron
Freeland's Scope Stands, Inc.
Game Haven Gunstocks (Kevlar rifle
 stocks)
Garrett Accur-Lt. D.F.S. Co. (fiberglass)
Genecco Gun Works, K.
Goens, Dale W.
Goodling's Gunsmithing (custom)
Gordie's Gun Shop (custom)
Goudy, Gary (custom)
Grace, Charles E.
Green, Roger M. (custom)
Greene's Machine Carving (gunstock
 duplicating & machining serv.; custom)
Griffin & Howe
Guncraft, Inc.
Gun Parts Corp. (commercial)
Hanson's Gun Center
Harper's Custom Stocks
Hart & Son, Inc., Robert W. (custom)
Hecht, Hubert J., Waffen-Hecht (custom)
Heilmann, Stephen (custom)
Hensley, Darwin (custom)
Heppler, Keith M. (custom rifle)
Heydenberk, Warren
Hillmer Custom Gunstocks, Paul D.
Hiptmayer, Klaus
Hoenig & Rodman (stock duplicating
 machine)
Hollis Gun Shop
H-S Precision, Inc. (Fiberglass)
Huebner, Corey O. (custom)
Hughes, Steven Dodd (custom)
Intermountain Arms (custom)
Jaeger, Inc., Paul
Jamison, Robert L., Jr.
Jarrett Rifles, Inc. (custom)
Jim's Gun Shop (custom)
Johnson Wood Products (blanks only)
Johnson, Neal G.
Johnson, Peter S. (custom)
Kartak Gun Works (custom)
Ken's Rifle Blanks
Kilham & Co.
Klein, Don
Klingler, Kenneth J. (custom carving only)
Knippel, Richard (custom)
Kros Walnut, Inc. (Circassian walnut
 blanks)
Lawson Co., Harry
LeFever & Sons, Inc., Frank
Lind, Al (custom)
Logan Security Products Co., Harry M.
 (custom)
Mandarino, Monte
Manley Shooting Supplies, Lowell
Matthews, Larry
Mazur Restoration, Peter (custom)
McCament, Jay
McDonald, Dennis (custom)
McFarland, Stan
McGuire, Bill (custom)

Meadow Industries
Mercer, R.M. (custom)
Miller Arms, Inc.
Miller, S.A. (gun wood)
Milliron Custom Guns & Stocks, Earl
Mitchell Arms, Inc.
Mitch's Stock Shop, Inc. (Fibercomb
 stocks)
Monell Custom Guns (custom)
Morrison Custom Rifles, J.W.
MPI Stocks (fiberglass)
Nelson, Stephen E. (custom)
New England Arms Co.
New England Custom Gun Service (See
 Apel, Dietrich)
Nickels, Paul R.
Nicklas, Ted (custom)
Norman, Jim, Custom Gunstocks
Olson, Vic (custom)
Ottmar, Maurice
Pachmayr Ltd. (blanks and custom jobs)
Pasadena Gun Center
Paulsen Gunstocks (blanks)
Ranch Products
Reiswig, Wallace E. (Calif. walnut blanks)
Richards Micro-Fit Stocks (thumbhole)
R&J Gunshop (custom)
Robinson, Don (blanks only)
Rogers Gunsmithing, Bob
Royal Arms
Ryan, Chad (custom)
Sanders Custom Gun Serv. (blanks)
Schaefer, Roy V. (commercial blanks)
Schiffman, Curt (custom)
Schiffman, Norman H. (custom)
Schwartz, David W.
Shaw's (custom only)
Sherk, Dan A. (custom)
Shows, Hank
Sile Distributors
Sinclair International, Inc.

Six Enterprises (fiberglass)
Snider Stocks
Sowers, Ed (custom hydro-coil gunstocks)
Speiser, Fred D.
Sportsmen's Equipment Co. (carbine
 conversions)
Stegall, Keith
Swan, D.J. (custom)
Talmage, William G.
Tennessee Valley Mfg. (custom, ML only)
Tiger-Hunt (curly maple stock blanks)
Trevallion Gunstocks
Trinko's Gun Service
Tucker, James C. (custom)
Unick's Gunsmithing
Van Epps, Milton
Van Horn, Gil
Vest, John (classic rifles)
Vic's Gun Refinishing
Von Atzigen, Ed (custom)
Wallace, R.D. (custom)
Weatherby, Inc.
Weber Chris/Waffen-Weber
Weems, Cecil
Wells, Fred
Werth, Terry (custom)
West, Robert G.
Western Gunstock Mfg. Co.
Westminster Arms Ltd. (Bull-Pup kits)
Wiebe, Duane
Williams, Bob
Williamson-Pate Gunsmith Service
Wills, David W.
Windish, Jim (walnut blanks)
Winter, Robert M.
Wisner's Gun Shop, Inc.
Yee, Mike
York M-1 Conversions
Zeeryp, Russell R.
Zollinger, Dean A.

TARGETS, BULLET AND CLAYBIRD TRAPS

Aztec International Ltd. (Exploding
 Bullseye targets)
Beeman Precision Arms, Inc. (airguns)
Birchwood-Casey
Caswell International Corp., Inc. (target
 carriers; commercial shooting ranges)
Dapkus Co., J.G. (live bullseye targets)
Detroit-Armor Corp. (Shooting Ranges)
The Dutchman's Firearms, Inc.
Epps (Orillia) Northern Ltd., Ellwood (hand
 traps)
Hunterjohn
Jaro Manuf. (paper targets)
Kleen-Bore, Inc.

Maki Industries (X-Spand Target System)
MTM Molded Prods. Co.
Outers Laboratories (claybird traps)
Peterson Instant Targets, Inc. (See Lyman
 Products) (paste-ons; Targ-Dots)
Phillips Enterprises, Inc. (portable target
 holder)
Red Star Target Co.
Remington Arms Co. (claybird traps)
Rocky Mountain Target Co. (Data-Targ)
Sheridan Products, Inc. (traps)
Trius Products, Inc. (claybird, can thrower)
Winchester, Div. Olin Corp. (claybird traps)
World of Targets (targets)

TAXIDERMY

Jonas Bros., Inc.
Kulis Freeze-Dry Taxidermy

Parker, Mark D.

TRAP AND SKEET SHOOTERS EQUIP.

The American Import Co. (targetthrower;
 claybird traps)
Briley Mfg. Co. (choke tubes)
Caswell International Corp.
C&H Research (Mercury recoil suppressor)
Clymer Mfg. Co., Inc. (snap shell)
D&H Prods. Co., Inc. (snap shell)
Euroarms of America, Inc.
Eyster Heritage Gunsmiths, Inc., Ken
 (shotgun competition choking)
Frigon Guns
Griggs Products (recoil redirector)
Hall Plastics, Inc., John
Harper, William E.
Hastings
Hoppe's Division (Monte Carlo pad)
Hunter Co., Inc.
Krieghoff International, Inc.
Ljutic Industries, Inc.

Magnum Research, Inc.
Meadow Industries (stock pad, variable;
 muzzle rest)
Moneymaker Guncraft (free-floating,
 ventilated ribs)
MTM Molded Products Co. (claybird
 thrower)
Nittler, William J. (shotgun barrel repairs)
Noble Co., Jim
Outers Laboratories (trap, claybird)
Protektor Model Co.
Remington Arms Co. (trap, claybird)
Shurkatch Corp., Longhorn Div.
Titus Shooting Specialties, Daniel (hullbag)
Trius Products, Inc. (can thrower; trap,
 claybird)
Widener's Reloading & Shooting Supply
Winchester, Div. Olin Corp. (trap, claybird)
Zeus International

TRIGGERS, RELATED EQUIPMENT

Bell Design Corp. (rifle triggers)
B.M.F. Activator, Inc.
Brownells, Inc.
Canjar Co., M.H. (triggers)
Central Specialties Co. (trigger locks only)
Cycle Dynamics, Inc.
Dayton-Traister Co. (triggers)
Electronic Trigger Systems
Flaig's (trigger shoes)
Gun Parts Corp.
Hastings

Holmes Firearms Corp. (trigger release)
Jones, Neil A. (See Custom Products)
Meier Works (shotgun trigger guard)
Miller Single Trigger Mfg. Co.
Nettestad, Bruce A. (trigger guards)
Pachmayr Ltd. (trigger shoe)
Pacific Tool Co. (trigger shoe)
Penrod Precision (triggers for Ruger #1,3)
Timney Mfg., Inc. (triggers)
Tyler Mfg.-Dist., Melvin (trigger shoe)
Williams Gun Sight Co. (trigger shoe)

MANUFACTURERS' DIRECTORY

A

A.A. Arms, Inc., 8325 Fairview Rd., Mint Hill, NC 28227/704-545-5565
A&B Industries, Inc., 7920-28 Hamilton Ave., Cincinnati, OH 45231/513-522-2992
Abel Safe & File Co., 105 North Fourth St., Fairbury, IL 61739/815-346-9280
Acculube II, Inc., 22025 70th Ave. S., Kent, WA 98032/206-395-7171
Accupro Gun Care, Div. of RTI Research Ltd., 15512-109 Ave., Surrey, BC U3R 7E8, Canada/604-583-7807
Accuracy Gun Shop, Lance Martini, 3651 University Ave., San Diego, CA 92104/619-282-8500
Accuracy Systems, Inc., 15205 N. Cave Creek Rd., Phoenix, AZ 85032/602-971-1991
Accuracy Unlimited, Frank Glenn, 16036 N. 49th Ave., Glendale, AZ 85306/602-978-9089
Accurate Arms Co., Inc. (Propellents Div.), Rt. 1, P.O. Box 167, McEwen, TN, 37101/615-729-4207/4208
Accurate Plating & Weaponry, Inc., 1937 Calumet St., Clearwater, FL 34625/813-449-9112
Accu-Tek, 4525 Carter Ct., Chino, CA 91710/714-627-2404
Ackley, P.O. (See Bellm Contenders)
Acme Custom Bullets, 2414 Clara Lane, San Antonio, TX 78213/512-680-4828
Action Ammo Ltd., P.O. Box 19630, Philadelphia, PA 19124/215-744-0100
Action Arms Ltd., P.O. Box 9573, Philadelphia, PA 19124/215-744-0100
Action Products, Inc., 22 N. Mulberry St., Hagerstown, MD 21740/301-797-1414
ACTIV Industries, Inc., P.O. Box F, 1000 Zigor Rd., Kearneysville, WV 25430/304-725-0451
Ad Hominem, RR 3, Orillia, ON L3V 6H3, Canada/705-689-5303
Adams, John J., P.O. Box 167, Corinth, VT 05039/802-439-5904
Adco International, 1 Wyman St., Woburn, MA 01801/617-935-1799
Adkins, Luther, P.O. Box 281, Shelbyville, IN 46176/317-392-3795
Advance Car Mover Co., Inc., Rowell Div., P.O. Box 1181, 112 N. Outagamie St., Appleton, WI 54912/414-734-1878
Advance Scouts, Inc., 2741 Patton Rd., Roseville, MN 55113/612-639-1326
AFSCO Ammunition, 731 W. Third St., Owen, WI 54460/715-229-2516
Ahlman's, Inc., RR 1, P.O. Box 20, Morristown, MN 55052/507-685-4244
Aimpoint U.S.A., 203 Elden St., Suite 302, Herndon, VA 22070/703-471-6828
Aimtech Mount Systems, P.O. Box 223, 101 Inwood Acres, Thomasville, GA 31792/912-226-4313
Air Rifle Specialists, 311 East Water St., Elmira, NY 14901/607-734-7340
Ajax Custom Grips, Inc., Div. of A. Jack Rosenberg & Sons, 11311 Stemmons, Suite #5, Dallas, TX 75229/214-241-6302
Alaska Bullet Works, P.O. Box 54, Douglas, AK 99824/907-789-1576
Alcas Cutlery Corp., 1116 E. State St., Olean, NY 14760/716-372-3111
Alco Carrying Cases, 601 W. 26th St., New York, NY 10001/212-675-5820
Aldis, Riichard L., 3020 Hozoni Rd., Prescott, AZ 86301/602-445-6723
Alessi Holsters, Inc., 2465 Niagara Falls Blvd., Tonawanda, NY 14150/716-691-5615
Alfano, Sam, 36180 Henry Gaines Rd., Pearl River, LA 70452/504-863-3364
Allard, Gary, Creek Side Metal & Woodcrafters, Fishers Hill, VA 22626/703-465-3903
All's, The Jim J. Tembelis Co., Inc., 280 E. Fernau Ave., Oshkosh, WI 54901/414-426-1080
Allen Co.,Bob, 214 SW Jackson, Des Moines, IA 50315/515-283-2191/800-247-8048
Allen, Inc., Don, HC55, P.O. Box 326, Sturgis, SD 57785/605-347-5227
Alley Supply Co., P.O. Box 848, Gardnerville, NV 89410/702-782-3800
Allred Bullet Co., 932 Evergreen Dr., Logan, UT 84321/801-752-6983
Alpha Precision, Inc., Rt. 1, P.O. Box 35-1, Preston Rd., Good Hope, GA 30641/404-267-6163
Alpine's Precision Gunsmithing, 2401 Government Way, Coeur D'Alene, ID 83814/208-765-3559
Alsa Corp., The, 1245 McClellan, Suite 204, Los Angeles, CA 90025/213-207-4005
Altamont Mfg. Co., 510 N. Commercial St., P.O. Box 309, Thomasboro, IL 61878/217-643-3125
A&M Waterfowl, Inc., P.O. Box 69, Ripley, TN 38063/901-635-4003
AMAC (American Military Arms Corp.), 2202 Redmond Rd., Jacksonville, AR 72076/501-982-1633
American Arms, Inc., 715 E. Armour Rd., N. Kansas City, MO 64116/816-474-3161
American Bullets, 2190 C Coffee Rd., Lithonia, GA 30058
American Custom Gunmakers Guild, c/o Jan Melchert, Exec. Director, 22 Division St., Northfield, MN 55057/507-645-8811
American Derringer Corp., 127 N. Lacy Dr., Waco, TX 76705/817-799-9111
American Gas & Chemical Co., Ltd., 220 Pegasus Ave., Northvale, NJ 07647/201-767-7300
American Gripcraft, 3230 S. Dodge #2, Tucson, AZ 85713/602-790-1222
American Import Co., The, 1453 Mission St., San Francisco, CA 94103/415-863-1506
American Industries, Inc., P.O. Box 27163, Salt Lake City, UT 84127/801-971-5006
American Optical Corp., 14 Mechanic St., Southbridge, MA 01550/617-765-9711
American Pistolsmiths Guild, 3922 Madonna Rd., Jarrettsville, MD 21084/301-557-6545
American Products Co., 14729 Spring Valley Rd., Morrison, IL 61270/815-772-3336
American Sales & Mfg. Co., P.O. Box 677, Laredo, TX 78042/512-723-6893
Amherst Arms, P.O. Box 658, Mt. Airy, MD 21771/301-829-9544
Ammo Load, Inc., 1560 E. Edinger, Suite G, Santa Ana, CA 92705/714-558-8858
Ammo-O-Mart, Ltd., P.O. Box 125, Hawkesbury, Ont., Canada K6A 2R8/613-632-9300
Ammunition Consulting Serv., Inc., Richard Geer, 55 White Oak Circle, St. Charles, IL 60174/708-377-4625
Amrine's Gun Shop, 937 Luna Ave., Ojai, CA 93023/805-646-2376
AMT (Arcadia Machine & Tool, Inc.), 6226 Santos Diaz St., Irwindale, CA 91702/818-334-6629
Anderson Mfg. Co., P.O. Box 4218, Federal Way, WA 98063/206-838-4299/800-541-4242
Angelo & Little Custom Gun Stock Blanks, Chaffin Creek Rd., Darbey, MT 59827
Ann Arbor Rod and Gun Co., 1946 Packard Rd., Ann Arbor, MI 48104/313-769-7866
Anschutz (See Precision Sales Intl., Inc.)
Answer Products Co., 1519 Westbury Dr., Davison, MI 48423/313-653-2911

Antique Arms Co., David F. Saunders, 1110 Cleveland, Monett, MO 65708/417-235-6501
Antique Gun Parts, Inc., 1118 S. Braddock Ave., Pittsburgh, PA 15218/412-241-1811
AO Safety Prods., Div. of American Optical Corp., 14 Mechanic St., Southbridge, MA 01550/617-765-9711
Apel, Dietrich, RR 2 P.O. Box 122W, Brook Rd., W. Lebanon, NH 03784/603-469-3565
Apex Rifle Co., 115 12th Ave. SE, Valley City, ND 58072/701-845-5155
API Outdoors, Inc., P.O. Box 1432, Tallulah, LA 71284/318-574-4903
Aplan, James O., HC 80 P.O. Box 793-25, Piedmont, SD 57769/605-347-5016
Armament Gunsmithing Co., Inc., 525 Route 22, Hillside, NJ 07205/201-686-0960
Armament Systems and Procedures, Inc., P.O. Box 1794, Appleton, WI 54913/414-731-7075
Armes de Chasse, P.O. Box 827, Chadds Ford, PA 19317/215-388-1146
Armitage International, Ltd., 1635-A Blue Ridge Blvd., Seneca, SC 29678/803-882-5900
Armite Labs., 1845 Randolph St., Los Angeles, CA 90001/213-587-7747
Arkfeld Mfg. & Dist. Co., Inc., Hwy 81 & Monroe Ave., P.O. Box 54, Norfolk, NE 68702-0054/402-371-9430
Armoloy Co. of Ft. Worth, 204 E. Daggett St., Fort Worth, TX 76104/817-332-5604
Armor Metal Products, P.O. Box 4609, Helena, MT 59604/406-442-5560
Armor, Div. of Buck Stop, Inc., 3015 Grow Rd., Stanton, MI 48888
Armory Publications, P.O. Box 4206, Oceanside, CA 92054/619-757-3930
Armoury, Inc., The, Route 202, New Preston, CT 06777/203-868-0001
A.R.M.S., Inc. (Atlantic Research Marketing Systems), 375 West St., West Arms, 4851 SW Madrona St., Lake Oswego, OR 97035/503-697-0533
Arms & Armour Press, Ltd., Villiers House, 41/47 Strand, London WC2N 5JE England
Arms Corp. of America, Inc., 4424 John Ave., Baltimore, MD 21227/301-247-6200
Arms Corp. of the Philippines (See Armscor Precision)
Arms Craft Gunsmithing, 1106 Linda Dr., Arroyo Grande, CA 93420/805-481-2830
Arms Ingenuity Co., P.O. Box 1, 51 Canal St., Weatogue, CT 06089/203-658-5624
Arms Services Corp., 33 Lockhouse Rd., Westfield, MA 01085/413-562-4196
Armscor Precision, 1875 S. Grant Rd., Suite 640, San Mateo, CA 94402/415-349-3592
Armson, Inc. (See Trijicon, Inc.)
Armsport, Inc., 3950 NW 49th St., Miami, FL 33142/305-635-7850
Armstec, Inc., 339 East Ave., Rochester, NY 14604/800-262-2832
Armurier Hiptmayer, P.O. Box 136, Eastman, Que. JOE 1P0, Canada/514-297-2492
Arratoonian, Andy, The Cottage, Sharow, Ripon HG4 5BP, England (0765)-5858
Art Jewel Enterprises Ltd., Eagle Business Ctr., 460 Randy Rd., Carol Stream, IL 60188/708-260-0400
ASI, 6226 Santos Diaz St., Irwindale, CA 91702/818-334-6629
A-Square Co., Inc., Rt. 4, Simmons, Rd., Madison, IN 47250/812-273-3633
Atlanta Cutlery, 2143 Geesmill Rd., Conyers, GA 30208/404-922-3700
Atlanta Discount Ammo, P.O. Box 258, Clarkesville, GA 30523/404-754-9000
Atlantic Mills, Inc., 1325 Washington Ave., Asbury Park, NJ 07712/201-774-4882
Atzigen, Ed von, The Custom Shop, 890 Cochrane Crescent, Peterborough, Ont., K9H 5N3 Canada/705-742-6693
Auto-Ordnance Corp., Williams Lane, West Hurley, NY 12491/914-679-7225
Autumn Sales, Inc., 1320 Lake St., Fort Worth, TX 76102/817-335-1634
A&W Repair, 2930 Schneider Dr., Arnold, MO 63010/314-287-3725
Aztec International Ltd., P.O. Box 1384, Clarkesville, GA 30523/404-754-8282

B

Bachman, Rick M. (See Old West Reproductions)
Badger Shooter's Supply, 106 S. Harding, Owen, WI 54460/715-229-2101
Baer Custom Guns, 1725 Minesite Rd., Allentown, PA 18103/215-398-2362
Baiar, Jim, 490 Halfmoon Rd., Columbia Falls, MT 59912/406-892-4409
Bain & Davis, Inc., 307 E. Valley Blvd., San Gabriel, CA 91776/213-283-7449
Baker, Stan, 10000 Lake City Way, Seattle, WA 98125/206-522-4575
Balaance Co., 340-39 Ave. SE, P.O. Box 505, Calgary, AB T2G 1X6, Canada/403-279-0334
Balickie Custom Stocks, Joe J., 408 Trelawney Lane, Apex, NC 27502/919-362-5185
Ballistic Products, Inc., P.O. Box 408, 2105 Daniels St., Long Lake, MN 55356/612-473-1550
Ballistic Research Industries (BRI), 953 Tower Place #A, Santa Cruz, CA 95062/408-476-7981
Ballistic Research, Tom Armbrust, 1108 W. May Ave., McHenry, IL 60050/815-385-0037
Bandcor Industries, Div. of Man-Sew Corp., 6108 Sherwin Dr., Port Richey, FL 34668/813-848-0432
Bang-Bang Boutique, 720 N. Flagler Dr., Fort Lauderdale, FL 33304/305-463-7910
Barami Corp., 6250 East 7 Mile Rd., Detroit, MI 48234/313-891-2536
Barbour Inc., Meadowbrook Rd., Milford, NH 03055/603-673-1313
Barnes Bullets, Inc., P.O. Box 215, American Fork, UT 84003/801-756-4222
Barnes Custom Shop (See Barnes Bullets, Inc.)
Barnett International, P.O. Box 934, 1967 Gunn Highway, Odessa, FL 33556/813-920-2241
Baron Technology, 62 Spring Hill Rd., Trumbull, CT 06611/203-452-0515
Barrett Firearms Mfg., Inc., P.O. Box 1077, Murfreesboro, TN 37133/615-896-2938
Bar-Sto Precision Machine, 73377 Sullivan Rd., P.O. Box 1838, Twentynine Palms, CA 92277/619-367-2747
Barta's Gunsmithing, 10231 US Hwy. #10, Cato, WI 54206/414-732-4472
Bartlett, Donald, 31829-32nd Pl. SW, Federal Way, WA 98023/206-927-0726
Bates, Jim, 2905 Lynnwood Circle SW, Decatur, AL 35603/205-355-3690
Bauer, Eddie, 15010 NE 36th St., Redmond, WA 98052
Bausch & Lomb, Inc., 42 East Ave., Rochester, NY 14603/800-828-5423
Beal's Bullets, 170 W. Marshall Rd., Lansdowne, PA 19050/215-259-1220
Beal, R. S., Jr., 170 W. Marshall Rd., Lansdowne, PA 19050/215-259-1220 (SASE f. inquiry)
Bean, L.L., 386 Main St., Freeport, ME 04032/207-865-3111
Bear Archery, RR 4, 4600 Southwest 41st Blvd., Gainesville, FL 32601/904-376-2327
Bear Hug Grips, Inc., P.O. Box 25944, Colorado Springs, CO 80936/719-598-5675

Beaver Lodge, 9245 16th Ave. SW, Seattle, WA 98106/206-763-1698
Beeman Precision Arms, Inc., 3440-GD Airway Dr., Santa Rosa, CA 95403/707-578-7900
Behlert Precison, Route 611 P.O. Box 63, Pipersville, PA 18947/215-766-8681
Beitzinger, George, 116-20 Atlantic Ave., Richmond Hill, NY 11419/718-847-7661
Belding & Mull, Inc., P.O. Box 428, 100 N. 4th St., Phillipsburg, PA 16866/814-342-0607
Belding's Custom Gun Shop, 10691 Sayers Rd., Munith, MI 49259/517-596-2388
B.E.L.L. (See Eldorado Cartridge Corp.)
Bell & Carlson, Inc., 509 N. 5th St., Atwood, KS 67730/913-626-3204
Bell's Custom Shop, 3315 Mannheim Rd., Franklin Park, IL 60131/708-678-1900
Bell Design Corp., 718 S. 2nd/P.O. Box 64, Atwood, KS 67730/913-626-3270
Bell Design Gun Services, 718 South 2nd, Atwood, KS 67730/913-626-3270
Bell Originals, Sid, Inc., R.D. 2, P.O. Box 219, Tully, NY 13159/607-842-6431
Bellm Contenders, P.O. Box 429, Cleveland, UT 84518 (price list $3)
Belltown, Ltd., 11 Camps Rd., Kent, CT 06757/203-354-5750
Benchmark Guns, 1265 5th Ave., Yuma, AZ 85364/602-783-5161
Benchmark Knives (See Gerber Legendary Blades)
Benelli Armi, S.p.A. (See Sile Distributors—handguns; Heckler & Koch—shotguns)
Benjamin Air Rifle Co., 2600 Chicory Rd., Racine, WI 53403/414-554-7900
Berdon Machine Co., 2011 W. Washington Ave., Yakima, WA 98902/509-453-0374
Beretta U.S.A., 17601 Beretta Drive, Accokeek, MD 20607/301-283-2191
Berger Bullets, 4234 N. 63rd Ave., Phoenix, AZ 85033/602-846-5791
Bergmann & Williams, 2450 Losee Rd., Suite F, N. Las Vegas, NV 89030/702-642-1091
Bertram Bullet Co. (See Huntington Die Specialties)
Bess, Gordon, 708 River St., Canon City, CO 81212/303-275-1073
Betz, Harold A., 6117 N. 27th Terrace, St. Joseph, MO 64505/816-279-2182
BF Arms, 1123 S. Locust, Grand Island, NE 68801/308-382-1121
Bianchi International, Inc., 100 Calle Cortez, Temecula, CA 92390/714-676-5621
Biesen, Al, 5021 Rosewood, Spokane, WA 99208/509-328-9340
Biesen, Roger, 5021 W. Rosewood, Spokane, WA 99208/509-328-9340
Big Beam (See Teledyne Co.)
Big Spring Enterprise "Bore Stores," P.O. Box 1115, Yellville, AR 72687/501-449-5297
Bilal, Mustafa, 5429 Russell Ave. NW, Suite 202, Seattle, WA 98107/206-782-4164
Billeb, Stephen L., 1259 S. Main, Burlington, IA 52601/319-753-2110
Billings Gunsmiths, Inc., Stan Wright, 1940 Grand Ave., Billings, MT 59102/406-652-3140
Billingsley, Ross, P.O. Box 25, Dayton, WY 82836/307-655-9344 (brochure $1)
Bill's Gun Repair, 1007 Burlington St., Mendota, IL 61342/815-539-5786
Bilsom Interntl., Inc., 109 Carpenter Dr., Sterling, VA 22170/703-834-1070
Birchwood-Casey, 7900 Fuller Rd., Eden Prairie, MN 55344/612-937-7933
Bishop & Son, Inc., E.C., 119 Main St., P.O. Box 7, Warsaw, MO 65355/816-438-5121
Bitterroot Bullet Co., P.O. Box 412, Lewiston, ID 83501/208-743-5635 (brochure: USA, Can. & Mexico $1 plus legal size env., intl. $2; lit. pkg.: USA, Can. & Mexico $7.75, Intl. $10.75)
Black Mountain Bullets, Rt. 3, P.O. Box 297, Warrenton, VA 22186/703-347-1199
Blackhawk East, P.O. Box 2274, Loves Park, IL 61131
Blackhawk Mtn., P.O. Box 210, Conifer, CO 80433
Blackhawk West, P.O. Box 285, Hiawatha, KS 66434
Black Hills Ammunition, 3401 S. Hwy. 79, Rapid City, SD 57701/605-348-5150
Blackinton & Co., V.H., P.O. Box 1300, 221 John L. Dietsch Blvd., Attleboro Falls, MA 02763/617-699-4436
Blackjack Knives, 7210 Jordan Ave., #D72, Canoga Park, CA 91303/818-902-9853
Blacksmith Corp., P.O. Box 1752, Chino Valley, AZ 86323/800-531-2665
Blacktail Mountain Books, 42 First Ave. West, Kalispell, MT 59901/406-257-5573
Blackwell, W.W., 9826 Sagedale, Houston, TX 77089/713-484-0935
Bledsoe, Weldon, 6812 Park Place Dr., Fort Worth, TX 76118/817-589-1704
Bleile, C. Roger, 5040 Ralph Ave., Cincinnati, OH 45238/513-251-0249
Blocker's Custom Holsters, Ted, 5360 NE 112th, Portland, OR 97220/503-254-9950
Blount Sporting Equipment Division, P.O. Box 856, Lewiston, ID 83501/208-746-2351
Blue and Gray Prods., Inc., 34 West Main St., Milo, ME 04463/800-637-5579
Blue Ridge Machinery and Tools, Inc., P.O. Box 536-GD, 2806 Putnam Ave., Hurricane, WV 25526/304-562-3538/800-872-6500
B.M.F. Activator, Inc., P.O. Box 262364, Houston, TX 77207/713-477-8442
Bochenski, Rudolph V., 11640 N. 51 Ave. #232, Glendale, AZ 85304/602-878-4327
Boeke, Gregg, Rt. 2, P.O. Box 149, Cresco, IA 52136/319-547-3746
Boessler, Erich, Gun Engraving Intl., Am Vogeltal 3, 8732 Munnerstadt, W. Germany/9733-9443
Boggs, Wm., 827 Copeland Rd., Columbus, OH 43212/614-486-6965
Boker USA, Inc., 14818 West 6th Ave., Suite #17A, Golden, CO 80401/303-279-5997
Bolden, Duane, 1295 Lassen Dr., Hanford, CA 93230/209-582-6937
Boltin, John M., P.O. Box 644, Estill, SC 29918/803-625-2185
Bo-Mar Tool & Mfg. Co., Rt. 12, P.O. Box 405, Longview, TX 75605/214-759-4784
Bonanza (See Forster Products, Inc.)
Bone, Ralph P., 718 N. Atlanta, Owasso, OK 74055/918-272-9745
Bonham, Henry "Hank", P.O. Box 242, Brownsville, ME 04414/207-965-2891
Boone's Custom Ivory Grips, Inc., 562 Coyote Rd., Brinnon, WA 98320/206-796-4330
Border Guns & Leather, P.O. Box 1423, Deming, NM 88031/505-546-2151
Boswell, Charles, Div. of Saxon Arms Ltd., 615 Jasmine Ave. N., Unit J, Tarpon Springs, FL 34689/813-938-4882
Bourne Co., Inc., Richard A., P.O. Box 141, Hyannis Port, MA 02647/617-775-0797
Bowen Classic Arms Corp., P.O. Box 67, Louisville, TN 37777/615-984-3583
Bowen Knife Co., P.O. Box 590, Blackshear, GA 31516/912-449-4794
Bowerly, Kent, Metolious Meadows Dr., H.C.R. P.O. Box 1903, Camp Sherman, OR 97730/503-595-6028
Boyd's Gunstock Industries, Inc., 3rd & Main, P.O. Box 305, Geddes, SD 57342/605-337-2125
Boyt Co., Div. of Welsh Sporting Goods, P.O. Drawer 668, Iowa Falls, IA 50126/515-648-4826
Brace, Larry D., 771 Blackfoot Ave., Eugene, OR 97404/503-688-1278
Brass Eagle, Inc., 7050A Bramalea Rd., Unit 19, Mississauga, Ont. L4Z 1C7, Canada/416-848-4844
Bratcher, Dan, 311 Belle Air Pl., Carthage, MO 64836/417-358-1518
Brauer Bros. Mfg. Co., 2020 Delmar Blvd., St. Louis, MO 63103/314-231-2864
Braun, M., 32, rue Notre-Dame, 2440 Luxembourg, Luxembourg
Brazos Arms Co., 17423 Autumn Trails, Houston, TX 77084/713-463-0598
Break-Free, P.O. Box 25020, Santa Ana, CA 92799/714-953-1900
Bretton, 19 rue Victor Grignard, Z.I. Montreynaud, 42-St. Etienne, France
Brgoch, Frank, 1580 S. 1500 East, Bountiful, UT 84010/801-295-1885
BRI (See Ballistic Research Industries)
Brian, C.T., 1101 Indiana Ct., Decatur, IL 62521/217-429-2290
Briganti Custom Gunsmith, P.O. Box 56, Highland Mills, NY 10930/914-928-9573
Briley Mfg. Co., 1085-B Gessner, Houston, TX 77055/713-932-6995
BRNO (See T.D. Arms)
Brobst, Jim, 299 Poplar St., Hamburg, PA 19526/215-562-2103
Brooker, Dennis B., Rt. 1, P.O. Box 12A, Derby, IA 50068/515-533-2103
Brown Precision, Inc., P.O. Box 270W, 7786 Molinos Ave., Los Molinos, CA 96055/800-543-2506/916-384-2506
Brown Products, Ed, Rt. 2, P.O. Box 2922, Perry, MO 63462/314-565-3261
Brownell Checkering Tools, W.E., 3356 Moraga Place, San Diego, CA 92117/619-276-6146
Brownells, Inc., 222 W. Liberty, Montezuma, IA 50171/515-623-5401
Browning (Gen. Offices), Rt. 1, Morgan, UT 84050/801-876-2711
Browning (Parts & Service), Rt. 4, P.O. Box 624-B, Arnold, MO 63010/314-287-6800
Bruno Bullets/Shooters Supply, 10 Fifth St., Kelayres, PA 18231/717-929-1791
Brunton USA, 620 East Monroe Ave., Riverton, WY 82501/307-856-6559
Bryco Arms (Distributed by Jennings Firearms, Inc.)
B-Square Co., P.O. Box 11281, Ft. Worth, TX 76110/817-923-0964
Bucheimer, Co., J.M., P.O. Box 280, Airport Rd., Frederick, MD 21701/301-662-5101
Buck Knives, Inc., P.O. Box 1267, 1900 Weld Blvd., El Cajon, CA 92022/619-449-1100/800-854-2557
Buck Stop Lure Co., Inc., 3600 Grow Rd., P.O. Box 636, Stanton, MI 48888/517-762-5091
Budin, Dave, Main St., Margaretville, NY 12455/914-568-4103
Buehler Scope Mounts, 17 Orinda Way, Orinda, CA 94563/415-254-3201
Buenger Enterprises, P.O. Box 5286, Oxnard, CA 93030/805-985-0541
Buffalo Bullet Co., Inc., 7352 S. Whittier Ave., Whittier, CA 90602/213-696-5738
Buffalo Rock Shooters Supply, R. Rt. 1, Ottawa, IL 61350/815-433-2471
Bull-Pup Industries, Inc., P.O. Box 187, Pioneertown, CA 92268/619-228-1949
Bullet Swaging Supply, Inc., P.O. Box 1056, 303 McMillan Rd., West Monroe, LA 71291/318-387-7257
Burgess, Byron, 710 Bella Vista Dr., Morro Bay, CA 93442/805-772-3974
Burgess, Ida I., Sam's Gun Shop, 25 Squam Rd., Rockport, MA 01966/617-546-6839
Burkhart, Don, P.O. Box 1306, Berthoud, CO 80513/303-532-0318
Burnham Bros., P.O. Box 669, 912 Main St., Marble Falls, TX 78654/512-693-3112
Burres, Jack, 10333 San Fernando Road, Pacoima, CA 91331/818-899-8000
Burris Co., Inc., 331 E. 8th St., P.O. Box 1747, Greeley, CO 80632/303-356-1670
Burt, Robert B., 106 Powder Mill Rd., P.O. Box 924, Canton, CT 06019/203-693-1117
Bushmaster Firearms Co., 999 Roosevelt Trail, Bldg. #3, Windham, ME 04062
Bushnell, 300 N. Lone Hill Ave., San Dimas, CA 91773/714-592-8000
Bustani, Leo, P.O. Box 8125, W. Palm Beach, FL 33407/305-622-2710 (SASE f. reply)
Butler Creek Corp., 290 Arden Dr., Belgrade, MT 59714/406-388-1356
Butterfield & Butterfield, 220 San Bruno Ave., San Francisco, CA 94103/415-861-7500

C

Cabela's, 812-13th Ave., Sidney, NE 69160/308-254-5505
Cabinet Mtn. Outfitter, P.O. Box 766, Plains, MT 59859/406-826-3970
Cache La Poudre Rifleworks, 140 N. College, Ft. Collins, CO 80524/303-482-6913
Calico (California Instrument Co.), 405 E. 19th St., Bakersfield, CA 93305/805-323-1327
Calico Hardwoods, Inc., 1648 Airport Blvd., Windsor, CA 95492/707-546-4045
Camdex, Inc., 2330 Alger, Troy, MI 48083/313-528-2300
Cameron's, 16690 W. 11th Ave., Golden, CO 80401/303-279-7365
Camilli, Lou, 4700 Oahu Dr. NE, Albuquerque, NM 87111/505-293-5259
Camillus Cutlery Co., 54 Main St., Camillus, NY 13031/315-672-8111/800-344-0456
Campbell, Dick, 20000 Silver Ranch Rd., Conifer, CO 80433/303-697-0150
Can Am Enterprises, 350 Jones Rd., Fruitland, Ont. LOR ILO, Canada/416-643-4357 (catalog $2)
Canjar Co., M.H., 500 E. 45th Ave., Denver, CO 80216/303-295-2638
Cannavaro, Brian V., 600 Farm Rd., Kalispell, MT 59901/406-756-8851
Cape Outfitters, Rt. 2 P.O. Box 437C, Cape Girardeau, MO 63701/314-335-4103
Carbide Die & Mfg. Co., Inc., 15615 E. Arrow Hwy., Covina, CA 91706/818-337-2518
Carry-Lite, Inc., 5203 W. Clinton Ave., Milwaukee, WI 53223/414-355-3520
Carter Gun Works, 2211 Jefferson Pk. Ave., Charlottesville, VA 22903
Carter, Ralph L., Carter's Gun Shop, 225 G St., Penrose, CO 81240/719-372-6240
Carter's Wildlife Calls, Inc., Garth, P.O. Box 821, Cedar City, UT 84720/801-586-7639
Cartridges Unlimited, 190 Bull's Bridge Rd., South Kent, CT 06785/203-927-3053
Cascade Cartridge, Inc. (See Blount Sporting Equipment Division)
Cascade Fabrication, 1090 Bailey Hill Rd. Unit A, Eugene, OR 97402/503-485-3433
Case & Sons Cutlery Co., W.R., P.O. Box 4000, Owens Way, Bradford, PA 16701/814-368-4123
Caspian Arms, 14 North Main St., Hardwick, VT 05843/802-472-6454
Caswell International Corp., 1221 Marshall St. NE, Minneapolis, MN 55413/612-379-2000
Cathey Enterprises, Inc., 3423 Milam Dr., P.O. Box 2202, Brownwood, TX 76804/915-643-2553
Cattle Baron Leather Co., P.O. Box 100724, Dept. GD, San Antonio, TX 78201/512-697-8900 (catalog $3)
Caudill, Larry T., 1025A Palomas Dr. SE, Albuquerque, NM 87108/505-255-2515
Caywood, Shane, P.O. Box 321, Minocqua, WI 54548/715-356-5414
CCI (See Blount Sporting Equipment Division)
Cedar Hill Game Call Co., Rt. 2 P.O. Box 236, Downsville, LA 71234/318-982-5632
Celestron International, P.O. Box 3587, Torrance, CA 90503
Cellini, Vito, Francesca, Inc., 3115 Old Ranch Rd., San Antonio, TX 78217/512-826-2584
Centaur Systems, Inc., 15127 NE 24th, C-3, Suite 114, Redmond, WA 98052/206-392-8472
Central Specialties Co., 200 Lexington Dr., Buffalo Grove, IL 60089/708-537-3300
Century Gun Dist., Inc., 1467 Jason Rd., Greenfield, IN 46140/317-462-4524
Century Intl. Arms, Inc., 80 N. Main St., St. Albans, VT 05478/802-527-1252
C&H Research, 155 Sunnyside Dr., Lewis, KS 67552/316-324-5445
C-H Tool & Die Corp., 106 N. Harding St., Owen, WI 54460/715-229-2146
Chace Leather Prods., 507 Alden St., Fall River, MA 02722/508-678-7556
Champion's Choice, Inc., 223 Space Park South, Nashville, TN 37211/615-834-6666
Champlin Firearms, Inc., P.O. Box 3191, Woodring Airport, Enid, OK 73701/405-237-7388
Champlin, R. MacDonald, P.O. Box 693, Manchester, NH 03105/603-483-8557

Chapman Mfg. Co., P.O. Box 250, Rt. 17 at Saw Mill Rd., Durham, CT 06422/203-349-9228

Chapuis Armes, 23 rue de Montorcier, BP15, 42380 St. Bonnet-le-Chateau, France/(33)77.50.06.96

Charter Arms Corp., 430 Sniffens Ln., Stratford, CT 06497/203-377-8080

Cheney Firearms Co., 915 E. 1050 N., Bountiful, UT 84010/801-295-4396

Cherokee Gun Accessories, 4127 Bay St. Suite 226, Fremont, CA 94538/415-471-5770

CheVron Bullets, RR 1, Ottawa, IL 61350/815-433-2471

Chevron Case Master, RR 1, Ottawa, IL 61350

Chicago Cutlery Co., 5420 N. County Rd. 18, Minneapolis, MN 55428/612-533-0472

Chinasports, Inc., 2010 S. Balboa Ave., Ontario, CA 91761/714-923-1411

Chipmunk (See Oregon Arms, Inc.)

Chippewa Shoe Co., P.O. Box 2521, Ft. Worth, TX 76113/817-332-4385

Chopie Mfg., Inc., 700 Copeland Ave., LaCrosse, WI 54603/608-784-0926

Christie's East, 219 E. 67th St., New York, NY 10021/212-606-0400

Christopher Firearms Co., Inc., E., Route 128 & Ferry St., Miamitown, OH 45041/513-353-1321

Chu Tani Industries, Inc., P.O. Box 3782, Chula Vista, CA 92011

Chuck's Gun Shop, P.O. Box 597, Waldo, FL 32694/904-468-2264

Churchill Glove Co., James P.O. Box 298, Centralia, WA 98531

Churchill, Winston, Twenty Mile Stream Rd., RFD P.O. Box 29B, Proctorsville, VT 05153/802-226-7772

Cimarron Arms, 9439 Katy Freeway, Houston, TX 77024

Clark Custom Guns, Inc., James E. Clark, Rt. 2, P.O. Box 22A, Keithville, LA 71047/318-915-0836

Clark Firearms Engraving, P.O. Box 80746, San Marino, CA 91118/818-287-1652

Clark Co., Inc., David, 360 Franklin St., P.O. Box 15054, Worcester, MA 01615/508-756-6216

Clark, Frank, 3714-27th St., Lubbock, TX 79410/806-799-1187

Classic Arms Corp., P.O. Box 8, Dunsmuir, CA 96025/916-235-2000

Classic Doubles International, Inc., 1982 Innerbelt Business Center Dr., St. Louis, MO 63114/314-423-6191

Clearview Mfg. Co., Inc., 413 South Oakley St., Fordyce, AR 71742/501-352-8557

Clements, Chas, Handicrafts Unltd., 1741 Dallas St., Aurora, CO 80010/303-364-0403

Clenzoil Corp., P.O. Box 1226, Sta. C, Canton, OH 44708/216-833-9758

Clerke Co., J.A., P.O. Box 627, Pearblossom, CA 93553/805-945-0713

Clift Mfg., L.R., 3821 Hammonton Rd., Marysville, CA 95901

Clifton Arms, Inc., P.O. Box 531258, Grand Prairie, TX 75053/214-647-2500

Clinton River Gun Serv., Inc., 30016 S. River Rd., Mt. Clemens, MI 48045/313-468-1090

Clymer Mfg. Co., Inc., 1645 W. Hamlin Rd., Rochester Hills, MI 48309-3368/313-853-5555

Coats, Mrs. Lester, 300 Luman Rd., Space 125, Phoenix, OR 97535/503-535-1611

Coffin, Charles H., 3719 Scarlet Ave., Odessa, TX 79762/915-366-4729

Coffin, Jim, 250 Country Club Lane, Albany, OR 97321/503-928-4391

Coleman Co., Inc., 250 N. St. Francis, Wichita, KS 67201

Collins Brothers Div. (See Bowen Knife Co.)

Colonial Knife Co., P.O. Box 3327, Providence, RI 02909/401-421-1600

Colorado School of Trades, 1575 Hoyt St., Lakewood, CO 80215/303-233-4697

Colorado Shooter's Supply, P.O. Box 132, Fruita, CO 80446/303-887-2813

Colorado Sutlers Arsenal, P.O. Box 991, Granby, CO 80446/303-887-2813

Colt Firearms, P.O. Box 1868, Hartford, CT 06101/203-236-6311

Command Post, Inc., The, P.O. Box 1500, Crestview, FL 32536/904-682-2492

Compass Industries, Inc., 104 East 25th St., New York, NY 10010/212-473-2614

Competition Bullets, Inc., 9996-29 Ave., Edmonton, Alb. T6N 1A2, Canada/403-463-2817

Competition Electronics, Inc., 3460 Precision Dr., Rockford, IL 61109/815-874-8001

Competition Limited, 1664 S. Research Loop Rd., Tucson, AZ 85710/602-722-6455

Competitive Pistol Shop, The, John Henderson, 5233 Palmer Dr., Ft. Worth, TX 76117/817-834-8479

Component Concepts, Inc., 20955 SW Regal Court, Aloha, OR 97006/503-642-3967

Condon, Inc., David, P.O. Box 312, 14502-G Lee Rd., Chatilly, VA 22021/703-631-7748 or 109 E. Washington St., Middleburg, VA 22117/703-687-5642

Condor Mfg. Co., 418 W. Magnolia Ave., Glendale, CA 91204/818-240-3173

Conetrol Scope Mounts, Hwy. 123 South, Seguin, TX 78155

Connecticut Valley Arms Co.(CVA), 5988 Peachtree Corners East, Norcross, GA 30071/404-449-4687

Conrad, C.A., 3964 Ebert St., Winston-Salem, NC 27127/919-788-5469

Container Development Corp., 424 Montgomery St., Watertown, WI 53094

Continental Kite & Key Co. (CONKKO), P.O. Box 40, Broomall, PA 19008/215-356-0711

Cook, Dave, 5831-26th Lane, Brampton, MI 49837/906-428-1235

Coonan Arms, Inc., 830 Hampden Ave., St. Paul, MN 55114/612-646-6672

Cooper-Woodward, 8073 Canyon Ferry Rd., Helena, MT 59601/406-375-3321

Corbin Applied Technology, P.O. Box 2171, White City, OR 97503/503-826-5211

Corbin Mfg. & Supply, Inc., 600 Industrial Circle, P.O. Box 2659, White City, OR 97503/503-826-5211

Cor-Bon, Inc., P.O. Box 10126, Detroit, MI 48210/313-894-2373

Corkys Gun Clinic, 111 North 11th Ave., Greeley, CO 80631/303-330-0516

Corry, John, 628 Martin Lane, Deerfield, IL 60015/708-541-6250

Costa, David, Cougar Optics, 94 Orient Ave., Arlington, MA 02174/617-643-9571

Country Armourer, The, P.O. Box 308, Ashby, MA 01431/508-386-7789

Cox, C. Ed, 166 W. Wylie Ave., Washington, PA 15301/412-228-2932

Crandall Tool & Machine Co., 1545 N. Mitchell St., Cadillac, MI 49601/616-775-5562

Cravener's Gun Shop, 1627-5th Ave., Ford City, PA 16226/412-763-8312

Creative Cartridge Co., 56 Morgan Rd., Canton, CT 06019/203-693-2529

Crocker Engraving, 1510-42nd St., Los Alamos, NM 87544

Crocker, Gordon D., 1510-42nd St., Los Alamos, NM 87544/505-667-9117

Crosman Airguns (a Coleman Co.), Routes 5 and 20, E. Bloomfield, NY 14443/716-657-6161

Crosman Blades, The Coleman Co., 250 N. St. Francis, Wichita, KS 67201

Crouse's Country Cover, P.O. Box 160, Storrs, CT 06268/203-429-3720

Cubriel, Reggie, 15610 Purple Sage, San Antonio, TX 78255/512-695-3364

Cullity Restoration, Daniel, 209 Old County Rd., East Sandwich, MA 02537/508-888-1147

Cumberland Arms, Rt. 1, P.O. Box 1150, Shafer Rd., Blantons Chapel, Manchester, TN 37355

Cumberland Knife & Gun Works, 5661 Bragg Blvd., Fayetteville, NC 28303/919-867-0009

Cureton, Earl T., Rt. 2, P.O. Box 388, Willoughby Rd., Bulls Gap, TN 37711/615-235-2854

Custom Chronograph, Inc., 5305 Reese Hill Rd., Sumas, WA 98295/206-988-7801

Custom Gun Guild, Frank Wood, 2646 Church Dr., Doraville, GA 30340/404-455-0346

Custom Hunting Ammo & Arms, 2900 Fisk Rd., Howell, MI 48843/517-546-9498

Custom Knifemaker's Supply (Bob Schrimsher), P.O. Box 308, Emory, TX 75440/214-473-3330

Custom Products, Neil A. Jones, RD #1, P.O. Box 483A, Saegertown, PA 16443/814-763-2769

Custom Shooting Prods., 8505 K St., Omaha, NE 68127

Custom Tackle & Ammo, P.O. Box 1886, Farmington, NM 87499/505-632-3539

CVA (See Connecticut Valley Arms Co.)

Cycle Dynamics, Inc., 74 Garden St., Feeding Hills, MA 01030/413-786-0141

D

Dahl's Custom Stocks, Rt. 4, P.O. Box 558, Lake Geneva, WI 53147/414-248-2464

Daisy Mfg. Co., P.O. Box 220, Rogers, AR 72756/501-636-1200

Dakota Arms, Inc., HC 55, P.O. Box 326, Sturgis, SD 57785/605-347-5227

Daly, Charles (See Outdoor Sports HQ)

Damascus-U.S.A., P.O. Box 448, Edenton, NC 27932/919-793-3415

Dangler, Homer L., P.O. Box 254, Addison, MI 49220/517-547-6745 (brochure $3)

Danner Shoe Mfg. Co., P.O. Box 30148, 12722 NE Airport Way, Portland, OR 97230/503-251-1100

Dapkus Co., J.G., P.O. Box 180, Cromwell, CT 06416/203-632-2308

Dara-Nes, Inc. (See Nesci Enterprises, Inc.)

Dart Mfg. Co., 4012 Bronze Way, Dallas, TX 75237/214-333-4221

Davenport, Sterling, 9611 E. Walnut Tree Dr., Tucson, AZ 85715/602-749-5590

Davidson Products For Shooters, 2020 Huntington Dr., Las Cruces, NM 88001/505-522-5612

Davis Service Center, Bill, 10173 Croydon Way #9, Sacramento, CA 95827/916-369-6789

Davis Industries, 15150 Sierra Bonita Lane, Chino, CA 91710/714-591-4726

Davis Leather Co., G. Wm. Davis, 3930 Valley Blvd., Unit F, Walnut, CA 91789/714-598-5620

Day & Sons, Inc., Leonard, P.O. Box 122, Flagg Hill Rd., Heath, MA 01346/413-337-8369

Dayton Traister Co., 4778 N. Monkey Hill Rd., Oak Harbor, WA 98277/206-675-3421

DBI Books, Inc., 4092 Commercial Ave., Northbrook, IL 60062/708-272-6310

Decker Shooting Products, 1729 Laguna Ave., Schofield, WI 54476/715-359-5873

D&D Gunsmiths, Ltd., 363 E. Elmwood, Troy, MI 48083/313-583-1512

D&E Magazines Mfg., P.O. Box 4876-D, Sylmar, CA 91342

Deer Me Products Co., P.O. Box 34, 1208 Park St., Anoka, MN 55303/612-421-8971

Defense Moulding Enterprises, 16781 Daisey Ave., Fountain Valley, CA 92708/714-842-5062

DeHaas Barrels, Mark DeHaas, Rt. 3, P.O. Box 77, Ridgeway, MO 64481/816-872-6308

DeHaas, Frank, 122 Albany Av., SE, Orange City, IA 51041/712-737-2759

Delorge, Ed, 2231 Hwy. 308, Thibodaux, LA 70301/504-447-1633

Del Rey Products, P.O. Box 91561, Los Angeles, CA 90009/213-823-0494

Del-Sports, Inc., Main St., Margaretville, NY 12455/914-586-4103

Delta Ltd., P.O. Box 777, Mt. Ida, AR 71957

Delta Vectors, Inc., 7119 W. 79th St., Overland Park, KS 66204/913-642-0307

Dem-Bart Hand Checkering Tools, Inc., 6807 Hiway #2, Snohomish, WA 98290/206-568-7356

Denver Arms, Ltd., P.O. Box 4640, Pagosa Springs, CO 81157/303-731-2295 (SASE)

DeSantis Holster & Leather Co., 140 Denton Ave., New Hyde Park, NY 11040/516-354-8000

Desert Industries, Inc., 3261 Patrick Ln., Las Vegas, NV 89120/702-795-3100

Detonics (See New Detonics Mfg. Corp.)

Detroit-Armor Corp., Detroit Bullet Trap Div., 2233 N. Palmer Dr., Schaumburg, IL 60103/708-397-4070

Dever, Jack, 8520 NW 90th, Oklahoma City, OK 73132/405-721-6393

Devereaux, R.H. "Dick", D.D. Custom Rifles, 5240 Mule Deer Dr., Colorado Springs, CO 80919/719-548-8468

Dewey Mfg. Co., J., 186 Skyview Dr., Southbury, CT 06488/203-264-3064

D&H Precision Tooling, 7522 Barnard Mill Rd., Ringwood, IL 60072/815-653-4011

D&H Prods. Co., Inc., 465 Denny Rd., Valencia, PA 16059/412-898-2840

Dibble, Derek A., 555 John Downey Dr., New Britain, CT 06051/203-224-2630

Dickson (See The American Import Co.)

Dilling Engravers, W.R., Rod Dilling, 105 N. Ridgewood Dr., Sebring, FL 33870/813-385-0647

Dilliott Gunsmithing, Inc., Rt. 3 P.O. Box 340, Scarlett Rd., Dandridge, TN 37725/615-397-9204

Dillon Precision Prods., Inc., 7442 E. Butherus Dr., Scottsdale, AZ 85260/602-948-8009

DiStefano, Dominic, 4303 Friar Lane, Colorado Springs, CO 80907/303-599-3366

Dixie Gun Works, Inc., P.O. Box 130, Union City, TN 38261/901-885-0700

Dixon Muzzleloading Shop, Inc., RD 1 P.O. Box 175, Kempton, PA 19529/215-756-6271

Dixon, William, Buckhorn Gun Works, Rt. 6 P.O. Box 2230, Rapid City, SD 57702/605-787-6289

D.O.C. Specialists (Doc & Bud Ulrich), 2209 S. Central Ave., Cicero, IL 60650/708-652-3606

Donnelly-Siskiyou Gun Works, C.P., 405 Kubli Rd., Grants Pass, OR 97527/503-846-6604

Doskocil Mfg. Co., Inc., P.O. Box 1246, Arlington, TX 76004/817-467-5116

Douglas Barrels, Inc., 5504 Big Tyler Rd., Charleston, WV 25313/304-776-1341

Dowtin Gunworks (DGW), Rt. 4 P.O. Box 930A, Flagstaff, AZ 86001/602-779-1898

Drain, Mark, SE 3211 Kamilche Point Rd., Shelton, WA 98584/206-426-5452

Dremel Mfg. Co., 4915-21st St., Racine, WI 53406

Dressel, Paul G., Jr., 209 N. 92nd Ave., Yakima, WA 98908/509-966-9233

Dri-Slide, Inc., 411 N. Darling, Fremont, MI 49412/616-924-3950

Dr. O's Products Ltd., P.O. Box 111, Niverville, NY 12130/518-784-3333

Dubber, Michael W., 5325 W. Mill Rd., Evansville, IN 47712/812-963-6156

DuBiel Arms Co., 1724 Baker Rd., Sherman, TX 75090/214-893-7313

Duds Ammo & Supply Co., P.O. Box 393, Barton, VT 05822/802-525-3835

Duffy, Charles E., Williams Lane, West Hurley, NY 12491/914-679-2997

Duncan's Gunworks, Inc., 1619 Grand Ave., San Marcos, CA 92069/619-727-0515

Dunham Co., P.O. Box 813, Brattleboro, VT 05301/802-254-2316

Dunn, Tom M., 1342 South Poplar, Casper, WY 82601/307-237-3207

DuPont (See IMR Powder Co.)

Durango Boot (See Northlake Boot Co.)

Dutchman's Firearms, Inc., The, 4143 Taylor Blvd., Louisville, KY 40215/502-366-0555

Dwyer, Dan, 915 W. Washington St., San Diego, CA 92103/619-296-1501
Dynamit Nobel-RWS, Inc., 105 Stonehurst Court, Northvale, NJ 07647/201-767-1995
Dyson & Son Ltd., Peter, 29-31 Church St., Honley, Huddersfield, W. Yorksh. HD7 2AH, England/44-484-661062

E

Eagle Imports, Inc., 1907 Highway #35, Ocean, NJ 07712/201-531-8375
Eagle International, Inc., 5195 W. 58th Ave., Suite 300, Arvada, CO 80002/303-426-8100
E-A-R Div., Cabot Corp., 5457 West 79th St., Indianapolis, IN 46268/317-872-6666
East Enterprises, Inc., 2208 Mallory Place, Monroe, LA 71201/318-325-1761
Echols, D'Arcy A., 164 W. 580 S., Providence, UT 84332/801-753-2367
Ed's Gun House, Ed Kukowski, Route 1, P.O. Box 62, Minnesota City, MN 55952/507-689-2925
Edmund Scientific Co., 101 E. Gloucester Pike, Barrington, NJ 08033/609-543-6250
Edwards Recoil Reducer, 1104 Milton Rd., Alton, IL 62002/618-462-3257
Eezox, Inc., P.O. Box 772, Waterford, CT 06385/203-447-8282
Efemes Enterprises, P.O. Box 691, Colchester, VT 05446
Eggleston, Jere, P.O. Box 50238, Columbia, SC 29250/803-799-3402
Ek Commando Knife Co., 601 N. Lombardy St., Richmond, VA 23220/804-257-7272
Eldorado Cartridge Corp., P.O. Box 308, Boulder City, NV 89005/702-294-0025
Eldorado Custom Shop, P.O. Box 308, Boulder City, NV 89005/702-294-0025
Electronic Trigger Systems, 4124 Thrushwood Lane, Minnetonka, MN 55345/612-935-7829
Elite Ammunition, P.O. Box 3251, Oakbrook, IL 60522/708-366-9006
Elko Arms, Dr. L. Kortz, 28 rue Ecole Moderne, B-7400 Soignies, H.T., Belgium/32-67.33.29.34
E&L Mfg., Inc., 39042 N. School House, Cave Creek, AZ 85331/602-488-2598
Ellett Bros., 267 Columbia Ave., Chapin, SC 29036/803-345-3751
Ellis Sport Shop, E.W., RD 1, Route 9N, P.O. Box 315, Corinth, NY 12822/518-654-6444
El Paso Saddlery, P.O. Box 27194, El Paso, TX 79926/915-544-2233
Emerging Technologies, Inc., P.O. Box 581, Little Rock, AR 72203/501-375-2227
EMF, Co., Inc., 1900 East Warner Ave. 1-D, Santa Ana, CA 92705/714-261-6611
Emmons, Bob, 11748 Robson Rd., Grafton, OH 44044/216-458-5890
Emsco Variable Shotgun Chokes, 101 Second Ave., SE, Waseca, MN 56093/507-835-1481
Encom America, Inc., P.O. Box 5314, Atlanta, GA 30307/404-525-2801
Engineered Accessories, 1804 S. Elm Grove Rd., New Berlin, WI 53151/414-797-0901
Englishtown Sporting Goods Co., Inc., David J. Maxham, 38 Main St., Englishtown, NJ 07726/201-446-7717
Epps (Orillia) Northern Ltd., Ellwood, RR 3, Hwy. 11 North, Orillia, Ont. L3V 6H3, Canada/705-689-5333
Erhardt, Dennis, 3280 Green Meadow Dr., Helena, MT 59601/406-368-2298
Essex Arms, P.O. Box 345, Island Pond, VT 05846/802-723-4313
Estate Cartridge, Inc., P.O. Box 3702, Conroe, TX 77305/409-856-7277
Euroarms of America, Inc., 1501 Lenoir Dr., P.O. Box 3277, Winchester, VA 22601/703-662-1863
Europtik, Ltd., P.O. Box 319, Dunmore, PA 18512/717-347-6049
Eutaw Company, Inc., P.O. Box 608, U.S. Hwy. 176 West, Holly Hill, SC 29059/803-496-3341
Evans, Robert, 332 Vine St., Oregon City, OR 97045/503-656-5693
Eversull & Co., Inc., K., Tracemont Farm, 4800 Hwy. 121, Boyce, LA 71409/318-793-8728
Excaliber Wax, Inc., P.O. Box 432, Kenton, OH 43326/419-673-0512
Excam, Inc., 4480 E. 11 Ave., P.O. Box 3483, Hialeah, FL 33013/305-681-4661
Eyster Heritage Gunsmiths, Inc., Ken, 6441 Bishop Rd., Centerburg, OH 43011/614-625-6131
Eze-Lap Diamond Prods., P.O. Box 2229, 15164 Weststate St., Westminster, CA 92683/714-847-1555

F

Fabian Bros. Sporting Goods, Inc., 1510 Morena Blvd., Suite "G," San Diego, CA 92110/619-275-0816
Fagan & Co., William, 22952 E. 15 Mile Rd., Mt. Clemens, MI 48043/313-465-4637
Fajen, Inc., Reinhart, 1000 Red Bud Dr., P.O. Box 338, Warsaw, MO 65355/816-438-5111
Falling Block Works, P.O. Box 3087, Fairfax, VA 22038/703-476-0043
Fanzoj, John, P.O. Box 25, Ferlach, Austria 9170
Farm Form, Inc., 7730 Chantilly, Galveston, TX 77551/409-744-0762
Farmer-Dressel, Sharon, 209 N. 92nd Ave., Yakima, WA 98908/509-966-9233
Farr Studio, 1231 Robinhood Rd., Greenville, TN 37743/615-638-8825
Fautheree, Andy, P.O. Box 4607, Pagosa Springs, CO 81157/303-731-5003 (must send SASE)
Favre, Jacqueline, 3111 S. Valley View Blvd., Suite B-214, Las Vegas, NV 89102/702-876-6278
Feather Industries, Inc., 2500 Central Ave.#K, Boulder, CO 80301/303-442-7021
Federal Cartridge Co., 900 Ehlen Dr., Anoka, MN 55303/612-422-2840
Federal Eng. Corp., 2335 S. Michigan Ave., Chicago, IL 60616/312-842-1063
Federal Ordnance, Inc., 1443 Potrero Ave., S. El Monte, CA 91733/818-350-4161
Fellowes, Ted, Beaver Lodge, 9245 16th Ave. SW, Seattle, WA 98106/206-763-1698
Fenwal, Inc., Resins Systems Div., 50 Main St., Ashland, MA 01721/508-881-2000 Ext. 2372
FERLIB, Armi di Ferraglio Libero, 46 Via Costa, 25063 Gardone V.T. (Brescia), Italy/030-83.75.86
Ferris Firearms, Gregg Ferris, 1827 W. Hildebrand, San Antonio, TX 78201/512-734-0304
Fiberpro, Inc., 3636 California St., San Diego, CA 92101/619-295-7703
F.I.E. Corp. (See Firearms Import & Export Corp.)
Fiocchi of America, Inc., Rt. 2, P.O. Box 90-8, Ozark, MO 65721/417-725-4118
Firearms Engravers Guild of America, Robert Evans, Secy., 332 Vine St., Oregon City, OR 97045/503-656-5693
Firearms Imp. & Exp. Corp., (F.I.E.), P.O. Box 4866, Hialeah Lakes, Hialeah, FL 33014/305-685-5966
First Distributors, Inc., Jack, 44633 Sierra Highway, Lancaster, CA 93534/805-945-6981
Fish, Marshall F., Rt. 22 N., P.O. Box 2439, Westport, NY 12993/518-962-4897
Fisher Enterprises, 655 Main St. #305, Edmonds, WA 98020/206-776-4365
Fisher, Jerry A., P.O. Box 652, 38 Buffalo Buttes, Dubois, WY 82513/307-455-2722
Fishpaw, Roy C., 101 Primrose Lane, Lynchburg, VA 24501/804-385-6667 ($2 for brochure)

Fiskars (See Gerber Legendary Blades)
Fitz Pistol Grip Co., P.O. Box 171, Douglas City, CA 96024/916-778-3136
Flaig's, 2200 Evergreen Rd., Millvale, PA 15209/412-821-1717
Flambeau Prods. Corp., 15981 Valplast Rd., Middlefield, OH 44062/216-632-1631
Flannery Engraving Co., Jeff W., 11034 Riddles Run Rd., Union, KY 41091/606-384-3127 (color catalog $5)
Flashette Co., 4725 S. Kolin Ave., Chicago, IL 60632/312-927-1302
Flayderman & Co., N., P.O. Box 2446, Ft. Lauderdale, FL 33303/305-761-8855
Flents Products Co., Inc., P.O. Box 2109, Norwalk, CT 06852/203-866-2581
Flint Creek Arms Co., David Demasi, P.O. Box 205, 136 Spring St., Phillipsburg, MT 59858
Flintlock Muzzle Loading Gun Shop, The, 1238 "G" S. Beach Blvd., Anaheim, CA 92804/714-821-6655
Floatstone Mfg. Co., 106 Powder Mill Rd., P.O. Box 765, Canton, CT 06019/203 -693-1977
Flouramics, Inc., 103 Pleasant Ave., Upper Saddle River, NJ 07458/201-825-8110
Flynn's Cust. Guns, P.O. Box 7461, Alexandria, LA 71301/318-455-7130
Fogle, James W., RR 2, P.O. Box 258, Herrin, IL 62948/618-988-1795
Folks, Donald E., 205 W. Lincoln St., Pontiac, IL 61764/815-844-7901
Force 10, Inc., 3029 Fairfield Ave., Suite 223, Bridgeport, CT 06605/203-334-8282
Forgett, Valmore J., Jr., 689 Bergen Blvd., Ridgefield, NJ 07657/201-945-2500
Forster Products, Inc., 82 E. Lanark Ave., Lanark, IL 61046/815-493-6360
Forster, Larry L., P.O. Box 212, 220 First St. NE, Gwinner, ND 58040/701-678-2475
Fort Knox Security Products, 1051 N. Industrial Park Rd., Orem, UT 84057/801-224-7233
Forthofer's Gunsmithing, Pete, 711 Spokane Ave., Whitefish, MT 59937/406-862-2674
Fortress Publications, Inc., P.O. Box 9241, Stoney Creek, Ont. L8G 3X9, Canada/416-662-3505
Forty-Five Ranch Enterprises, 119 S. Main St., Miami, OK 74354/918-542-9307
Forty-Niner Trading Co., P.O. Box 792, Manteca, CA 95336/209-823-7263
Fountain Products, 492 Prospect Ave., West Springfield, MA 01089/413-781-4651
Fowler Bullets, 4144 S. New Hope Rd., Gastonia, NC 28054/704-824-0026
Francis Tool Co., P.O. Box 7861, Eugene, OR 97401/503-345-7457
Francolini, Leonard, 56 Morgan Rd., Canton, CT 06019/203-693-2529
Francotte, Auguste & Cie, S.A., rue du Trois Juin 109, 4400 Herstal-Liege, Belgium/41-48.13.18
Frank, Henry, P.O. Box 984, Whitefish, MT 59937/406-862-2681
Frank Custom Guns, Ron, 7131 Richland Rd., Ft. Worth, TX 76118/817-284-4426
Frankonia Jagd, Hofmann & Co., Postfach 6780, D-8700 Wurzburg 1, West Germany
Frazier Brothers Sporting Goods, 1118 N. Main St., Franklin, IN 46131/317-736-4000
Fredrick Gun Shop, 10 Elson Drive, Riverside, RI 02915/401-433-2805
Freedom Arms, Inc., P.O. Box 1776, Freedom, WY 83120/307-883-2468
Freeland's Scope Stands, Inc., 3737 14th Ave., Rock Island, IL 61201/309-788-7449
Freshour Mfg., 1914-15th Ave. North, Texas City, TX 77590/713-945-7726
Frielich Police Equipment, 396 Broome St., New York, NY 10013/212-254-3045
Frielich, R.S., 211 East 21st St., New York, NY 10010/212-777-4477
Frigon Guns, 627 W. Crawford, Clay Center, KS 67432/913-632-5607
Frontier, 2910 San Bernardino, Laredo, TX 78040/512-723-5409
Frontier Arms Co., 2760 Tucson Hwy., Nogales, AZ 85621/602-281-0322
Frontier Cartridge Division-Hornady Mfg. Co., P.O. Box 1848, Grand Island, NE 68801/308-382-1390
Fullmer, Geo. M., 2499 Mavis St., Oakland, CA 94601/415-533-4193
Fulmer Antique Firearms, Chet, P.O. Box 792, (Rt. 2, Buffalo Lake), Detroit Lakes, MN 56502/218-847-7712
Furr Arms, Karl J. Furr, 91 N. 970 W., Orem, UT 84057/801-226-3877

G

Galati International, P.O. Box 326, Catawissa, MO 63015/314-257-4837
Galaxy Imports, Ltd., Inc., P.O. Box 3361, Victoria, TX 77903/512-573-4867
GALCO International, Ltd., 2019 West Quail Ave., Phoenix, AZ 85027/602-233-0956
Gamba, Renato, S.p.A., P.O. Box 48, Via Artigiani n.89, I-25063 Gardone V.T. (Brescia), Italy
Game Haven Gunstocks, 13750 Shire Rd., Wolverine, MI 49799/616-525-8257
Game-Winner, Inc., 2625 Cumberland Parkway, Suite 220, Atlanta, GA 30339/404-434-9210
Gammog, Gregory B.Gally, 16009 Kenny Rd., Laurel, MD 20707/301-725-3838
Gander Mountain, Inc., P.O. Box 128, Hwy. "W," Wilmot, WI 53192/414-862-2331, Ext. 6425
Garbi, Armas Urki, #12-14, 20.600 Eibar (Guipuzcoa) Spain/43-11.38.73
Garcia National Gun Traders, Inc., 225 SW 22nd Ave., Miami, FL 33135/305-642-2355
Garrett Accur-Lt. D.F.S.Co., P.O. Box 8675, Ft. Collins, CO 80524/303-224-3067
Gator Guns & Repair, 6255 Spur Hwy., Kenai, AK 99611/907-283-7947
Genecco Gun Works, K., 10512 Lower Sacramento Rd., Stockton, CA 95210/209-951-0706
Gentry Custom Gunmaker, David, 314 N. Hoffman, Belgrade, MT 59714/406-388-4867
Gerber Legendary Blades, 14200 SW 72nd Ave., Portland, OR 97223/503-639-6161
Getz Barrel Co., P.O. Box 88, Beavertown, PA 17813/717-658-7263
Gilbert Equipment Co., Inc., 960 Downtowner Rd., Mobile, AL 36609/205-344-3322
Gillman, Edwin, 33 Valley View Dr., Hanover, PA 17331/717-632-1662
Gilman-Mayfield, 1552 N. 1st, Fresno, CA 93703/209-237-2500
Giron, Robert E., 1328 Pocono St., Pittsburg, PA 15218/412-731-6041
Glacier Glove, 4890 Aircenter Circle #206, Reno, NV 89502/702-825-8225
Glaser Safety Slug, Inc., P.O. Box 8223, Foster City, CA 94404/415-345-7677
Glass, Herb, P.O. Box 25, Bullville, NY 10915/914-361-3021
Glimm, Jerome C., 19 S. Maryland, Conrad, MT 59425/406-278-3574
Glock, Inc., 6000 Highlands Parkway, Smyrna, GA 30082/404-432-1202
GML Products, Inc., 1634-A Montgomery Hwy., Suite 196, Birmingham, AL 35216/205-979-4867
G96 Designtech, Inc., 100 Sixth Ave., Paterson, NJ 07524
Goens, Dale W., P.O. Box 224, Cedar Crest, NM 87008/505-281-5419
Goergen, James, Rt. 2, P.O. Box 182BB, Austin, MN 55912/507-433-9280
GOEX, Inc., 1002 Springbrook Ave., Moosic, PA 18507/717-457-6724
Golden Powder International Sales, Inc., 8300 Douglas Ave., Suite 729, Dallas, TX 75225/214-373-3350
Göncz Armament, Inc., 11225 Magnolia Blvd. Suite 278, North Hollywood, CA 91601/818-503-4810
Gonic Arms, Inc., 134 Flagg Rd., Gonic, NH 03867/603-332-8456
Gonzalez, Ramon B., P.O. Box 370, Monticello, NY 12701/914-794-4515

Goode, A.R., 4125 NE 28th Terr., Ocala, FL 32670/904-622-9575
Goodling's Gunsmithing, R.D. #1, P.O. Box 1007, Spring Grove, PA 17632/717-225-3350
Goodwin, Fred, Goodwin's Gun Shop, Silver Ridge, Sherman Mills, ME 04776/207-365-4451
Gordie's Gun Shop, Gordon C. Mulholland, 1401 Fulton St., Streator, IL 61364/815-672-7202
Goudy, Gary, 263 Hedge Rd., Menlo Park, CA 94025/415-322-1338
Gould & Goodrich Leather, Inc., 709 E. McNeil St., P.O. Box 1479, Lillington, NC 27546/919-893-2071
Gournet, Geoffroy G., 820 Paxinosa Ave., Easton, PA 18042/215-559-0710
Grace, Charles E., 10144 Elk Lake Rd., Williamsburg, MI 49690/616-264-9483
Grace Metal Products, Inc., 115 Ames St., P.O. Box 67, Elk Rapids, MI 49629/616-264-8133
"Gramps" Antique Cartridges, Ellwood Epps, P.O. Box 341, Washago, Ont. L0K 2B0 Canada/705-689-5348
Granger, Georges, 66 cours Fauriel, 42100 Saint Etienne, France/77-25.14.73
Grant, Howard V., Hiawatha 153, Woodruff, WI 54568/715-356-7146
Graybill, Gene, 1035 Ironville Pike, Columbia, PA 17512/717-684-6220
Great Lakes Airguns, 6175 S. Park Ave., Hamburg, NY 14075/716-648-6666
Green, Arthur S., 485 S. Robertson Blvd., Suite 5, Beverly Hills, CA 90211/213-274-1283
Green Bay Bullets, P.O. Box 10446, 1486 Servais St., Green Bay, WI 54307-54304/414-497-2949
Greene's Machine Carving, 17200 W. 57th Ave., Golden, CO 80403/303-279-2383
Green Head Corp., RR 1 P.O. Box 33, Lacon, IL 61540/309-246-2155
Green, Roger M., P.O. Box 984, 435 East Birch, Glenrock, WY 82637/307-436-9804
Greenwald, Leon E. "Bud", 2553 S. Quitman St., Denver, CO 80219/303-935-3850
Greg Gunsmithing Repair, 3732 26th Ave. North, Robbinsdale, MN 55422/612-529-8103
Gremmel Enterprises, 271 Sterling Dr., Eugene, OR 97404/503-688-3319
Grendel, Inc., P.O. Box 908, Rockledge, FL 32955/305-636-1211
Griffin & Howe, 36 W. 44th St., Suite 1011, New York, NY 10036/212-921-0980
Griffin & Howe, Inc., 33 Claremont Rd., Bernardsville, NJ 07924/201-766-2287
Griffin's Guns & Antiques, RR 4, Peterboro, Ont., Canada K9J 6X5/705-745-7022
Griggs Products, P.O. Box 789, 270 S. Main St., Suite 103, Bountiful, UT 84010/801-295-9696
Grizzly Bullets, 2137 Hwy. 200, Trout Creek, MT 59874/406-847-2627
GRS Corp., (Glendo), P.O. Box 748, 900 Overlander St., Emporia, KS 66801/316-343-1084
GSI, Inc., 108 Morrow Ave., P.O. Box 129, Trussville, AL 35173/205-655-8299
GTS Enterprises, Inc. (Dynaray Marketing Div.), 50 W. Hillcrest Dr., Suite 215, Thousand Oaks, CA 91360/805-373-0921
Gun City, 212 West Main Ave., Bismarck, ND 58501/701-223-2304
Gun Club Sportswear, P.O. Box 477, Des Moines, IA 50302
Guncraft Books, Div. of Guncraft Sports, Inc., 125 E. Tyrone Rd., Oak Ridge, TN 378301/615-483-4024
Guncraft, Inc., 117 W. Pipeline, Hurst, TX 76053/817-282-1464
Guncraft Sports, Inc., 125 E. Tyrone Rd., Oak Ridge, TN 37830/615-483-4024
Gun Doctor, The, 435 East Maple, Roselle, IL 60172/708-894-0668
Gunfitters, The, P.O. Box 29005, Brooklyn Center, MN 55429/612-560-3008
Gun-Ho Sports Cases, 110 E. 10th St., St. Paul, MN 55101/612-224-9491
Gun Hunter Books, Div. of Gun Hunter Trading Co., 5075 Heisig St., Beaumont, TX 77705/409-835-3006
Gunline Tools, 2970 Saturn St., Brea, CA 92621/714-528-5252
Gunnerman Books, P.O. Box 4292, Auburn Hills, MI 48057/313-879-2779
Gun Parts Corp., P.O. Box 2, West Hurley, NY 12491/914-679-2417
Gun Room Press, The, 127 Raritan Ave., Highland Park, NJ 08904/201-545-4344
Guns, 81 E. Streetsboro St., Hudson, OH 44236/216-650-4563
Gunsite Gunsmithy, P.O. Box 451, Paulden, AZ 86334/602-636-4104
Gun South, Inc. (See GSI, Inc.)
Gun-Tec, P.O. Box 8125, W. Palm Beach, FL 33407 (SASE for reply)
Gun Works, The, 236 Main St., Springfield, OR 97477/503-741-4118
Gurney Engraving Method, #513-620 View St., Victoria, B.C. V8W 1J6 Canada/604-383-5243
Gusdorf Corp., 11440 Lackland Rd., St. Louis, MO 63146/314-567-5249
Gutmann Cutlery Co., Inc., 120 S. Columbus Ave., Mt. Vernon, NY 10553/914-699-4044
Gwinnell, Bryson J., P.O. Box 998, Southwick, MA 01077
Hagn Rifles & Actions, Martin Hagn, P.O. Box 444, Carnbrook, B.C. VIC 4H9, Canada/604-489-4861

H

Half Moon Rifle Shop, 490 Halfmoon Rd., Columbia Falls, MT 59912/406-892-4409
Hall Manufacturing, 1801 Yellow Leaf Rd., Clanton, AL 35045/205-755-4094
Hall Plastics, Inc., John, P.O. Box 1526, Alvin, TX 77512/713-489-9709
Hall's Shooting Products, Inc., Joe, 443 Wells Rd., Doylestown, PA 18901/215-345-6354
Hallberg, Fritz, 833 SW 30th, P.O. Box 322, Ontario, OR 97914/503-889-7052
Hallowell & Co., 340 West Putnam Ave., Greenwich, CT 06830/203-869-2190
Hamilton, Keith, P.O. Box 871, Gridley, CA 95948/916-846-2316
Hammans, Charles E., P.O. Box 788, 2022 McCracken, Stuttgart, AR 72106/501-673-1388
Hammond, Guy, 619 S. Pandora, Gilbert, AZ 85234/602-892-3437
Hand Engravers Supply Co., 601 Springfield Dr., Albany, GA 31707/912-432-9683
Handgun Press, P.O. Box 406, Glenview, IL 60025/708-724-8816
Hanned Precision, P.O. Box 2888, Sacramento, CA 95812
Hansen Cartridge Co., 244 Old Post Rd., Southport, CT 06490/203-259-6222
Hanson's Gun Center, Dick Hanson, 521 S. Circle Dr., Colorado Springs, CO 80910/719-634-4220
Hanusin, John, 3306 Commercial, Northbrook, IL 60062/708-564-2706
Hardin Specialty Distr., P.O. Box 338, Radcliff, KY 40160/502-351-6649
Harkrader's Cust. Gun Shop, 825 Radford St., Christiansburg, VA 24073/703-382-8809
Harper's Custom Stocks, 928 Lombrano St., San Antonio, TX 78207/512-732-5780
Harper, William E., The Great 870 Co., P.O. Box 6309, El Monte, CA 91734/213-579-3077
Harrington Cutlery, Inc., Russell, Subs. of Hyde Mfg. Co., 44 River St., Southbridge, MA 01550/617-765-0201
Harris Engineering, Inc., Barlow, KY 42024/502-334-3633
Harris Hand Engraving, Paul A., 10630 Janet Lee, San Antonio, TX 78230/512-391-5121
Harrison Bullet Works, 6437 E. Hobart, Mesa, AZ 85205/602-985-7844
Hart Rifle Barrels, Inc., RD 2, Lafayette, NY 13084/315-677-9841

Hart & Son, Inc., Robert W., 401 Montgomery St., Nescopeck, PA 18635/717-752-3655
Hartmann & Weiss GmbH, Rahistedter Bahnhofstr. 47, 2000 Hamburg 73, W. Germany/040-677.55.85
Harwood, Jack O., 1191 S. Pendlebury Lane, Blackfoot, ID 83221/208-785-5368
Hastings, P.O. Box 224, Clay Center, KS 67432/913-632-3169
Hatfield International, Inc.,224 N. 4th St., St. Joseph, MO 64484/816-279-8688
Haydel's Game Calls, Inc., 5018 Hazel Jones Rd., Bossier City, LA 71111/318-746-3586
H&B Forge Co., Rt. 2 Geisinger Rd., Shiloh, OH 44878/419-895-1856
Hebard Guns, Gil, 125-129 Public Square, P.O. Box 1, Knoxville, IL 61448
Hecht, Hubert J., Waffen-Hecht, P.O. Box 2635, Fair Oaks, CA 95628/916-966-1020
Heckler & Koch, Inc., 21480 Pacific Blvd., Sterling, VA 22170/703-450-1900
Heilmann, Stephen, P.O. Box 657, Grass Valley, CA 95945/916-272-8758
Heinie, Richard, 821 E. Adams, Havana, IL 62644/309-543-4535
Heller & Levin Associates, Inc., 88 Marlborough Court, Rockville Center, NY 11570/516-764-9349
Henckels Zwillingswerk, Inc., J.A., 9 Skyline Dr., Hawthorne, NY 10532/914-592-7370
Hendricks, Frank E., Master Engravers, Inc., Star Rt. 1A, P.O. Box 334, Dripping Springs, TX 78620/512-858-7828
Henigson & Associates, Steve, 2049 Kerwood Ave., Los Angeles, CA 90025/213-305-8288
Henriksen, Iver, 1211 S. 2nd St. W, Missoula, MT 59801
Henriksen Tool Co., Inc., 8515 Wagner Creek Rd., Talent, OR 97540/503-535-2309
Hensley, Darwin, P.O. Box 179, Brightwood, OR 97011/503-622-5411
Hensley & Gibbs, P.O. Box 10, Murphy, OR 97533/503-862-2341
Heppler, Keith M., 540 Banyan Circle, Walnut Creek, CA 94598/415-934-3509
Heppler's Machining, 2238 Calle Del Mundo, Santa Clara, CA 95054/408-748-9166
Hercules, Inc., Hercules Plaza, Wilmington, DE 19894/302-594-5000
Hermann Leather Co., H.J., Rt. 1, P.O. Box 525, Skiatook, OK 74070/918-396-1226
Herrett's Stocks, Inc., P.O. Box 741, Twin Falls, ID 83303/208-733-1498
Heydenberk, Warren R.O., 1059 W. Sawmill Rd., Quakertown, PA 18951/215-538-2682
Heym, Friedrich Wilh. (See Heckler & Koch, Inc.)
Hidalgo, Tony, 12701 SW 9th Pl., Davie, FL 33325/305-476-7645
High Bridge Arms, Inc., 3185 Mission St., San Francisco, CA 94110/415-282-8358
High North Products, P.O. Box 2, Antigo, WI 54409/715-623-5117
High-Tech Speciality Lubricants, 11 Finley Rd., Brampton, ON L6T 1B1, Canada/416-455-4050
Hill Speed Leather, Ernie, 4507 N. 195th Ave., Litchfield Park, AZ 85340/602-853-9222
Hillmer Custom Gunstocks, Paul D., 7251 Hudson Heights, Hudson, IA 50643/319-988-3941
Hindman, Ace, 1880 1/2 Upper Turtle Creek Rd., Kerrville, TX 78028/512-257-4290
Hinman Outfitters, Bob, 1217 W. Glen, Peoria, IL 61614/309-691-8132
Hiptmayer, Heidemarie, RR 112, #750, P.O. Box 136, Eastman, Que. J0E 1PO, Canada/514-297-2492
Hiptmayer, Klaus, P.O. Box 136, RR 112 #750, Eastman, Que. J0E 1P0, Canada/514-297-2492
Hirtenberger Patronen-, Zundhutchen- & Metallwarenfabrik, A.G., Leobersdorfer Str. 33, A2552 Hirtenberg, Austria
H.K.S. Products, 7841 Foundation Dr., Florence, KY 41042/606-342-7841
Hoag, James W., 8523 Canoga Ave., Suite C, Canoga Park, CA 91304/818-998-1510
Hobaugh, Wm. H., The Rifle Shop, P.O. Box M, Philipsburg, MT 59858/406-859-3515
Hobbie Gunsmithing, Duane A., 2412 Pattie Ave., Wichita, KS 67216/316-264-8266
Hodgdon Powder Co., Inc., 6231 Robinson, Shawnee Mission, KS 66202/913-362-9455
Hodgson, Richard, 9081 Tahoe Lane, Boulder, CO 80301
Hoenig & Rodman, 6521 Morton Dr., Boise, ID 83705/208-375-1116
Hofer, Peter, F. Lang-Str. 13, A9170 Ferlach, Austria/0-42-27-3683
Hogue Grips, P.O. Box 2038, Atascadero, CA 93423/805-466-6266
Holden Co., J.B., P.O. Box 320, Plymouth, MI 48170/313-455-4850
Holland, Dick, 422 NE 6th St., Newport, OR 97365/503-265-7556
Hollis Gun Shop, 917 Rex St., Carlsbad, NM 88220/505-835-3782
Hollywood Loading Tools (See M&M Engineering)
Holmes Firearms Corp., Bill Holmes, 1100 E. Township, Fayetteville, AR 72703
Holster Outpost, 649 Herbert St., El Cajon, CA 92020/619-588-1222
Hopkins & Allen Arms, P.O. Box 217, Hawthorne, NJ 07507
Hoppe's Div., Penguin Industries, Inc., Airport Industrial Mall, Coatesville, PA 19320/251-384-6000
Hornady Mfg. Co., P.O. Drawer 1848, Grand Island, NE 68802/308-382-1390
Horsehoe Leather Prods. (See Arratoonian, Andy)
Horst, Alan K., 3221 2nd Ave., N., Great Falls, MT 59401/406-545-1831
Horton Dist. Co. Inc., Lew, 15 Walkup Drive, Westboro, MA 01581/508-366-7400
House of Muskets, Inc., The, P.O. Box 4640, Pagosa Springs, CO 81157/303-731-2295 (catalog $3)
Hoyt Holster Co., Inc., P.O. Box 69, Coupeville, WA 98239/206-678-6640
H-S Precision, Inc., 112 N. Summit Ave., Prescott, AZ 86301/602-445-0607
Huebner, Corey O., 3604 S. 3rd W., Missoula, MT 59801/406-721-9647
Huey Gun Cases, Marvin, P.O. Box 22456, Kansas City, MO 64113/816-444-1637
Hugger Hooks Co., 3900 Easley Way, Golden, CO 80403/303-279-0600
Hughes, Steven Dodd, P.O. Box 11455, Eugene, OR 97440/503-485-8869 (catalog $3)
Hulme (See Marshall Enterprises)
Hume, Don, P.O. Box 351, Miami, OK 74355/918-542-6604
Hunkeler, A., Buckskin Machine Works, 3235 S. 358th St., Auburn, WA 98001/206-927-5412
Hunter Co., Inc., 3300 W. 71st Ave., Westminster, CO 80030/303-427-4626
Hunterjohn, P.O. Box 477, St. Louis, MO 63166/314-531-7250
Hunter's Specialties, Inc., 5285 Rockwell Dr. NE, Cedar Rapids, IA 52402/319-395-0321
Hunters Specialty, Inc., 130 Orchard Dr., Pittsburgh, PA 15235/412-795-8885
Huntington Die Specialties, 601 Oro Dam Blvd., Oroville, CA 95965/916-534-1210
Hutton Rifle Ranch, P.O. Box 45236, Boise, ID 83711/208-345-8781
Hydrosorbent Products, P.O. Box 437, Ashley Falls, MA 01222/413-229-2967
Hyper-Single, Inc., 520 E. Beaver, Jenks, OK 74037/918-299-2391

I

IAI (Irwindale Arms, Inc.), 6226 Santos Diaz St., Irwindale, CA 91702/818-334-1200
ICI-America, P.O. Box 751, Wilmington, DE 19897/302-575-3000
Idaho Ammunition Service, 2816 Mayfair Dr., Lewiston, ID 83501/208-743-0270
Imatronic, Inc., 1275 Paramount Pkwy., P.O. Box 520, Batavia, IL 60510/708-406-1920
IMR Powder Co., Rt. 5 P.O. Box 247E, Plattsburgh, NY 12901/518-561-9530

I.N.C., Inc., P.O. Box 12767, Wichita, KS 67277/316-721-9570
Incor, Inc., P.O. Box 132, Addison, TX 75001/214-931-3500
Indian Ridge Traders (See Koval Knives/IRT)
Ingle, Ralph W., Master Engraver, #4 Missing Link, Rossville, GA 30741/404-866-5589 (color brochure $5)
Innovision Enterprises, 728 Skinner Dr., Kalamazoo, MI 49001/616-382-1681
Interarmco (See Interarms/Walther)
Interarms, 10 Prince St., Alexandria, VA 22313/703-548-1400
Intermountain Arms, 105 E. Idaho Ave., Meridian, ID 83649/208-888-4911
Intl. Photographic Assoc., Inc., 4500 E. Speedway, Suite 90, Tucson, AZ 85712/602-326-2941
Intratec, 12405 SW 130th St., Miami, FL 33186/305-232-1821
Iron Sight Gunworks, Inc., 458 Corte Blanco, Upland, CA 91786
Irwin, Campbell H., Hartland Blvd. (Rt. 20), P.O. Box 152, East Hartland, CT 06027/203-653-3901
Irwindale Arms, Inc. (See IAI)
Ithaca Aquisition Corp./Ithaca Gun Co., 891 Route 34B, King Ferry, NY 13081/315-364-7171

J

J.A. Blades, Inc. (See Christopher Firearms Co., Inc., E.)
Jackalope Gun Shop, 1048 S. 5th St., Douglas, WY 82633/307-358-3441
Jaeger, Inc., Paul, P.O. Box 449, 1 Madison Ave., Grand Junction, TN 38039/901-764-6909
Jamison, R.L., Jr., Route 4, P.O. Box 200, Moses Lake, WA 98837/509-762-2659
Jantz Supply, Ken, 222 E. Main, Davis, OK 73030/405-369-2316
Jaro Manuf., P.O. Box 6125, 206 E. Shaw, Pasadena, TX 77506/713-472-0417
Jarrett Rifles, Inc., 383 Brown Rd., Jackson, SC 29831/803-471-3616
Jason Empire, Inc., 9200 Cody, P.O. Box 14930, Overland Park, KS 66214/913-888-0220
Javelina Products, P.O. Box 337, San Bernardino, CA 92402/714-882-5847
J-B Bore Cleaner, 299 Poplar St., Hamburg, PA 19526/215-562-2103
J/B Adventures & Safaris, Inc., P.O. Box 3397, Englewood, CO 80155/303-771-0977
Jennings Firearms, Inc., 3680 Research Way #1, Carson City, NV 89706/702-882-4007
Jensen's Custom Ammunition, 1146 E. Pima, Tucson, AZ 85712/602-325-3346
Jett & Co., Inc., RR #3 P.O. Box 167-B, Litchfield, IL 62056/217-324-3779
JGS Precision Tool Mfg., 1141 S. Sumner Rd., Coos Bay, OR 97420/503-267-4331
Jim's Gun Shop, James R. Spradlin, 113 Arthur, Pueblo, CO 80004/719-543-9462
John's Custom Leather, 525 S. Liberty St., Blairsville, PA 15717/412-459-6802
Johns, Bill, 1412 Lisa Rae, Round Rock, TX 78664/512-255-8246
Johnson Wood Products, I.D. Johnson & Sons, Rt. #1, Strawberry Point, IA 52076/319-933-4930
Johnson, Iver (See AMAC)
Johnson, Neal G., Gunsmithing, Inc., 111 Marvin Dr., Hampton, VA 23666/804-838-8091
Johnson, Peter S., c/o Orvis Co., 10 River Rd., Manchester, VT 05254/802-362-3622, Ext. 283
Johnston Brothers, 1889 Rte 9, Unit 22, Toms River, NJ 08756/201-240-6873
Jonas Bros., Inc., 1037 Broadway, Denver, CO 80203/303-534-7400 (catalog $2)
Jones, J.D., 721 Woodvue Lane, Wintersville, OH 43952/614-264-0176
Jones, Neil A. (See Custom Products)
Jones Munitions Systems, Paul (See Fitz Pistol Grip Co.)
Juenke, Vern, 25 Bitterbush Rd., Reno, NV 89523/702-345-0225
Jumbo Sports Prods., P.O. Box 280, Airport Rd., Frederick, MD 21701
Jungkind, Reeves C., 5805 N. Lamar Blvd., Austin, TX 78752/512-441-2000, Ext. 3325
Jurras, L.E., P.O. Box 680, Washington, IN 47501/812-254-7698
Just Brass, Inc., 121 Henry St., P.O. Box 112, Freeport, NY 11520/516-378-8588

K

KA-BAR Cutlery, Div. of American Consumer Prods., Inc., 31100 Solon Rd., Solon, OH 44139/216-248-7000
KA-BAR Knives, Collectors Division, 434 N. 9th St., Olean, NY 14760/716-372-5611
Kalispel Metal Prods. (KMP), P.O. Box 267, Cusick, WA 99119/509-445-1121
Kamyk, Steven, 9 Grandview Dr., Westfield, MA 01085/413-568-0457
Kane Products, Inc., 5572 Brecksville Rd., Cleveland, OH 44131/216-524-9962
Kartak Gun Works, David Kartak, 7525 S. Coast Hwy., South Beach, OR 97366/503-867-4951
Kasenit Co., Inc., P.O. Box 726, 3 King St., Mahwah, NJ 07430/201-529-3663
Kayusoft Intl., Star Route, Spray, OR 97874/503-462-3934
K.B.I., Inc., P.O. Box 6346, Harrisburg, PA 17112/717-540-8518
KDF, Inc., 2485 Hwy. 46 N., Seguin, TX 78155/512-379-8141
Keeler, R.H., KTW, Inc., 817 "N" St., Port Angeles, WA 98362/206-457-4702
Kehr, Roger, 7810 B Samurai Dr. SE, Olympia, WA 98503/206-456-0831
Kelley's, Harold Kelley, P.O. Box 125, Woburn, MA 01801/617-935-3389
Kellog's Professional Prods., Inc., 325 Pearl St., Sandusky, OH 44870/419-625-6551
Kelly, Lance, 1723 Willow Oak Dr., Edgewater, FL 32132/904-423-4933
Ken's Gun Specialties, Rt. 1 P.O. Box 147, Lakeview, AR 72642/501-431-5606
Ken's Rifle Blanks, Ken McCullough, Rt. 2 P.O. Box 85B, Weston, OR 97886/503-566-3879
Kenko Intl., Inc., 8141 West I-70 Frontage Rd. North, Arvada, CO 80002/303-425-1200
KenPatable Ent., Inc., P.O. Box 19422, Louisville, KY 40219/502-239-5447
Keowee Game Calls, 608 Hwy. 25 North, Travelers Rest, SC 29690/803-834-7204
Kershaw Knives/Kai Cutlery USA Ltd., Stafford Bus. Pk., 25300 SW Parkway, Wilsonville, OR 97070/503-636-0111
Kesselring Gun Shop, 400 Hwy. 99 North, Burlington, WA 98233/206-724-3113
Kilham & Co., Benjamin Kilham, Main St., P.O. Box 37, Lyme, NH 03768/603-795-4112
Kimber of Oregon, Inc., 9039 SE Jannsen Rd., Clackamas, OR 97015/503-656-6016
Kimel Industries, P.O. Box 335, Matthews, NC 28105/704-821-7663
King & Co., Edw. R. King, P.O. Box 1242 3800 Old Monroe Rd., Bloomington, IL 61701
King's Gun Works, 1837 W. Glenoaks Blvd., Glendale, CA 91201/818-956-6010
Kingyon, Paul L., 607 N. 5th St., Burlington, IA 52601/319-752-4465
Kirkpatrick Leather Co., P.O. Box 3150, Laredo, TX 78044/512-723-6631
Kiss Sights, 355 N. Lantana Ave., Suite 505, Camarillo, CA 93010/805-492-4007
K&K Ammo Wrist Band, R.D. #1, P.O. Box 448-CA18, Lewistown, PA 17044/717-242-2329
Kleen-Bore, Inc., 20 Ladd Ave., Northhampton, MA 01060/413-586-7240
Klein, Don, 433 Murray Park Dr., Ripon, WI 54971/414-748-2931
Kleinendorst, K.W., RR #1, P.O. Box 1500, Hop Bottom, PA 18824/717-289-4687

Klingler, Kenneth J., P.O. Box 141, Thistle Hill, Cabot, VT 05647/802-426-3811
KLP Mfg., 215 Charles Dr., Holland, MI 49424/616-396-2575
Knight & Hale Game Calls, P.O. Box 468, Cadiz, KY 42211/502-522-3651
Knippel, Richard, 825 Stoddard Ave., Modesto, CA 95350/209-529-6205
Knock on Wood Antiques, 355 Post Rd., P.O. Box 1710, Darien, CT 06820/203-655-9031
Kodiak Custom Bullets, 8261 Henry Circle, Anchorage, AK 99507/907-349-2282
Koevenig Engraving Service, E.J., P.O. Box 55, Rabbit Gulch, Hill City, SD 57745/605-574-2239
KOGOT Octagon Barrels, John Pell, 410 College Ave., Trinidad, CO 81082/719-846-9406
Kolpin Mfg., Inc., P.O. Box 107, Fox Lake, WI 53933/414-928-3118
Kopp Publishing Co., Div. of Koppco Industries, 1301 Franklin, Lexington, MO 64067/816-259-2636
Kopp, Terry K., 1301 Franklin, Lexington, MO 64067/816-259-2636
Korzinek, J., R.D. #2, P.O. Box 73, Canton, PA 17724/717-673-8512 (catalog $3)
Koval Knives/IRT, 460 Schrock Rd. #D, Columbus, OH 43229/614-888-6486
Kowa Optimed, Inc., 20001 S. Vermont Ave., Torrance, CA 90502/213-327-1913
Krieger Barrels, Inc., N114 W18697 Clinton Dr., Germantown, WI 53022/414-255-9593
Krieghoff International, Inc., P.O. Box 549, Ottsville, PA 18942/215-847-5173
Kris Mounts, 108 Lehigh St., Johnstown, PA 15905/814-539-9751
Kros Walnut, Inc., 6304 Rabbit Ears Circle, Colorado Springs, CO 80919/719-598-4929
KTW, Inc. (See Keeler, R.H.)
Kudlas, John, 622-14th St. SE, Rochester, MN 55904/507-288-5579
Kulis Freeze-Dry Taxidermy, 725 Broadway Ave., Bedford, OH 44146
Kwik Mount Corp., P.O. Box 19422, Louisville, KY 40259/502-239-5447
Kwik-Site, 5555 Treadwell, Wayne, MI 48184/313-326-1500

L

LaBounty Precision Reboring, P.O. Box 186, 7968 Silver Lk. Rd., Maple Falls, WA 98266/206-599-2047
LaCrosse Footwear, Inc., P.O. Box 1328, La Crosse, WI 54602/608-782-3020
LaFrance Specialties, P.O. Box 178211, San Diego, CA 92117/619-293-3373
Lage Uniwad, Inc., P.O. Box 446, Victor, IA 52327/319-647-3232
Lair, Sam, 520 E. Beaver, Jenks, OK 74037/918-299-2391
Lakefield Arms Ltd., P.O. Box 129, Lakefield, Ont. K0L 2H0, Canada/705-652-6735
Lampert, Ron L., Rt. 1, P.O. Box 177, Guthrie, MN 56461/218-854-7345
Lamson & Goodnow Mfg. Co., 45 Conway St., Shelburne Falls, MA 03170/413-625-6331
Lane Bullets, Larry Clay, 1011 S. 10th St., Kansas City, KS 66105/800-444-7468
Langenberg Hat Co., P.O. Box 1860, Washington, MO 63090/314-239-1860
Lansky Sharpeners, P.O. Box 800, Buffalo, NY 14221/716-634-6333
Large Gun & Mach. Shop, Wm., James W. McKenzie, RR1, P.O. Box 188, Ironton, OH 45638/614-532-5298
Largent, Nelson H., Silver Shield's, Inc., 4464-D Chinden Blvd., Boise, ID 83714/208-323-8991
Laser Aim, Inc., 100 S. Main St., P.O. Box 581, Little Rock, AR 72203
Laser Devices, Inc., 2 Harris Ct., A4, Monterey, CA 93940/408-373-0701
Lassen Community College, P.O. Box 3000, Hiway 139, Susanville, CA 96130/916-257-6181
Laughridge, William R., Cylinder & Slide, Inc., P.O. Box 937, Fremont, NE 68025/402-721-4277
Laurona Shotguns (See Galaxy Imports Ltd., Inc.)
Lawrence Leather Co., 1435 NW Northrup, Portland, OR 97209/503-228-8244
Lawson Co., Harry, 3328 N. Richey Blvd., Tucson, AZ 85716/602-326-1117
Lawson, John G. (The Sight Shop), 1802 E. Columbia Ave., Tacoma, WA 98404/206-474-5465
Lea Mfg. Co., 237 E. Aurora St., Waterbury, CT 06720/203-753-5116
LeClear Industries, 1126 Donald Ave., P.O. Box 484, Royal Oak, MI 48068/313-588-1025
Lee Precision, Inc., 4275 Hwy. U, Hartford, WI 53027/414-673-3075
Lee's Red Ramps, P.O. Box 1249, Phelan, CA 92371/619-868-5731
Lee, Mark, Mark Lee Supplies, 9901 France Court, Lakeville, MN 55044/612-461-2114
LeFever & Sons, Inc., Frank, RD #2, P.O. Box 31, Lee Center, NY 13363/315-337-6722
Leibowitz, Leonard, 1205 Murrayhill Ave., Pittsburgh, PA 15217/412-361-5455
Leica USA, 156 Ludlow Ave., Northvale, NJ 07647/201-767-7500
Leitz (See Leica USA)
LEM Gun Specialties, P.O. Box 87031, College Park, GA 30337
Letschnig, Franz, Master-Engraver, 620 Cathcard, Rm. 422, Montreal, Queb. H3B 1M1, Canada/514-875-4989
Leupold & Stevens, Inc., P.O. Box 688, Beaverton, OR 97075/503-646-9171
Lever Arms Service Ltd., 2131 Burrard St., Vancouver, B.C., V6J 3H7 Canada/604-736-0004
Liberty Antique Gunworks, 19 Key St., P.O. Box 183, Eastport, ME 04631/207-853-2327 (catalog $5)
Liberty Trouser Co., 2301 First Ave. North, Birmingham, AL 35203/205-251-9143
Lilja Precision Rifle Barrels, Inc., 245 Compass Creek Rd., P.O. Box 372, Plains, MT 59859/406-826-3084
Lind, Al, 7821 76th Ave. SW, Tacoma, WA 98498/206-584-6361
Linder Solingen Knives, 4401 Sentry Dr., Tucker, GA 30084/404-939-6915
Lindsay, Steve, RR 2 Cedar Hills, Kearney, NE 68847/308-236-7885
Lindsley Arms Cartridge Co., Inc., P.O. Box 757, 20 Crescent St., Henniker, NH 03242/603-428-3127 (for inquiries send SASE, brochure $1)
"Little John's" Antique Arms, 1740 W. Laveta, Orange, CA 92668
Littleton, J.F., 22 Service St., Oroville, CA 95966/916-533-6084
Ljutic Industries, Inc., P.O. Box 2117, 732 N. 16th Ave., Yakima, WA 98907/509-248-0476
Llama (See Stoeger Industries)
Lock's Phila. Gun Exch., 6700 Rowland, Philadelphia, PA 19149/215-332-6225
Lodewick, Walter H., 2816 NE Halsey, Portland, OR 97232/503-284-2554
Lofland, James W., 2275 Larkin Rd., Boothwyn, PA 19061/215-485-0391
Logan, Harry M., Box 745, Honokaa, HI 96727/808-776-1644
Log Cabin Sport Shop, 8010 Lafayette Rd., Lodi, OH 44254/216-948-1082 (catalog $3)
Logan Security Products Co., P.O. Box 16206, Columbus, OH 43216/616-265-7386
Lomont Precision Bullets, Kent Lomont, 4236 West 700 South, Poneto, IN 46781/219-694-6792
London Guns Ltd., P.O. Box 3750, Santa Barbara, CA 93130/805-683-4141
Lone Pine Trading Post, Jct. Highways 61 and 248, Minnesota City, MN 55959/507-689-2922

Lone Star Gunleather, 1301 Brushy Bend Dr., Round Rock, TX 78681/512-255-1805
Long, George F., 1500 Rogue River Hwy., Ste. F, Grants Pass, OR 97527/503-476-7552
Long Island Gunsmith, Ltd., 573 Sunrise Hwy., West Babylon, NY 11704/516-321-0924
Lorcin Engineering Co., Inc., 6471 Mission Blvd., Riverside, CA 92509/714-682-7374
Lortone, Inc., 2856 NW Market St., Seattle, WA 98107/206-789-3100
Low, Paul E., Jr., RR 1, Dunlap, IL 61525/309-685-1392
LPS Chemical Prods., Holt Lloyd Corp., 4647 Hugh Howell Rd., P.O. Box 3050, Tucker, GA 30084/404-934-7800
L&S Technologies, Inc. (See Aimtech Mount Systems)
LT Industries, Inc., 31812 Bainbridge Rd., Solon, OH 44139/216-248-7550
Lucas, Edw. E., 32 Garfield Ave., East Brunswick, NJ 08816/201-251-5526
Lyman Products Corp., 147 West St., Middlefield, CT 06455/203-349-3421
Lynn's Specialty Gunsmithing (See McMurdo, Lynn)
Lynx-Line (See Williams Shootin' Iron Service)

M

Mac-1 Airgun Distributors, 13972 Van Ness Ave., Gardena, CA 90249/213-327-3582
Mac's .45 Shop, P.O. Box 2028, Seal Beach, CA 90740/213-438-5046
MacDonald, R. Champlin, P.O. Box 693, Manchester, NH 03105/603-483-8557
Mack's Sport Shop, P.O. Box 1155, Kodiak, AK 99615/907-486-4276
Madis, David, 2453 West Five Mile Pkwy., Dallas, TX 75233/214-330-7169
Magma Engineering Co., P.O. Box 161, Queen Creek, AZ 85242/602-987-9008
Mag-na-port International, Inc., 41302 Executive Dr., Mt. Clemens, MI 48045/313-469-6727
Mag-Na-Port of Canada, 1861 Burrows Ave., Winnipeg, Manitoba R2X 2V6, Canada
Magnolia Sports, Inc., 211 West Main, Magnolia, AR 71753/501-234-8117
Magnum Research, Inc., 7110 University Ave. NE, Minneapolis, MN 55432/612-574-1868
Magnus Bullet Co., Inc., P.O. Box 2225, Birmingham, AL 35201/205-785-3357
Mag-Pack, P.O. Box 846, Chesterland, OH 44026
MagSafe Ammo Co., 2725 Friendly Grove Rd. NE, Olympia, WA 98506/206-357-6383
Mahony, Phillip Bruce, 67 White Hollow Rd., Lime Rock, CT 06039/203-435-9341
Mains, Wm. H., 3111 S. Valley View Blvd., Suite B-214, Las Vegas, NV 89103/702-876-6278
Maki Industries, 26-10th St. SE, Medicine Hat, AB T1A 1P7 Canada/403-526-7997
Maki, Robert E., Hand Engravers Emporium, P.O. Box 947, Northbrook, IL 60065/708-724-8238
Makinson, Nick, RR #3, Komoka, Ont. N0L 1R0 Canada/519-471-5462
Mallardtone Game Calls, 2901 16th St., Moline, IL 61265/309-762-8089
Maloni, Russ (See Russwood Custom Pistol Grips)
M.A.M. Products, Inc., 153 B Cross Slope Court, Englishtown, NJ 07726/201-536-7268
Mandall Shooting Supplies, 3616 N. Scottsdale Rd., Scottsdale, AZ 85252/602-945-2553
Mandarino, Laura, 136 Fifth Ave. West, Kalispell, MT 59901/406-257-6208
Mandarino, Monte, 136 Fifth Ave. West, Kalispell, MT 59901/406-257-6208
Manley Shooting Supplies, Lowell, 3684 Pine St., Deckerville, MI 48427/313-376-3665
Mannlicher (See Gun South, Inc.)
Mar Knives, Inc., Al, P.O. Box 1626, 5755 SW Jean Rd., Suite 101, Lake Oswego, OR 97034/503-635-9229
Marathon Rubber Prods. Co., Inc., 510 Sherman St., Wausau, WI 54401/715-845-6255
Marble Arms Corp., 420 Industrial Park, P.O. Box 111, Gladstone, MI 49837/906-428-3710
Marek, George, 55 Arnold St., Westfield, MA 01085/413-562-5673
Marent, Rudolf, 9711 Tiltree, Houston, TX 77075/713-946-7028
Marksman Products, 5622 Engineer Dr., Huntington Beach, CA 92649/714-898-7535
Marlin Firearms Co., 100 Kenna Drive, New Haven, CT 06473
Marquart Precision Co., P.O. Box 1740, Prescott, AZ 86302/602-445-5646
Marsh, Johnny, 1007 Drummond Dr., Nashville, TN 37211/615-834-2103
Marsh, Mike, The Croft Cottage, Main St., Elton, Derbyshire DE4 2BY, England/062-988-669
Martin, Elwyn H., Martin's Gun Shop, 937 S. Sheridan Blvd., Lakewood, CO 80226/303-922-2184
Martz, John V., 8060 Lakeview Lane, Lincoln, CA 95648/916-645-2250
Marvel, Alan, 3922 Madonna Rd., Jarretsville, MD 21084/301-557-6545
Maryland Gun Works, Ltd., TEC Bldg., 10097 Tyler Pl. #8, Ijamsville, MD 21754/301-831-8456
Masker Custom Rifles, Seely, 54 Woodshire S., Getzville, NY 14068/716-689-8894
Master Lock Co., 2600 N. 32nd St., Milwaukee, WI 53245/414-444-2800
Master Products, Inc., P.O. Box 8474, Van Nuys, CA 91409/818-365-0864
Matco, Inc., 1003-2nd St., N. Manchester, IN 46962/219-982-8282
Mathews and Son, Inc., Geo. E., 10224 S. Paramount Blvd., Downey, CA 90241
Matthews Cutlery, 4401 Sentry Dr., Tucker, GA 30084/404-939-6915
Matthews, Larry, 7525 S. Coast Hwy., South Beach, OR 97366/503-867-4951
Mauser-Werke Oberndorf, P.O. Box 1349, 7238 Oberndorf/Neckar, West Germany
Maverick Arms, Inc., Idustrial Blvd., P.O. Box 586, Eagle Pass, TX 78853/512-773-9007
Mayville Engineering Co., 715 South St., Mayville, WI 53050/414-387-4500
Mazur Restoration, Pete, 13083 Drummer Way, Grass Valley, CA 95949/916-268-2412
McCament, Jay, 1730-134th St. Ct. S., Tacoma, WA 98444/206-531-8832
McCann's Muzzle-Gun Works, 200 Federal City Rd., Pennington, NJ 08534/609-737-1707
McConnellstown Reloading & Cast Bullets, Inc., R.D. 3, P.O. Box 40, Huntingdon, PA 16652/814-627-5402
McCormick's Custom Gun Bluing, 609 NE 10th Ave., Vancouver, WA 98664/206-256-0579
McDonald, Dennis, 8359 Brady St., Peosta, IA 52068/319-556-7940
McFarland, Stan, 2221 Idella Ct., Grand Junction, CO 81505/303-243-4704
McGowen Rifle Barrels, Rt. 3., St. Anne, IL 60964/815-937-9816
McGuire, Bill, 1600 N. Eastmont Ave., East Wenatchee, WA 98802/509-884-6021
McKee, Arthur, 121 Eatons Neck Rd., Northport, NY 11768/516-757-8850
McKee Publications, 121 Eatons Neck Rd., Northport, NY 11768/516-575-5334
McKenzie, Lynton S.M., 6940 N. Alvernon Way, Tucson, AZ 85718/602-299-5090
McKillen & Heyer, Inc., 37603 Arlington Dr., P.O. Box 627, Willoughby, OH 44094/216-942-2491
McMillan Rifle Barrels, U.S. International, P.O. Box 3427, Bryan, TX 77805/409-846-3990
McMurdo, Lynn, P.O. Box 404, Afton, WY 83110/307-886-5535
McMurray & Son (See Mac-1 Airgun Distributors)
MCS, Inc. (See Mo's Competitor Supplies)
M&D Munitions Ltd., 127 Verdi St., Farmingdale, NY 11735/516-752-1038
MDS, Inc., 1640 Central Ave., St. Petersburg, FL 33712/813-894-3512
Meadow Industries, P.O. Box 450, Marlton, NJ 08053/609-953-0922
MEC, Inc. (See Mayville Engineering Co.)

Meier Works, Steve Hines, P.O. Box 328, 2102-2nd Ave., Canyon, TX 79015/806-655-7806
Mele, Frank, Rt. 1 P.O. Box 349, Springfork Rd., Granville, TN 38564/615-653-4414
Meprolight, 2821 Greenville Rd., LaGrange, GA 30240/404-884-7967
Mercer, R. M., 216 S. Whitewater Ave., Jefferson, WI 53549/414-674-3839
Merit Corp., Dept. GD, P.O. Box 9044, Schenectady, NY 12309/518-346-1420
Merkuria, FTC, Argentinska 38, 17005 Prague 7, Czechoslovakia
Merrill Pistol (See RPM)
Metalife Industries, P.O. Box 53, Mong Ave., Reno, PA 16343/814-436-7747
Metallic Casting & Copper Corp. (MCC), 214 E. Third St., Mt. Vernon, NY 10550/914-664-1311
Michael's Antiques, P.O. Box 591, Waldoboro, ME 04572
Michaels of Oregon Co., P.O. Box 13010, Portland, OR 97213/503-255-6890
Micro-Lube, Rt. 2, P.O. Box 201, Deming, NM 88030/505-546-9116
Micro Sight Co., 242 Harbor Blvd., Belmont, CA 94002/415-591-0769
Midway Arms, Inc., P.O. Box 1483, Columbia, MO 65205/314-445-2400
Midwest Gun Sport, 1108 Herbert Dr., Zebulon, NC 27597/919-269-5570
Military Armament Corp., P.O. Box 111, Mt. Zion Rd., Lingleville, TX 76461/817-965-3077
Miller Arms, Inc., D.E. Miller, P.O. Box 260, St. Onge, SD 57779/605-578-1790
Miller Co., David, 3131 E. Greenlee Rd., Tucson, AZ 85716/602-326-3117
Miller, S.A., Point Roberts Sports Ltd., P.O. Box 1053, 1440 Peltier Dr., Point Roberts, WA 98281/206-945-7014
Miller Single Trigger Mfg. Co., R.D. 1, P.O. Box 99, Millersburg, PA 17061/717-692-3704
Miller, Tom, c/o Huntington's Sportsman's Store, 601 Oro Dam Blvd., Oroville, CA 95965/916-534-1210
Miller Trading Co., 1103 Chestnut St., Wilmington, NC 28401
Millett Industries, 16131 Gothard St., Huntington Beach, CA 92647/714-842-5575
Milliron Custom Guns & Stocks, Earl, 1249 NE 166th Ave., Portland, OR 97230/503-252-3725
Mills, Hugh B., Jr., 3615 Canterbury Rd., New Bern, NC 28560/919-637-4631
Miniature Machine Co. (MMC), 210 E. Poplar St., Deming, NM 88030/505-546-2151
Mirador Optical Corp., 4051 Glencoe Ave., Marina Del Rey, CA 90292/213-821-5587
Mitchell Arms, Inc., 3400 W. MacArthur Blvd., Suite I, Santa Ana, CA 92704/714-957-5711
Mitch's Stock Shop, Inc., 115 12th Ave. SE, Valley City, ND 58072/701-845-5155
Mittermeier, Frank, 3577 E. Tremont Ave., New York, NY 10465/212-828-3843
MK Arms, Inc., P.O. Box 16411, Irvine, CA 92713/714-261-2767
M&M Engineering, 10642 Arminta St., Sun Valley, CA 91352/818-842-8376
MMC, Inc. (See Miniature Machine Co.)
MMP, RR 6 P.O. Box 384, Harrison, AR 72601/501-741-5019
M&N Bullet Lube, P.O. Box 495, 151 NE Jefferson St., Madras, OR 97741/503-255-3750
M.O.A. Corp., 175 Carr Dr., Brookville, OH 45309/513-833-5559
Mo's Competitor Supplies, 34 Delmar Dr., Brookfield, CT 06804/203-775-1013
Modern Gun Repair School, 2538 N. 8th St., Phoenix, AZ 85006/602-990-8346
Modern Muzzleloading, Inc., RR 1, P.O. Box 234A, Centerville, IA 52544/515-856-2633
Monell Custom Guns, Red Mill Road, RD #2, P.O. Box 96, Pine Bush, NY 12566/914-744-3021
Moneymaker Guncraft, 1420 Military Ave., Omaha, NE 68131/402-556-0226
Monogrip (See Hogue Grips)
Monte Kristo Pistol Grip Co., P.O. Box 171, Douglas City, CA 96024/916-778-3136
Montgomery Technical College, P.O. Box 787, Troy, NC 27371/919-572-3691
Moore & Co., Wm. Larkin, 31360 Via Colinas, Suite 109, Westlake Village, CA 91360/818-889-4160
Morrison Custom Rifles, J.W., 4015 W. Sharon, Phoenix, AZ 85029/602-978-3754
Moschetti, Mitch, P.O. Box 27065, Denver, CO 80227/303-936-1184
Mossberg & Sons, Inc., O.F., 7 Grasso St., N. Haven, CT 06473
Mountain Bear Rifle Works, Inc., Wm. Scott Bickett, 100-B Ruritan Rd., Sterling, VA 22170/703-430-0420
Mountain Hollow Game Calls, P.O. Box 121, Rt. 550 Military Rd., Cascade, MD 21719/301-241-4101
Mountain State Muzzleloading Supplies, Inc., P.O. Box 154-1, Rt. #2, Williamstown, WV 26187/304-375-7842
MPI Stocks, 5655 NW St. Helens Rd., Portland, OR 97210/503-226-1215
Mrock, Larry, R.F.D. 3, P.O. Box 207, Woodhill-Hooksett Rd., Bow, NH 03301/603-224-4096 (brochure $3)
MTM Molded Products Co., P.O. Box 14117, Dayton, OH 45414/513-890-7461
Mullis Guncraft, 3518 Lawyers Road East, Monroe, NC 28110/704-283-8789
Multi-Scale Charge Ltd., 2446 Cawthra Rd., Bldg. 1, Unit 10, Mississauga, Ont. L5A 3K6 Canada/416-566-1255
Munger, Robert D. (See Rusteprufe Laboratories)
Munsch Gunsmithing, Tommy, Rt. 2, P.O. Box 248, Little Falls, MN 56345/612-632-6695 (list $2; other inq. SASE)
Murphy Co., Inc., R., 13 Groton-Harvard Rd., P.O. Box 376, Ayer, MA 01432/617-772-3481
Murray State College, Gunsmithing Program, 1100 S. Murray, Tishomingo, OK 73460/405-371-2371
Museum of Historical Arms, Inc., 1038 Alton Rd., Miami Beach, FL 33139/305-672-7480 (catalog $5)
Mushroom Express Bullet Co., 3147 W. U.S. 40, Greenfield, IN 46140
Mustang Custom Pistol Grips (See Renner Co., R.J.)
Muzzle Loaders Etc., Inc., 9901 Lyndale Ave. S., Bloomington, MN 55420/612-884-1161
Muzzleload Magnum Products (See MMP)
Muzzleloaders Etc., Inc., Jim Westberg, 9901 Lyndale Ave. S., Bloomington, MN 55420/612-884-1161

N

NAI/Ballistek, 1260 Oro Grande #8, Lake Havasu City, AZ 86403
Nastoff's 45 Shop, Steve Nastoff, 1057 Laverne Ave., Youngtown, OH 44511/216-799-8870
National Survival Game, Inc., P.O. Box 1439, New London, NH 03257/603-526-4567
Navy Arms Co., 689 Bergen Blvd., Ridgefield, NJ 07657/201-945-2500
Necromancer Industries, Inc., 14 Communications Way, West Newton, PA 15089/412-872-8722
NEI, 9330 NE Halsey, Portland, OR 97220/503-255-3750
Neighbor, William (See Bill's Gun Repair)
Nelson Combat Leather, Bruce, P.O. Box 8691 CRB, Tucson, AZ 85738/602-825-9042 (catalog $3)

Nelson, Gary K., 975 Terrace Dr., Oakdale, CA 95361/209-847-4590
Nelson, Stephen E., P.O. Box 1478, Albany, OR 97321/503-745-5232
Nesci Enterprises, Inc., P.O. Box 119, Summit St., East Hampton, CT 06424/203-267-2588
Nettestad, Bruce A., RR 1, P.O. Box 140, Pelican Rapids, MN 56572/218-863-4301
Newbern Glove, 301 Jefferson St., Newbern, TN 38059/901-627-2557
New Detonics Mfg. Corp., 21438 N. 7th Ave. #F, Phoenix, AZ 85027/602-582-4867
Newell, Robert H., 55 Coyote, Los Alamos, NM 87544/505-662-7135 (brochure $2)
New England Arms Co., P.O. Box 278, Lawrence Lane, Kittery Point, ME 03905/207-439-0593
New England Custom Gun Service (See Apel, Dietrich)
New England Firearms Co., Inc., Industrial Rowe, Gardner, MA 01440/508-632-9393
New Orleans Arms Co., 5001 Treasure St., New Orleans, LA 70186/504-944-3371
New Orleans Jewelers Supply, 206 Chartres St., New Orleans, LA 70130/504-523-3839
Newman Gunshop, 119 Miller Rd., Agency, IA 52530/515-937-5775
NgraveR Co., 879 Raymond Hill Rd., Oakdale, CT 06370/203-848-8031
Nickels, Paul R., P.O. Box 71043, Las Vegas, NV 89170/702-435-5318
Nicklas, Ted, 5504 Hegel Rd., Goodrich, MI 48438/313-797-4493
Nikon, Inc., 623 Stewart Ave., Garden City, NY 11530/516-222-0200
Nitex, Inc., Ed House, P.O. Box 1706, Uvalde, TX 78801/512-278-8843
Nittler, William J., 290 More Dr., Boulder Creek, CA 95006/408-338-3376 or 408-438-7731
N&J Sales, Co., Lime Kiln Rd., Northford, CT 06472/203-484-0247
Noble Co., Jim, 1305 Columbia St., Vancouver, WA 98660/206-695-1309
Noreen, Peter H., Rt.2 P.O. Box 49, Herman, MN 56248/612-677-2682
Norinco (See Chinasports, Inc.)
NORMA (See Federal Cartridge Co.)
Norman, Jim, Custom Gunstocks, 14281 Cane Rd., Valley Center, CA 92082/619-749-6252
Normark Corp., 1710 E. 78th St., Minneapolis, MN 55423/612-869-3291
North American Arms, 1800 North 300 West, Spanish Fork, UT 84660/801-798-7401
North American Correspondence Schools, The Gun Pro School, Oak & Pawnee St., Scranton, PA 18515/717-342-7701
North American Specialties, 25422 Trabuco Rd. #105-328, El Toro, CA 92630/714-979-4867
North Consumer Prods. Div., 2664-B Saturn St., Brea, CA 92621/714-524-1665
Northeast Industrial, Inc. (See NEI)
North Fork Custom Gunsmithing, 428 Del Rio Rd., Roseburg, OR 97470/503-673-4467
Northlake Boot Co., 1810 Columbia Ave., Franklin, TN 37064/615-794-1556
North Wing Decoys Co., P.O. Box 1001, Fergus Falls, MN 56538/218-736-4378
No-Sho Mfg. Co., 10727 Glenfield Ct., Houston, TX 77096/713-723-5332
Nosler Bullets, Inc., 107 SW Columbia, Bend, OR 97702/503-382-3921
Novak, Wayne, 1206 1/2 30th St., Parkersburg, WV 26101/304-485-9295
N.S.G., Inc. (See National Survival Game, Inc.)
Nu-Line Guns, 1053 Caulks Hill Rd., Harvester, MO 63303/314-441-4500 or 441-4501
Null Holsters Ltd., Kenneth L., Hill City Station, Resaca, GA 30735
Nygord Precision Products, P.O. Box 8394, La Crescenta, CA 91214/818-352-3027

O

Oakland Custom Arms, Inc., 9191 Pine Knob Rd., Clarkston, MI 48016/313-625-1150
Oakman Turkey Calls, RD 1 P.O. Box 545E, McConnelsburg, PA 17233/717-485-4620
Obermeyer Rifled Barrels, 23122 60th St., Bristol, WI 53104/414-843-3537
October Country, P.O. Box 969, Hayden Lake, ID 83835/208-772-2068
Oehler Research, Inc., P.O. Box 9135, Austin, TX 78766/512-327-6900
Oker's Engraving, 365 Bell Rd., Bellford Mtn. Hts., P.O. Box 126, Shawnee, CO 80475/303-838-6062
Oklahoma Leather Products, Inc., 402 Newman Rd., Miami, OK 74354/918-542-6651
Old Dominion Engravers, Rt. 2 P.O. Box 74, Goode, VA 24556/703-586-5402
Old West Reproductions, R.M. Bachman, 1840 Stag Lane, Kalispell, MT 59901/406-755-6902 (catalog $3)
Old Western Scrounger, Inc., 12924 Hwy. A-12, Montague, CA 96064/916-459-5445 (write for list; $2)
Old World Oil Products, 3827 Queen Ave. N., Minneapolis, MN 55412/612-522-5037
Olson, Eric, 12721 E. 11th Ave., Spokane, WA 99216
Olson, Vic, 5002 Countryside Dr., Imperial, MO 63052/314-296-8086
Olt Co., Phil S., P.O. Box 550, Pekin, IL 61554/309-348-3633
Olympic Arms, Inc. (See Safari Arms/SGW)
Omark Industries (See Blount Sporting Equipment Division)
Omega Sales, Inc., P.O. Box 1066, Mt. Clemens, MI 48043/313-469-6727
Ontario Knife, Queen Cutlery Co., P.O. Box 500, Franklinville, NY 14737/716-676-5527
Orchard Park Enterprise, P.O. Box 563, Orchard Park, NY 14127/716-662-0356
Oregon Arms, Inc., 164 Schulz Rd., Central Point, OR 97502/503-664-5586
Oregon Trail Riflesmiths, Inc., P.O. Box 51, Mackay, ID 83251/208-588-2527
Orient-Western, P.O. Box 27573, San Francisco, CA 94127
Orion Bullets, P.O. Box 264, Franklin, ID 83237/208-646-2373
Original Mink Oil, Inc., P.O. Box 20191, 11021 NE Beach St., Portland, OR 97220/503-255-2814
Orvis Co., Inc., The, 10 River Rd., Manchester, VT 05254/802-362-3622
Ottmar, Maurice, P.O. Box 657, 113 E. Fir, Coulee City, WA 99115/509-632-5717
Outdoor Edge Cutlery Corp., 2888 Bluff St., Suite 130, Boulder, CO 80301/303-444-0937
Outdoor Sports Headquarters, Inc., 967 Watertower Lane, Dayton, OH 45449/513-865-5855
Outdoorsman's Bookstore, The, Llangorse, Brecon, County Powys LD3 7UE,(England) U.K.
Outers Laboratories, Div. of Blount, Route 2, Onalaska, WI 54650/608-781-5800
Owen, Harry (See Sport Specialties)
Ox-Yoke Originals, Inc., 34 Main St., Milo, ME 04463/207-943-2171

P

Pachmayr Ltd., 1875 S. Mountain Ave., Monrovia, CA 91016/818-357-7771
Pacific Intl. Merch. Corp., 2215 "J" St., Sacramento, CA 95816/916-446-2737
Pacific Tool Co., P.O. Box 2048, Ordnance Plant Rd., Grand Island, NE 68801/308-384-2308
P.A.C.T., Inc., P.O. Box 531525, Grand Prairie, TX 75053/214-641-0049
Pagel Gun Works, Jay A. Pagel, 1407 4th St. NW, Grand Rapids, MN 55744/218-326-3003
Paladin Press, P.O. Box 1307, Boulder, CO 80306/303-443-7250

Palcher Ammunition, Techstar Engineering, Inc., 2239 S. Huron Ave., Santa Ana, CA 92704/714-556-7384
Palmgren Steel Prods., Chicago Tool & Engineering Co., 8383 South Chicago Ave., Chicago, IL 60617/312-721-9675
Panavise Prods., Inc., 2850 E. 29th St., Long Beach, CA 90806/213-595-7621
Para-Ordnance Mfg.,Inc., 3411 McNicoll Ave., Unit #14, Scarborough, Ont. M1V 2V6, Canada/416-297-7855
Paragon Sales, Inc., P.O. Box 2022, Joliet, IL 60434/815-725-9212
Paris, Frank J., 13945 Minock Dr., Redford, MI 48239/313-255-0888
Parke-Bernet (See Sotheby's)
Parker-Case, P.O. Box 4000, Owens Way, Bradford, PA 16701/814-368-4123
Parker Reproductions, 124 River Rd., Middlesex, NJ 08846/201-469-0100
Parker-Hale, Bisleyworks, Golden Hillock Rd., Sparbrook, Birmingham B11 2PZ, England
Parker-Hale (See Precision Sports)
Parker, Mark D., 1240 Florida Ave. #7, Longmont, CO 80501/303-772-0214
Pasadena Gun Center, 206 E. Shaw, Pasadena, TX 77506/713-472-0417
P.A.S.T. Corp., 210 Park Ave., Columbia, MO 65205/314-449-7278
Paterson Gunsmithing, 438 Main St., Paterson, NJ 07502/201-345-4100
Pathfinder Sports Leather, 2920 E. Chambers St., Phoenix, AZ 85040/602-276-0016
Patriot Distribution Co., 2872 S. Wentworth Ave., Milwaukee, WI 53207/414-769-0760
Patriot Mfg. & Sales, 2163 Oak Beach Blvd., P.O. Box 2041, Sebring, FL 33871/813-655-1798
Pattern Control, 114 N. 3rd St., Garland, TX 75040/214-494-3551
Paulsen Gunstocks, Rt. 71, P.O. Box 11, Chinook, MT 59523/406-357-3403
PC Co., 5942 Secor Rd., Toledo, OH 43623/419-472-6222
Pease Accuracy, Bob, P.O. Box 787, Zipp Rd., New Braunfels, TX 78131/512-625-1342
Pedersen & Son, C.R., 2717 S. Pere Marquette, Ludington, MI 49431/616-843-2061
Pence Precision Barrels, RR #2 P.O. Box 179, S. Whitley, IN 46787/219-839-4745
Pendleton Woolen Mills, 218 SW Jefferson St., Portland, OR 97201/503-226-4801
Penguin Industries, Inc., Airport Industrial Mall, Coatesville, PA 19320/215-384-6000
Penn's Woods Products, Inc., 19 W. Pittsburgh St., Delmont, PA 15626/412-468-8311
Pennsylvania Gunsmith School, 812 Ohio River Blvd., Avalon, Pittsburgh, PA 15202/412-766-1812
Penrod Precision, 312 College Ave., P.O. Box 307, N. Manchester, IN 46962/219-981-8385
Pentax Corp., 35 Inverness Dr. E., Englewood, CO 80112/303-799-8000
Perazzi U.S.A., Inc., 1207 S. Shamrock Ave., Monrovia, CA 91016/818-303-0068
Personal Protection Systems Ltd., Aberbeen Rd., RD #5 P.O. Box 5027-A, Moscow, PA 18444/717-842-1766
Perugini Visini & Co. s.r.l., Via Camprelle, 126, 25080 Nuvolera (Bs.), Italy
Peters, E. Larry, c/o Kimber, 9039 SE Janssen Rd., Clackamas, OR 97015/503-656-6016
Petersen Publishing Co., 8490 Sunset Blvd., Los Angeles, CA 99069
Peterson Instant Targets, Inc. (See Lyman Products Corp.)
Peterson Gun Shop, A.W., 1693 Old Hwy. 441 N., Mt. Dora, FL 32757
Pettinger Arms Books, Gerald, Route 2, Russell, IA 50238/515-535-2239
Pflumm Gun Mfg. Co., 6139 Melrose Lane, Shawnee, KS 66203/913-268-3105
PFRB Company, P.O. Box 1242, Bloomington, IL 61701/309-473-3964
Phelps Mfg. Co., P.O. Box 2266, Evansville, IN 47714/812-423-2599
Phillips & Bailey, Inc., 815A Yorkshire St., Houston, TX 77022/713-699-4288
Phillips Enterprises, Inc., 3600 Sunset Ave., Ocean, NJ 07712/201-493-3191
Phoenix Arms Co. Ltd., Hy-Score Works, 40 Stonar Industrial Estate, Sandwich, Kent CT13 9LN, England/0304-61.12.21
Phyl-Mac, 609 NE 104th Ave., Vancouver, WA 98664/206-256-0579
Piedmont Community College, P.O. Box 1197, Roxboro, NC 27573/919-599-1181
Pilgrim Pewter, Inc., RD 2, P.O. Box 219, Tully, NY 13159/607-842-6431
Pilkington Gun Co., P.O. Box 1296, Muskogee, OK 74402/918-683-9418
Pilkington, Scott, P.O. Box 97, Monteagle, TN 37356/615-924-3475
Pine Technical Institute, 1100 Fourth St., Pine City, MN 55063/612-629-6764
Pioneer Guns, 5228 Montgomery Rd., Norwood, OH 45212/513-631-4871
Pioneer Marketing & Research, Inc., 216 Haddon Ave., Suite 522, Westmont, NJ 08108/609-854-2424
Piquette, Paul R., 80 Bradford Dr., Feeding Hills, MA 01030/413-786-5811
Pitzer Gun Tool Co., RR #1, P.O. Box 200, Earlham, IA 50272/515-462-3547
Plante, Eugene T., Gene's Custom Guns, 3890 Hill Ave., P.O. Box 10534, White Bear Lake, MN 55110/612-429-5105
Plaxco, J. Michael, Rt. 1, P.O. Box 203, Roland, AR 72135/501-868-9787
Plaza Cutlery, Inc., 3333 Bristol #161, South Coast Plaza, Costa Mesa, CA 92626/714-549-3932
Plum City Ballistics Range, Norman E. Johnson, Rt. 1, P.O. Box 29A, Plum City, WI 54761/715-647-2539
P&M Sales and Service, 5724 Gainsborough Pl., Oak Forest, IL 60452/708-687-7149
PMC-Eldorado Cartridge Co., P.O. Box 308, Boulder City, NV 89005/702-294-0025
PMI (See Pursuit Marketing, Inc.)
Poly Choke Div. (See Marble Arms Corp.)
Poly Technologies, Inc. (See PTK International, Inc.)
Polywad, Inc., P.O. Box 7916, Macon, GA 31209
Pomeroy, Robert, RR 1 P.O. Box 50, Morison Ave., East Corinth, ME 04427/207-285-7721
Ponsness-Warren, P.O. Box 8, Rathdrum, ID 83858/208-687-2231
Pony Express Sport Shop, Inc., 16606 Schoenborn St., Sepulveda, CA 91343/818-895-1231
Potts, Wayne E., 912 Poplar St., Denver, CO 80220/303-355-5462
Power Custom, Inc., RR 2 P.O. Box 756AB, Gravois Mills, MO 65037/314-372-5684
Power Plus Enterprises, Inc., P.O. Box 6070, Columbus, GA 31907/404-561-1717
P&P Tool Co., 125 W. Market St., Morrison, IL 61270/815-772-7618
P.P.C. Corp., 625 E. 24th St., Paterson, NJ 07514
Pranger, Ed, 1414-7th St., Anacortes, WA 98221/206-293-3488
Pre-64 Winchester Parts Co., P.O. Box 8125, West Palm Beach, FL 33407 (SASE w/ request list)
Precise Chambering Co., 2499 Mavis St., Oakland, CA 94601/415-533-4193
Precise International, 3 Chestnut St., Suffern, NY 10901/914-357-6200
Precise Metalsmithing Enterprises, James L. Wisner, 146 Curtis Hill Rd., Chehalis, WA 98532/206-748-3743
Precision Castings & Equipment, Inc., P.O. Box 135, Jasper, IN 47547/812-634-9167
Precision Imports, Inc., 5040 Space Center Dr., San Antonio, TX 78218/512-666-3033

Precision Munitions, Inc., P.O. Box 326, Jasper, IN 47547
Precision Prods. of Wash., Inc., N. 311 Walnut Rd., Spokane, WA 99206/509-928-0604
Precision Sales Intl., Inc., PSI, P.O. Box 1776, Westfield, MA 01086/413-562-5055
Precision Small Parts, Inc., 155 Carlton Rd., Charlottesville, VA 22901/804-293-6124
Precision Specialties Ltd., 131 Hendom Dr., Feeding Hills, MA 01030/413-786-3365
Precision Sport Optics, 7340 Firestone Blvd., Suite 222, Downey, CA 90241/213-937-7990
Precision Sports, P.O. Box 708, Kellogg Rd., Cortland, NY 13045/607-756-2851
Preston Pittman Game Calls, Inc., P.O. Box 568, Lucedale, MS 39465/601-947-4417
Primos Wild Game Calls, Inc., 4436 N. State St., A-7, P.O. Box 12785, Jackson, MS 39206
Professional Gunsmiths of America, 1301 Franklin, P.O. Box 224E, Lexington, MO 64067/816-259-2636
Professional Hunter Supplies, P.O. Box 608, 660 Berding St., Ferndale, CA 95536/707-786-4040
Proline Handgun Leather, Greg Kramer, 809 S. Geiger St., Tacoma, WA 98465/206-564-6652
Pro Load Ammunition, Inc., 1120 S. Varney St., Burbank, CA 91502/818-842-6978
Pro-Mark (Div. of Wells Lamont), 6640 W. Touhy, Chicago, IL 60648/312-647-8200
Prometheus/Titan Black (See Fisher Enterprises)
Pro-Port Ltd., 41302 Executive Dr., Mt. Clemens, MI 48045/313-469-7323
Protecto Plastics, Div. of Penguin Ind., Airport Industrial Mall, Coatesville, PA 19320/215-384-6000
Protektor Model Co., 7 Ash St., Galeton, PA 16922/814-435-2442
PSI (See Precision Sales Intl., Inc.)
PTK International, Inc., 6030 Hwy. 85, Suite 614, Riverdale, GA 30274/404-997-5811
Puccinelli Design, Leonard, 5580 La Jolla Blvd., Suite 323, La Jolla, CA 92037/619-551-2629
Pursuit Marketing, Inc. (PMI), 1980 Raymond Dr., Northbrook, IL 60062/708-272-4765
Pyrodex (See Hodgdon Powder Co., Inc.)
Pyramid, Inc., 3292 S. Highway 97, Redmond, OR 97786

Q

Quack Decoy Corp., 4 Mill St., Cumberland, RI 02864/401-723-8202
Quaker Boy, Inc., 5455 Webster Rd., Orchard Parks, NY 14127/716-662-3979
Quality Arms, Inc., P.O. Box 19477, Houston, TX 77224/713-870-8377
Quality Parts Co., 999 Roosevelt Trail, Bldg. 3, Windham, ME 04062/800-556-SWAT
Quartz-Lok, 13137 N. 21st Lane, Phoenix, AZ 85029/602-863-2729
Queen Cutlery Co., 507 Chestnut St., Titusville, PA 16354/800-222-5233
Quinetics Corp., P.O. Box 29007, San Antonio, TX 78229/516-684-8561

R

Rabeno, Martin, Spook Hollow Trading Co., P.O. Box 37F, RD #1, Ellenville, NY 12428/914-647-4567
Rahn Gun Works, Inc., 3700 Anders Rd., P.O. Box 2, Hastings, MI 49058/616-945-9894
Raida Intertraders S.A., Raida House, 1-G Ave. de la Couronne, B1050 Brussels, Belgium
Ram-Line, Inc., 15611 W. 6th Ave., Golden, CO 80401/303-279-0886
Ramos, Jesse, P.O. Box 7105, La Puente, CA 91744/818-369-6384
Ranch Products, P.O. Box 145, Malinta, OH 43535/313-277-3118
Randall-Made Knives, P.O. Box 1988, Orlando, FL 32802/407-855-8075 (catalog $1)
Ranger Mfg. Co., Inc., 1536 Crescent Dr., Augusta, GA 30919/404-738-3469
Ranging, Inc., Routes 5 & 20, East Bloomfield, NY 14443/716-657-6161
Ransom Intl. Corp., P.O. Box 3845, 1040 Sandretto Dr., Suite J, Prescott, AZ 86302/602-778-7899
Rapine Bullet Mfg. Co., P.O. Box 1119, East Greenville, PA 18041
Raven Arms, 1300 Bixby Dr., City of Industry, CA 91745/818-961-2511
R&C Knives and Such, P.O. Box 1047, Manteca, CA 95336/209-239-3722 (catalog $2)
RCBS (See Blount Sporting Equipment Division)
R.D.P. Tool Co., Inc., 49162 McCoy Ave., East Liverpool, OH 43920/216-385-5129
Reardon Products, P.O. Box 126, Morrison, IL 61270/815-772-3155
Red Ball, 100 Factory St., Nashua, NH 03060/603-881-4420
Red Head, Inc., P.O. Box 7100, Springfield, MO 65801/417-864-5430
Red Star Target Co., 4519 Brisebois Dr. NW, Calgary, AB T2L 2G3, Canada/403-289-7939
Redding, Inc., 1089 Starr Rd., Cortland, NY 13045/607-753-3331
Redfield, Inc., 5800 E. Jewell Ave., Denver, CO 80224/303-757-6411
Redman's Rifling & Reboring, Rt. 3, P.O. Box 330A, Omak, WA 98841/509-826-5512
Redwood Bullet Works, 3559 Bay Rd., Redwood City, CA 94063/415-367-6741
Reed Choke (See Clinton River Gun Serv., Inc.)
Refrigiwear, Inc., 71 Inip Dr., Inwood, Long Island, NY 11696
Re-Heater, Inc., 15828 S. Broadway, Gardena, CA 90248
Reiswig, Wallace E., Claro Walnut Gunstock Co., 1235 Stanley Ave., Chico, CA 95928/916-342-5188
Remington Arms Co., 1007 Market St., Wilmington, DE 19898/302-773-5291
Remington Footwear Co., 1810 Columbia Ave., Franklin, TN 37604/800-332-2688
Renegade, P.O. Box 31546, Phoenix, AZ 85046/602-482-6777
Renner Co., R.J., P.O. Box 3543, Glendale, CA 91221-0543/818-892-8008
Retting, Inc., Martin B., 11029 Washington, Culver City, CA 90232/213-837-2412
Rhino Replacement Parts, P.O. Box 669, Seneca, SC 29679/803-882-0788
Rice Protective Gun Coatings, 235-30th St., West Palm Beach, FL 33407/407-848-7771
Richards Classic Oil Finish, Rt. 2, P.O. Box 325, Bedford, KY 40006/502-255-7222
Richards Micro-Fit Gun Stocks, P.O. Box 1066, Sun Valley, CA 91352/818-767-6097
Richards, John, Rt. 2, P.O. Box 325, Bedford, KY 40006/502-255-7222
Rickard, Inc., Pete, RD 1, Cobleskill, NY 12043/800-282-5663
Ridgetop Sporting Goods, P.O. Box 306, 42907 Hilligoss Ln. East, Eatonville, WA 98328/206-832-6422
Rifle Shop, P.O. Box M, Philipsburg, MT 59858
RIG Products, 87 Coney Island Dr., Sparks, NV 89431/703-331-5666
Riggs, Jim, 206 Azalea, Boerne, TX 78006/512-249-8567
Riling Arms Books Co., Ray, 6844 Gorsten St., P.O. Box 18925, Philadelphia, PA 19119/215-438-2456
R&J Gunshop, Bob Kerr, 133 W. Main St., John Day, OR 97845/503-575-2130
Roberts Custom Guns (See Dayton Traister Co.)
Roberts, J.J., 166 Manassas Dr., Manassas Park, VA 22111/703-330-0448
Roberts Products, 25238 SE 32nd, Issaquah, WA 98027/206-392-8172
Roberts, Wm. A., Jr., Rt. 14, P.O. Box 75, Athens, AL 35611/205-232-7027
Robinson, Don, Pennsylvania Hse., 36 Fairfax Crescent, Southowram, Halifax, W. Yorkshire HX3 9SW, England

Rochester Lead Works, 76 Anderson Ave., Rochester, NY 14607/716-442-8500
Rocky Mountain Rifle Works Ltd., 1707 14th St., Boulder, CO 80302/303-443-9189
Rocky Mountain Target Co., P.O. Box 700, Black Hawk, SD 57718/605-787-5946
Rogers Gunsmithing, Bob, P.O. Box 305, 344 S. Walnut St., Franklin Grove, IL 61031/815-456-2685
Rohner, John R. and Hans, 710 Sunshine Canyon, Boulder, CO 80302/303-444-3841
Rolston, Fred, Jr., 210 East Cummins, Tecumseh, MI 49286/517-423-6002
Rooster Laboratories, P.O. Box 412514, Kansas City, MO 64141/816-474-1622
Rorschach Precision Products, P.O. Box 151613, Irving, TX 75015/214-790-3487
Rosenberg & Sons, Jack A., 12229 Cox Lane, Dallas, TX 75234/214-241-6302
Rosser, Bob, 142 Ramsey Dr., Albertville, AL 35950/205-878-5388
Roto/Carve, 6509 Indian Hills Rd., Minneapolis, MN 55435/612-944-5150
Roy's Custom Leather Goods, Hwy. 132S & Rawhide Rd., P.O. Box 893, Magnolia, AR 71753/501-234-1599
Royal Arms, 1934 John Towers Ave. #A, El Cajon, CA 92020/619-448-5466
Royal Ordnance Works Ltd., P.O. Box 3245, Wilson, NC 27893/919-237-0515
RPM (R&R Sporting Arms, Inc.), 15481 N. Twin Lakes Dr., Tucson, AZ 85337/602-725-1233
R&S Industries Corp., 1312 Washington Ave., St. Louis, MO 63103/314-241-8464
Rubright Bullets, 1008 S. Quince Rd., Walnutport, PA 18088/215-767-1339
Ruger (See Sturm, Ruger & Co.)
Rundell, Joe, 6198 Frances Rd., Clio, MI 48420/313-687-0559
Runge, Robert P., 94 Grove St., Ilion, NY 13357/315-894-3036
Rupert's Gun Shop, 2202 Dick Rd., Suite B, Fenwick, MI 48834/517-248-3252
Russell's Rifle Shop, Rt. 5, P.O. Box 92, Georgetown, TX 78626/512-778-5338
Russell Co., A.G., 1705 Hwy. 71 North, Springdale, AR 72764/501-751-7341
Russwood Custom Pistol Grips, 580 Main St., P.O. Box 460, East Aurora, NY 14052/716-652-7131
Rust Guardit (See Kleen-Bore, Inc.)
Rusteprufe Laboratories, 1319 Jefferson Ave., Sparta, WI 54656/608-269-4144
Rutgers Book Center, Mark Aziz, 127 Raritan Ave., Highland Park, NJ 08904/201-545-4344
Rutgers Gun & Boat Center, 127 Raritan Ave., Highland Park, NJ 08904/201-545-4344
R.V.I., P.O. Box 1439 Stn. A, Vancouver, B.C. V6C 1AO, Canada/604-524-3214; U.S.: P.O. Box 1864, Bellingham, WA 98227
RWS (See Dynamit Nobel-RWS, Inc.)
Ryan, Chad, RR 3 Box 72, Cresco, IA 52136/319-547-4384
Rybka Custom Leather Equipment, Thad, 32 Havilah Hill, Odenville, AL 35120

S

SAECO (See Redding, Inc.)
Safari Arms/SGW, 624 Old Pacific Highway SE, Olympia, WA 98503/206-456-3472
Safari Gun Co., 6410 Brandon Ave., Springfield, VA 22150/703-569-1097
Safariland Leather Products, 1941 S. Walker Ave., Monrovia, CA 91016/818-357-7902
Safety Direct, 56 Coney Island Dr., Sparks, NV 89431/702-354-4451
Safety Speed Holster, 910 S. Vail Ave., Montebello, CA 90640/213-723-4140
Sailer, Anthony F. (See AFSCO Ammunition)
Saint Henri, Jean, 6525 Dume Dr., Malibu, CA 90265/213-457-7211
Salter Calls, Inc., Eddie, P.O. Box 872; Hwy. 31 South-Brewton Industrial Park, Brewton, AL 36427/205-867-2584
SAM, Inc. (See Special Service Arms Mfg., Inc.)
Samco Global Arms, Inc., 6995 NW 43rd St., Miami, FL 33166/305-593-9782
Sampson, Roger, 430 N. Grove, Mora, MN 55051/612-679-4868
San Angelo Mfg. Co., 909 West 14th St., San Angelo, TX 76904/915-655-7126
Sanders Custom Gun Serv., Bob Sanders, 2358 Tyler Lane, Louisville, KY 40205/502-454-3338
Sandia Die & Cartridge Co., Rt. 5, P.O. Box 5400, Albuquerque, NM 87123/505-298-5729
Sandy's Custom Gunshop, Rt. #1, P.O. Box 4, Rockport, IL 62370/217-437-4241
San Francisco Gun Exch., 124 Second St., San Francisco, CA 94105/415-982-6097
Sarco, Inc., 323 Union St., Stirling, NJ 07980/201-647-3800
SAS (See Corbin Mfg. & Supply, Inc.)
Sauer (See Sigarms, Inc.)
Saunders Sptg. Gds., 338 Somerset St., N. Plainfield, NJ 07060
Savage Industries, Inc., Springdale Rd., Westfield, MA 01085/413-568-7001
Scansport, Inc., P.O. Box 700, Enfield, NH 03748/603-632-7654
Schaefer, Roy V., 965 W. Hilliard Lane, Eugene, OR 97404/503-688-4333
Schiffman, Curt, 12237 Powhatan Trail, Conifer, CO 80433/303-838-7128
Schiffman, Norman H., 12237 Powhatan Trail, Conifer, CO 80433/303-838-7128
Schmidt & Bender (See Jaeger, Inc., Paul)
Schneider, Gary, 12202 N. 62nd Pl., Scottsdale, AZ 85254/602-948-2525
Schrade Cutlery Corp., Rt. 209 North, Ellenville, NY 12428/914-647-7600
Schulz Industries, 16247 Minnesota Ave., Paramount, CA 90723/213-439-5903
Schumakers Gun Shop, 512 Prouty Corner Lp., #A, Colville, WA 99114/509-684-4848
Schwartz Custom Guns, Wayne E., 9621 Coleman Rd., Haslett, MI 48840/517-339-8939
Schwartz Custom Guns, David W., 2505 Waller St., Eau Claire, WI 54703/715-832-1735
Scotch Hunting Products Co., Inc., 6619 Oak Orchard Rd., Elba, NY 14058/716-757-9958
Scott/McDougall Custom Gunsmiths, 880 Piner Rd., Suite 50, Santa Rosa, CA 95403/707-546-2264
Scott Fine Guns, Inc., Thad, P.O. Box 412, Indianola, MS 38751/601-887-5929
Scott, Inc., Tyler, 313 Rugby Ave., Suite 162, Terrace Park, OH 45174/513-831-7603
Seacliff International, Inc., 2210 Santa Anita, S. El Monte, CA 91733/818-350-0515
Seattle Binocular & Scope Repair Co., P.O. Box 46094, Seattle, WA 98146
Security Gun Chest (See Tread Corp.)
Sedco Industries, Inc., 506 Spring St., Unit E, Lake Elsinore, CA 92330/714-674-5957
Seecamp Co., Inc., L.W., P.O. Box 255, New Haven, CT 06502/203-877-3429
Semmer, Charles, 7885 Cyd Dr., Denver, CO 80221/303-429-6947
Seneca Run Iron Works, Inc., dba "Swagease," P.O. Box 3032, Greeley, CO 80633/303-352-1425
Servus Rubber Co., 1136 2nd St., P.O. Box 3610, Rock Island, IL 61204
Shane's Gunsmithing, P.O. Box 321, Hwy. 51 S., Minocqua, WI 54548/715-356-5414
Sharps Arms Co., Inc., C., P.O. Box 885, Big Timber, MT 59011/406-932-4353
Shaw's, Finest in Guns, 1201 La Mirada Ave., Escondido, CA 92026/619-746-2474
Shaw, Inc., E.R., Small Arms Mfg. Co., Thoms Run Rd. & Prestley, Bridgeville, PA 15017/412-221-4343

Sheffield Knifemakers Supply, P.O. Box 141, Deland, FL 32721/904-775-6453
Shell Shack, 113 E. Main, Laurel, MT 59044/406-628-8986
Shenandoah School of Gunsmithing, P.O. Box 300, Bentonville, VA 22610/703-743-5494
Shepherd Scope Ltd., P.O. Box 189, Waterloo, NE 68069/402-779-2424
Sheridan Products, Inc., 2600 Chicory Rd., Racine, WI 53403/414-554-7900
Sherk, Dan A., 9701-17th St., Dawson Creek, B.C. V1G 4H7, Canada/604-782-5630
Sherwood Intl. Export Corp., 18714 Parthenia St., Northridge, CA 91324/818-349-7600
Sherwood, George, 46 N. River Dr., Roseburg, OR 97470/503-672-3159
Shilen Rifles, Inc., P.O. Box 1300, 205 Metro Park Blvd., Ennis, TX 75119/214-875-5318
Shiloh Rifle Mfg. Co., Inc., P.O. Box 279, Big Timber, MT 59011/406-932-4454
Shirley & Co. Riflemakers, J.A., 33 Malmers Well Rd., High Wycombe, Bucks. HP13 6PD, England/0494-44.68.83
Shockley, Harold H., 204 E. Farmington Rd., Hanna City, IL 61536/309-565-4524
Shooter's Choice (See Venco Industries, Inc.)
Shooters Accessory Supply (SAS) (See Corbin Mfg. & Supply, Inc.)
Shooters Supply, 1120 Tieton Dr., Yakima, WA 98902/509-452-1181
Shootin' Shack, 1065 Silverbeach Rd. #1, Riviera Beach, FL 33403/407-842-0990
Shooting Chrony, Inc., 2480 Cawthra Rd., Unit 22, Mississauga, Ont. 65A 2X2, Canada/416-276-6292
Shootist Supply, John Cook, 622 5th Ave., Belle Fourche, SD 57717/605-892-2811
Shostle, Ben, The Gun Room, 1121 Burlington Dr., Muncie, IN 47302/317-282-9073
Shows, Hank, dba The Best, 1078 Alice Ave., Ukiah, CA 95482/707-462-9060
Shurkatch Corp., Longhorn Div., P.O. Box 858, 50 S. Elm St., Richfield Springs, NY 13439/315-858-1470
Sierra Bullets, 10532 S. Painter Ave., Santa Fe Springs, CA 90670/213-941-0251
Sigarms, Inc., Industrial Drive, Exeter, NH 03833/603-722-2302
Sile Distributors, 7 Centre Market Pl., New York, NY 10013/213-925-4389
Siler Locks, C.E., 7 Acton Woods Rd., Candler, NC 28715/704-667-9991
Silhouette Leathers, H.R. Brown, P.O. Box 280202, Memphis, TN 38124/901-372-5731
Silver Shields, Inc., 4464-D Chinden Blvd., Boise, ID 83714/208-323-8991
Simmons Outdoor Corp., 14530 SW 119 Ave., Miami, FL 33186/305-252-0477
Simmons Enterprises, Ernie, 709 East Elizabethtown Rd., Manheim, PA 17545/717-664-4040
Simmons, Jerry, 715 Middlebury St., Goshen, IN 46526/219-533-8546
Sinclair International, Inc., 718 Broadway, New Haven, IN 46774/219-493-1858
Sinclair, W.P., 46 Westbury Rd., Edington, Wiltshire BA13 4PG, England/0380-83.04.94
Sipes Gun Shop, 919 High St., Little Rock, AR 72202/501-376-8940
Six Enterprises, 6564 Hidden Creek Dr., San Jose, CA 95120/408-268-8296
S&K Mfg. Co., P.O. Box 247, Pittsfield, PA 16340/814-563-7808
Skaggs, Ron E., P.O. Box 34, 114 Miles Ct., Princeton, IL 61356/815-875-8207
SKB (See Simmons Enterprises, Ernie)
Skinner, John R. (See Orvis Co., The)
Sklany, Steve, 566 Birch Grove Dr., Kalispell, MT 59901/406-755-4257
Slezak, Jerome F., 1290 Marlowe, Lakewood (Cleveland), OH 44107/216-221-1668
Slug Site Co., Ozark Wilds, Rt. 2 P.O. Box 158, Versailles, MO 65084/314-378-6430
Smires, Clifford L., RD 1 P.O. Box 100, Columbus, NJ 08022/609-298-3158
Smith & Wesson, 2100 Roosevelt Ave., Springfield, MA 01101/413-781-8300
Smith & Wesson Leather (See Gould & Goodrich Leather, Inc.)
Smith, Art, 4124 Thrushwood Lane, Minnetonka, MN 55345/612-935-7829
Smith Saddlery, Jesse W., N. 1325 Division, Spokane, WA 99202/509-325-0622
Smith, John, 912 Lincoln, Carpentersville, IL 60110
Smith, Mark A., P.O. Box 182, 200 N. 9th, Sinclair, WY 82334/307-324-7929
Smith, Ron, 5869 Straley, Ft. Worth, TX 76114/817-732-6768
Snapp's Gunshop, 6911 E. Washington Rd., Clare, MI 48617/517-386-9226
Snider Stocks, Walter S. Snider, Rt. 2 P.O. Box 147, Denton, NC 27239
Sodia Jagdgewehrfabrik, Franz, Schulhausgasse 14, 9170 Ferlach, (Karnten) Austria
Sokolovsky Corp., P.O. Box 70113, Sunnyvale, CA 94086/408-738-1935
Sonderman, Robert, 735 W. Kenton, Charleston, IL 61920/217-345-5429
Sotheby's, 1334 York Ave. at 72nd St., New York, NY 10021
South Bend Replicas, Inc., 61650 Oak Rd., South Bend, IN 46614/219-289-4500 (catalog $7)
Southeastern Community College—North Campus, 1015 Gear Ave., P.O. Drawer F, West Burlington, IA 52655/319-752-2731
Southern Ammunition Co., Inc., Rt. 1, P.O. Box 6B, Latta, SC 29565/803-752-7751
Southern Armory, P.O. Box 879, Hillsville, VA 24343/703-236-7835
Southwind Sanctions, P.O. Box 445, Aledo, TX 76008/817-441-8917
Sowers, Ed, 8331 DeCelis Pl., Unit C, Sepulveda, CA 91343/818-893-1233
Sparks, Milt, P.O. Box 187, Idaho City, ID 83631/208-392-6695 (brochure $2)
Special Service Arms Mfg., Inc., P.O. Box 500, Aiken, SC 29802/803-642-2224
Speer Products (See Blount Sporting Equipment Division)
Spegel, Craig, P.O. Box 108, Bay City, OR 97107/503-377-2697
Speiser, Fred D., 2229 Dearborn, Missoula, MT 59801/406-549-8133
Spence, George W., 115 Locust St., Steele, MO 63877/314-695-4926
Spencer Reblue Service, 1820 Tupelo Trail, Holt, MI 48842/517-694-7474
Spokhandguns, Inc., Vern D. Ewer, P.O. Box 370, 1206 Fig St., Benton City, WA 99320/509-588-5255
Sport Flite Mfg., Inc., P.O. Box 1082, Bloomfield Hills, MI 48303/313-647-3747
Sport Specialties, Harry Owen, P.O. Box 5337, Hacienda Hts., CA 91745/213-968-5806 (catalog $3)
Sportarms of Florida, 5555 NW 36 Ave., Miami, FL 33142/305-635-2411
Sporting Arms, Mfg., P.O. Box 191, 311 E. 8th St., Littlefield, TX 79339/806-385-5665
Sportsmen's Equipment Co., 915 W. Washington, San Diego, CA 92103/619-296-1501
Sportsmen's Exchange & Western Gun Traders, Inc., P.O. Box 111, 560 S. "C" St., Oxnard, CA 93030/805-483-1917
Sports Support Systems, Inc., 27281 Las Ramblas, Suite 200, Mission Viejo, CA 92691/714-367-0343
Springfield Armory, Inc., 420 W. Main St., Geneseo, IL 61254/309-944-5131
Springfield Sporters, Inc., RD 1, Penn Run, PA 15765/412-254-2626
S&S Firearms, 74-11 Myrtle Ave., Glendale, NY 11385/718-497-1100
SSK Co., 220 N. Belvidere Ave., York, PA 17404/717-854-2897
SSK Industries, 721 Woodvue Lane, Wintersville, OH 43952/614-264-0176
Stackpole Books, Cameron & Kelker Sts., Telegraph Press Bldg., Harrisburg, PA 17105
Stalker, Inc., P.O. Box 21, Fishermans Wharf Rd., Malakoff, TX 75148/214-489-1010
Star Machine Works, 418 10th Ave., San Diego, CA 92101/619-232-3216
Starnes, Ken, Rt. 1 P.O. Box 269, Scroggins, TX 75480/214-365-2312
Starrett Co., L.S., 121 Crescent St., Athol, MA 01331/617-249-3551
State Arms Gun Co., 815 S. Division St., Waunakee, WI 53597/608-849-5800
Steelman's Gun Shop, 10465 Beers Rd., Swartz Creek, MI 48473/313-735-4884
Steffens, Ron, 18396 Mariposa Creek Rd., Willits, CA 95490/707-485-0873
Stegall, Keith, P.O. Box 696, Gunnison, CO 81230
Steger, James R., 1131 Dorsey Pl., Plainfield, NJ 07062
Steiner Binoculars (See Pioneer Marketing & Research)
Steves House of Guns, Rt. 1, Minnesota City, MN 55959/507-689-2573
Stewart Game Calls, Inc., Johnny, P.O. Box 7954, 5100 Fort Ave., Waco, TX 76714/817-772-3261
Steyr-Daimler-Puch (See GSI, Inc.)
Stoeger Industries, 55 Ruta Ct., S. Hackensack, NJ 07606/201-440-2700
Stoeger Publishing Co. (See Stoeger Industries)
Stone Enterprises Ltd., Rt. 609, P.O. Box 335, Wicomico Church, VA 22579/804-580-5114
Storey, Dale A., DGS, Inc., 305 N. Jefferson, Casper, WY 82601/307-237-2414
Stott's Creek Armory, Inc., RR1 P.O. Box 70, Morgantown, IN 46160/317-878-5489
Strawbridge, Victor W., 6 Pineview Dr., Dover Point, Dover, NH 03820/603-742-0013
Strong Holster Co., 105 Maplewood Ave., Gloucester, MA 01930/508-281-3300
Stroup, Earl R., 30506 Flossmoor Way, Hayward, CA 94544/415-471-1549
Strutz, W.C., Rifle Barrels, Inc., P.O. Box 611, Eagle River, WI 54521/715-479-4766
Stuart Products, Inc., P.O. Box 1587, Easley, SC 29641/803-859-9360
Sturm, Ruger & Co., Inc., Lacey Place, Southport, CT 06490/203-259-7843
Summit Specialties, Inc., P.O. Box 786, Decatur, AL 35602/205-353-0634
Sundance Industries, Inc., 8216 Lankershim Blvd., #11, North Hollywood, CA 91605/818-768-1083
Sunora Gun Shop, 22935 Watkins St., Buckeye, AZ 85326/602-386-3193
Super Six Limited, 13105 W. Blue Mound, Brookfield, WI 53005/414-785-9325
Supreme Lens Covers (See Butler Creek Corp.)
Swampfire Shop, The, 1693 Old Hwy. 441 N., Mt. Dora, FL 32757/904-383-0595
Swann, D.J., 5 Orsova Close, Eltham North, Vic. 3095, Australia/03-431-0323
Swarovski Optik, 2 Slater Rd., Cranston, RI 02920/401-463-3000
Sweet Home, Inc., Subs. of Will-Burt., P.O. Box 250, Sweet Home, OR 97386/503-367-5185
Swenson's 45 Shop, A.D., P.O. Box 606, Fallbrook, CA 92028
Swift Bullet Co., RR 1, P.O. Box 140A, Quinter, KS 67752/913-754-3959
Swift Instruments, Inc., 952 Dorchester Ave., Boston, MA 02125
Swiss Army Knives, Inc., P.O. Box 874, Shelton, CT 06484/203-929-6391

T

Talley, Dave, P.O. Box 821, Glenrock, WY 82637/307-436-8724
Talmage, William G., 451 Phantom Creek Lane, P.O. Box 512, Meadview, AZ 86444/602-564-2380
Tamarack Prods., Inc., P.O. Box 625, Wauconda, IL 60084/708-526-9333
Taracorp Industries, 16th & Cleveland Blvd., Granite City, IL 62040/618-451-4400
Tasco Sales, Inc., 7600 NW 26th St., Miami, FL 33122/305-591-3670
Taurus International, Inc., 1675 NW 49th Ave., Miami, FL 33014/305-624-1115
Taylor & Robbins, P.O. Box 164, Rixford, PA 16745
Taylor, Twyla, P.O. Box 252, #2 Engress Rd., Oracle, AZ 85623/602-896-2860
Taylor's & Co., Inc., 2645 Papermill Rd., Winchester, VA 22601/703-722-2017
T.D. Arms, 32464 #2 23 Mile Rd., New Baltimore, MI 48047/313-949-1890
TDP Industries, Inc., 603 Airport Blvd., Doylestown, PA 18901/215-345-8687
Tekna, 101 Twin Dolphin Dr., Redwood City, CA 94065/800-225-2075
Teledyne Co., Big Beam, 290 E. Prairie St., Crystal Lake, IL 60014
Tele-Optics, Inc., P.O. Box 176, 219 E. Higgins Rd., Gilberts, IL 60136/708-426-7444
Tele-Optics, 5514 W. Lawrence Ave., Chicago, IL 60630/312-283-7757
Tennessee Valley Mfg., P.O. Box 1175, Corinth, MS 38834/601-286-5014
Ten-Ring Precision, Inc., 1449 Blue Crest Lane, San Antonio, TX 78232/512-494-3063
10-X Products Group, 2915 Lyndon B. Johnson Freeway, Suite 133, Dallas, TX 75234/214-243-4016
Tepeco, P.O. Box 342, Friendswood, TX 77546/713-482-2702
Tertin, James A. (See Jaeger, Inc., Paul)
Texas Longhorn Arms, Inc., P.O. Box 703, Richmond, TX 77469/713-341-0775
Texas Platers Supply Co., 2453 W. Five Mile Parkway, Dallas, TX 75233/214-330-7168
Theis, Terry, P.O. Box 535, Fredericksburg, TX 78624/512-997-6778
Thermos Div., KST Co., Norwich, CT 06361
Thiewes, George W., 1846 Allen Lane, St. Charles, IL 60174/708-584-1383
Thirion, Denise, P.O. Box 408, Graton, CA 95444/707-829-1876
Thompson, Larry R., Larry's Gun Shop, 521 E. Lake Ave., Watsonville, CA 95076/408-724-5328
Thompson, Norm, 18905 NW Thurman St., Portland, OR 97209
Thompson, Randall, Highline Machine Co., 654 Lela Pl., Grand Junction, CO 81504/303-434-4971
Thompson/Center Arms, Farmington Rd., P.O. Box 5002, Rochester, NH 03867/603-332-2394
3-D Ammunition & Bullets, 112 Plum St., Doniphan, NE 68832/402-845-2285
3-Ten Corp., P.O. Box 269, Feeding Hills, MA 01030/413-789-2086
Thunderbird Cartridge Co., Inc., P.O. Box 302, Phoenix, AZ 85001/602-237-3823
Tiger-Hunt, Michael D. Barton, P.O. Box 214, Jerome, PA 15937/814-479-2215
Tillinghast, James C., P.O. Box 405GD, Hancock, NH 03449/603-525-6615 (list $2)
Timney Mfg., Inc., 3065 W. Fairmount Ave., Phoenix, AZ 85017/602-274-2999
Tink's Safariland Hunting Corp., P.O. Box 244, Madison, GA 30650/404-342-4915
Tippman Pneumatics, Inc., 4402 New Haven Ave., Fort Wayne, IN 46803/219-422-6448
Titus, Daniel, Shooting Specialties, 872 Penn St., Bryn Mawr, PA 19010/215-525-8829
TMI Products, 930 S. Plumer Ave., Tucson, AZ 85719/602-792-1075
Tom's Gunshop, Tom Gillman, 4201 Central Ave., Hot Springs, AR 71913/501-624-3856
Torel, Inc., 1053 N. South St., P.O. Box 592, Yoakum, TX 77995/512-293-2341
Totally Dependable Products (See TDP Industries, Inc.)
Tradewinds, Inc., P.O. Box 1191, Tacoma, WA 98401
Traditions, Inc., 500 Main St., P.O. Box 235, Deep River, CT 06417/203-526-9555
Trail Guns Armoury, 1422 E. Main St., League City, TX 77573/713-332-5833
Trammco, Inc., P.O. Box 1258, Bellflower, CA 90706/213-428-5250
Trapper Gun, Inc., 18717 East 14 Mile Rd., Fraser, MI 48026/313-792-0134
Tread Corp., 1764 Granby St. NE, Roanoke, VA 24012/703-982-6881
Treso, Inc., P.O. Box 4640, Pagosa Springs, CO 81157/303-731-2295

Trevallion Gunstocks, David Trevallion, 9 Old Mountain Rd., Cape Neddick, ME 03902/207-361-1130
Treville, Stan de, P.O. Box 33021, San Diego, CA 92103/619-298-3393
Trijicon, Inc., P.O. Box 2130, Farmington Hills, MI 48018/313-553-4960
Trinidad State Junior College, 600 Prospect, Trinidad, CO 81082/719-846-5631
Trinko's Gun Service, 1406 E. Main St., Watertown, WI 53094/414-261-5175
Triple-K Mfg. Co., 2222 Commercial St., San Diego, CA 92113/619-232-2066
Trius Products, Inc., P.O. Box 25, Cleves, OH 45002/513-941-5682
Trophy Bonded Bullets, Inc., P.O. Box 262348, Houston, TX 77207/713-645-4499
Trotman Ltd., Ken, 135 Ditton Walk, Unit 11, Cambridge CB5 8QD, England
Tru-Balance Knife Co., 2155 Tremont Blvd. NW, Grand Rapids, MI 49504/616-453-3679
Tru-Square Metal Products, 640 First St. SW, P.O. Box 585, Auburn, WA 98001/206-833-2310
True Flite Bullet Co., 57 North Mountain Blvd., Mountaintop, PA 18707/717-474-9904
T&S Industries, Inc., 1027 Skyview Dr., West Carrollton, OH 45449/513-865-4010
Tucker, James C., P.O. Box 38790, Sacramento, CA 95838/916-662-0503
Tyler Mfg.-Dist., Melvin, 1326 W. Britton Rd., Oklahoma City, OK 73114/405-842-8044

U

Uberti USA, Inc., 362 Limerock Rd., P.O. Box 469, Lakeville, CT 06039/203-435-8068
Ugartechea, Ignacio, Apartado 21, Eibar, Spain
Ulrich, Dennis A., "Doc" & Bud D.O.C. Specialists, 2209 S. Central Ave., Cicero, IL 60650/708-652-3606
Ultra Light Arms, Inc., P.O. Box 1270, 214 Price St., Granville, WV 26534/304-599-5687
Uncle Mike's (See Michaels of Oregon Co.)
Unertl Optical Co., John, 1224 Freedom Rd., Mars, PA 16046/412-776-9700
Unick's Gunsmithing, 5005 Center Rd., Lowellville, OH 44436/216-536-8015
United Binocular Co., 9043 S. Western Ave., Chicago, IL 60620
United States Ammunition Co. (USAC), Inc., 4500-15th St. East, Tacoma, WA 98424/206-922-7589
United States Products Co., 518 Melwood Ave., Pittsburgh, PA 15213/412-621-2130
Upper Missoui Trading Co., 304 Harold St., Crofton, NE 68730/402-388-4844
USAC (See United States Ammunition Co.)
U.S. Repeating Arms Co., P.O. Box 30-300, New Haven, CT 06511/203-789-5000
Utica Cutlery Co., 820 Noyes St., Utica, NY 13503/315-733-4663

V

Vais Arms, George Vais, 4120 Willowbend, Houston, TX 77025
Valade, Robert B., 931-3rd. Ave., Seaside, OR 97138/503-738-7672
Valmet (See Stoeger Industries)
Valor Corp., 5555 NW 36th Ave., Miami, FL 33142/305-633-0127
Van Epps, Milton, Rt. 69-A, Parish, NY 13131/315-625-7251
Van Gorden, C.S., 1815 Main St., Bloomer, WI 54724/715-568-2612
Van Horn, Gil, P.O. Box 207, Llano, CA 93544
Van Patten, J.W., P.O. Box 145, Foster Hill, Milford, PA 18337/717-296-7069
Varner Sporting Arms, Inc., 1004-F N. Cobb Pkwy., Marietta, GA 30062/404-422-5468
Venco Industries, Inc., 16770 Hilltop Park Pl., Chagrin Falls, OH 44022/216-543-8808
Verney-Carron, B.P. 72, 54 Boulevard Thiers, 42002 St.-Etienne Cedex 1, France/33-77.79.15.00
Vest, John, P.O. Box 1552, Susanville, CA 96130/916-257-7228
Vibra-Tek Co., 1844 Arroya Rd., Colorado Springs, CO 80906/719-634-8611
Vic's Gun Refinishing, 6 Pineview Dr., Dover, NH 03820/603-742-0013
Viking Leathercraft, Inc., 1579A Jayken Way, Chula Vista, CA 92011/619-429-8050
Viramontez, Ray, 601 Springfield Dr., Albany, GA 31707/912-432-9683
Vitt/Boos, 2178 Nichols Ave., Stratford, CT 06497/203-375-6859
Von Atzigen, Ed, The Custom Shop, 890 Cochrane Cres., Peterborough, Ont. K9H 5N3, Canada/705-742-6693

W

Waffen-Frankonia (See Frankonia Jagd, Hofmann & Co.)
Wagoner, Vernon G., 2325 E. Encanto, Mesa, AZ 85213/602-835-1307
Wahl Corp., Paul, P.O. Box 500, Bogota, NJ 07603-0500/201-261-9245
Waldron, Herman, P.O. Box 475, 80 N. 17th St., Pomeroy, WA 99347/509-843-1404
Walker Arms Co., Inc., Rt. 2, P.O. Box 73, Highway 80 West, Selma, AL 36701/205-872-6231
Walker Shoe Co., P.O. Box 1167, Asheboro, NC 27203-1167/919-625-1380
Wallace, R.D., Star, Rt.1 P.O. Box 76, Grandin, MO 63943/314-593-4773
Wallace, Terry, 385 San Marino, Vallejo, CA 94589/707-642-7041
Walters Industries, 6226 Park Lane, Dallas, TX 75225/214-691-6973
WAMCO, Inc., Mingo Loop, P.O. Box 337, Oquossoc, ME 04964-0337/207-864-3344
Ward & Van Valkenburg, 114-32nd Ave. N., Fargo, ND 58102/701-232-2351
Wardell Precision Handguns Ltd., 4132 New River Stage 1, New River, AZ 85029
Wardrop, R.A., P.O. Box 245, 409 E. Marble St., Mechanicsburg, PA 17055/717-766-9663
Warner, Glenn, Endicott Johnson, 1100 E. Main St., Endicott, NY 13760/607-770-7426
Warren Muzzleloading Co., Inc., Hwy. 21 North, Ozone, AR 72854/501-292-3268
Warren, Floyd E., 1273 State Rt. 305 NE, Cortland, OH 44410/216-638-4219
Warren, Kenneth W., Mountain States Engraving, P.O. Box 2842, Wenatchee, WA 98802/509-663-6123
Washita Mountain Whetstone Co., P.O. Box 378, Lake Hamilton, AR 71951/501-525-3914
Wasp Shooting Systems, P.O. Box 241, Lakeview, AR 72642/501-431-5606
Watson Trophy Match Bullets, Ed, 2404 Wade Hampton Blvd., Greenville, SC 29615/803-244-7948
Wayland Prec. Wood Prods., P.O. Box 1142, Mill Valley, CA 94942/415-381-3543
Wayne, James, 2608 N. Laurent, Victoria, TX 77901/512-578-1258
WD-40 Co., P.O. Box 80607, San Diego, CA 92138-9021/619-275-1400
Weather Shield Sports Equipment, Inc., Rt. #3, Petoskey Rd., Charlevoix, MI 49720
Weatherby, Inc., 2781 Firestone Blvd., South Gate, CA 90280/213-569-7186
Weaver Arms Corp., P.O. Box 8, Dexter, MO 63841/314-568-3800
Weaver Scope Repair Service, 1121 Larry Mahan Dr., Suite B, El Paso, TX 79925/915-593-1005
Weaver (See Blount Sporting Equipment Division)
Weber, Chris/Waffen-Weber, #6-1691 Powick Rd., Kelowna, BC V1X 4L1, Canada/604-762-7575

Webster Scale Mfg. Co., P.O. Box 188, Sebring, FL 33870/813-385-6362
Weems, Cecil, P.O. Box 657, Mineral Wells, TX 76067/817-325-1462
Weisz Antique Gun Parts, P.O. Box 311, Arlington, VA 22210/703-243-9161
Welch, Sam, CVSR, P.O. Box 2110, Moab, UT 84532/801-259-8131
Wells, Fred, Wells Sport Store, 110 N. Summit St., Prescott, AZ 86301/602-445-3655
Wells Ltd., R.A., 3452 N. 1st Ave., Racine, WI 53402/414-639-5223
Wells, Rachel, 110 N. Summit St., Prescott, AZ 86301/602-445-3655
Wenoka/Seastyle, P.O. Box 8238, West Palm Beach, FL 33407/407-845-6155
Werth, Terry, 1203 Woodlawn Rd., Lincoln, IL 62656/217-732-9314
Wescombe, P.O. Box 488, Glencoe, CA 95232/209-293-7010
Wesson Arms, Dan, 293 Main St., Monson, MA 01057/413-267-4081
West, Robert G., 3973 Pam St., Eugene, OR 97402/503-344-3700
Western Cutlery (See Coleman Co., Inc.)
Western Gunstock Mfg. Co., 550 Valencia School Rd., Aptos, CA 95003/408-688-5884
Westminster Arms Ltd., P.O. Box 60260, Reno, CA 89506/916-827-2179
Westrom, John, Precise Firearms Finishing, 25 NW 44th Ave., Des Moines, IA 50313/515-288-8680
Weyer International, 333-14th St., Toledo, OH 43624/419-241-5454
Whinnery, Walt, Walt's Custom Leather, 1947 Meadow Creek Dr., Louisville, KY 40218/502-458-4361
White Laboratory, Inc., H.P., 3114 Scarboro Rd., Street, MD 21154/301-838-6550
Whitetail Design & Engineering Ltd., 9421 E. Mannsiding Rd., Clare, MI 48617/517-386-3932
Wichita Arms, Inc., 444 Ellis St., Wichita, KS 67211/316-265-0661
Wide View Scope Mount Corp., 26110 Michigan Ave., Inkster, MI 48141/313-274-1238
Widener's Reloading & Shooting Supply, Inc., P.O. Box 3009 CRS, Johnson City, TN 37602/615-282-6786
Wiebe, Duane, P.O. Box 497, Lotus, CA 95651/916-626-6240 or P.O. Box 1518, Casper, WY 82602/307-237-0615
Wiest, M.C., 125 E. Tyrone Rd., Oak Ridge, TN 37830/615-483-4024
Wild Bill Cleaver, Rt. 4, P.O. Box 462, Vashon, WA 98070/206-463-5738
Wildey, Inc., P.O. Box 475, Brookfield, CT 06804/203-355-9000
Wilkinson Arms, 26884 Pearl Rd., Parma, ID 83660/208-722-6771
Will-Burt Co., 169 S. Main, Orrville, OH 44667
Williams Gun Sight Co., 7389 Lapeer Rd., Davison, MI 48423/313-653-2131
Williams, Inc., Boyd, 8701-14 Mile Rd. (M-57),Cedar Springs, MI 49319
Williams Shootin' Iron Service, Rt. 1 P.O. Box 151A, Bennett Hill Rd., Central Lake, MI 49622/616-544-6615
Williamson-Pate Gunsmith Serv., 117 W. Pipeline, Hurst, TX 76053/817-282-1464
Willig, Claus, Siedlerweg 17, 8720 Schweinfurt, West Germany/01149-9721-41446
Wills, David W., 2776 Brevard Ave., Montgomery, AL 36109/205-272-8446
Willson Safety Prods. Div., P.O. Box 622, Reading, PA 19603
Wilson, Inc., L.E., P.O. Box 324, 404 Pioneer Ave., Cashmere, WA 98815/509-782-1328
Wilson Arms Co., 63 Leetes Island Rd., Branford, CT 06405/203-488-7297
Wilson Case Co., P.O. Box 1106, Hastings, NE 68902/800-322-5493
Wilson's Gun Shop, P.O. Box 578, Rt. 3, Box 211-D, Berryville, AR 72616/501-545-3618
Winchester Div., Olin Corp., 427 N. Shamrock St., East Alton, IL 62024
Winchester Press, 220 Old New Brunswick Rd., Piscataway, NJ 08854/201-981-0820
Winchester Sutler, Inc., HC 38 P.O. Box 1000, Winchester, VA 22601/703-888-3595
Windish, Jim, 2510 Dawn Dr., Alexandria, VA 22306/703-765-1994
Winter & Associates, 239 Hillary Dr., Verona, PA 15147/412-795-4124
Winter, Robert M., RR 2, P.O. Box 484, Menno, SD 57045/605-387-5322
Wisconsin Platers Supply Co. (See Texas Platers Supply Co.)
Wiseman, Bob (See McMillan Rifle Barrels)
Wisner's Gun Shop, Inc., P.O. Box 58, Hwy. G, Adna, WA 98552/206-748-8942
Wolfe Publishing Co., 6471 Air Park Dr., Prescott, AZ 86301/602-445-7810
Wolfe, Bernie, 2025 E. Yandall, El Paso, TX 79903
Wolff Co., W.C., P.O. Box I, Newtown Square, PA 19073/215-359-9600
Wolverine Boots & Shoes Div., Wolverine World Wide, 9341 Courtland Dr., Rockford, MI 49351/616-866-1561
Womack, Lester, 512 Westwood Dr., Prescott, AZ 86301/602-778-9624
Wood, Mel, P.O. Box 1255, Sierra Vista, AZ 85636/602-455-5541
Woodland Bullets, 638 Woodland Dr., Manheim, PA 17545/717-665-4332
Woolrich Woolen Mills, Mill St., Woolrich, PA 17779/717-769-6464
World of Targets, Div. of Steidle Corp., 9200 Floral Ave., Cincinnati, OH 45242/513-791-0917
Worthy Products, Inc., RR I, P.O. Box 213, Martville, NY 13111
Wyoming Armory, Inc., Route 1, Afton, WY 83110/307-886-9024
Wyoming Knife Corp., 101 Commerce Dr., Ft. Collins, CO 80524/303-224-3454

Y

Yavapai College, 1100 East Sheldon St., Prescott, AZ 86301/602-445-7300
Yearout, Lewis, 308 Riverview Dr. East, Great Falls, MT 59404/406-761-0589
Yee, Mike, 29927-56 Pl. S., Auburn, WA 98001/206-839-3991
Yellowstone Wilderness Supply, P.O. Box 129, West Yellowstone, MT 59758/406-646-7613
York M-1 Conversions, P.O. Box 262364, Houston, TX 77217/800-527-2881

Z

Z-Coat Co., 3915 U.S. Hwy. 98 S., Lakeland, FL 33801/813-665-1734
Zavodi Crvena Zastava (See Interarms)
Zeeryp, Russ, 1601 Foard Dr., Lynn Ross Manor, Morristown, TN 37814/615-586-2357
Zeiss Optical, Inc., Carl, 1015 Commerce St., Petersburg, VA 23803/804-861-0033
Zeitz Optics, U.S.A., 1501 E. Chapman Ave., Suite 306, Fullerton, CA 92631/714-879-8922
Zero Ammunition Co., Inc., 1601 22nd St. SE, P.O. Box 1188, Cullman, AL 35056/205-739-1606
Zeus International, P.O. Box 953, Tarpon Springs, FL 34688/813-863-5029
Zip Aerosol Prods. (See RIG Products)
Zoli USA, Inc., Antonio, P.O. Box 6190, Fort Wayne, IN 46896/219-447-4603
Zollinger, Dean A., Rt. 2, P.O. Box 135-A, Rexburg, ID 83440/208-356-6167